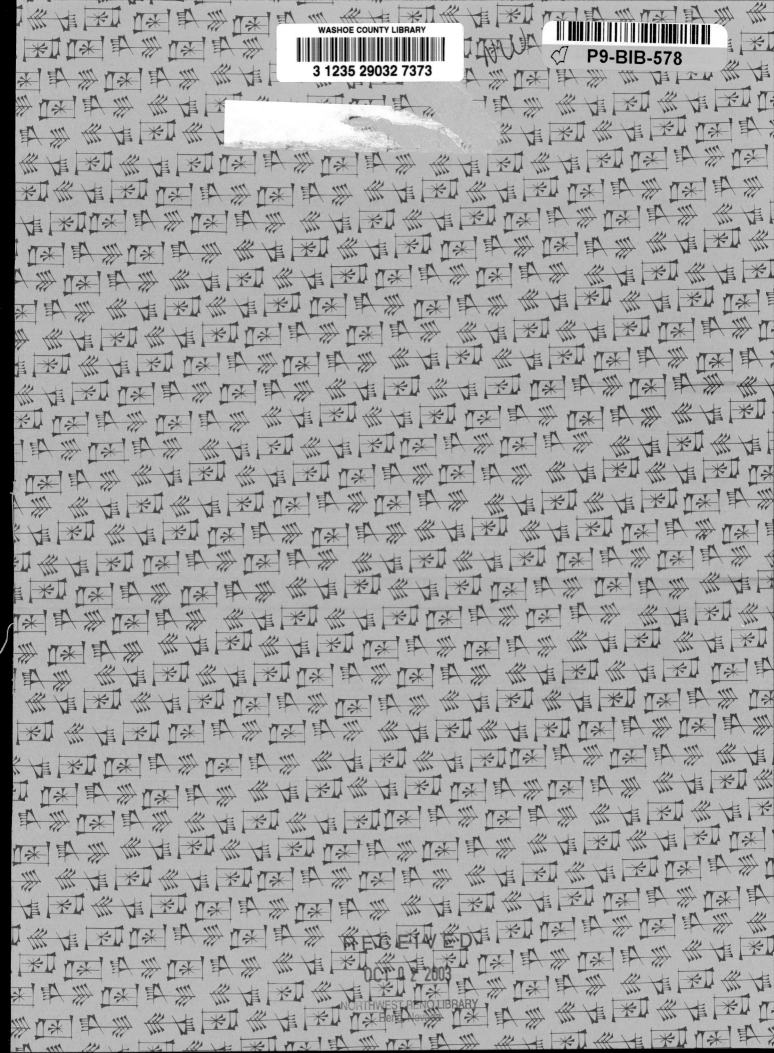

The American Republic

Editorial Board

The American Republic

PRIMARY SOURCES

Edited by Bruce Frohnen

Liberty Fund

INDIANAPOLIS

This book is published by Liberty Fund, Inc., a foundation
established to encourage study of the ideal of a society of free
and responsible individuals.

𒀀𒈚 𒊬𒄑

The cuneiform inscription that serves as our logo and as the
design motif for our endpapers is the earliest-known written
appearance of the word "freedom" (*amagi*), or "liberty." It is
taken from a clay document written about 2300 B.C. in the
Sumerian city-state of Lagash.

© 2002 Liberty Fund, Inc.
Printed in the United States of America

06   05   04   03   02   C   5   4   3   2
06   05   04   03   02   P   5   4   3   2

Library of Congress Cataloging-in-Publication Data

The American Republic: primary sources/edited
by Bruce Frohnen.
        p.   cm.
Includes bibliographical references.
ISBN 0-86597-332-6 (alk. paper)—ISBN 0-86597-333-4 (pbk.:
alk. paper)
1. United States—History—Colonial period, ca. 1600–
1775—Sources.   2. United States—History—Revolution,
1775–1783—Sources.   3. United States—History—1783–
1865—Sources.   I. Frohnen, Bruce.

E173.A7535   2002
973—dc21
2001038925

Liberty Fund, Inc.
8335 Allison Pointe Trail, Suite 300
Indianapolis, Indiana 46250-1684

Contents

9 Prelude to War

Alphabetical Table of Contents

Alphabetical List of Authors

Adams, John
Blyfield, Nathanael
Boucher, Jonathan
"Brutus" [Robert Yates?]
Bryan, Robert
Calhoun, John C.
"Centinel" [Samuel Bryan?]
Cotton, John
Crockett, Davy
Dickinson, John
Dwight, Timothy
"Federal Farmer, The" [Melancton Smith]
Hamilton, Alexander
Hayne, Robert Y.
Jackson, Andrew
Jay, John
Jefferson, Thomas
Kent, James
Leggett, William
Leland, John

Lincoln, Abraham
Madison, James
Marshall, John
Mather, Richard
Otis, James
Paine, Thomas
Partridge, Ralph
Sawyer, George S.
"Son of Liberty, A" [Silas Downer]
Story, Joseph
Stowe, Harriet Beecher
Taney, Roger
Taylor, John, of Caroline
Washington, George
Webster, Daniel
Webster, Noah
Williams, John
Williams, Roger
Wilson, James
Winthrop, John

Illustrations

Introduction

In the latter decades of the twentieth century scholars working in various subfields of American history brought a great deal of formerly neglected material to light. This material concerns issues ranging from the role of religious arguments and leaders in public life, to the breadth of historical understanding characterizing public debate, to the specifically British memories and sensibilities of Americans, to the importance of early constitutional documents and Americans' constitutional sophistication. In each of these areas the new material has made it possible for scholars to reexamine and reevaluate existing theories regarding the development of American politics. These new discoveries have opened vast new areas for fruitful research concerning the influences and concerns motivating those who have helped shape the character of American politics and the American people. Unfortunately, very little of this material is available in a form suitable for classroom use. This has left teachers to seek out half-measures—summarizing on their own or assigning works they know will not be read—in attempting to present American history in something approaching its true diversity and depth.

Collections by Belz; Hall, Leder, and Kammen; Hyneman and Lutz; Lutz; McDonald; Morgan; Sandoz; and White,[1] among others; have allowed scholars increased access to constitutional documents, declarations, sermons, and other public writings showing the factors that shaped public life in America, both before and after the War for Independence. Without diminishing the role accorded specifically ideological concerns and philosophical writings, these new materials have helped scholars better evaluate the sources and meanings of public acts ranging from co-

lonial settlement to the War for Independence, to the Constitution, and to the Civil War.

No single course, whether in high school, college, or even graduate school, could deal adequately with all the important materials unearthed in recent decades. However, by bringing together, in one manageable volume, key original documents and other writings that throw light on the cultural, religious, and historical concerns that have been raised, this volume aims to provide the means by which students and teachers may begin examining the diversity of issues and influences that characterize American history.

We now have access to crucial materials attesting to the importance of the context in which Americans spoke of practices such as liberty and religious freedom. A hitherto neglected literature now can enable scholars and students to discuss the American drive for liberty, not merely as a political concept, but as a religious idea, a historical practice, and a constitutional concern to be guaranteed and given substance through both national institutions and local customs.

The readings selected here represent opposite sides of important debates concerning, for example, American independence, religious establishment, and slavery. Conclusions regarding America's nature and development as a nation and as a people will vary, not least because American history is one of religious, ideological, and cultural conflict. Such conflicts have pitted the drive for community against the drive for individual autonomy, the call of God against the call of a wild nature to be confronted in near isolation, the desire for wealth against the desire to be held virtuous, and the demand for equality against respect for established authority. But exposure to the principal public acts and arguments engaged in these conflicts will provide a deeper and more nuanced understanding of their nature and sources—and of their influence on American history.

America's history has been characterized by both continuity and change. Even before the Civil War, at which point this volume leaves off, American traditions, with their roots deep in the histories of Great Britain, Rome, Greece,

---

1. Belz, *The Webster-Hayne Debate on the Nature of the Union;* Hall, Leder, and Kammen, *The Glorious Revolution in America;* Hyneman and Lutz, *American Political Writing during the Founding Era: 1760–1805;* Lutz, *Colonial Origins of the American Constitution;* McDonald, *Empire and Nation;* Edmund Sears Morgan, ed., *Prologue to Revolution: Sources and Documents on the Stamp Act Crisis, 1764–1766* (Chapel Hill: University of North Carolina Press, 1959); Sandoz, *Political Sermons of the American Founding Era: 1730–1805;* and White, *Democratick Editorials.*

and Israel, had been markedly transformed by changes in circumstances and public understanding.[2] But even traditions that have been transformed or weakened over time continue to influence public conduct, and with it the shape of both nations and peoples. By presenting readings from the perspectives of America's varied traditions, this volume seeks to help students learn how they might judge the strengths and weaknesses of the conflicting visions that have shaped American history.

ORGANIZATION OF THE WORK

This work is in nine sections, each composed of selections of public writings intended to illustrate the major philosophical, cultural, and policy positions at issue during crucial eras of American political and cultural development.

The first section, "Colonial Settlements and Societies," will provide documentary evidence of the purposes behind European settlement and the nature of settlements in practice. The second section, "Religious Society and Religious Liberty in Early America," will provide materials showing the pervasive public role of religion in early American public life as well as arguments concerning the importance of religious conscience and the limits that conscience should place on government support for religious orthodoxy. The third section, "Defending the Charters," will provide materials showing the American response to English acts—ranging from James II's revocation of colonial charters during the 1680s to parliamentary taxation during the 1750s—which Americans interpreted as attacks on their chartered, English liberties. The fourth section, "The War for Independence," will provide materials from all perspectives in the debate over independence—those centered on the chartered rights of Englishmen, those focusing on universal human rights, and those emphasizing loyalty and duty to Great Britain. The fifth section, "A New Constitution," will provide materials showing the roots of American constitutionalism in earlier English and colonial codes and charters, as well as the Articles of Confederation. In addition, it will provide important selections dealing with various "plans" or proposed constitutions, debates in the Constitutional Convention, and subsequent debates over ratification. The sixth section, "The Bill of Rights," will include Federalist and Anti-Federalist arguments concerning

the need to protect common law rights as well as the Anti-Federalist insistence that structural changes were needed in the proposed Constitution. The seventh section, "State versus Federal Authority," will present materials from both sides of issues related to the question of whether the states or the federal government held final authority in determining the course of public policy in America. The eighth section, "Forging a Nation," will provide materials regarding the debate over internal improvements and other federal measures aimed at binding the nation more closely together, particularly in the area of commerce. The final section, "Prelude to War," will focus on the political, cultural, and legal issues underlying the sectional differences that led to the Civil War. Debates concerning the morality and necessity of slavery, as well as attempts to secure political compromise regarding the status of "the peculiar institution," will be highlighted; their character and relative importance will be further illuminated by selections focusing on the relative power and position of various regions within the United States.

The volume ends with the prelude to the Civil War, stopping at that point for three interconnected reasons: (1) the need to produce a volume that does not reach an ungainly length, (2) the prevalence of courses on American history that split that history into the pre–Civil War era and the era commencing with the Civil War, and (3) recognition of the revolutionary changes wrought by the Civil War, making that event the natural stopping point for courses and this volume.

The placement of specific selections within this volume is intended to answer two pedagogical needs: that of chronological consistency and that of issue focus, so that students may see particular topics of importance in sufficient depth to give them serious examination. Consequently, while the sections into which the volume is divided generally follow a chronological order, materials within them at times overlap. For example, most writings presenting the Anti-Federalist critique of the Constitution are found in the section on the Bill of Rights rather than that on the Constitution. This has been done because the strongest Anti-Federalist arguments took the form of calls for revisions to the Constitution—revisions taken up under the rubric of amendments intended to protect the rights of the people. Not all Anti-Federalist concerns were addressed by the first Congress as it considered these

---

2. The classic work dealing with America's cultural inheritance is Russell Kirk, *The Roots of American Order* (Washington, 1991).

amendments. A key question in American history, however, concerns whether Anti-Federalist fears were addressed at all in that Congress or by those amendments we now call the Bill of Rights. Lincoln's relatively late "Address to the Wisconsin State Agricultural Society" also might be seen as coming at an "unchronological" place in the volume—in this case in the section on "Forging a Nation," before that on the "Prelude to War." Again, the reasoning is thematic. In this address Lincoln lays out his vision of America and the cultural as well as the economic promise of industrialization. Such issues are closely tied to debates over internal improvements and other concerns separating American regions. These concerns helped polarize the nation, but only after the slavery issue came to the forefront and exacerbated regional polarizations did they help to precipitate the Civil War.

Thanks are owed to the members of this volume's advisory board. I also thank James McClellan for important suggestions during the early development of this volume and Donald Livingston, Clyde Wilson, and Robert Waters for helpful suggestions. Any mistakes in judgment, selection, or performance are mine alone. Finally, I owe a special debt of gratitude to my wife, Antonia, for her patience and support.

Note on the Texts

The editor has sought to make only a bare minimum of changes to the texts included in this volume, so as to convey the flavor as well as content of the writings. Changes are limited to the following: The use of asterisks to mark deleted text has been replaced with the use of ellipses. Asterisks inserted without clear meaning or intent have been deleted, as have marginalia, extraneous quotation marks, and page numbers from previous editions that had been inserted in various texts. The letters "f" and "s" have been properly distinguished. Some of the longer titles have been shortened in accordance with modern usage. Headings in which the original text used anachronistic fonts or, for example, all capital letters, have been modernized and standardized.

The work of preceding editors in modernizing punctuation and spelling has not been tampered with. The editors of these previous volumes all expressed a desire to maintain strict fidelity to the original text and thereby incorporated only such minor modernizations in spelling, grammar, and punctuation as were absolutely necessary to promote readability and consistency. Those readers seeking specifics on such issues may find them in the relevant source volumes in the bibliography.

The principal issue of concern to the lay reader will be the inclusion of material in brackets. Such brackets denote material filled in by the editor, material questionable as to its true authorship, or in some instances text missing from the original.

Only those footnotes deemed necessary for understanding of the text have been reproduced here. However, in some instances (e.g., selections from Dickinson, Boucher, Noah Webster, and Story) footnotes are integral to the text, and in others explanatory notes are necessary. Footnotes of earlier editors are marked "Ed." and those few footnotes added by the current editor are marked "B. F."

In reproducing the fifth Lincoln-Douglas debate it was necessary to standardize fonts and to eliminate headings and subheadings inserted by the previous editors.

The American Republic

PART ONE Colonial Settlements and Societies

The FRAME of the

GOVERNMENT

OF THE

Province of Pennsilvania

IN

AMERICA:

Together with certain

L A W S

Agreed upon in England

BY THE

GOVERNOUR

AND

Divers FREE-MEN of the aforesaid
PROVINCE.

To be further Explained and Confirmed there by the first
Provincial Council and *General Assembly* that shall
be held, if they see meet.

Printed in the Year MDCLXXXII.

FAC-SIMILE OF TITLE PAGE OF PENN'S "FRAME OF GOVERNMENT, 1682."

Title page of Colonial Constitution of Pennsylvania. © Bettmann/CORBIS

No people has a true "beginning." Just as individuals come from families and neighborhoods, which instill them with certain beliefs and habits from an early age, so peoples come from other places and communities; they do not simply assemble and form themselves out of thin air. But the study of a people's inheritance must end somewhere. There must come a point at which we say, "Here are the basic, fundamental events and actions that set members of one community on their way to forming another." With Americans that point is the beginning of formal settlement in the New World.

Settlers brought to America a wealth of traditions, beliefs, habits, and motivations. They did not come to the New World as clean slates, nor did they write upon clean slates in forming new communities. Whether fleeing persecution, seeking wealth, or striving to establish a more godly community, they had to operate within the restrictions established by their charters or grants from the British king. Most obviously, these charters set down what authority would rule over settlers in each colony, whether it was a single proprietor, a governor answerable to the king, or a corporation set up under the king's auspices that also had to answer to the royal power. But troubles in Great Britain and the difficulties of long-distance travel in an era of wind-powered ships gave the settlers vast leeway in establishing local political, economic, and religious communities. This is not to say that events in Great Britain were irrelevant to those in the New World. The time of settlement was one of great unrest; it included the era of constitutional conflict between King James I and Parliament, followed by the English Civil War (1842–49), which

resulted in the beheading of Charles I and was itself followed by more than a decade of dictatorship under Oliver Cromwell and his Puritan army. But settlers in America exercised great freedom in establishing rules by which to govern themselves.

GOVERNING DOCUMENTS
For many centuries, the English people have had a particular faith in the power of the written word, and especially in the power of written documents to establish the means by which they were to be governed. Thus, despite the varying reasons for which English settlers came to America, written documents played a crucial role in the founding of the English colonies. And, despite many differences, these documents share important characteristics: an emphasis on the community's duties to God and on God's role as protector and judge of the community; a call on members of the community to serve the public good; and a reliance on written laws to enforce virtue and good order. In addition, by 1638, with the restoration of power to the Virginia House of Burgesses, legislative deliberation and consent were established as central governing principles in the American colonies. Documents in this section include frames of government that spell out how authority and lawmaking power shall be determined and list laws detailing rights, duties, and penalties for law-breaking. They also include more generalized covenants binding communities together in pursuit of a virtuous, religious life as well as more specific acts aimed at establishing workable township governance and securing the loyalty of the governors and the governed.

Virginia Articles, Laws, and Orders

1610–11

Virginia, the first English colony in America, was set up with a view toward economic profit. In the early years there were no profits. Life was harsh, and many people died from disease, hunger, and skirmishes with the Indians. The governing council, appointed in England, could not keep order, and the governor declared martial law. The following articles, issued by decree, were intended to restore order. Religion was accorded a crucial role in teaching the habits of good conduct during this era, and there was a common reliance in England and the other nations of Europe as well as in Virginia on the death penalty for a large number of offenses.

Articles, Laws, and Orders, Divine, Politic, and Martial for the Colony in Virginia

Articles, Lawes, and Orders, Divine, Politique, and Martiall for the Colony in Virginea: first established by Sir Thomas Gates Knight, Lieutenant Generall, the 24th of May 1610, exemplified and approved by the Right Honourable Sir Thomas West Knight, Lord Lawair, Lord Governor and Captaine Generall the 12th day of June 1610. Againe exemplified and enlarged by Sir Thomas Dale Knight, Marshall, and Deputie Governour, the 22nd of June, 1611.

Whereas his Majestie like himselfe a most zealous Prince hath in his owne Realmes a principall care of true Religion, and reverence to God, and hath alwaies strictly commaunded his Generals and Governours, with all his forces wheresoever, to let their waies be like his ends for the glorie of God.

And forasmuch as no good service can be performed, or warre well managed, where militarie discipline is not observed, and militarie discipline cannot be kept, where the rules or chiefe parts thereof, be not certainely set downe, and generally knowne, I have (with the advise and counsell of Sir Thomas Gates Knight, Lieutenant Generall) adhered unto the lawes divine, and orders politique, and martiall of his Lordship (the same exemplified) an addition of such others, as I have found either the necessitie of the present State of the Colonie to require, or the infancie, and weaknesses of the body thereof, as yet able to digest, and doe now publish them to all persons in the Colonie, that they may as well take knowledge of the Lawes themselves, as of the penaltie and punishment, which without partialitie shall be inflicted upon the breakers of the same.

1. First since we owe our highest and supreme duty, our greatest, and all our allegeance to him, from whom all power and authoritie is derived, and flowes as from the first, and onely fountaine, and being especiall souldiers emprest in this sacred cause, we must alone expect our success from him, who is only the blesser of all good attempts, the King of kings, the commaunder of commaunders, and Lord of Hostes, I do strictly commaund and charge all Captaines and Officers, of what qualitie or nature soever, whether commanders in the field, or in towne, or townes, forts or fortresses, to have a care that the Almightie God bee duly and daily served, and that they call upon their people to heare Sermons, as that also they diligently frequent Morning and Evening praier themselves by their owne exemplar and daily life, and duties herein, encouraging others thereunto, and that such, who shall often and wilfully absent themselves, be duly punished according to the martiall law in that case provided.

2. That no man speake impiously or maliciously, against the holy and blessed Trinitie, or any of the three persons, that is to say, against God the Father, God the Son, and God the holy Ghost, or against the knowne Articles of the Christian faith, upon paine of death.

3. That no man blaspheme Gods holy name upon paine of death, or use unlawful oathes, taking the name of God in vaine, curse, or banne,[1] upon paine of severe punishment for the first offence so committed, and for the sec-

---

1. Calling down evil upon a person.—Ed.

ond, to have a bodkin[2] thrust through his tongue, and if he continues the blaspheming of Gods holy name, for the third time so offending, he shall be brought to a martiall court, and there receive censure of death for his offence.

4. No man shall use any traiterous words against his Majesties Person, or royall authority upon paine of death.

5. No man shall speake any word, or do any act, which may tend to the derision, or despight[3] of Gods holy word upon paine of death: Nor shall any man unworthily demeane himself unto any Preacher, or Minister of the same, but generally hold them in all reverent regard, and dutiful intreatie,[4] otherwise he the offender shall openly be whipt three times, and ask publike forgivenesse in the assembly of the congregation three several Saboth Daies.

6. Everie man and woman duly twice a day upon the first towling of the Bell shall upon the working daies repaire unto the Church, to hear divine Service upon pain of losing his or her dayes allowance for the first omission, for the second to be whipt, and for the third to be condemned to the Gallies for six Moneths. Likewise no man or woman shall dare to violate or breake the Sabboth by any gaming, publique or private abroad, or at home, but duly sanctifie and observe the same, both himselfe and his familie, by preparing themselves at home with private prayer, that they may be the better fitted for the publique, according to the commandements of God, and the orders of our Church, as also every man and woman shall repaire in the morning to the divine service, and Sermons preached upon the Saboth day, and in the afternoon to divine service, and Catechising, upon paine for the first fault to lose their provision, and allowance for the whole weeke following, for the second to lose the said allowance, and also to be whipt, and for the third to suffer death.

7. All Preachers or Ministers within this our Colonie, or Colonies, shall in the Forts, where they are resident, after divine Service, duly preach every Sabbath day in the forenoone, and Catechise in the afternoone, and weekly say the divine service, twice every day, and preach every Wednesday, likewise every Minister where he is resident, within the same Fort, or Fortresse, Townes or Towne, shall chuse unto him, foure of the most religious and better dis-

posed as well to informe of the abuses and neglects of the people in their duties, and service to God, as also to the due reparation, and keeping of the Church handsome, and fitted with all reverent observances thereunto belonging: likewise every Minister shall keepe a faithful and true Record, or Church Booke of all Christnings, Marriages, and deaths of such our people, as shall happen within their Fort, or Fortresses, Townes or Towne at any time, upon the burthen of a neglectfull conscience, and upon paine of losing their Entertainment.[5]

8. He that upon pretended malice, shall murther or take away the life of any man, shall bee punished with death.

9. No man shal commit the horrible, and detestable sins of Sodomie upon pain of death; and he or she that can be lawfully convict of Adultery shall be punished with death. No man shall ravish or force any woman, maid or Indian, or other, upon pain of death, and know that he or shee, that shall commit fornication, and evident proofe made thereof, for their first fault shall be whipt, for the second they shall be whipt, and for their third they shall be whipt three times a weeke for one month, and aske publique forgivenesse in the Assembly of the Congregation.

10. No man shall bee found guilty of Sacriledge, which is a Trespasse as well committed in violating the abusing any sacred ministry, duty or office of the Church, irreverently, or prophanely, as by beeing a Church robber, to filch, steale or carry away anything out of the Church appertaining thereunto, or unto any holy, and consecrated place, to the divine Service of God, which no man should doe upon paine of death: likewise he that shall rob the store of any commodities therein, of what quality soever, whether provisions of victuals, or of arms, Trucking stuffe,[6] Apparrell, Linnen, or Wollen, Hose or Shooes, Hats or Caps, Instruments or Tooles of Steele, Iron, etc. or shall rob from his fellow souldier, or neighbor, any thing that is his, victuals, apparell, household stuffe, toole, or what necessary else soever, by water or land, out of boate, house, or knapsack, shall bee punished with death.

11. Hee that shall take an oath untruly, or beare false witnesse in any cause, or against any man whatsoever, shall be punished with death.

12. No manner of person whatsoever, shall dare to de-

2. A small dagger or stiletto.—Ed.
3. Open defiance.—Ed.
4. Treatment.—Ed.

5. Provisions.—Ed.
6. Materials for barter or exchange.—Ed.

tract, slaunder, columniate, or utter unseemly, and unfitting speeches, either against his Majesties Honourable Councell for this Colony, resident in England, or against the Committees, Assistants unto the said Councell, or against the zealous indeavors, and intentions of the whole body of Adventurers for this pious and Christian Plantation, or against any publique book, or bookes, which by their mature advise, and grave wisdomes, shall be thought fit, to be set foorth and publisht, for the advancement of the good of this Colony, and the felicity thereof, upon paine for the first time so offending, to be whipt three severall times, and upon his knees to acknowledge his offence and to aske forgivenesse upon the Saboth day in the assembly of the congregation, and for the second time so offending to be condemned to the Galley for three yeares, and for the third time so offending to be punished with death.

13. No manner of person whatsoever, contrarie to the word of God (which tyes every particular and private man, for conscience sake to obedience), and duty of the Magistrate, and such as shall be placed in authoritie over them, shall detract, slaunder, calumniate, murmur, mutenie, resist, disobey, or neglect the commaundments, either of the Lord Governour, and Captaine Generalle, the Lieutenant Generall, the Martiall, the Councell, or any authorised Captaine, Commaunder or publike Officer, upon paine for the first time so offending to be whipt three severall times, and upon his knees to acknowledge his offence, with asking forgivenesse upon the Saboth day in the assembly of the congregation, and for the second time so offending to be condemned to the Gally for three yeares: and for the third time so offending to be punished with death.

14. No man shall give any disgraceful words, or commit any act to the disgrace of any person in this Colonie, or any part thereof, upon paine of being tied head and feete together, upon the guard everie night for the space of one moneth, besides to bee publikely disgraced himselfe, and be made incapable ever after to possesse any place, or execute any office in this imployment.

15. No man of what condition soever shall barter, trucke, or trade with the Indians, except he be thereunto appointed by lawful authority upon paine of death.

16. No man shall rifle or dispoile, by force or violence, take away any thing from any Indian coming to trade, or otherwise, upon paine of death.

17. No Cape Marchant,[7] or Provant Master,[8] or Munition Master, or Truck Master, or keeper of any store, shall at any time imbezell, sell, or give away any thing under his Charge to any Favorite, of his, more than unto any other, whome necessity shall require in that case to have extraordinary allowance of provisions, nor shall they give a false accompt unto the Lord Governour, and Captaine Generall, unto the Lieutenant Generall, unto the Marshall, or any deputed Governor, at any time having the commaund of the Colony, with intent to defraud the said Colony, upon paine of death.

18. No man shall imbezel or take away the goods of any man that dyeth, or is imployed from the town or Fort where he dwelleth in any other occasioned remote service, for the time, upon pain of whipping three severall times, and restitution of the said goods againe, and in danger of incurring the penalty of the tenth Article, if so it may come under the construction of theft. And if any man die and make a will, his goods shall be accordingly disposed; if hee die intestate, his goods shall bee put into the store, and being valued by two sufficient praisors, his next of kinne (according to the common Lawes of England), shall from the Company, Committees, or adventurers, receive due satisfaction in moneys, according as they were praised, by which means the Colonie shall be better furnished; and the goods more carefully preserved, for the right heire, and the right heire receive content for the same in England.

19. There shall be no Capttain, Master, Marriner, saylor, or any else of what quality or condition soever, belonging to any Ship or Ships, at this time remaining, or which shall hereafter arrive within this our River, bargaine, buy, truck, or trade with any one member in this Colony, man, woman, or child, for any toole or instrument of iron, steel, or what else, whether appertaining to Smith Carpenter, Joyner, Shipwright, or any manuall occupation, or handicraft man whatsoever, resident within our Colonie, nor shall they buy or bargaine, for any apparell, linnen, or wollen, householdstuffe, bedde, bedding, sheete towels, napkins, brasse, pewter, or such like, eyther for ready money, or provisions, nor shall they exchange their provisions, of what quality soever, whether Butter, Cheese,

7. An officer who supervised the provision house of a fort.—Ed.
8. The master of the provisions, who also provided the soldiers' allowance.—Ed.

Bisket, meal, Oatmele, Aquavite,[9] oyle, Bacon, any kind of Spice, or such like, for any such aforesaid instruments, or tooles, apparell, or householdstuffe, at any time, or so long as they shall here remain, from the date of these presents upon paine of losse of their wages in England, confiscation and forfeiture of such their monies and provisions, and upon peril beside of such corporall punishment as shall be inflicted upon them by verdict and censure of a martiall Court: Nor shall any officer, souldier, or Trades man, or any else of what sort soever, members of this Colony, dare to sell any such Toole, or instruments, necessary and usefull, for the businesse of the Colonie, or trucke, sell, exchange, or give away his apparell, or household stuffe of what sort soever, unto any such Seaman, either for mony, or any such foresaid provisions, upon paine of 3 times severall whipping, for the one offender, and the other upon perill of incurring censure, whether of disgrace, or addition of such punishment, as shall bee thought fit by a Court martiall.

20. Whereas sometimes heeretofore the covetous and wide affections of some greedy and ill disposed Seamen, Saylers, and Marriners, laying hold upon the advantage of the present necessity, under which the Colony sometimes suffered, have sold unto our people, provisions of Meale, Oatmeale, Bisket, Butter, Cheese etc., at unreasonable rates, and prises unconscionable: for avoiding the like to bee now put in practise, there shall no Captain, Master, Marriner, or Saylor, or what Officer else belonging to any ship, or shippes, now within our river, or heereafter which shall arrive, shall dare to bargaine, exchange, barter, truck, trade, or sell, upon paine of death, unto any one Landman[10] member of this present Colony, any provisions of what kind soever, above the determined valuations, and prises, set downe and proclaimed, and sent therefore unto each of your severall ships, to bee fixed uppon your Maine mast, to the intent that want of due notice, and ignorance in this case, be no excuse, or plea, for any offender herein.

21. Sithence[11] we are not to bee a little carefull, and our young Cattell, and Breeders may be cherished, that by the preservation, and incrase of them, the Colony heere may receive in due time assured and great benefite, and the adventurers at home may be eased of so great a burthen, by sending unto us yeerely supplies of this kinde, which now heere for a while, carefully attended, may turne their supplies unto us into provisions of other qualities, when of these wee shall be able to subsist our selves, and which wee may in short time, be powerful enough to doe, if we wil according to our owne knowledge of what is good for our selves, forbeare to work into our own wants, againe, by over hasty destroying, and devouring the stockes, and authors of so profitable succeeding a Commodity, as increase of Cattell, Kine, Hogges, Goates, Poultrie etc. must of necessity bee granted, in every common mans judgement, to render unto us: Now know thee therefore, these promises carefully considered, that it is our will and pleasure, that every one, of what quality or condition soever hee bee, in this present Colony, to take due notice of this our Edict, whereby wee do strictly charge and command, that no man shall dare to kill, or destroy any Bull, Cow, Calfe, Mare, Horse, Colt, Goate, Swine, Cocke, Henne, Chicken, Dogge, Turkie, or any tame Cattel, or Poultry, of what condition soever; whether his owne, or appertaining to another man, without leave from the Generall, upon paine of death in the Principall, and in the accessary, burning in the Hand, and losse of his eares, and unto the concealer of the same four and twenty houres of whipping, with addition of further punishment, as shall be thought fitte by the censure, and verdict of a Martiall Court.

22. There shall no man or woman, Launderer or Launderesse, dare to wash any uncleane Linnen, drive bucks,[12] or throw out the water or sudes of fowle cloathes, in the open streete, within the Pallizadoes,[13] or within forty foote of the same, nor rench,[14] and make cleane, any kettle, pot, or pan, or such like vessell within twenty foote of the olde well, or new pump; nor shall any one aforesaid, within less than a quarter of one mile from the pallizadoes, dare to doe the necessities of nature, since by these unmanly, slothfull, and loathsome immodesties, the whole Fort may bee choaked, and poisoned with ill aires, and so corrupt (as in all reason cannot but much infect the same) and this shall they take notice of, and avoide, upon paine of whip-

9. Spirits or alcoholic beverages.—Ed.
10. Literally a man of the land—not a sailor.—Ed.
11. Seeing that.—Ed.

12. Bleach clothes.—Ed.
13. Pallisades.—Ed.
14. Rinse.—Ed.

ping and further punishment, as shall be thought meete, by the censure of a martiall Court.

23. No man shall imbezell, lose, or willingly breake, or fraudulently make away, either Spade, Shovell, Hatchet, Axe, Mattocke,[15] or other toole or instrument upon paine of whipping.

24. Any man that hath any edge toole, either of his owne, or which hath heeretofore beene belonging to the store, see that he bring it instantly to the storehouse, where he shall receive it againe by a particular note, both of the toole, and of his name taken, that such a toole unto him appertaineth, at whose hands, upon any necessary occasion, the said toole may be required, and this shall he do, upon paine of severe punishment.

25. Every man shall have an especiall and due care, to keepe his house sweete and cleane, as also so much of the streete, as lieth before his door, and especially he shall so provide, and set his bedstead whereon he lieth, that it may stand three foote at least from the ground, as will answere the contrarie at a martiall Court.

26. Every tradesman in their severall occupation, trade and function, shall duly and daily attend his worke upon his said trade or occupation, upon perill for his first fault, and negligence therein, to have his entertainment checkt for one moneth, for his second fault three moneth, for his third one yeare, and if he continue still unfaithfull and negligent therein, to be condemned to the Gally for three yeare.

27. All overseers of workemen, shall be carefull in seeing that performed, which is given them in charge, upon paine of such punishment as shall be inflicted upon him by a martiall Court.

28. No souldier or tradesman, but shall be readie, both in the morning, and in the afternoone, upon the beating of the Drum, to goe out unto his worke, nor shall hee return home, or from his worke, before the Drum beate againe, and the officer appointed for that business, bring him of, upon perill for the first fault to lie upon the Guard head and heeles together all night, for the second time so faulting to be whipt, and for the third time so offending to be condemned to the Gallies for a yeare.

29. No man or woman, (upon paine of death) shall runne away from the Colonie, to Powhathan, or any savage Weroance[16] else whatsoever.

15. A tool used to remove trees.—Ed.
16. A powerful chief of an Indian confederation south of the Potomac River.—Ed.

30. He that shall conspire any thing against the person of the Lord Governour, and Captaine Generall, against the Lieutenant Generall, or against the Marshall, or against any publike service commaunded by them, for the dignitie, and advancement of the good of the Colony, shall be punished with death: and he that shall have knowledge of any such pretended act of disloyalty or treason, and shall not reveale the same unto his Captaine, or unto the Governour of that fort or Towne wherein he is, within the space of one houre, shall for the concealing of the same after that time, be not onely held an accessary, but alike culpable as the principall traitor or conspirer, and for the same likewise he shall suffer death.

31. What man or woman soever, shall rob any garden, publike or private, being set to weed the same, or wilfully pluck up therein any roote, herbe, or flower, to spoile and wast or steale the same, or robbe any vineyard, or gather up the grapes, or steale any eares of the corne growing, whether in the ground belonging to the same fort or towne where he dwelleth, or in any other, shall be punished with death.

32. Whosoever Seaman, or Landman or what qualitie, or in what place of commaund soever, shall be imployed upon any discovery, trade, or fishing voiage into any of the rivers within the precincts of our Colonie, shall for the safety of those men who are committed to his commaund, stand upon good and carefull guard, for the prevention of any treachery in the Indian, and if they touch upon any shore, they shal be no less circumspect, and warie, with good and carefull guard day and night, putting forth good Centinell, and observing the orders and discipline of watch and ward, and when they have finished the discovery, trade, or fishing, they shall make hast with all speed, with such Barke or Barkes, Pinisse, Gallie, Ship. etc. as they shall have the commaund of, for the same purpose, to James towne againe, not presuming to goe beyond their commission, or to carry any such Barke or Barkes, Gally, Pinnice, Ship. etc. for England or any other countrey in the actual possession of any Christian Prince, upon perill to be held an enemie to this plantation, and traitor thereunto, and accordingly to lie liable unto such censure of punishment (if they arrive in England) as shall be thought fit by the Right Honourable Lords, his Majesties Councell for this Colonie, and if it shall so happen, that he or they shall be prevented, and brought backe hither againe into the Colonie, their trecherous flight to be punished with death.

33. There is not one man nor woman in this Colonie now present, or hereafter to arrive, but shall give up an account of his and their faith, and religion, and repaire unto the Minister, that by his conference with them, hee may understand, and gather, whether heretofore they have beene sufficiently instructed, and catechised in the principles and grounds of Religion, whose weaknesse and ignorance herein, the Minister finding, and advising them in all love and charitie, to repaire often unto him, to receive therein a greater measure of knowledge, if they shal refuse so to repaire unto him, and he the Minister give notice thereof unto the Governour, or that chiefe officer of that towne or fort, wherein he or she, the parties so offending shall remaine, the Governour shall cause the offender for his first time of refusall to be whipt, for the second time to be whipt twice, and to acknowledge his fault upon the Saboth day, in the assembly of the congregation, and for the third time to be whipt every day until he heath made the same acknowledgement, and asked forgivenesse for the same, and shall repaire unto the Minister, to be further instructed as aforesaid: and upon the Saboth when the Minister shall catechise, and of him demaund any question concerning his faith and knowledge, he shall not refuse to make answere upon the same perill.

34. What man or woman soever, Laundrer or Laundresse appointed to wash the foule linnen of any one labourer or souldier, or any one else as it is their duties so to doe, performing little, or no other service for their allowance out of the store, and daily provisions, and supply of other necessaries unto the Colonie, and shall from the said labourer or souldier, or any one else of what qualitie whatsoever, either take any thing for washing, or withhold or steale from him any such linnen committed to her to wash, or change the same willingly and wittingly, with purpose to give him worse, old and torne linnen for his good, and proofe shall be made thereof, she shall be whipped for the same, and lie in prison till she make restitution of such linnen, withheld or changed.

35. No Captaine, Master, or Mariner, of what condition soever, shall depart or carry out of the river, any Ship, Barke, Barge, Gally, Pinnace etc. Roaders[17] belonging to the Colonie, either now therein, or hither arriving, without leave and commission from the Generall or chiefe Commaunder of the Colonie upon paine of death.

36. No man or woman whatsoever, members of this Colonie, shall sell or give unto any Captine, Marriner, Master, or Sailer, etc. any commoditie of this countrey, of what quality soever, to be transported out of the Colonie, for his or their owne private uses, upon paine of death.

37. If any souldier indebted, shall refuse to pay his debts unto his creditor, his creditor shall informe his Captaine, if the Captaine cannot agree the same, the creditor shall informe the Marshals civill and principall officer, who shall preferre for the creditor a bill of complaint at the Marshals Court, where the creditor shal have Justice.

All such Bakers as are appointed to bake bread, or what else, either for the store to be given out in generall, or for any one in particular, shall not steale nor imbezell, loose, or defraud any man of his due and proper weight and measure, nor use any dishonest and deceiptfull tricke to make the bread weight heavier, or make it courser upon purpose to keepe backe any part or measure of the flower or meale committed unto him, nor aske, take, or detaine any one loafe more or lesse for his hire or paines for so baking, since whilest he who delivered unto him such meale or flower, being to attend the businesse of the Colonie, such baker or bakers are imposed upon no other service or duties, but onely so to bake for such as do worke, and this shall hee take notice of, upon paine for the first time offending herein of losing his eares, and for the second time to be condemned a yeare to the Gallies, and for the third time offending, to be condemned to the Gallies for three yeares.

All such cookes as are appointed to seeth,[18] bake or dresse any manner of way, flesh, fish, or what else, of what kind soever, either for the generall company, or for any private man, shall not make lesse, or cut away any part or parcel of such flesh, fish, etc. Nor detaine or demaund any party or parcell, as allowance or hire for his so dressing the same, since as aforesaid of the baker, hee or they such Cooke or Cookes, exempted from other publike works abroad, are to attend such seething and dressing of such publike flesh, fish, or other provisions of what kind soever, as their service and duties expected from them by the Colony, and this shall they take notice of, upon paine for the first time offending herein, of losing his eares, and for the second time to be condemned a yeare to the Gallies: and for the third time offending to be condemned to the Gallies for three years.

---

17. A vessel used in sheltered water near the shore.—Ed.

18. Boil.—Ed.

All fishermen, dressers of Sturgeon or such like appointed to fish, or to cure the said Sturgeon for the use of the Colonie, shall give a just and true account of all such fish as they shall take by day or night, of what kinds soever, the same to bring unto the Governour: As also of all such kegges of Sturgeon or Caviare as they shall prepare and cure upon perill for the first time offending heerein, of loosing his eares, and for the second time to be condemned a yeare to the Gallies, and for the third time offending, to be condemned to the Gallies for three yeares. Every Minister or Preacher shall every Sabboth day before Catechising, read all these lawes and ordinances, publikely in the assembly of the congregation upon paine of his entertainment checkt for that weeke.

The Mayflower Compact

November 11, 1620

The Puritans originally sought to settle near preexisting communities in the colony of Virginia. Their ship, the *Mayflower*, was blown off course, and they landed far to the north. But they had intended from the first to establish a separate community devoted to a pious life lived in common. They self-consciously formed this community among themselves, without looking to a higher temporal authority, through the Mayflower Compact.

The Mayflower Compact

In the Name of God, Amen. We whose Names are underwritten, the Loyal Subjects of our dread Soveraign Lord King *James,* by the grace of God of *Great Britain, France* and *Ireland,* King, *Defendor of the Faith &c.* Having undertaken for the glory of God, and advancement of the Christian Faith, and the Honour of our K[i]ng and Countrey, a Voyage to plant the first Colony in the Northern parts of *Virginia;* Do by these Presents, solemnly and mutually, in the presence of God and one another, Covenant and Combine our selves together into a Civil Body Politick, for our better ordering and preservation, and furtherance of the ends aforesaid: and by virtue hereof do enact, constitute, and frame, such just and equal Laws, Ordinances, Acts, Constitutions and Officers, from time to time, as shall be thought most meet and convenient for the general good of the Colony; unto which we promise all due submission and obedience. In witness whereof we have hereunto subscribed our Names at *Cape Cod,* the eleventh of *November,* in the Reign of our Soveraign Lord King *James,* of *England, France* and *Ireland* the eighteenth, and of *Scotland* the fifty fourth, *Anno Dom.* 1620.

John Carver,
William Bradford,
Edward Winslow,
William Brewster,
Isaac Allerton,
Myles Standish,
John Alden,
John Turner,
Francis Eaton,
James Chilton,
John Craxton,
John Billington,
Joses Fletcher,
John Goodman,
Samuel Fuller,
Christopher Martin,
William Mullins,
William White,
Richard Warren,
John Howland,
Steven Hopkins

Digery Priest,
Thomas Williams,
Gilbert Winslow,
Edmund Margesson,
Peter Brown,
Richard Britteridge,
George Soule,
Edward Tilly,
John Tilly,
Francis Cooke,
Thomas Rogers,
Thomas Tinker,
John Ridgdale,
Edward Fuller,
Richard Clark,
Richard Gardiner,
John Allerton,
Thomas English,
Edward Doten,
Edward Liester.

Fundamental Orders of Connecticut

January 14, 1639

English settlements were formed with the official sanction, and under the English-written rules, of colonial charters. But these charters were often undermined by events in the New World—most particularly by the movement of people seeking better land, safety, and other considerations important to their survival and way of life. In 1639, communities officially falling under the authority of the charters for Connecticut and the separate colony of New Haven found it in their interest to combine their governments. The result was the Fundamental Orders of Connecticut, one of the first written constitutions in America. It was essentially ratified in 1662 by the king, made the state constitution in 1776 (references to the king being omitted), and remained in effect until it was finally replaced in 1816.

Fundamental Orders of Connecticut

Forasmuch as it hath pleased the Allmighty God by the wise disposition of his diuyne[1] pruidence so to Order and dispose of things that we the Inhabitants and Residents of Windsor, Harteford and Wethersfield are now cohabiting and dwelling in and vppon the River of Conectecotte and the Lands thereunto adioyneing; and Well knowing where a people are gathered togather the word of God requires that to mayntayne the peace and vnion of such a people there should be an orderly and decent Gouerment established according to God, to order and dispose of the affayres of the people at all seasons as occation shall require; doe therefore assotiate and conioyne our selues to be as one Publike State or Commonwelth; and doe, for our selues and our Successors and such as shall be adioyned to vs att any tyme hereafter, enter into Combination and Confederation togather, to mayntayne and prsearue the liberty and purity of the gospell of our Lord Jesus wch we now prfesse, as also the disciplyne of the Churches, wch according to the truth of the said gospell is now practised amongst vs; As also in o[u]r Cieuell[2] Affaires to be guided and gouerned according to such Lawes, Rules, Orders and decrees as shall be made, ordered & decreed, as followeth:—

1. It is Ordered, sentenced and decreed, that there shall be yerely two generall Assemblies or Courts, the [first] on the second thursday in Aprill, the other the second thursday in September, following; the first shall be called the Courte of Election, wherein shall be yerely Chosen fro[m] tyme to tyme soe many Magestrats and other publike Officers as shall be found requisitte: Whereof one to be chosen Gouernour for the yeare ensueing and vntill another be chosen, and noe other Magestrate to be chosen for more then one yeare; pruided allwayes there be six chosen besids the Gouernour; wch being chosen and sworne according to an Oath recorded for that purpose shall haue power to administer iustice according to the Lawes here established, and for want thereof according to the rule of the word of God, wch choise shall be made by all that are admitted freemen and haue taken the Oath of Fidellity, and doe cohabitte wthin this Jurisdiction, (Hauing been admitted Inhabitants by the major prt of the Towne wherein they liue,) or the mayor prte of such as shall be then prsent.

2. It is Ordered, sentensed and decreed, that the Election of the aforesaid Magestrats shall be on this manner: euery prson prsent and quallified for choyse shall bring in (to the prsons deputed to receaue them) one single papr wth the name of him written in yt whome he desires to haue Gouernour, and he that hath the greatest number of papers shall be Gouernor for that yeare. And the rest of the Magestrats or publike Officers to be chosen in this manner: The Secrtary for the tyme being shall first read the names of all that are to be put to choise and then shall seuerally nominate them distinctly, and euery one that would haue the prson nominated to be chosen shall bring in one single paper written vppon, and he that would not haue him chosen shall bring in a blanke: and euery one that hath more written papers than blanks shall be a Magistrat for that yeare; wch papers shall be receaued and told by one or more

---

1. In this document, as in others, the letters *u* and *v* are often interchanged. Divine is here effectively rendered divyne. The letters *i* and *j* are likewise often interchanged.—Ed.

2. Civil.—Ed.

that shall be then chosen by the court and sworne to be faythfull therein; but in case there should not be sixe chosen as aforesaid, besids the Gouernor, out of those wch are nominated, then he or they wch haue the most written paprs shall be a Magestrate or Magestrats for the ensueing yeare, to make vp the aforesaid number.

3. It is Ordered, sentenced and decreed, that the Secretary shall not nominate any prson, nor shall any prson be chosen newly into the Magestracy wch was not prpownded in some Generall Courte before, to be nominated the next Election; and to that end yt shall be lawfull for ech of the Townes aforesaid by their deputyes to nominate any two who they conceaue fitte to be put to election; and the Courte may ad so many more as they iudge requisitt.

4. It is Ordered, sentenced and decreed that noe prson be chosen Gouernor aboue once in two years, and that the Gouernor be always a member of some approved congregation, and formerly of the Magestracy wthin this Jurisdiction; and all the Magestrats Freemen of this Comonwelth: and that no Magestrate or other publike officer shall execute any prte of his or their Office before they are seuerally sworne, wch shall be done in the face of the Courte if they be prsent, and in case of absence by some deputed for that purpose.

5. It is Ordered, sentenced and decreed, that to the aforesaid Courte of Election the seurall Townes shall send their deputyes, and when the Elections are ended they may prceed in any publike searuice as at other Courts. Also the other Generall Courte in September shall be for makeing of lawes, and any other publike occation, wch conserns the good of the Commonwealth.

6. It is Ordered, sentenced and decreed, that the Gournor shall, ether by himselfe or by the secretary, send out summons to the Constables of eur[3] Towne for the cauleing of these two standing Courts, on month at lest before their seurall tymes: And also if the Gournor and the gretest prte of the Magestrats see cause vppon any spetiall occation to call a generall Courte, they may giue order to the secretary soe to do wthin fowerteene dayes warneing; and if vrgent necessity so require, vppon a shorter notice, giueing sufficient grownds for yt to the deputyes when they meete, or else be questioned for the same; And if the Gournor and Mayor[4] prte of Magestrats shall ether neglect

or refuse to call the two Generall standing Courts or ether of them, as also at other tymes when to occations of the Commonwelth require, the Freemen thereof, or the Mayor prte of them, shall petition to them soe to doe: if then yt be ether denyed or neglected the said Freemen or the Mayor prte of them shall haue power to giue order to the Constables of the seuerall Townes to doe the same, and so may meete togather, and chuse to themselues a Moderator, and may prceed to do any Acte of power, wch any other Generall Courte may.

7. It is Ordered, sentenced and decreed that after there are warrants giuen out for any of the said Generall Courts, the Constable or Constables of ech Towne shall forthwth give notice distinctly to the inhabitants of the same, in some Publike Assembly or by goeing or sending from howse to howse, that at a place and tyme by him or them lymited and sett, they meet and assemble themselues togather to elect and chuse certen deputyes to be att the Generall Courte then following to agitate the afayres of the comonwelth; wch said Deputyes shall be chosen by all that are admitted Inhabitants in the seurall Townes and haue taken the oath of fidellity; pruided that non be chosen a Deputy for any Generall Courte wch is not a Freeman of this Commonwelth.

The a-foresaid deputyes shall be chosen in manner following: euery prson that is prsent and quallified as before exprssed, shall bring the names of such, written in seurall papers, as they desire to haue chosen for that Imployment, and these 3 or 4, more or lesse, being the number agreed on to be chosen for that tyme, that haue greatest number of papers written for them shall be dputyes for that Courte; whose names shall be endorsed on the backe side of the warrant and returned into the Courte, wth the Constable or Constables hand vnto the same.

8. It is Ordered, sentenced and decreed, that Wyndsor, Hartford and Wethersfield shall haue power, ech Towne, to send fower of their freemen as deputyes to euery Generall Courte; and whatsoeuer other Townes shall be hereafter added to this Jurisdiction, they shall send so many deputyes as the Courte shall judge meete, a resonable prportion to the number of Freemen that are in the said Townes being to be attended therein; wch deputyes shall have the power of the whole Towne to giue their voats and alowance to all such lawes and orders as may be for the publike good, and unto wch the said Townes are to be bownd.

9. It is ordered and decreed, that the deputyes thus cho-

3. Every.—Ed.
4. Major.—Ed.

sen shall haue power and liberty to appoynt a tyme and a place of meeting togather before any Generall Courte to aduise and consult of all such things as may concerne the good of the publike, as also to examine their owne Elections, whether according to the order, and if they or the gretest prte of them find any election to be illegall they may seclud such for prsent from their meeting, and returne the same and their resons to the Courte; and if yt proue true, the Courte may fyne the prty or prtyes so intruding and the Towne, if they see cause, and giue out a warrant to goe to a newe election in a legall way, either whole or in prte. Also the said deputyes shall haue power to fyne any that shall be disorderly at their meetings, or for not comeing in due tyme or place according to appoyntment; and they may return the said fynes into the Courte if yt be refused to be paid, and the tresurer to take notice of yt, and to estreete or levy the same as he doth other fynes.

10. It is Ordered, sentenced and decreed, that euery Generall Courte, except such as through neglecte of the Gournor and the greatest prte of Magestrats the Freemen themselves doe call, shall consist of the Gouernor, or some one chosen to moderate the Court, and fower other Magestrats at lest, wth the mayor prte of the deputyes of the seuerall Townes legally chosen; and in case the Freemen or mayor prte of them through neglect or refusall of the Gouernor and mayor prte of the magestrats, shall call a Courte, that yt shall consist of the mayor prte of Freemen that are prsent or their deputyes, wth a Moderator chosen by them: *In wch said Generall Courts shall consist the supreme power of the Commonwelth,* and they only shall haue power to make laws or repeale them, to graunt leuyes, to admitt of Freemen, dispose of lands vndisposed of, to seuerall Townes or prsons, and also shall haue power to call ether Courte or Magestrate or any other prson whatsoeuer into question for any misdemeanour, and may for just causes displace or deale otherwise according to the nature of the offence; and also may deale in any other matter that concerns the good of this commonwelth, excepte election of Magestrats, wch shall be done by the whole boddy of Freemen: In wch Courte the Gouernour or Moderator shall

haue power to order the Courte to giue liberty of spech, and silence vnceasonable and disorderly speakeings, to put all things to voate, and in case the vote be equall to haue the casting voice. But non of these Courts shall be adiorned or dissolued wthout the consent of the major prte of the Court.

11. It is ordered, sentenced and decreed, that when any Generall Courte vppon the occations of the Commonwelth haue agreed vppon any sume or somes of mony to be leuyed vppon the seuerall Townes wthin this Jurisdiction, that a Committee be chosen to sett out and appoynt wt shall be the prportion of euery Towne to pay of the said leuy, prvided the Committees be made vp of an equall number out of each Towne.

14th January, 1638, the 11 Orders abouesaid are voted.

The Oath of the Gournor, for the Prsent

I N.W. being now chosen to be Gournor wthin this Jurisdiction, for the yeare ensueing, and vntil a new be chosen, doe sweare by the greate and dreadful name of the everliueing God, to prmote the publicke good and peace of the same, according to the best of my skill; as also will mayntayne all lawfull priuiledges of this Commonwealth: as also that all wholsome lawes that are or shall be made by lawfull authority here established, be duly executed; and will further the execution of Justice according to the rule of Gods word; so helpe me God, in the name of the Lo: Jesus Christ.

The Oath of a Magestrate, for the Prsent

I, N.W. being chosen a Magestrate wthin this Jurisdiction for the yeare ensueing, doe sweare by the great and dreadfull name of the euerliueing God, to prmote the publike good and peace of the same, according to the best of my skill, and that I will mayntayne all the lawfull priuiledges therof according to my vnderstanding, as also assist in the execution of all such wholsome lawes as are made or shall be made by lawfull authority heare established, and will further the execution of Justice for the tyme aforesaid according to the righteous rule of Gods word; so helpe me God, etc.

The Massachusetts Body of Liberties

December 1641

The Puritan leader and former lawyer Nathaniel Ward proposed this code summarizing and systematizing laws already enacted in Massachusetts. Based on principles derived from biblical, or Mosaic, law and England's common, or judge-made, law, this code intentionally served as a check on political power. It forbade the authorities to take certain actions against individuals and set forth judicial and other procedures intended to protect them in their property and customary actions. The Massachusetts Body of Liberties is generally seen as an important source of rights recognized in the first ten amendments to the American Constitution, or Bill of Rights.

The Massachusetts Body of Liberties

A Coppie of the Liberties of the Massachusets Collonie in New England

The free fruition of such liberties Immunities and priveledges as humanitie, Civilitie, and Christianitie call for as due to every man in his place and proportion; without impeachment and Infringement hath ever bene and ever will be the tranquillitie and Stabilitie of Churches and Commonwealths. And the deniall or deprivall thereof, the disturbance if not the ruine of both.

We hould it therefore our dutie and safetie whilst we are about the further establishing of this Government to collect and express all such freedomes as for present we foresee may concerne us, and our posteritie after us, And to ratify them with our sollemne consent.

Wee doe therefore this day religiously and unanimously decree and confirme these following Rites, liberties, and priveledges concerneing our Churches, and Civill State to be respectively impartiallie and inviolably enjoyed and observed throughout our Jurisdiction for ever.

1. No mans life shall be taken away, no mans honour or good name shall be stayned, no mans person shall be arested, restrayned, banished, dismembred, nor any wayes punished, no man shall be deprived of his wife or children, no mans goods or estaite shall be taken away from him, nor any way indammaged under Coulor of law, or Countenance of Authoritie, unlesse it be by vertue or equitie of some expresse law of the Country warranting the same, established by a generall Court and sufficiently published, or in case of the defect of a law in any partecular case by the word of god. And in Capitall cases, or in cases concerning dismembring or banishment, according to that word to be judged by the Generall Court.

2. Every person within Jurisdiction, whether Inhabitant or forreiner shall enjoy the same justice and law, that is generall for the plantation, which we constitute and execute one towards another, without partialitie or delay.

3. No man shall be urged to take any oath or subscribe any articles, covenants or remonstrance, of a publique and Civill nature, but such as the Generall Court hath considered, allowed, and required.

4. No man shall be punished for not appearing at or before any Civill Assembly, Court, Councell, Magistrate, or officer, nor for the omission of any office or service, if he shall be necessarily hindred, by any apparent Act or providenc of god, which he could neither foresee nor avoid. Provided that this law shall not prejudice any person of his just cost or damage in any civill action.

5. No man shall be compelled to any publique worke or service unlesse the presse be grounded upon some act of the generall Court, and have reasonable allowance therefore.

6. No man shall be pressed in person to any office, worke, warres, or other publique service, that is necessarily and suffitiently exempted by any naturall or personall impediment, as by want of yeares, greatnes of age, defect of minde, fayling of sences, or impotencie of Lymbes.

7. No man shall be compelled to goe out of the limits of this plantation upon any offensive warres which this Commonwealth or any of our freinds or confederats shall volentarily undertake. But onely upon such vindictive and defensive warres in our owne behalfe, or the behalfe of our freinds, and confederats as shall be enterprized by the Counsell and consent of a Court generall, or by Authority derived from the same.

8. No mans Cattell or goods of what kinde soever shall

be pressed or taken for any publique use or service, unless it be by warrant grounded upon some act of the generall Court, nor without such reasonable prices and hire as the ordinarie rates of the Countrie do afford. And if his Cattle or goods shall perish or suffer damage in such service, the owner shall be suffitiently recompenced.

9. No monoplies shall be granted or allowed amongst us, but of such new Inventions that are profitable to the Countrie, and that for a short time.

10. All our lands and heritages shall be free from all finds and licences upon Alienations, and from all hariotts,[1] wardships, Liveries,[2] Primerseisens,[3] yeare day and wast, Escheates,[4] and forfeitures, upon the deaths of parents, or Ancestors, be they naturall, casuall, or Juditiall.

11. All persons which are of the age of 21 yeares, and of right understanding and meamories, whether excommunicate or condemned shall have full power and libertie to make theire wills and testaments, and other lawfull alienations of theire lands and estates.

12. Every man whether Inhabitant or fforreiner, free or not free shall have libertie to come to any publique Court, Councell, or Towne meeting, and either by speech or writeing to move any lawful, seasonable, and materiall question, or to present any necessary motion, complaint, petition, Bill or information, whereof that meeting hath proper cognizance, so it be done in convenient time, due order, and respective manner.

[13.] No man shall be rated here for any estaite or revenue he hath in England, or in any forreine parties till it be transported hither.

[14.] Any conveyance or Alienation of land or other estaite what so ever, made by any woman that is married, any childe under age, Ideott, or distracted person, shall be good, if it be passed and ratified by the consent of a generall Court.

15. All Covenous or fraudulent Alienations or Conveyances of lands, tenements, or any hereditaments, shall be of no validitie to defeat any man from due debts or legacies, or from any just title, clame or possession, of that which is so fradulently conveyed.

16. Every Inhabitant that is an howse holder shall have free fishing and fowling in any great ponds and Bayes, Coves and Rivers, so farre as the sea ebbes and flowes within the presincts of the towne where they dwell, unless the freemen of the same Towne or the Generall Court have otherwise appropriated them, provided that this shall not be extended to give leave to any man to come upon other proprietie without there leave.

17. Every man of or within this Jurisdiction shall have free libertie, not with standing any Civill power to remove both himselfe, and his familie at their pleasure out of the same, provided there be no legall impediment to the contrarie.

18. No mans person shall be restrained or imprisoned by any Authority what so ever, before the law hath sentenced him thereto, If he can put in sufficient securitie, bayle, or mainprise, for his appearance, and good behaviour in the meane time, unless it be in Crimes Capitall, and Contempts in open Court, and in such cases where some expresse act of Court doth allow it.

19. If in a generall Court any miscariage shall be amongst the Assistants when they are by themselves that may deserve an Admonition or fine under 20 sh, it shall be examined and sentenced amongst themselves, If amongst the Deputies when they are by themselves, It shall be examined and sentenced amongst themselves, If it be when the whole Court is togeather, it shall be judged by the whole Court, and not severallie as before.

20. If any which are to sit as Judges in any other Court shall demeane themselves offensively in the Court, the rest of the Judges present shall have power to censure him for it, if the cause be of a high nature it shall be presented to and censured at the next superior Court.

21. In all cases where the first summons are not served six dayes before the Court, and the cause briefly specified in the warrant, where appearance is to be made by the partie summoned, it shall be at his libertie whether he will appeare or not, except all cases that are to be handled in Courts suddainly called upon extraordinary occasions, In all cases where there appeares present and urgent cause Any Assistant or officer apointed shal have power to make out Attaichments for the first summons.

22. No man in any suit or action against an other shall falsely pretend great debts or damages to vex his Adversary, if it shall appeare any doth so, The Court shall have power to set a reasonable fine on his head.

23. No man shall be adjudged to pay for detaining any Debt from any Crediter above eight pounds in the hundred for one yeare, And not above that rate proportionable

---

1. Provision of military equipment by a fief.—Ed.
2. Maintenance allowance provided by a fief.—Ed.
3. A tax paid by the eldest to retain title to property.—Ed.
4. Inheritance tax.—Ed.

for all somes what so ever, neither shall this be a couleur or countenance to allow any usurie amongst us contrarie to the law of god.

24. In all Trespasses or damages done to any man or men, If it can be proved to be done by the meere default of him or them to whome the trespasse is done, It shall be judged no trespasse, nor any damage given for it.

25. No Summons pleading Judgement, or any kinde of proceeding in Court or course of Justice shall be abated, arested, or reversed, upon any kinde of cercumstantiall errors or mistakes, If the person and cause be rightly understood and intended by the Court.

26. Every man that findeth himselfe unfit to plead his owne cause in any Court, shall have Libertie to imploy any man against whom the Court doth not except, to helpe him, Provided he give him noe fee, or reward for his paines. This shall not exempt the partie him selfe from Answering such Questions in person as the Court shall thinke meete to demand of him.

27. If any plaintife shall give into any Court a declaration of his cause in writeing, The defendant shall also have libertie and time to give in his answer in writeing, And so in all further proceedings betwene partie and partie, So it doth not further hinder the dispach of Justice then the Court shall be willing unto.

28. The plaintife in all Actions brought in any Court shall have libertie to withdraw his Action, or to be nonsuited before the Jurie hath given in their verdict, in which case he shall alwaies pay full cost and chardges to the defendant, and may afterwards renew his suite at an other Court if he please.

29. In all Actions at law it shall be the libertie of the plaintife and defendant by mutual consent to choose whether they will be tryed by the Bench or by a Jurie, unlesse it be where the law upon just reason hath otherwise determined. The like libertie shall be granted to all persons in Criminall cases.

30. It shall be in the libertie both of plaintife and defendant, and likewise every delinquent (to be judged by a Jurie) to challenge any of the Jurors. And if his challenge be found just and reasonable by the Bench, or the rest of the Jurie, as the challenger shall choose it shall be allowed him, and tales de cercumstantibus impaneled in their room.

31. In all cases where evidence is so obscure or defective that the Jurie cannot clearly and safely give a positive verdict, whether it be a grand or petit Jurie, It shall have libertie to give a non Liquit, or a speciall verdict, in which last, that is in a speciall veredict, the Judgement of the cause shall be left to the Court, and all Jurors shall have libertie in matters of fact if they cannot finde the maine issue, yet to finde and present in their verdict so much as they can, If the Bench and Jurors shall so differ at any time about their verdict that either of them can not proceed with peace of conscience the case shall be referred to the Generall Court, who shall take the question from both and determine it.

32. Every man shall have libertie to replevy his Cattell or goods impounded, distreined, seised, or extended, unlesse it be upon execution after Judgement, and in paiment of fines. Provided he puts in good securitie to prosecute his replevin, And to satisfie such demands as his Adversary shall recover against him in Law.

33. No mans person shall be Arrested, or imprisoned upon execution or judgment for any debt or fine, if the law can finde competent meanes of satisfaction otherwise from his estaite, And if not his person may be arrested and imprisoned where he shall be kept at his owne charge, not the plaintife's till satisfaction be made: unlesse the Court that had cognizance of the cause or some superior Court shall otherwise provide.

34. If any man shall be proved and Judged a common Barrator vexing others with unjust frequent and endlesse suites, It shall be in the power of Courts both to denie him the benefit of the law, and to punish him for his Barratry.

35. No mans Corne nor hay that is in the field or upon the Cart, nor his garden stuffe, nor any thing subject to present decay, shall be taken in any distresse, unles he that takes it doth presently bestow it where it may not be imbesled nor suffer spoile or decay, or give securitie to satisfie the worth thereof if it comes to any harme.

36. It shall be in the libertie of every man cast condemned or sentenced in any cause in any Inferior Court, to make their Appeale to the Court of Assistants, provided they tender their appeale and put in securitie to prosecute it before the Court be ended wherein they were condemned, And within six dayes next ensuing put in good securitie before some Assistant to satisfie what his Adversarie shall recover against him; And if the cause be of a Criminall nature, for his good behaviour and appearance, And everie man shall have libertie to complaine to the Generall Court of any Injustice done him in any Court of Assistants or other.

37. In all cases where it appeares to the Court that the plaintife hath willingly and witingly done wronge to the defendant in commenceing and prosecuting any action or complaint against him, They shall have power to impose upon him a proportionable fine to the use of the defendant, or accused person, for his false complaint or clamor.

38. Everie man shall have libertie to Record in the publique Rolles of any Court any Testimony give[n] upon oath in the same Court, or before two Assistants, or any Deede or evidence legally confirmed there to remaine in perpetuam rei memoriam, that is for perpetuall memoriall or evidence upon occasion.

39. In all Actions both reall and personall betweene partie and partie, the Court shall have power to respite execution for a convenient time, when in their prudence they see just cause so to doe.

40. No Conveyance, Deede, or promise what so ever shall be of validitie, If it be gotten by Illegal violence, imprisonment, threatenings, or any kinde of forcible compulsion called Dures.

41. Everie man that is to Answere for any Criminall cause, whether he be in prison or under bayle, his cause shall be heard and determined at the next Court that hath proper Cognizance thereof, And may be done without prejudice of Justice.

42. No man shall be twise sentenced by Civill Justice for one and the same Crime, offence, or Trespasse.

43. No man shall be beaten with above 40 stripes, nor shall any true gentleman, nor any man equall to a gentleman be punished with whipping, unless his crime be very shamefull, and his course of life vitious and profligate.

44. No man condemned to dye shall be put to death within fower dayes next after his condemnation, unles the Court see speciall cause to the contrary, or in case of martiall law, nor shall the body of any man so put to death be unburied 12 howers, unlesse it be in case of Anatomie.

45. No man shall be forced by Torture to confesse any Crime against himselfe nor any other unlesse it be in some Capitall case where he is first fullie convicted by cleare and suffitient evidence to be guilty, After which if the cause be of that nature, That it is very apparent there be other conspiratours, or confederates with him, Then he may be tortured, yet not with such Tortures as be Barbarous and inhumane.

46. For bodilie punishments we allow amongst us none that are inhumane Barbarous or cruell.

47. No man shall be put to death without the testimony of two or three witnesses, or that which is equivalent there unto.

48. Every Inhabitant of the Countrie shall have free libertie to search and veewe any Rooles, Records, or Regesters of any Court or office except the Councell, And to have a transcript or exemplification thereof written examined, and signed by the hand of the officer of the office paying the appointed fees therefore.

49. No free man shall be compelled to serve upon Juries above two Courts in a yeare, except grand Jurie men, who shall hould two Courts together at the least.

50. All Jurors shall be chosen continuallie by the freemen of the Towne where they dwell.

51. All Associates selected at any time to Assist the Assistants in Inferior Courts, shall be nominated by the Townes belonging to that Court, by orderly agreement amonge themselves.

52. Children, Idiots, Distracted persons, and all that are strangers, or new commers to our plantation, shall have such allowances and dispensations in any cause whether Criminall or other as religion and reason require.

53. The age of discretion of passing away of lands or such kinde of herediments, or for giveing of votes, verdicts or Sentence in any Civill Courts or causes, shall be one and twentie yeares.

54. When so ever anything is to be put to vote, any sentence to be pronounced, or any other matter to be proposed, or read in any Court or Assembly, If the president or moderator thereof shall refuse to performe it, the Major parte of the members of that Court or Assembly shall have power to appoint any other meete man of them to do it, And if there be just cause to punish him that should and would not.

55. In all suites or Actions in any Court, the plaintife shall have libertie to make all the titles and claims to that he sues for he can. And the Defendant shall have libertie to plead all the pleas he can in answere to them, and the Court shall judge according to the intire evidence of all.

56. If any man shall behave himselfe offensively at any Towne meeting, the rest of the freemen then present, shall have power to sentence him for his offence, So be it the mulct or penaltie exceed not twentie shilings.

57. When so ever any person shall come to any very suddaine untimely and unnaturall death, Some Assistant, or the Constables of that Towne shall forthwith sumon a Jury of twelve free men to inquire of the cause and man-

ner of their death, and shall present a true verdict thereof to some neere Assistant, or the next Court to be helde for that Towne upon their oath.

LIBERTIES MORE PECULIARLIE
CONCERNING THE FREE MEN

58. Civill Authoritie hath power and libertie to see the peace, ordinances and Rules of Christ observed in every church according to his word, so it be done in a Civill and not in an Ecclesiastical way.

59. Civill Authoritie hath power and libertie to deale with any Church member in a way of Civill Justice, notwithstanding any Church relation, office, or interest.

60. No church censure shall degrade or depose any man from any Civill dignitie, office, or Authoritie he shall have in the Commonwealth.

61. No Magestrate, Juror, Officer, or other man shall be bound to informe present or reveale any private crim or offence, wherein there is no perill or danger to this plantation or any member thereof, when any necessarietye of conscience binds him to secresie grounded upon the word of god, unlesse it be in case of testimony lawfully required.

62. Any Shire or Towne shall have libertie to choose their Deputies whom and where they please for the General Court, So be it they be free men, and have taken there oath of fealtie, and Inhabiting in this Jurisdiction.

63. No Governor, Deputie Governor, Assistant, Associate, or grand Jury man at any Court, nor any Deputie for the Generall Court, shall at any time beare his owne chardges at any Court, but their necessary expences shall be defrayed either by the Towne, or Shire on whose service they are, or by the Country in generall.

64. Everie Action betweene partie and partie, and proceedings against delinquents in Criminall causes shall be briefly and destinctly entered in the Rolles of every Court by the Recorder thereof. That such actions be not afterwards brought againe to the vexation of any man.

65. No custome or prescription shall ever prevaile amongst us in any morall cause, our meaneing is maintaine anythinge that can be proved to bee morrallie sinfull by the word of god.

66. The Freemen of everie Towneship shall have power to make such by laws and constitutions as may concerne the wellfare of their Towne, provided they be not of a Criminall, but onely of a prudentiall nature. And that their penalties exceede not 20 sh. for one offence. And that they be not repugnant to the publique laws and orders of the Countrie. And if any Inhabitant shall neglect or refuse to observe them, they shall have power to levy the appointed penalties by distresse.

67. It is the constant libertie of the freemen of this plantation to choose yearly at the Court of Election out of the freemen all the Generall officers of this Jurisdiction. If they please to dischardge them at the day of Election by way of vote. They may do it without shewing cause. But if at any other generall Court, we hould it due justice, that the reasons thereof be alleadged and proved. By Generall officers we meane, our Governor, Deputie Governor, Assistants, Treasurer, Generall of our warres. And our Admiral at Sea, and such as are or hereafter may be of the like generall nature.

68. It is the libertie of the freemen to choose such deputies for the Generall Court out of themselves, either in their owne Townes or elsewhere as they judge fittest, And because we cannot foresee what varietie and weight of occasions may fall into future consideration, And what counsells we may stand in neede of, we decree. That the Deputies (to attend the Generall Court in the behalfe of the Countrie) shall not any time be stated or inacted, but from Court to Court, or at the most but for one yeare. that the Countrie may have an Annuall libertie to do in that case what is most behoofefull for the best welfare thereof.

69. No Generall Court shall be desolved or adjourned without the consent of the Major parte thereof.

70. All Freemen called to give any advise, vote, verdict, or sentence in any Court, Counsell, or Civill Assembly, shall have full freedome to doe it according to their true Judgments and Consciences, So it be done orderly and inofensively for the manner.

71. The Governor shall have a casting voice whensoever an Equi vote shall fall out of the Court of Assistants, or generall assembly, So shall the presendent or moderator have in all Civill Courts or Assemblies.

72. The Governor and Deputie Governor Joyntly consenting or any three Assistants concurring in consent shall have power out of Court to reprive a condemned malefactour, till the next quarter or generall Court. The generall Court onely shall have power to pardon a condemned malefactor.

73. The Generall Court hath libertie and Authoritie to send out any member of the Comanwealth of what quali-

tie, condition or office whatsoever into forreine parts about any publique message or Negotiation. Provided the partie sent be acquainted with the affaire he goeth about, and be willing to undertake the service.

74. The freemen of every Towne or Towneship, shall have full power to choose yearly or for lesse time out of themselves a convenient number of fitt men to order the planting or prudential occasions of that Towne, according to Instructions given them in writeing, Provided nothing be done by them contrary to the publique laws and orders of the Countrie, provided also the number of such select persons be not above nine.

75. It is and shall be the libertie of any member or members of any Court, Councell or Civill Assembly in cases of makeing or executing any order or law, that properlie concerne religion, or any cause capitall or warres, or Subscription to any publique Articles or Remonstrance, in case they cannot in Judgement and conscience consent to that way the Major vote or suffrage goes, to make their contra Remonstrance or protestation in speech or writeing, and upon request to have their dissent recorded in the Rolles of that Court. So it be done Christianlie and respectively for the manner. And their dissent onely be entered without the reasons thereof, for the avoiding of tediousness.

76. When so ever any Jurie of trialls or Jurours are not cleare in their Judgments or consciences conserneing any cause wherein they are to give their verdict, They shall have libertie in open Court to advise with any man they thinke fitt to resolve or direct them, before they give in their verdict.

77. In all cases wherein any freeman is to give his vote, be it in point of Election, makeing constitutions and orders, or passing sentence in any case of Judicature or the like, if he cannot see reason to give it positively one way or an other, he shall have libertie to be silent, and not pressed to a determined vote.

78. The Generall or publique Treasure or any parte thereof shall never be exspended but by the appointment of a Generall Court, nor any Shire Treasure, but by the appointment of the freemen thereof, nor any Towne Treasurie but by freemen of that Towneship.

LIBERTIES OF WOEMEN

79. If any man at his death shall not leave his wife a competent portion of his estaite, upon just complaint made to the Generall Court she shall be relieved.

80. Everie marryed woeman shall be free from bodilie correction or stripes by her husband, unlesse it be in his owne defence upon her assault. If there be any just cause of correction complaint shall be made to Authoritie assembled in some Court, from which onely she shall receive it.

LIBERTIES OF CHILDREN

81. When Parents dye intestate, the Elder sonne shall have a doble portion of his whole estate reall and personall, unlesse the Generall Court upon just cause alleadged shall Judge otherwise.

82. When parents dye intestate, haveing noe heires males of their bodies their Daughters shall inherit as Copartners, unles the Generall Court upon just reason shall judge otherwise.

83. If any parents shall wilfullie and unreasonably deny any childe timely or convenient mariage, or shall exercise any unnaturall severitie towards them, Such children shall have free libertie to complain to Authoritie for redresse.

84. No Orphan dureing their minoritie which was not committed to tuition or service by the parents in their life time, shall afterwards be absolutely disposed of by any kindred, friend, Executor, Towneship, or Church, nor by themselves without the consent of some Court, wherein two Assistants at least shall be present.

LIBERTIES OF SERVANTS

85. If any servants shall flee from the Tiranny and crueltie of their masters to the howse of any freeman of the same Towne, they shall be there protected and susteyned till due order be taken for their relife. Provided due notice thereof be speedily given to their masters from whom they fled. And the next Assistant or Constable where the partie flying is harboured.

86. No servant shall be put of for above a yeare to any other neither in the life of their master nor after their death by their Executors or Administrators unlesse it be by consent of Authoritie assembled in some Court, or two Assistants.

87. If any man smite out the eye or tooth of his man servant, or maid servant, or otherwise mayme or much disfigure him, unlesse it be by meere casualtie, he shall let them goe free from his service. And shall have such further recompense as the Court shall allow him.

88. Servants that have served diligentlie and faithfully to the benefitt of their maisters seaven yeares, shall not be

sent away emptie. And if any have bene unfaithfull, negligent or unprofitable in their service, notwithstanding the good usage of their maisters, they shall not be dismissed till they have made satisfaction according to the Judgement of Authoritie.

LIBERTIES OF FORREINERS AND STRANGERS

89. If any people of other Nations professing the true Christian Religion shall flee to us from the Tiranny or oppression of their persecutors, or from famyne, warres, or the like necessary and compulsarie cause, They shall be entertayned and succoured amongst us, according to that power and prudence god shall give us.

90. If any ships or other vessels, be it freind or enemy, shall suffer shipwrack upon our Coast, there shall be no violence or wrong offered to their persons or goods. But their persons shall be harboured, and relieved, and their goods preserved in safety till Authoritie may be certified thereof, and shall take further order therein.

91. There shall never be any bond slaverie villinage or Captivitie amongst us, unles it be lawfull Captives taken in just warres, and such strangers as willingly belie themselves or are sold to us. And these shall have all the liberties and Christian usages which the law of god established in Israell concerning such persons doeth morally require. This exempts none from servitude who shall be Judged thereto by Authoritie.

OFF THE BRUITE CREATURE

92. No man shall exercise any Tirranny or Crueltie towards any bruite Creature which are usuallie kept for mans use.

93. If any man shall have occasion to leade or drive Cattel from place to place that is far of, So that they be weary, or hungry, or fall sick, or lambe, It shall be lawful to rest or refresh them, for a competent time, in any open place that is not Corne, meadow, or inclosed for some peculiar use.

94.

1. If any man after legall conviction shall have or worship any other god, but the lord god, he shall be put to death. DUT. 13.6.10, DUT. 17.2.6, EX. 22.20

2. If any man or woeman be a witch, (that is hath or consulteth with a familiar spirit,) They shall be put to death. EX. 22.18, LEV. 20.27, DUT. 18.10

3. If any person shall Blaspheme the name of God, the father, Sonne, or Holie ghost, with direct expresse, presumptuous or high handed blasphemie, or shall curse god in the like manner, he shall be put to death. LEV. 24.15.16

4. If any person committ any wilfull murther, which is manslaughter, committed upon premeditated mallice, hatred, or Crueltie, not in a mans necessarie and just defence, nor by meere casualtie against his will, he shall be put to death. EX. 21.12, NUMB. 35.13.14, 30.31

5. If any person slayeth an other suddainely in his anger or Crueltie of passion, he shall be put to death. NUMB. 25.20.21, LEV. 24.17

6. If any person shall slay an other through guile, either by poysoning or other such divelish practice, he shall be put to death. EX. 21.14

7. If any man or woman shall lye with any beast or brute creature by Carnall Copulation, They shall surely be put to death. And the beast shall be slaine and buried and not eaten. LEV. 19.23

8. If any man lyeth with mankinde as he lyeth with a woeman, both of them have committed abhomination, they both shall surely be put to death. LEV. 19.22

9. If any person committeth Adultery with a married or espoused wife, the Adulterer and Adulteresse shall surely be put to death. EX. 20.14

10. If any man stealeth a man or mankinde, he shall surely be put to death. EX. 21.16

11. If any man rise up by false witnes, wittingly and of purpose to take away any man's life, he shall be put to death. DUT. 19.16, 18.19

12. If any man shall conspire and attempt any invation, insurrection, or publique rebellion against our commonwealth, or shall indeavour to surprize any Towne or Townes, fort or forts therein, or shall treacherously and perfediouslie attempt the alteration and subversion of our frame of politie or Government fundamentallie, he shall be put to death.

95. A declaration of the Liberties the Lord Jesus hath given to the Churches.

1. All the people of god within this Jurisdiction who are not in a church way, and be orthodox in Judgement, and not scandalous in life, shall have full libertie to gather themselves into a Church Estaite. Provided they doe it in a Christian way, with due observation of the rules of Christ revealed in his word.

2. Every Church hath full libertie to exercise all the ordinances of god, according to the rules of Scripture.

3. Every Church hath free libertie of Election and ordination of all their officers from time to time, provided they be able pious and orthodox.

4. Every Church hath free libertie of Admission, Recommendation, Dismission, and Expulsion, or deposall of their offi-

cers, and members, upon due cause, with free exercise of the Discipline and Censures of Christ according to the rules of his word.

5. No Injunctions are to be put upon any Church, Church Officers or member in point of Doctrine, worship or Discipline, whether for substance or cercumstance besides the Institutions of the lord.

6. Every Church of Christ hath freedome to celebrate dayes of fasting and prayer, and of thanksgiveing according to the word of god.

7. The Elders of Churches have free libertie to meete monthly, Quarterly, or otherwise, in convenient numbers and places, for conferences, and consultations about Christian and Church questions and occasions.

8. All Churches have libertie to deale with any of their members in a church way that are in the hand of Justice. So it be not to retard or hinder the course thereof.

9. Every Church hath libertie to deal with any magestrate, Deputie of Court or other officer what soe ever that is a member in a church way in case of apparent and just offence given in their places. so it be done with due observance and respect.

10. Wee allowe private meetings for edification in religion amongst Christians of all sortes of people. So it be without just offence both for number, time, place, and other cercumstances.

11. For the preventing and removeing of errour and offence that may grow and spread in any of the Churches in this Jurisdiction. And for the preserveing of trueith and peace in the severall churches within them selves, and for the maintenance and exercise of brotherly communion, amongst all the churches in the Countrie, It is allowed and ratified, by the Authoritie of this Generall Court as a lawfull libertie of the Churches of Christ. That once in every month of the yeare (when the season will beare it) It shall be lawfull for the minesters and Elders, of the Churches neere adjoyneing together, with any other of the breetheren with the consent of the churches to assemble by course in each severall Church one after an other. To the intent after the preaching of the word by such a minister as shall be requested thereto by the Elders of the church where the Assembly is held, The rest of the day may be spent in publique Christian Conference about the discussing and resolveing of any such doubts and cases of conscience concerning matter of doctrine or worship or government of the church as shall be propounded by any of the Breetheren of that church, with leave also to any other Brother to propound his objections or answeres for further satisfaction according to the word of god. Provided that the whole action be guided and moderated by the Elders of the Church where the Assemblie is helde, or

by such others as they shall appoint. And that no thing be concluded and imposed by way of Authoritie from one or more Churches upon an other, but onely by way of Brotherly conference and consultations. That the trueth may be searched out to the satisfying of every man's Conscience in the sight of god according to his worde. And because such an Assembly and the worke their of can not be duely attended to if other lectures be held in the same weeke. It is therefore agreed with the consent of the Churches. That in that weeke when such an Assembly is held. All the lectures in all the neighbouring Churches for the weeke shall be forborne. That so the publique service of Christ in this more solemne Assembly may be transacted with greater deligence and attention.

96. How so ever these above specified rites, freedomes, Immunities, Authorities and priveledges, both Civill and Ecclesiasticall are expressed onely under the name and title of Liberties, and not in the exact forme of Laws, or Statutes, yet we do with one consent fullie Authorise, and earnestly intreate all that are and shall be in Authoritie to consider them as laws, and not to faile to inflict condigne and proportionable punishments upon every man impartiallie, that shall infringe or violate any of them.

97. Wee likewise give full power and libertie to any person that shall at any time be denyed or deprived of any of them, to commence and prosecute their suite, Complaint, or action against any man that shall so doe, in any Court that hath proper Cognizance or judicature thereof.

98. Lastly because our dutie and desire is to do nothing suddainlie which fundamentally concerne us, we decree that these rites and liberties, shall be Audably read and deliberately weighed at ever Generall Court that shall be held, within three yeares next insueing, And such of them as shall not be altered or repealed they shall stand so ratified, That no man shall infringe them without due punishment.

And if any General Court within these next thre yeares shall faile or forget to reade and consider them as abovesaid. The Governor and Deputie Governor for the time being, and every Assistant present at such Courts shall forfeite 20 sh. a man, and everie Deputie 10 sh. a man for each neglect, which shall be paid out of their proper estate, and not by the Country or the Townes which choose them. And when so ever there shall arise any question in any Court amonge the Assistants and Associates thereof about the explanation of these Rites and liberties, The Generall Court onely shall have power to interprett them.

Charter of Liberties and Frame of Government of the Province of Pennsylvania in America

May 5, 1682

William Penn was the royal proprietor of the colony or province of Pennsylvania. He had the power to set up a government with almost no checks on his own power. Yet the Charter of Liberties he issued set up a government that would rule by and through the consent of the colonists. Its formal bill of rights included religious liberty for anyone professing belief in a deity and provided for legislative government based on election by the people. The document also includes a number of important innovations in the structure of government, including staggered terms for certain officeholders and a formal process for amendment.

Charter of Liberties and Frame of Government

The frame of the government of the province of Pensilvania, in America: together with certain laws agreed upon in England, by the Governor and divers freemen of the aforesaid province. To be further explained and confirmed there, by the first provincial Council that shall be held, if they see meet.

THE PREFACE

When the great and wise God had made the world, of all his creatures, it pleased him to chuse man his Deputy to rule it: and to fit him for so great a charge and trust, he did not only qualify him with skill and power, but with integrity to use them justly. This native goodness was equally his honour and his happiness; and whilst he stood here, all went well; there was no need of coercive or compulsive means; the precept of divine love and truth, in his bosom, was the guide and keeper of his innocency. But lust prevailing against duty, made a lamentable breach upon it; and the law, that before had no power over him, took place upon him, and his disobedient posterity, that such as would not live comfortable to the holy law within, should fall under the reproof and correction of the just law without, in a judicial administration.

This the Apostle teaches in divers of his epistles: "The law (says he) was added because of transgression," In another place, "Knowing that the law was not made for the righteous man, but for the disobedient and ungodly, for sinners, for unholy and prophane, for murderers, for whoremongers, for them that defile themselves with mankind, and for man-stealers, for lyers, for perjured persons," &c., but this is not all, he opens and carries the matter of government a little further: "Let every soul be subject to the higher powers; for there is no power but of God. The powers that be are ordained of God: whosoever therefore resisteth the power, resisteth the ordinance of God. For rulers are not a terror to good works, but to evil: wilt thou then not be afraid of the power? do that which is good, and thou shalt have praise of the same." "He is the minister of God to thee for good." "Wherefore ye must needs be subject, not only for wrath, but for conscience sake."

This settles the divine right of government beyond exception, and that for two ends: first, to terrify evil doers: secondly, to cherish those that do well; which gives government a life beyond corruption, and makes it as durable in the world, as good men shall be. So that government seems to me a part of religion itself, a thing sacred in its institution and end. For, if it does not directly remove the cause, it crushes the effects of evil, and is as such, (though a lower, yet) an emanation of the same Divine Power, that is both author and object of pure religion; the difference lying here, that the one is more free and mental, the other more corporal and compulsive in its operations: but that is only to evil doers; government itself being otherwise as capable of kindness, goodness and charity, as a more private society. They weakly err, that think there is no other use of government, than correction, which is the coarsest part of it: daily experience tells us, that the care and regulation of many other affairs, more soft, and daily necessary, makeup much of the greatest part of government; and which must have followed the peopling of the world, had Adam never fell, and will continue among men, on earth, under the highest attainments they may arrive at, by the coming of the blessed *Second Adam,* the Lord from heaven. Thus much of government in general, as to its rise and end.

For particular frames and models it will become me to say little; and comparatively I will say nothing. My reasons are:

First. That the age is too nice and difficult for it; there being nothing the wits of men are more busy and divided upon. It is true, they seem to agree to the end, to wit, happiness; but, in the means, they differ, as to divine, so to this human felicity; and the cause is much the same, not always want of light and knowledge, but want of using them rightly. Men side with their passions against their reason, and their sinister interests have so strong a bias upon their minds, that they lean to them gainst the good of the things they know.

Secondly. I do not find a model in the world, that time, place, and some singular emergences have not necessarily altered; nor is it easy to frame a civil government, that shall serve all places alike.

Thirdly. I know what is said by the several admirers of *monarchy, aristocracy* and *democracy,* which are the rule of one, a few, and many, and are the three common ideas of government, when men discourse on the subject. But I chuse to solve the controversy with this small distinction, and it belongs to all three: *Any government is free to the people under it* (whatever be the frame) *where the laws rule, and the people are a party to those laws,* and more than this is tyranny, oligarchy, or confusion.

But, lastly, when all is said, there is hardly one frame of government in the world so ill designed by its first founders, that, in good hands, would not do well enough; and [hi]story tells us, the best, in ill ones, can do nothing that is great or good; witness the said states. Governments, like clocks, go from the motion men give them; and as governments are made and moved by men, so by them they are ruined too. Wherefore governments rather depend upon men, than men upon governments. Let men be good, and the government cannot be bad; if it be ill, they will cure it. But, if men be bad, let the government be never so good, they will endeavor to warp and spoil it to their turn.

I know some say, let us have good laws, and no matter for the men that execute them: but let them consider, that though good laws do well, good men do better: for good laws may want good men, and be abolished or evaded[1] by ill men; but good men will never want good laws, nor suffer ill ones. It is true, good laws have some awe upon ill ministers, but that is where they have not power to escape or

abolish them, and the people are generally wise and good: but a loose and depraved people (which is the question) love laws and an administration like themselves. That, therefore, which makes a good constitution, must keep it, viz: men of wisdom and virtue, qualities, that because they descend not with worldly inheritances, must be carefully propagated by a virtuous education of youth; for which after ages will owe more to the care and prudence of founders, and the successive magistracy, than to their parents, for their private patrimonies.

These considerations of the weight of government, and the nice and various opinions about it, made it uneasy to me to think of publishing the ensuing frame and conditional laws, foreseeing both the censures, they will meet with, from men of differing humours and engagements, and the occasion they may give of discourse beyond my design.

But, next to the power of necessity, (which is a solicitor, that will take no denial) this induced me to a compliance, that we have (with reverence to God, and good conscience to men) to the best of our skill, contrived and composed the frame and laws of this government, to the great end of all government, viz: *To support power in reverence with the people, and to secure the people from the abuse of power;* that they may be free by their just obedience, and the magistrates honourable, for their just administration: for liberty, without obedience is confusion, and obedience without liberty is slavery. To carry this evenness is partly owing to the constitution, and partly to the magistracy: where either of these fail, government will be subject to convulsions; but where both are wanting, it must be totally subverted; then where both meet, the government is like to endure.

Which I humbly pray and hope *God* will please to make the lot of this Pensilvania. Amen.

WILLAM PENN

THE FRAME, &C—APRIL 25, 1682

To all Persons, to whom these presents may come. Whereas king Charles the Second, by his letters patents, under the great seal of England bearing date the fourth day of March in the Thirty and Third Year of the King, for divers consideration therein mentioned, hath been graciously pleased to give and grant unto me William Penn, by the name of William Penn, Esquire, son and heir of Sir William Penn, deceased, and to my heirs and assigns forever, all that tract of land, or Province called Pennsylvania, in America, with divers great powers, preheminences, royalties, jurisdictions,

---

1. Invaded in Franklin's print.—Ed.

and authorities, necessary for the well-being and government thereof: Now know ye, that for the well-being and government of the said province, and for the encouragement of all the freemen and planters that may be therein concerned, in pursuance of the powers aforementioned, I, the said William Penn have declared, granted, and confirmed, and by these presents, for me, my heirs and assigns, do declare, grant, and confirm unto all the freemen, planters and adventurers of, in and to the said province, these liberties, franchise, and properties, to be held, enjoyed and kept by the freemen, planters, and inhabitants of the said province of Pennsylvania for ever.

Imprimis. That the government of this province shall, according to the powers of the patent, consist of the Governor and freemen of the said province, in form of a provincial Council and General Assembly, by whom all laws shall be made, officers chosen, and public affairs transacted, as is hereafter respectively declared, that is to say—

II. That the freemen of the said province shall, on the twentieth day of the twelfth month, which shall be in the present year one thousand six hundred eighty and two, meet and assemble in some fit place, of which timely notice shall be before hand given by the Governor or his Deputy; and then, and there, shall chuse out of themselves seventy-two persons of most note for their wisdom, virtue and ability, who shall meet, on the tenth day of the first month next ensuing, and always be called, and act as, the provincial Council of the said province.

III. That, at the first choice of such provincial Council, one-third part of the said provincial Council shall be chosen to serve for three years, then next ensuing; one-third party, for two years then next ensuing; and one-third party, for one year then next ensuing each election, and no longer; and that the said third part shall go out accordingly; and on the twentieth day of the twelfth month, as aforesaid, yearly for ever afterwards, the freemen of the said province shall, in like manner, meet and assemble together, and then chuse twenty-four persons, being one-third of the said number, to serve in provincial Council for three years: it being intended, that one-third part of the whole provincial Council (always consisting, and to consist, of seventy-two persons, as aforesaid) falling off yearly, it shall be yearly supplied by such new yearly elections, as aforesaid; and that no one person shall continue therein longer than three years: and, in case any member shall decease before the last election during his time, that then at the next election ensuing his decease, another shall be chosen to supply his place, for the remaining time, he has to have served, and no longer.

IV. That, after the first seven years, every one of the said third parts, that goeth yearly off, shall be uncapable of being chosen again for one whole year following: that so all may be fitted for government and have experience of the care and burden of it.

V. That the provincial Council, in all cases and matters of moment, as their arguing upon bills to be passed into laws, erecting courts of justice, giving judgment upon criminals impeached, and choice of officers, in such manner as is hereinafter mentioned, not less than two-thirds of the whole provincial Council shall make a quorum and that the consent and approbation of two-thirds of such quorum shall be had in all such cases and matters of moment. And moreover that, in all cases and matters of lesser moment, twenty-four Members of the said provincial Council shall make a quorum the majority of which twenty-four shall, and may, always determine in such cases and causes of lesser moment.

VI. That, in this provincial Council, the Governor or his Deputy, shall or may, always preside, and have a treble voice; and the said provincial Council shall always continue, and sit upon its own adjournments and committees.

VII. That the Governor and provincial Council shall prepare and propose to the General Assembly, herafter mentioned, all bills, which they shall, at any time, think fit to be passed into laws, within the said province; which bills shall be published and affixed to the most noted places, in the inhabited parts thereof, thirty days before the meeting of the General Assembly, in order to the passing them into laws or rejecting of them, as the General Assembly shall see meet.

VIII. That the Governor and provincial Council shall take care, that all laws, statutes and ordinances, which shall at any time be made within the said province, be duly and diligently executed.

IX. That the Governor and provincial Council shall, at all times, have the care of the peace and safety of the province, and that nothing be by any person attempted to the subversion of this frame of government.

X. That the Governor and provincial Council shall, at all times, settle and order the situation of all cities, ports, and market towns in every county, modelling therein all public buildings, streets, and market places, and shall appoint all necessary roads, and high-ways in the province.

XI. That the Governor and provincial Councill shall, at all times, have power to inspect the management of the public treasury, and punish those who shall convert any part thereof to any other use, than what hath been agreed upon by the Governor, provincial Council, and General Assembly.

XII. That the Governor and provincial Council, shall erect and order all public schools, and encourage and reward the authors of useful sciences and laudable inventions in the said province.

XIII. That, for the better management of the power and trust aforesaid, the provincial Council shall, from time to time, divide itself into four distinct and proper committees, for the more easy administration of the affairs of the Province, which divides the seventy-two into four eighteens, every one of which eighteens shall consist of six out of each of the three orders, or yearly elections, each of which shall have a distinct portion of business, as followeth: *First,* a committee of plantations, to situate and settle cities, ports, and market towns, and high-ways, and to hear and decide all suits and controversies relating to plantations. *Secondly,* a committee of justice and safety, to secure the peace of the Province, and punish the mal-administration of those who subvert justice to the prejudice of the public, or private, interest. *Thirdly,* a committee of trade and treasury, who shall regulate all trade and commerce, according to law, encourage manufacture and country growth, and defray the public charge of the Province. And, *Fourthly,* a committee of manners, education, and arts, that all wicked and scandalous living may be prevented, and that youth may be successively trained up in virtue and useful knowledge and arts: the *quorum* of each of which committees being six, that is, two out of each of the three orders, or yearly elections, as aforesaid, make a constant and standing Council of *twenty-four* which will have the power of the provincial Council, being the quorum of it, in all cases not excepted in the fifth article; and in the said committees, and standing Council of the Province, the Governor, or his Deputy, shall, or may preside, as aforesaid; and in the absence of the Governor, or his Deputy, if no one is by either of them appointed, the said committees or Council shall appoint a President for that time, and not otherwise; and what shall be resolved at such committees, shall be reported to the said Council of the province, and shall be by them resolved and confirmed before the same shall be put in execution; and that these respective committees shall not sit at one and the same time, except in cases of necessity.

XIV. And, to the end that all laws prepared by the Governor and provincial Council aforesaid, may yet have the more full concurrence of the freemen of the province, it is declared, granted and confirmed, that, at the time and place or places, for the choices of a provincial council, as aforesaid, the said freemen shall yearly chuse Members to serve in a General Assembly, as their representatives, not exceeding two hundred persons, who shall yearly meet on the twentieth day of the second month, which shall be in the year one thousand six hundred eighty and three following, in the capital town, or city, of the said province, where, during eight days, the several Members may freely confer with one another; and, if any of them see meet, with a committee of the provincial Council (consisting of three out of each of the four committees aforesaid, being twelve in all) which shall be, at that time, purposely appointed to receive from any of them proposals, for the alterations or amendment of any of the said proposed and promulgated bills: and on the ninth day from their so meeting, the said General Assembly, after reading over the proposed bills by the Clerk of the provincial Council, and the occasions and motives for them being opened by the Governor or his Deputy, shall give their affirmative or negative, which to them seemeth best, in such manner as hereinafter is expressed. But not less than two-thirds shall make a *quorum* in the passing of laws, and choice of such officers as are by them to be chosen.

XV. That the laws so prepared and proposed, as aforesaid, that are assented to by the General Assembly, shall be enrolled as laws of the Province, with this stile: *By the Governor, with the assent and approbation of the freemen in provincial Council and General Assembly.*

XVI. That, for the establishment of the government and laws of this province, and to the end there may be an universal satisfaction in the laying of the fundamentals thereof: the General Assembly shall, or may, for the first year, consist of all the freemen of and in the said province; and ever after it shall be yearly chosen, as aforesaid; which number of two hundred shall be enlarged as the country shall increase in people, so as it do not exceed five hundred, at any time; the appointment and proportioning of which, as also the laying and methodizing of the choice of the provincial Council and General Assembly, in future times most equally to the divisions of the hundreds and counties, which the country shall hereafter be divided into, shall be in the power of the provincial Council to propose, and the General Assembly to resolve.

XVII. That the Governor and the provincial Council shall erect, from time to time, standing courts of justice, in such places and number as they shall judge convenient for the good government of the said province. And that the provincial Council shall, on the thirteenth day of the first month, yearly, elect and present to the Governor, or his Deputy, a double number of persons, to serve for Judges, Treasurers, Masters of Rolls, within the said province, for the year next ensuing; and the freemen of the said province, in the county courts, when they shall be erected, and till then, in the General Assembly, shall, on the three and twentieth day of the second month, yearly, elect and present to the Governor, or his Deputy, a double number of persons, to serve for Sheriffs, Justices of the Peace, and Coroners, for the year next ensuing; out of which respective elections and presentments, the Governor or his Deputy shall nominate and commissionate the proper number for each office, the third day after the said presentments, or else the first named in such presentment, for each office, shall stand and serve for that office the year ensuing.

XVIII. But forasmuch as the present condition of the province requires some immediate settlement, and admits not of so quick a revolution of officers; and to the end the said Province may, with all convenient speed, be well ordered and settled, I, William Penn, do therefore think fit to nominate and appoint such persons for Judges, Treasurers, Masters of the Rolls, Sheriffs, Justices of the Peace, and Coroners, as are most fitly qualified for those employments; to whom I shall make and grant commissions for the said offices, respectively, to hold to them, to whom the same shall be granted, for so long time as every such person shall well behave himself in the office, or place, to him respectively granted, and no longer. And upon the decease or displacing of any of the said officers, the succeeding officer, or officers, shall be chosen, as aforesaid.

XIX. That the General Assembly shall continue so long as may be needful to impeach criminals, fit to be there impeached, to pass bills into laws, that they shall think fit to pass into laws, and till such time as the Governor and provincial Council shall declare that they have nothing further to propose unto them, for their assent and approbation: and that declaration shall be a dismiss to the General Assembly for that time; which General Assembly shall be, notwithstanding, capable of assembling together into laws, and till such time as the Governor and provincial Council shall declare that they have nothing further to propose unto them, for their assent and approbation: and that declaration

shall be a dismiss to the General Assembly for that time; which General Assembly shall be, notwithstanding, capable of assembling together upon the summons of the provincial Council, at any time during that year, if the said provincial Council shall see occasion for their so assembling.

XX. That all the elections of members, or representatives of the people, to serve in provincial Council and General Assembly, and all questions to be determined by both, or either of them, that relate to passing of bills into laws, to the choice of officers, to impeachments by the General Assembly, and judgment of criminals upon such impeachments by the provincial Council, and to all other cases by them respectively judged of importance, shall be resolved and determined by the ballot, and unless on sudden and indispensible occasions, no business in provincial Council, or its respective committees, shall be finally determined the same day that it is moved.

XXI. That at all times when, and so often as it shall happen that the Governor shall or may be an infant, under the age of one and twenty years, and no guardians or commissioners are appointed in writing, by the father of the said infant, or that such guardians or commissioners shall be deceased; that during such minority, the provincial Council shall, from time to time, as they shall see meet, constitute and appoint guardians or commissioners, not exceeding three, one of which three shall preside as deputy and chief guardian, during such minority, and shall have and execute, with the consent of the other two, all the power of a Governor, in all the public affairs and concerns of the said province.

XXII. That, as often as any day of the month, mentioned in any article of this charter, shall fall upon the first day of the week, commonly called the Lord's Day, the business appointed for that day shall be deferred till the next day, unless in case of emergency.

XXIII. That no act, law, or ordinance whatsoever, shall at any time hereafter, be made or done by the Governor of this province, his heirs or assigns, or by the freemen in the provincial Council, or the General Assembly, to alter, change, or diminish the form, or effect, of this charter, or any part, or clause thereof, without the consent of the Governor, his heirs, or assigns, and six parts of seven of the said freemen in provincial Council and General Assembly.

XXIV. And lastly, that I, the said for myself, my heirs and assigns, have solemnly declared, granted and confirmed, and do hereby solemnly declare, grant and confirm, that neither I, my heirs, nor assigns, shall procure to do any thing or things, whereby the liberties, in this charter contained and expressed, shall be infringed or broken; and if any thing be procured by any person or persons contrary to these premises, it shall be held of no force or effect. In witness whereof, I, the said William Penn, have unto this present character of liberties set my hand and broad seal, this five and twentieth day of the second month, vulgarly called April, in the year of our Lord one thousand six hundred and eighty-two.

WILLIAM PENN

LAWS AGREED UPON IN ENGLAND, &C.

I. That the charter of liberties, declared, granted and confirmed the five and twentieth day of the second month, called April, 1682, before divers witnesses, by William Penn, Governor and chief Proprietor of Pennsylvania, to all the freemen and planters of the said province, is hereby declared and approved, and shall be for ever held for fundamental in the government thereof, according to the limitations mentioned in the said charter.

II. That every inhabitant in the said province, that is or shall be, a purchaser of one hundred acres of land, or upwards, his heirs and assigns, and every persons who shall have paid his passage, and taken up one hundred acres of land, at one penny an acre, and have cultivated ten acres threof, and every person, that hath been a servant, or bondsman, and is free by his service, that shall have taken up his fifty acres of land, and cultivated twenty thereof, and every inhabitant, artificer, or other resident in the said province, that pays scot and lot to the government; shall be deemed and accounted a freeman of the said province: and every such person shall, and may, be capable of electing, or being elected, representatives of the people, in provincial Council, or General Assembly, in the said province.

III. That all elections of members, or representatives of the people and freemen of the province of Pennsylvania, to serve in provincial Council, or General Assembly, to be held within the said province, shall be free and voluntary: and that the elector, that shall receive any reward or gift, in meat, drink, monies, or otherwise, shall forfeit his right to elect: and such person as shall directly or indirectly give, promise, or bestow any such reward as aforesaid, to be elected, shall forfeit his election, and be thereby incapable to serve as aforesaid: and the provincial Council and General Assembly shall be the sole judges of the regularity, or irregularity of the elections of their own respective Members.

IV. That no money or goods shall be raised upon, or paid by, any of the people of this province by way of public tax, custom or contribution, but by a law, for that purpose made; and whoever shall levy, collect, or pay any money or goods contrary thereunto, shall be held a public enemy to the province and a betrayer of the liberties of the people thereof.

V. That all courts shall be open, and justice shall neither be sold, denied or delayed.

VI. That, in all courts all persons of all persuasions may freely appear in their own way, and acording to their own manner, and there personally plead their own cause themselves; or, if unable, by their friends: and the first process shall be the exhibition of the complaint in court, fourteen days before the trial; and that the party, complained against, may be fitted for the same, he or she shall be summoned, no less than ten days before, and a copy of the complaint delivered him or her, at his or her dwelling house. But before the complaint of any person be received, he shall solemnly declare in court that he believes, in his conscience, his cause is just.

VII. That all pleadings, processes and records in courts, shall be short, and in English, and in an ordinary and plain character, that they may be understood, and justice speedily administered.

VIII. That all trials shall be by twelve men, and as near as may be, peers or equals, and of the neighborhood, and men without just exception; in cases of life, there shall be first twenty-four returned by the sheriffs, for a grand inquest, of whom twelve, at least, shall find the complaint to be true; and then the twelve men, or peers, to be likewise returned by the sheriff, shall have the final judgment. But reasonable challenges shall be always admitted against the said twelve men, or any of them.

IX. That all fees in all cases shall be moderate, and settled by the provincial Council, and General Assembly, and be hung up in a table in every respective court; and whosoever, shall be convicted of taking more, shall pay twofold, and be dismissed his employment; one moiety of which shall go to the party wronged.

X. That all prisons shall be work-houses, for felons, vagrants, and loose and idle persons; whereof one shall be in every county.

XI. That all prisoners shall be bailable by sufficient sureties, unless for capital offences, where the proof is evident, or the presumption great.

XII. That all persons wrongfully imprisoned, or prosecuted at law, shall have double damages against the informer, or prosecutor.

XIII. That all prisons shall be free, as to fees, food, and lodging.

XIV. That all lands and goods shall be liable to pay debts, except where there is legal issue, and then all the goods, and one-third of the land only.

XV. That all wills, in writing, attested by two witnesses, shall be of the same force as to lands, as other conveyances, being legally proved within forty days, either within or without the said province.

XVI. That seven years quiet possession shall give an unquestionable right, except in cases of infants, lunatics, married women, or persons beyond the seas.

XVII. That all briberies and extortion whatsoever shall be severely punished.

XVIII. That all fines shall be moderate, and saving men's contenements, merchandize, or wainage.

XIX. That all marriages (not forbidden by the law of God, as to nearness of blood and affinity by marriage) shall be encouraged; but the parents, or guardians, shall be first consulted, and the marriage shall be published before it be solemnized; and it shall be solemnized by taking one another as husband and wife, before credible witnesses; and a certificate of the whole, under the hands of parties and witnesses, shall be brought to the proper register of that county, and shall be registered in his office.

XX. And, to prevent frauds and vexatious suits within the said province, that all charters, gifts, grants, and conveyances (except leases for a year or under) and all bills, bonds, and specialties above five pounds, and not under three months, made in the said province, shall be enrolled, or registered in the public enrolment office of the said province, within the space of two months next after the making thereof, else to be void in law, and all deeds, grants, and conveyances of land (except as aforesaid) within the said province, and made out of the said province, shall be enrolled or registered, as aforesaid, within six months next after the making thereof, and settling and constituting an enrolment office or registry within the said province, else to be void in law against all persons whatsoever.

XXI. That all defacers or corrupters of charters, gifts, grants, bonds, bills, wills, contracts, and conveyances, or that shall deface or falsify any enrolment, registry or record, within this province, shall make double satisfaction for the same; half whereof shall go to the party wronged, and they shall be dismissed of all places of trust, and be publicly disgraced as false men.

XXII. That there shall be a register for births, marriages, burials, wills, and letters of administration, distinct from the other registry.

XXIII. That there shall be a register for all servants, where their names, time, wages, and days of payment shall be registered.

XXIV. That all lands and goods of felons shall be liable, to make satisfaction to the party wronged twice the value; and for want of lands or goods, the felons shall be bondmen to work in the common prison, or work-house, or otherwise, till the party injured be satisfied.

XXV. That the estates of capital offenders, as traitors and murderers, shall go, one-third to the next of kin to the sufferer, and the remainder to the next of kin to the criminal.

XXVI. That all witnesses, coming, or called, to testify their knowledge in or to any matter or thing, in any court, or before any lawful authority, within the said province, shall there give or delivery in their evidence, or testimony, by solemnly promising to speak the truth, the whole truth, and nothing but the truth, to the matter, or thing in question. And in case any person so called to evidence, shall be convicted of wilful falsehood, such person shall suffer and undergo such damage or penalty, as the person, or persons, against whom he or she bore false witness, did, or should, undergo; and shall also make satisfaction to the party wronged, and be publicly exposed as a false witness, never to be credited in any court, or before any Magistrate, in the said province.

XXVII. And, to the end that all officers chosen to serve within this province, may, with more care and dilligence, answer the trust reposed in them, it is agreed, that no such person shall enjoy more than one public office, at one time.

XXVIII. That all children, within this province, of the age of twelve years, shall be taught some useful trade or skill, to the end none may be idle, but the poor may work to live, and the rich, if they become poor may not want.

XXIX. That servants be not kept longer than their time, and such as are careful, be both justly and kindly used in their service, and put in fitting equipage at the expiration thereof, according to custom.

XXX. That all scandalous and malicious reporters, backbiters, defamers and spreaders of false news, whether against Magistrates, or private persons, shall be accordingly severely punished, as enemies to the peace and concord of this province.

XXXI. That for the encouragement of the planters and traders in this province, who are incorporated into a society, the patent granted to them by William Penn, Governor of the said province, is hereby ratified and confirmed.

XXXII. . . .

XXXIII. That all factors or correspondents in the said province, wronging their employers, shall make satisfaction, and one-third over, to their said employers: and in case of the death of any such factor or correspondent, the committee of trade shall take care to secure so much of the deceased party's estate as belongs to his said respective employers.

XXXIV. That all Treasurers, Judges, Masters of the Rolls, Sheriffs, Justices of the Peace, and other officers and persons whatsoever, relating to courts, or trials of causes, or any other service in the government; and all Members elected to serve in provincial Council and General Assembly, and all that have right to elect such Members, shall be such as possess faith in Jesus Christ, and that are not convicted of ill fame, or unsober and dishonest conversation, and that are of one and twenty years of age, at least; and that all such so qualified, shall be capable of the said several employments and privileges, as aforesaid.

XXXV. That all persons living in this province, who confess and acknowledge the one Almighty and eternal God, to be the Creator, Upholder and Ruler of the world; and that hold themselves obliged in conscience to live peaceable and justly in civil society, shall, in no ways, be molested or prejudiced for their religious persuasion, or practice, in matters of faith and worship, nor shall they be compelled, at any time, to frequent or maintain any religious worship, place or ministry whatever.

XXXVI. That, according to the good example of the primitive Christians, and the case of the creation, every first day of the week, called the Lord's day, people shall abstain from their common daily labour, that they may better dispose themselves to worship God according to their understandings.

XXXVII. That as a careless and corrupt administration of justice draws the wrath of God upon magistrates, so the wildness and looseness of the people provoke the indignation of God against a country: therefore, that all such offences against God, as swearing, cursing, lying, prophane talking, drunkenness, drinking of healths, obscene words, incest, sodomy, rapes, whoredom, fornication, and other uncleanness (not to be repeated) all treasons, misprisions, murders, duels, felony, seditions, maims, forcible entries, and other violences, to the persons and estates of the inhabitants within this province; all prizes, stage-plays, cards, dice, May-games, gamesters, masques, revels, bull-baitings, cock-fightings, bear-baitings, and the like, which excite the people to rudeness, cruelty, looseness, and irreligion, shall be respectively discouraged, and severely punished, according to the appointment of the Governor and freemen in provincial Council and General Assembly; as also all proceedings contrary to these laws, that are not here made expressly penal.

XXXVIII. That a copy of these laws shall be hung up in the provincial Council, and in public courts of justice: and that they shall be read yearly at the opening of every provincial Council and General Assembly, and court of justice; and their assent shall be testified, by their standing up after the reading thereof.

XXXIX. That there shall be, at no time, any alteration of any of these laws, without the consent of the Governor, his heirs, or assigns, and six parts of seven of the freemen, met in provincial Council and General Assembly.

XL. That all other matters and things not herein provided for, which shall, and may, concern the public justice, peace, or safety of the said province; and the raising and imposing taxes, customs, duties, or other charges whatsoever, shall be, and are, hereby referred to the order, prudence and determination of the Governor and freemen, in Provincial Council and General Assembly, to be held, from time to time, in the said province.

Signed and sealed by the Governor and freemen aforesaid, the fifth day of the third month, called one thousand six hundred and eighty-two.

Dorchester Agreement

October 8, 1633

The New England town meeting, so often seen as the heart of American democratic practice, was often a quite formal affair. Rules of order were developed over time, and the institution itself was often grounded in official documents. The township of Dorchester was among the first to formally provide for a smaller body of selectmen to carry on the business of the town meeting when it was not in session. This set the stage for further developments in governmental forms and for local conflicts between the people and their representatives.

Dorchester Agreement

An agreement made by the whole consent and vote of the plantation made Mooneday 8th of October, 1633

Inprimus it is ordered that for the generall good and well ordering of the affayres of the Plantation their shall be every Mooneday before the Court by eight of the Clocke in the morning, and prsently upon the beating of the drum, a generall meeting of the inhabitants of the Plantation att the meeteing house, there to settle (and sett downe) such orders as may tend to the generall good as aforesayd; and every man to be bound thereby without gaynesaying or resistance. It is also agreed that there shall be twelve men selected out of the Company that may or the greatest p't of them meete as aforesayd to determine as aforesayd, yet so as it is desired that the most of the Plantation will keepe the meeting constantly and all that are there although none of the Twelve shall have a free voyce as any of the 12 and that the greate[r] vote both of the 12 and the other shall be of force and efficasy as aforesayd. And it is likewise ordered that all things concluded as aforesayd shall stand in force and be obeyed vntill the next monethly meeteing and afterwardes if it be not contradicted and otherwise ordered upon the sayd monethly meete[ing] by the greatest p'te of those that are prsent as aforesayd. Moreover, because the Court in Winter in the vacansy of the sayd [   ] this said meeting to continue till the first Mooneday in the moneth mr Johnson, mr Eltwid Pummery (mr. Richards), John Pearce, George Hull, William Phelps, Thom. ffoard.

Maryland Act for Swearing Allegiance
1638

Plymouth Oath of Allegiance and Fidelity
1625

Current American oaths, including that demanded of witnesses giving testimony at trial and the so-called Pledge of Allegiance, constitute remnants of a centuries-long tradition demanding that citizens and subjects bind themselves to their political communities and leaders. England's Henry VIII used this tradition, among other means, to force the conversion of his people from the Catholic Church by demanding that they swear the Oath of Supremacy to him as head of the English Church. James I later required an oath to himself, but not as head of the church. Charles I, who reigned between 1625 and 1649, required both oaths of his subjects. However, because they were governed according to derivative charters, not all colonists were called on to swear them. Maryland, settled in large measure by Catholics fleeing English laws forbidding the practice of their religion, sought a more lenient oath. Protestant dissenters, likewise alienated from the hierarchy of the Church of England, also sought to avoid swearing oaths they thought impious. Local conditions—including provisions in the Massachusetts Bay charter, Plymouth plantation's existence beyond the borders of any chartered colony, and actions by local authorities—allowed for compromise. Maryland's Catholics were not required to recognize the king as head of their church, so long as they agreed to serve him as their temporal sovereign. The Puritans of Plymouth went further, using the oath swearing as a means by which to bind community members to the colony itself. In this way they undergirded the colonial government's legitimacy and provided a means by which to bring in new members as time went by.

Maryland Act for Swearing Allegiance

Be it Enacted and ordeined by the Lord Proprietarie of this Province by and with the Consent and approbation of the ffreemen of the same that all and every person or persons of the age of eighteen years and upwards Inhabitants or that Shall come hereafter to Inhabite within this Province shall within one month next after this present Assembly shall be dissolved or within one month after such person or persons shall land or come into this Province take an oath to our Soveraigne Lord King Charles his heirs and Successors in these words following (I: A B doe truly acknowledge professe testifie and declare in my concience before God and the World that our Soveraigne Lord King Charles is lawfull and rightfull King of England and of all other his Majesties Dominions and Countries and I will bear true faith and allegeance to his Majestie his heirs and lawfull Successors and him and them will defend to the uttermost of my power against all conspiracies and such attempts whatsoever which shall be made against his or their Crowne or dignity and shall and will doe my best endeavour to disclose and make known to his Majestie his heirs and lawfull Successors all Treasons and traiterous consperacies which I shall know or heare to be intended against his Majestie his heirs and lawfull Successors And I doe make this recognition and acknowledgement heartily willingly and truely upon the faith of a Christian So help me God) And Be it further Enacted By the authority aforesaid that if any person or persons to whom the Said oaths Shall be tendred by Virtue of this present act Shall willfully refuse to take the same that then Upon such tender and refusall the said person or persons so refuseing to take the said Oath shall be imprisoned till the next County Court or hundred Court of Kent and if at such Court such partie shall upon the Second tender refuse again to take the said oath the partie or parties so refuseing shall forfeit and lose all his Lands goods and Chattells within this Province to the Lord Proprietarie and his heirs and Shall be banished the said Province for ever (except women covert who Shall be committed only to prison untill such time as they will take the same oath).

To which end Be it further Enacted by the authority aforesaid that the Lieutent Generall or other officer Governour or Governours (for the time being) of this Province or two of the Councill or the Secretary of the Province for the time being or any Judge sitting in Court or the Commander of the Isle of Kent for persons being or that Shall be in the Ile of Kent Shall have full power to administer the said oath in manner aforesaid according to the intention of this present act This Act to continue till the end of the next assembly

Plymouth Oath of Allegiance and Fidelity

FORM OF OATH FOR ALL INHABITANTS
You shall sweare by the name of the great God . . . & earth & in his holy fear, & presence that you shall not speake, or doe, devise, or advise, anything or things, acte or acts, directly, or indirectly, By land, or water, that doth, shall, or may, tend to the destruction or overthrowe of this present plantation, Colonie, or Corporation of this towne Plimouth in New England.

Neither shall you suffer the same to be spoken, or done, but shall hinder & opposse the same, by all due means you can.

You shall not enter into any league, treaty, Confederace or combination, with any, within the said Colonie or without the same that shall plote, or contrive any thing to the hurte & ruine of the growth, and good of the said plantation.

You shall not consente to any such confederation, nor conceale any known unto you certainly, or by conje but shall forthwith manifest & make knowne by same, to the Governours of this said towne for the time being.

And this you promise & swear, simply & truly, & faithfully to performe as a true christian [you hope for help from God, the God of truth & punisher of falshoode].

FORM OF THE OATH GIVEN THE GOVERNOR
AND COUNCIL AT EVERY ELECTION
You shall swear, according to that wisdom, and measure of discerning given unto you; faithfully, equally & indifrently without respect of persons; to administer Justice, in all causes coming before you. And shall labor, to advance, & furder the good of this Colony, & plantation, to the utmost of your power; and oppose any thing that may hinder the same. So help you God.

Little Speech on Liberty

JOHN WINTHROP

1645

John Winthrop (1588–1649) was the son of a lawyer and himself practiced law until 1629 when, after the death of his second wife, his disillusionment with religious and political life in England caused him to seek a better life in New England. Already prominent among Puritan leaders, Winthrop was elected governor of Massachusetts Bay colony prior to his arrival in 1630. His speech on board the ship *Arrabella,* "A Modell of Christian Charity" (1630), provides a famous picture of Puritan community life and the call to be as "a City upon a Hill," providing an example of godly virtue for all nations. Winthrop served as governor for twelve of his remaining nineteen years, but his authority was not unquestioned. He presided over the trial and expulsion of Anne Hutchinson for preaching her antinomian views and in 1645 suffered impeachment (though he was acquitted) arising from charges that he showed too little respect for the judgment, desires, and liberties of the common people of his colony. In his "Little Speech on Liberty," delivered on his acquittal, Winthrop distinguishes between the natural liberty shared by all creatures to do what they desire and the civil liberty that allows a people to do what God demands.

Governor Winthrop's Speech

I suppose something may be expected from me, upon this charge that is befallen me, which moves me to speak now to you; yet I intend not to intermeddle in the proceedings of the court, or with any of the persons concerned therein. Only I bless God, that I see an issue of this troublesome business. I also acknowledge the justice of the court, and, for mine own part, I am well satisfied, I was publicly charged, and I am publicly and legally acquitted, which is all I did expect or desire. And though this be sufficient for my justification before men, yet not so before the God, who hath seen so much amiss in my dispensations (and even in this affair) as calls me to be humble. For to be publicly and criminally charged in this court, is matter of humiliation, (and I desire to make a right use of it,) notwithstanding I

be thus acquitted. If her father had spit in her face, (saith the Lord concerning Miriam,) should she not have been ashamed seven days? Shame had lien upon her, whatever the occasion had been. I am unwilling to stay you from your urgent affairs, yet give me leave (upon this special occasion) to speak a little more to this assembly. It may be of some good use, to inform and rectify the judgments of some of the people, and may prevent such distempers as have arisen amongst us. The great questions that have troubled the country, are about the authority of the magistrates and the liberty of the people. It is yourselves who have called us to this office, and being called by you, we have our authority from God, in way of an ordinance, such as hath the image of God eminently stamped upon it, the contempt and violation whereof hath been vindicated with examples of divine vengeance. I entreat you to consider, that when you choose magistrates, you take them from among yourselves, men subject to like passions as you are. Therefore when you see infirmities in us, you should reflect upon your own, and that would make you bear the more with us, and not be severe censurers of the failings of your magistrates, when you have continual experience of the like infirmities in yourselves and others. We account him a good servant, who breaks not his covenant. The covenant between you and us is the oath you have taken of us, which is to this purpose, that we shall govern you and judge your causes by the rules of God's laws and our own, according to our best skill. When you agree with a workman to build you a ship or house, etc., he undertakes as well for his skill as for his faithfulness, for it his profession, and you pay him for both. But when you call one to be a magistrate, he doth not profess nor undertake to have sufficient skill for that office, nor can you furnish him with gifts, etc., therefore you must run the hazard of his skill and ability. But if he fail in faithfulness, which by his oath he is bound unto, that he must answer for. If it fall out that the case be clear to common apprehension, and the rule clear also, if he transgress here, the error is not in the skill, but in the evil of the will: it must be required of him. But if the case be doubtful, or the rule doubtful, to men of such understanding and parts as your magistrates are, if your magistrates should err here, yourselves must bear it.

For the other point concerning liberty, I observe a great mistake in the country about that. There is a twofold liberty, natural (I mean as our nature is now corrupt) and civil or federal. The first is common to man with beasts and other creatures. By this, man, as he stands in relation to man simply, hath liberty to do what he lists; it is a liberty to evil as well as to good. This liberty is incompatible and inconsistent with authority, and cannot endure the least restraint of the most just authority. The exercise and maintaining of this liberty makes men grow more evil, and in time to be worse than brute beasts: *omnes sumus licentiâ deteriores.* This is that great enemy of truth and peace, that wild beast, which all the ordinances of God are bent against, to restrain and subdue it. The other kind of liberty I call civil or federal; it may also be termed moral, in reference to the covenant between God and man, in the moral law, and the politic covenants and constitutions amongst men themselves. This liberty is the proper end and object of authority, and cannot subsist without it; and it is a liberty to that only which is good, just, and honest. This liberty you are to stand for, with the hazard (not only of your goods, but) of your lives, if need be. Whatsoever crosseth this, is not authority, but a distemper thereof. This liberty is maintained and exercised in a way of subjection to authority; it is of the same kind of liberty wherewith Christ hath made us free. The woman's own choice makes such a man her husband; yet being so chosen, he is her lord, and she is to be subject to him, yet in a way of liberty, not of bondage; and a true wife accounts her subjection her honor and freedom, and would not think her condition safe and free, but in her subjection to her husband's authority. Such is the liberty of the church under the authority of Christ, her king and husband; his yoke is so easy and sweet to her as a bride's ornaments; and if through frowardness or wantonness, etc., she shake it off, at any time, she is at no rest in her spirit, until she take it up again; and whether her lord smiles upon her, and embraceth her in his arms, or whether he frowns, or rebukes, or smites her, she apprehends the sweetness of his love in all, and is refreshed, supported, and instructed by every such dispensation of his authority over her. On the other side, ye know who they are that complain of this yoke and say, let us break their bands, etc., we will not have this man to rule over us. Even so, brethren, it will be between you and your magistrates. If you stand for your natural corrupt liberties, and will do what is good in your own eyes, you will not endure the least weight of authority, but will murmur, and oppose, and be always striving to shake off that yoke; but if you will be satisfied to enjoy such civil and lawful liberties, such as Christ allows you, then will you quietly and cheerfully submit unto that authority which is set over you, in all the administrations of it, for your good. Wherein, if we fail at any time, we hope we shall be willing (by God's assistance) to hearken to good advice from any of you, or in any other way of God; so shall your liberties be preserved, in upholding the honor and power of authority amongst you.

Copy of a Letter from Mr. Cotton to Lord Say and Seal

JOHN COTTON

1636

John Cotton (1584–1652), the son of a successful lawyer, was a prominent minister in England until 1633. In that year, his skills and connections finally failed to protect him from a hostile Anglican hierarchy, and he was dismissed from his post for failing to conform to Church of England doctrines. He left for New England, where he became a leading teacher and minister. The letter to Lord Say and Seal was written in response to a Puritan nobleman who expressed an interest in emigrating to America. Lord Say and Seal was concerned that Puritan practice in the colonies would not guarantee that the social position held by his friends and himself would automatically gain them citizenship, church membership, and leading positions in the community. Cotton responded by defending the Puritan reliance on church membership as a sign of godly virtue both necessary and sufficient for full citizenship. The nobleman did not move to New England.

Copy of a Letter from Mr. Cotton to Lord Say and Seal in the Year 1636

Right honourable,

What your Lordship writeth of Dr. Twisse his works *de scientiâ mediâ,* and of the sabbath, it did refresh me to read, that his labors of such arguments were like to come to light; and it would refresh me much more to see them here: though (for my owne particular) till I gett some release from some constant labors here (which the church is desirous to procure) I can get litle, or noe oppertunity to reade any thing, or attend to any thing, but the dayly occurrences which presse in upon me continually, much beyond my strength either of body or minde. Your Lordships advertisement touching the civill state of this colony, as they doe breath forth your singular wisdome, and faithfulness, and tender care of the peace, so wee have noe reason to misinterprite, or undervalue your Lordships eyther directions, or intentions therein. I know noe man under heaven (I speake in Gods feare without flattery) whose counsell I should rather depend upon, for the wise administration of a civill state according to God, than upon your Lordship, and such confidence have I (not in you) but in the Lords presence in Christ with you, that I should never feare to betrust a greater commonwealth than this (as much as in us lyeth) under such a *perpetuâ dictaturâ* as your lordship should prescribe. For I nothing doubt, but that eyther your Lordship would prescribe all things according to the rule, or be willing to examine againe, and againe, all things according to it. I am very apt to believe, what Mr. Perkins hath, in one of his prefatory pages to his golden chaine, that the word, and scriptures of God doe conteyne a short *upoluposis,* or platforme, not onely of theology, but also of other sacred sciences (as he calleth them) attendants, and hand maids thereunto, which he maketh ethicks, eoconomicks, politicks, church-government, prophecy, academy. It is very suitable to Gods all-sufficient wisdome, and to the fulnes and perfection of Holy Scriptures, not only to prescribe perfect rules for the right ordering of a private mans soule to everlasting blessednes with himselfe, but also for the right ordering of a mans family, yea, of the commonwealth too, so farre as both of them are subordinate to spiritual ends, and yet avoide both the churches usurpation upon civill jurisdictions, *in ordine ad spiritualia,* and the commonwealths invasion upon ecclesiasticall administrations, *in ordine* to civill peace, and conformity to the civill state. Gods institutions (such as the government of church and of commonwealth be) may be close and compact, and coordinate one to another, and yet not confounded. God hath so framed the state of church government and ordinances, that they may be compatible to any commonwealth, though never so much disordered in his frame. But yet when a commonwealth hath liberty to mould his owne frame (*scripturae plenitudinem adoro*) I conceyve the scripture hath given full direction for the right ordering of the same, and that, in such sort as may best mainteyne the *eu-*

exia of the church. Mr. Hooker doth often quote a saying out of Mr. Cartwright (though I have not read it in him) that noe man fashioneth his house to his hangings, but his hangings to his house. It is better that the commonwealth be fashioned to the setting forth of Gods house, which is his church: than to accommodate the church frame to the civill state. Democracy, I do not conceyve that ever God did ordeyne as a fitt government eyther for church or commonwealth. If the people be governors, who shall be governed? As for monarchy, and aristocracy, they are both of them clearely approved, and directed in scripture, yet so as referreth the soveraigntie to himselfe, and setteth up Theocracy in both, as the best forme of government in the commonwealth, as well as in the church.

The law, which your Lordship instanceth in [that none shall be chosen to magistracy among us, but a church member] was made and enacted before I came into the countrey; but I have hitherto wanted sufficient light to plead against it. 1st. The rule that directeth the choice of supreame governors, is of like aequitie and weight in all magistrates, that one of their brethren (not a stranger) should be set over them. Deut. 17.15. and Jethroes counsell to Moses was approved of God, that the judges, and officers to be set over the people, should be men fearing God. Exod. 18. 21. and Solomon maketh it the joy of a commonwealth, when the righteous are in authority, and their mourning when the wicked rule, Prov. 29. 21. Job 34. 30. Your Lordship's feare, that this will bring in papal excommunicatjon, is iust, and pious; but let your Lordship be pleased againe to consider whether the consequence be necessary. *Turpius ejicitur quam non admittitur:* nonmembership may be a iust cause of non-admission to the place of magistracy, but yet, ejection out of his membership will not be a iust cause of ejecting him out of his magistracy. A godly woman, being to make choice of an husband, may iustly refuse a man that is eyther cast out of church fellowship, or is not yet receyved into it, but yet, when shee is once given to him, shee may not reject him then, for such defect. Mr. Humfrey was chosen for an assistant (as I heare) before the colony came over hither: and, though he be not as yet ioyned into church fellowship (by reason of the unsetlednes of the congregation where he liveth) yet the commonwealth doe still continue his magistracy to him, as knowing he waiteth for oppertunity of enioying church-fellowship shortly.

When your Lordship doubteth, that this corse will draw all things under the determination of the church, *in ordine ad spiritualia* (seeing the church is to determine who shall be members, and none but a member may have to doe in the government of a commonwealth) be pleased (I pray you) to conceyve, that magistrates are neyther chosen to office in the church, nor doe governe by directions from the church, but by civill lawes, and those enacted in generall corts, and executed in corts of iustice, by the governors and assistants. In all which, the church (as the church) hath nothing to doe: onely, it prepareth fitt instruments both to rule, and to choose rulers, which is no ambition in the church, nor dishonor to the commonwealth, the apostle, on the contrary, thought it a great dishonor and reproach to the church of Christ, if it were not able to yield able judges to heare and determine all causes amongst their brethren. i. Cor, 6. i. to 5. which place alone seemeth to me fully to decide this question: for it plainely holdeth forth this argument: It is a shame to the church to want able judges of civill matters and an audacious act in any church member voluntarily to go for judgment, other where than before the saints (as v. i.) then it will be noe arrogance nor folly in church members, nor preiudice to the commonwealth, if voluntarily they never choose any civill judges but from amongst the saints, such as church members are called to be. But the former is cleare: and how then can the latter be avoyded. If this therefore be (as your Lordship rightly conceyveth one of the maine objections if not the onely one) which hindereth this commonwealth from the entertainment of the propositions of those worthy gentlemen, wee intreate them, in the name of the Lord Jesus, to consider, in meeknes of wisdome, it is not any conceite, or will of ours, but the holy counsell and will of the Lord Jesus (whom they seeke to serve as well as wee) that overruleth us in this case: and we trust will overrule them also, that the Lord onely may be exalted amongst all his servants. What pittie and griefe were it, that the observance of the will of Christ should hinder good things from us!

But your Lordship doubteth, that if such a rule were necessary, then the church estate and the best ordered commonwealth in the world were not compatible. But let not your Lordship so conceyve. For, the church submitteth it selfe to all the lawes and ordinances of men, in what commonwealth soever they come to dwell. But it is one thing, to submit unto what they have noe calling to reforme: another thing, voluntarily to ordeyne a forme of government, which to the best discerning of many of us (for I speake not of myselfe) is expressly contrary to rule. Nor neede your Lordship feare (which yet I speake with submission to your Lordships better judgment) that this corse will lay such a foundation, as nothing but a mere democracy can be built upon it. Bodine confesseth, that though it be *status popularis,* where a people choose their owne governors; yet the government is not a democracy, if it be administred, not by the people, but by the governors, whether one (for then it is a monarchy, though elective) or by many, for then (as you know) it is aristocracy. In which respect it is, that church government is iustly denied (even by Mr. Robinson) to be democratical, though the people choose their owne officers and rulers.

Nor neede wee feare, that this course will, in time, cast the commonwealth into distractions, and popular confusions. For (under correction) these three things doe not undermine, but doe mutually and strongly mainteyne one another (even those three which wee principally aime at) authority in magistrates, liberty in people, purity in the church. Purity, preserved in the church, will preserve well ordered liberty in the people, and both of them establish well-ballanced authority in the magistrates. God is the author of all these three, and neyther is himselfe the God of confusion, nor are his wayes the wayes of confusion, but of peace.

What our brethren (magistrates or ministers, or leading freeholders) will answer to the rest of the propositions, I shall better understand before the gentlemans returne from Connecticutt, who brought them over. Mean while, two of the principall of them, the generall cort hath already condescended unto. 1. In establishing a standing councell, who, during their lives, should assist the governor in managing the chiefest affayres of this little state. They have chosen, for the present, onely two (Mr. Winthrope and Mr. Dudley) not willing to choose more, till they see what further better choyse the Lord will send over to them, that so they may keep an open doore, for such desireable gentlemen as your Lordship mentioneth. 2. They have graunted the governor and assistants a negative voyce, and reserved to the freemen the like liberty also. Touching other things, I hope to give your Lordship further account, when the gentleman returneth.

He being now returned, I have delivered to him an answer to the rest of your demands, according to the mindes of such leading men amongst us, as I thought meete to consult withall, concealing your name from any, except 2 or 3, who alike doe concurr in a joynt desire of yeilding to any such propositions, as your Lordship demandeth, so farre as with allowance from the word they may, beyond which I know your Lordship would not require any thing.

Now the Lord Jesus Christ (the prince of peace) keepe and bless your Lordship, and dispose of all your times and talents to his best advantage: and let the covenant of his grace and peace rest upon your honourable family and posterity, throughout all generations.

Thus, humbly craving pardon for my boldnesse and length, I take leave and rest,

Your Honours to serve in Christ Jesus,

J. C.

PART TWO Religious Society and Religious
Liberty in Early America

Portrait of George Washington by John Trumbull. © Bettmann/CORBIS

Throughout America, as throughout Europe, religious life and political life were intimately tied during the seventeenth and eighteenth centuries. Debates over religious toleration generally concerned whether people holding minority beliefs—be they Catholics in a Protestant country, Protestants in a Catholic nation, or dissenting Protestant groups within either—should be allowed to practice their religion without criminal sanction.

The modern liberal state, set up to protect individual choice against the demands of political, religious, and sometimes economic pressure, did not yet exist. Violent conflict still arose over religious disagreements. One cause of the English Civil War was opposition to Charles I's drive to bring dissenters to heel within the Anglican Church, which Charles was making more "Catholic" in its ceremonies. Religious disagreements could become violent because all sides considered them important. Civil government rested on religious faith and would crumble without it. Moreover, in a time during which people took seriously the possibility of both salvation and damnation, the tendency of particular belief systems to promote or undermine salvation was considered crucial, as was the tendency of particular political institutions to promote or undermine good religion.

The Bloody Tenent, of Persecution, for Cause of Conscience

ROGER WILLIAMS

1644

Roger Williams (1603–83) began his career as a minister in the Church of England. His Puritan ideas caused him to immigrate to New England in 1631, where his religious beliefs continued to change. He first became a kind of Baptist, then refused to adhere to any single Christian doctrine. He was banished from Massachusetts Bay in 1636 for preaching his beliefs. Soon thereafter, Williams helped found the colony of Rhode Island. This colony lacked a charter, so, in 1643, Williams returned to England to secure one. He also set about writing *The Bloody Tenent, of Persecution, for Cause of Conscience, discussed, in a Conference betweene Truth and Peace.* The "conference" between Truth and Peace (with Truth speaking for Williams) begins after the portion reproduced here. This portion is taken up with Williams's dedication to the English parliament and a "letter" that Williams sent to Puritan leader John Cotton, which was purportedly written by a man who had been imprisoned for his religious beliefs. The letter seeks Cotton's opinion as to whether the persecution of religious dissent can ever be properly imposed. Williams's book begins with this letter, which is followed by Cotton's reply, which in turn is followed by the conference between Truth and Peace.

The Bloody Tenent, of Persecution, for Cause of Conscience

To the Right Honorable, both Houses of the High Court of Parliament

Right Honourable and Renowned Patriots:

Next to the saving of your own *soules* (in the lamentable *shipwrack* of *Mankind*) your taske (as *Christians*) is to save the *Soules,* but as *Magistrates,* the *Bodies* and *Goods* of others.

Many excellent *Discourses* have been presented to your *Fathers* hands and Yours in former and present *Parliaments:* I shall be humbly bold to say, that (in what concernes your duties as *Magistrates,* towards others) a more necessary and seasonable *debate* was never yet presented.

Two things your *Honours* here may please to view (in this Controversie of *Persecution* for cause of *Conscience*) beyond what's extant.

First the whole *Body* of this *Controversie* form'd & pitch'd in true *Battalia.*

Secondly (although in respect of my selfe it be *impar congressus,* yet in the power of that *God* who is *Maximus in Minimis,* Your Honours shall see the Controversie is discussed with men as able as most, eminent for *abilitie* and *pietie,* Mr. *Cotton,* and the *New English Ministers.*

When the *Prophets* in Scripture have given their *Coats of Armes* and *Escutchions* to *Great Men,* Your *Honours* know the *Babylonian Monarch* hath the *Lyon,* the *Persian* the *Beare,* the *Grecian* the *Leopard,* the *Romane* a *compound* of the former 3. most strange and dreadfull, *Dan.* 7.

Their oppressing, plundring, ravishing, murthering, not only of the *bodies,* but the *soules* of Men are large explaining *commentaries* of such similitudes.

Your *Honours* have been famous to the end of the World, for your unparallel'd *wisdome, courage, justice, mercie,* in the vindicating your Civill *Lawes, Liberties,* &c. Yet let it not be grievous to your *Honours* thoughts to ponder a little, why all the *Prayers* and *Teares* and *Fastings* in this Nation have not pierc'd the *Heavens,* and quench'd these *Flames,* which yet who knowes how far they'll spread, and when they'll out!

Your *Honours* have broke the jawes of the *Oppressour,* and taken the prey out of their Teeth (*Iob.* 29.) For which Act I believe it hath pleased the most High *God* to set a *Guard* (not only of Trained Men, but) of mighty *Angels,* to secure your sitting and the Citie.

I feare we are not *pardoned,* though *reprieved:* O that there may be a lengthning of *Londons* tranquilitie, of the *Parliaments* safetie, by *mercy* to the *poore!* Dan. 4.

Right Honorable, *Soule yokes, Soule oppression, plundrings, ravishings, &c.* are of a *crimson* and *deepest dye,* and I believe the chiefe of *Englands* sins, unstopping the Viols of *Englands* present sorrowes.

This glasse presents your *Honours* with *Arguments* from *Religion, Reason, Experience,* all proving that the greatest yoakes yet lying upon *English necks,* (the *peoples* and Your *own*) are of a *spirituall* and *soule* nature.

All former *Parliaments* have changed these yoakes according to their *consciences,* (*Popish* or *Protestant*) 'Tis now your *Honours* turne at *helme,* and (as your *task,* so I hope your *resolution,* not to change (for that is but to turne the wheele, which another *Parliament,* and the very next may turne againe:) but to ease the Subjects and Your selves from a *yoake* (as was once spoke in a case not unlike *Act.* 15.) which neither You nor your Fathers were ever able to beare.

Most *Noble Senatours,* Your *Fathers* (whose *seats* You fill) are mouldred, and mouldring their *braines,* their *tongues,* &c. to *ashes* in the pit of *rottenesse:* They and You must shortly (together with two *worlds* of men) appeare at the great *Barre:* It shall then be no griefe of heart that you have now attended to the *cries* of *Soules, thousands oppressed, millions ravished* by the *Acts* and *Statutes* concerning *Soules,* not yet *repealed.*

Of *Bodies impoverished, imprisoned,* &c. for their *soules* beliefe, yea slaughtered on heapes for *Religions* controversies in the *Warres* of present and former Ages.

"Notwithstanding the success of later times, (wherein sundry opinions have been hatched about the subject of *Religion*) a man may clearly discerne with his eye, and as it were touch with his finger that according to the verity of holy Scriptures, &c. mens *consciences* ought in no sort to be violated, urged or constrained. And whensoever men have attempted any thing by this violent course, whether openly or by secret meanes, the issue hath beene pernicious, and the cause of great and *wonderfull innovations* in the principallest and mightiest *Kingdomes* and *Countries,* &c.

It cannot be denied to be a pious and prudentiall *act* for Your *Honours* (according to your conscience) to call for the advice of faithfull *Councellours* in the high debates concerning Your owne, and the soules of others.

Yet let it not be imputed as a *crime* for any *suppliant* to the *God* of *Heaven* for You, if in the humble sense of what their soules beleeve, they powre forth (amongst others) these three *requests* at the *Throne* of *Grace.*

First, That neither Your *Honours,* nor those excellent and worthy persons, whose advice you seek, limit the holy *One* of *Israel* to their *apprehensions, debates, conclusions,* rejecting or neglecting the humble and faithfull suggestions of any, though as base as spittle and clay, with which sometimes *Christ Iesus* opens the *eyes* of them that are borne blinde.

Secondly, That the present and future *generations* of the Sons of Men may never have cause to say that such a *Parliament* (as *England* never enjoyed the like) should modell the *worship* of the *living, eternall* and *invisible God* after the *Bias* of any earthly *interest,* though of the highest concernment under the Sunne: And yet, faith that learned Sir *Francis Bacon* (how ever otherwise perswaded, yet thus he confesseth:) "Such as hold *pressure* of *Conscience,* are guided therein by some private *interests* of their owne."

Thirdly, What ever way of *worshipping God* Your owne *Consciences* are perswaded to walke in, yet (from any *bloody act* of violence to the consciences of others) it may bee never told at *Rome* nor *Oxford,* that the *Parliament* of *England* hath committed a greater *rape,* then if they had forced or ravished the bodies of all the women in the *World.*

And that *Englands Parliament* (so famous throughout all Europe and the World) should at last turne *Papists, Prelatists, Presbyterians, Independents, Socinians, Familists, Antinomians,* &c. by confirming all these sorts of Consciences, by Civill force and violence to their Consciences.

Scriptures and Reasons written long since by a Witnesse of Jesus Christ, close Prisoner in Newgate, against Persecution in cause of Conscience; and sent some while since to Mr. Cotton, by a Friend who thus wrote:

In the multitude of Councellours there is safety: It is therefore humbly desired to be instructed in this point: viz.

Whether Persecution for cause of Conscience be not against the Doctrine of Jesus Christ the King of Kings. The Scriptures and Reasons are these.

Because *Christ* commandeth that the *Tares* and *Wheat* (which some understand are those that walke in the *Truth,* and those that walke in *Lies*) should be *let alone* in the *World,* and not *plucked* up untill the *Harvest,* which is the end of the *World, Matth.* 13. 30. 38. &c.

The same commandeth *Matth.* 15. 14. that they that are *Blinde* (as some interpret, led on in false *Religion,* and are offended with him for teaching true *Religion*) should be *let alone,* referring their punishment unto their falling into the *Ditch.*

Againe, *Luke* 9. 54, 55. hee reproved his *Disciples* who would have had *Fire* come downe from Heaven and devoure those *Samaritanes* who would not receive Him, in these words: Ye know not of what *Spirit* ye are, the son of Man is not come to destroy *Mens lives,* but to save them.

Paul the Apostle of our Lord teacheth, 2 *Tim.* 24. 2. That the servant of the Lord must not *strive,* but must be *gentle* toward *all Men,* suffering the Evill Men, instructing them with *meeknesse* that are contrary minded, proving if *God* at any time will give them *repentance,* that they may acknowledge the Truth, and come to *amendment* out of that snare of the *devill,* &c.

According to these blessed *Commandements,* the holy *Prophets* foretold, that when the *Law* of *Moses* (concerning *Worship*) should cease, and *Christs Kingdome* be established, *Esa.* 2. 4. *Mic.* 4. 3, 4. They shall breake their *Swords* into *Mathookes,* and their *Speares* into *Sithes.* And *Esa.* 11. 9. Then shall none hurt or destroy in all the *Mountaine* of my Holinesse, &c. And when he came, the same he *taught* and *practised,* as before: so did his *Disciples* after him, for the *Weapons* of his *Warfare* are not *carnall* (saith the Apostle) 2 *Cor.* 10. 4.

But he chargeth straitly that his Disciples should be so far from persecuting those that would not bee of their Religion, that when they were *persecuted* they should *pray* (*Matth.* 5.) when they were *cursed* they should *blesse,* &c.

And the Reason seemes to bee, because they who now are *Tares,* may hereafter become *Wheat;* they who are now *blinde,* may hereafter *see;* they that now *resist* him, may hereafter *receive* him; they that are now in the *devils snare,* in *adversenesse* to the *Truth,* may hereafter come to *repentance;* they that are now *blasphemers* and *persecutors* (as *Paul* was) may in time become *faithfull* as he; they that are now *idolators* as the *Corinths* once were (1 *Cor.* 6. 9.) may hereafter become *true worshippers* as they; they that are now *no people* of *God,* nor under *mercy* (as the Saints sometimes were, 1 *Pet.* 2. 20.) may hereafter become the people of *God,* and obtaine *mercy,* as they.

Some come not till the 11. houre, *Matth.* 20. 6. if those that come not till the *last houre* should be *destroyed,* because they come not at the *first,* then should they never come but be prevented.

All which *premises* are in all humility referred to your godly wise *consideration.*

Because this *persecution* for cause of *conscience* is against the *profession* and *practice* of *famous Princes.*

First, you may please to consider the speech of *King James,* in his *Majesties Speech* at *Parliament,* 1609. He saith, it is a sure *Rule* in *divinity,* that God never loves to plant his *Church* by *violence* and *bloodshed.*

And in his *Highnesse Apologie,* pag. 4. speaking of such *Papists* that tooke the Oath, thus:

"I gave good proofe that I intended no *persecution* against them for *conscience* cause, but onely desired to bee secured for *civill obedience,* which for *conscience* cause they are bound to performe."

And pag. 60. speaking of *Blackwell*[1] (the *Arch-priest*) his *Majesty* saith, "It was never my intention to lay any thing to the said *Arch-Priests* charge (as I have never done to any) for *cause of conscience.*" And in his *Highnesse Exposition* on *Revel.* 20. printed 1588. and after [in] 1603. his *Majesty* writeth thus: "Sixthly, the compassing of the *Saints* and the besieging of the *beloved City,* declareth unto us a certaine *note* of a *false Church,* to be *Persecution,* for they come to seeke the *faithfull,* the *faithfull* are them that are sought: the *wicked* are the *besiegers,* the *faithfull* are the *besieged.*"

Secondly, the saying of *Stephen* King of *Poland:*[2] "I am *King* of *Men,* not of *Consciences,* a Commander of *Bodies,* not of *Soules.*"

Thirdly, the *King* of *Bohemia* hath thus written:

"And notwithstanding the successe of the later times (wherein sundry *opinions* have beene hatched about the subject of *Religion*) may make one clearly discerne with his *eye,* and as it were to touch with his *Finger,* that according to the veritie of *Holy Scriptures,* and a *Maxime* heretofore

1. George Blackwell, a Roman Catholic divine, was commissioned to act as archpriest over the secular clergy in England by Cardinal Cajetan, March 7, 1598, in order to meet some of the difficulties arising from the lack of a Romish episcopate, and was confirmed and approved by a bull from Pope Clement VIII, April 6, 1599. He took the oath of allegiance enacted in consequence of the Gunpowder Plot, and openly expressed his approbation of it, though Paul V. had condemned it. His superiors at Rome could not endure his attempts to induce Roman Catholics to take the oath, and he was superseded in 1508. Rose, Biog. Dict., IV; Wood's Athenae Oxonienses, ii: 122.— Ed.

2. Stephen Bathori was King of Poland 1575–1586. Though a convert to the Roman Church he used no intolerance towards his Protestant subjects. He said, "I reign over persons; but it is God who rules the conscience. Know that God has reserved three things to himself; the creation of something out of nothing, the knowledge of futurity, and the government of the conscience." *Lardner's Cabinet Cyclopedia, Poland,* p. 167.—Ed.

told and maintained, by the ancient Doctors of the *Church;* That *mens consciences* ought in no sort to bee *violated, urged, or constrained;* and whensoever men have attempted any thing by this *violent course,* whether openly or by secret meanes, the issue hath beene *pernicious,* and the cause of great and wonderfull *Innovations* in the principallest and mightiest *Kingdomes* and *Countries* of all Christendome."

And further his *Majesty* saith: "So that once more we doe professe before *God* and the *whole World,* that from this time forward wee are firmly resolved not to *persecute* or *molest,* or suffer to be *persecuted* or *molested,* any person whosoever for *matter of Religion,* no not they that professe *themselves* to be of the *Romish Church,* neither to trouble or disturbe them in the exercise of their *Religion,* so they live conformable to the *Lawes* of the *States,* &c."[3]

And for the practice of this, where is *persecution* for cause of *conscience* except in *England* and where *Popery* reignes, and there neither in all places, as appeareth by *France, Poland,* and other places.

Nay, it is not practised amongst the *Heathen* that acknowledge not the *true God,* as the *Turke, Persian,* and others.

Thirdly, because *persecution* for cause of conscience is condemned by the ancient and later *Writers,* yea and *Papists* themselves.

Hilarie against *Auxentius*[4] saith thus: The *Christian Church* doth not *persecute,* but is *persecuted.* And lamentable it is to see the great folly of these times, and to sigh at the foolish opinion of this world, in that men thinke by humane aide to helpe *God,* and with worldly pompe and power to undertake to defend the *Christian Church.* I aske you *Bishops,* what helpe used the *Apostles* in the publishing of the *Gospel?* with the aid of what power did they preach *Christ,* and converted the *Heathen* from their *idolatry* to *God?* When they were in *prisons,* and lay in *chaines,* did they praise and give thankes to God for any *dignities, graces,* and *favours* received from the *Court?* Or do you thinke that *Paul* went about with *Regall Mandates,* or *Kingly authority,* to gather and establish the *Church* of *Christ?* sought he *protection* from *Nero, Vespasian?*

The *Apostles* wrought with their *hands* for their owne *maintenance,* travailing by *land* and *water* from *Towne* to *Citie,* to preach *Christ:* yea the more they were *forbidden,* the more they *taught* and preached *Christ.* But now alas, *humane helpe* must *assist* and *protect* the *Faith,* and give the same countenance to and by vaine and *worldly honours.*[5] Doe men seek to defend the *Church of Christ?* as if hee by his power were unable to performe it.

The same against the *Arrians.*

The *Church* now, which formerly by induring *misery* and *imprisonment* was knowne to be a *true Church,* doth now terrifie others by *imprisonment, banishment,* and *misery,* and boasteth that she is highly esteemed of the *world,* when as the true *Church* [she] cannot but be hated of the same.

Tertull. ad Scapulam:[6] It agreeth both with *humane reason,* and *naturall equity,* that every man *worship* God uncompelled, and beleeve what he will; for it neither hurteth nor profiteth any one another mans *Religion* and *Beleefe:* Neither beseemeth it any *Religion* to compell another to be of their *Religion,* which willingly and freely should be imbraced, and not by constraint: for as much as the *offerings* were required of those that freely and with good will offered, and not from the *contrary.*

Jerom. in proaem. lib. 4. in Jeremiam.[7] Heresie must be cut off with the *Sword* of the *Spirit:* let us strike through with the *Arrowes* of the *Spirit* all *Sonnes* and *Disciples* of mis-led *Heretickes,* that is, with *Testimonies* of holy *Scriptures.* The slaughter of *Heretickes* is by the word of God.

---

3. This paragraph, quoted also in the Address to Parliament, p. 7, is from the manifesto issued by the Elector Palatine, Frederick the Fifth, who had been elected King of Bohemia against Ferdinand the Second, Archduke of Austria and Emperor of Germany, at the beginning of the Thirty Years War. Schiller, *Thirty Years War,* Book I. James the First, whose daughter he married, was entirely opposed to his taking the crown, and refused to recognise him. Hume, *History of England,* Chap. 48. It was in the same year (1620) in which he was defeated that this "Humble Supplication" from which these "Scriptures and Reasons" are taken was printed. The Commons had boldly declared their sympathy with his misfortunes, and so circumstances gave significance to opinions uttered by one who was considered a representative of the Protestant cause, and which were so much in advance of those of James. Brandt, *The History of the Reformation in and about the Low Countries,* iv: lib. 52, p. 200.—Ed.

4. S. Hilarii Opera, Lib. I, Contra Arianos vel Auxentium, Cap. 3, 4, pp. 465, 466; Venetiis, 1749.—Ed.

5. This sentence may be read with a period after "countenance," the remaining words being connected with the following interrogation: or by changing the order of the words, thus, "and give countenance to the same by vaine and worldly honours."—Ed.

6. Tertulliani Opera, Tom. 1, Cap. 2, p. 152, Antverpiae, 1583; Lib'ry of Fathers, Tertullian, i: 143, Oxford, 1842.—Ed.

7. S. Hieronymi Opera, in praemium lib. 4, in Jeremiam, pp. 615–616, Parisiis, 1704. Only the first member of this sentence is found in the place cited. "*Quod si cavendum nobis est, ne veterem laedere videamur necessitudinem, si superbissimam haeresim spirituali mucrone truncemus.*"—Ed.

Brentius[8] upon 1 *Cor.* 3. No man hath power to make or give *Lawes* to *Christians,* whereby to binde their *consciences;* for willingly, freely, and uncompelled, with a ready desire and cheerfull minde, must those that come, run unto *Christ.*

Luther in his Booke of the *Civill Magistrate*[9] saith; The *Lawes* of the *Civill Magistrates* government extends no further then over the *body* or *goods,* and to that which is *externall:* for over the *soule God* will not suffer any man to *rule:* only he *himselfe* will rule there. Wherefore whosoever doth undertake to give *Lawes* unto the *Soules* and *Consciences* of Men, he usurpeth that *government* himselfe which appertaineth unto *God,* &c.

Therefore upon 1 *Kings* 5.[10] In the building of the *Temple* there was no *sound* of *Iron* heard, to signifie that *Christ* will have in his *Church* a *free* and a *willing* People, not compelled and constrained by *Lawes* and *Statutes.*

Againe he saith upon *Luk.* 22.[11] It is not the true *Catholike Church,* which is defended by the *Secular Arme* or humane Power, but the *false* and *feigned Church,* which although it carries the *Name* of a *Church* yet it denies the power thereof.

And upon *Psal.* 17.[12] he saith: For the true *Church* of *Christ* knoweth not *Brachium saeculare,* which the *Bishops* now adayes, chiefly use.

Againe, in *Postil. Dom.* 1. *post Epiphan.*[13] he saith: Let not *Christians* be *commanded,* but *exhorted:* for, He that willingly will not doe that, whereunto he is friendly exhorted, he is no *Christian:* wherefore they that doe compell those that are not willing, shew thereby that they are not *Christian Preachers,* but *Worldly Beadles.*

Againe, upon 1 *Pet.* 3.[14] he saith: If the *Civill Magistrate*

shall command me to believe thus and thus: I should answer him after this manner: *Lord,* or *Sir,* Looke you to your *Civill* or *Worldly Government,* Your Power extends not so farre as to command any thing in *Gods Kingdome:* Therefore herein I may not heare you. For if you cannot beare it, that any should usurpe *Authoritie* where you have to Command, how doe you thinke that *God* should suffer you to thrust him from his Seat, and to seat your selfe therein?

Lastly, the Papists, the *Inventors of Persecution,* in a wicked Booke of theirs set forth in *K. James* his *Reigne,* thus:

Moreover, the *Meanes* which *Almighty God* appointed his Officers to use in the Conversion of *Kingdomes* and *Nations,* and People, was *Humilitie, Patience, Charitie;* saying, Behold I send you as *Sheepe* in the midst of *Wolves,* Mat. 10. 16. He did not say, Behold I send you as *Wolves* among *Sheepe,* to kill, imprison, spoile and devoure those unto whom they were sent.

Againe *vers.* 7. he saith: They to whom I send you, will deliver you up into *Councells,* and in their *Synagogues* they will scourge you; and to *Presidents* and to *Kings* shall you be led for my sake. He doth not say: You whom I send, shall deliver the people (whom you ought to convert) unto *Councells,* and put them in Prisons, and lead them to *Presidents,* and *Tribunall Seates,* and make their *Religion Felony* and *Treason.*

Againe he saith, *vers.* 32. When ye enter into an House, salute it, saying, Peace be unto this House: he doth not say, You shall send *Pursevants* to ransack or spoile his House.

Againe he said, *John* 10. The good *Pastour* giveth his life for his Sheep, the *Thiefe* commeth not but to steale, kill and destroy. He doth not say, The *Theefe* giveth his life for his Sheep, and the Good *Pastour* commeth not but to steale, kill and destroy.

So that we holding our peace, our *Adversaries* themselves speake for us, or rather for the Truth.

To Answer Some Maine Objections

And first, that it is no *prejudice* to the *Common wealth,* if *Libertie of Conscience* were suffred to such as doe feare *God* indeed, as is or will be manifest in such mens lives and conversations.

Abraham abode among the *Canaanites* a long time, yet contrary to them in *Religion,* Gen. 13. 7. & 16. 13. Againe he sojourned in *Gerar,* and *K. Abimelech* gave him leave to abide in his Land, *Gen.* 20. 21. 23. 24.

---

8. The works of Brentius, 8 vols. folio, Tubingen, 1575–1590, are not within the Editor's reach, nor on the catalogues of any of the public libraries of the country, so far as examined.—Ed.

9. Luther's Sämtliche Schriften, herausgegeben J. G. Walch, 10ʳ Theil, 452. Halle. 1744.—Ed.

10. Schriften, x: 438.—Ed.

11. Schriften, xiii: 2818. Auslegung des Evangelii am Bartholomews Tag, Luke xxii: 24–30. "God will keep and govern his Church only by his Word, and not by human power." It may be that the reference is to some other passage.—Ed.

12. This passage is not found in his explanation of the 117th Psalm, Theil 4ʳ, 1261.—Ed.

13. Schriften, xii: 429. Auslegung der Epistel am ersten Sonntage nach Epiphania.—Ed.

14. Schriften, ix: 740. Auslegung der ersten Ep. Petri, cap. 2, v. 17. —Ed.

Isaack also dwelt in the same Land, yet contrary in *Religion,* Gen. 26.

Jacob lived 20 yeares in one House with his Unkle *Laban,* yet differed in *Religion,* Gen. 31.

The people of *Israel* were about 430 yeares in that infamous land of *Egypt,* and afterwards 70 yeares in *Babylon,* all which time they differed in *Religion* from the States, *Exod.* 12. & 2 *Chron.* 36.

Come to the time of *Christ,* where *Israel* was under the *Romanes,* where lived divers Sects of *Religion,* as *Herodians, Scribes* and *Pharises, Saduces* and *Libertines, Thudaeans* and *Samaritanes,* beside the Common Religion of the *Jewes, Christ* and his *Apostles.* All which differed from the Common *Religion* of the State, which was like the Worship of *Diana,* which almost the whole world then worshipped, *Acts* 19. 20.

All these lived under the Government of *Caesar,* being nothing hurtfull unto the *Common-wealth,* giving unto *Caesar* that which was his. And for their *Religion* and Consciences towards God, he left them to themselves, as having no Dominion over their *Soules* and *Consciences.* And when the Enemies of the Truth raised up any *Tumults,* the wisedome of the *Magistrate* most wisely appeased them, *Acts* 18 14. & 19. 35.

A Platform of Church Discipline

JOHN COTTON, RICHARD MATHER, AND RALPH PARTRIDGE

1649

This "Platform of Church Discipline" was drawn up by John Cotton, Richard Mather, and Ralph Partridge at the request of a synod, or convocation of church leaders, in Massachusetts held in 1648. The General Court, the highest political body in that colony, subsequently adopted it. Approval by a political body of a church document was considered natural in a colony that saw itself founded in a "covenant"—as a community formed for the purpose of following the will of God in its common life—and in which church membership was the key to political participation. The document also reflects the concern to provide for local autonomy among the colony's churches.

A Platform of Church Discipline, Gathered out of the Word of God, and Agreed upon by the Elders and Messengers of the Churches Assembled in the Synod, at Cambridge, in New-England
To Be Presented to the Churches and General Court for Their Consideration and Acceptance in the Lord, the 8th Month, Anno 1649

CHAPTER I

Of the Form of Church-Government; and That It Is One, Immutable, and Prescribed in the Word

1. Ecclesiastical polity, or church-government or discipline, is nothing else but that form and order that is to be observed in the church of Christ upon earth, both for the constitution of it, and all the administrations that therein are to be performed.

2. Church-government is considered in a double respect, either in regard of the parts of government themselves, or necessary circumstances thereof. The parts of government are prescribed in the word, because the Lord Jesus Christ, (Heb. iii. 5, 6; Exo. xxv. 40; 2 Tim. iii. 16,) the King and Law-giver in his church, is no less faithful in the house of God, than was Moses, who from the Lord delivered a form and pattern of government to the children of Israel in the Old Testament; and the holy Scriptures are now also so perfect as they are able to make the man of God perfect, and thoroughly furnished unto every good work; and therefore doubtless to the well-ordering of the house of God.

3. The parts of church-government are all of them exactly described in the word of God, (1 Tim. iii. 15; 1 Chr. xv. 13; Exod. ii. 4; 1 Tim. vi. 13. 16; Heb. xii. 27, 28; 1 Cor. xv. 24,) being parts or means of instituted worship according to the second commandment, and therefore to continue one and the same unto the appearing of our Lord Jesus Christ, as a kingdom that cannot be shaken, until he shall deliver it up unto God, even to the Father. (Deut. xii. 32; Ezek. xlv. 8; 1 Kin. xii. 31, 32, 33.) So that it is not left in the power of men, officers, churches, or any state in the world, to add, or diminish, or alter any thing in the least measure therein.

4. The necessary circumstances, as time and place, &c., belonging unto order and decency, are not so left unto men, as that, under pretence of them, they may thrust their own inventions upon the churches, (2 Kin. xii.; Exo. xx. 19; Isa. xxviii. 13; Col. i. 22, 23,) being circumscribed in the word with many general limitations, where they are determined with respect to the matter to be neither worship it self, nor circumstances separable from worship. (Acts xv. 28; Mat. xv. 9; 1 Cor. xi. 23, and viii. 34.) In respect of their end, they must be done unto edification; in respect of the manner, decently and in order, according to the nature of the things themselves, and civil and church custom. Doth not even nature its self teach you? Yea, they are in some sort determined particularly—namely, that they be done in such a manner as, all circumstances considered, is most expedient for edification: (1 Cor. xiv. 26, and xiv. 40, and xi. 14. 16, and xiv. 12. 19; Acts xv. 28.) So as, if there be no error

of man concerning their determination, the determining of them is to be accounted as if it were divine.

CHAPTER II

Of the Nature of the Catholick Church in General, and in Special of a Particular Visible Church

1. The catholick church is the whole company of those that are elected, redeemed, and in time effectually called from the state of sin and death unto a state of grace and salvation in Jesus Christ.

2. This church is either triumphant or militant. Triumphant, the number of them who are glorified in heaven; militant, the number of them who are conflicting with their enemies upon earth.

3. This militant church is to be consider'd as invisible and visible. (2 Tim. ii. 19; Rev. ii. 17; 1 Cor. vi. 17; Eph. iii. 17; Rom. i. 8; 1 Thes. i. 8; Isa. ii. 2; 1 Tim. vi. 12.) Invisible, in respect to their relation, wherein they stand to Christ as a body unto the head, being united unto him by the Spirit of God and faith in their hearts. Visible, in respect of the profession of their faith, in their persons, and in particular churches. And so there may be acknowledged an universal visible church.

4. The members of the militant visible church, considered either as not yet in church order, or walking according to the church order of the gospel. (Acts xix. 1; Col. ii. 5; Mat. xviii. 17; 1 Cor. v. 12.) In order, and so besides the spiritual union and communion common to all believers, they enjoy moreover an union and communion ecclesiastical, political. So we deny an universal visible church.

5. The state of the members of the militant visible church, walking in order, was either before the law, (Gen. xviii. 19; Exod. xix. 6,) economical, that is, in families; or under the law, national; or since the coming of Christ, only congregational (the term *independent,* we approve not): therefore neither national, provincial, nor classical.

6. A congregational church is by the institution of Christ a part of the militant visible church, consisting of a company of saints by calling, united into one body by an holy covenant, for the publique worship of God, and the mutual edification of one another in the fellowship of the Lord Jesus. (1 Cor. xiv. 23. 36, and i. 2, and xii. 27; Ex. xix. 5, 6; Deut. xxix. 1, and 9 to 15; Acts ii. 42; 1 Cor. xiv. 26.)

CHAPTER III

Of the Matter of the Visible Church, Both in Respect of Quality and Quantity

1. The matter of the visible church are saints by calling.

2. By saints, we understand—1, Such as have not only attained the knowledge of the principles of religion, and are free from gross and open scandals, but also do, together with the profession of their faith and repentance, walk in blameless obedience to the word, so as that in charitable discretion they may be accounted saints by calling, (tho' perhaps some or more of them be unsound and hypocrites inwardly) because the members of such particular churches are commonly by the Holy Ghost called "saints and faithful brethren in Christ;" and sundry churches have been reproved for receiving, and suffering such persons to continue in fellowship among them, as have been offensive and scandalous; the name of God also, by this means, is blasphemed, and the holy things of God defiled and profaned, the hearts of the godly grieved, and the wicked themselves hardened and holpen forward to damnation. (1 Cor. i. 2; Eph. i. 1; Heb. vi. 1; 1 Cor. i. 5; Ro. xv. 14; Psalm l. 16, 17; Acts viii. 37; Mat. iii. 6; Ro. vi. 17; 1 Cor. i. 2; Phil. i. 2; Col. i. 2; Eph. i. 1; 1 Cor. v. 2. 13; Rev. ii. 14, 15. 20; Ezek. xliv. 7. 9, and xxiii. 38, 39; Numb. xix. 20; Hag. ii. 13, 14; 1 Cor. xi. 27. 29; Psa. xxxvii. 21; 1 Cor. v. 6; 2 Cor. vii. 14.) The example of such doth endanger the sanctity of others, a little leaven leaveneth the whole lump. 2, The children of such who are also holy.

3. The members of churches, tho' orderly constituted, may in time degenerate, and grow corrupt and scandalous, which, tho' they ought not to be tolerated in the church, yet their continuance therein, thro' the defect of the execution of discipline and just censures, doth not immediately dissolve the being of a church, as appears in the church of Israel, and the churches of Galatia and Corinth, Pergamos and Thyatira. (Rev. ii. 14, 15; and xxi. 21.)

4. The matter of the church, in respect of its *quantity,* ought not to be of greater number than may ordinarily meet together conveniently in one place; (1 Cor. xiv. 21; Mat. xviii. 17,) nor ordinarily fewer than may conveniently carry on church-work. Hence, when the holy Scripture makes mention of the saints combined into a church estate in a town or city, where was but one congregation, it

usually calleth those saints ["the church"] in the singular number, as "the church of the Thessalonians," "the church of Smyrna, Philadelphia," &c.; (Rom. xvi. 1; 1 Thes. i. 1; Rev. ii. 28, and iii. 7,) but when it speaketh of the saints in a nation or province, wherein there were sundry congregations, it frequently and usually calleth them by the name of ["churches"] in the plural number, as the "churches of Asia, Galatia, Macedonia," and the like: (1 Cor. xvi. 1. 19; Gal. i. 2; 2 Cor. viii. 1; Thes. ii. 14,) which is further confirmed by what is written of sundry of those churches in particular, how they were assembled and met together the whole church in one place, as the church at Jerusalem, the church at Antioch, the church at Corinth and Cenchrea, tho' it were more near to Corinth, it being the port thereof, and answerable to a village; yet being a distinct congregation from Corinth, it had a church of its own, as well as Corinth had. (Acts ii. 46, and v. 12, and vi. 2, and xiv. 27, and xv. 38; 1 Cor. v. 4, and xiv. 23; Rom. xvi. 1.)

5. Nor can it with reason be thought but that every church appointed and ordained by Christ, had a ministry appointed and ordained for the same, and yet plain it is that there were no ordinary officers appointed by Christ for any other than congregational churches; (Acts xx. 28,) elders being appointed to feed not all flocks, but the particular flock of God, over which the Holy Ghost had made them overseers, and that flock they must attend, even the whole flock: and one congregation being as much as any ordinary elders can attend, therefore there is no greater church than a congregation which may ordinarily meet in one place.

CHAPTER IV

Of the Form of the Visible Church,
and of Church Covenant

1. Saints by calling must have a visible political union among themselves, or else they are not yet a particular church, (1 Cor. xii. 27; 1 Tim. iii. 15; Eph. ii. 22; 1 Cor. xii. 15, 16, 17,) as those similitudes hold forth, which the Scripture makes use of to shew the nature of particular churches; as a *body*, a *building, house, hands, eyes, feet* and other members, must be united, or else (remaining separate) are not a body. Stones, timber, tho' squared, hewen and polished, are not an house, until they are compacted and united:

(Rev. ii.) so saints or believers in judgment of charity, are not a church unless orderly knit together.

2. Particular churches cannot be distinguished one from another but by their forms. Ephesus is not Smyrna, nor Pergamos Thyatira; but each one a distinct society of itself, having officers of their own, which had not the charge of others; virtues of their own, for which others are not praised; corruptions of their own, for which others are not blamed.

3. This form is the *visible covenant,* agreement or consent, whereby they give up themselves unto the Lord, to the observing of the ordinances of Christ together in the same society, which is usually call'd the "church covenant." (Ex. xix. 5. 8; Deut. xxix. 12, 13; Zec. xi. 14, and ix. 11,) for we see not otherwise how members can have church-power over one another mutually. The comparing of each particular church to a *city,* and unto a *spouse,* (Eph. ii. 19; 2 Cor. xi. 2,) seemeth to conclude not only a form, but that that form is by way of covenant. The covenant, as it was that which made the family of Abraham and children of Israel to be a church and people unto God, (Gen. xvii. 7; Eph. ii. 12. 18,) so is it that which now makes the several societies of Gentile believers to be churches in these days.

4. This voluntary agreement, consent or covenant—for all these are here taken for the same—altho' the more express and plain it is, the more fully it puts us in mind of our mutual duty; and stirreth us up to it, and leaveth less room for the questioning of the truth of the church-estate of a company of professors, and the truth of membership of particular persons; yet we conceive the substance of it is kept where there is real agreement and consent of a company of faithful persons to meet constantly together in one congregation, for the publick worship of God, and their mutual edification: which real agreement and consent they do express by their constant practice in coming together for the publick worship of God and by their religious subjection unto the ordinances of God there: (Exod. xix. 5, and xx. 8, and xxiv. 3. 17; Josh. xxiv. 18 to 24; Psal. l. 5; Neh. ix. 38, and x. 1; Gen. xvii.; Deut. xxix.) the rather, if we do consider how Scripture-covenants have been entred into, not only expressly by word of mouth, but by sacrifice, by hand-writing and seal; and also sometimes by silent consent, without any writing or expression of words at all.

5. This form being by mutual covenant, it followeth, it is not faith in the heart, nor the profession of that faith, nor cohabitation, nor baptism. 1, Not *faith in the heart,* be-

cause that is invisible. 2, Not *a bare profession,* because that declareth them no more to be members of one church than another. 3, Not *cohabitation:* Atheists or Infidels may dwell together with believers. 4, Not *Baptism,* because it presupposeth a church-estate, as circumcision in the Old Testament, which gave no being to the church, the church being before it, and in the wilderness without it. Seals presuppose a covenant already in being. One person is a compleat subject of baptism, but one person is uncapable of being a church.

6. All believers ought, as God giveth them opportunity thereunto, to endeavour to join themselves unto a particular church, and that in respect of the honour of Jesus Christ, in his example and institution, by the professed acknowledgment of and subjection unto the order and ordinances of the gospel: (Acts ii. 47, and ix. 26; Mat. iii. 13, 14, 15, and xxviii. 19, 20; Psa. cxxxiii. 2, 3, and lxxxvii. 7; Mat. xviii. 20; 1 John i. 3,) as also in respect of their good communion founded upon their visible union, and contained in the promises of Christ's special presence in the church; whence they have fellowship with him, and in him, one with another: also in the keeping of them in the way of God's commandments, and recovering of them in case of wandering, (which all Christ's sheep are subject to in this life,) being unable to return of themselves; together with the benefit of their mutual edification, and of their posterity, that they may not be cut off from the privilege of the covenant. (Psa. cxix. 176; 1 Pet. ii. 25; Eph. iv. 16; Job xxii. 24, 25; Mat. xviii. 15, 16, 17.) Otherwise, if a believer offends, he remains destitute of the remedy provided in that behalf. And should all believers neglect this duty of joining to all particular congregations, it might follow thereupon that Christ should have no visible, political churches upon earth.

CHAPTER V

Of the First Subject of Church-Power;
Or, to Whom Church-Power Doth First Belong

1. The first subject of church-power is either supreme, or subordinate and ministerial. The supreme (by way of gift from the Father) is the Lord Jesus Christ. (Mat. xviii. 18; Rev. iii. 7; Isa. ix. 6; Joh. xx. 21. 23; 1 Cor. xiv. 32; Tit. i. 5; 1 Cor. v. 12.) The ministerial is either extraordi-

nary, as the apostles, prophets and evangelists; or ordinary, as every particular Congregational church.

2. Ordinary church power is either power of office—that is, such as is proper to the eldership—or power of privilege, such as belongs to the brotherhood. (Rom. xii. 4. 8; Acts i. 23, and vi. 3, and xiv. 23; 1 Cor. x. 29, 30.) The latter is in the brethren formally and immediately from Christ—that is, so as it may be acted or exercised immediately by themselves; the former is not in them formally or immediately, and therefore cannot be acted or exercised immediately by them, but is said to be in them, in that they design the persons unto office, who only are to act or to exercise this power.

CHAPTER VI

Of the Officers of the Church,
And Especially of Pastors and Teachers

1. A church being a company of people combined together by covenant for the worship of God, it appeareth thereby that there may be the essence and being of a church without any officers, seeing there is both the form and matter of a church; which is implied when it is said, "the apostles ordained elders in every church." (Acts xiv. 23.)

2. Nevertheless, tho' officers be not absolutely necessary to the simple being of churches, when they be called; yet ordinarily to their calling they are, and to their well-being: (Rom. x. 17; Jer. iii. 15; 1 Cor. xii. 28,) and therefore the Lord Jesus Christ, out of his tender compassion, hath appointed and ordained officers, which he would not have done, if they had not been useful and needful to the church; (Eph. iii. 11; Psa. lxviii. 18; Eph. iv. 8. 11,) yea, being ascended up to heaven, he received gifts for men; whereof officers for the church are justly accounted no small parts, they being to continue to the end of the world, and for the perfecting of all the saints.

3. These officers were either extraordinary or ordinary: extraordinary, as apostles, prophets, evangelists; ordinary, as elders and deacons. The apostles, prophets, and evangelists, as they were called extraordinarily by Christ, so their office ended with themselves: (1 Cor. xii. 28; Eph. iv. 11; Acts viii. 6. 16. 19, and xi. 28; Rom. xi. 13; 1 Cor. iv. 9,) whence it is that Paul, directing Timothy how to carry along church-administration, giveth no direction about the choice or course of apostles, prophets or evangelists,

but only of elders and deacons; and when Paul was to take his last leave of the church of Ephesus, he committed the care of feeding the church to no other, but unto the elders of that church. The like charge does Peter commit to the elders. (1 Tim. iii. 1, 2. 8 to 13; Tit. i. 5; Acts xx. 17. 28; 1 Pet. v. 1, 2, 3.)

4. Of elders (who are also in Scripture called *bishops*) some attend chiefly to the ministry of the word, as the pastors and teachers; (1 Tim. ii. 3; Phil. i. 1; Acts xx. 17. 28,) others attend especially unto rule, who are, therefore, called *ruling-elders.* (1 Tim. v. 17.)

5. The office of pastor and teacher appears to be distinct. The pastor's special work is, to attend to *exhortation,* and therein to administer a word of *wisdom:* (Eph. iv. 11; Rom. xii. 7, 8; 1 Cor. xii. 8,) the teacher is to attend to *doctrine,* and therein to administer a word of *knowledge:* (1 Tim. iv. 1, 2. Tit. i. 9,) and either of them to administer the seals of that covenant, unto the dispensation whereof they are alike called; as also to execute the censures, being but a kind of application of the word: the preaching of which, together with the application thereof, they are alike charged withal.

6. Forasmuch as both pastors and teachers are given by Christ for the perfecting of the saints and edifying of his body; (Eph. iv. 11, 12, and i. 22, 23,) which saints and body of Christ is his church: and therefore we account pastors and teachers to be both of them church-officers, and not the pastor for the church, and the teacher only for the schools: (1 Sam. x. 12., 19, 20,) tho' this we gladly acknowledge, that schools are both lawful, profitable, and necessary, for the training up of such in good literature or learning as may afterwards be called forth unto office of pastor or teacher in the church. (2 Kings ii. 3. 15.)

CHAPTER VII

Of Ruling Elders and Deacons

1. The ruling elder's office is distinct from the office of pastor and teacher; (Rom. xii. 7, 8, 9; 1 Tim. v. 17; 1 Cor. xii. 28; Heb. xiii. 17; 1 Tim. v. 17,) the ruling elders are not so called to exclude the pastors and teachers from ruling, because ruling and governing is common to these with the other; whereas attending to teach and preach the word is peculiar unto the former.

2. The ruling elder's work is to join with the pastor and teacher in those acts of spiritual rule, which are distinct from the ministry of the word and sacraments committed to them: (1 Tim. v. 17; 2 Chron. xxiii. 19; Rev. xxi. 12; 1 Tim. iv. 14; Matth. xviii. 17; 2 Cor. ii. 7, 8; Acts ii. 6; Acts xxi. 18. 22, 23.) Of which sort these be as followeth: 1, To open and shut the doors of God's house, by the admission of members approved by the church; by ordination of officers chosen by the church, and by excommunication of notorious and obstinate offenders renounced by the church, and by restoring of penitents forgiven by the church. 2, To call the church together when there is occasion, (Acts vi. 2, 3; and xiii. 15,) and seasonably to dismiss them again. 3, To prepare matters in private, that in publick they may be carried an end with less trouble, and more speedy dispatch. (2 Cor. viii. 19; Heb. xiii. 7, 17; 2 Thess. ii. 10, 11, 12.) 4, To moderate the carriage of all matters in the church assembled, as to propound matters to the church. To order the season of speech and silence, and to pronounce sentence according to the mind of Christ, with the consent of the church. 5, To be guides and leaders to the church in all matters whatsoever pertaining to church-administrations and actions. 6, To see that none in the church live inordinately, out of rank and place without a *calling,* or idly in their calling. (Acts xx. 28. 32; 1 Thess. v. 12; Jam. v. 14; Acts xx. 20.) 7, To prevent and heal such offences in life or in doctrine as might corrupt the church. 8, To feed the flock of God with a word of admonition. 9, And, as they shall be sent for, to visit and pray over their sick brethren. 10, And at other times, as opportunity shall serve thereunto.

3. The office of a deacon is instituted in the church by the Lord Jesus: (Acts vi. 3. 6; Phil. i. 1; 1 Tim. iii. 8; 1 Cor. xii. 28; 1 Tim. iii. 8, 9; Acts iv. 35, and vi. 2, 3; Rom. xii. 8.) Sometimes they are called *helps.* The Scripture telleth us how they should be qualified: "Grave, not double-tongued, not given to much wine, not given to filthy lucre." They must first be proved, and then use the office of a deacon, being found blameless. The office and work of a deacon is to receive the offerings of the church, gifts given to the church, and to keep the treasury of the church, and therewith to serve the tables, which the church is to provide for; as the Lord's table, the table of the ministers, and of such as are in necessity, to whom they are to distribute in simplicity.

4. The office, therefore, being limited unto the care of the temporal good things of the church, (1 Cor. vii. 17,) it

extends not to the attendance upon, and administration of the spiritual things thereof, as the word, and sacraments, and the like.

5. The ordinance of the apostle, (1 Cor. xvi. 1, 2, 3,) and practice of the church, commends the Lord's-day as a fit time for the contributions of the saints.

6. The instituting of all these officers in the church is the work of God himself, of the Lord Jesus Christ, of the Holy Ghost: (1 Cor. xii. 28; Eph. iv. 8. 11; Acts xx. 28.) And therefore such officers as he hath not appointed, are altogether unlawful, either to be placed in the church or to be retained therein, and are to be looked at as humane creatures, meer inventions and appointments of man, to the great dishonour of Christ Jesus, the Lord of his, the King of his church, whether popes, cardinals, patriarchs, archbishops, lord-bishops, arch-deacons, officials, commissaries, and the like. These and the rest of that hierarchy and retinue, not being plants of the Lord's planting, shall all be certainly rooted out and cast forth. (Matth. xv. 13).

7. The Lord hath appointed ancient widows (1 Tim. v. 9, 10,) (where they may be had) to minister in the church, in giving attendance to the sick, and to give succour unto them and others in the like necessities.

CHAPTER VIII

Of the Election of Church Officers

1. No man may take the honour of a church-officer unto himself but he that was called of God, as was Aaron. (Heb. v. 4.)

2. Calling unto office is either *immediate,* by Christ himself—such was the *call* of the apostles and prophets; (Gal. i. 1; Acts xiv. 23, and vi. 3,) this manner of calling ended with them, as hath been said—or *mediate,* by the church.

3. It is meet that, before any be ordained or chosen officers, they should first be tried and proved, because hands are not suddenly to be laid upon any, and both elders and deacons must be of both honest and good report. (1 Tim. v. 22, and vii. 10; Acts xvi. 2, and vi. 3.)

4. The things in respect of which they are to be tried, are those gifts and vertues which the Scripture requireth in men that are to be elected unto such places, viz: That elders must be "blameless, sober, apt to teach," and endued with such other qualifications as are laid down: 1 Tim. iii.

2; Tit. i. 6 to 9. Deacons to be fitted as is directed: Acts vi. 3; 1 Tim. iii. 8 to 11.

5. Officers are to be called by such churches whereunto they are to minister. Of such moment is the preservation of this power, that the churches exercised it in the presence of the apostles. (Acts xiv. 23, and i. 23, and vi. 3, 4, 5.)

6. A church being free, cannot become subject to any but by a free election; yet when such a people do chuse any to be over them in the Lord, then do they become subject, and most willingly submit to their ministry in the Lord, whom they have chosen. (Gal. v. 13; Heb. xiii. 17.)

7. And if the church have power to chuse their officers and ministers, (Rom. xvi. 17,) then, in case of manifest unworthiness and delinquency, they have power also to depose them: for to open and shut, to chuse and refuse, to constitute in office, and to remove from office, are acts belonging to the same power.

8. We judge it much conducing to the well-being and communion of the churches, (Cant. viii. 8, 9,) that, where it may conveniently be done, neighbour churches be advised withal, and their help be made use of in trial of church-officers, in order to their choice.

9. The choice of such church-officers belongeth not to the civil magistrate as such, or diocesan bishops, or patrons: for of these, or any such like, the Scripture is wholly silent, as having any power therein.

CHAPTER IX

Of Ordination and Imposition of Hands

1. Church-officers are not only to be chosen by the church, (Acts xiii. 3, and xiv. 23,) but also to be ordained by imposition of hands and prayer, with which at the ordination of elders, fasting also is to be joined. (1 Tim. v. 22.)

2. This ordination (Numb. viii. 10; Acts vi. 5, 6, and xiii. 2, 3,) we account nothing else but the solemn putting a man into his place and office in the church, whereunto he had right before by election; being like the installing of a magistrate in the common-wealth. Ordination therefore is not to go before, but to follow election, (Acts vi. 5, 6, and xiv. 23.) The essence and substance of the outward calling of an ordinary officer in the church does not consist in his ordination, but in his voluntary and free election by the church, and his accepting of that election; whereupon is founded that relation between pastor and flock,

between such a minister and such a people. Ordination does not constitute an officer, nor give him the essentials of his office. The apostles were elders, without imposition of hands by men: Paul and Barnabas were officers before that imposition of hands, (Acts xiii. 3.) The posterity of Levi were priests and Levites before hands were laid on them by the children of Israel.

3. In such churches where there are elders, imposition of hands in ordination is to be performed by those elders. (1 Tim. iv. 10; Acts xiii. 3; 1 Tim. v. 22.)

4. In such churches where there are no elders, (Numb. iii. 10,) imposition of hands may be performed by some of the brethren orderly chosen by the *church* thereunto. For, if the people may elect officers, which is the greater, and wherein the substance of the office doth consist, they may much more (occasion and need so requiring) impose hands in ordination; which is less, and but the accomplishment of the other.

5. Nevertheless, in such churches where there are no elders, and the church so desire, we see not why imposition of hands may not be performed by the elders of other churches. Ordinary officers laid hands upon the officers of many churches: the presbytery at Ephesus laid hands upon Timothy an evangelist; (1 Tim. iv. 14; Acts xiii. 3,) the presbytery at Antioch laid hands upon Paul and Barnabas.

6. Church-officers are officers to one church, even that particular over which the Holy Ghost hath made them overseers. Insomuch as elders are commanded to feed not all flocks, but the flock which is committed to their faith and trust, and dependeth upon them. Nor can constant residence at one congregation be necessary for a minister—no, nor yet lawful—if he be not a minister to one congregation only, but to the church universal; (1 Pet. v. 2; Acts xx. 28,) because he may not attend one part only of the church to which he is a minister, but he is called to attend unto all the flock.

7. He that is clearly released from his office relation unto that church whereof he was a minister, cannot be looked at as an officer, nor perform any act of office in any other church, unless he be again orderly called unto office: which, when it shall be, we know nothing to hinder; but imposition of hands also in his ordination (Acts xx. 28,) ought to be used towards him again: for so Paul the apostle received imposition of hands twice at least from Ananias, (Acts ix. 17, and xiii. 3.)

CHAPTER X

Of the Power of the Church and Its Presbytery

1. Supreme and Lordly power over all the churches upon earth doth only belong to Jesus Christ, who is king of the church, and the head thereof (Ps. ii. 6; Eph. i. 21, 22; Isa. ix. 6; Mat. xxviii. 18.) He hath the government upon his shoulders, and hath all power given to him, both in heaven and earth.

2. A company of professed believers, ecclesiastically confederate, as they are a church before they have officers, and without them; so, even in that estate, subordinate church-power (Acts i. 23, and xiv. 23, and vi. 3, 4; Mat. xviii. 17; 1 Cor. v. 4, 5,) under Christ delegated to them by him, doth belong to them in such a manner as is before expressed, Chap. V. Sec. 2, and as flowing from the very nature and essence of a church; it being natural unto all bodies, and so unto a church-body, to be furnished with sufficient power for its own preservation and subsistence.

3. This government of the church (Rev. iii. 7; 1 Cor. v. 12,) is a mixt government (and so has been acknowledged, long before the term of *independency* was heard of); in respect of Christ, the head and king of the church, and the Sovereign Power residing in him, and exercised by him, it is a *monarchy;* in respect of the body or brotherhood of the church, and power from Christ granted unto them (1 Tim. v. 27,) it resembles a *democracy;* in respect of the presbytery and power committed unto them, it is an *aristocracy.*

4. The Sovereign Power, which is peculiar unto Christ, is exercised—1, In calling the church out of the world into an holy fellowship with himself. (Gal. i. 4; Rev. v. 8, 9; Mat. xxviii. 20; Eph. iv. 8. 11; Jam. iv. 12; Is. xxxiii. 22; 1 Tim. iii. 15; 2 Cor. x. 4, 5; Is. xxxii. 2; Luke i. 71.) 2, In instituting the ordinances of his worship, and appointing his ministers and officers for the dispensing of them. 3, In giving laws for the ordering of all our ways, and the ways of his house. 4, In giving power and life to all his institutions, and to his people by them. 5, In protecting and delivering his church against and from all the enemies of their peace.

5. The power granted by Christ unto the body of the church and brotherhood, is a *prerogative* or *priviledge* which the church doth exercise—1, In *choosing* their own officers, whether elders or deacons. (Acts vi. 3. 5. and xiv. 23, and

ix. 26; Mat. xviii. 15, 16, 17.) 2, In *admission* of these members; and therefore there is great reason they should have power to remove any from their fellowship again. Hence, in case of offence, any brother hath power to convince and admonish an offending brother: and, in case of not hearing him, to take one or two more to set on the admonition: and in case of not hearing them, to proceed to tell the church: and as his offence may require, the whole church has power to proceed to the censure of him, whether by admonition or excommunication: (Tit. iii. 10; Col. iv. 17; Mat. xviii. 17; 2 Cor. ii. 7, 8,) and upon his repentance to restore him again unto his former communion.

6. In case an elder offend incorrigibly, the matter so requiring, as the church had power to call him to office, so they have power according to order (the counsel of other churches, where it may be had, directing thereto) to remove him from his office, and being now but a member, (Col. iv. 17; Ro. xvi. 17; Mat. xviii. 17,) in case he add contumacy to his sin, the church, that had power to receive him into their fellowship, hath also the same power to cast him out that they have concerning any other member.

7. Church-government or rule is placed by Christ in the officers of the church, (1 Tim. v. 17; Heb. xiii. 17; 1 Thes. v. 12,) who are therefore called *rulers,* while they rule with God: yet, in case of male-administration, they are subject to the power of the church, as hath been said before. (Rom. xii. 8; 1 Tim. v. 17; 1 Cor. xii. 28, 29; Heb. xiii. 7. 17.) The Holy Ghost frequently—yea, always—where it mentioneth church-rule and church government, ascribeth it to elders: whereas the work and duty of the people is expressed in the phrase of "obeying their elders," and "submitting themselves unto them in the Lord." So as it is manifest that an organick or compleat church is a body politick, consisting of some that are governours and some that are governed in the Lord.

8. The power which Christ hath committed to the elders is to feed and rule the church of God, and accordingly to call the church together upon any weighty occasion; (Acts xx. 28, and vi. 2; Numb. xvi. 12; Ezek. xlvi. 10; Acts xiii. 15; Hos. iv. 4,) when the members so called, without just cause, may not refuse to come, nor when they are come, depart before they are dismissed, nor speak in the church, before they have leave from the elders, nor continue so doing when they require silence; nor may they oppose or contradict the judgment or sentence of the elders,

without sufficient and weighty cause, because such practices are manifestly contrary unto order and government, and inlets of disturbance, and tend to confusion.

9. It belongs also unto the elders before to examine any officers or members before they be received of the church, (Rev. ii. 2; 1 Tim. v. 19; Acts xxi. 18. 22, 23; 1 Cor. v. 4, 5,) to receive the accusations brought to the church, and to prepare them for the churches hearing. In handling of offences and other matters before the church, they have power to declare and publish the will of God touching the same, and to pronounce sentence with the consent of the church. (Numb. vi. 23 to 26.) Lastly, They have power, when they dismiss the people, to bless them in the name of the Lord.

10. This power of government in the elders doth not any wise prejudice the power of privilege in the brotherhood; as neither the power of privilege in the brethren, doth prejudice the power of government in the elders, (Acts xiv. 15. 23, and vi. 2; 1 Cor. v. 4; 2 Cor. ii. 6, 7,) but they may sweetly agree together; as we may see in the example of the apostles, furnished with the greatest church-power, who took in the *concurrence* and *consent* of the brethren in church-administrations. Also that Scripture (2 Cor. ii. 9, and x. 6) doth declare that what the churches were to *act* and to *do* in these matters, they were to do in a way of obedience, and that not only to the direction of the apostles, but also of their ordinary elders. (Heb. xiii. 17.)

11. From the promises, namely, that the ordinary power of government belonging only to the elders, power of privilege remaining with the brotherhood, (as the power of judgment in matters of censure and power of liberty in matters of liberty,) it followeth that in an organick church and right administration, all church-acts proceed after the manner of a mixt administration, so as no church-act can be consummated or perfected without the consent of both.

CHAPTER XI

Of the Maintenance of Church-Officers

1. The apostle concludes that necessary and sufficient maintenance is due unto the ministers of the word from the law of nature and nations, from the law of Moses, the equity thereof, as also the rule of common reason. Moreover, the Scripture doth not only call elders labourers and workmen, (Gal. vi. 6,) but also, speaking of them, doth say

that "the labourer is worthy of his hire:" (1 Cor. ix. 9. 14; 1 Tim. v. 18,) and requires that he which is taught in the word, should communicate to him in all good things, and mention it, as an ordinance of the Lord, that they which preach the gospel, should live of the gospel, and forbiddeth the muzzling of the mouth of the ox that treadeth out the corn.

2. The Scriptures alledged requiring this maintenance as a bounden duty, and due debt, and not as a matter of alms and free gift, therefore people are not at liberty to do or not to do, what and when they please in this matter, no more than in any other commanded duty and ordinance of the Lord; (Rom. xv. 27; 1 Cor. ix. 21,) but ought of duty to minister of their "carnal things" to them that labour among them in word and doctrine, as well as they ought to pay any other workmen their wages, and to discharge and satisfie their debts, or to submit themselves to observe any other ordinance of the Lord.

3. The apostle (Gal. vi. 6) enjoying that he which is taught communicate to him that teacheth "in all good things," doth not leave it arbitrary, (1 Cor. xvi. 2,) what or how much a man shall give, or in what proportion, but even the latter, as well as the former, is prescribed and appointed by the Lord.

4. Not only members of churches, but "all that are taught in the word," are to contribute unto him that teacheth in all good things. In case that congregations are defective in their contributions, the deacons are to call upon them to do their duty: (Acts vi. 3, 4,) if their call sufficeth not, the church by her power is to require it of their members; and where church power, thro' the corruption of men, doth not or cannot attain the end, the magistrate is to see that the ministry be duly provided for, as appears from the commended example of Nehemiah. (Neh. xiii. 11; Isa. xliv. 23; 2 Cor. viii. 13, 14.) The magistrates are nursing-fathers and nursing-mothers, and stand charged with the custody of both tables; because it is better to prevent a scandal, that it may not come, and easier also, than to remove it, when it is given. It's most suitable to rule, that by the church's care each man should know his proportion according to rule, what he should do before he do it, that so his judgment and heart may be satisfied in what he doth, and just offence prevented in what is done.

CHAPTER XII

Of the Admission of Members into the Church

1. The doors of the churches of Christ upon earth do not by God's appointment stand so wide open, that all sorts of people, good and bad, may freely enter therein at their pleasure, (2 Chr. xxix. 19; Mat. xiii. 25, and xxii. 12,) but such as are admitted thereto, as members, ought to be examin'd and tryed first, whether they be fit and meet to be received into church-society or not. The Eunuch of Ethiopia, before his admission, was examined by Philip, (Acts viii. 37,) whether he did believe on Jesus Christ with all his heart. The angel of the church at Ephesus (Rev. ii. 2; Acts ix. 26,) is commended for trying such as said they were apostles, and were not. There is like reason for trying of them that profess themselves to be believers. The officers are charged with the keeping of the doors of the church, and therefore are in a special manner to make tryal of the fitness of such who enter. Twelve angels are set at the gates of the temple, (Rev. xxi. 12; 2 Chr. xxiii. 19,) lest such as were "ceremonially unclean" should enter thereunto.

2. The things which are requisite to be found in all church-members, are *repentance* from sin, and *faith* in Jesus Christ: (Acts ii. 38 to 42, and viii. 37,) and therefore these are the things whereof men are to be examined at their admission into the church, and which then they must profess and hold forth in such sort as may satisfie "rational charity" that the things are indeed. John Baptist admitted men to baptism confessing and bewailing their sins: (Mat. iii. 6; Acts xix. 18,) and of others it is said that "they came and confessed, and shewed their deeds."

3. The weakest measure of faith is to be accepted in those that desire to be admitted into the church, (Rom. xiv. 1,) if *sincere,* have the substance of that faith, repentance and holiness, which is required in church members; and such have most need of the ordinances for their confirmation and growth in grace. The Lord Jesus would not quench the smoaking flax, nor break the bruised reed, (Mat. xii. 20; Isa. xl. 11,) but gather the tender lambs in his arms, and carry them gently in his bosom. Such charity and tenderness is to be used, as the weakest Christian, if sincere, may not be excluded nor discouraged. Severity of examination is to be avoided.

4. In case any, thro' excessive fear or other infirmity, be unable to make their personal relation of their spiritual

estate in publick, it is sufficient that the elders, having received private satisfaction, make relation thereof in publick before the church, they testifying their assents thereunto: this being the way that tendeth most to edification. But whereas persons are of greater abilities, there it is most expedient that they make their relations and confessions personally with their own mouth, as David professeth of himself. (Psal. lxvi. 6.)

5. A personal and publick confession and declaring of God's manner of working upon the soul, is both lawful, expedient and useful, in sundry respects and upon sundry grounds. Those three thousand, (Acts ii. 37. 41.) before they were admitted by the apostles, did manifest that they were pricked at the heart by Peter's sermon, together with earnest desire to be delivered from their sins, which now wounded their consciences, and their ready receiving of the word of promise and exhortation. We are to be ready to "render a reason of the hope that is in us, to every one that asketh us;" (1 Pet. iii. 15; Heb. xi. 1; Eph. i. 18,) therefore we must be able and ready upon any occasion to declare and shew our *repentance* for sin, *faith* unfeigned, and *effectual calling*, because these are the *reason* of a well-grounded *hope*. "I have not hidden thy righteousness from the great congregation." (Psalm xl. 10.)

6. This profession of faith and repentance, as it must be made by such at their admission that were never in church society before; so nothing hindereth but the same way also be performed by such as have formerly been members of some other church, (Mat. iii. 5, 6; Gal. ii. 4; 1 Tim. v. 24,) and the church to which they now join themselves as members may lawfully require the same. Those three thousand (Acts ii.) which made their confession, were members of the church of the Jews before; so were those that were baptised by John. Churches may err in their admission; and persons regularly admitted may fall into offence. Otherwise, if churches might obtrude their members, or if church members might obtrude themselves upon other churches without due trial, the matter so requiring, both the liberty of the churches would thereby be infringed, in that they might not examine those, concerning whose fitness for communion they were unsatisfied; and besides the infringing of their liberty, the churches themselves would unavoidably be corrupted, and the ordinances defiled: whilst they might not refuse, but must receive the unworthy, which is contrary unto the Scripture, teaching that all churches are sisters, and therefore equal. (Cant. viii. 8.)

7. The like trial is to be required from such members of the church as were born in the same, or received their membership, or were baptised in their infancy or minority by virtue of the covenant of their parents, when being grown up into years of discretion, they shall desire to be made partakers of the Lord's Supper; unto which, because holy things must not be given unto the unworthy, therefore it is requisite (Mat. vii. 6; 1 Cor. xi. 27,) that these, as well as others, should come to their trial and examination, and manifest their faith and repentance by an open profession thereof, before they are received to the Lord's Supper, and otherwise not to be admitted thereunto. Yet these church members that were so born, or received in their childhood, before they are capable of being made partakers of full communion, have many priviledges which others (not church members) have not; they are in covenant with God, have the seal thereof upon them, viz: baptism; and so, if not regenerated, yet are in a more hopeful way of attaining regenerating grace, and all the spiritual blessings, both of the covenant and seal; they are also under church-watch, and consequently subject to the reprehensions, admonitions and censures thereof, for their healing and amendment, as need shall require.

CHAPTER XIII

Of Church-Members, Their Removal from One Church to Another, and of Recommendation and Dismission

1. Church-members may not remove or depart from the church, and so one from another as they please, nor without just and weighty cause, but ought to live and dwell together, (Heb. x. 25,) forasmuch as they are commanded not to forsake the assembling of themselves together. Such departure tends to the dissolution and ruine of the body, as the pulling of stones and pieces of timber from the building, and of members from the natural body, tend to the destruction of the whole.

2. It is, therefore, the duty of church-members, in such times and places, where counsel may be had, to consult with the church whereof they are members (Pro. xi. 16,) about their removal, that, accordingly, they having their approbation, may be encouraged, or otherwise desist. They who are joined with consent, should not depart without consent, except forced thereunto.

3. If a member's departure be manifestly unsafe and sinful, the church may not consent thereunto; for in so doing, (Ro. xiv. 23,) they should not act in faith, and should partake with him in his sin. (1 Tim. v. 22.) If the case be doubtful and the person not to be persuaded, (Acts xxi. 14,) it seemeth best to leave the matter unto God, and not forcibly to detain him.

4. Just reasons for a member's removal of himself from the church, are—1, If a man cannot continue without partaking in sin. (Eph. v. 11.) 2, In case of personal persecution: (Acts ix. 25, 29, 30, and viii. 1,) so Paul departed from the disciples at Damascus; also, in case of general persecution, when all are scattered. In case of real, and not only pretended want of competent subsistence, a door being opened for better supply in another place, (Neh. xiii. 20,) together with the means of spiritual edification. In these or like cases, a member may lawfully remove, and the church cannot lawfully detain him.

5. To separate from a church, either out of contempt of their holy fellowship, (2 Tim. iv. 10,) or out of covetousness, or for greater enlargements, with just grief to the church, or out of schism, or want of love, and out of a spirit of contention in respect of some unkindness, or some evil only *conceived* or *indeed* in the church, which might and should be tolerated and healed with a spirit of meekness, and of which evil the church is not yet convinced (tho' perhaps himself be) nor admonished; for these or the like reasons, to withdraw from publique communion in word or seals, or censures, is unlawful and sinful.

6. Such members as have orderly moved their habitation, ought to join themselves unto the church in order (Isa. lvi. 8,) where they do inhabit, (Acts ix. 26,) if it may be; otherwise, they can neither perform the duties nor receive the priviledges of members. Such an example, tolerated in some, is apt to corrupt others, which, if many should follow, would threaten the dissolution and confusion of churches, contrary to the Scripture. (1 Cor. xiv. 33.)

7. Order requires that a member thus removing, have letters testimonial and of dismission from the church (Act. xviii. 27,) whereof he yet is, unto the church whereunto he desireth to be joined, lest the church should be deluded; that the church may receive him in faith, and not be corrupted in receiving deceivers and false brethren. Until the person dismissed be received unto another church, he ceaseth not by his letters of dismission to be a member of the church whereof he was. The church cannot make *a* member *no* member but by excommunication.

8. If a member be called to remove only for a time where a church is, (Rom. xvi. 1, 2,) letters of recommendation are requisite and sufficient for communion with that church (2 Cor. iii. 1) in the ordinances and in their watch; as Phoebe, a servant of the church at Cenchrea, had a letter written for her to the church at Rome, that she might be received as becometh saints.

9. Such letters of recommendation and dismission (Acts xviii. 27) were written for Apollos, for Marcus to the Colossians, (Col. iv. 10,) for Phoebe to the Romans, (Rom. xvi. 1,) for sundry other churches. (2 Cor. iii. 5.) And the apostle tells us that some persons, not sufficiently known otherwise, have special need of such letters, tho' he, for his part, had no need thereof. The use of them is to be a benefit and help to the party for whom they are written, and for the furthering of his receiving among the saints, in the place whereto he goeth, and the due satisfaction of them in their receiving of him.

CHAPTER XIV

Of Excommunication and Other Censures

1. The censures of the church are appointed by Christ for the preventing, removing and healing of offences in the church; (1 Tim. v. 20; Jude 19; Deu. xiii. 11: 1 Cor. v. 6; Rom. ii. 24; Rev. ii. 14, 15, 16. 20,) for the reclaiming and gaining of offending brethren; for the deterring others from the like offences; for purging out the leaven which may infect the whole lump; for vindicating the honour of Christ and of his church, and the holy profession of the gospel; and for preventing of the wrath of God, that may justly fall upon the church, if they should suffer his covenant and the seals thereof to be profaned by notorious and obstinate offenders.

2. If an offence be private, (Mat. v. 23, 24,) (one brother offending another) the offender is to go and acknowledge his repentance for it unto his offended brother, who is then to forgive him; but if the offender neglect or refuse to do it, the brother offended is to go, and convince and admonish him of it, between themselves privately: if therefore the offender be brought to repent of his offence, the admonisher has won his brother: but if the offender hear

not his brother, the brother of the offended is to take with him one or two more, (verse 16,) that in the mouth of two or three witnesses every word may be established, (whether the word of admonition, if the offender receive it; or the word of complaint, if he refuse it,) for if he refuse it, (verse 17,) the offended brother is by the mouth of the elders to tell the church, and if he hear the church, and declare the same by penitent confession, he is recovered and gained: And if the church discern him to be willing to hear, yet not fully convinced of his offence, as in case of heresie, they are to dispence to him a publick admonition; which, declaring the offender to lye under the publick offence of the church, doth thereby with-hold or suspend him from the holy fellowship of the Lord's Supper, till his offence be removed by penitent confession. If he still continue obstinate, they are to cast him out by excommunication.

3. But if the offence be more publick at first, and of a more hainous and criminal nature, (1 Cor. v. 4. 8, 11,) to wit, such as are condemned by the light of nature; then the church, without such gradual proceeding, is to cast out the offender from their holy communion, for the further mortifying of his sin, and the healing of his soul in the day of the Lord Jesus.

4. In dealing with an offender, great care is to be taken that we be neither over-strict or rigorous, nor too indulgent or remiss: our proceeding herein ought to be with a spirit of meekness, considering ourselves, lest we also be tempted, (Gal. vi. 1,) and that the best of us have need of much forgiveness from the Lord. (Math. xviii. 34, 35.) Yet the winning and healing of the offender's soul being the end of these endeavours, (Ezek. xiii. 10,) we must not daub with untempered mortar, nor heal the wounds of our brethren slightly. On some, have compassion; others, save with fear.

5. While the offender remains excommunicate, (Mat. xviii. 17,) the church is to refrain from all member-like communion with him in spiritual things, (1 Cor. v. 11,) and also from all familiar communion with him in civil things, (2 Thes. iii. 6. 14,) farther than the necessity of natural or domestical or civil relations do require; and are therefore to forbear to eat and drink with him, that he may be ashamed.

6. Excommunication being a spiritual punishment, it doth not prejudice the excommunicate in, or deprive him of his civil rights, and therefore toucheth not princes or magistrates in respect of their civil dignity or authority;

(1 Cor. xiv. 24, 25,) and the excommunicate being but as a publican and a heathen, (2 Thes. iii. 14,) heathens being lawfully permitted to hear the *word* in church-assemblies, we acknowledge therefore the like liberty of hearing the word may be permitted to persons excommunicate that is permitted unto heathen. And because we are not without hope of his recovery, we are not to account him as an enemy, but to admonish him as a brother.

7. If the Lord sanctifie the censure to the offender, so as by the grace of Christ, he doth testifie his repentance with humble confession of his sin, and judging of himself, giving glory unto God, (2 Cor. ii. 7, 8,) the church is then to forgive him, and to comfort him, and to restore him to the wonted brotherly communion, which formerly he enjoyed with 'em.

8. The suffering of prophane or scandalous livers to continue in fellowship, and partake in the sacraments, (Rev. ii. 14, 15. 20,) is doubtless a great sin in those that have power in their hands to redress it, and do it not: Nevertheless, in so much as Christ, and his apostles in their times, and the prophets and other *godly men* in theirs, (Mat. xxiii. 3; Acts iii. 1,) did lawfully partake of the Lord's commanded ordinances in the Jewish church, and neither taught nor practised separation from the same, though unworthy ones were permitted therein: and inasmuch as the faithful in the church of Corinth, wherein were many unworthy persons and practises, (1 Cor. vi. and xv. 12,) are never commanded to absent themselves from the sacraments, because of the same; therefore the godly, in like cases, are not to separate.

9. As separation from such a church wherein profane and scandalous persons are tolerated, is not presently necessary; so for the members thereof, otherwise unworthy, hereupon to abstain from communicating with such a church in the participation of the sacraments, is unlawful. (2 Chr. xxx. 18; Gen. xviii. 25.) For as it were unreasonable for an innocent person to be punished for the faults of others, wherein he hath no hand, and whereunto he gave no consent; so is it more unreasonable that a godly man should neglect duty, and punish himself, in not coming for his portion in the blessing of the seals, as he ought, because others are suffered to come that ought not; especially considering that himself doth neither consent to their sin, nor to their approaching to the ordinance in their sin, nor to the neglect of others, who should put them away, and do

not, but, on the contrary, doth heartily mourn for these things, (Ezek. ix. 4,) modestly and seasonably stir up others to do their duty. If the church cannot be reformed, they may use their liberty, as is specified, Chap. XIII. Sect. 4. But this all the godly are bound unto, even every one to his endeavour, according to his power and place, that the unworthy may be duly proceeded against by the church, to whom this matter doth pertain.

CHAPTER XV

Of the Communion of Churches One with Another

1. Altho' *churches* be distinct, and therefore may not be confounded one with another, and equal, and therefore have not dominion one over another; (Rev. i. 4; Cant. viii. 8; Rom. xvi. 16; 1 Cor. xvi. 19; Acts xv. 23; Rev. ii. 1,) yet all the churches ought to preserve *church-communion* one with another, because they are all united unto Christ, not only as a mystical, but as a political head: whence is derived a communion suitable thereunto.

2. The communion of churches is exercised several ways. (Cant. viii. 8.) 1, By way of *mutual care* in taking thought for one another's welfare. 2, By way of *consultation* one with another, when we have occasion to require the judgment and counsel of other churches, touching any person or cause, wherewith they may be better acquainted than our selves; (Acts xv. 2,) as the church of Antioch consulted with the Apostles and elders of the church at Jerusalem, about the question of circumcision of the Gentiles, and about the false teachers that broached that doctrine. In which case, when any church wanteth light or peace among themselves, it is a way of communion of the churches, according to the word, to meet together by their elders and other messengers in a synod, (ver. 22, 23,) to consider and argue the point in doubt or difference; and, having found out the way of truth and peace, to commend the same by their letters and messengers to the churches whom the same may concern. But if a church be rent with divisions among themselves, or lye under any open scandal, and yet refuse to consult with other churches for healing or removing of the same, it is matter of just offence, both to the Lord Jesus and to other churches, (Ezek. xxxiv. 4,) as bewraying too much want of mercy and faithfulness, not to seek to bind up the breaches and wounds of the church and brethren; And therefore the state of such a church calleth aloud upon other churches to exercise a fuller act of brotherly communion, to wit, by way of admonition. 3, A way, then, of communion of churches, is by way of *admonition;* to wit, in case any public offence be found in a church, which they either discern not, or are slow in proceeding to use the means for the removing and healing of. Paul had no authority over Peter, yet when he saw Peter not walking with a right foot, he publickly rebuked him before the church. (Gal. ii. 11 to 14.) Tho' churches have no more authority one over another, than one apostle had over another, yet, as one apostle might admonish another, so may one church admonish another, and yet without usurpation. (Math. xviii. 15, 16, 17, by proportion.) In which case, if the church that lieth under offence, do not hearken to the church that doth admonish her, the church is to acquaint other neighbour churches with that offence, which the offending church still lieth under, together with the neglect of their brotherly admonition given unto them: Whereupon those other churches are to join in seconding the admonition formerly given: and if still the offending church continue in obstinacy and impenitency, they may forbear communion with them, and are to proceed to make use of the help of a synod or counsel of neighbour churches, walking orderly (if a greater cannot conveniently be had) for their conviction. If they hear not the synod, the synod having declared them to be obstinate, particular churches accepting and approving of the judgment of the synod, are to declare the sentence of *non-communion* respectively concerning them; and thereupon, out of religious care to keep their own communion pure, they may justly withdraw themselves from participation with them at the Lord's table, and from such other acts of holy communion, as the communion of churches doth otherwise allow and require. Nevertheless, if any members of such a church as live under public offence, do not consent to the offence of the church, but do in due sort bear witness against it, (Gen. xviii. 25,) they are still to be received to wonted communion, for it is not equal that the innocent should suffer with the offensive. Yea, furthermore, if such innocent members, after due waiting in the use of all due means for the healing of the offence of their own church, shall at last (with the allowance of the counsel of neighbour churches,) withdraw from the fellowship of their own church, and offer themselves to the fellowship of another, we judge it lawful for the other church to receive them (being otherwise fit) as if they had been orderly dismissed to them from their

own church. 4, A fourth way of communion with churches, is by way of *participation:* the members of one church occasionally coming to another, we willingly admit them to partake with them at the Lord's table, (1 Cor. xii. 13,) it being the seal of our communion not only with Christ, not only with the members of our own church, but also of all the churches of the saints: In which regard we refuse not to baptize their children presented to us, if either their own minister be absent, or such a fruit of holy fellowship be desired with us. In like cases, such churches as are furnished with more ministers than one, do willingly afford one of their own ministers to supply the absence or place of a sick minister of another church for a needful season. 5, A fifth way of church communion is by *recommendation,* (Rom. xvi. 1,) when the member of one church hath occasion to reside in another church, if but for a season, we commend him to their watchful fellowship by letters of recommendation: But if he be called to settle his abode there, we commit him, according to his desire, to the fellowship of their covenant by letters of dismission. 6, A sixth way of church communion, (Acts xviii. 27,) is in case of *need* to minister succour one unto another, (Acts xi. 22,) either of able members to furnish them with officers, or of outward support to the necessities of poorer churches, (verse 29,) as did the churches of the Gentiles contribute liberally to the poor saints at Jerusalem. (Rom. xiii. 26, 27.)

3. When a company of believers purpose to gather into church-fellowship, it is requisite for their safer proceeding and the mentioning of the communion of churches, that they signifie their intent unto the neighbouring churches, walking according to the order of the gospel, and desire their presence and help, and right hand of fellowship; (Gal. ii. 1, 2, and ix., by proportion,) which they ought readily to give unto them, when there is no just cause to except against their proceedings.

4. Besides these several ways of communion, there is also a way of *propagation of churches:* When a church shall grow too numerous, it is a way, and fit season to propagate one church out of another, by sending forth such of their members as are willing to remove, and to procure some officers to them, (Isa. xl. 20; Cant. viii. 8, 9,) as may enter with them into church estate among themselves. As bees, when the hive is too full, issue out by swarms, and are gathered into other hives, so the churches of Christ may do the same upon the like necessity; and therein hold forth to them the right hand of fellowship, both in their gathering into a church and in the ordination of their officers.

CHAPTER XVI

Of Synods

1. Synods, orderly assembled, (Acts xv. 2 to 15,) and rightly proceeding according to the pattern, (Acts xv.) we acknowledge as the ordinance of Christ: and tho' not absolutely necessary to the being, yet many times, thro' the iniquity of men and perverseness of times, necessary to the well-being of churches, for the establishment of truth and peace therein.

2. Synods being spiritual and ecclesiastical assemblies, are therefore made up of spiritual and ecclesiastical causes. The next efficient cause of them, under Christ, is the power of the churches sending forth their elders and other messengers, (Acts xv. 2, 3,) who being met together in the name of Christ, are the matter of a synod; and they in arguing and debating and determining matters of religion, (verse 6,) according to the word, and publishing the same to the churches it concerneth, (verse 7 to 23,) do put forth the proper and formal acts of a synod, (verse 31,) to the conviction of errors, and heresies, and the establishment of truth and peace in the churches, which is the end of a synod. (Acts xvi. 4. 15.)

3. Magistrates have power to call a synod, by calling to the churches to send forth their elders and other messengers to counsel and assist them in matters of religion; (2 Chr. xxix. 4, 5 to 11,) but yet the constituting of a synod is a church-act, and may be transacted by the churches, (Acts xv.) even when civil magistrates may be enemies to churches and to church-assemblies.

4. It belongeth unto synods and councils to debate and determine controversies of faith and cases of conscience; (Acts xv. 1, 2. 6, 7; 1 Chr. xv. 13; 2 Chr. xxix. 6, 7; Acts xv. 24. 28, 29,) to clear from the word holy directions for the holy worship of God and good government of the church; to bear witness against mal-administration and corruption in doctrine or manners, in any particular church; and to give directions for the reformation thereof; not to exercise church-censures in way of discipline, nor any other act of church-authority or jurisdiction which that presidential synod did forbear.

5. The synod's directions and determinations, so far as

consonant to the word of God, are to be received with reverence and submission; not only for their agreement therewith, (Acts xv.) (which is the principal ground thereof, and without which they bind not at all,) but also, secondarily, for the power whereby they are made, as being an ordinance of God appointed thereunto in his word.

6. Because it is difficult, if not impossible, for many churches to come together in one place, in their members universally; therefore they may assemble by their delegates or messengers, as the church at Antioch went not all to Jerusalem, but some select men for that purpose. (Acts xv. 2.) Because none are or should be more fit to know the state of the churches, nor to advise of ways for the good thereof, than elders; therefore it is fit that, in the choice of the messengers for such assemblies, they have special respect unto such; yet, inasmuch as not only Paul and Barnabas, but certain others also, (Acts xv. 2. 22, 23,) were sent to Jerusalem from Antioch, (Acts xv.) and when they were come to Jerusalem, not only the apostles and elders, but other bretheren, also do assemble and meet about the matter; therefore synods are to consist both of elders and other church-members, endued with gifts, and sent by the churches, not excluding the presence of any bretheren in the churches.

CHAPTER XVII

Of the Civil Magistrate's Power in Matters Ecclesiastical

1. It is lawful, profitable and necessary for Christians to gather themselves together into church estate, and therein to exercise all the ordinances of Christ, according unto the word, (Acts ii. 41. 47, and iv. 1, 2, 3,) although the consent of the magistrate could not be had thereunto; because the apostles and Christians in their time did frequently thus practise, when the magistrates, being all of them Jewish and Pagan, and most persecuting enemies, would give no countenance or consent to such matters.

2. Church-government stands in no opposition to civil government of commonwealths, nor any way intrencheth upon the authority of civil magistrates in their jurisdictions; nor any whit weakeneth their hands in governing, but rather strengtheneth them, and furthereth the people in yielding more hearty and conscionable obedience to them, whatsoever some ill affected persons to the ways of Christ

have suggested, to alienate the affections of kings and princes from the ordinances of Christ; as if the kingdom of Christ in his church could not rise and stand, without the falling and weakening of their government, which is also of Christ, (Isa. xlix. 23,) whereas the contrary is most true, that they may both stand together and flourish, the one being helpful unto the other, in their distinct and due administrations.

3. The power and authority of magistrates is not for the restraining of churches (Rom. xiii. 4; 1 Tim. ii. 2,) or any other good works, but for helping in and furthering thereof; and therefore the consent and countenance of magistrates, when it may be had, is not to be slighted, or lightly esteemed; but, on the contrary, it is part of that honor due to Christian magistrates to desire and crave their consent and approbation therein; which being obtained, the churches may then proceed in their way with much more encouragement and comfort.

4. It is not in the power of magistrates to compel their subjects to become church-members, and to partake of the Lord's Supper; (Ezek. xliv. 7. 9,) for the priests are reproved that brought unworthy ones into the sanctuary: (1 Cor. v. 11;) then it was unlawful for the priests, so it is as unlawful to be done by civil magistrates; those whom the church is to cast out, if they were in, the magistrate ought not to thrust them into the church, nor to hold them therein.

5. As it is unlawful for church-officers to meddle with the sword of the magistrate, (Mat. ii. 25, 26,) so it is unlawful for the magistrate to meddle with the work proper to church-officers. The acts of Moses and David, who were not only princes but prophets, were extraordinary, therefore not inimitable. Against such usurpation the Lord witnessed by smiting Uzziah with leprosie for presuming to offer incense. (2 Chr. xxvi. 16, 17.)

6. It is the duty of the magistrate to take care of matters of religion, and to improve his civil authority for the observing of the duties commanded in the first, as well as for observing of the duties commanded in the second table. They are called *gods*. (Psa. lxxxviii. 8.) The end of the magistrate's office is not only the quiet and peaceable life of the subject in matters of righteousness and honesty, but also in matters of godliness; yea, of all godliness. (1 Tim. ii. 1, 2; 1 Kings xv. 14, and xxii. 43; 2 Kings xii. 3, and xiv. 4, and xv. 35.) Moses, Joshua, David, Solomon, Asa, Jehoshaphat, Hezekiah, Josiah, are much commended by the Holy Ghost, for the putting forth their authority in matters of

religion; on the contrary, such kings as have been failing this way, are frequently taxed and reproved of the Lord. (1 Kings xx. 42; Job xxix. 25, and xxxi. 26. 28; Neh. xiii.; Jonah iii. 7; Ezra vii.; Dan. iii. 29.) And not only the kings of Juda, but also Job, Nehemiah, the king of Nineveh, Darius, Artaxerxes, Nebuchadnezzar, whom none looked at as types of Christ, (tho' were it so there were no place for any just objection) are commended in the books of God for exercising their authority this way.

7. The objects of the power of the magistrate are not things meerly inward, and so not subject to his cognizance and views: as unbelief, hardness of heart, erroneous opinions not vented, but only such things as are acted by the outward man: neither their power to be exercised in commanding such acts of the outward man, and punishing the neglect thereof, as are but meer inventions and devices of men, (1 Kings xx. 28. 42,) but about such acts as are commanded and forbidden in the word: yea, such as the word doth clearly determine, tho' not always clearly to the judgment of the magistrate or others, yet clearly in its self. In these he, of right, ought to put forth his authority, tho' ofttimes actually he doth it not.

8. Idolatry, blasphemy, heresie, (Deut. xiii.; 1 Kings xx. 28. 42,) venting corrupt and pernicious opinions, that destroy the foundation, (Dan. iii. 29,) open contempt of the word preached, (Zech. xiii. 3,) prophanation of the Lord's-Day, (Neh. xiii. 31,) disturbing the peaceable administration and exercise of the worship and holy things of God, (1 Tim. ii. 2,) and the like, (Rom. xiii. 4,) are to be restrained and punished by civil authority.

9. If any church, one or more, shall grow schismatical, rending itself from the communion of other churches, or shall walk incorrigibly and obstinately in any corrupt way of their own, contrary to the rule of the word; in such case, the magistrate (Josh. xxii.) is to put forth his coercive power, as the matter shall require. The tribes on this side Jordan intended to make war against the other tribes for building the altar of witness, whom they suspected to have turned away therein from following of the Lord.

FINIS

Providence Agreement
August 20, 1637

Maryland Act for Church Liberties
1638

Pennsylvania Act for Freedom of Conscience
December 7, 1682

Providence Agreement

Banished from Salem, Massachusetts, for his democratic views of church government, Roger Williams went to Rhode Island to found its earliest settlement at Providence. One of the first political compacts, the Providence Agreement also contains the first expression of the separation of church and state in America, binding members to obey only political authorities, and then only in regard to civil matters.

We whose names are hereunder, desirous to inhabit in the town of Providence, do promise to subject ourselves in active and passive obedience to all such orders or agreements as shall be made for the public good of the body in an orderly way, by the major consent of present inhabitants, masters of families, incorporated together in a Towne fellowship, and others whom they shall admit unto them only in civil things.

Maryland Act for Church Liberties

Maryland took a road toward religious toleration very different from Williams's. Lord Calvert, the colony's proprietor (and as such endowed with powers from the king to rule largely as he saw fit, subject to the king's wishes), was Catholic. Thus, colonists in Maryland, despite their representation in an assembly, and whatever their personal beliefs, had little power by which to oppose toleration specifically aimed at protecting Catholics. Nonetheless, Catholic rights would suffer periodic reversals in Maryland, which had a Protestant majority throughout most of its colonial existence.

Be it enacted by the Lord Proprietarie of this Province by and with the Advice and approbation of the ffreemen of the same that Holy Church within this Province shall have all her rights liberties and immunities safe whole and inviolable in all things. This act to continue till the end of the next Generall Assembly and then with the Consent of the Lord Proprietarie to be perpetuall.

Pennsylvania Act for Freedom of Conscience

Pennsylvania's proprietor, William Penn, held an expansive view of religious toleration, extending it to all who professed belief in a deity. However, Penn shared the common view that liberty, order, and justice depend upon virtue, which itself rests on Christian piety. Thus, his grant of religious liberties distinguishes between toleration for non-Christians and rights of political participation, which are reserved for Christians, and, further, continues traditional laws respecting Sabbath-keeping and punishment for sacrilegious speech and conduct.

Wheras the glory of almighty God and the good of mankind is the reason and end of government and, therefore, government in itself is a venerable ordinance of God. And forasmuch as it is principally desired and intended by the Proprietary and Governor and the freemen of the province of Pennsylvania and territories thereunto belonging to make and establish such laws as shall best preserve true christian and civil liberty in opposition to all unchristian, licentious, and unjust practices, whereby God may have his due, Caesar his due, and the people their due, from tyranny and oppression on the one side and insolence and licentiousness on the other, so that the best and firmest foundation may be laid for the present and future happiness of both the Governor and people of the province and territories aforesaid and their posterity.

Be it, therefore, enacted by William Penn, Proprietary and Governor, by and with the advice and consent of the deputies of the freemen of this province and counties aforesaid in assembly met and by the authority of the same, that these following chapters and paragraphs shall be the laws of Pennsylvania and the territories thereof.

Chap. I. Almighty God, being only Lord of conscience, father of lights and spirits, and the author as well as object of all divine knowledge, faith, and worship, who can only enlighten the mind and persuade and convince the understandings of people. In due reverence to his sovereignty over the souls of mankind;

Be it enacted, by the authority aforesaid, that no person now or at any time hereafter living in this province, who shall confess and acknowledge one almighty God to be the creator, upholder, and ruler of the world, and who professes him or herself obliged in conscience to live peaceably and quietly under the civil government, shall in any case be molested or prejudiced for his or her conscientious persuasion or practice. Nor shall he or she at any time be compelled to frequent or maintain any religious worship, place, or ministry whatever contrary to his or her mind, but shall freely and fully enjoy his, or her, christian liberty in that respect, without any interruption or reflection. And if any person shall abuse or deride any other for his or her different persuasion and practice in matters of religion, such person shall be looked upon as a disturber of the peace and be punished accordingly.

But to the end that looseness, irreligion, and atheism may not creep in under pretense of conscience in this province,

be it further enacted, by the authority aforesaid, that, according to the example of the primitive Christians and for the ease of the creation, every first day of the week, called the Lord's day, people shall abstain from their usual and common toil and labor that, whether masters, parents, children, or servants, they may the better dispose themselves to read the scriptures of truth at home or frequent such meetings of religious worship abroad as may best suit their respective persuasions.

Chap. II. And be it further enacted by, etc., that all officers and persons commissioned and employed in the service of the government in this province and all members and deputies elected to serve in the Assembly thereof and all that have a right to elect such deputies shall be such as profess and declare they believe in Jesus Christ to be the son of God, the savior of the world, and that are not convicted of ill-fame or unsober and dishonest conversation and that are of twenty-one years of age at least.

Chap. III. And be it further enacted, etc., that whosoever shall swear in their common conversation by the name of God or Christ or Jesus, being legally convicted thereof, shall pay, for every such offense, five shillings or suffer five days imprisonment in the house of correction at hard labor to the behoof of the public and be fed with bread and water only during that time.

Chap. V. And be it further enacted, etc., for the better prevention of corrupt communication, that whosoever shall speak loosely and profanely of almighty God, Christ Jesus, the Holy Spirit, or the scriptures of truth, and is legally convicted thereof, shall pay, for every such offense, five shillings or suffer five days imprisonment in the house of correction at hard labor to the behoof of the public and be fed with bread and water only during that time,

Chap. VI. And be it further enacted, etc., that whosoever shall, in their conversation, at any time curse himself or any other and is legally convicted thereof shall pay for every such offense five shillings or suffer five days imprisonment as aforesaid.

Worcestriensis

1776

The anonymous author of *Worcestriensis* ("From Worcester") addressed himself to the legislature of Massachusetts in the midst of the War for Independence. This was also a time during which citizens of the new state of Massachusetts were making modifications in their form of government. *Worcestriensis* stresses the need for the government officially to tolerate dissenting religious views in order to keep peace among denominations, prevent hypocrisy, and encourage wide-ranging or "catholic" inquiry into religious truths. But *Worcestriensis* also stresses the need for government to support religious teaching and practice so that the people will learn the virtues they need in order to maintain peace and support free government.

Worcestriensis

Number IV

To the Hon. Legislature of the State of Massachusetts-Bay

The subject of this disquisition (begun in my last) which is humbly offered to your consideration, is the promotion and establishment of religion in the State. In the course of the reasoning, it was suggested that a toleration of all religious principles (in other words, of all professions, modes & forms of worship) which do not sap the foundation of good government, is consistent with equity and the soundest policy. To establish this, as well as the general doctrine is my present design.

We live in [an] age of the world, in which the knowledge of the arts and sciences, calm and dispassionate enquiries and sound reasoning have been carried to surprising lengths, much to the honor of mankind. The rights of men and things, as well in an intellectual as a civil view, have by able writers, friends of human nature, been ascertained with great degrees of precision. Therefore it now becomes us in all our words and action to do nothing ungenerous, nothing unworthy the dignity of our *rational nature*.

In a well regulated state, it will be the business of the Legislature to prevent sectaries of different denominations from molesting and disturbing each other; to ordain that no part of the community shall be permitted to perplex and harrass the other for any supposed heresy, but that each individual shall be allowed to have and enjoy, profess and maintain his own system of religion, provided it does not issue in *overt acts* of treason against the state undermining the peace and good order of society.

To allow one part of a society to lord it over the faith and consciences of the other, in religious matters is the ready way to set the whole community together by the ears. It is laying a foundation for persecution in the abstract; for (as the judicious MONTESQUIEU observes) "it is a principle that every religion which is persecuted, becomes itself persecuting; for as soon as by some accidental turn it arises from persecution, it attacks the religion that persecuted it; not as a religion but as a tyranny."

It is necessary then that the laws require from the several religions, not only that they shall not embroil the State, but that they shall not raise disturbances among themselves. A citizen does not fulfill the laws by not disturbing the government; it is requisite that he should not trouble any citizen whomever.

Compulsion, instead of making men religious, generally has a contrary tendency, it works not conviction, but most naturally leads them into hypocrisy. If they are honest enquirers after truth; if their articles of belief differ from the creed of their *civil* superiors, compulsion will bring them into a sad *dilemma*. If they are conformists to what they do not believe, great uneasiness of mind must continuously perplex them. If they stand out and persist in nonconformity, they subject themselves to pains and penalties. There is further this ill consequence resulting from the establishment of religious dominion, viz. That an endeavor to suppress nonconformists, will increase, rather than diminish their number: For, however strange it may appear, yet indubitable facts prove that mankind [is] naturally compassionate [toward] those who are subjected to pains and hardships for the sake of their religion, and very frequently join with them and espouse their cause, raise sedition and faction, and endanger the public peace.

Whoever will read the history of Germany (not to mention the mother of harlots) will find this exemplified, in a manner and degree sufficient to shock any one who is not destitute of every spark of humanity. Calvinists and remonstrants made the religious divisions of the people: sometimes one party then the other was superior in their bloody disputes.

The fire first began among and between the congregations of different persuasions (calvinistic and arminian) the women and children came to blows and women pulled each others caps and hair as they passed and repassed the streets after (what they called divine) service was over in the several congregations, and the children gave each other bloody noses. This brought on civil dissention and altercation, until at length, rivers of blood in quarrels about things entirely immaterial and useless, relative either to this world or the other were shed; the nearest kindred embrued their hands in each others blood, subjects withdrew their allegiance and tumbled their rulers from their seats.

This is a true representation of facts, and is sufficient to deter any legislature from enacting laws requiring conformity to any particular mode or profession of religion, under pains of persecution in case of refusal.

This is not suggested because a *persecuting spirit* has of late years been conspicuous among the inhabitants of this state. On the contrary, a candid, catholic, and benevolent disposition has increased and prevailed. The principle reason why this is exhibited is, that as the GOOD PEOPLE of this and its sister states had just cause to alter and amend their civil constitution, so also, it is probable, the legislature of this State will take into consideration the eclesiastical discipline and government, and make such alterations and amendments in the constitution of the churches, as by them, in their wisdom shall be thought proper. We would therefore guard against everything that might be construed to have the least colour of a persecuting tendency, that so the law, relative to religion, may be the most candid, catholic and rational, that the nature of human society will admit of.

Perhaps some sticklers for establishments, requiring conformity to the prevailing religion, may now enquire whether, upon the principles above laid down, any legal establishment at all can take place? and if any, what? In answer to such querists, I would say that if by an establishment they intend the enacting and ordaining laws obliging dissenters from any certain religion to conform thereto, and, in case of nonconformity, subjecting them to pains,

penalties and disabilities, in this sense there can and ought to be none. The establishment contended for in this disquisition, is of a different kind, and must result from a different legal Procedure.

It must proceed only from the benign frames of the legislature from an encouragement of the GENERAL PRINCIPLES of religion and morality, recommending free inquiry and examination of the doctrines said to be divine; using all possible and lawful means to enable its subjects to discover the truth, and to entertain good and rational sentiments, and taking mild and parental measures to bring about the design; these are the most probable means to bring about that establishment of religion which is recommended, and a settlement on an immoveable BASIS. It is lawful for the directors of a state to give preference to that profession of religion which they take to be true, and they have right to inflict penalties on those who notoriously violate the laws of natural religion, and thereby disturb the public peace. The openly profane come within their penal jurisdiction. There is no stronger cement of society than a sacred regard to OATHS; nothing binds stronger to the observation of the laws, therefore the public safety, and the *honor* of the SUPREME BEING require that public *profaneness,* should bring down the public vengeance upon those who dare hurl profanities at the throne of OMNIPOTENCE, and thereby *lessen* the reverence of the people for oaths, and solemn appeals to almighty God, and so shaking the foundation of good order and security in society. The same may be said of all Profaneness, and also of debauchery, which strike a fatal blow at the root of good regulation, and the well-being of the state.

And now with regard to the positive interposition of civil magistracy in behalf of religion, I would say, that what has been above suggested with respect to *toleration,* will not disprove the right of the legislature to exert themselves in favor of one religious profession rather than another, they have a right of private judgment as well as others, and are BOUND to do their *utmost* to propagate *that* which they esteem to be true. This they are to do by providing *able* and *learned* TEACHERS, to instruct the people in the knowledge of what they deem the truth, maintaining them by the public money, though at the same time they have no right in the least degree to endeavor the depression of professions of any religious denomination. Nor let it be said (in order to a perfect toleration) that all religious denominations have an equal right to public countenance, for this would be an evident infringement on the right of private judgment in the members of the legislature.

If the greatest part of the people, coincide with the public authority of the State in giving the prefference to any one religious system and creed, the dissenting few, though they cannot conscientiously conform to the prevailing religion, yet ought to acquiesce and rest satisfied that their religious Liberty is not *diminished*.

This suggestion starts a question, which has caused much debate among persons of different religious sentiments, viz. Whether a minor part of a parish or other corporation, are, or can be consistently obliged to contribute to the maintenance and support of a minister to them disagreeable, who is approved by the majority.

This is answered by a very able writer in the following manner, viz. "that this will stand upon the same footing with their contributing towards the expence of a war, which they think not necessary or prudent. If no such power were admitted, covetousness would drive many into dissenting parties in order to save their money.

So that none can reasonably blame a government for requiring such a *general Contribution*, and in this case it seems fit it should be yielded to, as the determination of those to whose guardianship the minority have committed themselves and their possessions.

We hope and trust that you, Hon. directors of this State, will exert yourselves in the cultivation and promotion of pure and RATIONAL RELIGION among your constituents. If there were no arguments to be drawn from the consideration of a *future* world, yet those drawn from the great influence of religion upon the LAWS and the *observance* of them, must, and ought to prevail."

I would add, that our Legislature of the last year have declared that "a Government so popular can be supported only by universal Knowledge and VIRTUE, in the body of the people."

In addition to this, I shall produce the opinion of the above cited *Montesquieu* (a great *authority!*) and so conclude this number.

"Religion may support a state, when the laws themselves are incapable of doing it.

"Thus when a kingdom is frequently agitated by civil wars, religion may do much by obliging one part of the state to remain always quiet.

"A prince who loves and fears religion, is a lion, who stoops to the hand that strokes or to the voice that appeases him. He who fears and hates religion, is like the savage beast, that growls and bites the chain which prevents his flying on the passenger. He who has no religion at all, is that terrible animal; who perceives his liberty only when he tears in pieces, and when he devours."

Thanksgiving Proclamation and Letters to Religious Associations

GEORGE WASHINGTON

Thanksgiving Proclamation

October 3, 1789

Letter to the United Baptist Churches in Virginia

May 10, 1789

Letter to the Roman Catholics in the United States of America

March 15, 1790

Letter to the Hebrew Congregation in Newport

August 1790

Thanksgiving Proclamation

It was common practice in America, both before and after the Revolution, for political leaders to call for days of thanksgiving, as well as days of fasting and prayer, to mark great events and significant tragedies affecting the American republic. Here, Washington proclaims a Day of Thanksgiving, calling on Americans to acknowledge God's role in bringing them through the Revolution to the founding of their free government.

Whereas it is the duty of all Nations to acknowledge the providence of Almighty God, to obey his will, to be grateful for his benefits, and humbly to implore his protection and favor, and Whereas both Houses of Congress have by their joint Committee requested me "to recommend to the People of the United States a day of public thanks-giving and prayer to be observed by acknowledging with grateful hearts the many signal favors of Almighty God, especially by affording them an opportunity peaceably to establish a form of government for their safety and happiness."

Now therefore I do recommend and assign Thursday the 26th. day of November next to be devoted by the People of these States to the service of that great and glorious Being, who is the beneficent Author of all the good that was, that is, or that will be. That we may then all unite in rendering unto him our sincere and humble thanks, for his kind care and protection of the People of this country previous to their becoming a Nation, for the signal and manifold mercies, and the favorable interpositions of his providence, which we experienced in the course and conclusion of the late war, for the great degree of tranquillity, union, and plenty, which we have since enjoyed, for the peaceable and rational manner in which we have been enabled to establish constitutions of government for our safety and happiness, and particularly the national One now lately instituted, for the civil and religious liberty with which we are blessed, and the means we have of acquiring and diffusing useful knowledge and in general for all the great and various favors which he hath been pleased to confer upon us.

And also that we may then unite in most humbly offering our prayers and supplications to the great Lord and Ruler of Nations and beseech him to pardon our national and other transgressions, to enable us all, whether in public or private stations, to perform our several and relative duties properly and punctually, to render our national government a blessing to all the People, by constantly being a government of wise, just and constitutional laws, discreetly and faithfully executed and obeyed, to protect and guide all Sovereigns and Nations (especially such as have shown kindness unto us) and to bless them with good government, peace, and concord. To promote the knowledge and practice of true religion and virtue, and the encrease of science among them and Us, and generally to grant unto all Mankind such a degree of temporal prosperity as he alone knows to be best.

Letters to Religious Associations

In his replies to letters from various religious organizations representing minority faiths in America, Washington consistently maintains that those who hold dissenting religious views ought to be left alone to practice their beliefs and accorded decent respect in public, provided they conduct themselves as good citizens and supporters of the American republic.

To the United Baptist Churches in Virginia

Gentlemen:

I request that you will accept my best acknowledgements for your congratulation on my appointment to the first office in the nation. The kind manner in which you mention my past conduct equally claims the expression of my gratitude.

After we had, by the smiles of Heaven on our exertions, obtained the object for which we contended, I retired at the conclusion of the war, with an idea that my country would have no farther occasion for my services, and with the intention of never entering again into public life. But when the exigence of my country seemed to require me once more to engage in public affairs, an honest conviction of duty superseded my former resolution, and became my apology for deviating from the happy plan which I had adopted.

If I could have entertained the slightest apprehension that the Constitution framed in the Convention, where I had the honor to preside, might possibly endanger the religious rights of any ecclesiastical society, certainly I would never have placed my signature to it; and if I could now conceive that the general government might ever be so administered as to render the liberty of conscience insecure, I beg you will be persuaded that no one would be more zealous than myself to establish effectual barriers against the horrors of spiritual tyranny, and every species of religious persecution. For you, doubtless, remember that I have often expressed my sentiment, that every man, conducting himself as a good citizen, and being accountable to God alone for his religious opinions, ought to be protected in

worshipping the Deity according to the dictates of his own conscience.

While I recollect with satisfaction that the religious society of which you are members, have been, throughout America, uniformly, and almost unanimously, the firm friends to civil liberty, and the persevering promoters of our glorious revolution; I cannot hesitate to believe that they will be the faithful supporters of a free, yet efficient general government. Under this pleasing reflection I rejoice to assure them that they may rely on my best wishes and endeavors to advance their prosperity.

In the meantime be assured, Gentlemen, that I entertain a proper sense of your fervent supplications to God for my temporal and eternal happiness.

G. WASHINGTON

To the Roman Catholics in the United States of America

Gentlemen:

While I now receive with much satisfaction your congratulations on my being called, by an unanimous vote, to the first station in my country; I cannot but duly notice your politeness in offering an apology for the unavoidable delay. As that delay has given you an opportunity of realizing, instead of anticipating, the benefits of the general government, you will do me the justice to believe, that your testimony of the increase of the public prosperity, enhances the pleasure which I should otherwise have experienced from your affectionate address.

I feel that my conduct, in war and in peace, has met with more general approbation than could reasonably have been expected and I find myself disposed to consider that fortunate circumstance, in a great degree, resulting from the able support and extraordinary candour of my fellow-citizens of all denominations.

The prospect of national prosperity now before us is truly animating, and ought to excite the exertions of all good men to establish and secure the happiness of their country, in the permanent duration of its freedom and independence. America, under the smiles of a Divine Providence, the protection of a good government, and the cultivation of manners, morals, and piety, cannot fail of attaining an uncommon degree of eminence, in literature, commerce, agriculture, improvements at home and respectability abroad.

As mankind become more liberal they will be more apt to allow that all those who conduct themselves as worthy members of the community are equally entitled to the protection of civil government. I hope ever to see America among the foremost nations in examples of justice and liberality. And I presume that your fellow-citizens will not forget the patriotic part which you took in the accomplishment of their Revolution, and the establishment of their government; or the important assistance which they received from a nation in which the Roman Catholic faith is professed.

I thank you, gentlemen, for your kind concern for me. While my life and my health shall continue, in whatever situation I may be, it shall be my constant endeavour to justify the favourable sentiments which you are pleased to express of my conduct. And may the members of your society in America, animated alone by the pure spirit of Christianity, and still conducting themselves as the faithful subjects of our free government, enjoy every temporal and spiritual felicity.

G. WASHINGTON

To the Hebrew Congregation in Newport

Gentlemen:

While I received with much satisfaction your address replete with expressions of esteem, I rejoice in the opportunity of assuring you that I shall always retain grateful remembrance of the cordial welcome I experienced on my visit to Newport from all classes of citizens.

The reflection on the days of difficulty and danger which are past is rendered the more sweet from a consciousness that they are succeeded by days of uncommon prosperity and security.

If we have wisdom to make the best use of the advantages with which we are now favored, we cannot fail, under the just administration of a good government, to become a great and happy people.

The citizens of the United States of America have a right to applaud themselves for having given to mankind examples of an enlarged and liberal policy—a policy worthy of imitation. All possess alike liberty of conscience and immunities of citizenship.

It is now no more that toleration is spoken of as if it were the indulgence of one class of people that another enjoyed the exercise of their inherent natural rights, for, happily, the Government of the United States, which gives to bigotry no sanction, to persecution no assistance, requires only that they who live under its protection should demean themselves as good citizens in giving it on all occasions their effectual support.

It would be inconsistent with the frankness of my character not to avow that I am pleased with your favorable opinion of my administration and fervent wishes for my felicity.

May the children of the stock of Abraham who dwell in this land continue to merit and enjoy the good will of the other inhabitants—while every one shall sit in safety under his own vine and fig tree and there shall be none to make him afraid.

May the father of all mercies scatter light, and not darkness, upon our paths, and make us all in our several vocations useful here, and in His own due time and way everlastingly happy.

G. WASHINGTON

Farewell Address

GEORGE WASHINGTON

September 19, 1796

Throughout his public career and well after, Washington presented himself as the citizen soldier who gave up the quiet life he loved in order to serve his country in time of need. This model of virtue, which Washington believed he had a duty to both follow and exemplify, rested on a moral code grounded in religious faith. Men would recognize their public duty only if they were taught from a young age that they had duties to God and, from that, to their fellow men. In his parting words as president, Washington seeks to make clear the reliance of public liberty on private virtue and the reliance of both on religious faith. Furthermore, Washington self-consciously repeats the view, going back to the Puritans and beyond, that liberty itself is of small use to a people that does not recognize its higher duty to worship and live according to the commands of God.

Farewell Address

Friends, and Fellow-Citizens:

The period for a new election of a Citizen, to Administer the Executive government of the United States, being not far distant, and the time actually arrived, when your thoughts must be employed in designating the person, who is to be cloathed with that important trust, it appears to me proper, especially as it may conduce to a more distinct expression of the public voice, that I should now apprise you of the resolution I have formed, to decline being considered among the number of those, out of whom a choice is to be made.

I beg you, at the same time, to do me the justice to be assured, that this resolution has not been taken, without a strict regard to all the considerations appertaining to the relation, which binds a dutiful citizen to his country, and that, in with drawing the tender of service which silence in my situation might imply, I am influenced by no diminution of zeal for your future interest, no deficiency of grate-

ful respect for your past kindness; but am supported by a full conviction that the step is compatible with both.

The acceptance of, and continuance hitherto in, the office to which your Suffrages have twice called me, have been a uniform sacrifice of inclination to the opinion of duty, and to a deference for what appeared to be your desire. I constantly hoped, that it would have been much earlier in my power, consistently with motives, which I was not at liberty to disregard, to return to that retirement, from which I had been reluctantly drawn. The strength of my inclination to do this, previous to the last Election, had even led to the preparation of an address to declare it to you; but mature reflection on the then perplexed and critical posture of our Affairs with foreign Nations, and the unanimous advice of persons entitled to my confidence, impelled me to abandon the idea.

I rejoice, that the state of your concerns, external as well as internal, no longer renders the pursuit of inclination incompatible with the sentiment of duty, or propriety; and am persuaded whatever partiality may be retained for my services, that in the present circumstances of our country, you will not disapprove my determination to retire.

The impressions, with which I first undertook the arduous trust, were explained on the proper occasion. In the discharge of this trust, I will only say, that I have, with good intentions, contributed towards the Organization and Administration of the government, the best exertions of which a very fallible judgment was capable. Not unconscious, in the outset, of the inferiority of my qualifications, experience in my own eyes, perhaps still more in the eyes of others, has strengthned the motives to diffidence of myself; and every day the encreasing weight of years admonishes me more and more, that the shade of retirement is as necessary to me as it will be welcome. Satisfied that if any circumstances have given peculiar value to my services, they were temporary, I have the consolation to believe, that while choice and prudence invite me to quit the political scene, patriotism does not forbid it.

In looking forward to the moment, which is intended to terminate the career of my public life, my feelings do not permit me to suspend the deep acknowledgment of that debt of gratitude wch. I owe to my beloved country, for the many honors it has conferred upon me; still more for the stedfast confidence with which it has supported me; and for the opportunities I have thence enjoyed of manifesting my inviolable attachment, by services faithful and persevering, though in usefulness unequal to my zeal. If benefits have resulted to our country from these services, let it always be remembered to your praise, and as an instructive example in our annals, that, under circumstances in which the Passions agitated in every direction were liable to mislead, amidst appearances sometimes dubious, viscissitudes of fortune often discouraging, in situations in which not unfrequently want of Success has countenanced the spirit of criticism, the constancy of your support was the essential prop of the efforts, and a guarantee of the plans by which they were effected. Profoundly penetrated with this idea, I shall carry it with me to my grave, as a strong incitement to unceasing vows that Heaven may continue to you the choicest tokens of its beneficence; that your Union and brotherly affection may be perpetual; that the free constitution, which is the work of your hands, may be sacredly maintained; that its Administration in every department may be stamped with wisdom and Virtue; that, in fine, the happiness of the people of these States, under the auspices of liberty, may be made complete, by so careful a preservation and so prudent a use of this blessing as will acquire to them the glory of recommending it to the applause, the affection, and adoption of every nation which is yet a stranger to it.

Here, perhaps, I ought to stop. But a solicitude for your welfare, which cannot end but with my life, and the apprehension of danger, natural to that solicitude, urge me on an occasion like the present, to offer to your solemn contemplation, and to recommend to your frequent review, some sentiments, which are the result of much reflection, of no inconsiderable observation, and which appear to me all important to the permanency of your felicity as a People. These will be offered to you with the more freedom, as you can only see in them the disinterested warnings of a parting friend, who can possibly have no personal motive to biass his counsel. Nor can I forget, as an encouragement to it, your endulgent reception of my sentiments on a former and not dissimilar occasion.

Interwoven as is the love of liberty with every ligament of your hearts, no recommendation of mine is necessary to fortify or confirm the attachment.

The Unity of Government which constitutes you one people is also now dear to you. It is justly so; for it is a main Pillar in the Edifice of your real independence, the support of your tranquility at home; your peace abroad; of your safety; of your prosperity; of that very Liberty which you so highly prize. But as it is easy to foresee, that from different causes and from different quarters, much pains will be taken, many artifices employed, to weaken in your minds the conviction of this truth; as this is the point in your political fortress against which the batteries of internal and external enemies will be most constantly and actively (though often covertly and insidiously) directed, it is of infinite moment, that you should properly estimate the immense value of your national Union to your collective and individual happiness; that you should cherish a cordial, habitual and immoveable attachment to it; accustoming yourselves to think and speak of it as of the Palladium of your political safety and prosperity; watching for its preservation with jealous anxiety; discountenancing whatever may suggest even a suspicion that it can in any event be abandoned, and indignantly frowning upon the first dawning of every attempt to alienate any portion of our Country from the rest, or to enfeeble the sacred ties which now link together the various parts.

For this you have every inducement of sympathy and interest. Citizens by birth or choice, of a common country, that country has a right to concentrate your affections. The name of AMERICAN, which belongs to you, in your national capacity, must always exalt the just pride of Patriotism, more than any appellation derived from local discriminations. With slight shades of difference, you have the same Religion, Manners, Habits and political Principles. You have in a common cause fought and triumphed together. The independence and liberty you possess are the work of joint councils, and joint efforts; of common dangers, sufferings and successes.

But these considerations, however powerfully they address themselves to your sensibility are greatly outweighed by those which apply more immediately to your Interest.

Here every portion of our country finds the most commanding motives for carefully guarding and preserving the Union of the whole.

The *North,* in an unrestrained intercourse with the *South,* protected by the equal Laws of a common government, finds in the productions of the latter, great additional resources of Maritime and commercial enterprise and precious materials of manufacturing industry. The *South* in the same Intercourse, benefitting by the Agency of the *North,* sees its agriculture grow and its commerce expand. Turning partly into its own channels the seamen of the *North,* it finds its particular navigation envigorated; and while it contributes, in different ways, to nourish and increase the general mass of the National navigation, it looks forward to the protection of a Maritime strength, to which itself is unequally adapted. The *East,* in a like intercourse with the *West,* already finds, and in the progressive improvement of interior communications, by land and water, will more and more find a valuable vent for the commodities which it brings from abroad, or manufactures at home. The *West* derives from the *East* supplies requisite to its growth and comfort, and what is perhaps of still greater consequence, it must of necessity owe the *secure* enjoyment of indispensable *outlets* for its own productions to the weight, influence, and the future Maritime strength of the Atlantic side of the Union, directed by an indissoluble community of Interest as *one Nation.* Any other tenure by which the *West* can hold this essential advantage, whether derived from its own seperate strength, or from an apostate and unnatural connection with any foreign Power, must be intrinsically precarious.

While then every part of our country thus feels an immediate and particular Interest in Union, all the parts combined cannot fail to find in the united mass of means and efforts greater strength, greater resource, proportionably greater security from external danger, a less frequent interruption of their Peace by foreign Nations; and, what is of inestimable value! they must derive from Union an exemption from those broils and Wars between themselves, which so frequently afflict neighbouring countries, not tied together by the same government; which their own rivalships alone would be sufficient to produce, but which opposite foreign alliances, attachments and intriegues would stimulate and imbitter. Hence likewise they will avoid the necessity of those overgrown Military establishments, which under any form of Government are inauspicious to liberty, and which are to be regarded as particularly hostile to Republican Liberty: In this sense it is, that your Union ought to be considered as a main prop of your liberty, and that the love of the one ought to endear to you the preservation of the other.

These considerations speak a persuasive language to every reflecting and virtuous mind, and exhibit the continuance of the UNION as a primary object of Patriotic desire. Is there a doubt, whether a common government can embrace so large a sphere? Let experience solve it. To listen to mere speculation in such a case were criminal. We are authorized to hope that a proper organization of the whole, with the auxiliary agency of governments for the respective Subdivisions, will afford a happy issue to the experiment. 'Tis well worth a fair and full experiment. With such powerful and obvious motives to Union, affecting all parts of our country, while experience shall not have demonstrated its impracticability, there will always be reason, to distrust the patriotism of those, who in any quarter may endeavor to weaken its bands.

In contemplating the causes wch. may disturb our Union, it occurs as matter of serious concern, that any ground should have been furnished for characterizing parties by *Geographical* discriminations: *Northern* and *Southern; Atlantic* and *Western;* whence designing men may endeavour to excite a belief that there is a real difference of local interests and views. One of the expedients of Party to acquire influence, within particular districts, is to misrepresent the opinions and aims of other Districts. You cannot shield yourselves too much against the jealousies and heart burnings which spring from these misrepresentations. They tend to render Alien to each other those who ought to be bound together by fraternal affection. The Inhabitants of our Western country have lately had a useful lesson on this head. They have seen, in the Negociation by the Executive, and in the unanimous ratification by the Senate, of the Treaty with Spain, and in the universal satisfaction at that event, throughout the United States, a decisive proof how unfounded were the suspicions propagated among them of a policy in the General Government and in the Atlantic States unfriendly to their Interests in regard to the Mississippi. They have been witnesses to the formation of two Treaties, that with G: Britain and that with Spain, which secure to them every thing they could desire, in respect to our Foreign relations, towards confirming their prosperity. Will it not be their wisdom to rely for the preservation of these advantages on the Union by wch. they were procured? Will they not henceforth be deaf to those advisers, if such there are, who would sever them from their Brethren and connect them with Aliens?

To the efficacy and permanency of Your Union, a Government for the whole is indispensable. No Alliances however strict between the parts can be an adequate substitute. They must inevitably experience the infractions and interruptions which all Alliances in all times have experienced. Sensible of this momentous truth, you have improved upon your first essay, by the adoption of a Constitution of Government, better calculated than your former for an intimate Union, and for the efficacious management of your common concerns. This government, the offspring of our own choice uninfluenced and unawed, adopted upon full investigation and mature deliberation, completely free in its principles, in the distribution of its powers, uniting security with energy, and containing within itself a provision for its own amendment, has a just claim to your confidence and your support. Respect for its authority, compliance with its Laws, acquiescence in its measures, are duties enjoined by the fundamental maxims of true Liberty. The basis of our political systems is the right of the people to make and to alter their Constitutions of Government. But the Constitution which at any time exists, 'till changed by an explicit and authentic act of the whole People, is sacredly obligatory upon all. The very idea of the power and the right of the People to establish Government presupposes the duty of every Individual to obey the established Government.

All obstructions to the execution of the Laws, all combinations and Associations, under whatever plausible character, with the real design to direct, controul, counteract, or awe the regular deliberation and action of the Constituted authorities are distructive of this fundamental principle and of fatal tendency. They serve to organize faction, to give it an artificial and extraordinary force; to put in the place of the delegated will of the Nation, the will of a party; often a small but artful and enterprizing minority of the Community; and, according to the alternate triumphs of different parties, to make the public administration the Mirror of the ill concerted and incongruous projects of faction, rather than the organ of consistent and wholesome plans digested by common councils and modefied by mutual interests. However combinations or Associations of the above description may now and then answer popular ends, they are likely, in the course of time and things, to become potent engines, by which cunning, ambitious and unprincipled men will be enabled to subvert the Power of the People, and to usurp for themselves the reins of Government; destroying afterwards the very engines which have lifted them to unjust dominion.

Towards the preservation of your Government and the permanency of your present happy state, it is requisite, not only that you steadily discountenance irregular oppositions to its acknowledged authority, but also that you resist with care the spirit of innovation upon its principles however specious the pretexts. One method of assault may be to effect, in the forms of the Constitution, alterations which will impair the energy of the system, and thus to undermine what cannot be directly overthrown. In all the changes to which you may be invited, remember that time and habit are at least as necessary to fix the true character of Governments, as of other human institutions; that experience is the surest standard, by which to test the real tendency of the existing Constitution of a country; that facility in changes upon the credit of mere hypotheses and opinion exposes to perpetual change, from the endless variety of hypotheses and opinion: and remember, especially, that for the efficient management of your common interests, in a country so extensive as ours, a Government of as much vigour as is consistent with the perfect security of Liberty is indispensable. Liberty itself will find in such a Government, with powers properly distributed and adjusted, its surest Guardian. It is indeed little else than a name, where the Government is too feeble to withstand the enterprises of faction, to confine each member of the Society within the limits prescribed by the laws and to maintain all in the secure and tranquil enjoyment of the rights of person and property.

I have already intimated to you the danger of Parties in the State, with particular reference to the founding of them on Geographical discriminations. Let me now take a more comprehensive view, and warn you in the most solemn manner against the baneful effects of the Spirit of Party, generally.

This spirit, unfortunately, is inseperable from our nature, having its root in the strongest passions of the human Mind. It exists under different shapes in all Governments, more or less stifled, controuled, or repressed; but, in those of the popular form it is seen in its greatest rankness and is truly their worst enemy.

The alternate domination of one faction over another, sharpened by the spirit of revenge natural to party dissention, which in different ages and countries has perpetrated the most horrid enormities, is itself a frightful despotism. But this leads at length to a more formal and permanent despotism. The disorders and miseries, which result, gradually incline the minds of men to seek security and repose in the absolute power of an Individual: and sooner or later the chief of some prevailing faction more able or more fortunate than his competitors, turns this disposition to the purposes of his own elevation, on the ruins of Public Liberty.

Without looking forward to an extremity of this kind (which nevertheless ought not to be entirely out of sight) the common and continual mischiefs of the spirit of Party are sufficient to make it the interest and the duty of a wise People to discourage and restrain it.

It serves always to distract the Public Councils and enfeeble the Public administration. It agitates the Community with ill founded jealousies and false alarms, kindles the animosity of one part against another, foments occasionally riot and insurrection. It opens the door to foreign influence and corruption, which find a facilitated access to the government itself through the channels of party passions. Thus the policy and the will of one country, are subjected to the policy and will of another.

There is an opinion that parties in free countries are useful checks upon the Administration of the Government and serve to keep alive the spirit of Liberty. This within certain limits is probably true, and in Governments of a Monarchical cast Patriotism may look with endulgence, if not with favour, upon the spirit of party. But in those of the popular character, in Governments purely elective, it is a spirit not to be encouraged. From their natural tendency, it is certain there will always be enough of that spirit for every salutary purpose. And there being constant danger of excess, the effort ought to be, by force of public opinion, to mitigate and assuage it. A fire not to be quenched; it demands a uniform vigilance to prevent its bursting into a flame, lest instead of warming it should consume.

It is important, likewise, that the habits of thinking in a free Country should inspire caution in those entrusted with its administration, to confine themselves within their respective Constitutional spheres; avoiding in the exercise of the Powers of one department to encroach upon another. The spirit of encroachment tends to consolidate the powers of all the departments in one, and thus to create whatever the form of government, a real despotism. A just estimate of that love of power, and proneness to abuse it, which predominates in the human heart is sufficient to satisfy us of the truth of this position. The necessity of reciprocal checks in the exercise of political power; by dividing and distributing it into different depositories, and constituting each the Guardian of the Public Weal against invasions by the others, has been evinced by experiments ancient and modern; some of them in our country and under our own eyes. To preserve them must be as necessary as to institute them. If in the opinion of the People, the distribution or modification of the Constitutional powers be in any particular wrong, let it be corrected by an amendment in the way which the Constitution designates. But let there be no change by usurpation; for though this, in one instance, may be the instrument of good, it is the customary weapon by which free governments are destroyed. The precedent must always greatly overbalance in permanent evil any partial or transient benefit which the use can at any time yield.

Of all the dispositions and habits which lead to political prosperity, Religion and morality are indispensable supports. In vain would that man claim the tribute of Patriotism, who should labour to subvert these great Pillars of human happiness, these firmest props of the duties of Men and citizens. The mere Politician, equally with the pious man ought to respect and to cherish them. A volume could not trace all their connections with private and public felicity. Let it simply be asked where is the security for property, for reputation, for life, if the sense of religious obligation *desert* the oaths, which are the instruments of investigation in Courts of Justice? And let us with caution indulge the supposition, that morality can be maintained without religion. Whatever may be conceded to the influence of refined education on minds of peculiar structure, reason and experience both forbid us to expect that National morality can prevail in exclusion of religious principle.

'Tis substantially true, that virtue or morality is a necessary spring of popular government. The rule indeed extends with more or less force to every species of free Government. Who that is a sincere friend to it, can look with indifference upon attempts to shake the foundation of the fabric.

Promote then as an object of primary importance, Institutions for the general diffusion of knowledge. In proportion as the structure of a government gives force to public opinion, it is essential that public opinion should be enlightened.

As a very important source of strength and security, cherish public credit. One method of preserving it is to use it as sparingly as possible: avoiding occasions of expence by cultivating peace, but remembering also that timely disbursements to prepare for danger frequently prevent much greater disbursements to repel it; avoiding likewise the accumulation of debt, not only by shunning occasions of expence, but by vigorous exertions in time of Peace to discharge the Debts which unavoidable wars may have occasioned, not ungenerously throwing upon posterity the burthen which we ourselves ought to bear. The execution of these maxims belongs to your Representatives, but it is necessary that public opinion should cooperate. To facilitate to them the performance of their duty, it is essential that you should practically bear in mind, that towards the payment of debts there must be Revenue; that to have Revenue there must be taxes; that no taxes can be devised which are not more or less inconvenient and unpleasant; that the intrinsic embarrassment inseperable from the selection of the proper objects (which is always a choice of difficulties) ought to be a decisive motive for a candid construction of the Conduct of the Government in making it, and for a spirit of acquiescence in the measures for obtaining Revenue which the public exigencies may at any time dictate.

Observe good faith and justice towds. all Nations. Cultivate peace and harmony with all. Religion and morality enjoin this conduct; and can it be that good policy does not equally enjoin it? It will be worthy of a free, enlightened, and, at no distant period, a great Nation, to give to mankind the magnanimous and too novel example of a People always guided by an exalted justice and benevolence. Who can doubt that in the course of time and things the fruits of such a plan would richly repay any temporary advantages wch. might be lost by a steady adherence to it? Can it be, that Providence has not connected the permanent felicity of a Nation with its virtue? The experiment, at least, is recommended by every sentiment which ennobles human Nature. Alas! is it rendered impossible by its vices?

In the execution of such a plan nothing is more essential than that permanent, inveterate antipathies against particular Nations and passionate attachments for others should be excluded; and that in place of them just and am-

icable feelings towards all should be cultivated. The Nation, which indulges towards another an habitual hatred, or an habitual fondness, is in some degree a slave. It is a slave to its animosity or to its affection, either of which is sufficient to lead it astray from its duty and its interest. Antipathy in one Nation against another, disposes each more readily to offer insult and injury, to lay hold of slight causes of umbrage, and to be haughty and intractable, when accidental or trifling occasions of dispute occur. Hence frequent collisions, obstinate envenomed and bloody contests. The Nation, prompted by ill will and resentment sometimes impels to War the Government, contrary to the best calculations of policy. The Government sometimes participates in the national propensity, and adopts through passion what reason would reject; at other times, it makes the animosity of the Nation subservient to projects of hostility instigated by pride, ambition and other sinister and pernicious motives. The peace often, sometimes perhaps the Liberty, of Nations has been the victim.

So likewise, a passionate attachment of one Nation for another produces a variety of evils. Sympathy for the favourite nation, facilitating the illusion of an imaginary common interest, in cases where no real common interest exists, and infusing into one the enmities of the other, betrays the former into a participation in the quarrels and Wars of the latter, without adequate inducement or justification: It leads also to concessions to the favourite Nation of priviledges denied to others, which is apt doubly to injure the Nation making the concessions; by unnecessarily parting with what ought to have been retained; and by exciting jealousy, ill will, and a disposition to retaliate, in the parties from whom eql. priviledges are withheld: And it gives to ambitious, corrupted, or deluded citizens (who devote themselves to the favourite Nation) facility to betray, or sacrifice the interests of their own country, without odium, sometimes even with popularity; gilding with the appearances of a virtuous sense of obligation a commendable deference for public opinion, or a laudable zeal for public good, the base or foolish compliances of ambition corruption or infatuation.

As avenues to foreign influence in innumerable ways, such attachments are particularly alarming to the truly enlightened and independent Patriot. How many opportunities do they afford to tamper with domestic factions, to practice the arts of seduction, to mislead public opinion, to influence or awe the public Councils! Such an attachment of a small or weak, towards a great and powerful Nation, dooms the former to be the satellite of the latter.

Against the insidious wiles of foreign influence, (I conjure you to believe me fellow citizens) the jealousy of a free people ought to be *constantly* awake; since history and experience prove that foreign influence is one of the most baneful foes of Republican Government. But that jealousy to be useful must be impartial; else it becomes the instrument of the very influence to be avoided, instead of a defence against it. Excessive partiality for one foreign nation and excessive dislike of another, cause those whom they actuate to see danger only on one side, and serve to veil and even second the arts of influence on the other. Real Patriots, who may resist the intriegues of the favourite, are liable to become suspected and odious; while its tools and dupes usurp the applause and confidence of the people, to surrender their interests.

The Great rule of conduct for us, in regard to foreign Nations is in extending our commercial relations to have with them as little *political* connection as possible. So far as we have already formed engagements let them be fulfilled, with perfect good faith. Here let us stop. . . .

In offering to you, my Countrymen these counsels of an old and affectionate friend, I dare not hope they will make the strong and lasting impression, I could wish; that they will controul the usual current of the passions, or prevent our Nation from running the course which has hitherto marked the Destiny of Nations: But if I may even flatter myself, that they may be productive of some partial benefit, some occasional good; that they may now and then recur to moderate the fury of party spirit, to warn against the

mischiefs of foreign Intriegue, to guard against the Impostures of pretended patriotism; this hope will be a full recompence for the solicitude for your welfare, by which they have been dictated.

How far in the discharge of my Official duties, I have been guided by the principles which have been delineated, the public Records and other evidences of my conduct must Witness to You and to the world. To myself, the assurance of my own conscience is, that I have at least believed myself to be guided by them. . . .

Though in reviewing the incidents of my Administration, I am unconscious of intentional error, I am nevertheless too sensible of my defects not to think it probable that I may have committed many errors. Whatever they may be I fervently beseech the Almighty to avert or mitigate the evils to which they may tend. I shall also carry with me the hope that my Country will never cease to view them with indulgence; and that after forty five years of my life dedicated to its Service, with an upright zeal, the faults of incompetent abilities will be consigned to oblivion, as myself must soon be to the Mansions of rest.

Relying on its kindness in this as in other things, and actuated by that fervent love towards it, which is so natural to a Man, who views in it the native soil of himself and his progenitors for several Generations; I anticipate with pleasing expectation that retreat, in which I promise myself to realize, without alloy, the sweet enjoyment of partaking, in the midst of my fellow Citizens, the benign influence of good Laws under a free Government, the ever favourite object of my heart, and the happy reward, as I trust, of our mutual cares, labours and dangers.

The Rights of Conscience Inalienable

JOHN LELAND

1791

John Leland (1754–1841) was a Baptist minister, a political ally of James Madison, and a tireless advocate of religious disestablishment. Among the most radical proponents of eliminating restrictions on political rights for religious dissenters, he worked against the Episcopal Church in Virginia and the Congregational Church in New England, both of which enjoyed privileged status in their particular colony or state. His influence was in part responsible for the defeat of taxes proposed to support Episcopal Church teachings in Virginia (1785) and for eliminating public taxation in support of Congregationalist activities in Massachusetts (1833). This statement of views concerning the need to separate religious from political establishments was, in fact, delivered from a pulpit—it is a sermon. This sermon was written probably in 1791, after the United States had begun life under its new Constitution, and soon after Leland returned to New England from Virginia. Its original title was "The rights of Conscience inalienable, and therefore Religious Opinions not cognizable by Law: Or, The high-flying Churchman, stript of his legal Robe, appears a Yaho."

The Rights of Conscience Inalienable

There are four principles contended for, as the foundation of civil government, viz. birth, property, grace, and compact. The first of these is practised upon in all hereditary monarchies, where it is believed that the son of a monarch is entitled to dominion upon the decease of his father, whether he be a wise man or a fool. The second principle is built upon in all aristocratical governments, where the rich landholders have the sole rule of all their tenants, and make laws at pleasure which are binding upon all. The third principle is adopted by those kingdoms and states that require a religious test to qualify an officer of state, proscribing all non-conformists from civil and religious liberty. This was the error of Constantine's government, who first established the christian religion by law, and then proscribed

the pagans and banished the Arian heretics. This error also filled the heads of the anabaptists in Germany (who were re-sprinklers): they supposed that none had a right to rule but gracious men. The same error prevails in the see of Rome, where his holiness exalts himself above all who are called gods (i.e. kings and rulers), and where no protestant heretic is allowed the liberty of a citizen. This principle is also plead for in the Ottoman empire, where it is death to call in question the divinity of Mahomet or the authenticity of the Alcoran.

The same evil has twisted itself into the British form of government; where, in the state-establishment of the church of England, no man is eligible to any office, civil or military, without he subscribes to the 39 articles and book of common-prayer; and even then, upon receiving a commission for the army the law obliges him to receive the sacrament of the Lord's supper; and no non-conformist is allowed the liberty of his conscience without he subscribes to all the 39 articles but about 4. And when that is done his purse-strings are drawn by others to pay preachers in whom he has no confidence and whom he never hears.

This was the case with several of the southern states (until the revolution) in which the church of England was established.

The fourth principle (compact) is adopted in the American states as the basis of civil government. This foundation appears to be a just one by the following investigation.

Suppose a man to remove to a desolate island and take a peaceable possession of it without injuring any, so that he should be the honest inheritor of the isle. So long as he is alone he is the absolute monarch of the place, and his own will is his law, which law is as often altered or repealed as his will changes. In process of time from this man's loins ten sons are grown to manhood and possess property. So long as they are all good men each one can be as absolute, free, and sovereign as his father; but one of the ten turns vagrant, by robbing the rest; this villain is equal to if not an overmatch for any one of the nine—not one of them durst engage him in single combat: reason and safety both dictate to the nine the necessity of a confederation to unite their strength together to repel or destroy the plundering knave. Upon entering into confederation some compact or agreement would be stipulated by which each would be bound to do his equal part in fatigue and expence; it would be neccessary for these nine to meet at stated times to consult means of safety and happiness; a shady tree or small cabin would answer their purpose; and in case of disagreement four must give up to five.

In this state of things their government would be perfectly democratical, every citizen being a legislator.

In a course of years, from these nine there arises nine thousand; their government can be no longer democratical, prudence would forbid it. Each tribe or district must chuse their representative, who (for the term that he is chosen) has the whole political power of his constituents. These representatives, meeting in assembly, would have power to make laws binding on their constituents; and while their time was spent in making laws for the community each one of the community must advance a little of his money as a compensation therefor. Should these representatives differ in judgment the minor must submit to the major, as in the case above.

From this simple parable the following things are demonstrated:

1. That the law was not made for a righteous man, but for the disobedient. 2. That righteous men have to part with a little of their liberty and property to preserve the rest. 3. That all power is vested in and consequently derived from the people. 4. That the law should rule over rulers, and not rulers over the law. 5. That government is founded on compact. 6. That every law made by the legislators inconsistent with the compact, modernly called a constitution, is usurpive in the legislators and not binding on the people. 7. That whenever government is found inadequate to preserve the liberty and property of the people they have an indubitable right to alter it so as to answer those purposes. 8. That legislators in their legislative capacity cannot alter the constitution, for they are hired servants of the people to act within the limits of the constitution.

From these general observations I shall pass on to examine a question, which has been the strife and contention of ages. The question is, *"Are the rights of conscience alienable, or inalienable?"*

The word *conscience* signifies *common science,* a court of judicature which the Almighty has erected in every human breast; a *censor morum* over all his actions. Conscience will ever judge right when it is rightly informed, and speak the truth when it understands it. But to advert to the question—"Does a man upon entering into social compact surrender his conscience to that society to be controled by the laws thereof, or can he in justice assist in making laws to bind his children's consciences before they are born?" I judge not, for the following reasons:

1. Every man must give an account of himself to God, and therefore every man ought to be at liberty to serve God in that way that he can best reconcile it to his conscience. If government can answer for individuals at the day of judgment, let men be controled by it in religious matters; otherwise let men be free.

2. It would be sinful for a man to surrender that to man which is to be kept sacred for God. A man's mind should be always open to conviction, and an honest man will receive that doctrine which appears the best demonstrated; and what is more common than for the best of men to change their minds? Such are the prejudices of the mind, and such the force of tradition, that a man who never alters his mind is either very weak or very stubborn. How painful then must it be to an honest heart to be bound to observe the principles of his former belief after he is convinced of their imbecility? and this ever has and ever will be the case while the rights of conscience are considered alienable.

3. But supposing it was right for a man to bind his own conscience, yet surely it is very iniquitous to bind the consciences of his children; to make fetters for them before they are born is very cruel. And yet such has been the conduct of men in almost all ages that their children have been bound to believe and worship as their fathers did, or suffer shame, loss, and sometimes life; and at best to be called dissenters, because they dissent from that which they never joined voluntarily. Such conduct in parents is worse than that of the father of Hannibal, who imposed an oath upon his son while a child never to be at peace with the Romans.

4. Finally, religion is a matter between God and individuals, religious opinions of men not being the objects of civil government nor any ways under its control.

It has often been observed by the friends of religious establishment by human laws, that no state can long continue without it; that religion will perish, and nothing but infidelity and atheism prevail.

Are these things facts? Did not the christian religion prevail during the three first centuries, in a more glorious manner than ever it has since, not only without the aid of law, but in opposition to all the laws of haughty monarchs? And did not religion receive a deadly wound by being fostered in the arms of civil power and regulated by law? These things are so.

From that day to this we have but a few instances of religious liberty to judge by; for in almost all states civil rulers (by the instigation of covetous priests) have undertaken to steady the ark of religion by human laws; but yet we have a few of them without leaving our own land.

The state of Rhode-Island has stood above 160 years without any religious establishment. The state of New-York never had any. New-Jersey claims the same. Pennsylvania has also stood from its first settlement until now upon a liberal foundation; and if agriculture, the mechanical arts and commerce, have not flourished in these states equal to any of the states I judge wrong.

It may further be observed, that all the states now in union, saving two or three in New-England, have no legal force used about religion, in directing its course or supporting its preachers. And moreover the federal government is forbidden by the constitution to make any laws establishing any kind of religion. If religion cannot stand, therefore, without the aid of law, it is likely to fall soon in our nation, except in Connecticut and Massachusetts.

To say that "religion cannot stand without a state establishment" is not only contrary to fact (as has been proved already) but is a contradiction in phrase. Religion must have stood a time before any law could have been made about it; and if it did stand almost three hundred years without law it can still stand without it.

The evils of such an establishment are many.

1. Uninspired fallible men make their own opinions tests of orthodoxy, and use their own systems, as Procrustes used his iron bedstead, to stretch and measure the consciences of all others by. Where no toleration is granted to non-conformists either ignorance and superstition prevail or persecution rages; and if toleration is granted to restricted non-conformists the minds of men are biassed to embrace that religion which is favored and pampered by law (and thereby hypocrisy is nourished) while those who cannot stretch their consciences to believe any thing and every thing in the established creed are treated with contempt and opprobrious names; and by such means some

are pampered to death by largesses and others confined from doing what good they otherwise could by penury. The first lie under a temptation to flatter the ruling party, to continue that form of government which brings the sure bread of idleness; the last to despise that government and those rulers that oppress them. The first have their eyes shut to all further light that would alter the religious machine; the last are always seeking new light, and often fall into enthusiasm. Such are the natural evils of establishment in religion by human laws.

2. Such establishments not only wean and alienate the affections of one from another on account of the different usages they receive in their religious sentiments, but are also very impolitic, especially in new countries; for what encouragement can strangers have to migrate with their arts and wealth into a state where they cannot enjoy their religious sentiments without exposing themselves to the law? when at the same time their religious opinions do not lead them to be mutinous. And further, how often have kingdoms and states been greatly weakened by religious tests! In the time of the persecution in France not less than twenty thousand people fled for the enjoyment of religious liberty.

3. These establishments metamorphose the church into a creature, and religion into a principle of state; which has a natural tendency to make men conclude that bible religion is nothing but a trick of state. Hence it is that the greatest part of the well informed in literature are overrun with deism and infidelity: nor is it likely it will ever be any better while preaching is made a trade of emolument. And if there is no difference between bible religion and state religion I shall soon fall into infidelity.

4. There are no two kingdoms or states that establish the same creed or formularies of faith (which alone proves their debility). In one kingdom a man is condemned for not believing a doctrine that he would be condemned for believing in another kingdom. Both of these establishments cannot be right—but both of them can be, and surely are, wrong.

5. The nature of such establishments, further, is to keep from civil office the best of men. Good men cannot believe what they cannot believe; and they will not subscribe to what they disbelieve, and take an oath to maintain what they conclude is error: and as the best of men differ in judgment there may be some of them in any state: their talents and virtue entitle them to fill the most important

posts, yet because they differ from the established creed of the state they cannot—will not fill those posts. Whereas villains make no scruple to take any oath.

If these and many more evils attend such establishments—what were and still are the causes that ever there should be a state establishment of religion?

The causes are many—some of them follow.

1. The love of importance is a general evil. It is natural to men to dictate for others; they choose to command the bushel and use the whip-row, to have the halter around the necks of others to hang them at pleasure.

2. An over-fondness for a particular system or sect. This gave rise to the first human establishment of religion, by Constantine the Great. Being converted to the christian system, he established it in the Roman empire, compelled the pagans to submit, and banished the christian heretics, built fine chapels at public expence, and forced large stipends for the preachers. All this was done out of love to the christian religion: but his love operated inadvertently; for he did the christian church more harm than all the persecuting emperors did. It is said that in his day a voice was heard from heaven, saying, "Now is the poison spued into the churches." If this voice was not heard, it nevertheless was a truth; for from that day to this the christian religion has been made a stirrup to mount the steed of popularity, wealth, and ambition.

3. To produce uniformity in religion. Rulers often fear that if they leave every man to think, speak and worship as he pleases, that the whole cause will be wrecked in diversity; to prevent which they establish some standard of orthodoxy to effect uniformity. But is uniformity attainable? Millions of men, women and children, have been tortured to death to produce uniformity, and yet the world has not advanced one inch towards it. And as long as men live in different parts of the world, have different habits, education and interests, they will be different in judgment, humanly speaking.

Is conformity of sentiments in matters of religion essential to the happiness of civil government? Not at all. Government has no more to do with the religious opinions of men than it has with the principles of the mathematics. Let every man speak freely without fear—maintain the principles that he believes—worship according to his own faith, either one God, three Gods, no God, or twenty Gods; and let government protect him in so doing, i.e. see

that he meets with no personal abuse or loss of property for his religious opinions. Instead of discouraging of him with proscriptions, fines, confiscation or death; let him be encouraged, as a free man, to bring forth his arguments and maintain his points with all boldness; then if his doctrine is false it will be confuted, and if it is true (though ever so novel) let others credit it. When every man has this liberty what can he wish for more? A liberal man asks for nothing more of government.

The duty of magistrates is not to judge of the divinity or tendency of doctrines, but when those principles break out into overt acts of violence then to use the civil sword and punish the vagrant for what he has done and not for the religious phrenzy that he acted from.

It is not supposable that any established creed contains the whole truth and nothing but truth; but supposing it did, which established church has got it? All bigots contend for it—each society cries out "The temple of the Lord are we." Let one society be supposed to be in possession of the whole—let that society be established by law—the creed of faith that they adopt be so consecrated by government that the man that disbelieves it must die—let this creed finally prevail over the whole world. I ask what honor *truth* gets by all this? None at all. It is famed of a Prussian, called John the Cicero, that by one oration he reconciled two contending princes actually in war; but, says the historian, "it was his six thousand horse of battle that had the most persuasive oratory." So when one creed or church prevails over another, being armed with (a coat of mail) law and sword, truth gets no honor by the victory. Whereas if all stand upon one footing, being equally protected by law as citizens (not as saints) and one prevails over another by cool investigation and fair argument, then truth gains honor, and men more firmly believe it than if it was made an essential article of salvation by law.

Truth disdains the aid of law for its defence—it will stand upon its own merits. The heathens worshipped a goddess called truth, stark naked; and all human decorations of truth serve only to destroy her virgin beauty. It is error, and error alone, that needs human support; and whenever men fly to the law or sword to protect their system of religion and force it upon others, it is evident that they have something in their system that will not bear the light and stand upon the basis of truth.

4. The common objection "that the ignorant part of the

community are not capacitated to judge for themselves" supports the popish hierarchy, and all protestant as well as Turkish and pagan establishments, in idea.

But is this idea just? Has God chosen many of the wise and learned? Has he not hidden the mystery of gospel truth from them and revealed it unto babes? Does the world by wisdom know God? Did many of the rulers believe in Christ when he was upon earth? Were not the learned clergy (the scribes) his most inveterate enemies? Do not great men differ as much as little men in judgment? Have not almost all lawless errors crept into the world through the means of wise men (so called)? Is not a simple man, who makes nature and reason his study, a competent judge of things? Is the bible written (like Caligula's laws) so intricate and high that none but the letter-learned (according to common phrase) can read it? Is not the vision written so plain that he that runs may read it? Do not those who understand the original languages which the bible was written in differ as much in judgment as others? Are the identical copies of Matthew, Mark, Luke and John, together with the epistles, in every university, and in the hands of every master of arts? If not, have not the learned to trust to a human transcription, as much as the unlearned have to a translation? If these questions and others of a like nature can be confuted, then I will confess that it is wisdom for a conclave of bishops or a convocation of clergy to frame a system out of the bible and persuade the legislature to legalise it. No. It would be attended with so much expence, pride, domination, cruelty and bloodshed, that let me rather fall into infidelity; for no religion at all is better than that which is worse than none.

5. The ground work of these establishments of religion is clerical influence. Rulers, being persuaded by the clergy that an establishment of religion by human laws would promote the knowledge of the gospel, quell religious disputes, prevent heresy, produce uniformity, and finally be advantageous to the state, establish such creeds as are framed by the clergy; and this they often do the more readily when they are flattered by the clergy that if they thus defend the truth they will become nursing fathers to the church and merit something considerable for themselves.

What stimulates the clergy to recommend this mode of reasoning is,

1. Ignorance—not being able to confute error by fair argument.

2. Indolence—not being willing to spend any time to confute the heretical.

3. But chiefly covetousness, to get money—for it may be observed that in all these establishments settled salaries for the clergy recoverable by law are sure to be interwoven; and was not this the case, I am well convinced that there would not be many if any religious establishments in the christian world.

Having made the foregoing remarks, I shall next make some observations on the religion of Connecticut.

If the citizens of this state have any thing in existence that looks like a religious establishment, they ought to be very cautious; for being but a small part of the world they can never expect to extend their religion over the whole of it, without it is so well founded that it cannot be confuted.

If one third part of the face of the globe is allowed to be seas, the earthy parts would compose 4550 such states as Connecticut. The American empire would afford above 200 of them. And as there is no religion in this empire of the same stamp of the Connecticut standing order, upon the Saybrook platform, they may expect 199 against 1 at home, and 4549 against 1 abroad.

Connecticut and New-Haven were separate governments till the reign of Charles II when they were incorporated together by a charter, which charter is still considered by some as the basis of government.

At present (1791) there are in the state about 168 presbyterial, congregational and consociated preachers, 35 baptists, 20 episcopalians, 10 separate congregationals, and a few of other denominations. The first are the standing order of Connecticut, to whom all others have to pay obeisance. Societies of the standing order are established by law; none have right to vote therein but men of age who possess property to the amount of 40*l*, or are in full communion in the church. Their choice of ministers is by major vote; and what the society agree to give him annually is levied upon all within the limits of the society-bounds, except they bring a certificate to the clerk of the society that they attend worship elsewhere and contribute to the satisfaction of the society where they attend. The money being levied on the people is distrainable by law, and perpetually binding on the society till the minister is dismissed by a council or by death from his charge.

It is not my intention to give a detail of all the tumults, oppression, fines and imprisonments, that have heretofore been occasioned by this law-religion. These things are partly dead and buried, and if they do not rise of themselves let them sleep peaceably in the dust forever. Let it suffice on this head to say, that it is not possible in the nature of things to establish religion by human laws without perverting the design of civil law and oppressing the people.

The certificate that a dissenter produces to the society clerk (1784) must be signed by some officer of the dissenting church, and such church must be protestant-christian, for heathens, deists, Jews and papists, are not indulged in the certificate law; all of them, as well as Turks, must therefore be taxed to the standing order, although they never go among them or know where the meeting-house is.

This certificate law is founded on this principle, "that it is the duty of all persons to support the gospel and the worship of God." Is this principle founded in justice? Is it the duty of a deist to support that which he believes to be a threat and imposition? Is it the duty of a Jew to support the religion of Jesus Christ, when he really believes that he was an impostor? Must the papists be forced to pay men for preaching down the supremacy of the pope, whom they are sure is the head of the church? Must a Turk maintain a religion opposed to the alcoran, which he holds as the sacred oracles of heaven? These things want better confirmation. If we suppose that it is the duty of all these to support the protestant christian religion, as being the best religion in the world—yet how comes it to pass that human legislatures have right to force them so to do? I now call for an instance where Jesus Christ, the author of his religion, or the apostles, who were divinely inspired, ever gave orders to or intimated that the civil powers on earth ought to force people to observe the rules and doctrine of the gospel.

Mahomet called in the use of law and sword to convert people to his religion; but Jesus did not, does not.

It is the duty of men to love God with all their hearts, and their neighbors as themselves; but have legislatures authority to punish men if they do not? So there are many things that Jesus and the apostles taught that men ought to obey which yet the civil law has no concerns in.

That it is the duty of men who are taught in the word to communicate to the teacher is beyond controversy, but that it is the province of the civil law to force men to do so is denied.

The charter of Charles II is supposed to be the basis of government in Connecticut; and I request any gentleman to point out a single clause in that charter which authorises the legislature to make any religious laws, establish any religion, or force people to build meeting-houses or pay preachers. If there is no constitutional clause, it follows that the laws are usurpasive in the legislators and not binding on the people. I shall here add, that if the legislature of Connecticut have authority to establish the religion which they prefer to all religions, and force men to support it, then every legislature or legislator has the same authority; and if this be true, the separation of the christians from the pagans, the departure of the protestants from the papists, and the dissention of the presbyterians from the church of England, were all schisms of a criminal nature; and all the persecution that they have met with is the just effect of their stubbornness.

The certificate law supposes, 1. That the legislature have power to establish a religion: this is false. 2. That they have authority to grant indulgence to non-conformists: this is also false, for religious liberty is a *right* and not a *favor*. 3. That the legitimate power of government extends to force people to part with their money for religious purposes. This cannot be proved from the new testament.

The certificate law has lately passed a new modification. Justices of the peace must now examine them; this gives ministers of state a power over religious concerns that the new testament does not. To examine the law part by part would be needless, for the whole of it is wrong.

From what is said this question arises, "Are not contracts with ministers, i.e. between ministers and people, as obligatory as any contracts whatever?" The simple answer is, Yes. Ministers should share the same protection of the law that other men do, and no more. To proscribe them from seats of legislation, &c. is cruel. To indulge them with an exemption from taxes and bearing arms is a tempting emolument. The law should be silent about them; protect them as citizens (not as sacred officers) for the civil law knows no sacred religious officers.

In Rhode-Island, if a congregation of people agree to give a preacher a certain sum of money for preaching the bond is not recoverable by law.*

This law was formed upon a good principle, but, un-

* Some men, who are best informed in the laws of Rhode Island, say, that if ever there was such an act in that state there is nothing like it in existence at this day; and perhaps it is only cast upon them as a stigma because they have ever been friends to religious liberty. However, as the principle is supposable I have treated it as a real fact; and this I have done the more willingly because nine tenths of the people believe it is a fact.

happy for the makers of that law, they were incoherent in the superstructure.

The principle of the law is, that the gospel is not to be supported by law; that civil rulers have nothing to do with religion in their civil capacities. What business had they then to make that law? The evil seemed to arise from a blending religious right and religious opinions together. Religious right should be protected to all men, religious opinion to none; i.e. government should confirm the first unto all—the last unto none; each individual having a right to differ from all others in opinion if he is so persuaded. If a number of people in Rhode-Island or elsewhere are of opinion that ministers of the gospel ought to be supported by law, and chuse to be bound by a bond to pay him, government has no just authority to declare that bond illegal; for in so doing they interfere with private contracts, and deny the people the liberty of conscience. If these people bind nobody but themselves, who is injured by their religious opinions? But if they bind an individual besides themselves, the bond is fraudulent, and ought to be declared illegal. And here lies the mischief of Connecticut religion. My lord, major vote, binds all the minor part, unless they submit to idolatry, i.e. pay an acknowledgment to a power that Jesus Christ never ordained in his church; I mean produce a certificate. Yea, further, Jews, Turks, heathens, papists and deists, if such there are in Connecticut, are bound, and have no redress: and further, this bond is not annually given, but for life, except the minister is dismissed by a number of others, who are in the same predicament with himself.

Although it is no abridgment of religious liberty for congregations to pay their preachers by legal force, in the manner prescribed above, yet it is antichristian; such a church cannot be a church of Christ, because they are not governed by Christ's laws, but by the laws of state; and such ministers do not appear like ambassadors of Christ, but like ministers of state.

The next question is this: "Suppose a congregation of people have agreed to give a minister a certain sum of money annually for life, or during good behaviour, and in a course of time some or all of them change their opinions and verily believe that the preacher is in a capital error, and really from conscience dissent from him—are they still bound to comply with their engagements to the preacher?" This question is supposable, and I believe there have been a few instances of the kind.

If men have bound themselves, honor and honesty call upon them to comply, but God and conscience call upon them to come out from among them and let such blind guides* alone. Honor and honesty are amiable virtues; but God and conscience call to perfidiousness. This shows the impropriety of such contracts, which always may, and sometimes do lead into such labyrinths. It is time enough to pay a man after his labour is over. People are not required to communicate to the teacher before they are taught. A man called of God to preach, feels a necessity to preach, and a woe if he does not. And if he is sent by Christ, he looks to him and his laws for support; and if men comply with their duty, he finds relief; if not, he must go to his field, as the priests of old did. A man cannot give a more glaring proof of his covetousness and irreligion, than to say, "If you will give me so much, then I will preach, but if not be assured I will not preach to you."

So that in answering the question, instead of determining which of the evils to chuse, either to disobey God and conscience, or break honor and honesty, I would recommend an escape of both evils, by entering into no such contracts: for the natural evils of imprudence, that men are fallen into, neither God nor man can prevent.

A minister must have a hard heart to wish men to be forced to pay him when (through conscience, enthusiasm, or a private pique) they dissent from his ministry. The spirit of the gospel disdains such measures.

The question before us is not applicable to many cases in Connecticut: the dissenting churches make no contracts for a longer term than a year, and most of them make none at all. Societies of the standing order rarely bind themselves in contract with preachers, without binding others beside themselves; and when that is the case the bond is fraudulent: and if those who are bound involuntarily can get clear, it is no breach of honor or honesty.

A few additional remarks shall close my piece.

I. The church of Rome was at first constituted according to the gospel, and at that time her faith was spoken of through the whole world. Being espoused to Christ, as a chaste virgin, she kept her bed pure for her husband, almost three hundred years; but afterwards she played the whore with the kings and princes of this world, who with

*The phrase of *blind guides,* is not intended to cast contempt upon any order of religious preachers; for, let a preacher be orthodox or heterodox, virtuous or vicious, he is always a blind guide to those who differ from him in opinion.

their gold and wealth came in unto her, and she became a strumpet: and as she was the first christian church that ever forsook the laws of Christ for her conduct and received the laws of his rivals, i.e. was established by human law, and governed by the legalised edicts of councils, and received large sums of money to support her preachers and her worship by the force of civil power—she is called the *mother of harlots:* and all protestant churches, who are regulated by law, and force people to support their preachers, build meeting-houses and otherwise maintain their worship, are daughters of this holy mother.

II. I am not a citizen of Connecticut—the religious laws of the state do not oppress me, and I expect never will personally; but a love to religious liberty in general induces me thus to speak. Was I a resident in the state, I could not give or receive a certificate to be exempted from ministerial taxes; for in so doing I should confess that the legislature had authority to pamper one religious order in the state, and make all others pay obeisance to that sheef. It is high time to know whether all are to be free alike, and whether ministers of state are to be lords over God's heritage.

And here I shall ask the citizens of Connecticut, whether, in the months of April and September, when they chuse their deputies for the assembly, they mean to surrender to them the rights of conscience, and authorise them to make laws binding on their consciences. If not, then all such acts are contrary to the intention of constituent power, as well as unconstitutional and antichristian.

III. It is likely that one part of the people in Connecticut believe in conscience that gospel preachers should be supported by the force of law; and the other part believe that it is not in the province of civil law to interfere or any ways meddle with religious matters. How are both parties to be protected by law in their conscientious belief?

Very easily. Let all those whose consciences dictate that they ought to be taxed by law to maintain their preachers bring in their names to the society-clerk by a certain day, and then assess them all, according to their estates, to raise the sum stipulated in the contract; and all others go free. Both parties by this method would enjoy the full liberty of conscience without oppressing one another, the law use no force in matters of conscience, the evil of Rhode-Island law be escaped, and no persons could find fault with it (in a political point of view) but those who fear the consciences of too many would lie dormant, and therefore wish to force them to pay. Here let it be noted, that there are many in the world who believe in conscience that a minister is not entitled to any acknowledgment for his services without he is so poor that he cannot live without it (and thereby convert a gospel debt to alms). Though this opinion is not founded either on reason or scripture, yet it is a better opinion than that which would force them to pay a preacher by human law.

IV. How mortifying must it be to foreigners, and how far from conciliatory is it to citizens of the American states, who, when they come into Connecticut to reside must either conform to the religion of Connecticut or produce a certificate? Does this look like religious liberty or human friendship? Suppose that man (whose name need not be mentioned) that fills every American heart with pleasure and awe, should remove to Connecticut for his health, or any other cause—what a scandal would it be to the state to tax him to a presbyterian minister unless he produced a certificate informing them that he was an episcopalian?

V. The federal constitution certainly had the advantage, of any of the state constitutions, in being made by the wisest men in the whole nation, and after an experiment of a number of years trial, upon republican principles; and that constitution forbids Congress ever to establish any kind of religion, or require any religious test to qualify any officer in any department of the federal government. Let a man be pagan, Turk, Jew or Christian, he is eligible to any post in that government. So that if the principles of religious liberty, contended for in the foregoing pages, are supposed to be fraught with deism, fourteen states in the Union are now fraught with the same. But the separate states have not surrendered that (supposed) right of establishing religion to Congress. Each state retains all its power, saving what is given to the general government by the federal constitution. The assembly of Connecticut, therefore, still undertake to guide the helm of religion: and if Congress were disposed yet they could not prevent it by any power vested in them by the states. Therefore, if any of the people of Connecticut feel oppressed by the certificate law, or any other of the like nature, their proper mode of procedure will be to remonstrate against the oppression and petition the assembly for a redress of grievance.

VI. Divines generally inform us that there is such a time to come (called the Latter-Day Glory) when the knowledge of the Lord shall cover the earth as the waters do the sea, and that this day will appear upon the destruction of antichrist. If so, I am well convinced that Jesus will first remove all the hindrances or religious establishments, and cause all men to be free in matters of religion. When this is effected, he will say to the kings and great men of the earth, "Now see what I can do; ye have been afraid to leave the church and gospel in my hands alone, without steadying the ark by human law; but now I have taken the power and kingdom to myself, and will work for my own glory."

Here let me add, that in the southern states, where there has been the greatest freedom from religious oppression, where liberty of conscience is entirely enjoyed, there has been the greatest revival of religion; which is another proof that true religion can and will prevail best where it is left entirely to Christ.

Letter to the Danbury Baptist Association

THOMAS JEFFERSON

January 1, 1802

Jefferson's letter to the Danbury Baptist Association expresses the belief that religious and public life should be kept strictly separate. In the letter, Jefferson articulates only one of several American views on the proper relationship between religion and politics.

Letter to the Danbury Baptist Association

To Messrs. Nehemiah Dodge, Ephram Robbins,
and Stephen S. Nelson, a Committee of the Danbury
Baptist Association, in the State of Connecticut

January 1, 1802

Gentlemen,—The affectionate sentiments of esteem and approbation which you are so good as to express towards me, on behalf of the Danbury Baptist Association, give me the highest satisfaction. My duties dictate a faithful and zealous pursuit of the interests of my constituents, and in proportion as they are persuaded of my fidelity to those duties, the discharge of them becomes more and more pleasing.

Believing with you that religion is a matter which lies solely between man and his God, that he owes account to none other for his faith or his worship, that the legislative powers of government reach actions only, and not opinions, I contemplate with sovereign reverence that act of the whole American people which declared that their legislature should "make no law respecting an establishment of religion, or prohibiting the free exercise thereof," thus building a wall of separation between church and State. Adhering to this expression of the supreme will of the nation in behalf of the rights of conscience, I shall see with sincere satisfaction the progress of those sentiments which tend to restore to man all his natural rights, convinced he has no natural right in opposition to his social duties.

I reciprocate your kind prayers for the protection and blessing of the common Father and Creator of man, and tender you for yourselves and your religious association, assurances of my high respect and esteem.

PART THREE Defending the Charters

Portrait of John Adams, colonial leader and second president of the
United States. © Bettmann/CORBIS

Immigrants to America brought with them a long tradition of chartered rights. In determining the limits of political authority, they looked to a rich history, encapsulated in several important documents, of social and political custom. From Magna Charta, or the "Great Charter," of 1215 through the English Bill of Rights, Englishmen had won successive victories in their battles (sometimes literally fought with fire and sword) to limit their king's ability to imprison subjects indefinitely without trial, try subjects in arbitrary ways, quarter troops in subjects' homes, and otherwise do as he wished with those whom he ruled.

The colonists ruled themselves under their own charters, or grants from the king. These charters gave them certain rights and reserved others for the king, his ministers, or other governing persons or bodies (for example, a proprietary or royal governor). Americans believed that these charters established their rights, as English subjects, to all the other rights derived from Magna Charta. The king and parliament of Great Britain did not accept this view. The result was a long history of tension between colonials and the government in the mother country. It was during this time of tension that Americans developed a distinctive reading of their history and their rights as English subjects and human beings.

Magna Charta

1215

Magna Charta was the result of victory on the battlefield by barons (local lords) opposed to England's King John. Negotiated in the days following the battle at Runnemede, it was no theoretical document. It lists numerous specific, customary rights that the barons asserted they had held from time immemorial, but that John had violated. Among these were the rights to be taxed only at certain times and under certain conditions, and to be tried by a jury of one's peers. Following the preamble, Magna Charta begins by outlining the rights of the church. John had fought, as had many kings before him, to reserve for himself the right to appoint bishops. The Catholic Church and other opponents of unlimited royal power responded that the servants of God must be independent from service to the temporal authority.

Magna Charta

The great charter of King John, granted June 15, A.D. 1215. John, by the Grace of God, King of England, Lord of Ireland, Duke of Normandy, Aquitaine, and Count of Anjou, to his Archbishops, Bishops, Abbots, Earls, Barons, Justiciaries, Foresters, Sheriffs, Governors, Officers, and to all Bailiffs, and his faithful subjects, greeting. Know ye, that we, in the presence of God, and for the salvation of our soul, and the souls of all our ancestors and heirs, and unto the honour of God and the advancement of Holy Church, and amendment of our Realm, by advice of our venerable Fathers, Stephen, Archbishop of Canterbury, Primate of all England and Cardinal of the Holy Roman Church; Henry, Archbishop of Dublin; William, of London; Peter, of Winchester; Jocelin, of Bath and Glastonbury; Hugh, of Lincoln; Walter, of Worcester; William, of Coventry; Benedict, of Rochester—Bishops: of Master Pandulph, Sub-Deacon and Familiar of our Lord the Pope; Brother Aymeric, Master of the Knights-Templar in England; and the noble Persons, William Marescall, Earl of Pembroke; William, Earl of Salisbury; William, Earl of Warren; William, Earl of Arundel; Alan de Galloway, Constable of Scotland; Warin FitzGerald, Peter FitzHerbert, and Hubert de Burgh, Seneschal of Poitou; Hugh de Neville, Matthew FitzHerbert, Thomas Basset, Alan Basset, Philip of Albiney, Robert de Roppell, John Mareschal, John Fitz-Hugh, and others, our liegemen, have, in the first place, granted to God, and by this our present Charter confirmed, for us and our heirs for ever:

1. *Rights of the church.* That the Church of England shall be free, and have her whole rights, and her liberties inviolable; and we will have them so observed that it may appear thence that the freedom of elections, which is reckoned chief and indispensable to the English Church, and which we granted and confirmed by our Charter, and obtained the confirmation of the same from our Lord and Pope Innocent III, before the discord between us and our barons, was granted of mere free will; which Charter we shall observe, and we do will it to be faithfully observed by our heirs for ever.

2. *Grant of liberty to freemen.* We also have granted to all the freemen of our kingdom, for us and for our heirs for ever, all the underwritten liberties, to be had and holden by them and their heirs, of us and our heirs for ever: If any of our earls, or barons, or others, who hold of us in chief by military service, shall die, and at the time of his death his heir shall be of full age, and owe a relief, he shall have his inheritance by the ancient relief—that is to say, the heir or heirs of an earl, for a whole earldom, by a hundred pounds; the heir or heirs of a baron, for a whole barony, by a hundred pounds; their heir or heirs of a knight, for a whole knight's fee, by a hundred shillings at most; and whoever oweth less shall give less according to the ancient custom of fees. . . .

12. *No tax (scutage) except by the general council.* No scutage or aid shall be imposed in our kingdom, unless by the general council of our kingdom; except for ransoming our person, making our eldest son a knight, and once for marrying our eldest daughter; and for these there shall be paid no more than a reasonable aid. In like manner it shall be concerning the aids of the City of London.

13. *Liberties of London and other towns.* And the City of London shall have all its ancient liberties and free customs, as well by land as by water; furthermore, we will and grant that all other cities and boroughs, and towns and ports, shall have all their liberties and free customs.

14. *General council shall consent to assessment of taxes.* And for holding the general council of the kingdom concerning the assessment of aids, except in the three cases aforesaid, and for the assessing of scutages, we shall cause to be summoned the archbishops, bishops, abbots, earls, and greater barons of the realm, singly by our letters, and furthermore, we shall cause to be summoned generally, by our sheriffs and bailiffs, all others who hold of us in chief, for a certain day, that is to say, forty days before their meeting at least, and to a certain place; and in all letters of such summons we will declare the cause of such summons, and, summons being thus made the business shall proceed on the day appointed, according to the advice of such as shall be present, although all that were summoned come not. . . .

17. *Courts shall administer justice in a fixed place.* Common pleas shall not follow our court, but shall be holden in some place certain.

18. *Land disputes shall be tried in their proper counties.* Trials upon the Writs of Novel Disseisin, and of Mort d'ancestor, and of Darrein Presentment, shall not be taken but in their proper counties, and after this manner: We, or if we should be out of the realm, our chief justiciary, will send two justiciaries through every county four times a year, who, with four knights of each county, chosen by the county, shall hold the said assizes in the county, on the day, and at the place appointed.

19. *Keeping the assize courts open.* And if any matters cannot be determined on the day appointed for holding the assizes in each county, so many of the knights and freeholders as have been at the assizes aforesaid shall stay to decide them as is necessary, according as there is more or less business.

20. *Fines against freemen to be measured by the offense.* A freeman shall not be amerced for a small offence, but only according to the degree of the offence; and for a great crime according to the heinousness of it, saving to him his contentment; and after the same manner a merchant, saving to him his merchandise. And a villein shall be amerced after the same manner, saving to him his wainage, if he falls under our mercy; and none of the aforesaid amerciaments shall be assessed but by the oath of honest men in the neighbourhood.

21. *Same for nobles.* Earls and barons shall not be amerced but by their peers, and after the degree of the offence.

22. *Same for clergymen.* No ecclesiastical person shall be amerced for his tenement, but according to the proportion of the others aforesaid, and not according to the value of his ecclesiastical benefice.

23. Neither a town nor any tenant shall be distrained to make bridges or embankments, unless that anciently and of right they are bound to do it.

24. No sheriff, constable, coroner, or other of our bailiffs, shall hold "Pleas of the Crown."

25. All counties, hundreds, wapentakes, and trethings, shall stand at the old rents, without any increase, except in our demesne manors.

26. If any one holding of us a lay fee die, and the sheriff, or our bailiffs, show our letters patent of summons for debt which the dead man did owe to us, it shall be lawful for the sheriff or our bailiff to attach and register the chattels of the dead, found upon his lay fee, to the amount of the debt, by the view of lawful men, so as nothing be removed until our whole clear debt be paid; and the rest shall be left to the executors to fulfil the testament of the dead; and if there be nothing due from him to us, all the chattels shall go to the use of the dead, saving to his wife and children their reasonable shares.

27. If any freeman shall die intestate, his chattels shall be distributed by the hands of his nearest relations and friends, by view of the Church, saving to every one his debts which the deceased owed to him.

28. *Compensation for the taking of private property.* No constable or bailiff of ours shall take corn or other chattels of any man unless he presently give him money for it, or hath respite of payment by the good-will of the seller.

29. No constable shall distrain any knight to give money for castle-guard, if he himself will do it in his person, or by another able man, in case he cannot do it through any reasonable cause. And if we have carried or sent him into the army, he shall be free from such guard for the time he shall be in the army by our command.

30. *No taking of horses or carts without consent.* No sher-

iff or bailiff of ours, or any other, shall take horses or carts of any freeman for carriage, without the assent of the said freeman.

31. *No taking of trees for timber without consent.* Neither shall we nor our bailiffs take any man's timber for our castles or other uses, unless by the consent of the owner of the timber.

32. We will retain the lands of those convicted of felony only one year and a day, and then they shall be delivered to the lord of the fee.

33. All kydells (wears) for the time to come shall be put down in the rivers of Thames and Medway, and throughout all England, except upon the seacoast.

34. The writ which is called *proecipe*, for the future, shall not be made out to any one, of any tenement, whereby a freeman may lose his court.

35. *Uniform weights and measures.* There shall be one measure of wine and one of ale through our whole realm; and one measure of corn, that is to say, the London quarter; and one breadth of dyed cloth, and russets, and haberjects, that is to say, two ells within the lists; and it shall be of weights as it is of measures.

36. *Nothing from henceforth shall be given or taken for a writ of inquisition of life or limb, but it shall be granted freely, and not denied.*

37. If any do hold of us by fee-farm, or by socage, or by burgage, and he hold also lands of any other by knight's service, we will have the custody of the heir or land, which is holden of another man's fee by reason of that fee-farm, socage, or burgage; neither will we have the custody of the fee-farm, or socage, or burgage, unless knight's service was due to us out of the same fee-farm. We will not have the custody of an heir, nor of any land which he holds of another by knight's service, by reason of any petty serjeanty by which he holds of us, by the service of paying a knife, an arrow, or the like.

38. No bailiff from henceforth shall put any man to his law upon his own bare saying, without credible witnesses to prove it.

39. *Guarantee of judgment by one's peers and of proceedings according to the "law of the land."* No freeman shall be taken or imprisoned, or disseised, or outlawed, or banished, or any ways destroyed, nor will we pass upon him, nor will we send upon him, unless by the lawful judgment of his peers, or by the law of the land.

40. *Guarantee of equal justice (equality before the law).* We will sell to no man, we will not deny or delay to any man, either justice or right.

41. *Freedom of movement for merchants.* All merchants shall have safe and secure conduct, to go out of, and to come into England, and to stay there and to pass as well by land as by water, for buying and selling by the ancient and allowed customs, without any unjust tolls; except in time of war, or when they are of any nation at war with us. And if there be found any such in our land, in the beginning of the war, they shall be attached, without damage to their bodies or goods, until it be known unto us, or our chief justiciary, how our merchants be treated in the nation at war with us; and if ours be safe there, the others shall be safe in our dominions.

42. *Freedom to leave and reenter the kingdom.* It shall be lawful, for the time to come, for any one to go out of our kingdom, and return safely and securely by land or by water, saving his allegiance to us; unless in time of war, by some short space, for the common benefit of the realm, except prisoners and outlaws, according to the law of the land, and people in war with us, and merchants who shall be treated as is above mentioned.

43. If any man hold of any escheat as of the honour of Wallingford, Nottingham, Boulogne, Lancaster, or of other escheats which be in our hands, and are baronies, and die, his heir shall give no other relief, and perform no other service to us than he would to the baron, if it were in the baron's hand; and we will hold it after the same manner as the baron held it.

44. Those men who dwell without the forest from henceforth shall not come before our justiciaries of the forest, upon common summons, but such as are impleaded, or as sureties for any that are attached for something concerning the forest.

45. *Appointment of those who know the law.* We will not make any justices, constables, sheriffs, or bailiffs, but of such as know the law of the realm and mean duly to observe it.

46. All barons who have founded abbeys, which they hold by charter from the kings of England, or by ancient tenure, shall have the keeping of them, when vacant, as they ought to have.

47. All forests that have been made forests in our time shall forthwith be disforested; and the same shall be done with the water-banks that have been fenced in by us in our time.

48. All evil customs concerning forests, warrens, foresters, and warreners, sheriffs and their officers, water-banks and their keeper, shall forthwith be inquired into in each county, by twelve sworn knights of the same county chosen by creditable persons of the same county; and within forty days after the said inquest be utterly abolished, so as never to be restored: so as we are first acquainted therewith, or our justiciary, if we should not be in England.

49. We will immediately give up all hostages and charters delivered unto us by our English subjects, as securities for their keeping the peace, and yielding us faithful service.

50. We will entirely remove from their bailiwicks the relations of Gerard de Atheyes, so that for the future they shall have no bailiwick in England; we will also remove from their bailiwicks the relations of Gerard de Atheyes, so that for the future they shall have no bailiwick in England; we will also remove Engelard de Cygony, Andrew, Peter, and Gyon, from the Chancery; Gyon de Cygony, Geoffrey de Martyn, and his brothers; Philip Mark, and his brothers, and his nephew, Geoffrey, and their whole retinue.

51. As soon as peace is restored, we will send out of the kingdom all foreign knights, cross-bowmen, and stipendiaries, who are come with horses and arms to the molestation of our people.

52. If any one has been dispossessed or deprived by us, without the lawful judgment of his peers, of his lands, castles, liberties, or rights, we will forthwith restore them to him; and if any dispute arise upon this head, let the matter be decided by the five-and-twenty barons hereafter mentioned, for the preservation of the peace. And for all those things of which any person has, without the lawful judgment of his peers, been dispossessed or deprived, either by our father King Henry, or our brother King Richard, and which we have in our hands, or are possessed by others, and we are bound to warrant and make good, we shall have a respite till the term usually allowed the crusaders; excepting those things about which there is a plea depending, or whereof an inquest hath been made, by our order before we undertook the crusade; but as soon as we return from our expedition, or if perchance we tarry at home and do not make our expedition, we will immediately cause full justice to be administered therein.

53. The same respite we shall have, and in the same manner, about administering justice, disafforesting or letting continue the forests, which Henry our father, and our

brother Richard, have afforested; and the same concerning the wardship of the lands which are in another's fee, but the wardship of which we have hitherto had, by reason of a fee held of us by knight's service; and for the abbeys founded in other fee than our own, in which the lord of the fee says he has a right; and when we return from our expedition, or if we tarry at home, and do not make our expedition, we will immediately do full justice to all the complainants in this behalf.

54. No man shall be taken or imprisoned upon the appeal of a woman, for the death of any other than her husband.

55. All unjust and illegal fines made by us, and all amerciaments imposed unjustly and contrary to the law of the land, shall be entirely given up, or else be left to the decision of the five-and-twenty barons hereafter mentioned for the preservation of the peace, or of the major part of them, together with the foresaid Stephen, Archbishop of Canterbury, if he can be present, and others whom he shall think fit to invite; and if he cannot be present, the business shall notwithstanding go on without him; but so that if one or more of the aforesaid five-and-twenty barons be plaintiffs in the same cause, they shall be set aside as to what concerns this particular affair, and others be chosen in their room, out of the said five-and-twenty, and sworn by the rest to decide the matter.

56. If we have disseised or dispossessed the Welsh of any lands, liberties, or other things, without the legal judgment of their peers, either in England or in Wales, they shall be immediately restored to them; and if any dispute arise upon this head, the matter shall be determined in the Marches by the judgment of their peers; for tenements in England according to the law of England, for tenements in Wales according to the law of Wales, for tenements of the Marches according to the law of the Marches: the same shall the Welsh do to us and our subjects.

57. As for all those things of which a Welshman hath, without the lawful judgment of his peers, been disseised or deprived of by King Henry our father, or our brother King Richard, and which we either have in our hands or others are possessed of, and we are obliged to warrant it, we shall have a respite till the time generally allowed the crusaders; excepting those things about which a suit is depending, or whereof an inquest has been made by our order, before we undertook the crusade: but when we return, or if we stay at home without performing our expedition, we will im-

mediately do them full justice, according to the laws of the Welsh and of the parts before mentioned.

58. We will without delay dismiss the son of Llewellin, and all the Welsh hostages, and release them from the engagements they have entered into with us for the preservation of the peace.

59. We will treat with Alexander, King of Scots, concerning the restoring of his sisters and hostages, and his right and liberties, in the same form and manner as we shall do to the rest of our barons of England; unless by the charters which we have from his father, William, late King of Scots, it ought to be otherwise; and this shall be left to the determination of his peers in our court.

60. *Liberties to be granted to all subjects.* All the foresaid customs and liberties, which we have granted to be holden in our kingdom, as much as it belongs to us, all people of our kingdom, as well clergy as laity, shall observe, as far as they are concerned, towards their dependents.

61. *Oath to observe rights of the church and the people.* And whereas, for the honour of God and the amendment of our kingdom, and for the better quieting the discord that has arisen between us and our barons, we have granted all these things aforesaid; willing to render them firm and lasting, we do give and grant our subjects the underwritten security, namely, that the barons may choose five-and-twenty barons of the kingdom, whom they think convenient; who shall take care, with all their might, to hold and observe, and cause to be observed, the peace and liberties we have granted them, and by this our present Charter confirmed in this manner; that is to say, that if we, our justiciary, our bailiffs, or any of our officers, shall in any circumstance have failed in the performance of them towards any person, or shall have broken through any of these articles of peace and security, and the offence be notified to four barons chosen out of the five-and-twenty before mentioned, the said four barons shall repair to us, or our justiciary, if we are out of the realm, and, laying open the grievance, shall petition to have it redressed without delay: and if it be not redressed by us, or if we should chance to be out of the realm, if it should not be redressed by our justiciary within forty days, reckoning from the time it been notified to us, or to our justiciary (if we should be out of the realm), the four barons aforesaid shall lay the cause before the rest of the five-and-twenty barons; and the said five-and-twenty barons, together with the community of the whole kingdom, shall distrain and distress us in all the ways in which they shall be able, by seizing our castles, lands, possessions, and in any other manner they can, till the grievance is redressed, according to their pleasure; saving harmless our own person, and the persons of our Queen and children; and when it is redressed, they shall behave to us as before. And any person whatsoever in the kingdom may swear that he will obey the orders of the five-and-twenty barons aforesaid in the execution of the premises, and will distress us, jointly with them, to the utmost of his power; and we give public and free liberty to any one that shall please to swear to this, and never will hinder any person from taking the same oath.

62. As for all those of our subjects who will not, of their own accord, swear to join the five-and-twenty barons in distraining and distressing us, we will issue orders to make them take the same oath as aforesaid. And if any one of the five-and-twenty barons dies, or goes out of the kingdom, or is hindered any other way from carrying the things aforesaid into execution, the rest of the said five-and-twenty barons may choose another in his room, at their discretion, who shall be sworn in like manner as the rest. In all things that are committed to the execution of these five-and-twenty barons, if, when they are all assembled about any matter, and some of them, when summoned, will not or cannot come, whatever is agreed upon, or enjoined, by the major part of those that are present shall be reputed as firm and valid as if all the five-and-twenty had given their consent; and the aforesaid five-and-twenty shall swear that all the premises they shall faithfully observe, and cause with all their power to be observed. And we will procure nothing from any one, by ourselves nor by another, whereby any of these concessions and liberties may be revoked or lessened; and if any such thing shall have been obtained, let it be null and void; neither will we ever make use of it either by ourselves or any other. And all the ill-will, indignations, and rancours that have arisen between us and our subjects, of the clergy and laity, from the first breaking out of the dissensions between us, we do fully remit and forgive: moreover, all trespasses occasioned by the said dissensions, from Easter in the sixteenth year of our reign till the restoration of peace and tranquility, we hereby entirely remit to all, both clergy and laity, and as far as in us lies do fully forgive. We have, moreover, caused to be made for them the letters patent testimonial of Stephen, Lord Arch-

bishop of Canterbury, Henry, Lord Archbishop of Dublin, and the bishops aforesaid, as also of Master Pandulph, for the security and concessions aforesaid.

63. Wherefore we will and firmly enjoin, that the Church of England be free, and that all men in our kingdom have and hold all the aforesaid liberties, rights, and concessions, truly and peaceably, freely and quietly, fully and wholly to themselves and their heirs, of us and our heirs, in all things and places, for ever, as is aforesaid. It is also sworn, as well on our part as on the part of the barons, that all the things aforesaid shall be observed in good faith, and without evil subtilty. Given under our hand, in the presence of the witnesses above named, and many others, in the meadow called Runingmede, between Windsor and Staines, the 15th day of June, in the 17th year of the reign.

Petition of Right

1628

The unpopular foreign wars waged by England's Charles I had led his Parliament to refuse to grant him increased tax monies. Charles had responded by forcing wealthy subjects to lend money to his government, quartering his troops in private homes, and arbitrarily arresting and imprisoning important figures who publicly opposed his policies. In response, Parliament, led by the famous lawyer Sir Edward Coke, drafted and sent to the king the Petition of Right. In this document, Parliament sets forth its view that long-standing law and custom established its right to consent to all taxes, and the right of the people to be free from arbitrary imprisonment, the forced quartering of soldiers, and martial law during time of peace. In return for Charles's assent to this Petition, Parliament granted him increased subsidies.

Petition of Right

The Petition exhibited to his Majesty by the Lords Spiritual and Temporal, and Commons, in this present Parliament assembled, concerning divers Rights and Liberties of the Subjects, with the King's Majesty's royal answer thereunto in full Parliament

To the King's Most Excellent Majesty,

Humbly show unto our Sovereign Lord the King, the Lords Spiritual and Temporal, and Commons in Parliament assembled, that whereas it is declared and enacted by a statute made in the time of the reign of King Edward I., commonly called *Statutum de Tallagio non concedendo,* that no tallage or aid shall be laid or levied by the king or his heirs in this realm, without the good will and assent of the archbishops, bishops, earls, barons, knights, burgesses, and other the freemen of the commonalty of this realm; and by authority of Parliament holden in the five-and-twentieth year of the reign of King Edward III., it is declared and enacted, that from thenceforth no person shall be compelled to make any loans to the king against his will, because such loans were against reason and the franchise of the land; and by other laws of this realm it is provided, that none should

be charged by any charge or imposition, called a benevolence, nor by such like charge; by which the statutes before mentioned, and other the good laws and statutes of this realm, your subjects have inherited this freedom, that they should not be compelled to contribute to any tax, tallage, aid, or other like charge not set by common consent, in Parliament:

II. Yet nevertheless of late divers commissions directed to sundry commissioners in several counties, with instructions, have issued; by means whereof your people have been in divers places assembled, and required to lend certain sums of money unto your Majesty, and many of them, upon their refusal so to do, have had an oath administered unto them not warrantable by the laws or statutes of this realm, and have been constrained to become bound and make appearance and give utterance before your Privy Council, and in other places, and others of them have been therefore imprisoned, confined, and sundry other ways molested and disquieted; and divers other charges have been laid and levied upon your people in several counties by lord lieutenants, deputy lieutenants, commissioners for musters, justices of peace and others, by command or direction from your Majesty or your Privy Council, against the laws and free customs of the realm.

III. And whereas also by the statute called "The Great Charter of the liberties of England," it is declared and enacted that no freeman may be taken or imprisoned or be disseised of his freeholds or liberties, or his free customs, or be outlawed or exiled, or in any manner destroyed, but by the lawful judgment of his peers, or by the law of the land.

IV. And in the eight-and-twentieth year of the reign of King Edward III., it was declared and enacted by authority of Parliament, that no man, of what estate or condition that he be, should be put out of his lands or tenements, nor taken, nor imprisoned, nor disherited, nor put to death without being brought to answer by due process of law.

V. Nevertheless, against the tenor of the said statutes, and other the good laws and statutes of your realm to that end provided, divers of your subjects have of late been imprisoned without any cause showed; and when for their deliverance they were brought before your justices, by your Majesty's writs of *habeas corpus,* there to undergo and receive as the court should order, and their keepers commanded to certify the causes of their detainer, no cause was certified, but that they were detained by your Majesty's special command, signified by the lords of your Privy Council, and yet were returned back to several prisons, without being charged with anything to which they might make answer according to the law.

VI. And whereas of late great companies of soldiers and mariners have been dispersed into divers counties of the realm, and the inhabitants against their wills have been compelled to receive them into their houses, and there to suffer them to sojourn against the laws and customs of this realm, and to the great grievance and vexation of the people.

VII. And whereas also by authority of Parliament, in the five-and-twentieth year of the reign of King Edward III, it is declared and enacted, that no man shall be forejudged of life or limb against the form of the Great Charter and the law of the land; and by the said Great Charter, and other the laws and statutes of this your realm, no man ought to be adjudged to death but by the laws established in this your realm, either by the customs of the same realm or by acts of Parliament: and whereas no offender of what kind soever is exempted from the proceedings to be used, and punishments to be inflicted by the laws and statutes of this your realm; nevertheless of late time divers commissions under your Majesty's great seal have issued forth, by which certain persons have been assigned and appointed commissioners with power and authority to proceed within the land, according to the justice of martial law, against such soldiers or mariners, or other dissolute persons joining with them, as should commit any murder, robbery, felony, mutiny, or other outrage or misdemeanour whatsoever, and by such summary course and order as is agreeable to martial law, and as is used in armies in time of war, to proceed to the trial and condemnation of such offenders, and them to cause to be executed and put to death according to the law martial.

VIII. By pretext whereof some of your Majesty's subjects have been by some of the said commissioners put to death, when and where, if by the laws and statutes of the land they had deserved death, by the same laws and statutes also they might, and by no other ought to have been, judged and executed.

IX. And also sundry grievous offenders, by colour thereof claiming an exemption, have escaped the punishments due to them by the laws and statutes of this your realm, by reason that divers of your officers and ministers of justice have unjustly refused or forborne to proceed against such offenders according to the same laws and statutes, upon pretence that the said offenders were punishable only by martial law, and by authority of such commissions as aforesaid; which commissioners, and all other of like nature, are wholly and directly contrary to the said laws and statutes of this your realm.

X. They do therefore humbly pray your most excellent Majesty, that no man hereafter be compelled to make or yield any gift, loan, benevolence, tax, or such like charge, without common consent by act of Parliament; and that none be called to make, answer, or take such oath, or to give attendance, or be confined, or otherwise molested or disquieted concerning the same or for refusal thereof; and that no freeman, in any such manner as is before mentioned, be imprisoned or detained; and that your Majesty would be pleased to remove the said soldiers and mariners, and that your people may not be so burdened in time to come; and that the foresaid commissions, for proceeding by martial law, may be revoked and annulled; and that hereafter no commissions of like nature may issue forth to any person or persons whatsoever to be executed as aforesaid, lest by colour of them any of your Majesty's subjects be destroyed or put to death contrary to the laws and franchise of the land.

XI. All which they most humbly pray of your most excellent Majesty as their rights and liberties, according to the laws and statutes of this realm; and that your Majesty would also vouchsafe to declare, that the awards, doings, and proceedings, to the prejudice of your people in any of the premises, shall not be drawn hereafter into consequence or example; and that your Majesty would be also graciously pleased, for the further comfort and safety of your people, to declare your royal will and pleasure, that in the things aforesaid all your officers and ministers shall serve you according to the laws and statutes of this realm, as they tender the honour of your Majesty, and the prosperity of this kingdom.

[Which Petition being read the 2nd of June, 1628, the King's answer was thus delivered unto it.

The King willeth that right be done according to the laws and customs of the realm; and that the statutes be put in due execution, that his subjects may have no cause to complain of any wrong or oppressions, contrary to their just rights and liberties, to the preservation whereof he holds himself as well obliged as of his prerogative.

This form was unusual and was therefore thought to be an evasion; therefore on June 7 the King gave a second answer in the formula usual for approving bills: *Soit droit fait comme il est désire.*]

An Account of the Late Revolution in New England and Boston Declaration of Grievances

NATHANAEL BLYFIELD

April 18, 1689

James II was the younger son of the beheaded Charles I. In 1685, James succeeded his brother, Charles II, who had been restored to the throne in 1660. Unlike his brother, James did not believe it necessary to limit his claims to unchecked power in the light of parliamentary power and authority. In England, James set about legislating without parliamentary consent and withdrawing the charters by which townships traditionally had governed their own affairs. In America, he revoked colonial charters in an attempt to consolidate royal power and administration. Throughout the empire, James's opponents were subjected to arbitrary imprisonment. In England, the result was the Glorious Revolution of 1688, which brought William of Orange and his army to London, causing James to flee the country and his throne. Unrest also erupted in America, bringing down numerous governments imposed on the colonists from London. Blyfield, an English merchant, provides a narrative of the insurrection in Boston, which was part of a more general revolt throughout the colonies, as well as a copy of the Declaration of Boston's prominent citizens, which set forth their reasons for revolt.

An Account of the Late Revolution In New-England

Written by Mr. Nathanael Byfield,
to his Friends, &c.

Gentlemen,

Here being an opportunity of sending for *London,* by a Vessel that loaded at *Long-Island,* and for want of a Wind put in here; and not knowing that there will be the like from this Country suddenly, I am willing to give you some brief Account of the most remarkable things that have happened here within this Fortnight last past; concluding that till about that time, you will have received *per Carter,* a full Account of the management of Affairs here. Upon the *Eighteenth* Instant, about Eight of the Clock in the Morning, in *Boston,* it was reported at the *South* end of the Town, That at the *North* end they were all in Arms; and the like Report was at the *North* end, respecting the *South* end: Whereupon Captain *John George* was immediately seized, and about nine of the clock the Drums beat thorough the Town; and an Ensign was set up upon the Beacon. Then Mr. *Bradstreet,* Mr. *Dantforth,* Major *Richards,* Dr. *Cooke,* and Mr. *Addington* & c. were brought to the Council-house by a Company of Soldiers under the Command of Captain *Hill.* The mean while the People in Arms, did take up and put in to Gaol, Justice *Bullivant,* Justice *Foxcroft,* Mr. *Randolf,* Sheriff *Sherlock,* Captain *Ravenscroft,* Captain *White, Farewel, Broadbent, Crafford, Larkin, Smith,* and many more, as also *Mercey* the then Goal-keeper, and put *Scates* the Bricklayer in his place. About Noon, in the Gallery at the Council-house, was read the Declaration here inclosed. Then a Message was sent to the Fort to Sir *Edmund Andros,* By Mr. *Oliver* and Mr. *Eyres,* signed by the Gentlemen then in the Council-Chamber, (which is here also inclosed); to inform him how unsafe he was like to be if he did not deliver up himself, and Fort and Government forthwith, which he was loath to do. By this time, being about two of the Clock (the Lecture being put by) the Town was generally in Arms, and so many of the Countrey came in, that there was Twenty Companies in *Boston,* besides a great many that appeared at *Charles Town* that could not get over (some say Fifteen Hundred). There then came information to the Soldiers, That a Boat was come from the Frigat that made towards the Fort, which made them haste thither, and come to the Sconce soon after the Boat got thither; and 'tis said that Governor *Andros,* and about half a score Gentlemen, were coming down out of the Fort; but the Boat being seized, wherein were small

Arms, Hand-Granadoes, and a quantity of Match, the Governour and the rest went in again; whereupon Mr. *John Nelson,* who was at the head of the Soldiers, did demand the Fort and the Governor, who was loath to submit to them; but at length did come down, and was with the Gentlemen that were with him, conveyed to the Council-house, where Mr. *Bradstreet* and the rest of the Gentlemen waited to receive him; to whom Mr. *Stoughton* first spake, telling him, He might thank himself for the present disaster that had befallen him, &c. He was then confined for that night to Mr. *John Usher's* house under strong Guards, and the next day conveyed to the Fort, (where he yet remains, and with him Lieutenant Collonel *Ledget*) which is under the Command of Mr. *John Nelson;* and at the Castle, which is under the Command of Mr. *John Fairweather,* is Mr. *West,* Mr. *Graham,* Mr. *Palmer,* and Captaine *Tryfroye.* At that time Mr. *Dudley* was out upon the Circuit, and was holding a Court at *Southold* on *Long-Island.* And on the 21st. Instant he arrived at *Newport,* where he heard the News. The next day Letters came to him, advising him not to come home; he thereupon went over privately to Major *Smith's* at *Naraganzett,* and advice is this day come hither, that yesterday about a dozen young men, most of their own heads, went thither to demand him; and are gone with him down to *Boston.* We have also advice, that on *Fryday* last towards evening, Sir *Edmond Andross* did attempt to make an escape in Womans Apparel, and pass'd two Guards, and was stopped at the third, being discovered by his Shoes, not having changed them. We are here ready to blame you sometimes, that we have not to this day received advice concerning the great Changes in *England,* and in particular how it is like to fair with us here; who do hope and believe that all these things will work for our Good; and that you will not be wanting to promote the Good of a Country that stands in such need as *New-England* does at this day. The first day of *May,* according to former Usage, is the Election-day at *Road Island;* and many do say they intend their choice there then. I have not farther to trouble you with at present, but recommending you, and all our affairs with you, to the Direction and Blessing of our most Gracious God: I remain

 Gentlemen,

  Your Most Humble Servant at Command,

   Nathanael Byfield

Bristol, *April 29*
1689

Through the Goodness of God, there hath been no Blood shed. Nath. Clark *is in* Plymouth Gaol, *and* John Smith *in Gaol here, all waiting for News from* England.

Boston Declaration of Grievances

The Declaration of the Gentlemen, Merchants, and Inhabitants of Boston, and the Country Adjacent. April *18. 1689*

§. I. We have seen more than a decad of Years rolled away, since the *English* World had the Discovery of an horrid *Popish Plot;* wherein the bloody *Devotoes* of *Rome* had in their Design and Prospect no less than the extinction of the *Protestant Religion:* which mighty work they called *the utter subduing of a Pestilent Hersey;* wherein (they said) there never were such hopes of Success since the Death of Queen *Mary,* as now in our days. And we were of all men the most insensible, if we should apprehend a Countrey so remarkable for the true Profession and pure Exercise of the Protestant Religion as *New-England* is, wholly unconcerned in the Infamous Plot. To crush and break a Countrey so entirely and signally made up of *Reformed Churches,* and at length to involve it in the miseries of an utter Extirpation, must needs carry even a Supererogation of merit with it among such as were intoxicated with a Bigotry inspired into them by the great *Scarlet Whore.*

§. II. To get us within the reach of the desolation desired for us, it was no improper thing that we should first have our *Charter* Vacated, and the hedge which kept us from the wild Beasts of the field, effectually broken down. The accomplishment of this was hastened by the unwearied sollicitations, and slanderous accusations of a man, for his *Malice* and *Falshood,* well known unto us all. Our *Charter* was with a most injurious pretence (and scarce that) of Law, condemned before it was possible for us to appear at *Westminster* in the legal defence of it; and without a fair leave to answer for our selves, concerning the Crimes falsly laid to our charge, we were put under a *President* and *Council,* without any liberty for an Assembly, which the other *American Plantations* have, by a Commission from His *Majesty.*

§. III. The Commission was as *Illegal* for the form of it, as the way of obtaining it was *Malicious* and *unreasonable:* yet we made no Resistance thereunto as we could easily have done; but chose to give all *Mankind* a Demonstration of our being a people sufficiently dutiful and loyal to our King: and this with yet more Satisfaction, because we took pains to make our selves believe as much as ever we could of the Whedle then offer'd unto us; That his *Magesty's* desire was no other than the happy encrease and advance of these *Provinces* by their more immediate Dependance on the *Crown* of *England*. And we were convinced of it by the courses immediately taken to damp and spoyl our *Trade;* whereof decayes and complaints presently filled all the Country; while in the mean time neither the Honour nor the Treasure of the King was at all advanced by this new Model of our Affairs, but a considerable Charge added unto the Crown.

§. IV. In little more than half a Year we saw this Commission superseded by another, yet more Absolute and Arbitrary, with which Sir *Edmond Andross* arrived as our Governour: who besides his Power, with the Advice and Consent of his Council, to make Laws and raise Taxes as he pleased; had also Authority by himself to Muster and Imploy all Persons residing in the Territory as occasion shall serve; and to transfer such Forces to any English Plantation in *America,* as occasion shall require. And several Companies of Souldiers were now brought from *Europe,* to support what was to be imposed upon us, not without repeated Menaces that some hundreds more were intented for us.

§. V. The Government was no sooner in these Hands, but care was taken to load Preferments principally upon such Men as were strangers to, and haters of the People: and every ones Observation hath noted, what Qualifications recommended a Man to publick Offices and Employments, only here and there a *good Man* was used, where others could not easily be had; the Governour himself, with Assertions now and then falling from him, made us jealous that it would be thought for his Majesties Interest, if this People were removed and another succeeded in their room: And his far-fetch'd Instruments that were growing rich among us, would gravely inform us, that it was not for his Majesties Interest that we should thrive. But of all our oppressors we were chiefly *squeez'd* by a crew of abject Persons, fetched from *New-York,* to be the Tools of the Adversary, standing at our right hand; by these were extraordinary and intollerable Fees extorted from every one upon all occasions, without any Rules but those of their own insatiable Avarice and Beggary; and even the probate of a Will must now cost as many *Pounds* perhaps as it did *Shillings* heretofore; nor could a small Volume contain the other Illegalities done by these *Horse-Leeches* in the two or three Years that they have been sucking of us; and what Laws they made it was as impossible for us to know, as dangerous for us to break; but we shall leave the Men of *Ipswich* and of *Plimouth* (among others) to tell the story of the kindness which has been shown them upon this account. Doubtless a Land so ruled as once *New-England* was, has not without many fears and sighs beheld the wicked walking on every side, and the vilest Men exalted.

§. VI. It was now plainly affirmed, both by some in open Council, and by the same in private converse, that the people in *New-England* were all *Slaves,* and the only difference between them and *Slaves* is their not being bought and sold; and it was a maxim delivered in open Court unto us by one of the Council, *that we must not think the Priviledges of Englishmen would follow us to the end of the World:* Accordingly we have been treated with multiplied contradictions to *Magna Charta,* the rights of which we laid claim unto. Persons who did but peaceably object against the raising of Taxes without an Assembly, have been for it fined, some twenty, some thirty, and others fifty Pounds. Packt and pickt Juries have been very common things among us, when, under a pretended form of Law, the trouble of some honest and worthy Men has been aimed at: but when some of this Gang have been brought upon the Stage, for the most detestable Enormities that ever the Sun beheld, all Men have with Admiration seen what methods have been taken that they might not be treated according to their Crimes. Without a Verdict, yea, without a Jury sometimes have People been fined most unrighteously; and some not of the meanest Quality have been kept in long and close Imprisonment without any the least Information appearing against them, or an *Habeas Corpus* allowed unto them. In short, when our Oppressors have been a little out of Mony, 'twas but pretending some Offence to be enquired into, and the most innocent of Men were continually put into no small Expence to answer the Demands of the Officers, who must have Mony of them, or a prison for them tho none could accuse them of any Misdemeanour.

§. VII. To plunge the poor People every where into deeper Incapacities, there was one very comprehensive Abuse given to us; Multitudes of pious and sober Men through the Land, scrupled the Mode of Swearing on the

Book, desiring that they might Swear with an uplifted Hand, agreeable to the ancient Custom of the Colony; and though we think we can prove that the Common Law amongst us (as well as in some other places under the *English Crown*) not only indulges, but even commands and enjoins the Rite of lifting the Hand in *Swearing;* yet they that had this Doubt, were still put by from serving upon any Juries; and many of them were most unaccountably Fined and Imprisoned. Thus one Grievance is a *Trojan Horse,* in the Belly of which it is not easy to recount how many insufferable Vexations have been contained.

§. VIII. Because these things could not make us miserable fast enough, there was a notable Discovery made of we know not what *flaw* in all our *Titles to our Lands;* and, tho *besides* our purchase of them from the Natives; and, *besides* our actual peaceable unquestioned possession of them for near threescore Years, and besides the Promise of K. *Charles* II. in his Proclamation sent over to us in the Year 1683, *That no Man here shall receive any Prejudice in his Free-hold or Estate:* We had the Grant of our Lands, under the Seal of the *Council* of *Plimouth:* which Grant was Renewed and Confirmed unto us by King *Charles* I. under the Great Seal of *England;* and the *General Court* which consisted of the Patentees and their Associates, had made particular Grants hereof to the several *Towns* (though 'twas now deny'd by the Governour, that there was any such Thing as a *Town*) among us; to all which Grants the *General Court* annexed for the further securing of them, *A General Act,* published under the Seal of the Colony, in the Year 1684. Yet we were every day told, *That no man was owner of a Foot of Land in all the Colony.* Accordingly, *Writs of Intrusion* began every where to be served on People, that after all their Sweat and their Cost upon their formerly purchased Lands, thought themselves *Free-holders* of what they had. And the Governor caused the Lands pertaining to these and those *particular Men,* to be measured out for his Creatures to take possession of; and the *Right Owners,* for pulling up the Stakes, have passed through Molestations enough to tire all the patience in the World. They are more than a few, that were by Terrors driven to take *Patents* for their Lands at excessive rates, to save them from the next that might petition for them: and we fear that the forcing of the People at the *Eastward* hereunto, gave too much Rise to the late unhappy Invasion made by the *Indians* on them. *Blanck Patents* were got ready for the rest of us, to be sold at a Price, that all the Mony and Moveables

in the Territory could scarce have paid. And several *Towns* in the Country had their *Commons* begg'd by Persons (even by some of the Council themselves) who have been privately encouraged thereunto, by those that sought for Occasions to impoverish a Land already *Peeled, Meeted out and Trodden down.*

§. IX. All the Council were not ingaged in these ill Actions, but those of them which were true Lovers *of their Country,* were seldom admitted to, and seldomer consulted at the Debates which produced these unrighteous Things: Care was taken to keep them under Disadvantages; and the Governor, with five or six more, did what they would. We bore all these, and many more such Things, without making any attempt for any Relief; only Mr. *Mather,* purely out of respect unto the Good of his Afflicted Country, undertook a Voyage into *England;* which when these Men suspected him to be preparing for, they used all manner of Craft and Rage, not only to interrupt his *Voyage,* but to ruin his *Person* too. God having through many Difficulties given him to arrive at *White-hall,* the King, more than once or twice, promised him a certain *Magna Charta* for a speedy Redress of many things which we were groaning under: and in the mean time said, *That our Governor should be written unto, to forbear the Measures that he was upon.* However, after this, we were injured in those very Things which were complained of; and besides what Wrong hath been done in our Civil Concerns, we suppose the *Ministers,* and the *Churches* every where have seen our Sacred Concerns apace going after them: How they have been Discountenanced, has had a room in the reflections of every man, that is not a stranger *in our Israel.*

§. X. And yet that our Calamity might not be terminated here, we are again Briar'd in the Perplexities of another *Indian War;* how, or why, is a mystery too deep for us to unfold. And tho' 'tis judged that our *Indian* Enemies are not above 100. in number, yet an Army of *One thousand* English hath been raised for the Conquering of them; which Army of our poor Friends and Brethren now under *Popish Commanders* (for in the Army as well as in the Council, Papists are in Commission) has been under such a conduct, that not one *Indian* hath been kill'd, but more English are supposed to have died through sickness and hardship, than we have adversaries there alive; and the whole War hath been so managed, that we cannot but suspect in it, a branch of the Plot *to bring us low;* which we leave to be further enquir'd into in due time.

§. XI. We did nothing against these Proceedings, but only cry to our God; they *have caused the cry of the Poor to come unto him, and he hears the cry of the Afflicted.* We have been quiet hitherto, and so still we should have been, had not the Great God at this time laid us under a *double engagement* to do something for our security: besides, what we have in the strangely unanimous inclination, which our Countrymen by extreamest necessities are driven unto. For first, we are informed that the rest of the English *America* is Alarmed with just and great fears, that they may be attaqu'd by the *French,* who have lately ('tis said) already treated many of the English with worse then *Turkish* Cruelties; and while we are in equal danger of being surprised by them, it is high time we should be better guarded, than we are like to be while the Government remains in the hands by which it hath been held of late. Moreover, we have understood, (though the *Governour* has taken all imaginable care to keep us all ignorant thereof) that the Almighty God hath been pleased to prosper the noble undertaking of the Prince of *Orange,* to preserve the three Kingdoms from the horrible brinks of Popery and Slavery, and to bring to a Condign punishment those *worst of men,* by whom *English Liberties* have been destroy'd; in compliance with which Glorious Action, we ought surely to follow the Patterns which the Nobility, Gentry and Commonalty in several parts of those Kingdoms have set before us, though *they* therein chiefly proposed to prevent what *we* already endure.

§. XII. We do therefore seize upon the Persons of those few *Ill men* which have been (next to our Sins) the grand Authors of our Miseries; resolving to secure them, for what Justice, Orders from his Highness, with the *English Parliament* shall direct, lest, ere we are aware, we *find* (what we may *fear,* being on all sides in danger) our selves to be by them given away to a Forreign *Power,* before such Orders can reach unto us; for which Orders we now humbly wait. In the mean time firmly believing, that we have endeavoured nothing but what meer Duty to God and our *Country* calls for at our Hands: We commit our *Enterprise* unto the Blessing of Him, *who hears the cry of the Oppressed,* and advise all our Neighbours, for whom we have thus ventured our selves, to joyn with us in Prayers and all just Actions, for the Defence of the Land.

FINIS

The English Bill of Rights

1689

After James II fled his throne, frightened by the army brought to England by William of Orange and the lack of support he found among his own people, a convention was called to determine who would succeed him and under what terms. The first term agreed upon was that Catholics would no longer be eligible to rule. Other terms were agreed upon by the convention, which was called by William as a representation of the English people and consisted of all those still living who had served in Parliament. Like Magna Charta and the Petition of Right, the Bill of Rights is a "declaration" in that its authors believed that they were merely declaring, or making clear, preexisting, customary rights. It did, however, have long-reaching effects by further establishing Parliament's role in legislation, limiting the king's power to raise and keep armies without Parliament's approval, and establishing further checks on the king's power to prosecute opponents in an arbitrary manner. It also established a firm line of royal succession to William's wife Mary (daughter of James II, who officially ruled jointly with William until her death) and her line, and excluded Catholics. The document does not include prohibitions against *quo warranto* proceedings, by means of which James had in essence revoked town charters, because James had given up his claim to that right before leaving the throne.

The English Bill of Rights

An Act for Declaring the Rights and Liberties of the Subject, and Settling the Succession of the Crown

Whereas the Lords Spiritual and Temporal, and Commons, assembled at Westminster, lawfully, fully, and freely representing all the estates of the people of this realm, did upon the Thirteenth day of February, in the year of our Lord One Thousand Six Hundred Eighty-eight, present unto their Majesties, then called and known by the names and style of William and Mary, Prince and Princess of Orange, being present in their proper persons, a certain Declaration in writing, made by the said Lords and Commons, in the words following, viz.:—

"Whereas the late King James II., by the assistance of divers evil counsellors, judges, and ministers employed by him, did endeavour to subvert and extirpate the Protestant religion, and the laws and liberties of this kingdom:—

1. By assuming and exercising a power of dispensing with and suspending of laws, and the execution of laws, without consent of Parliament.

2. By committing and prosecuting divers worthy prelates, for humbly petitioning to be excused from concurring to the said assumed power.

3. By issuing and causing to be executed a commission under the Great Seal for erecting a court, called the Court of Commissioners for Ecclesiastical Causes.

4. By levying money for and to the use of the Crown by pretence of prerogative, for other time and in other manner than the same was granted by Parliament.

5. By raising and keeping a standing army within this kingdom in time of peace, without consent of Parliament, and quartering soldiers contrary to law.

6. By causing several good subjects, being Protestants, to be disarmed, at the same time when Papists were both armed and employed contrary to law.

7. By violating the freedom of election of members to serve in Parliament.

8. By prosecutions in the Court of King's Bench for matters and causes cognizable only in Parliament; and by divers other arbitrary and illegal causes.

9. And whereas of late years, partial, corrupt, and unqualified persons have been returned, and served on juries in trials, and particularly diverse jurors in trials for high treason, which were not freeholders.

10. And excessive bail hath been required of persons committed in criminal cases, to elude the benefit of the laws made for the liberty of the subjects.

11. And excessive fines have been imposed; and illegal and cruel punishments inflicted.

12. And several grants and promises made of fines and forfeitures, before any conviction or judgment against the persons upon whom the same were to be levied.

All which are utterly and directly contrary to the known laws and statutes, and freedom of this realm.

And whereas the said late King James II, having abdicated the government, and the throne being thereby vacant, his Highness the Prince of Orange (whom it hath pleased Almighty God to make the glorious instrument of delivering this kingdom from Popery and arbitrary power) did (by the advice of the Lords Spiritual and Temporal, and diverse principal persons of the Commons) cause letters to be written to the Lords Spiritual and Temporal, being Protestants, and other letters to the several counties, cities, universities, boroughs, and cinque ports, for the choosing of such persons to represent them, as were of right to be sent to Parliament, to meet and sit at Westminster upon the two-and-twentieth day of January, in this year one thousand six hundred eighty and eight, in order to such an establishment, as that their religion, laws, and liberties might not again be in danger of being subverted; upon which letters elections have been accordingly made.

And thereupon the said Lords Spiritual and Temporal, and Commons, pursuant to their respective letters and elections, being now assembled in a full and free representation of this nation, taking into their most serious consideration the best means for attaining the ends aforesaid, do in the first place (as their ancestors in like case have usually done), for the vindicating and asserting their ancient rights and liberties, declare:—

1. That the pretended power of suspending of laws, or the execution of laws, by regal authority, without consent of Parliament, is illegal.

2. That the pretended power of dispensing with laws, or the execution of laws by regal authority, as it hath assumed and exercised of late, is illegal.

3. That the commission for erecting the late Court of Commissioners for Ecclesiastical causes, and all other commissions and courts of like nature, are illegal and pernicious.

4. That levying money for or to the use of the Crown by pretence of prerogative, without grant of Parliament, for longer time or in other manner than the same is or shall be granted, is illegal.

5. That it is the right of the subjects to petition the King, and all commitments and prosecutions for such petitioning are illegal.

6. That the raising or keeping a standing army within the kingdom in time of peace, unless it be with consent of Parliament, is against law.

7. That the subjects which are Protestants may have arms for their defence suitable to their conditions, and as allowed by law.

8. That election of members of Parliament ought to be free.

9. That the freedom of speech, and debates or proceedings in Parliament, ought not to be impeached or questioned in any court or place out of Parliament.

10. That excessive bail ought not to be required, nor excessive fines imposed; nor cruel and unusual punishments inflicted.

11. That jurors ought to be duly impanelled and returned, and jurors which pass upon men in trials for high treason ought to be freeholders.

12. That all grants and promises of fines and forfeitures of particular persons before conviction are illegal and void.

13. And that for redress of all grievances, and for the amending, strengthening, and preserving of the laws, Parliament ought to be held frequently.

And they do claim, demand, and insist upon all and singular the premises, as their undoubted rights and liberties; and that no declarations, judgments, doings or proceedings, to the prejudice of the people in any of the said premises, ought in any wise to be drawn hereafter into consequence or example.

To which demand of their rights they are particularly encouraged by the declaration of his Highness the Prince of Orange, as being the only means for obtaining a full redress and remedy therein.

Having therefore an entire confidence that his said Highness the Prince of Orange will perfect the deliverance so far advanced by him, and will still preserve them from the violation of their rights, which they have here asserted, and from all other attempts upon their religion, rights, and liberties,

II. The said Lords Spiritual and Temporal, and Commons, assembled at Westminster, do resolve, that William and Mary, Prince and Princess of Orange, be, and be declared, King and Queen of England, France, and Ireland, and the dominions thereunto belonging, to hold the crown and royal dignity of the said kingdoms and dominions to them the said Prince and Princess during their lives, and the life of the survivor of them; and that the sole and full exercise of the regal power be only in, and executed by, the said Crown and royal dignity of the said kingdoms and dominions to be to the heirs of the body of the said Princess; and for default of such issue to the Princess Anne of Denmark, and the heirs of her body; and for default of such issue to the heirs of the body of the said Prince of Orange. And the Lords Spiritual and Temporal, and Commons, do pray the said Prince and Princess to accept the same accordingly.

III. And that the oaths hereafter mentioned be taken by all persons of whom the oaths of allegiance and supremacy might be required by law, instead of them; and that the said oaths of allegiance and supremacy be abrogated.

"I, A. B., do sincerely promise and swear, That I will be faithful and bear true allegiance to their Majesties King William and Queen Mary:

"So help me God."

"I, A. B., do swear, That I do from my heart abhor, detest, and abjure as impious and heretical that damnable doctrine and position, that Princes excommunicated or deprived by the Pope, or any authority of the See of Rome, may be deposed or murdered by their subjects, or any other whatsoever. And I do declare, that no foreign prince, person, prelate, state, or potentate hath, or ought to have, any jurisdiction, power, superiority, preeminence, or authority, ecclesiastical or spiritual, within this realm:

"So help me God!"

IV. Upon which their said Majesties did accept the Crown and royal dignity of the kingdoms of England, France, and Ireland, and the dominions thereunto belonging, according to the resolution and desire of the said Lords and Commons contained in the said declaration.

V. And thereupon their Majesties were pleased, that the said Lords Spiritual and Temporal, and Commons, being the two Houses of Parliament, should continue to sit, and with their Majesties' royal concurrence make effectual provision for the settlement of the religion, laws and liberties of this kingdom, so that the same for the future might not be in danger again of being subverted, to which the said Lords Spiritual and Temporal, and Commons, did agree and proceed to act accordingly.

VI. Now in pursuance of the premises, the said Lords Spiritual and Temporal, and Commons, in Parliament assembled, for the ratifying, confirming, and establishing the said declaration, and the articles, clauses, matters, and things therein contained, by the force of a law made in due form by authority of Parliament, do pray that it may be declared and enacted, That all and singular the rights and liberties asserted and claimed in the said declaration are the true, ancient, and indubitable rights and liberties of the people of this kingdom, and so shall be esteemed, allowed, adjudged, deemed, and taken to be, and that all and every of the particulars aforesaid shall be firmly and strictly holden and observed, as they are expressed in the said declaration; and all officers and ministers whatsoever shall serve their Majesties and their successors according to the same in all times to come.

VII. And the said Lords Spiritual and Temporal, and Commons, seriously considering how it hath pleased Almighty God, in his marvellous providence, and merciful goodness to this nation, to provide and preserve their said Majesties' royal persons most happily to reign over us upon the throne of their ancestors, for which they render unto Him from the bottom of their hearts their humblest thanks and praises, do truly, firmly, assuredly, and in the sincerity of their hearts, think, and do hereby recognize, acknowledge, and declare, that King James II, having abdicated the Government, and their Majesties having accepted the Crown and royal dignity aforesaid, their said Majesties did become, were, are, and of right ought to be, by the laws of this realm, our sovereign liege Lord and Lady, King and Queen of England, France, and Ireland, and the dominions thereunto belonging, in and to whose princely persons the royal state, crown, and dignity of the same realms, with all honours, styles, titles, regalties, prerogatives, powers, jurisdictions, and authorities to the same belonging and appertaining, are most fully, rightfully, and entirely invested and incorporated, united, and annexed.

VIII. And for preventing all questions and divisions in this realm, by reason of any pretended titles to the Crown, and for preserving a certainty in the succession thereof, in and upon which the unity, peace, tranquility, and safety of this nation doth, under God, wholly consist and depend, the said Lords Spiritual and Temporal, and Commons, do beseech their Majesties that it may be enacted, established, and declared, that the Crown and regal government of the said kingdoms and dominions, with all and singular the premises thereunto belonging and appertaining, shall be and continue to their said Majesties, and the survivor of them, during their lives, and the life of the survivor of them. And that the entire, perfect, and full exercise of the regal power and government be only in, and executed by, his Majesty, in the names of both their Majesties, during their joint lives; and after their deceases the said Crown and premises shall be and remain to the heirs of the body of her Majesty: and for default of such issue, to her Royal Highness the Princess Anne of Denmark, and the heirs of her body; and for default of such issue, to the heirs of the body of his said Majesty: And thereunto the said Lords Spiritual and Temporal, and Commons, do, in the name of all the people aforesaid, most humbly and faithfully submit themselves, their heirs and posterities, forever: and do faithfully promise, that they will stand to, maintain, and defend their said Majesties, and also the limitation and succession of the Crown herein specified and contained, to the utmost of their powers, with their lives and estates, against all persons whatsoever that shall attempt anything to the contrary.

IX. And whereas it hath been found by experience, that it is inconsistent with the safety and welfare of this Protestant kingdom, to be governed by a Popish prince, or by any king or queen marrying a Papist, the said Lords Spiritual and Temporal, and Commons, do further pray that it may be enacted, That all and every person and persons that is, are, or shall be reconciled to, or shall hold communion with, the See or Church of Rome, or shall profess the Popish religion, or shall marry a Papist, shall be excluded, and be for ever incapable to inherit, possess, or enjoy the Crown and Government of this realm, and Ireland, and the dominions thereunto belonging, or any part of the same, or to have, use, or exercise any regal power, authority, or jurisdiction within the same; and in all and every such case or cases the people of these realms shall be and are hereby absolved of their allegiance; and the said Crown and Government shall from time to time descend to, and be enjoyed by, such person or persons, being Protestants, as should have inherited and enjoyed the same, in case the said person or persons so reconciled, holding communion, or professing, or marrying, as aforesaid, were naturally dead.

X. And that every King and Queen of this realm, who at any time hereafter shall come to and succeed in the Imperial Crown of this kingdom, shall, on the first day of the meeting of the first Parliament, next after his or her com-

ing to the Crown, sitting in his or her throne in the House of Peers, in the presence of the Lords and Commons therein assembled, or at his or her coronation, before such person or persons who shall administer the coronation oath to him or her, at the time of his or her taking the said oath (which shall first happen), make, subscribe, and audibly repeat the declaration mentioned in the statute made in the thirteenth year of the reign of King Charles II., intituled "An act for the more effectual preserving the King's person and Government, by disabling Papists from sitting in either House of Parliament." But if it shall happen, that such King or Queen, upon his or her succession to the Crown of this realm, shall be under the age of twelve years, then every such King or Queen shall make, subscribe, and audibly repeat the said declaration at his or her coronation, or the first day of meeting of the first Parliament as aforesaid, which shall first happen after such King or Queen shall have attained the said age of twelve years.

XI. All which their Majesties are contented and pleased shall be declared, enacted, and established by authority of this present Parliament, and shall stand, remain, and be the law of this realm for ever; and the same are by their said Majesties, by and with the advice and consent of the Lords Spiritual and Temporal, and Commons, in Parliament assembled, and by the authority of the same, declared, enacted, or established accordingly.

XII. And be it further declared and enacted by the authority aforesaid, that from and after this present session of Parliament, no dispensation by *non obstante* of or to any statute, or any part thereof, shall be allowed, but that the same shall be held void and of no effect, except a dispensation be allowed of in such statute, and except in such cases as shall be specially provided for by one or more bill or bills to be passed during this present session of Parliament.

XIII. Provided that no charter, or grant, or pardon granted before the three-and-twentieth day of October, in the year of our Lord One thousand six hundred eighty-nine, shall be any ways impeached or invalidated by this Act, by that the same shall be and remain of the same force and effect in law, and no other, than as if this Act had never been made.

The Stamp Act

March 22, 1765

After fighting several wars against France during the eighteenth century, Great Britain found itself with vast new territories in North America and a vast public debt. Seeking new sources to tax, Parliament hit upon the colonists in America. The justification for taxing Americans was that they had not been paying their fair share of public expenses even though British troops had been defending their homes for decades. Americans had always been "taxed" through trade regulations that restricted domestic manufacturing and decreed that all goods must go through British ports on British ships, but Americans had not paid specific taxes on specific goods. And colonists had avoided much of the expense of trade regulations by engaging in widespread smuggling. Thus, in addition to its taxes, the Stamp Act also called for the use of harsh admiralty courts to ferret out smugglers. Yet Parliament was unprepared for the violent reaction its legislation would bring.

The Stamp Act

An act for granting and applying certain stamp duties, and other duties, in the British *colonies and plantations in* America, *towards further defraying the expences of defending, protecting, and securing the same; and for amending such parts of the several acts of parliament relating to the trade and revenues of the said colonies and plantations, as direct the manner of determining and recovering the penalties and forfeitures therein mentioned.*

Whereas *by an act made in the last session of parliament, several duties were granted, continued, and appropriated, towards defraying the expences of defending, protecting, and securing, the* British *colonies and plantations in* America: *and whereas it is just and necessary, that provision be made for raising a further revenue within your Majesty's dominions in* America, *towards defraying the said expences:* we, your Majesty's most dutiful and loyal subjects, the commons of *Great Britain* in parliament assembled, have therefore resolved to give and grant unto your Majesty the several rates and duties herein after mentioned; and do most humbly beseech your Majesty that it may be enacted, and be it enacted by

the King's most excellent majesty, by and with the advice and consent of the lords spiritual and temporal, and commons, in this present parliament assembled, and by the authority of the same, That from and after the first day of *November,* one thousand seven hundred and sixty five, there shall be raised, levied, collected, and paid unto his Majesty, his heirs, and successors, throughout the colonies and plantations in *America* which now are, or hereafter may be, under the dominion of his Majesty, his heirs and successors,

For every skin or piece of vellum or parchment, or sheet or piece of paper, on which shall be ingrossed, written or printed, any declaration, plea, replication, rejoinder, demurrer, or other pleading, or any copy thereof, in any court of law within the *British* colonies and plantations in *America,* a stamp duty of three pence.

For every skin or piece of vellum or parchment, or sheet or piece of paper, on which shall be ingrossed, written or printed, any special bail and appearance upon such bail in any such court, a stamp duty of two shillings.

For every skin or piece of vellum or parchment, or sheet or piece of paper, on which shall be ingrossed, written, or printed, any petition, bill, answer, claim, plea, replication, rejoinder, demurrer, or other pleading in any court of chancery or equity within the said colonies and plantations, a stamp duty of one shilling and six pence.

For every skin or piece of vellum or parchment, or sheet or piece of paper, on which shall be ingrossed, written, or printed, any copy of any petition, bill, answer, claim, plea, replication, rejoinder, demurrer, or other pleading in any such court, a stamp duty of three pence.

For every skin or piece of vellum or parchment, or sheet or piece of paper, on which shall be ingrossed, written, or printed, any monition, libel, answer, allegation, inventory, or renunciation in ecclesiastical matters in any court of probate, court of the ordinary, or other court exercising ecclesiastical jurisdiction within the said colonies and plantations, a stamp duty of one shilling.

For every skin or piece of vellum or parchment, or sheet or piece of paper, on which shall be ingrossed, written, or printed, any copy of any will (other than the probate thereof) monition, libel, answer, allegation, inventory, or renunciation in ecclesiastical matters in any such court, a stamp duty of six pence.

For every skin or piece of vellum or parchment, or sheet or piece of paper, on which shall be ingrossed, written, or printed, any donation, presentation, collation, or institution of or to any benefice, or any writ or instrument for the like purpose, or any register, entry, testimonial, or certificate of any degree taken in any university, academy, college, or seminary of learning, within the said colonies and plantations, a stamp duty of two pounds.

For every skin or piece of vellum or parchment, or sheet or piece of paper, on which shall be ingrossed, written, or printed, any monition, libel, claim, answer, allegation, information, letter of request, execution, renunciation, inventory, or other pleading, in any admiralty court within the said colonies and plantations, a stamp duty of one shilling.

For every skin or piece of vellum or parchment, or sheet or piece of paper, on which any copy of any such monition, libel, claim, answer, allegation, information, letter of request, execution, renunciation, inventory, or other pleading shall be ingrossed, written, or printed, a stamp duty of six pence.

For every skin or piece of vellum or parchment, or sheet or piece of paper, on which shall be ingrossed, written, or printed, any appeal, writ of error, writ of dower, *Ad quod damnum,* certiorari, statute merchant, statute staple, attestation, or certificate, by any officer, or exemplification of any record or proceeding in any court whatsoever within the said colonies and plantations (except appeals, writs of error, certiorari, attestations, certificates, and exemplifications, for or relating to the removal of any proceedings from before a single justice of the peace) a stamp duty of ten shillings.

For every skin or piece of vellum or parchment, or sheet or piece of paper, on which shall be ingrossed, written, or printed, any writ of covenant for levying of fines, writ of entry for suffering a common recovery, or attachment issuing out of, or returnable into, any court within the said colonies and plantations, a stamp duty of five shillings.

For every skin or piece of vellum or parchment, or sheet or piece of paper, on which shall be ingrossed, written, or printed, any judgment, decree, sentence, or dismission, or any record of *Nisi Prius* or *Postea,* in any court within

the said colonies and plantations, a stamp duty of four shillings.

For every skin or piece of vellum or parchment, or sheet or piece of paper, on which shall be ingrossed, written, or printed, any affidavit, common bail or appearance, interrogatory deposition, rule, order, or warrant of any court, or any *Dedimus Potestatem, Capias, Subpoena,* summons, compulsory citation, commission, recognizance, or any other writ, process, or mandate, issuing out of, or returnable into, any court, or any office belonging thereto, or any other proceeding therein whatsoever, or any copy thereof, or of any record not herein before charged, within the said colonies and plantations (except warrants relating to criminal matters, and proceeding thereon or relating thereto) a stamp duty of one shilling.

For every skin or piece of vellum or parchment, or sheet or piece of paper, on which shall be ingrossed, written, or printed, any licence, appointment, or admission of any counsellor, solicitor, attorney, advocate, or proctor, to practise in any court, or of any notary within the said colonies and plantations, a stamp duty of ten pounds.

For every skin or piece of vellum or parchment, or sheet or piece of paper, on which shall be ingrossed, written, or printed, any note or bill of lading, which shall be signed for any kind of goods, wares, or merchandize, to be exported from, or any cocket or clearance granted within the said colonies and plantations, a stamp duty of four pence. . . .

For every skin or piece of vellum or parchment, or sheet or piece of paper, on which any grant of any liberty, privilege, or franchise, under the seal of any of the said colonies or plantations, or under the seal or sign manual of any governor, proprietor, or publick officer alone, or in conjunction with any other person or persons, or with any council, or any council and assembly, or any exemplification of the same, shall be ingrossed, written, or printed, within the said colonies and plantations, a stamp duty of six pounds.

For every skin or piece of vellum or parchment, or sheet or piece of paper, on which shall be ingrossed, written, or printed, any licence for retailing of spirituous liquors, to be granted to any person who shall take out the same, within the said colonies and plantations, a stamp duty of twenty shillings. . . .

For every skin or piece of vellum or parchment, or sheet or piece of paper, on which shall be ingrossed, written or printed, any such probate, letters of administration or of guardianship, within all other parts of the *British* dominions in *America,* a stamp duty of ten shillings. . . .

For every skin or piece of vellum or parchment, or sheet or piece of paper, on which shall be ingrossed, written, or printed, any indenture, lease, conveyance, contract, stipulation, bill of sale, charter party, protest, articles of apprenticeship, or covenant (except for the hire of servants not apprentices, and also except such other matters as are herein before charged) within the *British* colonies and plantations in *America,* a stamp duty of two shillings and six pence.

For every skin or piece of vellum or parchment, or sheet or piece of paper, on which any warrant or order for auditing any publick accounts, beneficial warrant, order, grant, or certificate, under any publick seal, or under the seal or sign manual of any governor, proprietor, or publick officer alone, or in conjunction with any other person or persons, or with any council, or any council and assembly, not herein before charged, or any passport or let-pass, surrender of office, or policy of assurance, shall be ingrossed, written, or printed, within the said colonies and plantations (except warrants or orders for the service of the navy, army, ordnance, or militia, and grants of offices under twenty pounds *per annum* in salary, fees, and perquisites) a stamp duty of five shillings.

For every skin or piece of vellum or parchment, or sheet or piece of paper, on which shall be ingrossed, written, or printed, any notarial act, bond, deed, letter of attorney, procuration, mortgage, release, or other obligatory instrument, not herein before charged, within the said colonies and plantations, a stamp duty of two shillings and three pence. . . .

And for and upon every pack of playing cards, and all dice, which shall be sold or used within the said colonies and plantations, the several stamp duties following (that is to say)

For every pack of such cards, the sum of one shilling.

And for every pair of such dice, the sum of ten shillings.

And for and upon every paper, commonly called a *pamphlet,* and upon every news paper, containing publick news, intelligence, or occurrences, which shall be printed, dispersed, and made publick, within any of the said colonies and plantations, and for and upon such advertisements as are herein after mentioned, the respective duties following (that is to say)

For every such pamphlet and paper contained in half

a sheet, or any lesser piece of paper, which shall be so printed, a stamp duty of one halfpenny, for every printed copy thereof.

For every such pamphlet and paper (being larger than half a sheet, and not exceeding one whole sheet) which shall be so printed, a stamp duty of one penny, for every printed copy thereof.

For every pamphlet and paper being larger than one whole sheet, and not exceeding six sheets in octavo, or in a lesser page, or not exceeding twelve sheets in quarto, or twenty sheets in folio, which shall be so printed, a duty after the rate of one shilling for every sheet of any kind of paper which shall be contained in one printed copy thereof.

For every advertisement to be contained in any gazette, news paper, or other paper, or any pamphlet which shall be so printed, a duty of two shillings.

For every almanack or calendar, for any one particular year, or for any time less than a year, which shall be written or printed on one side only of any one sheet, skin, or piece of paper parchment, or vellum, within the said colonies and plantations, a stamp duty of two pence.

For every other almanack or calendar for any one particular year, which shall be written or printed within the said colonies and plantations, a stamp duty of four pence.

And for every almanack or calendar written or printed within the said colonies and plantations, to serve for several years, duties to the same amount respectively shall be paid for every such year.

For every skin or piece of vellum or parchment, or sheet or piece of paper, on which any instrument, proceeding, or other matter or thing aforesaid, shall be ingrossed, written, or printed, within the said colonies and plantations, in any other than the *English* language, a stamp duty of double the amount of the respective duties before charged thereon.

And there shall be also paid in the said colonies and plantations, a duty of six pence for every twenty shillings, in any sum not exceeding fifty pounds sterling money, which shall be given, paid, contracted, or agreed for, with or in relation to any clerk or apprentice, which shall be put or placed to or with any master or mistress to learn any profession, trade, or employment. . . .

LIV. And be it further enacted by the authority aforesaid, That all the monies which shall arise by the several rates and duties hereby granted (except the necessary charges of raising, collecting, recovering, answering, paying, and accounting for the same, and the necessary charges from time to time incurred in relation to this act, and the execution thereof) shall be paid into the receipt of his Majesty's exchequer, and shall be entered separate and apart from all other monies, and shall be there reserved to be from time to time disposed of by parliament, towards further defraying the necessary expences of defending, protecting, and securing, the said colonies and plantations. . . .

LVIII. And it is hereby further enacted and declared by the authority aforesaid, That all sums of money granted and imposed by this act as rates or duties, and also all sums of money imposed as forfeitures or penalties, and all sums of money required to be paid, and all other monies herein mentioned, shall be deemed and taken to be sterling money of *Great Britain,* and shall be collected, recovered, and paid, to the amount of the value which such nominal sums bear in *Great Britain;* and that such monies shall and may be received and taken, according to the proportion and value of five shillings and six pence the ounce in silver; and that all the forfeitures and penalties hereby inflicted, and which shall be incurred, in the said colonies and plantations, shall and may be prosecuted, sued for, and recovered, in any court of record, or in any court of admiralty, in the respective colony or plantation where the offence shall be committed, or in any court of vice admiralty appointed or to be appointed, and which shall have jurisdiction within such colony, plantation, or place, (which courts of admiralty or vice admiralty are hereby respectively authorized and required to proceed, hear, and determine the same,) at the election of the informer or prosecutor; and that from and after the twenty ninth day of *September,* one thousand seven hundred and sixty five, in all cases, where any suit or prosecution shall be commenced and determined for any penalty or forfeiture inflicted by this act, or by the said act made in the fourth year of his present Majesty's reign, or by any other act of parliament relating to the trade or revenues of the said colonies or plantations, in any court of admiralty in the respective colony or plantation where the offence shall be committed, either party, who shall think himself aggrieved by such determination, may appeal from such determination to any court of vice admiralty appointed or to be appointed, and which shall have jurisdiction within such colony, plantation, or place, (which court of vice admiralty is hereby authorized and required to proceed, hear, and determine such appeal) any law, custom, or usage, to the contrary notwithstanding;

and the forfeitures and penalties hereby inflicted, which shall be incurred in any other part of his Majesty's dominions, shall and may be prosecuted, sued for, and recovered, with full costs of suit, in any court of record within the kingdom, territory, or place, where the offence shall be committed, in such and the same manner as any debt or damage, to the amount of such forfeiture or penalty, can or may be sued for and recovered.

LIX. And it is hereby further enacted, That all the forfeitures and penalties hereby inflicted shall be divided, paid, and applied, as follows; (that is to say) one third part of all such forfeitures and penalties recovered in the said colonies and plantations, shall be paid into the hands of one of the chief distributors of stamped vellum, parchment, and paper, residing in the colony or plantation wherein the offender shall be convicted, for the use of his Majesty, his heirs, and successors; one third part of the penalties and forfeitures, so recovered, to the governor or commander in chief of such colony or plantation; and the other third part thereof, to the person who shall inform or sue for the same; and that one moiety of all such penalties and forfeitures recovered in any other part of his Majesty's dominions, shall be to the use of his Majesty, his heirs, and successors, and the other moiety thereof, to the person who shall inform or sue for the same.

LX. And be it further enacted by the authority aforesaid, That all the offences which are by this act made felony [counterfeiting or forging a stamped paper], and shall be committed within any part of his Majesty's dominions, shall and may be heard, tried, and determined, before any court of law within the respective kingdom, territory, colony, or plantation, where the offence shall be committed, in such and the same manner as all other felonies can or may be heard, tried, and determined, in such court.

LXI. And be it further enacted by the authority aforesaid, That all the present governors or commanders in chief of any *British* colony or plantation, shall, before the said first day of *November,* one thousand seven hundred and sixty five, and all who hereafter shall be made governors or commanders in chief of the said colonies or plantations, or any of them, before their entrance into their government, shall take a solemn oath to do their utmost, that all and every the clauses contained in this present act be punctually and *bona fide* observed, according to the true intent and meaning thereof, so far as appertains unto the said governors or commanders in chief respectively, under the like penalties, forfeitures, and disabilities, either for neglecting to take the said oath, or for wittingly neglecting to do their duty accordingly, as are mentioned and expressed in an act made in the seventh and eighth year of the reign of King *William* the Third, intituled, *An act for preventing frauds, and regulating abuses, in the plantation trade;* and the said oath hereby required to be taken, shall be administered by such person or persons as hath or have been, or shall be, appointed to administer the oath required to be taken by the said act made in the seventh and eighth year of the reign of King *William* the Third.

LXII. And be it further enacted by the authority aforesaid, That all records, writs, pleadings, and other proceedings in all courts whatsoever, and all deeds, instruments, and writings whatsoever, hereby charged, shall be ingrossed and written in such manner as they have been usually accustomed to be ingrossed and written, or are now ingrossed and written within the said colonies and plantations.

LXIII. And it is hereby further enacted, That if any person or persons shall be sued or prosecuted, either in *Great Britain* or *America,* for any thing done in pursuance of this act, such person and persons shall and may plead the general issue, and give this act and the special matter in evidence; and if it shall appear so to have been done, the jury shall find for the defendant or defendants: and if the plaintiff or plaintiffs shall become non-suited, or discontinue his or their action after the defendant or defendants shall have appeared, or if judgement shall be given upon any verdict or demurrer against the plaintiff or plaintiffs, the defendant or defendants shall recover treble costs, and have the like remedy for the same, as defendants have in other cases by law.

Braintree Instructions

JOHN ADAMS

1765

John Adams (1735–1826) was only thirty-one years old when he penned these instructions from his township to their colonial representative, but they were accepted unanimously and without amendment by his neighbors. In the instructions, the future revolutionary leader and second president of the United States sets out the colonists' objections to the Stamp Act, focusing on the burdensome nature of its unaccustomed tax and the danger to liberty from its extension of military justice into tax proceedings against colonists. Well before independence, Americans had developed a system of legislative representation that allowed for significant input from local citizens. Thus, it would have been no surprise to Mr. Thayer, the representative to whom these instructions are addressed, that his constituents should "instruct" him of their desire that he express their opposition to the Stamp Act and work to see it repealed.

Instructions of the Town of Braintree to Their Representative, 1765

To Ebenezer Thayer, Esq.

Sir,—In all the calamities which have ever befallen this country, we have never felt so great a concern, or such alarming apprehensions, as on this occasion. Such is our loyalty to the King, our veneration for both houses of Parliament, and our affection for all our fellow-subjects in Britain, that measures which discover any unkindness in that country towards us are the more sensibly and intimately felt. And we can no longer forbear complaining, that many of the measures of the late ministry, and some of the late acts of Parliament, have a tendency, in our apprehension, to divest us of our most essential rights and liberties. We shall confine ourselves, however, chiefly to the act of Parliament, commonly called the Stamp Act, by which a very burthensome, and, in our opinion, unconstitutional tax, is to be laid upon us all; and we subjected to numerous and enormous penalties, to be prosecuted, sued for, and recovered, at the option of an informer, in a court of admiralty, without a jury.

We have called this a burthensome tax, because the duties are so numerous and so high, and the embarrassments to business in this infant, sparsely-settled country so great, that it would be totally impossible for the people to subsist under it, if we had no controversy at all about the right and authority of imposing it. Considering the present scarcity of money, we have reason to think, the execution of that act for a short space of time would drain the country of its cash, strip multitudes of all their property, and reduce them to absolute beggary. And what the consequence would be to the peace of the province, from so sudden a shock and such a convulsive change in the whole course of our business and subsistence, we tremble to consider. We further apprehend this tax to be unconstitutional. We have always understood it to be a grand and fundamental principle of the constitution, that no freeman should be subject to any tax to which he has not given his own consent, in person or by proxy. And the maxims of the law, as we have constantly received them, are to the same effect, that no freeman can be separated from his property but by his own act or fault. We take it clearly, therefore, to be inconsistent with the spirit of the common law, and of the essential fundamental principles of the British constitution, that we should be subject to any tax imposed by the British Parliament; because we are not represented in that assembly in any sense, unless it be by a fiction of law, as insensible in theory as it would be injurious in practice, if such a taxation should be grounded on it.

But the most grievous innovation of all, is the alarming extension of the power of courts of admiralty. In these courts, one judge presides alone! No juries have any concern there! The law and the fact are both to be decided by the same single judge, whose commission is only during pleasure, and with whom, as we are told, the most mischievous of all customs has become established, that of taking commissions on all condemnations; so that he is under a pecuniary temptation always against the subject. Now, if the wisdom of the mother country has thought the independency of the judges so essential to an impartial administration of justice, as to render them independent of every power on earth,—independent of the King, the Lords, the Commons, the people, nay, independent in hope and expectation of the heir-apparent, by continuing their commissions after a demise of the crown, what justice and impartiality are we, at three thousand miles distance from the fountain, to expect from such a judge of admiralty? We have all along thought the acts of trade in this respect a grievance; but the Stamp Act has opened a vast number of sources of new crimes, which may be committed by any man, and cannot but be committed by multitudes, and prodigious penalties are annexed, and all these are to be tried by such a judge of such a court! What can be wanting, after this, but a weak or wicked man for a judge, to render us the most sordid and forlorn of slaves?—we mean the slaves of a slave of the servants of a minister of state. We cannot help asserting, therefore, that this part of the act will make an essential change in the constitution of juries, and it is directly repugnant to the Great Charter itself; for, by that charter, "no amerciament shall be assessed, but by the oath of honest and lawful men of the vicinage;" and, "no freeman shall be taken, or imprisoned, or disseized of his freehold, or liberties of free customs, nor passed upon, nor condemned, but by lawful judgment of his peers, or by the law of the land." So that this act will "make such a distinction, and create such a difference between" the subjects in Great Britain and those in America, as we could not have expected from the guardians of liberty in "both."

As these, sir, are our sentiments of this act, we, the freeholders and other inhabitants, legally assembled for this purpose, must enjoin it upon you, to comply with no measures or proposals for countenancing the same, or assisting in the execution of it, but by all lawful means, consistent with our allegiance to the King, and relation to Great Britain, to oppose the execution of it, till we can hear the success of the cries and petitions of America for relief.

We further recommend the most clear and explicit assertion and vindication of our rights and liberties to be entered on the public records, that the world may know, in the present and all future generations, that we have a clear knowledge and a just sense of them, and, with submission to Divine Providence, that we never can be slaves.

Nor can we think it advisable to agree to any steps for the protection of stamped papers or stamp-officers. Good and wholesome laws we have already for the preservation of the peace; and we apprehend there is no further danger of tumult and disorder, to which we have a well-grounded aversion; and that any extraordinary and expensive exertions would tend to exasperate the people and endanger the public tranquillity, rather than the contrary. Indeed, we cannot too often inculcate upon you our desires, that all extraordinary grants and expensive measures may, upon all occasions, as much as possible, be avoided. The public money of this country is the toil and labor of the people, who are under many uncommon difficulties and distresses at this time, so that all reasonable frugality ought to be observed. And we would recommend particularly, the strictest care and the utmost firmness to prevent all unconstitutional draughts upon the public treasury.

Resolutions of the Virginia House of Burgesses

June 1765

Declarations of the Stamp Act Congress

October 24, 1765

Opposition to the Stamp Act was strong, wide, and at times violent throughout the American colonies. For centuries, English subjects had responded to unpopular acts and legislation by petitioning the king for redress of their grievances. The colonists had been enthusiastic participants in this tradition since the founding of settlements in America. They continued that tradition during the Stamp Act crisis, further underlining their attachment to local, colonial legislatures by acting through bodies such as the House of Burgesses, the lower house of Virginia's legislature. In addition, however, colonists called a special congress of representatives from throughout the colonies to address the Stamp Act. This Stamp Act Congress issued its own statement of colonial grievances. The stated grievances were consistent: colonists were being taxed without their consent, in violation of ancient chartered rights, and they were being subjected to unfair and unaccustomed legal proceedings through the extension of admiralty court jurisdiction to tax cases in the colonies.

Resolutions of the Virginia House of Burgesses

Resolved, That the first Adventurers and Settlers of this his Majesty's Colony and Dominion of *Virginia* brought with them, and transmitted to their Posterity, and all other his Majesty's Subjects since inhabiting in this his Majesty's said Colony, all the Liberties, Privileges, Franchises, and Immunities, that have at any Time been held, enjoyed, and possessed, by the people of *Great Britain.*

Resolved, That by two royal Charters, granted by King *James* the First, the Colonists aforesaid are declared entitled to all Liberties, Privileges, and Immunities of Denizens and natural Subjects, to all Intents and Purposes, as if they had been abiding and born within the Realm of *England.*

Resolved, That the Taxation of the People by themselves, or by Persons chosen by themselves to represent them, who can only know what Taxes the People are able to bear, or the easiest Method of raising them, and must themselves be affected by every Tax laid on the People, is the only Security against a burthensome Taxation, and the distinguishing Characteristick of *British* Freedom, without which the ancient Constitution cannot exist.

Resolved, That his Majesty's liege People of this his most ancient and loyal Colony have without Interruption enjoyed the inestimable Right of being governed by such Laws, respecting their internal Polity and Taxation, as are derived from their own Consent, with the Approbation of their Sovereign, or his Substitute; and that the same hath never been forfeited or yielded up, but hath been constantly recognized by the Kings and People of *Great Britain.*

Declarations of the Stamp Act Congress

The Members of this Congress, sincerely devoted, with the warmest Sentiments of Affection and Duty to his Majesty's Person and Government, inviolably attached to the present happy Establishment of the Protestant Succession, and with Minds deeply impressed by a Sense of the present and impending Misfortunes of the *British* Colonies on this Continent; having considered as maturely as Time will permit, the Circumstances of the said Colonies, esteem it our indispensable Duty, to make the following Declarations of our humble Opinion, respecting the most Essential Rights and Liberties of the Colonists, and of the Grievances under which they labour, by Reason of several late Acts of Parliament.

I. That his Majesty's Subjects in these Colonies, owe the same Allegiance to the Crown of *Great-Britain,* that is owing from his Subjects born within the Realm, and all due Subordination to that August Body the Parliament of *Great-Britain.*

II. That his Majesty's Liege Subjects in these Colonies, are entitled to all the inherent Rights and Liberties of his Natural born Subjects, within the Kingdom of *Great-Britain.*

III. That it is inseparably essential to the Freedom of a People, and the undoubted Right of *Englishmen,* that no Taxes be imposed on them, but with their own Consent, given personally, or by their Representatives.

IV. That the People of these Colonies are not, and from their local Circumstances cannot be, Represented in the House of Commons in *Great-Britain.*

V. That the only Representatives of the People of these Colonies, are Persons chosen therein by themselves, and that no Taxes ever have been, or can be Constitutionally imposed on them, but by their respective Legislature.

VI. That all Supplies to the Crown, being free Gifts of the People, it is unreasonable and inconsistent with the Principles and Spirit of the *British* Constitution, for the People of *Great-Britain,* to grant to his Majesty the Property of the Colonists.

VII. That Trial by Jury, is the inherent and invaluable Right of every *British* Subject in these Colonies.

VIII. That the late Act of Parliament, entitled, *An Act for granting and applying certain Stamp Duties, and other Duties, in the* British *Colonies and Plantations in* America, *&c.* by imposing Taxes on the Inhabitants of these Colonies, and the said Act, and several other Acts, by extending the Jurisdiction of the Courts of Admiralty beyond its ancient Limits, have a manifest Tendency to subvert the Rights and Liberties of the Colonists.

IX. That the Duties imposed by several late Acts of Parliament, from the peculiar Circumstances of these Colonies, will be extremely Burthensome and Grievous; and from the scarcity of Specie, the Payment of them absolutely impracticable.

X. That as the Profits of the Trade of these Colonies ultimately center in *Great-Britain,* to pay for the Manufactures which they are obliged to take from thence, they eventually contribute very largely to all Supplies granted there to the Crown.

XI. That the Restrictions imposed by several late Acts of Parliament, on the Trade of these Colonies, will render them unable to purchase the Manufactures of *Great-Britain.*

XII. That the Increase, Prosperity, and Happiness of these Colonies, depend on the full and free Enjoyment of their Rights and Liberties, and an Intercourse with *Great-Britain* mutually Affectionate and Advantageous.

XIII. That it is the Right of the *British* Subjects in these Colonies, to Petition the King, or either House of Parliament.

Lastly, That it is the indispensable Duty of these Colonies, to the best of Sovereigns, to the Mother Country, and to themselves, to endeavour by a loyal and dutiful Address to his Majesty, and humble Applications to both Houses of Parliament, to procure the Repeal of the Act for granting and applying certain Stamp Duties, of all Clauses of any other Acts of Parliament, whereby the Jurisdiction of the Admiralty is extended as aforesaid, and of the other late Acts for the Restriction of *American* Commerce.

The Rights of the British Colonies
Asserted and Proved

JAMES OTIS

1763

James Otis (1725–83) was a lawyer, colonial official, and leading advocate for the rights of his fellow American colonists. In 1761, he resigned his post as advocate general of the Vice Admiralty Court to protest the issuance of writs of assistance by the Massachusetts superior court. These writs essentially gave authorities the right to search wherever they pleased for smuggled goods; Otis argued that they violated the rights of Englishmen. Soon thereafter, Otis was instrumental in calling for the Stamp Act Congress, in which he served. His public career was cut short when, in 1769, he suffered a blow to the head in an argument with a customs commissioner; the injury resulted in Otis's eventually going insane. In arguing against the Stamp Act, Otis in this selection restates his argument that colonists in America were entitled to the same rights as Englishmen.

The Rights of the British Colonies
Asserted and Proved

Of the Political and Civil Rights
of the British Colonists

Here indeed opens to view a large field; but I must study brevity—Few people have extended their enquiries after the foundation of any of their rights, beyond a charter from the crown. There are others who think when they have got back to old *Magna Charta*, that they are at the beginning of all things. They imagine themselves on the borders of Chaos (and so indeed in some respects they are) and see creation rising out of the unformed mass, or from nothing. Hence, say they, spring all the rights of men and of citizens. . . . But liberty was better understood, and more fully enjoyed by our ancestors, before the coming in of the first Norman Tyrants than ever after, 'till it was found necessary, for the salvation of the kingdom, to combat the arbitrary and wicked proceedings of the Stuarts.

The present happy and most righteous establishment is justly built on the ruins, which those Princes bro't on their Family; and two of them on their own heads—The last of the name sacrificed three of the finest kingdoms in Europe, to the councils of bigotted old women, priests and more weak and wicked ministers of state: He afterward went a grazing in the fields of St. Germains, and there died in disgrace and poverty, a terrible example of God's vengeance on arbitrary princes!

The deliverance under God wrought by the prince of Orange, afterwards deservedly made King Wm. 3rd. was as joyful an event to the colonies as to Great-Britain: In some of them steps were taken in his favour as soon as in England.

They all immediately acknowledged King William and Queen Mary as their lawful Sovereign. And such has been the zeal and loyalty of the colonies ever since for that establishment, and for the protestant succession in his Majesty's illustrious family, that I believe there is not one man in an hundred (except in Canada) who does not think himself under the best national civil constitution in the world.

Their loyalty has been abundantly proved, especially in the late war. Their affection and reverence for their mother country is unquestionable. They yield the most chearful and ready obedience to her laws, particularly to the power of that august body the parliament of Great-Britain, the supreme legislative of the kingdom and in dominions. These I declare are my own sentiments of duty and loyalty. I also hold it clear that the act of Queen Anne, which makes it high treason to deny "that the King with and by the authority of parliament, is able to make laws and statutes of sufficient force and validity to *limit and bind* the crown, and the descent, limitation, inheritance and *government* thereof" is founded on the principles of liberty and the British constitution: And he that would palm the doctrine of unlimited passive obedience and non-resistance upon mankind, and thereby or by any other means serve the cause of the Pretender, is not only a fool and a knave, but a rebel against common sense, as well as the laws of God, of Nature, and his Country.

—I also lay it down as one of the first principles from whence I intend to deduce the civil rights of the British colonies, that all of them are subject to, and dependent on Great-Britain; and that therefore as over subordinate governments, the parliament of Great-Britain has an undoubted power and lawful authority to make acts for the general good, that by naming them, shall and ought to be equally binding, as upon the subjects of Great-Britain within the realm. This principle, I presume will be readily granted on the other side of the Atlantic. It has been practiced upon for twenty years to my knowledge, in the province of the *Massachusetts-Bay;* and I have ever received it, that it has been so from the beginning, in this and the sister provinces, thro' the continent.*

I am aware, some will think it is time for me to retreat, after having expressed the power of the British parliament in quite so strong terms. But 'tis from and under this very power and its acts, and from the common law, that the political and civil rights of the Colonists are derived: And upon those grand pillars of liberty shall my defence be rested. At present therefore, the reader may suppose, that there is not one provincial charter on the continent; he may, if he pleases, imagine all taken away, without fault, without forfeiture, without tryal or notice. All this really happened to some of them in the last century. I would have the reader carry his imagination still further, and suppose a time may come, when instead of a process at common law, the parliament shall give a decisive blow to every charter in America, and declare them all void. Nay it shall also be granted, that 'tis barely possible, the time may come, when the real interest of the whole may require an act of parliament to annihilate all those charters. What could follow from all this, that would shake one of the essential, natural, civil or religious rights of the Colonists? Nothing. They would be men, citizens and british subjects after all. No act of parliament can deprive them of the liberties of such, unless any will contend that an act of parliament can make slaves not only of one, but of two millions of the commonwealth. And if so, why not of the whole? I freely own, that I can find nothing in the laws of my country, that would justify the parliament in making one slave, nor did they ever professedly undertake to make one.

Two or three innocent colony charters have been threatned with destruction an hundred and forty years past. I wish the present enemies of those harmless charters would reflect a moment, and be convinced that an act of parliament that should demolish those bugbears to the foes of liberty, would not reduce the Colonists to a state of absolute slavery. The worst enemies of the charter governments are by no means to be found in England. 'Tis a piece of justice due to Great-Britain to own, they are and have ever been natives of or residents in the colonies. A set of men in America, without honour or love to their country, have been long grasping at powers, which they think unattainable while these charters stand in the way. But they will meet with insurmountable obstacles to their project for enslaving the British colonies, should those, arising from provincial charters be removed. It would indeed seem very hard and severe, for those of the colonists, who have charters, with peculiar priviledges, to loose them. They were given to their ancestors, in consideration of their sufferings and merit, in discovering and settling America. Our forefathers were soon worn away in the toils of hard labour on their little plantations, and in war with the Savages. They thought they were earning a sure inheritance for their posterity. Could they imagine it would ever be tho't just to deprive them or theirs of their charter priviledges! Should this ever be the case, there are, thank God, natural, inherent and inseperable rights as men, and as citizens, that would remain after the so much wished for catastrophe, and which, whatever became of charters, can never be abolished *de jure,* if *de facto,* till the general conflagration.† Our rights as men and free born British subjects, give all the Colonists enough to make them very happy in comparison with the subjects of any other prince in the world.

Every British subject born on the continent of America, or in any other of the British dominions, is by the law of God and nature, by the common law, and by act of parliament, (exclusive of all charters from the Crown) entitled to all the natural, essential, inherent and inseparable rights of

---

*This however was formally declared as to Ireland, but so lately as the reign of G. 1. Upon the old principles of conquest the Irish could not have so much to say for an exemption, as the unconquered Colonists.

†The fine defence of the provincial charters of *Jeremy Dummer,* Esq.; the late very able and learned agent for the province of the *Massachusetts Bay,* makes it needless to go into a particular consideration of charter priviledges. That piece is unanswerable, but by power and might, and other arguments of that kind.

our fellow subjects in Great Britain. Among those rights are the following, which it is humbly conceived no man or body of men, not excepting the parliament, justly equitably and consistently with their own rights and the constitution, can take away.

1st. *That the supreme and subordinate powers of the legislation should be free and sacred in the hands where the community have once rightfully placed them.*

2dly. *The supreme national legislative cannot be altered justly 'till the commonwealth is dissolved, nor a subordinate legislative taken away without forfeiture or other good cause.* Nor then can the subjects in the subordinate government be reduced to a state of slavery, and subject to the despotic rule of others. A state has no right to make slaves of the conquered. Even when the subordinate right of legislature is forfeited, and so declared, this cannot affect the natural persons either of those who were invested with it, or the inhabitants,* so far as to deprive them of the rights of subjects and of men—The colonists will have an equitable right notwithstanding any such forfeiture of charter, to be represented in Parliament, or to have some new subordinate legislature among themselves. It would be best if they had both. Deprived however of their common rights as subjects, they cannot lawfully be, while they remain such. A representation in Parliament from the several Colonies, since they are become so large and numerous, as to be called on not to maintain provincial government, civil and military among themselves, for this they have chearfully done, but to contribute towards the support of a national standing army, by reason of the heavy national debt, when they themselves owe a large one, contracted in the common cause, can't be tho't an unreasonable thing, nor if asked, could it be called an immodest request. *Qui sentis commodum sentire debet et onus,* has been tho't a maxim of equity. But that a man should bear a burthen for other people, as well as himself, without a return, never long found a place in any law-book or decrees, but those of the most despotic princes. Besides the equity of an American representation in parliament, a thousand advantages would result from it. It would be the most effectual means of giving those of both countries a thorough knowledge of each others interests; as well as that of the whole, which are inseparable.

Were this representation allowed; instead of the scanda-

lous memorials and depositions that have been sometimes, in days of old, privately cooked up in an inquisitorial manner, by persons of bad minds and wicked views, and sent from America to the several boards, persons of the first reputation among their countrymen, might be on the spot, from the several colonies, truly to represent them. Future ministers need not, like some of their predecessors, have recourse for information in American affairs, to every vagabond stroller, that has run or rid post thro' America, from his creditors, or to people of no kind of reputation from the colonies; some of whom, at the time of administring their sage advice, have been as ignorant of the state of the country, as of the regions in Jupiter and Saturn.

No representation of the Colonies in parliament alone, would however be equivalent to a subordinate legislative among themselves; nor so well answer the ends of increasing their prosperity and the commerce of Great-Britain. It would be impossible for the parliament to judge so well, of their abilities to bear taxes, impositions on trade, and other duties and burthens, or of the local laws that might be really needful, as a legislative here.

3dly. *No legislative, supreme or subordinate, has a right to make itself arbitrary.*

It would be a most manifest contradiction, for a free legislative, like that of Great-Britain, to make itself arbitrary.

4thly. *The supreme legislative cannot justly assume a power of ruling by extempore arbitrary decrees, but is bound to dispense justice by known settled rules, and by duly authorized independant judges.*

5thly. *The supreme power cannot take from any man any part of his property, without his consent in person, or by representation.*

6thly. *The legislature cannot transfer the power of making laws to any other hands.*

These are their bounds, which by God and nature are fixed, hitherto have they a right to come, and no further.

1. *To govern by stated laws.*

2. *Those laws should have no other end ultimately, but the good of the people.*

3. *Taxes are not to be laid on the people, but by their consent in person, or by deputation.*

4. *Their whole power is not transferable.[†]*

These are the first principles of law and justice, and the great barriers of a free state, and of the British constitution in particular. I ask, I want no more —Now let it be shown

*See Magna Charta, the Bill of Rights. 3 Mod. 152 2. Salkeld 411. Vaughan 300.

†See Locke on Government. B. II. C. xi.

how 'tis reconcileable with these principles, or to many other fundamental maxims of the British constitution, as well as the natural and civil rights, which by the laws of their country, all British subjects are intitled to, as their best inheritance and birth-right, that all the northern colonies, who are without one representative in the house of Commons, should be taxed by the British parliament.

That the colonists, black and white, born here, are free born British subjects, and entitled to all the essential civil rights of such, is a truth not only manifest from the provincial charters, from the principles of the common law, and acts of parliament; but from the British constitution, which was reestablished at the revolution, with a professed design to lecture the liberties of all the subjects to all generations.*

In the 12 and 13 of Wm. cited above, the liberties of the subject are spoken of as their best birth-rights—No one ever dreamt, surely, that these liberties were confined to the realm. At that rate, no British subjects in the dominions could, without a manifest contradiction, be declared entitled to all the privileges of subjects born within the realm, to all intents and purposes, which are rightly given foreigners, by parliament, after residing seven years. These expressions of parliament, as well as of the charters, must be vain and empty sounds, unless we are allowed the essential rights of our fellow-subjects in Great-Britain.

Now can there be any liberty, where property is taken away without consent? Can it with any colour of truth, justice or equity, be affirmed, that the northern colonies are represented in parliament? Has this whole continent of near three thousand miles in length, and in which and his other American dominions, his Majesty has, or very soon will have, some millions of as good, loyal and useful subjects, white and black, as any in the three kingdoms, the election of one member of the house of commons?

Is there the least difference, as to the consent of the Colonists, whether taxes and impositions are laid on their trade, and other property, by the crown alone, or by the parliament? As it is agreed on all hands, the Crown alone cannot impost them. We should be justifiable in refusing to pay them, but must and ought to yield obedience to an act of parliament, tho' erroneous, 'till repealed.

I can see no reason to doubt, but that the imposition of taxes, whether on trade, or on land, or houses, or ships, on

real or personal, fixed or floating property, in the colonies, is absolutely irreconcileable with the rights of the Colonists, as British subjects, and as men. I say men, for in a state of nature, no man can take my property from me, without my consent: If he does, he deprives me of my liberty, and makes me a slave. If such a proceeding is a breach of the law of nature, no law of society can make it just— The very act of taxing, exercised over those who are not represented, appears to me to be depriving them of one of their most essential rights, as freemen; and if continued, seems to be in effect an entire disfranchisement of every civil right. For what one civil right is worth a rush, after a man's property is subject to be taken from him at pleasure, without his consent? If a man is not his *own assessor* in person, or by deputy, his liberty is gone, or lays intirely at the mercy of others.

I think I have heard it said, that when the Dutch are asked why they enslave their colonies, their answer is, that the liberty of Dutchmen is confined to Holland; and that it was never intended for Provincials in America, or anywhere else. A sentiment this, very worthy of modern Dutchmen; but if their brave and worthy ancestors had entertained such narrow ideas of liberty, seven poor and distressed provinces would never have asserted their rights against the whole Spanish monarchy, of which the present is but a shadow. It is to be hoped, none of our fellow subjects of Britain, great or small, have borrowed this Dutch maxim of plantation politics; if they have, they had better return it from whence it came; indeed they had. Modern Dutch or French maxims of state, never will suit with a British constitution. It is a maxim, that the King can do no wrong; and every good subject is bound to believe his King is not inclined to do any. We are blessed with a prince who has given abundant demonstrations, that in all his actions, he studies the good of his people, and the true glory of his crown, which are inseparable. It would therefore, be the highest degree of impudence and disloyalty to imagine that the King, at the head of his parliament, could have any, but the most pure and perfect intentions of justice, goodness and truth, that human nature is capable of. All this I say and believe of the King and parliament, in all their acts; even in that which so nearly affects the interest of the colonists; and that a most perfect and ready obedience is to be yielded to it, while it remains in force. I will go further, and readily admit, that the intention of the ministry was not only to promote the public good, by this act; but that

*See the convention, and acts confirming it.

Mr. Chancellor of the Exchequer had therein a particular view to the "ease, the quiet, and the good will of the Colonies," he having made this declaration more than once. Yet I hold that 'tis possible he may have erred in his kind intentions towards the Colonies, and taken away our fish and given us a stone. With regard to the parliament, as infallability belongs not to mortals, 'tis possible *they* may have been misinformed and deceived. The power of parliament is uncontroulable, but by themselves, and we must obey. They only can repeal their own acts. There would be an end of all government, if one or a number of subjects or subordinate provinces should take upon them so far to judge of the justice of an act of parliament, as to refuse obedience to it. If there was nothing else to restrain such a step, prudence ought to do it, for forceably resisting the parliament and the King's laws, is high treason. Therefore let the parliament lay what burthens they please on us, we must, it is our duty to submit and patiently bear them, till they will be pleased to relieve us. And tis to be presumed, the wisdom and justice of that august assembly, always will afford us relief by repealing such acts, as through mistake, or other human infirmities, have been suffered to pass, if they can be convinced that their proceedings are not constitutional, or not for the common good.

The parliament may be deceived, they may have been misinformed of facts, and the colonies may in many respects be misrepresented to the King, his parliament, and his ministry. In some instances, I am well assured the colonies have been very strangely misrepresented in England. I have now before me a pamphlet, called the "administration of the colonies," said to be written by a gentleman who formerly commanded in chief in one of them. I suppose this book was designed for public information and use. There are in it many good regulations proposed, which no power can enforce but the parliament. From all which I infer, that if our hands are tied by the passing of an act of parliament, our mouths are not stoped, provided we speak of that transcendent body with decency, as I have endeavoured always to do; and should any thing have escaped me, or hereafter fall from my pen, that bears the least aspect but that of obedience, duty and loyalty to the King & parliament, and the highest respect for the ministry, the candid will impute it to the agony of my heart, rather than to the pravity of my will. If I have one ambitious wish, 'tis to see Great-Britain at the head of the world, and to see my King, under God, the father of mankind. I pretend neither to the spirit of prophecy, nor any uncommon skill in predicting a Crisis, much less to tell when it begins to be "*nascent*" or is fairly midwiv'd into the world. But if I were to fix a meaning to the two first paragraphs of the *administrations of the colonies,* tho' I do not collect it from them, I should say the world was at the eve of the highest scene of earthly power and grandeur that has been ever yet displayed to the view of mankind. The cards are shuffling fast thro' all Europe. Who will win the prize is with God. This however I know *detur digniori.* The next universal monarchy will be favourable to the human race, for it must be founded on the principles of equity, moderation and justice. No country has been more distinguished for these principles than Great-Britain, since the revolution. I take it, every subject has a right to give his sentiments to the public, of the utility or inutility of any act whatsoever, even after it is passed, as well as while it is pending.—The equity and justice of a bill may be questioned, with perfect submission to the legislature. Reasons may be given, why an act ought to be repeal'd, & yet obedience must be yielded to it till that repeal takes place. If the reasons that can be given against an act, are such as plainly demonstrate that it is against *natural* equity, the executive courts will adjudge such acts void. It may be questioned by some, tho' I make no doubt of it, whether they are not obliged by their oaths to adjudge such acts void. If there is not a right of private judgement to be exercised, so far at least as to petition for a repeal, or to determine the expediency of risking a trial at law, the parliament might make itself arbitrary, which it is conceived it can not by the constitution.—I think every man has a right to examine as freely into the origin, spring and foundation of every power and measure in a commonwealth, as into a piece of curious machinery, or a remarkable phenomenon in nature; and that it ought to give no more offence to say, the parliament have erred, or are mistaken, in a matter of fact, or of right, than to say it of a private man, if it is true of both. If the assertion can be proved with regard to either, it is a kindness done them to show them the truth. With regard to the public, it is the duty of every good citizen to point out what he thinks erroneous in the commonwealth.

I have waited years in hopes to see some one friend of the colonies pleading in publick for them. I have waited in vain. One priviledge is taken away after another, and where we shall be landed, God knows, and I trust will protect and provide for us even should we be driven and persecuted into a more western wilderness, on the score of liberty, civil and religious, as many of our ancestors were, to these once inhospitable shores of America. I had formed great expectations from a gentleman, who published his first volume in quarto on the rights of the colonies two years since; but, as he foresaw, the state of his health and affairs have prevented his further progress. The misfortune is, gentlemen in America, the best qualified in every respect to state the rights of the colonists, have reasons that prevent them from engaging: Some of them have good ones. There are many infinitely better able to serve this cause than I pretend to be; but from indolence, from timidity, or by necessary engagements, they are prevented. There has been a most profound, and I think shameful silence, till it seems almost too late to assert our indisputable rights as men and as citizens. What must posterity think of us. The trade of the whole continent taxed by parliament, stamps and other internal duties and taxes as they are called, talked of, and not one petition to the King and Parliament for relief.

I cannot but observe here, that if the parliament have an equitable right to tax our trade, 'tis indisputable that they have as good an one to tax the lands, and every thing else. The taxing trade furnishes one reason why the other should be taxed, or else the burdens of the province will be unequally born, upon a supposition that a tax on trade is not a tax on the whole. But take it either way, there is no foundation for the distinction some make in England, between an internal and an external tax on the colonies. By the first is meant a tax on trade, by the latter a tax on land, and the things on it. A tax on trade is either a tax of every man in the province, or 'tis not. If 'tis not a tax on the whole, 'tis unequal and unjust, that a heavy burden should be laid on the trade of the colonies, to maintain an army of soldiers, custom-house officers, and fleets of guard-ships; all which, the incomes of both trade and land would not furnish means to support so lately as the last war, when all was at stake, and the colonies were reimbursed in part by parliament. How can it be supposed that all of a sudden the trade of the colonies alone can bear all this terrible burden. The late acquisitions in America, as glorious as they have been, and as beneficial as they are to Great-Britain, are only a security to these colonies against the ravages of the French and Indians. Our trade upon the whole is not, I believe, benefited by them one groat. All the time the

French Islands were in our hands, the fine sugars, &c. were all shipped home. None as I have been informed were allowed to be bro't to the colonies. They were too delicious a morsel for a North American palate. If it be said that a tax on the trade of the colonies is an equal and just tax on the whole of the inhabitants: What then becomes of the notable distinction between external and internal taxes? Why may not the parliament lay stamps, land taxes, establish tythes to the church of England, and so indefinitely. I know of no bounds. I do not mention the tythes out of any disrespect to the church of England, which I esteem by far the best *national* church, and to have had as ornaments of it many of the greatest and best men in the world. But to those colonies who in general dissent from a principle of conscience, it would seem a little hard to pay towards the support of a worship, whose modes they cannot conform to.

If an army must be kept in America, at the expence of the colonies, it would not seem quite so hard if after the parliament had determined the sum to be raised, and apportioned it, to have allowed each colony to assess its quota, and raise it as easily to themselves as might be. But to have the whole levied and collected without our consent is extraordinary. 'Tis allowed even to *tributaries,* and those laid under *military* contribution, to assess and collect the sums demanded. The case of the provinces is certainly likely to be the hardest that can be instanced in story. Will it not equal any thing but down right military execution? Was there ever a tribute imposed even on the conquered? A fleet, an army of soldiers, and another of taxgatherers kept up, and not a single office either for securing or collecting the duty in the gift of the tributary state.

I am aware it will be objected, that the parliament of *England,* and of Great Britain, since the union, have from early days to this time, made acts to bind if not to tax Ireland: I answer, Ireland is a *conquered* country. I do not, however, lay so much stress on this; for it is my opinion, that a *conquered* country has, upon submission and good behaviour, the same right to be free, under a conqueror, as the rest of his subjects. But the old notion of the *right of conquest,* has been, in most nations, the cause of many severities and heinous breaches of the law of nature: If any such have taken place with regard to *Ireland,* they should form no precedent for the colonies. The subordination and dependency of *Ireland* to Great Britain, is expresly declared by act of parliament, in the reign of G. 1st. The subordination of the *Colonies* to Great Britain, never was doubted, by a Lawyer, if at all; unless perhaps by the author of the administration of the colonies: He indeed seems to make a moot point of it, whether the colony legislative power is as independent "as the legislative Great Britain holds by its constitution, and under the great charter." —The *people* hold under the great charter, as 'tis vulgarly expressed from our law-books: But that the King and parliament should be said to hold under *Magna Charta,* is as new to me, as it is to question whether the colonies are *subordinate* to Great Britain. The provincial legislative is unquestionably subordinate to that of Great Britain. I shall endeavour more fully to explain the nature of that subordination, which has puzzled so many in their enquiries. It is often very difficult for great lovers of power and great lovers of liberty, neither of whom may have been used to the study of law, in any of its branches, to see the difference between subordination, absolute slavery and subjection, on one side; and liberty, independence and licenciousness, on the other. We should endeavour to find the middle road, and confine ourselves to it. The laws, the proceedings of parliament, and the decisions of the judges, relating to *Ireland,* will reflect light on this subject, rendered intricate only by art.

"Ireland being of itself a distinct dominion, and no part of the kingdom of England (as directly appeareth by many authorities in Calvin's case) was to have Parliaments holden there as in England." 4 INST. 349.

Why should not the colonies have, why are they not entitled to their assemblies, or parliaments, at least, as well as a conquered dominion?

"Wales, after the conquest of it, by Edward, the first, was annexed to England, jure proprietatis, 12 Ed. 1. by the statute of Rutland only, and after, more really by 27 H. 8. and 34, but at first received laws from England, as Ireland did; but writs proceeded not out of the English chancery, but they had a Chancery of their own, as Ireland hath; was not bound by the laws of England, unnamed until 27 H. 8. no more than Ireland is.

Ireland in nothing differs from it, but having a parliament *gratia Regis* (i.e. upon the old notion of conquest) subject (truly however) to the parliament of England. None doubts Ireland as much conquered as it; *and as much subject to the parliament of England, if it please.*"

VAUGHAN. 300.

A very strong argument arises from this authority, in favour of the *unconquered* plantations. If since Wales was annexed to England, they have had a representation in parliament, as they have to this day; and if the parliament of England does not tax *Ireland,* can it be right they should tax *us,* who have never been *conquered,* but came from England to *colonize,* and have always remained *good subjects* to this day?

I cannot find any instance of a tax laid by the English parliament on *Ireland.* "Sometimes the King of England called his Nobles of Ireland, to come to his parliament of England, &c. and by special words, the parliament of England may bind the subjects of Ireland"—3 INST. 350—.

The following makes it clear to me, the parliament of Great Britain do not tax *Ireland,* "The parliament of Ireland having been prorogued to the month of August *next, before they had provided for the maintenance of the government in that kingdom, a project* was set on foot here to supply that defect, by retrenching the drawbacks upon goods exported thither from England. According to this scheme, the 22d, the house in a grand committee, considered the present laws with respect to drawbacks upon tobaccoes, muslins, and East India silks, carried to Ireland; and came to two resolutions, which were reported the next day, and with an amendment to one of them agreed to by the house, as follows, Viz. 1. That three pence pr pound, part of the drawback on tobacco to be exported from Great Britain for Ireland, be taken off.

2. That the said diminution of the drawback do take effect upon all tobacco exported for Ireland, after the 24 of March 1713, and continue until the additional duty of three pence half penny per pound upon tobacco in Ireland, expiring on the said 24th of March, be *regranted:* And ordered a bill to be brought in, upon the said resolutions."

Proceedings of House of Commons, Vol. 5. 72.

This was constitutional; there is an infinite difference between taking off British drawbacks, and imposing Irish or other Provincial duties.

"Ireland is considered as a provincial government, subordinate to, but no part of the Realm of England," Mich. 11. G. 2. in case of Otway and Ramsay—"Acts of parliament made here, (i.e. in England) extend not to Ireland, unless particularly named; much less judgments obtained in the courts here; nor is it possible they should, because we have no officers to carry them into execution there." *ib.*

The first part seems to be applicable to the plantations in general, the latter is not; for by reason of charter reservations and particular acts of parliament, some judgments in England may be executed here, as final judgments, before his Majesty in council on a plantation appeal, and so from the admiralty.

It seems to have been disputed in Ireland, so lately as the 6 Geo. 1. Whether any act of the British parliament bound Ireland; or at least it was apprehended, that the undoubted right of the British parliament to bind Ireland, was in danger of being shaken: This, I presume, occasioned the act of that year, which declares, that "the kingdom of Ireland ought to be subordinate unto and dependent upon the Imperial Crown of Great Britain, as being inseparably united thereto. And the King's Majesty, with the consent of the lords and commons of Great Britain in parliament, hath power to make laws to bind the people of Ireland."—This parliamentary power must have some bounds, even as to *Ireland,* as well as the colonies who are admitted to be subordinate *ab initio* to Great Britain; not as *conquered,* but as *emigrant* subjects. If this act should be said to be a declaration not only of the general, but of the universal power of parliament, and that they may tax Ireland, I ask, Why it has never been done? If it had been done a thousand times, it would be a contradiction to the principles of a free government; and what is worse, destroy all subordination consistent with *freedom,* and reduce the people to *slavery.*

To say the parliament is absolute and arbitrary, is a contradiction. The parliament cannot make 2 and 2, 5; Omnipotency cannot do it. The supreme power in a state, is *jus dicere* only;—*jus dare,* strictly speaking, belongs alone to God. Parliaments are in all cases to *declare* what is parliament that makes it so: There must be in every instance, a higher authority, viz. GOD. Should an act of parliament be against any of *his* natural laws, which are *immutably* true, their declaration would be contrary to eternal truth, equity and justice, and consequently void: and so it would be adjudged by the parliament itself, when convinced of their mistake. Upon this great principle, parliaments repeal such acts, as soon as they find they have been mistaken, in having declared them to be for the public good, when in fact they were not so. When such mistake is evident and palpable, as in the instances in the appendix, the judges of the executive courts have declared the act "of a whole parliament void." See here the grandeur of the British constitution! See the wisdom of our ancestors! The supreme *legislative,* and the supreme *executive,* are a perpetual check and balance to each other. If the supreme executive errs, it is informed by the supreme legislative in parliament: If the supreme legislative errs, it is informed by the supreme executive in the King's courts of law. —Here, the King appears, as represented by his judges, in the highest lustre and majesty, as supreme executor of the commonwealth; and he never shines brighter, but on his Throne, at the head of the supreme legislative. This is government! This, is a constitution! to preserve which, either from foreign or domestic foes, has cost oceans of blood and treasure in every age; and the blood and the treasure have upon the whole been well spent. British America, hath been bleeding in this cause from its settlement: We have spent all we could raise, and more; for notwithstanding the parliamentary reimbursement of part, we still remain much in debt. The province of the *Massachusetts,* I believe, has expended more men and money in war since the year 1620, when a few families first landed at Plymouth, in proportion to their ability, than the three Kingdoms together. The same, I believe, may be truly affirmed, of many of the other colonies; tho' the *Massachusetts* has undoubtedly had the heaviest burthen. This may be thought incredible: but materials are collecting; and tho' some are lost, enough may remain, to demonstrate it to the world. I have reason to hope at least, that the public will soon see such proofs exhibited, as will show, that I do not speak quite at random.

Why then is it thought so heinous by the author of the administration of the colonies, and others, that the colonists should aspire after "a one whole legislative power" not independent of, but subordinate to the laws and parliament of Great-Britain? . . . It is a mistake in this author, to bring so heavy a charge as *high treason* against some of the colonists, which he does in effect in this place,* by representing them as "claiming in fact or indeed, the same full free independent unrestrained power and legislative will, in their several corporations, and under the King's commission, and their respective charters, as the government and legislature of Great-Britain holds by its constitution and under the great charter." No such claim was ever tho't of by any of the colonists. They are all better men and better subjects; and many of them too well versed in the laws of nature and nations, and the law and constitution of Great-Britain, to think they have a right to more than a *provin-*

---

*Page 39 of the administration.

cial subordinate legislative. All power is of GOD. Next and only subordinate to him, in the present state of the well-formed, beautifully constructed British monarchy, standing where I hope it ever will stand, for the pillars are fixed in judgment, righteousness and truth, is the King and Parliament. Under these, it seems easy to conceive subordinate powers in gradation, till we descend to the legislative of a town council, or even a private social club. These have each "a one whole legislative" subordinate, which, when it don't conteract the laws of any of its superiors, is to be indulged. Even when the laws of subordination are transgressed, the superior does not destroy the subordinate, but will negative its acts, as it may in all cases when disapproved. This right of negative is essential, and may be inforced: But in no case are the essential rights of the subjects, inhabiting the subordinate dominions, to be destroyed. This would put it in the power of the superior to reduce the inferior to a state of slavery; which cannot be rightfully done, even with *conquered* enemies and *rebels.* After satisfaction and security is obtained of the former, and examples are made of so many of the latter, as the ends of government require, the rest are to be restored to all the essential rights of men and of citizens. This is the great law of nature: and agreeable to this law, is the constant practice of all good and mild governments. This lenity and humanity has no where been carried further than in Great Britain. The Colonies have been so remarkable for loyalty, that there never has been any instance of rebellion or treason in them. This loyalty is in very handsome terms acknowledged by the author of the administration of the colonies. "It has been often suggested that care should be taken in the administration of the plantations, lest, in some future time, these colonies should become independent of the mother country. But perhaps it may be proper on this occasion, and, it is justice to say it, that if, by becoming independent, is meant a revolt, nothing is further from their nature, their interest, their thoughts. If a defection from the *alliance* of the mother country be suggested, it ought to be, and can be truly said, that their spirit abhors the sense of such; their attachment to the protestant succession in the house of Hanover, will ever stand unshaken; and nothing can eradicate from their hearts their natural and almost mechanical, affection to Great Britain, which they conceive under no other sense nor call by any other name than that of *home.* Any such suggestion, therefore, is a false and unjust aspersion on their principles and affec-

tions; and can arise from nothing but an intire ignorance of their circumstances."* After all this loyalty, it is a little hard to be charged with claiming, and represented as aspiring after, independency. The inconsistency of this I leave. We have said that the loyalty of the colonies has never been suspected; this must be restricted to a just suspicion. For it seems there have long been groundless suspicions of us in the minds of individuals. And there have always been those who have endeavoured to magnify these chimerical fears. I find Mr. Dummer complaining of this many years since.

"There is, says he, one thing more I have heard often urged against the charter colonies, and indeed tis what one meets with from people of all conditions and qualities, tho' with due respect to their better judgments, I can see neither reason nor colour for it. 'Tis said that their increasing numbers and wealth, joined to their great distance from Britain, will give them an opportunity, in the course of some years, to throw off their dependence on the nation, and declare themselves a free state, if not curb'd in time, by being made *entirely subject to the crown.*"[†]

This jealousy has been so long talked of, that many seems to believe it really well grounded. Not that there is danger of a "revolt," even in the opinion of the *author of the administration,* but that the colonists will by fraud or force avail themselves, in "fact or in deed," of an independent legislature. This, I think, would be a revolting with a vengeance. What higher revolt can there be, than for a province to assume the right of an independent legislative, or state? I must therefore think this a greater aspersion on the Colonists, than to charge them with a design to revolt, in the sense in which the Gentleman allows they have been abused: It is a more artful and dangerous way of attacking our liberties, than to charge us with being in open rebellion. That could be confuted instantly: but this seeming indirect way of charging the colonies, with a desire of throwing off their dependency, requires more pains to confute it than the other, therefore it has been recurred to. The truth is, Gentlemen have had departments in America, the functions of which they have not been fortunate in executing. The people have by these means been rendered uneasy, at bad Provincial measures. They have been represented as factious, seditious, and inclined to democracy whenever they have refused passive obedience to provincial man-

* Administration, p. 25, 26.
† Defence. 60.

dates, as arbitrary as those of a Turkish Bashaw: I say, Provincial mandates; for to the King and Parliament they have been ever submissive and obedient.

These representations of us, many of the good people of England swallow with as much ease, as they would a bottle-bubble, or any other story of a cock and a bull; and the worst of it is, among some of the most credulous, have been found Stars and Garters. However, they may all rest assured, the Colonists, who do not pretend to understand themselves so well as the people of England; tho' the author of the Administration makes them the fine compliment, to say, they "know their business much better," yet, will never think of independency. Were they inclined to it, they know the blood and the treasure it would cost, if ever effected; and when done, it would be a thousand to one if their liberties did not fall a sacrifice to the victor.

We all think ourselves happy under Great-Britain. We love, esteem and reverence our mother country, and adore our King. And could the choice of independency be offered the colonies, or subjection to Great-Britain upon any terms above absolute slavery, I am convinced they would accept the latter. The ministry, in all future generations may rely on it, that British America will never prove undutiful, till driven to it, as the last fatal resort against ministerial oppression, which will make the wisest mad, and the weakest strong.

These colonies are and always have been, "entirely subject to the crown," in the legal sense of the terms. But if any politician of "*tampering activity, of wrongheaded inexperience, misted to be meddling," means, by "curbing the colonies in time," and by "being made entirely subject to the crown;" that this subjection should be absolute, and confined to the crown, he had better have suppressed his wishes. This never will nor can be done, without making the colonists vassals of the crown. Subjects they are; their lands they hold of the crown, by common soccage, the freest feudal tennure, by which any hold their lands in England, or any where else. Would these gentlemen carry us back to the state of the Goths and Vandals, and revive all the military tenures and bondage which our fore-fathers could not bear? It may be worth nothing here, that few if any instances can be given, where colonies have been disposed to forsake or disobey a tender mother: But history is full of examples, that armies, stationed as guards over prov-

inces, have seized the prey for their general, and given him a crown at the expence of his master. Are all ambitious generals dead? Will no more rise up hereafter? The danger of a standing army in remote provinces is much greater to the metropolis, than at home. Rome found the truth of this assertion, in her Sylla's, her Pompey's and Caesars; but she found it too late: Eighteen hundred years have roll'd away since her ruin. A continuation of the same liberties that have been enjoyed by the colonists since the revolution, and the same moderation of government exercised towards them, will bind them in perpetual lawful and willing subjection, obedience and love to Great-Britain: She and her colonies will both prosper and flourish: The monarchy will remain in sound health and full vigor at that blessed period, when the proud arbitrary tyrants of the continent shall either unite in the deliverance of the human race, or resign their crowns. Rescued, human nature must and will be, from the general slavery that has so long triumphed over the species. Great-Britain has done much towards it: What a Glory will it be for her to complete the work throughout the world!

The author of the Administration (page 54) "describes" the defects of the "provincial courts," by a "very description," the first trait of which is, "The ignorance of the judges." Whether the description, or the description of the description, are *verily* true, either as applied by Lord Hale, or the Administrator, is left to the reader. I only ask, who makes the judges in the provinces? I know of but two colonies, viz. Connecticut and Rhode-Island, where they are chosen by the people. In all other colonies, they are either immediately appointed by the crown, or by his Majesty's governor, with the advice of what the Administrator calls, the "governor's council of state." And if they are in general such ignorant creatures, as the Administrator describes them, 'tis the misfortune, not the fault, of the people, in the colonies. However, I believe, justice in general, is as well administered in the colonies, as it will be when every thing is devolved upon a court of admiralty, general or provincial. The following is very remarkable. "In those popular governments, and where every executive officer is under a dependence for a temporary, wretched, and I had almost said arbitrary support, on the deputies of the people."†

Why is the temporary support found fault with? Would it be wise to give a governor a salary for a longer time than

---

*Administration. 34.

†Administ. 56.

his political life? As this is quite as uncertain as his natural life, it has been granted annually. So every governor has the chance of one year's salary after he is dead. All the King's officers, are not even in the charter provinces "dependent on the people" for support. The judges of the admiralty, those mirrors of justice, to be trusted, when none of the common law courts are, have all their commissions from home. These, besides other fees, have so much per cent on all they condemn, be it right or wrong, *and this by act of parliament.* Yet so great is their integrity, that it never was suspected that 50 per cent, if allowed, would have any influence on their decrees.

Custom-house officers universally, and Naval-officers, in all but two or three of the colonies, are, I believe, appointed directly from home, or by instruction to the Governor: and take just what they please, for any restraint they are under by the provincial acts. But on whom should a Governor depend for his honorable support, but the people? Is not the King fed from the field, and from the labor of his people? Does not his Majesty himself receive his aids from the free grant of his parliament? Do not all these originate in the house of commons? Did the house of Lords ever originate a grant? Do not our law books inform us that the Lords only assent or dissent, but never so much as propose an amendment, on a money bill? The King can take no more than the Parliament will give him, and yet some of his Governors have tho't it an insufferable hardship, that they could not take what they pleased. To take leave of the administrator, there are in his book some good hints, but a multiplicity of mistakes in fact, and errors in matters of right, which I have not time to mention particularly.

Ireland is a conquered kingdom; and yet have tho't they received very hard measure in some of the prohibitions and restrictions of their trade. But were the colonies ever conquered? Have they not been subjects and obedient, and loyal from their settlement? Were not the settlements made under the British laws and constitution? But if the colonies were all to be considered as conquered, they are entitled to the essential rights of men and citizens. And therefore admitting the right of prohibition, in its utmost extent and latitude; a right of taxation can never be infer'd from that. It may be for the good of the whole, that a certain commodity should be prohibited: But this power should be exercised, with great *moderation* and impartiality, over dominions, which are not *represented,* in the national parliament. I had however rather see this carried with a high

hand, to the utmost rigor, than have a tax of one shilling taken from me without my consent. A people may be very happy; free and easy among themselves, without a particular branch of foreign trade: I am sure these colonies have the natural means of every manufacture in *Europe,* and some that are out of their power to make or produce. It will scarcely be believed a hundred years hence, that the American manufactures could have been brought to such perfection, as they will then probably be in, if the present measures are pushed. One single act of parliament, we find has set people a thinking, in six months, more than they had done in their whole lives before. It should be remembered, that the most famous and flourishing manufactures, of wool, in *France,* were begun by *Lewis* 14, not an hundred years ago; and they now bid fair to rival the *English,* in every port abroad. All the manufactures that Great-Britain could make, would be consumed in America, and in her own plantations, if put on a right footing; for which a greater profit in return would be made, than she will ever see again for woollen sent to any part of Europe.

But tho' it be allow'd, that liberty may be enjoy'd in a comfortable measure, where *prohibitions* are laid on the trade of a kingdom or province; yet if *taxes* are laid on either, *without* consent, they cannot be said to be free. This barrier of liberty being once broken down, all is lost. If a shilling in the pound may be taken from me against my will, why may not twenty shillings; and if so, why not my liberty or my life? Merchants were always *particularly* favor'd by the common law—"All merchants, except enemies, may safely come into *England,* with their goods and merchandize"—2 Inst. 28.—And why not as well to the *plantations?* Are they not entitled to all the British privileges? No. they must be confined in their imports and exports to the good of the metropolis. Very well, we have submitted to this. The act of navigation is a good act, so are all that exclude foreign manufactures from the plantations, and every honest man will readily subscribe to them. Moreover, "Merchant strangers, are also to come into the realm and depart at pleasure; and they are to be friendly entertained." 2 Ri. C. 1. But to promote the manufactures of *England,* 'tis tho't best to shut up the *colonies* in a manner from all the world. Right as to Europe: But for God's sake, must we have no trade with other colonies? In some cases the trade betwen *British* colony and colony is prohibited, as in wool, &c. Granting all this to be right, is it not enough? No. duties and taxes must be paid without any *consent* or *representation* in parliament. The common law, that inestimable privilege of a jury, is also taken away in all trials in the colonies, relating to the revenue, if the informers have a mind to go the admiralty; as they ever have done, and ever will do, for very obvious reasons. "It has ever been boasted, says Mr. Dummer in his defence of the charters, as the peculiar privilege of an Englishman, and the security of his property, to be tryed by his country, and the laws of the land: Whereas this admiralty method deprives him of both, as it puts his estate in the disposal of a single person, and makes the civil law the rule of judgment; which tho' it may not properly be called foreign being the law of nations, yet 'tis what he has not consented to himself, nor his representative for him. A jurisdiction therefore so founded, ought not to extend beyond what *necessity* requires"—"If some bounds are not set to the jurisdiction of the admiralty, beyond which it shall not pass, it may in time, like the element to which it ought to be confin'd, grow outrageous, and overflow the banks of all the other courts of justice." I believe it has never been doubted by one sound, common lawyer of England, whether a court of admiralty ever answer'd many good ends; "the court of King's bench has a power to restrain the court of admiralty in England; and the reasons for such restraining power are as strong in New England as in Great-Britain," and in some respects more so; Yet Mr. Dummer mentions, a clamour that was raised at home by a judge of the admiralty for New England, who complain'd "that the common law courts by granting prohibitions, weaken, and in a manner suppress the authority of this court, and all the good ends for which it was constituted." Thus we see, that the court of admiralty long ago discover'd, no very friendly disposition towards the common law courts here; and the records of the house of Representatives afford us a notable instance of one, who was expelled the house, of which he had been an unworthy member, for the abusive misrepresentations of the province, by him secretly made.

Trade and traffick, says Lord Coke, "is the livelihood of a merchant, the life of the commonwealth, wherein the King and every subject hath interest; for the merchant is the good Bailiff of the realm, to export and vent the native commodities of the realm, and to import and bring in, the necessary commodities for the defence and benefit of the Realm—2 Inst. 28. reading on Magna Charta. C. 15—And are not the merchants of British America entitled to a livelihood also? Are they not British subjects? Are not an

infinity of commodities carried from hence for the *benefit of the realm,* for which in return come an infinity of *trifles,* which we could do without? Manufactures we must go into if our trade is cut off; our country is too cold to go naked in, and we shall soon be unable to make returns to England even for necessaries.

"When any law or custom of parliament is broken, and the crown possessed of a precedent, how difficult a thing is it to restore the subject again to his former freedom and safety?" 2. Inst. *on the confirmation of the great charter* —which provides in these words: "And for so much as divers people of our realm, are in fear, that the aids and talks which they have given to us before time, towards our wars, and other business of their own grant and good will (howsoever they were made) might *turn to a bondage* to them and their heirs, because they might be at another time found in the rolls, and likewise for the prices taken throughout the realm by our ministers; We have granted for us and our heirs, that we shall not draw such aids, talks nor prices *into a custom,* for any thing that hath been done heretofore, be it by roll, or any other precedent that may be founden."

By the first chapter of this act, the great charter is declared to be the common law. I would ask, whether we have not reason to fear, that the great aids, freely given by these provinces in the late war, will in like manner turn *to our bondage,* if they are to be kept on and *increased* during a *peace,* for the maintenance of a *standing army* here?—If tis said those aids were given for *our own* immediate defence, and that England spent millions in the same cause; I answer: The names of his present Majesty, and his royal Grand-father, will be ever dear to every loyal British American, for the protection they afforded us, and the salvation, under God, effected by their arms; but with regard to our fellow-subjects of Britain, we never were a whit behind hand with them. The New England Colonies in particular, were not only settled without the least expence to the mother country, but they have all along defended themselves against the frequent incursions of the most inhuman Salvages, perhaps on the face of the whole earth, at *their own cost:* Those more than brutal *men,* spirited and directed by the most inveterate, as well as most powerful enemy of Great Britain, have been constantly annoying our infant settlements for more than a century; spreading terror and desolation and sometimes depopulating whole villages in a night: yet amidst the fatigues of labor, and the horrors of war and bloodshed, Heaven vouchsaf'd its smiles. Behold, an extensive territory, settled, defended, and secured to his Majesty, I repeat it, *without the least expence to the mother country,* till within twenty years past! —When *Louisbourg* was reduced to his late Majesty, by the valor of his *New-England subjects,* the parliament, it must be own'd, saw meet to refund *part* of the charges: And every one knows the importance of *Louisbourg,* in the consultations of *Aix la Chapple;* but for the loss of our young men, the riches and strength of a country, not indeed slain by the enemy, but overborn by the uncommon hardships of the siege, and their confinement in garrison afterwards, there could be no recompence made.—In the late war, the *northern colonies* not only rais'd their full quota of men, but they went even beyond their ability: they are still deeply in debt, notwithstanding the parliamentary grants, annually made them, *in part* of their expences, in the common, *national, cause:* Had it not been for those grants, they had all been bankrupt long ago; while the *sugar colonies,* have born little or no share in it: They indeed sent a company or two of *Negroes* and *Molattoes,* if this be worth mentioning, to the sieges of Gaudaloupe, Martineco and the Havanna: I do not recollect any thing else that they have done; while the flower of *our* youth were annually pressed by ten thousands into the service, and there treated but little better, as we have been told, than hewers of wood and drawers of water. Provincial acts for impressing were obtained, only by letters of requisition from a secretary of state to a Governor; requiring him to use his influence to raise men; and sometimes, more than were asked for or wanted, were pressed, to give a figure to the Governor, and shew his influence; a remarkable instance of which might be mentioned. I would further observe, that Great-Britain was as immediately interested in the late war in America, as the colonies were. Was she not threatned with an invasion at the same time we were? Has she not an immense trade to the colonies? The British writers say, more than half her profitable trade is to *America:* All the profits of our trade center there, and is little enough to pay for the goods we import. A prodigious revenue arises to the Crown on American exports to Great-Britain, which in general is not murmured at: No manufacture of Europe besides British, can be lawfully bro't here; and no honest man desires they ever should, if the laws were put in execution upon all. With regard to a few Dutch imports that have made such a noise, the truth is, very little has been or could be run, before the appara-

tus of guardships; for the officers of some ports did their duty, while others may have made a monopoly of smuggling, for a few of their friends, who probably paid them large contributions; for it has been observed, that a very small office in the customs in America has raised a man a fortune sooner than a Government. The truth is, the acts of trade have been too often evaded; but by whom? Not by the American merchants in general, but by some former custom-house officers, their friends and partizans. I name no man, not being about to turn informer: But it has been a notorious grievance, that when the King himself cannot dispense with an act of parliament, there have been custom-house officers who have practiced it for years together, in favor of those towards whom they were graciously disposed. But to return to the subject of taxation: I find that

"the lords and commons cannot be charged with any-thing for the defence of the realm, for the safe-guard of the sea, &c. unless by their *will* in parliament."

Ld. Coke, on Magna Charta, Cap. 30.

"Impositions neither in time of war, or other the greatest necessity or occasion, that may be, much less in the time of peace, neither upon foreign or inland commodities, of what nature soever, be they never so superfluous or unnecessary, neither upon merchants, strangers, nor denizens, may be laid by the King's absolute power, without assent of parliament, be it never for so short a time."

Viner Prerogative of the King.
Ea. 1. cites 2 Molloy. 320. Cap. 12 sec. 1.

"In the reign of Edward 3, the black Prince of Wales having *Aquitain* granted to him, did lay an imposition of suage or socage a *soco,* upon his subjects of that dukedom, viz. a shilling for every fire, called hearth silver, which was of so great discontentment and odious to them, that it made them revolt. And nothing since this time has been imposed by pretext of any prerogative, upon merchandizes, imported into or exported out of this realm, until Queen Mary's time."　　　　　　　2 Inst. 61.

Nor has any thing of that kind taken place since the revolution. King Charles 1. his ship-money every one has heard of.

It may be said that these authorities will not serve the colonists, because the duties laid on them are by parliament. I acknowledge the difference of fact; but cannot see the great difference in equity, while the colonists are not represented in the house of commons: And therefore with all humble deference I apprehend, that 'till the colonists are so represented, the spirit of all these authorities will argue strongly in their favour. When the parliament shall think fit to allow the colonists a representation in the house of commons, the equity of their taxing the colonies, will be as clear as their power is at present of doing it without, if they please. When Mr. Dummer wrote his defence of the charters, there was a talk of taking them away, by act of parliament. This defence is dedicated to the right honourable the Ld. Carteret, then one of this Majesty's principal secretaries of state, since Earl of Granville. His third proposition is, that "it is not for the interest of the crown to resume the charters, if forfeited." This he proves; as also that it would be more for the interest of Great Britain to enlarge rather than diminish, the privilege of all the colonists. His last proposition is, that it "seems inconsistent with justice to disfranchise the charter colonies by an act of parliament."

"It seems therefore, says he, a severity without a precedent, that a people, who have the misfortune of being a thousand leagues distant from their sovereign, a misfortune great enough in itself, should, unsummoned, unheard, in one day, be deprived of their valuable privileges, which they and their fathers have enjoyed for near a hundred years." 'Tis true, as he observes, "the legislative power is absolute and unaccountable, and King, lords and commons, may do what they please; but the question here is not about *power*, but *right*" (or rather equity) "and shall not the supreme judicature of all the nation do right?" "One may say, that what the parliament cannot do justly, they cannot do at all. *In maximis minima est licentia.* The higher the power is, the greater caution is to be used in the execution of it; because the sufferer is helpless and without resort." I never heard that this reasoning gave any offence. Why should it? Is it not exactly agreable to the decisions of parliament and the determinations of the highest executive courts? But if it was thought hard that charter privileges should be taken away by act of parliament, is it not much harder to be in part, or in whole, disfranchised of rights, that have been always tho't inherent to a British subject, namely, to be free from all taxes, but what he consents to in person, or by his representative? This right, if it could be traced no higher

than Magna Charta, is part of the common law, part of a British subjects birthright, and as inherent and perpetual, as the duty of allegiance; both which have been bro't to these colonies, and have been hitherto held sacred and inviolable, and I hope and trust ever will. 'Tis humbly conceived, that the British colonists (except only the conquered, if any) are, by Magna Charta, as well entitled to have a voice in their taxes, as the subjects within the realm. Are we not as really deprived of that right, by the parliament assessing us before we are represented in the house of commons, as if the King should do it by his prerogative? Can it be said with any colour of truth or justice, that we are represented in parliament?

As to the colonists being represented by the provincial agents, I know of no power ever given them but to appear before his Majesty, and his ministry. Sometimes they have been directed to petition the parliament: But they none of them have, and I hope never will have, a power given them, by the colonists, to act as representatives, and to consent to taxes; and if they should make any concessions to the ministry, especially without order, the provinces could not by that be considered as represented in parliament.

Hibernia habet Parliamenta et faciunt leges et nostra statuta non ligant eos quia non mittant milites ad Parliamentum, sed personae eorum sunt subjecti Regis, sicut inhabitantes Calinae Gasconiae et Guienae.

12 Rep. III. cites R. 3. 12.—

"Ireland hath parliaments, and makes laws, and our statutes do not bind them, *because they send no Knights to parliament;* but their persons are subjects, of the King, as the inhabitants of Guiene, Gascony, &c."

Yet, if specially named, or by general words included as within any of the King's dominions, Ireland, says Ld. Coke, might be bound.   4 Inst. 351.

From all which, it seems plain, that the reason why Ireland and the plantations are not bound, unless named by an Act of Parliament, is, because they are *not represented* in the British parliament. Yet, in special cases, the British parliament has an undoubted right, as well as power, to bind both by their acts. But whether this can be extended to an indefinite taxation of both, is the greater question. I conceive the spirit of the British constitution must make an exception of all taxes, until it is tho't fit to unite a dominion to the realm. Such taxation must be considered either as uniting the dominions to the realm, or disfranchising them. If they are united, they will be intitled to a representation, as well as Wales; if they are so taxed without a union, or representation, they are so far disfranchised.

I don't find anything that looks like a duty on the colonies before the 25th of C. 2. c. 7. imposing a duty on enumerated commodities. The liberty of the subject was little attended to in that reign. If the nation could not fully assert their rights till the revolution, the colonies could not expect to be heard. I look on this act rather as a precedent of power, than of right and equity; if 'tis such, it will not affect my argument. The act appointing a tax on all mariners, of a certain sum per month, to be deducted out of their wages, is not to be compared with this. Mariners are not inhabitants of any part of the dominions: The sea is their element, till they are decrepit, and then the hospital is open for all mariners who are British subjects without exception. The general post-office established thro' the dominions, is for the convenience of trade and commerce: It is not laying any burthen upon it; for besides that it is upon the whole cheaper to correspond in this way than any other, every one is at liberty to send his own letters by a friend. The act of the 6th of his late Majesty, tho' it imposes a *duty* in terms, has been said to be designed for a *prohibition;* which is probable from the sums imposed; and 'tis pity it had not been so expressed, as there is not the least doubt of the just and equitable right of the parliament to lay prohibitions thro' the dominions, when they think the good of the whole requires it. But as has been said, there is an infinite difference between that and the exercise of unlimited power of taxation, over the dominions, without allowing them a representation:—It is said that the duties imposed by the new act will amount to a prohibition: Time only can ascertain this. The utility of this act is so fully examined in the appendix that I shall add nothing on that head here. It may be said that the colonies ought to bear their proportion of the national burdens: 'Tis just they should, and I think I have proved they have always done it freely and chearfully, and I know no reason to doubt but that they ever will.

Sometimes we have been considered only as the corporations in England: And it may be urged that it is no harder upon us to be taxed by parliament for the general cause than for them, who besides are at the expence of their corporate subordinate government.* I answer. 1. Those corporations are *represented* in parliament. 2. The colonies are

and have been at great expence in raising men, building forts, and supporting the King's civil government here. Now I read of no governors and other officers of his Majesty's nomination, that the city of London taxes its inhabitants to support; I know of no forts and garrisons that the city of London has lately built at its own expence, or of any annual levies that they have raised for the King's service and the common cause. These are things very fitting and proper to be done by a subordinate dominion, and tis their duty to do all they are able; but it seems but equal they should be allowed to assess the charges of it themselves. The rules of equity and the principles of the constitution seem to require this. Those who judge of the reciprocal rights that subsist between a supreme and subordinate state or dominion, by no higher rules than are applied to a corporation of button-makers, will never have a very comprehensive view of them. Yet sorry am I to say it, many elaborate writers on the *administration* of the *colonies,* seem to me never to rise higher in their notions, than what might be expected from a secretary to one of the *quorum.* If I should be ranked among this number, I shall have this consolation, that I have fallen into what is called very good company, and among some who have seen very high life below stairs. I agree with the Administrator, that of whatever revenues raised in the colonies, if they must be raised without our consent, "*the first and special appropriation of them ought to be to the paying the Governors, and all the other Crown officers;*" for it would be hard for the Colonists to be obliged to pay them after this. It was on this principle that at the last assembly of this province, I moved to stop every grant to the officers of the crown; more especially as I know some who have built very much upon the fine salaries they shall receive from the plantation branch of the revenue. Nor can I think it "injustice to the frame of human nature,"† to suppose, if I did not know it, that with similar views several officers of the Crown in some of the colonies have been pushing for such an act for many years. They have obtained their wish, and much good it will do them: But I would not give much for all that will center neat in the exchequer, after deducting the costs attending the execution of it, and the appropriations to the several officers proposed by the Administrator. What will be the unavoidable consequence of all this, suppose another war should happen, and it should be necessary to employ as many provincials in America as in the last? Would it be

---

* See Administration of the Colonies.

† Adm. p. 57.

possible for the colonies, after being burthened in their trade, perhaps after it is ruined, to raise men? Is it probable that they would have spirit enough to exert themselves? If 'tis said the French will never try for America, or if they should, regular troops are only to be employed, I grant our regular troops are the best in the world, and that the experience of the present officers shews that they are capable of every species of American service; yet we should guard against the worst. If another tryal for Canada should take place, which from the known temper of France, we may judge she will bring on the first fair opportunity, it might require 30 or 40,000 regulars to secure his Majesty's just rights. If it should be said, that other American duties must then be levied, besides the impossibility of our being able to pay them, the danger recurs of a large standing army so remote from home. Whereas a good provincial militia, with such occasional succours from the mother country, as exigencies may require, never was, and never will be attended with hazard. The experience of past times will show, that an army of 20 or 30,000 veterans, half 3000 miles from *Rome,* were very apt to proclaim *Cesars.* The first of the name, the assassin of his country owed his false glory, to stealing the affections of an army from the commonwealth. I hope these hints will not be taken amiss; they seem to occur from the nature of the subject I am upon: They are delivered in pure affection to my King and country, and amount to no reflection on any man. The best army, and the best men, we may hereafter have, may be led into temptation; all I think is, that a prevention of evil is much easier than a deliverance from it.

The sum of my argument is, That civil government is of God: That the administrators of it were originally the whole people: That they might have devolved it on whom they pleased: That this devolution is fiduciary, for the good of the whole; That by the British constitution, this devolution is on the King, lords and commons, the supreme, sacred and uncontroulable legislative power, not only in the realm, but thro' the dominions: That by the abdication, the original compact was broken to pieces: That by the revolution, it was renewed, and more firmly established, and the rights and liberties of the subject in all parts of the dominions, more fully explained and confirmed: That in consequence of this establishment, and the acts of succession and union his Majesty GEORGE III. is rightful king and sovereign, and with his parliament, the supreme legislative of Great Britain; France and Ireland, and the dominions thereto belonging: That this constitution is the most free one, and by far the best, now existing on earth: That by this constitution, every man in the dominion is a free man: That no parts of his Majesty's dominions can be taxed without their consent: That every part has a right to be represented in the supreme or some subordinate legislature: That the refusal of this, would seem to be a contradiction in practice to the theory of the constitution: That the colonies are subordinate dominions, and are now in such a state, as to make it best for the good of the whole, that they should not only be continued in the enjoyment of subordinate legislation, but be also represented in some proportion to their number and estates, in the grand legislature of the nation: That this would firmly unite all parts of the British empire, in the greatest peace and prosperity; and render it invulnerable and perpetual.

The Act Repealing the Stamp Act

March 18, 1766

The Declaratory Act

March 18, 1766

American opposition to the Stamp Act, particularly the boycotts of taxed goods in which merchants and common colonials engaged with enthusiasm, caused a significant decline in British-colonial trade. By 1766, Parliament decided that the taxes were costing more in reduced trade than they were bringing in through taxes, and the Stamp Act was repealed. However, Parliament at the same time passed what it called the Declaratory Act, by which it declared its absolute right to legislate for the colonies as it saw fit. This statement, and Parliament's decision to act in accordance with it, would spark the American Revolution.

The Act Repealing the Stamp Act

Whereas *an act was passed in the last session of parliament, intituled,* An act for granting and applying certain stamp duties, and other duties, in the *British* colonies and plantations in *America,* towards further defraying the expences of defending, protecting, and securing the same; and for amending such parts of the several acts of parliament relating to the trade and revenues of the said colonies and plantations, as direct the manner of determining and recovering the penalties and forfeitures therein mentioned: *and whereas the continuance of the said act would be attended with many inconveniencies, and may be productive of consequences greatly detrimental to the commercial interests of these kingdoms;* may it therefore please your most excellent Majesty, that it may be enacted; and be it enacted by the King's most excellent Majesty, by and with the advice and consent of the lords spiritual and temporal, and commons, in this present parliament assembled, and by the authority of the same, that from and after the first day of *May,* one thousand seven hundred and sixty six, the above-mentioned act,

and the several matters and things therein contained, shall be, and is and are hereby repealed and made void to all intents and purposes whatsoever.

The Declaratory Act

An act for the better securing the dependency of his Majesty's dominions in America *upon the crown and parliament of* Great Britain.

Whereas *several of the houses of representatives in his Majesty's colonies and plantations in* America, *have of late, against law, claimed to themselves, or to the general assemblies of the same, the sole and exclusive right of imposing duties and taxes upon his Majesty's subjects in the said colonies and plantations; and have, in pursuance of such claim, passed certain votes, resolutions, and orders, derogatory to the legislative authority of parliament, and inconsistent with the dependency of the said colonies and plantations upon the crown of* Great Britain: may it therefore please your most excellent Majesty, that it may be declared; and be it declared by the King's most excellent majesty, by and with the advice and consent of the lords spiritual and temporal, and commons, in this present parliament assembled, and by the authority of the same, That the said colonies and plantations in *America* have been, are, and of right ought to be, subordinate unto, and dependent upon the imperial crown and parliament of *Great Britain;* and that the King's majesty, by and with the advice and consent of the lords spiritual and temporal, and commons of *Great Britain,* in parliament assembled, had, hath, and of right ought to have, full power and authority to make laws and statutes of sufficient force and validity to bind the colonies and people of

America, subjects of the crown of *Great Britain,* in all cases whatsoever.

II. And be it further declared and enacted by the authority aforesaid, That all resolutions, votes, orders, and proceedings, in any of the said colonies or plantations, whereby the power and authority of the parliament of *Great Britain,* to make laws and statutes as aforesaid, is denied, or drawn into question, are, and are hereby declared to be, utterly null and void to all intents and purposes whatsoever.

PART FOUR The War for Independence

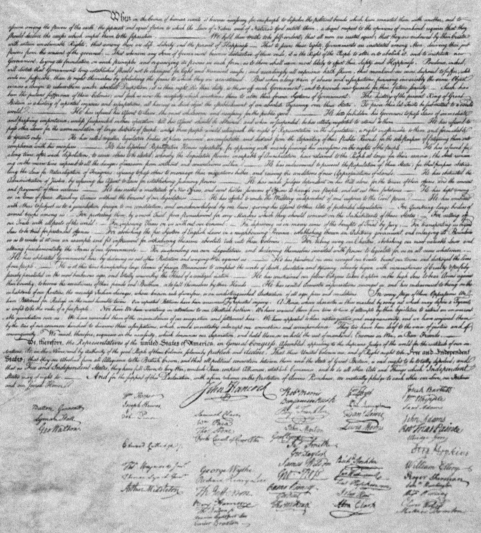

The original Declaration of Independence. © Joseph Sohm; Visions of America/CORBIS

The relative peace achieved after Parliament's repeal of the Stamp Act was short-lived. In 1767, Parliament passed the Townshend Acts, which reinstituted direct taxation on the colonies and imposed antismuggling regulations and legal proceedings at least as troublesome to the colonists as those that led to the Stamp Act Congress. Opposition quickly developed. Readings in this section illustrate the increasingly wide gulf between Americans' views of their rights and the British view of the status of any colony or subordinate people within the Empire.

A Discourse at the Dedication of the Tree of Liberty

"A SON OF LIBERTY" [SILAS DOWNER]

1768

Silas Downer (1729–85) was a prominent lawyer who was active in Rhode Island politics and was among the more prominent figures opposed to the Townshend Acts. The speech reproduced here (published under the pseudonym "A Son of Liberty") was delivered at the dedication of a Tree of Liberty. Ceremonies dedicating such trees went back to the days before the Norman conquest of Britain, when Saxon clans would assemble for town meetings under a large tree. Saxons had continued this tradition under Norman rule in remembrance of their lost liberty, and their descendants continued the tradition as a sign of their willingness to defend their chartered rights. The practice was common in America long before the Revolution and was part of a wider tradition of public speaking that included sermons delivered on election days by prominent local ministers.

A Discourse at the Dedication of the Tree of Liberty

Dearly beloved Countrymen,

We His Majesty's subjects, who live remote from the throne, and are inhabitants of a new world, are here met together to dedicate the *Tree of Liberty.* On this occasion we chearfully recognize our allegiance to our sovereign Lord, *George* the third, King of *Great-Britain,* and supreme Lord of these dominions, but utterly deny any other dependence on the inhabitants of that island, than what is mutual and reciprocal between all mankind.—It is good for us to be here, to confirm one another in the principles of liberty, and to renew our obligations to contend earnestly therefor.

Our forefathers, with the permission of their sovereign, emigrated from *England,* to avoid the unnatural oppressions which then took place in that country. They endured all sorts of miseries and hardships, before they could establish any tolerable footing in the new world. It was then hoped and expected that the blessing of freedom would be the inheritance of their posterity, which they preferred to every other temporal consideration. With the extremest toil, difficulty, and danger, our great and noble ancestors founded in *America* a number of colonies under the allegiance of the crown of *England.* They forfeited not the privileges of *Englishmen* by removing themselves hither, but brought with them every right, which they could or ought to have enjoyed had they abided in *England.*— They had fierce and dreadful wars with savages, who often poured their whole force on the infant plantations, but under every difficulty and discouragement, by the good providence of God they multiplied exceedingly and flourished, without receiving any protection or assistance from *England.* They were free from impositions. Their kings were well disposed to them, and their fellow subjects in *Great Britain* had not then gaped after *Naboth's* vineyard. Never were people so happy as our forefathers, after they had brought the land to a state of inhabitancy, and procured peace with the natives. They sat every man under his own vine, and under his own fig tree. They had but few wants; and luxury, extravagance, and debauchery, were known only by the names, as the things signified thereby, had not then arrived from the old world. The public worship of God, and the education of children and youth, were never more encouraged in any part of the globe. The laws which they made for the general advantage were exactly carried into execution. In fine, no country ever experienced more perfect felicity. Religion, learning, and a pure administration of justice were exceeding conspicuous, and kept even pace with the population of the country.

When we view this country in its extent and variety of climates, soils, and produce, we ought to be exceeding thankful to divine goodness in bestowing it upon our forefathers, and giving it as an heritage for their children.—We may call it the promised land, a good land and a large— a land of hills and vallies, of rivers, brooks, and springs of water—a land of milk and honey, and wherein we may eat bread to the full. A land whose stones are iron, the most useful material in all nature, and of other choice mines and minerals; and a land whose rivers and adjacent seas are stored with the best of fish. In a word, no part of the habitable world can boast of so many natural advantages as this northern part of *America.*

But what will all these things avail us, if we be deprived of that liberty which the GOD of nature hath given us. View the miserable condition of the poor wretches, who inhabit countries once the most fertile and happy in the world, where the blessings of liberty have been removed by the hand of arbitrary power. Religion, learning, arts, and industry, vanished at the deformed appearance of tyranny. Those countries are depopulated, and the scarce and thin inhabitants are fast fixed in chains and slavery. They have nothing which they can call their own; even their lives are at the absolute disposal of the monsters who have usurped dominion over them.

The dreadful scenes of massacre and bloodshed, the cruel tortures and brutal barbarities, which have been committed on the image of GOD, with all the horrible miseries which have overflowed a great part of the globe, have proceeded from wicked and ambitious men, who usurped an absolute dominion over their fellows. If this country should experience such a shocking change in their affairs, or if despotic sway should succeed the fair enjoyment of liberty, I should prefer a life of freedom in *Nova-Zembla, Greenland,* or in the most frozen regions in the world, even where the use of fire is unknown, rather than to live here to be tyrannized over by any of the human race.

Government is necessary. It was instituted to secure to individuals that natural liberty, which no human creature hath a right to deprive them of. For which end the people have given power unto the rulers to use as there may be occasion for the good of whole community, and not that the civil magistrate, who is only the peoples trustee, should make use of it for the hurt of the governed. If a commander of a fortress, appointed to make defence against the approaches of an enemy, should breech about his guns and fire upon his own town, he would commence tyrant and ought to be treated as an enemy to mankind.

The ends of civil government have been well answered in *America,* and justice duly administred in general, while we were governed by laws of our own make, and consented to by the Crown. It is of the very essence of the *British* con-stitution, that the people shall not be governed by laws, in the making of which they had no hand, or have their monies taken away without their own consent. This privilege is *inherent,* and cannot be *granted* by any but the Almighty. It is a natural right which no creature can *give,* or hath a right to take away. The great charter of liberties, commonly called *Magna Charta,* doth not *give* the privileges therein mentioned, nor doth our *Charters,* but must be considered as only declaratory of our rights, and in affirmance of them. The formation of legislatures was the first object of attention in the colonies. They all recognized the King of *Great-Britain,* and a government of each was erected, as like to that in *England,* as the nature of the country, and local circumstances, would admit. Assemblies or parliaments were instituted, wherein were present the King by his substitutes, with a council of great men, and the people, by their representatives. Our distant situation from *Great-Britain,* and other attendant circumstances, make it impossible for us to be represented in the parliament of that country, or to be governed from thence. The exigencies of state often require the immediate hand of governments and confusion and misrule would ensue if government was not topical. From hence it will follow that our legislatures were *compleat,* and that the parliamentary authority of *Great-Britain* cannot be extended over us without involving the greatest contradiction: For if we are to be controuled by their parliament, our own will be useless. In short, I cannot be perswaded that the parliament of *Great-Britain* have any lawful right to make *any laws whatsoever* to bind us, because there can be no fountain from whence such right can flow. It is universally agreed amongst us that they cannot tax us, because we are not represented there. Many other acts of legislation may affect us as nearly as taking away our monies. There are many kinds of property as dear to us as our money, and in which we may be greatly injured by allowing them a power in, or to direct about. Suppose the parliament of *Great-Britain* should undertake to prohibit us from walking in the streets and highways on certain saints days, or from being abroad after a certain time in the evening, or (to come nearer to the matter) to restrain us from working up and manufacturing materials of our own growth, would not our liberty and property be as much affected by such regulations as by a tax act? It is the very spirit of the constitution that the King's subjects shall not be governed by laws, in the making of which they had no share; and this principle is the greater barrier against tyranny and oppression. If this bulwark be thrown down, nothing will remain to us but a dreadful expectation of certain slavery. If any acts of the *British* parliament are found suitable and commensurate to the nature of the country, they may be introduced, or adopted, by special acts of our own parliaments, which would be equivalent to making them anew; and without such introduction or adoption, our allowance of the validity or force of *any* act of the *English* or *British* parliament in these dominions of the King, must and will operate as a concession on our part, that our fellow subjects in another country can choose a set of men among themselves, and impower them to make laws to bind us, as well in the matter of taxes as in every other case. It hath been fully proved, and is a point not to be controverted, that in our constitution the having of property, especially a landed estate, entitles the subject to a share in government and framing of laws. The *Americans* have such property and estate, but are not, and never can be represented in the *British* parliament. It is therefore clear that that assembly cannot pass *any* laws to bind us, but that we must be governed by our own parliaments, in which we can be in person, or by representation.

But of late a new system of politics hath been adopted in *Great-Britain,* and the *common people* there claim a sovereignty over us although they be only fellow subjects. The more I consider the nature and tendency of this claim, the more I tremble for the liberties of my country: For although it hath been unanswerably proved that they have no more power over us than we have over them, yet relying on the powerful logic of guns and cutlery ware, they cease not to make laws injurious to us; and whenever we expostulate with them for so doing, all the return is a discharge of threats and menaces.

It is now an established principle in *Great-Britain,* that we are subject to the *people* of that country, in the same manner as they are subject to the Crown. They expressly call us their subjects. The language of every paultry scribler, even of those who pretend friendship for us in some things, is after this lordly stile, *our colonies—our western dominions —our plantations—our islands—our subjects in America —our authority—our government*—with many more of the like imperious expressions. Strange doctrine that we should be the subjects of subjects, and liable to be controuled at their will! It is enough to break every measure of patience, that fellow subjects should assume such power over us. They are so possessed with the vision of the pleni-

tude of their power, that they call us rebels and traitors for denying their authority. If the King was an absolute monarch and ruled us according to his absolute will and pleasure, as some kings in *Europe* do their subjects, it would not be in any degree so humiliating and debasing, as to be governed by one part of the Kings subjects who are but equals. From every part of the conduct of the administration, from the acts, votes, and resolutions of the parliament, and from all the political writings in that country, and libels on *America,* this appears to be their claim, which I think may be said to be an invasion of the rights of the King, and an unwarrantable combination against the liberties of his subjects in *America.*

Let us now attend a little to the conduct of that country towards us, and see if it be possible to doubt of their principles. In the 9th. of *Anne,* the post-office act was made, which is a tax act, and which annually draws great sums of money from us. It is true that such an establishment would have been a great use, but then the regulation ought to have been made among ourselves. And it is a clear point to me that let it be ever so much to the advantage of this country, the parliament had no more right to interfere, than they have to form such an establishment in the electorate of *Hanover,* the King's *German* dominions.

They have prohibited us from purchasing any kind of goods or manufactures of *Europe* except from *Great-Britain,* and from selling any of our own goods or manufactures to foreigners, a few inconsiderable articles excepted, under pain of confiscation of vessel and cargo, and other heavy penalties. If they were indeed our sovereign lords and masters, as they pretend to be, such regulations would be in open violation of the laws of nature. But what adds to this grievance is, that in the trade between us they can set their own prices both on our and their commodities, which is in effect a tax and of which they have availed themselves: And moreover, duties are laid on divers enumerated articles on their import, for the express purpose of a revenue. They freely give and grant away our monies without our consent, under the specious pretence of defending, protecting, and securing *America,* and for the charges of the administration of justice here, when in fact, we are not indebted to them one farthing for any defence or protection from the first planting the country to this moment, but on the contrary, a balance is due to us for our exertion in the general cause; and besides, the advantages which have accrued to them in their trade with us hath put millions in their pockets. As to the administration of justice, no country in the world can boast of a purer one than this, the charges of which have been always chearfully provided for and paid without their interposition. There is reason to fear that if the *British* people undertake the business of the administration of justice amongst us it will be worse for us, as it may cause an introduction of their fashionable corruptions, whereby our pure streams of justice will be tainted and polluted. But in truth, by the administration of justice is meant the keeping up an outfit of officers to rob us of our money, to keep us down and humble, and to frighten us out of our undoubted rights.

And here it may be proper to mention the grievances of the custom house. Trade is the natural right of all men, but it is so restrained, perplexed and fettered that the officers of the customs, where there happens a judge of admiralty to their purpose, can seize and get condemned any vessel or goods they see fit. They will seize a vessel without shewing any other cause than their arbitrary will, and keep her a long time without exhibiting any libel, during all which time the owner knows not on what account she is seized, and when the trial comes on, he is utterly deprived of one by a jury, contrary to the usages among our fellow subjects in *Britain,* and perhaps all his fortune is determinable by a single, base, and infamous tool of a violent, corrupt, and wicked administration. Besides, these officers, who seem to be born with long claws, like eagles, exact most exorbitant fees, even from small coasting vessels, who pass along shore, and carry from plantation to plantation, bread, meat, firewood, and other necessaries, and without the intervention of which the country would labour under great inconveniencies, directly contrary to the true intent and meaning of one of the acts of trade, by which they pretend to govern themselves, such vessels by that act not being obliged to have so much as a register. It is well known that their design in getting into office is to enrich themselves by fleecing the merchants, and it is thought that very few have any regard to the interest of the Crown, which is only a pretence they make in order to accomplish their avaricious purposes.

The *common people* of *Great-Britain* very liberally give and grant away the property of the *Americans* without their consent, which if yielded to by us must fix us in the lowest bottom of slavery: For if they can take away one penny from us against our wills, they can take all. If they have such power over our properties they must have a pro-

portionable power over our persons; and from hence it will follow, that they can demand and take away our lives, whensoever it shall be agreeable to their sovereign wills and pleasure.

This claim of the commons to a sovereignty over us, is founded by them on their being the *Mother Country.* It is true that the first emigrations were from *England;* but upon the whole, more settlers have come from *Ireland, Germany,* and other parts of *Europe,* than from *England.* But if every soul came from *England,* it would not give them any title to sovereignty or even to superiority. One spot of ground will not be sufficient for all. As places fill up, mankind must disperse, and go where they can find a settlement; and being born free, must carry with them their freedom and independence on their fellows, go where they will. Would it not be thought strange if the commonalty of the *Massachusetts Bay* should require our obedience, because this colony was first settled from that dominion? By the best accounts, *Britain* was peopled from *Gaul,* now called *France,* wherefore according to their principles the parliaments of *France* have a right to govern them. If this doctrine of the maternal authority of one country over another be a little examined, it will be found to be the greatest absurdity that ever entered into the head of a politician.— In the time of *Nimrod,* all mankind lived together on the plains of *Shinar,* from whence they were dispersed at the building of *Babel.* From that dispersion all the empires, kingdoms, and states in the world are derived. That this doctrine may be fully exposed, let us suppose a few *Turks* or *Arabs* to be the present inhabitants of the plains of *Shinar,* and that they should demand the obedience of every kingdom, state, and country in the world, on account of their being the *Mother Country,* would it be one jot more ridiculous than the claim made by the parliament of *Great-Britain* to rule and reign over us? It is to be hoped that in future the words *Mother Country* will not be so frequently in our mouths, as they are only sounds without meaning.

Another grievance to be considered, is the alarming attempt of the people of *Old England* to restrain our manufactures. This country abounds in iron, yet there is an act of parliament, passed in the late King's reign to restrain us from manufacturing it into plates and rods by mill work, the last of which forms are absolutely necessary for the making of nails, the most useful article in a new country that can be conceived.—Be astonished all the world, that the people of a country who call themselves Christians and a civilized nation, should imagine that any principles of policy will be a sufficient excuse, for their permitting their fellow subjects on a distant part of the earth from making use of the blessings of the GOD of nature. There would be just as much reason to prohibit us from spinning our wool and flax, or making up our cloaths. Such prohibitions are infractions on the natural rights of men and are utterly void.

They have undertook, at the distance of three thousand miles, to regulate and limit our trade with the natives round about us, and from whom our lands were purchased—a trade which we opened ourselves, and which we ought to enjoy unrestricted. Further, we are prohibited by a people, who never set foot here from making any more purchases from the *Indians,* and even of settling those which we have made. The truth is, they intend to take into their own hands the whole of the back lands, witness the patents of immense tracts continually solicited and making out to their own people. The consequence will be shocking, and we ought to be greatly alarmed at such a procedure. All new countries ought to be free to settlers, but instead thereof every settler on these patent lands, and their descendants forever will be as compleat slaves to their landlords, as the common people of *Poland* are to their lords.

A standing army in time of profound peace is cantoned and quartered about the country to awe and intimidate the people.—Men of war and cutters are in every port, to the great distress of trade. In time of war we had no station ships, but were obliged to protect our trade, but now in time of full peace, when there are none to make us afraid we are visited with the plague of men of war, who commit all manner of disorders and irregularities; and behave in as hostile a manner as if they were open and declared enemies. In open defiance of civility, and the laws of *Great-Britain,* which they protest to be governed by, they violently seize and forcibly carry on board their ships the persons of the King's loving subjects. What think ye my brethren, of a military government in each town?—Unless we exert ourselves in opposition to their plan of subjecting us, we shall all have soldiers quartered about upon us, who will take the absolute command of our families. Centry boxes will be set up in all the streets and passages, and none of us will be able to pass without being brought too by a soldier with his fixed bayonet, and giving him a satisfactory account of ourselves and business. Perhaps it will be ordered that we shall put out fire and candle at eight of the clock at night, for fear of conspiracy. From which tearful calamities may the GOD of our fathers deliver us!

But after all, nothing which has yet happened ought to alarm us more than their suspending government here, because our parliaments or assemblies (who ought to be free) do not in their votes and resolutions please the populace of *Great Britain.* Suppose a parcel of mercenary troops in *England* should go to the parliament house, and order the members to vote as they directed under pain of dissolution, how much liberty would be left to them? In short, this dissolving of government upon such pretences as are formed, leaves not the semblance of liberty to the people. —We all ought to resent the treatment which the *Massachusetts Bay* hath had, as their case may soon come to be our own.

We are constantly belied and misrepresented in our gracious sovereign, by the officers who are sent hither, and others who are in the cabal of ruining this country. They are the persons who ought to be called rebels and traitors, as their conduct is superlatively injurious to the King and his faithful subjects.

Many other grievances might be enumerated, but the time would fail.—Upon the whole, the conduct of *Great-Britain* shews that they have formed a plan to subject us so effectually to their absolute commands, that even the freedom of speech will be taken from us. This plan they are executing as fast as they can; and almost every day produces some effect of it. We are insulted and menaced only for petitioning. Our prayers are prevented from reaching the royal ear, and our humble supplications to the throne are wickedly and maliciously represented as so many marks of faction and disloyalty. If they can once make us afraid to speak or write, their purpose will be finished.— Then farewel liberty.—Then those who were crouded in narrow limits in *England* will take possession of our extended and fertile fields, and set us to work for them.

Wherefore, dearly beloved, let us with unconquerable resolution maintain and defend that liberty wherewith GOD hath made us free. As the total subjection of a people arises generally from gradual encroachments, it will be our indispensable duty manfully to oppose every invasion of our rights in the beginning. Let nothing discourage us from this duty to ourselves and our posterity. Our fathers fought and found freedom in the wilderness; they cloathed themselves with the skins of wild beasts, and lodged under trees and among bushes; but in that state they were happy because they were free.—Should these our noble ancestors arise from the dead, and find their posterity trucking away that liberty, which they purchased at so dear a rate, for the mean trifles and frivolous merchandize of *Great Britain,* they would return to the grave with a holy indignation against us. In this day of danger let us exert every talent, and try every lawful mean, for the preservation of our liberties. It is thought that nothing will be of more avail, in our present distressed situation, than to stop our imports from *Britain.* By such a measure this little colony would save more than 173,000 pounds, lawful money, in one year, besides the advantages which would arise from the industry of the inhabitants being directed to the raising of wool and flax, and the establishment of manufactures. Such a measure might distress the manufacturers and poor people in *England,* but that would be their misfortune. Charity begins at home, and we ought primarily to consult our own interest; and besides, a little distress might bring the people of that country to a better temper, and a sense of their injustice towards us. No nation or people in the world ever made any figure, who were dependent on any other country for their food or cloathing. Let us then in justice to ourselves and our children, break off a trade so pernicious to our interest, and which is likely to swallow up both our estates and liberties.—A trade which hath nourished the people, in idleness and dissipation.—We cannot, we will not, betray the trust reposed in us by our ancestors, by giving up the least of our liberties.—We will be freemen, or we will die—we cannot endure the thought of be-

ing governed by subjects, and we make no doubt but the Almighty will look down upon our righteous contest with gracious approbation. We cannot bear the reflection that this country should be yielded to them who never had any hand in subduing it. Let our whole conduct shew that we know what is due to ourselves. Let us act prudently, peaceably, firmly, and jointly. Let us break off all trade and commerce with a people who would enslave us, as the only means to prevent our ruin. May we strengthen the hands of the civil government here, and have all our exertions tempered with the principles of peace and order, and may we by precept and example encourage the practice of virtue and morality, without which no people can be happy.

It only remains now, that we dedicate the *Tree of Liberty.*

We do therefore, in the name and behalf of all the true Sons *of* Liberty *in* America, Great-Britain, Ireland, Corsica, *or wheresoever they are dispersed throughout the world,* dedicate *and* solemnly devote *this tree, to be a* Tree *of* Liberty— *May all our councils and deliberations under it's venerable branches be guided by wisdom, and directed to the support and maintenance of that liberty, which our renowned forefathers sought out and found under trees and in the wilderness.—May it long flourish, and may the* Sons *of* Liberty *often repair hither, to confirm and strengthen each other.— When they look towards this sacred* Elm, *may they be penetrated with a sense of their duty to themselves, their country, and their posterity:— And may they, like the house of* David, *grow stronger and stronger, while their enemies, like the house of* Saul, *grow weaker and weaker.* Amen.

Letters from a Farmer in Pennsylvania, Letters V and IX

JOHN DICKINSON

1767–68

John Dickinson (1732–1808) was a lawyer, a member of the Pennsylvania Assembly, and a leading spokesman against parliamentary power in America. His argument, that Parliament's acts constituted dangerous innovations violating ancient chartered rights, became the centerpiece of colonial opposition to the Stamp Act and subsequent parliamentary conduct. His "Letters from a Farmer in Pennsylvania to the Inhabitants of the British Colonies" were highly influential and widely read throughout the colonies. Dickinson wrote the Resolutions of the Stamp Act Congress but would later refuse to sign the Declaration of Independence, on the grounds that independence was a radical step he could not approve.

Letter V

My dear Countrymen,

Perhaps the objection to the late act, imposing duties upon paper, etc. might have been safely rested on the argument drawn from the universal conduct of parliaments and ministers, from the first existence of these colonies, to the administration of Mr. *Greenville.*

What but the indisputable, the acknowledged exclusive right of the colonies to tax themselves, could be the reason, that in this long period of more than one hundred and fifty years, no statute was ever passed for the sole purpose of raising a revenue on the colonies? And how clear, how cogent must that reason be, to which every parliament, and every minister, for so long a time submitted, without a single attempt to innovate?

England, in part of that course of years, and *Great Britain,* in other parts, was engaged in several fierce and expensive wars; troubled with some tumultuous and bold parliaments; governed by many daring and wicked minis-

ters; yet none of them ever ventured to touch the *Palladium* of *American* liberty. Ambition, avarice, faction, tyranny, all revered it. Whenever it was necessary to raise money on the colonies, the requisitions of the crown were made, and dutifully complied with. The parliament, from time to time, regulated their trade, and that of the rest of the empire, to preserve their dependence, and the connection of the whole in good order.

The people of *Great Britain,* in support of their privileges, boast much of their antiquity. It is true they are ancient; yet it may well be questioned, if there is a single privilege of a *British* subject, supported by longer, more solemn, or more uninterrupted testimony, than the exclusive right of taxation in these colonies. The people of *Great Britain* consider that kingdom as the sovereign of these colonies, and would now annex to that sovereignty a prerogative never heard of before. How would they bear this, was the case their own? What would they think of a *new* prerogative claimed by the crown? We may guess what their conduct would be, from the transports of passion into which they fell about the late embargo, tho' laid to relieve the most emergent necessities of state, admitting of no delay; and for which there were numerous precedents. Let our liberties be treated with the same tenderness and it is all we desire.

Explicit as the conduct of parliaments, for so many ages, is, to prove that no money can be levied on these colonies by parliament, for the purpose of raising a revenue, yet it is not the only evidence in our favor.

Every one of the most material arguments against the legality of the *Stamp Act,* operates with equal force against the act now objected to; but as they are well known, it seems unnecessary to repeat them here.

This general one only shall be considered at present: That tho' these colonies are dependent on *Great Britain;*

and tho' she has a legal power to make laws for preserving that dependence; yet it is not necessary for this purpose, nor essential to the relation between a mother country and her colonies, as was eagerly contended by the advocates for the *Stamp Act,* that she should raise money on them without their consent.

Colonies were formerly planted by warlike nations, to keep their enemies in awe; to relieve their country, over-burdened with inhabitants; or to discharge a number of discontented and troublesome citizens. But in more modern ages, the spirit of violence being, in some measure, if the expression may be allowed, sheathed in commerce, colonies have been settled by the nations of *Europe* for the purposes of trade. These purposes were to be attained, by the colonies raising for their mother country those things which she did not produce herself; and by supplying themselves from her with things they wanted. These were the *national objects* in the commencement of our colonies, and have been uniformly so in their promotion.

To answer these grand purposes, perfect liberty was known to be necessary; all history proving, that trade and freedom are nearly related to each other. By a due regard to this wise and just plan, the infant colonies, exposed in the unknown climates and unexplored wildernesses of this new world, lived, grew, and flourished.

The parent country, with undeviating prudence and virtue, attentive to the first principles of colonization, drew to herself the benefits she might reasonably expect, and preserved to her children the blessings on which those benefits were founded. She made laws, obliging her colonies to carry to her all those products which she wanted for her own use; and all those raw materials which she chose herself to work up. Besides this restriction, she forbade them to procure *manufactures* from any other part of the globe, or even the *products* of *European* countries, which alone could rival her, without being first brought to her. In short, by a variety of laws, she regulated their trade in such a manner as she thought most conducive to their mutual advantage, and her own welfare. A power was reserved to the crown of *repealing* any laws that should be enacted: The *executive* authority of government was also lodged in the crown, and its representatives; and an *appeal* was secured to the crown from all judgments in the administration of justice.

For all these powers, established by the mother country

over the colonies; for all these immense emoluments derived by her from them; for all their difficulties and distresses in fixing themselves, what was the recompense made them? A communication of her rights in general, and particularly of that great one, the foundation of all the rest—that their property, acquired with so much pain and hazard, should be disposed of by none but themselves*—or, to use the beautiful and emphatic language of the sacred scriptures,† "that they should sit *every man* under his vine, and under his fig-tree, and NONE SHOULD MAKE THEM AFRAID."

Can any man of candor and knowledge deny, that these institutions form an affinity between *Great Britain* and her colonies, that sufficiently secures their dependence upon her? Or that for her to levy taxes upon them, is to reverse the nature of things? Or that she can pursue such a measure, without reducing them to a state of vassalage?

If any person cannot conceive the supremacy of *Great Britain* to exist, without the power of laying taxes to levy money upon us, the history of the colonies, and of *Great Britain,* since their settlement, will prove the contrary. He will there find the amazing advantages arising to her from them—the constant exercise of her supremacy—and their filial submission to it, without a single rebellion, or even the thought of one, from their first emigration to this moment—And all these things have happened, without one instance of *Great Britain's* laying taxes to levy money upon them.

How many *British*‡ *authors* have demonstrated that the

---

*"The power of *taxing themselves,* was the privilege of which the *English* were, with reason, *particularly jealous.*" (Hume's *Hist. of England*)
† Mic. iv. 4.
‡ It has been said in the House of Commons, when complaints have been made of the decay of trade to any part of *Europe,* "That such things were not worth regard, as *Great Britain* was possessed of colonies that could consume more of her manufactures than she was able to supply them with." "As the case now stands, we shall show that the plantations are a spring of *wealth* to this nation, that they work for us, that their TREASURE CENTERS ALL HERE, and that the laws have tied them fast enough to us; so that it must be through our own fault and mismanagement, if they become independent of *England.*" (Davenant *on the Plantation Trade*)
"It is better that the islands should be supplied from the Northern Colonies than from *England;* for this reason, the provisions we might send to *Barbados, Jamaica,* etc. would be *unimproved* product of the earth, as grain of all kinds, or such product where there is little got by the improvement, as malt, salt beef and pork; indeed the exportation of salt first thither would be more advantageous, but the goods which

present wealth, power and glory of their country, are founded upon these colonies? As constantly as streams tend to the ocean, have they been pouring the fruits of all their labors into their mother's lap. Good heaven! and shall a total oblivion of former tendernesses and blessings, be spread over the minds of a good and wise nation, by the

sordid arts of intriguing men, who, covering their selfish projects under pretenses of public good, first enrage their countrymen into a frenzy of passion, and then advance their own influence and interest, by gratifying the passion, which they themselves have basely excited.

Hitherto *Great Britain* has been contented with her

---

we send to the *Northern Colonies,* are such, whose *improvement* may be justly said, one with another, to be near *four fifths* of the value of the *whole commodity,* as apparel, household furniture, and many other things." (*Idem*)

"*New England* is the most prejudicial plantation to the kingdom of *England;* and yet, to do right to that most industrious *English* colony, I must confess, that though we lose by their unlimited trade with other foreign plantations, yet we are very great gainers by their direct trade to and from *Old England.* Our yearly exportations of *English* manufactures, malt and other goods, from hence thither, amounting, in my opinion, to *ten times* the value of what is imported from there; which calculation I do not make at random, but upon *mature consideration,* and, peradventure, upon *as much experience in this very trade,* as any other person will pretend to; and therefore, whenever reformation of our correspondency in trade with that people shall be thought on, it will, in my poor judgment, require GREAT TENDERNESS, and VERY SERIOUS CIRCUMSPECTION." (Sir Josiah Child's *Discourse on Trade*)

"Our plantations spend mostly our *English* manufactures, and those *of all sorts almost imaginable,* in *egregious quantities,* and employ nearly *two thirds of all our* English *shipping; so that we have more people in En-gland,* by reason of our plantations in *America.*" (*Idem*)

Sir Josiah Child says, in another part of his work, "That not more than fifty families are maintained in *England* by the refining of sugar." From whence, and from what *Davenant* says, it is plain, that the advantages here said to be derived from the plantations by *England,* must be meant chiefly of the continental colonies.

"I shall sum up my whole remarks in our *American* colonies, with this observation, that as they are a certain annual revenue of SEVERAL MILLIONS STERLING to their mother country, they ought carefully to be protected, duly encouraged, and at every opportunity that presents itself, improved for their increment and advantage, as every one they can possibly reap, must at last return to us with interest." (BEAWES'S Lex Merc. Red.)

"We may safely advance, that our trade and navigation are greatly increased by our colonies, and that they really are a source of treasure and naval power to this kingdom, since THEY WORK FOR US, AND THEIR TREASURE CENTERS HERE. Before their settlement, our manufactures were few, and those but indifferent; the number of *English* merchants very small, and the whole shipping of the nation much inferior to what now belongs to the Northern Colonies only. *These are certain facts.* But since their establishment, our condition has altered for the better, almost to a degree beyond credibility—Our MANUFACTURES are prodigiously increased, chiefly by the demand for them in the plantations, where they AT LEAST TAKE OFF ONE HALF, and supply us with many valuable commodities for exportation, which is as great an emolument to the mother kingdom, as to the plantations themselves." (POSTLETHWAYT's *Univ. Dict. of Trade and Commerce*)

"Most of the nations of *Europe* have interfered with us, more or less,

in divers of our staple manufactures, within half a century, not only in our woolen, but in our lead and tin manufactures, as well as our fisheries." (POSTLETHWAYT, *ibid.*)

"The inhabitants of our colonies, by carrying on a trade with their *foreign neighbors,* do not only occasion a *greater quantity of the goods and merchandises* of Europe *being sent from hence to them,* and a greater quantity of the product of America to be sent from them hither, *which would otherwise be carried from, and brought* to Europe *by foreigners,* but an increase of the seamen and navigation in those parts, which is of great strength and security, as well as of great advantage to our plantations in general. And though *some of our colonies* are not only for preventing the *importations of all goods of the same species they produce,* but suffer particular planters to *keep great runs of land in their possession uncultivated,* with design to prevent new settlements, whereby they imagine the prices of their commodities may be affected; yet if it be considered, that the markets of *Great Britain* depend on the markets of ALL *Europe* in general, and that the *European* markets in *general* depend on the proportion between the *annual consumption* and the *whole quantity* of each species *annually produced* by ALL *nations;* it must follow, that whether we or foreigners are the producers, carriers, importers and exporters of *American* produce, yet their respective prices in *each colony* (the difference of freight, customs and importations considered) will always bear proportion to the *general consumption* of the *whole quantity* of each sort, *produced in all colonies,* and *in all parts,* allowing only for the usual contingencies that trade and commerce, agriculture and manufacturers, are liable to in all countries." (POSTLETHWAYT, *ibid.*)

"It is certain, that from the very time *Sir Walter Raleigh,* the father of our *English* colonies, and his associates, first projected these establishments, there have been persons who have found an interest, in *misrepresenting,* or lessening the value of them—The attempts were called *chimerical* and dangerous. Afterwards many malignant suggestions were made about sacrificing so many *Englishmen* to the obstinate desire of settling colonies in countries which then produced very little advantage. But as these difficulties were gradually surmounted, those complaints vanished. No sooner were *these lamentations* over, but *others* arose in their stead; when it could be no longer said, that the colonies were *useless,* it was alleged that they were not *useful enough* to their mother country; that while we were loaded with taxes, they were absolutely free; that the *planters* lived like *princes,* while the inhabitants of *England* labored hard for a tolerable subsistence." (POSTLETHWAYT, *ibid.*)

"Before the settlement of these colonies," says *Postlethwayt,* "our manufactures were few, and those but indifferent. In those days we had not only our naval stores, but our ships from our neighbors. *Germany* furnished us with all things of metal, even to nails. Wine, paper, linens, and a thousand other things, came from *France. Portugal* supplied us with sugar; all the products of *America* were poured into us from *Spain;* and the *Venetians* and *Genoese* retailed to us the commodities of the *East Indies,* at their own price."

prosperity. Moderation has been the rule of her conduct. But now, a general humane people, that so often has protected the liberty of strangers, is inflamed into an attempt to tear a privilege from her own children, which, if executed, must, in their opinion, sink them into slaves: AND FOR WHAT? For a pernicious power, not necessary to her, as her own experience may convince her; but horribly dreadful and detestable to them.

It seems extremely probable, that when cool, dispassionate posterity, shall consider the affectionate intercourse, the reciprocal benefits, and the unsuspecting confidence, that have subsisted between these colonies and their parent country, for such a length of time, they will execrate, with the bitterest curses, the infamous memory of those men, whose pestilential ambition unnecessarily, wantonly, cruelly, first opened the forces of civil discord between them; first turned their love into jealousy; and first taught these provinces, filled with grief and anxiety, to inquire—

> *Mens ubi materna est?*
> Where is maternal affection?
> *A Farmer*

Letter IX

My dear Countrymen,

I have made some observations on the PURPOSES for which money is to be levied upon us by the late act of parliament. I shall now offer to your consideration some further reflections on that subject: And, unless I am greatly mistaken, if these purposes are accomplished according to the *expressed* intention of the act, they will be found effectually to *supersede* that authority in our respective assemblies, which is essential to liberty. The question is not,

---

"If it be asked whether foreigners, for what goods they take of us, do not pay on *that consumption* a great portion of our taxes? It is admitted they do." (POSTLETHWAYT'S *Great Britain's True System*)

"If we are afraid that one day or other the colonies will revolt, and set up for themselves, as some seem to apprehend, let us not *drive* them to a *necessity* to *feel* themselves independent of us; as they *will* do, the moment they perceive that THEY CAN BE SUPPLIED WITH ALL THINGS FROM WITHIN THEMSELVES, and do not need our assistance. If we would keep them still dependent upon their mother country, and, in some respects, *subservient* to her *views* and welfare; let us make it their INTEREST always to be so." (TUCKER *on Trade*)

"Our colonies, while they have *English* blood in their veins, and have relations in *England,* and WHILE THEY CAN GET BY TRADING WITH US, the *stronger* and *greater* they grow, the *more* this *crown* and *kingdom* will *get* by them; and nothing but such an arbitrary power as shall make them desperate, can bring them to rebel." (DAVENANT *on the Plantation Trade*)

"The Northern colonies are not upon the same footing as those of the South; and having a worse soil to improve, they must find the recompense some other way, which only can be in property and dominion: Upon which score, any INNOVATIONS in the form of government there, should be cautiously examined, for fear of entering upon measures, by which the industry of the inhabitants be quite discouraged. 'Tis ALWAYS UNFORTUNATE for a people, either by CONSENT, or upon COMPULSION, to depart from their PRIMITIVE INSTITUTIONS, and THOSE FUNDAMENTALS, by which they were FIRST UNITED TOGETHER." (*Idem*) The most effectual way of *uniting* the colonies, is to make it their common interest to oppose the designs and attempts of *Great Britain.*

"All wise states will well consider how to preserve the advantages arising from colonies, and avoid the evils. And I conceive that there can be but TWO ways in nature to hinder them from throwing off their dependence; *one,* to keep it out of their *power;* and the *other,* out of their *will.* The *first* must be by *force;* and the *latter,* by *using them well,* and keeping them employed in such productions, and making such manufactures, as will support themselves and their families comfortably, *and procure them wealth too,* and at least not prejudice their mother country.

"*Force* can never be used effectually to answer the end, *without destroying the colonies themselves.* Liberty and encouragement are necessary to carry people thither, and to keep them together when they are there; and violence will hinder both. Any body of troops, considerable enough to awe them, and keep them in subjection, under the direction too of a needy governor, often sent thither to make his fortune, and at such a distance from any application for redress, will soon put an end to all planting, and leave the country to the soldiers alone, and if it did not, *would eat up all the profit of the colony.* For this reason, arbitrary countries have not been equally successful in planting colonies with free ones; and what they have done in that kind, has either been by force, at a vast expense, or *by departing from the nature of their government,* and *giving such privileges to planters as were denied to their other subjects.* And I dare say, that a few prudent laws, and a little prudent conduct, would soon give us far the greatest share of the riches of all *America,* perhaps drive many of the other nations out of it, or into our colonies for shelter.

"There are *so many exigencies* in all states, *so many foreign wars,* and *domestic disturbances,* that these colonies CAN NEVER WANT OPPORTUNITIES, if they watch for them, *to do what they shall find their interest to do;* and therefore we ought to take all the precautions in our power, that it shall never be *their interest* to act against that of their native country; an evil which can no other-wise be averted, than by keeping them *fully employed* in such trades *as will increase their own* as well as our wealth; for it is much to be feared, if we do not find employment for them, they may find it for us; the interest of the mother country, is always to keep them dependent, and so employed; and it requires all her addresses to do it; and it is certainly more *easily* and *effectually* done by *gentle* and *insensible* methods, than by *power* alone." (CATO's *Letters*)

whether some branches shall be lopped off—The axe is laid to the root of the tree; and the whole body must infallibly perish, if we remain idle spectators of the work.

No free people ever existed, or can ever exist, without keeping, to use a common, but strong expression, "the purse strings," in their own hands. Where this is the case, *they* have a *constitutional check* upon the administration, which may thereby be brought into order *without violence:* But where such a power is not lodged in the *people,* oppression proceeds uncontrolled in its career, till the governed, transported into rage, seek redress in the midst of blood and confusion.

The elegant and ingenious Mr. *Hume,* speaking of the *Anglo-Norman* government, says—"Princes and Ministers were too ignorant, to be themselves sensible of the advantage attending an equitable administration, and there was no established council or *assembly,* WHICH COULD PROTECT THE PEOPLE, and BY WITHDRAWING SUPPLIES, regularly and PEACEABLY admonish the king of his duty, and ENSURE THE EXECUTION OF THE LAWS."

Thus this great man, whose political reflections are so much admired, makes *this power* one of the foundations of liberty.

The *English* history abounds with instances, proving that *this* is the proper and successful way to obtain redress to grievances. How often have kings and ministers endeavored to throw off this legal curb upon them, by attempting to raise money by a variety of inventions, under pretense of law, without having recourse to parliament? And how often have they been brought to reason, and peaceably obliged to do justice, by the exertion of this constitutional authority of the people, vested in their representatives?

The inhabitants of these colonies have, on numberless occasions, reaped the benefit of this authority *lodged in their assemblies.*

It has been for a long time, and now is, a constant instruction to all governors, *to obtain* a PERMANENT *support for the offices of government.* But as the author of "the administration of the colonies" says, "this order of the crown is generally, if not universally, rejected by the legislatures of the colonies."

They perfectly know *how much* their grievances would be regarded, if they had *no other* method of engaging attention, than by *complaining.* Those who rule, are extremely apt to think well of the constructions made by themselves in support of their own power. *These* are frequently erroneous, and pernicious to those they govern. Dry remonstrances, to show that such constructions are wrong and oppressive, carry very little weight with them, in the opinion of persons who gratify their own inclinations in making these constructions. *They* CANNOT understand the reasoning that opposes *their* power and desires. But let it be made *their interest* to understand such reasoning—and a *wonderful light* is instantly thrown upon the matter; and then, rejected remonstrances become as clear as "proofs of holy writ."*

The three most important articles that our assemblies, or any legislatures can provide for, are, First—the defense of the society: Secondly—the administration of justice: And thirdly—the support of civil government.

Nothing can properly regulate the expense of making provision for these occasions, but the *necessities* of the society; its *abilities;* the *conveniency* of the modes of levying money in it; the *manner* in which the laws have been executed; and the *conduct* of the officers of government: *All which* are circumstances, that *cannot* possibly be properly *known,* but by the society itself; or if they should be known, *will not* probably be properly *considered* but by that society.

If money be raised upon us by *others,* without our consent, for our "defense," those who are the judges in *levying* it, must also be the judges in *applying* it. Of consequence the money *said* to be taken from us for our defense, *may be employed* to our injury. We may be chained in by a line of fortifications—obliged to pay for the building and maintaining them—and be told, that they are for our defense. With what face can we dispute the fact, after having granted that those who *apply* the money, had a right to *levy* it? For surely, it is much easier for their wisdom to understand how to apply it in the best manner, than how to levy it in the best manner. Besides, the *right of levying* is of infinitely more consequence than *that of applying.* The people of *England,* who would burst out into a fury, if the crown should attempt to *levy* money by its own authority, have always assigned to the crown the *application* of money.

As to "the administration of justice"—the judges ought, in a well regulated state, to be equally independent of the executive and legislative powers. Thus in *England,* judges hold their commissions from the crown "*during good be-*

* Shakespeare.

havior," and have salaries, suitable to their dignity, *settled* on them by parliament. The purity of the courts of law since this establishment, is a proof of the wisdom with which it was made.

But in these colonies, how fruitless has been every attempt to have the judges appointed "*during good behavior*"? Yet whoever considers the matter will soon perceive, that *such commissions* are beyond all comparison more necessary in these colonies, than they were in *England.*

The chief danger to the subject *there,* arose from the arbitrary *designs of the crown;* but *here,* the time may come, when we may have to contend with the *designs of the crown, and of a mighty kingdom.* What then must be our chance, when the laws of life and death are to be spoken by judges totally dependent on *that crown,* and *that kingdom*—sent over perhaps *from thence*—filled with *British prejudices* —and *backed by a* STANDING *army*—supported out of OUR OWN pockets, to "assert and maintain" OUR OWN "dependence and obedience"?

But supposing that through the extreme lenity that will prevail in the government *through all future ages,* these colonies will never behold any thing like the campaign of chief justice *Jeffereys,* yet what innumerable acts of injustice may be committed, and how fatally may the principles of liberty be sapped, by a succession of judges *utterly independent of the people?* Before such judges, the supple wretches, who cheerfully join in avowing sentiments inconsistent with freedom, will always meet with smiles; while the honest and brave men, who disdain to sacrifice their native land to their own advantage, but on every occasion boldly vindicate her cause, will constantly be regarded with frowns.

There are two other considerations relating to this head, that deserve the most serious attention.

By the late act, the officers of the customs are "impowered to enter into any HOUSE, warehouse, shop, cellar, or other place, in the *British* colonies or plantations in *America,* to search for or seize prohibited or unaccustomed goods," etc. on "writs granted by the superior or supreme court of justice, having jurisdiction within such colony or plantation respectively."

If we only reflect, that the judges of these courts are to be *during pleasure*—that they are to have "*adequate provision*" made for them, which is to continue *during their complaisant behavior*—that they may be *strangers* to these colonies—what an engine of oppression may this authority be in such hands?

I am well aware, that writs of this kind may be granted at home, under the seal of the court of exchequer: But I know also, that the greatest asserters of the rights of *Englishmen* have always strenuously contended, that *such a power* was dangerous to freedom, and expressly contrary to the common law, which ever regarded a man's *house* as his castle, or a place of perfect security.

If such power was in the least degree dangerous *there,* it must be utterly destructive to liberty *here.* For the people there have two securities against the undue exercise of this power by the crown, which are wanting with us, if the late act takes place. In the first place, if any injustice is done *there,* the person injured may bring his action against the offender, and have it tried before INDEPENDENT JUDGES, who are NO PARTIES IN COMMITTING THE INJURY. *Here* he must have it tried before DEPENDENT JUDGES, being the men WHO GRANTED THE WRIT.*

To say, that the cause is to be tried by a jury, can never reconcile men who have any idea of freedom, to *such a power.* For we know that sheriffs in almost every colony on this continent, are totally dependent on the crown; and packing of juries has been frequently practised even in the capital of the *British* empire. Even if juries are well inclined, we have too many instances of the influence of overbearing unjust judges upon them. The brave and wise men who accomplished the revolution, thought the *independency of judges* essential to freedom.

The other security which the people have at home, but which we shall want here, is this.

If this power is abused *there,* the parliament, the grand resource of the oppressed people, is ready to afford relief. Redress of grievances must precede grants of money. But what regard can *we* expect to have paid to our assemblies, when they will not hold even the puny privilege of *French* parliaments—that of registering, before they are put in execution, the edicts that take away our money.

The second consideration above hinted at, is this. There is a confusion in our laws, that is quite unknown in *Great Britain.* As this cannot be described in a more clear or exact manner, than has been done by the ingenious author of the history of *New York,* I beg leave to use his words. "The

---

*The writs for searching houses in *England,* are to be granted "under the seal of the court of exchequer," according to the statute—and that seal is kept by the chancellor of the exchequer. 4th Inst. p. 104.

state of our laws opens a door to much controversy. The *uncertainty,* with respect to them, RENDERS PROPERTY PRECARIOUS, and GREATLY EXPOSES US TO THE ARBITRARY DECISION OF BAD JUDGES. The common law of *England* is generally received, together with such statutes as were enacted before we had a legislature of our own; but our COURTS EXERCISE A SOVEREIGN AUTHORITY, in determining *what parts of the common and statute law* ought to be extended: For it must be admitted, that the *difference of circumstances* necessarily requires us, in some cases, *to* REJECT *the determination* of both. In many instances, they have also extended even acts of parliament, passed since we had a distinct legislature, *which is greatly adding to our confusion.* The practice of our courts is no less *uncertain than* the law. Some of the *English* rules are adopted, others rejected. Two things therefore seem to be ABSOLUTELY NECESSARY for the PUBLIC SECURITY. First, the passing an act for settling the extent of the *English* laws. Secondly, that the courts ordain a general set of rules for the regulation of the practice."

How easy it will be, under this "state of our laws," for an artful judge, to act in the most arbitrary manner, and yet cover his conduct under specious pretences; and how difficult it will be for the injured people to obtain relief, may be readily perceived. We may take a voyage of 3000 miles to complain; and after the trouble and hazard we have undergone, we may be told, that the collection of the revenue, and maintenance of the prerogative, must not be discouraged—and if the misbehavior is so gross as to admit of no justification, it may be said, that it was an error in judgment only, arising from the confusion of our laws, and the zeal of the King's servants to do their duty.

If the commissions of judges are *during the pleasure of the crown,* yet if their salaries are *during the pleasure of the people,* there will be *some check* upon their conduct. Few men will consent to draw on themselves the hatred and contempt of those among whom they live, for the empty honor of being judges. It is the sordid love of gain, that tempts men to turn their backs on virtue, and pay their homage where they ought not.

As to the third particular, "the support of civil government"— few words will be sufficient. Every man of the least understanding must know, that the executive power may be exercised in a manner so disagreeable and harassing to the people, that it is absolutely requisite, that *they* should be enabled by the gentlest method which human

policy has yet been ingenious enough to invent, that is, by *shutting their hands,* to "ADMONISH" (as Mr. *Hume* says) certain persons "OF THEIR DUTY."

What shall we now think when, upon looking into the late act, we find the assemblies of these provinces thereby stripped of their authority *on these several heads?* The *declared* intention of the act is, "that a revenue should be raised IN HIS MAJESTY'S DOMINIONS IN AMERICA, for making a more certain and adequate provision *for defraying the charge of* THE ADMINISTRATION OF JUSTICE, and *the support of* CIVIL GOVERNMENT in such provinces where it shall be found necessary, and *toward further defraying the expenses of* DEFENDING, PROTECTING AND SECURING THE SAID DOMINIONS."

Let the reader pause here one moment—and reflect—whether the colony in which *he* lives, has not made such "certain and adequate provision" *for these purposes,* as is *by the colony judged suitable to its abilities, and all other circumstances.* Then let him reflect—whether if this act takes place, money is not to be raised on *that* colony *without its consent,* to make "provision" *for these purposes, which it does not judge to be suitable to its abilities, and all other circumstances.* Lastly, let him reflect—whether the people of that country are not in a state of the most abject slavery, *whose property may be taken from them* under the notion of right, *when they have refused to give it.*

For my part, I think I have good reason for vindicating the honor of the assemblies on this continent, by publicly asserting, that THEY *have made as "certain and adequate provision" for the purposes above mentioned, as they ought to have made,* and that it should not be presumed, that they will not do it hereafter. Why then should *these most important trusts* be wrested out of their hands? Why should they not now be permitted to enjoy that authority, which they have exercised from the first settlement of these colonies? Why should they be scandalized by this innovation, when their respective provinces are now, and will be, for several years, laboring under loads of debt, imposed on them for the very purpose now spoken of? Why should all the inhabitants of these colonies be, with the utmost indignity, treated as a herd of despicable stupid wretches, so utterly void of common sense, that they will not even make "adequate provision" for the "administration of justice, and the support of civil government" among them, or for their own "defense"—though without such "provision" every people must inevitably be overwhelmed with anarchy and destruction? Is it possible to form an idea of a slavery more *complete,* more *miserable,* more *disgraceful,* than that of a people, where *justice is administered, government exercised,* and a *standing army maintained,* AT THE EXPENSE OF THE PEOPLE, and yet WITHOUT THE LEAST DEPENDENCE UPON THEM? If we can find no relief from this infamous situation, it will be fortunate for us, if Mr. *Greenville,* setting his fertile fancy again at work, can, as by one exertion of it he has stripped us of our *property* and *liberty,* by another deprive us of so much of our *understanding;* that, unconscious of what we *have been* or *are,* and ungoaded by tormenting reflections, we may bow down our necks, with all the stupid serenity of servitude, to any drudgery, which our lords and masters shall please to command.

When the charges of the "administration of justice," the "support of civil government," and the "expenses of defending, protecting and securing" us, are provided for, I should be glad to know, upon *what occasions* the crown will ever call our assemblies together? Some few of them may meet of their own accord, by virtue of their charters. But what will they have to do, when they are met? To what shadows will they be reduced? The men, whose deliberations heretofore had an influence on every matter relating to the *liberty* and *happiness* of themselves and their constituents, and whose authority in domestic affairs at least, might well be compared to that of *Roman* senators, will *now* find their deliberations of no more consequence, than those of *constables.* They may *perhaps* be allowed to make laws *for the yoking of hogs,* or *pounding of stray cattle.* Their influence will hardly be permitted to extend *so high,* as the *keeping roads in repair,* as *that business* may more properly be executed by those who receive the public cash.

One most memorable example in history is so applicable to the point now insisted on, that it will form a just conclusion of the observations that have been made.

Spain was once *free.* Their *cortes* resembled our parliaments. No *money* could be raised on the subject, *without their consent.* One of their Kings having received a grant from them, to maintain a war against the *Moors,* desired, that if the sum which they had given, should not be sufficient, he might be allowed, *for that emergency only,* to raise more money *without assembling the Cortes.* The request was violently opposed by the best and wisest men in the assembly. It was, however, complied with by the votes of a majority; and this single concession was a PRECEDENT for other concessions of the like kind, until at last the crown obtained a general power of raising money, in cases of necessity. From that period the *Cortes* ceased to be *useful*—the *people* ceased to be *free.*

Venienti occurrite morbo.
Oppose a disease at its beginning.
A Farmer

Declaration and Resolves of the First Continental Congress

October 14, 1774

Americans responded to the Townshend Acts as they had responded to the Stamp Act—with declarations of grievances and through boycotts and occasional violence. But Parliament's reaction was significantly harsher than it had been during the Stamp Act crisis, particularly after the Boston Tea Party in 1773 resulted in the destruction of tea belonging to the East India Company. That year, Parliament passed the Coercive Acts, closing ports, extending military justice, closing local legislatures, and giving increased power to royal authorities acting in the colonies. Colonists responded, in turn, through more violence and through the calling of a Continental Congress, much like the Stamp Act Congress, bringing various colonial representatives together to express opposition and plan common strategies. The Declaration and Resolves of this Congress states colonial grievances and calls for a restoration of comity through repeal of Parliament's arbitrary actions.

Declaration and Resolves of the First Continental Congress

Whereas, since the close of the last war, the British parliament, claiming a power of right to bind the people of America by statute in all cases whatsoever, hath, in some acts expressly imposed taxes on them, and in others, under various pretenses, but in fact for the purpose of raising a revenue, hath imposed rates and duties payable in these colonies, established a board of commissioners with unconstitutional powers, and extended the jurisdiction of courts of Admiralty not only for collecting the said duties, but for the trial of causes merely arising within the body of a county.

And whereas, in consequence of other statutes, judges who before held only estates at will in their offices, have been made dependent on the Crown alone for their salaries, and standing armies kept in times of peace. And it has lately been resolved in Parliament, that by force of a statute made in the thirty-fifth year of the reign of King Henry the Eighth, colonists may be transported to England, and tried there upon accusations for treasons and misprisions, or concealments of treasons committed in the colonies; and by a late statute, such trials have been directed in cases therein mentioned:

And whereas, in the last session of Parliament, three statutes were made . . . [the Boston Port Act, the Massachusetts Government Act, the Administration of Justice Act], and another statute was then made [the Quebec Act] . . . All which statutes are impolitic, unjust, and cruel, as well as unconstitutional, and most dangerous and destructive of American rights.

And whereas, Assemblies have been frequently dissolved, contrary to the rights of the people, when they attempted to deliberate on grievances; and their dutiful, humble, loyal, & reasonable petitions to the crown for redress, have been repeatedly treated with contempt, by His Majesty's ministers of state:

The good people of the several Colonies of New-hampshire, Massachusetts-bay, Rhode-island and Providence plantations, Connecticut, New-York, New-Jersey, Pennsylvania, Newcastle, Kent and Sussex on Delaware, Maryland, Virginia, North-Carolina, and South-Carolina, justly alarmed at these arbitrary proceedings of parliament and administration, have severally elected, constituted, and appointed deputies to meet, and sit in general Congress, in the city of Philadelphia, in order to obtain such establishment, as that their religion, laws, and liberties, may not be subverted:

Whereupon the deputies so appointed being now assembled, in a full and free representation of these Colonies, taking into their most serious consideration the best means of attaining the ends aforesaid, do in the first place, as Englishmen their ancestors in like cases have usually done, for asserting and vindicating their rights and liberties, declare,

That the inhabitants of the English Colonies in North America, by the immutable laws of nature, the principles of the English constitution, and the several charters or compacts, have the following Rights:

Resolved, N. C. D.

1. That they are entitled to life, liberty, and property, & they have never ceded to any sovereign power whatever, a right to dispose of either without their consent.

2. That our ancestors, who first settled these colonies, were at the time of their emigration from the mother country, entitled to all the rights, liberties, and immunities of free and natural-born subjects within the realm of England.

3. That by such emigration they by no means forfeited, surrendered, or lost any of those rights, but that they were, and their descendants now are entitled to the exercise and enjoyment of all such of them, as their local and other circumstances enable them to exercise and enjoy.

4. That the foundation of English liberty, and of all free government, is a right in the people to participate in their legislative council: and as the English colonists are not represented, and from their local and other circumstances, cannot properly be represented in the British parliament, they are entitled to a free and exclusive power of legislation in their several provincial legislatures, where their right of representation can alone be preserved, in all cases of taxation and internal polity, subject only to the negative of their sovereign, in such manner as has been heretofore used and accustomed. But, from the necessity of the case, and a regard to the mutual interest of both countries, we cheerfully consent to the operation of such acts of the British parliament, as are bona fide restrained to the regulation of our external commerce, for the purpose of securing the commercial advantages of the whole empire to the mother country, and the commercial benefits of its respective members excluding every idea of taxation, internal or external, for raising a revenue on the subjects in America without their consent.

5. That the respective colonies are entitled to the common law of England, and more especially to the great and inestimable privilege of being tried by their peers of the vicinage, according to the course of that law.

6. That they are entitled to the benefit of such of the English statutes, as existed at the time of their colonization; and which they have, by experience, respectively found to be applicable to their several local and other circumstances.

7. That these, his majesty's colonies, are likewise entitled to all the immunities and privileges granted and confirmed to them by royal charters, or secured by their several codes of provincial laws.

8. That they have a right peaceably to assemble, consider of their grievances, and petition the King; and that all prosecutions, prohibitory proclamations, and commitments for the same, are illegal.

9. That the keeping a Standing army in these colonies, in times of peace, without the consent of the legislature of that colony in which such army is kept, is against law.

10. It is indispensably necessary to good government, and rendered essential by the English constitution, that the constituent branches of the legislature be independent of each other; that, therefore, the exercise of legislative power in several colonies, by a council appointed during pleasure, by the crown, is unconstitutional, dangerous, and destructive to the freedom of American legislation.

All and each of which the aforesaid deputies, in behalf of themselves, and their constituents, do claim, demand, and insist on, as their indubitable rights and liberties; which cannot be legally taken from them, altered or abridged by any power whatever, without their own consent, by their representatives in their several provincial legislatures.

In the course of our inquiry, we find many infringements and violations of the foregoing rights, which, from an ardent desire that harmony and mutual intercourse of affection and interest may be restored, we pass over for the present, and proceed to state such acts and measures as have been adopted since the last war, which demonstrate a system formed to enslave America.

Resolved, That the following acts of Parliament are infringements and violations of the rights of the colonists; and that the repeal of them is essentially necessary, in order to restore harmony between Great Britain and the American colonies, . . . viz.:

The several Acts of 4 Geo. 3, ch. 15 & ch. 34, 5 Geo. 3, ch. 25; 6 Geo. 3, ch. 52; 7 Geo. 3, ch. 41 & 46; 8 Geo. 3, ch. 22; which impose duties for the purpose of raising a revenue in America, extend the powers of the admiralty courts beyond their ancient limits, deprive the American subject of trial by jury, authorize the judges' certificate to indemnify the prosecutor from damages that he might otherwise be liable to, requiring oppressive security from a claimant of ships and goods seized before he shall be allowed to defend his property; and are subversive of American rights.

Also the 12 Geo. 3, ch. 24, entitled "An act for the better preserving his Majesty's dockyards, magazines, ships, ammunition, and stores," which declares a new offense in America, and deprives the American subject of a constitutional trial by jury of the vicinage, by authorizing the trial of any person charged with the committing any offense described in the said act, out of the realm, to be indicted and tried for the same in any shire or county within the realm.

Also the three acts passed in the last session of parliament, for stopping the port and blocking up the harbour of Boston, for altering the charter & government of the Massachusetts-bay, and that which is entitled "An Act for the better administration of Justice," &c.

Also the act passed the same session for establishing the Roman Catholic Religion in the province of Quebec, abolishing the equitable system of English laws, and erecting a tyranny there, to the great danger, from so great a dissimilarity of Religion, law, and government, of the neighboring British colonies. . . .

Also the act passed the same session for the better providing suitable quarters for officers and soldiers in his Majesty's service in North America.

Also, that the keeping a standing army in several of these colonies, in time of peace, without the consent of the legislature of that colony in which the army is kept, is against law.

To these grievous acts and measures Americans cannot submit, but in hopes that their fellow subjects in Great-Britain will, on a revision of them, restore us to that state in which both countries found happiness and prosperity, we have for the present only resolved to pursue the following peaceable measures: 1st. To enter into a non-importation, non-consumption, and non-exportation agreement or association. 2. To prepare an address to the people of Great-Britain, and a memorial to the inhabitants of British America, & 3. To prepare a loyal address to his Majesty, agreeable to resolutions already entered into.

Virginia Bill of Rights

June 12, 1776

Opposition to Britain in the colonial legislatures was intense. The Bill of Rights passed by the Virginia House of Burgesses presents arguments foreshadowing the soon-to-be-issued Declaration of Independence, asserting colonists' equality with all other British subjects and calling on Parliament to recognize their inalienable rights.

Virginia Bill of Rights

A Declaration of Rights

Made by the Representatives of the good People of Virginia, assembled in full and free Convention, which rights to pertain to them and their posterity as the basis and foundation of government.

I. That all men are by nature equally free and independent, and have certain inherent rights, of which, when they enter into a state of society, they cannot by any compact, deprive or divest their posterity; namely, the enjoyment of life and liberty with the means of acquiring and possessing property, and pursuing and obtaining happiness and safety.

II. That all power is vested in, and consequently derived from, the people; that magistrates are their trustees and servants, and at all times amendable to them.

III. That government is, or ought to be, instituted for the common benefit, protection and security of the people, nation, or community; of all the various modes and forms of government, that is best which is capable of producing the greatest degree of happiness and safety, and is most effectually secured against the danger of maladministration; and that, when a government shall be found inadequate or contrary to these purposes, a majority of the community hath an indubitable, unalienable and indefeasible right to reform, alter or abolish it, in such manner as shall be judged most conducive to the public weal.

IV. That no man, or set of men, are entitled to exclusive or separate emoluments or privileges from the community but in consideration of public services, which not being descendible, neither ought the offices of magistrate, legislator, or judge to be hereditary.

V. That the legislative, executive and judicial powers should be separate and distinct; and that the members thereof may be restrained from oppression, by feeling and participating the burdens of the people, they should, at fixed periods, be reduced to a private station, return into that body from which they were originally taken, and the vacancies be supplied by frequent, certain and regular elections, in which all, or any part of the former members to be again eligible or ineligible, as the laws shall direct.

VI. That all elections ought to be free, and that all men having sufficient evidence of permanent common interest with, and attachment to the community have the right of suffrage, and cannot be taxed, or deprived of their property for public uses, without their own consent, or that of their representatives so elected, nor bound by any law to which they have not in like manner assented, for the public good.

VII. That all power of suspending laws, or the execution of laws, by any authority, without consent of the representatives of the people, is injurious to their rights, and ought not to be exercised.

VIII. That in all capital or criminal prosecutions, a man hath a right to demand the cause and nature of his accusation, to be confronted with the accusers and witnesses, to call for evidence in his favor, and to speedy trial by an impartial jury of twelve men of his vicinage, without whose unanimous consent he cannot be found guilty; nor can he be compelled to give evidence against himself; that no man be deprived of his liberty, except by the law of the land or the judgment of his peers.

IX. That excessive bail ought not to be required, nor excessive fines imposed, nor cruel and unusual punishments inflicted.

X. That general warrants, whereby an officer or messenger may be commanded to search suspected places without evidence of a fact committed, or to seize any person or persons not named, or whose offence is not particularly described and supported by evidence, are grievous and oppressive, and ought not to be granted.

XI. That in controversies respecting property, and in suits between man and man, the ancient trial by jury of twelve men is preferable to any other, and ought to be held sacred.

XII. That the freedom of the press is one of the great bulwarks of liberty, and can never be restrained but by despotic governments.

XIII. That a well regulated militia, composed of the body of the people, trained to arms, is the proper, natural, and safe defence of a free State; that standing armies in time of peace should be avoided as dangerous to liberty; and that in all cases the military should be under strict subordination to, and governed by, the civil power.

XIV. That the people have a right to uniform government; and therefore, that no government separate from or independent of the government of Virginia, ought to be erected or established within the limits thereof.

XV. That no free government, or the blessing of liberty, can be preserved to any people, but by a firm adherence to justice, moderation, temperance, frugality and virtue, and by a frequent recurrence to fundamental principles.

XVI. That religion, or the duty which we owe to our Creator, and the manner of discharging it, can be directed only by reason and conviction, not by force or violence; and therefore all men are equally entitled to the free exercise of religion, according to the dictates of conscience; and that it is the duty of all to practice Christian forbearance, love and charity towards each other.

On Civil Liberty, Passive Obedience, and Non-resistance

JONATHAN BOUCHER

1775

Jonathan Boucher (1738–1804) was an Episcopal minister and tutor to, among others, the stepson of George Washington. A loyalist, or "Tory," who believed the colonists had no right to rebel against the acts of Parliament, Boucher preached non-resistance to an increasingly hostile audience until 1775 when, fearing for his life, he returned to England. In 1797, he published thirteen of his sermons against colonial resistance under the title *A View of the Causes and Consequences of the American Revolution*. The sermon reprinted here, the twelfth in the series, was given as an answer to a 1775 sermon preached on the same subjects and biblical texts by a Reverend Duché.

On Civil Liberty, Passive Obedience, and Non-resistance*

Galatians, ch. v. ver. 1
Stand fast, therefore, in the liberty wherewith Christ hath made us free.

It is not without much sincere concern that I find myself thus again constrained to animadvert on the published opinions of another Clergyman, of great worth and amiableness of character—a Clergyman whom I have the pleasure to know, and who, I believe, is not more generally known than he is beloved. If his opinions had been confined to points of little moment, and on which even mistakes could have done no great harm, I could have been well contented to have let this pass down the stream of time, with a long list of similar patriotic publications, without any animadversions of mine. But if what he has published, even with good intentions, be, as I think it clearly is, of a pernicious and dangerous tendency, (and the more

*Preached in the parish of Queen Anne, in Maryland: in answer to a Sermon, on the same text and same subjects, by the Rev. Mr. Duché, preached and printed in Philadelphia in 1775.

so, perhaps, from it's being delivered in the form of a sermon,) I owe no apology either to him, or to any man, for thus endeavouring to furnish you with an antidote to the poison which has been so industriously dispersed among you.

To have become noted either as a political writer or preacher, as some (who at least are unacquainted with my preaching) are pleased to tell you I now am, is a circumstance that gives me no pleasure. I was sorry to hear the observation; not (I thank God!) from any consciousness of my having ever written or preached any thing, of which (at least in point of principle) I have reason to be ashamed; but because it is painful to reflect, that it should have fallen to my lot to live in times, and in a country, in which such subjects demand the attention of every man. Convinced in my judgment that it is my duty to take the part which I have taken, though I cannot but lament it's not having produced all the beneficial consequences which I fondly flattered myself it might, I dare not allow myself to discontinue it. The time, I know, has been, when addresses of this sort from English pulpits were much more frequent than they now are. Even now, however, they are not wholly discontinued: sermons on political topics, on certain stated days, are still preached, and with the authority of Government. This is mentioned to obviate a charge, that I am singular in continuing this practice; as it proves that such preaching is not yet proscribed from our pulpits. That a change, indeed, in this respect, as well in the principles as in the conduct of modern preachers, has taken place among us, is readily confessed: but that it is a change for the better, has no where yet been proved. A comparison of the 30th of January sermons of the present times, with those of our older Divines, might suggest many not uninteresting reflections: but as it is no part of my purpose to seat myself in a censorial chair, I enter not into the disquisition; but shall content myself with cursorily observing, that if the political sermons of the present day be more popular than those of our predecessors, it is owing, too probably, to their being also more frivolous (not to say more unsound, and less learned) than such compositions used to be.

But, without being influenced by the principles or the practices of other preachers, I must, for myself, be permitted to think it incumbent on me to watch and attend to circumstances as they arise; such, more especially, as nearly concern the welfare of the people committed to my charge. In any such politics as do not touch the conscience, nor trench upon duty, I hope I neither feel nor take more interest than mankind in general do: but there is a sense in which politics, properly understood, form an essential branch of Christian duty. These politics take in a very principal part, if not the whole, of the second table of the Decalogue, which contains our duty to our neighbour.

It is from this second table that the compilers of our Catechism have very properly deduced the great duty of *honouring and obeying the king, and all that are put in authority under him.* Reverently to submit ourselves to *all our governors, teachers, spiritual pastors, and masters,* is indeed a duty so essential to the peace and happiness of the world, that St. Paul thinks no Christian could be ignorant of it: and therefore, when he recommends it to Titus as a topic on which he should not fail frequently to insist, he supposes it would be sufficient if his converts were *put in mind to be subject to principalities and powers, to obey magistrates, and to be ready to every good work.* This, however, is as direct and clear a commission for a Christian minister's preaching on politics, in the just sense of the word, on all proper occasions, as can be produced for our preaching at all on any subject. Let me hope, then, that I now stand sufficiently vindicated as a preacher of politics (if such an one I am to be deemed) by having proved, that, in thus preaching, I do no more than St. Paul enjoined: all I pretend to, all I aim at, is to *put you in mind* only of your *duty to your neighbour*.*

---

*A very vehement protest against political sermons in general has lately been delivered by a person of great eminence in the political world, which (though aimed perhaps only at one individual Divine, yet being general, and, as such, equally affecting the loyal and the disloyal preacher) it would be unpardonable in the writer of a volume of political sermons to pass over wholly without notice.

. . . "Politics and the pulpit are terms that have little agreement. No sound ought to be heard in the church, but the healing voice of Christian charity. The cause of Civil Liberty and Civil Government gains as little as that of Religion by this confusion of duties. Those who quit

It is, however, not a little mortifying to the few friends of the good old principles of the Church of England yet left among us to observe (as it is impossible they should fail to observe) that offence is taken, not so much because some of us preach on politics, as because we preach what are called unpopular politics. Preachers who are less anx-

---

their proper character, to assume what does not belong to them, are, for the greater part, ignorant both of the character they leave, and of the character they assume. Wholly unacquainted with the world, in which they are so fond of meddling, and inexperienced in all it's affairs, on which they pronounce with so much confidence, they have nothing of politics but the passions they excite. Surely the church is a place where one day's truce ought to be allowed to the dissensions and animosities of mankind."—Reflections on the Revolution in France, p. 14.

The whole force of this striking passage seems to rest on the term *politics* being understood in it's vague and vulgar acceptation, and merely as referring to the wrangling debates of modern assemblies; debates which, far too often, turn entirely on the narrow, selfish and servile views of party. The term has been, and in such a disquisition ought to have been, used in a much more extended and more dignified sense; comprehending all that long list of duties which every man owes to society in it's public capacity. Every man is at least as much concerned to be a good subject, as he is to be a good neighbour: and so far is a preacher from being chargeable with being guilty of "a confusion of duties," or of "assuming a character which does not belong to him," that he acts strictly within the line of his profession, when he explains, as well as he is able, and enforces on the people committed to his care, their public as well as their private duties. Such politics are, literally, the "healing voice of Christian charity."

For weak and wicked politics, whether in or out of the pulpit, no plea is here offered: I would humbly suggest only, that, as the Clergy are far from claiming to be more enlightened than others on these topics, there seems to be no reason for supposing that they are less so. Their "unacquaintance with the world, and inexperience in all it's affairs," even admitting the fact, cannot fairly be esteemed a disadvantage to them: and their habits of study and reflection are certainly in their favour. So far have English Divines in general been from giving any countenance to "the dissensions and animosities of mankind," that in their writings chiefly (which form a large portion of English literature) are any effectual checks to these foul passions to be found: and so little, in general, have they merited the character of being "ignorant," either as Divines or Politicians, that men of the first-rate abilities might easily be named, who have distinguished themselves in both capacities. Who is he that will take upon him to say, that the late Dean of St. Patrick's, or the present Dean of Gloucester, were either unlearned Divines, or shallow Politicians?

The peremptory tone with which we of the Clergy are so often interdicted from meddling with politics in our pulpits, has long appeared to me to be more dictatorial than, as the free subjects of a free government, it is incumbent on us to bear. We, surely, are not less at liberty than other men to use our own discretion: nor can it, I bless God! with any shew of justice, be objected to the Clergy of the Church of England, that they have ever in general either preached or written any such politics as are hostile to the interests either of good government or good men.

This is not the first time that Statesmen have shewn an unaccountable jealousy of the Clergy's interfering in political disquisitions. At the

ious to *speak right,* than *smooth things,* are now hardly less numerous among us, in proportion to our population, than such men were among the puritans in the last century: and their discourses are not only preached, but published, "at the request of battalions, generals, and commanders in chief." But, wo unto that people who studiously place temptations in the way of the ministers of God to *handle the word of God deceitfully!* and wo unto those ministers who are thus tempted to *cause the people to err, by their lies and their lightness!*

Let me humbly hope, then, that, whilst I thus continue to plead in behalf of Government, I may continue to experience the same indulgence which those persons do who speak against it. The ground I have taken, I am aware, is deemed untenable; but, having now just gone over that ground with great care, I feel a becoming confidence that I shall not easily be driven from it. The same diligence, the same plain honest course of proceeding which I have taken, will, I trust, produce the same effects with all of you, who, not being yet absorbed within the vortex of party, are still happy in the possession of minds open to conviction. With no others do I presume to argue. That I am persevering in the pursuit of this unpopular course, I readily own; yet I feel I want spirits to enter on any such discussions with those persons among us, who, settling controverted points with their hands rather than with their tongues, demonstrate with tar and feathers, fetch arguments from prisons, and confute by confiscation and exile.

To find out the true and precise meaning of any passage of Scripture, it is in general necessary to know the circumstances of the writer, and his end and aim in writing. St. Paul, the author of my text, was deeply involved in that very natural but perplexing dispute which soon arose among the first converts, and even among the Disciples, concerning the observance of the ritual services; and how far they were, or were not, obligatory on Christians. There are few of his writings, in some part or other of which this

<hr>

accession of the present Family, wishing to discountenance all investigations of their title to the throne, and most afraid of the Clergy, it is said, some eminent infidel writers were employed and paid by Government expressly to write against religion, not because the King's ministers either disbelieved or disliked religion, but because they thought it the most likely means to draw the attention of the Clergy off from politics, and in confidence that their answers would be a sufficient antidote to the poison of the infidels. It is believed that, in the public offices, proofs might be obtained of individuals receiving pensions for writing both against and for religion.

great question does not come forward. It evidently runs through the whole of this epistle to the Galatians, as well as through this particular verse.

The Jewish zealots (like their ancestors in the wilderness, who ever and anon murmured for want of the flesh-pots in Egypt) were perpetually troubling the infant church on the subject of this question. It became our Apostle, then, diligently to labour after the removal of this difficulty. This he undertakes to do; and very satisfactorily obviates the difficulty by a comparison of the two dispensations, the former of which he proves to have been *a yoke of bondage* when put in competition with that perfect *law of liberty* now promulged to the world. The law of Moses was no doubt well contrived and adapted to the singular circumstances of the people to whom it was given; yet, when a revelation still better adapted to the general circumstances of mankind was made known, it was a most unaccountable instance of folly and perverseness in that people to wish to be again *entangled* in a yoke which neither they nor their forefathers were well able to bear. Emancipated as they now were from so burthensome a service, it was to act the part of madmen still to hug their chains.

Freely offered, however, as the Gospel of uncircumcision now was *to the Jew first and also to the Gentile,* it behoved the latter also (who, as well as their brethren of the law, were *called unto liberty*) to stand fast. It is true they were not, as the Jews were, *made free* from the servile observance of *days, and months, and times, and years;* to which they had never been subjected. But there was another kind of subjection or slavery, not less oppressive, from which they were now released; I mean the slavery of sin. Heretofore they were *the servants of sin;* but now, they were *no more servants, but sons; and if sons, then heirs of God through Christ.* Admitted to this blessed privilege, and no longer the children of Hagar and of Ishmael, but of Sarah and of Isaac, the exhortation is with great propriety addressed to them also: *Stand fast in the liberty wherewith Christ hath made you free.*

As the liberty here spoken of respected the Jews, it denoted an exemption from the burthensome services of the ceremonial law: as it respected the Gentiles, it meant a manumission from bondage under the *weak and beggarly elements of the world,* and an admission into the covenant of grace: and as it respected both in common, it meant a freedom from the servitude of sin. Every sinner is, literally, a slave; for, *his servants ye are, to whom ye obey:*—and the only true liberty is the liberty of being the servants of God;

for, *his service is perfect freedom.* The passage cannot, without infinite perversion and torture, be made to refer to any other kind of liberty; much less to that liberty of which every man now talks, though few understand it. However common this term has been, or is, in the mouths chiefly of those persons who are as little distinguished for the accuracy as they are for the paucity of their words; and whatever influence it has had on the affairs of the world, it is remarkable that it is never used (at least not in any such sense as it is elsewhere used) in any of the laws either of God or men. Let a minister of God, then, stand excused if (taught by him who knoweth what is fit and good for us better than we ourselves, and is *wont also to give us more than either we desire or deserve*) he seeks not to amuse you by any flowery panegyrics on liberty. Such panegyrics are the productions of ancient heathens and modern patriots: nothing of the kind is to be met with in the Bible, nor in the Statute Book. The word *liberty,* as meaning civil liberty, does not, I believe, occur in all the Scriptures. With the aid of a concordance I find only two or three passages, in two apocryphal writers, that look at all like it. In the xivth chapter and 26th verse of the 1st of Maccabees, the people are said to owe much gratitude to Simon, the high-priest, for having renewed a friendship and league with the Lacedemonians, confirmed the league with the Romans, established Israel, and *confirmed their liberty.* But it is evident that this expression means, not that the Jews were then to be exempted from any injunctions, or any restraints, imposed upon them by their own lawful government; but only that they were delivered from a foreign jurisdiction and from tributary payments, and left free to live under the law of Moses. The only circumstance relative to government, for which the Scriptures seem to be particularly solicitous, is in inculcating obedience to lawful governors, as well knowing where the true danger lies. Nevertheless, as occasion has lately been taken from this text, on which I am now to discourse, to treat largely on civil liberty and government, (though for no other reason that appears but that the word *liberty* happens to stand in the text,) I entreat your indulgence, whilst, without too nicely scrutinizing the propriety of deducing from a text a doctrine which it clearly does not suggest, I once more adopt a plan already chalked out for me, and deliver to you what occurs to me as proper for a Christian audience to attend to on the subject of Liberty.

It has just been observed, that the liberty inculcated in the Scriptures, (and which alone the Apostle had in view in this text,) is wholly of the spiritual or religious kind. This liberty was the natural result of the new religion in which mankind were then instructed; which certainly gave them no new civil privileges. They remained subject to the governments under which they lived, just as they had been before they became Christians, and just as others were who never became Christians; with this difference only, that the duty of submission and obedience to Government was enjoined on the converts to Christianity with new and stronger sanctions. The doctrines of the Gospel make no manner of alteration in the nature or form of Civil Government; but enforce afresh, upon all Christians, that obedience which is due to the respective Constitutions of every nation in which they may happen to live. Be the supreme power lodged in one or in many, be the kind of government established in any country absolute or limited, this is not the concern of the Gospel. It's single object, with respect to these public duties, is to enjoin obedience to the laws of every country, in every kind or form of government.

The only liberty or freedom which converts to Christianity could hope to gain by becoming Christians, was the being exempted from sundry burthensome and servile Jewish ordinances, on the one hand; and, on the other, from Gentile blindness and superstition. They were also in some measure perhaps made more *free* in the *inner man;* by being endowed with greater firmness of mind in the cause of truth, against the terrors and the allurements of the world; and with such additional strength and vigour as enabled them more effectually to resist the natural violence of their lusts and passions. On all these accounts it was that our Saviour so emphatically told the Jews, that *the truth* (of which himself was now the preacher) would *make them free**. And on the same principle St. James terms the Gospel *the perfect law of liberty.*

In the infancy of Christianity, it would seem that some rumour had been spread (probably by Judas of Galilee, who is mentioned in the Acts[†]) that the Gospel was designed to undermine kingdoms and commonwealths; as if the intention of our Saviour's first coming had been the same with that which is reserved for the second, viz. to *put down all rule, and all authority, and all power.* On this supposition the apparent solicitude of our Saviour and his

*John, ch. viii. ver. 32.
[†]Ch. v. ver. 37.

Apostles, in their frequent and earnest recommendation of submission to *the higher powers,* is easily and naturally accounted for. Obedience to Government is every man's duty, because it is every man's interest: but it is particularly incumbent on Christians, because (in addition to it's moral fitness) it is enjoined by the positive commands of God: and therefore, when Christians are disobedient to human ordinances, they are also disobedient to God. If the form of government under which the good providence of God has been pleased to place us be mild and free, it is our duty to enjoy it with gratitude and with thankfulness; and, in particular, to be careful not to abuse it by licentiousness. If it be less indulgent and less liberal than in reason it ought to be, still it is our duty not to disturb and destroy the peace of the community, by becoming refractory and rebellious subjects, and *resisting the ordinances of God.* However humiliating such acquiescence may seem to men of warm and eager minds, the wisdom of God in having made it our duty is manifest. For, as it is the natural temper and bias of the human mind to be impatient under restraint, it was wise and merciful in the blessed Author of our religion not to add any new impulse to the natural force of this prevailing propensity, but, with the whole weight of his authority, altogether to discountenance every tendency to disobedience.

If it were necessary to vindicate the Scriptures for this their total unconcern about a principle which for many other writings seem to regard as the first of all human considerations, it might be observed, that, avoiding the vague and declamatory manner of such writings, and avoiding also the useless and impracticable subtleties of metaphysical definitions, these Scriptures have better consulted the great general interests of mankind, by summarily recommending and enjoining a conscientious reverence for law whether human or divine. To respect the laws, is to respect liberty in the only rational sense in which the term can be used; for liberty consists in a subserviency to law*. "Where there is no law," says Mr. Locke, "there is no freedom."

The mere man of nature (if such an one there ever was) has no freedom: *all his lifetime he is subject to bondage.* It is by being included within the pale of civil polity and government that he takes his rank in society as a free man.

Hence it follows, that we are free, or otherwise, as we are governed by law, or by the mere arbitrary will, or wills, of any individual, or any number of individuals. And liberty is not the setting at nought and despising established laws —much less the making our own wills the rule of our own actions, or the actions of others—and not bearing (whilst yet we dictate to others) the being dictated to, even by the laws of the land; but it is the being governed by law, and by law only. The Greeks described Eleutheria, or Liberty, as the daughter of Jupiter, the supreme fountain of power and law. And the Romans, in like manner, always drew her with the pretor's wand, (the emblem of legal power and authority,) as well as with the cap. Their idea, no doubt, was, that liberty was the fair fruit of just authority, and that it consisted in men's being subjected to law. The more carefully well-devised restraints of law are enacted, and the more rigorously they are executed in any country, the greater degree of civil liberty does that country enjoy. To pursue liberty, then, in a manner not warranted by law, whatever the pretence may be, is clearly to be hostile to liberty: and those persons who thus *promise you liberty,* are themselves *the servants of corruption.*

"Civil liberty (says an excellent writer[†]) is a severe and a restrained thing; implies, in the notion of it, authority, settled subordinations, subjection, and obedience; and is altogether as much hurt by too little of this kind, as by too much of it. And the love of liberty, when it is indeed the love of liberty, which carries us to withstand tyranny, will as much carry us to reverence authority, and to support it; for this most obvious reason, that one is as necessary to the being of liberty, as the other is destructive of it. And, therefore, the love of liberty which does not produce this effect, the love of liberty which is not a real principle of dutiful behaviour towards authority, is as hypocritical as the religion which is not productive of a good life. Licentiousness is, in truth, such an excess of liberty as is of the same nature with tyranny. For, what is the difference betwixt them, but that one is lawless power exercised under pretence of authority, or by persons vested with it; the other, lawless

---

*. . . . "Multo esse indignius in eâ civitate, quae legibus teneatur, discedi à legibus: hoc enim vinculum est hujus dignitatis quâ fruimur in republicâ; *hoc fundamentum libertatis;* hic fons aequitatis. Mens et animus, et sententia civitatis posita est in legibus. Ut corpora nostra sine mente, sic civitas sine lege, suis partibus, ut nervis, ac sanguine et membris uti non potest. Legum ministri, mâgistratus; legum interpretes, judices; legum denique idcirco omnes servi sumus, ut liberi esse possimus." —Cicero Orat. pro A. Cluentio. sect. 53.

†Bishop Butler, in his Sermon before the House of Lords, January 30, 1740.

power exercised under pretence of liberty, or without any pretence at all? A people, then, must always be less free in proportion as they are more licentious; licentiousness being not only different from liberty, but directly contrary to it—a direct breach upon it."

True liberty, then, is a liberty to do every thing that is right, and the being restrained from doing any thing that is wrong. So far from our having a right to do every thing that we please, under a notion of liberty, liberty itself is limited and confined—but limited and confined only by laws which are at the same time both it's foundation and it's support. It can, however, hardly be necessary to inform you, that ideas and notions respecting liberty, very different from these, are daily suggested in the speeches and the writings of the times; and also that some opinions on the subject of government at large, which appear to me to be particularly loose and dangerous, are advanced in the sermon now under consideration; and that, therefore, you will acknowledge the propriety of my bestowing some farther notice on them both.

It is laid down in this sermon, as a settled maxim that the end of government is "the common good of mankind." I am not sure that the position itself is indisputable*; but,

if it were, it would by no means follow that, "this common good being matter of common feeling, government must therefore have been instituted by common consent." There is an appearance of logical accuracy and precision in this statement; but it is only an appearance. The position is vague and loose; and the assertion is made without an attempt to prove it. If by men's "common feelings" we are to understand that principle in the human mind called common sense, the assertion is either unmeaning and insignificant, or it is false. In no instance have mankind ever yet agreed as to what is, or is not, "the common good." A form or mode of government cannot be named, which these "common feelings" and "common consent," the sole arbiters, as it seems, of "common good," have not, at one time or another, set up and established, and again pulled down and reprobated. What one people in one age have concurred in establishing as the "common good," another in another age have voted to be mischievous and big with ruin. The premises, therefore, that "the common good is matter of common feeling," being false, the consequence drawn from it, viz. that government was instituted by "common consent," is of course equally false.

This popular notion, that government was originally formed by the consent or by a compact of the people, rests on, and is supported by, another similar notion, not less popular, nor better founded. This other notion is, that the whole human race is born equal; and that no man is natu-

---

*"This, which is commonly affirmed, that the end of government is *the good of the inferiors,* must be understood *cum grano salis.* For, from this principle, misunderstood, some have collected that because the end is above the means, and more noble, therefore subjects are above their governors; and so may call them to account for their misgovernment, and judge, and punish, and remove them, if they see cause. From which false collections, made by seditious and turbulent persons, infinite troubles, confusions, rebellions, and desolations, have followed. We must know, therefore,

"First, That, to procure the good of inferiors, is indeed the duty of superiors, and one end why God committed the people to them; but not the sole or principal end of their authority. For, princes receive their power only from God; and are by him constituted and entrusted with government of others, chiefly for his own glory and honour, as his deputies and vicegerents upon earth: for, *they are his ministers,* Rom. xiii. So that the principal end of their government is the advancement of God's honour, who is the supreme King and Lord of all the world: and therefore, if they fail in the performance of this trust, they are accountable only to him, who entrusted them; and not to the people, whom he hath put under them, and whom he never authorised to call them to account, but to appeal to him only.

"Secondly, It is not generally true that all government is only for the benefit of those who are governed: for, some government there is merely for the benefit of the superior; as that of a lord or master over his servants."—Bishop Andrews on the Commandments, 1650, folio 331.

The learned Mr. Selden observes of the maxim, *Salus populi suprema lex,* that "there is not any thing in the world more abused. For, we apply it as if we ought to forsake the known laws, when it may be for the ad-

vantage of the people so to do: whereas it means no such thing. For, it is not *salus populi suprema lex est,* but ESTO; it being one of the twelve tables. And after divers laws made, some for punishment, and some for reward, then follows this, i.e. *In all the laws you make, have a special eye to the good of the people."*—Table Talk, p. 40.

That most famous casuist, Bishop Sanderson, also says, "There is no man will deny, that *the safety of the people,* i.e. of the whole community, as that word comprehends the king together with the subjects, *is the supreme law.* But, that *the safety of the people,* i.e. of the subjects, the king being excluded, is *the supreme law,* there is no man will affirm it, unless he be a fool, or an impostor; a fool, if he doth believe what he himself saith—and an impostor, if he doth not believe it. But, if any man will seriously look into the original of this aphorism, I do believe he will easily grant that it ought more precisely to be understood of the safety of the prince, than of the safety of the subjects. This saying came to us from the Romans, and was then used by them when their republic did flourish most of all under a popular state. And there is no wonder that *the people's safety* was *the supreme law* with them, with whom the people themselves were the supreme power. In the judgment, therefore, of those wise ancients, who were the first authors of this aphorism, *the safety of the people* was the *supreme law* of the people in a democracy, but of the king in a monarchy."—Cases of Conscience, Lecture the 9th, § xvii. p. 330. edit. 1660.

rally inferior, or, in any respect, subjected to another; and that he can be made subject to another only by his own consent. The position is equally ill-founded and false both in it's premises and conclusions. In hardly any sense that can be imagined is the position strictly true; but, as applied to the case under consideration, it is demonstrably not true. Man differs from man in every thing that can be supposed to lead to supremacy and subjection, *as one star differs from another star in glory.* It was the purpose of the Creator, that man should be social: but, without government, there can be no society; nor, without some relative inferiority and superiority, can there be any government. A musical instrument composed of chords, keys, or pipes, all perfectly equal in size and power, might as well be expected to produce harmony, as a society composed of members all perfectly equal to be productive of order and peace. If (according to the idea of the advocates of this chimerical scheme of equality) no man could rightfully *be compelled to come in* and be a member even of a government to be formed by a regular compact, but by his own individual consent; it clearly follows, from the same principles, that neither could he rightfully be made or compelled to submit to the ordinances of any government already formed, to which he has not individually or actually consented. On the principle of equality, neither his parents, nor even the vote of a majority of the society, (however virtuously and honourably that vote might be obtained,) can have any such authority over any man. Neither can it be maintained that acquiescence implies consent; because acquiescence may have been extorted from impotence or incapacity. Even an explicit consent can bind a man no longer than he chooses to be bound. The same principle of equality that exempts him from being governed without his own consent, clearly entitles him to recall and resume that consent whenever he sees fit; and he alone has a right to judge when and for what reasons it may be resumed.

Any attempt, therefore, to introduce this fantastic system into practice, would reduce the whole business of social life to the wearisome, confused, and useless task of mankind's first expressing, and then withdrawing, their consent to an endless succession of schemes of government. Governments, though always forming, would never be completely formed: for, the majority to-day, might be the minority tomorrow; and, of course, that which is now fixed might and would be soon unfixed. Mr. Locke indeed says, that, "by consenting with others to make one body-politic under government, a man puts himself under an obligation to every one of that society to submit to the determination of the majority, and to be concluded by it." For the sake of the peace of society, it is undoubtedly reasonable and necessary that this should be the case: but, on the principles of the system now under consideration, before Mr. Locke or any of his followers can have authority to say that it actually is the case, it must be stated and proved that every individual man, on entering into the social compact, did first consent, and declare his consent, to be concluded and bound in all cases by the vote of the majority. In making such a declaration, he would certainly consult both his interest and his duty; but at the same time he would also completely relinquish the principle of equality, and eventually subject himself to the possibility of being governed by ignorant and corrupt tyrants*. Mr. Locke himself afterwards disproves his own position respecting this supposed obligation to submit to the "determination of the majority," when he argues that a right of resistance still exists in the governed: for, what is resistance but a recalling and resuming the consent heretofore supposed to have been given, and in fact refusing to submit to the "determination of the majority?" It does not clearly appear what Mr. Locke exactly meant by what he calls "the determination of the majority:" but the only rational and practical public manner of declaring "the determination of the majority," is by law: the laws, therefore, in all countries, even in those that are despotically governed, are to be regarded as the declared "determination of a majority" of the members of that community; because, in such cases, even acquiescence only must be looked upon as equivalent to a declaration. A right of resistance, therefore, for which

*The present government of France, having largely experienced the folly and the danger of being consistent in pursuing this system of equality to it's full extent, have now abandoned it; but so, however, as still to make a shew of it's being retained. They now, very justly, thus define their principle: "L'egalité consiste en ce, que la loi est la même pour tous, soit qu'elle protège, soit qu'elle punisse." Art. 3. Droits. But, after all the pomp and parade they have made about the liberality of their reforms, what is there in this more liberal than all mankind, in all ages, have thought and said, when they drew Justice blind, and balancing her even-poised scales; or indeed more liberal than we find more pointedly expressed in the well-known clause of our own Magna Charta? "Nullus liber homo capiatur, vel imprisonetur, aut dissosietur de libero tenemento suo, vel liberis consuetudinibus suis, aut utlagetur, aut exuletur, aut aliquo alio modo destruatur: nec super eum ibimus, nec super eum mittemus nisi per legale judicium parium suorum, vel per legem terrae. Nulli vendemus, nulli negabimus, aut differemus rectum aut judicium." —Magna Charta, sect. 35.

Mr. Locke contends, is incompatible with the duty of submitting to the determination of "the majority," for which he also contends.

It is indeed impossible to carry into effect any government which, even by compact, might be framed with this reserved right of resistance. Accordingly there is no record that any such government ever was so formed. If there had, it must have carried the seeds of it's decay in it's very constitution. For, as those men who make a government (certain that they have the power) can have no hesitation to vote that they also have the right to unmake it; and as the people, in all circumstances, but more especially when trained to make and unmake governments, are at least as well disposed to do the latter as the former, it is morally impossible that there should be any thing like permanency or stability in a government so formed. Such a system, therefore, can produce only perpetual dissensions and contests, and bring back mankind to a supposed state of nature; arming every man's hand, like Ishmael's, against every man, and rendering the world an *aceldama,* or field of blood.—Such theories of government seem to give something like plausibility to the notions of those other modern theorists, who regard all governments as invasions of the natural rights of men, usurpations, and tyranny. On this principle it would follow, and could not be denied, that government was indeed fundamentally, as our people are sedulously taught it still is, an evil. Yet it is to government that mankind owe their having, after their fall and corruption, been again reclaimed, from a state of barbarity and war, to the conveniency and the safety of the social state: and it is by means of government that society is still preserved, the weak protected from the strong, and the artless and innocent from the wrongs of proud oppressors. It was not without reason, then, that Mr. Locke asserted, that a greater wrong cannot be done to prince and people, than is done by "propagating wrong notions concerning government."

Ashamed of this shallow device, that government originated in superior strength and violence, another party, hardly less numerous, and certainly not less confident than the former, fondly deduce it from some imaginary compact. They suppose that, in the decline perhaps of some fabulous age of gold, a multitude of human beings, who, like their brother beasts, had hitherto ranged the forests, *without guide, overseer, or ruler*—at length convinced, by experience, of the impossibility of living either alone with any degree of comfort or security, or together in society, with peace, without government, had (in some lucid interval of reason and reflection) met together in a spacious plain, for the express purpose of framing a government. Their first step must have been the transferring to some individual, or individuals, some of those rights which are supposed to have been inherent in each of them: of these it is essential to government that they should be divested; yet can they not, rightfully, be deprived of them, otherwise than by their own consent. Now, admitting this whole supposed assembly to be perfectly equal as to rights, yet all agreed as to the propriety of ceding some of them, on what principles of equality is it possible to determine, either who shall relinquish such a portion of his rights, or who shall be invested with such new accessory rights? By asking another to exercise jurisdiction over me, I clearly confess that I do not think myself his equal; and by his consenting to exercise such authority, he also virtually declares that he thinks himself superior. And, to establish this hypothesis of a compact, it is farther necessary that the whole assembly should concur in this opinion—a concurrence so extremely improbable, that it seems to be barely possible. The supposition that a large concourse of people, in a rude and imperfect state of society, or even a majority of them, should thus rationally and unanimously concur to subject themselves to various restrictions, many of them irksome and unpleasant, and all of them contrary to all their former habits, is to suppose them possessed of more wisdom and virtue than multitudes in any instance in real life have ever shewn. Another difficulty respecting this notion may yet be mentioned. Without a power of life and death, it will, I presume, be readily admitted that there could be no government. Now, admitting it to be possible that men, from motives of public and private utility, may be induced to submit to many heavy penalties, and even to corporal punishment, inflicted by the sentence of the law, there is an insuperable objection to any man's giving to another a power over his life: this objection is, that no man has such a power over his own life; and cannot therefore transfer to another, or to others, be they few or many, on any conditions, a right which he does not himself possess. He only who gave life, can give the authority to take it away: and as such authority is essential to government, this argument seems very decidedly to prove, not only that government did not originate in any compact, but also that it was originally from God*.

* Grotius's definition of the supreme magistrate, or "summa potestas," whether vested in one or in many, is, that it is "solius Dei imperio subditus." This agrees with that of our Church; which describes our supreme magistrate, or sovereign, to be "*next under God, supreme,* over all

This visionary idea of a government by compact was, as Filmer says, "first hatched in the schools; and hath, ever since, been fostered by Papists, for good divinity." For some time, the world seemed to regard it merely as another Utopian fiction; and it was long confined to the disciples of Rome and Geneva, who, agreeing in nothing else, yet agreed in this. In an evil hour it gained admittance into the Church of England; being first patronized by her during the civil wars, by "a few miscreants, who were as far from being true Protestants, as true Subjects." Mankind have listened, and continue to listen to it with a predilection and partiality, just as they do to various other exceptionable notions, which are unfavourable to true religion and sound morals; merely from imagining, that if such doctrines be true, they shall no longer be subjected to sundry restraints, which, however wholsome and proper, are too often unpalatable to our corrupt natures. What we wish to be true, we easily persuade ourselves is true. On this principle it is not difficult to account for our thus eagerly following these *ignes fatui* of our own fancies or "feelings," rather than the sober steady light of the word of God; which (in this instance as well as in others) lies under this single disadvantage, that it proposes no doctrines which may conciliate our regards by flattering our pride.

If, however, we can even resolve no longer to be bewildered by these vain imaginations, still the interesting question presses on us, "Where," in the words of Plato*, "where shall we look for the origin of government?" Let Plato himself instruct us. Taught then by this oracle of Heathen wisdom, "we will take our stations there, where the prospect of it is most easy and most beautiful." Of all the theories respecting the origin of government with which the world has ever been either puzzled, amused, or instructed, that of the Scriptures alone is accompanied by no insuperable difficulties.

It was not to be expected from an all-wise and all-merciful Creator, that, having formed creatures capable of order and rule, he should turn them loose into the world under the guidance only of their own unruly wills; that, like so many wild beasts, they might tear and worry one another in their mad contests for preeminence. His purpose from the first, no doubt, was, that men should *live godly and sober lives*. But, such is the sad estate of our corrupted nature, that, ever since the Fall, we have been averse from good, and prone to evil. We are, indeed, so disorderly and unmanageable, that, were it not for the restraints and the terrors of human laws, it would not be possible for us to dwell together. But as men were clearly formed for society, and to dwell together, which yet they cannot do without the restraints of law, or, in other words, without government, it is fair to infer that government was also the original intention of God†, who never decrees the end, without also decreeing the means. Accordingly, when man was made, his Maker did not turn him adrift into a shoreless ocean, without star or compass to steer by. As soon as there were some to be governed, there were also some to govern: and the first man, by virtue of that paternal claim, on which all subsequent governments have been founded, was first invested with the power of government. For, we are not to judge of the Scriptures of God, as we do of some other writings; and so, where no express precept appears,

---

† "To him that shall diligently read the Scriptures, it will be plain and evident, that the Son of God, having created our first parents, and purposing to multiply their seed into many generations, for the replenishing of the world with their posterity, did give to Adam for his time, and to the rest of the Patriarchs and Chief Fathers successively before the Flood, authority, power, and dominion over their children and offspring, to rule and govern them; ordaining, by the very law of Nature, that their said children and offspring (begotten and brought up by them) should fear, reverence, honour, and obey them. Which power and authority before the Flood resting in the Patriarchs and in the Chief Fathers, because it had a very long extent, not only for the education of their said children and offspring whilst they were young, but likewise for the ordering, governing, and ruling of them afterwards when they came to man's estate; and for that also it had no superior power or authority over or above it on earth appearing in the Scriptures: although it be called either patriarchal, regal, or imperial, and that we only term it "potestas regia;" yet, being well considered how far it did reach, we may truly say that it was in a sort "potestas regia;" as now, in a right and true construction, "potestas regia" may justly be called potestas patria.

"If any man shall therefore affirm, that men at the first, without all good education or civility, ran up and down in woods and fields as wild creatures, resting themselves in caves and dens, and acknowledging no superiority over one another, until they were taught by experience the necessity of government; and that thereupon they chose some among themselves to order and rule the rest, giving them power and authority so to do; and that, consequently, all civil power, jurisdiction and authority was first derived from the people and disordered multitude; or either is originally still in them, or else is deduced by their consents naturally from them; and is not God's ordinance, originally descending from him, and depending upon him,—He doth greatly err." "Placet eis."—Bishop Overall's Convocation Book, MDCVI, cap. 2. can. 2.

---

causes, persons, &c." Now, on the principle of those who, without rejecting Grotius's definition, found government on compact, and derive power mediately from God, and immediately from the people, these strange consequences must follow; viz. that this supremacy is, and is not, "*next under God;*" that it is superior and inferior, above and below the people, supreme and dependent.

*Plato, of Laws, book iii.

hastily to conclude that none was given. On the contrary, in commenting on the Scriptures, we are frequently called upon to find out the precept from the practice. Taking this rule, then, for our direction in the present instance, we find, that, copying after the fair model of heaven itself, wherein there was government even among the angels, the families of the earth were subjected to rulers, at first set over them by God: *for, there is no power, but of God; the powers that be are ordained of God.* The first father was the first king: and if (according to the rule just laid down) the law may be inferred from the practice, it was thus that all government originated; and monarchy is it's most ancient form.

Little risque is run in affirming, that this idea of the patriarchal origin of government has not only the most and best authority of history, as far as history goes, to support it; but that it is also by far the most natural, most consistent, and most rational idea. Had it pleased God not to have interfered at all in the case, neither directly nor indirectly, and to have left mankind to be guided only by their own uninfluenced judgments, they would naturally have been led to the government of a community, or a nation, from the natural and obvious precedent of the government of a family. In confirmation of this opinion, it may be observed, that the patriarchal scheme is that which always has prevailed, and still does prevail, among the most enlightened people *: and (what is no slight attestation of it's truth)

---

*"To fathers within their private families Nature hath given a supreme power: for which cause we see, throughout the world, even from the first foundation thereof, all men have ever been taken as lords and lawful kings in their own houses."—Hooker's Ecclesiastical Polity, book i. p. 20.

"From earliest times the people were accustomed to look up to one family, as presiding over national concerns, religious equally and political; by an hereditary right partaking, in public opinion, of divine authority."—Mitford's Hist. of Greece, vol. i. p. 64.

It is the general sentiment of Homer, that Jupiter hath entrusted the sceptre and the laws to kings, that he may govern by them: just as it is the prevailing sentiment of the Scriptures, that, through God, *kings reign, and princes decree justice.* The passages are innumerable, in which Homer calls kings the *shepherds* and *fathers* of their people. Referred merely to Homer, the opinion of those etymologists who derive πατηρ from τηρεω—ut de Deo sit, ὁ το παν τηρων; de homine verò, ως τους παιδας τηρων, though unusual, is by no means to be scorned. Homer's common phrase for kings, as fathers, is, πατηρ ὡς ἤπιος ηεν; intimating, that the authority of kings was of the genuine and legitimate kind. i.e. paternal; or strict, yet tender.

"Aristotle's opinion on this point is, that the power of government did originally arise from the right of fatherhood; which cannot possibly consist with that natural equality which men dream of: for, in the first of his

---

it has also prevailed, and still does prevail, among the most unenlightened †. According to Vitruvius, the rudiments of architecture are to be found in the cottage: and, according to Aristotle, the first principles of government are to be traced to private families. Kingdoms and empires are but so many larger families: and hence it is that our Church,

---

politics, he agrees exactly with the Scripture, and lays this foundation of government. The first society, saith he, made of many houses, is a village, which seems most naturally to be a colony of families, or foster-brethren of children and children's children."—Filmer's Patriarcha, p. 28.

That the Romans also (at least in the early period of their history) considered government as patriarchal, or as derived from, and analogous to, that of fathers over children, is probable from Romulus's having given the name of *patres* and *patricians* to those citizens, to whom the chief share of power was allotted.

†"Le gouvernement Chinois nous rappelle celui des patriarches. L'autorité que ceux-ci avoient sur leur famille, l'empereur de la Chine l'exerce pleinement sur ses sujets. Tout annonce d'ailleurs, que le gouvernement patriarchal est le source du gouvernement monarchique, pris dans toute son etendue."—Description de la Chine, par M. l'Abbé Grosier, tom. ii. p. 1.

"Their government and their laws" (viz. those of some savage tribes of Africans) "appear to have been originally of the patriarchal kind, where the elder of every family was priest and judge."—Matthews's Voyage to Sierra Leone, p. 73.

"The word Mungo, which the Europeans translate King, signifies only Head-man: and he is always addressed by the title of Fasiè, or *father.*" Ibid. p. 74.

A more striking testimony in favour of the universality of the opinion, that government is indeed (as was said of John the Baptist) *not of men, but of God,* could not well have been given, than has been given by the elegant historian of America. It is the more striking, and more forcible, from it's not having been so intended: for, certainly, nothing could be farther from Dr. Robertson's thoughts than it must have been to give any countenance or support to an *unpopular* obsolete doctrine, espoused by Filmer, and run down by Locke.

"The dominion of the Incas, though the most absolute of all despotisms, was mitigated by it's alliance with religion. The mind was not humbled and depressed by the idea of a forced subjection to the will of a superior; obedience paid to one who was *believed to be cloathed with divine authority,* was willingly yielded, and implied no degradation. The sovereign, conscious that the submissive reverence of his people flowed from their *belief of his heavenly descent,* was continually reminded of a distinction which prompted him to imitate that beneficent power which he was supposed to represent. In consequence of these impressions, there hardly occurs, in the traditional history of Peru, *any instance of rebellion* against the reigning prince; and among twelve successive monarchs, there was not one tyrant."—Robertson's History of America, vol. ii. p. 310, 4to edit.

The intelligent reader is requested to compare this pleasing account of this sensible, good, and happy people, with the same author's description of their fiercer and more heroical brethren of the North, who were distinguished by a rampant spirit of liberty; or, as our gentler author (softened no doubt by the mild spirit of whiggism) is pleased to term that spirit, "the pride of independence, impatience under any spein perfect conformity with the doctrine here inculcated, in her explication of the fifth commandment, from the obedience due to parents, wisely derives the congenial duty of *honouring the king and all that are put in authority under him*.

It is from other passages of Scripture, from the nature of the thing, from the practice of Adam, and from the practice of all nations (derived from and founded on this precedent) that we infer that Adam had and exercised sovereign power over all his issue. But the first instance of power exercised by one human being over another is in the subjection of Eve to her husband. This circumstance suggests

---

cies of restraint, and a disdain to acknowledge any superior."—Ibid. vol. i. p. 404.

As the idea of a patriarchal government adopted in this Discourse is now very generally rejected, chiefly on the authority of Mr. Locke's answer to a treatise on the subject by Sir Robert Filmer; and as that book is now antiquated, and, where known at all, known only through the medium of the answer to it; and as also I have lately perused the book, and did not find it deserving of all that extreme contempt with which it is now the fashion to mention it, I could not easily reconcile to myself the neglect of this opportunity to recommend it to my readers also to peruse the book, and to judge for themselves.

The chief point in debate between these two authors relates to "the beginning of Political Societies," or the origin of Government. Filmer's opinion is, that every human being is born the political subject of some other human being; that infants, the moment they are born, are the natural subjects of their parents; and that the State, or supreme power of any country, is the parent, or in the place of a parent, to all who are born within it's jurisdiction, entitled to their allegiance, but bound to provide for their guardianship and protection. Mr. Locke's very different opinion is, that all men being born free, equal, and independent, no one could be put out of this estate, and subjected to the political power of another, without his own consent. And that nothing short of the consent of a number of free men, capable of a majority to unite and incorporate into a society, ever did, or could, give beginning to any lawful government in the world. My opinion on both these points has been briefly, and perhaps unsatisfactorily, but very sincerely, delivered in the body of the sermon: to which, as I am not now engaged to write either a direct answer to Mr. Locke, or a defence of Sir Robert Filmer, all that I am solicitous to add, is, that my opinion is the same that it was, as to this point, two-and-twenty years ago.

Mr. Locke, with a great shew of candour, treats Filmer pretty much as controversial writers in general treat their opponents. Even in his preface, and before it was possible he could have shewn that his censures were well founded, unmindful of his own excellent rule, that "railing should not be taken for arguments," he endeavours to excite a prejudice against the author, by rudely taxing him with "glib nonsense." There are, no doubt, in several of Sir Robert Filmer's Treatises, many weak things; for, he does not appear to have been an author by profession—of course he was not so careful in the selection either of his arguments or his style, as more experienced writers usually are, and as no doubt he ought to have been. Many are the imperfections of this nature which his answerer has detected, and exposed with very little remorse: whilst he passes over, without noticing, or at least with a very slight notice, those parts of the Treatise he answers, which alone are of great moment, and which (it is believed) are unanswerable. The leading idea, or principle, of Sir Robert Filmer's Patriarcha is, that government is not of human, but divine origin; and that the government of a family is the basis, or pattern, of all other government. And this principle, notwithstanding Mr. Locke's answer, is still (in the opinion of the author of these ser-

mons) unrefuted, and still true. Some weak arguments, which were unwarily used to defend it, were indeed very satisfactorily refuted: this, however, proved no more than that the answerer was strong only where the first writer was weak.

It is allowed, that the author of the Patriarcha entertained some very extravagant notions on monarchy, and the sacredness of kings: and (what is perhaps still less pardonable) some disparaging and unjust opinions respecting the supremacy of law. On these points his cooler antagonist, who was a bigot (if a bigot at all) to more popular opinions, attacks, and even ridicules him with success. This success would have been greater, had it not been tarnished by many ungentleman-like sneers, which were ever and anon thrown out, on the knight's having been a courtier. This was a low artifice, which Mr. Locke should have disdained; and which, whether he disdained or no, he would probably have forborne, had he recollected that, in the age of Sir Robert Filmer, the being a courtier was a truly honourable distinction.

And all that he has written, as well as all that has been written concerning him, shews, that Sir Robert Filmer, though certainly not so careful and close a reasoner as Mr. Locke, was neither less learned, nor of a less elevated and liberal mind. He was also, if not a profound, yet a fair, candid, and gentlemanly writer. Nor should it be omitted, because it is much to his credit, that he appears to have been actuated by two as noble and as dignified sentiments as can warm the human breast; I mean, loyalty and piety.

Mr. Locke had the good fortune to enjoy a pre-eminent reputation for political wisdom longer than most men who have degraded great abilities by employing them to promote the temporary purposes of a party. Till the American war, he was looked up to as an oracle: and the whole nation implicitly pinned their faith, in politics, on his dogmas. But, when that great controversy between the Parent State and her Colonies came to be agitated, men were under a necessity of examining, thinking, and judging for themselves. One consequence of their doing so was, that the high degree of infallibility, which, till then, had been ascribed to the name and the works of Mr. Locke, was greatly lessened. At length, in 1781, Dr. Tucker, the celebrated Dean of Gloucester, wrote a Treatise (and one of the best he ever did write) on purpose to "consider, examine, and confute the notions of Mr. Locke and his followers, concerning the origin, extent, and end of civil government." Since that time writers in general venture to read Mr. Locke, as they do other authors, without being overawed by the unmerited popularity attached to his name. One of the last, and not least eminent of our political writers, boldly calls him (yet not with more freedom than justice)—"that arch propagator of wild conceits, that wholesale fabricator of fantastical systems of polity, (accuse me not of political blasphemy!) John Locke, who had scarcely given birth to this shapeless abortion, when he crushed it at a stroke, by proving the impossibility of it's existence. He was compelled to acknowledge, that the coming into society upon such terms would be—only to go out again."—See a Letter to the Hon. Tho. Erskine, by John Gifford, Esq. p. 56.

sundry reflections, of some moment in this argument. In the first place, it shews that power is not a natural right. Adam could not have assumed, nor could Eve have submitted to it, had it not been so ordained of God. It is, therefore, equally an argument against the domineering claims of despotism, and the fantastic notion of a compact. It proves too, that there is a sense in which it may, with truth, be asserted, that government was originally founded in weakness and in guilt: that it may and must be submitted to by a fallen creature, even when exercised by a fallen creature, lost both to wisdom and goodness. The equality of nature (which, merely as it respects an ability to govern, may be admitted, only because God, had he so seen fit, might have ordained that the man should be subjected to the woman) was superseded by the actual interference of the Almighty, to whom alone original underived power can be said to belong.

Even where the Scriptures are silent, they instruct: for, in general, whatever is not therein commanded is actually forbidden. Now, it is certain that mankind are no where in the Scriptures commanded to resist authority; and no less certain that, either by direct injunction, or clear implication, they are commanded to *be subject to the higher powers:* and this subjection is said to be enjoined, not for our sakes only, but also *for the Lord's sake.* The glory of God is much concerned, that there should be good government in the world: it is, therefore, the uniform doctrine of the Scriptures, that it is under the deputation and authority of God alone that *kings reign and princes decree justice.* Kings and princes (which are only other words for supreme magistrates) were doubtless created and appointed, not so much for their own sakes, as for the sake of the people committed to their charge: yet are they not, therefore, the creatures of the people. So far from deriving their authority from any supposed consent or suffrage of men, they receive their commission from Heaven; they receive it from God, the source and original of all power. However obsolete, therefore, either the sentiment or the language may now be deemed, it is with the most perfect propriety that the supreme magistrate, whether consisting of one or of many, and whether denominated an emperor, a king, an archon, a dictator, a consul, or a senate, is to be regarded and venerated as the vicegerent of God.

But were the texts usually appealed to on this topic more dubious than (we bless God!) they are, the example of the Christian legislator may, at least to Christians, well stand in the place of all precepts. There are not many questions, in which the interests of mankind are more nearly concerned than they are in ascertaining their duty as subjects. It is therefore very improbable, that the Saviour of the world should have left the world in the dark, in an affair of so much moment: but that he should have misled his followers, and that Christians should have been exposed to the hazard of becoming bad subjects even through the inadvertence of their founder, it is little less than blasphemy to suppose. We are therefore deeply interested to find out, if we can, what it was that our Saviour really thought, said, and did, in the case; and for what purpose.

It is readily acknowledged, that his history (in which alone his laws are contained) does not dwell copiously on the duties of sovereigns and subjects. This appearance of inattention, we may be assured, was not permitted without design: nor, in fact, is our duty on this point (any more than it is in others) the less forcibly inculcated by our having been left to find out the precept from his practice. On one point, however, of great moment in this discussion, the gospel history, when properly understood, is full and decided; viz. that every thing our blessed Lord either said or did, pointedly tended to discourage the disturbing a settled government. Hence it is fair to infer the judgment of Jesus Christ to have been, that the most essential duty of subjects with respect to government was (in the phraseology of a prophet) *to be quiet, and to sit still.* Yet, had he judged of

---

Mr. Locke, however, and his followers, in presenting these principles to the public in their most popular form, have the demerit only of having new-dressed principles which are at least as old as the rebellion of Korah, Dathan, and Abiram. In the unhappy reign of the first Charles, those principles were industriously revived and brought forward with great zeal: and there is hardly a principle or project of any moment in Mr. Locke's Treatise, of which the rudiments may not be traced in some of the many political pieces which were then produced. In a collection of "Original Papers relative to the History of the Colony of Massachusetts Bay," which Governor Hutchinson had printed, but which were never published, I find the following passages; containing, if I mistake not, the very essence of Mr. Locke's system. The Paper, from which these passages are taken, is intitled "Libertye and the Weale Publick reconciled, in a Declaration to the late Court of Elections at Newtown, the 17th of the 3d Month, 1637." In this declaration Liberty is thus defined: "That the people may not be subjected to any lawe, or power, amonge themselves, *without theire consent:* whatsoever is more than this, is neither lawful nor durable, and insteade of libertye, may prove bondage, or licentiousnesse." This is farther defended from some exceptions made by Mr. Vane, afterwards Sir Henry Vane, thus: "It is clearly agreed by all, that the care of safety and wellfare was the original cause or occasion of common weales, and of many families subjecting themselves to rulers and lawes: for *no man hath lawfulle power over another but by consent;* so likewise, by the lawe of proprietie, *no man can have just interest in that which belongeth to another, without his consent.*"

questions of this nature as we do, he certainly did not want motives to induce him to excite commotions in the government of Judea; and such motives too as (according to human reckoning) are highly meritorious and honourable. At the time when he was upon earth, his country groaned under an unjust and most oppressive bondage. It had just been subdued by a people, whose chief motive for overrunning the world with their conquests was a lust of dominion: and it was as arbitrarily governed, as it had been iniquitously acquired. The Jews, it is true, were not then eminent, at least as a nation, for their virtues: but they were not chargeable with that "un-Roman spirit," as one of our orators expressed himself, or (to borrow the congenial phraseology of another) that "degeneracy of soul," which led them tamely to submit to their oppressors. A general opinion prevailed in the nation, that the expected Messiah would deliver them from this galling vassalage; that he was to be, not a spiritual, but a temporal, prince—a prince who should restore to Israel the supremacy, of which the Romans had deprived it—who should reign in all secular pomp and power in the throne of David—and, having subdued the rest of the world, make Jerusalem the seat of an universal monarchy. The very name given to him imports royalty and sovereignty: and he really was the legal heir to the crown of Judea.

In support of this assertion, it is to be observed, that the Jews had two ways of tracing their genealogies, by a kind of double descent; the one natural, the other legal. The natural descent was when a person, by natural generation, descends from another; the legal, when one not naturally descended from another, yet succeeded, as nearest of kin, to the inheritance. St. Luke deduces the natural line of Christ from David; and shews how Christ, by Nathan, is the son of David, according to the flesh, by natural descent: whereas St. Matthew deduces the legal line of Christ also from David, shewing how Christ, as Solomon's heir, and lawful king of the Jews, succeeded, as nearest of kin, to sit upon the throne of David his father: and the Evangelist is so satisfied with the legality of this genealogy, that he calls Christ, "*the born* king of the Jews," that is to say, the person who was their king by birth*. The Jews themselves could name none of their nation who was nearer than he was. None of them ever produced any legal exception against him; and therefore, whilst a large party, convinced of the validity of his title to the throne by birth, wished to

confirm it by election, and to make him a king, all that the friends of the Power who was in possession, or his enemies, could do to defeat his claim, was to get the Romans on their side, by artfully insinuating that the best of all titles was that which had been obtained by conquest: hence, their cry was, *We will have no king but Caesar!*

Add to this—It is well known that in no instance whatever did our Saviour give greater offence to his countrymen than he did by not gratifying them in their expectations of a temporal deliverance. For this opinion of his title to the throne was not taken up at random; nor only by a few persons, merely to serve some bye-ends of their own. The idea pervades his whole history. It was one of the chief grounds of the enmity of his countrymen towards him, and the only plausible pretence on which he could be arraigned. And, notwithstanding his repeated declarations that his *kingdom was not of this world,* yet it was on this account that at last he was *brought as a lamb to the slaughter.*

When it is asserted that Christianity made no alteration in the civil affairs of the world, the assertion should neither be made, nor understood, without some qualification. The injunction to *render unto Caesar the things that are Caesar's,* is no doubt very comprehensive; implying that unless we are good Subjects, we cannot be good Christians: but then we are to *render unto Caesar,* or the supreme magistrate, that obedience only to which God has given him a just claim: our paramount duty is to God, to whom we are to render *the things that are God's.* If, therefore, in the course of human affairs, a case should occur (and no doubt such cases do often occur) in which the performance of both these obligations becomes incompatible, we cannot long be at a loss in determining that it is our duty to obey God rather than men. The worship of idols, as well as sacrifices and auguries, certainly entered into, and made a part of, the civil policy of ancient Rome. Temples dedicated to a variety of false deities were under the peculiar care of the Senate. The office of Pontifex Maximus, or High Priest, was annexed to the title of Emperor. Now, surely, it was the intention of the Founder of Christianity, and it is the natural tendency of it's doctrines, to produce some alteration in things of this sort. In Mahometan countries, a plurality of wives is allowed by law: in many countries still Pagan, the worship of images is enjoined by the State: in several parts of Africa, parents who are past labour are, by the laws of the land, exposed by their children to be torn in pieces by wild beasts: and even in so civilized a country as China, children are thus exposed by their parents, with

*See Matth. ch. ii. ver. 2.

the sanction and authority of the laws. Would Christianity endure such shocking outrages against all that is humane, moral, or pious, though supported by Government? It certainly would not: for the spirit of St. Paul, when he saw the city of Athens *wholly given to idolatry,* was so *stirred in him,* that, for disputing publicly with *certain philosophers of the Epicureans and of the Stoics,* they carried him unto Areopagus; where, far from shrinking from his duty, he openly arraigned all the people of Athens, of being *too superstitious.* This charge he founded on his having seen *an altar with this inscription, To the unknown God;* which yet was not set up contrary to law. Sundry improprieties, sanctioned by legal authority, were censured by Christ himself. Was it not by virtue of his regal power that, as *one having authority,* he cast the buyers and sellers out of the temple; who yet were there, and pursuing their usual callings, with the public permission? Still, though they certainly were not restrained by any idea that all interference with the civil affairs of the world was contrary to Christianity, it no where appears, that either our Saviour, or any of his apostles, ever did interfere with the affairs of any government, or the administration of any government, otherwise than by submitting to them. Yet, let it not be said, that he who could have commanded *more than twelve legions of angels,* wanted power or means to have *resisted,* and with effect, that pusillanimous Roman governor, who, from the basest of all motives, *gave sentence,* that a person in whom he declared he *found no fault,* should be put to death, merely to gratify a senseless, malicious, and clamorous multitude. Let it not be said, that his pretensions to sovereignty were either romantic or dubious: *a great multitude* of his cotemporaries and countrymen, *being in number about five thousand,* thought so favourably of them, that they would have set him on their throne in that way by which alone we are now told authority over a free people can properly be obtained, viz. by the suffrages of the people. To assert his claim *de jure* against those who held it *de facto,* they would fain have *taken him by force* (that is, no doubt, in opposition to the Romans and their adherents) *to make him a king.* That he was not restrained from gratifying these natural wishes of so large a number of his impatient countrymen, by any apprehensions of his being evil-spoken of, as *a pestilent fellow,* one who *perverted the people, forbidding to give tribute to Caesar, and saying that he himself was king,* may very rationally be inferred from his having submitted to no less unmerited aspersions with invincible fortitude: and his yielding at last

to the ignominy of the cross, proves that he was not to be deterred from doing any thing which he knew would redound either to the glory of God, or the good of mankind, by the dread of any calumnies, or the terrors of any sufferings*.

His constant discouragement, therefore, of a scheme so well calculated not only to promote his own elevation, but to emancipate his country (had he estimated either worldly grandeur, or the condition of subjects under government, according to our ideas) would have been inconsistent with that love to mankind which he manifested in every other action of his life. The only rational conclusion, therefore, that the case will admit of, is, that he thought it would be better, both for Judea in particular, and for the world in general, that in the former case the people should not be distracted by a revolution, and in the latter that there should be no precedent to which revolutionists might appeal: his words were not meant to bear merely a local and circumscribed, but a general and extended application, when he directed his followers to *render unto Caesar the things that are Caesar's:* his practice was conformable to this precept; and so would ours be, were we but practically convinced that *it is enough for the disciple to be as his master, and the servant as his lord.* As Christians, solicitous to tread in the steps in which our Saviour trod, the tribute of civil obedience is as much due to our civil rulers, even

*This extreme reluctance of the Jews to pay tribute to any Foreign Power was sanctioned by their religion: for, in Deuteron. ch. xvii. ver. 15. they are expressly enjoined to choose a king *from among their brethren, and not a stranger.* It was natural, therefore, that they should regard the paying tribute to the Romans as a badge of slavery; and natural also, that they should very generally dislike the publicans, who were the persons appointed by the Romans to collect such tribute. Judas the Gaulonite, taking advantage of this national prepossession, with the avowed purpose of shaking off this yoke, excited an insurrection: and so numerous were his adherents, that even after they were crushed as a civil party, they seem to have existed as a religious sect, under the name of *Zealots.* Persons of this order appear to have acted as public censors, or as societies for the reformation of manners; and, as such, were sometimes called The Just. Of this order, it is probable, those persons were, whom the Chief Priests and Scribes employed to *watch* and *to take hold of the words* of our Saviour: and therefore the expression in St. Luke, ch. xx. ver. 20. *which should feign themselves just men,* would be more accurately translated, if rendered, who feigned themselves, or pretended to be, *the Just;* that is to say, of the order of *the Just.* Jesus Christ himself was accused of being of this order; because, as it was alleged, he *forbade the people to give tribute* unto Caesar. To this circumstance of his being of that sect, which originated in his country of Galilee, the wife of Pilate may be supposed to have alluded, when she sent to her husband, saying, *Have thou nothing to do with that Just Man!*

though they should happen to be invaders like the Romans, and though, like Herod, the ministers of government should chance to be oppressors, as the duty of religious obedience is a debt which we owe to *the King of kings, and Lord of lords.*

Nor let this be deemed a degrading and servile principle: it is the very reverse; and it is this it's superior dignity which proves it's celestial origin. For, whilst other doctrines and other systems distract the world with disputes and debates which admit of no decision, and of *wars and fightings* which are almost as endless as they are useless, it is the glory of Christianity to teach her votaries patiently to bear imperfections, inconveniences and evils in government, as in every thing else that is human. This patient acquiescence under some remediless evils is not more our duty than it is our interest: for, the only very intolerable grievance in government is, when men allow themselves to disturb and destroy the peace of the world, by vain attempts to render that perfect, which the laws of our nature have ordained to be imperfect. And there is more magnanimity, as well as more wisdom, in enduring some present and certain evils, than can be manifested by any projects of redress that are uncertain; but which, if they fail, may bring down irretrievable ruin on thousands of others, as well as on ourselves: since to suffer nobly indicates more greatness of mind than can be shewn even by acting valiantly. Wise men, therefore, in the words of a noted philosopher,* will "rather choose to brook with patience some inconveniences under government (because human affairs cannot possibly be without some) than self-opinionatedly disturb the quiet of the public." And, weighing the justice of those things you are about, not by the persuasion and advice of private men, but by the laws of the realm, you will no longer suffer ambitious men, through the streams of your blood, to wade to their own power; but esteem it better to enjoy yourselves in the present state, though perhaps not the best, than, by waging war, endeavour to procure a reformation in another age, yourselves "in the meanwhile either killed, or consumed with age."

This long enquiry concerning the divine origin and authority of government might perhaps have been deemed rather curious than useful, were it not of acknowledged moment, that some dangerous inferences which are usually drawn from the contrary opinion should be obviated.

*Hobbes.

One of these dangerous inferences it seems to have been the aim of the sermon now before me to inculcate. Government being assumed to be a mere human ordinance, it is thence inferred, that "rulers are the servants of the public": and, if they be, no doubt it necessarily follows, that they may (in the coarse phrase of the times) be *cashiered* or continued in pay, be reverenced or resisted, according to the mere whim or caprice of those over whom they are appointed to rule. Hence the author of this sermon also takes occasion to enter his protest against "passive obedience and non-resistance."

It really is a striking feature in our national history, that, ever since the Revolution, hardly any person of any note has preached or published a sermon, into which it was possible to drag this topic, without declaring against this doctrine. It seems to have been made a kind of criterion or test of principle, and the watch-word of a party. For, it cannot well be said, that the circumstances of the times, or the temper of men's minds, either lately have been, or now are, such as particularly to call for these studied and repeated protestations. What is not less remarkable is, that whilst the right of resistance has thus incessantly been delivered from the pulpit, insisted on by orators, and inculcated by statesmen, the contrary position is still (I believe) the dictate of religion, and certainly the doctrine of the established Church, and still also the law of the land.

You are not now to learn my mind on this point. As, however, the subject has again been forced on me, let me be permitted again to obviate, if I can, some fresh misrepresentations, and again to correct some new mistakes.

All government, whether lodged in one or in many, is, in it's nature, absolute and irresistible. It is not within the competency even of the supreme power to limit itself; because such limitation can emanate only from a superior. For any government to make itself irresistible, and to cease to be absolute, it must cease to be supreme; which is but saying, in other words, that it must dissolve itself, or be destroyed. If, then, to resist government be to destroy it, every man who is a subject must necessarily owe to the government under which he lives an obedience either active or passive: active, where the duty enjoined may be performed without offending God; and passive, (that is to say, patiently to submit to the penalties annexed to disobedience,) where that which is commanded by man is forbidden by God. No government upon earth can rightfully compel any one of it's subjects to an active compliance with any thing that is, or that appears to his conscience to be, inconsistent with, or contradictory to, the known laws of God: because every man is under a prior and superior obligation to *obey God in all things.* When such cases of incompatible demands of duty occur, every well-informed person knows what he is to do; and every well-principled person will do what he ought, viz. he will submit to the ordinances of God, rather than comply with the commandments of men. In thus acting he cannot err; and this alone is "passive obedience," which I entreat you to observe is so far from being "unlimited obedience," (as it's enemies wilfully persist to miscall it,) that it is the direct contrary. Resolute not to disobey God, a man of good principles determines, in case of competition, as the lesser evil, to disobey man: but he knows that he should also disobey God, were he not, at the same time, patiently to submit to any penalties incurred by his disobedience to man.

With the fancies or the follies of the injudicious defenders of this doctrine, who, in the heat of controversy, have argued for the exclusive irresistibility of kings, merely in their personal capacity, I have no concern. Such arguments are now to be met with only in the answers of those equally injudicious, but less candid, opposers of the doctrine, who (as though there were any gallantry in taking a fortress that is no longer defended) persist to combat a phantom which, now at least, may be said to be of their own creating. In the present state of things, when a resistance is recommended, it must be, not against the king alone, but against the laws of the land. To encourage undistinguishing multitudes, by the vague term of resistance, to oppose all such laws as happen not to be agreeable to certain individuals, is neither more nor less than, by a regular plan, to attempt the subversion of the government: and I am not sure but that such attacks are more dangerous to free than to absolute governments.

Even the warmest advocates for resistance acknowledge, that, like civil liberty, the term is incapable of any accurate definition*. Particular cases of injury and oppression are imagined: on which arguments are founded, to shew that

mankind must be determined and governed, not by any known and fixed laws, but "by a law antecedent and paramount to all positive laws of men;" "by their natural sense and feelings." These unwritten, invisible, and undefinable "antecedent laws;" this indescribable "natural sense and feelings;" these "hidden powers and mysteries" in our Constitution, are points too refined and too subtle for argument. Indeed it can be to little purpose to argue, either on resistance or on any other subject, with men who are so weak as to declaim, when it is incumbent on them to reason.

Without any encouragement, mankind, alas! are, of themselves, far too *prone to be presumptuous and self-willed;* always disposed and ready to *despise dominion,* and *to speak evil of dignities.* There is, says a learned writer[†], such a "witchcraft in rebellion, as to tempt men to be rebels, even though they are sure to be damned for it." What dreadful confusions and calamities must have been occasioned in the world, had such strong and dangerous natural propensities been directly encouraged by any positive law! It was surely, then, merciful and wise in the Almighty Ruler of the world, to impose on his creatures the general law of obedience without any exceptions. A non-resisting spirit never yet made any man a bad subject. And if men of such mild and yielding tempers have shewn less ardour, than many others do, in the pursuit of that liberty which makes so conspicuous a figure in the effusions of orators and poets, it can be only for this reason, that they think it is precisely that kind of liberty which has so often set the world in an uproar, and that therefore it would be better for the world if it were never more heard of[‡]. If they are mis-

---

[†] Dean Sherlock, in his Case of Resistance.

[‡] To men of plain sense, who (having no party purposes to serve) in any controverted question are anxious only to find the truth, it is wearisome to have, instead of a fair attempt to illustrate or clear up any of the great difficulties which embarrass, and must for ever embarrass, the subject of government, in all political discussions, this one unvaried topic of declamation for ever dinned in their ears. But it is particularly irksome to find such stale and thread-bare sophistry adopted and brought forward by so elegant and classical a writer as Lord Lyttelton.

In his first Dialogue of the Dead, he makes Hampden say, "It is a disgrace to our Church to have taken up such opinions; and I will venture to prophesy, that our Clergy must in future times renounce them, or they will be turned against them by those who mean their destruction. Suppose a Popish king on the throne: will the Clergy then adhere to passive obedience and non-resistance? If they do, they deliver up their religion to Rome: if they do not, their practice will confute their own doctrines."

By having taken no care to refute these sentiments; and by the artful compliment thus paid, at the expence of their predecessors, to the Clergy

---

*The Marquis of Halifax confesses, that the right of resistance, which yet he contends is the life and soul of our Constitution, cannot be defined:

"It is," he says, "an *hidden power* in the Constitution, which would be lost if it were defined: a certain *mystery,* by virtue of which a nation may, at some critical times, be secured from ruin; but then it must be kept a *mystery.* It is rendered useless when touched by unskilful hands: and no people ever had or deserved to have that power, which was so unwary as to anticipate their claim to it."

taken, their mistakes are at least harmless: and there is much justice, as well as great good sense, in Bishop Hall's remark, that "some quiet errors are better than some unruly truths."

When, not long since, a noted patriot* declared, in his place in Parliament, that he knew no difference between a revolution and a rebellion, excepting that in the former an attempt to alter the form of government succeeded, and in the latter it did not, the sentiment was objected to as licentious and seditious. Yet, on the principles of the advocates of resistance, he said no more than he might easily have defended: nor am I sure but that (notwithstanding the pains which the public men of that period took to guard against such an inference, in their debates on the word *ab-*

─────────

of his day, who, he was well aware, had pretty generally renounced what he affected to prophesy they would renounce, it is too evident this noble author was not unwilling to have them regarded as his own.

There must be a total subversion of every thing that relates to our present Constitution, before we can again have a Popish king on the throne. But, should the Almighty (as a punishment for our great sin in not being sufficiently thankful for the blessing of having long had our throne filled by a mild and patriotic race of Protestant kings) see fit once more to permit a Popish monarch to sit on the throne, God forbid the Clergy should not *adhere* to doctrines enjoined by the law of the land, by the authority of their Church, and by the word of God! Had the noble historian forgotten, or did he only affect to forget, what part the Clergy of the Church of England did in general take when (themselves being Protestants) there actually was a Popish king upon the throne? The seven bishops whom James the Second committed to the Tower, and whom King William deprived for not renouncing King James, did, in neither of their opposite trials, "renounce the doctrines of passive obedience and non-resistance:" yet neither "did they deliver up their religion to Rome, nor confute their own doctrines by their own practice." So far from this, no one circumstance contributed so much to defeat the mad purpose of this bigoted monarch to introduce Popery into the kingdom, as the objections made to it by these persecuted bishops: and unless the principle of resistance may be promoted by an exemplary recommendation of non-resistance, their doctrines were not confuted by their practice. The conduct of these memorable men, on this memorable occasion, is not only a very satisfactory illustration of the true principles of this much misrepresented doctrine, but a complete vindication of it.

Had he been so disposed, Lord Lyttelton might have seen a cloud of witnesses in favour of these exploded doctrines among our older divines. There is a very interesting catalogue of them, together with extracts evincing what their sentiments on this point were, in the history of Sacheverell's trial. He might also have seen, and he is inexcusable if he did not see (and perhaps still more inexcusable if, having seen, he did not learn more from) a most masterly Sermon on Passive Obedience, by Bishop Berkley. I hope I shall neither be regarded as dictatorial, nor unreasonable, in expressing an earnest wish, that no one may hereafter presume to shoot these random arrows against this venerable doctrine, till he has read and considered, and is also able to answer, this Discourse by this eminent Prelate.

*Mr. Wilkes.

dication) on these principles the promoters of the revolution itself, emphatically so called, must submit to the imputation of having effected it by resistance. It was clearly a successful revolution. If, then, this was the case as to the revolution, how, it may be asked, did it differ, in point of principle, either from the grand rebellion that preceded it, or either of the subsequent rebellions for the purpose of restoring the abdicated family? and how, on the same principles, can we condemn the murder of the father, and vindicate the expulsion of the son?—Mr. Locke, like many inferior writers, when defending resistance, falls into inconsistencies, and is at variance with himself. "Rebellion being," as he says, "an opposition not to persons, but to authority, which is founded only in the constitution and laws of the government, those, whoever they be, who by force break through, and by force justify their violation of them, are truly and properly rebels." To this argument no one can object: but it should be attended to, that, in political consideration, it is hardly possible to dissociate the ideas of authority in the abstract from persons vested with authority. To resist a person legally vested with authority, is, I conceive, to all intents and purposes, the same thing as to resist authority. Nothing, but it's success, could have rescued the revolution from this foul imputation, had it not been for the abdication. Accordingly this great event has always hung like a mill-stone on the necks of those who must protest against rebellions; whilst yet their system of politics requires that they should approve of resistance, and the revolution.

The resistance which your political counsellors urge you to practise, (and which no doubt was intended to be justified by the sermon which I have now been compelled to notice,) is not a resistance exerted only against the persons invested with the supreme power either legislative or executive, but clearly and literally against *authority*. Nay, if I at all understand the following declaration made by those who profess that they are the disciples of Mr. Locke, you are encouraged to resist not only all authority over us as it now exists, but any and all that it is possible to constitute. "Can men who exercise their reason believe, that the Divine Author of our existence intended a part of the human race to hold an absolute property in, and an unbounded power over, others marked out by his infinite wisdom and goodness as the objects of a legal domination never rightfully resistible, however severe and oppressive?" It might be hazardous, perhaps, for me, even under the shelter of a Scripture phrase, to call these words *great swelling words;*

because they are congressional words. That they have excited a very general panic, and many apprehensions of a real impending slavery, is no more than might have been expected in a country where there is literally "absolute property in, and unbounded power over, human beings." How far this was intended, I presume not to judge. But, involved and obscure as the language (in which these extraordinary sentiments are couched) must be confessed to be, the declaration certainly points at all government: and it's full meaning amounts to a denial of that just supremacy which "the Divine Author of our existence" has beyond all question given to "one part of the human race" to hold over another. Without some paramount and irresistible power, there can be no government. In our Constitution, this supremacy is vested in the King and the Parliament; and, subordinate to them, in our Provincial Legislatures. If you were now released from this constitutional power, you must differ from all others "of the human race," if you did not soon find yourselves under a necessity of submitting to a power no less absolute, though vested in other persons, and a government differently constituted. And much does it import you to consider, whether those who are now so ready to promise to make *the grievous yoke of your fathers lighter,* may not themselves verify Rehoboam's assertion, and make you feel that *their little fingers are thicker than your father's loins.*

Be it (for the sake of argument) admitted, that the government under which till now you have lived happily, is, most unaccountably, all at once become *oppressive and severe;* did you, of yourselves, make the discovery? No: I affirm, without any apprehension of being contradicted, that you are acquainted with these oppressions only from the report of others. For what, then, (admitting you have a right to resist in any case,) are you now urged to resist and rise against those whom you have hitherto always regarded (and certainly not without reason) as your *nursing fathers and nursing mothers?* Often as you have already heard it repeated without expressing any disapprobation, I assure myself it will afford you no pleasure to be reminded, that it is on account of an insignificant duty on tea, imposed by the British Parliament; and which, for aught we know, may or may not be constitutionally imposed; but which, we well know, two thirds of the people of America can never be called on to pay. Is it the part of an *understanding people,* of loyal subjects, or of good Christians, instantly to resist and rebel for a cause so trivial? O my brethren, consult your

own hearts, and follow your own judgments! and learn not your "measures of obedience" from men who weakly or wickedly imagine there can be liberty unconnected with law—and whose aim it is to drive you on, step by step, to a resistance which will terminate, if it does not begin, in rebellion! On all such trying occasions, learn the line of conduct which it is your duty and interest to observe, from our Constitution itself: which, in this particular, is a fair transcript or exemplification of the ordinance of God. Both the one and the other warn you against resistance: but you are not forbidden either to remonstrate or to petition. And can it be humiliating to any man, or any number of men, to ask, when we have but to *ask and it shall be given?* Is prayer an abject duty; or do men ever appear either so great, or so amiable, as when they are modest and humble? However meanly this privilege of petitioning may be regarded by those who claim every thing as a right, they are challenged to shew an instance, in which it has failed, when it ought to have succeeded. If, however, our grievances, in any point of view, be of such moment as that other means of obtaining redress should be judged expedient, happily we enjoy those means. In a certain sense, some considerable portion of legislation is still in our own hands. We are supposed to have chosen "fit and able" persons to represent us in the great council of our country: and they only can constitutionally interfere either to obtain the enacting of what is right, or the repeal of what is wrong*. If

---

*"Our Assemblies are the true, proper, legal guardians of our rights, privileges, and liberties. If any laws of the British Parliament are thought oppressive; or if, in the administration of the British government, any unnecessary or unreasonable burthen be laid upon us, they are the proper persons to seek for redress, and they are the most likely to succeed. They have the legal and constitutional means in their hands. They are the *real,* not the *pretended,* representatives of the people. They are bodies known and acknowledged by the public laws of the empire. Their representations will be attended to, and their remonstrances heard." — See "A View of the Controversy between Great Britain and her Colonies, p. 25, by A. W. Farmer;" that is, by the late Bishop Seabury of Connecticut.

The fate of the excellent author of this well-written piece, and several others of not inferior merit under the same signature, might well discourage any man who attempts to serve the public, if animated only by the hopes of temporal rewards. When a missionary in the service of the Society for propagating the Gospel in Foreign Parts, whilst the revolt was still in it's infancy, he wrote several seasonable pieces, adapted to the capacities of the people, under the assumed character of a Farmer. They were generally acknowledged to have done much good. But, being attributed to another Gentleman, he alone derived any personal advantage from them: for, to him the British government granted an hand-

we, and our fellow-subjects, have been conscientiously faithful in the discharge of our duty, we can have no reason to doubt that our delegates will be equally faithful in the discharge of theirs. Our Provincial Assemblies, it is true, are but one part of our Colonial Legislature: they form, however, that part which is the most efficient. If the present general topic of complaint be, in their estimation, well founded, and a real and great grievance, what reason have you to imagine that all the Assemblies on the Continent will not concur and be unanimous in so representing it? And if they should all concur so to represent it, it is hardly within the reach of supposition that all due attention will not be paid to their united remonstrances. So many and such large concessions have often been made, at the instance only of individual Assemblies, that we are warranted in relying, that nothing which is reasonable and proper will ever be withheld from us, provided only it be asked for with decency, and that we do not previously forfeit our title to attention by becoming refractory and rebellious.

Let it be supposed, however, that even the worst may happen, which can happen; that our remonstrances are disregarded, our petitions rejected, and our grievances unredressed: what, you will naturally ask—what, in such a case, would I advise you to do?—Advice, alas! is all I have to give; which, however, though you may condescend to ask and to regard it, will neither be asked, nor accepted, by those who alone can give it great effect. Yet, circumscribed as our sphere of influence is, we are not wholly without influence; and therefore, even in our humble department, we have some duties to perform. To your question, therefore, I hesitate not to answer, that I wish and advise you to act the part of reasonable men, and of Christians. You will be pleased to observe, however, that I am far from thinking that your virtue will ever be brought to so severe a test and trial. The question, I am aware, was an ensnaring one, suggested to you by those who are as little solicitous about your peace, as they are for my safety: the answer which, in condescension to your wishes, I have given to it, is direct and plain; and not more applicable to you, than it is to all the people of America. If you think the duty of threepence a pound upon tea, laid on by the British Parliament, a grievance, it is your duty to instruct your members to take all the constitutional means in their power to obtain redress: if those means fail of success, you cannot but be sorry and grieved; but you will better bear your disappointment, by being able to reflect that it was not owing to any misconduct of your own. And, what is the whole history of human life, public or private, but a series of disappointments? It might be hoped that Christians would not think it grievous to be doomed to submit to disappointments and calamities, as their Master submitted, even if they were as innocent. His disciples and first followers shrunk from no trials nor dangers[*]. Treading in the steps of him who, *when he was reviled, blessed, and when he was persecuted, suffered it,* they willingly laid down their lives, rather than resist some of the worst tyrants that ever disgraced the annals of history. Those persons are as little acquainted with general history, as they are with the particular doctrines of Christianity, who represent such submission as abject and servile. I affirm, with great authority, that "there can be no better way of asserting the people's lawful rights, than the disowning unlawful commands, by thus patiently suffering." When this doctrine was more gener-

---

some pension, whilst the real Author never received a farthing. All the return that all his exertions procured for him, was imprisonment, persecution, and exile. By this country he was neglected and abandoned; and by that which gave him birth, disowned: though a man of such transcendent abilities as would have been an ornament and a blessing to any country that had seen fit to patronize him. At length, thankful to be forgiven, he was permitted to return to his native country, where, as the bishop of Connecticut, he was supported by an humble eleemosynary pittance contributed by a few private friends in England; and, in February 1796, died as unnoticed as he had lived. Farewell, poor Seabury!—however neglected in life, there still lives one at least who knew thy worth, and honours thy memory!

"His saltem accumulem donis, & fungar inani

"Munere————"

See an Account of his Consecration in Scotland, in Mr. Skinner's very valuable Ecclesiastical History of Scotland, vol. ii. p. 683. See also the Obituary of the Gentleman's Magazine, p. 442, for May 1797.

Before the troubles, the University of Oxford was pleased to confer on him the honorary degree of D. D.; and in 1793 he published, at New York, two volumes of Discourses, which are such as might have brought credit to any Prelate in any age and in any country. Books of any kind, however, (and, perhaps, Sermons least of all,) not being in much demand in America, he wished to have had them republished in England; and for that purpose furnished the Author of this Volume with six more Discourses, in MS. to be added to them. But, such is the obscurity, or possibly the unpopularity, of a man of unquestionable learning and piety, that no Bookseller has yet ventured to undertake the work.

[*]"Humanity cannot be degraded by humiliation. It is it's very character to submit to such things. There is a consanguinity between benevolence and humility. They are virtues of the same stock."—Burke's Two Letters, 1796, p. 27.

ally embraced, our holy religion gained as much by submission, as it is now in a fair way of losing for want of it.

Having, then, my brethren, thus long been *tossed to and fro* in a wearisome circle of *uncertain traditions,* or in speculations and projects still more uncertain, concerning government, what better can you do than, following the Apostle's advice, *to submit yourselves to every ordinance of man, for the Lord's sake; whether it be to the King as supreme,* *or unto GOVERNORS, as unto them that are SENT by him for the punishment of evil-doers, and for the praise of them that do well? For, so is the will of God, that with well-doing ye may put to silence the ignorance of foolish men: as free, and not using your liberty for a cloke of maliciousness, but as the servants of God. Honour all men: love the brotherhood: fear God: honour the king.*

Common Sense

THOMAS PAINE

January 10, 1776

Thomas Paine (1737–1809) was born in England but frequently referred to himself as a "citizen of the world." He moved to America in 1774, where he was soon involved in the struggle with Great Britain. Paine's powerful rhetoric had a significant effect on the course of events in America. *Common Sense* was by far the most widely read pamphlet of its day and was credited by George Washington, among others, with swaying public opinion in favor of separation from Great Britain. Paine's advocacy of American independence and republicanism represents the most radical edge of thought during this time. In addition to his writings urging revolution in America, he took an active part in the early days of the French Revolution, before being imprisoned by France's revolutionary government. He was saved from execution only by the fall from power (and execution) of the French revolutionary leader Robespierre. His revolutionary activities and frequent attacks against Christian ministers and churches made him many enemies, including in America, and he spent his last years in relative isolation and poverty.

Common Sense

On the Origin and Design of Government in General, with Concise Remarks on the English Constitution

Some writers have so confounded society with government, as to leave little or no distinction between them; whereas they are not only different, but have different origins. Society is produced by our wants and government by our wickedness; the former promotes our happiness *positively* by uniting our affections, the latter *negatively* by restraining our vices. The one encourages intercourse, the other creates distinctions. The first is a patron, the last a punisher.

Society in every state is a blessing, but government, even in its best state, is but a necessary evil; in its worst state an intolerable one: for when we suffer, or are exposed to the same miseries *by a government,* which we might expect in a country *without government,* our calamity is heightened by reflecting that we furnish the means by which we suffer. Government, like dress, is the badge of lost innocence; the palaces of kings are built upon the ruins of the bowers of paradise. For were the impulses of conscience clear, uniform and irresistibly obeyed, man would need no other law-giver; but that not being the case, he finds it necessary to surrender up a part of his property to furnish means for the protection of the rest; and this he is induced to do by the same prudence which in every other case advises him, out of two evils to choose the least. Wherefore, security being the true design and end of government, it unanswerably follows that whatever form thereof appears most likely to ensure it to us, with the least expence and greatest benefit, is preferable to all others.

In order to gain a clear and just idea of the design and end of government, let us suppose a small number of persons settled in some sequestered part of the earth, unconnected with the rest; they will then represent the first peopling of any country, or of the world. In this state of natural liberty, society will be their first thought. A thousand motives will excite them thereto; the strength of one man is so unequal to his wants, and his mind so unfitted for perpetual solitude, that he is soon obliged to seek assistance and relief of another, who in his turn requires the same. Four or five united would be able to raise a tolerable dwelling in the midst of a wilderness, but one man might labor out the common period of life without accomplishing any thing; when he had felled his timber he could not remove it, nor erect it after it was removed; hunger in the mean time would urge him to quit his work, and every different want would call him a different way. Disease, nay even misfortune, would be death; for though neither might be mortal, yet either would disable him from living, and reduce him to a state in which he might rather be said to perish than to die.

Thus necessity, like a gravitating power, would soon form our newly arrived emigrants into society, the reciprocal blessings of which would supercede, and render the obligations of law and government unnecessary while they remained perfectly just to each other; but as nothing but

Heaven is impregnable to vice, it will unavoidably happen that in proportion as they surmount the first difficulties of emigration, which bound them together in a common cause, they will begin to relax in their duty and attachment to each other: and this remissness will point out the necessity of establishing some form of government to supply the defect of moral virtue.

Some convenient tree will afford them a State House, under the branches of which the whole colony may assemble to deliberate on public matters. It is more than probable that their first laws will have the title only of regulations and be enforced by no other penalty than public disesteem. In this first parliament every man by natural right will have a seat.

But as the colony increases, the public concerns will increase likewise, and the distance at which the members may be separated, will render it too inconvenient for all of them to meet on every occasion as at first, when their number was small, their habitations near, and the public concerns few and trifling. This will point out the convenience of their consenting to leave the legislative part to be managed by a select number chosen from the whole body, who are supposed to have the same concerns at stake which those have who appointed them, and who will act in the same manner as the whole body would act were they present. If the colony continue increasing, it will become necessary to augment the number of representatives, and that the interest of every part of the colony may be attended to, it will be found best to divide the whole into convenient parts, each part sending its proper number: and that the *elected* might never form to themselves an interest separate from the *electors,* prudence will point out the propriety of having elections often: because as the *elected* might by that means return and mix again with the general body of the *electors* in a few months, their fidelity to the public will be secured by the prudent reflection of not making a rod for themselves. And as this frequent interchange will establish a common interest with every part of the community, they will mutually and naturally support each other, and on this, (not on the unmeaning name of king,) depends the *strength of government, and the happiness of the governed.*

Here then is the origin and rise of government; namely, a mode rendered necessary by the inability of moral virtue to govern the world; here too is the design and end of government, viz. freedom and security. And however our eyes may be dazzled with show, or our ears deceived by sound; however prejudice may warp our wills, or interest darken

our understanding, the simple voice of nature and reason will say, 'tis right.

I draw my idea of the form of government from a principle in nature which no art can overturn, viz. that the more simple any thing is, the less liable it is to be disordered, and the easier repaired when disordered; and with this maxim in view I offer a few remarks on the so much boasted Constitution of England. That it was noble for the dark and slavish times in which it was erected, is granted. When the world was overrun with tyranny the least remove therefrom was a glorious rescue. But that it is imperfect, subject to convulsions, and incapable of producing what it seems to promise, is easily demonstrated.

Absolute governments, (though the disgrace of human nature) have this advantage with them, they are simple; if the people suffer, they know the head from which their suffering springs; know likewise the remedy; and are not bewildered by a variety of causes and cures. But the Constitution of England is so exceedingly complex, that the nation may suffer for years together without being able to discover in which part the fault lies; some will say in one and some in another, and every political physician will advise a different medicine.

I know it is difficult to get over local or long standing prejudices, yet if we will suffer ourselves to examine the component parts of the English Constitution, we shall find them to be the base remains of two ancient tyrannies, compounded with some new Republican materials.

First.—The remains of monarchical tyranny in the person of the king.

Secondly.—The remains of aristocratical tyranny in the persons of the peers.

Thirdly.—The new Republican materials, in the persons of the Commons, on whose virtue depends the freedom of England.

The two first, by being hereditary, are independent of the people; wherefore in a *constitutional sense* they contribute nothing towards the freedom of the State.

To say that the Constitution of England is an *union* of three powers, reciprocally *checking* each other, is farcical; either the words have no meaning, or they are flat contradictions.

To say that the Commons is a check upon the king, presupposes two things.

First.—That the king is not to be trusted without being looked after; or in other words, that a thirst for absolute power is the natural disease of monarchy.

Secondly.— That the Commons, by being appointed for that purpose, are either wiser or more worthy of confidence than the crown.

But as the same constitution which gives the Commons a power to check the king by withholding the supplies, gives afterwards the king a power to check the Commons, by empowering him to reject their other bills; it again supposes that the king is wiser than those whom it has already supposed to be wiser than him. A mere absurdity!

There is something exceedingly ridiculous in the composition of monarchy; it first excludes a man from the means of information, yet empowers him to act in cases where the highest judgment is required. The state of a king shuts him from the world, yet the business of a king requires him to know it thoroughly; wherefore the different parts, by unnaturally opposing and destroying each other, prove the whole character to be absurd and useless.

Some writers have explained the English Constitution thus: the king, say they, is one, the people another; the peers are a house in behalf of the king, the Commons in behalf of the people; but this hath all the distinctions of a house divided against itself; and though the expressions be pleasantly arranged, yet when examined they appear idle and ambiguous; and it will always happen, that the nicest construction that words are capable of, when applied to the description of something which either cannot exist, or is too incomprehensible to be within the compass of description, will be words of sound only, and though they may amuse the ear, they cannot inform the mind: for this explanation includes a previous question, viz. *how came the king by a power which the people are afraid to trust, and always obliged to check?* Such a power could not be the gift of a wise people, neither can any power, *which needs checking,* be from God; yet the provision which the Constitution makes supposes such a power to exist.

But the provision is unequal to the task; the means either cannot or will not accomplish the end, and the whole affair is a *Felo de se:* for as the greater weight will always carry up the less, and as all the wheels of a machine are put in motion by one, it only remains to know which power in the constitution has the most weight, for that will govern: and though the others, or a part of them, may clog, or, as the phrase is, check the rapidity of its motion, yet so long as they cannot stop it, their endeavours will be ineffectual: The first moving power will at last have its way, and what it wants in speed is supplied by time.

That the crown is this overbearing part in the English Constitution needs not be mentioned, and that it derives its whole consequence merely from being the giver of places and pensions is self-evident; wherefore, though we have been wise enough to shut and lock a door against absolute Monarchy, we at the same time have been foolish enough to put the crown in possession of the key.

The prejudice of Englishmen, in favor of their own government, by king, lords and Commons, arises as much or more from national pride than reason. Individuals are undoubtedly safer in England than in some other countries: but the will of the king is as much the law of the land in Britain as in France, with this difference, that instead of proceeding directly from his mouth, it is handed to the people under the formidable shape of an act of Parliament. For the fate of Charles the First hath only made kings more subtle—not more just.

Wherefore, laying aside all national pride and prejudice in favor of modes and forms, the plain truth is that *it is wholly owing to the constitution of the people, and not to the constitution of the government* that the crown is not as oppressive in England as in Turkey.

An inquiry into the *constitutional errors* in the English form of government, is at this time highly necessary; for as we are never in a proper condition of doing justice to others, while we continue under the influence of some leading partiality, so neither are we capable of doing it to ourselves while we remain fettered by any obstinate prejudice. And as a man who is attached to a prostitute is unfitted to choose or judge of a wife, so any prepossession in favor of a rotten constitution of government will disable us from discerning a good one. . . .

Thoughts on the Present State of American Affairs

In the following pages I offer nothing more than simple facts, plain arguments, and common sense: and have no other preliminaries to settle with the reader, than that he will divest himself of prejudice and prepossession, and suffer his reason and his feelings to determine for themselves: that he will put on, or rather that he will not put off, the true character of a man, and generously enlarge his views beyond the present day.

Volumes have been written on the subject of the struggle between England and America. Men of all ranks have embarked in the controversy, from different motives, and with various designs; but all have been ineffectual, and the period of debate is closed. Arms as the last resource decide the contest; the appeal was the choice of the king, and the continent has accepted the challenge.

It hath been reported of the late Mr. Pelham (who though an able minister was not without his faults) that on his being attacked in the House of Commons on the score that his measures were only of a temporary kind, replied, *"they will last my time."* Should a thought so fatal and unmanly possess the colonies in the present contest, the name of ancestors will be remembered by future generations with detestation.

The sun never shone on a cause of greater worth. 'Tis not the affair of a city, a county, a province, or a kingdom; but of a continent—of at least one eighth part of the habitable globe. 'Tis not the concern of a day, a year, or an age; posterity are virtually involved in the contest, and will be more or less affected even to the end of time, by the proceedings now. Now is the seed-time of continental union, faith and honor. The least fracture now will be like a name engraved with the point of a pin on the tender rind of a young oak; the wound would enlarge with the tree, and posterity read it in full grown characters.

By referring the matter from argument to arms, a new era for politics is struck—a new method of thinkings has arisen. All plans, proposals, &c. prior to the nineteenth of April, *i.e.* to the commencement of hostilities, are like the almanacks of the last year; which though proper then, are superceded and useless now. Whatever was advanced by the advocates on either side of the question then, terminated in one and the same point, viz. a union with Great Britain; the only difference between the parties was the method of effecting it; the one proposing force, the other friendship; but it has so far happened that the first has failed, and the second has withdrawn her influence.

As much has been said of the advantages of reconciliation, which, like an agreeable dream, has passed away and left us as we were, it is but right that we should examine the contrary side of the argument, and inquire into some of the many material injuries which these colonies sustain, and always will sustain, by being connected with and dependant on Great Britain. To examine that connection and dependance, on the principles of nature and common sense, to see what we have to trust to, if separated, and what we are to expect, if dependant.

I have heard it asserted by some, that as America has flourished under her former connection with Great Britain, the same connection is necessary towards her future happiness, and will always have the same effect. Nothing can be more fallacious than this kind of argument. We may as well assert that because a child has thrived upon milk, that it is never to have meat, or that the first twenty years of our lives is to become a precedent for the next twenty. But even this is admitting more than is true; for I answer roundly, that America would have flourished as much, and probably much more, had no European power taken any notice of her. The commerce by which she hath enriched herself are the necessaries of life, and will always have a market while eating is the custom of Europe.

But she has protected us, say some. That she hath engrossed us is true, and defended the continent at our expense as well as her own, is admitted; and she would have defended Turkey from the same motive, *viz.* for the sake of trade and dominion.

Alas! we have been long led away by ancient prejudices and made large sacrifices to superstition. We have boasted the protection of Great Britain, without considering, that her motive was *interest* not *attachment;* and that she did not protect us from *our enemies* on *our account;* but from *her enemies* on *her own account,* from those who had no quarrel with us on any *other account,* and who will always be our enemies on the *same account.* Let Britain waive her pretensions to the continent, or the continent throw off the dependance, and we should be at peace with France and Spain, were they at war with Britain. The miseries of Hanover's last war ought to warn us against connections.

It hath lately been asserted in Parliament, that the colonies have no relation to each other but through the parent country, *i.e.* that Pennsylvania and the Jerseys, and so on for the rest, are sister colonies by the way of England; this is certainly a very roundabout way of proving relationship, but it is the nearest and only true way of proving enmity (or enemyship, if I may so call it.) France and Spain never were, nor perhaps ever will be, our enemies as *Americans,* but as our being the *subjects of Great Britain.*

But Britain is the parent country, say some. Then the more shame upon her conduct. Even brutes do not devour their young, nor savages make war upon their families; wherefore, the assertion, if true, turns to her reproach; but it happens not to be true, or only partly so, and the phrase *parent* or *mother country* hath been jesuitically adopted by the king and his parasites, with a low papistical design of gaining an unfair bias on the credulous weakness of our minds. Europe, and not England, is the parent country of

America. This new world hath been the asylum for the persecuted lovers of civil and religious liberty from *every part* of Europe. Hither have they fled, not from the tender embraces of the mother, but from the cruelty of the monster; and it is so far true of England, that the same tyranny which drove the first emigrants from home, pursues their descendants still.

In this extensive quarter of the globe, we forget the narrow limits of three hundred and sixty miles (the extent of England) and carry our friendship on a larger scale; we claim brotherhood with every European Christian, and triumph in the generosity of the sentiment.

It is pleasant to observe by what regular gradations we surmount the force of local prejudices, as we enlarge our acquaintance with the world. A man born in any town in England divided into parishes, will naturally associate most with his fellow parishioners (because their interests in many cases will be common) and distinguish him by the name of *neighbor;* if he meet him but a few miles from home, he drops the narrow idea of a street, and salutes him by the name of *townsman;* if he travel out of the county and meet him in any other, he forgets the minor divisions of street and town, and calls him *countryman, i.e. countyman;* but if in their foreign excursions they should associate in France, or any other part of *Europe,* their local remembrance would be enlarged into that of *Englishman.* And by a just parity of reasoning, all Europeans meeting in America, or any other quarter of the globe, are *countrymen;* for England, Holland, Germany, or Sweden, when compared with the whole, stand in the same places on the larger scale, which the divisions of street, town, and county do on the smaller ones; distinctions too limited for continental minds. Not one third of the inhabitants, even of this province, [Pennsylvania], are of English descent. Wherefore, I reprobate the phrase of parent or mother country applied to England only, as being false, selfish, narrow and ungenerous.

But, admitting that we were all of English descent, what does it amount to? Nothing. Britain, being now an open enemy, extinguishes every other name and title: and to say that reconciliation is our duty, is truly farcical. The first king of England, of the present line (William the Conqueror) was a Frenchman, and half the peers of England are descendants from the same country; wherefore, by the same method of reasoning, England ought to be governed by France.

Much hath been said of the united strength of Britain and the colonies, that in conjunction they might bid defiance to the world. But this is mere presumption; the fate of war is uncertain, neither do the expressions mean any thing; for this continent would never suffer itself to be drained of inhabitants, to support the British arms in either Asia, Africa or Europe.

Besides, what have we to do with setting the world at defiance? Our plan is commerce, and that, well attended to, will secure us the peace and friendship of all Europe; because it is the interest of all Europe to have America a free port. Her trade will always be a protection, and her barrenness of gold and silver secure her from invaders.

I challenge the warmest advocate for reconciliation to show a single advantage that this continent can reap by being connected with Great Britain. I repeat the challenge; not a single advantage is derived. Our corn will fetch its price in any market in Europe, and our imported goods must be paid for, buy them where we will.

But the injuries and disadvantages which we sustain by that connection, are without number; and our duty to mankind at large, as well as to ourselves, instruct us to renounce the alliance: because, any submission to, or dependence on, Great Britain, tends directly to involve this continent in European wars and quarrels, and set us at variance with nations who would otherwise seek our friendship, and against whom we have neither anger nor complaint. As Europe is our market for trade, we ought to form no partial connection with any part of it. It is the true interest of America to steer clear of European contentions, which she never can do, while, by her dependence on Britain, she is made the make-weight in the scale of British politics.

Europe is too thickly planted with kingdoms to be long at peace, and whenever a war breaks out between England and any foreign power, the trade of America goes to ruin, *because of her connection with Britain.* The next war may not turn out like the last, and should it not, the advocates for reconciliation now will be wishing for separation then, because neutrality in that case would be a safer convoy than a man of war. Every thing that is right or reasonable pleads for separation. The blood of the slain, the weeping voice of nature cries, 'TIS TIME TO PART. Even the distance at which the Almighty hath placed England and America is a strong and natural proof that the authority of the one over the other, was never the design of heaven. The time likewise at which the continent was discovered, adds weight to the argument, and the manner in which it was peopled, increases the force of it. The Reformation was preceded by the discovery of America: As if the Almighty graciously meant to open a sanctuary to the persecuted in future years, when home should afford neither friendship nor safety.

The authority of Great Britain over this continent, is a form of government, which sooner or later must have an end. And a serious mind can draw no true pleasure by looking forward, under the painful and positive conviction that what he calls "the present constitution" is merely temporary. As parents, we can have no joy, knowing that this government is not sufficiently lasting to insure any thing which we may bequeath to posterity. And by a plain method of argument, as we are running the next generation into debt, we ought to do the work of it, otherwise we use them meanly and pitifully. In order to discover the line of our duty rightly, we should take our children in our hand, and fix our station a few years farther into life; that eminence will present a prospect which a few present fears and prejudices conceal from our sight.

Though I would carefully avoid giving unnecessary offence, yet I am inclined to believe, that all those who espouse the doctrine of reconciliation, may be included within the following descriptions.

Interested men, who are not to be trusted, weak men who *cannot* see, prejudiced men who will not see, and a certain set of moderate men who think better of the European world than it deserves; and this last class, by an ill-judged deliberation, will be the cause of more calamities to this continent than all the other three.

It is the good fortune of many to live distant from the scene of present sorrow; the evil is not sufficiently brought to their doors to make them feel the precariousness with which all American property is possessed. But let our imaginations transport us a few moments to Boston; that seat of wretchedness will teach us wisdom, and instruct us for ever to renounce a power in whom we can have no trust. The inhabitants of that unfortunate city who but a few months ago were in ease and affluence, have now no other alternative than to stay and starve, or turn out to beg. Endangered by the fire of their friends if they continue within the city, and plundered by the soldiery if they leave it, in their present situation they are prisoners without the hope of redemption, and in a general attack for their relief they would be exposed to the fury of both armies.

Men of passive tempers look somewhat lightly over the offences of Great Britain, and, still hoping for the best, are apt to call out, *Come, come, we shall be friends again for all this.* But examine the passions and feelings of mankind: bring the doctrine of reconciliation to the touchstone of nature, and then tell me whether you can hereafter love, honor, and faithfully serve the power that hath carried fire and sword into your land? If you cannot do all these, then are you only deceiving yourselves, and by your delay bringing ruin upon posterity. Your future connection with Britain, whom you can neither love nor honor, will be forced and unnatural, and being formed only on the plan of present convenience, will in a little time fall into a relapse more wretched than the first. But if you say, you can still pass the violations over, then I ask, hath your house been burnt? Hath your property been destroyed before your face? Are your wife and children destitute of a bed to lie on, or bread to live on? Have you lost a parent or a child by their hands, and yourself the ruined and wretched survivor? If you have not, then are you not a judge of those who have. But if you have, and can still shake hands with the murderers, then are you unworthy the name of husband, father, friend, or lover, and whatever may be your rank or title in life, you have the heart of a coward, and the spirit of a sycophant.

This is not inflaming or exaggerating matters, but trying them by those feelings and affections which nature justifies, and without which we should be incapable of discharging the social duties of life, or enjoying the felicities of it. I mean not to exhibit horror for the purpose of provoking revenge, but to awaken us from fatal and unmanly slumbers, that we may pursue determinately some fixed object. 'Tis not in the power of Britain or of Europe to conquer America, if she doth not conquer herself by delay and timidity. The present winter is worth an age if rightly employed, but if lost or neglected the whole continent will partake of the misfortune; and there is no punishment which that man doth not deserve, be he who, or what, or where he will, that may be the means of sacrificing a season so precious and useful.

'Tis repugnant to reason, to the universal order of things, to all examples from former ages, to suppose that this continent can long remain subject to any external power. The most sanguine in Britain doth not think so. The utmost stretch of human wisdom cannot, at this time, compass a plan, short of separation, which can promise the continent even a year's security. Reconciliation is *now* a fallacious dream. Nature has deserted the connection, and art cannot supply her place. For, as Milton wisely expresses, "never can true reconcilement grow where wounds of deadly hate have pierced so deep."

Every quiet method for peace hath been ineffectual. Our prayers have been rejected with disdain; and hath tended to convince us that nothing flatters vanity or confirms obstinacy in kings more than repeated petitioning—and nothing hath contributed more than that very measure to make the kings of Europe absolute. Witness Denmark and Sweden. Wherefore, since nothing but blows will do, for God's sake let us come to a final separation, and not leave the next generation to be cutting throats under the violated unmeaning names of parent and child.

To say they will never attempt it again is idle and visionary; we thought so at the repeal of the Stamp Act, yet a year or two undeceived us; as well may we suppose that nations which have been once defeated will never renew the quarrel.

As to government matters, 'tis not in the power of Britain to do this continent justice: the business of it will soon be too weighty and intricate to be managed with any tolerable degree of convenience, by a power so distant from us, and so very ignorant of us; for if they cannot conquer us, they cannot govern us. To be always running three or four thousand miles with a tale or a petition, waiting four or five months for an answer, which, when obtained, requires five or six more to explain it in, will in a few years be looked upon as folly and childishness. There was a time when it was proper, and there is a proper time for it to cease.

Small islands not capable of protecting themselves are the proper objects for government to take under their care; but there is something absurd, in supposing a Continent to be perpetually governed by an island. In no instance hath nature made the satellite larger than its primary planet; and as England and America, with respect to each other, reverse the common order of nature, it is evident that they belong to different systems. England to Europe: America to itself.

I am not induced by motives of pride, party or resentment to espouse the doctrine of separation and independence; I am clearly, positively, and conscientiously persuaded that it is the true interest of this continent to be so; that everything short of *that* is mere patchwork, that it can afford no lasting felicity,—that it is leaving the sword to our children, and shrinking back at a time when a little more, a little further, would have rendered this continent the glory of the earth.

As Britain hath not manifested the least inclination towards a compromise, we may be assured that no terms can be obtained worthy the acceptance of the continent, or any ways equal to the expence of blood and treasure we have been already put to.

The object contended for, ought always to bear some just proportion to the expense. The removal of North, or the whole detestable junto, is a matter unworthy the millions we have expended. A temporary stoppage of trade was an inconvenience, which would have sufficiently balanced the repeal of all the acts complained of, had such repeals been obtained; but if the whole continent must take up arms, if every man must be a soldier, 'tis scarcely worth our while to fight against a contemptible ministry only. Dearly, dearly do we pay for the repeal of the acts, if that is all we fight for; for, in a just estimation 'tis as great a folly to pay a Bunker Hill price for law as for land. As I have always considered the independency of this continent, as an event which sooner or later must arrive, so from the late rapid progress of the continent to maturity, the event cannot be far off. Wherefore, on the breaking out of hostilities, it was not worth the while to have disputed a matter which time would have finally redressed, unless we meant to be in earnest: otherwise it is like wasting an estate on a suit at law, to regulate the trespasses of a tenant whose lease is just expiring. No man was a warmer wisher for a reconciliation than myself, before the fatal nineteenth of April, 1775, but the moment the event of that day was made known, I rejected the hardened, sullen-tempered Pharaoh of England for ever; and disdain the wretch, that with the pretended title of FATHER OF HIS PEOPLE can unfeelingly hear of their slaughter, and composedly sleep with their blood upon his soul.

But admitting that matters were now made up, what would be the event? I answer, the ruin of the continent. And that for several reasons.

First. The powers of governing still remaining in the hands of the king, he will have a negative over the whole legislation of this continent. And as he hath shown himself such an inveterate enemy to liberty, and discovered such a thirst for arbitrary power, is he, or is he not, a proper person to say to these colonies, *You shall make no laws but what I please!?* And is there any inhabitant of America so ignorant as not to know, that according to what is called the *present Constitution,* this continent can make no laws but what the king gives leave to; and is there any man so unwise as not to see, that (considering what has happened) he will suffer no law to be made here but such as suits *his* purpose? We may be as effectually enslaved by the want of laws in America, as by submitting to laws made for us in England. After matters are made up (as it is called) can there be any doubt, but the whole power of the crown will be exerted to keep this continent as low and humble as possible? Instead of going forward we shall go backward, or be perpetually quarrelling, or ridiculously petitioning. We are already greater than the king wishes us to be, and will he not hereafter endeavor to make us less? To bring the matter to one point, Is the power who is jealous of our prosperity, a proper power to govern us? Whoever says *No,* to this question, is an independent for independency means no more than this, whether we shall make our own laws, or, whether the king, the greatest enemy this continent hath, or can have, shall tell us *there shall be no laws but such as I like.*

But the king, you will say, has a negative in England; the people there can make no laws without his consent. In point of right and good order, it is something very ridiculous that a youth of twenty-one (which hath often happened) shall say to several millions of people older and wiser than himself, "I forbid this or that act of yours to be law." But in this place I decline this sort of reply, though I will never cease to expose the absurdity of it, and only answer that England being the king's residence, and America not so, makes quite another case. The king's negative here is ten times more dangerous and fatal than it can be in England; for there he will scarcely refuse his consent to a bill for putting England into as strong a state of defense as possible, and in America he would never suffer such a bill to be passed.

America is only a secondary object in the system of British politics. England consults the good of this country no further than it answers her own purpose. Wherefore, her own interest leads her to suppress the growth of ours in every case which doth not promote her advantage, or in the least interferes with it. A pretty state we should soon be in under such a second hand government, considering what has happened! Men do not change from enemies to friends by the alteration of a name: And in order to show that reconciliation now is a dangerous doctrine, I affirm, *that it would be policy in the king at this time to repeal the acts, for the sake of reinstating himself in the government of*

the provinces; In order that HE MAY ACCOMPLISH BY CRAFT AND SUBTLETY, IN THE LONG RUN, WHAT HE CANNOT DO BY FORCE AND VIOLENCE IN THE SHORT ONE. Reconciliation and ruin are nearly related.

Secondly. That as even the best terms which we can expect to obtain can amount to no more than a temporary expedient, or a kind of government by guardianship, which can last no longer than till the colonies come of age, so the general face and state of things in the interim will be unsettled and unpromising. Emigrants of property will not choose to come to a country whose form of government hangs but by a thread, and who is every day tottering on the brink of commotion and disturbance; and numbers of the present inhabitants would lay hold of the interval to dispose of their effects, and quit the continent.

But the most powerful of all arguments is, that nothing but independence, *i.e.* a continental form of government, can keep the peace of the continent and preserve it inviolate from civil wars. I dread the event of a reconciliation with Britain now, as it is more than probable that it will be followed by a revolt some where or other, the consequences of which may be far more fatal than all the malice of Britain.

Thousands are already ruined by British barbarity; (thousands more will probably suffer the same fate). Those men have other feelings than us who have nothing suffered. All they now possess is liberty; what they before enjoyed is sacrificed to its service, and having nothing more to lose they disdain submission. Besides, the general temper of the colonies, towards a British government will be like that of a youth who is nearly out of his time; they will care very little about her: And a government which cannot preserve the peace is no government at all, and in that case we pay our money for nothing; and pray what is it that Britain can do, whose power will be wholly on paper, should a civil tumult break out the very day after reconciliation? I have heard some men say, many of whom I believe spoke without thinking, that they dreaded an independence, fearing that it would produce civil wars: It is but seldom that our first thoughts are truly correct, and that is the case here; for there is ten times more to dread from a patched up connection than from independence. I make the sufferer's case my own, and I protest, that were I driven from house and home, my property destroyed, and my circumstances ruined, that as a man, sensible of injuries, I could never relish the doctrine of reconciliation, or consider myself bound thereby.

The colonies have manifested such a spirit of good order and obedience to continental government, as is sufficient to make every reasonable person easy and happy on that head. No man can assign the least pretence for his fears, on any other grounds, than such as are truly childish and ridiculous, viz., that one colony will be striving for superiority over another.

Where there are no distinctions there can be no superiority; perfect equality affords no temptation. The Republics of Europe are all (and we may say always) in peace. Holland and Switzerland are without wars, foreign or domestic: Monarchical governments, it is true, are never long at rest: the crown itself is a temptation to enterprising ruffians at home; and that degree of pride and insolence ever attendant on regal authority, swells into a rupture with foreign powers in instances where a republican government, by being formed on more natural principles, would negociate the mistake.

If there is any true cause of fear respecting independence, it is because no plan is yet laid down. Men do not see their way out. Wherefore, as an opening into that business I offer the following hints; at the same time modestly affirming, that I have no other opinion of them myself, than that they may be the means of giving rise to something better. Could the straggling thoughts of individuals be collected, they would frequently form materials for wise and able men to improve into useful matter.

Let the assemblies be annual, with a president only. The representation more equal, their business wholly domestic, and subject to the authority of a Continental Congress.

Let each colony be divided into six, eight, or ten, convenient districts, each district to send a proper number of delegates to Congress, so that each colony send at least thirty. The whole number in Congress will be at least 390. Each Congress to sit and to choose a President by the following method. When the delegates are met, let a colony be taken from the whole thirteen colonies by lot, after which let the Congress choose (by ballot) a President from out of the delegates of that province. In the next Congress, let a colony be taken by lot from twelve only, omitting that colony from which the president was taken in the former Congress, and so proceeding on till the whole thirteen shall have had their proper rotation. And in order that nothing may pass into a law but what is satisfactorily just, not less than three-fifths of the Congress to be called a majority. He that will promote discord, under a government so equally formed as this, would have joined Lucifer in his revolt.

But as there is a peculiar delicacy from whom, or in what manner, this business must first arise, and as it seems most agreeable and consistent that it should come from some intermediate body between the governed and the governors, that is, between the Congress and the people, let a continental conference be held in the following manner, and for the following purpose,

A committee of twenty-six members of Congress, *viz.* Two for each colony. Two members from each House of Assembly, or Provincial Convention; and five representatives of the people at large, to be chosen in the capital city or town of each province, for, and in behalf of the whole province, by as many qualified voters as shall think proper to attend from all parts of the province for that purpose; or, if more convenient, the representatives may be chosen in two or three of the most populous parts thereof. In this conference, thus assembled, will be united the two grand principles of business, *knowledge* and *power*. The Members of Congress, Assemblies, or Conventions, by having had experience in national concerns, will be able and useful counsellors, and the whole, being impowered by the people, will have a truly legal authority.

The conferring members being met, let their business be to frame a Continental Charter, or Charter of the United Colonies; (answering to what is called the Magna Charta of England) fixing the number and manner of choosing Members of Congress, Members of Assembly, with their date of sitting; and drawing the line of business and jurisdiction between them: Always remembering, that our strength is continental, not provincial. Securing freedom and property to all men, and above all things, the free exercise of religion, according to the dictates of conscience; with such other matter as it is necessary for a charter to contain. Immediately after which, the said conference to dissolve, and the bodies which shall be chosen conformable to the said charter, to be the legislators and governors of this continent for the time being: Whose peace and happiness, may GOD preserve. AMEN.

Should any body of men be hereafter delegated for this or some similar purpose, I offer them the following extracts from that wise observer on governments, Dragonetti. "The science," says he, "of the politician consists in fixing the true point of happiness and freedom. Those men would deserve the gratitude of ages, who should discover a mode of government that contained the greatest sum of individual happiness, with the least national expense." (Dragonetti on "Virtues and Reward.")

But where, say some, is the king of America? I'll tell you, friend, he reigns above, and doth not make havoc of mankind like the royal brute of Great Britain. Yet that we may not appear to be defective even in earthly honors, let a day be solemnly set apart for proclaiming the charter; let it be brought forth placed on the divine law, the Word of God; let a crown be placed thereon, by which the world may know, that so far as we approve of monarchy, that in America the law is king. For as in absolute governments the king is law, so in free countries the law ought to be king; and there ought to be no other. But lest any ill use should afterwards arise, let the crown at the conclusion of the ceremony be demolished, and scattered among the people whose right it is.

A government of our own is our natural right: and when a man seriously reflects on the precariousness of human affairs, he will become convinced, that it is infinitely wiser and safer, to form a Constitution of our own in a cool deliberate manner, while we have it in our power, than to trust such an interesting event to time and chance. If we omit it now, some Massanello may hereafter arise, who, laying hold of popular disquietudes, may collect together the desperate and the discontented, and by assuming to themselves the powers of government, finally sweep away the liberties of the continent like a deluge. Should the government of America return again into the hands of Britain, the tottering situation of things will be a temptation for some desperate adventurer to try his fortune; and in such a case, what relief can Britain give? Ere she could hear the news, the fatal business might be done; and ourselves suffering like the wretched Britons under the oppression of the conqueror. Ye that oppose independence now, ye know not what ye do: ye are opening a door to eternal tyranny, by keeping vacant the seat of government. There are thousands and tens of thousands, who would think it glorious to expel from the continent, that barbarous and hellish power, which hath stirred up the Indians and the Negroes to destroy us; the cruelty hath a double guilt, it is dealing brutally by us, and treacherously by them.

To talk of friendship with those in whom our reason forbids us to have faith, and our affections wounded through a thousand pores instruct us to detest, is madness and folly. Every day wears out the little remains of kindred between us and them; and can there be any reason to hope, that as the relationship expires, the affection will increase, or that we shall agree better when we have ten times more and greater concerns to quarrel over than ever?

Ye that tell us of harmony and reconciliation, can ye restore to us the time that is past? Can ye give to prostitution its former innocence? neither can ye reconcile Britain and America. The last cord now is broken, the people of England are presenting addresses against us. There are injuries which nature cannot forgive; she would cease to be nature if she did. As well can the lover forgive the ravisher of his mistress, as the continent forgive the murders of Britain. The Almighty hath implanted in us these unextinguishable feelings for good and wise purposes. They are the guardians of his image in our hearts. They distinguish us from the herd of common animals. The social compact would dissolve, and justice be extirpated from the earth, or have only a casual existence were we callous to the touches of affection. The robber and the murderer would often escape unpunished, did not the injuries which our tempers sustain, provoke us into justice.

O! ye that love mankind! Ye that dare oppose not only the tyranny but the tyrant, stand forth! Every spot of the old world is overrun with oppression. Freedom hath been hunted round the globe. Asia and Africa have long expelled her. Europe regards her like a stranger, and England hath given her warning to depart. O! receive the fugitive, and prepare in time an asylum for mankind.

The Declaration of Independence

July 4, 1776

By the time the Continental Congress had decided to declare independence from Great Britain, armed conflict had been raging for more than a year. Soldiers on both sides were dying, and it was becoming increasingly clear that Parliament would not accede to American colonists' demands. Armed resistance would die out, however, without financial and material assistance—most prominently available from Britain's old enemy, France. In order to secure such aid, and to solidify support among opponents of parliamentary authority in America, the Continental Congress determined to officially declare the independence of the thirteen colonies from Great Britain. Jefferson's preamble to the Declaration, with its seemingly abstract statements of inalienable rights, is often quoted. Less quoted is the main body of the text, in which the Congress details the abuses committed by King George against his people in America. The charges are levelled against the king rather than Parliament. The principal reason for this is that Americans believed that their rights were secured through charters granted by the king. In the American view, it was the king alone, acting through colonial governments, through whom they were connected with the people and government of Great Britain.

The Declaration of Independence

In Congress, July 4, 1776,

The Unanimous Declaration of the
Thirteen United States of America

When in the Course of human events, it becomes necessary for one people to dissolve the political bands which have connected them with another, and to assume among the powers of the earth, the separate and equal station to which the Laws of Nature and of Nature's God entitle them, a decent respect to the opinions of mankind requires that they should declare the causes which impel them to the separation.

We hold these truths to be self-evident, that all men are created equal, that they are endowed by their Creator with certain unalienable Rights, that among these are Life, Liberty and the pursuit of Happiness. That to secure these rights, Governments are instituted among Men, deriving their just powers from the consent of the governed. That whenever any Form of Government becomes destructive of these ends, it is the Right of the People to alter or to abolish it, and to institute new Government, laying its foundation on such principles and organizing its powers in such form, as to them shall seem most likely to effect their Safety and Happiness. Prudence, indeed, will dictate that Governments long established should not be changed for light and transient causes; and accordingly all experience hath shown, that mankind are more disposed to suffer, while evils are sufferable, than to right themselves by abolishing the forms to which they are accustomed. But when a long train of abuses and usurpations, pursuing invariably the same Object evinces a design to reduce them under absolute Despotism, it is their right, it is their duty, to throw off such Government, and to provide new Guards for their future security.—Such has been the patient sufferance of these Colonies; and such is now the necessity which constrains them to alter their former Systems of Government. The history of the present King of Great Britain is a history of repeated injuries and usurpations, all having in direct object the establishment of an absolute Tyranny over these States. To prove this, let Facts be submitted to a candid world.

He has refused his Assent to Laws, the most wholesome and necessary for the public good.

He has forbidden his Governors to pass Laws of immediate and pressing importance, unless suspended in their operation till his Assent should be obtained; and when so suspended, he has utterly neglected to attend to them.

He has refused to pass other Laws for the accommodation of large districts of people, unless those people would relinquish the right of Representation in the Legislature, a right inestimable to them and formidable to tyrants only.

He has called together legislative bodies at places unusual, uncomfortable, and distant from the depository of their Public Records, for the sole purpose of fatiguing them into compliance with his measures.

He has dissolved Representative Houses repeatedly, for

opposing with manly firmness his invasions on the rights of the people.

He has refused for a long time, after such dissolutions, to cause others to be elected; whereby the Legislative Powers, incapable of Annihilation, have returned to the People at large for their exercise; the State remaining in the mean time exposed to all the dangers of invasion from without, and convulsions within.

He has endeavoured to prevent the population of these States; for that purpose obstructing the Laws of Naturalization of Foreigners; refusing to pass others to encourage their migration hither, and raising the conditions of new Appropriations of Lands.

He has obstructed the Administration of Justice, by refusing his Assent to Laws for establishing Judiciary Powers.

He has made Judges dependent on his Will alone, for the tenure of their offices, and the amount and payment of their salaries.

He has erected a multitude of New Offices, and sent hither swarms of Officers to harass our People, and eat out their substance.

He has kept among us, in times of peace, Standing Armies without the Consent of our legislatures.

He has affected to render the Military independent of and superior to the Civil power.

He has combined with others to subject us to a jurisdiction foreign to our constitution, and unacknowledged by our laws; giving his Assent to their acts of pretended Legislation:

For Quartering large bodies of armed troops among us:

For protecting them, by a mock Trial, from punishment for any Murders which they should commit on the Inhabitants of these States:

For cutting off our Trade with all parts of the world:

For imposing taxes on us without our Consent:

For depriving us in many cases, of the benefits of Trial by Jury:

For transporting us beyond Seas to be tried for pretended offenses:

For abolishing the free System of English Laws in a neighboring Province, establishing therein an Arbitrary government, and enlarging its Boundaries so as to render it at once an example and fit instrument for introducing the same absolute rule into these Colonies:

For taking away our Charters, abolishing our most valuable Laws, and altering fundamentally the Forms of our Governments:

For suspending our own Legislatures, and declaring themselves invested with power to legislate for us in all cases whatsoever.

He has abdicated Government here, by declaring us out of his Protection and waging War against us.

He has plundered our seas, ravaged our Coasts, burnt our towns, and destroyed the lives of our people.

He is at this time transporting large armies of foreign mercenaries to complete the works of death, desolation and tyranny, already begun with circumstances of Cruelty & perfidy scarcely paralleled in the most barbarous ages, and totally unworthy the Head of a civilized nation.

He has constrained our fellow Citizens taken Captive on the high Seas to bear Arms against their Country, to become the executioners of their friends and Brethren, or to fall themselves by their Hands.

He has excited domestic insurrections amongst us, and has endeavoured to bring on the inhabitants of our frontiers, the merciless Indian Savages, whose known rule of warfare, is an undistinguished destruction of all ages, sexes and conditions.

In every stage of these Oppressions We have Petitioned for Redress in the most humble terms: Our repeated petitions have been answered only by repeated injury. A Prince, whose character is thus marked by every act which may define a Tyrant, is unfit to be the ruler of a free people.

Nor have We been wanting in attention to our British brethren. We have warned them from time to time of attempts by their legislature to extend an unwarrantable jurisdiction over us. We have reminded them of the circumstances of our emigration and settlement here. We have appealed to their native justice and magnanimity, and we have conjured them by the ties of our common kindred to disavow these usurpations, which would inevitably interrupt our connections and correspondence. They too have been deaf to the voice of justice and of consanguinity. We must, therefore, acquiesce in the necessity, which denounces our Separation, and hold them, as we hold the rest of mankind, Enemies in War, in Peace Friends.

We, therefore, the Representatives of the United States of America, in General Congress Assembled, appealing to the Supreme Judge of the world for the rectitude of our intentions, do, in the Name and by Authority of the good People of these Colonies, solemnly publish and declare, That these United Colonies are, and of Right ought to be Free and Independent States; that they are Absolved from all Allegiance to the British Crown, and that all political connection between them and the State of Great Britain, is and ought to be totally dissolved; and that as Free and Independent States, they have full Power to levy War, conclude Peace, contract Alliances, establish Commerce, and to do all other Acts and Things which Independent States may of right do. And for the support of this Declaration, with a firm reliance on the protection of divine Providence, we mutually pledge to each other our Lives, our Fortunes and our sacred Honor.

John Hancock

New Hampshire
Josiah Bartlett
William Whipple
Matthew Thornton

Massachusetts
John Hancock
Samuel Adams
John Adams
Robert Treat Paine
Elbridge Gerry

Rhode Island
Stephen Hopkins
William Ellery

Connecticut
Roger Sherman
Samuel Huntington
William Williams
Oliver Wolcott

New York
William Floyd
Philip Livingston
Francis Lewis
Lewis Morris

New Jersey
Richard Stockton
John Witherspoon
Francis Hopkinson
John Hart
Abraham Clark

Pennsylvania
Robert Morris
Benjamin Rush
Benjamin Franklin
John Morton
George Clymer
James Smith
George Taylor
James Wilson
George Ross

Delaware
Caesar Rodney
George Read
Thomas McKean

Maryland
Samuel Chase
William Paca
Thomas Stone
Charles Carroll of
   Carrollton

Virginia
George Wythe
Richard Henry Lee
Thomas Jefferson
Benjamin Harrison
Thomas Nelson, Jr.
Francis Lightfoot Lee
Carter Braxton

North Carolina
William Hooper
Joseph Hewes
John Penn

South Carolina
Edward Rutledge
Thomas Heyward, Jr.
Thomas Lynch, Jr.
Arthur Middleton

Georgia
Button Gwinnett
Lyman Hall
George Walton

PART FIVE A New Constitution

Fourth U.S. president and *Federalist* author, James Madison, by Gilbert Stuart. © Bettmann/CORBIS

Painting of Alexander Hamilton, American statesman and *Federalist* author. © Bettmann/CORBIS

John Jay, first chief justice and *Federalist* author; head-and-shoulders engraving by Hall. © Bettmann/CORBIS

By the time the American Revolution came to its close, Americans had a great deal of experience in drafting frames of government or constitutions. Inheritors of a long tradition of charter writing, Americans had drafted their own governing documents since the earliest days of settlement in the New World. Various colonies adapted existing documents or drew up new ones in their early days of independence, and the newly independent states had formed a confederation to tend their common concerns. But the task of forming a "more perfect union" to better handle the economic and political uncertainties of life free from British rule was nonetheless monumental. Documents and essays here, building on those presented earlier, highlight the various plans and arguments put forth to secure ordered liberty for the American people, as a nation and in their various states and localities.

Thoughts on Government

JOHN ADAMS

1776

Adams was among the most influential leaders of the founding generation. He helped draft the Declaration of Independence and the Articles of Confederation and was the primary author of the Massachusetts Constitution of 1780, which is still in effect at this writing. Richard Henry Lee published Adams's "Thoughts on Government" as a pamphlet, drawn from a letter Adams had written to George Wythe and, with slight variations, several other delegates to the First Continental Congress. In it, Adams makes the case for republican government and, more particularly, for the separation of powers among legislative, executive, and judicial branches. "Thoughts on Government" was highly influential, particularly among those drafting state constitutions.

Thoughts on Government

My dear Sir,

If I was equal to the task of forming a plan for the government of a colony, I should be flattered with your request, and very happy to comply with it; because, as the divine science of politics is the science of social happiness, and the blessings of society depend entirely on the constitutions of government, which are generally institutions that last for many generations, there can be no employment more agreeable to a benevolent mind than a research after the best.

Pope flattered tyrants too much when he said,

For forms of government let fools contest,
That which is best administered is best.

Nothing can be more fallacious than this. But poets read history to collect flowers, not fruits; they attend to fanciful images, not the effects of social institutions. Nothing is more certain, from the history of nations and nature of man, than that some forms of government are better fitted for being well administered than others.

We ought to consider what is the end of government, before we determine which is the best form. Upon this point all speculative politicians will agree, that the happiness of society is the end of government, as all divines and moral philosophers will agree that the happiness of the individual is the end of man. From this principle it will follow, that the form of government which communicates ease, comfort, security, or, in one word, happiness, to the greatest number of persons, and in the greatest degree, is the best.

All sober inquirers after truth, ancient and modern, pagan and Christian, have declared that the happiness of man, as well as his dignity, consists in virtue. Confucius, Zoroaster, Socrates, Mahomet, not to mention authorities really sacred, have agreed in this.

If there is a form of government, then, whose principle and foundation is virtue, will not every sober man acknowledge it better calculated to promote the general happiness than any other form?

Fear is the foundation of most governments; but it is so sordid and brutal a passion, and renders men in whose breasts it predominates so stupid and miserable, that Americans will not be likely to approve of any political institution which is founded on it.

Honor is truly sacred, but holds a lower rank in the scale of moral excellence than virtue. Indeed, the former is but a part of the latter, and consequently has not equal pretensions to support a frame of government productive of human happiness.

The foundation of every government is some principle or passion in the minds of the people. The noblest principles and most generous affections in our nature, then, have the fairest chance to support the noblest and most generous models of government.

A man must be indifferent to the sneers of modern Englishmen, to mention in their company the names of Sidney, Harrington, Locke, Milton, Nedham, Neville, Burnet, and Hoadly. No small fortitude is necessary to confess that one has read them. The wretched condition of this country, however, for ten or fifteen years past, has frequently reminded me of their principles and reasonings. They will convince any candid mind, that there is no good government but what is republican. That the only valuable part of the British constitution is so; because the very definition of a republic is "an empire of laws, and not of men." That, as a republic is the best of governments, so that particular arrangement of the powers of society, or, in other words, that form of government which is best contrived to secure an impartial and exact execution of the laws, is the best of republics.

Of republics there is an inexhaustible variety, because the possible combinations of the powers of society are capable of innumerable variations.

As good government is an empire of laws, how shall your laws be made? In a large society, inhabiting an extensive country, it is impossible that the whole should assemble to make laws. The first necessary step, then, is to depute power from the many to a few of the most wise and good. But by what rules shall you choose your representatives? Agree upon the number and qualifications of persons who shall have the benefit of choosing, or annex this privilege to the inhabitants of a certain extent of ground.

The principle difficulty lies, and the greatest care should be employed in constituting this representative assembly. It should be in miniature an exact portrait of the people at large. It should think, feel, reason and act like them. That it may be the interest of this assembly to do strict justice at all times, it should be an equal representation, or, in other words, equal interests among the people should have equal interests in it. Great care should be taken to effect this, and to prevent unfair, partial, and corrupt elections. Such regulations, however, may be better made in times of greater tranquillity than the present; and they will spring up themselves naturally, when all the powers of government come to be in the hands of the people's friends. At present, it will be safest to proceed in all established modes, to which the people have been familiarized by habit.

A representation of the people in one assembly being obtained, a question arises, whether all the powers of government, legislative, executive, and judicial, shall be left in this body? I think a people cannot be long free, nor ever happy, whose government is in one assembly. My reasons for this opinion are as follow:—

1. A single assembly is liable to all the vices, follies, and frailties of an individual; subject to fits of humor, starts of passion, flights of enthusiasm, partialities, or prejudice, and consequently productive of hasty results and absurd judgments. And all these errors ought to be corrected and defects supplied by some controlling power.

2. A single assembly is apt to be avaricious, and in time will not scruple to exempt itself from burdens, which it will lay, without compunction, on its constituents.

3. A single assembly is apt to grow ambitious, and after a time will not hesitate to vote itself perpetual. This was one fault of the Long Parliament; but more remarkably of Holland, whose assembly first voted themselves from annual to septennial, then for life, and after a course of years, that all vacancies happening by death or otherwise, should be filled by themselves, without any application to constituents at all.

4. A representative assembly, although extremely well qualified, and absolutely necessary, as a branch of the legislative, is unfit to exercise the executive power, for want of two essential properties, secrecy and despatch.

5. A representative assembly is still less qualified for the judicial power, because it is too numerous, too slow, and too little skilled in the laws.

6. Because a single assembly, possessed of all the powers of government, would make arbitrary laws for their own interest, execute all laws arbitrarily for their own interest, and adjudge all controversies in their own favor.

But shall the whole power of legislation rest in one assembly? Most of the foregoing reasons apply equally to prove that the legislative power ought to be more complex; to which we may add, that if the legislative power is wholly in one assembly, and the executive in another, or in a single person, these two powers will oppose and encroach upon each other, until the contest shall end in war, and the whole power, legislative and executive, be usurped by the strongest.

The judicial power, in such case, could not mediate, or hold the balance between the two contending powers, because the legislative would undermine it. And this shows the necessity, too, of giving the executive power a negative upon the legislative, otherwise this will be continually encroaching upon that.

To avoid these dangers, let a distinct assembly be constituted, as a mediator between the two extreme branches of the legislature, that which represents the people, and that which is vested with the executive power.

Let the representative assembly then elect by ballot, from among themselves or their constituents, or both, a distinct assembly, which, for the sake of perspicuity, we will call a council. It may consist of any number you please, say twenty or thirty, and should have a free and independent exercise of its judgment, and consequently a negative voice in the legislature.

These two bodies, thus constituted, and made integral parts of the legislature, let them unite, and by joint ballot choose a governor, who, after being stripped of most of those badges of domination, called prerogatives, should have a free and independent exercise of his judgment, and be made also an integral part of the legislature. This, I know, is liable to objections; and, if you please, you may make him only president of the council, as in Connecticut. But as the governor is to be invested with the executive power, with consent of council, I think he ought to have a negative upon the legislative. If he is annually elective, as he ought to be, he will always have so much reverence and affection for the people, their representatives and counsellors, that, although you give him an independent exercise of his judgment, he will seldom use it in opposition to the two houses, except in cases the public utility of which would be conspicuous; and some such cases would happen.

In the present exigency of American affairs, when, by an act of Parliament, we are put out of the royal protection, and consequently discharged from our allegiance, and it has become necessary to assume government for our immediate security, the governor, lieutenant-governor, secretary, treasurer, commissary, attorney-general, should be chosen by joint ballot of both houses. And these and all other elections, especially of representatives and counsellors, should be annual, there not being in the whole circle of the sciences a maxim more infallible than this, "where annual elections end, there slavery begins."

These great men, in this respect, should be, once a year,

> Like bubbles on the sea of matter borne,
> They rise, they break, and to that sea return.

This will teach them the great political virtues of humility, patience, and moderation, without which every man in power becomes a ravenous beast of prey.

This mode of constituting the great offices of state will answer very well for the present; but if by experiment it should be found inconvenient, the legislature may, at its leisure, devise other methods of creating them, by elections of the people at large, as in Connecticut, or it may

enlarge the term for which they shall be chosen to seven years, or three years, or for life, or make any other alterations which the society shall find productive of its ease, its safety, its freedom, or, in one word, its happiness.

A rotation of all offices, as well as of representatives and counsellors, has many advocates, and is contended for with many plausible arguments. It would be attended, no doubt, with many advantages; and if the society has a sufficient number of suitable characters to supply the great number of vacancies which would be made by such a rotation, I can see no objection to it. These persons may be allowed to serve for three years, and then be excluded three years, or for any longer or shorter term.

Any seven or nine of the legislative council may be made a quorum, for doing business as a privy council, to advise the governor in the exercise of the executive branch of power, and in all acts of state.

The governor should have the command of the militia and of all your armies. The power of pardons should be with the governor and council.

Judges, justices, and all other officers, civil and military, should be nominated and appointed by the governor, with the advice and consent of council, unless you choose to have a government more popular; if you do, all officers, civil and military, may be chosen by joint ballot of both houses; or, in order to preserve the independence and importance of each house, by ballot of one house, concurred in by the other. Sheriffs should be chosen by the freeholders of counties; so should registers of deeds and clerks of counties.

All officers should have commissions, under the hand of the governor and seal of the colony.

The dignity and stability of government in all its branches, the morals of the people, and every blessing of society depend so much upon an upright and skillful administration of justice, that the judicial power ought to be distinct from both the legislative and executive, and independent upon both, that so it may be a check upon both, as both should be checks upon that. The judges, therefore, should be always men of learning and experience in the laws, of exemplary morals, great patience, calmness, coolness, and attention. Their minds should not be distracted with jarring interests; they should not be dependent upon any man, or body of men. To these ends, they should hold estates for life in their offices; or, in other words, their commissions should be during good behavior, and their salaries ascertained and established by law. For misbehavior, the grand inquest of the colony, the house of representatives, should impeach them before the governor and council, where they should have time and opportunity to make their defence; but, if convicted, should be removed from their offices, and subjected to such other punishment as shall be proper.

A militia law, requiring all men, or with very few exceptions besides cases of conscience, to be provided with arms and ammunition, to be trained at certain seasons; and requiring counties, towns, or other small districts, to be provided with public stocks of ammunition and intrenching utensils, and with some settled plans for transporting provisions after the militia, when marched to defend their country against sudden invasions; and requiring certain districts to be provided with field-pieces, companies of matrosses, and perhaps some regiments of light-horse, is always a wise institution, and, in the present circumstances of our country, indispensable.

Laws for liberal education of youth, especially of the lower class of people, are so extremely wise and useful, that, to a humane and generous mind, no expense for this purpose would be thought extravagant.

The very mention of sumptuary laws will excite a smile. Whether our countrymen have wisdom and virtue enough to submit to them, I know not; but the happiness of the people might be greatly promoted by them, and a revenue saved sufficient to carry on this war forever. Frugality is a great revenue, besides curing us of vanities, levities, and fopperies, which are real antidotes to all great, manly, and warlike virtues.

But must not all commissions run in the name of a king? No. Why may they not as well run thus, "The colony of _____ to A.B. greeting," and be tested by the governor?

Why may not writs, instead of running in the name of the king, run thus, "The colony of _____ to the sheriff," &c., and be tested by the chief justice?

Why may not indictments conclude, "against the peace of the colony of _____ and the dignity of the same?"

A constitution founded on these principles introduces knowledge among the people, and inspires them with a conscious dignity becoming freemen; a general emulation takes place, which causes good humor, sociability, good manners, and good morals to be general. That elevation of sentiment inspired by such a government, makes the common people brave and enterprising. That ambition which is inspired by it makes them sober, industrious, and frugal. You will find among them some elegance, perhaps, but more solidity; a little pleasure, but a great deal of business; some politeness, but more civility. If you compare such a country with the regions of domination, whether monarchical or aristocratical, you will fancy yourself in Arcadia or Elysium.

If the colonies should assume governments separately, they should be left entirely to their own choice of the forms; and if a continental constitution should be formed, it should be a congress, containing a fair and adequate representation of the colonies, and its authority should sacredly be confined to those cases, namely, war, trade, disputes between colony and colony, the post-office, and the unappropriated lands of the crown, as they used to be called.

These colonies, under such forms of government, and in such a union, would be unconquerable by all the monarchies of Europe.

You and I, my dear friend, have been sent into life at a time when the greatest lawgivers of antiquity would have wished to live. How few of the human race have ever enjoyed an opportunity of making an election of government, more than of air, soil, or climate, for themselves or their children! When, before the present epocha, had three millions of people full power and a fair opportunity to form and establish the wisest and happiest government that human wisdom can contrive? I hope you will avail yourself and your country of that extensive learning and indefatigable industry which you possess, to assist her in the formation of the happiest governments and the best character of a great people. For myself, I must beg you to keep my name out of sight; for this feeble attempt, if it should be known to be mine, would oblige me to apply to myself those lines of the immortal John Milton, in one of his sonnets:—

I did but prompt the age to quit their clogs
By the known rules of ancient liberty,
When straight a barbarous noise environs me
Of owls and cuckoos, asses, apes, and dogs.

Articles of Confederation

1778

Still embroiled in a life-or-death struggle with Great Britain, the new United States by 1778 had determined to formalize their relationship with one another and to set up a formal means by which to deal with their common concerns—of which the war was, of course, the most important. These Articles set up a confederacy, that is, a coalition of sovereign states, which would act on behalf of those states only in certain limited areas and only when the states were unanimous in approving a course of action. There was very little central government under the Articles of Confederation. The Continental Congress existed primarily to conduct diplomatic relations and oversee the conduct of the war. As to funding the war, taxes were collected by the states and granted to the Continental Congress only on a fitful basis. It was dissatisfaction with the Articles, and with the government that they established, that brought about the Constitutional Convention.

Articles of Confederation

To all to whom these Presents shall come, we the undersigned Delegates of the States affixed to our names send greeting. Whereas the Delegates of the United States of America in Congress assembled did on the fifteenth day of November in the Year of our Lord One Thousand Seven Hundred and Seventy seven, and in the Second Year of the Independence of America agree to certain articles of Confederation and perpetual Union between the States of New Hampshire, Massachusetts-bay, Rhode Island and Providence Plantations, Connecticut, New York, New Jersey, Pennsylvania, Delaware, Maryland, Virginia, North-Carolina, South-Carolina, and Georgia in the Words following, viz. "Articles of Confederation and perpetual Union between the States of New Hampshire, Massachusetts-bay, Rhode Island and Providence Plantations, Connecticut, New-York, New-Jersey, Pennsylvania, Delaware, Maryland, Virginia, North-Carolina, South-Carolina and Georgia.

Art. I. The Stile of this confederacy shall be "The United States of America."

Art. II. Each State retains its sovereignty, freedom and independence, and every Power, Jurisdiction and right, which is not by this confederation expressly delegated to the United States, in Congress assembled.

Art. III. The said States hereby severally enter into a firm league of friendship with each other, for their common defence, the security of their Liberties, and their mutual and general welfare, binding themselves to assist each other, against all force offered to, or attacks made upon them, or any of them, on account of religion, sovereignty, trade, or any other pretence whatever.

Art. IV. The better to secure and perpetuate mutual friendship and intercourse among the people of the different States in this union, the free inhabitants of each of these States, paupers, vagabonds and fugitives from Justice excepted, shall be entitled to all privileges and immunities of free citizens in the several States; and the people of each State shall have free ingress and regress to and from any other State, and shall enjoy therein all the privileges of trade and commerce, subject to the same duties, impositions and restrictions as the inhabitants thereof respectively, provided that such restriction shall not extend so far as to prevent the removal of property imported into any State, to any other State of which the owner is an inhabitant; provided also that no imposition, duties or restriction shall be laid by any State, on the property of the United States, or either of them.

If any Person guilty of, or charged with treason, felony, or other high misdemeanor in any State, shall flee from Justice, and be found in any of the United States, he shall upon demand of the Governor or executive power, of the State from which he fled, be delivered up and removed to the State having jurisdiction of his offence.

Full faith and credit shall be given in each of these States to the records, acts and judicial proceedings of the courts and magistrates to every other State.

Art. V. For the more convenient management of the general interests of the United States, delegates shall be annually appointed in such manner as the legislature of each State shall direct, to meet in Congress on the first Monday in November, in every year, with a power reserved to each State, to recall its delegates, or any of them, at any time within the year, and to send others in their stead, for the remainder of the Year.

No State shall be represented in Congress by less than two, nor by more than seven Members; and no person shall be capable of being a delegate for more than three years in any term of six years; nor shall any person, being a delegate, be capable of holding any office under the United States, for which he, or another for his benefit receives any salary, fees or emolument of any kind.

Each State shall maintain its own delegates in a meeting of the States, and while they act as members of the committee of the States.

In determining questions in the United States, in Congress assembled, each State shall have one vote.

Freedom of speech and debate in Congress shall not be impeached or questioned in any Court, or place out of Congress, and the members of Congress shall be protected in their persons from arrests and imprisonments, during the time of their going to and from, and attendance of Congress, except for treason, felony, or breach of the peace.

Art. VI. No State without the consent of the United States in Congress assembled, shall send any embassy to, or receive any embassy from, or enter into any conference, agreement, or alliance or treaty with any King, Prince or State; nor shall any person holding any office of profit or trust under the United States, or any of them, accept of any present, emolument, office or title of any kind whatever from any King, Prince or foreign State; nor shall the United States in Congress assembled, or any of them, grant any title of nobility.

No two or more States shall enter into any treaty, confederation or alliance whatever between them, without the consent of the United States in Congress assembled, specifying accurately the purposes for which the same is to be entered into, and how long it shall continue.

No State shall lay any imposts or duties, which may interfere with any stipulations in treaties, entered into by the United States in Congress assembled, with any King, Prince or State, in pursuance of any treaties already proposed by Congress, to the courts of France and Spain.

No vessels of war shall be kept up in time of peace by any State, except such number only, as shall be deemed necessary by the United States in Congress assembled, for the defence of such State, or its trade; nor shall any body of forces be kept up by any State in time of peace, except such number only, as in the judgment of the United States, in Congress assembled, shall be deemed requisite to garrison the forts necessary for the defence of such State; but every State shall always keep up a well regulated and disciplined militia, sufficiently armed and accoutered, and shall provide and constantly have ready for use, in public stores, a due number of field pieces and tents, and a proper quantity of arms, ammunition and camp equipage.

No State shall engage in any war without the consent of the United States in Congress assembled, unless such State be actually invaded by enemies, or shall have received certain advice of a resolution being formed by some nation of Indians to invade such State, and the danger is so imminent as not to admit of a delay, till the United States in Congress assembled can be consulted: nor shall any State grant commissions to any ships or vessels of war, nor letters of marque or reprisal, except it be after a declaration of war by the United States in Congress assembled, and then only against the kingdom or State and the subjects thereof, against which war has been so declared, and under such regulations as shall be established by the United States in Congress assembled, unless such State be infested by pirates, in which case vessels of war may be fitted out for that occasion, and kept so long as the danger shall continue, or until the United States in Congress assembled shall determine otherwise.

Art. VII. When land-forces are raised by any State for the common defence, all officers of or under the rank of colonel, shall be appointed by the legislature of each State respectively by whom such forces shall be raised, or in such manner as such State shall direct, and all vacancies shall be filled up by the State which first made the appointment.

Art. VIII. All charges of war, and all other expenses that shall be incurred for the common defence or general welfare, and allowed by the United States in Congress assembled, shall be defrayed out of a common treasury, which shall be supplied by the several States, in proportion to the value of all land within each State, granted to or surveyed for any person, as such land and the buildings and improvements thereon shall be estimated according to such mode as the United States in Congress assembled, shall from time to time direct and appoint. The taxes for paying that proportion shall be laid and levied by the authority and direction of the legislatures of the several States within the time agreed upon by the United States in Congress assembled.

Art. IX. The United States in Congress assembled shall have the sole and exclusive right and power of determining on peace and war, except in the cases mentioned in the sixth article—of sending and receiving ambassadors—entering into treaties and alliances, provided that no treaty of commerce shall be made whereby the legislative power of the respective States shall be restrained from imposing such imposts and duties on foreigners, as their own people are subjected to, or from prohibiting the exportation or importation of any species of goods or commodities whatsoever—of establishing rules for deciding in all cases, what captures on land or water shall be legal, and in what manner prizes taken by land or naval forces in the service of the United States shall be divided or appropriated—of granting letters of marque and reprisal in times of peace—appointing courts for the trial of piracies and felonies committed on the high seas and establishing courts for receiving and determining finally appeals in all cases of captures, provided that no member of Congress shall be appointed a judge of any of the said courts.

The United States in congress assembled shall also be the last resort on appeal in all disputes and differences now subsisting or that hereafter may arise between two or more States concerning boundary, jurisdiction or any other cause whatever; which authority shall always be exercised in the manner following: Whenever the legislative or executive authority or lawful agent of any State in controversy with another shall present a petition to Congress, stating the matter in question and praying for a hearing, notice thereof shall be given by order of Congress to the legislative or executive authority of the other State in controversy, and a day assigned for the appearance of the parties by their lawful agents, who shall then be directed to appoint, by joint consent, commissioners or judges to constitute a court for hearing and determining the matter in question; but if they cannot agree, Congress shall name three persons out of each of the United States, and from the list of such persons each party shall alternately strike out one, the petitioners beginning, until the number shall be reduced to thirteen; and from that number not less than seven, nor more than nine names as Congress shall direct, shall in the presence of Congress be drawn out by lot, and the persons whose names shall be so drawn or any five of them, shall be commissioners or judges, to hear and finally determine the controversy, so always as a major part of the judges who shall hear the cause shall agree in the determination; and if either party shall neglect to attend at the day appointed, without showing reasons which Congress shall judge sufficient, or being present shall refuse to strike, the Congress shall proceed to nominate three persons out of each State, and the secretary of Congress shall strike in behalf of such party absent or refusing; and the judgment and sentence of the court to be appointed, in the manner before prescribed, shall be final and conclusive; and if any of the parties shall refuse to submit to the authority of such court, or to appear to defend their claim or cause, the court shall nevertheless proceed to pronounce sentence, or judgment, which shall in like manner be final and decisive, the judgment or sentence and other proceedings being in either case transmitted to Congress, and lodged among the Acts of Congress for the security of the parties concerned: provided that every commissioner, before he sits in judgment, shall take an oath to be administered by one of the judges of the supreme or superior court of the State, where the cause shall be tried, "well and truly to hear and determine the matter in question, according to the best of his judgment, without favor, affection or hope of reward": provided also that no State shall be deprived of territory for the benefit of the United States.

All controversies concerning the private right of soil claimed under different grants of two or more States, whose jurisdictions as they may respect such lands, and the States which passed such grants are adjusted, the said grants or either of them being at the same time claimed to have originated antecedent to such settlement of jurisdiction, shall on the petition of either party to the Congress of the United States, be finally determined as near as may be in the same manner as is before prescribed for deciding disputes respecting territorial jurisdiction between different States.

The United States in Congress assembled shall also have the sole and exclusive right and power of regulating the alloy and value of coin struck by their own authority, or by that of the respective States—fixing the standard of weights and measures throughout the United States.—regulating the trade and managing all affairs with the Indians, not members of any of the States, provided that the legislative right of any State within its own limits be not infringed or violated—establishing and regulating post-offices from one State to another, throughout all the

United States, and exacting such postage on the papers passing thro' the same as may be requisite to defray the expenses of the said office—appointing all officers of the land forces, in the service of the United States, excepting regimental officers—appointing all the officers of the naval forces, and commissioning all officers whatever in the service of the United States—making rules for the government and regulation of the said land and naval forces, and directing their operations.

The United States in Congress assembled shall have authority to appoint a committee, to sit in the recess of Congress, to be denominated "A Committee of the States," and to consist of one delegate from each State; and to appoint such other committees and civil officers as may be necessary for managing the general affairs of the United States under their direction—to appoint one of their number to preside, provided that no person be allowed to serve in the office of president more than one year in any term of three years; to ascertain the necessary sums of money to be raised for the service of the United States, and to appropriate and apply the same for defraying the public expenses—to borrow money, or emit bills on the credit of the United States, transmitting every half year to the respective States an account of the sums of money so borrowed or emitted—to build and equip a navy—to agree upon the number of land forces, and to make requisitions from each State for its quota, in proportion to the number of white inhabitants in such State; which requisition shall be binding, and thereupon the legislature of each State shall appoint the regimental officers, raise the men and cloath, arm and equip them in a soldier like manner, at the expense of the United States, and the officers and men so cloathed, armed and equipped shall march to the place appointed, and within the time agreed on by the United States in Congress assembled. But if the United States in Congress assembled shall, on consideration of circumstances, judge proper that any State should not raise men, or should raise a smaller number than its quota, and that any other State should raise a greater number of men than the quota thereof, such extra number shall be raised, officered, cloathed, armed and equipped in the same manner as the quota of such State, unless the legislature of such State shall judge that such extra number cannot be safely spared out of the same, in which case they shall raise officers, cloath, arm and equip as many of such extra number as they judge can be safely spared. And the officers and men so cloathed, armed and equipped, shall march to the place appointed, and within the time agreed on by the United States in Congress assembled.

The United States in Congress assembled shall never engage in a war, nor grant letters of marque and reprisal in time of peace, nor enter into any treaties or alliances, nor coin money, nor regulate the value thereof, nor ascertain the sums and expenses necessary for the defence and welfare of the United States, or any of them, nor emit bills, nor borrow money on the credit of the United States, nor appropriate money, nor agree upon the number of vessels of war, to be built or purchased, or the number of land or sea forces to be raised, nor appoint a commander in chief of the army or navy, unless nine States assent to the same; nor shall a question on any other point, except for adjourning from day to day be determined, unless by the votes of a majority of the United States in Congress assembled.

The Congress of the United States shall have power to adjourn to any time within the year, and to any place within the United States, so that no period of adjournment be for a longer duration than the space of six months, and shall publish the Journal of their proceedings monthly, except such parts thereof relating to treaties, alliances or military operations as in their judgment require secrecy; and the yeas and nays of the delegates of each State on any question shall be entered on the Journal, when it is desired by any delegate; and the delegates of a State, or any of them, at his or their request shall be furnished with a transcript of the said Journal, except such parts as are above excepted, to lay before the legislatures of the several States.

Art. X. The Committee of the States, or any nine of them, shall be authorized to execute, in the recess of Congress, such of the powers of Congress as the United States in Congress assembled, by the consent of nine States, shall from time to time think expedient to vest them with; provided that no power be delegated to the said committee, for the exercises of which, by the articles of confederation, the voice of nine States in the Congress of the United States assembled is requisite.

Art. XI. Canada acceding to this confederation, and joining in the measures of the United States, shall be admitted into, and entitled to all the advantages of this union; but no other colony shall be admitted into the same, unless such admission be agreed to by nine States.

Art. XII. All bills of credit emitted, monies borrowed

and debts contracted by, or under the authority of Congress, before the assembling of the United States, in pursuance of the present confederation, shall be deemed and considered as a charge against the United States, for payment and satisfaction whereof the said United States, and the public faith are hereby solemnly pledged.

Art. XIII. Every State shall abide by the determinations of the United States in Congress assembled, on all questions which by this confederation are submitted to them. And the Articles of this confederation shall be inviolably observed by every State, and the union shall be perpetual; nor shall any alteration at any time hereafter be made in any of them; unless such alteration be agreed to in a Congress of the United States, and be afterwards confirmed by the legislatures of every State.

And whereas it hath pleased the Great Governor of the World to incline the hearts of the legislatures we respectively represent in Congress, to approve of, and to authorize us to ratify the said articles of confederation and perpetual union. KNOW YE that we the undersigned delegates, by virtue of the power and authority to us given for that purpose, do by these presents, in the name and in behalf of our respective constituents, fully and entirely ratify and confirm each and every of the said articles of confederation and perpetual union, and all and singular the matters and things therein contained. And we do further solemnly plight and engage the faith of our respective constituents, that they shall abide by the determinations of the United States in Congress assembled, on all questions, which by the said confederation are submitted to them. And that the articles thereof shall be inviolably observed by the States we respectively represent, and that the union shall be perpetual. In Witness whereof we have hereunto set our hands in Congress. Done at Philadelphia in the State of Pennsylvania the ninth Day of July in the Year of our Lord one Thousand seven Hundred and Seventy-eight, and in the third year of the independence of America.

The Essex Result

April 29, 1778

The constitution eventually adopted by the state of Massachusetts in 1780 was very much the product of local participation. A proposed draft was sent to the various counties and, in several cases, rejected. The most eloquent response came from Essex County, which, under the leadership of Theophilus Parsons, set forth both its objections and its views on the proper grounding and form of state government. While concerned specifically with the Massachusetts state constitution, the Essex Result provides an important example of the workings of local conventions more generally, and the reasoning on which they acted.

The Essex Result

In Convention of Delegates from the several towns of Lynn, Salem, Danvers, Wenham, Manchester, Gloucester, Ipswich, Newbury-Port, Salisbury, Methuen, Boxford, and Topsfield, holden by adjournment at Ipswich, on the twenty-ninth day of April, one thousand seven hundred and seventy-eight

Peter Coffin Esq; in the Chair.

The Constitution and form of Government framed by the Convention of this State, was read paragraph by paragraph, and after debate, the following votes were passed.

1. That the present situation of this State renders it best, that the framing of a Constitution therefor, should be postponed 'till the public affairs are in a more peaceable and settled condition.

2. That a bill of rights, clearly ascertaining and defining the rights of conscience, and that security of person and property, which every member in the State hath a right to expect from the supreme power thereof, ought to be settled and established, previous to the ratification of any constitution for the State.

3. That the executive power in any State, ought not to have any share or voice in the legislative power in framing the laws, and therefore, that the second article of the Constitution is liable to exception.

4. That any man who is chosen Governor, ought to be properly qualified in point of property—that the qualification therefor, mentioned in the third article of the Constitution, is not sufficient—nor is the same qualification directed to be ascertained on fixed principles, as it ought to be, on account of the fluctuation of the nominal value of money, and of property.

5. That in every free Republican Government, where the legislative power is rested in an house or houses of representatives, all the members of the State ought to be equally represented.

6. That the mode of representation proposed in the sixth article of the constitution, is not so equal a representation as can reasonably be devised.

7. That therefore the mode of representation in said sixth article is exceptionable.

8. That the representation proposed in said article is also exceptionable, as it will produce an unwieldy assembly.

9. That the mode of election of Senators pointed out in the Constitution is exceptionable.

10. That the rights of conscience, and the security of person and property each member of the State is entitled to, are not ascertained and defined in the Constitution, with a precision sufficient to limit the legislative power—and therefore, that the thirteenth article of the constitution is exceptionable.

11. That the fifteenth article is exceptionable, because the numbers that constitute a quorum in the House of Representatives and Senate, are too small.

12. That the seventeenth article of the constitution is exceptionable, because the supreme executive officer is not vested with proper authority—and because an independence between the executive and legislative body is not preserved.

13. That the nineteenth article is exceptionable, because a due independence is not kept up between the supreme legislative, judicial, and executive powers, nor between any two of them.

14. That the twentieth article is exceptionable, because

the supreme executive officer hath a voice, and must be present in that Court, which alone hath authority to try impeachments.

15. That the twenty second article is exceptionable, because the supreme executive power is not preserved distinct from, and independent of, the supreme legislative power.

16. That the twenty third article is exceptionable, because the power of granting pardons is not solely vested in the supreme executive power of the State.

17. That the twenty eighth article is exceptionable, because the delegates for the Continental Congress may be elected by the House of Representatives, when all the Senators may vote against the election of those who are delegated.

18. That the thirty fourth article is exceptionable, because the rights of conscience are not therein clearly defined and ascertained; and further, because the free exercise and enjoyment of religious worship is there said to be *allowed* to all the protestants in the State, when in fact, that free exercise and enjoyment is the natural and uncontroulable right of every member of the State.

A committee was then appointed to attempt the ascertaining of the true principles of government, applicable to the territory of the Massachusetts-Bay; to state the nonconformity of the constitution proposed by the Convention of this State to those principles, and to delineate the general outlines of a constitution conformable thereto; and to report the same to this Body.

This Convention was then adjourned to the twelfth day of May next, to be holden at Ipswich.

The Convention met pursuant to adjournment, and their committee presented the following report.

The committee appointed by this Convention at their last adjournment, have proceeded upon the service assigned them. With diffidence have they undertaken the several parts of their duty, and the manner in which they have executed them, they submit to the candor of this Body. When they considered of what vast consequence, the forming of a Constitution is to the members of this State, the length of time that is necessary to canvass and digest any proposed plan of government, before the establishment of it, and the consummate coolness, and solemn deliberation which should attend, not only those gentlemen who have, reposed in them, the important trust of delineating the several lines in which the various powers of government are to move, but also all those, who are to form an opinion of the execution of that trust, your committee must be excused when they express a surprise and regret, that so short a time is allowed the freemen inhabiting the territory of the Massachusetts-Bay, to revise and comprehend the form of government proposed to them by the convention of this State, to compare it with those principles on which every free government ought to be founded, and to ascertain it's conformity or nonconformity thereto. All this is necessary to be done, before a true opinion of it's merit or demerit can be formed. This opinion is to be certified within a time which, in our apprehension, is much too short for this purpose, and to be certified by a people, who, during that time, have had and will have their minds perplexed and oppressed with a variety of public cares. The committee also beg leave to observe, that the constitution proposed for public approbation, was formed by gentlemen, who, at the same time, had a large share in conducting an important war, and who were employed in carrying into execution almost all the various powers of government.

The committee however proceeded in attempting the task assigned them, and the success of that attempt is now reported.

The reason and understanding of mankind, as well as the experience of all ages, confirm the truth of this proposition, that the benefits resulting to individuals from a free government, conduce much more to their happiness, than the retaining of all their natural rights in a state of nature. These benefits are greater or less, as the form of government, and the mode of exercising the supreme power of the State, are more or less conformable to those principles of equal impartial liberty, which is the property of all men from their birth as the gift of their Creator, compared with the manners and genius of the people, their occupations, customs, modes of thinking, situation, extent of country, and numbers. If the constitution and form of government are wholly repugnant to those principles, wretched are the subjects of that State. They have surrendered a portion of their natural rights, the enjoyment of which was in some degree a blessing, and the consequence is, they find themselves stripped of the remainder. As an anodyne to compose the spirits of these slaves, and to lull them into a passively obedient state, they are told, that tyranny is preferable to no government at all; a proposition which is to be doubted, unless considered under some limitation. Surely a state of nature is more excellent than that, in which men are meanly submissive to the haughty will of an imperious tyrant, whose savage passions are not bounded by the laws of reason, religion, honor, or a regard to his subjects, and the point to which all his movements center, is the gratification of a brutal appetite. As in a state of nature much happiness cannot be enjoyed by individuals, so it has been conformable to the inclinations of almost all men, to enter into a political society so constituted, as to remove the inconveniences they were obliged to submit to in their former state, and, at the same time, to retain all those natural rights, the enjoyment of which would be consistent with the nature of a free government, and the necessary subordination to the supreme power of the state.

To determine what form of government, in any given case, will produce the greatest possible happiness to the subject, is an arduous task, not to be compassed perhaps by any human powers. Some of the greatest geniuses and most learned philosophers of all ages, impelled by their sollicitude to promote the happiness of mankind, have nobly dared to attempt it: and their labours have crowned them with immortality. A Solon, a Lycurgus of Greece, a Numa of Rome are remembered with honor, when the wide extended empires of succeeding tyrants, are hardly important enough to be faintly sketched out on the map, while their superb thrones have long since crumbled into dust. The man who alone undertakes to form a constitution, ought to be an unimpassioned being; one enlightened mind; biassed neither by the lust of power, the allurements of pleasure, nor the glitter of wealth; perfectly acquainted with all the alienable and unalienable rights of mankind; possessed of this grand truth, that all men are born equally free, and that no man ought to surrender any part of his natural rights, without receiving the greatest possible equivalent; and influenced by the impartial principles of rectitude and justice, without partiality for, or prejudice against the interest or professions of any individuals or class of men. He ought also to be master of the histories of all the empires and states which are now existing, and all those which have figured in antiquity, and thereby able to collect and blend their respective excellencies, and avoid those defects which experience hath pointed out. Rousseau, a learned foreigner, a citizen of Geneva, sensible of the importance and difficulty of the subject, thought it impossible for any body of people, to form a free and equal constitution for themselves, in

which, every individual should have equal justice done him, and be permitted to enjoy a share of power in the state, equal to what should be enjoyed by any other. Each individual, said he, will struggle, not only to retain all his own natural rights, but to acquire a controul over those of others. Fraud, circumvention, and an union of interest of some classes of people, combined with an inattention to the rights of posterity, will prevail over the principles of equity, justice, and good policy. The Genevans, perhaps the most virtuous republicans now existing, thought like Rousseau. They called the celebrated Calvin to their assistance. He came, and, by their gratitude, have they embalmed his memory.

The freemen inhabiting the territory of the Massachusetts-Bay are now forming a political society for themselves. Perhaps their situation is more favorable in some respects, for erecting a free government, than any other people were ever favored with. That attachment to old forms, which usually embarrasses, has not place amongst them. They have the history and experience of all States before them. Mankind have been toiling through ages for their information; and the philosophers and learned men of antiquity have trimmed their midnight lamps, to transmit to them instruction. We live also in an age, when the principles of political liberty, and the foundation of governments, have been freely canvassed, and fairly settled. Yet some difficulties we have to encounter. Not content with removing our attachment to the old government, perhaps we have contracted a prejudice against some part of it without foundation. The idea of liberty has been held up in so dazzling colours, that some of us may not be willing to submit to that subordination necessary in the freest States. Perhaps we may say further, that we do not consider ourselves united as brothers, with an united interest, but have fancied a clashing of interests amongst the various classes of men, and have acquired a thirst of power, and a wish of domination, over some of the community. We are contending for freedom—Let us all be equally free— It is possible, and it is just. Our interests when candidly considered are one. Let us have a constitution founded, not upon party or prejudice—not one for to-day or to-morrow—but for posterity. Let *Esto perpetua* be it's motto. If it is founded in good policy; it will be founded in justice and honesty. Let all ambitious and interested views be discarded, and let regard be had only to the good of the whole, in which the situation and rights of posterity must be considered: and let equal justice be done to all the members of the community; and we thereby imitate our common father, who at our births, dispersed his favors, not only with a liberal, but with an equal hand.

Was it asked, what is the best form of government for the people of the Massachusetts-Bay? we confess it would be a question of infinite importance: and the man who could truly answer it, would merit a statue of gold to his memory, and his fame would be recorded in the annals of late posterity, with unrivalled lustre. The question, however, must be answered, and let it have the best answer we can possibly give it. Was a man to mention a despotic government, his life would be a just forfeit to the resentments of an affronted people. Was he to hint monarchy, he would deservedly be hissed off the stage, and consigned to infamy. A republican form is the only one consonant to the feelings of the generous and brave Americans. Let us now attend to those principles, upon which all republican governments, who boast any degree of political liberty, are founded, and which must enter into the spirit of a FREE republican constitution. For all republics are not FREE.

All men are born equally free. The rights they possess at their births are equal, and of the same kind. Some of those rights are alienable, and may be parted with for an equivalent. Others are unalienable and inherent, and of that importance, that no equivalent can be received in exchange. Sometimes we shall mention the surrendering of a power to controul our natural rights, which perhaps is speaking with more precision, than when we use the expression of parting with natural rights—but the same thing is intended. Those rights which are unalienable, and of that importance, are called the rights of conscience. We have duties, for the discharge of which we are accountable to our Creator and benefactor, which no human power can cancel. What those duties are, is determinable by right reason, which may be, and is called, a well informed conscience. What this conscience dictates as our duty, is so; and that power which assumes a controul over it, is an usurper; for no consent can be pleaded to justify the controul, as any consent in this case is void. The alienation of some rights, in themselves alienable, may be also void, if the bargain is of that nature, that no equivalent can be received. Thus, if a man surrender all his alienable rights, without reserving a controul over the supreme power, or a right to resume in certain cases, the surrender is void, for

he becomes a slave; and a slave can receive no equivalent. Common equity would set aside this bargain.

When men form themselves into society, and erect a body politic or State, they are to be considered as one moral whole, which is in possession of the supreme power of the State. This supreme power is composed of the powers of each individual collected together, and VOLUNTARILY parted with by him. No individual, in this case, parts with his unalienable rights, the supreme power therefore cannot controul them. Each individual also surrenders the power of controuling his natural alienable rights, ONLY WHEN THE GOOD OF THE WHOLE REQUIRES it. The supreme power therefore can do nothing but what is for the good of the whole; and when it goes beyond this line, it is a power usurped. If the individual receives an equivalent for the right of controul he has parted with, the surrender of that right is valid; if he receives no equivalent, the surrender is void, and the supreme power as it respects him is an usurper. If the supreme power is so directed and executed that he does not enjoy political liberty, it is an illegal power, and he is not bound to obey. Political liberty is by some defined, a liberty of doing whatever is not prohibited by law. The definition is erroneous. A tyrant may govern by laws. The republic's of Venice and Holland govern by laws, yet those republic's have degenerated into insupportable tyrannies. Let it be thus defined; political liberty is the right every man in the state has, to do whatever is not prohibited by laws, TO WHICH HE HAS GIVEN HIS CONSENT. This definition is in unison with the feelings of a free people. But to return—If a fundamental principle on which each individual enters into society is, that he shall be bound by no laws but those to which he has consented, he cannot be considered as consenting to any law enacted by a minority: for he parts with the power of controuling his natural rights, only when the good of the whole requires it; and of this there can be but one absolute judge in the State. If the minority can assume the right of judging, there may then be two judges; for however large the minority may be, there must be another body still larger, who have the same claim, if not a better, to the right of absolute determination. If therefore the supreme power should be so modelled and exerted, that a law may be enacted by a minority, the inforcing of that law upon an individual who is opposed to it, is an act of tyranny. Further, as every individual, in entering into the society, parted with a power of controuling his natural rights equal to that parted with by any other, or in other words, as all the members of the society contributed an equal portion of their natural rights, towards the forming of the supreme power, so every member ought to receive equal benefit from, have equal influence in forming, and retain an equal controul over, the supreme power.

It has been observed, that each individual parts with the power of controuling his natural alienable rights, only when the good of the whole requires it, he therefore has remaining, after entering into political society, all his unalienable natural rights, and a part also of his alienable natural rights, provided the good of the whole does not require the sacrifice of them. Over the class of unalienable rights the supreme power hath no controul, and they ought to be clearly defined and ascertained in a BILL OF RIGHTS, previous to the ratification of any constitution. The bill of rights should also contain the equivalent every man receives, as a consideration for the rights he has surrendered. This equivalent consists principally in the security of his person and property, and is also unassailable by the supreme power: for if the equivalent is taken back, those natural rights which were parted with to purchase it, return to the original proprietor, as nothing is more true, than that ALLEGIANCE AND PROTECTION ARE RECIPROCAL.

The committee also proceeded to consider upon what principles, and in what manner, the supreme power of the state thus composed of the powers of the several individuals thereof, may be formed, modelled, and exerted in a republic, so that every member of the state may enjoy political liberty. This is called by some, *the ascertaining of the political law of the state.* Let it now be called *the forming of a constitution.*

The reason why the supreme governor of the world is a rightful and just governor, and entitled to the allegiance of the universe is, because he is infinitely good, wise, and powerful. His goodness prompts him to the best measures, his wisdom qualifies him to discern them, and his power to effect them. In a state likewise, the supreme power is best disposed of, when it is so modelled and balanced, and rested in such hands, that it has the greatest share of goodness, wisdom, and power, which is consistent with the lot of humanity.

That state, (other things being equal) which has reposed the supreme power in the hands of one or a small number of persons, is the most powerful state. An union, expedition, secrecy and dispatch are to be found only here. Where power is to be executed by a large number, there will not probably be either of the requisites just mentioned. Many men have various opinions: and each one will be tenacious of his own, as he thinks it preferable to any other; for when he thinks otherwise, it will cease to be his opinion. From this diversity of opinions results disunion; from disunion, a want of expedition and dispatch. And the larger the number to whom a secret is entrusted, the greater is the probability of it's disclosure. This inconvenience more fully strikes us when we consider that want of secrecy may prevent the successful execution of any measures, however excellently formed and digested.

But from a single person, or a very small number, we are not to expect that political honesty, and upright regard to the interest of the body of the people, and the civil rights of each individual, which are essential to a good and free constitution. For these qualities we are to go to the body of the people. The voice of the people is said to be the voice of God. No man will be so hardy and presumptuous, as to affirm the truth of that proposition in it's fullest extent. But if this is considered as the intent of it, that the people have always a disposition to promote their own happiness, and that when they have time to be informed, and the necessary means of information given them, they will be able to determine upon the necessary measures therefor, no man, of a tolerable acquaintance with mankind, will deny the truth of it. The inconvenience and difficulty in forming any free permanent constitution are, that such is the lot of humanity, the bulk of the people, whose happiness is principally to be consulted in forming a constitution, and in legislation, (as they include the majority) are so situated in life, and such are their laudable occupations, that they cannot have time for, nor the means of furnishing themselves with proper information, but must be indebted to some of their fellow subjects for the communication. Happy is the man, and blessings will attend his memory, who shall improve his leisure, and those abilities which heaven has indulged him with, in communicating that true information, and impartial knowledge, to his fellow subjects, which will insure their happiness. But the artful demagogue, who to gratify his ambition or avarice, shall, with the gloss of false patriotism, mislead his countrymen, and meanly snatch from them the golden glorious opportunity of forming a system of political and civil liberty, fraught with blessings for themselves, and remote posterity, what language can paint his demerit? The execrations of ages will be a punishment inadequate; and his name, though ever blackening as it rolls down the stream of time, will not catch its proper hue.

Yet, when we are forming a Constitution, by deductions that follow from established principles, (which is the only good method of forming one for futurity,) we are to look further than to the bulk of the people, for the greatest wisdom, firmness, consistency, and perseverance. These qualities will most probably be found amongst men of education and fortune. From such men we are to expect genius cultivated by reading, and all the various advantages and assistances, which art, and a liberal education aided by wealth, can furnish. From these result learning, a thorough knowledge of the interests of their country, when considered abstractedly, when compared with the neighbouring States, and when with those more remote, and an acquaintance with it's produce and manufacture, and it's exports and imports. All these are necessary to be known, in order to determine what is the true interest of any state; and without that interest is ascertained, impossible will it be to discover, whether a variety of certain laws may be beneficial or hurtful. From gentlemen whose private affairs compel them to take care of their own household, and deprive them of leisure, these qualifications are not to be generally expected, whatever class of men they are enrolled in.

Let all these respective excellencies be united. Let the supreme power be so disposed and ballanced, that the laws may have in view the interest of the whole; let them be wisely and consistently framed for that end, and firmly adhered to; and let them be executed with vigour and dispatch.

Before we proceed further, it must be again considered, and kept always in view, that we are not attempting to form a temporary constitution, one adjusted only to our present circumstances. We wish for one founded upon such principles as will secure to us freedom and happiness, however our circumstances may vary. One that will smile amidst the declensions of European and Asiatic empires, and survive the rude storms of time. It is not therefore to be understood, that all the men of fortune of the present day, are men of wisdom and learning, or that they are not. Nor that the bulk of the people, the farmers, the merchants, the tradesmen, and labourers, are all honest and

upright, with single views to the public good, or that they are not. In each of the classes there are undoubtedly exceptions, as the rules laid down are general. The proposition is only this. That among gentlemen of education, fortune and leisure, we shall find the largest number of men, possessed of wisdom, learning, and a firmness and consistency of character. That among the bulk of the people, we shall find the greatest share of political honesty, probity, and a regard to the interest of the whole, of which they compose the majority. That wisdom and firmness are not sufficient without good intentions, nor the latter without the former. The conclusion is, let the legislative body unite them all. The former are called the excellencies that result from an aristocracy; the latter, those that result from a democracy.

The supreme power is considered as including the legislative, judicial, and executive powers. The nature and employment of these several powers deserve a distinct attention.

The legislative power is employed in making laws, or prescribing such rules of action to every individual in the state, as the good of the whole requires, to be conformed to by him in his conduct to the governors and governed, with respect both to their persons and property, according to the several relations he stands in. What rules of action the good of the whole requires, can be ascertained only by the majority, for a reason formerly mentioned. Therefore the legislative power must be so formed and exerted, that in prescribing any rule of action, or, in other words, enacting any law, the majority must consent. This may be more evident, when the fundamental condition on which every man enters into society, is considered. No man consented that his natural alienable rights should be wantonly controuled: they were controulable, only when that controul should be subservient to the good of the whole; and that subserviency, from the very nature of government, can be determined but by one absolute judge. The minority cannot be that judge, because then there may be two judges opposed to each other, so that this subserviency remains undetermined. Now the enacting of a law, is only the exercise of this controul over the natural alienable rights of each member of the state; and therefore this law must have the consent of the majority, or be invalid, as being contrary to the fundamental condition of the original social contract. In a state of nature, every man had the sovereign controul over his own person. He might also have, in that state, a qualified property. Whatever lands or chattels he had acquired the peaceable possession of, were exclusively his, by right of occupancy or possession. For while they were unpossessed he had a right to them equally with any other man, and therefore could not be disturbed in his possession, without being injured; for no man could lawfully dispossess him, without having a better right, which no man had. Over this qualified property every man in a state of nature had also a sovereign controul. And in entering into political society, he surrendered this right of controul over his person and property, (with an exception to the rights of conscience) to the supreme legislative power, to be exercised by that power, *when the good of the whole demanded it.* This was all the right he could surrender, being all the alienable right of which he was possessed. The only objects of legislation therefore, are the person and property of the individuals which compose the state. If the law affects only the persons of the members, the consent of a majority of any members is sufficient. If the law affects the property only, the consent of those who hold a majority of the property is enough. If it affects, (as it will very frequently, if not always,) both the person and property, the consent of a majority of the members, and of those members also, who hold a majority of the property is necessary. If the consent of the latter is not obtained, their interest is taken from them against their consent, and their boasted security of property is vanished. Those who make the law, in this case give and grant what is not theirs. The law, in it's principles, becomes a second stamp act. Lord Chatham very finely ridiculed the British house of commons upon that principle. "You can give and grant, said he, only your own. Here you give and grant, what? The property of the Americans." The people of the Massachusetts-Bay then thought his Lordship's ridicule well pointed. And would they be willing to merit the same? Certainly they will agree in the principle, should they mistake the application. The laws of the province of Massachusetts-Bay adopted the same principle, and very happily applied it. As the votes of proprietors of common and undivided lands in their meetings, can affect only their property, therefore it is enacted, that in ascertaining the majority, the votes shall be collected according to the respective interests of the proprietors. If each member, without regard to his property, has equal influence in legislation with any other, it follows, that some members enjoy greater benefits and powers in legislation than others,

when these benefits and powers are compared with the rights parted with to purchase them. For the property-holder parts with the controul over his person, as well as he who hath no property, and the former also parts with the controul over his property, of which the latter is destitute. Therefore to constitute a perfect law in a free state, affecting the persons and property of the members, it is necessary that the law be for the good of the whole, which is to be determined by a majority of the members, and that majority should include those, who possess a major part of the property in the state.

The judicial power follows next after the legislative power; for it cannot act, until after laws are prescribed. Every wise legislator annexes a sanction to his laws, which is most commonly penal, (that is) a punishment either corporal or pecuniary, to be inflicted on the member who shall infringe them. It is the part of the judicial power (which in this territory has always been, and always ought to be, a court and jury) to ascertain the member who hath broken the law. Every man is to be presumed innocent, until the judicial power hath determined him guilty. When that decision is known, the law annexes the punishment, and the offender is turned over to the executive arm, by whom it is inflicted on him. The judicial power hath also to determine what legal contracts have been broken, and what member hath been injured by a violation of the law, to consider the damages that have been sustained, and to ascertain the recompense. The executive power takes care that this recompense is paid.

The executive power is sometimes divided into the external executive, and internal executive. The former comprehends war, peace, the sending and receiving ambassadors, and whatever concerns the transactions of the state with any other independent state. The confederation of the United States of America hath lopped off this branch of the executive, and placed it in Congress. We have therefore only to consider the internal executive power, which is employed in the peace, security and protection of the subject and his property, and in the defence of the state. The executive power is to marshal and command her militia and armies for her defence, to enforce the law, and to carry into execution all the orders of the legislative powers.

A little attention to the subject will convince us, that these three powers ought to be in different hands, and independent of one another, and so ballanced, and each having that check upon the other, that their independence shall be preserved—If the three powers are united, the government will be absolute, *whether these powers are in the hands of one or a large number.* The same party will be the legislator, accuser, judge and executioner; and what probability will an accused person have of an acquittal, however innocent he may be, when his judge will be also a party.

If the legislative and judicial powers are united, the maker of the law will also interpret it; and the law may then speak a language, dictated by the whims, the caprice, or the prejudice of the judge, with impunity to him—And what people are so unhappy as those, whose laws are uncertain. It will also be in the breast of the judge, when grasping after his prey, to make a retrospective law, which shall bring the unhappy offender within it; and this also he can do with impunity—The subject can have no peaceable remedy—The judge will try himself, and an acquittal is the certain consequence. He has it also in his power to enact any law, which may shelter him from deserved vengeance.

Should the executive and legislative powers be united, mischiefs the most terrible would follow. The executive would enact those laws it pleased to execute, and no others—The judicial power would be set aside as inconvenient and tardy—The security and protection of the subject would be a shadow—The executive power would make itself absolute, and the government end in a tyranny—Lewis the eleventh of France, by cunning and treachery compleated the union of the executive and legislative powers of that kingdom, and upon that union established a system of tyranny. France was formerly under a free government.

The assembly or representatives of the united states of Holland, exercise the executive and legislative powers, and the government there is absolute.

Should the executive and judicial powers be united, the subject would then have no permanent security of his person and property. The executive power would interpret the laws and bend them to his will; and, as he is the judge, he may leap over them by artful constructions, and gratify, with impunity, the most rapacious passions. Perhaps no cause in any state has contributed more to promote internal convulsions, and to stain the scaffold with it's best blood, than this unhappy union. And it is an union which the executive power in all states, hath attempted to form:

if that could not be compassed, to make the judicial power dependent upon it. Indeed the dependence of any of these powers upon either of the others, which in all states has always been attempted by one or the other of them, has so often been productive of such calamities, and of the shedding of such oceans of blood, that the page of history seems to be one continued tale of human wretchedness.

The following principles now seem to be established.

1. That the supreme power is limited, and cannot controul the unalienable rights of mankind, nor resume the equivalent (that is, the security of person and property) which each individual receives, as a consideration for the alienable rights he parted with in entering into political society.

2. That these unalienable rights, and this equivalent, are to be clearly defined and ascertained in a BILL OF RIGHTS, previous to the ratification of any constitution.

3. That the supreme power should be so formed and modelled, as to exert the greatest possible power, wisdom, and goodness.

4. That the legislative, judicial, and executive powers, are to be lodged in different hands, that each branch is to be independent, and further, to be so ballanced, and be able to exert such checks upon the others, as will preserve it from a dependence on, or an union with them.

5. That government can exert the greatest power when it's supreme authority is vested in the hands of one or a few.

6. That the laws will be made with the greatest wisdom, and best intentions, when men, of all the several classes in the state concur in the enacting of them.

7. That a government which is so constituted, that it cannot afford a degree of political liberty nearly equal to all it's members, is not founded upon principles of freedom and justice, and where any member enjoys no degree of political liberty, the government, so far as it respects him, is a tyranny, for he is controuled by laws to which he has never consented.

8. That the legislative power of a state hath no authority to controul the natural rights of any of it's members, unless the good of the whole requires it.

9. That a majority of the state is the only judge when the general good does require it.

10. That where the legislative power of the state is so formed, that a law may be enacted by the minority, each member of the state does not enjoy political liberty. And

11. That in a free government, a law affecting the person and property of it's members, is not valid, unless it has the consent of a majority of the members, which majority should include those, who hold a major part of the property in the state.

It may be necessary to proceed further, and notice some particular principles, which should be attended to in forming the three several powers in a free republican government.

The first important branch that comes under our consideration, is the legislative body. Was the number of the people so small, that the whole could meet together without inconvenience, the opinion of the majority would be more easily known. But, besides the inconvenience of assembling such numbers, no great advantages could follow. Sixty thousand people could not discuss with candor, and determine with deliberation. Tumults, riots, and murder would be the result. But the impracticability of forming such an assembly, renders it needless to make any further observations. The opinions and consent of the majority must be collected from persons, delegated by every freeman of the state for that purpose. Every freeman, who hath sufficient discretion, should have a voice in the election of his legislators. To speak with precision, in every free state where the power of legislation is lodged in the hands of one or more bodies of representatives elected for that purpose, the person of every member of the state, and all the property in it, ought to be represented, because they are objects of legislation. All the members of the state are qualified to make the election, unless they have not sufficient discretion, or are so situated as to have no wills of their own. Persons not twenty one years old are deemed of the former class, from their want of years and experience. The municipal law of this country will not trust them with the disposition of their lands, and consigns them to the care of their parents or guardians. Women what age soever they are of, are also considered as not having a sufficient acquired discretion; not from a deficiency in their mental powers, but from the natural tenderness and delicacy of their minds, their retired mode of life, and various domestic duties. These concurring, prevent that promiscuous intercourse with the world, which is necessary to qualify them for electors. Slaves are of the latter class and have no wills. But are slaves members of a free government? We feel the absurdity, and would to God, the situation of America

and the tempers of it's inhabitants were such, that the slave-holder could not be found in the land.

The rights of representation should be so equally and impartially distributed, that the representatives should have the same views, and interests with the people at large. They should think, feel, and act like them, and in fine, should be an exact miniature of their constituents. They should be (if we may use the expression) the whole body politic, with all it's property, rights, and priviledges, reduced to a smaller scale, every part being diminished in just proportion. To pursue the metaphor: If in adjusting the representation of freemen, any ten are reduced into one, all the other tens should be alike reduced: or if any hundred should be reduced to one, all the other hundreds should have just the same reduction. The representation ought also to be so adjusted, that it should be the interest of the representatives at all times, to do justice, therefore equal interest among the people, should have equal interest among the body of representatives. The majority of the representatives should also represent a majority of the people, and the legislative body should be so constructed, that every law affecting property, should have the consent of those who hold a majority of the property. The law would then be determined to be for the good of the whole by the proper judge, the majority, and the necessary consent thereto would be obtained: and all the members of the State would enjoy political liberty, and an equal degree of it. If the scale to which the body politic is to be reduced, is but a little smaller than the original, or, in other words, if a small number of freemen should be reduced to one, that is, send one representative, the number of representatives would be too large for the public good. The expences of government would be enormous. The body would be too unwieldy to deliberate with candor and coolness. The variety of opinions and oppositions would irritate the passions. Parties would be formed and factions engendered. The members would list under the banners of their respective leaders: address and intrigue would conduct the debates, and the result would tend only to promote the ambition or interest of a particular party. Such has always been in some degree, the course and event of debates instituted and managed by a large multitude.

For these reasons, some foreign politicians have laid it down as a rule, that no body of men larger than an hundred, would transact business well: and Lord Chesterfield called the British house of commons a mere mob, because of the number of men which composed it.

Elections ought also to be free. No bribery, corruption, or undue influence should have place. They stifle the free voice of the people, corrupt their morals, and introduce a degeneracy of manners, a supineness of temper, and an inattention to their liberties, which pave the road for the approach of tyranny, in all it's frightful forms.

The man who buys an elector by his bribes, will sell him again, and reap a profit from the bargain; and he thereby becomes a dangerous member of society. The legislative body will hold the purse strings, and men will struggle for a place in that body to acquire a share of the public wealth. It has always been the case. Bribery will be attempted, and the laws will not prevent it. All states have enacted severe laws against it, and they have been ineffectual. The defect was in their forms of government. They were not so contrived, as to prevent the practicability of it. If a small corporation can place a man in the legislative body, to bribe will be easy and cheap. To bribe a large corporation would be difficult and expensive, if practicable. In Great-Britain, the representatives of their counties and great cities are freely elected. To bribe the electors there, is impracticable: and their representatives are the most upright and able statesmen in parliament. The small boroughs are bought by the ministry and opulent men; and their representatives are the mere tools of administration or faction. Let us take warning.

A further check upon bribery is, when the corrupter of a people knows not the electors. If delegates were first appointed by a number of corporations, who at a short day were to elect their representatives, these blood-hounds in a state would be at fault. They would not scent their game. Besides, the representatives would probably be much better men — they would be double refined.

But it may be said, the virtuous American would blast with indignation the man, who should proffer him a bribe. Let it now be admitted as a fact. We ask, will that always be the case? The most virtuous states have become vicious. The morals of all people, in all ages, have been shockingly corrupted. The rigidly virtuous Spartans, who banished the use of gold and silver, who gloried in their poverty for centuries, at last fell a prey to luxury and corruption. The Romans, whose intense love to their country, astonishes a modern patriot, who fought the battles of the republic for three hundred years without pay, and who, as volunteers, extended her empire over Italy, were at last dissolved in luxury, courted the hand of bribery, and finally sold themselves as slaves, and prostrated their country to tyrants the most ignominious and brutal. Shall we alone boast an exemption from the general fate of mankind? Are our private and political virtues to be transmitted untainted from generation to generation, through a course of ages? Have we not already degenerated from the pure morals and disinterested patriotism of our ancestors? And are not our manners becoming soft and luxurious, and have not our vices began to shoot? Would one venture to prophecy, that in a century from this period, we shall be a corrupt luxurious people, perhaps the close of that century would stamp this prophecy with the title of history.

The rights of representation should also be held sacred and inviolable, and for this purpose, representation should be fixed upon known and easy principles; and the constitution should make provision, that recourse should constantly be had to those principles within a very small period of years, to rectify the errors that will creep in through lapse of time, or alteration of situations. The want of fixed principles of government, and a stated regular recourse to them, have produced the dissolution of all states, whose constitutions have been transmitted to us by history.

But the legislative power must not be trusted with one assembly. A single assembly is frequently influenced by the vices, follies, passions, and prejudices of an individual. It is liable to be avaricious, and to exempt itself from the burdens it lays upon it's constituents. It is subject to ambition, and after a series of years, will be prompted to vote itself perpetual. The long parliament in England voted itself perpetual, and thereby, for a time, destroyed the political liberty of the subject. Holland was governed by one representative assembly annually elected. They afterwards voted themselves from annual to septennial; then for life; and finally exerted the power of filling up all vacancies, without application to their constituents. The government of Holland is now a tyranny *though a republic.*

The result of a single assembly will be hasty and indigested, and their judgments frequently absurd and inconsistent. There must be a second body to revise with coolness and wisdom, and to controul with firmness, independent upon the first, either for their creation, or existence. Yet the first must retain a right to a similar revision and controul over the second.

Let us now ascertain some particular principles which should be attended to, in forming the executive power.

When we recollect the nature and employment of this power, we find that it ought to be conducted with vigour and dispatch. It should be able to execute the laws without opposition, and to controul all the turbulent spirits in the state, who should infringe them. If the laws are not obeyed, the legislative power is vain, and the judicial is mere pageantry. As these laws, with their several sanctions, are the only securities of person and property, the members of the state can confide in, if they lay dormant through failure of execution, violence and oppression will erect their heads, and stalk unmolested through the land. The judicial power ought to discriminate the offender, as soon after the commission of the offence, as an impartial trial will admit; and the executive arm to inflict the punishment immediately after the criminal is ascertained. This would have an happy tendency to prevent crimes, as the commission of them would awaken the attendant idea of punishment; and the hope of an escape, which is often an inducement, would be cut off. The executive power ought therefore in these cases, to be exerted with union, vigour, and dispatch. Another duty of that power is to arrest offenders, to bring them to trial. This cannot often be done, unless secrecy and expedition are used. The want of these two requisites, will be more especially inconvenient in repressing treasons, and those more enormous offences which strike at the happiness, if not existence of the whole. Offenders of these classes do not act alone. Some number is necessary to the compleating of the crime. Cabals are formed with art, and secrecy presides over their councils; while measures the most fatal are the result, to be executed by desperation. On these men the thunder of the state should be hurled with rapidity; for if they hear it roll at a distance, their danger is over. When they gain intelligence of the process, they abscond, and wait a more favourable opportunity. If that is attended with difficulty, they destroy all the evidence of their guilt, brave government, and deride the justice and power of the state.

It has been observed likewise, that the executive power is to act as Captain-General, to marshal the militia and armies of the state, and, for her defence, to lead them on to battle. These armies should always be composed of the militia or body of the people. Standing armies are a tremendous curse to a state. In all periods in which they have existed, they have been the scourge of mankind. In this de-partment, union, vigour, secrecy, and dispatch are more peculiarly necessary. Was one to propose a body of militia, over which two Generals, with equal authority, should have the command, he would be laughed at. Should one pretend, that the General should have no controul over his subordinate officers, either to remove them or to supply their posts, he would be pitied for his ignorance of the subject he was discussing. It is obviously necessary, that the man who calls the militia to action, and assumes the military controul over them in the field, should previously know the number of his men, their equipments and residence, and the talents and tempers of the several ranks of officers, and their respective departments in the state, that he may wisely determine to whom the necessary orders are to be issued. Regular and particular returns of these requisites should be frequently made. Let it be enquired, are these returns to be made only to the legislative body, or a branch of it, which necessarily moves slow?—Is the General to go to them for information? intreat them to remove an improper officer, and give him another they shall chuse? and in fine is he to supplicate his orders from them, and constantly walk where their leading-strings shall direct his steps? If so, where are the power and force of the militia—where the union—where the dispatch and profound secrecy? Or shall these returns be made to him?—when he may see with his own eyes—be his own judge of the merit, or demerit of his officers—discern their various talents and qualifications, and employ them as the service and defence of his country demand. Besides, the legislative body or a branch of it is local—they cannot therefore personally inform themselves of these facts, but must judge upon trust. The General's opinion will be founded upon his own observations—the officers and privates of the militia will act under his eye: and, if he has it in his power immediately to promote or disgrace them, they will be induced to noble exertions. It may further be observed here, that if the subordinate civil or military executive officers are appointed by the legislative body or a branch of it, the former will become dependent upon the latter, and the necessary independence of either the legislative or executive powers upon the other is wanting. The legislative power will have that undue influence over the executive which will amount to a controul, for the latter will be their creatures, and will fear their creators. . . .

We are next to fix upon some general rules which should govern us in forming the judicial power. This power is to be independent upon the executive and legislative. The judicial power should be a court and jury, or as they are commonly called, the Judges and jury. The jury are the peers or equals of every man, and are to try all facts. The province of the Judges is to preside in and regulate all trials, and ascertain the law. We shall only consider the appointment of the Judges. The same power which appoints them, ought not to have the power of removing them, not even for misbehavior. That conduct only would then be deemed misbehavior which was opposed to the will of the power removing. A removal in this case for proper reasons, would not be often attainable: for to remove a man from an office, because he is not properly qualified to discharge the duties of it, is a severe censure upon that man or body of men who appointed him—and mankind do not love to censure themselves. Whoever appoints the judges, they ought not to be removable at pleasure, for they will then feel a dependence upon that man or body of men who hath the power of removal. Nor ought they to be dependent upon either the executive or legislative power for their sallaries; for if they are, that power on whom they are thus dependent, can starve them into a compliance. One of these two powers should appoint, and the other remove. The legislative will not probably appoint so good men as the executive, for reasons formerly mentioned. The former are composed of a large body of men who have a numerous train of friends and connexions, and they do not hazard their reputations, which the executive will. It has often been mentioned that where a large body of men are responsible for any measures, a regard to their reputations, and to the public opinion, will not prompt them to use that care and precaution, which such regard will prompt one or a few to make use of. Let one more observation be now introduced to confirm it. Every man has some friends and dependents who will endeavor to snatch him from the public hatred. One man has but a few comparatively, they are not numerous enough to protect him, and he falls a victim to his own misconduct. When measures are conducted by a large number, their friends and connexions are numerous and noisy—they are dispersed through the State—their clamors stifle the execrations of the people, whose groans cannot even be heard. But to resume, neither will the executive body be the most proper judge when to remove. If this body is judge, it must also be the accuser, or the legislative body, or a branch of it, must be—If the executive body complains, it will be both accuser and judge—If the complaint is preferred by the legislative body, or a branch of it, when the judges are appointed by the legislative body, then a body of men who were concerned in the appointment, must in most cases complain of the impropriety of their own appointment. Let therefore the judges be appointed by the executive body—let their salaries be independent—and let them hold their places during good behaviour—Let their misbehaviour be determinable by the legislative body—Let one branch thereof impeach, and the other judge. Upon these principles the judicial body will be independent so long as they behave well and a proper court is appointed to ascertain their mal-conduct.

The Committee afterwards proceeded to consider the Constitution framed by the Convention of this State. They have examined that Constitution with all the care the shortness of the time would admit. And they are compelled, though reluctantly to say, that some of the principles upon which it is founded, appeared to them inconsonant, not only to the natural rights of mankind, but to the fundamental condition of the original social contract, and the principles of a free republican government. In that form of government the governor appears to be the supreme executive officer, and the legislative power is in an house of representatives and senate. It may be necessary to descend to a more particular consideration of the several articles of that constitution.

The second article thereof appears exceptionable upon the principles we have already attempted to establish, because the supreme executive officer hath a seat and voice in one branch of the legislative body, and is assisting in originating and framing the laws, the Governor being entitled to a seat and voice in the Senate, and to preside in it, and may thereby have that influence in the legislative body, which the supreme executive officer ought not to have.

The third article among other things, ascertains the qualifications of the Governor, Lieutenant Governor, Senators and Representatives respecting property—The estate sufficient to qualify a man for Governor is so small, it is hardly any qualification at all. Further, the method of ascertaining the value of the estates of the officers aforesaid is vague and uncertain as it depends upon the nature and quantity of the currency, and the encrease of property, and not upon any fixed principles. This article therefore appears to be exceptionable.

The sixth article regulates the election of representatives. So many objections present themselves to this article, we are at a loss which first to mention. The representation is grossly unequal, and it is flagrantly unjust. It violates the fundamental principle of the original social contract, and introduces an unweildy and expensive house. Representation ought to be equal upon the principles formerly mentioned. By this article any corporation, however small, may send one representative, while no corporation can send more than one, unless it has three hundred freemen. Twenty corporations (of three hundred freemen in each) containing in the whole six thousand freemen, may send forty representatives, when one corporation, which shall contain six thousand two hundred and twenty, can send but nineteen. One third of the state may send a majority of the representatives, and all the laws may be enacted by a minority—Do all the members of the state then, enjoy political liberty? Will they not be controuled by laws enacted against their consent? When we go further and find, that sixty members make an house, and that the concurrence of thirty one (which is about one twelfth of what may be the present number of representatives) is sufficient to bind the persons and properties of the members of the State, we stand amazed, and are sorry that any well disposed Americans were so inattentive to the consequences of such an arrangement.

The number of representatives is too large to debate with coolness and deliberation, the public business will be protracted to an undue length and the pay of the house is enormous. As the number of freemen in the State encreases, these inconveniences will encrease; and in a century, the house of representatives will, from their numbers, be a mere mob. Observations upon this article croud upon us, but we will dismiss it, with wishing that the mode of representation there proposed, may be candidly compared with the principles which have been already mentioned in the course of our observations upon the legislative power, and upon representation in a free republic.

The ninth article regulates the election of Senators, which we think exceptionable. As the Senators for each district will be elected by all the freemen in the state properly qualified, a trust is reposed in the people which they are unequal to. The freemen in the late province of Main, are to give in their votes for senators in the western district, and so, on the contrary. Is it supposeable that the freemen in the county of Lincoln can judge of the political merits of a senator in Berkshire? Must not the several corpora-

tions in the state, in a great measure depend upon their representatives for information? And will not the house of representatives in fact chuse the senators? That independence of the senate upon the house, which the constitution seems to have intended, is visionary, and the benefits which were expected to result from a senate, as one distinct branch of the legislative body, will not be discoverable.

The tenth article prescribes the method in which the Governor is to be elected. This method is open to, and will introduce bribery and corruption, and also originate parties and factions in the state. The Governor of Rhode-Island was formerly elected in this manner, and we all know how long a late Governor there, procured his re-election by methods the most unjustifiable. Bribery was attempted in an open and flagrant manner.

The thirteenth article ascertains the authority of the general court, and by that article we find their power is limited only by the several articles of the constitution. We do not find that the rights of conscience are ascertained and defined, unless they may be thought to be in the thirty fourth article. That article we conceive to be expressed in very loose and uncertain terms. What is a *religious* profession and worship of God, has been disputed for sixteen hundred years, and the various sects of christians have not yet settled the dispute. What is a free exercise and enjoyment of religious worship has been, and still is, a subject of much altercation. And this free exercise and enjoyment is said to be *allowed* to the protestants of this state by the constitution, when we suppose it to be an unalienable right of all mankind, which no human power can wrest from them. We do not find any bill of rights either accompanying the constitution, or interwoven with it, and no attempt is made to define and secure that protection of the person and property of the members of the state, which the legislative and executive bodies cannot withhold, unless the general words *of confirming the right to trial by jury,* should be considered as such definition and security. We think a bill of rights ascertaining and clearly describing the rights of conscience, and that security of person and property, the supreme power of the state is bound to afford to all the members thereof, ought to be fully ratified, before, or at the same time with, the establishment of any constitution.

The fifteenth article fixes the number which shall constitute a quorum in the senate and house of representatives—We think these numbers much too small—This constitution will immediately introduce about three hundred and sixty mumbers into the house. If sixty make a quorum, the house may totally change its members six different times; and it probably will very often in the course of a long session, be composed of such a variety of members, as will retard the public business, and introduce confusion in the debates, and inconsistency in the result. Besides the number of members, whose concurrence is necessary to enact a law, is so small, that the subjects of the state will have no security, that the laws which are to controul their natural rights, have the consent of a majority of the freemen. The same reasoning applies to the senate, though not so strikingly, as a quorum of that body must consist of nearly a third of the senators.

The eighteenth article describes the several powers of the Governor or the supreme executive officer. We find in comparing the several articles of the constitution, that the senate are the only court to try impeachments. We also conceive that every officer in the state ought to be amenable to such court. We think therefore that the members of that court ought never to be advisory to any officer in the state. If their advice is the result of inattention or corruption, they cannot be brought to punishment by impeachment, as they will be their own judges. Neither will the officer who pursues their advice be often, if ever, punishable, for a similar reason. To condemn this officer will be to reprobate their own advice—consequently a proper body is not formed to advise the Governor, when a sudden emergency may render advice expedient: for the senate advise, and are the court to try impeachments. We would now make one further observation, that we cannot discover in this article or in any part of the constitution that the executive power is entrusted with a check upon the legislative power, sufficient to prevent the encroachment of the latter upon the former—Without this check the legislative power will exercise the executive, and in a series of years the government will be as absolute as that of Holland.

The nineteenth article regulates the appointment of the several classes of officers. And we find that almost all the officers are appointed by the Governor and Senate. An objection formerly made occurs here. The Senate with the Governor are the court to remove these officers for misbehaviour. Those officers, in general, who are guilty of maleconduct in the execution of their office, were improper men to be appointed. Sufficient care was not taken in ascertaining their political military or moral qualifications. Will the senators therefore if they appoint, be a proper court to remove. Will not a regard to their own characters have an undue bias upon them. This objection will grow stronger, if we may suppose that the time will come when a man may procure his appointment to office by bribery. The members of that court therefore who alone can remove for misbehaviour, should not be concerned in the appointment. Besides, if one branch of the legislative body appoint the executive officers, and the same branch alone can remove them, the legislative power will acquire an undue influence over the executive.

The twenty second article describes the authority the Governor shall have in all business to be transacted by him and the Senate. The Governor by this article must be present in conducting an impeachment. He has it therefore in his power to rescue a favourite from impeachment, so long as he is Governor, by absenting himself from the Senate, whenever the impeachment is to be brought forwards.

We cannot conceive upon what principles the twenty third article ascertains the speaker of the house to be one of the three, the majority of whom have the power of granting pardons. The speaker is an officer of one branch of the legislative body, and hourly depends upon them for his existence in that character—he therefore would not probably be disposed to offend any leading party in the house, by consenting to, or denying a pardon. An undue influence might prevail and the power of pardoning be improperly exercised.—When the speaker is guilty of this improper exercise, he cannot be punished but by impeachment, and as he is commonly a favourite of a considerable party in the house, it will be difficult to procure the accusation; for his party will support him.

The judges by the twenty fourth article are to hold their places during good behaviour, but we do not find that their salaries are any where directed to be fixed. The house of representatives may therefore starve them into a state of dependence.

The twenty-eighth article determines the mode of electing and removing the delegates for Congress. It is by joint ballot of the house and Senate. These delegates should be some of the best men in the State. Their abilities and characters should be thoroughly investigated. This will be more effectually done, if they are elected by the legislative body, each branch having a right to originate or negative the choice, and removal. And we cannot conceive why they should not be elected in this manner, as well as all officers who are annually appointed with annual grants of their sallaries, as is directed in the nineteenth article. By the mode of election now excepted against, the house may choose their delegates, altho' every Senator should vote against their choice.

The thirty-fourth article respecting liberty of conscience, we think exceptionable, but the observations necessary to be made thereon, were introduced in animadverting upon the thirteenth article. . . .

The Committee, in obedience to the direction of this body, afterwards proceeded to delineate the general outlines of a Constitution, conformable to what have been already reported by them, as the principles of a free republican government, and as the natural rights of mankind.

They first attempted to delineate the legislative body. It has already been premised, that the legislative power is to be lodged in two bodies, composed of the representatives of the people. That representation ought to be equal. And that no law affecting the person and property of the members of the state ought to be enacted, without the consent of a majority of the members, and of those also who hold a major part of the property.

In forming the first body of legislators, let regard be had only to the representation of persons, not of property. This body we call the house of representatives. Ascertain the number of representatives. It ought not to be so large as will induce an enormous expence to government, nor too unwieldy to deliberate with coolness and attention; nor so small as to be unacquainted with the situation and circumstances of the state. One hundred will be large enough, and perhaps it may be too large. We are persuaded that any number of men exceeding that, cannot do business with such expedition and propriety a smaller number could. However let that at present be considered as the number. Let us have the number of freemen in the several counties in the state; and let these representatives be apportioned among the respective counties, in proportion to their number of freemen. The representation yet remains equal. Let the representatives for the several counties be elected in this manner. Let the several towns in the respective counties, the first wednesday in May annually, choose delegates to meet in county convention on the thursday next after the second wednesday in May annually, and there elect the representatives for the county—Let the number of delegates each town shall send to the county

convention be regulated in this manner. Ascertain that town which hath the smallest number of freemen; and let that town send one. Suppose the smallest town contains fifty. All the other towns shall then send as many members as they have fifties. If after the fifties are deducted, there remains an odd number, and that number is twenty five, or more, let them send another, if less, let no notice be taken of it. We have taken a certain for an uncertain number. Here the representation is as equal as the situation of a large political society will admit. No qualification should be necessary for a representative, except residence in the county the two years preceding his election, and the payment of taxes those years. Any freeman may be an elector who hath resided in the county the year preceeding. The same qualification is requisite for a delegate, that is required of a representative. The representatives are designed to represent the persons of the members, and therefore we do not consider a qualification in point of property necessary for them.

These representatives shall be returned from the several parts of the county in this manner—Each county convention shall divide the county into as many districts as they send representatives, by the following rule—As we have the number of freemen in the county, and the number of county representatives, by dividing the greater by the less we have the number of freemen entitled to send one representative. Then add as many adjoining towns together as contain that number of freemen, or as near as may be, and let those towns form one district, and proceed in this manner through the county. Let a representative be chosen out of each district, and let all the representatives be elected out of the members who compose the county convention. In this house we find a proportionate representation of persons. If a law passes this house it hath the consent of a majority of the freemen; and here we may look for political honesty, probity and upright intentions to the good of the whole. Let this house therefore originate money-bills, as they will not have that inducement to extravagant liberality which an house composed of opulent men would, as the former would feel more sensibly the consequences. This county convention hath other business to do, which shall be mentioned hereafter. We shall now only observe, that this convention, upon a proper summons, is to meet again, to supply all vacancies in it's representation, by electing other representatives out of the district in which the vacancy falls. The formation of the second body of legislators next came under consideration, which may be called the senate. In electing the members for this body, let the representation of property be attended to. The senators may be chosen most easily in a county convention, which may be called the senatorial convention. Ascertain the number of senators. Perhaps thirty three will be neither too large nor too small. Let seven more be added to the thirty three which will make forty—these seven will be wanted for another pupose to be mentioned hereafter—Apportion the whole number upon the several counties, in proportion to the state-tax each county pays. Each freeman of the state, who is possessed of a certain quantity of property, may be an elector of the senators. To ascertain the value of a man's estate by a valuation is exceedingly difficult if possible, unless he voluntarily returns a valuation—To ascertain it by oath would be laying snares for a man's conscience, and would be a needless multiplication of oaths if another method could be devised—To fix his property at any certain sum, would be vague and uncertain, such is the fluctuation of even the best currency, and such the continual alteration of the nominal value of property—Let the state-tax assessed on each freeman's estate decide it—That tax will generally bear a very just proportion to the nominal value of a currency, and of property. Let every freeman whose estate pays such a proportion of the state-tax that had been last assessed previous to his electing, as three pounds is to an hundred thousand pounds, be an elector—The senatorial convention may be composed of delegates from the several towns elected in this manner. Ascertain the town which contains the smallest number of freemen whose estates pay such tax, and ascertain that number. Suppose it to be thirty. Let that town send one, and let all the other towns in the county send as many delegates as they have thirties. If after the thirties are deducted, there remains an odd number, and that number is fifteen, or more, let them send another, if it is less than fifteen let no notice be taken of it. Let the delegates for the senatorial convention be chosen at the same time with the county delegates, and meet in convention the second wednesday in May annually, which is the day before the county convention is to meet—and let no county delegate be a senatorial delegate the same year—We have here a senate (deducting seven in the manner and for the purpose hereafter to be mentioned) which more peculiarly represents the property of the state; and no act will pass both branches of the legislative body, without having the con-

sent of those members who hold a major part of the property of the state. In electing the senate in this manner, the representation will be as equal as the fluctuation of property will admit of, and it is an equal representation of property so far as the number of senators are proportioned among the several counties. Such is the distribution of intestate estates in this country, the inequality between the estates of the bulk of the property holders is so inconsiderable, and the tax necessary to qualify a man to be an elector of a senator is so moderate, it may be demonstrated, that a law which passes both branches will have the consent of those persons who hold a majority of the property in the state. No freeman should be a delegate for the senatorial convention unless his estate pays the same tax which was necessary to qualify him to elect delegates for that convention; and no freeman shall be an elector of a delegate for that convention, nor a delegate therefor, unless he has been an inhabitant of the county for the two years next preceeding. No person shall be capable of an election into the senate unless he has been an inhabitant of the county for three years next preceeding his election—His qualification in point of estate is also to be considered. Let the state tax which was assessed upon his estate for the three years next preceeding his election be upon an average, at the rate of six pounds in an hundred thousand annually.

This will be all the duty of the senatorial convention unless there should be a vacancy in the senate when it will be again convened to fill up the vacancy. These two bodies will have the execution of the legislative power; and they are composed of the necessary members to make a just proportion of taxes among the several counties. This is all the discretionary power they will have in apportioning the taxes.

Once in five years at least, the legislative body shall make a valuation for the several counties in the State, and at the same time each county shall make a county valuation, by a county convention chosen for that purpose only, by the same rules which the legislative body observed in making the State valuation—and whenever a State valuation is made, let the several county valuations be also made. The legislative body after they have proportioned the State tax among the several counties, shall also proportion the tax among the several plantations and towns, agreeably to the county valuation, to be filed in the records of the General Court for that purpose. It may be observed that this county valuation will be taken and adjusted in county convention, in which persons only are to be equally represented: and it may also be objected that property ought also to be represented for this purpose. It is answered that each man in the county will pay at least a poll tax, and therefore ought to be represented in this convention—that it is impracticable in one convention to have persons and property both represented, with any degree of equality, without great intricacy—and that, where both cannot be represented without great intricacy, the representation of property should yield the preference to that of persons. The counties ought not to be compelled to pay their own representatives—if so, the counties remote from the seat of government would be at a greater charge than the other counties, which would be unjust—for they have only an equal influence in legislation with the other counties, yet they cannot use that influence but at a greater expence—They therefore labor under greater disadvantages in the enjoyment of their political liberties, than the other counties. If the remote counties enjoyed a larger proportional influence in legislation than the other counties, it would be just they should pay their own members, for the enhanced expence would tend to check this inequality of representation.

All the representatives should attend the house, if possible, and all the senators the senate. A change of faces in the course of a session retards and perplexes the public business. No man should accept of a seat in the legislative body without he intends a constant attendance upon his duty. Unavoidable accidents, necessary private business, sickness and death may, and will prevent a general attendance: but the numbers requisite to constitute a quorum of the house and senate should be so large as to admit of the absence of members, only for the reasons aforesaid. If members declined to attend their duty they should be expelled, and others chosen who would do better. Let seventy five constitute a quorum of the house, and twenty four of the senate. However no law ought to be enacted at any time, unless it has the concurrence of fifty one representatives, and seventeen senators.

We have now the legislative body (deducting seven of the senators.) Each branch hath a negative upon the other —and either branch may originate any bill or propose any amendment, except a money bill, which should be concurred or nonconcurred by the senate in the whole. The legislative body is so formed and ballanced that the laws will be made with the greatest wisdom and the best intentions; and the proper consent thereto is obtained. Each man enjoys political liberty, and his civil rights will be taken care of. And all orders of men are interested in government, will put confidence in it, and struggle for it's support. As the county and senatorial delegates are chosen the same day throughout the State, as all the county conventions are held at the same time, and all the senatorial conventions on one day, and as these delegates are formed into conventions on a short day after their election, elections will be free, bribery will be impracticable, and party and factions will not be formed. As the senatorial conventions are held the day before the county conventions, the latter will have notice of the persons elected senators, and will not return them as representatives—The senatorial convention should after it's first election of senators be adjourned without day, but not dissolved, and to be occasionally called together by the supreme executive officer to keep the senate full, should a senator elected decline the office, or afterwards resign, be expelled, or die. The county convention in the same way are to keep the representation full, and also supply all vacancies in the offices they will be authorised to appoint to and elect as will be presently mentioned. By making provision in the constitution that recourse be had to these principles of representation every twenty years, by taking new lists of the freemen for that purpose, and by a new distribution of the number of representatives agreeably thereto, and of the senators in proportion to the State tax, representation will be always free and equal. These principles easily accommodate themselves to the erection of new counties and towns. Crude and hasty determinations of the house will be revised or controuled by the senate; and those views of the senate which may arise from ambition or a disregard to civil liberty will be frustrated. Government will acquire a dignity and firmness, which is the greatest security of the subject: while the people look on, and observe the conduct of their servants, and continue or withdraw their favour annually, according to their merit or demerit.

The forming of the executive power came next in course. Every freeman in the State should have a voice in this formation; for as the executive power hath no controul over property, but in pursuance of established laws, the consent of the property-holders need not be considered as necessary. Let the head of the executive power be a Governor (or in his absence, or on his death, a Lieutenant Governor) and let him be elected in the several county conventions by ballot, on the same day the representatives are chosen. Let a return be made by each man fixed upon by the several conventions, and the man who is returned by any county shall be considered as having as many votes, as that county sends representatives. Therefore the whole number of votes will be one hundred. He who hath fifty one or more votes is Governor. Let the Lieutenant-Governor be designated in the same way. This head of the supreme executive power should have a privy council, or a small select number (suppose seven) to advise with. Let him not chuse them himself—for he might then, if wickedly disposed, elect no persons who had integrity enough to controul him by their advice. Let the legislative body elect them in this manner. The house shall chuse by ballot seven out of the senate. These shall be a privy council, four of whom shall constitute a quorum. Let the Governor alone marshal the militia, and regulate the same, together with the navy, and appoint all their officers, and remove them at pleasure. The temper, use, and end of a militia and navy require it. He should likewise command the navy and militia, and have power to march the latter any where within the state. Was this territory so situated, that the militia could not be marched out of it, without entering an enemy's country, he should have no power to march them out of the state. But the late province of Main militia must march through New-Hampshire to enter Massachusetts, and so, on the contrary. The neighbouring states are all friends and allies, united by a perpetual confederacy. Should Providence or Portsmouth be attacked suddenly, a day's delay might be of most pernicious consequence. Was the consent of the legislative body, or a branch of it, necessary, a longer delay would be unavoidable. Still the Governor should be under a controul. Let him march the militia without the state with the advice of his privy council, and his authority be continued for ten days and no longer, unless the legislative body in the mean time prolong it. In these ten days he may convene the legislative body, and take their opinion. If his authority is not continued, the legislative body may controul him, and order the militia back. If his conduct is disapproved, his reputation, and that of his advisers is ruined. He will never venture on the measure, unless the general good requires it, and then he will be applauded. Remember the election of Governor and council is annual. But the legislative body must have a check upon the Captain General. He is best qualified to appoint his subordinate officers, but he may appoint improper ones—He has the sword, and may wish to form cabals amongst his officers to perpetuate his power—The legislative body should therefore have a power of removing any militia officer at pleasure—Each branch should have this power. The Captain General will then be effectually controuled. The Governor with his privy council may also appoint the following executive officers, viz The attorney General and the justices of the peace, who shall hold their places during good behaviour—This misbehaviour shall be determined by the senate on impeachment of the house. On this scheme a mutual check is thus far preserved in both the powers. The supreme executive officer as he is annually removeable by the people, will for that, and the other reasons formerly mentioned, probably appoint the best officers: and when he does otherwise the legislative power will remove them. The militia officers which are solely appointed, and removeable at pleasure, by the Governor, are removeable at pleasure by either branch of the legislative. Those executive officers which are removeable only for misbehaviour, the consent of the privy council, chosen by the legislative body, is first necessary to their appointment, and afterwards they are removeable by the senate, on impeachment of the house. We now want only to give the executive power a check upon the legislative, to prevent the latter from encroaching on the former, and stripping it of all it's rights. The legislative in all states hath attempted it where this check was wanting, and have prevailed, and the freedom of the state was thereby destroyed. This attempt hath resulted from that lust of domination, which in some degree influences all men, and all bodies of men. The Governor therefore with the consent of the privy council, may negative any law, proposed to be enacted by the legislative body. The advantages which will attend the due use of this negative are, that thereby the executive power will be preserved entire—the encroachments of the legislative will be repelled, and the powers of both be properly balanced. All the business of the legislative body will be brought into one point, and subject to an impartial consideration on a regular consistent plan. As the Governor will have it in charge to state the situation of the government to the legislative body at the opening of every session, as far as his information will qualify him therefor, he will now know officially, all that has been done, with what design the laws were enacted, how far they have answered the proposed end, and what still remains to compleat the intention of the legislative body. The reasons why he will not make an improper use of his negative are—his annual election—the annual election of the privy council, by and out of the legislative body—His political character and honour are at stake—If he makes a proper use of his negative by preserving the executive powers entire, by pointing out any mistake in the laws which may escape any body of men through inattention, he will have the smiles of the people. If on the contrary, he makes an improper use of his negative, and wantonly opposes a law that is for the public good, his reputation, and that of his privy council are forfeited, and they are disgracefully tumbled from their seats. This Governor is not appointed by a King, or his ministry, nor does he receive instructions from a party of men, who are pursuing an interest diametrically opposite to the good of the state. His interest is the same with that of every man in the state; and he knows he must soon return, and sink to a level with the rest of the community.

The danger is, he will be too cautious of using his negative for the interest of the state. His fear of offending may prompt him, if he is a timid man, to yield up some parts of the executive power. The Governor should be thus qualified for his office—He shall have been an inhabitant of the state for four years next preceeding his election, and paid public taxes those years—Let the state tax assessed upon his estate those years be, upon an average, at the rate of sixteen pounds in an hundred thousand annually. . . .

Let us also consider in whose hands the power of pardoning should be lodged. If the legislative body or a branch of it are entrusted with it, the same body which made or were concerned in making the law, will excuse the breach of it. This body is so numerous that most offenders will have some relation or connexion with some of it's members, undue influence for that reason may take place, and if a pardon should be issued improperly, the public blame will fall upon such members, it would not have the weight of a feather; and no conviction upon an impeachment could follow—The house would not impeach themselves, and the senators would not condemn the senate. If this power of pardoning is lodged with the Governor and privy council, the number is so small, that all can personally inform themselves of the facts, and misinformation will be detected. Their own reputation would guard them against undue influence, for the censure of the people will hang on their necks with the weight of a mill-stone—And impeachments will stare them in the face, and conviction strike them with terror. Let the power of pardoning be therefore lodged with the Governor and privy council.

The right of convening, adjourning, proroguing, and dissolving the legislative body deserves consideration. The constitution will make provision for their convention on the last wednesday in May annually. Let each branch of the legislative, have power to adjourn itself for two days—Let the legislative body have power to adjourn or prorogue itself to any time within the year. Let the Governor and privy council have authority to convene them at pleasure, when the public business calls for it, for the assembling of the legislative body may often be necessary, previous to the day to which that body had adjourned or prorogued itself, as the legislative body when dispersed cannot assemble itself. And to prevent any attempts of their voting a continuance of their political existence, let the constitution make provision, that some time in every year, on or before the wednesday preceeding the last wednesday in May, the Governor shall dissolve them. Before that day, he shall not have power to do it, without their consent.

As the principles which should govern in forming the judicial power have been already mentioned, a few observations only, are necessary to apply those principles.

Let the judges of the common law courts, of the admiralty, and probate, and the register of probate, be appointed by the Governor and privy council; let the stipends of these judges be fixed; and let all those officers be removeable only for misbehaviour. Let the senate be the judge of that misbehaviour, on impeachment of the house.

The committee have now compleated the general out lines of a constitution, which they suppose may be conformable to the principles of a free republican government—They have not attempted the description of the less important parts of a constitution, as they naturally and obviously are determinable by attention to those principles—Neither do they exhibit these general out lines, as the only ones which can be consonant to the natural rights of mankind, to the fundamental terms of the original social contract, and to the principles of political justice; for they do not assume to themselves infallibility. To compleat the task assigned them by this body, this constitution is held up in a general view, to convince us of the practicability of enjoying a free republican government, in which our natural rights are attended to, in which the original social contract is observed, and in which political justice governs; and also to justify us in our objections to the constitution proposed by the convention of this state, which we have taken the liberty to say is, in our apprehension, in some degree deficient in those respects.

To balance a large society on republican or general laws, is a work of so great difficulty, that no human genius, however comprehensive, is perhaps able, by the mere dint of reason and reflection, to effect it. The penetrating and dispassionate judgments of many must unite in this work: experience must guide their labour: time must bring it to perfection: and the feeling of inconveniencies must correct the mistakes which they will probably fall into, in their first trials and experiments. . . .

This was at least the task enjoined upon the committee, and whether it has been successfully executed, they presume not to determine. They aimed at modelling the three branches of the supreme power in such a manner, that the government might act with the greatest vigour and wisdom, and with the best intentions—They aimed that each of those branches should retain a check upon the others, sufficient to preserve it's independence—They aimed that no member of the state should be controuled by any law, or be deprived of his property, against his consent— They aimed that all the members of the state should enjoy political liberty, and that their civil liberties should have equal care taken of them—and in fine, that they should be a free and an happy people—The committee are sensible, that the spirit of a free republican constitution, or the moving power which should give it action, ought to be political virtue, patriotism, and a just regard to the natural rights of mankind. This spirit, if wanting, can be obtained only from that Being, who infused the breath of Life into our first parent.

The committee have only further to report, that the inhabitants of the several towns who deputed delegates for this convention, be seriously advised, and solemnly exhorted, as they value the political freedom and happiness of themselves and of their posterity, to convene all the freemen of their several towns in town meeting, for this purpose regularly notified, and that they do unanimously vote their disapprobation of the constitution and form of government, framed by the convention of this state; that a regular return of the same be made to the secretary's office, that it may there remain a grateful monument to our posterity of that consistent, impartial and persevering attachment to political, religious, and civil liberty, which actuated their fathers, and in defence of which, they bravely fought, chearfully bled, and gloriously died.

The above report being read was accepted.

Attest, PETER COFFIN, *Chairman.*

Northwest Ordinance

1787

The Northwest Ordinance made it clear to the world that the thirteen states would soon multiply through settlement in the area north of the Ohio and east of the Mississippi Rivers. Already populated by increasing numbers of settlers, these areas represented vast room for expansion—room that the British government had made off-limits to colonists. This ordinance commits the central government to providing, within the Northwest Territory, the means for education, including religious education. It also commits the government to maintaining the rights for which the American war for independence had been fought.

Northwest Ordinance

An ordinance for the Government of the Territory of the United States, north-west of the River Ohio be it ordained by the United States in Congress assembled, That the said territory, for the purposes of temporary government, be one district; subject, however, to be divided into two districts, as future circumstances may in the opinion of Congress, make it expedient.

Be it ordained by the authority aforesaid, That the estates, both of resident and non-resident proprietors in the said territory, dying intestate, shall descend to, and be distributed among their children, and the descendants of a deceased child in equal parts; the descendants of a deceased child or grandchild, to take the share of their deceased parent in equal parts among them: And where there shall be no children or descendants, then in equal parts to the next of kin, in equal degree; and among collaterals, the children of a deceased brother or sister of the intestate, shall have in equal parts among them, their deceased parents' share; and there shall in no case be a distinction between kindred of the whole and half blood; saving in all cases to the widow of the intestate, her third part of the real estate for life, and one third part of the personal estate; and this law relative to descents and dower, shall remain in full force until altered by the legislature of the district.—And until the governor and judges shall adopt laws as herein af-

ter mentioned, estates in the said territory may be devised or bequeathed by wills in writing, signed and sealed by him or her, in whom the estate may be (being of full age) and attested by three witnesses;—and real estates may be conveyed by lease and release, or bargain and sale, signed, sealed, and delivered by the person being of full age, in whom the estate may be, and attested by two witnesses, provided such wills be duly proved, and such conveyances be acknowledged, or the execution thereof duly proved, and be recorded within one year after proper magistrates, courts, and registers shall be appointed for that purpose; and personal property may be transferred by delivery; saving, however, to the French and Canadian inhabitants, and other settlers of the Kaskaskies, Saint Vincent's, and the neighboring villages, who have heretofore professed themselves citizens of Virginia, their laws and customs now in force among them, relative to the descent and conveyance of property.

Be it ordained by the authority aforesaid, That there shall be appointed from time to time, by Congress, a governor, whose commission shall continue in force for the term of three years, unless sooner revoked by Congress; he shall reside in the district, and have a freehold estate therein, in one thousand acres of land, while in the exercise of his office.

There shall be appointed from time to time, by Congress, a secretary, whose commission shall continue in force for four years, unless sooner revoked; he shall reside in the district, and have a freehold estate therein, in five hundred acres of land, while in the exercise of his office; it shall be his duty to keep and preserve the acts and laws passed by the legislature, and the public records of the district, and the proceedings of the governor in his executive department; and transmit authentic copies of such acts and proceedings, every six months, to the secretary of Congress. There shall also be appointed a court to consist of three judges, any two of whom to form a court, who shall have a common law jurisdiction, and reside in the district, and have each therein a freehold estate in five hundred acres of land, while in the exercise of their offices; and their commissions shall continue in force during good behavior.

The governor and judges, or a majority of them, shall adopt and publish in the district, such laws of the original States, criminal and civil, as may be necessary, and best suited to the circumstances of the district, and report them to Congress, from time to time; which laws shall be in force in the district until the organization of the General Assembly therein, unless disapproved of by Congress; but afterwards the Legislature shall have authority to alter them as they shall think fit.

The governor, for the time being, shall be commander-in-chief of the militia, appoint and commission all officers in the same below the rank of general officers; all general officers shall be appointed and commissioned by Congress.

Previous to the organization of the general assembly, the governor shall appoint such magistrates and other civil officers, in each county or township, as he shall find necessary for the preservation of the peace and good order in the same. After the general assembly shall be organized, the powers and duties of magistrates and other civil officers shall be regulated and defined by the said assembly; but all magistrates and other civil officers, not herein otherwise directed, shall, during the continuance of this temporary government, be appointed by the governor.

For the prevention of crimes and injuries, the laws to be adopted or made shall have force in all parts of the district, and for the execution of process, criminal and civil, the governor shall make proper divisions thereof—and he shall proceed from time to time, as circumstances may require, to lay out the parts of the district in which the Indian titles shall have been extinguished, into counties and townships, subject, however, to such alterations as may thereafter be made by the legislature.

So soon as there shall be five thousand free male inhabitants, of full age, in the district, upon giving proof thereof to the governor, they shall receive authority, with time and place, to elect representatives from their counties or townships, to represent them in the general assembly; *Provided,* That for every five hundred free male inhabitants, there shall be one representative, and so on progressively with the number of free male inhabitants shall the right of representation increase, until the number of representatives shall amount to twenty-five; after which, the number and proportion of representatives shall be regulated by the legislature: *Provided* that no person be eligible or qualified to act as a representative, unless he shall have been a citizen of one of the United States three years, and be a resident in the district, or unless he shall have resided in the district three years; and, in either case, shall likewise hold in his own right, in fee simple, two hundred acres of land within the same: *Provided* also, That a freehold in fifty acres of land in the district, having been a citizen of one of the States, and being resident in the district, or the like freehold and two years residence in the district shall be necessary to qualify a man as an elector of a representative.

The representatives thus elected shall serve for the term of two years; and in case of the death of a representative, or removal from office, the governor shall issue a writ to the county or township, for which he was a member, to elect another in his stead, to serve for the residue of the term.

The general assembly or legislature shall consist of the Governor, Legislative Council, and House of Representatives. The Legislative Council shall consist of five members, to continue in office five years, unless sooner removed by Congress; any three of whom to be a quorum: and the members of the Council shall be nominated and appointed in the following manner, to wit: As soon as representatives shall be elected, the Governor shall appoint a time and place for them to meet together, and, when met, they shall nominate ten persons, residents in the district, and each possessed of a freehold in five hundred acres of land, and return their names to Congress; five of whom Congress shall appoint and commission to serve as aforesaid; and, whenever a vacancy shall happen in the council, by death or removal from office, the House of Representatives shall nominate two persons, qualified as aforesaid, for each vacancy, and return their names to Congress; one of whom Congress shall appoint and commission for the residue of the term. And every five years, four months at least before the expiration of the time of service of the members of Council, the said House shall nominate ten persons, qualified as aforesaid, and return their names to Congress; five of whom Congress shall appoint and commission to serve as members of the Council five years, unless sooner removed. And the Governor, Legislative Council, and House of Representatives, shall have authority to make laws, in all cases, for the good government of the district, not repugnant to the principles and articles in this ordinance established and declared. And all bills having passed by a majority in the House, and by a majority in the Council, shall be referred to the Governor for his assent; but no bill, or legislative Act whatever, shall be of any force without his assent. The governor shall have power to convene, prorogue and dissolve the General Assembly, when, in his opinion, it shall be expedient.

The Governor, judges, Legislative Council, Secretary, and such other officers as Congress shall appoint in the district, shall take an oath or affirmation of fidelity, and of office; the Governor before the President of Congress, and all other officers before the Governor. As soon as a legislature shall be formed in the district, the Council and House assembled, in one room, shall have authority, by joint ballot, to elect a delegate to Congress, who shall have a seat in Congress, with a right of debating, but not of voting during this temporary government.

And for extending the fundamental principles of civil and religious liberty, which form the basis whereon these republics, their laws and constitutions are erected; to fix and establish those principles as the basis of all laws, constitutions, and governments, which forever hereafter shall be formed in the said territory: to provide also for the establishment of States, and permanent government therein, and for their admission to a share in the federal councils on an equal footing with the original States, at as early periods as may be consistent with the general interest:

It is hereby ordained and declared by the authority aforesaid, That the following articles shall be considered as articles of compact between the original States, and the people and States in the said territory, and forever remain unalterable, unless by common consent, to wit:

Article the first. No person, demeaning himself in a peaceable and orderly manner, shall ever be molested on account of his mode of worship or religious sentiments, in the said territory.

Article the second. The inhabitants of the said territory, shall always be entitled to the benefits of the writ of *habeas corpus,* and of the trial by jury; of a proportionate representation of the people in the legislature; and of judicial proceedings according to the course of the common law. All persons shall be bailable, unless for capital offenses, where the proof shall be evident or the presumption great. All fines shall be moderate; and no cruel or unusual punishments shall be inflicted. No man shall be deprived of his liberty or property, but by the judgment of his peers, or the law of the land, and, should the public exigencies make it

necessary, for the common preservation, to take any person's property, or to demand his particular services, full compensation shall be made for the same. And, in the just preservation of rights and property, it is understood and declared, that no law ought ever to be made, have force in the said territory, that shall, in any manner whatever, interfere with or affect private contracts or engagements, *bona fide,* and without fraud, previously formed.

Article the third. Religion, morality, and knowledge, being necessary to good government and the happiness of mankind, schools and the means of education shall forever be encouraged. The utmost good faith shall always be observed towards the Indians; their lands and property shall never be taken from them without their consent; and, in their property, rights, and liberty, they never shall be invaded or disturbed, unless in just and lawful wars authorized by Congress; but laws founded in justice and humanity shall from time to time be made for preventing wrongs being done to them, and for preserving peace and friendship with them.

Article the fourth. The said territory, and the States which may be formed therein, shall forever remain a part of this Confederacy of the United States of America, subject to the Articles of Confederation, and to such alterations therein as shall be constitutionally made; and to all the Acts and ordinances of the United States in Congress assembled, conformable thereto. The inhabitants and settlers in the said territory, shall be subject to pay a part of the federal debts contracted or to be contracted, and a proportional part of the expenses of government, to be appointed on them by Congress according to the same common rule and measure by which apportionments thereof shall be made on the other States; and the taxes for paying their proportion shall be laid and levied by the authority and direction of the legislatures of the district or districts, or new States, as in the original States, within the time agreed upon by the United States in Congress assembled. The legislatures of those districts or new States shall never interfere with the primary disposal of the soil by the United States in Congress assembled, nor with any regulations Congress may find necessary for securing the title in such soil to the *bona fide* purchasers. No tax shall be imposed on lands the property of the United States; and, in no case, shall non-resident proprietors be taxed higher than residents. The navigable waters leading into the Mississippi and St. Lawrence, and the carrying places between the same, shall be common highways and forever free, as well to the inhabitants of the said territory as to the citizens of the United States, and those of any other States that may be admitted into the confederacy, without any tax, impost, or duty therefor.

Article the fifth. There shall be formed in the said territory, not less than three, nor more than five States; and the boundaries of the States, as soon as Virginia shall alter her act of cession, and consent to the same, shall become fixed and established as follows, to wit: The western State in the said territory, shall be bounded by the Mississippi, the Ohio and Wabash rivers; a direct line drawn from the Wabash and Post Vincents due north to the territorial line between the United States and Canada; and by the said territorial line to the lake of the Woods and Mississippi. The middle State shall be bounded by the said direct line, the Wabash from Post Vincents to the Ohio; by the Ohio, by a direct line drawn due north from the mouth of the Great Miami, to the said territorial line, and by the said territorial line. The eastern States shall be bounded by the last mentioned direct line, the Ohio, Pennsylvania, and the said territorial line: *Provided* however, and it is further understood and declared, that the boundaries of these three States shall be subject so far to be altered, that if Congress shall hereafter find it expedient, they shall have authority to form one or two States in that part of the said territory which lies north of an east and west line drawn through the southerly bend or extreme of Lake Michigan. And whenever any of the said States shall have sixty thousand free inhabitants therein, such State shall be admitted, by its delegates, into the Congress of the United States, on an equal footing with the original States, in all respects whatever; and shall be at liberty to form a permanent constitution and State government: provided the constitution and government so to be formed, shall be republican, and in conformity with the principles contained in these articles; and so far as it can be consistent with the general interest of the confederacy, such admission shall be allowed at an earlier period, and when there may be a less number of free inhabitants in the State than sixty thousand.

Article the sixth. There shall be neither slavery nor involuntary servitude in the said territory, otherwise than in the punishment of crimes whereof the party shall have been duly convicted: *Provided, always,* That any person escaping into the same, from whom labor or service is lawfully claimed in any one of the original States, such fugitive may be lawfully reclaimed, and conveyed to the person claiming his or her labor or service as aforesaid.

Be it ordained by the authority aforesaid, That the resolutions of the 23rd of April, 1784, relative to the subject of this ordinance, be, and the same are hereby repealed and declared null and void.

Albany Plan of Union

July 10, 1754

Great Britain's frequent wars with France often produced violent conflicts within or near the American colonies. These conflicts, combined with frequent skirmishes between settlers and native American Indians, caused Americans to fear for their safety. The Albany Plan of Union, so called because it was drawn up at a convention held in that city, was an attempt to foster American cooperation in preventing and coping with these dangers. Principally drafted by longtime colonial leader Benjamin Franklin, this is an early example of a political union set up to achieve limited goals, without turning member colonies into mere subordinate creatures of the union.

Albany Plan of Union

Plan of a Proposed Union of the Several Colonies of Masachusets-bay, New Hampshire, Coneticut, Rhode Island, New York, New Jerseys, Pensilvania, Maryland, Virginia, North Carolina, and South Carolina, For their Mutual Defence and Security, and for Extending the British Settlements in North America.

That humble Application be made for an Act of the Parliament of Great Britain, by Virtue of which, one General Government may be formed in America, including all the said Colonies, within and under which Government, each Colony may retain its present Constitution, except in the Particulars wherein a Change may be directed by the said Act, as hereafter follows.

That the said General Government be administred by a President General, To be appointed and Supported by the Crown, and a Grand Council to be Chosen by the Representatives of the People of the Several Colonies, met in their respective Assemblies.

That within   Months after the passing of such Act, The House of Representatives in the Several Assemblies, that Happen to be Sitting within that time or that shall be Specially for that purpose Convened, may and Shall Choose Members for the Grand Council in the following Proportions, that is to say.

Masachusets-Bay	7.
New Hampshire	2.
Coneticut	5.
Rhode-Island	2.
New-York	4.
New-Jerseys	3.
Pensilvania	6.
Maryland	4.
Virginia	7.
North-Carolina	4.
South-Carolina	4.
	48.

Who shall meet for the first time at the City of Philadelphia, in Pensilvania, being called by the President General as soon as conveniently may be, after his Appointment.

That there shall be a New Election of Members for the Grand Council every three years; And on the Death or Resignation of any Member his Place shall be Supplyed by a New Choice at the next Sitting of the Assembly of the Colony he represented.

That after the first three years, when the Proportion of Money arising out of each Colony to the General Treasury can be known, The Number of Members to be Chosen, for each Colony shall from time to time in all ensuing Elections be regulated by that proportion (yet so as that the Number to be Chosen by any one Province be not more than Seven nor less than Two).

That the Grand Council shall meet once in every Year, and oftner if Occasion require, at such Time and place as they shall adjourn to at the last preceeding meeting, or as they shall be called to meet at by the President General, on any Emergency, he having first obtained in Writing the Consent of seven of the Members to such call, and sent due and timely Notice to the whole.

That the Grand Council have Power to Chuse their Speaker, and shall neither be Dissolved, prorogued nor Continue Sitting longer than Six Weeks at one Time without their own Consent, or the Special Command of the Crown.

That the Members of the Grand Council shall be Allowed for their Service ten shillings Sterling per Diem, during their Sessions or Journey to and from the Place of Meeting; Twenty miles to be reckoned a days Journey.

That the Assent of the President General be requisite, to all Acts of the Grand Council, and that it be His Office, and Duty to cause them to be carried into Execution.

That the President General with the Advice of the Grand Council, hold or Direct all Indian Treaties in which the General Interest or Welfare of the Colony's may be Concerned; And make Peace or Declare War with the Indian Nations. That they make such Laws as they Judge Necessary for regulating all Indian Trade. That they make all Purchases from Indians for the Crown, of Lands not within the Bounds of Particular Colonies, or that shall not be within their Bounds when some of them are reduced to more Convenient Dimensions. That they make New Settlements on such Purchases, by Granting Lands in the Kings Name, reserving a Quit Rent to the Crown, for the use of the General Treasury. That they make Laws for regulating and Governing such new Settlements, till the Crown shall think fit to form them into Particular Governments.

That they raise and pay Soldiers, and build Forts for the Defence of any of the Colonies, and equip Vessels of Force to Guard the Coasts and Protect the Trade on the Ocean, Lakes, or Great Rivers; But they shall not Impress Men in any Colonies, without the Consent of its Legislature. That for these purposes they have Power to make Laws And lay and Levy such General Duties, Imposts, or Taxes, as to them shall appear most equal and Just, Considering the Ability and other Circumstances of the Inhabitants in the Several Colonies, and such as may be Collected with the least Inconvenience to the People, rather discouraging Luxury, than Loading Industry with unnecessary Burthens. That they may Appoint a General Treasurer and a Particular Treasurer in each Government, when Necessary, And from Time to Time may Order the Sums in the Treasuries of each Government, into the General Treasury, or draw on them for Special payments as they find most Con-venient; Yet no money to Issue, but by joint Orders of the President General and Grand Council Except where Sums have been Appropriated to particular Purposes, And the President General is previously impowered By an Act to draw for such Sums.

That the General Accounts shall be yearly Settled and Reported to the Several Assembly's.

That a Quorum of the Grand Council impower'd to Act with the President General, do consist of Twenty-five Members, among whom there shall be one, or more from a Majority of the Colonies. That the Laws made by them for the Purposes aforesaid, shall not be repugnant but as near as may be agreeable to the Laws of England, and Shall be transmitted to the King in Council for Approbation, as Soon as may be after their Passing and if not disapproved within Three years after Presentation to remain in Force.

That in case of the Death of the President General The Speaker of the Grand Council for the Time Being shall Succeed, and be Vested with the Same Powers, and Authority, to Continue until the King's Pleasure be known.

That all Military Commission Officers Whether for Land or Sea Service, to Act under this General Constitution, shall be Nominated by the President General But the Approbation of the Grand Council, is to be Obtained before they receive their Commissions, And all Civil Officers are to be Nominated, by the Grand Council, and to receive the President General's Approbation, before they Officiate; But in Case of Vacancy by Death or removal of any Officer Civil or Military under this Constitution, The Governor of the Province, in which such Vacancy happens, may Appoint till the Pleasure of the President General and Grand Council can be known. That the Particular Military as well as Civil Establishments in each Colony remain in their present State, this General Constitution Notwithstanding. And that on Sudden Emergencies any Colony may Defend itself, and lay the Accounts of Expence thence Arisen, before the President General and Grand Council, who may allow and order payment of the same As far as they Judge such Accounts Just and reasonable. . . .

Virginia and New Jersey Plans

1787

Virginia was a prime mover behind calls for a convention to alter the Articles of Confederation. As the Constitutional Convention met in Philadelphia, the Virginia delegation, led by Edmund Randolph, sought to seize the initiative by quickly dispensing with the stated plan of merely reforming the Articles. Virginia instead presented a detailed plan for a new constitution. This draft, penned in large measure by James Madison, sets forth the so-called large-state view that legislative representatives should be chosen on the basis of population, rather than granting each state an equal vote. William Paterson drafted the New Jersey Plan as the so-called small-state alternative to the Virginia Plan. It increased powers in the central government but, by failing to mention any revisions for legislative representation, in essence continued the practice of one state, one vote. The Great Compromise between these views allowed the convention to continue by providing for a lower House with representatives apportioned by population and a Senate in which each state would have an equal voice.

Virginia Plan

1. Resolved, that the Articles of Confederation ought to be so corrected and enlarged as to accomplish the objects proposed by their institution, namely *common Defence, Security of Liberty* and *general welfare.*

2. Resolved therefore, that the rights of Suffrage in the National Legislature ought to be proportioned to the Quotas of contribution, or to the number of free inhabitants, as the one or the other rule may seem best in different cases.

3. Resolved, that the National Legislature ought to consist of *two branches.*

4. Resolved, that the Members of the first Branch of the National Legislature ought to be elected by the people of the several States every _____ for the term of _____ years, to be of the age of at least _____, to receive liberal stipends, by which they may be compensated for the devotion of their time to public service—to be ineligible to any office established by a particular State, or under the authority of the United States, (except those peculiarly belonging to the functions of the first Branch) during the term of service, and for the space _____ after its expiration; to be incapable of re-election for the space of _____ after the expiration of their term of service, and to be subject to recall.

5. Resolved, that the members of the second branch of the National Legislature ought to be elected by those of the first, out of a proper number of persons nominated by the individual Legislatures, to be of the age of _____ years at least; to hold their offices for a term sufficient to ensure their independency; to receive liberal Stipends by which they may be compensated for the devotion of their time to the public service; and to be in-eligible to any office established by a particular State, or under the authority of the United States (except those peculiarly belonging to the functions of the second Branch) during the term of service, and for the space of _____ after the expiration thereof.

6. Resolved, that each Branch ought to possess the right of originating Acts, that the National Legislature ought to be empowered to enjoy, the *Legislative rights vested in Congress* by the Confederation, and moreover to Legislate in all cases to which the Separate States are incompetent; or in which the harmony of the United States may be interrupted, by the exercise of individual Legislation—to negative all Laws passed by the several States, contravening, in the opinion of the National Legislature, the articles of Union; and to call forth the force of the Union against any Member of the Union, failing to fulfil its duty under the articles thereof.

7. Resolved, that a National Executive be instituted; to be chosen by the National Legislature, for the term of _____ years—to receive punctually at stated times a fixed compensation for the services rendered, in which no increase or diminution shall be made so as to affect the Magistracy, existing at the time of such increase or diminution, and to be ineligible a second time; and that beside

a general authority to execute the National laws, it ought to enjoy the Executive rights vested in Congress by the Confederation.

8. Resolved, that the Executive and a convenient number of the National Judiciary, ought to compose a *Council of revision,* with authority to examine every act of the National Legislature before it shall operate, and every act of a particular Legislature before a negative thereon shall be final; and that the dissent of the said council shall amount to a rejection, unless the act of the National Legislature be again passed, or that of a particular Legislature be again negatived by _____ of the Members of each Branch.

9. Resolved, that a National Judiciary be established to Consist of one or more supreme tribunals, and of inferior tribunals to be chosen by the National Legislature; to hold their Offices during good behavior, and to receive punctually at stated times fixed compensation for their services, in which no increase or diminution shall be made, so as to affect the persons actually in office at the time of such increase or diminution.

That the jurisdiction of the inferior Tribunals shall be to hear and determine in the first instance, and of the supreme tribunal to hear and determine in the dernier resort; all piracies and felonies on the high Seas, captures from an enemy; cases in which foreigners or citizens of other States applying to such jurisdictions may be interested, or which respect the collection of the National revenue; impeachments of any National officers and questions which may involve the national peace and harmony.

10. Resolved, that provision ought to be made for the *admission of States* lawfully arising within the limits of the United States, whether from a voluntary junction of Government and Territory or otherwise, with the consent of a number of voices in the National Legislatures less than the whole.

11. Resolved, that a Republican Government and the territory of each State (except in the instance of a voluntary junction of Government and Territory) ought to be guaranteed by the United States to each State.

12. Resolved, that provision ought to be made for the continuance of Congress and their authorities and privileges, until a given day after the reform of the Articles of Union shall be adopted, and for the completion of all their engagements.

13. Resolved, that provision ought to be made for the amendment of the Articles of Union whensoever it shall

seem necessary (and that the assent of the National Legislature ought not to be required thereto).

14. Resolved, that the Legislative, Executive and Judiciary powers within the several States ought to be bound by oath to support the Articles of Union.

15. Resolved, that the amendments which shall be offered to the Confederation, by the Convention, ought at a proper time, or times, after the approbation of Congress, to be submitted to an assembly or assemblies of Representatives, recommended by the several Legislatures, to be expressly chosen by the people, to consider and decide thereon.

New Jersey Plan

1. Resolved, that the Articles of Confederation ought to be so revised, corrected, and enlarged as to render the federal Constitution adequate to the exigencies of Government, and the preservation of the Union.

2. Resolved, that in addition to the Powers vested in the United States in Congress by the present existing Articles of Confederation, they be authorized to pass Acts for raising a Revenue by levying a duty or duties on all goods or merchandise of foreign growth or manufacture, imported into any part of the United States,—by Stamps on Paper vellum or parchment,—and by a postage on all letters or packages passing through the general Post Office, to be applied to such federal purposes as they shall deem proper and expedient; to make rules and regulations for the collection thereof, and the same from time to time, to alter and amend in such manner as they shall think proper: to pass Acts for the regulation of trade and commerce, as well with foreign Nations, as with each other; provided that all punishments, fines, forfeitures and penalties to be incurred for contravening such acts, rules, and regulations shall be adjudged by the common Law Judiciarys of the State in which any offence contrary to the true intent and meaning of such acts and regulations shall have been committed or perpetrated; with liberty of commencing in the first instance all suits and prosecutions for that purpose in the superior Common Law Judiciary of such State, subject nevertheless, for the correction of all errors, both in law and fact, in rendering judgment, to an appeal to the Judiciary of the United States.

3. Resolved, that whenever requisitions shall be neces-

sary, instead of the rule for making requisition mentioned in the Articles of Confederation, the United States in Congress be authorized to make such requisitions in proportion to the whole number of white and other free citizens and Inhabitants of every age, sex and condition, including those bound to servitude for a term of years, and three fifths of all other persons not comprehended in the foregoing description—(except Indians not paying Taxes); that if such requisitions be not complied with, in the time to be specified therein, to direct the collection thereof in the non-complying States and for that purpose to devise and pass Acts directing and authorizing the same; provided that none of the powers hereby vested in the United States in congress shall be exercised without the consent of at least _____ States, and in that proportion, if the number of confederated States should be hereafter increased or diminished.

4. Resolved, that the United States in Congress be authorized to elect a federal Executive to consist of persons, to continue in office for the Term of years; to receive punctually at stated times a fixed compensation for their services in which no increase or diminution shall be made so as to affect the persons composing the Executive at the time of such increase or diminution; to be paid out of the Federal Treasury; to be incapable of holding any other office or appointment during their time of service, and for _____ years thereafter; to be ineligible a second time, and removable by Congress on application by a majority of the Executives of the several States; that the Executive, besides their general authority to execute the federal Acts, ought to appoint all federal officers not other wise provided for, and to direct all military operations; provided that none of the persons composing the federal Executive shall on any occasion take command of any troops so as personally to conduct any enterprise as General or in any other capacity.

5. Resolved, that a federal Judiciary be established, to consist of a supreme Tribunal, the Judges of which to be appointed by the Executive, and to hold their Offices during good behavior, to receive punctually at stated times a fixed compensation for their services, in which no increase or diminution shall be made so as to affect the persons actually in office at the time of such increase or diminution;— That the Judiciary so established shall have authority to hear and determine in the first instance on all impeachments of federal officers, and by way of appeal in the dernier resort in all cases touching the rights of Ambassadors, in all cases of captures from an enemy, in all cases of piracies and felonies on the high Seas, in all cases in which foreigners may be interested in the construction of any treaty or treaties, or which may arise on any of the Acts for regulation of trade, or the collection of the federal Revenue: that none of the Judiciary shall during the time they remain in Office be capable of receiving or holding any other Office or appointment during their time of service, or for _____ thereafter.

6. Resolved, that all Acts of the United States in Congress made by virtue and in pursuance of the powers hereby vested in them, and all Treaties made and ratified under the authority of the United States, shall be the supreme law of the respective States, as far as those Acts or Treaties shall relate to the said States or their Citizens, and that the Judiciary of the several States shall be bound thereby in their decisions, anything in the respective laws of the Individual States to the contrary notwithstanding; and that if any State, or any body of men in any State, shall oppose or prevent the carrying into execution such acts or treaties, the federal Executive shall be authorized to call forth the power of the Confederated States, or so much thereof as may be necessary to enforce and compel an obedience to such Acts, or an Observance of such Treaties.

7. Resolved, that provision be made for the admission of new States into the Union.

8. Resolved, that the Rule for naturalization ought to be the same in every State.

9. Resolved, that a Citizen of one State committing an offence in another State of the Union, shall be deemed guilty of the same offence, as if it had been committed by a Citizen of the State in which the Offence was committed.

The Constitution of the United States of America

1787

The U.S. Constitution is the world's oldest written national constitution still in effect. It sets forth the structure of the new government, assigning powers and establishing procedures for election and appointment among the legislative, executive, and judicial branches—in descending order of power and importance.

Constitution of the United States of America

WE THE PEOPLE of the United States, in Order to form a more perfect Union, establish Justice, insure domestic Tranquility, provide for the common defence, promote the general Welfare, and secure the Blessings of Liberty to ourselves and our Posterity, do ordain and establish this CONSTITUTION for the United States of America.

Article I

SECTION 1. All legislative Powers herein granted shall be vested in a Congress of the United States, which shall consist of a Senate and House of Representatives.

SECTION 2. The House of Representatives shall be composed of Members chosen every second Year by the People of the several States, and the Electors in each State shall have the Qualifications requisite for Electors of the most numerous Branch of the State Legislature.

No Person shall be a Representative who shall not have attained to the Age of twenty five Years, and been seven Years a Citizen of the United States, and who shall not, when elected, be an Inhabitant of that State in which he shall be chosen.

Representatives and direct Taxes shall be apportioned among the several States which may be included within this Union, according to their respective Numbers, which shall be determined by adding to the whole Number of free Persons, including those bound to Service for a Term of Years, and excluding Indians not taxed, three fifths of all other Persons. The actual Enumeration shall be made within three Years after the first Meeting of the Congress of the United States, and within every subsequent Term of ten Years, in such Manner as they shall by Law direct. The Number of Representatives shall not exceed one for every thirty Thousand, but each State shall have at Least one Representative; and until such enumeration shall be made, the State of New Hampshire shall be entitled to chuse three, Massachusetts eight, Rhode-Island and Providence Plantations one, Connecticut five, New-York six, New Jersey four, Pennsylvania eight, Delaware one, Maryland six, Virginia ten, North Carolina five, South Carolina five, and Georgia three.

When vacancies happen in the Representation from any State, the Executive Authority thereof shall issue Writs of Election to fill such Vacancies.

The House of Representatives shall chuse their Speaker and other Officers; and shall have the sole Power of Impeachment.

SECTION 3. The Senate of the United States shall be composed of two Senators from each State, chosen by the Legislature thereof, for six Years; and each Senator shall have one Vote.

Immediately after they shall be assembled in Consequence of the first Election, they shall be divided as equally as may be into three Classes. The Seats of the Senators of the first Class shall be vacated at the Expiration of the Second Year, of the second Class at the Expiration of the fourth Year, and of the third Class at the Expiration of the sixth Year; so that one-third may be chosen every second Year; and if Vacancies happen by Resignation, or otherwise, during the Recess of the Legislature of any State, the Executive thereof may make temporary Appointments until the next Meeting of the Legislature, which shall then fill such Vacancies.

No Person shall be a Senator who shall not have attained to the Age of thirty Years, and been nine Years a Citizen of the United States, and who shall not, when elected, be an Inhabitant of that State for which he shall be chosen.

The Vice President of the United States shall be President of the Senate, but shall have no Vote, unless they be equally divided.

The Senate shall chuse their other Officers, and also a President pro tempore, in the absence of the Vice President, or when he shall exercise the Office of President of the United States.

The Senate shall have the sole Power to try all Impeachments. When sitting for that Purpose, they shall be on Oath or Affirmation. When the President of the United States is tried, the Chief Justice shall preside: And no Person shall be convicted without the Concurrence of two-thirds of the Members present.

Judgment in Cases of Impeachment shall not extend further than to removal from Office, and disqualification to hold and enjoy any Office of honor, Trust, or Profit under the United States: but the Party convicted shall nevertheless be liable and subject to Indictment, Trial, Judgment, and Punishment, according to Law.

SECTION 4. The Time, Places and Manner of holding Elections for Senators and Representatives, shall be prescribed in each State by the Legislature thereof; but the Congress may at any time by Law make or alter such Regulations, except as to the Places of chusing Senators.

The Congress shall assemble at least once in every Year, and such Meeting shall be on the first Monday in December, unless they shall by Law appoint a different Day.

SECTION 5. Each House shall be the Judge of the Elections, Returns, and Qualifications of its own Members, and a Majority of each shall constitute a Quorum to do Business; but a smaller Number may adjourn from day to day, and may be authorized to compel the Attendance of absent Members, in such Manner, and under such Penalties as each House may provide.

Each House may determine the Rules of its Proceedings, punish its Members for disorderly Behavior, and, with the Concurrence of two thirds, expel a Member.

Each House shall keep a Journal of its Proceedings, and from time to time publish the same, excepting such Parts as may in their Judgment require Secrecy; and the Yeas and Nays of the Members of either House on any question shall, at the Desire of one fifth of those Present be entered on the Journal.

Neither House, during the Session of Congress, shall, without the Consent of the other, adjourn for more than three days, nor to any other Place than that in which the two Houses shall be sitting.

SECTION 6. The Senators and Representatives shall receive a Compensation for their Services, to be ascertained by Law, and paid out of the Treasury of the United States. They shall in all Cases, except Treason, Felony and Breach of the Peace, be privileged from Arrest during their Attendance at the Session of their respective Houses, and in going to and returning from the same; and for any Speech or Debate in either House, they shall not be questioned in any other Place.

No Senator or Representative shall, during the Time for which he was elected, be appointed to any civil Office under the Authority of the United States, which shall have been created, or the Emoluments whereof shall have been encreased during such time; and no Person holding any Office under the United States, shall be a Member of either House during his Continuance in Office.

SECTION 7. All Bills for raising Revenue shall originate in the House of Representatives; but the Senate may propose or concur with Amendments as on other Bills.

Every Bill which shall have passed the House of Representatives and the Senate, shall, before it become a Law, be presented to the President of the United States; if he approve he shall sign it, but if not he shall return it, with his Objections to that House in which it shall have originated, who shall enter the Objections at large on their Journal, and proceed to reconsider it. If after such Reconsideration two thirds of that House shall agree to pass the Bill, it shall be sent, together with the Objections, to the other House, by which it shall likewise be reconsidered, and if approved by two thirds of that House, it shall become a Law. But in all such Cases the Votes of both Houses shall be determined by yeas and Nays, and the Names of the Persons voting for and against the Bill shall be entered on the Journal of each House respectively. If any Bill shall not be returned by the President within ten Days (Sundays excepted) after it shall have been presented to him, the Same shall be a Law, in like Manner as if he had signed it, unless the Congress by their Adjournment prevent its Return, in which Case it shall not be a Law.

Every Order, Resolution, or Vote to which the Concurrence of the Senate and House of Representatives may be necessary (except on a question of Adjournment) shall be presented to the President of the United States; and before the Same shall take Effect, shall be approved by him, or being disapproved by him, shall be repassed by two thirds of the Senate and House of Representatives, according to the Rules and Limitations prescribed in the Case of a Bill.

Section 8. The Congress shall have Power To lay and collect Taxes, Duties, Imposts and Excises, to pay the Debts and provide for the common Defense and general Welfare of the United States; but all Duties, Imposts and Excises shall be uniform throughout the United States;

To borrow money on the credit of the United States;

To regulate Commerce with foreign Nations, and among the several States, and with the Indian Tribes;

To establish an uniform Rule of Naturalization, and uniform Laws on the subject of Bankruptcies throughout the United States;

To coin Money, regulate the Value thereof, and of foreign Coin, and fix the Standard of Weights and Measures;

To provide for the Punishment of counterfeiting the Securities and current Coin of the United States;

To establish Post Offices and post Roads;

To promote the Progress of Science and useful Arts, by securing for limited Times to Authors and Inventors the exclusive Right to their respective Writings and Discoveries;

To constitute Tribunals inferior to the supreme Court;

To define and punish Piracies and Felonies committed on the high Seas, and Offenses against the Law of Nations;

To declare War, grant Letters of Marque and Reprisal and make Rules concerning Captures on Land and Water;

To raise and support Armies, but no Appropriation of Money to that Use shall be for a longer Term than two Years;

To provide and maintain a Navy;

To make Rules for the Government and Regulation of the land and naval Forces;

To provide for calling forth the Militia to execute the Laws of the Union, suppress Insurrections and repel Invasions;

To provide for organizing, arming, and disciplining the Militia, and for governing such Part of them as may be employed in the Service of the United States, reserving to the States respectively, the Appointment of the Officers, and the Authority of training the Militia according to the discipline prescribed by Congress;

To exercise exclusive Legislation in all Cases whatsoever, over such District (not exceeding ten Miles square) as may, by Cession of particular States, and the acceptance of Congress, become the Seat of the Government of the United States, and to exercise like Authority over all Places purchased by the Consent of the Legislature of the State in which the Same shall be, for the Erection of Forts, Magazines, Arsenals, dock-Yards, and other needful Buildings;—And

To make all Laws which shall be necessary and proper for carrying into Execution the foregoing Powers, and all other Powers vested by this Constitution in the Government of the United States, or in any Department or Officer thereof.

Section 9. The Migration or Importation of Such Persons as any of the States now existing shall think proper to admit, shall not be prohibited by the Congress prior to the Year one thousand eight hundred and eight, but a tax or duty may be imposed on such Importation, not exceeding ten dollars for each Person.

The privilege of the Writ of Habeas Corpus shall not be suspended, unless when in Cases of Rebellion or Invasion the public Safety may require it.

No Bill of Attainder or ex post facto Law shall be passed.

No capitation, or other direct, Tax shall be laid, unless in Proportion to the Census or Enumeration herein before directed to be taken.

No Tax or Duty shall be laid on Articles exported from any State.

No preference shall be given by any Regulation of Commerce or Revenue to the Ports of one State over those of another: nor shall Vessels bound to, or from, one State be obliged to enter, clear, or pay Duties in another.

No money shall be drawn from the Treasury, but in Consequence of Appropriations made by Law; and a regular Statement and Account of the Receipts and Expenditures of all public Money shall be published from time to time.

No Title of Nobility shall be granted by the United States: And no Person holding any Office of Profit or Trust under them, shall, without the Consent of the Congress, accept of any present, Emolument, Office, or Title, of any kind whatever, from any King, Prince, or foreign State.

Section 10. No State shall enter into any Treaty, Alliance, or Confederation; grant Letters of Marque and Reprisal; coin Money; emit Bills of Credit; make any

Thing but gold and silver Coin a Tender in Payment of Debts; pass any Bill of Attainder, ex post facto Law, or Law impairing the Obligation of Contracts, or grant any Title of Nobility.

No State shall, without the Consent of the Congress, lay any Imposts or Duties on Imports or Exports, except what may be absolutely necessary for executing its inspection Laws: and the net Produce of all Duties and Imposts, laid by any State on Imports or Exports, shall be for the Use of the Treasury of the United States; and all such Laws shall be subject to the Revision and Control of the Congress.

No State shall, without the Consent of Congress, lay any duty of Tonnage, keep Troops, or Ships of War in time of Peace, enter into any Agreement or Compact with another State, or with a foreign Power, or engage in War, unless actually invaded, or in such imminent Danger as will not admit of delay.

Article II

SECTION 1. The executive Power shall be vested in a President of the United States of America. He shall hold his Office during the Term of four years, and, together with the Vice-President, chosen for the same Term, be elected, as follows:

Each State shall appoint, in such Manner as the Legislature thereof may direct, a Number of Electors, equal to the whole Number of Senators and Representatives to which the State may be entitled in the Congress: but no Senator or Representative, or Person holding an Office of Trust or Profit under the United States, shall be appointed an Elector.

The Electors shall meet in their respective States, and vote by Ballot for two persons, of whom one at least shall not be an Inhabitant of the same State with themselves. And they shall make a List of all the Persons voted for, and of the Number of Votes for each; which List they shall sign and certify, and transmit sealed to the Seat of the Government of the United States, directed to the President of the Senate. The President of the Senate shall, in the Presence of the Senate and House of Representatives, open all the Certificates, and the Votes shall then be counted. The Person having the greatest Number of Votes shall be the President, if such Number be a Majority of the whole Number of Electors appointed; and if there be more than one who

have such Majority, and have an equal Number of Votes, then the House of Representatives shall immediately chuse by Ballot one of them for President; and if no Person have a Majority, then from the five highest on the List the said House shall in like Manner chuse the President. But in chusing the President, the Votes shall be taken by States, the Representation from each State having one Vote; A quorum for this Purpose shall consist of a Member or Members from two-thirds of the States, and a Majority of all the States shall be necessary to a Choice. In every Case, after the Choice of the President, the Person having the greatest Number of Votes of the Electors shall be the Vice-President. But if there should remain two or more who have equal Votes, the Senate shall chuse from them by Ballot the Vice-President.

The Congress may determine the Time of chusing the Electors, and the Day on which they shall give their Votes; which Day shall be the same throughout the United States.

No person except a natural born Citizen, or a Citizen of the United States, at the time of the Adoption of this Constitution, shall be eligible to the Office of President; neither shall any Person be eligible to that Office who shall not have attained to the Age of thirty-five Years, and been fourteen Years a Resident within the United States.

In case of the Removal of the President from Office, or of his Death, resignation, or Inability to discharge the Powers and Duties of the said Office, the same shall devolve on the Vice President, and the Congress may by Law provide for the Case of Removal, Death, Resignation or Inability, both of the President and Vice President, declaring what Officer shall then act as President, and such Officer shall act accordingly, until the Disability be removed, or a President shall be elected.

The President shall, at stated Times, receive for his Services, a Compensation, which shall neither be encreased nor diminished during the Period for which he shall have been elected, and he shall not receive within that Period any other Emolument from the United States, or any of them.

Before he enter on the Execution of his Office, he shall take the following Oath or Affirmation:—"I do solemnly swear (or affirm) that I will faithfully execute the Office of President of the United States, and will to the best of my Ability, preserve, protect and defend the Constitution of the United States."

SECTION 2. The President shall be Commander in Chief of the Army and Navy of the United States, and of the Militia of the several States, when called into the actual Service of the United States; he may require the Opinion, in writing, of the principal Officer in each of the executive Departments, upon any subject relating to the Duties of their respective Offices, and he shall have Power to grant Reprieves and Pardons for Offenses against the United States, except in Cases of Impeachment.

He shall have Power, by and with the Advice and Consent of the Senate, to make Treaties, provided two-thirds of the Senators present concur; and he shall nominate, and by and with the Advice and Consent of the Senate, shall appoint Ambassadors, other public Ministers and Consuls, Judges of the supreme Court, and all other Officers of the United States, whose Appointments are not herein otherwise provided for, and which shall be established by law; but the Congress may by Law vest the Appointment of such inferior Officers, as they think proper, in the President alone, in the Courts of Law, or in the Heads of Departments.

The President shall have Power to fill up all Vacancies that may happen during the Recess of the Senate, by granting Commissions which shall expire at the End of their next Session.

SECTION 3. He shall from time to time give to the Congress Information of the State of the Union, and recommend to their Consideration such Measures as he shall judge necessary and expedient; he may, on extraordinary Occasions, convene both Houses, or either of them, and in Case of Disagreement between them, with Respect to the Time of Adjournment, he may adjourn them to such Time as he shall think proper; he shall receive Ambassadors and other public Ministers; he shall take Care that the Laws be faithfully executed, and shall Commission all the Officers of the United States.

SECTION 4. The President, Vice President and all civil Officers of the United States, shall be removed from Office on Impeachment for, and Conviction of, Treason, Bribery, or other high Crimes and Misdemeanors.

Article III

SECTION 1. The judicial Power of the United States, shall be vested in one supreme Court, and in such inferior Courts as the Congress may from time to time ordain and establish. The Judges, both of the supreme and inferior Courts, shall hold their offices during good Behaviour, and shall, at stated Times, receive for their Services a Compensation which shall not be diminished during their Continuance in Office.

SECTION 2. The judicial Power shall extend to all Cases, in Law and Equity, arising under this Constitution, the Laws of the United States, and Treaties made, or which shall be made, under their Authority;—to all Cases affecting Ambassadors, other public Ministers and Consuls;—to all Cases of admiralty and maritime Jurisdiction;—to Controversies to which the United States shall be a Party;—to Controversies between two or more States;—between a State and Citizens of another State;—between Citizens of different States;—between Citizens of the same State claiming Lands under Grants of different States, and between a State, or the Citizens thereof, and foreign States, Citizens or Subjects.

In all Cases affecting Ambassadors, other public Ministers and Consuls, and those in which a State shall be Party, the supreme Court shall have original Jurisdiction. In all the other Cases before mentioned, the supreme Court shall have appellate Jurisdiction, both as to Law and Fact, with such Exceptions, and under such Regulations as the Congress shall make.

The trial of all Crimes, except in Cases of Impeachment, shall be by Jury; and such Trial shall be held in the State where the said Crimes shall have been committed; but when not committed within any State, the Trial shall be at such Place or Places as the Congress may by Law have directed.

SECTION 3. Treason against the United States, shall consist only in levying War against them, or in adhering to their Enemies, giving them Aid and Comfort. No Person shall be convicted of Treason unless on the Testimony of two Witnesses to the same overt Act, or on Confession in open Court.

The Congress shall have power to declare the Punishment of Treason, but no Attainder of Treason shall work Corruption of Blood, or Forfeiture except during the Life of the Person attainted.

Article IV

SECTION 1. Full Faith and Credit shall be given in each State to the public Acts, Records, and judicial Proceedings of every other State. And the Congress may by general Laws prescribe the Manner in which such Acts, Records and Proceedings shall be proved, and the Effect thereof.

SECTION 2. The Citizens of each State shall be entitled to all Privileges and Immunities of Citizens in the several States.

A Person charged in any State with Treason, Felony, or other Crime, who shall flee from Justice, and be found in another State, shall on demand of the executive Authority of the State from which he fled, be delivered up, to be removed to the State having Jurisdiction of the Crime.

No Person held to Service or Labour in one State, under the Laws thereof, escaping into another, shall, in Consequence of any Law or Regulation therein, be discharged from such Service or Labour, but shall be delivered up on Claim of the Party to whom such Service or Labour may be due.

SECTION 3. New States may be admitted by the Congress into this Union; but no new State shall be formed or erected within the Jurisdiction of any other State; nor any State be formed by the Junction of two or more States, or parts of States, without the Consent of the Legislatures of the States concerned as well as of the Congress.

The Congress shall have Power to dispose of and make all needful Rules and Regulations respecting the Territory of other Property belonging to the United States; and nothing in this Constitution shall be so construed as to Prejudice any Claims of the United States, or of any particular State.

SECTION 4. The United States shall guarantee to every State in this Union a Republican Form of Government, and shall protect each of them against Invasion; and on Application of the Legislature, or of the Executive (when the Legislature cannot be convened) against domestic Violence.

Article V

The Congress, whenever two-thirds of both Houses shall deem it necessary, shall propose Amendments to this Constitution, or, on the Application of the Legislatures of two-thirds of the several States, shall call a Convention for proposing Amendments, which, in either Case, shall be valid to all Intents and Purposes, as part of this Constitution, when ratified by the Legislatures of three-fourths of the several States, or by Conventions in three-fourths thereof, as the one or the other Mode of Ratification may be proposed by the Congress; Provided that no Amendment which may be made prior to the Year One thousand eight hundred and eight shall in any Manner affect the first and fourth Clauses in the Ninth Section of the first Article, and that no State without its Consent, shall be deprived of its equal Suffrage in the Senate.

Article VI

All Debts contracted and Engagements entered into, before the Adoption of this Constitution shall be as valid against the United States under this Constitution, as under the Confederation.

This Constitution, and the Laws of the United States which shall be made in Pursuance thereof, and all Treaties made, or which shall be made, under Authority of the United States, shall be the supreme Law of the Land, and the Judges in every State shall be bound thereby, any Thing in the Constitution or Laws of any State to the Contrary notwithstanding.

The Senators and Representatives before mentioned, and the Members of the several State Legislatures, and all executive and judicial Officers, both of the United States and of the several States, shall be bound by Oath or Affirmation, to support this constitution; but no religious Test shall ever be required as a Qualification to any Office or public Trust under the United States.

Article VII

The Ratification of the Conventions of nine States shall be sufficient for the Establishment of this Constitution between the States so ratifying the Same. Done in Convention by the Unanimous Consent of the States present the Seventeenth Day of September in the Year of our Lord one thousand seven hundred and Eighty seven and of the Independence of the United States of America the Twelfth. In witness whereof We have here unto subscribed our Names,

Go WASHINGTON
Presidt. and deputy from Virginia.

New Hampshire
John Langdon,
Nicholas Gilman.

Massachusetts
Nathaniel Gorham,
Rufus King.

Connecticut
Wm. Saml. Johnson,
Roger Sherman.

New York
Alexander Hamilton.

New Jersey
Wil: Livingston,
David Brearley,
Wm. Paterson,
Jona. Dayton.

Pennsylvania
B. Franklin,
Robt. Morris,
Tho: Fitzsimons,
James Wilson,
Thomas Mifflin,
Geo: Clymer,
Jared Ingersoll,
Gouv: Morris.

Delaware
Geo: Read,
John Dickinson,
Jaco: Broom,
Gunning Bedford, Jun'r,
Richard Bassett.

Maryland
James M'Henry,
Danl Carroll,
Dan: of St. Thos. Jenifer.

Virginia
John Blair,
James Madison, Jr.

North Carolina
Wm. Blount,
Hu. Williamson,
Rich'd Dobbs Spaight.

South Carolina
J. Rutledge,
Charles Pinckney,
Charles Cotesworth
    Pinckney,
Pierce Butler.

Georgia
William Few,
William Jackson, Secretary.

    Attest:
Abr. Baldwin.

The Federalist, Papers 1, 9, 10, 39, 47–51, 78

ALEXANDER HAMILTON, JAMES MADISON, AND JOHN JAY

1787

The new Constitution was not easily ratified. Rhode Island refused even to send delegates to the Constitutional Convention. A number of powerful political figures, including Virginia's firebrand Patrick Henry and New York governor George Clinton, lined up early to oppose it. Even a number of prominent convention delegates expressed opposition to the new governing document. Thus, after the Constitution was submitted to state conventions for ratification, there was significant uncertainty whether it would gain acceptance from the necessary three-quarters of the states.

Alexander Hamilton, former aide to Gen. George Washington, member of the New York Assembly, and future secretary of the treasury, was particularly concerned about the Constitution's prospects in his state, which had Anti-Federalist George Clinton for its governor. Hamilton sought to answer the charges being levelled against the Constitution in numerous pamphlets—principally that it would set up a centralized government that would invade the liberties of the states and of the people. Hamilton recruited James Madison, leading architect of the Constitution, and the jurist and future Supreme Court justice John Jay to write a series of newspaper articles explaining and justifying the new form of government. Whether the ensuing articles, published under the pseudonym "Publius," changed any votes is largely unknown, but the essays have become recognized as important statements of the principles of the Constitution and of republican government in general.

No. 1

ALEXANDER HAMILTON

Introduction

After full experience of the insufficiency of the existing federal government, you are invited to deliberate upon a New Constitution for the United States of America. The subject speaks its own importance; comprehending in its consequences, nothing less than the existence of the UNION, the safety and welfare of the parts of which it is composed, the fate of an empire, in many respects, the most interesting in the world. It has been frequently remarked, that it seems to have been reserved to the people of this country to decide, by their conduct and example, the important question, whether societies of men are really capable or not, of establishing good government from reflection and choice, or whether they are forever destined to depend, for their political constitutions, on accident and force. If there be any truth in the remark, the crisis at which we are arrived may, with propriety, be regarded as the period when that decision is to be made; and a wrong election of the part we shall act, may, in this view, deserve to be considered as the general misfortune of mankind.

This idea, by adding the inducements of philanthropy to those of patriotism, will heighten the solicitude which all considerate and good men must feel for the event. Happy will it be if our choice should be directed by a judicious estimate of our true interests, uninfluenced by considerations foreign to the public good. But this is more ardently to be wished for, than seriously to be expected. The plan offered to our deliberations, affects too many particular interests, innovates upon too many local institutions, not to involve in its discussion a variety of objects extraneous to its merits, and of views, passions and prejudices little favourable to the discovery of truth.

Among the most formidable of the obstacles which the new constitution will have to encounter, may readily be distinguished the obvious interest of a certain class of men in every state to resist all changes which may hazard a diminution of the power, emolument and consequence of the offices they hold under the state establishments . . . and the perverted ambition of another class of men, who will either hope to aggrandize themselves by the confusions of their country, or will flatter themselves with fairer prospects of elevation from the subdivision of the empire into several partial confederacies, than from its union under one government.

It is not, however, my design to dwell upon observations of this nature. I am aware that it would be disingenuous to resolve indiscriminately the opposition of any set of men into interested or ambitious views, merely because their situations might subject them to suspicion. Candour will oblige us to admit, that even such men may be actuated by upright intentions; and it cannot be doubted, that much of the opposition, which has already shown itself, or that may hereafter make its appearance, will spring from sources blameless at least, if not respectable . . . the honest errors of minds led astray by preconceived jealousies and fears. So numerous indeed and so powerful are the causes which serve to give a false bias to the judgement, that we, upon many occasions, see wise and good men on the wrong as well as on the right side of questions, of the first magnitude to society. This circumstance, if duly attended to, would always furnish a lesson of moderation to those, who are engaged in any controversy, however well persuaded of being in the right. And a further reason for caution, in this respect, might be drawn from the reflection, that we are not always sure, that those who advocate the truth are actuated by purer principles than their antagonists. Ambition, avarice, personal animosity, party opposition, and many other motives, not more laudable than these, are apt to operate as well upon those who support, as upon those who oppose, the right side of a question. Were there not even these inducements to moderation, nothing could be more ill judged than that intolerant spirit, which has, at all times, characterized political parties. For, in politics as in religion, it is equally absurd to aim at making proselytes by fire and sword. Heresies in either can rarely be cured by persecution.

And yet, just as these sentiments must appear to candid men, we have already sufficient indications, that it will happen in this, as in all former cases of great national discussion. A torrent of angry and malignant passions will be let loose. To judge from the conduct of the opposite parties, we shall be led to conclude, that they will mutually hope to evince the justness of their opinions, and to increase the number of their converts, by the loudness of their declamations, and by the bitterness of their invectives. An enlightened zeal for the energy and efficiency of government, will be stigmatized as the offspring of a temper fond of power, and hostile to the principles of liberty. An over scrupulous jealousy of danger to the rights of the people, which is more commonly the fault of the head than of the heart, will be represented as mere pretence and artifice . . . the stale bait for popularity at the expense of public good. It will be forgotten, on the one hand, that jealousy is the usual concomitant of violent love, and that the noble enthusiasm of liberty is too apt to be infected with a spirit of narrow and illiberal distrust. On the other hand, it will be equally forgotten, that the vigour of government is essential to the security of liberty; that, in the contemplation of a sound and well informed judgment, their interests can never be separated; and that a dangerous ambition more often lurks behind the specious mask of zeal for the rights of the people, than under the forbidding appearances of zeal for the firmness and efficiency of government. History will teach us, that the former has been found a much more certain road to the introduction of despotism, than the latter, and that of those men who have overturned the liberties of republics, the greatest number have begun their career, by paying an obsequious court to the people . . . commencing demagogues, and ending tyrants.

In the course of the preceding observations it has been my aim, fellow citizens, to put you upon your guard against all attempts, from whatever quarter, to influence your decision in a matter of the utmost moment to your welfare, by any impressions, other than those which may result from the evidence of truth. You will, no doubt, at the same time, have collected from the general scope of them, that they proceed from a source not unfriendly to the new constitution. Yes, my countrymen, I own to you, that, after having given it an attentive consideration, I am clearly of opinion, it is your interest to adopt it. I am convinced, that this is the safest course for your liberty, your dignity, and your happiness. I affect not reserves, which I do not feel. I will not amuse you with an appearance of deliberation, when I have decided. I frankly acknowledge to you my convictions, and I will freely lay before you the reasons on which they are founded. The consciousness of good intentions disdains ambiguity. I shall not however multiply professions on this head. My motives must remain in the depository of my own breast: my arguments will be open to all, and may be judged of by all. They shall at least be offered in a spirit, which will not disgrace the cause of truth.

I propose, in a series of papers, to discuss the following interesting particulars . . . *The utility of the UNION to your political prosperity . . . The insufficiency of the present confederation to preserve that Union . . . The necessity of a government at least equally energetic with the one proposed, to the attainment of this object . . . The conformity of the proposed constitution to the true principles of republican government . . . Its analogy to your own state constitution . . . and lastly, The additional security, which its adoption will afford to the preservation of that species of government, to liberty and to property.*

In the progress of this discussion, I shall endeavour to give a satisfactory answer to all the objections which shall have made their appearance, that may seem to have any claim to attention.

It may perhaps be thought superfluous to offer arguments to prove the utility of the UNION, a point, no doubt, deeply engraved on the hearts of the great body of the people in every state, and one which, it may be imagined, has no adversaries. But the fact is, that we already hear it whispered in the private circles of those who oppose the new constitution, that the Thirteen States are of too great extent for any general system, and that we must of necessity resort to separate confederacies of distinct portions of the whole.* This doctrine will, in all probability, be gradually propagated, till it has votaries enough to countenance its open avowal. For nothing can be more evident, to those who are able to take an enlarged view of the subject, than the alternative of an adoption of the constitution, or a dismemberment of the Union. It may, therefore, be essential to examine particularly the advantages of that Union, the certain evils, and the probable dangers, to which every state will be exposed from its dissolution. This shall accordingly be done.

PUBLIUS

No. 9

ALEXANDER HAMILTON

The Utility of the Union as a Safeguard against Domestic Faction and Insurrection

A firm union will be of the utmost moment to the peace and liberty of the states, as a barrier against domestic faction and insurrection.

It is impossible to read the history of the petty republics of Greece and Italy, without feeling sensations of hor-

*The same idea, tracing the arguments to their consequences, is held out in several of the late publications against the New Constitution.

ror and disgust at the distractions with which they were continually agitated, and at the rapid succession of revolutions, by which they were kept perpetually vibrating between the extremes of tyranny and anarchy. If they exhibit occasional calms, these only serve as short-lived contrasts to the furious storms that are to succeed. If now and then intervals of felicity open themselves to view, we behold them with a mixture of regret arising from the reflection, that the pleasing scenes before us are soon to be overwhelmed by the tempestuous waves of sedition and party rage. If momentary rays of glory break forth from the gloom, while they dazzle us with a transient and fleeting brilliancy, they at the same time admonish us to lament, that the vices of government should pervert the direction, and tarnish the lustre, of those bright talents and exalted endowments, for which the favoured soils that produced them have been so justly celebrated.

From the disorders that disfigure the annals of those republics, the advocates of despotism have drawn arguments, not only against the forms of republican government, but against the very principles of civil liberty. They have decried all free government, as inconsistent with the order of society, and have indulged themselves in malicious exultation over its friends and partisans. Happily for mankind, stupendous fabrics reared on the basis of liberty, which have flourished for ages, have in a few glorious instances refuted their gloomy sophisms. And, I trust, America will be the broad and solid foundation of other edifices not less magnificent, which will be equally permanent monuments of their error.

But it is not to be denied, that the portraits they have sketched of republican government, were too just copies of the originals from which they were taken. If it had been found impracticable to have devised models of a more perfect structure, the enlightened friends of liberty would have been obliged to abandon the cause of that species of government as indefensible. The science of politics, however, like most other sciences, has received great improvement. The efficacy of various principles is now well understood, which were either not known at all, or imperfectly known to the ancients. The regular distribution of power into distinct departments; the introduction of legislative balances and checks; the institution of courts composed of judges, holding their offices during good behaviour; the representation of the people in the legislature, by deputies of their own election; these are either wholly new discoveries, or have made their principal progress towards perfection in modern times. They are means, and powerful means, by which the excellencies of republican government may be retained, and its imperfections lessened or avoided. To this catalogue of circumstances, that tend to the amelioration of popular systems of civil government, I shall venture, however novel it may appear to some, to add one more, on a principle which has been made the foundation of an objection to the new constitution; I mean the ENLARGEMENT of the ORBIT within which such systems are to revolve, either in respect to the dimensions of a single state, or to the consolidation of several smaller states into one great confederacy. The latter is that which immediately concerns the object under consideration. It will, however, be of use to examine the principle in its application to a single state, which shall be attended to in another place.

The utility of a confederacy, as well to suppress faction, and to guard the internal tranquillity of states, as to increase their external force and security, is in reality not a new idea. It has been practised upon in different countries and ages, and has received the sanction of the most approved writers on the subjects of politics. The opponents of the PLAN proposed have with great assiduity cited and circulated the observations of Montesquieu on the necessity of a contracted territory for a republican government. But they seem not to have been apprised of the sentiments of that great man expressed in another part of his work, nor to have adverted to the consequences of the principle to which they subscribe with such ready acquiescence.

When Montesquieu recommends a small extent for republics, the standards he had in view were of dimensions, far short of the limits of almost every one of these states. Neither Virginia, Massachusetts, Pennsylvania, New York, North Carolina, nor Georgia, can by any means be compared with the models from which he reasoned, and to which the terms of his description apply. If we therefore receive his ideas on this point, as the criterion of truth, we shall be driven to the alternative, either of taking refuge at once in the arms of monarchy, or of splitting ourselves into an infinity of little, jealous, clashing, tumultuous commonwealths, the wretched nurseries of unceasing discord, and the miserable objects of universal pity or contempt. Some of the writers, who have come forward on the other side of the question, seem to have been aware of the dilemma; and have even been bold enough to hint at the division of the larger states, as a desirable thing. Such an

infatuated policy, such a desperate expedient, might, by the multiplication of petty offices, answer the views of men, who possess not qualifications to extend their influence beyond the narrow circles of personal intrigue; but it could never promote the greatness or happiness of the people of America.

Referring the examination of the principle itself to another place, as has been already mentioned, it will be sufficient to remark here, that in the sense of the author who has been most emphatically quoted upon the occasion, it would only dictate a reduction of the SIZE of the more considerable MEMBERS of the union; but would not militate against their being all comprehended in one confederate government. And this is the true question, in the discussion of which we are at present interested.

So far are the suggestions of Montesquieu from standing in opposition to a general union of the states, that he explicitly treats of a CONFEDERATE REPUBLIC as the expedient for extending the sphere of popular government, and reconciling the advantages of monarchy with those of republicanism.

"It is very probable, says he, that mankind would have been obliged, at length, to live constantly under the government of a SINGLE PERSON, had they not contrived a kind of constitution, that has all the internal advantages of a republican, together with the external force of a monarchical government. I mean a CONFEDERATE REPUBLIC.

"This form of government is a convention by which several smaller *states* agree to become members of a larger *one*, which they intend to form. It is a kind of assemblage of societies, that constitute a new one, capable of increasing by means of new associations, till they arrive to such a degree of power as to be able to provide for the security of the united body.

"A republic of this kind, able to withstand an external force, may support itself without any internal corruption. The form of this society prevents all manner of inconveniences.

"If a single member should attempt to usurp the supreme authority, he could not be supposed to have an equal authority and credit in all the confederate states. Were he to have too great influence over one, this would alarm the rest. Were he to subdue a part, that which would still remain free might oppose him with forces, independent of those which he had usurped, and overpower him before he could be settled in his usurpation.

"Should a popular insurrection happen in one of the

confederate states, the others are able to quell it. Should abuses creep into one part, they are reformed by those that remain sound. The state may be destroyed on one side, and not on the other; the confederacy may be dissolved, and the confederates preserve their sovereignty.

"As this government is composed of small republics, it enjoys the internal happiness of each, and with respect to its external situation, it is possessed, by means of the association, of all the advantages of large monarchies."

I have thought it proper to quote at length these interesting passages, because they contain a luminous abridgement of the principal arguments in favour of the union, and must effectually remove the false impressions, which a misapplication of the other parts of the work was calculated to produce. They have, at the same time, an intimate connexion with the more immediate design of this paper, which is to illustrate the tendency of the union to repress domestic faction and insurrection.

A distinction, more subtle than accurate, has been raised between a *confederacy* and a *consolidation* of the states. The essential characteristic of the first, is said to be the restriction of its authority to the members in their collective capacities, without reaching to the individuals of whom they are composed. It is contended, that the national council ought to have no concern with any object of internal administration. An exact equality of suffrage between the members, has also been insisted upon as a leading feature of a confederate government. These positions are, in the main, arbitrary; they are supported neither by principle nor precedent. It has indeed happened, that governments of this kind have generally operated in the manner which the distinction taken notice of supposes to be inherent in their nature; but there have been in most of them extensive exceptions to the practice, which serve to prove, as far as example will go, that there is no absolute rule on the subject. And it will be clearly shown, in the course of this investigation, that, as far as the principle contended for has prevailed, it has been the cause of incurable disorder and imbecility in the government.

The definition of a *confederate republic* seems simply to be, "an assemblage of societies," or an association of two or more states into one state. The extent, modifications, and objects, of the federal authority, are mere matters of discretion. So long as the separate organization of the members be not abolished, so long as it exists by a constitutional necessity for local purposes, though it should be in perfect subordination to the general authority of the union, it would still be, in fact and in theory, an association of states, or a confederacy. The proposed constitution, so far from implying an abolition of the state governments, makes them constituent parts of the national sovereignty, by allowing them a direct representation in the senate, and leaves in their possession certain exclusive, and very important, portions of the sovereign power. This fully corresponds, in every rational import of the terms, with the idea of a federal government.

In the Lycian confederacy, which consisted of twenty-three CITIES, or republics, the largest were entitled to *three* votes in the COMMON COUNCIL, those of the middle class to *two,* and the smallest to *one.* The COMMON COUNCIL had the appointment of all the judges and magistrates of the respective CITIES. This was certainly the most delicate species of interference in their internal administration; for if there be any thing that seems exclusively appropriated to the local jurisdictions, it is the appointment of their own officers. Yet Montesquieu, speaking of this association, says, "were I to give a model of an excellent confederate republic, it would be that of Lycia." Thus we perceive, that the distinctions insisted upon, were not within the contemplation of this enlightened writer; and we shall be led to conclude, that they are the novel refinements of an erroneous theory.

PUBLIUS

No. 10

JAMES MADISON

The same Subject continued

Among the numerous advantages promised by a well constructed union, none deserves to be more accurately developed, than its tendency to break and control the violence of faction. The friend of popular governments, never finds himself so much alarmed for their character and fate, as when he contemplates their propensity to this dangerous vice. He will not fail, therefore, to set a due value on any plan which, without violating the principles to which he is attached, provides a proper cure for it. The instability, injustice, and confusion, introduced into the public councils, have, in truth, been the mortal diseases under which popular governments have every where perished; as they continue to be the favourite and fruitful topics from which the adversaries to liberty derive their most specious declamations. The valuable improvements made by the American constitutions on the popular models, both ancient and modern, cannot certainly be too much admired; but it would be an unwarrantable partiality, to contend that they have as effectually obviated the danger on this side, as was wished and expected. Complaints are every where heard from our most considerate and virtuous citizens, equally the friends of public and private faith, and of public and personal liberty, that our governments are too unstable; that the public good is disregarded in the conflicts of rival parties; and that measures are too often decided, not according to the rules of justice, and the rights of the minor party, but by the superior force of an interested and overbearing majority. However anxiously we may wish that these complaints had no foundation, the evidence of known facts will not permit us to deny that they are in some degree true. It will be found, indeed, on a candid review of our situation, that some of the distresses under which we labour, have been erroneously charged on the operation of our governments; but it will be found, at the same time, that other causes will not alone account for many of our heaviest misfortunes; and, particularly, for that prevailing and increasing distrust of public engagements, and alarm for private rights, which are echoed from one end of the continent to the other. These must be chiefly, if not wholly, effects of the unsteadiness and injustice, with which a factious spirit has tainted our public administrations.

By a faction, I understand a number of citizens, whether amounting to a majority or minority of the whole, who are united and actuated by some common impulse of passion, or of interest, adverse to the rights of other citizens, or to the permanent and aggregate interests of the community.

There are two methods of curing the mischiefs of faction: The one, by removing its causes; the other, by controling its effects.

There are again two methods of removing the causes of faction: The one, by destroying the liberty which is essential to its existence; the other, by giving to every citizen the same opinions, the same passions, and the same interests.

It could never be more truly said, than of the first remedy, that it is worse than the disease. Liberty is to faction, what air is to fire, an aliment, without which it instantly expires. But it could not be a less folly to abolish liberty, which is essential to political life, because it nourishes faction, than it would be to wish the annihilation of air,

which is essential to animal life, because it imparts to fire its destructive agency.

The second expedient is as impracticable, as the first would be unwise. As long as the reason of man continues fallible, and he is at liberty to exercise it, different opinions will be formed. As long as the connection subsists between his reason and his self-love, his opinions and his passions will have a reciprocal influence on each other; and the former will be objects to which the latter will attach themselves. The diversity in the faculties of men, from which the rights of property originate, is not less an insuperable obstacle to an uniformity of interests. The protection of these faculties, is the first object of government. From the protection of different and unequal faculties of acquiring property, the possession of different degrees and kinds of property immediately results; and from the influence of these on the sentiments and views of the respective proprietors, ensues a division of the society into different interests and parties.

The latent causes of faction are thus sown in the nature of man; and we see them every where brought into different degrees of activity, according to the different circumstances of civil society. A zeal for different opinions concerning religion, concerning government, and many other points, as well of speculation as of practice; an attachment to different leaders, ambitiously contending for pre-eminence and power; or to persons of other descriptions, whose fortunes have been interesting to the human passions, have, in turn, divided mankind into parties, inflamed them with mutual animosity, and rendered them much more disposed to vex and oppress each other, than to co-operate for their common good. So strong is this propensity of mankind, to fall into mutual animosities, that where no substantial occasion presents itself, the most frivolous and fanciful distinctions have been sufficient to kindle their unfriendly passions, and excite their most violent conflicts. But the most common and durable source of factions, has been the various and unequal distribution of property. Those who hold, and those who are without property, have ever formed distinct interests in society. Those who are creditors, and those who are debtors, fall under a like discrimination. A landed interest, a manufacturing interest, a mercantile interest, a monied interest, with many lesser interests, grow up of necessity in civilized nations, and divide them into different classes, actuated by different sentiments and views. The regulation of these various and interfering interests, forms the principal task of modern legislation, and involves the spirit of party and faction in the necessary and ordinary operations of government.

No man is allowed to be a judge in his own cause; because his interest would certainly bias his judgment, and, not improbably, corrupt his integrity. With equal, nay, with greater reason, a body of men are unfit to be both judges and parties, at the same time; yet, what are many of the most important acts of legislation, but so many judicial determinations, not indeed concerning the rights of single persons, but concerning the rights of large bodies of citizens? and what are the different classes of legislators, but advocates and parties to the causes which they determine? Is a law proposed concerning private debts? It is a question to which the creditors are parties on one side, and the debtors on the other. Justice ought to hold the balance between them. Yet the parties are, and must be, themselves the judges; and the most numerous party, or, in other words, the most powerful faction, must be expected to prevail. Shall domestic manufactures be encouraged, and in what degree, by restrictions on foreign manufactures? are questions which would be differently decided by the landed and the manufacturing classes; and probably by neither with a sole regard to justice and the public good. The apportionment of taxes, on the various descriptions of property, is an act which seems to require the most exact impartiality; yet there is, perhaps, no legislative act in which greater opportunity and temptation are given to a predominant party, to trample on the rules of justice. Every shilling with which they over-burden the inferior number, is a shilling saved to their own pockets.

It is in vain to say, that enlightened statesmen will be able to adjust these clashing interests, and render them all subservient to the public good. Enlightened statesmen will not always be at the helm: nor, in many cases, can such an adjustment be made at all, without taking into view indirect and remote considerations, which will rarely prevail over the immediate interest which one party may find in disregarding the rights of another, or the good of the whole.

The inference to which we are brought, is, that the *causes* of faction cannot be removed; and that relief is only to be sought in the means of controlling its *effects.*

If a faction consists of less than a majority, relief is supplied by the republican principle, which enables the majority to defeat its sinister views, by regular vote. It may clog the administration, it may convulse the society; but it will be unable to execute and mask its violence under the forms of the constitution. When a majority is included in a faction, the form of popular government, on the other hand, enables it to sacrifice to its ruling passion or interest, both the public good and the rights of other citizens. To secure the public good, and private rights, against the danger of such a faction, and at the same time to preserve the spirit and the form of popular government, is then the great object to which our inquiries are directed. Let me add, that it is the great desideratum, by which alone this form of government can be rescued from the opprobrium under which it has so long laboured, and be recommended to the esteem and adoption of mankind.

By what means is this object attainable? Evidently by one of two only. Either the existence of the same passion or interest in a majority, at the same time, must be prevented; or the majority, having such co-existent passion or interest, must be rendered, by their number and local situation, unable to concert and carry into effect schemes of oppression. If the impulse and the opportunity be suffered to coincide, we well know, that neither moral nor religious motives can be relied on as an adequate control. They are not found to be such on the injustice and violence of individuals, and lose their efficacy in proportion to the number combined together; that is, in proportion as their efficacy becomes needful.

From this view of the subject, it may be concluded, that a pure democracy, by which I mean, a society consisting of a small number of citizens, who assemble and administer the government in person, can admit of no cure for the mischiefs of faction. A common passion or interest will, in almost every case, be felt by a majority of the whole; a communication and concert, results from the form of government itself; and there is nothing to check the inducements to sacrifice the weaker party, or an obnoxious individual. Hence it is, that such democracies have ever been spectacles of turbulence and contention; have ever been found incompatible with personal security, or the rights of property; and have, in general, been as short in their lives, as they have been violent in their deaths. Theoretic politicians, who have patronised this species of government, have erroneously supposed, that, by reducing mankind to a perfect equality in their political rights, they would, at the same time, be perfectly equalized and assimilated in their possessions, their opinions, and their passions.

A republic, by which I mean a government in which the scheme of representation takes place, opens a different prospect, and promises the cure for which we are seeking. Let us examine the points in which it varies from pure democracy, and we shall comprehend both the nature of the cure and the efficacy which it must derive from the union.

The two great points of difference, between a democracy and a republic, are, first, the delegation of the government, in the latter, to a small number of citizens elected by the rest; secondly, the greater number of citizens, and greater sphere of country, over which the latter may be extended.

The effect of the first difference is, on the one hand, to refine and enlarge the public views, by passing them through the medium of a chosen body of citizens, whose wisdom may best discern the true interest of their country, and whose patriotism and love of justice, will be least likely to sacrifice it to temporary or partial considerations. Under such a regulation, it may well happen, that the public voice, pronounced by the representatives of the people, will be more consonant to the public good, than if pronounced by the people themselves, convened for the purpose. On the other hand, the effect may be inverted. Men of factious tempers, of local prejudices, or of sinister designs, may by intrigue, by corruption, or by other means, first obtain the suffrages, and then betray the interests of the people. The question resulting is, whether small or extensive republics are most favourable to the election of proper guardians of the public weal; and it is clearly decided in favour of the latter by two obvious considerations.

In the first place, it is to be remarked, that however small the republic may be, the representatives must be raised to a certain number, in order to guard against the cabals of a few; and that, however large it may be, they must be limited to a certain number, in order to guard against the confusion of a multitude. Hence, the number of representatives in the two cases not being in proportion to that of the constituents, and being proportionally greatest in the small republic, it follows, that if the proportion of fit characters be not less in the large than in the small republic, the former will present a greater option, and consequently a greater probability of a fit choice.

In the next place, as each representative will be chosen by a greater number of citizens in the large than in the small republic, it will be more difficult for unworthy candidates to practise with success the vicious arts, by which elections are too often carried; and the suffrages of the people being more free, will be more likely to centre in men who possess the most attractive merit, and the most diffusive and established characters.

It must be confessed, that in this, as in most other cases, there is a mean, on both sides of which inconveniences will be found to lie. By enlarging too much the number of electors, you render the representative too little acquainted with all their local circumstances and lesser interests; as by reducing it too much, you render him unduly attached to these, and too little fit to comprehend and pursue great and national objects. The federal constitution forms a happy combination in this respect; the great and aggregate interests, being referred to the national, the local and particular to the state legislatures.

The other point of difference is, the greater number of citizens, and extent of territory, which may be brought within the compass of republican, than of democratic government; and it is this circumstance principally which renders factious combinations less to be dreaded in the former, than in the latter. The smaller the society, the fewer probably will be the distinct parties and interests composing it; the fewer the distinct parties and interests, the more frequently will a majority be found of the same party; and the smaller the number of individuals composing a majority, and the smaller the compass within which they are placed, the more easily will they concert and execute their plans of oppression. Extend the sphere, and you take in a greater variety of parties and interests; you make it less probable that a majority of the whole will have a common motive to invade the rights of other citizens; or if such a common motive exists, it will be more difficult for all who feel it to discover their own strength, and to act in unison with each other. Besides other impediments, it may be remarked, that where there is a consciousness of unjust or dishonourable purposes, communication is always checked by distrust, in proportion to the number whose concurrence is necessary.

Hence it clearly appears, that the same advantage, which a republic has over a democracy, in controling the effects of faction, is enjoyed by a large over a small republic . . . is enjoyed by the union over the states composing it. Does this advantage consist in the substitution of representatives, whose enlightened views and virtuous sentiments render them superior to local prejudices, and to schemes of injustice? It will not be denied, that the representation of the union will be most likely to possess these requisite endowments. Does it consist in the greater security afforded by a greater variety of parties, against the event of any one party being able to outnumber and oppress the rest? In an equal degree does the increased variety of parties, comprised within the union, increase this security. Does it, in fine, consist in the greater obstacles opposed to the concert and accomplishment of the secret wishes of an unjust and interested majority? Here, again, the extent of the union gives it the most palpable advantage.

The influence of factious leaders may kindle a flame within their particular states, but will be unable to spread a general conflagration through the other states: a religious sect may degenerate into a political faction in a part of the confederacy; but the variety of sects dispersed over the entire face of it, must secure the national councils against any danger from that source: a rage for paper money, for an abolition of debts, for an equal division of property, or for any other improper or wicked project, will be less apt to pervade the whole body of the union, than a particular member of it; in the same proportion as such a malady is more likely to taint a particular county or district, than an entire state.

In the extent and proper structure of the union, therefore, we behold a republican remedy for the diseases most incident to republican government. And according to the degree of pleasure and pride we feel in being republicans, ought to be our zeal in cherishing the spirit, and supporting the character of federalists.

PUBLIUS

No. 39

JAMES MADISON

The conformity of the plan to republican principles: an objection in respect to the powers of the convention, examined

The last paper having concluded the observations, which were meant to introduce a candid survey of the plan of government reported by the convention, we now proceed to the execution of that part of our undertaking.

The first question that offers itself is, whether the general form and aspect of the government be strictly republican? It is evident that no other form would be reconcileable with the genius of the people of America; with the fundamental principles of the revolution; or with that honourable determination which animates every votary of freedom, to rest all our political experiments on the capacity of mankind for self-government. If the plan of the convention, therefore, be found to depart from the republican character, its advocates must abandon it as no longer defensible.

What then are the distinctive characters of the republican form? Were an answer to this question to be sought, not by recurring to principles, but in the application of the term by political writers, to the constitutions of different states, no satisfactory one would ever be found. Holland, in which no particle of the supreme authority is derived from the people, has passed almost universally under the denomination of a republic. The same title has been bestowed on Venice, where absolute power over the great body of the people is exercised, in the most absolute manner, by a small body of hereditary nobles. Poland, which is a mixture of aristocracy and of monarchy in their worst forms, has been dignified with the same appellation. The government of England, which has one republican branch only, combined with a hereditary aristocracy and monarchy, has, with equal impropriety, been frequently placed on the list of republics. These examples, which are nearly as dissimilar to each other as to a genuine republic, show the extreme inaccuracy with which the term has been used in political disquisitions.

If we resort for a criterion, to the different principles on which different forms of government are established, we may define a republic to be, or at least may bestow that name on, a government which derives all its powers directly or indirectly from the great body of the people; and is administered by persons holding their offices during pleasure, for a limited period, or during good behaviour. It is *essential* to such a government, that it be derived from the great body of the society, not from an inconsiderable proportion, or a favoured class of it; otherwise a handful of tyrannical nobles, exercising their oppressions by a delegation of their powers, might aspire to the rank of republicans, and claim for their government the honourable title of republic. It is *sufficient* for such a government, that the persons administering it be appointed, either directly or indirectly, by the people; and that they hold their appointments by either of the tenures just specified; otherwise every government in the United States, as well as every other popular government that has been, or can be well organized or well executed, would be degraded from the republican character. According to the constitution of every state in the union, some or other of the officers of government are appointed indirectly only by the people. According to most of them, the chief magistrate himself is so appointed. And according to one, this mode of appointment is extended to one of the co-ordinate branches of the legislature. According to all the constitutions also, the tenure of the highest offices is extended to a definite period, and in many instances, both within the legislative and executive departments, to a period of years. According to the provisions of most of the constitutions, again, as well as according to the most respectable and received opinions on the subject, the members of the judiciary department are to retain their offices by the firm tenure of good behaviour.

On comparing the constitution planned by the convention, with the standard here fixed, we perceive at once, that it is, in the most rigid sense, conformable to it. The house of representatives, like that of one branch at least of all the state legislatures, is elected immediately by the great body of the people. The senate, like the present congress, and the senate of Maryland, derives its appointment indirectly from the people. The president is indirectly derived from the choice of the people, according to the example in most of the states. Even the judges, with all other officers of the union, will, as in the several states, be the choice, though a remote choice, of the people themselves. The duration of the appointments is equally conformable to the republican standard, and to the model of the state constitutions. The house of representatives is periodically elective, as in all the states; and for the period of two years, as in the state of South Carolina. The senate is elective, for the period of six years; which is but one year more than the period of the senate of Maryland; and but two more than that of the senates of New York and Virginia. The president is to continue in office for the period of four years; as in New York and Delaware, the chief magistrate is elected for three years, and in South Carolina for two years. In the other

states the election is annual. In several of the states, however, no explicit provision is made for the impeachment of the chief magistrate. And in Delaware and Virginia, he is not impeachable till out of office. The president of the United States is impeachable at any time during his continuance in office. The tenure by which the judges are to hold their places, is, as it unquestionably ought to be, that of good behaviour. The tenure of the ministerial offices generally, will be a subject of legal regulation, conformably to the reason of the case, and the example of the state constitutions.

Could any further proof be required of the republican complexion of this system, the most decisive one might be found in its absolute prohibition of titles of nobility, both under the federal and the state governments; and in its express guarantee of the republican form to each of the latter.

But it was not sufficient, say the adversaries of the proposed constitution, for the convention to adhere to the republican form. They ought, with equal care, to have preserved the *federal* form, which regards the union as a *confederacy* of sovereign states; instead of which, they have framed a *national* government, which regards the union as a *consolidation* of the states. And it is asked, by what authority this bold and radical innovation was undertaken? The handle which has been made of this objection requires, that it should be examined with some precision.

Without inquiring into the accuracy of the distinction on which the objection is founded, it will be necessary to a just estimate of its force, first, to ascertain the real character of the government in question; secondly, to inquire how far the convention were authorized to propose such a government: and thirdly, how far the duty they owed to their country, could supply any defect of regular authority.

First. In order to ascertain the real character of the government, it may be considered in relation to the foundation on which it is to be established; to the sources from which its ordinary powers are to be drawn; to the operation of those powers; to the extent of them; and to the authority by which future changes in the government are to be introduced.

On examining the first relation, it appears, on one hand, that the constitution is to be founded on the assent and ratification of the people of America, given by deputies elected for the special purpose; but on the other, that this assent and ratification is to be given by the people, not as individuals composing one entire nation, but as composing the distinct and independent states to which they respectively belong. It is to be the assent and ratification of the several states, derived from the supreme authority in each state . . . the authority of the people themselves. The act, therefore, establishing the constitution, will not be a *national,* but a *federal* act.

That it will be a federal, and not a national act, as these terms are understood by the objectors, the act of the people, as forming so many independent states, not as forming one aggregate nation, is obvious from this single consideration, that it is to result neither from the decision of a *majority* of the people of the union, nor from that of a *majority* of the states. It must result from the *unanimous* assent of the several states that are parties to it, differing no otherwise from their ordinary assent than in its being expressed, not by the legislative authority, but by that of the people themselves. Were the people regarded in this transaction as forming one nation, the will of the majority of the whole people of the United States would bind the minority; in the same manner as the majority in each state must bind the minority; and the will of the majority must be determined either by a comparison of the individual votes, or by considering the will of the majority of the states, as evidence of the will of a majority of the people of the United States. Neither of these rules has been adopted. Each state, in ratifying the constitution, is considered as a sovereign body, independent of all others, and only to be bound by its own voluntary act. In this relation, then, the new constitution will, if established, be a *federal,* and not a *national* constitution.

The next relation is, to the sources from which the ordinary powers of government are to be derived. The house of representatives will derive its powers from the people of America, and the people will be represented in the same proportion, and on the same principle, as they are in the legislature of a particular state. So far the government is *national,* not *federal.* The senate, on the other hand, will derive its powers from the states, as political and co-equal societies; and these will be represented on the principle of equality in the senate, as they now are in the existing congress. So far the government is *federal,* not *national.* The executive power will be derived from a very compound source. The immediate election of the president is to be made by the states in their political characters. The votes alloted to them are in a compound ratio, which considers them partly as distinct and co-equal societies; partly as unequal members of the same society. The eventual election, again, is to be made by that branch of the legislature which consists of the national representatives; but in this particular act, they are to be thrown into the form of individual delegations, from so many distinct and co-equal bodies politic. From this aspect of the government, it appears to be of a mixed character, presenting at least as many *federal* as *national* features.

The difference between a federal and national government, as it relates to the *operation of the government,* is, by the adversaries of the plan of the convention, supposed to consist in this, that in the former, the powers operate on the political bodies composing the confederacy, in their political capacities; in the latter, on the individual citizens composing the nation, in their individual capacities. On trying the constitution by this criterion, it falls under the *national,* not the *federal* character; though perhaps not so completely as has been understood. In several cases, and particularly in the trial of controversies to which states may be parties, they must be viewed and proceeded against in their collective and political capacities only. But the operation of the government on the people in their individual capacities, in its ordinary and most essential proceedings, will, on the whole, in the sense of its opponents, designate it in this relation, a *national* government.

But if the government be national, with regard to the *operation* of its powers, it changes its aspect again, when we contemplate it in relation to the *extent* of its powers. The idea of a national government involves in it, not only an authority over the individual citizens, but an indefinite supremacy over all persons and things, so far as they are objects of lawful government. Among a people consolidated into one nation, this supremacy is completely vested in the national legislature. Among communities united for particular purposes, it is vested partly in the general, and partly in the municipal legislatures. In the former case, all local authorities are subordinate to the supreme; and may be controled, directed, or abolished by it at pleasure. In the latter, the local or municipal authorities form distinct and independent portions of the supremacy, no more subject, within their respective spheres, to the general authority, than the general authority is subject to them within its own sphere. In this relation, then, the proposed government cannot be deemed a *national* one; since its jurisdiction extends to certain enumerated objects only, and leaves to the several states, a residuary and inviolable sovereignty over all other objects. It is true, that in controversies relating to the boundary between the two jurisdictions, the tribunal which is ultimately to decide, is to be established under the general government. But this does not change the principle of the case. The decision is to be impartially made, according to the rules of the constitution: and all the usual and most effectual precautions are taken to secure this impartiality. Some such tribunal is clearly essential to prevent an appeal to the sword, and a dissolution of the compact; and that it ought to be established under the general, rather than under the local governments; or, to speak more properly, that it could be safely established under the first alone, is a position not likely to be combated.

If we try the constitution by its last relation, to the authority by which amendments are to be made, we find it neither wholly *national*, nor wholly *federal*. Were it wholly national, the supreme and ultimate authority would reside in the majority of the people of the union; and this authority would be competent at all times, like that of a majority of every national society, to alter or abolish its established government. Were it wholly federal on the other hand, the concurrence of each state in the union would be essential to every alteration that would be binding on all. The mode provided by the plan of the convention, is not founded on either of these principles. In requiring more than a majority, and particularly, in computing the proportion by *states,* not by *citizens,* it departs from the *national,* and advances towards the *federal* character. In rendering the concurrence of less than the whole number of states sufficient, it loses again the *federal,* and partakes of the *national* character.

The proposed constitution, therefore, even when tested by the rules laid down by its antagonists, is, in strictness, neither a national nor a federal constitution; but a composition of both. In its foundation it is federal, not national; in the sources from which the ordinary powers of the government are drawn, it is partly federal, and partly national; in the operation of these powers, it is national, not federal; in the extent of them again, it is federal, not national; and finally, in the authoritative mode of introducing amendments, it is neither wholly federal, nor wholly national.

PUBLIUS

No. 47

JAMES MADISON

The meaning of the maxim, which requires a separation of the departments of power, examined and ascertained

Having reviewed the general form of the proposed government, and the general mass of power allotted to it; I proceed to examine the particular structure of this government, and the distribution of this mass of power among its constituent parts.

One of the principal objections inculcated by the more respectable adversaries to the constitution, is its supposed violation of the political maxim, that the legislative, executive, and judiciary departments, ought to be separate and distinct. In the structure of the federal government, no regard, it is said, seems to have been paid to this essential precaution in favour of liberty. The several departments of power are distributed and blended in such a manner, as at once to destroy all symmetry and beauty of form: and to expose some of the essential parts of the edifice to the danger of being crushed by the disproportionate weight of other parts.

No political truth is certainly of greater intrinsic value, or is stamped with the authority of more enlightened patrons of liberty, than that on which the objection is founded. The accumulation of all powers, legislative, executive, and judiciary, in the same hands, whether of one, a few, or many, and whether hereditary, self-appointed, or elective, may justly be pronounced the very definition of tyranny. Were the federal constitution, therefore, really chargeable with this accumulation of power, or with a mixture of powers, having a dangerous tendency to such an accumulation, no further arguments would be necessary to inspire a universal reprobation of the system. I persuade myself, however, that it will be made apparent to every one, that the charge cannot be supported, and that the maxim on which it relies has been totally misconceived and misapplied. In order to form correct ideas on this important subject, it will be proper to investigate the sense in which the preservation of liberty requires, that the three great departments of power should be separate and distinct.

The oracle who is always consulted and cited on this subject, is the celebrated Montesquieu. If he be not the author of this invaluable precept in the science of politics, he has the merit at least of displaying and recommending it most effectually to the attention of mankind. Let us endeavour, in the first place, to ascertain his meaning on this point.

The British constitution was to Montesquieu, what Homer has been to the didactic writers on epic poetry. As the latter have considered the work of the immortal bard, as the perfect model from which the principles and rules of the epic art were to be drawn, and by which all similar works were to be judged: so this great political critic appears to have viewed the constitution of England as the standard, or to use his own expression, as the mirror of political liberty; and to have delivered, in the form of elementary truths, the several characteristic principles of that particular system. That we may be sure then not to mistake his meaning in this case, let us recur to the source from which the maxim was drawn.

On the slightest view of the British constitution, we must perceive, that the legislative, executive, and judiciary departments, are by no means totally separate and distinct from each other. The executive magistrate forms an integral part of the legislative authority. He alone has the prerogative of making treaties with foreign sovereigns, which, when made, have, under certain limitations, the force of legislative acts. All the members of the judiciary department are appointed by him; can be removed by him on the address of the two houses of parliament, and form, when he pleases to consult them, one of his constitutional councils. One branch of the legislative department, forms also a great constitutional council to the executive chief; as, on another hand, it is the sole depository of judicial power in cases of impeachment, and is invested with the supreme appellate jurisdiction in all other cases. The judges again are so far connected with the legislative department, as often to attend and participate in its deliberations, though not admitted to a legislative vote.

From these facts, by which Montesquieu was guided, it may clearly be inferred, that in saying, "there can be no liberty, where the legislative and executive powers are united in the same person, or body of magistrates;" or, "if the power of judging, be not separated from the legislative and executive powers," he did not mean that these departments ought to have no *partial agency* in, or no *control* over the acts of each other. His meaning, as his own words import, and still more conclusively as illustrated by the example in his eye, can amount to no more than this, that where the *whole* power of one department is exercised by the same hands which possess the *whole* power of another department, the fundamental principles of a free constitution are subverted. This would have been the case in the constitution examined by him, if the king, who is the sole executive magistrate, had possessed also the complete legislative power, or the supreme administration of justice; or if the entire legislative body had possessed the supreme judiciary, or the supreme executive authority. This, however, is not among the vices of that constitution. The magistrate, in whom the whole executive power resides, cannot of himself make a law, though he can put a negative on every law; nor administer justice in person, though he has the appointment of those who do administer it. The judges can exercise no executive prerogative, though they are shoots from the executive stock; nor any legislative function, though they may be advised with by the legislative councils. The entire legislature, can perform no judiciary act; though by the joint act of two of its branches, the judges may be removed from their offices; and though one of its branches is possessed of the judicial power in the last resort. The entire legislature again can exercise no executive prerogative, though one of its branches* constitutes the supreme executive magistracy; and another, on the impeachment of a third, can try and condemn all the subordinate officers in the executive department.

The reasons on which Montesquieu grounds his maxim, are a further demonstration of his meaning. "When the legislative and executive powers are united in the same person or body," says he, "there can be no liberty, because apprehensions may arise lest *the same* monarch or senate should *enact* tyrannical laws, to *execute* them in a tyrannical manner." Again, "were the power of judging joined with the legislative, the life and liberty of the subject would be exposed to arbitrary control, for *the judge* would then be *the legislator*. Were it joined to the executive power, *the judge* might behave with all the violence of *an oppressor*." Some of these reasons are more fully explained in other passages; but briefly stated as they are here, they sufficiently establish the meaning which we have put on this celebrated maxim of this celebrated author.

If we look into the constitutions of the several states, we find that, notwithstanding the emphatical, and in some instances, the unqualified terms in which this axiom has been laid down, there is not a single instance in which the several departments of power have been kept absolutely

*The King.

separate and distinct. New Hampshire, whose constitution was the last formed, seems to have been fully aware of the impossibility and inexpediency of avoiding any mixture whatever of these departments; and has qualified the doctrine by declaring, "that the legislative, executive, and judiciary powers, ought to be kept as separate from, and independent of each other, *as the nature of a free government will admit; or as is consistent with that chain of connexion, that binds the whole fabric of the constitution in one indissoluble bond of unity and amity.*" Her constitution accordingly mixes these departments in several respects. The senate, which is a branch of the legislative department, is also a judicial tribunal for the trial of impeachments. The president, who is the head of the executive department, is the presiding member also of the senate; and besides an equal vote in all cases, has a casting vote in case of a tie. The executive head is himself eventually elective every year by the legislative department; and his council is every year chosen by and from the members of the same department. Several of the officers of state are also appointed by the legislature. And the members of the judiciary department are appointed by the executive department.

The constitution of Massachusetts has observed a sufficient, though less pointed caution, in expressing this fundamental article of liberty. It declares, "that the legislative department shall never exercise the executive and judicial powers, or either of them: the executive shall never exercise the legislative and judicial powers, or either of them: the judicial shall never exercise the legislative and executive powers, or either of them." This declaration corresponds precisely with the doctrine of Montesquieu, as it has been explained, and is not in a single point violated by the plan of the convention. It goes no farther than to prohibit any one of the entire departments from exercising the powers of another department. In the very constitution to which it is prefixed, a partial mixture of powers has been admitted. The executive magistrate has a qualified negative on the legislative body; and the senate, which is a part of the legislature, is a court of impeachment for members both of the executive and judiciary departments. The members of the judiciary department again, are appointable by the executive department, and removable by the same authority, on the address of the two legislative branches. Lastly, a number of the officers of government, are annually appointed by the legislative department. As the appointment to offices, particularly executive offices, is in its nature an executive function, the compilers of the constitution have,

in this last point at least, violated the rule established by themselves.

I pass over the constitutions of Rhode Island and Connecticut, because they were formed prior to the revolution: and even before the principle under examination had become an object of political attention.

The constitution of New York contains no declaration on this subject; but appears very clearly to have been framed with an eye to the danger of improperly blending the different departments. It gives, nevertheless, to the executive magistrate a partial control over the legislative department; and what is more, gives a like control to the judiciary department, and even blends the executive and judiciary departments in the exercise of this control. In its council of appointment, members of the legislative, are associated with the executive authority, in the appointment of officers, both executive and judiciary. And its court for the trial of impeachments and correction of errors, is to consist of one branch of the legislature and the principal members of the judiciary department.

The constitution of New Jersey has blended the different powers of government more than any of the preceding. The governor, who is the executive magistrate, is appointed by the legislature; is chancellor, and ordinary, or surrogate of the state; is a member of the supreme court of appeals, and president with a casting vote of one of the legislative branches. The same legislative branch acts again as executive council of the governor, and with him constitutes the court of appeals. The members of the judiciary department are appointed by the legislative department, and removeable by one branch of it on the impeachment of the other.

According to the constitution of Pennsylvania,* the president, who is head of the executive department, is annually elected by a vote in which the legislative department predominates. In conjunction with an executive council, he appoints the members of the judiciary department, and forms a court of impeachments for trial of all officers, judiciary as well as executive. The judges of the supreme court, and justices of the peace, seem also to be removable by the legislature; and the executive power of pardoning in certain cases to be referred to the same department. The members of the executive council are made EX OFFICIO justices of peace throughout the state.

---

*The constitutions of these states have been since altered.

In Delaware,* the chief executive magistrate is annually elected by the legislative department. The speakers of the two legislative branches are vice-presidents in the executive department. The executive chief, with six others, appointed three by each of the legislative branches, constitute the supreme court of appeals: he is joined with the legislative department in the appointment of the other judges. Throughout the states, it appears that the members of the legislature may at the same time be justices of the peace. In this state, the members of one branch of it are EX OFFICIO justices of the peace; as are also the members of the executive council. The principal officers of the executive department are appointed by the legislative; and one branch of the latter forms a court of impeachments. All officers may be removed on address of the legislature.

Maryland has adopted the maxim in the most unqualified terms; declaring that the legislative, executive, and judicial powers of government, ought to be for ever separate and distinct from each other. Her constitution, notwithstanding, makes the executive magistrate appointable by the legislative department; and the members of the judiciary, by the executive department.

The language of Virginia is still more pointed on this subject. Her constitution declares, "that the legislative, executive, and judiciary departments, shall be separate and distinct; so that neither exercise the powers properly belonging to the other; nor shall any person exercise the powers of more than one of them at the same time; except that the justices of county courts shall be eligible to either house of assembly." Yet we find not only this express exception, with respect to the members of the inferior courts; but that the chief magistrate, with his executive council, are appointable by the legislature; that two members of the latter, are triennially displaced at the pleasure of the legislature; and that all the principal officers, both executive and judiciary, are filled by the same department. The executive prerogative of pardoning, also, is in one case vested in the legislative department.

The constitution of North Carolina, which declares, "that the legislative, executive, and supreme judicial powers of government, ought to be forever separate and distinct from each other," refers at the same time to the legislative department, the appointment not only of the executive chief, but all the principal officers within both that and the judiciary department.

In South Carolina, the constitution makes the executive magistracy eligible by the legislative department. It gives to the latter, also, the appointment of the members of the judiciary department, including even justices of the peace and sheriffs; and the appointment of officers in the executive department, down to captains in the army and navy of the state.

In the constitution of Georgia, where it is declared, "that the legislative, executive, and judiciary departments, shall be separate and distinct, so that neither exercise the powers properly belonging to the other," we find that the executive department is to be filled by appointments of the legislature; and the executive prerogative of pardoning, to be finally exercised by the same authority. Even justices of the peace are to be appointed by the legislature.

In citing these cases in which the legislative, executive, and judiciary departments, have not been kept totally separate and distinct, I wish not to be regarded as an advocate for the particular organizations of the several state governments. I am fully aware, that among the many excellent principles which they exemplify, they carry strong marks of the haste, and still stronger of the inexperience, under which they were framed. It is but too obvious, that, in some instances, the fundamental principle under consideration, has been violated by too great a mixture, and even an actual consolidation of the different powers; and that in no instance has a competent provision been made for maintaining in practice the separation delineated on paper. What I have wished to evince is, that the charge brought against the proposed constitution, of violating a sacred maxim of free government, is warranted neither by the real meaning annexed to that maxim by its author, nor by the sense in which it has hitherto been understood in America. This interesting subject will be resumed in the ensuing paper.

PUBLIUS

No. 48

JAMES MADISON

The same subject continued, with a view to the means of giving efficacy in practice to that maxim

It was shown in the last paper, that the political apothegm there examined, does not require that the legislative, executive, and judiciary departments, should be wholly un-

*The constitutions of these states have been since altered.

connected with each other. I shall undertake in the next place to show, that unless these departments be so far connected and blended, as to give to each a constitutional control over the others, the degree of separation which the maxim requires, as essential to a free government, can never in practice be duly maintained.

It is agreed on all sides, that the powers properly belonging to one of the departments, ought not to be directly and completely administered by either of the other departments. It is equally evident, that neither of them ought to possess, directly or indirectly, an overruling influence over the others in the administration of their respective powers. It will not be denied, that power is of an encroaching nature, and that it ought to be effectually restrained from passing the limits assigned to it. After discriminating, therefore, in theory, the several classes of power, as they may in their nature be legislative, executive, or judiciary; the next, and most difficult task, is to provide some practical security for each, against the invasion of the others. What this security ought to be, is the great problem to be solved.

Will it be sufficient to mark, with precision, the boundaries of these departments, in the constitution of the government, and to trust to these parchment barriers against the encroaching spirit of power? This is the security which appears to have been principally relied on by the compilers of most of the American constitutions. But experience assures us, that the efficacy of the provision has been greatly overrated; and that some more adequate defence is indispensably necessary for the more feeble, against the more powerful members of the government. The legislative department is every where extending the sphere of its activity, and drawing all power into its impetuous vortex.

The founders of our republics have so much merit for the wisdom which they have displayed, that no task can be less pleasing than that of pointing out the errors into which they have fallen. A respect for truth, however, obliges us to remark, that they seem never for a moment to have turned their eyes from the danger to liberty, from the overgrown and all-grasping prerogative of an hereditary magistrate, supported and fortified by an hereditary branch of the legislative authority. They seem never to have recollected the danger from legislative usurpations, which, by assembling all power in the same hands, must lead to the same tyranny as is threatened by executive usurpations.

In a government where numerous and extensive prerogatives are placed in the hands of a hereditary monarch, the executive department is very justly regarded as the source of danger, and watched with all the jealousy which a zeal for liberty ought to inspire. In a democracy, where a multitude of people exercise in person the legislative functions, and are continually exposed, by their incapacity for regular deliberation and concerted measures, to the ambitious intrigues of their executive magistrates, tyranny may well be apprehended, on some favourable emergency, to start up in the same quarter. But in a representative republic, where the executive magistracy is carefully limited, both in the extent and the duration of its power; and where the legislative power is exercised by an assembly, which is inspired by a supposed influence over the people, with an intrepid confidence in its own strength; which is sufficiently numerous to feel all the passions which actuate a multitude; yet not so numerous as to be incapable of pursuing the objects of its passions, by means which reason prescribes; it is against the enterprising ambition of this department, that the people ought to indulge all their jealousy, and exhaust all their precautions.

The legislative department derives a superiority in our governments from other circumstances. Its constitutional powers being at once more extensive, and less susceptible of precise limits, it can, with the greater facility, mask under complicated and indirect measures, the encroachments which it makes on the co-ordinate departments. It is not unfrequently a question of real nicety in legislative bodies, whether the operation of a particular measure will, or will not extend beyond the legislative sphere. On the other side, the executive power being restrained within a narrower compass, and being more simple in its nature; and the judiciary being described by land-marks, still less uncertain, projects of usurpation by either of these departments, would immediately betray and defeat themselves. Nor is this all: as the legislative department alone has access to the pockets of the people, and has in some constitutions full discretion, and in all, a prevailing influence over the pecuniary rewards of those who fill the other departments; a dependence is thus created in the latter, which gives still greater facility to encroachments of the former.

I have appealed to our own experience for the truth of what I advance on this subject. Were it necessary to verify this experience by particular proofs, they might be multiplied without end. I might collect vouchers in abundance from the records and archives of every state in the union.

But as a more concise, and at the same time equally satisfactory evidence, I will refer to the example of two states, attested by two unexceptionable authorities.

The first example is that of Virginia, a state which, as we have seen, has expressly declared in its constitution, that the three great departments ought not to be intermixed. The authority in support of it is Mr. Jefferson, who, besides his other advantages for remarking the operation of the government, was himself the chief magistrate of it. In order to convey fully the ideas with which his experience had impressed him on this subject, it will be necessary to quote a passage of some length from his very interesting "Notes on the state of Virginia," (p. 195.) "All the powers of government, legislative, executive, and judiciary, result to the legislative body. The concentrating these in the same hands, is precisely the definition of despotic government. It will be no alleviation that these powers will be exercised by a plurality of hands, and not by a single one. One hundred and seventy-three despots would surely be as oppressive as one. Let those who doubt it, turn their eyes on the republic of Venice. As little will it avail us that they are chosen by ourselves. An *elective despotism* was not the government we fought for; but one which should not only be founded on free principles, but in which the powers of government should be so divided and balanced among several bodies of magistracy, as that no one could transcend their legal limits, without being effectually checked and restrained by the others. For this reason, that convention which passed the ordinance of government, laid its foundation on this basis, that the legislative, executive, and judiciary departments, should be separate and distinct, so that no person should exercise the powers of more than one of them at the same time. *But no barrier was provided between these several powers.* The judiciary and executive members were left dependent on the legislative for their subsistence in office, and some of them for their continuance in it. If, therefore, the legislature assumes executive and judiciary powers, no opposition is likely to be made; nor if made, can be effectual; because in that case, they may put their proceeding into the form of an act of assembly, which will render them obligatory on the other branches. They have accordingly, *in many* instances, *decided rights* which should have been left to *judiciary controversy; and the direction of the executive, during the whole time of their session, is becoming habitual and familiar.*"

The other state which I shall take for an example, is Pennsylvania; and the other authority the council of cen-

sors which assembled in the years 1783 and 1784. A part of the duty of this body, as marked out by the constitution, was "to inquire whether the constitution had been preserved inviolate in every part; and whether the legislative and executive branches of government, had performed their duty as guardians of the people, or assumed to themselves, or exercised other or greater powers than they are entitled to by the constitution." In the execution of this trust, the council were necessarily led to a comparison of both the legislative and executive proceedings, with the constitutional powers of these departments: and from the facts enumerated, and to the truth of most of which both sides in the council subscribed, it appears that the constitution had been flagrantly violated by the legislature in a variety of important instances.

A great number of laws had been passed violating, without any apparent necessity, the rule requiring that all bills of a public nature shall be previously printed for the consideration of the people; although this is one of the precautions chiefly relied on by the constitution against improper acts of the legislature.

The constitutional trial by jury had been violated; and powers assumed which had not been delegated by the constitution.

Executive powers had been usurped.

The salaries of the judges, which the constitution expressly requires to be fixed, had been occasionally varied; and cases belonging to the judiciary department, frequently drawn within legislative cognizance and determination.

Those who wish to see the several particulars falling under each of these heads, may consult the journals of the council which are in print. Some of them, it will be found, may be imputable to peculiar circumstances connected with the war: but the greater part of them may be considered as the spontaneous shoots of an ill constituted government.

It appears also, that the executive department had not been innocent of frequent breaches of the constitution. There are three observations, however, which ought to be made on this head. *First.* A great proportion of the instances, were either immediately produced by the necessities of the war, or recommended by congress or the commander in chief. *Second.* In most of the other instances, they conformed either to the declared or the known sentiments of the legislative department. *Third.* The executive department of Pennsylvania is distinguished from that of the other states, by the number of members composing it. In this respect it has as much affinity to a legislative assembly, as to an executive council. And being at once exempt from the restraint of an individual responsibility for the acts of the body, and deriving confidence from mutual example and joint influence; unauthorized measures would of course be more freely hazarded, than where the executive department is administered by a single hand, or by a few hands.

The conclusion which I am warranted in drawing from these observations is, that a mere demarkation on parchment of the constitutional limits of the several departments, is not a sufficient guard against those encroachments which lead to a tyrannical concentration of all the powers of government in the same hands.

PUBLIUS

No. 49

JAMES MADISON

The same subject continued, with the same view

The author of the "Notes on the state of Virginia," quoted in the last paper, has subjoined to that valuable work, the draught of a constitution, which had been prepared in order to be laid before a convention expected to be called in 1783, by the legislature, for the establishment of a constitution for that commonwealth. The plan, like every thing from the same pen, marks a turn of thinking original, comprehensive, and accurate; and is the more worthy of attention, as it equally displays a fervent attachment to republican government, and an enlightened view of the dangerous propensities against which it ought to be guarded. One of the precautions which he proposes, and on which he appears ultimately to rely as a palladium to the weaker departments of power, against the invasions of the stronger, is perhaps altogether his own, and as it immediately relates to the subject of our present inquiry, ought not to be overlooked.

His proposition is, "that whenever any two of the three branches of government shall concur in opinion each by the voices of two thirds of their whole number, that a convention is necessary for altering the constitution, or *correcting breaches of it,* a convention shall be called for the purpose."

As the people are the only legitimate fountain of power,

and it is from them that the constitutional charter, under which the several branches of government hold their power, is derived; it seems strictly consonant to the republican theory, to recur to the same original authority, not only whenever it may be necessary to enlarge, diminish, or new model the powers of government; but also whenever any one of the departments may commit encroachments on the chartered authorities of the others. The several departments being perfectly co-ordinate by the terms of their common commission, neither of them, it is evident, can pretend to an exclusive or superior right of settling the boundaries between their respective powers: and how are the encroachments of the stronger to be prevented, or the wrongs of the weaker to be redressed, without an appeal to the people themselves, who, as the grantors of the commission, can alone declare its true meaning, and enforce its observance?

There is certainly great force in this reasoning, and it must be allowed to prove, that a constitutional road to the decision of the people ought to be marked out and kept open, for certain great and extraordinary occasions. But there appear to be insuperable objections against the proposed recurrence to the people, as a provision in all cases for keeping the several departments of power within their constitutional limits.

In the first place, the provision does not reach the case of a combination of two of the departments against a third. If the legislative authority, which possesses so many means of operating on the motives of the other departments, should be able to gain to its interest either of the others, or even one-third of its members, the remaining department could derive no advantage from this remedial provision. I do not dwell, however, on this objection, because it may be thought to lie rather against the modification of the principle, than against the principle itself.

In the next place, it may be considered as an objection inherent in the principle, that, as every appeal to the people would carry an implication of some defect in the government, frequent appeals would, in a great measure, deprive the government of that veneration which time bestows on every thing, and without which perhaps the wisest and freest governments would not possess the requisite stability. If it be true that all governments rest on opinion, it is no less true, that the strength of opinion in each individual, and its practical influence on his conduct, depend much on the number which he supposes to have entertained the same opinion. The reason of man, like man himself, is timid and cautious when left alone; and acquires firmness and confidence, in proportion to the number with which it is associated. When the examples which fortify opinion, are *ancient,* as well as *numerous,* they are known to have a double effect. In a nation of philosophers, this consideration ought to be disregarded. A reverence for the laws would be sufficiently inculcated by the voice of an enlightened reason. But a nation of philosophers is as little to be expected, as the philosophical race of kings wished for by Plato. And in every other nation, the most rational government will not find it a superfluous advantage to have the prejudices of the community on its side.

The danger of disturbing the public tranquillity, by interesting too strongly the public passions, is a still more serious objection against a frequent reference of constitutional questions to the decision of the whole society. Notwithstanding the success which has attended the revisions of our established forms of government, and which does so much honour to the virtue and intelligence of the people of America, it must be confessed, that the experiments are of too ticklish a nature to be unnecessarily multiplied. We are to recollect, that all the existing constitutions were formed in the midst of a danger which repressed the passions most unfriendly to order and concord; of an enthusiastic confidence of the people in their patriotic leaders, which stifled the ordinary diversity of opinions on great national questions; of a universal ardour for new and opposite forms, produced by a universal resentment and indignation against the ancient government; and whilst no spirit of party, connected with the changes to be made, or the abuses to be reformed, could mingle its leaven in the operation. The future situations in which we must expect to be usually placed, do not present any equivalent security against the danger which is apprehended.

But the greatest objection of all is, that the decisions which would probably result from such appeals, would not answer the purpose of maintaining the constitutional equilibrium of the government. We have seen that the tendency of republican governments is, to an aggrandizement of the legislative, at the expense of the other departments. The appeals to the people, therefore, would usually be made by the executive and judiciary departments. But whether made by one side or the other, would each side enjoy equal advantages on the trial? Let us view their different situations. The members of the executive and judiciary departments, are few in number, and can be personally known to a small part only of the people. The latter, by the mode of their appointment, as well as by the nature and permanency of it, are too far removed from the people to share much in their prepossessions. The former are generally the objects of jealousy; and their administration is always liable to be discoloured and rendered unpopular. The members of the legislative department, on the other hand, are numerous. They are distributed and dwell among the people at large. Their connexions of blood, of friendship, and of acquaintance, embrace a great proportion of the most influential part of the society. The nature of their public trust implies a personal influence among the people, and that they are more immediately the confidential guardians of their rights and liberties. With these advantages, it can hardly be supposed, that the adverse party would have an equal chance for a favourable issue.

But the legislative party would not only be able to plead their cause most successfully with the people: they would probably be constituted themselves the judges. The same influence which had gained them an election into the legislature, would gain them a seat in the convention. If this should not be the case with all, it would probably be the case with many, and pretty certainly with those leading characters, on whom every thing depends in such bodies. The convention, in short, would be composed chiefly of men who had been, who actually were, or who expected to be members of the department whose conduct was arraigned. They would consequently be parties to the very question to be decided by them.

It might, however, sometimes happen, that appeals would be made under circumstances less adverse to the executive and judiciary departments. The usurpations of the legislature might be so flagrant and so sudden, as to admit of no specious colouring. A strong party among themselves might take side with the other branches. The executive power might be in the hands of a peculiar favourite of the people. In such a posture of things, the public decision might be less swayed by prepossessions in favour of the legislative party. But still it could never be expected to turn on the true merits of the question. It would inevitably be connected with the spirit of pre-existing parties, or of parties springing out of the question itself. It would be connected with persons of distinguished character, and extensive influence in the community. It would be pronounced by the very men who had been agents in, or opponents of the measures, to which the decision would relate. The *passions,* therefore, not the *reason,* of the public, would sit in judgment. But it is the reason of the public alone, that ought to control and regulate the government. The passions ought to be controled and regulated by the government.

We found in the last paper, that mere declarations in the written constitution, are not sufficient to restrain the several departments within their legal limits. It appears in this, that occasional appeals to the people would be neither a proper, nor an effectual provision for that purpose. How far the provisions of a different nature contained in the plan above quoted, might be adequate, I do not examine. Some of them are unquestionably founded on sound political principles, and all of them are framed with singular ingenuity and precision.

PUBLIUS

No. 50

JAMES MADISON

The same subject continued, with the same view

It may be contended, perhaps, that instead of *occasional* appeals to the people, which are liable to the objections urged against them, *periodical* appeals are the proper and adequate means of *preventing and correcting infractions of the constitution.*

It will be attended to, that in the examination of these expedients, I confine myself to their aptitude for *enforcing* the constitution, by keeping the several departments of power within their due bounds; without particularly considering them, as provisions for *altering* the constitution itself. In the first view, appeals to the people at fixed periods, appear to be nearly as ineligible, as appeals on particular occasions as they emerge. If the periods be separated by short intervals, the measures to be reviewed and rectified, will have been of recent date, and will be connected with all the circumstances which tend to vitiate and pervert the result of occasional revisions. If the periods be distant from each other, the same remark will be applicable to all recent measures; and in proportion as the remoteness of the others may favour a dispassionate review of them this advantage is inseparable from inconveniences which seem to counterbalance it. In the first place, a distant prospect of public censure would be a very feeble restraint on power

from those excesses, to which it might be urged by the force of present motives. Is it to be imagined, that a legislative assembly, consisting of a hundred or two hundred members, eagerly bent on some favourite object, and breaking through the restraints of the constitution in pursuit of it, would be arrested in their career, by considerations drawn from a censorial revision of their conduct at the future distance of ten, fifteen, or twenty years? In the next place, the abuses would often have completed their mischievous effects before the remedial provision would be applied. And in the last place, where this might not be the case, they would be of long standing, would have taken deep root, and would not easily be extirpated.

The scheme of revising the constitution, in order to correct recent breaches of it, as well as for other purposes, has been actually tried in one of the states. One of the objects of the council of censors, which met in Pennsylvania, in 1783 and 1784, was, as we have seen, to inquire "whether the constitution had been violated; and whether the legislative and executive departments had encroached on each other." This important and novel experiment in politics, merits, in several points of view, very particular attention. In some of them it may, perhaps, as a single experiment, made under circumstances somewhat peculiar, be thought to be not absolutely conclusive. But, as applied to the case under consideration, it involves some facts which I venture to remark, as a complete and satisfactory illustration of the reasoning which I have employed.

First. It appears, from the names of the gentlemen who composed the council, that some, at least, of its most active and leading members, had also been active and leading characters in the parties which pre-existed in the state.

Second. It appears that the same active and leading members of the council, had been active and influential members of the legislative and executive branches, within the period to be reviewed; and even patrons or opponents of the very measures to be thus brought to the test of the constitution. Two of the members had been vice-presidents of the state, and several others members of the executive council, within the seven preceding years. One of them had been speaker, and a number of others, distinguished members of the legislative assembly, within the same period.

Third. Every page of their proceedings witnesses the effect of all these circumstances on the temper of their deliberations. Throughout the continuance of the council, it was split into two fixed and violent parties. The fact is acknowledged and lamented by themselves. Had this not been the case, the face of their proceedings exhibit a proof equally satisfactory. In all questions, however unimportant in themselves, or unconnected with each other, the same names stand invariably contrasted on the opposite columns. Every unbiassed observer may infer, without danger of mistake, and at the same time without meaning to reflect on either party, or any individuals of either party, that unfortunately *passion*, not *reason*, must have presided over their decisions. When men exercise their reason coolly and freely on a variety of distinct questions, they inevitably fall into different opinions on some of them. When they are governed by a common passion, their opinions, if they are so to be called, will be the same.

Fourth. It is at least problematical, whether the decisions of this body do not, in several instances, misconstrue the limits prescribed for the legislative and executive departments, instead of reducing and limiting them within their constitutional places.

Fifth. I have never understood that the decisions of the council on constitutional questions, whether rightly or erroneously formed, have had any effect in varying the practice founded on legislative constructions. It even appears, if I mistake not, that in one instance, the cotemporary legislature denied the constructions of the council, and actually prevailed in the contest.

This censorial body, therefore, proves at the same time, by its researches, the existence of the disease; and by its example, the inefficacy of the remedy.

This conclusion cannot be invalidated by alleging, that the state in which the experiment was made, was at that crisis, and had been for a long time before, violently heated and distracted by the rage of party. Is it to be presumed, that at any future septennial epoch, the same state will be free from parties? Is it to be presumed that any other state, at the same, or any other given period, will be exempt from them? Such an event ought to be neither presumed nor desired; because an extinction of parties necessarily implies either a universal alarm for the public safety, or an absolute extinction of liberty.

Were the precaution taken of excluding from the assemblies elected by the people to revise the preceding administration of the government, all persons who should have been concerned in the government within the given period, the difficulties would not be obviated. The impor-

tant task would probably devolve on men, who, with inferior capacities, would in other respects be little better qualified. Although they might not have been personally concerned in the administration, and therefore not immediately agents in the measures to be examined; they would probably have been involved in the parties connected with these measures, and have been elected under their auspices.

PUBLIUS

No. 51

JAMES MADISON

The same subject continued, with the same view, and concluded

To what expedient then shall we finally resort, for maintaining in practice the necessary partition of power among the several departments, as laid down in the constitution? The only answer that can be given is, that as all these exterior provisions are found to be inadequate, the defect must be supplied, by so contriving the interior structure of the government, as that its several constituent parts may, by their mutual relations, be the means of keeping each other in their proper places. Without presuming to undertake a full developement of this important idea, I will hazard a few general observations, which may perhaps place it in a clearer light, and enable us to form a more correct judgment of the principles and structure of the government planned by the convention.

In order to lay a due foundation for that separate and distinct exercise of the different powers of government, which, to a certain extent, is admitted on all hands to be essential to the preservation of liberty, it is evident that each department should have a will of its own; and consequently should be so constituted, that the members of each should have as little agency as possible in the appointment of the members of the others. Were this principle rigorously adhered to, it would require that all the appointments for the supreme executive, legislative, and judiciary magistracies, should be drawn from the same fountain of authority, the people, through channels having no communication whatever with one another. Perhaps such a plan of constructing the several departments, would be less difficult in practice, than it may in contemplation appear. Some difficulties, however, and some additional expense, would attend the execution of it. Some deviations, therefore, from the principle must be admitted. In the constitution of the judiciary department in particular, it might be inexpedient to insist rigorously on the principle; first, because peculiar qualifications being essential in the members, the primary consideration ought to be to select that mode of choice which best secures these qualifications; secondly, because the permanent tenure by which the appointments are held in that department, must soon destroy all sense of dependence on the authority conferring them.

It is equally evident, that the members of each department should be as little dependent as possible on those of the others, for the emoluments annexed to their offices. Were the executive magistrate, or the judges, not independent of the legislature in this particular, their independence in every other, would be merely nominal.

But the great security against a gradual concentration of the several powers in the same department, consists in giving to those who administer each department, the necessary constitutional means, and personal motives, to resist encroachments of the others. The provision for defence must in this, as in all other cases, be made commensurate to the danger of attack. Ambition must be made to counteract ambition. The interest of the man, must be connected with the constitutional rights of the place. It may be a reflection on human nature, that such devices should be necessary to control the abuses of government. But what is government itself, but the greatest of all reflections on human nature? If men were angels, no government would be necessary. If angels were to govern men, neither external nor internal controls on government would be necessary. In framing a government which is to be administered by men over men, the great difficulty lies in this: you must first enable the government to control the governed; and in the next place oblige it to control itself. A dependence on the people is, no doubt, the primary control on the government; but experience has taught mankind the necessity of auxiliary precautions.

This policy of supplying, by opposite and rival interests, the defect of better motives, might be traced through the whole system of human affairs, private as well as public. We see it particularly displayed in all the subordinate distributions of power; where the constant aim is, to divide and arrange the several offices in such a manner as that each may be a check on the other; that the private interest of every individual may be a centinel over the public rights.

These inventions of prudence cannot be less requisite in the distribution of the supreme powers of the state.

But it is not possible to give to each department an equal power of self-defence. In republican government, the legislative authority necessarily predominates. The remedy for this inconveniency is, to divide the legislature into different branches; and to render them, by different modes of election, and different principles of action, as little connected with each other, as the nature of their common functions, and their common dependence on the society, will admit. It may even be necessary to guard against dangerous encroachments by still further precautions. As the weight of the legislative authority requires that it should be thus divided, the weakness of the executive may require, on the other hand, that it should be fortified. An absolute negative on the legislature, appears, at first view, to be the natural defence with which the executive magistrate should be armed. But perhaps it would be neither altogether safe, nor alone sufficient. On ordinary occasions, it might not be exerted with the requisite firmness; and on extraordinary occasions, it might be perfidiously abused. May not this defect of an absolute negative be supplied by some qualified connexion between this weaker department, and the weaker branch of the stronger department, by which the latter may be led to support the constitutional rights of the former, without being too much detached from the rights of its own department?

If the principles on which these observations are founded be just, as I persuade myself they are, and they be applied as a criterion to the several state constitutions, and to the federal constitution, it will be found, that if the latter does not perfectly correspond with them, the former are infinitely less able to bear such a test.

There are moreover two considerations particularly applicable to the federal system of America, which place that system in a very interesting point of view.

First. In a single republic, all the power surrendered by the people, is submitted to the administration of a single government; and the usurpations are guarded against, by a division of the government into distinct and separate departments. In the compound republic of America, the power surrendered by the people, is first divided between two distinct governments, and then the portion allotted to each subdivided among distinct and separate departments. Hence a double security arises to the rights of the people. The different governments will control each other; at the same time that each will be controled by itself.

Second. It is of great importance in a republic, not only to guard the society against the oppression of its rulers; but to guard one part of the society against the injustice of the other part. Different interests necessarily exist in different classes of citizens. If a majority be united by a common interest, the rights of the minority will be insecure. There are but two methods of providing against this evil: the one, by creating a will in the community independent of the majority, that is, of the society itself; the other, by comprehending in the society so many separate descriptions of citizens, as will render an unjust combination of a majority of the whole very improbable, if not impracticable. The first method prevails in all governments possessing an hereditary or self-appointed authority. This, at best, is but a precarious security; because a power independent of the society may as well espouse the unjust views of the major, as the rightful interests of the minor party, and may possibly be turned against both parties. The second method will be exemplified in the federal republic of the United States. Whilst all authority in it will be derived from, and dependent on the society, the society itself will be broken into so many parts, interests, and classes of citizens, that the rights of individuals, or of the minority, will be in little danger from interested combinations of the majority. In a free government, the security for civil rights must be the same as that for religious rights. It consists in the one case in the multiplicity of interests, and in the other, in the multiplicity of sects. The degree of security in both cases will depend on the number of interests and sects; and this may be presumed to depend on the extent of country and number of people comprehended under the same government. This view of the subject must particularly recommend a proper federal system to all the sincere and considerate friends of republican government: since it shows, that in exact proportion as the territory of the union may be formed into more circumscribed confederacies, or states, oppressive combinations of a majority will be facilitated; the best security under the republican form, for the rights of every class of citizens, will be diminished; and consequently, the stability and independence of some member of the government, the only other security, must be proportionally increased. Justice is the end of government. It is the end of civil society. It ever has been, and ever will be, pursued, until it be obtained, or until liberty be lost in the pursuit. In a society, under the forms of which the stronger faction can readily unite and oppress the weaker, anarchy may as truly be said to reign, as in a state of nature,

where the weaker individual is not secured against the violence of the stronger: and as, in the latter state, even the stronger individuals are prompted, by the uncertainty of their condition, to submit to a government which may protect the weak, as well as themselves: so, in the former state, will the more powerful factions or parties be gradually induced, by a like motive, to wish for a government which will protect all parties, the weaker as well as the more powerful. It can be little doubted, that if the state of Rhode Island was separated from the confederacy, and left to itself, the insecurity of rights under the popular form of government within such narrow limits, would be displayed by such reiterated oppressions of factious majorities, that some power altogether independent of the people, would soon be called for by the voice of the very factions whose misrule had proved the necessity of it. In the extended republic of the United States, and among the great variety of interests, parties, and sects, which it embraces, a coalition of a majority of the whole society could seldom take place upon any other principles, than those of justice and the general good: whilst there being thus less danger to a minor from the will of the major party, there must be less pretext also, to provide for the security of the former, by introducing into the government a will not dependent on the latter: or, in other words, a will independent of the society itself. It is no less certain than it is important, notwithstanding the contrary opinions which have been entertained, that the larger the society, provided it lie within a practicable sphere, the more duly capable it will be of self-government. And happily for the *republican cause,* the practicable sphere may be carried to a very great extent, by a judicious modification and mixture of the *federal principle.*

PUBLIUS

No. 78

ALEXANDER HAMILTON

A view of the constitution of the judicial department in relation to the tenure of good behaviour

We proceed now to an examination of the judiciary department of the proposed government.

In unfolding the defects of the existing confederation, the utility and necessity of a federal judicature have been clearly pointed out. It is the less necessary to recapitulate the considerations there urged, as the propriety of the institution in the abstract is not disputed: *the* only questions which have been raised being relative to the manner of constituting it, and to its extent. To these points, therefore, our observations shall be confined.

The manner of constituting it seems to embrace these several objects: 1st. The mode of appointing the judges. 2d. The tenure by which they are to hold their places. 3d. The partition of the judiciary authority between different courts, and their relations to each other.

First. As to the mode of appointing the judges: this is the same with that of appointing the officers of the union in general, and has been so fully discussed in the two last numbers, that nothing can be said here which would not be useless repetition.

Second. As to the tenure by which the judges are to hold their places: This chiefly concerns their duration in office; the provisions for their support; the precautions for their responsibility.

According to the plan of the convention, all the judges who may be appointed by the United States are to hold their offices *during good behaviour,* which is conformable to the most approved of the state constitutions . . . among the rest, to that of this state. Its propriety having been drawn into question by the adversaries of that plan, is no light symptom of the rage for objection, which disorders their imaginations and judgments. The standard of good behaviour for the continuance in office of the judicial magistracy is certainly one of the most valuable of the modern improvements in the practice of government. In a monarchy, it is an excellent barrier to the despotism of the prince: in a republic it is a no less excellent barrier to the encroachments and oppressions of the representative body. And it is the best expedient which can be devised in any government, to secure a steady, upright, and impartial administration of the laws.

Whoever attentively considers the different departments of power must perceive, that, in a government in which they are separated from each other, the judiciary, from the nature of its functions, will always be the least dangerous to the political rights of the constitution; because it will be least in a capacity to annoy or injure them. The executive not only dispenses the honours, but holds the sword of the community; the legislature not only commands the purse, but prescribes the rules by which the duties and rights of every citizen are to be regulated; the ju-

diciary, on the contrary, has no influence over either the sword or the purse; no direction either of the strength or of the wealth of the society; and can take no active resolution whatever. It may truly be said to have neither FORCE nor WILL, but merely judgment; and must ultimately depend upon the aid of the executive arm even for the efficacy of its judgments.

This simple view of the matter suggests several important consequences. It proves incontestably that the judiciary is beyond comparison the weakest of the three departments of power;* that it can never attack with success either of the other two; and that all possible care is requisite to enable it to defend itself against their attacks. It equally proves, that though individual oppression may now and then proceed from the courts of justice, the general liberty of the people can never be endangered from that quarter: I mean, so long as the judiciary remains truly distinct from both the legislature and the executive. For I agree that "there is no liberty, if the power of judging be not separated from the legislative and executive powers."† And it proves, in the last place, that as liberty can have nothing to fear from the judiciary alone, but would have everything to fear from its union with either of the other departments; that as all the effects of such a union must ensue from a dependence of the former on the latter, notwithstanding a nominal and apparent separation; that as from the natural feebleness of the judiciary, it is in continual jeopardy of being overpowered, awed or influenced by its coordinate branches; and that as nothing can contribute so much to its firmness and independence, as permanency in office, this quality may therefore be justly regarded as an indispensable ingredient in its constitution; and in a great measure as the citadel of the public justice and the public security.

The complete independence of the courts of justice is peculiarly essential in a limited constitution. By a limited constitution I understand one which contains certain specified exceptions to the legislative authority; such for instance as that it shall pass no bills of attainder, no *ex post facto* laws, and the like. Limitations of this kind can be preserved in practice no other way than through the medium

---

*The celebrated Montesquieu, speaking of them says, "of the three powers above mentioned, the JUDICIARY is next to nothing." Spirit of Laws, vol. 1, page 186.
†Idem. page 181.

of the courts of justice; whose duty it must be to declare all acts contrary to the manifest tenor of the constitution void. Without this, all the reservations of particular rights or privilege would amount to nothing.

Some perplexity respecting the rights of the courts to pronounce legislative acts void, because contrary to the constitution, has arisen from an imagination that the doctrine would imply a superiority of the judiciary to the legislative power. It is urged that the authority which can declare the acts of another void, must necessarily be superior to the one whose acts may be declared void. As this doctrine is of great importance in all the American constitutions, a brief discussion of the grounds on which it rests cannot be unacceptable.

There is no position which depends on clearer principles, than that every act of a delegated authority, contrary to the tenor of the commission under which it is exercised, is void. No legislative act therefore contrary to the constitution can be valid. To deny this would be to affirm that the deputy is greater than his principal; that the servant is above his master; that the representatives of the people are superior to the people themselves; that men acting by virtue of powers may do not only what their powers do not authorize, but what they forbid.

If it be said that the legislative body are themselves the constitutional judges of their own powers, and that the construction they put upon them is conclusive upon the other departments, it may be answered, that this cannot be the natural presumption, where it is not to be collected from any particular provisions in the constitution. It is not otherwise to be supposed that the constitution could intend to enable the representatives of the people to substitute their *will* to that of their constituents. It is far more rational to suppose that the courts were designed to be an intermediate body between the people and the legislature, in order, among other things, to keep the latter within the limits assigned to their authority. The interpretation of the laws is the proper and peculiar province of the courts. A constitution is in fact, and must be, regarded by the judges as a fundamental law. It therefore belongs to them to ascertain its meaning as well as the meaning of any particular act proceeding from the legislative body. If there should happen to be an irreconcilable variance between the two, that which has the superior obligation and validity ought of course to be preferred; or in other words, the constitution ought to be preferred to the statute, the intention of the people to the intention of their agents.

Nor does this conclusion by any means suppose a superiority of the judicial to the legislative power. It only supposes that the power of the people is superior to both; and that where the will of the legislature declared in its statutes, stands in opposition to that of the people declared in the constitution, the judges ought to be governed by the latter, rather than the former. They ought to regulate their decisions by the fundamental laws, rather than by those which are not fundamental.

This exercise of judicial discretion in determining between two contradictory laws, is exemplified in a familiar instance. It not uncommonly happens, that there are two statutes existing at one time, clashing in whole or in part with each other, and neither of them containing any repealing clause or expression. In such a case, it is the province of the courts to liquidate and fix their meaning and operation: So far as they can by any fair construction be reconciled to each other; reason and law conspire to dictate that this should be done. Where this is impracticable, it becomes a matter of necessity to give effect to one, in exclusion of the other. The rule which has obtained in the courts for determining their relative validity is that the last in order of time shall be preferred to the first. But this is a mere rule of construction, not derived from any positive law, but from the nature and reason of the thing. It is a rule not enjoined upon the courts by legislative provision, but adopted by themselves, as consonant to truth and propriety, for the direction of their conduct as interpreters of the law. They thought it reasonable, that between the interfering acts of an *equal* authority, that which was the last indication of its will, should have the preference.

But in regard to the interfering acts of a superior and subordinate authority, of an original and derivative power, the nature and reason of the thing indicate the converse of that rule as proper to be followed. They teach us that the prior act of a superior ought to be preferred to the subsequent act of an inferior and subordinate authority; and that, accordingly, whenever a particular statute contravenes the constitution, it will be the duty of the judicial tribunals to adhere to the latter, and disregard the former.

It can be of no weight to say, that the courts on the pretence of a repugnancy, may substitute their own pleasure to the constitutional intentions of the legislature. This might as well happen in the case of two contradictory statutes; or it might as well happen in every adjudication upon any single statute. The courts must declare the sense of the law; and if they should be disposed to exercise WILL instead of JUDGMENT, the consequence would equally be the substitution of their pleasure to that of the legislative body. The observation, if it proved anything, would prove that there ought to be no judges distinct from that body.

If then the courts of justice are to be considered as the bulwarks of a limited constitution against legislative encroachments, this consideration will afford a strong argument for the permanent tenure of judicial offices, since nothing will contribute so much as this to that independent spirit in the judges, which must be essential to the faithful performance of so arduous a duty.

This independence of the judges is equally requisite to guard the constitution and the rights of individuals from the effects of those ill humours which the arts of designing men, or the influence of particular conjunctures, sometimes disseminate among the people themselves, and which, though they speedily give place to better information and more deliberate reflection, have a tendency, in the mean time, to occasion dangerous innovations in the government, and serious oppressions of the minor party in the community. Though I trust the friends of the proposed constitution will never concur with its enemies, in questioning that fundamental principle of republican government, which admits the right of the people to alter or abolish the established constitution whenever they find it inconsistent with their happiness; yet it is not to be inferred from this principle, that the representatives of the people, whenever a momentary inclination happens to lay hold of a majority of their constituents incompatible with the provisions in the existing constitution, would, on that account, be justifiable in a violation of those provisions; or that the courts would be under a greater obligation to connive at infractions in this shape, than when they had proceeded wholly from the cabals of the representative body. Until the people have, by some solemn and authoritative act, annulled or changed the established form, it is binding upon themselves collectively, as well as individually: and no presumption, or even knowledge of their sentiments, can warrant their representatives in a departure from it, prior to such an act. But it is easy to see, that it would require an uncommon portion of fortitude in the judges to do their duty as faithful guardians of the constitution,

where legislative invasions of it had been instigated by the major voice of the community.

But it is not with a view to infractions of the constitution only, that the independence of the judges may be an essential safe-guard against the effects of occasional ill humours in the society. These sometimes extend no farther than to the injury of the private rights of particular classes of citizens, by unjust and partial laws. Here also the firmness of the judicial magistracy is of vast importance in mitigating the severity and confining the operation of such laws. It not only serves to moderate the immediate mischiefs of those which may have been passed, but it operates as a check upon the legislative body in passing them; who, perceiving that obstacles to the success of an iniquitous intention are to be expected from the scruples of the courts, are in a manner compelled, by the very motives of the injustice they meditate, to qualify their attempts. This is a circumstance calculated to have more influence upon the character of our governments, than but few may imagine. The benefits of the integrity and moderation of the judiciary have already been felt in more states than one; and though they may have displeased those whose sinister expectations they may have disappointed, they must have commanded the esteem and applause of all the virtuous and disinterested. Considerate men, of every description, ought to prize whatever will tend to beget or fortify that temper in the courts; as no man can be sure that he may not be tomorrow the victim of a spirit of injustice, by which he may be a gainer to-day. And every man must now feel, that the inevitable tendency of such a spirit is to sap the foundations of public and private confidence, and to introduce in its stead universal distrust and distress.

That inflexible and uniform adherence to the rights of the constitution, and of individuals, which we perceive to be indispensable in the courts of justice, can certainly not be expected from judges who hold their offices by a temporary commission. Periodical appointments, however regulated, or by whomsoever made, would, in some way or other, be fatal to their necessary independence. If the power of making them was committed either to the executive or legislature, there would be danger of an improper complaisance to the branch which possessed it; if to both, there would be an unwillingness to hazard the displeasure of either; if to the people, or to persons chosen by them for the special purpose, there would be too great a disposition to consult popularity, to justify a reliance that nothing would be consulted but the constitution and the laws.

There is yet a further and a weighty reason for the permanency of judicial offices; which is deducible from the nature of the qualifications they require. It has been frequently remarked, with great propriety, that a voluminous code of laws is one of the inconveniences necessarily connected with the advantages of a free government. To avoid an arbitrary discretion in the courts, it is indispensable that they should be bound down by strict rules and precedents, which serve to define and point out their duty in every particular case that comes before them; and it will readily be conceived, from the variety of controversies which grow out of the folly and wickedness of mankind, that the records of those precedents must unavoidably swell to a very considerable bulk, and must demand long and laborious study to acquire a competent knowledge of them. Hence it is, that there can be but few men in the society, who will have sufficient skill in the laws to qualify them for the stations of judges. And making the proper deductions for the ordinary depravity of human nature, the number must be still smaller of those who unite the requisite integrity with the requisite knowledge. These considerations apprize us, that the government can have no great option between fit characters; and that a temporary duration in office, which would naturally discourage such characters from quitting a lucrative line of practice to accept a seat on the bench, would have a tendency to throw the administration of justice into hands less able, and less well qualified, to conduct it with utility and dignity. In the present circumstances of this country, and in those in which it is likely to be for a long time to come, the disadvantages on this score would be greater than they may at first sight appear; but it must be confessed, that they are far inferior to those which present themselves under the other aspects of the subject.

Upon the whole, there can be no room to doubt, that the convention acted wisely in copying from the models of those constitutions which have established *good behaviour* as the tenure of judicial offices, in point of duration; and that, so far from being blameable on this account, their plan would have been inexcusably defective, if it had wanted this important feature of good government. The experience of Great Britain affords an illustrious comment on the excellence of the institution.

PUBLIUS

Address of the Minority of the Pennsylvania Convention

December 12, 1787

During debate over the Constitution's ratification by the Pennsylvania convention. The authors of "The Address and Reasons of Dissent of the Minority of the Convention of Pennsylvania to Their Constituents" were not allowed to have their views printed in the convention's official journal. The address was originally published in the *Pennsylvania Packet and Daily Advertiser* on December 18, 1787, and that is the version reprinted here. It narrates the troubles experienced by the Constitution's opponents in that state. It goes on to criticize the Constitution for failing to protect the rights of states and individuals, and proposes amendments to correct its flaws.

Address of the Minority of the Pennsylvania Convention

The Address and Reasons of Dissent of the Minority of the Convention of the State of Pennsylvania to their Constituents

It was not until after the termination of the late glorious contest, which made the people of the United States an independent nation, that any defect was discovered in the present confederation. It was formed by some of the ablest patriots in America. It carried us successfully through the war; and the virtue and patriotism of the people, with their disposition to promote the common cause, supplied the want of power in Congress.

The requisition of Congress for the five *per cent.* impost was made before the peace, so early as the first of February, 1781, but was prevented taking effect by the refusal of one state; yet it is probable every state in the union would have agreed to this measure at that period, had it not been for the extravagant terms in which it was demanded. The requisition was new moulded in the year 1783, and accompanied with an additional demand of certain supplementary funds for 25 years. Peace had now taken place, and the United States found themselves labouring under a considerable foreign and domestic debt, incurred during the war. The requisition of 1783 was commensurate with the interest of the debt, as it was then calculated; but it has been more accurately ascertained since that time. The domestic debt has been found to fall several millions of dollars short of the calculation, and it has lately been considerably diminished by large sales of the western-lands. The states have been called on by Congress annually for supplies until the general system of finance proposed in 1783 should take place.

It was at this time that the want of an efficient federal government was first complained of, and that the powers vested in Congress were found to be inadequate to the procuring of the benefits that should result from the union. The impost was granted by most of the states, but many refused the supplementary funds; the annual requisitions were set at nought by some of the states, while others complied with them by legislative acts, [but] were tardy in their payments, and Congress found themselves incapable of complying with their engagements, and supporting the federal government. It was found that our national character was sinking in the opinion of foreign nations. The Congress could make treaties of commerce, but could not enforce the observance of them. We were suffering from the restrictions of foreign nations, who had shackled our commerce, while we were unable to retaliate: and all now agreed that it would be advantageous to the union to enlarge the powers of Congress; that they should be enabled in the amplest manner to regulate commerce, and to lay and collect duties on the imports throughout the United States. With this view a convention was first proposed by Virginia, and finally recommended by Congress for the different states to appoint deputies to meet in convention, "for the purposes of revising and amending the present articles of confederation, so as to make them adequate to the exigencies of the union." This recommendation the legislatures of twelve states complied with so hastily as not to consult their constituents on the subject; and though the different legislatures had no authority from their constituents for the purpose, they probably apprehended the necessity would justify the measure; and none of them extended their ideas at that time further than "revising and amending the present articles of confederation." Pennsylvania by the act appointing deputies expressly confined their powers to this object; and though it is probable that some of the members of the assembly of this state had at that time in contemplation to annihilate the present confederation as well as the constitution of Pennsylvania, yet the plan was not sufficiently matured to communicate it to the public.

The majority of the legislature of this commonwealth, were at that time under the influence of the members from the city of Philadelphia. They agreed that the deputies sent by them to convention should have no compensation for their services, which determination was calculated to prevent the election of any member who resided at a distance from the city. It was in vain for the minority to attempt electing delegates to the convention, who understood the circumstances, and the feelings of the people, and had a common interest with them. They found a disposition in the leaders of the majority of the house to chuse themselves and some of their dependants. The minority attempted to prevent this by agreeing to vote for some of the leading members, who they knew had influence enough to be appointed at any rate, in hopes of carrying with them some respectable citizens of Philadelphia, in whose principles and integrity they could have more confidence; but even in this they were disappointed, except in one member; the eighth member was added at a subsequent session of the assembly.

The Continental convention met in the city of Philadelphia at the time appointed. It was composed of some men of excellent characters; of others who were more remarkable for their ambition and cunning, than their patriotism; and of some who had been opponents to the independence of the United States. The delegates from Pennsylvania were, six of them, uniform and decided opponents to the constitution of this commonwealth. The convention sat upwards of four months. The doors were kept shut, and the members brought under the most sol-

emn engagements of secrecy.* Some of those who opposed their going so far beyond their powers, retired, hopeless, from the convention, others had the firmness to refuse signing the plan altogether, and many who did sign it, did it not as a system they wholly approved, but as the best that could be then obtained, and notwithstanding the time spend on this subject, it is agreed on all hands to be a work of haste and accommodation.

Whilst the gilded chains were forging in the secret conclave, the meaner instruments of despotism without, were busily employed in alarming the fears of the people with dangers which did not exist, and exciting their hopes of greater advantages from the expected plan than even the best government on earth could produce.

The proposed plan had not many hours issued forth from the womb of suspicious secrecy, until such as were prepared for the purpose, were carrying about petitions for people to sign, signifying their approbation of the system, and requesting the legislature to call a convention. While every measure was taken to intimidate the people against opposing it, the public papers seemed with the most violent threats against those who should dare to think for themselves, and *tar and feathers* were liberally promised to all those who would not immediately join in supporting the proposed government be it what it would. Under such circumstances petitions in favour of calling a convention were signed by great numbers in and about the city, before they had leisure to read and examine the system, many of whom, now they are better acquainted with it, and have had time to investigate its principles, are heartily opposed to it. The petitions were speedily handed into the legislature.

Affairs were in this situation when on the 28th of September last a resolution was proposed to the assembly by a member of the house who had been also a member of the federal convention, for calling a state convention, to be elected within *ten* days for the purpose of examining and adopting the proposed constitution of the United States, though at this time the house had not received it from Congress. This attempt was opposed by a minority, who after offering every argument in their power to prevent the precipitate measure, without effect, absented themselves from the house as the only alternative left them, to prevent

*The Journals of the conclave are still concealed.

the measure taking place previous to their constituents being acquainted with the business—That violence and outrage which had been so often threatened was now practised; some of the members were seized the next day by a mob collected for the purpose, and forcibly dragged to the house, and there detained by force whilst the quorum of the legislature, *so formed,* compleated their resolution. We shall dwell no longer on this subject, the people of Pennsylvania have been already acquainted therewith. We would only further observe that every member of the legislature, previously to taking his seat, by solemn oath or affirmation, declares, "that he will not do or consent to any act or thing whatever that shall have a tendency to lessen or abridge their rights and privileges, as declared in the constitution of this state." And that constitution which they are so solemnly sworn to support cannot legally be altered but by a recommendation of the council of censors, who alone are authorised to propose alterations and amendments, and even these must be published at least *six months,* for the consideration of the people.—The proposed system of government for the United States, if adopted, will [alter] and may annihilate the constitution of Pennsylvania; and therefore the legislature had no authority whatever to recommend the calling a convention for that purpose. This proceeding could not be considered as binding on the people of this commonwealth. The house was formed by violence, some of the members composing it were detained there by force, which alone would have vitiated any proceedings, to which they were otherwise competent; but had the legislature been legally formed, this business was absolutely without their power.

In this situation of affairs were the subscribers elected members of the convention of Pennsylvania. A convention called by a legislature in direct violation of their duty, and composed in part of members, who were compelled to attend for that purpose, to consider of a constitution proposed by a convention of the United States, who were not appointed for the purpose of framing a new form of government, but whose powers were expressly confined to altering and amending the present articles of confederation.—Therefore the members of the continental convention in proposing the plan acted as individuals, and not as deputies from Pennsylvania.* The assembly who called the

state convention acted as individuals, and not as the legislature of Pennsylvania; nor could they or the convention chosen on their recommendation have authority to do any [act] or thing, that can alter or annihilate the constitution of Pennsylvania (both of which will be done by the new constitution) nor are their proceedings in our opinion, at all binding on the people.

The election for members of the convention was held at so early a period and the want of information was so great, that some of us did not know of it until after it was over, and we have reason to believe that great numbers of the people of Pennsylvania have not yet had an opportunity of sufficiently examining the proposed constitution—We apprehend that no change can take place that will affect the internal government or constitution of this commonwealth, unless a majority of the people should evidence a wish for such a change; but on examining the number of votes given for members of the present state convention, we find that of upwards of *seventy thousand* freemen who are intitled to vote in Pennsylvania, the whole convention has been elected by about *thirteen thousand* voters, and though *two thirds* of the members of the convention have thought proper to ratify the proposed constitution, yet those *two thirds* were elected by the votes of only *six thousand and eight hundred* freemen.

In the city of Philadelphia and some of the eastern counties, the junto that took the lead in the business agreed to vote for none but such as would solemnly promise to adopt the system in *toto,* without exercising their judgment. In many of the counties the people did not attend the elections as they had not an opportunity of judging of the plan. Others did not consider themselves bound by the call of a set of men who assembled at the state-house in Philadelphia, and assumed the name of the legislature of Pennsylvania; and some were prevented from voting by the violence of the party who were determined at all events to force down the measure. To such lengths did the tools of despotism carry their outrage, that in the night of the election for members of convention, in the city of Phila-

---

*The continental convention in direct violation of the 13th article of the confederation, have declared, "that the ratification of nine states

shall be sufficient for the establishment of this constitution, between the states so ratifying the same."—Thus has the plighted faith of the states been sported with! They had solemnly engaged that the confederation now subsisting should be inviolably preserved by each of them, and the union thereby formed, should be perpetual, unless the same should be altered by mutual consent.

delphia, several of the subscribers (being then in the city to transact your business) were grossly abused, ill-treated and insulted while they were quiet in their lodgings, though they did not interfere, nor had any thing to do with the said election, but, as they apprehend, because they were supposed to be adverse to the proposed constitution, and would not tamely surrender those sacred rights, which you had committed to their charge.

The convention met, and the same disposition was soon manifested in considering the proposed constitution, that had been exhibited in every other stage of the business. We were prohibited by an express vote of the convention, from taking any question on the separate articles of the plan, and reduced to the necessity of adopting or rejecting *in toto.*—'Tis true the majority permitted us to debate on each article, but restrained us from proposing amendments.—They also determined not to permit us to enter on the minutes our reasons of dissent against any of the articles, nor even on the final question our reasons of dissent against the whole. Thus situated we entered on the examination of the proposed system of government, and found it to be such as we could not adopt, without, as we conceived, surrendering up your dearest rights. We offered our objections to the convention, and opposed those parts of the plan, which, in our opinion, would be injurious to you, in the best manner we were able; and closed our arguments by offering the following propositions to the convention.

1. The right of conscience shall be held inviolable; and neither the legislative, executive nor judicial powers of the United States shall have authority to alter, abrogate, or infringe any part of the constitution of the several states, which provide for the preservation of liberty in matters of religion.

2. That in controversies respecting property, and in suits between man and man, trial by jury shall remain as heretofore, as well in the federal courts, as in those of the several states.

3. That in all capital and criminal prosecutions, a man has a right to demand the cause and nature of his accusation, as well in the federal courts, as in those of the several states; to be heard by himself and his counsel; to be confronted with the accusers and witnesses; to call for evidence in his favor, and a speedy trial by an impartial jury of his vicinage, without whose unanimous consent, he cannot be found guilty, nor can he be compelled to give evidence against himself; and that no man be deprived of his liberty, except by the law of the land or the judgment of his peers.

4. That excessive bail ought not to be required, nor excessive fines imposed, nor cruel nor unusual punishments inflicted.

5. That warrants unsupported by evidence, whereby any officer or messenger may be commanded or required to search suspected places, or to seize any person or persons, his or their property, not particularly described, are grievous and oppressive, and shall not be granted either by the magistrates of the federal government or others.

6. That the people have a right to the freedom of speech, of writing and publishing their sentiments, therefore, the freedom of the press shall not be restrained by any law of the United States.

7. That the people have a right to bear arms for the defense of themselves and their own state, or the United States, or for the purpose of killing game; and no law shall be passed for disarming the people or any of them, unless for crimes committed, or real danger of public injury from individuals; and as standing armies in the time of peace are dangerous to liberty, they ought not to be kept up: and that the military shall be kept under strict subordination to and be governed by the civil powers.

8. The inhabitants of the several states shall have liberty to fowl and hunt in seasonable times, on the lands they hold, and on all other lands in the United States not inclosed, and in like manner to fish in all navigable waters, and others not private property, without being restrained therein by any laws to be passed by the legislature of the United States.

9. That no law shall be passed to restrain the legislatures of the several states from enacting laws for imposing taxes, except imposts and duties on goods imported or exported, and that no taxes, except imposts and duties upon goods imported and exported, and postage on letters shall be levied by the authority of Congress.

10. That the house of representatives be properly increased in number; that elections shall remain free; that the several states shall have power to regulate the elections for senators and representatives, without being controuled either directly or indirectly by any interference on the part of the Congress; and that elections of representatives be annual.

11. That the power of organizing, arming and disciplin-

ing the militia (the manner of disciplining the militia to be prescribed by Congress) remain with the individual states, and that Congress shall not have authority to call or march any of the militia out of their own state, without the consent of such state, and for such length of time only as such state shall agree.

That the sovereignty, freedom and independency of the several states shall be retained, and every power, jurisdiction and right which is not by this constitution expressly delegated to the United States in Congress assembled.

12. That the legislative, executive, and judicial powers be kept separate; and to this end that a constitutional council be appointed, to advise and assist the president, who shall be responsible for the advice they give, hereby the senators would be relieved from almost constant attendance; and also that the judges be made completely independent.

13. That no treaty which shall be directly opposed to the existing laws of the United States in Congress assembled, shall be valid until such laws shall be repealed, or made conformable to such treaty; neither shall any treaties be valid which are in contradiction to the constitution of the United States, or the constitutions of the several states.

14. That the judiciary power of the United States shall be confined to cases affecting ambassadors, other public ministers and consuls; to cases of admiralty and maritime jurisdiction; to controversies to which the United States shall be a party; to controversies between two or more states—between a state and citizens of different states—between citizens claiming lands under grants of different states; and between a state or the citizens thereof and foreign states, and in criminal cases, to such only as are expressly enumerated in the constitution, & that the United States in Congress assembled, shall not have power to enact laws, which shall alter the laws of descents and distribution of the effects of deceased persons, the titles of lands or goods, or the regulation of contracts in the individual states.

After reading these propositions, we declared our willingness to agree to the plan, provided it was so amended as to meet those propositions, or something similar to them: and finally moved the convention to adjourn, to give the people of Pennsylvania time to consider the subject, and determine for themselves; but these were all rejected, and the final vote was taken, when our duty to you induced us to vote against the proposed plan, and to decline signing the ratification of the same.

During the discussion we met with many insults, and some personal abuse; we were not even treated with decency, during the sitting of the convention, by the persons in the gallery of the house; however, we flatter ourselves that in contending for the preservation of those invaluable rights you have thought proper to commit to our charge, we acted with a spirit becoming freemen, and being desirous that you might know the principles which actuated our conduct, and being prohibited from inserting our reasons of dissent on the minutes of the convention, we have subjoined them for your consideration, as to you alone we are accountable. It remains with you whether you will think those inestimable privileges, which you have so ably contended for, should be sacrificed at the shrine of despotism, or whether you mean to contend for them with the same spirit that has so often baffled the attempts of an aristocratic faction, to rivet the shackles of slavery on you and your unborn posterity.

Our objections are comprised under three general heads of dissent, viz.

We dissent, first, because it is the opinion of the most celebrated writers on government, and confirmed by uniform experience, that a very extensive territory cannot be governed on the principles of freedom, otherwise than by a confederation of republics, possessing all the powers of internal government; but united in the management of their general, and foreign concerns.

If any doubt could have been entertained of the truth of the foregoing principle, it has been fully removed by the concession of *Mr. Wilson,* one of majority on this question, and who was one of the deputies in the late general convention. In justice to him, we will give his own words; they are as follows, viz. "The extent of country for which the new constitution was required, produced another difficulty in the business of the federal convention. It is the opinion of some celebrated writers, that to a small territory, the democratical; to a middling territory (as Montesquieu has termed it) the monarchial; and to an extensive territory, the despotic form of government is best adapted. Regarding then the wide and almost unbounded jurisdiction of the United States, at first view, the hand of despotism seemed necessary to controul, connect, and protect it; and hence the chief embarrassment rose. For, we know that, altho' our constituents would chearfully submit to the legislative restraints of a free government, they would spure at every attempt to shackle them with despotic power."—And again in another part of his speech he continues.—"Is it probable that the dissolution of the state governments, and the establishment of one *consolidated empire* would be eligible in its nature, and satisfactory to the people in its administration? I think not, as I have given reasons to shew that so extensive a territory could not be governed, connected, and preserved, but by the *supremacy of despotic power.* All the exertions of the most potent emperors of Rome were not capable of keeping that empire together, which in extent was far inferior to the dominion of America."

We dissent, secondly, because the powers vested in Congress by this constitution, must necessarily annihilate and absorb the legislative, executive, and judicial powers of the several states, and produce from their ruins one consolidated government, which from the nature of things will be *an iron banded despotism,* as nothing short of the supremacy of despotic sway could connect and govern these United States under one government.

As the truth of this position is of such decisive importance, it ought to be fully investigated, and if it is founded to be clearly ascertained; for, should it be demonstrated, that the powers vested by this constitution in Congress will have such an effect as necessarily to produce one consolidated government, the question then will be reduced to this short issue, viz. whether satiated with the blessings of liberty; whether repenting of the folly of so recently asserting their unalienable rights, against foreign despots at the expence of so much blood and treasure, and such painful and arduous struggles, the people of America are now willing to resign every privilege of freemen, and submit to the dominion of an absolute government, that will embrace all America in one chain of despotism; or whether they will with virtuous indignation, sparn at the shackles prepared for them, and confirm their liberties by a conduct becoming freemen.

That the new government will not be a confederacy of states, as it ought, but one consolidated government, founded upon the destruction of the several governments of the states, we shall now shew.

The powers of Congress under the new constitution, are complete and unlimited over the *purse* and the *sword,* and are perfectly independent of, and supreme over, the state governments; whose intervention in these great points is entirely destroyed. By virtue of their power of taxation, Congress may command the whole, or any part of the property of the people. They may impose what imposts upon commerce; they may impose what land taxes, poll taxes, excises, duties on all written instruments, and duties on every other article that they may judge proper; in short, every species of taxation, whether of an external or internal nature is comprised in section the 8th, of article the 1st, viz. "The Congress shall have power to lay and collect taxes, duties, imposts, and excises, to pay the debts, and provide for the common defence and general welfare of the United States."

As there is no one article of taxation reserved to the state governments, the Congress may monopolise every source of revenue, and thus indirectly demolish the state governments, for without funds they could not exist, the taxes, duties and excises imposed by Congress may be so high as to render it impracticable to levy further sums on the same articles; but whether this should be the case or not, if the state governments should presume to impose taxes, duties or excises, on the same articles with Congress, the latter may abrogate and repeal the laws whereby they are imposed, upon the allegation that they interfere with the due collection of their taxes, duties or excises, by virtue of the following clause, part of section 8th, article 1st. viz. "To make all laws which shall be necessary and proper for carrying into execution the foregoing powers, and all other powers vested by this constitution in the government of the United States, or in any department or officer thereof[.]"

The Congress might gloss over this conduct by construing every purpose for which the state legislatures now lay taxes, to be for the "*general welfare,*" and therefore as of their jurisdiction.

And the supremacy of the laws of the United States is established by article 6th, viz. "That this constitution and the laws of the United States, which shall be made in pursuance thereof, and *all treaties* made, or which shall be made, under the authority of the United States, shall be the *supreme law of the land; and the judges in every state shall be bound thereby; any thing in the constitution or laws of any state to the contrary notwithstanding.*" It has been alledged that the words "pursuant to the constitution," are a restriction upon the authority of Congress; but when it is considered that by other sections they are invested with every efficient power of government, and which may be exercised to the absolute destruction of the state governments, without any violation of even the forms of the constitution, this seeming restriction, as well as every other restriction in it, appears to us to be nugatory and delusive; and only introduced as a blind upon the real nature of the government. In our opinion, "pursuant to the constitution," will be coextensive with the *will* and *pleasure* of Congress, which, indeed, will be the only limitation of their powers.

We apprehend that two co-ordinate sovereignties would be a solecism in politics. That therefore as there is no line of distinction drawn between the general, and state governments; as the sphere of their jurisdiction is undefined, it would be contrary to the nature of things, that both should exist together, one or the other would necessarily triumph in the fullness of dominion. However the contest could not be of long continuance, as the state governments are divested of every means of defence, and will be obliged by "the supreme law of the land" *to yield at discretion.*

It has been objected to this total destruction of the state governments, that the existence of their legislatures is made essential to the organization of Congress; that they must assemble for the appointment of the senators and president general of the United States. True, the state legislatures may be continued for some years, as boards of appointment, merely, after they are divested of every other function, but the framers of the constitution foreseeing that the people will soon be disgusted with this solemn mockery of a government without power and usefulness, have made a provision for relieving them from the imposition, in section 4th, of article 1st, viz. "The times, places, and manner of holding elections for senators and representatives, shall be prescribed in each state by the legislature thereof; *but the Congress may at any time, by law make or alter such regulations; except as to the place of chusing senators.*"

As Congress have the controul over the time of the appointment of the president general, of the senators and of the representatives of the United States, they may prolong their existence in office, for life, by postponing the time of their election and appointment, from period to period, under various pretences, such as an apprehension of invasion, the factious disposition of the people, or any other plausible presence that the occasion may suggest; and having thus obtained life-estates in the government, they may fill up the vacancies themselves, by their controul over the mode of appointment; with this exception in regard to the senators, that as the place of appointment for them, must, by the constitution, be in the particular state, they may depute some body in the respective states, to fill up the vacancies in the senate, occasioned by death, until they can venture to assume it themselves. In this manner, may the only restriction in this clause be evaded. By virtue of the foregoing section, when the spirit of the people shall be gradually broken; when the general government shall be firmly established, and when a numerous standing army shall render opposition vain, the Congress may compleat the system of despotism, in renouncing all dependence on the people, by continuing themselves and children in the government.

The celebrated *Montesquieu,* in his Spirit of Laws, vol. 1, page 12th, says, "That in a democracy there can be no exercise of sovereignty, but by the suffrages of the people, which are their will; now the sovereigns will is the sovereign himself; the laws therefore, which establish the right of suffrage, are fundamental to this government. In fact, it is as important to regulate in a republic in what manner, by whom, and concerning what suffrages are to be given, as it is in a monarchy to know who is the prince, and after what manner he ought to govern." The *time, mode* and *place* of the election of representatives, senators and president general of the United States, ought not to be under the controul of Congress, but fundamentally ascertained and established.

The new constitution, consistently with the plan of consolidation, contains no reservation of the rights and privileges of the state governments, which was made in the confederation of the year 1778, by article the 2d, viz. "That each state retains its sovereignty, freedom, and independence, and every power, jurisdiction and right, which is not by this confederation expressly delegated to the United States in Congress assembled."

The legislative power vested in Congress by the foregoing recited sections, is so unlimited in its nature; may be so comprehensive and boundless its exercise, that this alone would be amply sufficient to annihilate the state governments, and swallow them up in the grand vortex of general empire.

The judicial powers vested in Congress are also so various and extensive, that by legal ingenuity they may be extended to every case, and thus absorb the state judiciaries, and when we consider the decisive influence that a general judiciary would have over the civil polity of the several states, we do not hesitate to pronounce that this power, unaided by the legislative, would effect a consolidation of the states under one government.

The powers of a court of equity, vested by this constitution, in the tribunals of Congress; powers which do not exist in Pennsylvania, unless so far as they can be incorporated with jury trial, would, in this state, greatly contribute to this event. The rich and wealthy suitors would eagerly lay hold of the infinite makes, perplexities and delays, which a court of chancery, with the appellate powers of the supreme court in fact as well as law would furnish him with, and thus the poor man being plunged in the bottomless pit of legal discussion, would drop his demand in despair.

In short, consolidation pervades the whole constitution. It begins with an annunciation that such was the intention. The main pillars of the fabric correspond with it, and the concluding paragraph is a confirmation of it. The preamble begins with the words, "We the people of the United States," which is the style of a compact between individuals entering into a state of society, and not that of a confederation of states. The other features of consolidation, we have before noticed.

Thus we have fully established the position, that the powers vested by this constitution in Congress, will effect a consolidation of the states under one government, which even the advocates of this constitution admit, could not be done without the sacrifice of all liberty.

3. We dissent, Thirdly, Because if it were practicable to govern so extensive a territory as these United States includes, on the plan of a consolidated government, consistent with the principles of liberty and the happiness of the people, yet the construction of this constitution is not calculated to attain the object, for independent of the nature of the case, it would of itself, necessarily produce a despotism, and that not by the usual gradations, but with the celerity that has hitherto only attended revolutions effected by the sword.

To establish the truth of this position, a cursory investigation of the principles and form of this constitution will suffice.

The first consideration that this review suggests, is the emission of a BILL OF RIGHTS ascertaining and fundamentally establishing those unalienable and personal rights of men, without the full, free, and secure enjoyment of which there can be no liberty, and over which it is not necessary for a good government to have the controul. The principal of which are the rights of conscience, personal liberty by the clear and unequivocal establishment of the writ of *habeas corpus,* jury trial in criminal and civil cases, by an impartial jury of the vicinage or county, with the common law proceedings, for the safety of the accused in criminal prosecutions and the liberty of the press, that scourge of tyrants; and the grand bulwark of every other liberty and privilege; the stipulations heretofore made in saving of them in the state constitutions, are entirely superceded by this constitution.

The legislature of a free country should be so formed as to have a competent knowledge of its constituents, and enjoy their confidence. To produce these essential requisites, the representation ought to be fair, equal, and sufficiently numerous, to possess the same interests, feelings, opinions, and views, which the people themselves would possess, were they all assembled; and so numerous as to prevent bribery and undue influence, and so responsible to the people, by frequent and fair elections, as to prevent their neglecting or sacrificing the views and interests of their constituents, to their own pursuits.

We will now bring the legislature under this constitution to the test of the foregoing principles, which will demonstrate, that it is deficient in every essential quality of a just and fare representation.

The house of representatives is to consist of [65] members; that is one for about every 50,000 inhabitants, to be chosen every two years. Thirty-three members will form a quorum for doing business, and 17 of these, being the majority, determine the sense of the house.

The senate, the other constituent branch of the legislature, consists of 26 members, being *two* from each state, appointed by their legislatures every six years—fourteen senators make a quorum; the majority of whom, eight, determines the sense of the body; except in judging on impeachments, or in making treaties, or in expelling a member, when two thirds of the senators present, must concur.

The president is to have the controul over the enacting of laws, so far as to make the concurrence of *two* thirds of the representatives and senators present necessary, if he should object to the laws.

Thus it appears that the liberties, happiness, interests, and great concerns of the whole United States, may be dependent upon the integrity, virtue, wisdom, and knowledge of 25 or 26 men.—How unadequate and unsafe a representation! Inadequate, because the sense and views of 3 or 4 millions of people diffused over so extensive a territory comprising such various climates, products, habits, interests, and opinions, cannot be collected in so small a body; and besides, it is not a fair and equal representation of the people even in proportion to its number, for the smallest state has as much weight in the senate as the largest, and from the smallness of the number to be chosen for both branches of the legislature; and from the mode of election and appointment, which is under the controul of Congress; and from the nature of the thing, men of the most elevated rank in life will alone be chosen. The other orders in the society, such as farmers, traders, and mechanics, who all ought to have a competent number of their best informed men in the legislature, will be totally unrepresented.

The representation is unsafe, because in the exercise of such great powers and trusts, it is so exposed to corruption and undue influence, by the gift of the numerous places of honor and emolument, at the disposal of the executive; by the arts and address of the great and designing; and by direct bribery.

The representation is moreover inadequate and unsafe, because of the long terms for which it is appointed, and the mode of its appointment, by which Congress may not only controul the choice of the people, but may so manage as to divest the people of this fundamental right, and become self elected.

The number of members in the house of representatives *may* be encreased to one for every 30,000 inhabitants. But when we consider, that this cannot be done without the consent of the senate, who from their share in the legislative, in the executive, and judicial departments, and permanency of appointment, will be the great efficient body in this government, and whose weight and predominance would be abridged by an increase of the representatives, we are persuaded that this is a circumstance that cannot be expected. On the contrary, the number of representatives will probably be continued at 65, although the population of the country may swell to treble what it now is; unless a revolution should effect a change.

We have before noticed the judicial power as it would effect a consolidation of the states into one government; we will now examine it, as it would affect the liberties and welfare of the people, supposing such a government were practicable and proper.

The judicial power, under the proposed constitution, is founded on the well-known principles of the *civil law*, by which the judge determines both on law and fact, and appeals are allowed from the inferior tribunals to the superior, upon the whole question; so that *facts* as well as *law*, would be re-examined, and even new facts brought forward in the court of appeals and to use the words of a very eminent Civilian—"The cause is many times another thing before the court of appeals, than what it was at the time of the first sentence."

That this mode of proceeding is the one which must be adopted under this constitution, is evident from the following circumstances:—1st. That the trial by jury, which is the grand characteristic of the common law, is secured by the constitution, only in criminal cases.—2d. That the appeal from both *law* and *fact* is expressly established, which is utterly inconsistent with the principles of the common law, and trials by jury. The only mode in which an appeal from law and fact can be established, is, by adopting the principles and practice of the civil law; unless the United States should be drawn into the absurdity of calling and swearing juries, merely for the purpose of contradicting their verdicts, which would render juries contemptible and worse than useless.—3d. That the courts to be established would decide on all cases *of law and equity,* which is a well known characteristic of the civil law, and these courts would have conusance not only of the laws of the United States and of treaties, and of cases affecting ambassadors, but of all cases of *admiralty and maritime jurisdiction,* which last are matters belonging exclusively to the civil law, in every nation in Christendom.

Not to enlarge upon the loss of the invaluable right of trial by an unbiassed jury, so dear to every friend of liberty, the monstrous expence and inconveniences of the mode of proceeding to be adopted, are such as will prove intolerable to the people of this country. The lengthy proceedings of the civil law courts in the chancery of England, and in the courts of Scotland and France, are such that few men of moderate fortune can endure the expence of; the poor man must therefore submit to the wealthy. Length of purse will too often prevail against right and justice. For instance, we are told by the learned judge *Blackstone,* that a question only on the property of an ox[,] of the value of *three* guineas, originating under the civil law proceedings in Scotland, after many interlocutory orders and sentences below, was carried at length from the court of sessions, the highest court in that part of Great Britain, by way of *appeal* to the house of lords, where the question of law and fact was finally determined. He adds, that no pique or spirit could in the court of king's bench or common pleas at Westminster, have given continuance to such a cause for a tenth part of the time, nor have cost a twentieth part of the expence. Yet the costs in the courts of king's bench and common pleas in England, are infinitely greater than those which the people of this country have ever experienced. We abhor the idea of losing the transcendant privilege of trial by jury, with the loss of which, it is remarked by the same learned author, that in Sweden, the liberties of the commons were extinguished by an aristocratic senate; and that *trial by jury* and the liberty of the people went together. At the same time we regret the intolerable delay, the enormous expences and infinite vexation to which the people of this country will be exposed from the voluminous proceedings of the courts of civil law, and especially from the appellate jurisdiction, by means of which a man may be drawn from the utmost boundaries of this extensive country to the seat of the supreme court of the nation to contend, perhaps with a wealthy and powerful adversary. The consequence of this establishment will be an absolute confirmation of the power of aristocratical influence in the courts of justice; for the common people will not be able to contend or struggle against it.

Trial by jury in criminal cases may also be excluded by declaring that the libeller for instance shall be liable to an action of debt for a specified sum thus evading the common law prosecution by indictment and trial by jury. And the common course of proceeding against a ship for breach of revenue laws by information (which will be classed among civil causes) will at the civil law be within the resort of a court, where no jury intervenes. Besides, the benefit of jury trial, in cases of a criminal nature, which cannot be evaded, will be rendered of little value, by calling the accused to answer far from home; there being no provision that the trial be by a jury of the neighbourhood or country. Thus an inhabitant of Pittsburgh, on a charge of crime committed on the banks of the Ohio, may be obliged to defend himself at the side of the Delaware, and so *vice versa:* To conclude this head: we observe that the judges of the courts of Congress would not be independent, as they are not debarred from holding other offices, during the pleasure of the president and senate, and as they may derive their support in part from fees, alterable by the legislature.

The next consideration that the constitution presents, is the undue and dangerous mixture of the powers of government: the same body possessing legislative, executive, and judicial powers. The senate is a constituent branch of the legislature, it has judicial power in judging on impeachments, and in this case unites in some measure the characters of judge and party as all the principal officers are appointed by the president-general with the concurrence of the senate and therefore they derive their offices in part from the senate. This may bias the judgments of the senators, and tend to screen great delinquents from punishment. And the senate has, moreover, various and great executive powers, viz. in concurrence with the president-general, they form treaties with foreign nations, that may controul and abrogate the constitutions and laws of the several states. Indeed, there is no power, privilege or liberty of the state governments, or of the people, but what may be affected by virtue of this power. For all treaties, made by them, are to be the "supreme law of the land: any thing in the constitution or laws of any state, to the contrary notwithstanding."

And this great power may be exercised by the president and 10 senators (being two thirds of 14, which is a quorum of that body). What an inducement would this offer to the ministers of foreign powers to compass by bribery *such concessions* as could not otherwise be obtained. It is the unvaried usage of all free states, whenever treaties interfere with the positive laws of the land, to make the intervention of the legislature necessary to give them operation. This became necessary, and was afforded by the parliament of Great-Britain, in consequence of the late commercial treaty between that kingdom and France—As the senate judges on impeachments, who is to try the members of the senate for the abuse of this power! And none of the great appointments to office can be made without the consent of the senate.

Such various, extensive, and important powers combined in one body of men, are inconsistent with all freedom; the celebrated Montesquieu tells us, that "when the legislative and executive powers are united in the same person, or in the same body of magistrates, there can be no liberty, because apprehensions may arise, lest the same monarch or *senate* should enact tyrannical laws, to execute them in a tyrannical manner."

"Again, there is no liberty, if the power of judging be not separated from the legislative and executive powers. Were it joined with the legislative, the life and liberty of the subject would be exposed to arbitrary controul; for the judge would then be legislator. Were it joined to the executive power, the judge might behave with all the violence of an oppressor. There would be an end of every thing, were the same man, or the same body of the nobles, or of the people, to exercise those three powers; that of enacting laws; that of executing the public resolutions; and that of judging the crimes or differences of individuals."

The president general is dangerously connected with the senate; his coincidence with the views of the ruling junto in that body, is made essential to his weight and importance in the government, which will destroy the independency and purity in the executive department, and having the power of pardoning without the concurrence of a council, he may skreen from punishment the most [treasonable] attempts that may be made on the liberties of the people, when instigated by his enadjutors in the senate. Instead of this dangerous and improper mixture of the executive with the legislative and judicial, the supreme executive powers ought to have been placed in the president, with a small independent council, made personally responsible for every appointment to office or other act, by having their opinions recorded; and that without the concurrence of the majority of the quorum of this council, the president should not be capable of taking any step.

The power of direct taxation applies to every individual, as congress, under this government, is expressly vested with the authority of laying a capitation or poll tax upon every person to any amount. This is a tax that, however oppressive in its nature, and unequal in its operation, is certain as to its produce and simple in its collection; it cannot be evaded like the objects of imposts or excise, and will be paid, because all that a man hath will he give for his head. This tax is so congenial to the nature of despotism, that it has ever been a favorite under such governments. Some of those who were in the late general convention from this state, have long laboured to introduce a poll-tax among us.

The power of direct taxation will further apply to every individual as congress may tax land, cattle, trades, occupations &c. to any amount, and every object of internal taxation is of that nature that however oppressive, the people will have but this alternative, either to pay the tax, or let their property be taken, for all resistance will be vain. The standing army and select militia would enforce the collection.

For the moderate exercise of this power, there is no controul left in the state governments, whose intervention is destroyed. No relief, or redress of grievances can be extended, as heretofore by them. There is not even a declaration of RIGHTS to which the people may appeal for the vindication of their wrongs in the court of justice. They must therefore, implicitly, obey the most arbitrary laws, as the worst of them will be pursuant to the principles and form of the constitution, and that strongest of all checks upon the conduct of administration, *responsibility to the people,* will not exist in this government. The permanency of the appointments of senators and representatives, and the controul the congress have over their election, will place them independent of the sentiments and resentment of the people, and the administration having a greater interest in the government than in the community, there will be no consideration to restrain them from oppression and tyranny. In the government of this state, under the old confederation, the members of the legislature are taken from among the people, and their interests and welfare are so inseparably connected with those of their constituents, that they can derive no advantage from oppressive laws and taxes, for they would suffer in common with their fellow citizens; would participate in the burthens they impose on the community, as they must return to the common level, after a short period; and notwithstanding every exertion of influence, every means of corruption, a necessary rotation excludes them from permanency in the legislature.

This large state is to have but ten members in that Congress which is to have the liberty, property and dearest concerns of every individual in this vast country at absolute command and even these ten persons, who are to be our only guardians; who are to supercede the legislature of Pennsylvania, will not be of the choice of the people, nor amenable to them. From the mode of their election and appointment they will consist of the lordly and high-minded; of men who will have no congenial feelings with the people, but a perfect indifference for, and contempt of them; they will consist of those harpies of power, that prey upon the very vitals; that riot on the miseries of the community. But we will suppose, although in all probability it may never be realized in fact, that our deputies in Congress have the welfare of their constituents at heart, and will exert themselves in their behalf, what security could even this afford; what relief could they extend to their oppressed constituents? To attain this, the majority of the deputies of the twelve other states in Congress must be alike well disposed; must alike forego the sweets of power, and relinquish the pursuits of ambition which from the nature of things is not to be expected. If the people part with a responsible representation in the legislature, founded upon fair, certain and frequent elections, they have nothing left they can call their own. Miserable is the lot of that people whose every concern depends on the WILL and PLEASURE of their rulers. Our soldiers will become Janissaries, and our officers of government Bashaws; in short, the system of despotism will soon be compleated.

From the foregoing investigation, it appears that the Congress under this constitution will not possess the confidence of the people, which is an essential requisite in a good government; for unless the laws command the confidence and respect of the great body of the people so as to induce them to support them, when called on by the civil magistrate they must be executed by the aid of a numerous standing army, which would be inconsistent with every idea of liberty; for the same force that may be employed to compel obedience to good laws, might and probably would be used to wrest from the people their constitutional liberties. The framers of this constitution appear to have been aware of this great deficiency; to have been sensible that no dependence could be placed on the people for their support; but on the contrary, that the government must be executed by force. They have therefore made a provision for this purpose in a permanent STANDING ARMY, and a MILITIA that may be subjected to as strict discipline and government.

A standing army in the hands of a government placed so independent of the people, may be made a fatal instrument to overturn the public liberties; it may be employed to enforce the collection of the most oppressive taxes, and to carry into execution the most arbitrary measures. An ambitious man who may have the army at his devotion, may step up into the throne, and seize upon absolute power.

The absolute unqualified command that Congress have over the militia may be made instrumental to the destruc-

tion of all liberty, both public and private; whether of a personal, civil or religious nature.

First, the personal liberty of every man probably from sixteen to sixty years of age, may be destroyed by the power Congress have in organizing and governing of the militia. As militia they may be subjected to fines to any amount, levied in a military manner; they may be subjected to corporal punishments of the most disgraceful and humiliating kind, and to death itself, by the sentence of a court martial: To this our young men will be more immediately subjected, as a select militia, composed of them, will best answer the purposes of government.

Secondly, The rights of conscience may be violated, as there is no exemption of those persons who are conscientiously scrupulous of bearing arms. These compose a respectable proportion of the community in the state. This is the more remarkable, because even when the distresses of the late war, and the evident disaffection of many citizens of that description, inflamed our passions, and when every person, who was obliged to risque his own life, must have been exasperated against such as on any account kept back from the common danger, yet even then, when outrage and violence might have been expected, the rights of conscience were held sacred.

At this momentous crisis, the framers of our state constitution made the most express and decided declaration and stipulations in favour of the rights of conscience; but now when no necessity exists, those dearest rights of men are left insecure.

Thirdly, The absolute command of Congress over the militia may be destructive of public liberty; for under the guidance of an arbitrary government, they may be made the unwilling instruments of tyranny. The militia of Pennsylvania may be marched to New England or Virginia to quell an insurrection occasioned by the most galling oppression, and aided by the standing army, they will no doubt be successful in subduing their liberty and independency; but in so doing, although the magnanimity of their minds will be extinguished, yet the meaner passions of resentment and revenge will be increased, and these in turn will be the ready and obedient instruments of despotism to enslave the others; and that with an irritated vengeance. Thus, may the militia be made the instruments of crushing the last efforts of expiring liberty, of riveting the chains of despotism on their fellow citizens, and on one another. This power can be exercised not only without violating the constitution but in strict conformity with it; it is calculated for this express purpose, and will doubtless be executed accordingly.

As this government will not enjoy the confidence of the people, but be executed by force, it will be a very expensive and burthensome government. The standing army must be numerous, and as a further support, it will be the policy of this government to multiply officers in every department; judges, collectors, tax gatherers, excisemen and the whole host of revenue officers will swarm over the land, devouring the hard earnings of the industrious. Like the locusts of old, impoverishing and defolating all before them.

We have not noticed the smaller, nor many of the considerable blemishes, but have confined our objections to the great and essential defects; the main pillars of the constitution; which we have shewn to be inconsistent with the liberty and happiness of the people, as its establishment will annihilate the state governments, and produce one consolidated government, that will eventually and speedily issue in the supremacy of despotism.

In this investigation, we have not confined our views to the interests or welfare of this state, in preference to the others. We have overlooked all local circumstances—we have considered this subject on the broad scale of the general good: we have asserted the cause of the present and future ages; the cause of liberty and mankind.

Nathaniel Breading
John Smilie
Richard Baird
Adam Orth
John A. Hanna
John Whitehill
John Harris
Robert Whitehill
John Reynolds
Jonathan Hoge
Nicholas Lutz

John Ludwig
Abraham Lincoln
John Bishop
Joseph Heister
Joseph Powel
James Martin
William Findley
John Baird
James Edgar
William Todd.

The yeas and nays upon the final vote were as follows, viz.

YEAS.

George Latimer
Benjamin Rush
Hilary Baker
James Wilson
Thomas McKean
William McPherson
John Hunn
George Gray
Samuel Ashmead
Enoch Edwards
Henry Wynkoop
John Barclay
Thomas Yardley
Abraham Stout
Thomas Bull
Anthony Wayne
William Gibbons
Richard Downing
Thomas Cheyney
John Hannum
Stephen Chambers
Robert Coleman
Sebastian Grass

NAYS.

John Whitehill
John Harris
John Reynolds
Robert Whitehill
Jonathan Hoge
Nicholas Lutz
John Ludwig
Abraham Lincoln
John Bishop
Joseph Heister
James Martin
Joseph Powell

YEAS.

John Hubley
Jasper Yates
Henry Stagle
Thomas Campbell
Thomas Hartley
David Grier
John Black
Benjamin Pedan
John Arndt
Stephen Balliott
Joseph Horsefield
David Deshler
William Wilson
John Boyd
Thomas Scott
John Nevill
John Allison
Jonathan Roberts
John Richards
F. A. Muhlenberg
James Morris
Timothy Pickering
Benjamin Elliot

NAYS.

William Findley
John Baird
William Todd
James Marshall
James Edgar
Nathaniel Breading
John Smilie
Richard Baird
William Brown
Adam Orth
John Andre Hannah

Philadelphia, Dec. 12, 1787.

An Examination of the Leading Principles of the Federal Constitution

NOAH WEBSTER

October 10, 1787

Noah Webster (1758–1843) was an educator, an author of children's primers, and the compiler of the first American dictionary. This last project was taken on out of a concern, shared with Benjamin Franklin, to free Americans from cultural subservience to Great Britain. Webster, an ardent Federalist, would later edit several magazines and newspapers supporting greater powers for the central government in the United States.

An Examination of the Leading Principles of the Federal Constitution

To His Excellency Benjamin Franklin, Esq. President of the Commonwealth of Pennsylvania, and Member of the Late Convention, Held at Philadelphia for the Purpose of Devising a Constitution for the Government of the United States, the Following Remarks upon the System Recommended by That Convention

Of all the memorable aeras that have marked the progress of men from the savage state to the refinements of luxury, that which has combined them into society, under a wise system of government, and given form to a nation, has ever been recorded and celebrated as the most important. Legislators have ever been deemed the greatest benefactors of mankind—respected when living, and often deified after their death. Hence the fame of Fohi and Confucius—of Moses, Solon and Lycurgus—of Romulus and Numa—of Alfred, Peter the Great, and Mango Capac; whose names will be celebrated through all ages, for framing and improving constitutions of government, which introduced order into society and secured the benefits of law to millions of the human race.

This western world now beholds an aera important beyond conception, and which posterity will number with the age of Czar of Muscovy, and with the promulgation of the Jewish laws at Mount Sinai. The names of those men who have digested a system of constitutions for the American empire, will be enrolled with those of Zamolxis and Odin, and celebrated by posterity with the honors which less enlightened nations have paid to the fabled demi-gods of antiquity.

But the origin of the AMERICAN REPUBLIC is distinguished by peculiar circumstances. Other nations have been driven together by fear and necessity—the governments have generally been the result of a single man's observations; or the offspring of particular interests. In the formation of our constitution, the wisdom of all ages is collected—the legislators of antiquity are consulted—as well as the opinions and interests of the millions who are concerned. In short, it is *an empire of reason.*

In the formation of such a government, it is not only the *right,* but the indispensable *duty* of every citizen to examine the principles of it, to compare them with the principles of other governments, with a constant eye to our particular situation and circumstances, and thus endeavor to foresee the future operations of our own system, and its effects upon human happiness.

Convinced of this truth, I have no apology to offer for the following remarks, but an earnest desire to be useful to my country.

In attending to the proposed Federal Constitution, the first thing that presents itself to our consideration, is the division of the legislative into two branches. This article has so many advocates in America, that it needs not any vindication.*—But it has its opposers, among whom are some respectable characters, especially in Pennsylvania; for which reason, I will state some of the arguments and facts which incline me to favor the proposed division.

*A division of the legislature has been adopted in the new constitution of every state except Pennsylvania and Georgia.

On the first view of men in society, we should suppose that no man would be bound by a law to which he had not given his consent. Such would be our first idea of political obligation. But experience, from time immemorial, has proved it to be impossible to unite the opinions of all the members of a community, in every case; and hence the doctrine, that the opinions of a *majority* must give law to the *whole State:* a doctrine as universally received, as any intuitive truth.

Another idea that naturally presents itself to our minds, on a slight consideration of the subject, is, that in a perfect government, all the members of a society should be present, and each give his suffrage in acts of legislation, by which he is to be bound. This is impracticable in large states; and even were it not, it is very questionable whether it would be the *best* mode of legislation. It was however practised in the free states of antiquity; and was the cause of innumerable evils. To avoid these evils, the moderns have invented the doctrine of *representation,* which seems to be the perfection of human government.

Another idea, which is very natural, is, that to complete the mode of legislation, all the representatives should be collected into *one body,* for the purpose of debating questions and enacting laws. Speculation would suggest the idea; and the desire of improving upon the systems of government in the old world, would operate powerfully in its favor.

But men are ever running into extremes. The passions, after a violent constraint, are apt to run into licentiousness; and even the reason of men, who have experienced evils from the *defects* of a government, will sometimes coolly condemn the *whole system.*

Every person, moderately acquainted with human nature, knows that public bodies, as well as individuals, are liable to the influence of sudden and violent passions, under the operation of which, the voice of reason is silenced. Instances of such influence are not so frequent, as in individuals; but its effects are extensive in proportion to the numbers that compose the public body. This fact suggests the expediency of dividing the powers of legislation between the two bodies of men, whose debates shall be separate and not dependent on each other; that, if at any time, one part should appear to be under any undue influence, either from passion, obstinacy, jealousy of particular men, attachment to a popular speaker, or other extraordinary causes, there might be a power in the legislature sufficient

to check every pernicious measure. Even in a small republic, composed of men, equal in property and abilities, and all meeting for the purpose of making laws, like the old Romans in the field of Mars, a division of the body into two independent branches, would be a necessary step to prevent the disorders, which arise from the pride, irritability and stubborness of mankind. This will ever be the case, while men possess passions, easily inflamed, which may bias their reason and lead them to erroneous conclusions.

Another consideration has weight: A single body of men may be led astray by one person of abilities and address, who, on the first starting a proposition, may throw a plausible appearance on one side of the question, and give a lead to the whole debate. To prevent any ill consequence from such a circumstance, a separate discussion, before a different body of men, and taken up on new grounds, is a very eligible expedient.

Besides, the design of a senate is not merely to check the legislative assembly, but to collect wisdom and experience. In most of our constitutions, and particularly in the proposed federal system, greater age and longer residence are required to qualify for the senate, than for the house of representatives. This is a wise provision. The house of representatives may be composed of new and unexperienced members—strangers to the forms of proceeding, and the science of legislation. But either positive institutions, or customs, which may supply their place, fill the senate with men venerable for age and respectability, experienced in the ways of men, and in the art of governing, and who are not liable to the bias of passions that govern the young. If the senate of Rhode Island is an exception to this observation, it is a proof that the mass of the people are corrupted, and that the senate should be elected less frequently than the other house: Had the old senate in Rhode Island held their seats for three years; had they not been chosen, amidst a popular rage for paper money, the honor of that state would probably have been saved. The old senate would have stopped the measure for a year or two, till the people could have had time to deliberate upon its consequences. I consider it as a capital excellence of the proposed constitution, that the senate can be wholly renewed but once in six years.

Experience is the best instructor—it is better than a thousand theories. The history of every government on earth affords proof of the utility of different branches in a legislature. But I appeal only to our own experience in

America. To what cause can we ascribe the absurd measures of Congress, in times past, and the speedy recision of whole measures, but to the want of some check? I feel the most profound deference for that honorable body, and perfect respect for their opinions; but some of their steps betray a great want of consideration—a defect, which perhaps nothing can remedy, but a division of their deliberations. I will instance only their *resolution* to build a *Federal Town.* When we were involved in a debt, of which we could hardly pay the interest, and when Congress could not command a shilling, the very proposition was extremely absurd. Congress themselves became ashamed of the resolution, and rescinded it with as much silence as possible. Many other acts of that body are equally reprehensible—but respect forbids me to mention them.

Several states, since the war, have experienced the necessity of a division of the legislature. Maryland was saved from a most pernicious measure, by her senate. A rage for paper money, bordering on madness, prevailed in their house of delegates—an emission of £.500,000 was proposed; a sum equal to the circulating medium of the State. Had the sum been emitted, every shilling of specie would have been driven from circulation, and most of it from the state. Such a loss would not have been repaired in seven years—not to mention the whole catalogue of frauds which would have followed the measure. The senate, like honest, judicious men, and the protectors of the interests of the state, firmly resisted the rage, and gave the people time to cool and to think. Their resistance was effectual—the people acquiesced, and the honor and interest of the state were secured.

The house of representatives in Connecticut, soon after the war, had taken offence at a certain act of Congress. The upper house, who understood the necessity and expediency of the measure, better than the people, refused to concur in a remonstrance to Congress. Several other circumstances gave umbrage to the lower house; and to weaken or destroy the influence of the senate, the representatives, among other violent proceedings, resolved, not merely to remove the seat of government, but to make every county town in the state the seat of government, by rotation. This foolish resolution would have disgraced school-boys—the senate saved the honor of the state, by rejecting it with disdain—and within two months, every representative was ashamed of the conduct of the house. All public bodies have these fits of passion, when their con-

duct seems to be perfectly boyish; and in these paroxisms, a check is highly necessary.

Pennsylvania exhibits many instances of this hasty conduct. At one session of the legislature, an armed force is ordered, by a precipitate resolution, to expel the settlers at Wioming from their possessions—at a succeeding session, the same people are confirmed in their possessions. At one session, a charter is wrested from a corporation—at another, restored. The whole state is split into parties—everything is decided by party—any proposition from one side of the house, is sure to be damned by the other—and when one party perceives the other has the advantage, they play truant—and an officer or a mob hunt the absconding members in all the streets and alleys in town. Such farces have been repeated in Philadelphia—and *there alone.* Had the legislature been framed with some check upon rash proceedings, the honor of the state would have been saved—the party spirit would have died with the measures proposed in the legislature. But now, any measure may be carried by party in the house; it then becomes a law, and sows the seeds of dissension throughout the state.*

A thousand examples similar to the foregoing may be produced, both in ancient and modern history. Many plausible things may be said in favor of pure democracy—many in favor of uniting the representatives of the people in one single house—but uniform experience proves both to be inconsistent with the peace of society, and the rights of freemen. . . .

People who have heard and read of the European governments, founded on the different ranks of *monarch, nobility and people,* seem to view the *senate* in America, where

---

*I cannot help remarking the singular jealousy of the constitution of Pennsylvania, which requires that a bill shall be published for the consideration of the people, before it is enacted into a law, except in extraordinary cases. This annihilates the legislature, and reduces it to an advisory body. It almost wholly supersedes the uses of *representation,* the most excellent improvement in modern governments. Besides the absurdity of constituting a legislature, without supreme power, such a system will keep the state perpetually embroiled. It carries the spirit of discussion into all quarters, without the means of reconciling the opinions of men, who are not assembled to hear each others' arguments. They debate with themselves—form their own opinions, without the reasons which influence others, and without the means of information. Thus the warmth of different opinions, which, in other states, dies in the legislature, is diffused through the state of Pennsylvania, and becomes personal and permanent. The seeds of dissension are sown in the constitution, and no state, except Rhode Island, is so distracted by factions.

there is no difference of ranks and titles, as a useless branch—or as a servile imitation of foreign constitutions of government, without the same reasons. This is a capital mistake. Our senates, it is true, are not composed of a different order of men; but the same reasons, the same necessity for distinct branches of the legislature exists in all governments. But in most of our American constitutions, we have all the advantages of checks and balance, without the danger which may arise from a superior and independent order of men.

It is worth our while to institute a brief comparison between our American forms of government, and the two *best constitutions* that ever existed in Europe, the *Roman* and the *British.*

In England, the king or supreme executive officer, is hereditary. In America, the president of the United States, is elective. That this is an advantage will hardly be disputed.

In ancient Rome, the king was elective, and so were the consuls, who were the executive officers in the republic. But they were elected by the body of the people, in their public assemblies; and this circumstance paved the way for such excessive bribery and corruption as are wholly unknown in modern times. The president of the United States is also elective; but by a few men—chosen by the several legislatures—under their inspection—separated at a vast distance—and holding no office under the United States. Such a mode of election almost precludes the possibility of corruption. Besides, no state however large, has the power of chusing a president in that state; for each elector must choose at least one man, who is not an inhabitant of that State to which he belongs.

The crown of England is hereditary—the consuls of Rome were chosen annually—both these extremes are guarded against in our proposed constitution. The president is not dismissed from his office, as soon as he is acquainted with business—he continues four years, and is re-eligible, if the people approve his conduct. Nor can he canvass for his office, by reason of the distance of the electors; and the pride and jealousy of the states will prevent his continuing too long in office. . . .

The powers vested in the president resemble the powers of the supreme magistrates in Rome. They are not so extensive as those of the British king; but in one instance, the president, with concurrence of the senate, has powers exceeding those of the Roman consuls; I mean in the appointment of judges and other subordinate executive officers. The praetors or judges in Rome were chosen annually by the people. This was a defect in the Roman government. One half the evils in a state arise from a lax execution of the laws; and it is impossible that an executive officer can act with vigor and impartiality, when his office depends on the popular voice. An annual popular election of executive officers is the sure source of a negligent, partial and corrupt administration. The independence of the judges in England has produced a course of the most just, impartial and energetic judicial decisions, for many centuries, that can be exhibited in any nation on earth. In this point therefore I conceive the plan proposed in America to be an improvement on the Roman constitution. In all free governments, that is, in all countries, where *laws govern,* and not *men,* the supreme magistrate should have it in his power to execute any law, however unpopular, without hazarding his person or office. The laws are the sole *guardians* of right, and when the magistrate dares not act, every person is insecure.

Let us now attend to the constitution and the powers of the senate.

The house of lords in England is wholly independent on the people. The lords spiritual hold their seats by office; and the people at large have no voice in disposing of the ecclesiastical dignities. The temporal lords hold their seats by hereditary right or by grant from the king: And it is a branch of the king's prerogative to make what peers he pleases.

The senate in Rome was elective; but a senator held his seat for life.*

---

*I say the senate was *elective*—but this must be understood with some exceptions; or rather qualifications. The constitution of the Roman senate has been a subject of enquiry, with the first men in modern ages. Lord Chesterfield requested the opinion of the learned Vertot, upon the manner of chusing senators in Rome; and it was a subject of discussion between Lord Harvey and Dr. Middleton. The most probable account of the manner of forming the senate, and filling up vacancies, which I have collected from the best writers on this subject, is here abridged for the consideration of the reader.

Romulus chose one hundred persons, from the principal families in Rome, to form a council or senate; and reserved to himself the right of nominating their successors; that is of filling vacancies. "Mais comme Romulus avoit lui même choisi les premiers senateurs il se reserva le droit de nommer a son gré, leurs successeurs."—Mably, sur les Romains. Other well informed historians intimate that Romulus retained the right of nominating the president only. After the union of the Sabines with the Romans, Romulus added another hundred members

The proposed senate in America is constituted on principles more favorable to liberty: The members are elective, and by the separate legislatures: They hold their seats for six years—they are thus rendered sufficiently dependent on their constituents; and yet are not dismissed from their

---

to the senate, but by *consent of the people.* Tarquin, the *ancient,* added another hundred; but historians are silent as to the manner.

On the destruction of Alba by Hostilius, some of the principal Alban families were added to the senate, *by consent of the senate and people.*

After the demolition of the monarchy, Appius Claudius was admitted into the senate by *order of the people.*

Cicero testifies that, from the extinction of the monarchy, all the members of the senate were admitted by *command of the people.*

It is observable that the first creation of the senators was the act of the monarch; and the first patrician families claimed the sole right of admission into the senate. "Les familles qui descendoient des deux cent senateurs que Romulus avoit créés,—se crurent seules en droit d'entrer dans le senat."—Mably

This right however was not granted in its utmost extent; for many of the senators in the Roman commonwealth, were taken from plebian families. For sixty years before the institution of the *censorship,* which was A. U. C. 311, we are not informed how vacancies in the senate were supplied. The most probable method was this; to enrol, in the list of senators, the different magistrates; viz., the consuls, praetors, the two quaestors of patrician families, the five tribunes (afterwards ten) and the two aediles of plebian families: The office of quaestor gave an immediate admission into the senate. The tribunes were admitted two years after their creation. This enrollment seems to have been a matter of course; and likewise their confirmation by the people in their comitia or assemblies.

On extraordinary occasions, when the vacancies of the senate were numerous, the consuls used to nominate some of the most respectable of the equestrian order to be chosen by the people.

On the institution of the censorship, the censors were invested with full powers to inspect the manners of the citizens,—enrol them in their proper ranks according to their property,—make out lists of the senators and leave out the names of such as had rendered themselves unworthy of their dignity by any scandalous vices. This power they several times exercised; but the disgraced senators had an appeal to the people.

After the senate had lost half its members in the war with Hannibal, the dictator, M. Fabius Buteo, filled up the number with the magistrates, with those who had been honored with a civic crown, or others who were respectable for age and character. One hundred and seventy new members were added at once, with *the approbation of the people.* The vacancies occasioned by Sylla's proscriptions amounted to three hundred, which were supplied by persons nominated by Sylla and *chosen by the people.*

Before the time of the Gracchi, the number of senators did not exceed three hundred. But in Sylla's time, so far as we can collect from direct testimonies, it amounted to about five hundred. The age necessary to qualify for a seat in the senate is not exactly ascertained; but several circumstances prove it to have been about thirty years.

See Vertot, Mably, and Middleton on this subject.

In the last ages of Roman splendor, the property requisite to qualify a person for a senator, was settled by Augustus at eight hundred sestertia—more than six thousand pounds sterling.

office as soon as they become acquainted with the forms of proceeding.

It may be objected by the larger states, that the representation is not equal; the smallest states having the privilege of sending the same number of senators as the largest. To obviate this objection, I would suggest but two or three ideas.

1. If each state had a representation and a right in deciding questions, proportional to its property, three states would almost command the whole. Such a constitution would gradually annihilate the small states; and finally melt down the whole United States into one undivided sovereignty. The free states of Spain and the heptarchy in England, afford striking examples of this.

Should it be said that such an event is desirable, I answer; the states are all entitled to their respective sovereignties, and while they claim independence in international jurisdiction, the federal constitution ought to guarantee their sovereignty.

Another consideration has weight—There is, in all nations, a tendency toward an accumulation of power in some point. It is the business of the legislator to establish some barriers to check the tendency. In small societies, a man worth £.100,000 has but one vote, when his neighbors, who are worth but fifty pounds, have each one vote likewise. To make property the sole basis of authority, would expose many of the best citizens to violence and oppression. To make the number of inhabitants in a state, the rule of apportioning power, is more equitable; and were the United States one indivisible interest, would be a perfect rule for representation. But the detached situation of the states has created some separate interests—some local institutions, which they will not resign nor throw into the hands of other states. For these peculiar interests, the states have an *equal* attachment—for the preservation and enjoyment of these, an *equal* sovereignty is necessary; and the sovereignty of each state would not be secure, had each state, in both branches of the legislature an authority in passing laws, proportioned to its inhabitants.

3. But the senate should be considered as representing the confederacy in a body. It is a false principle in the vulgar idea of representation, that a man delegated by a particular district in a state, is the representative of that district only; whereas in truth a member of the legislature from any town or county, is the representative of the whole state. In passing laws, he is to view the whole collective in-

terest of the state, and act from that view; not from a partial regard to the interest of the town or county where he is chosen.

The same principle extends to the Congress of the United States. A delegate is bound to represent the true local interest of his constituents—to state in its true light to the whole body—but when each provincial interest is thus stated, every member should act for the *aggregate interest* of the whole confederacy. The design of representation is to bring the collective interest into view—a delegate is not the legislator of a single state—he is as much the legislator of the whole confederacy as of the particular state where he is chosen; and if he gives his vote for a law which he believes to be beneficial to his own state only, and pernicious to the rest, he betrays his trust and violates his oath. It is indeed difficult for a man to divest himself of local attachments and act from an impartial regard to the general good; but he who cannot for the most part do this, is not a good legislator.

These considerations suggest the propriety of continuing the senators in office, for a longer period, than the representatives. They gradually lose their partiality, generalize their views, and consider themselves as acting for the whole confederacy. Hence in the senate we may expect union and firmness—here we may find the *general good* the object of legislation, and a check upon the more partial and interested acts of the other branch.

These considerations obviate the complaint, that the representation in the senate is not equal; for the senators represent the whole confederacy; and all that is wanted of the members is information of the true situation and interest of each state. As they act under the direction of the several legislatures, two men may as fully and completely represent a state, as twenty; and when the true interest of each state is known, if the senators perform the part of good legislators, and act impartially for the whole collective body of the United States, it is totally immaterial where they are chosen.*

The house of representatives is the more immediate voice of the separate states—here the states are represented in proportion to their number of inhabitants—here the separate interests will operate with their full force, and the violence of parties and the jealousies produced by interfering interests, can be restrained and quieted only by a body of men, less local and dependent.

It may be objected that no separate interests should exist in a state; and a division of the legislature has a tendency to create them. But this objection is founded on mere jealousy, or a very imperfect comparison of the Roman and British governments, with the proposed federal constitution.

The house of peers in England is a body originally and totally independent on the people—the senate in Rome was mostly composed of patrician or noble families, and after the first election of a senator, he was no longer dependent on the people—he held his seat for life. But the senate of the United States can have no separate interests from the body of the people; for they live among them—they are chosen by them—they *must* be dismissed from their place once in six years and *may* at any time be impeached for mal-practices—their property is situated among the people, and with their persons, subject to the same laws. No title can be granted, but the temporary titles of office, bestowed by the voluntary election of the people; and no pre-eminence can be acquired but by the same means.

---

*It is a capital defect of most of the state-constitutions, that the senators, like the representatives, are chosen in particular districts, They are thus inspired with local views, and however wrong it may be to entertain them, yet such is the constitution of human nature, that men are almost involuntarily attached to the interest of the district which has reposed confidence in their abilities and integrity. Some partiality therefore for constituents is always expectable. To destroy it as much as possible, a political constitution should remove the grounds of local attachment. Connecticut and Maryland have wisely destroyed this attachment in their senates, by ordaining that the members shall be chosen in the *state at large*. The senators hold their seats by the suffrages of the state, *not of a district;* hence they have no particular number of men to fear or to oblige.—They represent *the state;* hence that union and firmness which the senates of those states have manifested on the most trying occasions, and by which they have prevented the most rash and iniquitous measures.

It may be objected, that when the election of senators is vested in the people, they must choose men in their own neighborhood, or else those with whom they are unacquainted. With respect to representatives, this objection does not lie; for they are chosen in small districts; and as to senators, there is, in every state, a small number of men, whose reputation for abilities, integrity and good conduct will lead the people to a very just choice. Old experienced statesmen should compose the senate; and people are generally, in this free country, acquainted with their characters. Were it possible, as it is in small states, it would be an improvement in the doctrine of representation, to give every freeman the right of voting for every member of the legislature, and the privilege of choosing the men in any part of the state. This would totally exclude bribery and undue influence; for no man can bribe a state; and it would almost annihilate partial views in legislation. But in large states it may be impracticable.

The separation of the legislature divides the power—checks—restrains—amends the proceedings—at the same time, it creates no division of interest, that can tempt either branch to encroach upon the other, or upon the people. In turbulent times, such restraint is our greatest safety—in calm times, and in measures obviously calculated for the general good, both branches must always be unanimous. . . .

The house of representatives is formed on very equitable principles; and is calculated to guard the privileges of the people. . . .

Some may object to their continuance in power *two years.* But I cannot see any danger arising from this quarter. On the contrary, it creates less trouble for the representatives, who by such choice are taken from their professions and obliged to attend Congress, some of them at the distance of at least seven hundred miles. While men are chosen by the people, and responsible to them, there is but little danger from ambition or corruption. . . .

The fourth section, article 1, of the new constitution declares that "The times, places, and manner of holding elections for senators and representatives, shall be prescribed in each state by the legislature thereof; *but the Congress may at any time by law make or alter such regulations, except as to the places of chusing senators.*" Here let us pause—What did the convention mean by giving Congress power to *make regulations,* prescribed by the legislatures? Is this expression accurate or intelligible? But the word *alter* is very intelligible, and the clause puts the election of representatives *wholly,* and the senators *almost wholly,* in the power of Congress.

The views of the convention I believe to be perfectly upright—They might mean to place the election of representatives and senators beyond the reach of faction—They doubtless had good reasons, in *their* minds, for the clause—But I see no occasion for any power in Congress to interfere with the choice of their own body—They will have power to suppress insurrections, as they ought to have; but the clause in *Italics* gives *needless* and *dangerous* powers—I hope the states will reject it with decency, and adopt the whole system, without altering another syllable. . . .

Every bill that passes a majority of both houses of Congress, must be sent to the president for his approbation; but it must be returned in ten days, whether approved by him or not; and the concurrence of two thirds of both houses passes the bill into a law, notwithstanding any ob-

jections of the president. The constitution therefore gives the supreme executive a check but no negative, upon the sense of Congress.

The powers lodged in Congress are extensive; but it is presumed that they are not too extensive. The first object of the constitution is to *unite* the states into one *compact society,* for the purpose of government. If such *union* must exist, or the states be exposed to foreign invasions, internal discord, reciprocal encroachments upon each others property—to weakness and infamy, which no person will dispute; what powers must be collected and lodged in the supreme head or legislature of these states. The answer is easy: This legislature must have exclusive jurisdiction in all matters in which the states have a mutual interest. There are some regulations in which all the states are equally concerned—there are others, which in their operation, are limited to one state. The first belongs to Congress—the last to the respective legislatures. No one state has a right to supreme control, in any affair in which the other states have an interest, nor should Congress interfere in any affair which respects one state only. This is the general line of division, which the convention have endeavored to draw, between the powers of Congress and the rights of the individual states. The only question therefore is, whether the new constitution delegates to Congress any powers which do not respect the general interest and welfare of the United States. If these powers intrench upon the present sovereignty of any *state,* without having for an object the *collective interest* of the whole, the powers are too extensive. But if they do not extend to all concerns, in which the states have a mutual interest, they are too limited. If in any instance, the powers necessary for protecting the *general* interest, interfere with the constitutional rights of an *individual* state, such state has assumed powers that are inconsistent with the safety of the United States, and which ought instantly to be resigned. Considering the states as individuals, on equal terms, entering into a social compact, no state has a right to any power which may prejudice its neighbors. If therefore the federal constitution has collected into the federal legislature no more power than is necessary for the *common defence and interest,* it should be recognized by the states, however particular clauses may supersede the exercise of certain powers by the individual states.

This question is of vast magnitude. The states have very high ideas of their separate sovereignty; altho' it is certain, that while each exists in its full latitude, we can have no

Federal sovereignty. However flattered each state may be by its independent sovereignty, we can have no union, no respectability, no national character, and what is more, no national justice, till the states resign to one *supreme head* the exclusive power of *legislating, judging and executing,* in all matters of a general nature. Every thing of a private or provincial nature, must still rest on the ground of the respective state-constitutions.

After examining the limits of the proposed congressional powers, I confess I do not think them too extensive—I firmly believe that the life, liberty and property of every man, and the peace and independence of each state, will be more fully secured under such a constitution of federal government, than they will under a constitution with more limited powers; and infinitely more safe than under our boasted distinct sovereignties. It appears to me that Congress will have no more power than will be necessary for our union and general welfare; and such power they must have or we are in a wretched state. On the adoption of this constitution, I should value real estate twenty per cent. higher than I do at this moment.

I will not examine into the extent of the powers proposed to be lodged in the supreme federal head; the subject would be extensive and require more time than I could bestow upon it. But I will take up some objections, that have been made to particular points of the new constitution.

Most of the objections I have yet heard to the constitution, consist in mere insinuations unsupported by reasoning or fact. They are thrown out to instil groundless jealousies into the minds of the people, and probably with a view to prevent all government; for there are, in every society, some turbulent geniuses whose importance depends solely on faction. To seek the insidious and detestable nature of these insinuations, it is necessary to mention, and to remark on a few particulars.

1. The first objection against the constitution is, that the legislature will be more expensive than our present confederation. This is so far from being true, that the money we actually lose by our present weakness, disunion and *want of government* would support the civil government of every state in the confederacy. Our public poverty does not proceed from the expensiveness of Congress, nor of the civil list; but from want of power to command our own advantages. We pay more money to foreign nations, in the course of business, and merely for *want of government,* than would, under an efficient government, pay the annual interest of our domestic debt. Every man in business knows this to be *truth;* and the objection can be designed only to delude the ignorant.

2. Another objection to the constitution, is the division of the legislature into two branches. Luckily this objection has no advocates but in Pennsylvania; and even here their number is dwindling. The factions that reign in this state, the internal discord and passions that disturb the government and the peace of the inhabitants, have detected the errors of the constitution, and will some time or other produce a reformation. The division of the legislature has been the subject of discussion in the beginning of this essay; and will be deemed, by nineteen-twentieths of the Americans, one of the principal excellencies of the constitution.

3. A third insinuation, is that the proposed federal government will annihilate the several legislatures. This is extremely disingenuous. Every person, capable of reading, must discover, that the convention have labored to draw the line between the federal and provincial powers—to define the powers of Congress, and limit them to those general concerns which *must* come under federal jurisdiction, and which *cannot* be managed in the separate legislatures—that in all internal regulations, whether of civil or criminal nature, the states retain their sovereignty, and have it guaranteed to them by this very constitution. Such a groundless insinuation, or rather mere surmise, must proceed from dark designs or extreme ignorance, and deserves the severest reprobation.

4. It is alledged that the liberty of the press is not guaranteed by the new constitution. But this objection is wholly unfounded. The liberty of the press does not come within the jurisdiction of federal government. It is firmly established in all the states either by law, or positive declarations in *bills of right;* and not being mentioned in the federal constitution, is not—and cannot be abridged by Congress. It stands on the basis of the respective state-constitutions. Should any state resign to Congress the exclusive jurisdiction of a certain district, which should include any town where presses are already established, it is in the power of the state to reserve the liberty of the press, or any other fundamental privilege, and make it an immutable condition of the grant, that such rights shall never be violated. All objections therefore on this score are "*baseless visions.*"

5. It is insinuated that the constitution gives Congress the power of levying internal taxes at pleasure. This insin-

uation seems founded on the eighth section of the first article, which declares, that "Congress shall have power to lay and collect taxes, duties, imposts and excises, to pay the debts and provide for the common defence and general welfare of the United States."

That Congress should have power to collect duties, imposts and excises, in order to render them uniform throughout the United States will hardly be controverted. The whole objection is to the right of levying internal taxes.

But it will be conceded that the supreme head of the states must have power, competent to the purposes of our union, or it will be, as it now is, a *useless body,* a mere expense, without any advantage. To pay our public debt, to support foreign ministers and our own civil government, money must be raised; and if the duties and imposts are not adequate to these purposes, where shall the money be obtained? It will be answered, let Congress apportion the sum to be raised, and leave the legislatures to collect the money. Well this is all that is intended by the clause under consideration; with the addition of a federal power that shall be sufficient to oblige a delinquent state to comply with the requisition. Such power must exist somewhere, or the debts of the United States can never be paid. For want of such power, our credit is lost and our national faith is a bye-word.

For want of such power, one state now complies fully with a requisition, another partially, and a third absolutely refuses or neglects to grant a shilling. Thus the honest and punctual are doubly loaded—and the knave triumphs in his negligence. In short, no honest man will dread a power that shall enforce an equitable system of taxation. The dishonest are ever apprehensive of a power that shall oblige them to do what honest men are ready to do voluntarily.

Permit me to ask those who object to this power of taxation, how shall money be raised to discharge our honest debts which are universally acknowledged to be just? Have we not already experienced the inefficacy of a system without power? Has it not been proved to demonstration, that a voluntary compliance with the demands of the union can never be expected? To what expedient shall we have recourse? What is the resort of all governments in cases of delinquency? Do not the states vest in the legislature, or even in the governor and council, a power to enforce laws, even with the militia of the states? And how rarely does there exist the necessity of exerting such a power? Why

should such a power be more dangerous in Congress than in a legislature? Why should more confidence be reposed in a member of one legislature than of another? Why should we choose the best men in the state to represent us in Congress, and the moment they are elected arm ourselves against them as against tyrants and robbers? Do we not, in this conduct, act the part of a man, who, as soon as he has married a woman of unsuspected chastity, locks her up in a dungeon? Is there any spell or charm, that instantly changes a delegate to Congress from an honest man into a knave—a tyrant? I confess freely that I am willing to trust Congress with any powers that I should dare lodge in a state-legislature. I believe life, liberty, and property is as safe in the hands of a federal legislature, organized in the manner proposed by the convention, as in the hands of any legislature, that has ever been or ever will be chosen in any particular state.

But the idea that Congress can levy taxes *at pleasure* is false, and the suggestion wholly unsupported. The preamble to the constitution is declaratory of the purposes of our union: and the assumption of any powers not necessary to *establish justice, insure domestic tranquility, provide for the common defence, promote the general welfare, and to secure the blessings of liberty to ourselves and our posterity,* will be unconstitutional, and endanger the existence of Congress. Besides, in the very clause which gives the power of levying duties and taxes, the purposes to which the money shall be appropriated are specified, viz. *to pay the debts and provide for the common defence and general welfare of the United States.** For these purposes money must be collected, and the power of collection must be lodged, sooner or later, in a federal head; or the common defence and general welfare must be neglected.

The states in their separate capacity, cannot provide for

---

*The clause may at first appear ambiguous. It may be uncertain whether we should read and understand it thus—"The Congress shall have power to lay and collect taxes, duties, imposts and excises *in order to pay the debts,*" &c. or whether the meaning is—"The Congress shall have power to lay and collect taxes, duties, imposts and excises, and *shall have power to pay the debts,*" &c. On considering the construction of the clause, and comparing it with the preamble, the last sense seems to be improbable and absurd. But it is not very material; for no powers are vested in Congress but what are included under the general expressions, of *providing for the common defence and general welfare of the United States.* Any powers not promotive of these purposes, will be unconstitutional;—consequently any appropriations of money to any other purpose will expose the Congress to the resentment of the states, and the members to impeachment and loss of their seats.

the *common* defence; nay in case of a civil war, a state cannot secure its own existence. The only question therefore is, whether it is necessary to unite, and provide for our *common defence and general welfare*. For this question being once decided in the affirmative, leaves no room to controvert the propriety of constituting a power over the whole United States, adequate to these general purposes.

The states, by granting such power, do not throw it out of their own hands—they only throw, each its proportion, into a common stock—they merely combine the powers of the several states into one point, where they *must* be collected, before they *can* be exerted. But the powers are still in their own hands; and cannot be alienated, till they create a body independent of themselves, with a force at their command, superior to the whole yeomanry of the country.

6. It is said there is no provision made in the new constitution against a standing army in time of peace. Why do not people object that no provision is made against the introduction of a body of Turkish Janizaries; or against making the Alcoran the rule of faith and practice, instead of the Bible? The answer to such objections is simply this—*no such provision is necessary*. The people in this country cannot forget their apprehensions from a British standing army, quartered in America; and they turn their fears and jealousies against themselves. Why do not the people of most of the states apprehend danger from standing armies from their own legislatures? Pennsylvania and North Carolina, I believe, are the only states that have provided against this danger at all events. Other states have declared that "no standing armies shall be kept up without the consent of the legislature." But this leaves the power entirely in the hands of the legislature. Many of the states however have made *no provision* against this evil. What hazards these states suffer! Why does not a man pass a law in his family, that no armed soldier shall be quartered in his house by his consent? The reason is very plain: no man will suffer his liberty to be abridged, or endangered—his disposition and his power are uniformly opposed to any infringement of his rights. In the same manner, the principles and habits, as well as the power of the Americans are directly opposed to standing armies: and there is as little necessity to guard against them by positive constitutions, as to prohibit the establishment of the Mahometan religion. But the constitution provides for our safety; and while it gives Congress power to raise armies, it declares that no appropriation of money to their support shall be for a longer term than two years.

Congress likewise are to have power to provide for organizing, arming and disciplining the militia, but have no other command of them, except when in actual service. Nor are they at liberty to call out the militia at pleasure—but only, to execute the laws of the union, suppress insurrections, and repel invasions. For these purposes, government must always be armed with a military force, if the occasion should require it; otherwise laws are nugatory, and life and property insecure.

7. Some persons have ventured to publish an intimation, that by the proposed constitution, the trial by jury is abolished in all *civil cases*. Others very modestly insinuate, that it is in *some cases* only. The fact is, that trial by jury is not affected in *any* case, by the constitution; except in cases of impeachment, which are to be tried by the senate. None but persons in office in or under Congress can be impeached; and even after a judgment upon an impeachment, the offender is liable to a prosecution, before a common jury, in a regular course of law. The insinuation therefore that trials by jury are to be abolished, is groundless, and beyond conception, wicked. It must be wicked, because the circulation of a barefaced falsehood, respecting a privilege, dear to freemen, can proceed only from a depraved heart and the worst intentions.

8. It is also intimated as a probable event, that the federal courts will absorb the judiciaries of the federal states. This is a mere suspicion, without the least foundation. The jurisdiction of the federal states is very accurately defined and easily understood. It extends to the cases mentioned in the constitution, and to the execution of the laws of Congress, respecting commerce, revenue, and other general concerns.

With respect to other civil and criminal actions, the powers and jurisdiction of the several judiciaries of each state, remain unimpaired. Nor is there anything novel in allowing appeals to the supreme court. Actions are mostly to be tried in the state where the crimes are committed—But appeals are allowed under our present confederation, and no person complains; nay, were there no appeal, every man would have reason to complain, especially when a final judgement, in an inferior court, should affect property to a large amount. But why is an objection raised against an appellate jurisdiction in the supreme court, respecting *fact* as well as *law?* Is it less safe to have the opinions of two juries than of one? I suspect many people will think this is no defect in the constitution. But perhaps it will destroy a material requisite of a good jury, viz. their vicinity to the cause of action. I have no doubt, that when causes were tried, in periods prior to the Christian aera, before twelve men, seated upon twelve stones, arranged in a circular form, under a huge oak, there was great propriety in submitting causes to men *in the vicinity*. The difficulty of collecting evidence, in those rude times, rendered it necessary that juries should judge mostly from their own knowledge of facts or from information obtained out of court. But in these polished ages, when juries depend almost wholly on the testimony of witnesses; and when a complication of interests, introduced by commerce and other causes, renders it almost impossible to collect men, in the vicinity of the parties, who are wholly disinterested, it is no disadvantage to have a cause tried by a jury of strangers. Indeed the latter is generally the most eligible.

But the truth is, the creation of all inferior courts is in the power of Congress; and the constitution provides that Congress may make such exceptions from the right of appeals as they shall judge proper. When these courts are erected, their jurisdictions will be ascertained, and in small actions, Congress will doubtless direct that a sentence in a subordinate court shall, to a certain amount, be definite and final. All objections therefore to the judicial powers of the federal courts appear to me as trifling as any of the preceding.

9. But, say the enemies of slavery, negroes may be imported for twenty-one years. This exception is addressed to the quakers; and a very pitiful exception it is.

The truth is, Congress cannot prohibit the importation of slaves during that period; but the laws against the importation into particular states, stand unrepealed. An immediate abolition of slavery would bring ruin upon the whites, and misery upon the blacks, in the southern states. The constitution has therefore wisely left each state to pursue its own measures, with respect to this article of legislation, during the period of twenty-one years.

Such are the principal objections that have yet been made by the enemies of the new constitution. They are mostly frivolous, or founded on false constructions, and a misrepresentation of the true state of facts. They are evidently designed to raise groundless jealousies in the minds of well meaning people, who have little leisure and opportunity to examine into the principles of government. But a little time and reflection will enable most people to detect such mischievous intentions; and the spirit and firmness which have distinguished the conduct of the Americans, during the conflict for independence, will eventually triumph over the enemies of union, and bury them in disgrace or oblivion.

But I cannot quit this subject without attempting to correct some of the erroneous opinions respecting *freedom* and *tyranny*, and the principles by which they are supported. Many people seem to entertain an idea, that liberty consists in *a power to act without any control*. This is more liberty than even the savages enjoy. But in civil society, political liberty consists in *acting conformably to a sense of a majority of the society*. In a free government every man binds himself to obey the *public voice*, or the opinions of a majority; and the *whole society* engages to *protect each individual*. In such a government a man is *free* and safe. But reverse the case; suppose every man to act without control or fear of punishment—every man would be free, but no man would be sure of his freedom one moment. Each would have the power of taking his neighbor's life, liberty, or property; and no man would command more than his own strength to repel the invasion. The case is the same with states. If the states should not unite into one compact society, every state may trespass upon its neighbor, and the injured state has no means of redress but its own military force.

The present situation of our American states is very little better than a state of nature—Our boasted state sovereignties are so far from securing our liberty and property, that they, every moment, expose us to the loss of both. That state which commands the heaviest purse and longest sword, may at any moment, lay its weaker neighbor under tribute; and there is no superior power now existing, that can regularly oppose the invasion or redress the injury. From such liberty, O Lord, deliver us!

But what is tyranny? Or how can a free people be deprived of their liberties? Tyranny is the exercise of some power over a man, which is not warranted by law, or necessary for the public safety. A people can never be deprived of their liberties, while they retain in their own hands, a power sufficient to any other power in the state. This position leads me directly to enquire, in what consists the power of a nation or of an order of men?

In some nations, legislators have derived much of their power from the influence of religion, or from that implicit belief which an ignorant and superstitious people entertain of the gods, and their interposition in every transaction of life. The Roman senate sometimes availed themselves of this engine to carry their decrees and maintain their authority. This was particularly the case, under the aristocracy which succeeded the abolition of the monarchy. The augurs and priests were taken wholly from patrician families. They constituted a distinct order of men—had power to negative any law of the people, by declaring that it was passed during the taking of the auspices. This influence derived from the authority of opinion, was less perceptible, but as tyrannical as a military force. The same influence constitutes, at this day, a principal support of federal governments on the Eastern continent, and perhaps in South America. But in North America, by a singular concurrence of circumstances, the possibility of establishing this influence, as a pillar of government is totally precluded.

Another source of power in government is a military force. But this, to be efficient, must be superior to any force that exists among the people, or which they can command; for otherwise this force would be annihilated, on the first exercise of acts of oppression. Before a standing army can rule, the people must be disarmed; as they are in almost every kingdom in Europe. The supreme power in America cannot enforce unjust laws by the sword; because the whole body of the people are armed, and constitute a force superior to any band of regular troops that can be, on any pretence, raised in the United States. A military force, at the command of Congress, can execute no laws, but such as the people perceive to be just and constitutional; for they will possess the *power*, and jealousy will instantly inspire the *inclination*, to resist the execution of a law which appears to them unjust and oppressive. In spite of all the nominal powers, vested in Congress by the constitution, were the system once adopted in its fullest latitude, still the actual exercise of them would be frequently interrupted by popular jealousy. I am bold to say, that *ten* just and constitutional measures would be resisted, where *one* unjust or oppressive law would be enforced. The powers vested in Congress are little more than *nominal;* nay *real* power cannot be vested in them, nor in any body, but in the *people*. The source of power is in the *people* of this country, and cannot for ages, and probably never will, be removed.

In what then does *real* power consist? The answer is short and plain—in *property*. Could we want any proofs of this, which are not exhibited in this country, the uniform testimony of history will furnish us with multitudes. But I will go no farther for proof, than the two governments already mentioned, the Roman and the British.

Rome exhibited a demonstrative proof of the insepara-

ble connexion between property and dominion. The first form of its government was an elective monarchy—its second, an aristocracy; but these forms could not be permanent, because they were not supported by property. The kings at first and afterwards the patricians had nominally most of the power; but the people, possessing most of the lands, never ceased to assert their privileges, till they established a commonwealth. And the kings and senate could not have held the reigns of government in their hands so long as they did, had they not artfully contrived to manage the established religion, and play off the superstitious credulity of the people against their own power. "Thus this weak constitution of government," says the ingenious Mr. Moyle, speaking of the aristocracy of Rome, "not founded on the true *center of dominion, land,* nor on any standing foundation of authority, nor rivetted in the esteem and affections of the people; and being attacked by strong passion, general interest and the joint forces of the people, mouldered away of course, and pined of a lingering consumption, till it was totally swallowed up by the prevailing faction, and the nobility were moulded into the mass of the people."* The people, notwithstanding the nominal authority of the patricians, proceeded regularly in enlarging their own powers. They first extorted from the senate, the right of electing *tribunes,* with a negative upon the proceedings of the senate. They obtained the right of proposing and debating laws; which before had been vested in the senate; and finally advanced to the power of enacting laws, without the authority of the senate. They regained the rights of election in their comitia, of which they had been deprived by Servius Tullius. They procured a permanent body of laws, collected from the Grecian institutions. They destroyed the influence of augurs, or diviners, by establishing the *tributa comitia,* in which they were not allowed to consult the gods. They increased their power by large accessions of conquered lands. They procured a repeal of the law which prohibited marriages between the patricians and plebians. The Licinian law limited all possessions to five hundred acres of land; which, had it been fully executed, would have secured the commonwealth.

The Romans proceeded thus step by step to triumph over the aristocracy, and to crown their privileges, they procured the right of being elected to the highest offices of the state. By acquiring *the property* of the plebians, the no-

*Essay on the Roman government.

bility, several times, held most of the power of the state; but the people, by reducing the interest of money, abolishing debts, or by forcing other advantages from the patricians, generally held the power of governing in their own hands.

In America, we begin our empire with more popular privileges than the Romans ever enjoyed. We have not to struggle against a monarch or an aristocracy—power is lodged in the mass of the people.

On reviewing the English history, we observe a progress similar to that in Rome—an incessant struggle for liberty from the date of Magna Charta, in John's reign, to the revolution. The struggle has been successful, by abridging the enormous power of the nobility. But we observe that the power of the people has increased in an exact proportion to their acquisitions of property. Wherever the right of primogeniture is established, property must accumulate and remain in families. Thus the landed property in England will never be sufficiently distributed, to give the powers of government wholly into the hands of the people. But to assist the struggle for liberty, commerce has interposed, and in conjunction with manufacturers, thrown a vast weight of property into the democratic scale. Wherever we cast our eyes, we see this truth, that *property* is the basis of *power;* and this, being established as a cardinal point, directs us to the means of preserving our freedom. Make laws, irrevocable laws in every state, destroying and barring entailments; leave real estates to revolve from hand to hand, as time and accident may direct; and no family influence can be acquired and established for a series of generations—no man can obtain dominion over a large territory—the laborious and saving, who are generally the best citizens, will possess each his share of property and power, and thus the balance of wealth and power will continue where it is, in the *body of the people.*

A general and tolerably equal distribution of landed property is the whole basis of national freedom: The system of the great Montesquieu will ever be erroneous, till the words *property or lands in fee simple* are substituted for *virtue,* throughout his *Spirit of Laws.*

Virtue, patriotism, or love of country, never was and never will be, till mens' natures are changed, a fixed, permanent principle and support of government. But in an agricultural country, a general possession of land in fee simple, may be rendered perpetual, and the inequalities introduced by commerce, are too fluctuating to endanger government. An equality of property, with a necessity of alienation, constantly operating to destroy combinations of powerful families, is the very *soul of a republic*—While this continues, the people will inevitably possess both *power* and *freedom;* when this is lost, power departs, liberty expires, and a commonwealth will inevitably assume some other form.

The liberty of the press, trial by jury, the Habeas Corpus writ, even Magna Charta itself, although justly deemed the palladia of freedom, are all inferior considerations, when compared with a general distribution of real property among every class of people.* The power of entailing estates is more dangerous to liberty and republican government, than all the constitutions that can be written on paper, or even than a standing army. Let the people

*Montesquieu supposed *virtue* to be the principle of a republic. He derived his notions of this form of government, from the astonishing firmness, courage and patriotism which distinguished the republics of Greece and Rome. But this *virtue* consisted in pride, contempt of strangers and a martial enthusiasm which sometimes displayed itself in defence of their country. These principles are never permanent—they decay with refinement, intercourse with other nations and increase of wealth. No wonder then that these republics declined, for they were not founded on fixed principles; and hence authors imagine that republics cannot be durable. None of the celebrated writers on government seems to have laid sufficient stress on a general possession of real property in fee-simple. Even the author of the *Political Sketches,* in the *Museum* for the month of September, seems to have passed it over in silence; although he combats Montesquieu's system, and to prove it false, enumerates some of the principles which distinguish our governments from others, and which he supposes constitutes the support of republics.

The English writers on law and government consider Magna Charta, trial by juries, the Habeas Corpus act, and the liberty of the press, as the bulwarks of freedom. All this is well. But in no government of consequence in Europe, is freedom established on its true and immoveable foundation. The property is too much accumulated, and the accumulations too well guarded, to admit the *true principle of republics.* But few centuries have elapsed, since the body of the people were vassals. To such men, the smallest extension of popular privileges, was deemed an invaluable blessing. Hence the encomiums upon trial by juries, and the articles just mentioned. But these people have never been able to mount to the source of *liberty, estates in fee,* or at least but partially; they are yet obliged to drink at the streams. Hence the English jealousy of certain rights, which are guaranteed by acts of parliament. But in America, and here alone, we have gone at once to the *fountain of liberty,* and raised the people to their true dignity. Let the lands be possessed by the people in fee-simple, let the fountain be kept pure, and the streams will be pure of course. Our jealousy of *trial by jury, the liberty of the press,* &c., is totally groundless. Such rights are inseparably connected with the *power* and *dignity* of the people, which rest on their *property.* They cannot be abridged. All *other* [free] nations have wrested *property* and *freedom* from *barons* and *tyrants; we* begin our empire with full possession of property and all its attending rights.

have property, and they *will* have power—a power that will for ever be exerted to prevent a restriction of the press, and abolition of trial by jury, or the abridgement of any other privilege. The liberties of America, therefore, and her forms of government, stand on the broadest basis. Removed from the fears of a foreign invasion and conquest, they are not exposed to the convulsions that shake other governments; and the principles of freedom are so general and energetic, as to exclude the possibility of a change in our republican constitutions.

But while *property* is considered as the *basis* of the freedom of the American yeomanry, there are other auxiliary supports; among which is the *information of the people.* In no country, is education so general—in no country, have the body of the people such a knowledge of the rights of men and the principles of government. This knowledge, joined with a keen sense of liberty and a watchful jealousy, will guard our constitutions, and awaken the people to an instantaneous resistance of encroachments.

But a principal bulwark of freedom is the *right of election.* An equal distribution of property is the *foundation* of a republic; but *popular elections* form the *great barrier,* which defends it from assault, and guards it from the slow and imperceptible approaches of corruption. Americans! never resign that right. It is not very material whether your representatives are elected for one year or two—but the *right* is the Magna Charta of your governments. For this reason, expunge that clause of the new constitution before mentioned, which gives Congress an influence in the election of their own body. The *time, place* and *manner* of chusing senators or representatives are of little or no consequence to Congress. The number of members and time of meeting in Congress are fixed; but the *choice* should rest with the several states. I repeat it—reject the clause with decency, but with unanimity and firmness.

Excepting that clause the constitution is good—it guarantees the *fundamental principles* of our several constitutions—it guards our rights—and while it vests extensive powers in Congress, it vests no more than are necessary for our union. Without powers lodged somewhere in a single body, fully competent to lay and collect equal taxes and duties—to adjust controversies between different states—to silence contending interests—to suppress insurrections—to regulate commerce—to treat with foreign nations, our confederation is a cobweb—liable to be blown asunder by every blast of faction that is raised in the remotest corner of the United States.

Every motive that can possibly influence men ever to unite under civil government, now urges the unanimous adoption of the new constitution. But in America we are urged to it by a singular necessity. By the local situation of the several states *a few* command *all* the advantages of commerce. Those states which have no advantages, made equal exertions for independence, loaded themselves with immense debts, and now are utterly unable to discharge them; while their richer neighbors are taxing them for their own benefit, merely because they *can.* I can prove to a demonstration that Connecticut, which has the heaviest internal or state debt, in proportion to its number of inhabitants, of any in the union, cannot discharge its debt, on any principles of taxation ever yet practised. Yet the state pays in duties, at least 100,000 dollars annually, on goods consumed by its own people, but imported by New York. This sum, could it be saved to the state by an equal system of revenue, would enable that state to gradually sink its debt.*

New Jersey and some other states are in the same situation, except that their debts are not so large, in proportion to their wealth and population.

The boundaries of the several states were not drawn with a view to independence; and while this country was subject to Great Britain, they produced no commercial or political inconveniences. But the revolution has placed things on a different footing. The advantages of some states, and the disadvantages of others are so great—and so materially affect the business and interest of each, that nothing but an equalizing system of revenue, that shall reduce the advantages to some equitable proportion, can prevent a civil war and save the national debt. Such a system of revenue is the *sine qua non* of public justice and tranquillity.

It is absurd for a man to oppose the adoption of the constitution, because *he* thinks some part of it defective or exceptionable. Let every man be at liberty to expunge what *he* judges to be exceptionable, and not a syllable of the constitution will survive the scrutiny. A painter, after exe-

*The state debt of Connecticut is about 3,500,000 dollars, its proportion of the federal debt about the same sum. The annual interest of the whole 420,000 dollars.

cuting a masterly piece, requested every spectator to draw a pencil mark over the part that did not please him; but to his surprise, he soon found the *whole piece* defaced. Let every man examine the most perfect building by his *own* taste, and like some microscopic critics, condemn the *whole* for small deviations from the rules of architecture, and not a part of the *best* constructed fabric would escape. But let *any* man take a *comprehensive view* of the whole, and he will be pleased with the general beauty and proportions, and admire the structure. The same remarks apply to the new constitution. I have no doubt that *every* member of the late convention has exceptions to *some part* of the system proposed. Their constituents have the same, and if *every* objection must be removed, before we have a national government, the Lord have mercy on us.

Perfection is not the lot of humanity. Instead of censuring the small faults of the constitution, I am astonished that so many clashing interests have been reconciled—and so many sacrifices made to the *general interest!* The mutual concessions made by the gentlemen of the convention, reflect the highest honor on their candor and liberality; at the same time, they prove that their minds were deeply impressed with a conviction, that such mutual sacrifices are *essential to our union.* They *must* be made sooner or later by every state; or jealousies, local interests and prejudices will unsheath the sword, and some Caesar or Cromwell will avail himself of our divisions, and wade to a throne through streams of blood.

It is not our duty as freemen, to receive the opinions of any men however great and respectable, without an examination. But when we reflect that some of the greatest men in America, with the venerable Franklin and the illustrious Washington at their head; *some* of them the *fathers* and *saviors* of their country, men who have labored at the helm during a long and violent tempest, and guided us to the haven of peace—and *all* of them distinguished for their abilities, their acquaintance with ancient and modern governments, as well as with the temper, the passions, the interests and the wishes of the Americans;—when we reflect on these circumstances, it is impossible to resist impressions of respect, and we are almost impelled to suspect our own judgements, when we call in question any part of the system, which they have recommended for adoption. Not having the same means of information, we are more liable to mistake the nature and tendency of particular articles of the constitution, or the reasons on which they were admitted. Great confidence therefore should be reposed in the abilities, the zeal and integrity of that respectable body. But after all, if the constitution should, in its future operation, be found defective or inconvenient, two-thirds of both houses of Congress or the application of two-thirds of the legislatures, may open the door for amendments. Such improvements may then be made, as experience shall dictate.

Let us then consider the *New Federal Constitution,* as it really is, an *improvement* on the *best* constitutions that the world ever saw. In the house of representatives, the people of America have an equal voice and suffrage. The choice of men is placed in the freemen or electors at large; and the frequency of elections, and the responsibility of the members, will render them sufficiently dependent on their constituents. The senate will be composed of older men; and while their regular dismission from office, once in six years, will preserve their dependence on their constituents, the duration of their existence will give firmness to their decisions, and temper the factions which must necessarily prevail in the other branch. The president of the United States is elective, and what is a capital improvement on the best governments, the mode of chusing him excludes the danger of faction and corruption. As the supreme executive, he is invested with power to enforce the laws of the union and give energy to the federal government.

The constitution defines the powers of Congress; and every power not expressly delegated to that body, remains in the several state-legislatures. The sovereignty and the republican form of government of each state is guaranteed by the constitution; and the bounds of jurisdiction between the federal and respective state governments, are marked with precision. In theory, it has all the energy and freedom of the British and Roman governments, without their defects. In short, the privileges of freemen are interwoven into the feelings and habits of the Americans; *liberty* stands on the immoveable basis of a general distribution of property and diffusion of knowledge; but the Americans must cease to contend, to fear, and to hate, before they can realize the benefits of independence and government, or enjoy the blessings, which heaven has lavished, in rich profusion, upon this western world.

PART SIX The Bill of Rights

Engraving of Joseph Story by J. Cheney, from a crayon drawing by
W. W. Story. *Life and Letters of Joseph Story* (Boston, 1851)

Opposition to the new Constitution was rooted in fear that the new, more powerful central government would invade the accustomed rights of the states and of the people. Whether as subjects of British colonies or citizens of independent states, Americans had always ruled themselves in most matters—looking first to small communities or townships, then to the colonial or state government, and only in more general, common matters beyond their state borders. Moreover, Americans' experience with the central government of Great Britain had been one in which their customary rights, guaranteed by their charters and codes of law, had been repeatedly violated. Thus, "Anti-Federalists" criticized the proposed Constitution as a danger to the people's ability to rule themselves and to live free from the kinds of impositions visited upon them by Great Britain.

Anti-Federalists spent most of their time and energy proposing amendments to the Constitution aimed at defending the rights of the states and of the people. A number of the changes they sought were structural. For example, Anti-Federalists often sought to take away the central government's right to tax citizens directly, rather than by requisitioning money from the states, which then would tax their citizens as they saw fit. In the end, the focus was on calls for guarantees that the central government would not violate certain individual rights or intrude upon certain policy areas considered appropriate only for state action. Selections here illustrate the debate on the purpose and nature of such guarantees when the central government has been given only certain specific powers to act, and only in certain defined policy areas.

The Federalist, Papers 84 and 85

ALEXANDER HAMILTON, JAMES MADISON, AND JOHN JAY

1787

In these selections we see the main line of Federalist argument: that a Bill of Rights was unnecessary and dangerous. It was unnecessary because the Constitution granted only certain clearly defined powers to the central government. It was dangerous because any attempt to reduce the traditional rights enjoyed by Americans to a few statements would leave out of the Constitution—and presumably without legal defense—many important rights and privileges.

No. 84

ALEXANDER HAMILTON

Concerning several miscellaneous objections

In the course of the foregoing review of the constitution, I have endeavoured to answer most of the objections which have appeared against it. There remain, however, a few which either did not fall naturally under any particular head, or were forgotten in their proper places. These shall now be discussed: but as the subject has been drawn into great length, I shall so far consult brevity, as to comprise all my observations on these miscellaneous points in a single paper.

The most considerable of the remaining objections is, that the plan of the convention contains no bill of rights. Among other answers given to this, it has been upon different occasions remarked, that the constitutions of several of the states are in a similar predicament. I add, that New York is of the number. And yet the persons who in this state oppose the new system, while they profess an unlimited admiration for our particular constitution, are among the most intemperate partizans of a bill of rights. To justify their zeal in this matter, they allege two things: one is, that though the constitution of New York has no bill of rights prefixed to it, yet it contains in the body of it, various provisions in favour of particular privileges and rights, which, in substance, amount to the same thing; the other is, that the constitution adopts, in their full extent, the common and statute law of Great Britain, by which many other rights, not expressed, are equally secured.

To the first I answer, that the constitution offered by the convention contains, as well as the constitution of this state, a number of such provisions.

Independent of those which relate to the structure of the government, we find the following: Article I, section 3, clause 7. "Judgment in cases of impeachment shall not extend further than to removal from office, and disqualification to hold and enjoy any office of honour, trust, or profit under the United States; but the party convicted shall, nevertheless, be liable and subject to indictment, trial, judgment, and punishment, according to law." Section 9. of the same article, clause 2. "The privilege of the writ of *habeas corpus* shall not be suspended, unless when in cases of rebellion or invasion the public safety may require it." Clause 3. "No bill of attainder or *ex post facto* law shall be passed." Clause 7. "No title of nobility shall be granted by the United States; and no person holding any office of profit or trust under them, shall, without the consent of the congress, accept of any present, emolument, office, or title, of any kind whatever, from any king, prince, or foreign state." Article II. section 2. clause 3. "The trial of all crimes, except in cases of impeachment, shall be by jury; and such trial shall be held in the state where the said crimes shall have been committed; but when not committed within any state, the trial shall be at such place or places as the congress may by law have directed." Section 3. of the same article: "Treason against the United States shall consist only in levying war against them, or in adhering to their enemies, giving them aid and comfort. No person shall be convicted of treason, unless on the testimony of two witnesses to the same overt act, or on confession in open court." And clause 3. of the same section: "The congress shall have power to declare the punishment of treason; but no attainder of treason shall work corruption of blood, or forfeiture, except during the life of the person attainted."

It may well be a question, whether these are not, upon the whole, of equal importance with any which are to be found in the constitution of this state. The establishment of the writ of *habeas corpus,* the prohibition of *ex post facto* laws, and of TITLES OF NOBILITY, *to which we have no corresponding provisions in our constitution,* are perhaps greater securities to liberty than any it contains. The creation of crimes after the commission of the fact, or, in other words, the subjecting of men to punishment for things which, when they were done, were breaches of no law; and the practice of arbitrary imprisonments have been, in all ages, the favourite and most formidable instruments of tyranny. The observations of the judicious Blackstone, in reference to the latter, are well worthy of recital: "To bereave a man of life (says he) or by violence to confiscate his estate, without accusation or trial, would be so gross and notorious an act of despotism, as must at once convey the alarm of tyranny throughout the whole nation; but confinement of the person, by secretly hurrying him to jail, where his sufferings are unknown or forgotten, is a less public, a less stricking, and therefore *a more dangerous engine* of arbitrary government." And as a remedy for this fatal evil, he is every where peculiarly emphatical in his encomiums on the *habeas corpus* act, which in one place he calls "the BULWARK of the British constitution."

Nothing need be said to illustrate the importance of the prohibition of titles of nobility. This may truly be denominated the corner stone of republican government for so long as they are excluded, there can never be serious danger that the government will be any other than that of the people.

To the second, that is, to the pretended establishment of the common and statute law by the constitution, I answer, that they are expressly made subject "to such alterations and provisions as the legislature shall from time to time make concerning the same." They are therefore at any moment liable to repeal by the ordinary legislative power, and of course have no constitutional sanction. The only use of the declaration was to recognize the ancient law, and to remove doubts which might have been occasioned by the revolution. This consequently can be considered as no part of a declaration of rights; which under our constitutions must be intended to limit the power of the government itself.

It has been several times truly remarked, that bills of rights are, in their origin, stipulations between kings and their subjects, abridgments of prerogative in favour of privilege, reservations of rights not surrendered to the prince. Such as MAGNA CHARTA, obtained by the Barons, sword in hand, from king John. Such were the subsequent confirmations of that charter by succeeding princes. Such was the *petition of right* assented to by Charles the First, in the beginning of his reign. Such also, was the declaration of right presented by the lords and commons to the prince of Orange in 1688, and afterwards thrown into the form of an act of parliament, called the bill of rights. It is evident, therefore, that according to their primitive signification, they have no application to constitutions professedly founded upon the power of the people, and executed by their immediate representatives and servants. Here, in strictness, the people surrender nothing; and as they retain every thing, they have no need of particular reservations. "WE THE PEOPLE of the United States, to secure the blessings of liberty to ourselves and our posterity, do *ordain* and *establish* this constitution for the United States of America:" this is a better recognition of popular rights, than volumes of those aphorisms, which make the principal figure in several of our state bills of rights, and which would sound much better in a treatise of ethics, than in a constitution of government.

But a minute detail of particular rights, is certainly far less applicable to a constitution like that under consideration, which is merely intended to regulate the general political interests of the nation, than to one which has the regulation of every species of personal and private concerns. If therefore the loud clamours against the plan of convention, on this score, are well founded, no epithets of reprobation will be too strong for the constitution of this state. But the truth is, that both of them contain all which, in relation to their objects, is reasonably to be desired.

I go further, and affirm, that bills of rights, in the sense and to the extent they are contended for, are not only unnecessary in the proposed constitution, but would even be dangerous. They would contain various exceptions to powers not granted; and on this very account, would afford a colourable pretext to claim more than were granted. For why declare that things shall not be done, which there is no power to do? Why, for instance, should it be said, that the liberty of the press shall not be restrained, when no power is given by which restrictions may be imposed? I will not contend that such a provision would confer a regulating power; but it is evident that it would furnish, to men disposed to usurp, a plausible pretence for claiming that power. They might urge with a semblance of reason, that the constitution ought not to be charged with the absurdity of providing against the abuse of an authority, which was not given, and that the provision against restraining the liberty of the press afforded a clear implication, that a right to prescribe proper regulations concerning it, was intended to be vested in the national government. This may serve as a specimen of the numerous handles which would be given to the doctrine of constructive powers, by the indulgence of an injudicious zeal for bills of rights.

On the subject of the liberty of the press, as much has been said, I cannot forbear adding a remark or two: in the first place, I observe that there is not a syllable concerning it in the constitution of this state; in the next, I contend that whatever has been said about it in that of any other state, amounts to nothing. What signifies a declaration, that "the liberty of the press shall be inviolably preserved?" What is the liberty of the press? Who can give it any definition which would not leave the utmost latitude for evasion? I hold it to be impracticable; and from this I infer, that its security, whatever fine declarations may be inserted in any constitution respecting it, must altogether depend on public opinion, and on the general spirit of the people and of the government.* And here, after all, as intimated upon

another occasion, must we seek for the only solid basis of all our rights.

There remains but one other view of this matter to conclude the point. The truth is, after all the declamation we have heard, that the constitution is itself, in every rational sense, and to every useful purpose, A BILL OF RIGHTS. The several bills of rights, in Great Britain, form its constitution, and conversely the constitution of each state is its bill of rights. In like manner the proposed constitution, if adopted, will be the bill of rights of the union. Is it one object of a bill of rights to declare and specify the political privileges of the citizens in the structure and administration of the government? This is done in the most ample and precise manner in the plan of the convention; comprehending various precautions for the public security, which are not to be found in any of the state constitutions. Is another object of a bill of rights to define certain immunities and modes of proceeding, which are relative to personal and private concerns? This we have seen has also been attended to, in a variety of cases, in the same plan. Adverting therefore to the substantial meaning of a bill of rights, it is absurd to allege that it is not to be found in the work of the convention. It may be said that it does not go far enough, though it will not be easy to make this appear; but it can with no propriety be contended that there is no such thing. It certainly must be immaterial what mode is observed as to the order of declaring the rights of the citizens, if they are provided for in any part of the instrument which establishes the government. Whence it must be apparent, that much of what has been said on this subject rests merely on verbal and nominal distinctions, entirely foreign to the substance of the thing.

Another objection, which, from the frequency of its repetition, may be presumed to be relied on, is of this nature: it is improper (say the objectors) to confer such large powers, as are proposed, upon the national government; because the seat of that government must of necessity be too remote from many of the states to admit of a proper knowledge on the part of the constituent, of the conduct of the representative body. This argument, if it proves any

*To show that there is a power in the constitution, by which the liberty of the press may be affected, recourse has been had to the power of taxation. It is said, that duties may be laid upon publications so high as to amount to a prohibition. I know not by what logic it could be maintained, that the declarations in the state constitutions, in favour of the freedom of the press, would be a constitutional impediment to the imposition of duties upon publications by the state legislatures. It cannot certainly be pretended that any degree of duties, however low, would be an abridgement of the liberty of the press. We know that newspapers are taxed in Great Britain, and yet it is notorious that the press no where enjoys greater liberty than in that country. And if duties of any kind may be laid without a violation of that liberty, it is evident that the extent must depend on legislative discretion, regulated by public opinion; so that after all general declarations respecting the liberty of the press, will give it no greater security than it will have without them. The same invasions of it may be effected under the state constitutions which contain those

declarations through the means of taxation, as under the proposed constitution, which has nothing of the kind. It would be quite as significant to declare, that government ought to be free, that taxes ought not to be excessive, &c. as that the liberty of the press ought not to be restrained.

thing, proves that there ought to be no general government whatever. For the powers which, it seems to be agreed on all hands, ought to be vested in the union, cannot be safely intrusted to a body which is not under every requisite control. But there are satisfactory reasons to show, that the objection is, in reality, not well founded. There is in most of the arguments which relate to distance, a palpable illusion of the imagination. What are the sources of information, by which the people in any distant county must regulate their judgment of the conduct of their representatives in the state legislature? Of personal observation they can have no benefit. This is confined to the citizens on the spot. They must therefore depend on the information of intelligent men, in whom they confide: and how must these men obtain their information? Evidently from the complexion of public measures, from the public prints, from correspondences with their representatives, and with other persons who reside at the place of their deliberations.

It is equally evident that the like sources of information would be open to the people, in relation to the conduct of their representatives in the general government: and the impediments to a prompt communication which distance may be supposed to create, will be overbalanced by the effects of the vigilance of the state governments. The executive and legislative bodies of each state will be so many sentinels over the persons employed in every department of the national administration; and as it will be in their power to adopt and pursue a regular and effectual system of intelligence, they can never be at a loss to know the behaviour of those who represent their constituents in the national councils, and can readily communicate the same knowledge to the people. Their disposition to apprize the community of whatever may prejudice its interests from another quarter, may be relied upon, if it were only from the rivalship of power. And we may conclude with the fullest assurance, that the people, through that channel, will be better informed of the conduct of their national representatives, than they can be by any means they now possess, of that of their state representatives.

It ought also to be remembered, that the citizens who inhabit the country at and near the seat of government will, in all questions that affect the general liberty and prosperity, have the same interest with those who are at a distance; and that they will stand ready to sound the alarm when necessary, and to point out the actors in any pernicious project. The public papers will be expeditious messengers of intelligence to the most remote inhabitants of the union.

Among the many curious objections which have appeared against the proposed constitution, the most extraordinary and the least colourable is derived from the want of some provision respecting the debts due *to* the United States. This has been represented as a tacit relinquishment of those debts, and as a wicked contrivance to screen public defaulters. The newspapers have teemed with the most inflammatory railings on this head; yet there is nothing clearer than that the suggestion is entirely void of foundation, the offspring of extreme ignorance or extreme dishonesty. In addition to the remarks I have made upon the subject in another place, I shall only observe, that as it is a plain dictate of common sense, so it is also an established doctrine of political law, that *"states neither lose any of their rights, nor are discharged from any of their obligations, by a change in the form of their civil government."*

The last objection of any consequence at present recollected, turns upon the article of expense. If it were even true, that the adoption of the proposed government would occasion a considerable increase of expense, it would be an objection that ought to have no weight against the plan. The great bulk of the citizens of America, are with reason convinced that union is the basis of their political happiness. Men of sense of all parties now, with few exceptions, agree that it cannot be preserved under the present system, nor without radical alterations; that new and extensive powers ought to be granted to the national head, and that these require a different organization of the federal government; a single body being an unsafe depository of such ample authorities. In conceding all this, the question of expense is given up; for it is impossible, with any degree of safety, to narrow the foundation upon which the system is to stand. The two branches of the legislature are, in the first instance, to consist of only sixty-five persons; the same number of which congress, under the existing confederation, may be composed. It is true that this number is intended to be increased; but this is to keep pace with the progress of the population and resources of the country. It is evident, that a less number would, even in the first instance, have been unsafe; and that a continuance of the present number would, in a more advanced stage of population, be a very inadequate representation of the people.

Whence is the dreaded augmentation of expense to

spring: One source indicated, is the multiplication of offices under the new government. Let us examine this a little.

It is evident that the principal departments of the administration under the present government, are the same which will be required under the new. There are now a secretary at war, a secretary for foreign affairs, a board of treasury consisting of three persons, a treasurer, assistants, clerks, &c. These offices are indispensable under any system, and will suffice under the new, as well as the old. As to ambassadors and other ministers and agents in foreign countries, the proposed constitution can make no other difference, than to render their characters, where they reside, more respectable, and their services more useful. As to persons to be employed in the collection of the revenues, it is unquestionably true that these will form a very considerable addition to the number of federal officers; but it will not follow, that this will occasion an increase of public expense. It will be in most cases nothing more than an exchange of state for national officers. In the collection of all duties, for instance, the persons employed will be wholly of the latter description. The states individually, will stand in no need of any for this purpose. What difference can it make in point of expense, to pay officers of the customs appointed by the state, or by the United States.

Where then are we to seek for those additional articles of expense, which are to swell the account to the enormous size that has been represented? The chief item which occurs to me, respects the support of the judges of the United States. I do not add the president, because there is now a president of congress, whose expenses may not be far, if any thing, short of those which will be incurred on account of the president of the United States. The support of the judges will clearly be an extra expense, but to what extent will depend on the particular plan which may be adopted in regard to this matter. But upon no reasonable plan can it amount to a sum which will be an object of material consequence.

Let us now see what there is to counterbalance any extra expense that may attend the establishment of the proposed government. The first thing which presents itself is, that a great part of the business, that now keeps congress sitting through the year, will be transacted by the president. Even the management of foreign negotiations will naturally devolve upon him, according to general principles concerted with the senate, and subject to their final concurrence. Hence it is evident, that a portion of the year will suffice for the session of both the senate and the house of representatives: we may suppose about a fourth for the latter, and a third, or perhaps half, for the former. The extra business of treaties and appointments may give this extra occupation to the senate. From this circumstance we may infer, that until the house of representatives shall be increased greatly beyond its present number, there will be a considerable saving of expense from the difference between the constant session of the present, and the temporary session of the future congress.

But there is another circumstance, of great importance in the view of economy, The business of the United States has hitherto occupied the state legislatures, as well as congress. The latter has made requisitions which the former have had to provide for. It has thence happened, that the sessions of the state legislatures have been protracted greatly beyond what was necessary for the execution of the mere local business. More than half their time has been frequently employed in matters which related to the United States. Now the members who compose the legislatures of the several states amount to two thousand and upwards; which number has hitherto performed what, under the new system, will be done in the first instance by sixty-five persons, and probably at no future period by above a fourth or a fifth of that number. The congress under the proposed government will do all the business of the United States themselves, without the intervention of the state legislatures, who thenceforth will have only to attend to the affairs of their particular states, and will not have to sit in any proportion as long as they have heretofore done. This difference, in the time of the sessions of the state legislatures, will be clear gain, and will alone form an article of saving, which may be regarded as an equivalent for any additional objects of expense that may be occasioned by the adoption of the new system.

The result from these observations is, that the sources of additional expense from the establishment of the proposed constitution, are much fewer than may have been imagined; that they are counterbalanced by considerable objects of saving; that that, while it is questionable on which side of the scale will preponderate, it is certain that a government less expensive would be incompetent to the purposes of the union.

PUBLIUS

No. 85

ALEXANDER HAMILTON

Conclusion

According to the formal division of the subject of these papers, announced in my first number, there would appear still to remain for discussion two points. . . . "the analogy of the proposed government to your own state constitution," and "the additional security which its adoption will afford to republican government, to liberty, and to property." But these heads have been so fully anticipated, and so completely exhausted in the progress of the work, that it would now scarcely be possible to do any thing more than repeat, in a more dilated form, which has been already said; which the advanced stage of the question, and the time already spent upon it, conspire to forbid.

It is remarkable, that the resemblance of the plan of the convention to the act which organizes the government of this state, holds, not less with regard to many of the supposed defects, than to the real excellencies of the former. Among the pretended defects, are the re-eligibility of the executive; the want of a council; the omission of a formal bill of rights; the omission of a provision respecting the liberty of the press: these, and several others, which have been noted in the course of our inquiries, are as much chargeable on the existing constitution of this state, as on the one proposed for the union: and a man must have slender pretensions to consistency, who can rail at the latter for imperfections which he finds no difficulty in excusing in the former. Nor indeed can there be a better proof of the insincerity and affectation of some of the zealous adversaries of the plan of the convention, who profess to be devoted admirers of the government of this state, than the fury with which they have attacked that plan, for matters in regard to which our own constitution is equally, or perhaps more vulnerable.

The additional securities to republican government, to liberty, and to property, to be derived from the adoption of the plan, consist chiefly in the restraints which the preservation of the union will impose upon local factions and insurrections, and upon the ambition of powerful individuals in single states, who might acquire credit and influence enough, from leaders and favourites, to become the despots of the people: in the diminution of the opportunities to foreign intrigue, which the dissolution of the confederacy would invite and facilitate; in the prevention of extensive military establishments, which could not fail to grow out of wars between the states in a disunited situation: in the express guarantee of a republican form of government to each; in the absolute and universal exclusion of titles of nobility; and in the precautions against the repetition of those practices on the part of the state governments, which have undermined the foundations of property and credit: have planted mutual distrust in the breasts of all classes of citizens: and have occasioned an almost universal prostration of morals.

Thus have I, fellow citizens, executed the task I had assigned to myself; with what success your conduct must determine. I trust, at least, you will admit, that I have not failed in the assurance I gave you respecting the spirit with which my endeavours should be conducted. I have addressed myself purely to your judgments, and have studiously avoided those asperities which are too apt to disgrace political disputants of all parties, and which have been not a little provoked by the language and conduct of the opponents of the constitution. The charge of a conspiracy against the liberties of the people, which has been indiscriminately brought against the advocates of the plan, has something in it too wanton and too malignant not to excite the indignation of every man who feels in his own bosom a refutation of the calumny. The perpetual changes which have been rung upon the wealthy, the well born, and the great, are such as to inspire the disgust of all sensible men. And the unwarrantable concealments and misrepresentations, which have been in various ways practised to keep the truth from the public eye, are of a nature to demand the reprobation of all honest men. It is possible that these circumstances may have occasionally betrayed me into intemperances of expression which I did not intend: it is certain that I have frequently felt a struggle between sensibility and moderation; and if the former has in some instances prevailed, it must be my excuse, that it has been neither often nor much.

Let us now pause, and ask ourselves whether, in the course of these papers, the proposed constitution has not been satisfactorily vindicated from the aspersions thrown upon it; and whether it has not been shown to be worthy of the public approbation, and necessary to the public safety and prosperity. Every man is bound to answer these questions to himself, according to the best of his conscience and understanding, and to act agreeably to the genuine and sober dictates of his judgment. This is a duty from which nothing can give him a dispensation. It is one that he is called upon, nay, constrained by all the obligations that form the bands on society, to discharge sincerely and honestly. No partial motive, no particular interest, no pride of opinion, no temporary passion or prejudice, will justify to himself, to his country, to his posterity, an improper election of the part he is to act. Let him beware of an obstinate adherence to party: let him reflect, that the object upon which he is to decide is not a particular interest of the community, but the very existence of the nation: and let him remember, that a majority of America has already given its sanction to the plan which he is to approve or reject.

I shall not dissemble, that I feel an entire confidence in the arguments which recommend the proposed system to your adoption; and that I am unable to discern any real force in those by which it has been assailed. I am persuaded, that it is the best which our political situation, habits, and opinions will admit, and superior to any the revolution has produced.

Concessions on the part of the friends of the plan, that it has not a claim to absolute perfection, have afforded matter of no small triumph to its enemies. Why, say they, should we adopt an imperfect thing? Why not amend it, and make it perfect before it is irrevocably established? This may be plausible, but it is plausible only. In the first place I remark, that the extent of these concessions has been greatly exaggerated. They have been stated as amounting to an admission, that the plan is radically defective; and that, without material alterations, the rights and the interests of the community cannot be safely confided to it. This, as far as I have understood the meaning of those who make the concessions, is an entire perversion of their sense. No advocate of the measure can be found, who will not declare as his sentiment, that the system, though it may not be perfect in every part, is, upon the whole, a good one; is the best that the present views and circumstances of the country will permit; and is such a one as promises every species of security which a reasonable people can desire.

I answer in the next place, that I should esteem it the extreme of imprudence to prolong the precarious state of our national affairs, and to expose the union to the jeopardy of successive experiments, in the chimerical pursuit of a perfect plan. I never expect to see a perfect work from imperfect man. The result of the deliberations of all collective bodies, must necessarily be a compound as well of the errors and prejudices, as of the good sense and wisdom of the individuals of whom they are composed. The compacts which are to embrace thirteen distinct states, in a common bond of amity and union, must as necessarily be a compromise of as many dissimilar interests and inclinations. How can perfection spring from such materials?

The reasons assigned in an excellent little pamphlet lately published in this city, unanswerably show the utter improbability of assembling a new convention, under circumstances in any degree so favourable to a happy issue, as those in which the late convention met, deliberated, and concluded. I will not repeat the arguments there used, as I presume the production itself has had an extensive circulation. It is certainly well worth the perusal of every friend to his country. There is however one point of light in which the subject of amendments still remains to be considered; and in which it has not yet been exhibited. I cannot resolve to conclude, without first taking a survey of it in this aspect.

It appears to me susceptible of complete demonstration, that it will be far more easy to obtain subsequent than previous amendments to the constitution. The moment an alteration is made in the present plan, it becomes, to the purpose of adoption, a new one, and must undergo a new decision of each state. To its complete establishment throughout the union, it will therefore require the concurrence of thirteen states. If, on the contrary, the constitution should once be ratified by all the states as it stands, alterations in it may at any time be effected by nine states. In this view alone the chances are as thirteen to nine* in favour of subsequent amendments, rather than of the original adoption of an entire system.

This is not all. Every constitution for the United States must inevitably consist of a great variety of particulars, in which thirteen independent states are to be accommodated in their interests or opinions of interest. We may of course expect to see, in any body of men charged with its original formation, very different combinations of the parts upon different points. Many of those who form the majority on one question, may become the minority on a second, and an association dissimilar to either, may constitute

*It may rather be said TEN, for though two-thirds may set on foot the measure, three-fourths must ratify.

the majority on a third. Hence the necessity of moulding and arranging all the particulars which are to compose the whole, in such a manner, as to satisfy all the parties to the compact; and hence also an immense multiplication of difficulties and casualties in obtaining the collective assent to a final act. The degree of that multiplication must evidently be in a ratio to the number of particulars and the number of parties.

But every amendment to the constitution, if once established, would be a single proposition, and might be brought forward singly. There would then be no necessity for management or compromise, in relation to any other point; no giving nor taking. The will of the requisite number, would at once bring the matter to a decisive issue. And consequently whenever nine, or rather ten states, were united in the desire of a particular amendment, that amendment must infallibly prevail. There can, therefore, be no comparison between the facility of affecting an amendment, and that of establishing in the first instance a complete constitution.

In opposition to the probability of subsequent amendments it has been urged, that the persons delegated to the administration of the national government, will always be disinclined to yield up any portion of the authority of which they were once possessed. For my own part, I acknowledge a thorough conviction that any amendments which may, upon mature consideration, be thought useful, will be applicable to the organization of the government, not to the mass of its powers; and on this account alone, I think there is no weight in the observation just stated. I also think there is little force in it on another account. The intrinsic difficulty of governing THIRTEEN STATES, independent of calculations upon an ordinary degree of public spirit and integrity, will, in my opinion, constantly *impose* on the national rulers, the *necessity* of a spirit of accommodation to the reasonable expectations of their constituents. But there is yet a further consideration, which proves beyond the possibility of doubt, that the observation is futile. It is this, that the national rulers, whenever nine states concur, will have no option upon the subject. By the fifth article of the plan the congress will be *obliged*, "on the application of the legislatures of two-thirds of the states, (which at present amount to nine) to call a convention for proposing amendments, which *shall be valid* to all intents and purposes as part of the constitution, when ratified by

the legislatures of three-fourths of the states or by conventions in three-fourths thereof." The words of this article are peremptory. The congress "*shall* call a convention." Nothing in this particular is left to discretion. Of consequence all the declamation about the disinclination to a change, vanishes in air. Nor, however difficult it may be supposed to unite two-thirds, or three-fourths of the state legislatures, in amendments which may affect local interests, can there be any room to apprehend any such difficulty in a union on points which are merely relative to the general liberty or security of the people. We may safely rely on the disposition of the state legislatures to erect barriers against the encroachments of the national authority.

If the foregoing argument be a fallacy, certain it is that I am myself deceived by it; for it is, in my conception, one of those rare instances in which a political truth can be brought to the test of mathematical demonstration. Those who see the matter in the same light, however zealous they may be for amendments, must agree in the propriety of a previous adoption, as the most direct road to their object.

The zeal for attempts to amend, prior to the establishment of the constitution, must abate in every man, who is ready to accede to the truth of the following observations of a writer, equally solid and ingenious: "to balance a large state or society (says he) whether monarchical or republican, on general laws, is a work of so great difficulty, that no human genius, however comprehensive, is able by the mere dint of reason and reflection, to effect it. The judgments of many must unite in the work: EXPERIENCE must guide their labour: TIME must bring it to perfection: and the FEELING of inconveniences must correct the mistakes which they *inevitably* fall into, in their first trials and experiments." These judicious reflections contain a lesson of moderation to all the sincere lovers of the union, and ought to put them upon their guard against hazarding anarchy, civil war, a perpetual alienation of the states from each other, and perhaps the military despotism of a victorious demagogue, in the pursuit of what they are not likely to obtain, but from TIME and EXPERIENCE. It may be in me a defect of political fortitude, but I acknowledge that I cannot entertain an equal tranquillity with those who affect to treat the dangers of a longer continuance in our present situation as imaginary. A NATION without a NATIONAL GOVERNMENT, is an awful spectacle. The establishment of a constitution, in time of profound peace, by the voluntary consent of a whole people, is a PRODIGY, to the completion of which I look forward with trembling anxiety. In so arduous an enterprise, I can reconcile it to no rules of prudence to let go the hold we now have, upon seven out of the thirteen states; and after having passed over so considerable a part of the ground, to re-commence the course. I dread the more the consequences of new attempts, because I KNOW THAT POWERFUL INDIVIDUALS, in this and in other states, are enemies to a general national government in every possible shape.

PUBLIUS

Letter I

"CENTINEL"

October 1787

The letters of "Centinel" were probably written by Samuel Bryan, son of Judge George Bryan, who was a leader of Pennsylvania Anti-Federalists. They first appeared in the Philadelphia *Independent Gazetteer* (from which this selection is taken) and the Philadelphia *Freeman's Journal.* Several were widely reprinted. Throughout these letters, Centinel seeks to live up to his name by warning Americans of the dangers to their liberties posed by the new Constitution. Centinel's first letter, the most successful, was cited for its defense of common law rights and its attack on the wisdom of political checks and balances.

Letter I

To the Freemen of Pennsylvania
  Friends, Countrymen and *Fellow Citizens,*
PERMIT one of yourselves to put you in mind of certain *liberties* and *privileges* secured to you by the constitution of this commonwealth, and to beg your serious attention to his uninterested opinion upon the plan of federal government submitted to your consideration, before you surrender these great and valuable privileges up forever. Your present frame of government, secures to you a right to hold yourselves, houses, papers and possessions free from search and seizure, and therefore warrants granted without oaths or affirmations first made, affording sufficient foundation for them, whereby any officer or messenger may be commanded or required to search your houses or seize your persons or property, not particularly described in such warrant, shall not be granted. Your constitution further provides "that in controversies respecting property, and in suits between man and man, the parties have a right *to trial by jury, which ought to be held sacred.*" It also provides and declares, *"that the people have a right of* FREEDOM OF SPEECH, *and of* WRITING *and* PUBLISHING *their sentiments, therefore* THE FREEDOM OF THE PRESS OUGHT NOT TO BE RESTRAINED." The constitution of Pennsylvania is *yet* in

existence, as *yet* you have the right to *freedom of speech, and of publishing your sentiments.* How long those rights will appertain to you, you yourselves are called upon to say, whether your *houses* shall continue to be your *castles;* whether your *papers,* your *persons* and your *property,* are to be held sacred and free from *general warrants,* you are now to determine. Whether the *trial by jury* is to continue as your birthright, the freemen of Pennsylvania, nay, of all America, are now called upon to declare.

Without presuming upon my own judgement, I cannot think it an unwarrantable presumption to offer my private opinion, and call upon others for their's; and if I use my pen with the boldness of a freeman, it is because I know that *the liberty of the press yet remains unviolated,* and *juries yet are judges.*

The late Convention have submitted to your consideration on a plan of a new, federal government—The subject is highly interesting to your future welfare—Whether it be calculated to promote the great ends of civil society, *viz.* the happiness and prosperity of the community; it behoves you well to consider, uninfluenced by the authority of names. Instead of that frenzy of enthusiasm, that has actuated the citizens of Philadelphia, in their approbation of the proposed plan, before it was possible that it could be the result of a rational investigation into its principles; it ought to be dispassionately and deliberately examined, and its own intrinsic merit the only criterion of your patronage. If ever free and unbiassed discussion was proper or necessary, it is on such an occasion.—All the blessings of liberty and the dearest privileges of freemen, are now at stake and dependent on your present conduct. Those who are competent to the task of developing the principles of government, ought to be encouraged to come forward, and thereby the better enable the people to make a proper judgment; for the science of government is so abstruse, that few are able to judge for themselves; without such assistance the people are too apt to yield an implicit assent to the opinions of those characters, whose abilities are held in the highest esteem, and to those in whose integrity and patriotism they can confide; not considering that the love of domination is generally in proportion to talents, abilities, and superior acquirements; and that the men of the greatest purity of intention may be made instruments of despotism in the hands of the *artful and designing*. If it were not for the stability and attachment which time and habit gives to forms of government, it would be in the power of the enlightened and aspiring few, if they should combine, at any time to destroy the best establishments, and even make the people the instruments of their own subjugation.

The late revolution having effaced in a great measure all former habits, and the present institutions are so recent, that there exists not that great reluctance to innovation, so remarkable in old communities, and which accords with reason, for the most comprehensive mind cannot foresee the full operation of material changes on civil polity; it is the genius of the common law to resist innovation.

The wealthy and ambitious, who in every community think they have a right to lord it over their fellow creatures, have availed themselves, very successfully, of this favorable disposition; for the people thus unsettled in their sentiments, have been prepared to accede to any extreme of government; all the distresses and difficulties they experience, proceeding from various causes, have been ascribed to the impotency of the present confederation, and thence they have been led to expect full relief from the adoption of the proposed system of government; and in the other event, immediately ruin and annihilation as a nation. These characters flatter themselves that they have lulled all distrust and jealousy of their new plan, by gaining the concurrence of the two men in whom America has the highest confidence, and now triumphantly exult in the completion of their long meditated schemes of power and aggrandisement. I would be very far from insinuating that the two illustrious personages alluded to, have not the welfare of their country at heart; but that the unsuspecting goodness and zeal of the one, has been imposed on, in a subject of which he must be necessarily inexperienced, from his other arduous engagements; and that the weakness and indecision attendant on old age, has been practised on in the other.

I am fearful that the principles of government inculcated in Mr. Adams's treatise, and enforced in the numerous essays and paragraphs in the news-papers, have misled some well designing members of the late Convention.—But it will appear in the sequel, that the construction of the proposed plan of government is infinitely more extravagant.

I have been anxiously expecting that some enlightened patriot would, ere this, have taken up the pen to expose the futility, and counteract the baneful tendency of such principles. Mr. Adams's *sine qua non* of a good government is three balancing powers, whose repelling qualities are to produce an equilibrium of interests, and thereby promote the happiness of the whole community. He asserts that the administrators of every government, will ever be actuated by views of private interest and ambition, to the prejudice of the public good; that therefore the only effectual method to secure the rights of the people and promote their welfare, is to create an opposition of interests between the members of two distinct bodies, in the exercise of the powers of government, and balanced by those of a third. This hypothesis supposes human wisdom competent to the task of instituting three co-equal orders in government, and a corresponding weight in the community to enable them respectively to exercise their several parts, and whose views and interests should be so distinct as to prevent a coalition of any two of them for the destruction of the third. Mr. Adams, although he has traced the constitution of every form of government that ever existed, as far as history affords materials, has not been able to adduce a single instance of such a government; he indeed says that the British constitution is such in theory, but this is rather a confirmation that his principles are chimerical and not to be reduced to practice. If such an organization of power were practicable, how long would it continue? not a day— for there is so great a disparity in the talents, wisdom and industry of mankind, that the scale would presently preponderate to one or the other body, and with every accession of power the means of further increase would be greatly extended. The state of society in England is much more favorable to such a scheme of government than that of America. There they have a powerful hereditary nobility, and real distinctions of rank and interests; but even there, for want of that perfect equallity of power and distinction of interests, in the three orders of government, they exist but in name; the only operative and efficient check, upon the conduct of administration, is the sense of the people at large.

Suppose a government could be formed and supported on such principles, would it answer the great purposes of civil society; If the administrators of every government are actuated by views of private interest and ambition, how is the welfare and happiness of the community to be the result of such jarring adverse interests?

Therefore, as different orders in government will not produce the good of the whole, we must recur to other principles. I believe it will be found that the form of government, which holds those entrusted with power, in the greatest responsibility to their constituents, the best calculated for freemen. A republican, or free government, can only exist where the body of the people are virtuous, and where property is pretty equally divided, in such a government the people are the sovereign and their sense or opinion is the criterion of every public measure; for when this ceases to be the case, the nature of the government is changed, and an aristocracy, monarchy or despotism will rise on its ruin. The highest responsibility is to be attained, in a simple struction of government, for the great body of the people never steadily attend to the operations of government, and for want of due information are liable to be imposed on.—If you complicate the plan by various orders, the people will be perplexed and divided in their sentiments about the source of abuses or misconduct, some will impute it to the senate, others to the house of representatives, and so on, that the interposition of the people may be rendered imperfect or perhaps wholly abortive. But if, imitating the constitution of Pennsylvania, you vest all the legislative power in one body of men (separating the executive and judicial) elected for a short period, and necessarily excluded by rotation from permanency, and guarded from precipitancy and surprise by delays imposed on its proceedings, you will create the most perfect responsibility, for then, whenever the people feel a grievance they cannot mistake the authors, and will apply the remedy with certainty and effect, discarding them at the next election. This tie of responsibility will obviate all the dangers apprehended from a single legislature, and will the best secure the rights of the people.

Having promised thus much, I shall now proceed to the examination of the proposed plan of government, and I trust, shall make it appear to the meanest capacity, that it has none of the essential requisites of a free government, that it is neither founded on those balancing restraining powers, recommended by Mr. Adams and attempted in the British constitution, or possessed of that responsibility to its constituents, which, in my opinion, is the only effectual security for the liberties and happiness of the people; but on the contrary, that it is a most daring attempt to establish a despotic aristocracy among freemen, that the world has ever witnessed.

I shall previously consider the extent of the powers intended to be vested in Congress, before I examine the construction of the general government.

It will not be controverted that the legislative is the highest delegated power in government, and that all others are subordinate to it. The celebrated *Montesquieu* establishes it as a maxim, that legislation necessarily follows the power of taxation. By sect. 8, of the first article of the proposed plan of government, "the Congress are to have power to lay and collect taxes, duties, imposts and excises, to pay the debts and provide for the common defence and *general welfare* of the United States; but all duties, imposts and excises, shall be uniform throughout the United States." Now what can be more comprehensive than these words; not content by other sections of this plan, to grant all the great executive powers of a confederation, and a STANDING ARMY IN TIME OF PEACE, that grand engine of oppression, and moreover the absolute controul over the commerce of the United States and all external objects of revenue, such as unlimited imposts upon imports, &c.—they are to be vested with every species of *internal* taxation;—whatever taxes, duties and excises that they may deem requisite for the *general welfare,* may be imposed on the citizens of these states, levied by the officers of Congress, distributed through every district in America; and the collection would be enforced by the standing army, however grievous or improper they may be. The Congress may construe every purpose for which the state legislatures now lay taxes, to be for the *general welfare,* and thereby seize upon every object of revenue.

The judicial power by 1st sect. of article 3 ["]shall extend to all cases, in law and equity, arising under this constitution, the laws of the United States, and treaties made or which shall be made under their authority; to all cases affecting ambassadors, other public ministers and consuls; to all cases of admiralty and maritime jurisdiction, to controversies to which the United States shall be a party, to controversies between two or more states, between a state and citizens of another state, between citizens of different states, between citizens of the same state claiming lands under grants of different states, and between a state, or the citizens thereof, and foreign states, citizens or subjects."

The judicial power to be vested in one Supreme Court, and in such Inferior Courts as the Congress may from time to time ordain and establish.

The objects of jurisdiction recited above, are so numerous, and the shades of distinction between civil causes are oftentimes so slight, that it is more than probable that the state judicatories would be wholly superceded, for in contests about jurisdiction, the federal court, as the most powerful, would ever prevail. Every person acquainted with the history of the courts in England, knows by what ingenious sophisms they have, at different periods, extended the sphere of their jurisdiction over objects out of the line of their institution, and contrary to their very nature; courts of a criminal jurisdiction obtaining cognizance in civil causes.

To put the omnipotency of Congress over the state government and judicatories out of all doubt, the 6th article ordains that "this constitution and the laws of the United States which shall be made in pursuance thereof, and all treaties made, or which shall be made under the authority of the United States, shall be the *Supreme law of the land*, and the judges in every state shall be bound thereby, any thing in the constitution or laws of any state to the contrary notwithstanding."

By these sections the all prevailing power of taxation, and such extensive legislative and judicial powers are vested in the general government, as must in their operation, necessarily absorb the state legislatures and judicatories; and that such was in the contemplation of the framers of it, will appear from the provision made for such event, in another part of it; (but that, fearful of alarming the people by so great an innovation, they have suffered the forms of the separate governments to remain, as a blind). By sect. 4th of the 1st article, "the times, places and manner of holding elections for senators and representatives, shall be prescribed in each state by the legislature thereof; *but the Congress may at any time, by law, make or alter such regulations, except as to the place of chusing senators.*" The plain construction of which is, that when the state legislatures drop out of sight, from the necessary operation of this government, then Congress are to provide for the election and appointment of representatives and senators.

If the foregoing be a just comment—if the United States are to be melted down into one empire, it becomes you to consider, whether such a government, however constructed, would be eligible in so extended a territory; and whether it would be practicable, consistent with freedom?

It is the opinion of the greatest writers, that a very extensive country cannot be governed on democratical principles, on any other plan, than a confederation of a number of small republics, possessing all the powers of internal government, but united in the management of their foreign and general concerns.

It would not be difficult to prove, that any thing short of despotism, could not bind so great a country under one government; and that whatever plan you might, at the first setting out, establish, it would issue in a despotism.

If one general government could be instituted and maintained on principles of freedom, it would not be so competent to attend to the various local concerns and wants, of every particular district; as well as the peculiar governments, who are nearer the scene, and possessed of superior means of information, besides, if the business of the *whole* union is to be managed by one government, there would not be time. Do we not already see, that the inhabitants in a number of larger states, who are remote from the seat of government, are loudly complaining of the inconveniencies and disadvantages they are subjected to on this account, and that, to enjoy the comforts of local government, they are separating into smaller divisions.

Having taken a review of the powers, I shall now examine the construction of the proposed general government.

Art. 1 sect. 1. "All legislative powers herein granted shall be vested in a Congress of the United States, which shall consist of a senate and house of representatives." By another section, the president (the principal executive officer) has a conditional controul over their proceedings.

Sec. 2. "The house of representatives shall be composed of members chosen every second year, by the people of the several states. The number of representatives shall not exceed one for every 30,000 inhabitants."

The senate, the other constituent branch of the legislature, is formed by the legislature of each state appointing two senators, for the term of six years.

The executive power by Art. 2, Sec. 1. is to be vested in a president of the United States of America, elected for four years: Sec. 2. gives him power, by and with the consent of the senate to make treaties, provided two thirds of the senators present concur; and he shall nominate, and by and with the advice and consent of the senate, shall appoint ambassadors, other public ministers and consuls, judges of the Supreme Court, and all other officers of the United States, whose appointments are not herein otherwise provided for, and which shall be established by law,

&c. And by another section he has the absolute power of granting reprievs and pardons for treason and all other high crimes and misdemeanors, except in case of impeachment.

The foregoing are the outlines of the plan.

Thus we see, the house of representatives, are on the part of the people to balance the senate, who I suppose will be composed of the *better sort*, the *well born*, &c. The number of the representatives (being only one for every 30,000 inhabitants) appears to be too few, either to communicate the requisite information, of the wants, local circumstances and sentiments of so extensive an empire, or to prevent corruption and undue influence, in the exercise of such great powers; the term for which they are to be chosen, too long to preserve a due dependence and accountability to their constituents; and the mode and places of their election not sufficiently ascertained, for as Congress have the controul over both, they may govern the choice, by ordering the *representatives* of a *whole* state, to be *elected* in *one* place, and that too may be the most *inconvenient*.

The senate, the great efficient body in this plan of government, is constituted on the most unequal principles. The smallest state in the union has equal weight with the great States of Virginia, Massachusetts, or Pennsylvania. —The Senate, besides its legislative functions, has a very considerable share in the Executive; none of the principal appointments to office can be made without its advice and consent. The term and mode of its appointment, will lead to permanency; the members are chosen for six years, the mode is under the controul of Congress, and as there is no exclusion by rotation, they may be continued for life, which, from their extensive means of influence, would follow of course. The President, who would be a mere pageant of state, unless he coincides with the views of the Senate, would either become the head of the aristocratic junto in that body, or its minion; besides, their influence being the most predominant, could the best secure his re election to office. And from his power of granting pardons, he might screen from punishment the most reasonable attempts on the liberties of the people, when instigated by the Senate.

From this investigation into the organization of this government, it appears that it is devoid of all responsibility or accountability to the great body of the people, and that so far from being a regular balanced government, it would be in practice a *permanent* ARISTOCRACY.

The framers of it; actuated by the true spirit of such a government, which ever abominates and suppresses all free enquiry and discussion, have made no provision for the *liberty of the press,* that grand *palladium of freedom,* and *scourge of tyrants;* but observed a total silence on that head. It is the opinion of some great writers, that if the liberty of the press, by an institution of religion, or otherwise, could be rendered *sacred,* even in *Turkey,* that despotism would fly before it. And it is worthy of remark, that there is no declaration of personal rights, premised in most free constitutions; and that trial by *jury* in *civil* cases is taken away; for what other construction can be put on the following, viz. Article III. Sect. 2d. "In all cases affecting ambassadors, other public ministers and consuls, and those in which a State shall be party, the Supreme Court shall have *original* jurisdiction. In all the other cases above mentioned, the Supreme Court shall have *appellate* jurisdiction, both as to *law and fact?*" It would be a novelty in jurisprudence, as well as evidently improper to allow an appeal from the verdict of a jury, on the matter of fact; therefore, it implies and allows of a dismission of the jury in civil cases, and especially when it is considered, that jury trial in criminal cases is expressly stipulated for, but not in civil cases.

But our situation is represented to be so *critically* dreadful, that, however reprehensible and exceptionable the proposed plan of government may be, there is no alternative, between the adoption of it and absolute ruin.—My fellow citizens, things are not at that crisis, it is the argument of tyrants; the present distracted state of Europe secures us from injury on that quarter, and as to domestic dissentions, we have not so much to fear from them, as to precipitate us into this form of government; without it is a safe and a proper one. For remember, of all *possible* evils, that of *despotism* is the *worst* and the most to be *dreaded.*

Besides, it cannot be supposed, that the first essay on so difficult a subject, is so well digested, as it ought to be;— if the proposed plan, after a mature deliberation, should meet the approbation of the respective States, the matter will end; but if it should be found to be fraught with dangers and inconveniencies, a future general Convention being in possession of the objections, will be the better enabled to plan a suitable government.

Who's here so base, that would a bond-man be?
If any, speak; for him have I offended.
Who's here so vile, that will not love his country?
If any, speak; for him have I offended.

CENTINEL

Essay I

"BRUTUS"

October 1787

The essays of "Brutus" were probably written by Robert Yates. Yates was a judge, a dissenting member of the Constitutional Convention, and an ally of Governor George Clinton of New York. The pseudonym was meant to remind readers of Marcus Junius Brutus, who assassinated the emperor Julius Caesar in the name of the Roman Republic. Brutus's essays ran in the New York *Journal* during the same time period as *The Federalist*. In his first essay Brutus sets forth a comprehensive critique of the government that would be established under the Constitution. He focuses on the likelihood that the new central government will take over powers properly belonging to the states, leaving the people with no defense for their customary rights.

Essay I

To the Citizens of the State of New-York

When the public is called to investigate and decide upon a question in which not only the present members of the community are deeply interested, but upon which the happiness and misery of generations yet unborn is in great measure suspended, the benevolent mind cannot help feeling itself peculiarly interested in the result.

In this situation, I trust the feeble efforts of an individual, to lead the minds of the people to a wise and prudent determination, cannot fail of being acceptable to the candid and dispassionate part of the community. Encouraged by this consideration, I have been induced to offer my thoughts upon the present important crisis of our public affairs.

Perhaps this country never saw so critical a period in their political concerns. We have felt the feebleness of the ties by which these United-States are held together, and the want of sufficient energy in our present confederation, to manage, in some instances, our general concerns. Various expedients have been proposed to remedy these evils, but none have succeeded. At length a Convention of the states has been assembled, they have formed a constitution which will now, probably, be submitted to the people to ratify or reject, who are the fountain of all power, to whom alone it of right belongs to make or unmake constitutions, or forms of government, at their pleasure. The most important question that was ever proposed to your decision, or to the decision of any people under heaven, is before you, and you are to decide upon it by men of your own election, [chosen] specially for this purpose. If the constitution, offered to [your acceptance], be a wise one, calculated to preserve the [invaluable blessings] of liberty, to secure the inestimable rights of mankind, and promote human happiness, then, if you accept it, you will lay a lasting foundation of happiness for millions yet unborn; generations to come will rise up and call you blessed. You may rejoice in the prospects of this vast extended continent becoming filled with freemen, who will assert the dignity of human nature. You may solace yourselves with the idea, that society, in this favoured land, will [full] advance to the highest point of perfection; the human mind will expand in knowledge and virtue, and the golden age be, in some measure, realised. But if, on the other hand, this form of government contains principles that will lead to the subversion of liberty —if it tends to establish a despotism, or, what is worse, a tyrannic aristocracy; then, if you adopt it, this only remaining assylum for liberty will be [shut] up, and posterity will execrate your memory.

Momentous then is the question you have to determine, and you are called upon by every motive which should influence a noble and virtuous mind, to examine it well, and to make up a wise judgment. It is insisted, indeed, that this constitution must be received, be it ever so imperfect. If it has its defects, it is said, they can be best amended when they are experienced. But remember, when the people once part with power, they can seldom or never resume it again but by force. Many instances can be produced in which the people have voluntarily increased the powers of their rulers; but few, if any, in which rulers have willingly abridged their authority. This is a sufficient reason to induce you to be careful, in the first instance, how you deposit the powers of government.

With these few introductory remarks I shall proceed to a consideration of this constitution.

The first question that presents itself on the subject is, whether a confederated government be the best for the United States or not? Or in other words, whether the thirteen United States should be reduced to one great republic, governed by one legislature, and under the direction of one executive and judicial; or whether they should continue thirteen confederated republics, under the direction and controul of a supreme federal head for certain defined national purposes only?

This enquiry is important, because, although the government reported by the convention does not go to a perfect and entire consolidation, yet it approaches so near to it, that it must, if executed, certainly and infallibly terminate in it.

This government is to possess absolute and uncontroulable power, legislative, executive and judicial, with respect to every object to which it extend, for by, the last clause of section 8th, article 1st, it is declared "that the Congress shall have power to make all laws which shall be necessary and proper for carrying into execution the foregoing powers, and all other powers vested by this constitution, in the government of the United States; or in any department or office thereof." And by the 6th article, it is declared "that this constitution, and the laws of the United States, which shall be made in pursuance thereof, and the treaties made, or which shall be made, under the authority of the United States, shall be the supreme law of the land; and the judges in every state shall be bound thereby, any thing in the constitution, or law of any state to the contrary notwithstanding." It appears from these articles that there is no need of any intervention of the state governments, between the Congress and the people, to execute any one power vested in the general government, and that the constitution and laws of every state are nullified and declared void, so far as they are or shall be inconsistent with this constitution, or the laws made in pursuance of it, or with treaties made under the authority of the United States.—The government then, so far as it extends, is a complete one, and not a confederation. It is as much one complete government as that of New-York or Massachusetts, has as absolute and perfect powers to make and execute all laws, to appoint officers, institute courts, declare offences, and annex penal-

ties, with respect to every object to which it extends, as any other in the world. So far therefore as its powers reach, all ideas of confederation are given up and lost. It is true this government is limited to certain objects, or to speak more properly, some small degree of power is still left to the states, but a little attention to the powers vested in the general government, will convince every candid man, that if it is capable of being executed, all that is reserved for the individual states [must] very soon be annihilated, except so far a [s they are] barely necessary to the organization of the general government. The powers of the general legislature extend to every case that is of the least importance—there is nothing valuable to human nature, nothing dear to freemen, but what is within its power. It has authority to make laws which will affect the lives, the liberty, and property of every man in the United States; nor can the constitution or laws of any state, in any way prevent or impede the full and complete execution of every power given. The legislative power is competent to lay taxes, duties, imposts, and excises;—there is no limitation to this power, unless it be said that the clause which directs the use to which those taxes, and duties shall be applied, may be said to be a limitation; but this is no restriction of the power at all, for by this clause they are to be applied to pay the debts and provide for the common defence and general welfare of the United States; but the legislature have authority to contract debts at their discretion; they are the sole judges of what is necessary to provide for the common defence, and they only are to determine what is for the general welfare: this power therefore is neither more nor less, than a power to lay and collect taxes, imposts, and excises, at their pleasure; not only the power to lay taxes unlimited, as to the amount they may require, but it is perfect and absolute to raise them in any mode they please. No state legislature, or any power in the state governments, have any more to do in carrying this into effect, than the authority of one state has to do with that of another. In the business therefore of laying and collecting taxes, the idea of confederation is totally lost, and that of one entire republic is embraced. It is proper here to remark, that the authority to lay and collect tax is the most important of any power that can be granted; it connects with it almost all other powers, or at least will in process of time draw all other after it; it is the great mean of protection, security, and defence, in a good government, and the great engine of oppression and tyranny in a bad one. This cannot fail of being the case, if we consider the contracted limits which are set by this constitution, to the late governments, on this article of raising money. No state can emit paper money—lay any duties, or imposts, on imports, or exports, but by consent of the Congress; and then the net produce shall be for the benefit of the United States. The only mean therefore left, for any state to support its government and discharge its debts, is by direct taxation; and the United States have also power to lay and collect taxes, in any way they please. Every one who has thought on the subject, must be convinced that but small sums of money can be collected in any country, by direct taxes, when the foederal government begins to exercise the right of taxation in all its parts, the legislatures of the several states shall find it impossible to raise monies to support their governments. Without money they cannot be supported, and they must dwindle away, and, as before observed, their powers absorbed in that of the general government.

It might be here shown, that the power of the federal legislative, to raise and support armies at pleasure, as well in peace as in war, and their controul over the militia, tend, not only to a consolidation of the government, but the destruction of liberty.—I shall not, however, dwell upon these, as a few observations upon the judicial power of this government, in addition to the preceding, will fully evince the truth of the position.

The judicial power of the United States is to be vested in a supreme court, and in such inferior courts as Congress may from time to time ordain and establish. The powers of these courts are very extensive; their jurisdiction comprehends all civil causes, except such as arise between citizens of the same state; and it extends to all cases in law and equity arising under the constitution. One inferior court must be established, I presume, in each state at least, with the necessary executive officers appendant thereto. It is easy to see, that in the common course of things, these courts will eclipse the dignity, and take away from the respectability, of the state courts. These courts will be, in themselves, totally independent of the states, deriving their authority from the United States, and receiving from them fixed salaries; and in the course of human events it is to be expected, that they will swallow up all the powers of the courts in the respective states.

How far the clause in the 8th section of the 1st article may operate to do away all idea of confederated states, and to effect an entire consolidation of the whole into one general government, it is impossible to say. The powers given by this article are very general and comprehensive, and it may receive a construction to justify the passing almost any law. A power to make all laws, which shall be *necessary and proper,* for carrying into execution, all powers vested by the constitution in the government of the United States, or any department or officer thereof, is a power very comprehensive and definite, and may, for ought I know, be exercised in such manner as entirely to abolish the state legislatures. Suppose the legislature of a state should pass a law to raise money to support their government and pay the state debt, may the Congress repeal this law, because it may prevent the collection of a tax which they may think proper and necessary to lay, to provide for the general welfare of the United States? For all laws made, in pursuance of this constitution, are the supreme law of the land, and the judges in every state shall be bound thereby, any thing in the constitution or laws of the different states to the contrary notwithstanding.—By such a law, the government of a particular state might be overturned at one stroke, and thereby be deprived of every means of its support.

It is not meant, by stating this case, to insinuate that the constitution would warrant a law of this kind; or unnecessarily to alarm the fears of the people, by suggesting, that the federal legislature would be more likely to pass the limits assigned them by the constitution, than that of an individual state, further than they are less responsible to the people. But what is meant is, that the legislature of the United States are vested with the great and uncontroulable powers, of laying and collecting taxes, duties, imposts, and excises; of regulating trade, raising and supporting armies, organizing, arming, and disciplining the militia, instituting courts, and other general powers. And are by this clause invested with the power of making all laws, *proper and necessary,* for carrying all these into execution; and they may so exercise this power as entirely to annihilate all the state governments, and reduce this country to one single government. And if they may do it, it is pretty certain they will; for it will be found that the power retained by individual states, small as it is, will be a clog upon the wheels of the government of the United States; the latter therefore will be naturally inclined to remove it out of the way. Besides, it is a truth confirmed by the unerring experience of ages, that every man, and every body of men, invested with power, are ever disposed to increase it, and to acquire a superiority over every thing that stands in their way. This disposition, which is implanted in human nature, will operate in the federal legislature to lessen and ultimately to subvert the state authority, and having such advantages, will most certainly succeed, if the federal government succeeds at all. It must be very evident then, that what this constitution wants of being a complete consolidation of the several parts of the union into one complete government, possessed of perfect legislative, judicial, and executive powers, to all intents and purposes, it will necessarily acquire in its exercise and operation.

Let us now proceed to enquire, as I at first proposed, whether it be best the thirteen United States should be reduced to one great republic, or not? It is here taken for granted, that all agree in this, that whatever government we adopt, it ought to be a free one; that it should be so framed as to secure the liberty of the citizens of America, and such an one as to admit of a full, fair, and equal representation of the people. The question then will be, whether a government thus constituted, and founded on such principles, is practicable, and can be exercised over the whole United States, reduced into one state?

If respect is to be paid to the opinion of the greatest and wisest men who have ever thought or wrote on the science of government, we shall be constrained to conclude, that a free republic cannot succeed over a country of such immense extent, containing such a number of inhabitants, and these encreasing in such rapid progression as that of the whole United States. Among the many illustrious authorities which might be produced to this point, I shall content myself with quoting only two. The one is the baron de Montesquieu, spirit of laws, chap. xvi. vol. I. "It is natural to a republic to have only a small territory, otherwise it cannot long subsist. In a large republic there are men of large fortunes, and consequently of less moderation; there are trusts too great to be placed in any single subject; he has interest of his own; he soon begins to think that he may be happy, great and glorious, by oppressing his fellow citizens; and that he may raise himself to grandeur on the ruins of his country. In a large republic, the public good is sacrificed to a thousand views; it is subordinate to exceptions, and depends on accidents. In a small one, the interest of the public is easier perceived, better understood, and more within the reach of every citizen; abuses are of less extent, and of course are less protected." Of the same opinion is the marquis Beccarari.

History furnishes no example of a free republic, any thing like the extent of the United States. The Grecian republics were of small extent; so also was that of the Romans. Both of these, it is true, in process of time, extended their conquests over large territories of country; and the consequence was, that their governments were changed from that of free governments to those of the most tyrannical that ever existed in the world.

Not only the opinion of the greatest men, and the experience of mankind, are against the idea of an extensive republic, but a variety of reasons may be drawn from the reason and nature of things, against it. In every government, the will of the sovereign is the law. In despotic governments, the supreme authority being lodged in one, his will is law, and can be as easily expressed to a large extensive territory as to a small one. In a pure democracy the people are the sovereign, and their will is declared by themselves; for this purpose they must all come together to deliberate, and decide. This kind of government cannot be exercised, therefore, over a country of any considerable extent; it must be confined to a single city, or at least limited to such bounds as that the people can conveniently assemble, be able to debate, understand the subject submitted to them, and declare their opinion concerning it.

In a free republic, although all laws are derived from the consent of the people, yet the people do not declare their consent by themselves in person, but by representatives, chosen by them, who are supposed to know the minds of their constituents, and to be possessed of integrity to declare this mind.

In every free government, the people must give their assent to the laws by which they are governed. This is the true criterion between a free government and an arbitrary one. The former are ruled by the will of the whole, expressed in any manner they may agree upon; the latter by the will of one, or a few. If the people are to give their assent to the laws, by persons chosen and appointed by them, the manner of the choice and the number chosen, must be such, as to possess, be disposed, and consequently qualified to declare the sentiments of the people; for if they do not know, or are not disposed to speak the sentiments of the people, the people do not govern, but the sovereignty is in a few. Now, in a large extended country, it is impossible to have a representation, possessing the sentiments, and of integrity, to declare the minds of the people, without having it so numerous and unwieldly, as to be subject in great measure to the inconveniency of a democratic government.

The territory of the United States is of vast extent; it now contains near three millions of souls, and is capable of containing much more than ten times that number. Is it practicable for a country, so large and so numerous as they will soon become, to elect a representation, that will speak their sentiments, without their becoming so numerous as to be incapable of transacting public business? It certainly is not.

In a republic, the manners, sentiments, and interests of the people should be similar. If this be not the case, there will be a constant clashing of opinions; and the representatives of one part will be continually striving against those of the other. This will retard the operations of government, and prevent such conclusions as will promote the public good. If we apply this remark to the condition of the United States, we shall be convinced that it forbids that we should be one government. The United States includes a variety of climates. The productions of the different parts of the union are very variant, and their interests, of consequence, diverse. Their manners and habits differ as much as their climates and productions; and their sentiments are by no means coincident. The laws and customs of the several states are, in many respects, very diverse, and in some opposite; each would be in favor of its own interests and customs, and, of consequence, a legislature, formed of representatives from the respective parts, would not only be too numerous to act with any care or decision, but would be composed of such heterogenous and discordant principles, as would constantly be contending with each other.

The laws cannot be executed in a republic, of an extent equal to that of the United States, with promptitude.

The magistrates in every government must be supported in the execution of the laws, either by an armed force, maintained at the public expence for that purpose; or by the people turning out to aid the magistrate upon his command, in case of resistance.

In despotic governments, as well as in all the monarchies of Europe, standing armies are kept up to execute the commands of the prince or the magistrate, and are employed for this purpose when occasion requires: But they have always proved the destruction of liberty, and [as] abhorrent to the spirit of a free republic. In England, where they depend upon the parliament for their annual support, they have always been complained of as oppressive and unconstitutional, and are seldom employed in executing of the laws; never except on extraordinary occasions, and then under the direction of a civil magistrate.

A free republic will never keep a standing army to execute its laws. It must depend upon the support of its citizens. But when a government is to receive its support from the aid of the citizens, it must be so constructed as to have the confidence, respect, and affection of the people. Men who, upon the call of the magistrate, offer themselves to execute the laws, are influenced to do it either by affection to the government, or from fear; where a standing army is at hand to punish offenders, every man is actuated by the latter principle, and therefore, when the magistrate casts, will obey: but, where this is not the case, the government must test for its support upon the confidence and respect which the people have for their government and laws. The body of the people being attached, the government will always be sufficient to support and execute its laws, and to operate upon the fears of any faction which may be opposed to it, not only to prevent an opposition to the execution of the laws themselves, but also to compel the most of them to aid the magistrate; but the people will not be likely to have such confidence in their rulers, in a republic so extensive as the United States, as necessary for these purposes. The confidence which the people have in their rulers, in a free republic, arises from their knowing them, from their being responsible to them for their conduct, and from the power they have of displacing them when they misbehave: but in a republic of the extent of this continent, the people in general would be acquainted with very few of their rulers: the people at large would know little of their proceedings, and it would be extremely difficult to change them. The people in Georgia and New-Hampshire would not know one another's mind, and therefore could not act in concert to enable them to effect a general change of representatives. The different parts of so extensive a country could not possibly be made acquainted with the conduct of their representatives, nor be informed of the reasons upon which measures were founded. The consequence will be, they will have no confidence in their legislature, suspect them of ambitious views, be jealous of every measure they adopt, and will not support the laws they pass. Hence the government will be nerveless and inefficient, and no way will be left to render it otherwise, but by establishing an armed force to execute the laws at the point of the bayonet—a government of all others the most to be dreaded.

In a republic of such vast extent as the United States, the legislature cannot attend to the various concerns and wants of its different parts. It cannot be sufficiently numerous to be acquainted with the local condition and wants of the different districts, and if it could, it is impossible it should have sufficient time to attend to and provide for all the variety of cases of this nature, that would be continually arising.

In so extensive a republic, the great officers of government would soon become above the controul of the people, and abuse their power to the purpose of aggrandizing themselves, and oppressing them. The trust committed to the executive offices, in a country of the extent of the United States, must be various and of magnitude. The command of all the troops and navy of the republic, the appointment of officers, the power of pardoning offences, the collecting of all the public revenues, and the power of expending them, with a number of other powers, must be lodged and exercised in every state, in the hands of a few. When these are attended with great honor and emolument, as they always will be in large states, so as greatly to interest men to pursue them, and to be proper objects for ambitious and designing men, such men will be ever restless in their pursuit after them. They will use the power, when they have acquired it, to the purposes of gratifying their own interest and ambition, and it is scarcely possible, in a very large republic, to call them to account for their misconduct, or to prevent their abuse of power.

These are some of the reasons by which it appears, that a free republic cannot long subsist over a country of the great extent of these states. If then this new constitution is calculated to consolidate the thirteen states into one, as it evidently is, it ought not to be adopted.

Though I am of opinion, that it is a sufficient objection to this government, to reject it, that it creates the whole union into one government, under the form of a republic, yet if this objection was obviated, there are exceptions to it, which are so material and fundamental, that they ought to determine every man, who is a friend to the liberty and happiness of mankind, not to adopt it. I beg the candid and dispassionate attention of my countrymen, while I state these objections—they are such as have obtruded themselves upon my mind upon a careful attention to the matter, and such as I sincerely believe are well founded. There are many objections, of small moment, of which I shall take no notice—perfection is not to be expected in any thing that is the production of man—and if I did not in my conscience believe that this scheme was defective in the fundamental principles—in the foundation upon which a free and equal government must rest, I would hold my peace.

BRUTUS

Letter III

For many years generally attributed to Virginia statesman Richard Henry Lee, *Letters from the Federal Farmer* have more recently been attributed to Melancton Smith, a New York merchant and opponent of Alexander Hamilton in the New York ratifying convention. The first set of letters was published as a pamphlet and enjoyed great popularity and influence, though a later set was not so successful. In his third letter, the "Federal Farmer" expresses concern that, under the Constitution, the common people will not be adequately represented, the central government will abuse its taxing power, and common law rights will not be secure.

Letter III

Dear Sir,

The great object of a free people must be so to form their government and laws, and so to administer them, as to create a confidence in, and respect for the laws; and thereby induce the sensible and virtuous part of the community to declare in favor of the laws, and to support them without an expensive military force. I wish, though I confess I have not much hope, that this may be the case with the laws of congress under the new constitution. I am fully convinced that we must organize the national government on different principals, and make the parts of it more efficient, and secure in it more effectually the different interests in the community; or else leave in the state governments some powers proposed to be lodged in it—at least till such an organization shall be found to be practicable. Not sanguine in my expectations of a good federal administration, and satisfied, as I am, of the impracticability of consolidating the states, and at the same time of preserving the rights of the people at large, I believe we ought still to leave some of those powers in the state governments, in which the people, in fact, will still be represented—to define some other powers proposed to be vested in the general government, more carefully, and to establish a few principles to secure a proper exercise of the powers given

it. It is not my object to multiply objections, or to contend about inconsiderable powers or amendments. I wish the system adopted with a few alterations; but those, in my mind, are essential ones; if adopted without, every good citizen will acquiesce, though I shall consider the duration of our governments, and the liberties of this people, very much dependant on the administration of the general government. A wise and honest administration, may make the people happy under any government; but necessity only can justify even our leaving open avenues to the abuse of power, by wicked, unthinking, or ambitious men, I will examine, first, the organization of the proposed government, in order to judge; 2d, with propriety, what powers are improperly, at least prematurely lodged in it. I shall examine, 3d, the undefined powers; and 4th, those powers, the exercise of which is not secured on safe and proper ground.

First. As to the organization—the house of representatives, the democrative branch, as it is called, is to consist of 65 members: that is, about one representative for fifty thousand inhabitants, to be chosen biennially—the federal legislature may increase this number to one for each thirty thousand inhabitants, abating fractional numbers in each state.—Thirty-three representatives will make a quorum for doing business, and a majority of those present determine the sense of the house.—I have no idea that the interests, feelings, and opinions of three or four millions of people, especially touching internal taxation, can be collected in such a house.—In the nature of things, nine times in ten, men of the elevated classes in the community only can be chosen—Connecticut, for instance, will have five representatives—not one man in a hundred of those who form the democrative branch in the state legislature, will, on a fair computation, be one of the five.—The people of this country, in one sense, may all be democratic; but if we make the proper distinction between the few men of wealth and abilities, and consider them, as we ought, as the natural aristocracy of the country, and the great body of the people, the middle and lower classes, as the democracy, this federal representative branch will have but very little democracy in it, even this small representation is not secured on proper principles.—The branches of the legislature are essential parts of the fundamental compact, and ought to be so fixed by the people, that the legislature cannot alter itself by modifying the elections of its own members. This, by a part of Art. 1, Sect. 4, the general legislature may do, it may evidently so regulate elections as to secure the choice of any particular description of men.—It may make the whole state one district—make the capital, or any places in the state, the place or places of election—it may declare that the five men (or whatever the number may be the state may chuse) who shall have the most votes shall be considered as chosen.—In this case it is easy to perceive how the people who live scattered in the inland towns will bestow their votes on different men—and how a few men in a city, in any order or profession, may unite and place any five men they please highest among those that may be voted for—and all this may be done constitutionally, and by those silent operations, which are not immediately perceived by the people in general.—I know it is urged, that the general legislature will be disposed to regulate elections on fair and just principles:—This may be true—good men will generally govern well with almost any constitution: but why in laying the foundation of the social system, need we unnecessarily leave a door open to improper regulations? —This is a very general and unguarded clause, and many evils may flow from that part which authorises the congress to regulate elections.—Were it omitted, the regulations of elections would be solely in the respective states, where the people are substantially represented; and where the elections ought to be regulated, otherwise to secure a representation from all parts of the community, in making the constitutions, we ought to provide for dividing each state into a proper number of districts, and for confining the electors in each district to the choice of some men, who shall have a permanent interest and residence in it; and also for this essential object, that the representative elected shall have a majority of the votes of those electors who shall attend and give their votes.

In considering the practicability of having a full and equal representation of the people from all parts of the union, not only distances and different opinions, customs and views, common in extensive tracts of country, are to be taken into view, but many differences peculiar to Eastern, Middle, and Southern States. These differences are not so perceivable among the members of congress, and men of general information in the states, as among the men who would properly form the democratic branch. The Eastern states are very democratic, and composed chiefly of moderate freeholders; they have but few rich men and no slaves; the Southern states are composed chiefly of rich planters and slaves; they have but few moderate freeholders, and the prevailing influence, in them is generally a dissipated aristocracy: The Middle states partake partly of the Eastern and partly of the Southern character.

Perhaps, nothing could be more disjointed, unweildly and incompetent to doing business with harmony and dispatch, than a federal house of representatives properly numerous for the great objects of taxation, &c. collected from the federal states; whether such men would ever act in concert; whether they would not worry along a few years, and then be the means of separating the parts of the union, is very problematical?—View this system in whatever form we can, propriety brings us still to this point, a federal government possessed of general and complete powers, as to those national objects which cannot well come under the cognizance of the internal laws of the respective states, and this federal government, accordingly, consisting of branches not very numerous.

The house of representatives is on the plan of consolidation, but the senate is entirely on the federal plan; and Delaware will have as much constitutional influence in the senate, as the largest state in the union: and in this senate are lodged legislative, executive and judicial powers: Ten states in this union urge that they are small states, nine of which were present in the convention.—They were interested in collecting large powers into the hands of the senate, in which each state still will have its equal share of power. I suppose it was impracticable for the three large states, as they were called, to get the senate formed on any other principles: But this only proves, that we cannot form one general government on equal and just principles— and proves, that we ought not to lodge in it such extensive powers before we are convinced of the practicability of organizing it on just and equal principles. The senate will consist of two members from each state, chosen by the state legislatures, every sixth year. The clause referred to, respecting the elections of representatives, empowers the general legislature to regulate the elections of senators also, "except as to the places of chusing senators."—There is, therefore, but little more security in the elections than in those of representatives: Fourteen senators make a quorum for business, and a majority of the senators present give the vote of the senate, except in giving judgment upon an impeachment, or in making treaties, or in expelling a member, when two-thirds of the senators present must agree —The members of the legislature are not excluded from being elected to any military offices, or any civil offices, except those created, or the emoluments of which shall be increased by themselves: two-thirds of the members present, of either house, may expel a member at pleasure. The senate is an independant branch of the legislature, a court for trying impeachments, and also a part of the executive, having a negative in the making of all treaties, and in appointing almost all officers.

The vice president is not a very important, if not an unnecessary part of the system—he may be a part of the senate at one period, and act as the supreme executive magistrate at another—The election of this officer, as well as of the president of the United States seems to be properly secured; but when we examine the powers of the president, and the forms of the executive, we shall perceive that the general government, in this part, will have a strong tendency to aristocracy, or the government of the few. The executive is, in fact, the president and senate in all transactions of any importance; the president is connected with, or tied to the senate; he may always act with the senate, but never can effectually counteract its views: The president can appoint no officer, civil or military, who shall not be agreeable to the senate; and the presumption is, that the will of so important a body will not be very easily controuled, and that it will exercise its powers with great address.

In the judicial department, powers ever kept distinct in well balanced governments, are no less improperly blended in the hands of the same men—in the judges of the supreme court is lodged the law, the equity and the fact. It is not necessary to pursue the minute organical parts of the general government proposed.—There were various interests in the convention, to be reconciled, especially of large and small states; of carrying and non-carrying states; and of states more and states less democratic—vast labour and attention were by the convention bestowed on the organization of the parts of the constitution offered; still it is acknowledged there are many things radically wrong in the essential parts of this constitution—but it is said that these are the result of our situation: On a full examination of the subject, I believe it; but what do the laborious inquiries and determination of the convention prove? If they prove anything, they prove that we cannot consolidate the states on proper principles: The organization of the government presented proves, that we cannot form a general government in which all power can be safely lodged; and a little attention to the parts of the one proposed will make it appear very evident, that all the powers proposed to be lodged in it, will not be then well deposited, either for the purposes of government, or the preservation of liberty. I will suppose no abuse of power in those cases, in which the abuse of it is not well guarded against—I will suppose the words authorizing the general government to regulate the elections of its own members struck out of the plan, or free district elections, in each state, amply secured.—That the small representation provided for shall be as fair and equal as it is capable of being made—I will suppose the judicial department regulated on pure principles, by future laws, as far as it can be by the constitution, and consist with the situation of the country—still there will be an unreasonable accumulation of powers in the general government if all be granted, enumerated in the plan proposed. The plan does not present a well balanced government: The senatorial branch of the legislative and the executive are substantially united, and the president, or the state executive magistrate, may aid the senatorial interest when weakest, but never can effectually support the democratic, however it may be opposed;—the excellency, in my mind, of a well-balanced government is that it consists of distinct branches, each sufficiently strong and independant to keep its own station, and to aid either of the other branches which may occasionally want aid.

The convention found that any but a small house of representatives would be expensive, and that it would be impracticable to assemble a large number of representatives. Not only the determination of the convention in this case, but the situation of the states, proves the impracticability of collecting, in any one point, a proper representation.

The formation of the senate, and the smallness of the house, being, therefore, the result of our situation, and the actual state of things, the evils which may attend the exercise of many powers in this national government may be considered as without a remedy.

All officers are impeachable before the senate only—before the men by whom they are appointed, or who are consenting to the appointment of these officers. No judgment of conviction, on an impeachment, can be given unless two thirds of the senators agree. Under these circumstances the right of impeachment, in the house, can be of but little importance; the house cannot expect often to convict the offender; and, therefore, probably, will but seldom or never exercise the right. In addition to the insecurity and inconveniences attending this organization beforementioned, it may be observed, that it is extremely difficult to secure the people against the fatal effects of corruption and influence. The power of making any law will be in the president, eight senators, and seventeen representatives, relative to the important objects enumerated in the constitution. Where there is a small representation a sufficient number to carry any measure, may, with ease, be influenced by bribes, offices and civilities; they easily form private juntoes, and out-door meetings, agree on measures, and carry them by silent votes.

Impressed, as I am, with a sense of the difficulties there are in the way of forming the parts of a federal government on proper principles, and seeing a government so unsubstantially organized, after so arduous an attempt has been made, I am led to believe, that powers ought to be given to it with great care and caution.

In the second place it is necessary, therefore, to examine the extent, and the probable operations of some of those extensive powers proposed to be vested in this government. These powers, legislative, executive, and judicial, respect internal as well as external objects. Those respecting external objects, as all foreign concerns, commerce, imposts, all causes arising on the seas, peace and war, and Indian affairs, can be lodged no where else, with any propriety, but in this government. Many powers that respect internal objects ought clearly to be lodged in it; as those to regulate trade between the states, weights and measures, the coin or current monies, post-offices, naturalization, &c. These powers may be exercised without essentially effecting the internal police of the respective states: But powers to lay and collect internal taxes, to form the militia, to make bankrupt laws, and to decide on appeals, questions arising on the internal laws of the respective states, are of a very serious nature, and carry with them almost all other powers. These taken in connection with the others, and powers to raise armies and build navies, proposed to be lodged in this government, appear to me to comprehend all the essential powers in this community, and those which will be left to the states will be of no great importance.

A power to lay and collect taxes at discretion, is, in itself, of very great importance. By means of taxes, the government may command the whole or any part of the subject's property. Taxes may be of various kinds; but there is a strong distinction between external and internal taxes. External taxes are import duties, which are laid on imported goods; they may usually be collected in a few seaport towns, and of a few individuals, though ultimately paid by the consumer; a few officers can collect them, and they can be carried no higher than trade will bear, or smuggling permit —that in the very nature of commerce, bounds are set to them. But internal taxes, as poll and land taxes, excises, duties on all written instruments, &c. may fix themselves on every person and species of property in the community; they may be carried to any lengths, and in proportion as they are extended, numerous officers must be employed to assess them, and to enforce the collection of them. In the United Netherlands the general government has compleat powers, as to external taxation; but as to internal taxes, it makes requisitions on the provinces. Internal taxation in this country is more important, as the country is so very extensive. As many assessors and collectors of federal taxes will be above three hundred miles from the seat of the federal government as will be less. Besides, to lay and collect taxes, in this extensive country, must require a great number of congressional ordinances, immediately operating upon the body of the people; these must continually interfere with the state laws, and thereby produce disorder and general dissatisfaction, till the one system of laws or the other, operating on the same subjects, shall be abolished. These ordinances alone, to say nothing of those respecting the milita, coin, commerce, federal judiciary, &c. &c. will probably soon defeat the operations of the state laws and governments.

Should the general government think it politic, as some administration (if not all) probably will, to look for a support in a system of influence, the government will take every occasion to multiply laws, and officers to execute them, considering these as so many necessary props for its own support. Should this system of policy be adopted, taxes more productive than the impost duties will, probably, be wanted to support the government, and to discharge foreign demands, without leaving any thing for the domestic creditors. The internal sources of taxation then must be called into operation, and internal tax laws and federal assessors and collectors spread over this immense country. All these circumstances considered, is it wise, prudent, or safe, to vest the powers of laying and collecting internal taxes in the general government, while imperfectly organized and inadequate; and to trust to amending it hereafter, and making it adequate to this purpose? It is not only unsafe but absurd to lodge power in a government before it is fitted to receive it? It is confessed that this power and representation ought to go together. Why give the power first? Why give the power to the few, who, when possessed of it, may have address enough to prevent the increase of representation? Why not keep the power, and, when necessary, amend the constitution, and add to its other parts this power, and a proper increase of representation at the same time? Then men who may want the power will be under strong inducements to let in the people, by their representatives, into the government, to hold their due proportion of this power. If a proper representation be impracticable, then we shall see this power resting in the states, where it at present ought to be, and not inconsiderately given up.

When I recollect how lately congress, conventions, legislatures, and people contended in the cause of liberty, and carefully weighed the importance of taxation, I can scarcely believe we are serious in proposing to vest the powers of laying and collecting internal taxes in a government so imperfectly organized for such purposes. Should the United States be taxed by a house of representatives of two hundred members, which would be about fifteen members for Connecticut, twenty-five for Massachusetts, &c. still the middle and lower classes of people could have no great share, in fact, in taxation. I am aware it is said, that the representation proposed by the new constitution is sufficiently numerous; it may be for many purposes; but to suppose that this branch is sufficiently numerous to guard the rights of the people in the administration of the government, in which the purse and sword is placed, seems to argue that we have forgot what the true meaning of representation is. I am sensible also, that it is said that congress will not attempt to lay and collect internal taxes; that it is necessary for them to have the power, though it cannot probably be exercised.—I admit that it is not probable that any prudent congress will attempt to lay and collect internal taxes, especially direct taxes: but this only proves, that the power would be improperly lodged in congress, and that it might be abused by imprudent and designing men.

I have heard several gentlemen, to get rid of objections to this part of the constitution, attempt to construe the powers relative to direct taxes, as those who object to it would have them; as to these, it is said, that congress will only have power to make requisitions, leaving it to the states to lay and collect them. I see but very little colour for this construction, and the attempt only proves that this part of the plan cannot be defended. By this plan there can be no doubt, but that the powers of congress will be complete as to all kinds of taxes whatever—Further, as to internal taxes, the state governments will have concurrent powers with the general government, and both may tax the same objects in the same year; and the objection that the general government may suspend a state tax, as a necessary measure for the promoting the collection of a federal tax, is not without foundation.—As the states owe large debts, and have large demands upon them individually, there clearly will be a propriety in leaving in their possession exclusively, some of the internal sources of taxation, at least until the federal representation shall be properly encreased: The power in the general government to lay and collect internal taxes, will render its powers respecting armies, navies and the militia, the more exceptionable. By the constitution it is proposed that congress shall have power "to raise and support armies, but no appropriation of money to that use shall be for a longer term than two years; to provide and maintain a navy; to provide for calling forth the militia to execute the laws of the union; suppress insurrections, and repel invasions: to provide for organizing, arming, and disciplining the militia"; reserving to the states the right to appoint the officers, and to train the militia according to the discipline prescribed by congress; congress will have unlimited power to raise armies, and to engage officers and men for any number of years; but a legislative act applying money for their support can have operation for no longer term than two years, and if a subsequent congress do not within the two years renew the appropriation, or further appropriate monies for the use of the army, the army will be left to take care of itself. When an army shall once be raised for a number of years, it is not probable that it will find much difficulty in getting congress to pass laws for applying monies to its support. I see so many men in America fond of a standing army, and especially among those who probably will have a large share in administering the federal system; it is very evident to me, that we shall have a large standing army as soon as the monies to support them can be possibly found. An army is not a very agreeable place of employment for the young gentlemen of many families. A power to raise armies must be lodged some where; still this will not justify the lodging this power in a bare majority of so few men without any checks; or in the government in which the great body of the people, in the nature of things, will be only nominally represented. In the state governments the great body of the people, the yeomanry, &c. of the country, are represented: It is true they will chuse the members of congress, and may now and then chuse a man of their own way of thinking; but it is not impossible for forty, or thirty thousand people in this country, one time in ten to find a man who can possess similar feelings, views, and interests with themselves: Powers to lay and collect taxes and to raise armies are of the greatest moment; for carrying them into effect, laws need not be frequently made, and the yeomanry, &c. of the country ought substantially to have a check upon the passing of these laws; this check ought to be placed in the legislatures, or at least, in the few men the common people of the country, will, probably, have in congress, in the true sense of the word, "from among themselves." It is true, the yeomanry of the country possess the lands, the weight of property, possess arms, and are too strong a body of men to be openly offended—and, therefore, it is urged, they will take care of themselves, that men who shall govern will not dare pay any disrespect to their opinions. It is easily perceived, that if they have not their proper negative upon passing laws in congress, or on the passage of laws relative to taxes and armies, they may in twenty or thirty years be by means imperceptible to them, totally deprived of that boasted weight and strength: This may be done in a great measure by congress, if disposed to do it, by modelling the militia. Should one fifth or one eighth part of the men capable of bearing arms, be made a select militia, as has been proposed, and those the young and ardent part of the community, possessed of but little or no property, and all the others put upon a plan that will render them of no importance, the former will answer all the purposes of an army, while the latter will be defenceless. The state must train the militia in such form and according to such systems and rules as congress shall prescribe: and the only actual influence the respective states will have respecting the militia will be in appointing the officers. I see no provision made for calling out the *posse comitatus* for executing the laws of the union, but provision is made for congress to call forth the militia for the execution of them—and the militia in general, or any select part of it, may be called out under military officers, instead of the sheriff to enforce an execution of federal laws, in the first instance, and thereby introduce an entire military execution of the laws. I know that powers to raise taxes, to regulate the military strength of the community on some uniform plan, to provide for

its defence and internal order, and for duly executing the laws, must be lodged somewhere; but still we ought not so to lodge them, as evidently to give one order of men in the community, undue advantages over others; or commit the many to the mercy, prudence, and moderation of the few. And so far as it may be necessary to lodge any of the peculiar powers in the general government, a more safe exercise of them ought to be secured, by requiring the consent of two-thirds or three-fourths of congress thereto—until the federal representation can be increased, so that the democratic members in congress may stand some tolerable chance of a reasonable negative, in behalf of the numerous, important, and democratic part of the community.

I am not sufficiently acquainted with the laws and internal police of all the states to discern fully, how general bankrupt laws, made by the union, would effect them, or promote the public good. I believe the property of debtors, in the several states, is held responsible for their debts in modes and forms very different. If uniform bankrupt laws can be made without producing real and substantial inconveniences, I wish them to be made by congress.

There are some powers proposed to be lodged in the general government in the judicial department, I think very unnecessarily, I mean powers respecting questions arising upon the internal laws of the respective states. It is proper the federal judiciary should have powers co-extensive with the federal legislature—that is, the power of deciding finally on the laws of the union. By Art. 3, Sec. 2. the powers of the federal judiciary are extended (among other things) to all cases between a state and citizens of another state—between citizens of different states—between a state or the citizens thereof, and foreign states, citizens or subjects. Actions in all these cases, except against a state government, are now brought and finally determined in the law courts of the states respectively and as there are no words to exclude these courts of their jurisdiction in these cases, they will have concurrent jurisdiction with the inferior federal courts in them; and, therefore, if the new constitution be adopted without any amendment in this respect, all those numerous actions, now brought in the state courts between our citizens and foreigners, between citizens of different states, by state governments against foreigners, and by state governments against citizens of other states, may also be brought in the federal courts; and an appeal will lay in them from the state courts or federal inferior courts to the supreme judicial court of the union. In almost all these cases, either party may have the trial by jury in the state courts; except paper money and tender laws, which are wisely guarded against in the proposed constitution; justice may be obtained in these courts on reasonable terms; they must be more competent to proper decisions on the laws of their respective states, than the federal states can possibly be. I do not, in any point of view, see the need of opening a new jurisdiction in these causes—of opening a new scene of expensive law suits, of suffering foreigners, and citizens of different states, to drag each other many hundred miles into the federal courts. It is true, those courts may be so organized by a wise and prudent legislature, as to make the obtaining of justice in them tolerably easy; they may in general be organized on the common law principles of the country: But this benefit is by no means secured by the constitution. The trial by jury is secured only in those few criminal cases, to which the federal laws will extend—as crimes committed on the seas, against the laws of nations, treason and counterfeiting the federal securities and coin: But even in these cases, the jury trial of the vicinage is not secured—particularly in the large states, a citizen may be tried for a crime committed in the state, and yet tried in some states 500 miles from the place where it was committed; but the jury trial is not secured at all in civil causes. Though the convention have not established this trial, it is to be hoped that congress, in putting the new system into execution, will do it by a legislative act, in all cases in which it can be done with propriety. Whether the jury trial is not excluded the supreme judicial court is an important question. By Art. 3, Sec. 2, all cases affecting ambassadors, other public ministers, and consuls, and in those cases in which a state shall be party, the supreme court shall have jurisdiction. In all the other cases beforementioned, the supreme court shall have appellate jurisdiction, both as to *law and fact,* with such exception, and under such regulations as the congress shall make. By court is understood a court consisting of judges; and the idea of a jury is excluded. This court, or the judges, are to have jurisdiction on appeals, in all the cases enumerated, as to law and fact; the judges are to decide the law and try the fact, and the trial of the fact being assigned to the judges by the constitution, a jury for trying the fact is excluded; however, under the exceptions and powers to make regulations, congress may, perhaps, introduce the jury, to try the fact in most necessary cases.

There can be but one supreme court in which the final jurisdiction will centre in all federal causes—except in cases where appeals by law shall not be allowed: The judicial powers of the federal courts extend in law and equity to certain cases: and, therefore, the powers to determine on the law, in equity, and as to the fact, all will concentrate in the supreme court:—These powers, which by this constitution are blended in the same hands, the same judges, are in Great-Britain deposited in different hands—to wit, the decision of the law in the law judges, the decision in equity in the chancellor, and the trial of the fact in the jury. It is a very dangerous thing to vest in the same judge power to decide on the law, and also general powers in equity; for if the law restrain him, he is only to step into his shoes of equity, and give what judgment his reason or opinion may dictate; we have no precedents in this country, as yet, to regulate the divisions in equity as in Great Britain; equity, therefore, in the supreme court for many years will be mere discretion. I confess in the constitution of this supreme court, as left by the constitution, I do not see a spark of freedom or a shadow of our own or the British common law.

This court is to have appellate jurisdiction in all the other cases before mentioned: Many sensible men suppose that cases before mentioned respect, as well the criminal cases as the civil ones mentioned antecedently in the constitution, if so an appeal is allowed in criminal cases—contrary to the usual sense of law. How far it may be proper to admit a foreigner or the citizen of another state to bring actions against state governments, which have failed in performing so many, promises made during the war is doubtful: How far it may be proper so to humble a state, as to oblige it to answer to an individual in a court of law, is worthy of consideration; the states are now subject to no such actions; and this new jurisdiction will subject the states, and many defendants to actions, and processes, which were not in the contemplation of the parties, when the contract was made; all engagements existing between citizens of different states, citizens and foreigners, states and foreigners; and states and citizens of other states were made the parties contemplating the remedies then existing on the laws of the states—and the new remedy proposed to be given in the federal courts, can be founded on no principle whatever.

Your's, &c,

THE FEDERAL FARMER

Memorial and Remonstrance against Religious Assessments

JAMES MADISON

1785

Virginia Bill for Establishing Religious Freedom

THOMAS JEFFERSON

1786

While the controversy over Virginia's proposed Bill for Religious Education took place before the Constitutional Convention, it is directly relevant to any informed reading of the First Amendment's language concerning religious freedom. The Virginia state legislature had proposed legislation imposing a tax on property holders, proceeds from which would be used to propagate the Christian religion. It was generally seen as a thinly veiled subsidy for the established Episcopal Church. James Madison, an important drafter of the Constitution and a principal drafter of the Bill of Rights, was also the principal author of the "Memorial and Remonstrance." Thomas Jefferson was the principal author of the Virginia Bill for Religious Freedom, first introduced in 1777 but not made law until 1786.

Memorial and Remonstrance against Religious Assessments

We, the subscribers, citizens of the said Commonwealth, having taken into serious consideration, a Bill printed by order of the last Session of General Assembly, entitled "A Bill establishing a provision for Teachers of the Christian Religion," and conceiving that the same, if finally armed with the sanctions of a law, will be a dangerous abuse of power, are bound as faithful members of a free State, to remonstrate against it, and to declare the reasons by which we are determined. We remonstrate against the said Bill,

1. Because we hold it for a fundamental and undeniable truth, "that religion or the duty which we owe to our Cre-

ator and the manner of discharging it, can be directed only by reason and conviction, not by force or violence." The religion then of every man must be left to the conviction and conscience of every man, and it is the right of every man to exercise it as these may dictate. This right is in its nature an unalienable right. It is unalienable because the opinions of men, depending only on the evidence contemplated by their own minds, cannot follow the dictates of other men. It is unalienable also because what is here a right towards men, is a duty towards the Creator. It is the duty of every man to render to the Creator such homage, and such only, as he believes to be acceptable to him. This duty is precedent, both in order of time and degree of obligation, to the claims of Civil Society. Before any man can be considered as a member of Civil Society, he must be considered as a subject of the Governor of the Universe. And if a member of Civil Society, who enters into any subordinate association, must always do it with a reservation of his duty to the general authority, much more must every man who becomes a member of any particular Civil Society do it with a saving of his allegiance to the Universal Sovereign. We maintain therefore that in matters of religion no man's right is abridged by the institution of Civil Society, and that religion is wholly exempt from its cognizance. True it is that no other rule exists, by which any question which may divide a society can be ultimately determined, but the will of the majority; but it is also true, that the majority may trespass on the rights of the minority.

2. Because if religion be exempt from the authority of the society at large, still less can it be subject to that of the

Legislative Body. The latter are but the creatures and vice-gerents of the former. Their jurisdiction is both derivative and limited. It is limited with regard to the co-ordinate departments; more necessarily is it limited with regard to the constituents. The preservation of a free government requires not merely that the metes and bounds which separate each department of power may be invariably maintained, but more especially that neither of them be suffered to overleap the great barrier which defends the rights of the people. The rulers who are guilty of such an encroachment, exceed the commission from which they derive their authority, and are tyrants. The People who submit to it are governed by laws made neither by themselves nor by an authority derived from them, and are slaves.

3. Because it is proper to take alarm at the first experiment on our liberties. We hold this prudent jealousy to be the first duty of citizens, and one of [the] noblest characteristics of the late Revolution. The freemen of America did not wait till usurped power had strengthened itself by exercise and entangled the question in precedents. They saw all the consequences in the principle, and they avoided the consequences by denying the principle. We revere this lesson too much, soon to forget it. Who does not see that the same authority which can establish Christianity in exclusion of all other religions, may establish with the same ease any particular sect of Christians in exclusion of all other sects? That the same authority which can force a citizen to contribute three pence only of his property for the support of any one establishment, may force him to conform to any other establishment in all cases whatsoever?

4. Because the bill violates that equality which ought to be the basis of every law. . . . If "all men are by nature equally free and independent," [then] all men are to be considered as entering into Society on equal conditions, as relinquishing no more and therefore retaining no less, one than another, of their natural rights. Above all are they to be considered as retaining an "*equal* title to the free exercise of religion according to the dictates of conscience." Whilst we assert for ourselves a freedom to embrace, to profess, and to observe the religion which we believe to be of divine origin, we cannot deny an equal freedom to those whose minds have not yielded to the evidence which has convinced us. If this freedom be abused, it is an offence against God, not against man. To God therefore, not to men, must an account of it be rendered. As the Bill violates

equality by subjecting some to peculiar burdens, so it violates the same principle by granting to other peculiar exemptions. Are the Quakers and Menonists [to whom exemptions are granted] the only sects who think a compulsive support of their religions unnecessary and unwarantable? Can their piety alone be intrusted with the care of public worship? Ought their religions to be endowed above all others with extraordinary privileges by which proselytes may be enticed from all others? We think too favorably of the justice and good sense of these denominations to believe that they either covet pre-eminences over their fellow citizens, or that they will be seduced by them from the common opposition to the measure.

5. Because the bill implies either that the Civil Magistrate is a competent judge of religious truth, or that he may employ religion as an engine of civil policy. The first is an arrogant pretension falsified by the contradictory opinions of rulers in all ages and throughout the world; the second an unhallowed perversion of the means of salvation.

6. Because the establishment proposed by the Bill is not requisite for the support of the Christian religion. To say that it is, is a contradiction to the Christian religion itself; for every page of it disavows a dependence on the powers of this world. It is a contradiction to fact, for it is known that this religion both existed and flourished, not only without the support of human laws, but in spite of every opposition from them; and not only during the period of miraculous aid, but long after it had been left to its own evidence and the ordinary care of Providence. Nay, it is a contradiction in terms, for a religion not invented by human policy must have pre-existed and been supported before it was established by human policy. It is moreover to weaken in those who profess this religion a pious confidence in its innate excellence and the patronage of its Author and to foster in those who still reject it, a suspicion that its friends are too conscious of its fallacies to trust it to its own merits.

7. Because experience witnesseth that ecclesiastical establishments, instead of maintaining the purity and efficacy or religion, have had a contrary operation. During almost fifteen centuries has the legal establishment of Christianity been on trial. What have been its fruits? More or less in all places, pride and indolence in the Clergy [and] ignorance and servility in the laity; in both, superstition, bigotry, and persecution. Enquire of the teachers

of Christianity for the ages in which it appeared in its greatest lustre; those of every sect point to the ages prior to its incorporation with Civil policy. Propose a restoration of this primitive state in which its teachers depended on the voluntary rewards of their flocks; many of them predict its downfall. On which side ought their testimony to have greatest weight, when for or when against their interest?

8. Because the establishment in question is not necessary for the support of Civil Government. If it be urged as necessary for the support of Civil Government only as it is a means of supporting religion, and it be not necessary for the latter purpose, it cannot be necessary for the former. If religion be not within [the] cognizance of Civil Government, how can its legal establishment be said to be necessary to civil Government? What influence in fact have ecclesiastical establishments had on Civil Society? In some instances they have been seen to erect a spiritual tyranny on the ruins of Civil authority; in many instances they have been seen upholding the thrones of political tyranny; in no instance have they been seen the guardians of the liberties of the people. Rulers who wished to subvert the public liberty may have found an established clergy convenient auxiliaries. A just government, instituted to secure and perpetuate it, needs them not. Such a government will be best supported by protecting every citizen in the enjoyment of his religion with the same equal hand which protects his person and his property; by neither invading the equal rights of any Sect nor suffering any Sect to invade those of another.

9. Because the proposed establishment is a departure from that generous policy which, offering an asylum to the persecuted and oppressed of every nation and religion, promised a lustre to our country and an accession to the number of its citizens. What a melancholy mark is the Bill of sudden degeneracy? Instead of holding forth an asylum to the persecuted, it is itself a signal of persecution. It degrades from the equal rank of citizens all those whose opinions in religion do not bend to those of the legislative authority. Distant as it may be, in its present form, from the Inquisition it differs from it only in degree. The one is the first step, the other the last in the career of intolerance. The magnanimous sufferer under the cruel scourge in foreign regions, must view the Bill as a beacon on our coast, warning him to seek some other haven where liberty and philanthropy in their due extent may offer a more certain repose from his troubles.

10. Because it will have a like tendency to banish our citizens. The allurements presented by other situations are every day thinning their number. To superadd a fresh motive to emigration, by revoking the liberty which they now enjoy, would be the same species of folly which has dishonoured and depopulated flourishing kingdoms.

11. Because it will destroy that moderation and harmony which the forbearance of our laws to intermeddle with religion has produced amongst its several sects. Torrents of blood have been spilt in the old world by vain attempts of the secular arm to extinguish religious discord by proscribing all difference in religious opinions. Time has at length revealed the true remedy. Every relaxation of narrow and rigorous policy, wherever it has been tried, has been found to assuage the disease. The American theatre has exhibited proofs that equal and complete liberty, if it does not wholly eradicate it, sufficiently destroys its malignant influence on the health and prosperity of the State. If, with the salutary effects of this system under our own eyes, we begin to contract the bonds of religious freedom, we know no name that will too severely reproach our folly. At least let warning be taken at the first fruits of the threatened innovation. The very appearance of the Bill has transformed that "Christian forbearance, love and charity," which of late mutually prevailed, into animosities and jealousies which may not soon be appeased. What mischiefs may not be dreaded should this enemy to the public quiet be armed with the force of a law?

12. Because the policy of the bill is adverse to the diffusion of the light of Christianity. The first wish of those who enjoy this precious gift ought to be that it may be imparted to the whole race of mankind. Compare the number of those who have as yet received it with the number still remaining under the dominion of false religions, and how small is the former! Does the policy of the Bill tend to lessen the disproportion? No; it at once discourages those who are strangers to the light of [revelation] from coming into the region of it; and [it] countenances, by example, the nations who continue in darkness in shutting out those who might convey it to them. . . .

13. Because attempts to enforce, by legal sanctions, acts obnoxious to so great a proportion of Citizens tend to enervate the laws in general and to slacken the bands of So-

ciety. If it be difficult to execute any law which is not generally deemed necessary or salutary, what must be the case where [the law] is deemed invalid and dangerous? And what may be the effect of so striking an example of impotency in the Government, on its general authority.

14. Because a measure of such singular magnitude and delicacy ought not to be imposed, without the clearest evidence that it is called for by a majority of citizens; and no satisfactory method is yet proposed by which the voice of the majority in this case may be determined, or its influence secured. "The people of the respective countries are indeed requested to signify their opinion respecting the adoption of the Bill to the next Session of Assembly." But the representation must be made equal before the voice either of the Representatives or of the Counties, will be that of the people. Our hope is that neither of the former will, after due consideration, espouse the dangerous principle of the Bill. Should the event disappoint us, it will still leave us in full confidence that a fair appeal to the latter will reverse the sentence against our liberties.

15. Because, finally, "the equal right of every citizen to the free exercise of his Religion according to the dictates of conscience" is held by the same tenure with all our other rights. If we recur to its origin, it is equally the gift of nature. If we weigh its importance, it cannot be less dear to us. If we consult the Declaration of those rights which pertain to the good people of Virginia as the "basis and foundation of Government," it is enumerated with equal solemnity, or rather studied emphasis. Either, then, we must say that the will of the Legislature is the only measure of their authority, and that in the plenitude of this authority, they may sweep away all our fundamental rights; or, that they are bound to leave this particular right untouched and sacred. Either we must say that they may controul the freedom of the press, may abolish the trial by jury, may swallow up the Executive and Judiciary powers of the State—nay that they may despoil us of our very right of suffrage and erect themselves into an independent and hereditary assembly—or we must say that they have no authority to enact into law the Bill under consideration. We the subscribers say, that the General Assembly of this Commonwealth have no such authority. And that no effort may be omitted on our part against so dangerous an usurpation, we oppose to it this remonstrance, earnestly praying, as we are in duty bound, that the Supreme Lawgiver of the Universe, by illuminating those to whom it is addressed, may on the one hand turn their councils from every act which would affront his holy prerogative or violate the trust committed to them, and on the other, guide them into every measure which may be worthy of his [blessing, may re] dound to their own praise, and may establish more firmly the liberties, the prosperity, and the happiness of the Commonwealth.

A Bill for Establishing Religious Freedom

Section I. Well aware that the opinions and belief of men depend not on their own will, but follow involuntarily the evidence proposed to their minds; that Almighty God hath created the mind free, and manifested his supreme will that free it shall remain by making it altogether insusceptible of restraint; that all attempts to influence it by temporal punishments, or burthens, or by civil incapacitations, tend only to beget habits of hypocrisy and meanness, and are a departure from the plan of the holy author of our religion, who being lord both of body and mind, yet choose not to propagate it by coercions on either, as was in his Almighty power to do, but to exalt it by its influence on reason alone; that the impious presumption of legislature and ruler, civil as well as ecclesiastical, who, being themselves but fallible and uninspired men, have assumed dominion over the faith of others, setting up their own opinions and modes of thinking as the only true and infallible, and as such endeavoring to impose them on others, hath established and maintained false religions over the greatest part of the world and through all time: That to compel a man to furnish contributions of money for the propagation of opinions which he disbelieves and abhors, is sinful and tyrannical; that even the forcing him to support this or that teacher of his own religious persuasion, is depriving him of the comfortable liberty of giving his contributions to the particular pastor whose morals he would make his pattern, and whose powers he feels most persuasive to righteousness; and is withdrawing from the ministry those temporary rewards, which proceeding from an approbation of their personal conduct, are an additional incitement to earnest and unremitting labours for the instruction of mankind; that our civil rights have no dependance on our religious opinions, any more than our opinions in physics or geometry; and therefore the proscribing any citizen as unworthy the public confidence by laying upon him an incapacity of being called to offices of trust or emolument, unless he profess or renounce this or that religious opinion, is depriving him injudiciously of those privileges and advantages to which, in common with his fellow-citizens, he has a natural right; that it tends also to corrupt the principles of that very religion it is meant to encourage, by bribing with a monopoly of worldly honours and emoluments, those who will externally profess and conform to it; that though indeed these are criminals who do not withstand such temptation, yet neither are those innocent who lay the bait in their way; that the opinions of men are not the object of civil government, nor under its jurisdiction; that to suffer the civil magistrate to intrude his powers into the field of opinion and to restrain the profession or propagation of principles on supposition of their ill tendency is a dangerous falacy, which at once destroys all religious liberty, because he being of course judge of that tendency will make his opinions the rule of judgment, and approve or condemn the sentiments of others only as they shall square with or suffer from his own; that it is time enough for the rightful purposes of civil government for its officers to interfere when principles break out into overt acts against peace and good order; and finally, that truth is great and will prevail if left to herself; that she is the proper and sufficient antagonist to error, and has nothing to fear from the conflict unless by human interposition disarmed of her natural weapons, free argument and debate; errors ceasing to be dangerous when it is permitted freely to contradict them.

Sect. II. We the General Assembly of Virginia do enact that no man shall be compelled to frequent or support any religious worship, place, or ministry whatsoever, nor shall be enforced, restrained, molested, or burthened in his body or goods; or shall otherwise suffer, on account of his religious opinions or belief; but that all men shall be free to profess, and by argument to maintain, their opinions in matters of religion, and that the same shall in no wise diminish, enlarge, or affect their civil capacities.

Sect. III. And though we well know that this Assembly, elected by the people for their ordinary purposes of legislation only, have no power to restrain the acts of succeeding Assemblies, constituted with powers equal to our own, and that therefore to declare this act to be irrevocable would be of no effect in law; yet we are free to declare, and do declare, that the rights hereby asserted are of the natural rights of mankind, and that if any act shall be hereafter passed to repeal the present or to narrow its operations, such act will be an infringement of natural right.

Speech Introducing Proposed Constitutional Amendments

JAMES MADISON

June 8, 1789

Debate over First Amendment Language

August 15, 1789

The First Ten Amendments to the Constitution, or the Bill of Rights

1789

Many of those who eventually voted to ratify the Constitution did so with the understanding, or at least the hope, that the document would be amended as soon as the new Congress met. James Madison was a principal member of the first House of Representatives to meet after ratification. He saw to it that among the first pieces of business considered by that body was a series of amendments designed to address the concerns of Anti-Federalists and others nervous about the new powers conferred on the federal government.

Speech Introducing Proposed Constitutional Amendments

Amendments to the Constitution

Mr. MADISON rose, and reminded the House that this was the day that he had heretofore named for bringing forward amendments to the Constitution, as contemplated in the fifth article of the Constitution. He then addressed the Speaker as follows: This day, Mr. Speaker, is the day assigned for taking into consideration the subject of amendments to the Constitution. As I considered myself bound in honor and in duty to do what I have done on this subject, I shall proceed to bring the amendments before you as soon as possible, and advocate them until they shall be

finally adopted or rejected by a Constitutional majority of this House. With a view of drawing your attention to this important object, I shall move that this House do now resolve itself into a Committee of the Whole on the state of the Union; by which an opportunity will be given, to bring forward some propositions, which I have strong hopes will meet with the unanimous approbation of this House, after the fullest discussion and most serious regard. I therefore move you, that the House now go into a committee on this business.

Mr. SMITH was not inclined to interrupt the measures which the public were so anxiously expecting, by going into a Committee of the Whole at this time. He observed there were two modes of introducing this business to the House. One by appointing a select committee to take into consideration the several amendments proposed by the State Conventions; this he thought the most likely way to shorten the business. The other was, that the gentleman should lay his propositions on the table, for the consideration of the members; that they should be printed, and taken up for discussion at a future day. Either of these modes would enable the House to enter upon business better prepared than could be the case by a sudden transition from other important concerns to which their minds were strongly bent. He therefore hoped that the honorable gentleman would consent to bring the subject forward in one of those ways, in preference to going into a Committee of the Whole. For, said he, it must appear extremely impolitic to go into the consideration of amending the Government, before it is organized, before it has begun to operate. Certainly, upon reflection, it must appear to be premature. I wish, therefore, gentlemen would consent to the delay: for the business which lies in an unfinished state—I mean particularly the collection bill—is necessary to be passed; else all we have hitherto done is of no effect. If we go into the discussion of this subject, it will take us three weeks or a month; and during all this time, every other business must be suspended, because we cannot proceed with either accuracy or despatch when the mind is perpetually shifted from one subject to another.

Mr. Jackson.—I am of opinion we ought not to be in a hurry with respect to altering the Constitution. For my part, I have no idea of speculating in this serious manner on theory. If I agree to alterations in the mode of administering this Government, I shall like to stand on the sure ground of experience, and not be treading air. What experience have we had of the good or bad qualities of this Constitution? Can any gentleman affirm to me one proposition that is a certain and absolute amendment? I deny that he can. Our Constitution, sir, is like a vessel just launched, and lying at the wharf; she is untried, you can hardly discover any one of her properties. It is not known how she will answer her helm, or lay her course; whether she will bear with safety the precious freight to be deposited in her hold. But, in this state, will the prudent merchant attempt alterations? Will he employ workmen to tear off the planking and take asunder the frame? He certainly will not. Let us, gentlemen, fit out our vessel, set up her masts, and expand her sails, and be guided by the experiment in our alterations. If she sails upon an uneven keel, let us right her by adding weight where it is wanting. In this way, we may remedy her defects to the satisfaction of all concerned; but if we proceed now to make alterations, we may deface a beauty, or deform a well proportioned piece of workmanship. In short, Mr. Speaker, I am not for amendments at this time; but if gentlemen should think it a subject deserving of attention, they will surely not neglect the more important business which is now unfinished before them. Without we pass the collection bill we can get no revenue, and without revenue the wheels of Government cannot move. I am against taking up the subject at present, and shall therefore be totally against the amendments, if the

Government is not organized, that I may see whether it is grievous or not.

When the propriety of making amendments shall be obvious from experience, I trust there will be virtue enough in my country to make them. Much has been said by the opponents to this Constitution, respecting the insecurity of jury trials, that great bulwark of personal safety. All their objections may be done away, by proper regulations on this point, and I do not fear but such regulations will take place. The bill is now before the Senate, and a proper attention is shown to this business. Indeed, I cannot conceive how it could be opposed; I think an almost omnipotent Emperor would not be hardy enough to set himself against it. Then why should we fear a power which cannot be improperly exercised?

We have proceeded to make some regulations under the Constitution; but have met with no inaccuracy, unless it may be said that the clause respecting vessels bound to or from one State be obliged to enter, clear, or pay duties in another, is somewhat obscure; yet that is not sufficient, I trust, in any gentleman's opinion to induce an amendment. But let me ask what will be the consequence of taking up this subject? Are we going to finish it in an hour? I believe not; it will take us more than a day, a week, a month—it will take a year to complete it! And will it be doing our duty to our country, to neglect or delay putting the Government in motion, when everything depends upon its being speedily done?

Let the Constitution have a fair trial; let it be examined by experience, discover by that test what its errors are, and then talk of amending; but to attempt it now is doing it at a risk, which is certainly imprudent. I have the honor of coming from a State that ratified the Constitution by the unanimous vote of a numerous convention: the people of Georgia have manifested their attachment to it, by adopting a State Constitution framed upon the same plan as this. But although they are thus satisfied, I shall not be against such amendments as will gratify the inhabitants of other States, provided they are judged of by experience and not merely on theory. For this reason, I wish the consideration of the subject postponed until the 1st of March, 1790.

Mr. Goodhue.—I believe it would be perfectly right in the gentleman who spoke last, to move a postponement to the time he has mentioned; because he is opposed to the consideration of amendments altogether. But I believe it will be proper to attend to the subject earlier; because it is the wish of many of our constituents, that something should be added to the Constitution, to secure in a stronger manner their liberties from the inroads of power. Yet I think the present time premature; inasmuch as we have other business before us, which is incomplete, but essential to the public interest. When that is finished, I shall concur in taking up the subject of amendments.

Mr. BURKE thought amendments to the Constitution necessary, but this was not the proper time to bring them forward. He wished the Government completely organized before they entered upon this ground. The law for collecting the revenue is immediately necessary; the Treasury Department must be established; till this, and other important subjects are determined, he was against taking this up. He said it might interrupt the harmony of the House, which was necessary to be preserved in order to despatch the great objects of legislation. He hoped it would be postponed for the present, and pledged himself to bring it forward hereafter, if nobody else would.

Mr. MADISON.—The gentleman from Georgia (Mr. JACKSON) is certainly right in his opposition to my motion for going into a Committee of the Whole, because he is unfriendly to the object I have in contemplation; but I cannot see that the gentlemen who wish for amendments to be proposed at the present session, stand on good ground when they object to the House going into committee on this business.

When I first hinted to the House my intention of calling their deliberations to this object, I mentioned the pressure of other important subjects, and submitted the propriety of postponing this till the more urgent business was despatched; but finding that business not despatched, when the order of the day for considering amendments arrived, I thought it a good reason for a farther delay; I moved the postponement accordingly. I am sorry the same reason still exists in some degree, but it operates with less force, when it is considered that it is not now proposed to enter into a full and minute discussion of every part of the subject, but merely to bring it before the House; that our constituents may see we pay a proper attention to a subject they have much at heart; and if it does not give that full gratification which is to be wished, they will discover that it proceeds from the urgency of business of a very important nature. But if we continue to postpone from time to time, and refuse to let the subject come into view, it may occasion suspicions, which, though not well founded, may tend to

inflame or prejudice the public mind against our decisions. They may think we are not sincere in our desire to incorporate such amendments in the Constitution as will secure those rights, which they consider as not sufficiently guarded. The applications for amendments come from a very respectable number of our constituents, and it is certainly proper for Congress to consider the subject, in order to quiet that anxiety which prevails in the public mind. Indeed, I think it would have been of advantage to the Government if it had been practicable to have made some propositions for amendments the first business we entered upon; it would have stifled the voice of complaint, and made friends of many who doubted the merits of the Constitution. Our future measures would then have been more generally agreeably supported; but the justifiable anxiety to put the Government into operation prevented that; it therefore remains for us to take it up as soon as possible. I wish then to commence the consideration at the present moment; I hold it to be my duty to unfold my ideas, and explain myself to the House in some form or other without delay. I only wish to introduce the great work, and, as I said before, I do not expect it will be decided immediately; but if some step is taken in the business, it will give reason to believe that we may come to a final result. This will inspire a reasonable hope in the advocates for amendments, that full justice will be done to the important subject; and I have reason to believe their expectation will not be defeated. I hope the House will not decline my motion for going into a committee.

Mr. SHERMAN.—I am willing that this matter should be brought before the House at a proper time. I suppose a number of gentlemen think it their duty to bring it forward; so that there is no apprehension it will be passed over in silence. Other gentlemen may be disposed to let the subject rest until the more important objects of Government are attended to; and I should conclude, from the nature of the case, that the people expect the latter from us in preference to altering the Constitution; because they have ratified that instrument, in order that the Government may begin to operate. If this was not their wish, they might as well have rejected the Constitution, as North Carolina has done, until the amendments took place. The State I have the honor to come from adopted this system by a very great majority, because they wished for the Government; but they desired no amendments. I suppose this was the case in other States; it will therefore be imprudent to neglect much more important concerns for this. The executive part of the Government wants organization; the business of the revenue is incomplete, to say nothing of the judiciary business. Now, will gentlemen give up these points to go into a discussion of amendments, when no advantage can arise from them? For my part, I question if any alteration which can be now proposed would be an amendment, in the true sense of the word; but, nevertheless, I am willing to let the subject be introduced. If the gentleman only desires to go into committee for the purpose of receiving his propositions, I shall consent; but I have strong objections to being interrupted in completing the more important business; because I am well satisfied it will alarm the fears of twenty of our constituents where it will please one.

Mr. WHITE.—I hope the House will not spend much time on this subject, till the more pressing business is despatched; but, at the same time, I hope we shall not dismiss it altogether, because I think a majority of the people who have ratified the Constitution, did it under the expectation that Congress would, at some convenient time, examine its texture and point out where it was defective, in order that it might be judiciously amended. Whether, while we are without experience, amendments can be digested in such a manner as to give satisfaction to a Constitutional majority of this House, I will not pretend to say; but I hope the subject may be considered with all convenient speed. I think it would tend to tranquilize the public mind; therefore I shall vote in favor of going into a Committee of the Whole, and, after receiving the subject, shall be content to refer it to a special committee to arrange and report. I fear, if we refuse to take up the subject, it will irritate many of our constituents, which I do not wish to do. If we cannot, after mature consideration, gratify their wishes, the cause of complaint will be lessened, if not removed. But a doubt on this head will not be a good reason why we should refuse to inquire. I do not say this as it affects my immediate constituents, because I believe a majority of the district which elected me do not require alterations; but I know there are people in other parts who will not be satisfied unless some amendments are proposed.

Mr. SMITH, of South Carolina, thought the gentleman who brought forward the subject had done his duty: he had supported his motion with ability and candor, and if he did not succeed, he was not to blame. On considering what had been urged for going into a committee, he was induced to join the gentleman; but it would be merely to receive his propositions, after which he would move something to this effect: That, however desirous this House may be to go into the consideration of amendments to the Constitution, in order to establish the liberties of the people of America on the securest foundation, yet the important and pressing business of the Government prevents their entering upon that subject at present.

Mr. PAGE.—My colleague tells you he is ready to submit to the Committee of the Whole his ideas on this subject. If no objection had been made to his motion, the whole business might have been finished before this. He has done me the honor of showing me certain propositions which he has drawn up; they are very important, and I sincerely wish the House may receive them. After they are published, I think the people will wait with patience till we are at leisure to resume them. But it must be very disagreeable to them to have it postponed from time to time, in the manner it has been for six weeks past; they will be tired out by a fruitless expectation. Putting myself into the place of those who favor amendments, I should suspect Congress did not mean seriously to enter upon the subject; that it was vain to expect redress from them. I should begin to turn my attention to the alternative contained in the fifth article, and think of joining the Legislatures of those States which have applied for calling a new convention. How dangerous such an expedient would be I need not mention; but I venture to affirm, that unless you take early notice of this subject, you will not have power to deliberate. The people will clamor for a new convention; they will not trust the House any longer. Those, therefore, who dread the assembling of a convention, will do well to acquiesce in the present motion, and lay the foundation of a most important work. I do not think we need consume more than half an hour in the Committee of the Whole; this is not so much time but we may conveniently spare it, considering the nature of the business. I do not wish to divert the attention of Congress from the organization of the Government, nor do I think it need be done, if we comply with the present motion.

Mr. VINING.—I hope the House will not go into a Committee of the Whole. It strikes me that the great amendment which the Government wants is expedition in the despatch of business. The wheels of the national machine cannot turn, until the impost and collection bill are perfected; these are the desiderata which the public mind is anxiously expecting. It is well known, that all we have hitherto done amounts to nothing, if we leave the business in its present state. True; but, say gentlemen, let us go into committee; it will take but a short time; yet may it not take a considerable proportion of our time? May it not be procrastinated into days, weeks, nay, months? It is not the most facile subject, that can come before the Legislature of the Union. Gentlemen's opinions do not run in a parallel on this topic; it may take up more time to unite or concentre them than is now imagined. And what object is to be attained by going into a committee? If information is what we seek after, cannot that be obtained by the gentleman's laying his propositions on the table; they can be read, or they can be printed. But I have two other reasons for opposing this motion; the first is, the uncertainty with which we must decide on questions of amendment, founded merely on speculative theory; the second is a previous question, how far it is proper to take the subject of amendments into consideration, without the consent of two-thirds of both Houses? I will submit it to gentlemen, whether the words of the Constitution, "the Congress, whenever two-thirds of both Houses shall deem it necessary, shall propose amendments," do not bear my construction, that it is as requisite for two-thirds to sanction the expediency of going into the measure at present, as it will be to determine the necessity of amending at all. I take it that the fifth article admits of this construction, and think that two-thirds of the Senate and House of Representatives must concur in the expediency as to the time and manner of amendments, before we can proceed to the consideration of the amendments themselves. For my part, I do not see the expediency of proposing amendments. I think, sir, the most likely way to quiet the perturbation of the public mind, will be to pass salutary laws; to give permanency and stability to Constitutional regulations, founded on principles of equity and adjusted by wisdom. Although hitherto we have done nothing to tranquillize that agitation which the adoption of the Constitution threw some people into, yet the storm has abated and a calm succeeds. The people are not afraid of leaving the question of amendments to the discussion of their representatives; but is this the juncture for discussing it? What have Congress done towards completing the business of their appointment? They have passed a law regulating certain oaths; they have passed the impost bill; but are not vessels daily arriving, and the revenue slipping through our fingers? Is it not very strange that we neglect the completion of the revenue system? Is the system of jurisprudence unnecessary? And here let me ask gentlemen how

they propose to amend that part of the Constitution which embraces the judicial branch of the Government, when they do not know the regulations proposed by the Senate, who are forming a bill on this subject?

If the honorable mover of the question before the House does not think he discharges his duty without bringing his propositions forward, let him take the mode I have mentioned, by which there will be little loss of time. He knows, as well as any gentleman, the importance of completing the business on your table, and that it is best to finish one subject before the introduction of another. He will not, therefore, persist in a motion which tends to distract our minds, and incapacitate us from making a proper decision on any subject. Suppose every gentleman who desires alterations to be made in the Constitution were to submit his propositions to a Committee of the Whole; what would be the consequence? We should have strings of them contradictory to each other, and be necessarily engaged in a discussion that would consume too much of our precious time.

Though the State I represent had the honor of taking the lead in the adoption of this Constitution, and did it by a unanimous vote; and although I have the strongest predilection for the present form of Government, yet I am open to information, and willing to be convinced of its imperfections. If this be done, I shall cheerfully assist in correcting them. But I cannot think this a proper time to enter upon the subject, because more important business is suspended; and, for want of experience we are as likely to do injury by our prescriptions as good. I wish to see every proposition which comes from that worthy gentleman on the science of Government; but I think it can be presented better by staying where we are, than by going into committee, and therefore shall vote against his motion.

Mr. MADISON.—I am sorry to be accessary to the loss of a single moment of time by the House. If I had been indulged in my motion, and we had gone into a Committee of the Whole, I think we might have rose and resumed the consideration of other business before this time; that is, so far as it depended upon what I proposed to bring forward. As that mode seems not to give satisfaction, I will withdraw the motion, and move, you, sir, that a select committee be appointed to consider and report such amendments as are proper for Congress to propose to the Legislatures of the several States, conformably to the fifth article of the Constitution.

I will state my reasons why I think it proper to propose

amendments, and state the amendments themselves, so far as I think they ought to be proposed. If I thought I could fulfil the duty which I owe to myself and my constituents, to let the subject pass over in silence, I most certainly should not trespass upon the indulgence of this House. But I cannot do this, and am therefore compelled to beg a patient hearing to what I have to lay before you. And I do most sincerely believe, that if Congress will devote but one day to this subject, so far as to satisfy the public that we do not disregard their wishes, it will have a salutary influence on the public councils, and prepare the way for a favorable reception of our future measures. It appears to me that this House is bound by every motive of prudence, not to let the first session pass over without proposing to the State Legislatures, some things to be incorporated into the Constitution, that will render it as acceptable to the whole people of the United States, as it has been found acceptable to a majority of them. I wish, among other reasons why something should be done, that those who had been friendly to the adoption of this Constitution may have the opportunity of proving to those who were opposed to it that they were as sincerely devoted to liberty and a Republican Government, as those who charged them with wishing the adoption of this Constitution in order to lay the foundation of an aristocracy or despotism. It will be a desirable thing to extinguish from the bosom of every member of the community, any apprehensions that there are those among his countrymen who wish to deprive them of the liberty for which they valiantly fought and honorably bled. And if there are amendments desired of such a nature as will not injure the Constitution, and they can be ingrafted so as to give satisfaction to the doubting part of our fellow-citizens, the friends of the Federal Government will evince that spirit of deference and concession for which they have hitherto been distinguished.

It cannot be a secret to the gentlemen in this House, that, notwithstanding the ratification of this system of Government by eleven of the thirteen United States, in some cases unanimously, in others by large majorities; yet still there is a great number of our constituents who are dissatisfied with it; among whom are many respectable for their talents and patriotism, and respectable for their talents and patriotism, and respectable for the jealousy they have for their liberty, which, though mistaken in its object, is laudable in its motive. There is a great body of the people falling under this description, who at present feel much inclined to join their support to the cause of Federalism, if they were satisfied on this one point. We ought not to disregard their inclination, but, on principles of amity and moderation, conform to their wishes, and expressly declare the great rights of mankind secured under this Constitution. The acquiescence which our fellow-citizens show under the Government, calls upon us for a like return of moderation. But perhaps there is a stronger motive than this for our going into a consideration of the subject. It is to provide those securities for liberty which are required by a part of the community; I allude in a particular manner to those two States that have not thought fit to throw themselves into the bosom of the Confederacy. It is a desirable thing, on our part as well as theirs, that a re-union should take place as soon as possible. I have no doubt, if we proceed to take those steps which would be prudent and requisite at this juncture, that in a short time we should see that disposition prevailing in those States which have not come in, that we have seen prevailing in those States which have embraced the Constitution.

But I will candidly acknowledge, that, over and above all these considerations, I do conceive that the Constitution may be amended; that is to say, if all power is subject to abuse, that then it is possible the abuse of the powers of the General Government may be guarded against in a more secure manner than is now done, while no one advantage arising from the exercise of that power shall be damaged or endangered by it. We have in this way something to gain, and, if we proceed with caution, nothing to lose. And in this case it is necessary to proceed with caution; for while we feel all these inducements to go into a revisal of the Constitution, we must feel for the Constitution itself, and make that revisal a moderate one. I should be unwilling to see a door opened for a reconsideration of the whole structure of the Government—for a re-consideration of the principles and the substance of the powers given; because I doubt, if such a door were opened, we should be very likely to stop at that point which would be safe to the Government itself. But I do wish to see a door opened to consider, so far as to incorporate those provisions for the security of rights, against which I believe no serious objection has been made by any class of our constituents: such as would be likely to meet with the concurrence of two-thirds of both Houses, and the approbation of three-fourths of the State Legislatures. I will not propose a single alteration which I do not wish to see take place, as intrinsically proper in itself, or proper because it is wished for by a respectable number of my fellow-citizens; and therefore I shall not propose a single alteration but is likely to meet the concurrence required by the Constitution. There have been objections of various kinds made against the Constitution. Some were levelled against its structure because the President was without a council; because the Senate, which is a legislative body, had judicial powers in trials on impeachments; and because the powers of that body were compounded in other respects, in a manner that did not correspond with a particular theory; because it grants more power than is supposed to be necessary for every good purpose, and controls the ordinary powers of the State Governments. I know some respectable characters who opposed this Government on these grounds; but I believe that the great mass of the people who opposed it, disliked it because it did not contain effectual provisions against the encroachments on particular rights, and those safeguards which they have been long accustomed to have interposed between them and the magistrate who exercises the sovereign power; nor ought we to consider them safe, while a great number of our fellow-citizens think these securities necessary.

It is a fortunate thing that the objection to the Government has been made on the ground I stated; because it will be practicable, on that ground, to obviate the objection, so far as to satisfy the public mind that their liberties will be perpetual, and this without endangering any part of the Constitution, which is considered as essential to the existence of the Government by those who promoted its adoption.

The amendments which have occurred to me, proper to be recommended by Congress to the State Legislatures, are these:

First. That there be prefixed to the Constitution a declaration, that all power is originally vested in, and consequently derived from, the people.

That Government is instituted and ought to be exercised for the benefit of the people; which consists in the enjoyment of life and liberty, with the right of acquiring and using property, and generally of pursuing and obtaining happiness and safety.

That the people have an indubitable, unalienable, and indefeasible right to reform or change their Government, whenever it be found adverse or inadequate to the purposes of its institution.

Secondly. That in article 1st, section 2, clause 3, these words be struck out, to wit: "The number of Representatives shall not exceed one for every thirty thousand, but each State shall have at least one Representative, and until such enumeration shall be made;" and that in place thereof be inserted these words, to wit: "After the first actual enumeration, there shall be one Representative for every thirty thousand, until the number amounts to———, after which the proportion shall be so regulated by Congress, that the number shall never be less than———, nor more than———, but each State shall, after the first enumeration, have at least two Representatives; and prior thereto."

Thirdly. That in article 1st, section 6, clause 1, there be added to the end of the first sentence, these words, to wit: "But no law varying the compensation last ascertained shall operate before the next ensuing election of Representatives."

Fourthly. That in article 1st, section 9, between clauses 3 and 4, be inserted these clauses, to wit: The civil rights of none shall be abridged on account of religious belief or worship, nor shall any national religion be established, nor shall the full and equal rights of conscience be in any manner, or on any pretext, infringed.

The people shall not be deprived or abridged of their right to speak, to write, or to publish their sentiments; and the freedom of the press, as one of the great bulwarks of liberty, shall be inviolable.

The people shall not be restrained from peaceably assembling and consulting for their common good; nor from applying to the Legislature by petitions, or remonstrances, for redress of their grievances.

The right of the people to keep and bear arms shall not be infringed; a well armed and well regulated militia being the best security of a free country: but no person religiously scrupulous of bearing arms shall be compelled to render military service in person.

No soldier shall in time of peace be quartered in any house without the consent of the owner; nor at any time, but in a manner warranted by law.

No person shall be subject, except in cases of impeachment, to more than one punishment or one trial for the same offence; nor shall be compelled to be a witness against himself; nor be deprived of life, liberty, or property, without due process of law; nor be obliged to relinquish his property, where it may be necessary for public use, without a just compensation.

Excessive bail shall not be required, nor excessive fines imposed, nor cruel and unusual punishments inflicted.

The rights of the people to be secured in their persons, their houses their papers, and their other property, from all unreasonable searches and seizures, shall not be violated by warrants issued without probable cause, supported by oath or affirmation, or not particularly describing the places to be searched, or the persons or things to be seized.

In all criminal prosecutions, the accused shall enjoy the right to a speedy and public trial, to be informed of the cause and nature of the accusation, to be confronted with his accusers, and the witnesses against him; to have a compulsory process for obtaining witnesses in his favor; and to have the assistance of counsel for his defence.

The exceptions here or elsewhere in the Constitution, made in favor of particular rights, shall not be so construed as to diminish the just importance of other rights retained by the people, or as to enlarge the powers delegated by the Constitution; but either as actual limitations of such powers, or as inserted merely for greater caution.

Fifthly. That in article 1st, section 10, between clauses 1 and 2, be inserted this clause, to wit:

No State shall violate the equal rights of conscience, or the freedom of the press, or the trial by jury in criminal cases.

Sixthly. That, in article 3d, section 2, be annexed to the end of clause 2d, these words, to wit:

But no appeal to such court shall be allowed where the value in controversy shall not amount to———dollars: nor shall any fact triable by jury, according to the course of common law, be otherwise re-examinable than may consist with the principles of common law.

Seventhly. That in article 3d, section 2, the third clause be struck out, and in its place be inserted the clauses following, to wit:

The trial of all crimes (except in cases of impeachments, and cases arising in the land or naval forces, or the militia when on actual service, in time of war or public danger) shall be by an impartial jury of freeholders of the vicinage, with the requisite of unanimity for conviction, of the right of challenge, and other accustomed requisites; and in all crimes punishable with loss of life or member, presentment or indictment by a grand jury shall be an essential preliminary, provided that in cases of crimes committed within any county which may be in possession of an enemy, or in which a general insurrection may prevail, the trial may by

law be authorized in some other county of the same State, as near as may be to the seat of the offence.

In cases of crimes committed not within any county, the trial may by law be in such county as the laws shall have prescribed. In suits at common law, between man and man, the trial by jury, as one of the best securities to the rights of the people, ought to remain inviolate.

Eighthly. That immediately after article 6th, be inserted, as article 7th, the clauses following, to wit:

The powers delegated by this Constitution are appropriated to the departments to which they are respectively distributed: so that the Legislative Department shall never exercise the powers vested in the Executive or Judicial, nor the Executive exercise the powers vested in the Legislative or Judicial, nor the Judicial exercise the powers vested in the Legislative or Executive Departments.

The powers not delegated by this Constitution, nor prohibited by it to the States, are reserved to the States respectively.

Ninthly. That article 7th be numbered as article 8th.

The first of these amendments relates to what may be called a bill of rights. I will own that I never considered this provision so essential to the Federal Constitution as to make it improper to ratify it, until such an amendment was added; at the same time, I always conceived, that in a certain form, and to a certain extent, such a provision was neither improper nor altogether useless. I am aware that a great number of the most respectable friends to the Government, and champions for republican liberty, have thought such a provision not only unnecessary, but even improper; nay, I believe some have gone so far as to think it even dangerous. Some policy has been made use of, perhaps, by gentlemen on both sides of the question: I acknowledge the ingenuity of those arguments which were drawn against the Constitution, by a comparison with the policy of Great Britain, in establishing a declaration of rights; but there is too great a difference in the case to warrant the comparison: therefore, the arguments drawn from that source were in a great measure inapplicable. In the declaration of rights which that country has established, the truth is, they have gone no farther than to raise a barrier against the power of the Crown; the power of the Legislature is left altogether indefinite. Although I know whenever the great rights, the trial by jury, freedom of the press, or liberty of conscience, come in question in that body, the invasion of them is resisted by able advocates, yet their

Magna Charta does not contain any one provision for the security of those rights, respecting which the people of America are most alarmed. The freedom of the press and rights of conscience, those choicest privileges of the people, are unguarded in the British Constitution.

But although the case may be widely different, and it may not be thought necessary to provide limits for the legislative power in that country, yet a different opinion prevails in the United States. The people of many States have thought it necessary to raise barriers against power in all forms and departments of Government, and I am inclined to believe, if once bills of rights are established in all the States as well as the Federal Constitution, we shall find, that, although some of them are rather unimportant, yet, upon the whole, they will have a salutary tendency. It may be said, in some instances, they do no more than state the perfect equality of mankind. This, to be sure, is an absolute truth, yet it is not absolutely necessary to be inserted at the head of a Constitution.

In some instances they assert those rights which are exercised by the people in forming and establishing a plan of Government. In other instances, they specify those rights which are retained when particular powers are given up to be exercised by the Legislature. In other instances, they specify positive rights, which may seem to result from the nature of the compact. Trial by jury cannot be considered as a natural right, but a right resulting from a social compact, which regulates the action of the community, but is as essential to secure the liberty of the people as any one of the pre-existent rights of nature. In other instances, they lay down dogmatic maxims with respect to the construction of the Government; declaring that the Legislative, Executive, and Judicial branches, shall be kept separate and distinct. Perhaps the best way of securing this in practice is, to provide such checks as will prevent the encroachment of the one upon the other.

But, whatever may be the form which the several States have adopted in making declarations in favor of particular rights, the great object in view is to limit and qualify the powers of Government, by excepting out of the grant of power those cases in which the Government ought not to act, or to act only in a particular mode. They point these exceptions sometimes against the abuse of the Executive power, sometimes against the Legislative, and, in some cases, against the community itself; or, in other words, against the majority in favor of the minority.

In our Government it is, perhaps, less necessary to guard against the abuse in the Executive Department than any other; because it is not the stronger branch of the system, but the weaker. It therefore must be levelled against the Legislative, for it is the most powerful, and most likely to be abused, because it is under the least control. Hence, so far as a declaration of rights can tend to prevent the exercise of undue power, it cannot be doubted but such declaration is proper. But I confess that I do conceive, that in a Government modified like this of the United States, the great danger lies rather in the abuse of the community than in the Legislative body. The prescriptions in favor of liberty ought to be levelled against that quarter where the greatest danger lies, namely, that which possesses the highest prerogative of power. But this is not found in either the Executive or Legislative departments of Government, but in the body of the people, operating by the majority against the minority.

It may be thought that all paper barriers against the power of the community are too weak to be worthy of attention. I am sensible they are not so strong as to satisfy gentlemen of every description who have seen and examined thoroughly the texture of such a defence; yet, as they have a tendency to impress some degree of respect for them, to establish the public opinion in their favor, and rouse the attention of the whole community, it may be one means to control the majority from those acts to which they might be otherwise inclined.

It has been said, by way of objection to a bill of rights, by many respectable gentlemen out of doors, and I find opposition on the same principles likely to be made by gentlemen on this floor, that they are unnecessary articles of a Republican Government, upon the presumption that the people have those rights in their own hands, and that is the proper place for them to rest. It would be a sufficient answer to say, that this objection lies against such provisions under the State Governments, as well as under the General Government; and there are, I believe, but few gentlemen who are inclined to push their theory so far as to say that a declaration of rights in those cases is either ineffectual or improper. It has been said, that in the Federal Government they are unnecessary, because the powers are enumerated, and it follows, that all that are not granted by the Constitution are retained; that the Constitution is a bill of powers, the great residuum being the rights of the people; and, therefore, a bill of rights cannot be so necessary as if the residuum was thrown into the hands of the Government. I admit that these arguments are not entirely without foundation; but they are not conclusive to the extent which has been supposed. It is true, the powers of the General Government are circumscribed, they are directed to particular objects; but even if Government keeps within those limits, it has certain discretionary powers with respect to the means, which may admit of abuse to a certain extent, in the same manner as the powers of the State Governments under their constitutions may to an indefinite extent; because in the Constitution of the United States, there is a clause granting to Congress the power to make all laws which shall be necessary and proper for carrying into execution all the powers vested in the Government of the United States, or in any department or officer thereof; this enables them to fulfil every purpose for which the Government was established. Now, may not laws be considered necessary and proper by Congress, (for it is for them to judge of the necessity and propriety to accomplish those special purposes which they may have in contemplation,) which laws in themselves are neither necessary nor proper; as well as improper laws could be enacted by the State Legislatures, for fulfilling the more extended objects of those Governments? I will state an instance, which I think in point, and proves that this might be the case. The General Government has a right to pass all laws which shall be necessary to collect its revenue; the means for enforcing the collection are within the direction of the Legislature: may not general warrants be considered necessary for this purpose, as well as for some purposes which it was supposed at the framing of their constitutions the State Governments had in view? If there was reason for restraining the State Governments from exercising this power, there is like reason for restraining the Federal Government.

It may be said, indeed it has been said, that a bill of rights is not necessary, because the establishment of this Government has not repealed those declarations of rights which are added to the several State constitutions; that those rights of the people which had been established by the most solemn act, could not be annihilated by a subsequent act of that people, who meant and declared at the head of the instrument, that they ordained and established a new system, for the express purpose of securing to themselves and posterity the liberties they had gained by an arduous conflict.

I admit the force of this observation, but I do not look upon it to be conclusive. In the first place, it is too uncer-

tain ground to leave this provision upon, if a provision is at all necessary to secure rights so important as many of those I have mentioned are conceived to be, by the public in general, as well as those in particular who opposed the adoption of this Constitution. Besides, some States have no bills of rights, there are others provided with very defective ones, and there are others whose bills of rights are not only defective, but absolutely improper; instead of securing some in the full extent which republican principles would require, they limit them too much to agree with the common ideas of liberty.

It has been objected also against a bill of rights, that, by enumerating particular exceptions to the grant of power, it would disparage those rights which were not placed in that enumeration; and it might follow by implication, that those rights which were not singled out, were intended to be assigned into the hands of the General Government, and were consequently insecure. This is one of the most plausible arguments I have ever heard urged against the admission of a bill of rights into this system; but, I conceive, that it may be guarded against. I have attempted it, as gentlemen may see by turning to the last clause of the fourth resolution.

It has been said that it is unnecessary to load the Constitution with this provision, because it was not found effectual in the constitution of the particular States. It is true, there are a few particular States in which some of the most valuable articles have not, at one time or other, been violated; but it does not follow but they may have, to a certain degree, a salutary effect against the abuse of power. If they are incorporated into the Constitution, independent tribunals of justice will consider themselves in a peculiar manner the guardians of those rights; they will be an impenetrable bulwark against every assumption of power in the Legislative or Executive; they will be naturally led to resist every encroachment upon rights expressly stipulated for in the Constitution by the declaration of rights. Besides this security, there is a great probability that such a declaration in the federal system would be enforced; because the State Legislatures will jealously and closely watch the operations of this Government, and be able to resist with more effect every assumption of power, than any other power on earth can do; and the greatest opponents to a Federal Government admit the State Legislatures to be sure guardians of the people's liberty. I conclude, from this view of the subject, that it will be proper in itself, and highly politic, for the tranquillity of the public mind, and the stability of the Government, that we should offer something, in the form I have proposed, to be incorporated in the system of Government, as a declaration of the rights of the people.

In the next place, I wish to see that part of the Constitution revised which declares that the number of Representatives shall not exceed the proportion of one for every thirty thousand persons, and allows one Representative to every State which rates below that proportion. If we attend to the discussion of this subject, which has taken place in the State conventions, and even in the opinion of the friends to the Constitution, an alteration here is proper. It is the sense of the people of America, that the number of Representatives ought to be increased, but particularly that it should not be left in the discretion of the Government to diminish them, below that proportion which certainly is in the power of the Legislature, as the Constitution now stands; and they may, as the population of the country increases, increase the House of Representatives to a very unwieldy degree. I confess I always thought this part of the Constitution defective, though not dangerous; and that it ought to be particularly attended to whenever Congress should go into the consideration of amendments.

There are several minor cases enumerated in my proposition, in which I wish also to see some alteration take place. That article which leaves it in the power of the Legislature to ascertain its own emolument, is one to which I allude. I do not believe this is a power which, in the ordinary course of Government, is likely to be abused. Perhaps of all the powers granted, it is least likely to abuse; but there is a seeming impropriety in leaving any set of men without control to put their hand into the public coffers, to take out money to put in their pockets; there is a seeming indecorum in such power, which leads me to propose a change. We have a guide to this alteration in several of the amendments which the different conventions have proposed. I have gone, therefore, so far as to fix it, that no law varying the compensation, shall operate until there is a change in the Legislature; in which case it cannot be for the particular benefit of those who are concerned in determining the value of the service.

I wish, also, in revising the Constitution, we may throw into that section, which interdicts the abuse of certain powers in the State Legislatures, some other provisions of equal, if not greater importance than those already made. The words, "No State shall pass any bill of attainder, *ex post*

facto law," &c., were wise and proper restrictions in the Constitution. I think there is more danger of those powers being abused by the State Governments than by the Government of the United States. The same may be said of other powers which they possess, if not controlled by the general principle, that laws are unconstitutional which infringe the rights of the community. I should, therefore, wish to extend this interdiction, and add, as I have stated in the 5th resolution, that no State shall violate the equal right of conscience, freedom of the press, or trial by jury in criminal cases; because it is proper that every Government should be disarmed of powers which trench upon those particular rights. I know, in some of the State constitutions, the power of the Government is controlled by such a declaration; but others are not. I cannot see any reason against obtaining even a double security on those points; and nothing can give a more sincere proof of the attachment of those who opposed this Constitution to these great and important rights, than to see them join in obtaining the security I have now proposed; because it must be admitted, on all hands, that the State Governments are as liable to attack these invaluable privileges as the General Government is, and therefore ought to be as cautiously guarded against.

I think it will be proper, with respect to the judiciary powers, to satisfy the public mind on those points which I have mentioned. Great inconvenience has been apprehended to suitors from the distance they would be dragged to obtain justice in the Supreme Court of the United States, upon an appeal on an action for a small debt. To remedy this, declare that no appeal shall be made unless the matter in controversy amounts to a particular sum; this, with the regulations respecting jury trials in criminal cases, and suits at common law, it is to be hoped, will quiet and reconcile the minds of the people to that part of the Constitution.

I find, from looking into the amendments proposed by the State conventions, that several are particularly anxious that it should be declared in the Constitution, that the powers not therein delegated should be reserved to the several States. Perhaps other words may define this more precisely than the whole of the instrument now does. I admit they may be deemed unnecessary; but there can be no harm in making such a declaration, if gentlemen will allow that the fact is as stated. I am sure I understand it so, and do therefore propose it.

These are the points on which I wish to see a revision of

the Constitution take place. How far they will accord with the sense of this body, I cannot take upon me absolutely to determine; but I believe every gentleman will readily admit that nothing is in contemplation, so far as I have mentioned, that can endanger the beauty of the Government in any one important feature, even in the eyes of its most sanguine admirers. I have proposed nothing that does not appear to me as proper in itself, or eligible as patronised by a respectable number of our fellow-citizens; and if we can make the Constitution better in the opinion of those who are opposed to it, without weakening its frame, or abridging its usefulness in the judgment of those who are attached to it, we act the part of wise and liberal men to make such alterations as shall produce that effect.

Having done what I conceived was my duty, in bringing before this House the subject of amendments, and also stated such as I wish for and approve, and offered the reasons which occurred to me in their support, I shall content myself, for the present, with moving "that a committee be appointed to consider of and report such amendments as ought to be proposed by Congress to the Legislatures of the States, to become, if ratified by three-fourths thereof, part of the Constitution of the United States." By agreeing to this motion, the subject may be going on in the committee, while other important business is proceeding to a conclusion in the House. I should advocate greater despatch in the business of amendments, if I were not convinced of the absolute necessity there is of pursuing the organization of the Government; because I think we should obtain the confidence of our fellow-citizens, in proportion as we fortify the rights of the people against the encroachments of the Government.

Mr. JACKSON.—The more I consider the subject of amendments, the more I am convinced it is improper. I revere the rights of my constituents as much as any gentleman in Congress, yet I am against inserting a declaration of rights in the Constitution, and that for some of the reasons referred to by the gentleman last up. If such an addition is not dangerous or improper, it is at least unnecessary: that is a sufficient reason for not entering into the subject at a time when there are urgent calls for our attention to important business. Let me ask gentlemen, what reason there is for the suspicions which are to be removed by this measure? Who are Congress, that such apprehensions should be entertained of them? Do we not belong to the mass of the people? Is there a single right that, if in-

fringed, will not affect us and our connexions as much as any other person? Do we not return at the expiration of two years into private life, and is not this a security against encroachments? Are we not sent here to guard those rights which might be endangered, if the Government was an aristocracy or a despotism? View for a moment the situation of Rhode Island, and say whether the people's rights are more safe under State Legislatures than under a Government of limited powers. Their liberty is changed to licentiousness. But do gentlemen suppose bills of rights necessary to secure liberty? If they do, let them look at New York, New Jersey, Virginia, South Carolina, and Georgia. Those States have no bills of rights, and is the liberty of the citizens less safe in those States, than in the other of the United States? I believe it is not.

There is a maxim in law, and it will apply to bills of rights, that when you enumerate exceptions, the exceptions operate to the exclusion of all circumstances that are omitted; consequently, unless you except every right from the grant of power, those omitted are inferred to be resigned to the discretion of the Government.

The gentleman endeavors to secure the liberty of the press; pray how is this in danger? There is no power given to Congress to regulate this subject as they can commerce, or peace, or war. Has any transaction taken place to make us suppose such an amendment necessary? An honorable gentleman, a member of this House, has been attacked in the public newspapers on account of sentiments delivered on this floor. Have Congress taken any notice of it? Have they ordered the writer before them, even for a breach of privilege, although the Constitution provides that a member shall not be questioned in any place for any speech or debate in the House? No; these things are offered to the public view, and held up to the inspection of the world. These are principles which will always prevail. I am not afraid, nor are other members, I believe, our conduct should meet the severest scrutiny. Where, then, is the necessity of taking measures to secure what neither is nor can be in danger?

I hold, Mr. Speaker, that the present is not a proper time for considering of amendments. The States of Rhode Island and North Carolina are not in the Union. As to the latter, we have every presumption that she will come in. But in Rhode Island I think the anti-federal interest yet prevails. I am sorry for it, particularly on account of the firm friends of the Union, who are kept without the embrace of the Confederacy by their countrymen. These persons are worthy of our patronage; and I wish they would apply to us for protection; they should have my consent to be taken into the Union upon such application. I understand there are some important mercantile and manufacturing towns in that State, who ardently wish to live under the laws of the General Government; if they were to come forward and request us to take measures for this purpose, I would give my sanction to any which would be likely to bring about such an event.

But to return to my argument. It being the case that those States are not yet come into the Union, when they join us, we shall have another list of amendments to consider, and another bill of rights to frame. Now, in my judgment, it is better to make but one work of it whenever we set about the business.

But in what a situation shall we be with respect to those foreign Powers with whom we desire to be in treaty? They look upon us as a nation emerging into figure and importance. But what will be their opinion, if they see us unable to retain the national advantages we have just gained? They will smile at our infantine efforts to obtain consequence, and treat us with the contempt we have hitherto borne by reason of the imbecility of our Government. Can we expect to enter into a commercial competition with any of them, while our system is incomplete? And how long it will remain in such a situation, if we enter upon amendments, God only knows. Our instability will make us objects of scorn. We are not content with two revolutions in less than fourteen years; we must enter upon a third, without necessity or propriety. Our faith will be like the *punica fides* of Carthage; and we shall have none that will repose confidence in us. Why will gentlemen press us to propose amendments, while we are without experience? Can they assure themselves that the amendments, as they call them, will not want amendments, as soon as they are adopted? I will not tax gentlemen with a desire of amusing the people; I believe they venerate their country too much for this; but what more can amendments lead to? That part of the Constitution which is proposed to be altered, may be the most valuable part of the whole; and perhaps those who now clamor for alterations, may, ere long, discover that they have marred a good Government, and rendered their own liberties insecure. I again repeat it, this is not the time for bringing forward amendments; and, notwithstanding the honorable gentleman's ingenious arguments on that point, I am now more strongly persuaded it is wrong.

If we actually find the Constitution bad upon experience, or the rights and privileges of the people in danger, I here pledge myself to step forward among the first friends of liberty to prevent the evil; and if nothing else will avail, I will draw my sword in the defence of freedom, and cheerfully immolate at that shrine my property and my life. But how are we now proceeding? Why, on nothing more than theoretical speculation, pursuing a mere *ignis fatuus,* which may lead us into serious embarrassments. The imperfections of the Government are now unknown; let it have a fair trial, and I will be bound they show themselves; then we can tell where to apply the remedy, so as to secure the great object we are aiming at.

There are, Mr. Speaker, a number of important bills on the table which require despatch; but I am afraid, if we enter on this business, we shall not be able to attend to them for a long time. Look, sir, over the long list of amendments proposed by some of the adopting States, and say, when the House could get through the discussion; and I believe, sir, every one of those amendments will come before us. Gentlemen may feel themselves called by duty or inclination to oppose them. How are we then to extricate ourselves from this labyrinth of business? Certainly we shall lose much of our valuable time, without any advantage whatsoever. I hope, therefore, the gentleman will press us no further; he has done his duty, and acquitted himself of the obligation under which he lay. He may now accede to what I take to be the sense of the House, and let the business of amendments lie over until next Spring; that will be soon enough to take it up to any good purpose.

Mr. GERRY.—I do not rise to go into the merits or demerits of the subject of amendments; nor shall I make any other observations on the motion for going into a Committee of the Whole on the state of the Union, which is now withdrawn, than merely to say, that, referring the subject to that committee, is treating it with the dignity its importance requires. But I consider it improper to take up this business, when our attention is occupied by other important objects. We should despatch the subjects now on the table, and let this lie over until a period of more leisure for discussion and attention. The gentleman from Virginia says it is necessary to go into a consideration of this subject, in order to satisfy the people. For my part, I cannot be of his opinion. The people know we are employed in the organization of the Government, and cannot expect that we should forego this business for any other. But I would not have it understood, that I am against entering upon amendments when the proper time arrives. I shall be glad to set about it as soon as possible, but I would not stay the operations of the Government on this account. I think with the gentleman from Delaware, (Mr. VINING,) that the great wheels of the political machine should first be set in motion; and with the gentleman from Georgia, (Mr. JACKSON,) that the vessel ought to be got under way, lest she lie by the wharf till she beat off her rudder, and run herself a wreck ashore.

I say I wish as early a day as possible may be assigned for taking up this business, in order to prevent the necessity which the States may think themselves under of calling a new convention. For I am not, sir, one of those blind admirers of this system, who think it all perfection; nor am I so blind as not to see its beauties. The truth is, it partakes of humanity; in it is blended virtue and vice, errors and excellence. But I think if it is referred to a new convention, we run the risk of losing some of its best properties; this is a case I never wish to see. Whatever might have been my sentiments of the ratification of the Constitution without amendments, my sense now is, that the salvation of America depends upon the establishment of this Government, whether amended or not. If the Constitution which is now ratified should not be supported, I despair of ever having a Government of these United States.

I wish the subject to be considered early for another reason. There are two States not in the Union; it would be a very desirable circumstance to gain them. I should therefore be in favor of such amendments as might tend to invite them and gain their confidence; good policy will dictate to us to expedite that event. Gentlemen say, that we shall not obtain the consent of two-thirds of both Houses to amendments. Are gentlemen willing then to throw Rhode Island and North Carolina into the situation of foreign nations? They have told you that they cannot accede to the Union, unless certain amendments are made to the Constitution; if you deny a compliance with their request in that particular, you refuse an accommodation to bring about that desirable event, and leave them detached from the Union.

I have another reason for going early into this business. It is necessary to establish an energetic Government. My idea of such a Government is, that due deliberation be had in making laws, and efficiency in the execution. I hope, in this country, the latter may obtain without the dread of despotism. I would wish to see the execution of good laws irresistible. But from the view which we have already had

of the disposition of the Government, we seem really to be afraid to administer the powers with which we are invested, lest we give offence. We appear afraid to exercise the Constitutional powers of the Government, which the welfare of the State requires, lest a jealousy of our powers be the consequence. What is the reason of this timidity? Why, because we see a great body of our constituents opposed to the Constitution as it now stands, who are apprehensive of the enormous powers of Government. But if this business is taken up, and it is thought proper to make amendments, it will remove this difficulty. Let us deal fairly and candidly with our constituents, and give the subject a full discussion; after that, I have no doubt but the decision will be such as, upon examination, we shall discover to be right. If it shall then appear proper and wise to reject the amendments, I dare to say the reasons for so doing will bring conviction to the people out of doors, as well as it will to the members of this House; and they will acquiesce in the decision, though they may regret the disappointment of their fondest hopes for the security of the liberties of themselves and their posterity. Thus, and thus only, the Government will have its due energy, and accomplish the end for which it was instituted.

I am against referring the subject to a select committee, because I conceive it would be disrespectful to those States which have proposed amendments. The conventions of the States consisted of the most wise and virtuous men of the community; they have ratified this Constitution, in full confidence that their objections would at least be considered; and shall we, sir, preclude them by the appointment of a special committee, to consider of a few propositions brought forward by an individual gentleman? Is it in contemplation that the committee should have the subject at large before them, or that they should report upon the particular amendments just mentioned, as they think proper? And are we to be precluded from the consideration of any other amendments but those the committee may report? A select committee must be considered improper, because it is putting their judgments against that of the conventions which have proposed amendments; but if the committee are to consider the matter at large, they will be liable to this objection, that their report will only be waste of time. For if they do not bring forward the whole of the amendments recommended, individual members will consider themselves bound to bring them forward for the decision of the House. I would therefore submit, if gentlemen are determined to proceed in the business at this time, whether it is not better that it should go, in the first instance, to a Committee of the Whole, as first proposed by the gentleman from Virginia?

Some gentlemen consider it necessary to do this to satisfy our constituents. I think referring the business to a special committee will be attempting to amuse them with trifles. Our fellow-citizens are possessed of too much discernment not to be able to discover the intention of Congress by such procedure. It will be the duty of their representatives to tell them, if they were not able to discover it of themselves, they require the subject to be fairly considered; and if it be found to be improper to comply with their reasonable expectations, to tell them so. I hope there is no analogy between federal and punic faith; but unless Congress shall candidly consider the amendments which have been proposed in confidence by the State conventions, federal faith will not be considered very different from the *punica fides* of Carthage. The ratification of the Constitution in several States would never have taken place, had they not been assured that the objections would have been duly attended to by Congress. And I believe many members of these conventions would never have voted for it, if they had not been persuaded that Congress would notice them with that candor and attention which their importance requires. I will say nothing respecting the amendments themselves; they ought to stand or fall on their own merits. If any of them are eligible, they will be adopted; if not, they will be rejected.

Mr. LIVERMORE was against this motion; not that he was against amendments at a proper time. It is enjoined on him to act a rational part in procuring certain amendments, and he meant to do so; but he could not say what amendments were requisite, until the Government was organized. He supposed the judiciary law would contain certain regulations that would remove the anxiety of the people respecting such amendments as related thereto, because he thought much of the minutiae respecting suits between citizens of different States, &c. might be provided for by law. He could not agree to make jury trials necessary on every occasion; they were not practised even at this time, and there were some cases in which a cause could be better decided without a jury than with one.

In addition to the judiciary business, there is that which relates to the revenue. Gentlemen had let an opportunity go through their hands of getting a considerable supply from the impost on the Spring importations. He reminded them of this; and would tell them now was the time to finish that business; for if they did not sow in seed-time, they would be beggars in harvest. He was well satisfied in his own mind, that the people of America did not look for amendments at present; they never could imagine it to be the first work of Congress.

He wished the concurrence of the Senate upon entering on this business, because if they opposed the measure, all the House did would be mere waste of time; and there was some little difficulty on this point, because it required the consent of two-thirds of both Houses to agree to what was proper on this occasion. He said, moreover, it would be better to refer the subject generally, if referred to them at all, than to take up the propositions of individual members.

Mr. SHERMAN.—I do not suppose the Constitution to be perfect, nor do I imagine if Congress and all the Legislatures on the continent were to revise it, that their united labors would make it perfect. I do not expect any perfection on this side the grave in the works of man; but my opinion is, that we are not at present in circumstances to make it better. It is a wonder that there has been such unanimity in adopting it, considering the ordeal it had to undergo; and the unanimity which prevailed at its formation is equally astonishing; amidst all the members from the twelve States present at the Federal Convention, there were only three who did not sign the instrument to attest their opinion of its goodness. Of the eleven States who have received it, the majority have ratified it without proposing a single amendment. This circumstance leads me to suppose that we shall not be able to propose any alterations that are likely to be adopted by nine States; and gentlemen know, before the alterations take effect, they must be agreed to by the Legislatures of three-fourths of the States in the Union. Those States which have not recommended alterations, will hardly adopt them, unless it is clear that they tend to make the Constitution better. Now, how this can be made out to their satisfaction I am yet to learn; they know of no defect from experience. It seems to be the opinion of gentlemen generally that this is not the time for entering upon the discussion of amendments: our only question therefore is, how to get rid of the subject. Now, for my own part, I would prefer to have it referred to a Committee of the Whole, rather than a special committee, and therefore shall not agree to the motion now before the House.

Mr. GERRY moved, that the business lie over until the 1st day of July next, and that it be the order for that day.

Mr. SUMTER.—I consider the subject of amendments of such great importance to the Union, that I shall be glad to see it undertaken in any manner. I am not, Mr. Speaker, disposed to sacrifice substance to form; therefore, whether the business shall originate in a Committee of the Whole or in the House, is a matter of indifference to me, so that it be put in train. Although I am seriously inclined to give this subject a full discussion, yet I do not wish it to be fully entered into at present, but am willing it should be postponed to a future day, when we shall have more leisure. With respect to referring to a select committee, I am rather against it; because I consider it as treating the applications of the State conventions rather slightly; and I presume it is the intention of the House to take those applications into consideration as well as any other. If it is not, I think it will give fresh cause for jealousy; it will rouse the alarm which is now suspended, and the people will become clamorous for amendments. They will decline any further application to Congress, and resort to the other alternative pointed out in the Constitution. I hope, therefore, this House, when they do go into the business, will receive those propositions generally. This, I apprehend, will tend to tranquilize the public mind, and promote that harmony which ought to be kept up between those in the exercise of the powers of Government, and those who have clothed them with the authority, or, in other words, between Congress and the people. Without a harmony and confidence subsist between them, the measures of Government will prove abortive, and we shall have still to lament that imbecility and weakness which have long marked our public councils.

Mr. VINING found himself in a delicate situation respecting the subject of amendments. He came from a small State, and therefore his sentiments would not be considered of so much weight as the sentiments of those gentlemen who spoke the sense of much larger States. Besides, his constituents had prejudged the question, by a unanimous adoption of the Constitution, without suggesting any amendments thereto. His sense accorded with the declared sense of the State of Delaware, and he was doubly bound to object to amendments which were either improper or unnecessary. But he had good reasons for opposing the consideration of even proper alterations at this time. He would ask the gentleman who pressed them, whether he would be responsible for the risk the Government would run of being injured by an *interregnum?* Proposing amendments at this time, is suspending the operations of Government, and may be productive of its ruin.

He would not follow the gentleman in his arguments, though he supposed them all answerable, because he would not take up the time of the House; he contented himself with saying, that a bill of rights was unnecessary in a Government deriving all its powers from the people; and the Constitution enforced the principle in the strongest manner by the practical declaration prefixed to that instrument; he alluded to the words, "We the people do ordain and establish."

There were many things mentioned by some of the State Conventions which he would never agree to, on any conditions whatever; they changed the principles of the Government, and were therefore obnoxious to its friends. The honorable gentleman from Virginia had not touched upon any of them; he was glad of it, because he could by no means bear the idea of an alteration respecting them; he referred to the mode of obtaining direct taxes, judging of elections, &c.

He found he was not speaking to the question; he would therefore return to it, and declare he was against committing the subject to a select committee; if it was to be committed at all, he preferred a Committee of the Whole, but hoped the subject would be postponed.

Mr. MADISON found himself unfortunate in not satisfying gentlemen with respect to the mode of introducing the business; he thought, from the dignity and peculiarity of the subject, that it ought to be referred to a Committee of the Whole. He accordingly made that motion first, but finding himself not likely to succeed in that way, he had changed his ground. Fearing again to be discomfited, he would change his mode, and move the propositions he had stated before, and the House might do what they thought proper with them. He accordingly moved the propositions by way of resolutions to be adopted by the House.

Mr. LIVERMORE objected to these propositions, because they did not take up the amendments of the several States.

Mr. PAGE was much obliged to his colleague for bringing the subject forward in the manner he had done. He conceived it to be just and fair. What was to be done when the House would not refer it to a committee of any sort, but bring the question at once before them? He hoped it would be the means of bringing about a decision.

Mr. LAWRENCE moved to refer Mr. MADISON's motion to the Committee of the Whole on the state of the Union.

Mr. LEE thought it ought to be taken up in that committee; and hoped his colleague would bring the propositions before the committee, when on the state of the Union, as he had originally intended.

Mr. BOUDINOT wished the appointment of a select committee, but afterwards withdrew his motion.

At length Mr. LAWRENCE's motion was agreed to, and Mr. MADISON's propositions were ordered to be referred to a Committee of the Whole. Adjourned.

Debate over First Amendment Language

Amendments to the Constitution

The House again went into a Committee of the Whole on the proposed amendments to the Constitution, Mr. BOUDINOT in the Chair.

The fourth proposition being under consideration, as follows:

Article 1. Section 9. Between paragraphs two and three insert "no religion shall be established by law, not shall the equal rights of conscience be infringed."

Mr. SYLVESTER had some doubts of the propriety of the mode of expression used in this paragraph. He apprehended that it was liable to a construction different from what had been made by the committee. He feared it might be thought to have a tendency to abolish religion altogether.

Mr. VINING suggested the propriety of transposing the two members of the sentence.

Mr. GERRY said it would read better if it was that no religious doctrine shall be established by law.

Mr. SHERMAN thought the amendment altogether unnecessary, inasmuch as Congress had no authority whatever delegated to them by the Constitution to make religious establishments; he would, therefore, move to have it struck out.

Mr. CARROLL.—As the rights of conscience are in their nature, of peculiar delicacy, and will little bear the gentlest touch of governmental hand: and as many sects have concurred in opinion that they are not well secured under the present Constitution, he said he was much in favor of adopting the words. He thought it would tend more towards conciliating the minds of the people to the Government than almost any other amendment he had heard proposed. He would not contend with gentlemen about the phraseology, his object was to secure the substance in such a manner as to satisfy the wishes of the honest part of the community.

Mr. MADISON said, he apprehended the meaning of the words to be, that Congress should not establish a religion, and enforce the legal observation of it by law, nor compel men to worship God in any manner contrary to their conscience. Whether the words are necessary or not, he did not mean to say, but they had been required by some of the State Conventions, who seemed to entertain an opinion that under the clause of the Constitution, which gave power to Congress to make all laws necessary and proper to carry into execution the Constitution, and the laws made under it, enabled them to make laws of such a nature as might infringe the rights of conscience, and establish a national religion; to prevent these effects he presumed the amendment was intended, and he thought it as well expressed as the nature of the language would admit.

Mr. HUNTINGTON said that he feared, with the gentleman first up on this subject, that the words might be taken in such latitude as to be extremely hurtful to the cause of religion. He understood the amendment to mean what had been expressed by the gentleman from Virginia; but others might find it convenient to put another construction upon it. The ministers of their congregations to the Eastward were maintained by the contributions of those who belonged to their society; the expense of building meeting-houses was contributed in the same manner. These things were regulated by by-laws. If an action was brought before a Federal Court on any of these cases, the person who had neglected to perform his engagements could not be compelled to do it; for a support of ministers or building of places of worship might be construed into a religious establishment.

By the charter of Rhode Island, no religion could be established by law; he could give a history of the effects of such a regulation; indeed the people were now enjoying the blessed fruits of it. He hoped, therefore, the amendment would be made in such a way as to secure the rights of conscience, and a free exercise of the rights of religion, but not to patronise those who professed no religion at all.

Mr. MADISON thought, if the word "national" was inserted before religion, it would satisfy the minds of honorable gentlemen. He believed that the people feared one sect might obtain a pre-eminence, or two combine together, and establish a religion to which they would compel others to conform. He thought if the word "national" was introduced, it would point the amendment directly to the object it was intended to prevent.

Mr. Livermore was not satisfied with that amendment; but he did not wish them to dwell long on the subject. He thought it would be better if it were altered, and made to read in this manner, that Congress shall make no laws touching religion, or infringing the rights of conscience.

Mr. Gerry did not like the term national, proposed by the gentleman from Virginia, and he hoped it would not be adopted by the House. It brought to his mind some observations that had taken place in the conventions at the time they were considering the present Constitution. It had been insisted upon by those who were called anti-federalists, that this form of Government consolidated the Union; the honorable gentleman's motion shows that he considers it in the same light. Those who were called anti-federalists at that time, complained that they had injustice done them by the title, because they were in favor of a Federal Government, and the others were in favor of a national one; the federalists were for ratifying the Constitution as it stood, and the others not until amendments were made. Their names then ought not to have been distinguished by federalists and anti-federalists, but rats and anti-rats.

Mr. Madison withdrew his motion, but observed that the words "no national religion shall be established by law," did not imply that the Government was a national one; the question was then taken on Mr. Livermore's motion, and passed in the affirmative, thirty-one for, and twenty against it.

The First Ten Amendments to the Constitution, or the Bill of Rights

Articles in Addition to, and Amendment of, the Constitution of the United States of America, Proposed by Congress, and Ratified by the Legislatures of the Several States, Pursuant to the Fifth Article of the Original Constitution

Amendment I

Congress shall make no law respecting an establishment of religion, or prohibiting the free exercise thereof; or abridging the freedom of speech, or of the press; or the right of the people peaceably to assemble, and to petition the Government for a redress of grievances.

Amendment II

A well regulated Militia, being necessary to the security of a free State, the right of the people to keep and bear Arms, shall not be infringed.

Amendment III

No Soldier shall, in time of peace be quartered in any house, without the consent of the Owner, nor in time of war, but in a manner to be prescribed by law.

Amendment IV

The right of the people to be secure in their persons, houses, papers, and effects, against unreasonable searches and seizures, shall not be violated, and no Warrants shall issue, but upon probable cause, supported by Oath or affirmation, and particularly describing the place to be searched, and the persons or things to be seized.

Amendment V

No person shall be held to answer for a capital, or other wise infamous crime, unless on a presentment or indictment of a Grand Jury, except in cases arising in the land or naval forces, or in the Militia, when in actual service in time of War or public danger; nor shall any person be subject for the same offenses to be twice put in jeopardy of life or limb; nor shall be compelled in any criminal case to be a witness against himself, nor be deprived of life, liberty, or property, without due process of law; nor shall private property be taken for public use, without just compensation.

Amendment VI

In all criminal prosecutions, the accused shall enjoy the right to a speedy and public trial, by an impartial jury of the State and district wherein the crime shall have been committed, which district shall have been previously ascertained by law, and to be informed of the nature and cause of the accusation; to be confronted with the witnesses against him; to have compulsory process for obtaining witnesses in his favor, and to have the Assistance of Counsel for his defence.

Amendment VII

In suits at common law, where the value in controversy shall exceed twenty dollars, the right of trial by jury shall be preserved, and no fact tried by a jury, shall be otherwise reexamined in any Court of the United States, than according to the rules of the common law.

Amendment VIII

Excessive bail shall not be required, nor excessive fines imposed, nor cruel and unusual punishments inflicted.

Amendment IX

The enumeration in the Constitution, of certain rights, shall not be construed to deny or disparage others retained by the people.

Amendment X

The powers not delegated to the United States by the Constitution, nor prohibited by it to the States, are reserved to the States respectively, or to the people.

Commentaries on the Constitution of the United States

JOSEPH STORY

1833

Joseph Story (1779–1845) was born in Marblehead, Massachusetts, a stronghold of Federalist sentiment. Nonetheless, he was a committed supporter of the Democratic-Republican Party. Elected to the House of Representatives before he had reached the age of thirty, at thirty-one he was named to the Supreme Court by President James Madison. Here he continued an established career publishing commentaries on American law and, in 1833, wrote the highly influential *Commentaries on the Constitution of the United States*. Despite Story's commitment to the Democratic-Republicans—long held to be the party of states' rights—he consistently upheld a reading of the Constitution emphasizing the supremacy of the central government and the requirements for well-ordered liberty. In this selection he discusses the context and limits of rights protected by several of the Constitution's first ten amendments.

Commentaries on the Constitution of the United States

Amendments to the Constitution

. . . §1863. Let us now enter upon the consideration of the amendments, which, it will be found, principally regard subjects properly belonging to a bill of rights.

§1864. The first is, "Congress shall make no law respecting an establishment of religion, or prohibiting the free exercise thereof; or abridging the freedom of speech, or of the press; or the right of the people peaceably to assemble, and to petition government for a redress of grievances."

§1865. And first, the prohibition of any establishment of religion, and the freedom of religious opinion and worship.

How far any government has a right to interfere in matters touching religion, has been a subject much discussed by writers upon public and political law. The right and the duty of the interference of government, in matters of religion, have been maintained by many distinguished authors, as well those, who were the warmest advocates of free governments, as those, who were attached to governments of a more arbitrary character.[1] Indeed, the right of a society or government to interfere in matters of religion will hardly be contested by any persons, who believe that piety, religion, and morality are intimately connected with the well being of the state, and indispensable to the administration of civil justice. The promulgation of the great doctrines of religion, the being, and attributes, and providence of one Almighty God; the responsibility to him for all our actions, founded upon moral freedom and accountability; a future state of rewards and punishments; the cultivation of all the personal, social, and benevolent virtues;—these never can be a matter of indifference in any well ordered community.[2] It is, indeed, difficult to conceive, how any civilized society can well exist without them. And at all events, it is impossible for those, who believe in the truth of Christianity, as a divine revelation, to doubt, that it is the especial duty of government to foster, and encourage it among all the citizens and subjects. This is a point wholly distinct from that of the right of private judgment in matters of religion, and of the freedom of public worship according to the dictates of one's conscience.

§1866. The real difficulty lies in ascertaining the limits, to which government may rightfully go in fostering and encouraging religion. Three cases may easily be supposed. One, where a government affords aid to a particular religion, leaving all persons free to adopt any other; another,

---

1. See Grotius, B. 2, ch. 20, § 44 to 51; Vattell, B. 1, ch. 12, § 125, 126; Hooker's Ecclesiastical Polity, B. 5, § 1 to 10; Bynkershoeck, 2 P. J. Lib. 2, ch. 18; Woodeson's Elem. Lect. 3, p. 49; Burlemaqui, Pt. 3, ch. 3, p. 171, and Montesq. B. 24, ch. 1 to ch. 8, ch. 14 to ch. 16, B. 25, ch. 1, 2, 9, 10, 11, 12.

2. See Burlemaqui, Pt. 3, ch. 3, p. 171, &c.; 4 Black. Comm. 43.

where it creates an ecclesiastical establishment for the propagation of the doctrines of a particular sect of that religion, leaving a like freedom to all others; and a third, where it creates such an establishment, and excludes all persons, not belonging to it, either wholly, or in part, from any participation in the public honours, trusts, emoluments, privileges, and immunities of the state. For instance, a government may simply declare, that the Christian religion shall be the religion of the state, and shall be aided, and encouraged in all the varieties of sects belonging to it; or it may declare, that the Catholic or Protestant religion shall be the religion of the state, leaving every man to the free enjoyment of his own religious opinions; or it may establish the doctrines of a particular sect, as of Episcopalians, as the religion of the state, with a like freedom; or it may establish the doctrines of a particular sect, as exclusively the religion of the state, tolerating others to a limited extent, or excluding all, not belonging to it, from all public honours, trusts, emoluments, privileges, and immunities.

§ 1867. Now, there will probably be found few persons in this, or any other Christian country, who would deliberately contend, that it was unreasonable, or unjust to foster and encourage the Christian religion generally, as a matter of sound policy, as well as of revealed truth. In fact, every American colony, from its foundation down to the revolution, with the exception of Rhode Island, (if, indeed, that state be an exception,) did openly, by the whole course of its laws and institutions, support and sustain, in some form, the Christian religion; and almost invariably gave a peculiar sanction to some of its fundamental doctrines. And this has continued to be the case in some of the states down to the present period, without the slightest suspicion, that it was against the principles of public law, or republican liberty.[3] Indeed, in a republic, there would seem to be a peculiar propriety in viewing the Christian religion, as the great basis, on which it must rest for its support and permanence, if it be, what it has ever been deemed by its truest friends to be, the religion of liberty. Montesquieu has remarked, that the Christian religion is a stranger to mere despotic power. The mildness so frequently recommended in the gospel is incompatible with the despotic rage, with which a prince punishes his subjects, and exercises himself in cruelty.[4] He has gone even further, and affirmed, that the Protestant religion is far more congenial with the spirit of political freedom, than the Catholic. "When," says he, "the Christian religion, two centuries ago, became unhappily divided into Catholic and Protestant, the people of the north embraced the Protestant, and those of the south still adhered to the Catholic. The reason is plain. The people of the north have, and will ever have, a spirit of liberty and independence, which the people of the south have not. And, therefore, a religion, which has no visible head, is more agreeable to the independency of climate, than that, which has one."[5] Without stopping to inquire, whether this remark be well founded, it is certainly true, that the parent country has acted upon it with a severe and vigilant zeal; and in most of the colonies the same rigid jealousy has been maintained almost down to our own times. Massachusetts, while she has promulgated in her BILL OF RIGHTS the importance and necessity of the public support of religion, and the worship of God, has authorized the legislature to require it only for Protestantism. The language of that bill of rights is remarkable for its pointed affirmation of the duty of government to support Christianity, and the reasons for it. "As," says the third article, "the happiness of a people, and the good order and preservation of civil government, essentially depend upon piety, religion, and morality; and as these cannot be generally diffused through the community, but by the institution of the public worship of God, and of public instructions in piety, religion, and morality; therefore, to promote their happiness and to secure the good order and preservation of their government, the people of this Common wealth have a right to invest their legislature with power to authorize, and require, and the legislature shall from time to time authorize and require, the several towns, parishes, &c. &c. to make suitable provision at their own expense for the institution of the public worship of God, and for the support and maintenance of public *protestant* teachers of piety, religion, and morality, in all cases where such provision shall not be made voluntarily." Afterwards there follow provisions, prohibiting any superiority of one sect over another, and securing to all citizens the free exercise of religion.

§ 1868. Probably at the time of the adoption of the con-

3. 2 Kent's Comm. Lect. 34, p. 35 to 37; Rawle on Const. ch. 10, p. 121, 122.

4. Montesq. Spirit of Laws, B. 24, ch. 3.

5. Montesq. Spirit of Laws, B. 24, ch. 5.

stitution, and of the amendment to it, now under consideration, the general, if not the universal, sentiment in America was, that Christianity ought to receive encouragement from the state, so far as was not incompatible with the private rights of conscience, and the freedom of religious worship. An attempt to level all religions, and to make it a matter of state policy to hold all in utter indifference, would have created universal disapprobation, if not universal indignation.[6]

§ 1869. It yet remains a problem to be solved in human affairs, whether any free government can be permanent, where the public worship of God, and the support of religion, constitute no part of the policy or duty of the state in any assignable shape. The future experience of Christendom, and chiefly of the American states, must settle this problem, as yet new in the history of the world, abundant, as it has been, in experiments in the theory of government.

§ 1870. But the duty of supporting religion, and especially the Christian religion, is very different from the right to force the consciences of other men, or to punish them for worshipping God in the manner, which, they believe, their accountability to him requires. It has been truly said, that "religion, or the duty we owe to our Creator, and the manner of discharging it, can be dictated only by reason and conviction, not by force or violence,"[7] Mr. Locke himself, who did not doubt the right of government to interfere in matters of religion, and especially to encourage Christianity, at the same time has expressed his opinion of the right of private judgment, and liberty of conscience, in a manner becoming his character, as a sincere friend of civil and religious liberty. "No man, or society of men," says he, "have any authority to impose their opinions or interpretations on any other, the meanest Christian; since, in matters of religion, every man must know, and believe, and give an account for himself."[8] The rights of conscience are, indeed, beyond the just reach of any human power. They are given by God, and cannot be encroached upon by human authority, without a criminal disobedience of the precepts of natural, as well as of revealed religion.

§ 1871. The real object of the amendment was, not to

countenance, much less to advance Mahometanism, or Judaism, or infidelity, by prostrating Christianity; but to exclude all rivalry among Christian sects, and to prevent any national ecclesiastical establishment, which should give to an hierarchy the exclusive patronage of the national government. It thus cut off the means of religious persecution, (the vice and pest of former ages,) and of the subversion of the rights of conscience in matters of religion, which had been trampled upon almost from the days of the Apostles to the present age.[9] The history of the parent country had afforded the most solemn warnings and melancholy instructions on this head;[10] and even New-England, the land of the persecuted puritans, as well as other colonies, where the Church of England had maintained its superiority, would furnish out a chapter, as full of the darkest bigotry and intolerance, as any, which could be found to disgrace the pages of foreign annals.[11] Apostacy, heresy, and nonconformity had been standard crimes for public appeals, to kindle the flames of persecution, and apologize for the most atrocious triumphs over innocence and virtue.[12]

§ 1872. Mr. Justice Blackstone, after having spoken with a manly freedom of the abuses in the Romish church respecting heresy; and, that Christianity had been deformed by the demon of persecution upon the continent, and that the island of Great Britain had not been *entirely* free from the scourge,[13] defends the final enactments against nonconformity in England, in the following set phrases, to which, without any material change, might be justly applied his own sarcastic remarks upon the conduct of the Roman ecclesiastics in punishing heresy.[14] "For noncon-

6. See 2 Lloyd's Deb. 195, 196.

7. Virginia Bill of Rights, 1 Tuck. Black. Comm. App. 296; 2 Tuck. Black. Comm. App. note G. p. 10, 11.

8. Lord King's Life of Locke, p. 373.

9. Lloyd's Deb. 195.

10. 4 Black. Comm. 41 to 59.

11. Ante, Vol. I. § 53, 72, 74.

12. See 4 Black. Comm. 43 to 59.

13. "*Entirely*"! Should he not have said, *never* free from the scourge, as more conformable to historical truth?

14. Black. Comm. 45, 46.—His words are: "It is true, that the sanctimonious hypocrisy of the Canonists went, at first, no further, than enjoining penance, excommunication, and ecclesiastical deprivation for heresy, though afterwards they proceeded to imprisonment by the ordinary, and confiscation of goods *in pios usus*. But in the mean time they had prevailed upon the weakness of bigotted princes to make the civil power subservient to their purposes, by making heresy not only a temporal, but even a capital offence; the Romish Ecclesiastics determining, without appeal, whatever they pleased, to be heresy, and shifting off to the secular arm the odium and the drudgery of executions, with which

formity to the worship of the church," (says he,) "there is much more to be pleaded than for the former, (that is, reviling the ordinances of the church,) being a matter of private conscience, to the scruples of which our *present* laws have shown a very just, and Christian indulgence. For undoubtedly all persecution and oppression of weak consciences, on the score of religious persuasions, are highly unjustifiable upon every principle of natural reason, civil liberty, or sound religion. But care must be taken not to carry this indulgence into such extremes, as may endanger the national church. There is always a difference to be made between toleration and establishment." [15] Let it be remembered, that at the very moment, when the learned commentator was penning these cold remarks, the laws of England merely tolerated protestant dissenters in their public worship upon certain conditions, at once irritating and degrading; that the test and corporation acts excluded them from public and corporate offices, both of trust and profit; that the learned commentator avows, that the object of the test and corporation acts was to exclude them from office, in common with Turks, Jews, heretics, papists, and other sectaries; [16] that to deny the Trinity, however conscientiously disbelieved, was a public offence, punishable by fine and imprisonment; and that, in the rear of all these disabilities and grievances, came the long list of acts against papists, by which they were reduced to a state of political and religious slavery, and cut off from some of the dearest privileges of mankind. [17]

§ 1873. It was under a solemn consciousness of the dangers from ecclesiastical ambition, the bigotry of spiritual pride, and the intolerance of sects, thus exemplified in our domestic, as well as in foreign annals, that it was deemed advisable to exclude from the national government all power to act upon the subject. [18] The situation, too, of the different states equally proclaimed the policy, as well as the necessity of such an exclusion. In some of the states, episcopalians constituted the predominant sect; in others, presbyterians; in others, congregationalists; in others, quakers; and in others again, there was a close numerical rivalry among contending sects. It was impossible, that there should not arise perpetual strife and perpetual jealousy on the subject of ecclesiastical ascendancy, if the national government were left free to create a religious establishment. The only security was in extirpating the power. But this alone would have been an imperfect security, if it had not been followed up by a declaration of the right of the free exercise of religion, and a prohibition (as we have seen) of all religious tests. Thus, the whole power over the subject of religion is left exclusively to the state governments, to be acted upon according to their own sense of justice, and the state constitutions; and the Catholic and the Protestant, the Calvinist and the Arminian, the Jew and the Infidel, may sit down at the common table of the national councils, without any inquisition into their faith, or mode of worship. [19]

§ 1874. The next clause of the amendment respects the liberty of the press. "Congress shall make no law abridging the freedom of speech, or of the press." [20] That this amendment was intended to secure to every citizen an absolute right to speak, or write, or print, whatever he might please, without any responsibility, public or private, therefor, is a supposition too wild to be indulged by any rational man. This would be to allow to every citizen a right to destroy, at his pleasure, the reputation, the peace, the property, and even the personal safety of every other citizen. A man might, out of mere malice and revenge, accuse another of the most infamous crimes; might excite against him the indignation of all his fellow citizens by the most atrocious

_____

they themselves were too tender and delicate to intermeddle. Nay, they presented to intercede, and pray in behalf of the convicted heretic, *ut citra mortis periculum sententia circum eum moderatur,* well knowing, at the same time, that they were delivering the unhappy victim to certain death." 4 Black. Comm. 45, 46. Yet the learned author, in the same breath, could calmly vindicate the outrageous oppressions of the Church of England upon Catholics and Dissenters with the unsuspecting satisfaction of a bigot.

15. 4 Black. Comm. 51, 52.

16. 1 Black. Comm. 58.

17. 1 Black. Comm. 51 to 59.—Mr. Tucker, in his Commentaries on Blackstone, has treated the whole subject in a manner of most marked contrast to that of Mr. J. Blackstone. His ardour is as strong, as the coolness of his adversary is humiliating, on the subject of religious liberty. 2 Tuck. Black. Comm. App. Note G. p. 3, &c. See also 4 Jefferson's Corresp. 103, 104; Jefferson's Notes on Virginia, 264 to 270; 1 Tuck. Black. Comm. App. 296.

18. 2 Lloyd's Debates, 195, 196, 197.—"The sectarian spirit," said the late Dr. Currie, "is uniformly selfish, proud, and unfeeling." (Edinburgh Review, April, 1832, p. 125.)

19. See 2 Kent's Comm. Lect. 24, (2d edition, p. 35 to 37); Rawle on Const. ch. 10, p. 121, 122; 2 Lloyd's Deb. 195. See also Vol. II. § 621.

20. In the convention a proposition was moved to insert in the constitution a clause, that "the liberty of the press shall be inviolably preserved;" but it was negatived by a vote of six states against five. Journal of Convention, p. 377.

calumnies; might disturb, nay, overturn all his domestic peace, and embitter his parental affections; might inflict the most distressing punishments upon the weak, the timid, and the innocent; might prejudice all a man's civil, and political, and private rights; and might stir up sedition, rebellion, and treason even against the government itself, in the wantonness of his passions, or the corruption of his heart. Civil society could not go on under such circumstances. Men would then be obliged to resort to private vengeance, to make up for the deficiencies of the law; and assassinations, and savage cruelties, would be perpetrated with all the frequency belonging to barbarous and brutal communities. It is plain, then, that the language of this amendment imports no more, than that every man shall have a right to speak, write, and print his opinions upon any subject whatsoever, without any prior restraint, so always, that he does not injure any other person in his rights, person, property, or reputation;[21] and so always, that he does not thereby disturb the public peace, or attempt to subvert the government.[22] It is neither more nor less, than an expansion of the great doctrine, recently brought into operation in the law of libel, that every man shall be at liberty to publish what is true, with good motives and for justifiable ends. And with this reasonable limitation it is not only right in itself, but it is an inestimable privilege in a free government. Without such a limitation, it might become the scourge of the republic, first denouncing the principles of liberty, and then, by rendering the most virtuous patriots odious through the terrors of the press, introducing despotism in its worst form.

§ 1875. A little attention to the history of other countries in other ages will teach us the vast importance of this right. It is notorious, that, even to this day, in some foreign countries it is a crime to speak on any subject, religious, philosophical, or political, what is contrary to the received opinions of the government, or the institutions of the country, however laudable may be the design, and however virtuous may be the motive. Even to animadvert upon the conduct of public men, of rulers, or representatives, in terms of the strictest truth and courtesy, has been, and is deemed, a scandal upon the supposed sanctity of their sta-

tions and characters, subjecting the party to grievous punishment. In some countries no works can be printed at all, whether of science, or literature, or philosophy, without the previous approbation of the government; and the press has been shackled, and compelled to speak only in the timid language, which the cringing courtier, or the capricious inquisitor, should license for publication. The Bible itself, the common inheritance not merely of Christendom, but of the world, has been put exclusively under the control of government; and not allowed to be seen, or heard, except in a language unknown to the common inhabitants of the country. To publish a translation in the vernacular tongue, has been in former times a flagrant offence.

§ 1876. The history of the jurisprudence of England, (the most free and enlightened of all monarchies,) on this subject, will abundantly justify this statement. The art of printing, soon after its introduction, (we are told,) was looked upon, as well in England, as in other countries, as merely a matter of state, and subject to the coercion of the crown. It was therefore regulated in England by the king's proclamations, prohibitions, charters of privilege, and licenses, and finally by the decrees of the court of Star Chamber; which limited the number of printers, and of presses, which each should employ, and prohibited new publications, unless previously approved by proper licensers. On the demolition of this odious jurisdiction, in 1641, the long parliament of Charles the First, after their rupture with that prince, assumed the same powers, which the Star Chamber exercised, with respect to licensing books; and during the commonwealth, (such is human frailty, and the love of power, even in republics!) they issued their ordinances for that purpose, founded principally upon a Star Chamber decree, in 1637. After the restoration of Charles the Second, a statute on the same subject was passed, copied, with some few alterations, from the parliamentary ordinances. The act expired in 1679, and was revived and continued for a few years after the revolution of 1688. Many attempts were made by the government to keep it in force; but it was so strongly resisted by parliament, that it expired in 1694, and has never since been revived.[23] To this very hour the liberty of the press in England stands upon this negative foundation. The power to restrain it is dormant, not dead.

21. Tuck. Black. Comm. App. 297 to 299; 2 Tuck. Black. Comm. App. 11; 2 Kent's Comm. Lect. 24, p. 16 to 26.

22. Rawle on Const. ch. 10, p. 123, 124; 2 Kent's Comm. Lect. 24, p. 16 to 26; De Lolme, B. 2, ch. 12, 13; 2 Lloyd's Deb. 197, 198.

23. 4 Black. Comm. 152, note; 2 Tucker's Black. Comm. App. Note G. p. 12, 13; De Lolme, B. 2, ch. 12, 13; 2 Kent's Comm. Lect. 24, (2d edition, p. 17, 18, 19.)

It has never constituted an article of any of her numerous bills of rights; and that of the revolution of 1688, after securing other civil and political privileges, left this without notice, as unworthy of care, or fit for restraint.

§ 1877. This short review exhibits, in a striking light, the gradual progress of opinion in favour of the liberty of publishing and printing opinions in England, and the frail and uncertain tenure, by which it has been held. Down to this very day it is a contempt of parliament, and a high breach of privilege, to publish the speech of any member of either house, without its consent.[24] It is true, that it is now silently established by the course of popular opinion to be innocent in practice, though not in law. But it is notorious, that within the last fifty years the publication was connived at, rather than allowed; and that for a considerable time the reports were given in a stealthy manner, covered up under the garb of speeches in a fictitious assembly.

§ 1878. There is a good deal of loose reasoning on the subject of the liberty of the press, as if its inviolability were constitutionally such, that, like the king of England, it could do no wrong, and was free from every inquiry, and afforded a perfect sanctuary for every abuse; that, in short, it implied a despotic sovereignty to do every sort of wrong, without the slightest accountability to private or public justice. Such a notion is too extravagant to be held by any sound constitutional lawyer, with regard to the rights and duties belonging to governments generally, or to the state governments in particular. If it were admitted to be correct, it might be justly affirmed, that the liberty of the press was incompatible with the permanent existence of any free government. Mr. Justice Blackstone has remarked, that the liberty of the press, properly understood, is essential to the nature of a free state; but that this consists in laying no *previous* restraints upon publications, and not in freedom from censure for criminal matter, when published. Every freeman has an undoubted right to lay what sentiments he pleases before the public; to forbid this is to destroy the freedom of the press. But, if he publishes what is improper, mischievous, or illegal, he must take the consequences of his own temerity. To subject the press to the restrictive power of a licenser, as was formerly done before, and since the revolution (of 1688), is to subject all freedom of sentiment to the prejudices of one man, and make him the arbitrary and infallible judge of all controverted points in

learning, religion, and government. But to punish any dangerous or offensive writings, which, when published, shall, on a fair and impartial trial, be adjudged of a pernicious tendency, is necessary for the preservation of peace and good order, of government and religion, the only solid foundations of civil liberty. Thus, the will of individuals is still left free; the abuse only of that free will is the object of legal punishment. Neither is any restraint hereby laid upon freedom of thought or inquiry; liberty of private sentiment is still left; the disseminating, or making public of bad sentiments, destructive of the ends of society, is the crime, which society corrects. A man may be allowed to keep poisons in his closet; but not publicly to vend them as cordials. And after some additional reflections, he concludes with this memorable sentence: "So true will it be found, that to censure the licentiousness, is to maintain the liberty of the press."[25]

§ 1879. De Lolme states the same view of the subject; and, indeed, the liberty of the press, as understood by all England, is the right to publish without any previous restraint, or license; so, that neither the courts of justice, nor other persons, are authorized to take notice of writings intended for the press; but are confined to those, which are printed. And, in such cases, if their character is questioned, whether they are lawful, or libellous, is to be tried by a jury, according to due proceedings at law.[26] The noblest patriots of England, and the most distinguished friends of liberty, both in parliament, and at the bar, have never contended for a total exemption from responsibility, but have asked only, that the guilt or innocence of the publication should be ascertained by a trial by jury.[27]

---

25. 1 Black. Comm. 152, 153; *Rex* v. *Burdett,* 4 Barn. & Ald. R. 95.— Mr. Justice Best in *Rex* v. *Burdett,* (4 Barn. & Ald. R. 95, 132,) said "my opinion of the liberty of the press is, that every man ought to be permitted to instruct his fellow subjects; that every man may fearlessly advance any new doctrines, provided he does so with proper respect to the religion and government of the country; that he may point out errors in the measures of public men; but, he must not impute criminal conduct to them. The liberty of the press cannot be carried to this extent, without violating another equally sacred right, the right of character. This right can only be attacked in a court of justice, where the party attacked has a fair opportunity of defending himself. Where vituperation begins, the liberty of the press ends."

26. De Lolme, B. 2, ch. 12, 291 to 297.

27. See also *Rex* v. *Burdett,* 4 Barn. & Ald. 95.—The celebrated act of parliament of Mr. Fox, giving the right to the jury, in trials for libels, to judge of the whole matter of the charge, and to return a general verdict, did not affect to go farther. The celebrated defence of Mr. Erskine,

24. See Comyn's Dig. *Parliament,* G. 9.

§ 1880. It would seem, that a very different view of the subject was taken by a learned American commentator, though it is not, perhaps, very easy to ascertain the exact extent of his opinions. In one part of his disquisitions, he seems broadly to contend, that the security of the freedom of the press requires, that it should be exempt, not only from previous restraint by the executive, as in Great Britain; but, from legislative restraint also; and that this exemption, to be effectual, must be an exemption, not only from the previous inspection of licensers, but from the subsequent penalty of laws.[28] In other places, he seems as explicitly to admit, that the liberty of the press does not include the right to do injury to the reputation of another, or to take from him the enjoyment of his rights or property, or to justify slander and calumny upon him, as a private or public man. And yet it is added, that every individual certainly has a right to speak, or publish his sentiments on the measures of government. To do this without restraint, control, or *fear of punishment for so doing,* is that which constitutes the genuine freedom of the press.[29] Perhaps the apparent contrariety of these opinions may arise from mixing up, in the same disquisitions, a discussion of the right of the state governments, with that of the national government, to interfere in cases of this sort, which may stand upon very different foundations. Or, perhaps, it is meant to be contended, that the liberty of the press, in all cases, excludes public punishment for public wrongs; but not civil redress for private wrongs, by calumny and libels.

§ 1881. The true mode of considering the subject is, to examine the case with reference to a state government, whose constitution, like that, for instance, of Massachusetts, declares, that "the liberty of the press is essential to the security of freedom in a state; it ought not, therefore, to be restrained in this commonwealth." What is the true interpretation of this clause? Does it prohibit the legislature from passing any laws, which shall control the licentiousness of the press, or afford adequate protection to individuals, whose private comfort, or good reputations are assailed, and violated by the press? Does it stop the legislature from passing any laws to punish libels and inflammatory publications, the object of which is to excite sedition against the government, to stir up resistance to its laws, to urge on conspiracies to destroy it, to create odium and indignation against virtuous citizens, to compel them to yield up their rights, or to make them the objects of popular vengeance? Would such a declaration in Viriginia (for she has, on more than one occasion, boldly proclaimed, that the liberty of the press ought not to be restrained,) prohibit the legislature from passing laws to punish a man, who should publish, and circulate writings, the design of which avowedly is to excite the slaves to general insurrection against their masters, or to inculcate upon them the policy of secretly poisoning, or murdering them? In short, is it contended, that the liberty of the press is so much more valuable, than all other rights in society, that the public safety, nay the existence of the government itself is to yield to it? Is private redress for libels and calumny more important, or more valuable, than the maintenance of the good order, peace, and safety of society? It would be difficult to answer these questions in favour of the liberty of the press, without at the same time declaring, that such a licentiousness belonged, and could belong only to a despotism; and was utterly incompatible with the principles of a free government.

§ 1882. Besides:—What is meant by restraint of the press, or an abridgment of its liberty? If to publish without control, or responsibility be its genuine meaning; is not that equally violated by allowing a private compensation for damages, as by a public fine? Is not a man as much restrained from doing a thing by the fear of heavy damages, as by public punishment? Is he not often as severely punished by one, as by the other? Surely, it can make no difference in the case, what is the nature or extent of the restraint, if all restraint is prohibited. The legislative power is just as much prohibited from one mode, as from an-

on the trial of the Dean of St. Asaph, took the same ground. Even Junius, with his severe and bitter assaults upon established authority and doctrines, stopped here. "The liberty of the press," (said he,) "is the palladium of all the civil, political, and religious rights of an Englishman, and the right of juries to return a general verdict in all cases whatsoever, is an essential part of our constitution." "The laws of England, provide as effectually, as any human laws can do, for the protection of the subject in his reputation, as well as in his person and property. If the characters of private men are insulted, or injured, a double remedy is open to them, by action and by indictment."—"With regard to strictures upon the characters of men in office, and the measures of government, the case is a *little* different. A *considerable* latitude must be allowed in the discussion of public affairs, or the liberty of the press will be of no benefit to society." But he no where contends for the right to publish seditious libels; and, on the contrary, through his whole reasoning he admits the duty to punish those, which are really so.

28. 2 Tuck. Black. Comm. App. 20; 1 Tuck. Black. Comm. App. 298, 299.

29. 2 Tuck. Black. Comm. App. 28 to 30; 1 Tuck. Black. Comm. App. 298, 299.

other. And it may be asked, where is the ground for distinguishing between public and private amesnability for the wrong? The prohibition itself states no distinction. It is general; it is universal. Why, then, is the distinction attempted to be made? Plainly, because of the monstrous consequences flowing from such a doctrine. It would prostrate all personal liberty, all private peace, all enjoyment of property, and good reputation. These are the great objects, for which government is instituted; and, if the licentiousness of the press must endanger, not only these, but all public rights and public liberties, is it not as plain, that the right of government to punish the violators of them (the only mode of redress, which it can pursue) flows from the primary duty of self-preservation? No one can doubt the importance, in a free government, of a right to canvass the acts of public men, and the tendency of public measures, to censure boldly the conduct of rulers, and to scrutinize closely the policy, and plans of the government. This is the great security of a free government. If we would preserve it, public opinion must be enlightened; political vigilance must be inculcated; free, but not licentious, discussion must be encouraged. But the exercise of a right is essentially different from an abuse of it. The one is no legitimate inference from the other. Common sense here promulgates the broad doctrine, *sic utere tuo, ut non alienum laedas;* so exercise your own freedom, as not to infringe the rights of others, or the public peace and safety.

§ 1883. The doctrine laid down by Mr. Justice Blackstone, respecting the liberty of the press, has not been repudiated (as far as is known) by any solemn decision of any of the state courts, in respect to their own municipal jurisprudence. On the contrary, it has been repeatedly affirmed in several of the states, notwithstanding their constitutions, or laws recognize, that "the liberty of the press ought not to be restrained," or more emphatically, that "the liberty of the press shall be inviolably maintained." This is especially true in regard to Massachusetts, South-Carolina, and Louisiana.[30] Nay; it has farther been held, that the truth of the facts is not alone sufficient to justify the publication, unless it is done from good motives, and for justifiable purposes, or, in other words, on an occasion, (as upon the canvass of candidates for public office,) when public duty, or private right requires it.[31] And the very circumstance, that, in the constitutions of several other states, provision is made for giving the truth in evidence, in prosecutions for libels for official conduct, when the matter published is proper for public information, is exceedingly strong to show, how the general law is understood. The exception establishes in all other cases the propriety of the doctrine. And Mr. Chancellor Kent, upon a large survey of the whole subject, has not scrupled to declare, that "it has become a constitutional principle in this country, that every citizen may freely speak, write, and publish his sentiments on all subjects, *being responsible for the abuse of that right;* and, that no law can rightfully be passed, to restrain, or abridge the freedom of the press."[32]

§ 1884. Even with these reasonable limitations, it is not an uncommon opinion among European statesmen of high character and extensive attainments, that the liberty of the press is incompatible with the permanent existence of any free government; nay, of any government at all. That, if it be true, that free governments cannot exist without it, it is quite as certain, that they cannot exist with it. In short, that the press is a new element in modern society; and likely, in a great measure, to control the power of armies, and the sovereignty of the people. That it works with a silence, a cheapness, a suddenness, and a force, which may break up, in an instant, all the foundations of society, and move public opinion, like a mountain torrent, to a general desolation of every thing within its reach.

§ 1885. Whether the national government possesses a power to pass any law, not restraining the liberty of the press, but punishing the licentiousness of the press, is a question of a very different nature, upon which the commentator abstains from expressing any opinion. In 1798, Congress, believing that they possessed a constitutional authority for that purpose, passed an act, punishing all unlawful combinations, and conspiracies, to oppose the measures of the government, or to impede the operation of the laws, or to intimidate and prevent any officer of the United States from undertaking, or executing his duty. The same act further provided, for a public presentation, and punishment by fine, and imprisonment, of all persons, who should write, print, utter, or publish any false, scandalous, and malicious writing, or writings against the government of the United States, or of either house of congress, or of the president, with an intent to defame them, or bring

---

30. *Commonwealth* v. *Clap,* 4 Mass. R. 163; *Commonwealth* v. *Blanding,* 3 Pick. R. 304; The *State* v. *Lehre,* 2 Rep. Const. Court, 809; 2 Kent's Comm. Lect. 24, (2d edition, p. 17 to 24.)

31. Ibid.

32. 1 Kent's Comm. Lect. 24, (2d edition, p. 17 to 24.) See also Rawle on Const. ch. 10, p. 123, 124.

them into contempt, or disrepute, or to excite against them the hatred of the good people of the United States; or to excite them to oppose any law, or act of the president, in pursuance of law of his constitutional powers; or to resist, or oppose, or defeat any law; or to aid, encourage, or abet any hostile designs of any foreign nation against the United States. And the same act authorized the truth to be given in evidence on any such prosecution; and the jury, upon the trial, to determine the law and the fact, as in other cases.[33]

§ 1886. This act was immediately assailed, as unconstitutional, both in the state legislatures, and the courts of law, where prosecutions were pending. Its constitutionality was deliberately affirmed by the courts of law; and in a report made by a committee of congress. It was denied by a considerable number of the states; but affirmed by a majority. It became one of the most prominent points of attack upon the existing administration; and the appeal thus made was, probably, more successful with the people, and more consonant with the feelings of the times, than any other made upon that occasion. The act, being limited to a short period, expired by its own limitation, in March, 1801; and has never been renewed. It has continued, down to this very day, to be a theme of reproach with many of those, who have since succeeded to power.[34]

§ 1886. The remaining clause secures "the right of the people peaceably to assemble and to petition the government for a redress of grievances."

§ 1887. This would seem unnecessary to be expressly

provided for in a republican government, since it results from the very nature of its structure and institutions. It is impossible, that it could be practically denied, until the spirit of liberty had wholly disappeared, and the people had become so servile and debased, as to be unfit to exercise any of the privileges of freemen.[35]

§ 1888. The provision was probably borrowed from the declaration of rights in England, on the revolution of 1688, in which the right to petition the king for a redress of grievances was insisted on; and the right to petition parliament in the like manner has been provided for, and guarded by statutes passed before, as well as since that period.[36] Mr. Tucker has indulged himself in a disparaging criticism upon the phraseology of this clause, as savouring too much of that style of condescension, in which favours are supposed to be granted.[37] But this seems to be quite overstrained; since it speaks the voice of the people in the language of prohibition, and not in that of affirmance of a right, supposed to be unquestionable, and inherent.

§ 1889. The next amendment is: "A well regulated militia being necessary to the security of a free state, the right of the people to keep and bear arms shall not be infringed."

§ 1890. The importance of this article will scarcely be doubted by any persons, who have duly reflected upon the subject. The militia is the natural defence of a free country against sudden foreign invasions, domestic insurrections, and domestic usurpations of power by rulers. It is against sound policy for a free people to keep up large military establishments and standing armies in time of peace, both from the enormous expenses, with which they are attended, and the facile means, which they afford to ambitious and unprincipled rulers, to subvert the government, or trample upon the rights of the people. The right of the citizens to keep and bear arms has justly been considered, as the palladium of the liberties of a republic; since it offers a strong moral check against the usurpation and arbitrary power of rulers; and will generally, even if these are successful in the first instance, enable the people to resist and triumph over them.[38] And yet, though this truth would seem so clear, and the importance of a well regulated militia would

33. Act of 14th July, 1798, ch. 91.
34. The learned reader will find the subject discussed at large in many of the pamphlets of that day, and especially in the Virginia Report, and Resolutions of the Virginia Legislature, in December, 1798, and January, 1800; in the Report of a Committee of congress on the Alien and Sedition laws, on the 25th of February, 1799; in the Resolutions of the legislatures of Massachusetts and Kentucky, in 1799; in Bayard's Speech on the Judiciary act, in 1802; in Addison's charges to the grand jury, in Pennsylvania, printed with his Reports; in 2 Tucker's Black. Comm. App. note G. p. 11 to 30. It is surprising, with what facility men glide into the opinion, that a measure is universally deemed unconstitutional, because it is so in their own opinion, especially if it has become unpopular. It has been often asserted, by public men, as the universal sense of the nation, that this act was unconstitutional; and that opinion has been promulgated recently, with much emphasis, by distinguished statesmen; as we have already had occasion to notice. What the state of public and professional opinion on this subject now is, it is, perhaps, difficult to determine. But it is well known, that the opinions then deliberately given by many professional men, and judges, and legislatures, in favour of the constitutionality of the law, have never been retracted. See Vol. III. § 1288, 1289, and note.

35. See 2 Lloyd's Debates, 197, 198, 199.
36. See 1 Black. Comm. 143; 5 Cobbett's Parl'y. Hist. p. 109, 110; Rawle on Const. ch. 10, p. 124; 3 Amer. Museum, 420; 2 Kent's Comm. Lect. 24, p. 7, 8.
37. 1 Tucker's Black. Comm. App. 299.
38. 1 Tucker's Black. Comm. App. 300; Rawle on Const. ch. 10, p. 125; 2 Lloyd's Debates, 219, 220.

seem so undeniable, it cannot be disguised, that among the American people there is a growing indifference to any system of militia discipline, and a strong disposition, from a sense of its burthens, to be rid of all regulations. How it is practicable to keep the people duly armed without some organization, it is difficult to see. There is certainly no small danger, that indifference may lead to disgust, and disgust to contempt; and thus gradually undermine all the protection intended by this clause of our national bill of rights.[39]

§ 1891. A similar provision in favour of protestants (for to them it is confined) is to be found in the bill of rights of 1688, it being declared, "that the subjects, which are protestants, may have arms for their defence suitable to their condition, and as allowed by law."[40] But under various pretences the effect of this provision has been greatly narrowed; and it is at present in England more nominal than real, as a defensive privilege.[41]

§ 1892. The next amendment is: "No soldier shall in time of peace be quartered in any house, without the consent of the owner, nor in time of war, but in a manner to be prescribed by law."

§ 1893. This provision speaks for itself. Its plain object is to secure the perfect enjoyment of that great right of the common law, that a man's house shall be his own castle, privileged against all civil and military intrusion. The billetting of soldiers in time of peace upon the people has been a common resort of arbitrary princes, and is full of inconvenience and peril. In the petition of right (4 Charles I.), it was declared by parliament to be a great grievance.[42]

§ 1894. The next amendment is: "The right of the people to be secure in their persons, houses, papers, and effects against unreasonable searches and seizures shall not be violated; and no warrants shall issue, but upon probable cause, supported by oath or affirmation, and particularly describing the place to be searched, and the person or things to be seized."

§ 1895. This provision seems indispensable to the full enjoyment of the rights of personal security, personal liberty, and private property. It is little more than the affirmance of a great constitutional doctrine of the common law. And its introduction into the amendments was doubtless occasioned by the strong sensibility excited, both in England and America, upon the subject of general warrants almost upon the eve of the American Revolution. Although special warrants upon complaints under oath, stating the crime, and the party by name, against whom the accusation is made, are the only legal warrants, upon which an arrest can be made according to the law of England;[43] yet a practice had obtained in the secretaries' office ever since the restoration, (grounded on some clauses in the acts for regulating the press,) of issuing general warrants to take up, without naming any persons in particular, the authors, printers, and publishers of such obscene, or seditious libels, as were particularly specified in the warrant. When these acts expired, in 1694, the same practice was continued in every reign, and under every administration, except the four last years of Queen Anne's reign, down to the year 1763. The general warrants, so issued, in general terms authorized the officers to apprehend all persons suspected, without naming, or describing any person in special. In the year 1763, the legality of these general warrants was brought before the King's Bench for solemn decision; and they were adjudged to be illegal, and void for uncertainty.[44]

43. And see *Ex parte Burford,* 3 Cranch, 447; 2 Lloyd's Deb. 226, 227.

44. *Money* v. *Leach,* 3 Burr, 1743; 4 Black. Comm. 291, 292, and note ibid. See also 15 Hansard's Parl. Hist. 1398 to 1418, (1764); *Bell* v. *Clapp,* 10 John. R. 263; *Sailly* v. *Smith,* 11 John. R. 500; 1 Tucker's Black. Comm. App. 301; Rawle on Const. ch. 10, p. 127.—It was on account of a supposed repugnance to this article, that a vehement opposition was made to the alien act of 1798, ch. 75, which authorized the president to order all such aliens, as he should judge dangerous to the peace and safety of the United States, or have reasonable grounds to suspect of any treasonable, or secret machinations against the government to depart out of the United States; and in case of disobedience, punished the refusal with imprisonment. That law having long since passed away, it is not my design to enter upon the grounds, upon which its constitutionality was asserted or denied. But the learned reader will find ample information on the subject in the report of a committee of congress, on the petitions for the repeal of the alien and sedition laws, 25th of February, 1799; the report and resolutions of the Virginia legislature of 7th of January, 1800; Judge Addison's charges to the grand jury in the Appendix to his reports; and 1 Tucker's Black. Comm. App. 301 to 304; Id. 306. See also Vol. III. § 1288, 1289, and note.

Mr. Jefferson has entered into an elaborate defence of the right and duty of public officers to disregard, in certain cases, the injunctions of the law, in a letter addressed to Mr. Colvin in 1810. (4 Jefferson's

39. It would be well for Americans to reflect upon the passage in Tacitus, (Hist. IV. ch. 74): "*Nam neque quies sine armis, neque arma sine stipendiis, neque stipendia sine tributis, haberi queunt.*" Is there any escape from a large standing army, but in a well disciplined militia? There is much wholesome instruction on this subject in 1 Black. Comm. ch. 13, p. 408 to 417.

40. 5 Cobbett's Parl. Hist. p. 110; 1 Black. Comm. 143, 144.

41. 1 Tucker's Black. Comm. App. 300.

42. 2 Cobbett's Parl. Hist. 375; Rawle on Const. ch. 10, p. 126, 127; 1 Tucker's Black. Comm. App. 300, 301; 2 Lloyd's Debates, 223.

A warrant, and the complaint, on which the same is founded, to be legal, must not only state the name of the party, but also the time, and place, and nature of the offence with reasonable certainty.[45]

§ 1896. The next amendment is: "Excessive bail shall not be required; nor excessive fines imposed; nor cruel and unusual punishments inflicted." This is an exact transcript of a clause in the bill of rights, framed at the revolution of 1688.[46] The provision would seem to be wholly unnecessary in a free government, since it is scarcely possible, that any department of such a government should authorize, or justify such atrocious conduct.[47] It was, however, adopted, as an admonition to all departments of the national government, to warn them against such violent proceedings, as had taken place in England in the arbitrary reigns of some of the Stuarts.[48] In those times, a demand of excessive bail was often made against persons, who were odious to the court, and its favourites; and on failing to procure it, they were committed to prison.[49] Enormous fines and amercements were also sometimes imposed, and cruel and vindictive punishments inflicted. Upon this subject Mr. Justice Blackstone has wisely remarked, that sanguinary laws are a bad symptom of the distemper of any state, or at least of its weak constitution. The laws of the Roman kings, and the twelve tables of the Decemviri, were full of cruel punishments; the Porcian law, which exempted all citizens from sentence of death, silently abrogated them all. In this period the republic flourished. Under the emperors severe laws were revived, and then the empire fell.[50]

§ 1897. It has been held in the state courts, (and the point does not seem ever to have arisen in the courts of the United States,) that this clause does not apply to punishments inflicted in a state court for a crime against such state; but that the prohibition is addressed solely to the national government, and operates, as a restriction upon its powers.[51]

§ 1898. The next amendment is: "The enumeration in the constitution of certain rights shall not be construed to deny, or disparage others retained by the people." This clause was manifestly introduced to prevent any perverse, or ingenious misapplication of the well known maxim, that an affirmation in particular cases implies a negation in all others; and é converso, that a negation in particular cases implies an affirmation in all others.[52] The maxim, rightly understood, is perfectly sound and safe; but it has often been strangely forced from its natural meaning into the support of the most dangerous political heresies. The amendment was undoubtedly suggested by the reasoning of the Federalist on the subject of a general bill of rights.[53]

§ 1899. The next and last amendment is: "The powers not delegated to the United States by the constitution, nor prohibited by it to the states, are reserved to the states respectively, or to the people."

§ 1900. This amendment is a mere affirmation of what, upon any just reasoning, is a necessary rule of interpret-

Corresp. 149, 151) On that occasion, he justified a very gross violation of this very article by General Wilkinson, (if, indeed, he did not authorize it,) in the seizure of two American citizens by military force, on account of supposed treasonable conspiracies against the United States, and transporting them, without any warrant, or order of any civil authority, from New-Orleans to Washington for trial. They were both discharged from custody at Washington by the Supreme Court, upon a full hearing of the case. (*Ex parte Bollman & Swartout,* 4 Cranch, 75 to 136) Mr. Jefferson reasons out the whole case, and assumes, without the slightest hesitation, the positive guilt of the parties. His language is: "Under these circumstances, was he (General Wilkinson) justifiable (1.) in seizing notorious conspirators? On this there can be but two opinions; *one, of the guilty, and their accomplices;* the *other, that of all honest men!!!* (2.) In sending them to the seat of government, when the *written law* gave them a right to TRIAL BY JURY? The danger of their rescue, of their continuing their machinations, *the tardiness and weakness of the law, apathy of the judges, active patronage of the whole tribe of lawyers, unknown disposition of the juries,* an hourly expectation of the enemy, salvation of the city, and of the Union itself, which would have been convulsed to its centre, had that conspiracy succeeded; *all these constituted a law of necessity and self-preservation; and rendered the salus populi supreme over the* WRITTEN *law!!!*" Thus, the constitution is to be wholly disregarded, because Mr. Jefferson has no confidence in judges, or juries, or laws. He first assumes the guilt of the parties, and then denounces every person connected with the courts of justice, as unworthy of trust. Without any warrant or lawful authority, citizens are dragged from their homes under military force, and exposed to the perils of a long voyage, against the plain language of this very article; and yet three years after they are discharged by the Supreme Court, Mr. Jefferson uses this strong language.

45. See *Ex parte Burford,* 3 Cranch, 447.
46. 5 Cobbett's Parl. Hist. 110.
47. 2 Elliot's Debates, 345.
48. See 2 Lloyd's Debates, 225, 226; 3 Elliot's Debates, 345.

49. Rawle on Const. ch. 10, p. 130, 131.
50. 4 Black. Comm. 17. See De Lolme, B. 2, ch. 16, p. 366, 367, 368, 369.
51. See *Barker* v. *The People,* 3 Cowen's R. 686; *James* v. *Commonwealth,* 12 Sergeant and Rawle's R. 220. See *Barron* v. *Mayor of Baltimore,* 7 Peters's R. (1833.)
52. See *ante,* Vol. I. § 448; The Federalist, No. 83.
53. The Federalist, No. 84; *ante,* Vol. III. § 1852 to 1857; 1 Lloyd's Debates, 433, 437; 1 Tucker's Black. Comm. App. 307, 308.

ing the constitution. Being an instrument of limited and enumerated powers, it follows irresistibly, that what is not conferred, is withheld, and belongs to the state authorities, if invested by their constitutions of government respectively in them; and if not so invested, it is retained BY THE PEOPLE, as a part of their residuary sovereignty.[54] When this amendment was before congress, a proposition was moved, to insert the word "expressly" before "delegated," so as to read "the powers not *expressly* delegated to the United States by the constitution," &c. On that occasion it was remarked, that it is impossible to confine a government to the exercise of express powers. There must necessarily be admitted powers by implication, unless the constitution descended to the most minute details.[55] It is a general principle, that all corporate bodies possess all powers incident to a corporate capacity, without being absolutely expressed. The motion was accordingly negatived.[56] Indeed, one of the great defects of the confederation was, (as we have already seen,) that it contained a clause, prohibiting the exercise of any power, jurisdiction, or right, not *expressly delegated*.[57] The consequence was, that congress were crippled at every step of their progress; and were often compelled by the very necessities of the times to usurp powers, which they did not constitutionally possess; and thus, in effect, to break down all the great barriers against tyranny and oppression.[58]

§ 1901. It is plain, therefore, that it could not have been the intention of the framers of this amendment to give it effect, as an abridgment of any of the powers granted under the constitution, whether they are express or implied, direct or incidental. Its sole design is to exclude any interpretation, by which other powers should be assumed beyond those, which are granted. All that are granted in the original instrument, whether express or implied, whether direct or incidental, are left in their original state. All pow-

ers not delegated, (not all powers not *expressly* delegated,) and not prohibited, are reserved.[59] The attempts, then, which have been made from time to time, to force upon this language an abridging, or restrictive influence, are utterly unfounded in any just rules of interpreting the words, or the sense of the instrument. Stripped of the ingenious disguises, in which they are clothed, they are neither more nor less, than attempts to foist into the text the word "expressly;" to qualify, what is general, and obscure, what is clear, and defined. They make the sense of the passage bend to the wishes and prejudices of the interpreter; and employ criticism to support a theory, and not to guide it. One should suppose, if the history of the human mind did not furnish abundant proof to the contrary, that no reasonable man would contend for an interpretation founded neither in the letter, nor in the spirit of an instrument. Where is controversy to end, if we desert both the letter and the spirit? What is to become of constitutions of government, if they are to rest, not upon the plain import of their words, but upon conjectural enlargements and restrictions, to suit the temporary passions and interests of the day? Let us never forget, that our constitutions of government are solemn instruments, addressed to the common sense of the people and designed to fix, and perpetuate their rights and their lberties. They are not to be frittered away to please the demagogues of the day. They are not to be violated to gratify the ambition of political leaders. They are to speak in the same voice now, and for ever. They are of no man's private interpretation. They are ordained by the will of the people; and can be changed only by the sovereign command of the people.

§ 1902. It has been justly remarked, that the erection of a new government, whatever care or wisdom may distinguish the work, cannot fail to originate questions of intricacy and nicety; and these may in a particular manner be expected to flow from the establishment of a constitution, founded upon the total, or partial incorporation of a number of distinct sovereignties. Time alone can mature and perfect so compound a system; liquidate the meaning of all the parts; and adjust them to each other in a harmonious and consistent whole.[60]

---

54. See 1 Tucker's Black. Comm. App. 307, 308, 309.

55. Mr. Madison added, that he remembered the word "expressly" had been moved in the Virginia Convention by the opponents to the ratification; and after a full and fair discussion, was given up by them, and the system allowed to retain its present form. 2 Lloyd's Debates, 234.

56. 2 Lloyd's Deb. 243, 244; *McCulloh* v. *Maryland,* 4 Wheat. R. 407; *Martin* v. *Hunter,* 1 Wheat. R. 325; *Houston* v. *Moore,* 5 Wheat. R. 49; *Anderson* v. *Dunn,* 6 Wheat. R. 225, 226.

57. Confederation, Article 2, *ante* Vol. I. § 230.

58. The Federalist, No. 33, 38, 42, 44; *ante* Vol. I. § 269.

59. *McCulloh* v. *Maryland,* 4 Wheat. R. 406, 407; *ante* Vol. I. § 433.

60. The Federalist, No. 82. See also Mr. Hume's Essays, Vol. I. *Essay on the Rise of Arts and Sciences.*

The People v. Ruggles

JAMES KENT

1811

At the time of America's break with Great Britain, most law on both sides of the Atlantic was not written in statute books. Instead, judges applied the common law in judging disputes and criminal cases brought before them. Common law was the tradition established by custom, interpreted by judges, and passed on through precedents or preceding judicial decisions. When the American states established their own constitutions and governments, they also adopted the common law for themselves. Thus, the United States explicitly adopted the traditions of British law and custom as bases for their own decisions regarding crimes and civil disputes. This did not mean that Americans sought to remain forever British in their law and custom. Through their statutes and constitutions, for example, they did away with the test oaths, fines, and other disabilities imposed on religious minorities by the establishment of the Church of England. But it did mean that statutes and constitutions would be read against a particular background of custom and tradition.

In *The People v. Ruggles,* Justice James Kent of New York's highest court considered the case of a man convicted of blasphemy. The defendant had claimed that New York's constitution established toleration for all kinds of religion and worship, except those promoting immoral behavior. This meant, he claimed, that Christianity was not part of New York's common law. Because Ruggles had not attacked religion in general (which all admitted would be a crime) and because his remarks—questioning the divinity of Christ—would not undermine morals or the ability of oaths to cause people to tell the truth, he could not be convicted of any crime. James Kent flatly disagreed with this argument, upholding the traditional view that Christianity was a crucial part of the common law.

The People v. Ruggles (8 Johns 225)

KENT, *Ch. J.:*

The offense charged is, that the defendant below did "wickedly, maliciously and blasphemously utter, in the presence and hearing of divers good and Christian people, these false, feigned, scandalous, malicious, wicked and blasphemous words, to wit, 'Jesus Christ was a bastard and his mother must be a whore'"; and the single question is, whether this be a public offense by the law of the land. After conviction we must intend that these words were uttered in a wanton manner, and, as they evidently import, with a wicked and malicious disposition, and not in a serious discussion upon any controverted point in religion. The language was blasphemous, not only in a popular, but in a legal sense; for blasphemy, according to the most precise definitions, consists in maliciously reviling God, or religion, and this was reviling Christianity through its author. (Emlyn's Preface to the State Trials, p. 8; see, also, Whitlock's Speech, State Trials, Vol. II. 273.) The jury have passed upon the intent or *quo animo,* and if those words spoken, in any case, will amount to a misdemeanor, the indictment is good.

Such words uttered with such a disposition, were an offense at common law. In *Taylor's* case (1 Vent., 293; 3 Keb., 607; Tremaine's Pleas of the Crown, 226, S. C.) the defendant was convicted upon information of speaking similar words, and the Court of K. B. said that Christianity was parcel of the law, and to cast contumelious reproaches upon it, tended to weaken the foundation of moral obligation, and the efficacy of oaths. And in the case of *Rex* v. *Woolston* (Str., 834; Fitzg., 64), on a like conviction, the court said they would not suffer it to be debated whether defaming Christianity in general was not an offense at common law, for that whatever strikes at the root of Christianity tends manifestly to the dissolution of civil government. But the court were careful to say that they did not intend to include disputes between learned men upon particular controverted points. The same doctrine was laid down in the late case of *The King* v. *Williams,* for the publication of Paine's "Age of Reason," which was tried before Lord Kenyon in July, 1797. The authorities show that blasphemy against God, and contumelious reproaches and profane ridicule of Christ or the Holy Scriptures (which are equally treated as blasphemy), are offenses punishable at common law, whether uttered by words or writings. (*Taylor's* case, 1 Vent., 293; 4 Bl. Com., 59; 1 Hawk., bk. 1, ch. 5; 1 East's P. C., 3; Tremaine's Entries, 225, *Rex* v. *Doyle*.) The consequences may be less extensively pernicious in the one case than in the other, but in both instances the reviling is still an offense, because it tends to corrupt the morals of the people, and to destroy good order. Such offenses have always been considered independent of any religious establishment or the rights of the Church. They are treated as affecting the essential interests of civil society.

And why should not the language contained in the indictment be still an offense with us? There is nothing in our manners or institutions which has prevented the application or the necessity of this part of the common law. We stand equally in need, now as formerly, of all the moral discipline, and of those principles of virtue, which help to bind society together. The people of this State, in common with the people of this country, profess the general doctrines of Christianity, as the rule of their faith and practice; and to scandalize the author of these doctrines is not only, in a religious point of view, extremely impious, but, even in respect to the obligations due to society, is a gross violation of decency and good order. Nothing could be more offensive to the virtuous part of the community, or more injurious to the tender morals of the young, than to declare such profanity lawful. It would go to confound all distinction between things sacred and profane; for, to use the words of one of the greatest oracles of human wisdom, "profane scoffing doth by little and little deface the reverence for religion;" and who adds, in another place, "two principal causes have I ever known of atheism — curious controversies and profane scoffing." (Lord Bacon's Works, Vol. II., 291, 503.) Things which corrupt moral sentiment, as obscene actions, prints and writings, and even gross instances of seduction, have, upon the same principle, been held indictable; and shall we form an exception in these particulars to the rest of the civilized world? No government among any of the polished nations of antiquity, and none of the institutions of modern Europe (a single and monitory case excepted), ever hazarded such a bold experiment upon the solidity of the public morals, as to permit with impunity, and under the sanction of their tribunals the general religion of the community to be openly insulted and defamed. The very idea of jurisprudence with

the ancient lawgivers and philosophers, embraced the religion of the country. *Jurisprudentia est divinarum atque humanurum rerum notitia* (Dig., bk. 1, 10, 2; Cic. De Legibus, bk. 2, *passim*.)

The free, equal, and undisturbed enjoyment of religious opinion, whatever it may be, and free and decent discussions on any religious subject, is granted and secured; but to revile, with malicious and blasphemous contempt, the religion professed by almost the whole community, is an abuse of that right. Nor are we bound, by any expressions in the constitution, as some have strangely supposed, either not to punish at all, or to punish indiscriminately the like attacks upon the religion of Mahomet or of the Grand Lama; and for this plain reason, that the case assumes that we are a Christian people, and the morality of the country is deeply ingrafted upon Christianity, and not upon the doctrines or worship of those imposters. Besides, the offense is *crimen malitiae* and the imputation of malice could not be inferred from any invectives upon superstitions equally false and unknown. We are not to be restrained from animadversion upon offenses against public decency, like those committed by Sir Charles Sedley (1 Sid., 168), or by one Rollo (Sayer, 158), merely because there may be savage tribes, and perhaps semi-barbarous nations, whose sense of shame would not be effected by what we should consider the most audacious outrages upon decorum. It is sufficient that the common law checks upon words and actions, dangerous to the public welfare, apply to our case, and are suited to the condition of this and every other people whose manners are refined, and whose morals have been elevated and inspired with a more enlarged benevolence, by means of the Christian religion.

Though the constitution has discarded religious establishments, it does not forbid judicial cognizance of those offenses against religion and morality which have no reference to any such establishment, or to any particular form of government, but are punishable because they strike at the root of moral obligation, and weaken the security of the social ties. The object of the 38th article of the constitution, was, to "guard against spiritual oppression and intolerance," by declaring that "the free exercise and enjoyment of religious profession and worship, without discrimination or preference, should forever thereafter be allowed within this State, to all mankind." This declaration (noble and magnanimous as it is, when duly understood) never meant to withdraw religion in general, and with it the best sanctions of moral and social obligation from all consideration and notice of the law. It will be fully satisfied by a free and universal toleration, without any of the tests, disabilities, or discriminations, incident to a religious establishment. To construe it as breaking down the common law barriers against licentious, wanton, and impious attacks upon Christianity itself, would be an enormous perversion of its meaning. The proviso guards the article from such dangerous latitude of construction, when it declares that "the liberty of conscience hereby granted shall not be so construed as to excuse acts of licentiousness, or justify practices inconsistent with the peace and safety of this State." The preamble and this proviso are a species of commentary upon the meaning of the article, and they sufficiently show that the framers of the constitution intended only to banish test oaths, disabilities and the burdens, and sometimes the oppressions, of church establishments; and to secure to the people of this State freedom from coercion, and an equality of right, on the subject of religion. This was no doubt the consummation of their wishes. It was all that reasonable minds could require, and it had long been a favorite object, on both sides of the Atlantic, with some of the most enlightened friends to the rights of mankind, whose indignation had been roused by infringements of the liberty of conscience, and whose zeal was inflamed in the pursuit of its enjoyment. That this was the meaning of the constitution is further confirmed by a paragraph in a preceding article, which specially provides that "such parts of the common law as might be construed to establish or maintain any particular denomination of Christians, or their ministers," were thereby abrogated.

The legislative exposition of the constitution is conformable to this view of it. Christianity, in its enlarged sense, as a religion revealed and taught in the Bible, is not unknown to our law. The statute for preventing immorality (Laws, Vol. I., 224); consecrates the first day of the week as holy time, and considers the violation of it as immoral. This was only the continuation, in substance, of a law of the colony which declared that the profanation of the Lord's day was "the great scandal of the Christian faith." The Act Concerning Oaths (Laws, Vol. I., p. 405) recognizes the common law mode of administering an oath, "by laying the hand on and kissing the gospels." Surely, then, we are bound to conclude, that wicked and malicious words, writings and actions which go to vilify those gospels, continue, as at common law, to be an offense against the public peace and safety. They are inconsistent with the reverence due to the administration of an oath, and among their other evil consequences, they tend to lessen, in the public mind, its religious sanction.

The court are accordingly of opinion that the judgment below must be affirmed.

Judgment affirmed.

Marbury v. Madison

JOHN MARSHALL

1803

Federalist president John Adams lost his 1800 bid for reelection to his political adversary, Thomas Jefferson, head of the new Democratic-Republican Party. After losing, but before Jefferson had replaced him in office, Adams and his Senate supporters pushed through a number of federal appointments. Their goal was to continue the Federalist Party influence by placing loyal followers in administrative and judicial posts. William Marbury was among these followers. Appointed a justice of the peace for the District of Columbia, Marbury was not allowed to take his post because James Madison, secretary of state under Thomas Jefferson, refused to deliver his commission. Marbury sued Madison, seeking to have the Supreme Court issue a writ of mandamus —an order telling Madison to deliver the commission. The suit went directly to the United States Supreme Court, where Chief Justice John Marshall (1755–1835) presided. Marshall, a former member of Congress from Virginia and secretary of state under John Adams, was also a staunch Federalist. He would serve as chief justice for several decades and be credited in later years with establishing a strong national judiciary that supported strong actions by the central government to bind the states to federal authority. In deciding *Marbury* he faced a dilemma. The Jefferson Administration would ignore any writ of mandamus, hurting the standing of the Supreme Court. But denying Marbury's request might itself be seen as a sign of fear and weakness in the face of presidential power. Marshall followed neither course. Instead, he ruled that, while Madison should have delivered the commission, the Supreme Court had no right to issue writs of mandamus. Marshall further ruled that the section of the Judiciary Act of 1789 granting the Court such powers violated the Constitution and so was null and void. By this act, Marshall has been credited with establishing the Supreme Court's power to declare acts of Congress unconstitutional and to play the pivotal role in interpreting the Constitution, which were critical steps in establishing the apportionment of powers within the federal government. In later decades, the Court's role as interpreter of the Constitution would result in the creation of sweeping new interpretations of the Constitution and the rights of individuals

and groups. After *Marbury*, it was not until 1857 that the Supreme Court declared another law null and void.

Marbury v. Madison (5 US 187)

Opinion of the Court

In the order in which the court has viewed this subject, the following questions have been considered and decided.

1st Has the applicant a right to the commission he demands?

2dly. If he has a right, and that right has been violated, do the laws of his country afford him a remedy?

3dly. If they do afford him a remedy, is it a *mandamus* issuing from this court?

The first object of enquiry is,

1st. Has the applicant a right to the commission he demands?

His right originates in an act of congress passed in February 1801, concerning the district of Columbia.

After dividing the district into two counties, the 11th section of this law, enacts, "that there shall be appointed in and for each of the said counties, such number of discreet persons to be justices of the peace as the president of the United States shall, from time to time, think expedient, to continue in office for five years.

It appears, from the affidavits, that in compliance with this law, a commission for William Marbury as a justice of peace for the county of Washington, was signed by John Adams, then president of the United States; after which the seal of the United States was affixed to it; but the commission has never reached the person for whom it was made out.

In order to determine whether he is entitled to this commission, it becomes necessary to enquire whether he has been appointed to the office. For if he has been appointed, the law continues him in office for five years, and he is entitled to the possession of those evidences of office, which, being completed, become his property.

The 2d section of the 2d article of the constitution, declares, that, "the president shall nominate, and, by and with the advice and consent of the senate, shall appoint ambassadors, other public ministers and consuls, and all other officers of the United States, whose appointments are not otherwise provided for."

The third section declares, that "he shall commission all the officers of the United States."

An act of congress directs the secretary of state to keep the seal of the United States, "to make out and record, and affix the said seal to all civil commissions to officers of the United States, to be appointed by the President, by and with the consent of the senate, or by the President alone; provided that the said seal shall not be affixed to any commission before the same shall have been signed by the President of the United States."

These are the clauses of the constitution and laws of the United States, which affect this part of the case. They seem to contemplate three distinct operations:

1st, The nomination. This is the sole act of the President, and is completely voluntary.

2d. The appointment. This is also the act of the President, and is also a voluntary act, though it can only be performed by and with the advice and consent of the senate.

3d. The commission. To grant a commission to a person appointed, might perhaps be deemed a duty enjoined by the constitution. "He shall," says that instrument, "commission all the officers of the United States. . . ."

This is an appointment made by the President, by and with the advice and consent of the senate, and is evidenced by no act but the commission itself. In such a case therefore the commission and the appointment seem inseparable; it being almost impossible to shew an appointment otherwise than by proving the existence of a commission; still the commission is not necessarily the appointment; though conclusive evidence of it.

But at what stage does it amount to this conclusive evidence?

The answer to this question seems an obvious one. The appointment being the sole act of the President, must be completely evidenced, when it is shewn that he has done every thing to be performed by him.

Should the commission, instead of being evidence of an appointment, even be considered as constituting the appointment itself; still it would be made when the last act to be done by the President was performed, or, at furthest, when the commission was complete.

The last act to be done by the President, is the signature of the commission. He has then acted on the advice and consent of the senate to his own nomination. The time for deliberation has then passed. He has decided. His judgment, on the advice and consent of the senate concurring with his nomination, has been made, and the officer is appointed. This appointment is evidenced by an open, unequivocal act; and being the last act required from the person making it, necessarily excludes the idea of its being, so far as respects the appointment, an inchoate and incomplete transaction.

Some point of time must be taken when the power of the executive over an officer, not removeable at his will, must cease. That point of time must be when the constitutional power of appointment has been exercised. And this power has been exercised when the last act, required from the person possessing the power, has been performed. This last act is the signature of the commission. This idea seems to have prevailed with the legislature, when the act passed, converting the department of foreign affairs into the department of state. By that act it is enacted, that the secretary of state shall keep the seal of the United States, "and shall make out and record, and shall affix the said seal to all civil commissions to officers of the United States, to be appointed by the President:" "Provided that the said seal shall not be affixed to any commission, before the same shall have been signed by the President of the United States; nor to any other instrument or act, without the special warrant of the President therefor."

The signature is a warrant for affixing the great seal to the commission; and the great seal is only to be affixed to an instrument which is complete. It attests, by an act supposed to be of public notoriety, the verity of the Presidential signature.

It is never to be affixed till the commission is signed, because the signature, which gives force and effect to the commission, is conclusive evidence that the appointment is made.

The commission being signed, the subsequent duty of the secretary of state is prescribed by law, and not to be guided by the will of the President. He is to affix the seal of the United States to the commission, and is to record it.

This is not a proceeding which may be varied, if the judgment of the executive shall suggest one more eligible; but is a precise course accurately marked out by law, and is to be strictly pursued. It is the duty of the secretary of state to conform to the law, and in this he is an officer of the United States, bound to obey the laws. He acts, in this respect, as has been very properly stated at the bar, under the authority of law, and not by the instructions of the President. It is a ministerial act which the law enjoins on a particular officer for a particular purpose.

If it should be supposed, that the solemnity of affixing the seal, is necessary not only to the validity of the commission, but even to the completion of an appointment, still when the seal is affixed the appointment is made, and the commission is valid. No other solemnity is required by law; no other act is to be performed on the part of government. All that the executive can do to invest the person with his office, is done; and unless the appointment be then made, the executive cannot make one without the co-operation of others. . . .

It is therefore decidedly the opinion of the court, that when a commission has been signed by the President, the appointment is made; and that the commission is complete, when the seal of the United States has been affixed to it by the secretary of state.

Where an officer is removeable at the will of the executive, the circumstance which completes his appointment is of no concern; because the act is at any time revocable; and the commission may be arrested, if still in the office. But when the officer is not removeable at the will of the executive, the appointment is not revocable, and cannot be annulled. It has conferred legal rights which cannot be resumed.

The discretion of the executive is to be exercised until the appointment has been made. But having once made the appointment, his power over the office is terminated in all cases, where, by law, the officer is not removeable by him. The right to the office is *then* in the person appointed, and he has the absolute, unconditional, power of accepting or rejecting it.

Mr. Marbury, then, since his commission was signed by the President, and sealed by the secretary of state, was appointed; and as the law creating the office, gave the officer a right to hold for five years, independent of the executive, the appointment was not revocable; but vested in the officer legal rights, which are protected by the laws of his country.

To withhold his commission, therefore, is an act deemed by the court not warranted by law, but violative of a vested legal right.

This brings us to the second enquiry; which is,

2dly. If he has a right, and that right has been violated, do the laws of his country afford him a remedy?

The very essence of civil liberty certainly consists in the right of every individual to claim the protection of the laws, whenever he receives an injury. One of the first duties of government is to afford that protection. In Great Britain the king himself is sued in the respectful form of a petition, and he never fails to comply with the judgment of his court. . . .

The government of the United States has been emphatically termed a government of laws, and not of men. It will certainly cease to deserve this high appellation, if the laws furnish no remedy for the violation of a vested legal right.

If this obloquy is to be cast on the jurisprudence of our country, it must arise from the peculiar character of the case.

It behoves us then to enquire whether there be in its composition any ingredient which shall exempt it from legal investigation, or exclude the injured party from legal redress. In pursuing this enquiry the first question which presents itself, is, whether this can be arranged with that class of cases which come under the description of *damnum absque injuria*—a loss without an injury.

This description of cases never has been considered, and it is believed never can be considered, as comprehending offices of trust, of honor or of profit. The office of justice of peace in the district of Columbia is such an office; it is therefore worthy of the attention and guardianship of the laws. It has received that attention and guardianship. It has been created by special act of congress, and has been secured, so far as the laws can give security to the person appointed to fill it, for five years. It is not then on account of the worthlessness of the thing pursued, that the injured party can be alleged to be without remedy.

Is it in the nature of the transaction? Is the act of delivering or withholding a commission to be considered as a mere political act, belonging to the executive department alone, for the performance of which, entire confidence is placed by our constitution in the supreme executive; and for any misconduct respecting which, the injured individual has no remedy.

That there may be such cases is not to be questioned; but that every act of duty, to be performed in any of the great departments of government, constitutes such a case, is not to be admitted. . . .

By the act passed in 1796, authorising the sale of the lands above the mouth of Kentucky river (vol. 3d. p. 299) the purchaser, on paying his purchase money, becomes completely entitled to the property purchased; and on producing to the secretary of state, the receipt of the treasurer upon a certificate required by the law, the president of the United States is authorised to grant him a patent. It is further enacted that all patents shall be countersigned by the secretary of state, and recorded in his office. If the secretary of state should choose to withhold this patent; or the patent being lost, should refuse a copy of it; can it be imagined that the law furnishes to the injured person no remedy?

It is not believed that any person whatever would attempt to maintain such a proposition.

It follows then that the question, whether the legality of an act of the head of a department be examinable in a court of justice or not, must always depend on the nature of that act.

If some acts be examinable, and others not, there must be some rule of law to guide the court in the exercise of its jurisdiction.

In some instances there may be difficulty in applying the rule to particular cases; but there cannot, it is believed, be much difficulty in laying down the rule.

By the constitution of the United States, the President is invested with certain important political powers, in the exercise of which he is to use his own discretion, and is accountable only to his country in his political character, and to his own conscience. To aid him in the performance of these duties, he is authorized to appoint certain officers, who act by his authority and in conformity with his orders.

In such cases, their acts are his acts; and whatever opinion may be entertained of the manner in which executive discretion may be used, still there exists, and can exist, no power to control that discretion. The subjects are political. They respect the nation, not individual rights, and being entrusted to the executive, the decision of the executive

is conclusive. The application of this remark will be perceived by adverting to the act of congress for establishing the department of foreign affairs. This officer, as his duties were prescribed by that act, is to conform precisely to the will of the President. He is the mere organ by whom that will is communicated. The acts of such an officer, as an officer, can never be examinable by the courts.

But when the legislature proceeds to impose on that officer other duties; when he is directed peremptorily to perform certain acts; when the rights of individuals are dependent on the performance of those acts; he is so far the officer of the law; is amenable to the laws for his conduct; and cannot at his discretion sport away the vested rights of others.

The conclusion from this reasoning is, that where the heads of departments are the political or confidential agents of the executive, merely to execute the will of the President, or rather to act in cases in which the executive possesses a constitutional or legal discretion, nothing can be more perfectly clear than that their acts are only politically examinable. But where a specific duty is assigned by law, and individual rights depend upon the performance of that duty, it seems equally clear that the individual who considers himself injured, has a right to resort to the laws of his country for a remedy.

If this be the rule, let us enquire how it applies to the case under the consideration of the court.

The power of nominating to the senate, and the power of appointing the person nominated, are political powers, to be exercised by the President according to his own discretion. When he has made an appointment, he has exercised his whole power, and his discretion has been completely applied to the case. If, by law, the officer be removable at the will of the President, then a new appointment may be immediately made, and the rights of the officer are terminated. But as a fact which has existed cannot be made never to have existed, the appointment cannot be annihilated; and consequently if the officer is by law not removable at the will of the President; the rights he has acquired are protected by the law, and are not resumable by the President. They cannot be extinguished by executive authority, and he has the privilege of asserting them in like manner as if they had been derived from any other source.

The question whether a right has vested or not, is, in its

nature, judicial, and must be tried by the judicial authority. If, for example, Mr. Marbury had taken the oaths of a magistrate, and proceeded to act as one; in consequence of which a suit had been instituted against him, in which his defence had depended on his being a magistrate; the validity of his appointment must have been determined by judicial authority.

So, if he conceives that, by virtue of his appointment, he has a legal right, either to the commission which has been made out for him, or to a copy of that commission, it is equally a question examinable in a court, and the decision of the court upon it must depend on the opinion entertained of his appointment.

That question has been discussed, and the opinion is, that the latest point of time which can be taken as that at which the appointment was complete, and evidenced, was when, after the signature of the president, the seal of the United States was affixed to the commission.

It is then the opinion of the court,

1st. That by signing the commission of Mr. Marbury, the president of the United States appointed him a justice of peace, for the county of Washington in the district of Columbia; and that the seal of the United States, affixed thereto by the secretary of state, is conclusive testimony of the verity of the signature, and of the completion of the appointment; and that the appointment conferred on him a legal right to the office for the space of five years.

2dly. That, having this legal title to the office, he has a consequent right to the commission; a refusal to deliver which, is a plain violation of that right, for which the laws of his country afford him a remedy.

It remains to be enquired whether,

3dly. He is entitled to the remedy for which he applies. This depends on,

1st. The nature of the writ applied for, and,

2dly. The power of this court.

1st. The nature of the writ.

Blackstone, in the 3d volume of his commentaries, page 110, defines a mandamus to be, "a command issuing in the king's name from the court of king's bench, and directed to any person, corporation, or inferior court of judicature within the king's dominions, requiring them to do some particular thing therein specified, which appertains to their office and duty, and which the court of king's bench has previously determined, or at least supposes, to be consonant to right and justice."

Lord Mansfield, in 3d Burrows 1266, in the case of the *King v. Baker, et al.* states with much precision and explicitness the cases in which this writ may be used.

"Whenever," says that very able judge, "there is a right to execute an office, perform a service, or exercise a franchise (more especially if it be in a matter of public concern, or attended with profit) and a person is kept out of possession, or dispossessed of such right, and has no other specific legal remedy, this court ought to assist by mandamus, upon reasons of justice, as the writ expresses, and upon reasons of public policy, to preserve peace, order and good government." In the same case he says, "this writ ought to be used upon all occasions where the law has established no specific remedy, and where in justice and good government there ought to be one." . . .

This writ, if awarded, would be directed to an officer of government, and its mandate to him would be, to use the words of Blackstone, "to do a particular thing therein specified, which appertains to his office and duty and which the court has previously determined, or at least supposes, to be consonant to right and justice." Or, in the words of Lord Mansfield, the applicant, in this case, has a right to execute an office of public concern, and is kept out of possession of that right.

These circumstances certainly concur in this case.

Still, to render the mandamus a proper remedy, the officer to whom it is to be directed, must be one to whom, on legal principles, such writ may be directed; and the person applying for it must be without any other specific and legal remedy.

1st. With respect to the officer to whom it would be directed. . . .

It is not by the office of the person to whom the writ is directed, but the nature of the thing to be done that the propriety or impropriety of issuing a mandamus, is to be determined. Where the head of a department acts in a case, in which executive discretion is to be exercised; in which he is the mere organ of executive will; it is again repeated, that any application to a court to control, in any respect, his conduct, would be rejected without hesitation.

But where he is directed by law to do a certain act affecting the absolute rights of individuals, in the performance of which he is not placed under the particular direction of the President, and the performance of which, the President cannot lawfully forbid, and therefore is never presumed to have forbidden; as for example, to record a commission, or a patent for land, which has received all the legal solemnities; or to give a copy of such record; in such cases, it is not perceived on what ground the courts of the country are further excused from the duty of giving judgment, that right be done to an injured individual, than if the same services were to be performed by a person not the head of a department. . . .

This, then, is a plain case for a mandamus, either to deliver the commission, or a copy of it from the record; and it only remains to be enquired,

Whether it can issue from this court.

The act to establish the judicial courts of the United States authorizes the supreme court "to issue writs of mandamus, in cases warranted by the principles and usages of law, to any courts appointed, or persons holding office, under the authority of the United States."

The secretary of state, being a person holding an office under the authority of the United States, is precisely within the letter of the description; and if this court is not authorized to issue a writ of mandamus to such an officer, it must be because the law is unconstitutional, and therefore absolutely incapable of conferring the authority, and assigning the duties which its words purport to confer and assign.

The constitution vests the whole judicial power of the United States in one supreme court, and such inferior courts as congress shall, from time to time, ordain and establish. This power is expressly extended to all cases arising under the laws of the United States; and consequently, in some form, may be exercised over the present case; because the right claimed is given by a law of the United States.

In the distribution of this power it is declared that "the supreme court shall have original jurisdiction in all cases affecting ambassadors, other public ministers and consuls, and those in which a state shall be a party. In all other cases, the supreme court shall have appellate jurisdiction."

It has been insisted, at the bar, that as the original grant of jurisdiction, to the supreme and inferior courts, is general, and the clause, assigning original jurisdiction to the supreme court, contains no negative or restrictive words; the power remains to the legislature, to assign original jurisdiction to that court in other cases than those specified in the article which has been recited; provided those cases belong to the judicial power of the United States.

If it had been intended to leave it in the discretion of the legislature to apportion the judicial power between the supreme and inferior courts according to the will of that body, it would certainly have been useless to have proceeded further than to have defined the judicial power, and the tribunals in which it should be vested. The subsequent part of the section is mere surplussage, is entirely without meaning, if such is to be the construction. If congress remains at liberty to give this court appellate jurisdiction, where the constitution has declared their jurisdiction shall be original; and original jurisdiction where the constitution has declared it shall be appellate; the distribution of jurisdiction, made in the constitution, is form without substance.

Affirmative words are often, in their operation, negative of other objects than those affirmed; and in this case, a negative or exclusive sense must be given to them or they have no operation at all.

It cannot be presumed that any clause in the constitution is intended to be without effect; and therefore such a construction is inadmissible, unless the words require it.

If the solicitude of the convention, respecting our peace with foreign powers, induced a provision that the supreme court should take original jurisdiction in cases which might be supposed to affect them; yet the clause would have proceeded no further than to provide for such cases, if no further restriction on the powers of congress had been intended. That they should have appellate jurisdiction in all other cases, with such exceptions as congress might make, is no restriction; unless the words be deemed exclusive of original jurisdiction.

When an instrument organizing fundamentally a judicial system, divides it into one supreme, and so many inferior courts as the legislature may ordain and establish; then enumerates its powers, and proceeds so far to distribute them, as to define the jurisdiction of the supreme court by declaring the cases in which it shall take original jurisdiction, and that in others it shall take appellate jurisdiction; the plain import of the words seems to be, that in one class of cases its jurisdiction is original, and not appellate; in the other it is appellate, and not original. If any other construction would render the clause inoperative, that is an additional reason for rejecting such other construction, and for adhering to their obvious meaning.

To enable this court then to issue a mandamus, it must be shewn to be an exercise of appellate jurisdiction, or to be necessary to enable them to exercise appellate jurisdiction.

It has been stated at the bar that the appellate jurisdiction may be exercised in a variety of forms, and that if it be the will of the legislature that a mandamus should be used for that purpose, that will must be obeyed. This is true, yet the jurisdiction must be appellate, not original.

It is the essential criterion of appellate jurisdiction, that it revises and corrects the proceedings in a cause already instituted, and does not create that cause. Although, therefore, a mandamus may be directed to courts, yet to issue such a writ to an officer for the delivery of a paper, is in effect the same as to sustain an original action for that paper, and therefore seems not to belong to appellate, but to original jurisdiction. Neither is it necessary in such a case as this, to enable the court to exercise its appellate jurisdiction.

The authority, therefore, given to the supreme court, by the act establishing the judicial courts of the United States, to issue writs of mandamus to public officers, appears not to be warranted by the constitution; and it becomes necessary to enquire whether a jurisdiction, so conferred, can be exercised.

The question, whether an act, repugnant to the constitution, can become the law of the land, is a question deeply interesting to the United States; but, happily, not of an intricacy proportioned to its interest. It seems only necessary to recognise certain principles, supposed to have been long and well established, to decide it.

That the people have an original right to establish, for their future government, such principles as, in their opinion, shall most conduce to their own happiness, is the basis, on which the whole American fabric has been erected. The exercise of this original right is a very great exertion; nor can it, nor ought it to be frequently repeated. The principles, therefore, so established, are deemed fundamental. And as the authority, from which they proceed, is supreme, and can seldom act, they are designed to be permanent.

This original and supreme will organizes the government, and assigns, to different departments, their respective powers. It may either stop here; or establish certain limits not to be transcended by those departments.

The government of the United States is of the latter description. The powers of the legislature are defined, and limited; and that those limits may not be mistaken, or forgotten, the constitution is written. To what purpose are powers limited, and to what purpose is that limitation committed to writing, if these limits may, at any time, be passed by those intended to be restrained? The distinction,

between a government with limited and unlimited powers, is abolished, if those limits do not confine the persons on whom they are imposed, and if acts prohibited and acts allowed, are of equal obligation. It is a proposition too plain to be contested, that the constitution controls any legislative act repugnant to it; or, that the legislature may alter the constitution by an ordinary act.

Between these alternatives there is no middle ground. The constitution is either a superior, paramount law, unchangeable by ordinary means, or it is on a level with ordinary legislative acts, and like other acts, is alterable when the legislature shall please to alter it.

If the former part of the alternative be true, then a legislative act contrary to the constitution is not law: if the latter part be true, then written constitutions are absurd attempts, on the part of the people, to limit a power, in its own nature illimitable.

Certainly all those who have framed written constitutions contemplate them as forming the fundamental and paramount law of the nation, and consequently the theory of every such government must be, that an act of the legislature, repugnant to the constitution, is void.

This theory is essentially attached to a written constitution, and is consequently to be considered, by this court, as one of the fundamental principles of our society. It is not therefore to be lost sight of in the further consideration of this subject.

If an act of the legislature, repugnant to the constitution, is void, does it, notwithstanding its invalidity, bind the courts, and oblige them to give it effect? Or, in other words, though it be not law, does it constitute a rule as operative as if it was a law? This would be to overthrow in fact what was established in theory; and would seem, at first view, an absurdity too gross to be insisted on. It shall, however, receive a more attentive consideration.

It is emphatically the province and duty of the judicial department to say what the law is. Those who apply the rule to particular cases, must of necessity expound and interpret that rule. If two laws conflict with each other, the courts must decide on the operation of each.

So if a law be in opposition to the constitution; if both the law and the constitution apply to a particular case, so that the court must either decide that case conformably to the law, disregarding the constitution; or conformably to the constitution, disregarding the law; the court must determine which of these conflicting rules governs the case. This is of the very essence of judicial duty.

If then the courts are to regard the constitution; and the constitution is superior to any ordinary act of the legislature; the constitution, and not such ordinary act, must govern the case to which they both apply.

Those then who controvert the principle that the constitution is to be considered, in court, as a paramount law, are reduced to the necessity of maintaining that courts must close their eyes on the constitution, and see only the law.

This doctrine would subvert the very foundation of all written constitutions. It would declare that an act, which, according to the principles and theory of our government, is entirely void; is yet, in practice, completely obligatory. It would declare, that if the legislature shall do what is expressly forbiden, such act, notwithstanding the express prohibition, is in reality effectual. It would be giving to the legislature a practical and real omnipotence, with the same breath which professes to restrict their powers within narrow limits. It is prescribing limits, and declaring that those limits may be passed at pleasure.

That it thus reduces to nothing what we have deemed the greatest improvement on political institutions—a written constitution—would of itself be sufficient, in America, where written constitutions have been viewed with so much reverence, for rejecting the construction. But the peculiar expressions of the constitution of the United States furnish additional arguments in favour of its rejection.

The judicial power of the United States is extended to all cases arising under the constitution.

Could it be the intention of those who gave this power, to say that, in using it, the constitution should not be looked into? That a case arising under the constitution should be decided without examining the instrument under which it arises?

This is too extravagant to be maintained.

In some cases then, the constitution must be looked into by the judges. And if they can open it at all, what part of it are they forbidden to read, or to obey?

There are many other parts of the constitution which serve to illustrate this subject.

It is declared that "no tax or duty shall be laid on articles exported from any state." Suppose a duty on the export of cotton, of tobacco, or of flour; and a suit instituted to re-cover it. Ought judgment to be rendered in such a case? ought the judges to close their eyes on the constitution, and only see the law.

The constitution declares that "no bill of attainder or *ex post facto* law shall be passed."

If, however, such a bill should be passed and a person should be prosecuted under it; must the court condemn to death those victims whom the constitution endeavours to preserve?

"No person," says the constitution, "shall be convicted of treason unless on the testimony of two witnesses to the same overt act, or on confession in open court."

Here the language of the constitution is addressed especially to the courts. It prescribes, directly for them, a rule of evidence not to be departed from. If the legislature should change that rule, and declare *one* witness, or a confession *out* of court, sufficient for conviction, must the constitutional principle yield to the legislative act?

From these, and many other selections which might be made, it is apparent, that the framers of the constitution contemplated that instrument, as a rule for the government of *courts,* as well as of the legislature.

Why otherwise does it direct the judges to take an oath to support it? This oath certainly applies, in an especial manner, to their conduct in their official character. How immoral to impose it on them, if they were to be used as the instruments, and the knowing instruments, for violating what they swear to support!

The oath of office, too, imposed by the legislature, is completely demonstrative of the legislative opinion on this subject. It is in these words, "I do solemnly swear that I will administer justice without respect to persons, and do equal right to the poor and to the rich; and that I will faithfully and impartially discharge all the duties incumbent on me as according to the best of my abilities and understanding, agreeably to *the constitution,* and laws of the United States."

Why does a judge swear to discharge his duties agreably to the constitution of the United States, if that constitution forms no rule for his government? if it is closed upon him, and cannot be inspected by him?

If such be the real state of things, this is worse than solemn mockery. To prescribe, or to take this oath, becomes equally a crime.

It is also not entirely unworthy of observation, that in

declaring what shall be the *supreme* law of the land, the *constitution* itself is first mentioned; and not the laws of the United States generally, but those only which shall be made in *pursuance* of the constitution, have that rank.

Thus, the particular phraseology of the constitution of the United States confirms and strengthens the principle, supposed to be essential to all written constitutions, that a law repugnant to the constitution is void; and that *courts,* as well as other departments, are bound by that instrument.

The rule must be discharged.

Barron v. the Mayor and City Council of Baltimore

JOHN MARSHALL

1833

The city of Baltimore undertook a number of road and harbor improvements to accommodate its expanding population and commercial activity. Between the years 1815 and 1821 these improvements, including diversion of area waterways, made the water shallower around a wharf owned by the company of Craig & Barron. The effect was to make the water near Craig & Barron's wharf too shallow for larger and more profitable cargo ships. John Barron, the surviving member of the corporation, sued the city for financial losses suffered by the business as a result of the decrease in water levels. The case eventually found its way to the U.S. Supreme Court. One of the points at issue here was whether the city had violated Barron's right under the Fifth Amendment to the United States Constitution not to have his property taken for public use without just compensation. In siding with the city (without even hearing their arguments), Chief Justice Marshall established the rule that the protections of the Bill of Rights would be applied against the national government, but not against the states that had joined in forming that government.

Barron v. the Mayor and City Council of Baltimore

The plaintiff in error contends that it comes within that clause in the fifth amendment to the constitution, which inhibits the taking of private property for public use, without just compensation. He insists that this amendment, being in favour of the liberty of the citizen, ought to be so construed as to restrain the legislative power of a state, as well as that of the United States. If this proposition be untrue, the court can take no jurisdiction of the cause.

The question thus presented is, we think, of great importance, but not of much difficulty.

The constitution was ordained and established by the people of the United States for themselves, for their own government, and not for the government of the individual states. Each state established a constitution for itself, and, in that constitution, provided such limitations and restrictions on the powers of its particular government as its judgment dictated. The people of the United States framed such a government for the United States as they supposed best adapted to their situation, and best calculated to promote their interests. The powers they conferred on this government were to be exercised by itself; and the limitations on power, if expressed in general terms, are naturally, and, we think, necessarily applicable to the government created by the instrument. They are limitations of power granted in the instrument itself; not of distinct governments, framed by different persons and for different purposes.

If these propositions be correct, the fifth amendment must be understood as restraining the power of the general government, not as applicable to the states. In their several constitutions they have imposed such restrictions on their respective governments as their own wisdom suggested; such as they deemed most proper for themselves. It is a subject on which they judge exclusively, and with which others interfere no farther than they are supposed to have a common interest.

The counsel for the plaintiff in error insists that the constitution was intended to secure the people of the several states against the undue exercise of power by their respective state governments; as well as against that which might be attempted by their general government. In support of this argument he relies on the inhibitions contained in the tenth section of the first article.

We think that section affords a strong if not a conclusive argument in support of the opinion already indicated by the court.

The preceding section contains restrictions which are obviously intended for the exclusive purpose of restraining the exercise of power by the departments of the general government. Some of them use language applicable only to congress: others are expressed in general terms. The third clause, for example, declares that "no bill of attainder or ex post facto law shall be passed." No language can be more general; yet the demonstration is complete that it applies solely to the government of the United States. In addition to the general arguments furnished by the instrument itself, some of which have been already suggested, the succeeding section, the avowed purpose of which is to restrain state legislation, contains in terms the very prohibition. It declares that "no state shall pass any bill of attainder or ex post facto law." This provision, then, of the ninth section, however comprehensive its language, contains no restriction on state legislation.

The ninth section having enumerated, in the nature of a bill of rights, the limitations intended to be imposed on the powers of the general government, the tenth proceeds to enumerate those which were to operate on the state legislatures. These restrictions are brought together in the same section, and are by express words applied to the states. "No state shall enter into any treaty," &c. Perceiving that in a constitution framed by the people of the United States for the government of all, no limitation of the action of government on the people would apply to the state government, unless expressed in terms; the restrictions contained in the tenth section are in direct words so applied to the states.

It is worthy of remark, too, that these inhibitions generally restrain state legislation on subjects entrusted to the general government, or in which the people of all the states feel an interest.

A state is forbidden to enter into any treaty, alliance or confederation. If these compacts are with foreign nations, they interfere with the treaty making power which is conferred entirely on the general government; if with each other, for political purposes, they can scarcely fail to interfere with the general purpose and intent of the constitution. To grant letters of marque and reprisal, would lead directly to war; the power of declaring which is expressly given to congress. To coin money is also the exercise of a power conferred on congress. It would be tedious to recapitulate the several limitations on the powers of the states which are contained in this section. They will be found, generally, to restrain state legislation on subjects entrusted to the government of the union, in which the citizens of all the states are interested. In these alone were the whole

people concerned. The question of their application to states is not left to construction. It is averred in positive words.

If the original constitution, in the ninth and tenth sections of the first article, draws this plain and marked line of discrimination between the limitations it imposes on the powers of the general government, and on those of the states; if in every inhibition intended to act on state power, words are employed which directly express that intent; some strong reason must be assigned for departing from this safe and judicious course in framing the amendments, before that departure can be assumed.

We search in vain for that reason.

Had the people of the several states, or any of them, required changes in their constitutions; had they required additional safeguards to liberty from the apprehended encroachments of their particular governments: the remedy was in their own hands, and would have been applied by themselves. A convention would have been assembled by the discontented state, and the required improvements would have been made by itself. The unwieldy and cumbrous machinery of procuring a recommendation from two-thirds of congress, and the assent of three-fourths of their sister states, could never have occurred to any human being as a mode of doing that which might be effected by the state itself. Had the framers of these amendments intended them to be limitations on the powers of the state governments, they would have imitated the framers of the original constitution, and have expressed that intention. Had congress engaged in the extraordinary occupation of improving the constitutions of the several states by affording the people additional protection from the exercise of power by their own governments in matters which concerned themselves alone, they would have declared this purpose in plain and intelligible language.

But it is universally understood, it is a part of the history of the day, that the great revolution which established the constitution of the United States, was not effected without immense opposition. Serious fears were extensively entertained that those powers which the patriot statesmen, who then watched over the interests of our country, deemed essential to union, and to the attainment of those invaluable objects for which union was sought, might be exercised in a manner dangerous to liberty. In almost every convention by which the constitution was adopted, amendments to guard against the abuse of power were recommended.

These amendments demanded security against the apprehended encroachments of the general government—not against those of the local governments.

In compliance with a sentiment thus generally expressed, to quiet fears thus extensively entertained, amendments were proposed by the required majority in congress, and adopted by the states. These amendments contain no expression indicating an intention to apply them to the state governments. This court cannot so apply them.

We are of opinion that the provision in the fifth amendment to the constitution, declaring that private property shall not be taken for public use without just compensation, is intended solely as a limitation on the exercise of power by the government of the United States, and is not applicable to the legislation of the states. We are therefore of opinion that there is no repugnancy between the several acts of the general assembly of Maryland, given in evidence by the defendants at the trial of this cause, in the court of that state, and the constitution of the United States. This court, therefore, has no jurisdiction of the cause; and it is dismissed.

PART SEVEN State versus Federal Authority

The Issue of Sovereignty. Lithograph by O. E. Woods. Courtesy of the Library of Congress

One of the central issues at the Constitutional Convention and at the conventions called to consider ratifying that Constitution was this: How could Americans form a government to address their common problems without losing the sovereignty of their individual states? Arguments over representation, the powers of the Supreme Court, congressional taxing power, and even the Bill of Rights in large measure grew out of Americans' concern to balance the needs of the nation with the rights of the states. Ratification and passage of the Constitution's first ten amendments did not end this debate. Indeed, it remained at the center of American public life up through the Civil War and, in some ways and in certain quarters, long after.

Questions concerning states' rights and federal authority erupted at various times before the Civil War. This occurred most explosively in regard to slavery, but two other issues raised tensions to dangerous levels. First, the Alien and Sedition Acts increased presidential powers concerning the status of foreign citizens suspected of fomenting unrest and limited certain forms of criticism of the national government. Second, the War of 1812 was politically unpopular and raised the issue of the central government's right to draft citizens of the states into military service. Both called the very existence of the states' union into question.

Beneath the immediate issues was a constitutional question: Was the United States the creature of its states—a compact among sovereignties—or was it a union of citizens, joined together in a national government, with the states subordinate members of that greater whole?

Essay V

"BRUTUS"

1787

In this essay, "Brutus" resurrects the American colonists' distinction between "internal" and "external" taxation. In effect likening the federal government to Great Britain's empire, Brutus argues that no central government can directly tax the goods or property of a people without taking away their rights. He is particularly concerned about the federal government's ability to claim authority under the Necessary and Proper Clause—that phrase in the Constitution giving Congress the right to use means "necessary and proper" to carry out its enumerated, specifically granted powers. In Brutus's view this power could lead to unlimited federal taxation, which would leave states dependent on the central government for their financial survival, effectively destroying state sovereignty.

Essay V

To the People of the State of New-York

It was intended in this Number to have prosecuted the enquiry into the organization of this new system; particularly to have considered the dangerous and premature union of the President and Senate, and the mixture of legislative, executive, and judicial powers in the Senate.

But there is such an intimate connection between the several branches in whom the different species of authority is lodged, and the powers with which they are invested, that on reflection it seems necessary first to proceed to examine the nature and extent of the powers granted to the legislature.

This enquiry will assist us the better to determine, whether the legislature is so constituted, as to provide proper checks and restrictions for the security of our rights, and to guard against the abuse of power—For the means should be suited to the end; a government should be framed with a view to the objects to which it extends: if these be few in number, and of such a nature as to give but small occasion or opportunity to work oppression in the exercise of authority, there will be less need of a numerous representation, and special guards against abuse, than

if the powers of the government are very extensive, and include a great variety of cases. It will also be found necessary to examine the extent of these powers, in order to form a just opinion how far this system can be considered as a confederation, or a consolidation of the states. Many of the advocates for, and most of the opponents to this system, agree that the form of government most suitable for the United States, is that of a confederation. The idea of a confederated government is that of a number of independent states entering into a compact, for the conducting certain general concerns, in which they have a common interest, leaving the management of their internal and local affairs to their separate governments. But whether the system proposed is of this nature cannot be determined without a strict enquiry into the powers proposed to be granted.

This constitution considers the people of the several states as one body corporate, and is intended as an original compact, it will therefore dissolve all contracts which may be inconsistent with it. This not only results from its nature, but is expressly declared in the *6th article* of it. The design of the constitution is expressed in the preamble, to be, "in order to form a more perfect union, to establish justice, insure domestic tranquility, provide for the common defence, promote the general welfare, and secure the blessings of liberty to ourselves and posterity." These are the ends this government is to accomplish, and for which it is invested, with certain powers, among these is the power "to make all laws which are *necessary and proper* for carrying into execution the foregoing powers, and *all other* powers vested by this constitution in the government of the United States, or in any department or officer thereof." It is a rule in construing a law to consider the objects the legislature had in view in passing it, and to give it such an explanation as to promote their intention. The same rule will apply in explaining a constitution. The great objects then are declared in this preamble in general and indefinite terms to be to provide for the common defence, promote the general welfare, and an express power being vested in the legislature to make all laws which shall be necessary and proper for carrying into execution all the powers vested in the general government. The inference is natural that the legislature will have an authority to make all laws which they shall judge necessary for the common safety, and to promote the general welfare. This amounts to a power to make laws at discretion: No terms can be found more indefinite than these, and it is obvious, that the legislature alone must judge what laws are proper and necessary for the purpose. It may be said, that this way of explaining the constitution, is torturing and making it speak what it never intended. This is far from my intention, and I shall not even insist upon this implied power, but join issue with those who say we are to collect the idea of the powers given from the express words of the clauses granting them; and it will not be difficult to shew that the same authority is expressly given which is supposed to be implied in the forgoing paragraphs.

In the 1st article, 8th section, it is declared, "that Congress shall have power to lay and collect taxes, duties, imposts and excises, to pay the debts, and provide for the common defence, and general welfare of the United States." In the preamble, the intent of the constitution, among other things, is declared to be to provide for the common defence, and promote the general welfare, and in this clause the power is in express words given to Congress "to provide for the common defence, and general welfare." —And in the last paragraph of the same section there is an express authority to make all laws which shall be necessary and proper for carrying into execution this power. It is therefore evident, that the legislature under this constitution may pass any law which they may think proper. It is true the 9th section restrains their power with respect to certain objects. But these restrictions are very limited, some of them improper, some unimportant, and others not easily understood, as I shall hereafter shew. It has been urged that the meaning I give to this part of the constitution is not the true one, that the intent of it is to confer on the legislature the power to lay and collect taxes, &c. in order to provide for the common defence and general welfare. To this I would reply, that the meaning and intent of the constitution is to be collected from the words of it, and I submit to the public, whether the construction I have given it is not the most natural and easy. But admitting the contrary opinion to prevail, I shall nevertheless, be able to shew, that the same powers are substantially vested in the general government, by several other articles in the constitution. It invests the legislature with authority to lay and collect taxes, duties, imposts and excises, in order to provide for the common defence, and promote the general welfare, and to pass all laws which may be necessary and proper for carrying this power into effect. To comprehend the extent of this authority, it will be requisite to examine 1st. what is included in this power to lay and collect taxes, duties, imposts and excises.

2d. What is implied in the authority, to pass all laws which shall be necessary and proper for carrying this power into execution.

3d. What limitation, if any, is set to the exercise of this power by the constitution.

1st. To detail the particulars comprehended in the general terms, taxes, duties, imposts and excises, would require a volume, instead of a single piece in a news-paper. Indeed it would be a task far beyond my ability, and to which no one can be competent, unless possessed of a mind capable of comprehending every possible source of revenue; for they extend to every possible way of raising money, whether by direct or indirect taxation. Under this clause may be imposed a poll-tax, a land-tax, a tax on houses and buildings, on windows and fire places, on cattle and on all kinds of personal property:—It extends to duties on all kinds of goods to any amount, to tonnage and poundage on vessels, to duties on written instruments, newspapers, almanacks, and books:—It comprehends an excise on all kinds of liquors, spirits, wines, cyder, beer, &c. and indeed takes in duty or excise on every necessary or conveniency of life; whether of foreign or home growth or manufactory. In short, we can have no conception of any way in which a government can raise money from the people, but what is included in one or other of these general terms. We may say then that this clause commits to the hands of the general legislature every conceivable source of revenue within the United States. Not only are these terms very comprehensive, and extend to a vast number of objects, but the power to lay and collect has great latitude; it will lead to the passing a vast number of laws, which may affect the personal rights of the citizens of the states, expose their property to fines and confiscation, and put their lives in jeopardy: it opens a door to the appointment of a swarm of revenue and excise officers to pray upon the honest and industrious part of the community, eat up their substance, and not on the spoils of the country.

2d. We will next enquire into what is implied in the authority to pass all laws which shall be necessary and proper to carry this power into execution.

It is, perhaps, utterly impossible fully to define this power. The authority granted in the first clause can only be understood in its full extent, by descending to all the particular cases in which a revenue can be raised; the number and variety of these cases are so endless, and as it were infinite, that no man living has, as yet, been able to reckon them up. The greatest geniuses in the world have been for ages employed in the research, and when mankind had supposed that the subject was exhausted they have been astonished with the refined improvements that have been made in modern times, and especially in the English nation on the subject—If then the objects of this power cannot be comprehended, how is it possible to understand the extent of that power which can pass all laws which shall be necessary and proper for carrying it into execution? It is truly incomprehensible. A case cannot be conceived of, which is not included in this power. It is well known that the subject of revenue is the most difficult and extensive in the science of government. It requires the greatest talents of a statesman, and the most numerous and exact provisions of the legislature. The command of the revenues of a state gives the command of every thing in it.—He that has the purse will have the sword, and they that have both, have every thing; so that the legislature having every source from which money can be drawn under their direction, with a right to make all laws necessary and proper for drawing forth all the resource of the country, would have, in fact, all power.

Were I to enter into the detail, it would be easy to shew how this power in its operation, would totally destroy all the powers of the individual states. But this is not necessary for those who will think for themselves, and it will be useless to such as take things upon trust, nothing will awaken them to reflection, until the iron hand of oppression compel them to it.

I shall only remark, that this power, given to the federal legislature, directly annihilates all the powers of the state legislatures. There cannot be a greater solecism in politics than to talk of power in a government, without the command of any revenue. It is as absurd as to talk of an animal without blood, or the subsistence of one without food. Now the general government having in their controul every possible source of revenue, and authority to pass any law they may deem necessary to draw them forth, or to fa-

cilitate their collection; no source of revenue is therefore left in the hands of any state. Should any state attempt to raise money by law, the general government may repeal or arrest it in the execution, for all their laws will be the supreme law of the land: If then any one can be weak enough to believe that a government can exist without having the authority to raise money to pay a door-keeper to their assembly, he may believe that the state government can exist, should this new constitution take place.

It is agreed by most of the advocates of this new system, that the government which is proper for the United States should be a confederated one; that the respective states ought to retain a portion of their sovereignty, and that they should preserve not only the forms of their legislatures, but also the power to conduct certain internal concerns. How far the powers to be retained by the states, [shall] extend, is the question; we need not spend much time on this subject, as it respects this constitution, for a government without the power to raise money is one only in name. It is clear that the legislatures of the respective states must be altogether dependent on the will of the general legislature, for the means of supporting their government. The legislature of the United States will have a right to exhaust every source of revenue in every state, and to annul all laws of the states which may stand in the way of effecting it; unless therefore we can suppose the state governments can exist without money to support the officers who execute them, we must conclude they will exist no longer than the general legislatures choose they should. Indeed the idea of any government existing, in any respect, as an independent one, without any means of support in their own hands, is an absurdity. If therefore, this constitution has in view, what many of its framers and advocates say it has, to secure and guarantee to the separate states the exercise of certain powers of government it certainly ought to have left in their hands some sources of revenue. It should have marked the line in which the general government should have raised money, and set bounds over which they should not pass, leaving to the separate states other means to raise supplies for the support of their governments, and to discharge their respective debts. To this it is objected, that the general government ought to have power competent to the purposes of the union; they are to provide for the common defence, to pay the debts of the United States, support foreign ministers, and the civil establishment of the union, and to do these they ought to have authority to raise money adequate to the purpose. On this I observe, that the state governments have also contracted debts, they require money to support their civil officers, and how this is to be done, if they give to the general government a power to raise money in every way in which it can possibly be raised, with such a controul over the state legislatures as to prohibit them, whenever the general legislature may think proper, from raising any money. It is again objected that it is very difficult, if not impossible, to draw the line of distinction between the powers of the general and state governments on this subject. The first, it is said, must have the power of raising the money necessary for the purposes of the union, if they are limited to certain objects the revenue may fall short of a sufficiency for the public exigencies, they must therefore have discretionary power. The line may be easily and accurately drawn between the powers of the two governments on this head. The distinction between external and internal taxes, is not a novel one in this country, it is a plain one, and easily understood. The first includes impost duties on all imported goods; this species of taxes it is proper should be laid by the general government; many reasons might be urged to shew that no danger is to be apprehended from their exercise of it. They may be collected in few places, and from few hands with certainty and expedition. But few officers are necessary to be imployed in collecting them, and there is no danger of oppression in laying them, because, if they are laid higher than trade will bear, the merchants will cease importing, or smuggle their goods. We have therefore sufficient security, arising from the nature of the thing, against burdonsome, and intolerable impositions from this kind of tax. But the case is far otherwise with regard to direct taxes; these include poll taxes, land taxes, excises, duties on written instruments, on every thing we eat, drink, or wear; they take hold of every species of property, and come home to every man's house and packet. These are often so oppressive, as to grind the face of the poor, and render the lives of the common people a burden to them. The great and only security the people can have against oppression from this kind of taxes, must rest in their representatives. If they are sufficiently numerous to be well informed of the circumstances, and ability of those who send them, and have a proper regard for the people, they will be secure. The general legislature, as I have shewn in a former paper, will not be thus qualified, and therefore, on this account, ought not to exercise the power of direct taxation. If the power of laying imposts will not be sufficient, some other specific mode of raising a revenue should have been assigned the general government; many may be suggested in which their power may be accurately defined and limited, and it would be much better to give them authority to lay and collect a duty on exports, not to exceed a certain rate per cent, than to have surrendered every kind of resource that the country has, to the complete abolition of the state governments, and which will introduce such an infinite number of laws and ordinances, fines and penalties, courts, and judges, collectors, and excisemen, that when a man can number them, he may enumerate the stars of Heaven.

I shall resume this subject in my next, and by an induction of particulars shew, that this power, in its exercise, will subvert all state authority, and will work to the oppression of the people, and that there are no restrictions in the constitution that will soften its rigour, but rather the contrary.

BRUTUS

Chisholm v. Georgia

JAMES WILSON

1793

U.S. Constitution, Eleventh Amendment

1787

In 1792, the executors of the estate of Alexander Chisholm, a citizen of South Carolina, sued the state of Georgia for failing to pay debts owed to Chisholm. Georgia refused to appear in court, claiming that, as a sovereign state, it could not be sued without its own consent. The Supreme Court held for Chisholm on the ground that the Constitution's Article 3, section 2, clearly said that states could be sued by citizens of other states. But the issues raised by *Chisholm* go beyond the language of the Constitution to the nature of the union. The federal government did not see itself as liable to being sued by just anyone at his own pleasure. It regulated when, how, and for what reasons it could be sued. In so doing, it followed the practice in Great Britain, where the king could be "sued" only in special courts that heard pleas as a favor or special grant. States extended federal practice in regard to suits from their own citizens.

In his opinion in *Chisholm,* Justice Wilson emphasized the sovereignty, not of any government, but of the people. According to Wilson, the real power in any free, republican government rested with the people themselves. And this included the right to give whatever powers they liked to whatever branch or level of government they saw fit. According to Wilson, it was self-evident that the people had *not* given states the power to refuse to be sued. When the *Chisholm* Court came to the conclusion that the states were less than sovereign parts of a sovereign union, the result was swift action in Congress and by the States—passing and ratifying the Eleventh Amendment in less than a year. This amendment revoked that constitutional language, reestablishing, for a time, the sovereignty of the states.

Chisholm v. Georgia (2 US 419)

WILSON, *Justice.*[1] This is a case of uncommon magnitude. One of the parties to it is a STATE; certainly respectable, claiming to be *sovereign.* The question to be determined is, whether this State, so respectable, and whose claim soars so high, is amenable to the jurisdiction of the Supreme Court of the *United States?* This question, important in itself, will depend on others, more important still; and may, perhaps, be ultimately resolved into one, no less *radical* than this—"do the people of the *United States* form a NATION?"

A cause so conspicuous and interesting, should be carefully and accurately viewed from every possible point of sight. I shall examine it; *1st.* By the principles of general jurisprudence. *2d.* By the laws and practice of particular States and *Kingdoms.* From the law of nations little or no illustration of this subject can be expected. By that law the several States and Governments spread over our globe, are considered as forming a *society,* not a NATION. It has only been by a very few comprehensive minds, such as those of *Elizabeth* and the *Fourth Henry,* that this last great idea has been even contemplated. *3dly.* and chiefly, I shall examine the important question before us, by the Constitution of the *United States,* and the legitimate result of that valuable instrument.

I. I am, first, to examine this question by the principles of general jurisprudence. What I shall say upon this head, I introduce by the observation of an original and profound writer, who, in the philosophy of *mind,* and all the sciences attendant on this *prime* one, has formed an aera not less

---

1. Justice Iredell issued what is now generally termed the opinion of the Court; Justice Wilson's more famous opinion was written separately but in concurrence with Iredell's.—B. F.

remarkable, and far more illustrious, than that formed by the justly celebrated *Bacon,* in another science, not prosecuted with less ability, but less dignified as to its object; I mean the philosophy of *matter.* Dr. *Reid,* in his excellent enquiry into the human mind, on the principles of *common sense,* speaking of the sceptical and illiberal philosophy, which under bold, but false, pretentions to liberality, prevailed in many parts of *Europe* before he wrote, makes the following judicious remark: "The language of philosophers, with regard to the original faculties of the mind, is so adapted to the prevailing system, that it cannot fit any other; like a coat that fits the man for whom it was made, and shews him to advantage, which yet will fit very aukward upon one of a different make, although as handsome and well proportioned. It is hardly possible to make any innovation in our philosophy concerning the mind and its operations, without using new words and phrases, or giving a different meaning to those that are received." With equal propriety may this solid remark be applied to the great subject, on the principles of which the decision of this Court is to be founded. The perverted use of *genus* and *species* in *logic,* and of *impressions* and *ideas* in *metaphysics,* have never done mischief so extensive or so *practically* pernicious, as has been done by *States* and *sovereigns,* in *politics* and *jurisprudence;* in the politics and jurisprudence even of those, who wished and meant to be free. In the place of those expressions I intend not to substitute new ones; but the expressions themselves I shall certainly use for purposes different from those, for which hitherto they have been frequently used; and one of them I shall apply to an object still more different from that, to which it has hitherto been more frequently, I may say almost universally, applied. In these purposes, and in this application, I shall be justified by example the most splendid, and by authority the most binding; the example of the most refined as well as the most free nation known to antiquity; and the authority of one of the best Constitutions known to modern times. With regard to one of the terms—State—this authority is declared: With regard to the other—sovereign—the authority is implied only: But it is equally strong: For, in an instrument well drawn, as in a poem well composed, silence is sometimes most expressive.

To the Constitution of the *United States* the term SOVEREIGN, is totally unknown. There is but one place where it could have been used with propriety. But, even in that place it would not, perhaps, have comported with the delicacy of those, who *ordained* and *established* that Constitution. They *might* have announced themselves "SOVEREIGN" people of the *United States:* But serenely conscious of the *fact,* they avoided the *ostentatious declaration.*

Having thus avowed my disapprobation of the purposes, for which the terms, *State* and *sovereign,* are frequently used, and of the object, to which the application of the last of them is almost universally made; it is now proper that I should disclose the meaning, which I assign to both, and the application, which I make of the latter. In doing this, I shall have occasion incidently to evince, how true it is, that States and Governments were made for man; and, at the same time, how true it is, that his *creatures* and *servants* have first *deceived,* next *vilified,* and, at last, *oppressed* their *master* and *maker.*

MAN, fearfully and wonderfully made, is the workmanship of his all perfect CREATOR: A *State;* useful and valuable as the contrivance is, is the *inferior* contrivance of *man;* and from his *native* dignity derives all its *acquired* importance. When I speak of a State as an inferior contrivance, I mean that it is a contrivance inferior only to that, which is *divine:* Of all *human* contrivances, it is certainly most transcendantly excellent. It is concerning this contrivance that *Cicero* says so sublimely, "Nothing, which is exhibited upon our globe, is more acceptable to that divinity, which governs the whole universe, than those communities and assemblages of men, which, lawfully associated, are denominated STATES."

Let a *State* be considered as subordinate to the PEOPLE: But let every thing else be subordinate to the *State.* The *latter* part of this position is equally necessary with the former. For in the practice, and even at length, in the science of politics there has very frequently been a strong current against the natural order of things, and an inconsiderate or an interested disposition to sacrifice the *end* to the *means.* As the *State* has claimed precedence of the people; so, in the same inverted course of things, the *Government* has often claimed precedence of the State; and to this perversion in the *second* degree, many of the volumes of confusion concerning sovereignty owe their existence. The *ministers,* dignified very properly by the appellation of the *magistrates,* have wished, and have succeeded in their wish, to be considered as the *sovereigns* of the State. This *second* degree of perversion is confined to the old world, and begins to diminish even there: but the *first* degree is still too prevalent, even in the several States, of which our union is composed. By a State I mean, a complete body of free persons united together for their common benefit, to enjoy peaceably what is their own, and to do justice to others. It is an *artificial* person. It has its affairs and its interests: It has its rules: It has its rights: And it has its obligations. It may acquire property distinct from that of its members: It may incur debts to be discharged out of the public stock, not out of the private fortunes of individuals. It may be bound by contracts; and for damages arising from the breach of those contracts. In all our contemplations, however, concerning this feigned and artificial person, we should never forget, that, in truth and nature, those, who think and speak, and act, are *men.*

Is the foregoing description of a State a true description? It will not be questioned but it is. Is there any part of this description, which intimates, in the remotest manner, that a State, any more than the men who compose it, ought not to do justice and fulfil engagements? It will not be pretended that there is. If justice is not done; if engagements are not fulfilled; is it upon general principles of right, less proper, in the case of a great number, than in the case of an individual, to secure, by compulsion, that, which will not be voluntarily performed? Less proper it surely cannot be. The only reason, I believe, why a free man is bound by human laws, is, *that he binds himself.* Upon the same principles, upon which he becomes bound *by the laws,* he becomes amenable to the *Courts of Justice,* which are formed and authorised by those laws. If one free man, an original sovereign, may do all this; why may not an aggregate of free men, a collection of original sovereigns, do this likewise? If the dignity of each *singly* is undiminished; the dignity of all *jointly* must be unimpaired. A State, like a merchant, makes a contract. A dishonest State, like a dishonest merchant, wilfully refuses to discharge it: The latter is amenable to a Court of Justice: Upon general principles of right, shall the former when summoned to answer the fair demands of its creditor, be permitted, proteus-like, to assume a new appearance, and to insult him and justice, by declaring *I am a* SOVEREIGN *State?* Surely not. Before a claim, so contrary, in its first appearance, to the general principles of right and equality, be sustained by a just and impartial tribunal, the person, natural or artificial, entitled to make such claim, should certainly be well known and authenticated. Who, or what, is a sovereignty? What is his or its sovereignty? On this subject, the errors and the mazes are endless and inexplicable. To

enumerate all, therefore, will not be expected: To take notice of some will be necessary to the full illustration of the present important cause. In one sense, the term *sovereign* has for its correlative, *subject,* In this sense, the term can receive no application; for it has no object in the Constitution of the *United States.* Under that Constitution there are *citizens,* but *no subjects.* "Citizen of the *United States.*" "Citizens of another State." "Citizens of different States." "A State or citizen thereof." The term, subject, occurs, indeed, once in the instrument; but to mark the contrast strongly, the epithet "foreign" is prefixed. In *this* sense, I presume the State of *Georgia* has no claim upon her own citizens: In this sense, I am certain, she can have no claim upon the citizens of another State.

In another sense, according to some writers, every State, which governs itself without any dependence on another power, is a sovereign State. Whether, with regard to her own citizens, this is the case of the State of *Georgia;* whether those citizens have done, as the individuals of *England* are said, by their late instructors, to have done, surrendered the Supreme Power to the State or Government, and reserved nothing to themselves; or whether, like the people of other States, and of the *United States,* the citizens of *Georgia* have reserved the Supreme Power in their own hands; and on that Supreme Power have made the State *dependent,* instead of being sovereign; these are questions, to which, as a Judge in this cause, I can neither know nor suggest the proper answers; though, as a citizen of the *Union,* I know, and am interested to know, that the most satisfactory answers can be given. As a citizen, I know the Government of that State to be republican; and my short definition of such a Government is,—one constructed on this principle, that the Supreme Power resides in the body of the people. As a Judge of this Court, I know, and can decide upon the knowledge, that the citizens of *Georgia,* when they acted upon the large scale of the *Union,* as a part of the "People of the *United States,*" did *not* surrender the Supreme or sovereign Power to that State; but, *as to the purposes of the Union,* retained it to themselves. *As to the purposes of the Union,* therefore, *Georgia is* NOT *a sovereign State.* If the Judicial decision of this case forms *one of those* purposes; the *allegation,* that *Georgia* is a sovereign State, is unsupported by the *fact.* Whether the judicial decision of this cause is, or is not, one of those purposes, is a question which will be examined particularly in a subsequent part of my argument.

There is a third sense, in which the term sovereign is frequently used, and which it is very material to trace and explain, as it furnishes a basis for what I presume to be one of the principal objections against the jurisdiction of this Court over the State of *Georgia.* In this sense, sovereignty is derived from a feudal source; and like many other parts of that system so degrading to man, still retains its influence over our sentiments and conduct, though the cause, by which that influence was produced, never extended to the *American* States. The accurate and well informed President *Henault,* in his excellent chronological abridgment of the History of *France,* tells us, that, about the end of the second race of *Kings,* a new kind of possession was acquired, under the name of *Fief.* The Governors of Cities and Provinces usurped equally the property of land, and the *administration of justice;* and established themselves as proprietary *Seigniors over* those places, in which they had been only civil magistrates or military officers. By this means, there was introduced into the State a new kind of authority, to which was assigned the appellation of sovereignty. In process of time the feudal system was extended over *France,* and almost all the other nations of *Europe:* And every *Kingdom* became, in fact, a large *fief.* Into *England* this system was introduced by the conqueror: and to this aera we may, probably, refer the *English* maxim, that the *King* or sovereign is the fountain of Justice. But, in the case of the *King,* the sovereignty had a double operation. While it vested him with jurisdiction over others, it excluded all others from jurisdiction over him. With regard to him, there was no superior power; and, consequently, on feudal principles, no right of jurisdiction. "The law, says Sir *William Blackstone,* ascribes to the *King* the attribute of sovereignty: he is sovereign and independent within his own dominions; and owes no kind of objection to any other potentate upon earth. Hence it is, that no *suit* or action can be brought against the *King,* even in civil matters; because no Court can have jurisdiction over him: for all jurisdiction implies superiority of power." This last position is only a branch of a much more extensive principle, on which a plan of systematic despotism has been lately formed in *England,* and prosecuted with unwearied assiduity and care. Of this plan the author of the Commentaries was, if not the introducer, at least the great supporter. He has been followed in it by writers later and less known; and his doctrines have, both on the other and *this* side of the Atlantic, been implicitly and generally received

by those, who neither examined their *principles* nor their *consequences,* The principle is, that all human law must be prescribed by a *superior.* This principle I mean not now to examine. Suffice it, at present to say, that another principle, very different in its nature and operations, forms, in my judgment, the basis of sound and genuine jurisprudence; laws derived from the pure source of equality and justice must be founded on the CONSENT of those, whose obedience they require. The *sovereign,* when traced to his source, must be found in the *man.*

I have now fixed, in the scale of things, the grade of a *State:* and have described its composure: I have considered the nature of sovereignty; and pointed its application to the proper object. I have examined the question before us, by the principles of general jurisprudence. In those principles I find nothing, which tends to evince an exemption of the State of *Georgia,* from the jurisdiction of the Court. I find every thing to have a contrary tendency.

II. I am, in the second place, to examine this question by the laws and practice of different States and *Kingdoms.* In ancient Greece, as we learn from *Isocrates,* whole nations defended their rights before crouded tribunals. Such occasions as these excited, we are told, all the powers of persuasion; and the vehemence and enthusiasm of the sentiment was gradually infused into the *Grecian* language, equally susceptible of strength and harmony. In those days, law, liberty, and refining science, made their benign progress in strict and graceful union: The rude and degrading league between the bar and feudal barbarism was not yet formed.

When the laws and practice of particular States have any application to the question before us; that application will furnish what is called an argument *a fortiori;* because all the instances produced will be instances of *subjects* instituting and supporting suits against those, who were deemed *their own sovereigns.* These instances are stronger than the present one; because between the present plaintiff and defendant no such unequal relation is alledged to exist.

Columbus atchieved the discovery of that country, which, perhaps, ought to bear his name. A contract made by *Columbus* furnished the first precedent for supporting, in his discovered country, the cause of injured merit against the claims and pretentions of haughty and ungrateful power. His son *Don Diego* wasted two years in incessant, but fruitless, solicitation at the Court of *Spain,* for the rights which descended to him in consequence of his father's original capitulation. He endeavoured, at length, to obtain, by a legal sentence, what he could not procure from the favour of an interested *Monarch.* He commenced a suit against *Ferdinand* before the Council, which managed *Indian* affairs: and that *Court,* with integrity which reflects honour on their proceedings, *decided* against the *King,* and *sustained Don Diego's* claim.

Other States have instituted officers to judge the proceedings of their *Kings:* Of this kind were the *Ephori* of *Sparta:* of this kind also was the mayor of the *Palace,* and afterwards the constable of *France.*

But of all the laws and institutions relating to the present question, none is so striking as that described by the famous *Hottoman,* in his book entitled *Francogallia.* When the *Spaniards* of *Arragon* elect a *King,* they represent a kind of play, and introduce a personage, whom they dignify by the name of LAW, *la Justiza,* of *Arragon.* This personage they declare, by a public decree, to be greater and more powerful than their *Kings* and then address him in the following remarkable expressions. "We, who are of as great worth as you, and can do more than you can do, elect you to be our *King,* upon the conditions stipulated: But between you and us there is *one* of greater authority than you."

In *England,* according to Sir *William Blackstone,* no suit can be brought against the *King,* even in civil matters. So, in that *Kingdom,* is the law, at *this* time, received. But it was not always so. Under the *Saxon* Government, a very different doctrine was held to be orthodox. Under that Government, as we are informed by the Mirror of Justice, a book said, by Sir *Edward Coke,* to have been written, in part, at least, before the conquest; under that Government it was ordained, that the *King's* Court should be open to all Plaintiffs, by which, without delay, they should have remedial writs, as well against the *King* or against the *Queen,* as against any *other* of the people. The law continued to be the same for some centuries after the conquest. Until the time of *Edward I.* the *King* might have been sued as a common person. The form of the process was even imperative. "*Praecipe Henrico Regi Angliae*" &c. "Command *Henry King* of *England*" &c. *Bracton,* who wrote in the time of *Henry III.* uses these very remarkable expressions concerning the *King* "*in justitia recipienda, minimo de regno suo comparetur*"—"in receiving justice, he should be placed on a level with the meanest person in the *Kingdom.*" True it is, that now in *England* the *King* must be sued in his Courts by *Petition,* but even now, the difference is only in the *form,* not in the *thing.* The judgments or decrees

of those Courts will substantially be the same upon a *precatory* as upon a *mandatory* process. In the Courts of Justice, says the very able author of the considerations on the laws of forfeiture, the *King* enjoys many privileges; yet not to deter the subject from contending with him freely. The Judge of the High Court of Admiralty in *England* made, in a very late cause, the following manly and independent declaration. "In any case, where the Crown is a party, it is to be observed, that the Crown can no more withhold evidence of documents in its possession, than a private person. If the Court thinks proper to *order* the production of any public instrument; that order *must* be *obeyed.* It wants no *Insignia* of an authority derived from the Crown."

"Judges ought to know, that the poorest peasant is a man as well as the *King* himself: all men ought to obtain justice; since in the estimation of justice, all men are *equal;* whether the Prince complain of a peasant, or a peasant complain of the Prince." These are the words of a *King,* of the late *Frederic* of *Prussia.* In his Courts of Justice, that great man stood his native greatness; and disdained to mount upon the artificial stilts of sovereignty.

Thus much concerning the laws and practice of other States and *Kingdoms.* We see nothing against, but much in favour of, the jurisdiction of this Court over the State of *Georgia,* a party to this cause.

III. I am, thirdly, and chiefly, to examine the important question now before us, by the Constitution of the *United States,* and the legitimate result of that valuable instrument. Under this view, the question is naturally subdivided into two others. 1. *Could* the Constitution of the *United States* vest a jurisdiction over the State of *Georgia?* 2. *Has* that Constitution vested such jurisdiction in this Court? I have already remarked, that in the *practice,* and even in the *science* of politics, there has been frequently a strong current against the *natural* order of things; and an *inconsiderate* or an *interested* disposition to sacrifice the *end* to the *means.* This remark deserves a more particular illustration. Even in almost every nation, which has been denominated *free,* the *state* has assumed a supercilious preeminence above the *people,* who have *formed* it: Hence the haughty notions of *state independence, state sovereignty* and *state supremacy.* In *despotic* Governments, the *Government* has usurped, in a similar manner, both upon the *state* and the *people:* Hence all arbitrary doctrines and pretensions concerning the Supreme, absolute, and incontrolable, power of *Government.* In *each, man* is degraded from the *prime* rank, which he ought to hold in human affairs: In the *latter,* the *state* as well as the *man* is degraded. Of *both* degradations, striking instances occur in history, in politics, and in common life. One of them is drawn from an anecdote, which is recorded concerning *Louis XIV.* who has been stiled the grand *Monarch* of *France.* This *Prince,* who diffused around him so much dazzling splendour, and so little vivifying heat, was vitiated by that inverted manner of teaching and of thinking, which forms *Kings* to be tyrants, without knowing or even suspecting that they are so. The oppression, under which he held his subjects during the whole course of his long reign, proceeded chiefly from the principles and habits of his erroneous education. By these, he had been accustomed to consider his *Kingdom* as his patrimony, and his power over his subjects as his rightful and undelegated inheritance. These sentiments were so deeply and strongly imprinted on his mind, that when one of his Ministers represented to him the miserable condition, to which those subjects were reduced, and, in the course of his representation, frequently used the word *L'Etat, the state,* the *King,* though he felt the truth and approved the substance of all that was said, yet was shocked at the frequent repetition of the expression *L'Etat;* and complained of it as an indecency offered to his person and character. And, indeed, that *Kings* should imagine themselves the *final causes,* for which *men* were made, and *societies* were formed, and *Governments* were instituted, will cease to be a matter of wonder or surprise, when we find that lawyers, and statesmen, and philosophers, have taught or favoured principles, which necessarily lead to the same conclusion. Another instance, equally strong, but still more astonishing, is drawn from the *British* Government, as described by Sir *William Blackstone* and his followers. As described by him and them, the *British* is a despotic Government. It is a Government without a people. In that Government, as so described, the *sovereignty* is possessed by the Parliament: In the Parliament, therefore, the supreme and absolute authority is vested: In the Parliament resides that incontrolable and despotic power, which, in all Governments, must reside somewhere. The constituent parts of the Parliament are the *King's* Majesty, the Lord's Spiritual, the Lord's Temporal, and the Commons. The *King* and these three Estates together form the great corporation or body politic of the *Kingdom.* All these sentiments are found; the last expressions are found *verbatim* in the commentaries upon the laws of *England.* The *Parliament* form the great *body poli-*

tic of *England! What,* then, or *where,* are the PEOPLE? *Nothing! No where!* They are not so much as even the "baseless fabric of a vision!" From legal contemplation they totally disappear! Am I not warranted in saying, that, if this is a just description; a Government, so and justly so described, is a despotic Government? Whether this description is or is not a just one, is a question of very different import.

In the *United States,* and in the several States, which compose the *Union,* we go not so far: but still we go *one step* farther than we ought to go in this unnatural and inverted order of things. The *states,* rather than the PEOPLE, for whose sakes the States exist, are frequently the objects which attract and arrest our principal attention. This, I believe, has produced much of the confusion and perplexity, which have appeared in several proceedings and several publications on state-politics, and on the pòlitics, too, of the *United States.* Sentiments and expressions of this inaccurate kind prevail in our common, even in our convivial, language. Is a toast asked? "The *United States,*" instead of the "People of the *United States,*" is the toast given. This is not *politically* correct. The toast is meant to present to view the *first* great object in the *Union:* It presents only the *second:* It presents only the *artificial* person, instead of the *natural* persons, who spoke it into existence. A *State* I cheerfully admit, is the noblest work of *Man:* But, *Man himself,* free and honest, is, I speak as to this world, the noblest work of GOD.

Concerning the prerogative of *Kings,* and concerning the sovereignty of States, much has been said and written; but little has been said and written concerning a subject much more dignified and important, the majesty of the people. The mode of expression, which I would substitute in the place of that generally used, is not only *politically,* but also (for between true liberty and true taste there is a close alliance) *classically* more correct. On the mention of *Athens,* a thousand refined and endearing associations rush at once into the memory of the *scholar,* the *philosopher,* and the *patriot.* When *Homer,* one of the most correct, as well as the oldest of human authorities, enumerates the *other* nations of *Greece,* whose forces acted at the siege of *Troy,* he arranges them under the names of their different *Kings* or *Princes:* But when he comes to the *Athenians,* he distinguishes them by the peculiar appellation of the PEOPLE of *Athens.* The well known address used by *Demosthenes,* when he harrangued and animated his assembled countrymen, was "O Men of *Athens.*" With the strictest propriety, therefore, *classical* and *political*, our national scene opens with the most magnificent object, which the nation could present. "The PEOPLE of the *United States*" are the first personages introduced. Who were those people? They were the citizens of thirteen States, each of which had a separate Constitution and Government, and all of which were connected together by articles of confederation. To the purposes of public strength and felicity, that confederacy was totally inadequate. A requisition on the several States terminated its *Legislative* authority: *Executive* or *Judicial* authority it had none. In order, therefore, to form a more perfect union, *to establish justice,* to ensure domestic tranquillity, to provide for common defence, and to secure the blessings of liberty, *those people,* among whom were the people of *Georgia,* ordained and established the present Constitution. By that Constitution Legislative power is vested, Executive power is vested, *Judicial* power is vested.

The question now opens fairly to our view, *could* the *people* of those States, among whom were those of *Georgia,* bind those *States,* and *Georgia* among the others, by the Legislative, Executive, and Judicial power so vested? If the principles, on which I have founded myself, are just and true; this question must unavoidably receive an affirmative answer. If those *States* were the *work* of those *people;* those people, and, that I may apply the case closely, the people of *Georgia,* in particular, could alter, as they pleased, their former work: To any given degree, they could *diminish* as well as enlarge it. *Any* or *all* of the former State-powers, they could *extinguish* or *transfer.* The inference, which necessarily results, is, that the Constitution ordained and established by *those* people; and, still closely to apply the case, in particular by the people of *Georgia, could* vest jurisdiction or judicial power over those States and over the State of *Georgia* in particular.

The next question under this head, is,—*Has* the Constitution done so? Did those people mean to exercise this, their undoubted power? These questions may be resolved, either by fair and conclusive deductions, or by direct and explicit declarations. In order, ultimately, to discover, whether the people of the *United States* intended to bind those States by the *Judicial* power vested by the national Constitution, a previous enquiry will naturally be: Did those *people* intend to bind those *states* by the *Legislative* power vested by that Constitution? The articles of confederation, it is well known, did not operate upon individual *citizens,* but operated only upon *states,* This defect was

remedied by the national Constitution, which, *as all allow,* has an operation on individual citizens. But if an opinion, which some seem to entertain, be just; the defect remedied, on one side, was balanced by a defect introduced on the other; For they seem to think, that the present Constitution operates only on individual citizens, and not on States. This opinion, however, appears to be altogether unfounded. When certain laws of the States are declared to be "subject to the revision and controul of the *Congress;*" * it cannot, surely, be contended that the *Legislative* power of the national Government was meant to have *no* operation on the several States. The *fact,* uncontrovertibly established in *one* instance, proves the *principle* in *all other* instances, to which the facts will be found to apply. We may then infer, that the people of the *United States* intended to bind the several States, by the *Legislative* power of the national Government.

In order to make the discovery, at which we ultimately aim, a *second* previous enquiry will naturally be—Did the people of the *United States* intend to bind the several States by the *Executive* power of the national Government? The affirmative answer to the former question directs, unavoidably, an affirmative answer to this. Ever since the time of *Bracton,* his maxim, I believe, has been deemed a good one —"*Supervacuum esset leges condere, nisi esset qui leges tueretur.*" "It would be superfluous to *make* laws, unless those laws, when made, were to be enforced." When the laws are plain, and the application of them is uncontroverted, they are enforced immediately by the *Executive* authority of Government. When the application of them is doubtful or intricate, the interposition of the *judicial* authority becomes necessary. The same principle, therefore, which directed us from the *first* to the *second* step, will direct us from the *second* to the third and *last* step of our deduction. Fair and conclusive deduction, then, evinces that the *people* of the *United States did* vest this Court with jurisdiction over the State of *Georgia.* The same truth may be deduced from the *declared objects,* and the general texture of the Constitution of the *United States.* One of its declared objects is, to form an union more perfect, than, before that time, had been formed. Before that time, the *Union* possessed Legislative, but *uninforced* Legislative power over the States. Nothing could be more natural than to *intend* that this Legislative power should be enforced by powers Exec-

*Ar. 1. s. 10.

utive and *Judicial.* Another declared object is, "to establish justice." This points, in a particular manner, to the *Judicial* authority. And when we view this object in conjunction with the declaration, "that no State shall pass a law impairing the obligation of contracts;" we shall probably think, that this object points, in a particular manner, to the jurisdiction of the Court over the several States. What good purpose could this Constitutional provision *secure,* if a State might pass a law impairing the obligation of *its own* contracts; and be amenable, for such a violation of right, to no controuling judiciary power? We have seen, that on the principles of general jurisprudence, a State, for the breach of a contract, may be liable for damages. A third declared object is—"to ensure domestic tranquillity." This tranquillity is most likely to be disturbed by controversies between States. These consequences will be most peaceably and effectually decided by the establishment and by the exercise of a superintending judicial authority. By such exercise and establishment, the law of nations; the rule between contending States; will be enforced among the several States, in the same manner as municipal law.

Whoever considers, in a combined and comprehensive view, the *general texture* of the Constitution, will be satisfied, that the people of the *United States* intended to form themselves into a nation for *national purposes.* They instituted, for *such* purposes, a national Government, complete in all its parts, with powers Legislative, Executive and Judiciary; and, in all those powers, extending over the whole nation. Is it congruous, that, with regard to *such* purposes, any man or body of men, any person natural or artificial, should be permitted to claim successfully an entire exemption from the jurisdiction of the national Government? Would not such claims, crowned with success, be repugnant to our very existence as a nation? When so many trains of deduction, coming from different quarters, converge and unite, at last, in the same point; we may safely conclude, as the *legitimate result* of this Constitution, that the State of *Georgia* is amenable to the jurisdiction of this Court.

But, in my opinion, this doctrine rests not upon the legitimate result of fair and conclusive deduction from the Constitution: It is confirmed, beyond all doubt, by the *direct* and *explicit declaration* of the Constitution itself. "The judicial power of the *United States* shall extend, to controversies between *two* States." *Two* States are supposed to have a controversy between them: This controversy is sup-

posed to be brought before those vested with the judicial power of the *United States:* Can the most consummate degree of professional ingenuity devise a mode by which this "controversy between two States" can be brought before a Court of law; and yet neither of those States be a Defendant? "The judicial power of the *United States* shall extend to controversies, between a *state* and *citizens* of *another* State." Could the strictest legal language; could even that language, which is peculiarly appropriated to an art, deemed, by a great master, to be one of the most honorable, laudable, and profitable things in our law; could this strict and appropriated language, describe, with more precise accuracy, the cause now depending before the tribunal? *Causes,* and not *parties* to causes, are weighed by justice, in her equal scales: On the former *solely,* her attention is fixed: To the latter, she *is,* as she is painted, blind.

I have now tried this question by all the touchstones, to which I proposed to apply it. I have examined it by the principles of general jurisprudence; by the laws and practice of States and *Kingdoms;* and by the Constitution of the *United States.* From all, the combined inference is; that the action lies.

CUSHING, *Justice.* The grand and principal question in this case is, whether a State can, by the Foederal Constitution, be sued by an individual citizen of another State?

The point turns not upon the law or practice of *England,* although perhaps it may be in some measure elucidated thereby, nor upon the law of any other country whatever; but upon the Constitution established by the people of the *United States;* and particularly upon the extent of powers given to the Foederal Judicial in the 2d section of the 3d article of the Constitution. It is declared that "the Judicial power shall extend to all cases in law and equity arising under the Constitution, the laws of the *United States,* or treaties made or which shall be made under their authority; to all cases affecting ambassadors or other public ministers and consuls; to all cases of admiralty and maritime jurisdiction; to controversies, to which the *United States* shall be a party; to controversies between two or more States and citizens of another State; between citizens of different States; between citizens of the same State claiming lands under grants of different States; and between a State and citizens thereof and foreign States, citizens or subjects." The judicial power, then, is expressly extended to *"controversies between a State and citizens of another State."* When a citizen makes a demand against a

State, of which he is not a citizen, it is as really a controversy between a State and a citizen of another State, as if such State made a demand against such citizen. The case, then, seems clearly to fall within the letter of the Constitution. It may be suggested that it could not be intended to subject a State to be a Defendant, because it would effect the sovereignty of States. If that be the case, what shall we do with the immediate preceding clause; "*controversies between two or more States,*" where a State must of necessity be Defendant? If it was not the intent, in the very next clause also, that a State might be made Defendant, why was it so expressed as naturally to lead to and comprehend that idea? Why was not an exception made if one was intended?

Again—what are we to do with the last clause of the section of judicial powers, viz. "*Controversies between a state, or the citizens thereof, and foreign states or citizens?*" Here again, States must be suable or liable to be made Defendants by this clause, which has a similar mode of language with the two other clauses I have remarked upon. For if the judicial power extends to a controversy between one of the *United States* and a foreign State, as the clause expresses, one of them must be Defendant. And then, what becomes of the sovereignty of States as far as suing affects it? But although the words appear reciprocally to affect the State here and a foreign State, and put them on the same footing as far as may be, yet ingenuity may say, that the State here may sue, but cannot be sued; but that the foreign State may be sued but cannot sue. We may touch foreign sovereignties but not our own. But I conceive the reason of the thing, as well as the words of the Constitution, tend to shew that the Foederal Judicial power extends to a suit brought by a foreign State against any one of the *United States*. One design of the general Government was for managing the great affairs of peace and war and the general defence, which were impossible to be conducted, with safety, by the States *separately*. Incident to these powers, and for preventing controversies between foreign powers or citizens from rising to extremeties and to an appeal to the sword, a national tribunal was necessary, amicably to decide them, and thus ward off such fatal, public calamity. Thus, States at home and their citizens, and foreign States and their citizens, are put together without distinction upon the same footing, as far as may be, as to controversies between them. So also, with respect to controversies between a State and citizens of another State (at home) comparing all the clauses together, the remedy is reciprocal; the claim to justice equal.

As controversies between State and State, and between a State and citizens of another State, might tend gradually to involve States in war and bloodshed, a disinterested civil tribunal was intended to be instituted to decide such controversies, and preserve peace and friendship. Further; if a State is entitled to Justice in the Foederal Court, against a citizen of another State, why not such citizen against the State, when the same language equally comprehends both? The rights of individuals and the justice due to them, are as dear and precious as those of States. Indeed the latter are founded upon the former; and the great end and object of them must be to secure and support the rights of individuals, or else vain is Government.

But still it may be insisted, that this will reduce States to mere corporations, and take away all sovereignty. As to corporations, all States whatever are corporations or bodies politic. The only question is, what are their powers? As to individual States and the *United States,* the Constitution marks the boundary of powers. Whatever power is deposited with the *Union* by the people for their own necessary security, is so far a curtailing of the power and prerogatives of States. This is, as it were, a self-evident proposition; at least it cannot be contested. Thus the power of declaring war, making peace, raising and supporting armies for public defence, levying duties, excises and taxes, if necessary, with many other powers, are lodged in *Congress;* and are a most essential abridgement of State sovereignty. Again; the restrictions upon States; "No State shall enter into any *treaty, alliance, or confederation, coin money, emit bills of credit, make any thing but gold and silver a tender in payment of debts, pass any law impairing the obligation of contracts;*" these, with a number of others, are important restrictions of the power of States, and were thought necessary to maintain the *Union;* and to establish some fundamental uniform principles of public justice, throughout the whole *Union.* So that, I think, no argument of force can be taken from the sovereignty of States. Where it has been abridged, it was thought necessary for the greater indispensable good of the whole. If the Constitution is found inconvenient in practice in this or any other particular, it is well that a regular mode is pointed out for amendment. But, while it remains, all offices Legislative, Executive, and Judicial, both of the States and of the *Union,* are bound by oath to support it.

One other objection has been suggested, that if a State may be sued by a citizen of another State, then the *United*

States may be sued by a citizen of any of the States, or, in other words, by any of their citizens. If this be a necessary consequence, it must be so. I doubt the consequence, from the different wording of the different clauses, connected with other reasons. When speaking of the *United States,* the Constitution says "*controversies to which the* UNITED STATES *shall be a party*" not controversies between the *United States* and any of their citizens. When speaking of States, it says, "*controversies between two or more states; between a state and citizens of another state.*" As to reasons for citizens suing a different State, which do not hold equally good for suing the *United States;* one may be, that as controversies between a State and citizens of another State, might have a tendency to involve both States in contest, and perhaps in war, a common umpire to decide such controversies, may have a tendency to prevent the mischief. That an object of this kind was had in view by the framers of the Constitution, I have no doubt, when I consider the clashing interfering laws which were made in the neighbouring States, before the adoption of the Constitution,

and some affecting the property of citizens of another State in a very different manner from that of their own citizens. But I do not think it necessary to enter fully into the question, whether the *United States* are liable to be sued by an individual citizen? In order to decide the point before us. Upon the whole, I am of opinion, that the Constitution warrants a suit against a State, by an individual citizen of another State. . . .

U.S. Constitution

Amendment XI

The Judicial power of the United States shall not be construed to extend to any suit in law or equity, commenced or prosecuted against one of the United States by Citizens of another State, or by Citizens or Subjects of any Foreign State.

The Alien and Sedition Acts

June 25, 1798

Virginia Resolutions

December 21, 1798

Kentucky Resolutions

November 10, 1798

Counter-resolutions of Other States

1799

Report of Virginia House of Delegates

1799

During 1797 and 1798, American diplomats met with officials of the French revolutionary government in an attempt to negotiate continued peace between the two countries. During these negotiations, the French officials demanded bribes totaling $1,250,000 from the Americans in exchange for continued cooperation. The French during this period were engaged in wars and attempts to overthrow governments throughout Europe. In addition, French immigrants to the United States—along with a number of immigrants from Ireland, where pro-French feeling was widespread—were engaged in political activities aimed at unseating Federalist politicians, President John Adams in particular. In response, in 1798 Adams and the Federalist-controlled legislature passed four laws, the most controversial of which were the Alien and Sedition Acts. The Alien Act authorized the president to deport aliens, in time of peace, whom he found to be "dangerous to the peace and safety of the United States." The Sedition Act made it a high misdemeanor, punishable by fine and imprisonment, to commit any treasonable activity, which was defined to include publishing false, scandalous, and malicious writing concerning the government of the United States. Twenty-five men were arrested under this last act, most of them editors of newspapers loyal to Thomas Jefferson's Democratic-Republican Party.

Amidst the outcry that ensued, Kentucky and Virginia passed resolutions condemning and refusing to abide by the Alien and Sedition Acts. Written, respectively, by Jefferson and his ally, James Madison, these resolutions once again raised the question of how far federal powers extended within the borders of the several states, and how far the states might go in opposing federal legislation. A number of states issued strongly worded counter-resolutions decrying what came to be called the doctrine of Nullification, according to which states could refuse to enforce or abide by particular federal laws. In response, Madison drafted a report in the Virginia legislature laying out his position on the proper relationship between state and federal sovereignty and authority.

The Alien and Sedition Acts

An Act Concerning Aliens

SECTION 1. *Be it enacted by the Senate and House of Representatives of the United States of America, in Congress assembled,* That it shall be lawful for the President of the United States, at any time during the continuance of this act, to *order* all such *aliens* as he shall judge dangerous to the peace and safety of the United States, or shall have reasonable grounds to suspect are concerned in any treasonable or secret machinations against the government thereof, to depart out of the territory of the United States within such time as shall be expressed in such order; which order shall be served on such alien, by delivering him a copy thereof, or leaving the same at his usual abode, and returned to the office of the Secretary of State, by the marshal, or other person, to whom the same shall be directed. And in case any alien, so ordered to depart, shall be found at large within the United States after the time limited in such order for his departure, and not having obtained a *license* from the President to reside therein, or having obtained such *license,* shall not have conformed thereto, every such alien shall, on conviction thereof, be imprisoned for a term not exceeding three years, and shall never after be admitted to become a citizen of the United States: *Provided always, and be it further enacted,* That if any alien so ordered to depart shall prove, to the satisfaction of the President, by evidence, to be taken before such person or persons as the President shall direct, who are for that purpose hereby authorized to administer oaths, that no injury or danger to the United States will arise from suffering such alien to reside therein, the President may grant a *license* to such alien to remain within the United States for such time as he shall judge proper, and at such place as he may designate. And the President may also require of such alien to enter into a bond to the United States, in such penal sum as he may direct, with one or more sufficient sureties, to the satisfaction of the person authorized by the President to take the same, conditioned for the good behaviour of such alien during his residence in the United States, and not violating his license, which license the President may revoke whenever he shall think proper.

Sᴇᴄᴛ. 2. *And be it further enacted,* That it shall be lawful for the President of the United States, whenever he may deem it necessary for the public safety, to order to be removed out of the territory thereof any alien who may or shall be in prison in pursuance of this act; and to cause to be arrested and sent out of the United States such of those aliens as shall have been ordered to depart therefrom, and shall not have obtained a license as aforesaid, in all cases where, in the opinion of the President, the public safety requires a speedy removal. And if any alien so removed or sent out of the United States by the President shall voluntarily return thereto, unless by permission of the President

of the United States, such alien, on conviction thereof, shall be imprisoned so long as, in the opinion of the President, the public safety may require.

Sᴇᴄᴛ. 3. *And be it further enacted,* That every master or commander of any ship or vessel which shall come into any port of the United States after the first day of July next shall, immediately on his arrival, make report in writing to the collector or other chief officer of the customs of such port, of all aliens, if any on board his vessel, specifying their names, age, the place of nativity, the country from which they shall have come, the nation to which they belong and owe allegiance, their occupation, and a description of their persons, as far as he shall be informed thereof, and on failure, every such master and commander shall forfeit and pay three hundred dollars, for the payment whereof, on default of such master or commander, such vessel shall also be holden, and may by such collector or other officer of the customs be detained. And it shall be the duty of such collector or other officer of the customs, forthwith to transmit to the office of the Department of State true copies of all such returns.

Sᴇᴄᴛ. 4. *And be it further enacted,* That the Circuit and District Courts of the United States shall respectively have cognizance of all crimes and offences against this act. And all marshals and other officers of the United States are required to execute all precepts and orders of the President of the United States, issued in pursuance or by virtue of this act.

Sᴇᴄᴛ. 5. *And be it further enacted,* That it shall be lawful for any alien who may be ordered to be removed from the United States, by virtue of this act, to take with him such part of his goods, chattels, or other property, as he may find convenient; and all property left in the United States, by any alien who may be removed as aforesaid, shall be and remain subject to his order and disposal, in the same manner as if this act had not been passed.

Sᴇᴄᴛ. 6. *And be it further enacted,* That this act shall continue and be in force for and during the term of two years from the passing thereof.

Sedition Act

Sᴇᴄᴛɪᴏɴ 1. *Be it enacted by the Senate and House of Representatives of the United States of America, in Congress assembled,* That if any persons shall unlawfully combine or conspire together, with intent to oppose any measure or measures of the government of the United States, which are or shall be directed by proper authority, or to impede the operation of any law of the United States, or to intimidate or prevent any person holding a place or office in or under the government of the United States, from undertaking, performing, or executing his trust or duty: and if any person or persons, with intent as aforesaid, shall counsel, advise, or attempt to procure any insurrection, riot, unlawful assembly, or combination, whether such conspiracy, threatening, counsel, advice, or attempt shall have the proposed effect or not, he or they shall be deemed guilty of a high misdemeanour, and on conviction before any court of the United States having jurisdiction thereof, shall be punished by a fine not exceeding five thousand dollars, and by imprisonment during a term of not less than six months, nor exceeding five years; and further, at the discretion of the court, may be holden to find sureties for his good behaviour, in such sum, and for such time, as the said court may direct.

Sect. 2. *And be it further enacted,* That if any person shall write, print, utter, or publish, or shall cause or procure to be written, printed, uttered, or published, or shall knowingly and willingly assist or aid in writing, printing, uttering, or publishing any false, scandalous and malicious writing or writings against the government of the United States, or either House of the Congress of the United States, or the President of the United States, with intent to defame the said government, or either House of the said Congress, or the said President, or to bring them, or either of them, into contempt or disrepute; or to excite against them, or either or any of them, the hatred of the good people of the United States, or to stir up sedition within the United States; or to excite any unlawful combinations therein, for opposing or resisting any law of the United States, or any act of the President of the United States, done in pursuance of any such law, or of the powers in him vested by the Constitution of the United States; or to resist, oppose, or defeat any such law or act; or to aid, encourage or abet any hostile designs of any foreign nation against the United States, their people or government, then such person, being thereof convicted before any court of the United States having jurisdiction thereof, shall be punished by a fine not exceeding two thousand dollars, and by imprisonment not exceeding two years.

Sect. 3. *And be it further enacted and declared,* That if any person shall be prosecuted under this act for the writing or publishing any libel aforesaid, it shall be lawful for the defendant, upon the trial of the cause, to give in evidence in his defence, the truth of the matter contained in the publication charged as a libel. And the jury who shall try the cause shall have a right to determine the law and the fact, under the direction of the court, as in other cases.

Sect. 4. *And be it further enacted,* That this act shall continue and be in force until the third day of March, one thousand eight hundred and one, and no longer: *Provided,* That the expiration of the act shall not prevent or defeat a prosecution and punishment of any offence against the law, during the time it shall be in force.

Virginia Resolutions

Resolutions, As Adopted by Both Houses of Assembly

1. *Resolved,* That the General Assembly of Virginia doth unequivocally express a firm resolution to maintain and defend the Constitution of the United States, and the Constitution of this State, against every aggression, either foreign or domestic, and that it will support the government of the United States in all measures warranted by the former.

2. That this Assembly most solemnly declares a warm attachment to the union of the States, to maintain which, it pledges all its powers; and that for this end it is its duty to watch over and oppose every infraction of those principles, which constitute the only basis of that union, because a faithful observance of them can alone secure its existence, and the public happiness.

3. That this Assembly doth explicitly and peremptorily declare that it views the powers of the Federal Government as resulting from the compact, to which the States are parties, as limited by the plain sense and intention of the instrument constituting that compact; as no further valid than they are authorized by the grants enumerated in that compact; and that in case of a deliberate, palpable, and dangerous exercise of other powers not granted by the said compact, the States, who are the parties thereto, have the right, and are in duty bound, to interpose for arresting the progress of the evil, and for maintaining within their respective limits, the authorities, rights, and liberties appertaining to them.

4. That the General Assembly doth also express its deep

regret that a spirit has in sundry instances been manifested by the Federal Government, to enlarge its powers by forced constructions of the constitutional charter which defines them; and that indications have appeared of a design to expound certain general phrases (which, having been copied from the very limited grant of powers in the former articles of confederation, were the less liable to be misconstrued), so as to destroy the meaning and effect of the particular enumeration, which necessarily explains and limits the general phrases, and so as to consolidate the States by degrees into one sovereignty, the obvious tendency and inevitable result of which would be to transform the present republican system of the United States into an absolute, or at best, a mixed monarchy.

5. That the General Assembly doth particularly protest against the palpable and alarming infractions of the Constitution, in the two late cases of the "alien and sedition acts," passed at the last session of Congress, the first of which exercises a power nowhere delegated to the Federal Government; and which by uniting legislative and judicial powers to those of executive, subverts the general principles of free government, as well as the particular organization and positive provisions of the federal Constitution; and the other of which acts exercises in like manner a power not delegated by the Constitution, but on the contrary expressly and positively forbidden by one of the amendments thereto; a power which more than any other ought to produce universal alarm, because it is levelled against that right of freely examining public characters and measures, and of free communication among the people thereon, which has ever been justly deemed the only effectual guardian of every other right.

6. That this State having by its convention which ratified the federal Constitution, expressly declared, "that among other essential rights, the liberty of conscience and of the press cannot be cancelled, abridged, restrained, or modified by any authority of the United States," and from its extreme anxiety to guard these rights from every possible attack of sophistry or ambition, having with other States recommended an amendment for that purpose, which amendment was in due time annexed to the Constitution, it would mark a reproachful inconsistency and criminal degeneracy, if an indifference were now shown to the most palpable violation of one of the rights thus declared and secured, and to the establishment of a precedent which may be fatal to the other.

7. That the good people of this commonwealth having ever felt, and continuing to feel the most sincere affection to their brethren of the other States, the truest anxiety for establishing and perpetuating the union of all, and the most scrupulous fidelity to that Constitution which is the pledge of mutual friendship, and the instrument of mutual happiness, the General Assembly doth solemnly appeal to the like dispositions of the other States, in confidence that they will concur with this commonwealth in declaring, as it does hereby declare, that the acts aforesaid are unconstitutional, and that the necessary and proper measure will be taken by each, for co-operating with this State in maintaining unimpaired the authorities, rights, and liberties reserved to the States respectively, or to the people.

8. That the Governor be desired to transmit a copy of the foregoing resolutions to the executive authority of each of the other States, with a request that the same may be communicated to the legislature thereof. And that a copy be furnished to each of the senators and representatives representing this state in the Congress of the United States.

Kentucky Resolutions

In the House of Representatives

The House, according to the standing order of the day, resolved itself into a committee of the whole on the state of the commonwealth, Mr. Caldwell in the chair; and after some time spent therein, the Speaker resumed the chair, and Mr. Caldwell reported that the committee had, according to order, had under consideration the Governor's address, and had come to the following resolutions thereupon, which he delivered in at the clerk's table, where they were twice read and agreed to by the House.

1. *Resolved,* That the several states composing the United States of America, are not united on the principle of unlimited submission to their general government; but that by compact, under the style and title of a Constitution for the United States, and of amendments thereto, they constituted a general government for special purposes, delegated to that government certain definite powers, reserving, each state to itself, the residuary mass of right to their own self-government; and that whensoever the general government assumes undelegated powers, its acts are unauthoritative, void, and of no force: That to this compact

each state acceded as a state, and is an integral party, its co-states forming as to itself, the other party: That the government created by this compact was not made the exclusive or final *judge* of the extent of the powers delegated to itself; since that would have made its discretion, and not the Constitution, the measure of its powers; but that, as in all other cases of compact among parties having no common judge, each party has an equal right to judge for itself, as well of infractions, as of the mode and measure of redress.

2. *Resolved,* That the Constitution of the United States having delegated to Congress a power to punish treason, counterfeiting the securities and current coin of the United States, piracies and felonies committed on the high seas, and offences against the laws of nations, and no other crimes whatever, and it being true as a general principle, and one of the amendments to the Constitution having also declared, "that the powers not delegated to the United States by the Constitution, nor prohibited by it to the states, are reserved to the states respectively, or to the people;" therefore, also, the same act of Congress, passed on the 14th day of July, 1798, and entitled, "an act in addition to the act entitled, an act for the punishment of certain crimes against the United States;" as also the act passed by them on the 27th day of June, 1798, entitled, "an act to punish frauds committed on the Bank of the United States," (and all other their acts which assume to create, define, or punish crimes other than those enumerated in the Constitution,) are altogether void, and of no force, and that the power to create, define, and punish such other crimes is reserved, and of right appertains, solely and exclusively, to the respective states, each within its own territory.

3. *Resolved,* That it is true as a general principle, and is also expressly declared by one of the amendments to the Constitution, that "the powers not delegated to the United States by the Constitution, nor prohibited by it to the states, are reserved to the states respectively, or to the people;" and that no power over the freedom of religion, freedom of speech, or freedom of the press, being delegated to the United States by the Constitution, nor prohibited by it to the states, all lawful powers respecting the same did of right remain, and were reserved to the states, or to the people; that thus was manifested their determination to retain to themselves the right of judging how far the licentiousness of speech and of the press may be abridged without lessening their useful freedom, and how far those

abuses which cannot be separated from their use, should be tolerated rather than the use be destroyed; and thus also they guarded against all abridgment by the United States of the freedom of religious opinions and exercises, and retained to themselves the right of protecting the same, as this state by a law passed on the general demand of its citizens, had already protected them from all human restraint or interference: and that in addition to this general principle and express declaration, another and more special provision has been made by one of the amendments to the Constitution, which expressly declares, that "Congress shall make no law respecting an establishment of religion, or prohibiting the free exercise thereof, or abridging the freedom of speech, or of the press," thereby guarding in the same sentence, and under the same words, the freedom of religion, of speech, and of the press, insomuch, that whatever violates either, throws down the sanctuary which covers the others, and that libels, falsehoods, and defamations, equally with heresy and false religion, are withheld from the cognizance of federal tribunals: that therefore the act of the Congress of the United States, passed on the 14th day of July, 1798, entitled, "an act in addition to the act for the punishment of certain crimes against the United States," which does abridge the freedom of the press, is not law, but is altogether void and of no effect.

4. *Resolved,* That alien-friends are under the jurisdiction and protection of the laws of the state wherein they are; that no power over them has been delegated to the United States, nor prohibited to the individual states distinct from their power over citizens; and it being true as a general principle, and one of the amendments to the Constitution having also declared, that "the powers not delegated to the United States by the Constitution, nor prohibited by it to the states, are reserved to the states respectively, or to the people," the act of the Congress of the United States, passed on the 22d day of June, 1798, entitled "an act concerning aliens," which assumes power over alien-friends not delegated by the Constitution, is not law, but is altogether void and of no force.

5. *Resolved,* That in addition to the general principle as well as the express declaration, that powers not delegated are reserved, another and more special provision inserted in the Constitution, from abundant caution, has declared, "that the *migration* or importation of such persons as any of the states now existing shall think proper to admit, shall not be prohibited by the Congress prior to the year 1808:"

that this commonwealth does admit the migration of alien-friends described as the subject of the said act concerning aliens; that a provision against prohibiting their migration, is a provision against all acts equivalent thereto, or it would be nugatory; that to remove them when migrated, is equivalent to a prohibition of their migration, and is therefore contrary to the said provision of the Constitution, and void.

6. *Resolved,* That the imprisonment of a person under the protection of the laws of this commonwealth, on his failure to obey the simple *order* of the President, to depart out of the United States, as is undertaken by the said act, entitled "an act concerning aliens," is contrary to the Constitution, one amendment to which has provided, that "no person shall be deprived of liberty without due process of law," and that another having provided, "that in all criminal prosecutions, the accused shall enjoy the right to a public trial by an impartial jury, to be informed of the nature and cause of the accusation, to be confronted with the witnesses against him, to have compulsory process for obtaining witnesses in his favour, and to have the assistance of counsel for his defence," the same act undertaking to authorize the President to remove a person out of the United States, who is under the protection of the law, on his own suspicion, without accusation, without jury, without public trial, without confrontation of the witnesses against him, without having witnesses in his favour, without defence, without counsel, is contrary to these provisions, also, of the Constitution, is therefore not law, but utterly void and of no force.

That transferring the power of judging any person who is under the protection of the laws, from the courts to the President of the United States, as is undertaken by the same act, concerning aliens, is against the article of the Constitution which provides, that "the judicial power of the United States shall be vested in courts, the judges of which shall hold their offices during good behaviour," and that the said act is void for that reason also; and it is further to be noted, that this transfer of judiciary power is to that magistrate of the General Government, who already possesses all the executive, and a qualified negative in all the legislative powers.

7. *Resolved,* That the construction applied by the General Government, (as is evinced by sundry of their proceedings,) to those parts of the Constitution of the United States which delegates to Congress a power to lay and collect taxes, duties, imposts, and excises; to pay the debts, and provide for the common defence and general welfare of the United States, and to make all laws which shall be necessary and proper for carrying into execution the powers vested by the Constitution in the Government of the United States, or any department thereof, goes to the destruction of all the limits prescribed to their power by the Constitution: that words meant by that instrument to be subsidiary only to the execution of the limited powers, ought not to be so construed as themselves to give unlimited powers, nor a part so to be taken, as to destroy the whole residue of the instrument: that the proceedings of the General Government under colour of these articles, will be a fit and necessary subject for revisal and correction at a time of greater tranquillity, while those specified in the preceding resolutions call for immediate redress.

8. *Resolved,* That the preceding resolutions be transmitted to the senators and representatives in Congress from this commonwealth, who are hereby enjoined to present the same to their respective houses, and to use their best endeavours to procure, at the next session of Congress, a repeal of the aforesaid unconstitutional and obnoxious acts.

9. *Resolved, lastly,* That the Governor of this commonwealth be, and is hereby authorized and requested to communicate the preceding resolutions to the legislatures of the several states, to assure them that this commonwealth considers union for specified national purposes, and particularly for those specified in their late federal compact, to be friendly to the peace, happiness, and prosperity of all the states: that, faithful to that compact, according to the plain intent and meaning in which it was understood and acceded to by the several parties, it is sincerely anxious for its preservation: that it does also believe, that to take from the states all the powers of self-government, and transfer them to a general and consolidated government, without regard to the special obligations and reservations solemnly agreed to in that compact, is not for the peace, happiness or prosperity of these states: and that therefore, this commonwealth is determined, as it doubts not its co-states are, tamely to submit to undelegated and consequently unlimited powers in no man or body of men on earth: that if the acts before specified should stand, these conclusions would flow from them; that the general government may place any act they think proper on the list of crimes, and punish it themselves, whether enumerated or not enumerated by the Constitution, as cognizable by them; that they may trans-

fer its cognizance to the President or any other person, who may himself be the accuser, counsel, judge and jury, whose *suspicions* may be the evidence, his order the sentence, his officer the executioner, and his breast the sole record of the transaction; that a very numerous and valuable description of the inhabitants of these states being, by this precedent, reduced as outlaws to the absolute dominion of one man, and the barrier of the Constitution thus swept away from us all, no rampart now remains against the passions and the power of a majority of Congress, to protect from a like exportation or other more grievous punishment the minority of the same body, the legislatures, judges, governors, and counsellors of the states, nor their other peaceable inhabitants who may venture to reclaim the constitutional rights and liberties of the states and people, or who, for other causes, good or bad, may be obnoxious to the views, or marked by the suspicions of the President, or be thought dangerous to his or their elections, or other interests public or personal: that the friendless alien has indeed been selected as the safest subject of a first experiment; but the citizen will soon follow, or rather has already followed; for, already has a sedition-act marked him as its prey: that these and successive acts of the same character, unless arrested on the threshold, may tend to drive these states into revolution and blood, and will furnish new calumnies against republican governments, and new pretexts for those who wish it to be believed, that man cannot be governed but by a rod of iron: that it would be a dangerous delusion, were a confidence in the men of our choice, to silence our fears for the safety of our rights: that confidence is everywhere the parent of despotism; free government is founded in jealousy, and not in confidence; it is jealousy and not confidence which prescribes limited constitutions to bind down those whom we are obliged to trust with power: that our Constitution has accordingly fixed the limits to which and no further our confidence may go; and let the honest advocate of confidence read the alien and sedition-acts, and say if the Constitution has not been wise in fixing limits to the government it created, and whether we should be wise in destroying those limits? Let him say what the government is if it be not a tyranny, which the men of our choice have conferred on the President, and the President of our choice has assented to and accepted, over the friendly strangers, to whom the mild spirit of our country and its laws had pledged hospitality

and protection: that the men of our choice have more respected the bare suspicions of the President, than the solid rights of innocence, the claims of justification, the sacred force of truth, and the forms and substance of law and justice. In questions of power, then, let no more be heard of confidence in man, but bind him down from mischief, by the chains of the Constitution. That this commonwealth does, therefore, call on its co-states for an expression of their sentiments on the acts concerning aliens, and for the punishment of certain crimes herein before specified, plainly declaring whether these acts are or are not authorized by the Federal compact. And it doubts not that their sense will be so announced, as to prove their attachment unaltered to limited government, whether general or particular, and that the rights and liberties of their co-states, will be exposed to no dangers by remaining embarked on a common bottom with their own: That they will concur with this commonwealth in considering the said acts as so palpably against the Constitution, as to amount to an undisguised declaration, that the compact is not meant to be the measure of the powers of the general government, but that it will proceed in the exercise over these states of all powers whatsoever: That they will view this as seizing the rights of the states, and consolidating them in the hands of the general government with a power assumed to bind the states, (not merely in cases made federal,) but in all cases whatsoever, by laws made, not with their consent, but by others against their consent: That this would be to surrender the form of government we have chosen, and to live under one deriving its powers from its own will, and not from our authority; and that the co-states, recurring to their natural right in cases not made federal, will concur in declaring these acts void and of no force, and will each unite with this commonwealth, in requesting their repeal at the next session of Congress.

EDMUND BULLOCK, *S. H. R.*

JOHN CAMPBELL, *S. S. P. T.*

Passed the House of Representatives, Nov. 10th, 1798. In Senate, November 13th, 1798, unanimously concurred in.

Approved November 16th, 1798.

JAMES GARRARD, *G. K.*

By the Governor.

HARRY TOULMIN,
Secretary of State

Counter-resolutions of Other States

State of Delaware.
In the House of Representatives

Resolved, By the Senate and House of Representatives of the state of Delaware, in General Assembly met, That they consider the resolutions from the state of Virginia, as a very unjustifiable interference with the general government and constituted authorities of the United States, and of dangerous tendency, and therefore not a fit subject for the further consideration of the General Assembly.

Isaac Davis,
Speaker of Senate.
Stephen Lewis,
Speaker of House of Representatives.

Resolved, That the above resolutions be signed by the Speaker of the Senate, and by the Speaker of the House of Representatives; and that the Governor of this state be requested to forward the same to the Governor of the state of Virginia.

State of Rhode Island and Providence Plantations.
In General Assembly

Certain resolutions of the legislature of Virginia, passed on the twenty-first day of December last, being communicated to this Assembly,

1. *Resolved,* That in the opinion of this legislature, the second section of the third article of the Constitution of the United States, in these words, to wit: *The judicial power shall extend to all cases arising under the laws of the United States,* vests in the federal courts exclusively, and in the Supreme Court of the United States ultimately, the authority of deciding on the constitutionality of any act or law of the Congress of the United States.

2. *Resolved,* That for any state legislature to assume that authority would be,

1st. Blending together legislative and judicial powers.

2d. Hazarding an interruption of the peace of the states by civil discord, in case of a diversity of opinions among the state legislatures; each state having, in that case, no resort for vindicating its own opinion, but to the strength of its own arm.

3d. Submitting most important questions of law, to less competent tribunals; and

4th. An infraction of the Constitution of the United States, expressed in plain terms.

3. *Resolved,* That although, for the above reasons, this legislature, in their public capacity, do not feel themselves authorized to consider and decide on the constitutionality of the sedition and alien-laws (so called), yet they are called upon by the exigency of this occasion, to declare, that in their private opinions, these laws are within the powers delegated to Congress, and promotive of the welfare of the United States.

4. *Resolved,* That the Governor communicate these resolutions to the supreme executive of the state of Virginia, and, at the same time, express to him, that this legislature cannot contemplate, without extreme concern and regret, the many evil and fatal consequences which may flow from the very unwarrantable resolutions aforesaid of the legislature of Virginia, passed on the twenty-first day of December last.

Commonwealth of Massachusetts. In Senate

The Legislature of Massachusetts, having taken into serious consideration the resolutions of the state of Virginia, passed the 21st day of December last, and communicated by his excellency the Governor, relative to certain supposed infractions of the Constitution of the United States, by the government thereof, and being convinced that the Federal Constitution is calculated to promote the happiness, prosperity and safety of the people of these United States, and to maintain that union of the several states, so essential to the welfare of the whole; and, being bound by solemn oath to support and defend that Constitution, feel it unnecessary to make any professions of their attachment to it, or of their firm determination to support it against every aggression, foreign or domestic.

But they deem it their duty solemnly to declare, that while they hold sacred the principle, that the consent of the people is the only pure source of just and legitimate power, they cannot admit the right of the state legislatures to denounce the administration of that government to which the people themselves, by a solemn compact, have exclusively committed their national concerns: That, although a liberal and enlightened vigilance among the people is always to be cherished, yet an unreasonable jealousy of the men of their choice, and a recurrence to measures of extremity, upon groundless or trivial pretexts, have a strong tendency to destroy all rational liberty at home, and to deprive the United States of the most essential advantages in their relations abroad: That this Legislature are persuaded, that the decision of all cases in law and equity, arising under the Constitution of the United States, and the construction of all laws made in pursuance thereof, are exclusively vested by the people in the judicial courts of the United States.

That the people in that solemn compact, which is declared to be the supreme law of the land, have not constituted the state legislatures the judges of the acts or measures of the Federal Government, but have confided to them the power of proposing such amendments of the Constitution, as shall appear to them necessary to the interests, or conformable to the wishes of the people whom they represent.

That by this construction of the Constitution, an amicable and dispassionate remedy is pointed out for any evil which experience may prove to exist, and the peace and prosperity of the United States may be preserved without interruption.

But, should the respectable state of Virginia persist in the assumption of the right to declare the acts of the national government unconstitutional, and should she oppose successfully her force and will to those of the nation, the Constitution would be reduced to a mere cypher, to the form and pageantry of authority, without the energy of power. Every act of the Federal Government which thwarted the views, or checked the ambitious projects of a particular state, or of its leading and influential members, would be the object of opposition and of remonstrance; while the people, convulsed and confused by the conflict between two hostile jurisdictions, enjoying the protection of neither, would be wearied into a submission to some bold leader, who would establish himself on the ruins of both.

The Legislature of Massachusetts, although they do not themselves claim the right, nor admit the authority, of any of the state governments to decide upon the constitutionality of the acts of the Federal Government, still, lest their silence should be construed into disapprobation, or at best into a doubt of the constitutionality of the acts referred to by the state of Virginia; and, as the General Assembly of Virginia has called for an expression of their sentiments, do explicitly declare, that they consider the acts of Con-

gress, commonly called "the alien and sedition-acts," not only constitutional, but expedient and necessary: That the former act respects a description of persons whose rights were not particularly contemplated in the Constitution of the United States, who are entitled only to a temporary protection, while they yield a temporary allegiance: a protection, which ought to be withdrawn whenever they become "dangerous to the public safety," or are found guilty of "treasonable machinations" against the government: That Congress having been especially entrusted by the people with the general defence of the nation, had not only the right but were bound to protect it against internal, as well as external foes.

That the United States, at the time of passing the *act concerning aliens,* were threatened with actual invasion, had been driven by the unjust and ambitious conduct of the French government into warlike preparations, expensive and burdensome, and had then, within the bosom of the country, thousands of aliens, who, we doubt not, were ready to co-operate in any external attack.

It cannot be seriously believed, that the United States should have waited till the poniard had in fact been plunged. The removal of aliens is the usual preliminary of hostility, and is justified by the invariable usages of nations. Actual hostility had unhappily long been experienced, and a formal declaration of it the government had reason daily to expect. The law, therefore, was just and salutary, and no officer could, with so much propriety be entrusted with the execution of it, as the one in whom the Constitution has reposed the executive power of the United States.

The sedition-act, so called, is, in the opinion of this Legislature, equally defensible. The General Assembly of Virginia, in their resolve under consideration, observe, that when that state, by its convention, ratified the Federal Constitution, it expressly declared, "That, among other essential rights, the liberty of conscience and of the press cannot be cancelled, abridged, restrained or modified by any authority of the United States," and from its extreme anxiety to guard these rights from every possible attack of sophistry or ambition, with other states, recommended an amendment for that purpose; which amendment was, in due time, annexed to the Constitution; but they did not surely expect that the proceedings of their state convention were to explain the amendment adopted by the union. The words of that amendment, on this subject, are, "Congress shall make no law abridging the freedom of speech, or of the press."

The act complained of is no abridgment of the freedom of either. The genuine liberty of speech and the press, is the liberty to utter and publish the truth; but the constitutional right of the citizen to utter and publish the truth, is not to be confounded with the licentiousness in speaking and writing, that is only employed in propagating falsehood and slander. This freedom of the press has been explicitly secured by most, if not all the state constitutions; and of this provision there has been generally but one construction among enlightened men; that it is a security for the rational use and not the abuse of the press; of which the courts of law, the juries and people will judge: this right is not infringed, but confirmed and established by the late act of Congress.

By the Constitution, the legislative, executive, and judicial departments of government are ordained and established; and general enumerated powers vested in them respectively, including those which are prohibited to the several states. Certain powers are granted in general terms by the people to their General Government, for the purposes of their safety and protection. That government is not only empowered, but it is made their duty, to repel invasions and suppress insurrections; to guarantee to the several states a republican form of government; to protect each state against invasion, and, when applied to, against domestic violence; to hear and decide all cases in law and equity, arising under the Constitution, and under any treaty or law made in pursuance thereof; and all cases of admiralty and maritime jurisdiction, and relating to the law of nations. Whenever, therefore, it becomes necessary to effect any of the objects designated, it is perfectly consonant to all just rules of construction to infer, that the usual means and powers necessary to the attainment of that object, are also granted: but the Constitution has left no occasion to resort to implication for these powers; it has made an express grant of them, in the eighth section of the first article, which ordains, "That Congress shall have power to make all laws which shall be necessary and proper for carrying into execution the foregoing powers, and all other powers vested by the Constitution in the Government of the United States, or in any department or officer thereof."

This Constitution has established a supreme court of the United States, but has made no provision for its protection, even against such improper conduct in its presence, as might disturb its proceedings, unless expressed in the section before recited. But as no statute has been passed on this subject, this protection is, and has been for nine years past, uniformly found in the application of the principles and usages of the common law. The same protection may unquestionably be afforded by a statute passed in virtue of the before-mentioned section, as necessary and proper, for carrying into execution the powers vested in that department. A construction of the different parts of the Constitution, perfectly just and fair, will, on analogous principles, extend protection and security against the offences in question, to the other departments of government, in discharge of their respective trusts.

The President of the United States is bound by his oath "to preserve, protect, and defend the Constitution," and it is expressly made his duty "to take care that the laws be faithfully executed;" but this would be impracticable by any created being, if there could be no legal restraint of those scandalous misrepresentations of his measures and motives, which directly tend to rob him of the public confidence. And equally impotent would be every other public officer, if thus left to the mercy of the seditious.

It is holden to be a truth most clear, that the important trusts before enumerated, cannot be discharged by the government to which they are committed, without the power to restrain or punish seditious practices and unlawful combinations against itself, and to protect the officers thereof from abusive misrepresentations. Had the Constitution withheld this power, it would have made the government responsible for the effects, without any control over the causes which naturally produce them, and would have essentially failed of answering the great ends for which the people of the United States declare, in the first clause of that instrument, that they establish the same, viz: "To form a more perfect union, establish justice, insure domestic tranquillity, provide for the common defence, promote the general welfare, and secure the blessings of liberty to ourselves and posterity."

Seditious practices and unlawful combinations against the federal government, or any officer thereof, in the performance of his duty, as well as licentiousness of speech and of the press, were punishable on the principles of common law in the courts of the United States, before the act in question was passed. This act, then, is an amelioration of that law in favour of the party accused, as it mitigates the punishment which that authorizes, and admits of any investigation of public men and measures which is regulated by truth. It is not intended to protect men in office, only as they are agents of the people. Its object is to afford legal security to public offices and trusts created for the safety and happiness of the people, and therefore the security derived from it is for the benefit of the people, and is their right.

This construction of the Constitution, and of the existing law of the land, as well as the act complained of, the legislature of Massachusetts most deliberately and firmly believe, results from a just and full view of the several parts of that Constitution; and they consider that act to be wise and necessary, as an audacious and unprincipled spirit of falsehood and abuse had been too long unremittingly exerted for the purpose of perverting public opinion, and threatened to undermine and destroy the whole fabric of the government.

The legislature further declare, that in the foregoing sentiments they have expressed the general opinion of their constituents, who have not only acquiesced without complaint in those particular measures of the federal government, but have given their explicit approbation by re-electing those men who voted for the adoption of them: nor is it apprehended, that the citizens of this state will be accused of supineness, or of an indifference to their constitutional rights; for, while on the one hand, they regard with due vigilance, the conduct of the government: on the other, their freedom, safety, and happiness require, that they should defend that government and its constitutional measures against the open or insidious attacks of any foe, whether foreign or domestic.

And lastly, that the Legislature of Massachusetts feel a strong conviction, that the several United States are connected by a common interest, which ought to render their union indissoluble, and that this state will always cooperate with its confederate states, in rendering that union productive of mutual security, freedom and happiness.

Sent down for concurrence.

SAMUEL PHILIPS, President.

In the House of Representatives, Feb. 13, 1799. Read and concurred.

EDWARD ROBBINS, Speaker.

State of New York. In Senate

Whereas the people of the United States have established for themselves a free and independent national govern-

ment. And whereas it is essential to the existence of every government, that it have authority to defend and preserve its constitutional powers inviolate, inasmuch as every infringement thereof tends to its subversion. And whereas the judicial power extends expressly to all cases of law and equity arising under the Constitution and the laws of the United States, whereby the interference of the legislatures of the particular states in those cases, is manifestly excluded. And whereas our peace, prosperity, and happiness eminently depend on the preservation of the Union, in order to which, a reasonable confidence in the constituted authorities and chosen representatives of the people is indispensable. And whereas every measure calculated to weaken that confidence, has a tendency to destroy the usefulness of our public functionaries, and to excite jealousies equally hostile to rational liberty and the principles of a good republican government. And whereas the Senate, not perceiving that the rights of the particular states have been violated, nor any unconstitutional powers assumed by the general government, cannot forbear to express the anxiety and regret with which they observe the inflammatory and pernicious sentiments and doctrines which are contained in the resolutions of the legislatures of Virginia and Kentucky; sentiments and doctrines no less repugnant to the Constitution of the United States, and the principles of their union, than destructive to the Federal Government, and unjust to those whom the people have elected to administer it: wherefore,

Resolved, That while the Senate feel themselves constrained to bear unequivocal testimony against such sentiments and doctrines, they deem it a duty no less indispensable, explicitly to declare their incompetency, as a branch of the legislature of this state, to supervise the acts of the general government.

Resolved, That his excellency the Governor be, and he is hereby requested to transmit a copy of the foregoing resolution to the executives of the states of Virginia and Kentucky, to the end that the same may be communicated to the legislatures thereof.

State of Connecticut

At a general assembly of the state of Connecticut, holden at Hartford, in the said state, on the second Thursday of May, Anno Domini, 1799, his excellency the Governor having communicated to this Assembly sundry resolutions of the legislature of Virginia, adopted in December 1798, which relate to the measures of the general government, and the said resolutions having been considered, it is

Resolved, That this Assembly views with deep regret, and explicitly disavows, the principles contained in the aforesaid resolutions; and particularly the opposition to the "alien and sedition-acts," acts, which the Constitution authorized; which the exigency of the country rendered necessary; which the constituted authorities have enacted, and which merit the entire approbation of this Assembly. They therefore decidedly refuse to concur with the legislature of Virginia, in promoting any of the objects attempted in the aforesaid resolutions.

And it is further *Resolved,* that his excellency the Governor be requested to transmit a copy of the foregoing resolution to the Governor of Virginia, that it may be communicated to the legislature of that state.

Passed in the House of Representatives unanimously.

Concurred unanimously, in the upper House.

State of New Hampshire.
In the House of Representatives

The committee to take into consideration the resolutions of the General Assembly of Virginia, dated December 21st, 1798; also certain resolutions of the Legislature of Kentucky, of the 10th November, 1798, report as follows:

The Legislature of New Hampshire having taken into consideration certain resolutions of the General Assembly of Virginia, dated December 21, 1798; also certain resolutions of the Legislature of Kentucky, of the 10th of November, 1798:

Resolved, That the Legislature of New Hampshire unequivocally express a firm resolution to maintain and defend the Constitution of the United States, and the Constitution of this state, against every aggression, either foreign or domestic, and that they will support the government of the United States in all measures warranted by the former.

That the state legislatures are not the proper tribunals to determine the constitutionality of the laws of the general government, that the duty of such decision is properly and exclusively confided to the judicial department.

That if the Legislature of New Hampshire, for mere speculative purposes, were to express an opinion on the acts of the general government, commonly called "the alien and sedition-bills," that opinion would unreservedly be, that those acts are constitutional, and in the present critical situation of our country, highly expedient.

That the constitutionality and expediency of the acts aforesaid, have been very ably advocated and clearly demonstrated by many citizens of the United States, more especially by the minority of the General Assembly of Virginia. The Legislature of New Hampshire, therefore, deem it unnecessary, by any train of arguments, to attempt further illustration of the propositions, the truth of which, it is confidently believed, at this day, is very generally seen and acknowledged.

Which report being read and considered, was unanimously received and accepted, one hundred and thirty-seven members being present.

Sent up for concurrence.

JOHN PRENTICE, Speaker

In Senate, the same day, read and concurred unanimously.

AMOS SHEPARD, President

Approved, June 15th, 1799.

J. T. GILMAN, Governor

State of Vermont.
In the House of Representatives

The House proceeded to take under their consideration, the resolutions of the General Assembly of Virginia, relative to certain measures of the general government, transmitted to the Legislature of this state, for their consideration: Whereupon,

Resolved, That the General Assembly of the state of Vermont do highly disapprove of the resolutions of the General Assembly of Virginia, as being unconstitutional in their nature, and dangerous in their tendency. It belongs not to state legislatures to decide on the constitutionality of laws made by the general government; this power being exclusively vested in the judiciary courts of the Union: That his excellency the Governor be requested to transmit a copy of this resolution to the executive of Virginia, to be communicated to the General Assembly of that state: And that the same be sent to the Governor and Council for their concurrence.

In Council, October 30, 1799.

Read and concurred unanimously.

Report of Virginia House of Delegates

Report of the committee to whom were referred the communications of various states relative to the resolutions of the General Assembly of this state, concerning the Alien and Sedition-Laws

Whatever room might be found in the proceedings of some of the states who have disapproved of the resolutions of the General Assembly of this commonwealth, passed on the 21st day of December, 1798, for painful remarks on the spirit and manner of those proceedings, it appears to the committee most consistent with the duty, as well as dignity of the General Assembly, to hasten an oblivion of every circumstance which might be construed into a diminution of mutual respect, confidence, and affection, among the members of the Union.

The committee have deemed it a more useful task, to revise, with a critical eye, the resolutions which have met with this disapprobation; to examine fully the several objections and arguments which have appeared against them; and to inquire whether there be any errors of fact, of principle, or of reasoning, which the candour of the General Assembly ought to acknowledge and correct.

The first of the resolutions is in the words following:

Resolved, That the General Assembly of Virginia doth unequivocally express a firm resolution to maintain and defend the Constitution of the United States, and the Constitution of this state, against every aggression, either foreign or domestic, and that they will support the government of the United States in all measures warranted by the former.

No unfavourable comment can have been made on the sentiments here expressed. To maintain and defend the Constitution of the United States, and of their own state, against every aggression, both foreign and domestic, and to support the government of the United States in all measures warranted by their Constitution, are duties which the General Assembly ought always to feel, and to which, on such an occasion, it was evidently proper to express its sincere and firm adherence.

In their next resolution—*The General Assembly most solemnly declares a warm attachment to the union of the states, to maintain which it pledges all its powers; and that, for this end, it is its duty to watch over and oppose every infraction of those principles, which constitute the only basis of that union, because a faithful observance of them can alone secure its existence and the public happiness.*

The observation just made is equally applicable to this solemn declaration, of warm attachment to the union, and this solemn pledge to maintain it; nor can any question arise among enlightened friends of the union, as to the duty of watching over and opposing every infraction of those principles which constitute its basis, and a faithful observance of which can alone secure its existence, and the public happiness thereon depending.

The third resolution is in the words following:

That this Assembly doth explicitly and peremptorily declare, that it views the powers of the Federal Government, as resulting from the compact, to which the states are parties, as limited by the plain sense and intention of the instrument constituting that compact; as no farther valid than they are authorized by the grants enumerated in that compact; and that in case of a deliberate, palpable and dangerous exercise of other powers, not granted by the said compact, the states who are parties thereto have the right, and are in duty bound, to interpose for arresting the progress of the evil, and for maintaining within their respective limits, the authorities, rights, and liberties appertaining to them.

On this resolution, the committee have bestowed all the attention which its importance merits; they have scanned it not merely with a strict, but with a severe eye; and they feel confidence in pronouncing, that, in its just and fair construction, it is unexceptionably true in its several positions, as well as constitutional and conclusive in its inferences.

The resolution declares, *first,* that "it views the powers of the Federal Government, as resulting from the compact to which the states are parties;" in other words, that the Federal powers are derived from the Constitution, and that the Constitution is a compact to which the states are parties.

Clear as the position must seem, that the federal powers are derived from the Constitution, and from that alone, the committee are not unapprised of a late doctrine, which opens another source of federal powers, not less extensive and important, than it is new and unexpected. The examination of this doctrine will be most conveniently connected with a review of a succeeding resolution. The committee satisfy themselves here with briefly remarking, that in all the cotemporary discussions and comments which the Constitution underwent, it was constantly justified and recommended, on the ground, that the powers not given to the government, were withheld from it; and that, if any doubt could have existed on this subject, under the original text of the Constitution, it is removed, as far as words could remove it, by the 12th amendment, now a part of the Constitution, which expressly declares, "that the powers not delegated to the United States, by the Constitution, nor prohibited by it to the states, are reserved to the states respectively, or to the people."

The other position involved in this branch of the resolution, namely, "that the states are parties to the Constitution or compact," is, in the judgment of the committee, equally free from objection. It is indeed true, that the term "states," is sometimes used in a vague sense, and sometimes in different senses, according to the subject to which it is applied. Thus, it sometimes means the separate sections of territory occupied by the political societies within each; sometimes the particular governments, established by those societies; sometimes those societies as organized into those particular governments; and, lastly, it means the people composing those political societies, in their highest sovereign capacity. Although it might be wished that the perfection of language admitted less diversity in the signification of the same words, yet little inconveniency is produced by it, where the true sense can be collected with certainty from the different applications. In the present instance, whatever different constructions of the term "states," in the resolution, may have been entertained, all will at least concur in that last mentioned; because, in that sense, the Constitution was submitted to the "states:" in that sense the "states" ratified it: and, in that sense of the term "states," they are consequently parties to the compact, from which the powers of the federal government result.

The next position is, that the General Assembly views the powers of the federal government, "as limited by the plain sense and intention of the instrument constituting that compact," and "as no farther valid than they are authorized by the grants therein enumerated." It does not seem possible, that any just objection can lie against either of these clauses. The first amounts merely to a declaration, that the compact ought to have the interpretation plainly intended by the parties to it; the other to a declaration, that it ought to have the execution and effect intended by them. If the powers granted, be valid, it is solely because they are granted: and, if the granted powers are valid, because granted, all other powers not granted, must not be valid.

The resolution, having taken this view of the federal compact, proceeds to infer, "that, in case of a deliberate, palpable, and dangerous exercise of other powers, not granted by the said compact, the states, who are parties thereto, have the right and are in duty bound to interpose for arresting the progress of the evil, and for maintaining within their respective limits, the authorities, rights, and liberties appertaining to them."

It appears to your committee to be a plain principle, founded in common sense, illustrated by common practice, and essential to the nature of compacts, that, where resort can be had to no tribunal, superior to the authority of the parties, the parties themselves must be the rightful judges in the last resort, whether the bargain made has been pursued or violated. The Constitution of the United States was formed by the sanction of the states, given by each in its sovereign capacity. It adds to the stability and dignity, as well as to the authority of the Constitution, that it rests on this legitimate and solid foundation. The states, then, being the parties to the constitutional compact, and in their sovereign capacity, it follows of necessity, that there can be no tribunal above their authority, to decide in the last resort, whether the compact made by them be violated; and, consequently, that, as the parties to it, they must themselves decide, in the last resort, such questions as may be of sufficient magnitude to require their interposition.

It does not follow, however, that because the states, as sovereign parties to their constitutional compact, must ultimately decide whether it has been violated, that such a decision ought to be interposed, either in a hasty manner, or on doubtful and inferior occasions. Even in the case of ordinary conventions between different nations, where, by the strict rule of interpretation, a breach of a part may be deemed a breach of the whole, every part being deemed a condition of every other part and of the whole, it is always laid down that the breach must be both wilful and material to justify an application of the rule. But in the case of an intimate and constitutional union, like that of the United States, it is evident that the interposition of the parties, in their sovereign capacity, can be called for by occasions only, deeply and essentially affecting the vital principles of their political system.

The resolution has accordingly guarded against any misapprehension of its object, by expressly requiring for such an interposition, "the case of a *deliberate, palpable,* and *dangerous* breach of the Constitution, by the exercise of *powers not granted* by it. It must be a case, not of a light and transient nature, but of a nature *dangerous* to the great purposes for which the Constitution was established. It must be a case, moreover, not obscure or doubtful in its construction, but plain and *palpable.* Lastly, it must be a case not resulting from a partial consideration, or hasty determination; but a case stamped with a final consideration and *deliberate* adherence. It is not necessary, because the resolution does not require that the question should be discussed, how far the exercise of any particular power, ungranted by the Constitution, would justify the interposition of the parties to it. As cases might easily be stated, which none would contend ought to fall within that description; cases, on the other hand, might, with equal ease, be stated, so flagrant and so fatal, as to unite every opinion in placing them within that description.

But the resolution has done more than guard against misconstruction, by expressly referring to cases of a *deliberate, palpable,* and *dangerous* nature. It specifies the object of the interposition which it contemplates, to be solely that of arresting the progress of the *evil* of usurpation, and of maintaining the authorities, rights, and liberties appertaining to the states, as parties to the Constitution.

From this view of the resolution, it would seem inconceivable that it can incur any just disapprobation from those who, laying aside all momentary impressions, and recollecting the genuine source and object of the Federal Constitution, shall candidly and accurately interpret the meaning of the General Assembly. If the deliberate exercise of dangerous powers, palpably withheld by the Constitution, could not justify the parties to it, in interposing even so far as to arrest the progress of the evil, and thereby to preserve the Constitution itself, as well as to provide for the safety of the parties to it, there would be an end to all relief from usurped power, and a direct subversion of the rights specified or recognised under all the state constitutions, as well as a plain denial of the fundamental principle on which our independence itself was declared.

But it is objected that the judicial authority is to be regarded as the sole expositor of the Constitution, in the last resort; and it may be asked for what reason, the declaration by the General Assembly, supposing it to be theoretically true, could be required at the present day and in so solemn a manner.

On this objection it might be observed, *first,* that there may be instances of usurped power, which the forms of the Constitution would never draw within the control of the judicial department; *secondly,* that if the decision of the judiciary be raised above the authority of the sovereign parties to the Constitution, the decisions of the other departments, not carried by the forms of the Constitution before the judiciary, must be equally authoritative and final with the decisions of that department. But the proper answer to the objection is, that the resolution of the General Assembly relates to those great and extraordinary cases, in which all the forms of the Constitution may prove ineffectual against infractions dangerous to the essential rights of the parties to it. The resolution supposes that dangerous powers, not delegated, may not only be usurped and executed by the other departments, but that the judicial department also may exercise or sanction dangerous powers beyond the grant of the Constitution; and, consequently, that the ultimate right of the parties to the Constitution, to judge whether the compact has been dangerously violated, must extend to violations by one delegated authority, as well as by another; by the judiciary, as well as by the executive, or the legislature.

However true, therefore, it may be, that the judicial department, is, in all questions submitted to it by the forms of the Constitution, to decide in the last resort, this resort must necessarily be deemed the last in relation to the authorities of the other departments of the government; not in relation to the rights of the parties to the constitutional compact, from which the judicial as well as the other departments hold their delegated trusts. On any other hypothesis, the delegation of judicial power would annul the authority delegating it; and the concurrence of this department with the others in usurped powers, might subvert for ever, and beyond the possible reach of any rightful remedy, the very Constitution which all were instituted to preserve.

The truth declared in the resolution being established, the expediency of making the declaration at the present day, may safely be left to the temperate consideration and candid judgment of the American public. It will be remembered that a frequent recurrence to fundamental principles, is solemnly enjoined by most of the state constitutions, and particularly by our own, as a necessary safeguard against the danger of degeneracy to which republics are liable, as well as other governments, though in a less degree than others. And a fair comparison of the political doctrines not unfrequent at the present day, with those which characterized the epoch of our revolution, and which form the basis of our republican constitutions, will best determine whether the declaratory recurrence here made to those principles, ought to be viewed as unseasonable and improper, or as a vigilant discharge of an important duty.

The authority of constitutions over governments, and of the sovereignty of the people over constitutions, are truths which are at all times necessary to be kept in mind; and at no time perhaps more necessary than at the present.

The fourth resolution stands as follows:

That the General Assembly doth also express its deep regret, that a spirit has in sundry instances, been manifested by the federal government, to enlarge its powers by forced constructions of the constitutional charter which defines them; and that indications have appeared of a design to expound certain general phrases, (which, having been copied from the very limited grant of powers in the former articles of confederation, were the less liable to be misconstrued,) so as to destroy the meaning and effect of the particular enumeration which necessarily explains, and limits the general phrases; and so as to consolidate the states, by degrees, into one sovereignty, the obvious tendency and inevitable result of which would be, to transform the present republican system of the United States into an absolute, or, at best, a mixed monarchy.

The *first* question here to be considered is, whether a spirit has in sundry instances been manifested by the Federal Government to enlarge its powers by forced constructions of the constitutional charter.

The General Assembly having declared its opinion merely by regretting in general terms that forced constructions for enlarging the federal powers have taken place, it does not appear to the committee necessary to go into a specification of every instance to which the resolution may allude. The alien and sedition-acts being particularly named in a succeeding resolution, are of course to be understood as included in the allusion. Omitting others which have less occupied public attention, or been less extensively regarded as unconstitutional, the resolution may be presumed to refer particularly to the bank law, which from the circumstances of its passage, as well as the latitude of construction on which it is founded, strikes the attention with singular force; and the carriage tax, distinguished also by circumstances in its history having a similar tendency. Those instances, alone, if resulting from forced construction and calculated to enlarge the powers of the Federal Government, as the committee cannot but conceive to be the case, sufficiently warrant this part of the resolution. The committee have not thought it incumbent on them to extend their attention to laws which have been objected to, rather as varying the constitutional distribution of powers in the Federal Government, than as an absolute

enlargement of them; because instances of this sort, however important in their principles and tendencies, do not appear to fall strictly within the text under review.

The other questions presenting themselves, are—
1. Whether indications have appeared of a design to expound certain general phrases copied from the "articles of confederation" so as to destroy the effect of the particular enumeration explaining and limiting their meaning. 2. Whether this exposition would by degrees consolidate the states into one sovereignty. 3. Whether the tendency and result of this consolidation would be to transform the republican system of the United States into a monarchy.

I. The general phrases here meant must be those "of providing for the common defence and general welfare."

In the "articles of confederation," the phrases are used as follows, in Art. VIII. "All charges of war, and all other expenses that shall be incurred *for the common defence and general welfare,* and allowed by the United States in Congress assembled, shall be defrayed out of a common treasury, which shall be supplied by the several states, in proportion to the value of all land within each state, granted to, or surveyed for any person, as such land and the buildings and improvements thereon shall be estimated, according to such mode as the United States in Congress assembled shall from time to time direct and appoint."

In the existing Constitution, they make the following part of Sec. 8, "The Congress shall have power to lay and collect taxes, duties, imposts, and excises, to pay the debts, and to provide for the common defence and general welfare of the United States."

This similarity in the use of these phrases in the two great federal charters, might well be considered, as rendering their meaning less liable to be misconstrued in the latter; because it will scarcely be said, that in the former they were ever understood to be either a general grant of power, or to authorize the requisition or application of money by the old Congress to the common defence and general welfare, except in the cases afterwards enumerated, which explained and limited their meaning; and if such was the limited meaning attached to these phrases in the very instrument revised and remodelled by the present Constitution, it can never be supposed that when copied into this Constitution, a different meaning ought to be attached to them.

That, notwithstanding this remarkable security against misconstruction, a design has been indicated to expound these phrases in the Constitution, so as to destroy the effect of the particular enumeration of powers by which it explains and limits them, must have fallen under the observation of those who have attended to the course of public transactions. Not to multiply proofs on this subject, it will suffice to refer to the debates of the federal legislature, in which arguments have on different occasions been drawn, with apparent effect, from these phrases, in their indefinite meaning.

To these indications might be added, without looking farther, the official report on manufactures, by the late Secretary of the Treasury, made on the 5th of December, 1791; and the report of a committee of Congress, in January, 1797, on the promotion of agriculture. In the first of these it is expressly contended to belong "to the discretion of the national legislature to pronounce upon the objects which concern the *general welfare,* and for which, under that description, an appropriation of money is requisite and proper. And there seems to be no room for a doubt, that whatever concerns the general interests of LEARNING, of AGRICULTURE, of MANUFACTURES, and of COMMERCE, are within the sphere of the national councils, *as far as regards the application of money.* The latter report assumes the same latitude of power in the national councils, and applies it to the encouragement of agriculture by means of a society to be established at the seat of government. Although neither of these reports may have received the sanction of a law carrying it into effect, yet, on the other hand, the extraordinary doctrine contained in both, has passed without the slightest positive mark of disapprobation from the authority to which it was addressed.

Now, whether the phrases in question be construed to authorize every measure relating to the common defence and general welfare, as contended by some; or every measure only in which there might be an application of money, as suggested by the caution of others; the effect must substantially be the same, in destroying the import and force of the particular enumeration of powers which follow these general phrases in the Constitution. For it is evident that there is not a single power whatever, which may not have some reference to the common defence, or the general welfare; nor a power of any magnitude, which, in its exercise, does not involve or admit an application of money. The government, therefore, which possesses power in either one or other of these extents, is a government without the lim-

itations formed by a particular enumeration of powers; and consequently, the meaning and effect of this particular enumeration is destroyed by the exposition given to these general phrases.

This conclusion will not be affected by an attempt to qualify the power over the "general welfare," by referring it to cases where the *general welfare* is beyond the reach of *separate* provisions by the *individual states;* and leaving to these their jurisdictions, in cases to which their separate provisions may be competent. For, as the authority of the individual states must in all cases be incompetent to general regulations operating through the whole, the authority of the United States would be extended to every object relating to the general welfare, which might, by any possibility, be provided for by the general authority. This qualifying construction, therefore, would have little, if any tendency, to circumscribe the power claimed under the latitude of the terms "general welfare."

The true and fair construction of this expression, both in the original and existing federal compacts, appears to the committee too obvious to be mistaken. In both, the Congress is authorized to provide money for the common defence and *general welfare.* In both, is subjoined to this authority, an enumeration of the cases to which their powers shall extend. Money cannot be applied to the *general welfare* otherwise than by an application of it to some *particular* measures, conducive to the general welfare. Whenever, therefore, money has been raised by the general authority, and is to be applied to a particular measure, a question arises whether the particular measure be within the enumerated authorities vested in Congress. If it be, the money requisite for it may be applied to it; if it be not, no such application can be made. This fair and obvious interpretation coincides with, and is enforced by the clause in the Constitution, which declares, that "no money shall be drawn from the treasury, but in consequence of appropriations by law." An appropriation of money to the general welfare would be deemed rather a mockery than an observance of this constitutional injunction.

2. Whether the exposition of the general phrases here combated would not, by degrees, consolidate the states into one sovereignty, is a question concerning which the committee can perceive little room for difference of opinion. To consolidate the states into one sovereignty, nothing more can be wanted, than to supersede their respective sov-

ereignties in the cases reserved to them, by extending the sovereignty of the United States, to all cases of the "general welfare," that is to say, to *all cases whatever.*

3. That the obvious tendency and inevitable result of a consolidation of the states into one sovereignty, would be to transform the republican system of the United States into a monarchy, is a point which seems to have been sufficiently decided by the general sentiment of America. In almost every instance of discussion, relating to the consolidation in question, its certain tendency to pave the way to monarchy seems not to have been contested. The prospect of such a consolidation has formed the only topic of controversy. It would be unnecessary, therefore, for the committee to dwell long on the reasons which support the position of the General Assembly. It may not be improper, however, to remark two consequences evidently flowing from an extension of the federal powers to every subject falling within the idea of the "general welfare."

One consequence must be, to enlarge the sphere of discretion allotted to the executive magistrate. Even within the legislative limits properly defined by the Constitution, the difficulty of accommodating legal regulations to a country so great in extent, and so various in its circumstances, has been much felt; and has led to occasional investments of power in the executive, which involve perhaps as large a portion of discretion as can be deemed consistent with the nature of the executive trust. In proportion as the objects of legislative care might be multiplied, would the time allowed for each be diminished, and the difficulty of providing uniform and particular regulations for all be increased. From these sources would necessarily ensue a greater latitude to the agency of that department which is always in existence, and which could best mould regulations of a general nature, so as to suit them to the diversity of particular situations. And it is in this latitude, as a supplement to the deficiency of the laws, that the degree of executive prerogative materially consists.

The other consequence would be that of an excessive augmentation of the offices, honours, and emoluments depending on the executive will. Add to the present legitimate stock, all those of every description which a consolidation of the states would take from them, and turn over to the Federal Government, and the patronage of the executive would necessarily be as much swelled in this case, as its prerogative would be in the other.

This disproportionate increase of prerogative and patronage must, evidently, either enable the chief magistrate of the Union, by quiet means, to secure his re-election from time to time, and finally, to regulate the succession as he might please; or, by giving so transcendent an importance to the office, would render the elections to it so violent and corrupt, that the public voice itself might call for an hereditary, in place of an elective succession. Whichever of these events might follow, the transformation of the republican system of the United States into a monarchy, anticipated by the General Assembly from a consolidation of the states into one sovereignty, would be equally accomplished; and whether it would be into a mixed or an absolute monarchy, might depend on too many contingencies to admit of any certain foresight.

The resolution next in order, is contained in the following terms:

That the General Assembly doth particularly protest against the palpable and alarming infractions of the Constitution, in the two late cases of the "alien and sedition-acts," passed at the last session of Congress; the first of which exercises a power nowhere delegated to the Federal Government; and which, by uniting legislative and judicial powers to those of executive, subverts the general principles of a free Government, as well as the particular organization and positive provisions of the Federal Constitution; and the other of which acts exercises, in like manner, a power not delegated by the Constitution; but, on the contrary, expressly and positively forbidden by one of the amendments thereto: a power which, more than any other, ought to produce universal alarm; because it is levelled against that right of freely examining public characters and measures, and of free communication among the people thereon, which has ever been justly deemed the only effectual guardian of every other right.

The subject of this resolution having, it is presumed, more particularly led the General Assembly into the proceedings which they communicated to the other states, and being in itself of peculiar importance, it deserves the most critical and faithful investigation; for the length of which no other apology will be necessary.

The subject divides itself into *first,* "The alien-act," *secondly,* "The sedition-act."

I. Of the "alien-act," it is affirmed by the resolution, 1st. That it exercises a power nowhere delegated to the Federal Government. 2d. That it unites legislative and judicial powers to those of the executive. 3d. That this union of power subverts the general principles of free government. 4th. That it subverts the particular organization and positive provisions of the Federal Constitution.

In order to clear the way for a correct view of the first position, several observations will be premised.

In the first place, it is to be borne in mind, that it being a characteristic feature of the Federal Constitution, as it was originally ratified, and an amendment thereto having precisely declared, "That the powers not delegated to the United States by the Constitution, nor prohibited by it to the states, are reserved to the states respectively, or to the people," it is incumbent in this, as in every other exercise of power by the Federal Government, to prove from the Constitution, that it grants the particular power exercised.

The next observation to be made is, that much confusion and fallacy have been thrown into question, by blending the two cases of *"aliens, members of a hostile nation; and aliens, members of friendly nations."* These two cases are so obviously and so essentially distinct, that it occasions no little surprise that the distinction should have been disregarded: and the surprise is so much the greater, as it appears that the two cases are actually distinguished by two separate acts of Congress, passed at the same session, and comprised in the same publication; the one providing for the case of "alien enemies;" the other "concerning aliens" indiscriminately; and consequently extending to aliens of every nation in peace and amity with the United States. With respect to alien enemies, no doubt has been intimated as to the federal authority over them; the Constitution having expressly delegated to Congress the power to declare war against any nation, and of course to treat it and all its members as enemies. With respect to aliens who are not enemies, but members of nations in peace and amity with the United States, the power assumed by the act of Congress is denied to be constitutional; and it is accordingly against this act, that the protest of the General Assembly is expressly and exclusively directed.

A third observation is, that were it admitted, as is contended, that the "act concerning aliens" has for its object not a *penal,* but a *preventive* justice, it would still remain to be proved that it comes within the constitutional power of the federal legislature; and if within its power, that the legislature has exercised it in a constitutional manner.

In the administration of preventive justice, the following principles have been held sacred: that some probable ground of suspicion be exhibited before some judicial authority; that it be supported by oath or affirmation; that the party may avoid being thrown into confinement, by finding pledges or sureties for his legal conduct sufficient in the judgment of some judicial authority; that he may have the benefit of a writ of *habeas corpus,* and thus obtain his release, if wrongfully confined; and that he may at any time be discharged from his recognizance, or his confinement, and restored to his former liberty and rights, on the order of the proper judicial authority, if it shall see sufficient cause.

All these principles of the only preventive justice known to American jurisprudence are violated by the alien-act. The ground of suspicion is to be judged of, not by any judicial authority, but by the executive magistrate alone; no oath or affirmation is required; if the suspicion be held reasonable by the President, he may order the suspected alien to depart the territory of the United States, without the opportunity of avoiding the sentence, by finding pledges for his future good conduct; as the President may limit the time of departure as he pleases, the benefit of the writ of *habeas corpus* may be suspended with respect to the party, although the Constitution ordains, that it shall not be suspended, unless when the public safety may require it in case of rebellion or invasion, neither of which existed at the passage of the act; and the party being under the sentence of the President, either removed from the United States, or being punished by imprisonment, or disqualification ever to become a citizen on conviction of not obeying the order of removal, he cannot be discharged from the proceedings against him, and restored to the benefits of his former situation, although the *highest judicial authority* should see the most sufficient cause for it.

But, in the last place, it can never be admitted, that the removal of aliens, authorized by the act, is to be considered, not as punishment for an offence, but as a measure of precaution and prevention. If the banishment of an alien from a country into which he has been invited, as the asylum most auspicious to his happiness; a country where he may have formed the most tender of connexions, where he may have vested his entire property, and acquired property of the real and permanent, as well as the movable and temporary kind; where he enjoys under the laws a greater share of the blessings of personal security and personal liberty than he can elsewhere hope for, and where he may have nearly completed his probationary title to citizenship; if, moreover, in the execution of the sentence against him, he is to be exposed, not only to the ordinary dangers of the sea, but to the peculiar casualties incident to a crisis of war, and of unusual licentiousness on that element, and possibly to vindictive purposes which his emigration itself may have provoked; if a banishment of this sort be not a punishment, and among the severest of punishments, it will be difficult to imagine a doom to which the name can be applied. And if it be a punishment, it will remain to be inquired, whether it can be constitutionally inflicted, on mere suspicion, by the single will of the executive magistrate, on persons convicted of no personal offence against the laws of the land, nor involved in any offence against the law of nations, charged on the foreign state of which they are members.

One argument offered in justification of this power exercised over aliens is, that the admission of them into the country being of favour, not of right, the favour is at all times revocable.

To this argument it might be answered, that allowing the truth of the inference, it would be no proof of what is required. A question would still occur, whether the Constitution had vested the discretionary power of admitting aliens in the federal government, or in the state governments.

But it cannot be a true inference, that because the admission of an alien is a favour, the favour may be revoked at pleasure. A grant of land to an individual may be of favour, not of right; but the moment the grant is made, the favour becomes a right, and must be forfeited before it can be taken away. To pardon a malefactor may be favour, but the pardon is not, on that account, the less irrevocable. To admit an alien to naturalization is as much a favour, as to admit him to reside in the country; yet it cannot be pretended, that a person naturalized can be deprived of the benefit, any more than a native citizen can be disfranchised.

Again, it is said, that aliens not being parties to the Constitution, the rights and privileges which it secures cannot be at all claimed by them.

To this reasoning, also, it might be answered, that although aliens are not parties to the Constitution, it does not follow that the Constitution has vested in Congress an absolute power over them. The parties to the Constitution may have granted, or retained, or modified the power over aliens, without regard to that particular consideration.

But a more direct reply is, that it does not follow, be-cause aliens are not parties to the Constitution, as citizens are parties to it, that whilst they actually conform to it, they have no right to its protection. Aliens are not more parties to the laws, than they are parties to the Constitution; yet, it will not be disputed, that as they owe, on one hand, a temporary obedience, they are entitled in return to their protection and advantage.

If aliens had no rights under the Constitution, they might not only be banished, but even capitally punished, without a jury or the other incidents to a fair trial. But so far has a contrary principle been carried, in every part of the United States, that except on charges of treason, an alien has, besides all the common privileges, the special one of being tried by a jury, of which one-half may be also aliens.

It is said, further, that by the law and practice of nations, aliens may be removed at discretion, for offences against the law of nations; that Congress are authorized to define and punish such offences; and that to be dangerous to the peace of society is, in aliens, one of those offences.

The distinction between alien enemies and alien friends, is a clear and conclusive answer to this argument. Alien enemies are under the law of nations, and liable to be punished for offences against it. Alien friends, except in the single case of public ministers, are under the municipal law, and must be tried and punished according to that law only.

This argument also, by referring the alien-act to the power of Congress to define and *punish* offences against the law of nations, yields the point that the act is of a *penal*, not merely of a preventive operation. It must, in truth, be so considered. And if it be a penal act, the punishment it inflicts, must be justified by some offence that deserves it.

Offences for which aliens, within the jurisdiction of a country, are punishable, are first, offences committed by the nation of which they make a part, and in whose offences they are involved: Secondly, offences committed by themselves alone, without any charge against the nation to which they belong. The first is the case of alien enemies; the second, the case of alien friends. In the first case, the offending nation can no otherwise be punished than by war, one of the laws of which authorizes the expulsion of such of its members, as may be found within the country, against which the offence has been committed. In the second case, the offence being committed by the individual, not by his nation, and against the municipal law, not against the law of nations, the individual only, and not the nation, is punishable; and the punishment must be conducted according to the municipal law, not according to the law of nations. Under this view of the subject, the act of Congress, for the removal of alien enemies, being conformable to the law of nations, is justified by the Constitution: and the "act," for the removal of alien friends, being repugnant to the constitutional principles of municipal law, is unjustifiable.

Nor is the act of Congress, for the removal of alien friends, more agreeable to the general practice of nations, than it is within the purview of the law of nations. The general practice of nations, distinguishes between alien friends and alien enemies. The latter it has proceeded against, according to the law of nations, by expelling them as enemies. The former it has considered as under a local and temporary allegiance, and entitled to a correspondent protection. If contrary instances are to be found in barbarous countries, under undefined prerogatives, or amid revolutionary dangers, they will not be deemed fit precedents for the government of the United States, even if not beyond its constitutional authority.

It is said, that Congress may grant letters of marque and reprisal; that reprisals may be made on persons, as well as property; and that the removal of aliens may be considered as the exercise in an inferior degree, of the general power of reprisal on persons.

Without entering minutely into a question that does not seem to require it, it may be remarked, that reprisal is a seizure of foreign persons or property, with a view to obtain that justice for injuries done by one state or its members, to another state or its members, for which, a refusal of the aggressor requires such a resort to force under the law of nations. It must be considered as an abuse of words to call the removal of persons from a country, a seizure or reprisal on them: nor is the distinction to be overlooked between reprisals on persons within the country and under the faith of its laws, and on persons out of the country.

But, laying aside these considerations, it is evidently impossible to bring the alien-act within the power of granting reprisals; since it does not allege or imply any injury received from any particular nation, for which this proceeding against its members was intended as a reparation. The proceeding is authorized against aliens *of every nation;* of nations charged neither with any similar proceeding against American citizens, nor with any injuries for which

justice might be sought, in the mode prescribed by the act. Were it true, therefore, that good causes existed for reprisals against one or more foreign nations, and that neither persons nor property of its members, under the faith of our laws, could plead an exemption, the operation of the act ought to have been limited to the aliens among us, belonging to such nations. To license reprisals against all nations, for aggressions charged on one only, would be a measure as contrary to every principle of justice and public law, as to a wise policy, and the universal practice of nations.

It is said, that the right of removing aliens is an incident to the power of war, vested in Congress by the Constitution.

This is a former argument in a new shape only; and is answered by repeating, that the removal of alien enemies is an incident to the power of war; that the removal of alien friends, is not an incident to the power of war.

It is said, that Congress are by the Constitution to protect each state against invasion; and that the means of *preventing* invasion are included in the power of protection against it.

The power of war in general, having been before granted by the Constitution, this clause must either be a mere specification for greater caution and certainty, of which there are other examples in the instrument, or be the injunction of a duty, superadded to a grant of the power. Under either explanation, it cannot enlarge the powers of Congress on the subject. The power and the duty to protect each state against an invading enemy, would be the same under the general power, if this regard to greater caution had been omitted.

Invasion is an operation of war. To protect against invasion is an exercise of the power of war. A power, therefore, not incident to war, cannot be incident to a particular modification of war. And as the removal of alien friends, has appeared to be no incident to a general state of war, it cannot be incident to a partial state, or a particular modification of war.

Nor can it ever be granted, that a power to act on a case when it actually occurs, includes a power over all the means that may *tend to prevent* the occurrence of the case. Such a latitude of construction would render unavailing every practicable definition of particular and limited powers. Under the idea of preventing war in general, as well as invasion in particular, not only an indiscriminate removal of all aliens might be enforced, but a thousand other things still more remote from the operations and precautions appurtenant to war, might take place. A bigoted or tyrannical nation might threaten us with war, unless certain religious or political regulations were adopted by us; yet it never could be inferred, if the regulations which would prevent war, were such as Congress had otherwise no power to make, that the power to make them would grow out of the purpose they were to answer. Congress have power to suppress insurrections, yet it would not be allowed to follow, that they might employ all the means tending to prevent them; of which a system of moral instruction for the ignorant, and of provident support for the poor, might be regarded as among the most efficacious.

One argument for the power of the general government to remove aliens, would have been passed in silence, if it had appeared under any authority inferior to that of a report, made during the last session of Congress, to the House of Representatives by a committee, and approved by the House. The doctrine on which this argument is founded, is of so new and so extraordinary a character, and strikes so radically at the political system of America, that it is proper to state it in the very words of the report.

"The act [concerning aliens] is said to be unconstitutional, because to remove aliens is a direct breach of the Constitution, which provides, by the 9th section of the 1st article, that the migration or importation of such persons as any of the states shall think proper to admit, shall not be prohibited by the Congress, prior to the year 1808."

Among the answers given to this objection to the constitutionality of the act, the following very remarkable one is extracted:

"Thirdly, that as the Constitution has *given to the states* no power to remove aliens, during the period of the limitation under consideration, in the mean time, on the construction assumed, there would be no authority in the country, empowered to send away dangerous aliens, which cannot be admitted."

The reasoning here used, would not in any view, be conclusive; because there are powers exercised by most other governments, which in the United States are withheld by the people, both from the general government, and from the state governments. Of this sort are many of the powers prohibited by the declarations of right prefixed to the constitutions, or by the clauses in the constitutions, in the nature of such declarations. Nay, so far is the political system

of the United States distinguishable from that of other countries, by the caution with which powers are delegated and defined, that in one very important case, even of commercial regulations and revenue, the power is absolutely locked up against the hands of both governments. A tax on exports can be laid by no constitutional authority whatever. Under a system thus peculiarly guarded, there could surely be no absurdity in supposing, that alien friends, who if guilty of treasonable machinations may be punished, or if suspected on probable grounds, may be secured by pledges or imprisonment, in like manner with permanent citizens, were never meant to be subjected to banishment by any arbitrary and unusual process, either under the one government or the other.

But, it is not the inconclusiveness of the general reasoning in this passage, which chiefly calls the attention to it. It is the principle assumed by it, that the powers held by the states, are given to them by the Constitution of the United States; and the inference from this principle, that the powers supposed to be necessary which are not so given to state governments, must reside in the government of the United States.

The respect, which is felt for every portion of the constituted authorities, forbids some of the reflections which this singular paragraph might excite; and they are the more readily suppressed, as it may be presumed, with justice perhaps, as well as candour, that inadvertence may have had its share in the error. It would be an unjustifiable delicacy, nevertheless, to pass by so portentous a claim, proceeding from so high an authority, without a monitory notice of the fatal tendencies with which it would be pregnant.

Lastly, it is said, that a law on the same subject with the alien-act, passed by this state originally in 1785, and re-enacted in 1792, is a proof that a summary removal of suspected aliens, was not heretofore regarded by the Virginia Legislature, as liable to the objections now urged against such a measure.

This charge against Virginia vanishes before the simple remark, that the law of Virginia relates to "suspicious persons being the subjects of any foreign power or state, who shall have *made a declaration of war,* or actually *commenced hostilities,* or from whom the President shall apprehend *hostile designs;*" whereas the act of Congress relates to aliens, being the subjects of foreign powers and states, who have *neither declared war, nor commenced hostilities, nor from whom hostile designs are apprehended.*

2. It is next affirmed of the alien act, that it unites legislative, judicial, and executive powers in the hands of the President.

However difficult it may be to mark, in every case, with clearness and certainty, the line which divides legislative power, from the other departments of power, all will agree, that the powers referred to these departments may be so general and undefined, as to be of a legislative, not of an executive or judicial nature; and may for that reason be unconstitutional. Details to a certain degree, are essential to the nature and character of a law; and on criminal subjects, it is proper, that details should leave as little as possible to the discretion of those who are to apply and to execute the law. If nothing more were required, in exercising a legislative trust, than a general conveyance of authority, without laying down any precise rules, by which the authority conveyed should be carried into effect; it would follow, that the whole power of legislation might be transferred by the legislature from itself, and proclamations might become substitutes for laws. A delegation of power in this latitude, would not be denied to be a union of the different powers.

To determine, then, whether the appropriate powers of the distinct departments are united by the act authorizing the executive to remove aliens, it must be inquired whether it contains such details, definitions and rules, as appertain to the true character of a law; especially, a law by which personal liberty is invaded, property deprived of its value to the owner, and life itself indirectly exposed to danger.

The alien-act declares, "that it shall be lawful for the President to order all such aliens as he shall judge *dangerous* to the peace and safety of the United States, or shall have reasonable ground to *suspect,* are concerned in any treasonable, or *secret machinations,* against the government thereof, to depart," &c.

Could a power be well given in terms less definite, less particular, and less precise? To be *dangerous to the public safety;* to be *suspected of secret machinations* against the government: these can never be mistaken for legal rules or certain definitions. They leave everything to the President. His will is the law.

But, it is not a legislative power only, that is given to the President. He is to stand in the place of the judiciary also. His suspicion is the only evidence which is to convict: his order, the only judgment which is to be executed.

Thus, it is the President whose will is to designate the offensive conduct; it is his will that is to ascertain the individuals on whom it is charged; and it is his will, that is to cause the sentence to be executed. It is rightly affirmed, therefore, that the act unites legislative and judicial powers to those of the executive.

3. It is affirmed, that this union of power subverts the general principles of free government.

It has become an axiom in the science of government, that a separation of the legislative, executive, and judicial departments, is necessary to the preservation of public liberty. Nowhere has this axiom been better understood in theory, or more carefully pursued in practice, than in the United States.

4. It is affirmed that such a union of powers subverts the particular organization and positive provisions of the Federal Constitution.

According to the particular organization of the Constitution, its legislative powers are vested in the Congress, its executive powers in the President, and its judicial powers in a supreme and inferior tribunals. The union of any two of these powers, and still more of all three, in any one of these departments, as has been shown to be done by the alien-act, must consequently subvert the constitutional organization of them.

That positive provisions, in the Constitution, securing to individuals the benefits of fair trial, are also violated by the union of powers in the alien-act, necessarily results from the two facts, that the act relates to alien friends, and that alien friends being under the municipal law only, are entitled to its protection.

II. The *second* object against which the resolution protests, is the sedition-act.

Of this act it is affirmed, 1. That it exercises in like manner a power not delegated by the Constitution. 2. That the power, on the contrary, is expressly and positively forbidden by one of the amendments to the Constitution. 3. That this is a power, which more than any other ought to produce universal alarm; because it is levelled against that right of freely examining public characters and measures, and of free communication thereon, which has ever been justly deemed the only effectual guardian of every other right.

1. That it exercises a power not delegated by the Constitution.

Here again, it will be proper to recollect, that the Federal Government being composed of powers specifically granted, with a reservation of all others to the states or to the people, the positive authority under which the sedition-act could be passed must be produced by those who assert its constitutionality. In what part of the Constitution, then, is this authority to be found?

Several attempts have been made to answer this question, which will be examined in their order. The committee will begin with one, which has filled them with equal astonishment and apprehension; and which, they cannot but persuade themselves, must have the same effect on all, who will consider it with coolness and impartiality, and with a reverence for our Constitution, in the true character in which it issued from the sovereign authority of the people. The committee refer to the doctrine lately advanced as a sanction to the sedition-act, "that the common or unwritten law," a law of vast extent and complexity, and embracing almost every possible subject of legislation, both civil and criminal, makes a part of the law of these states, in their united and national capacity.

The novelty and, in the judgment of the committee, the extravagance of this pretension, would have consigned it to the silence in which they have passed by other arguments, which an extraordinary zeal for the act has drawn into the discussion: But the auspices under which this innovation presents itself, have constrained the committee to bestow on it an attention, which other considerations might have forbidden.

In executing the task, it may be of use to look back to the colonial state of this country, prior to the Revolution; to trace the effects of the Revolution which converted the colonies into independent states; to inquire into the import of the articles of confederation, the first instrument by which the union of the states was regularly established; and finally, to consult the Constitution of 1788, which is the oracle that must decide the important question.

In the state, prior to the Revolution, it is certain that the common law, under different limitations, made a part of the colonial codes. But whether it be understood that the original colonists brought the law with them, or made it their law by adoption; it is equally certain, that it was the separate law of each colony within its respective limits, and was unknown to them, as a law pervading and operating through the whole, as one society.

It could not possibly be otherwise. The common law was not the same in any two of the colonies; in some, the modifications were materially and extensively different. There was no common legislature, by which a common will could be expressed in the form of a law; nor any common magistracy, by which such a law could be carried into practice. The will of each colony, alone and separately, had its organs for these purposes.

This stage of our political history furnishes no foothold for the patrons of this new doctrine.

Did then the principle or operation of the great event which made the colonies independent states, imply or introduce the common law as a law of the Union?

The fundamental principle of the Revolution was, that the colonies were co-ordinate members with each other, and with Great Britain, of an empire, united by a common executive sovereign, but not united by any common legislative sovereign. The legislative power was maintained to be as complete in each American parliament, as in the British parliament. And the royal prerogative was in force in each colony, by virtue of its acknowledging the king for its executive magistrate, as it was in Great Britain, by virtue of a like acknowledgment there. A denial of these principles by Great Britain, and the assertion of them by America, produced the Revolution.

There was a time, indeed, when an exception to the legislative separation of the several component and coequal parts of the empire obtained a degree of acquiescence. The British parliament was allowed to regulate the trade with foreign nations, and between the different parts of the empire. This was, however, mere practice without right, and contrary to the true theory of the Constitution. The conveniency of some regulations, in both those cases, was apparent; and as there was no legislature with power over the whole, nor any constitutional pre-eminence among the legislatures of the several parts, it was natural for the legislature of that particular part which was the eldest and the largest, to assume this function, and for the others to acquiesce in it. This tacit arrangement was the less criticised, as the regulations established by the British parliament operated in favour of that part of the empire which seemed to bear the principal share of the public burdens, and were regarded as an indemnification of its advances for the other parts. As long as this regulating power was confined to the two objects of conveniency and equity, it was not complained of, nor much inquired into. But, no sooner was it perverted to the selfish views of the party assuming it, than the injured parties began to feel and to reflect; and the moment the claim to a direct and indefinite power was ingrafted on the precedent of the regulating power, the whole

charm was dissolved, and every eye opened to the usurpation. The assertion by Great Britain of a power to make
laws for the other members of the empire *in all cases whatsoever,* ended in the discovery that she had a right to make
laws for them *in no cases whatsoever.*

Such being the ground of our Revolution, no support
nor colour can be drawn from it, for the doctrine that the
common law is binding on these states as one society. The
doctrine, on the contrary, is evidently repugnant to the
fundamental principle of the Revolution.

The articles of confederation are the next source of information on this subject.

In the interval between the commencement of the Revolution and the final ratification of these articles, the nature
and extent of the Union was determined by the circumstances of the crisis, rather than by any accurate delinea-
tion of the general authority. It will not be alleged, that the
"common law" could have had any legitimate birth as a law
of the United States during that state of things. If it came,
as such, into existence at all, the charter of confederation
must have been its parent.

Here again, however, its pretensions are absolutely destitute of foundation. This instrument does not contain a
sentence or syllable that can be tortured into a countenance of the idea, that the parties to it were, with respect
to the objects of the common law, to form one community.
No such law is named or implied, or alluded to as being in
force, or as brought into force by that compact. No provision is made by which such a law could be carried into operation; whilst, on the other hand, every such inference
or pretext is absolutely precluded by Article 2d, which declares, "that each state retains its sovereignty, freedom, and
independence, and every power, jurisdiction, and right,
which is not by this confederation expressly delegated to
the United States, in Congress assembled."

Thus far it appears that not a vestige of this extraordinary doctrine can be found in the origin or progress of
American institutions. The evidence against it has, on the
contrary, grown stronger at every step, till it has amounted
to a formal and positive exclusion, by written articles of
compact among the parties concerned.

Is this exclusion revoked, and the common law introduced as a national law, by the present Constitution of the
United States? This is the final question to be examined.

It is readily admitted, that particular parts of the common law may have a sanction from the Constitution, so
far as they are necessarily comprehended in the technical phrases which express the powers delegated to the
government; and so far also, as such other parts may be
adopted by Congress as necessary and proper for carrying into execution the powers expressly delegated. But, the
question does not relate to either of these portions of the
common law. It relates to the common law beyond these
limitations.

The only part of the Constitution which seems to have
been relied on in this case is the 2d Sect. of Art. III.
"The judicial power shall extend to all cases *in law and equity,* arising *under this Constitution,* the laws of the United
States, and treaties made or which shall be made under
their authority."

It has been asked what cases, distinct from those arising
under the laws and treaties of the United States, can arise
under the Constitution, other than those arising under the
common law; and it is inferred, that the common law is accordingly adopted or recognised by the Constitution.

Never, perhaps, was so broad a construction applied to
a text so clearly unsusceptible of it. If any colour for the
inference could be found, it must be in the impossibility of
finding any other cases in law and equity, within the provision of the Constitution, to satisfy the expression; and
rather than resort to a construction affecting so essentially
the whole character of the government, it would perhaps
be more rational to consider the expression as a mere pleo-
nasm, or inadvertence. But, it is not necessary to decide on
such a dilemma. The expression is fully satisfied, and its
accuracy justified, by two descriptions of cases, to which
the judicial authority is extended, and neither of which implies that the common law is the law of the United States.
One of these descriptions comprehends the cases growing
out of the restrictions on the legislative power of the states.
For example, it is provided that "no state shall emit bills
of credit," or "make anything but gold and silver coin a
tender in payment of debts." Should this prohibition be violated, and a suit *between citizens of the same state* be the
consequence, this would be a case arising under the Constitution, before the judicial power of the United States.
A second description comprehends suits between citizens
and foreigners, or citizens of different states, to be decided
according to the state or foreign laws; but submitted by the
Constitution to the judicial power of the United States;
the judicial power being, in several instances, extended beyond the legislative power of the United States.

To this explanation of the text, the following observations may be added:

The expression, "cases in law and equity," is manifestly confined to cases of a civil nature; and would exclude cases of criminal jurisdiction. Criminal cases in law and equity would be a language unknown to the law.

The succeeding paragraph of the same section is in harmony with this construction. It is in these words: "In all cases affecting ambassadors, other public ministers, and consuls, and those in which a state shall be a party, the Supreme Court shall have original jurisdiction. *In all* the other cases [including cases in law and equity arising under the Constitution] the Supreme Court shall have *appellate* jurisdiction both as to law and *fact;* with such exceptions, and under such regulations, as Congress shall make."

This paragraph, by expressly giving an *appellate* jurisdiction, in cases of law and equity arising under the Constitution, to *fact,* as well as to law, clearly excludes criminal cases, where the trial by jury is secured; because the fact, in such cases, is not a subject of appeal. And, although the appeal is liable to such *exceptions* and regulations as Congress may adopt, yet it is not to be supposed that an *exception* of *all* criminal cases could be contemplated; as well because a discretion in Congress to make or omit the exception would be improper, as because it would have been unnecessary. The exception could as easily have been made by the Constitution itself, as referred to the Congress.

Once more; the amendment last added to the Constitution, deserves attention, as throwing light on this subject. "The judicial power of the United States shall not be construed to extend to any suit in *law* or *equity,* commenced or prosecuted against one of the United States, by citizens of another state, or by citizens or subjects of any foreign power." As it will not be pretended that any criminal proceeding could take place against a state, the terms *law* or *equity,* must be understood as appropriate to *civil,* in exclusion of *criminal* cases.

From these considerations, it is evident, that this part of the Constitution, even if it could be applied at all to the purpose for which it has been cited, would not include any cases whatever of a criminal nature; and consequently, would not authorize the inference from it, that the judicial authority extends to *offences* against the common law, as offences arising under the Constitution.

It is further to be considered, that even if this part of the Constitution could be strained into an application to every common law case, criminal as well as civil, it could have no effect in justifying the sedition-act, which is an exercise of legislative, and not of judicial power: and it is the judicial power only, of which the extent is defined in this part of the Constitution.

There are two passages in the Constitution, in which a description of the law of the United States is found. The first is contained in Art. III. sect. 2, in the words following: "This Constitution, the laws of the United States, and treaties made, or which shall be made under their authority." The second is contained in the second paragraph of Art. VI. as follows: "This Constitution, and the laws of the United States which shall be made in pursuance thereof, and all treaties made, or which shall be made, under the authority of the United States, shall be the supreme law of the land." The first of these descriptions was meant as a guide to the judges of the United States; the second, as a guide to the judges in the several states. Both of them consist of an enumeration, which was evidently meant to be precise and complete. If the common law had been understood to be a law of the United States, it is not possible to assign a satisfactory reason why it was not expressed in the enumeration.

In aid of these objections, the difficulties and confusion inseparable from a constructive introduction of the common law, would afford powerful reasons against it.

Is it to be the common law with or without the British statutes?

If without the statutory amendments, the vices of the code would be insupportable.

If with these amendments, what period is to be fixed for limiting the British authority over our laws?

Is it to be the date of the eldest or the youngest of the colonies?

Or are the dates to be thrown together, and a medium deduced?

Or is our independence to be taken for the date?

Is, again, regard to be had to the various changes in the common law made by the local codes of America?

Is regard to be had to such changes, subsequent, as well as prior, to the establishment of the Constitution?

Is regard to be had to future, as well as past changes?

Is the law to be different in every state, as differently modified by its code; or are the modifications of any particular state to be applied to all?

And on the latter supposition, which among the state codes would form the standard?

Questions of this sort might be multiplied with as much ease, as there would be difficulty in answering them.

The consequences flowing from the proposed construction, furnish other objections equally conclusive; unless the text were peremptory in its meaning, and consistent with other parts of the instrument.

These consequences may be in relation to the legislative authority of the United States; to the executive authority; to the judicial authority; and to the governments of the several states.

If it be understood, that the common law is established by the Constitution, it follows that no part of the law can be altered by the legislature; such of the statutes already passed, as may be repugnant thereto would be nullified; particularly the "sedition-act" itself, which boasts of being a melioration of the common law; and the whole code, with all its incongruities, barbarisms, and bloody maxims, would be inviolably saddled on the good people of the United States.

Should this consequence be rejected, and the common law be held, like other laws, liable to revision and alteration, by the authority of Congress, it then follows, that the authority of Congress is co-extensive with the objects of common law; that is to say, with every object of legislation: for to every such object does some branch or other of the common law extend. The authority of Congress would, therefore, be no longer under the limitations marked out in the Constitution. They would be authorized to legislate in all cases whatsoever.

In the next place, as the President possesses the executive powers of the Constitution, and is to see that the laws be faithfully executed, his authority also must be coextensive with every branch of the common law. The additions which this would make to his power, though not readily to be estimated, claim the most serious attention.

This is not all; it will merit the most profound consideration, how far an indefinite admission of the common law, with a latitude in construing it, equal to the construction by which it is deduced from the Constitution, might draw after it the various prerogatives making part of the unwritten law of England. The English constitution itself is nothing more than a composition of unwritten laws and maxims.

In the third place, whether the common law be admitted as of legal or of constitutional obligation, it would con-fer on the judicial department a discretion little short of a legislative power.

On the supposition of its having a constitutional obligation, this power in the judges would be permanent and irremediable by the legislature. On the other supposition, the power would not expire, until the legislature should have introduced a full system of statutory provisions. Let it be observed, too, that besides all the uncertainties above enumerated, and which present an immense field for judicial discretion, it would remain with the same department to decide what parts of the common law would, and what would not, be properly applicable to the circumstances of the United States.

A discretion of this sort has always been lamented as incongruous and dangerous, even in the colonial and state courts; although so much narrowed by positive provisions in the local codes on all the principal subjects embraced by the common law. Under the United States, where so few laws exist on those subjects, and where so great a lapse of time must happen before the vast chasm could be supplied, it is manifest that the power of the judges over the law would, in fact, erect them into legislators; and that, for a long time, it would be impossible for the citizens to conjecture, either what was, or would be law.

In the last place, the consequence of admitting the common law as the law of the United States, on the authority of the individual states, is as obvious as it would be fatal. As this law relates to every subject of legislation, and would be paramount to the constitutions and laws of the states, the admission of it would overwhelm the residuary sovereignty of the states, and by one constructive operation, new-model the whole political fabric of the country.

From the review thus taken of the situation of the American colonies prior to their independence; of the effect of this event on their situation; of the nature and import of the articles of confederation; of the true meaning of the passage in the existing Constitution from which the common law has been deduced; of the difficulties and uncertainties incident to the doctrine; and of its vast consequences in extending the powers of the Federal Government, and in superseding the authorities of the state governments; the committee feel the utmost confidence in concluding, that the common law never was, nor, by any fair construction, ever can be, deemed a law for the American people as one community; and they indulge the strongest expectation that the same conclusion will finally be drawn, by all candid and accurate inquirers into the subject. It is indeed distressing to reflect, that it ever should have been made a question, whether the Constitution, on the whole face of which is seen so much labour to enumerate and define the several objects of federal power, could intend to introduce in the lump, in an indirect manner, and by a forced construction of a few phrases, the vast and multifarious jurisdiction involved in the common law; a law filling so many ample volumes; a law overspreading the entire field of legislation; and a law that would sap the foundation of the Constitution as a system of limited and specified powers. A severer reproach could not, in the opinion of the committee, be thrown on the Constitution, on those who framed, or on those who established it, than such a supposition would throw on them.

The argument, then, drawn from the common law, on the ground of its being adopted or recognised by the Constitution, being inapplicable to the sedition-act, the committee will proceed to examine the other arguments which have been founded on the Constitution.

They will waste but little time on the attempt to cover the act by the preamble to the Constitution; it being contrary to every acknowledged rule of construction, to set up this part of an instrument, in opposition to the plain meaning expressed in the body of the instrument. A preamble usually contains the general motives or reasons, for the particular regulations or measures which follow it; and is always understood to be explained and limited by them. In the present instance, a contrary interpretation would have the inadmissible effect, of rendering nugatory or improper every part of the Constitution which succeeds the preamble.

The paragraph in Art. I. sect. 8, which contains the power to lay and collect taxes, duties, imposts, and excise; to pay the debts, and provide for the common defence and general welfare, having been already examined, will also require no particular attention in this place. It will have been seen that in its fair and consistent meaning, it cannot enlarge the enumerated powers vested in Congress.

The part of the Constitution which seems most to be recurred to, in defence of the "sedition-act," is the last clause of the above section, empowering Congress "to make all laws which shall be necessary and proper for carrying into execution the foregoing powers, and all other powers vested

by this Constitution in the government of the United States, or in any department or officer thereof."

The plain import of this clause is, that Congress shall have all the incidental or instrumental powers necessary and proper for carrying into execution all the express powers; whether they be vested in the government of the United States, more collectively, or in the several departments or officers thereof. It is not a grant of new powers to Congress, but merely a declaration, for the removal of all uncertainty, that the means of carrying into execution, those otherwise granted, are included in the grant.

Whenever, therefore, a question arises concerning the constitutionality of a particular power, the first question is, whether the power be expressed in the Constitution. If it be, the question is decided. If it be not expressed, the next inquiry must be, whether it is properly an incident to an express power, and necessary to its execution. If it be, it may be exercised by Congress. If it be not, Congress cannot exercise it.

Let the question be asked, then, whether the power over the press, exercised in the "sedition-act," be found among the powers expressly vested in the Congress? This is not pretended.

Is there any express power, for executing which it is a necessary and proper power?

The power which has been selected, as least remote, in answer to this question, is that of "suppressing insurrections;" which is said to imply a power to *prevent* insurrections, by punishing whatever may *lead* or *tend* to them. But, it surely cannot, with the least plausibility, be said, that a regulation of the press, and a punishment of libels, are exercises of a power to suppress insurrections. The most that could be said, would be, that the punishment of libels, if it had the tendency ascribed to it, might prevent the occasion of passing or executing laws necessary and proper for the suppression of insurrections.

Has the Federal Government no power, then, to prevent as well as to punish resistance to the laws?

They have the power, which the Constitution deemed most proper, in their hands for the purpose. The Congress has power before it happens, to pass laws for punishing it; and the executive and judiciary have power to enforce those laws when it does happen.

It must be recollected by many, and could be shown to the satisfaction of all, that the construction here put on the terms "necessary and proper," is precisely the construction which prevailed during the discussions and ratifications of the Constitution. It may be added, and cannot too often be repeated, that it is a construction absolutely necessary to maintain their consistency with the peculiar character of the government, as possessed of particular and defined powers only; not of the general and indefinite powers vested in ordinary governments. For, if the power to *suppress insurrection,* includes a power to *punish libels;* or if the power to *punish,* includes a power to *prevent,* by all the means that may have that *tendency;* such is the relation and influence among the most remote subjects of legislation, that a power over a very few, would carry with it a power over all. And it must be wholly immaterial, whether unlimited powers be exercised under the name of unlimited powers, or be exercised under the name of unlimited means of carrying into execution limited powers.

This branch of the subject will be closed with a reflection which must have weight with all; but more especially with those who place peculiar reliance on the judicial exposition of the Constitution, as the bulwark provided against undue extensions of the legislative power. If it be understood that the powers implied in the specified powers, have an immediate and appropriate relation to them, as means, necessary and proper for carrying them into execution, questions on the constitutionality of laws passed for this purpose, will be of a nature sufficiently precise and determinate for judicial cognizance and control! If, on the other hand, Congress are not limited in the choice of means by any such appropriate relation of them to the specified powers; but may employ all such means as they may deem fitted to *prevent,* as well as to *punish,* crimes subjected to their authority; such as may have a *tendency* only to *promote* an object for which they are authorized to provide; every one must perceive, that questions relating to means of this sort, must be questions of mere policy and expediency, on which legislative discretion alone can decide, and from which the judicial interposition and control are completely excluded.

2. The next point which the resolution requires to be proved, is, that the power over the press exercised by the sedition-act, is positively forbidden by one of the amendments to the Constitution.

The amendment stands in these words—"Congress shall make no law respecting an establishment of religion, or prohibiting the free exercise thereof, *or abridging the freedom of speech or of the press;* or the right of the people peaceably to assemble, and to petition the government for a redress of grievances."

In the attempts to vindicate the "sedition-act," it has been contended, 1. That the "freedom of the press" is to be determined by the meaning of these terms in the common law. 2. That the article supposes the power over the press to be in Congress, and prohibits them only from *abridging* the freedom allowed to it by the common law.

Although it will be shown, in examining the second of these positions, that the amendment is a denial to Congress of all power over the press, it may not be useless to make the following observations on the first of them.

It is deemed to be a sound opinion, that the sedition-act, in its definition of some of the crimes created, is an abridgment of the freedom of publication, recognised by principles of the common law in England.

The freedom of the press under the common law, is, in the defences of the sedition-act, made to consist in an exemption from all *previous* restraint on printed publications, by persons authorized to inspect and prohibit them. It appears to the committee, that this idea of the freedom of the press, can never be admitted to be the American idea of it: since a law inflicting penalties on printed publications, would have a similar effect with a law authorizing a previous restraint on them. It would seem a mockery to say, that no law should be passed, preventing publications from being made, but that laws might be passed for punishing them in case they should be made.

The essential difference between the British government, and the American constitutions, will place this subject in the clearest light.

In the British government, the danger of encroachments on the rights of the people, is understood to be confined to the executive magistrate. The representatives of the people in the legislature, are not only exempt themselves, from distrust, but are considered as sufficient guardians of the rights of their constituents against the danger from the executive. Hence it is a principle, that the parliament is unlimited in its power; or, in their own language, is omnipotent. Hence, too, all the ramparts for protecting the rights of the people, such as their magna charta, their bill of rights, &c., are not reared against the parliament, but against the royal prerogative. They are merely legislative precautions against executive usurpations. Under such a government as this, an exemption of the press from previous restraint by licensers appointed by the king, is all the freedom that can be secured to it.

In the United States, the case is altogether different. The people, not the government, possess the absolute sovereignty. The legislature, no less than the executive, is under limitations of power. Encroachments are regarded as possible from the one, as well as from the other. Hence, in the United States, the great and essential rights of the people are secured against legislative, as well as against executive ambition. They are secured, not by laws paramount to prerogative, but by constitutions paramount to laws. This security of the freedom of the press requires, that it should be exempt, not only from previous restraint by the executive, as in Great Britain, but from legislative restraint also; and this exemption, to be effectual, must be an exemption not only from the previous inspection of licensers, but from the subsequent penalty of laws.

The state of the press, therefore, under the common law, cannot, in this point of view, be the standard of its freedom in the United States.

But there is another view, under which it may be necessary to consider this subject. It may be alleged, that although the security for the freedom of the press, be different in Great Britain and in this country; being a legal security only in the former, and a constitutional security in the latter; and although there may be a further difference, in an extension of the freedom of the press here, beyond an exemption from previous restraint, to an exemption from subsequent penalties also; yet that the actual legal freedom of the press, under the common law, must determine the degree of freedom which is meant by the terms, and which is constitutionally secured against both previous and subsequent restraints.

The committee are not unaware of the difficulty of all general questions, which may turn on the proper boundary between the liberty and licentiousness of the press. They will leave it therefore for consideration only, how far the difference between the nature of the British government, and the nature of the American governments, and the practice under the latter, may show the degree of rigour in the former to be inapplicable to, and not obligatory in the latter.

The nature of governments elective, limited, and responsible, in all their branches, may well be supposed to require a greater freedom of animadversion than might be tolerated by the genius of such a government as that of Great Britain. In the latter, it is a maxim, that the king, an hereditary, not a responsible magistrate, can do no wrong; and that the legislature, which in two-thirds of its composition, is also hereditary, not responsible, can do what it pleases. In the United States, the executive magistrates are not held to be infallible, nor the legislatures to be omnipotent; and both being elective, are both responsible. Is it not natural and necessary, under such different circumstances, that a different degree of freedom, in the use of the press, should be contemplated?

Is not such an inference favoured by what is observable in Great Britain itself? Notwithstanding the general doctrine of the common law, on the subject of the press, and the occasional punishment of those who use it with a freedom offensive to the government; it is well known, that with respect to the responsible members of the government, where the reasons operating here, become applicable there, the freedom exercised by the press, and protected by the public opinion, far exceeds the limits prescribed by the ordinary rules of law. The ministry, who are responsible to impeachment, are at all times animadverted on, by the press, with peculiar freedom; and during the elections for the House of Commons, the other responsible part of the government, the press is employed with as little reserve towards the candidates.

The practice in America must be entitled to much more respect. In every state, probably, in the Union, the press has exerted a freedom in canvassing the merits and measures of public men, of every description, which has not been confined to the strict limits of the common law. On this footing, the freedom of the press has stood; on this footing it yet stands. And it will not be a breach, either of truth or of candour, to say, that no persons or presses are in the habit of more unrestrained animadversions on the proceedings and functionaries of the state governments, than the persons and presses most zealous in vindicating the act of Congress for punishing similar animadversions on the government of the United States.

The last remark will not be understood as claiming for the state governments an immunity greater than they have heretofore enjoyed. Some degree of abuse is inseparable from the proper use of everything; and in no instance is this more true, than in that of the press. It has accordingly been decided by the practice of the states, that it is better to leave a few of its noxious branches to their luxuriant growth, than by pruning them away, to injure the vigour of those yielding the proper fruits. And can the wisdom of this policy be doubted by any who reflect, that to the press alone, chequered as it is with abuses, the world is indebted for all the triumphs which have been gained by reason and humanity, over error and oppression; who reflect, that to the same beneficent source, the United States owe much of the lights which conducted them to the rank of a free and independent nation; and which have improved their political system into a shape so auspicious to their happiness. Had "sedition-acts," forbidding every publication that might bring the constituted agents into contempt or disrepute, or that might excite the hatred of the people against the authors of unjust or pernicious measures, been uniformly enforced against the press, might not the United States have been languishing at this day, under the infirmities of a sickly confederation? Might they not possibly be miserable colonies, groaning under a foreign yoke?

To these observations, one fact will be added, which demonstrates that the common law cannot be admitted as the *universal* expositor of American terms, which may be the same with those contained in that law. The freedom of conscience, and of religion, are found in the same instruments which assert the freedom of the press. It will never be admitted, that the meaning of the former, in the common law of England, is to limit their meaning in the United States.

Whatever weight may be allowed to these considerations, the committee do not, however, by any means intend to rest the question on them. They contend that the article of amendment, instead of supposing in Congress a power that might be exercised over the press, provided its freedom was not abridged, was meant as a positive denial to Congress, of any power whatever on the subject.

To demonstrate that this was the true object of the article, it will be sufficient to recall the circumstances which led to it, and to refer to the explanation accompanying the article.

When the Constitution was under the discussions which preceded its ratification, it is well known, that great apprehensions were expressed by many, lost the omission of some positive exception from the powers delegated, of certain rights, and of the freedom of the press particularly, might expose them to the danger of being drawn by construction within some of the powers vested in Congress; more especially of the power to make all laws necessary and proper for carrying their other powers into execution. In reply to this objection, it was invariably urged to be a fundamental and characteristic principle of the Constitution, that all powers not given by it, were reserved; that no powers were given beyond those enumerated in the Constitution, and such as were fairly incident to them; that the power over the rights in question, and particularly over the press, was neither among the enumerated powers, nor incident to any of them; and consequently that an exercise of any such power, would be a manifest usurpation. It is painful to remark, how much the arguments now employed in behalf of the sedition-act, are at variance with the reasoning which then justified the Constitution, and invited its ratification.

From this posture of the subject, resulted the interesting question in so many of the conventions, whether the doubts and dangers ascribed to the Constitution, should be removed by any amendments previous to the ratification, or be postponed, in confidence that as far as they might be proper, they would be introduced in the form provided by the Constitution. The latter course was adopted; and in most of the states, the ratifications were followed by propositions and instructions for rendering the Constitution more explicit, and more safe to the rights not meant to be delegated by it. Among those rights, the freedom of the press, in most instances, is particularly and emphatically mentioned. The firm and very pointed manner, in which it is asserted in the proceedings of the convention of this state, will be hereafter seen.

In pursuance of the wishes thus expressed, the first Congress that assembled under the Constitution, proposed certain amendments which have since, by the necessary ratifications, been made a part of it; among which amendments, is the article containing, among other prohibitions on the Congress, an express declaration that they should make no law abridging the freedom of the press.

Without tracing farther the evidence on this subject, it would seem scarcely possible to doubt, that no power whatever over the press was supposed to be delegated by the Constitution, as it originally stood; and that the amendment was intended as a positive and absolute reservation of it.

But the evidence is still stronger. The proposition of amendment is made by Congress, is introduced in the following terms: "*The conventions of a number of the states having at the time of their adopting the Constitution expressed a desire, in order to prevent misconstructions or abuse of its powers, that further declaratory and restrictive clauses should be added; and as extending the ground of public confidence in the government, will best ensure the beneficent ends of its institutions."*

Here is the most satisfactory and authentic proof, that the several amendments proposed, were to be considered as either declaratory or restrictive; and whether the one or the other, as corresponding with the desire expressed by a number of the states, and as extending the ground of public confidence in the government.

Under any other construction of the amendment relating to the press, than that it declared the press to be wholly exempt from the power of Congress, the amendment could neither be said to correspond with the desire expressed by a number of the states, nor be calculated to extend the ground of public confidence in the government.

Nay more; the construction employed to justify the "sedition-act," would exhibit a phenomenon, without a parallel in the political world. It would exhibit a number of respectable states, as denying first that any power over the press was delegated by the Constitution; as proposing next, that an amendment to it, should explicitly declare that no such power was delegated; and finally, as concurring in an amendment actually recognising or delegating such a power.

Is then the federal government, it will be asked, destitute of every authority for restraining the licentiousness of the press, and for shielding itself against the libellous attacks which may be made on those who administer it?

The Constitution alone can answer this question. If no such power be expressly delegated, and it be not both necessary and proper to carry into execution an express power; above all, if it be expressly forbidden by a declaratory amendment to the Constitution, the answer must be, that the federal government is destitute of all such authority.

And might it not be asked in turn, whether it is not more probable, under all the circumstances which have been reviewed, that the authority should be withheld by the Constitution, than that it should be left to a vague and violent construction; whilst so much pains were bestowed in enumerating other powers, and so many less important powers are included in the enumeration?

Might it not be likewise asked, whether the anxious circumspection which dictated so many *peculiar* limitations on the general authority, would be unlikely to exempt the press altogether from that authority? The peculiar magnitude of some of the powers necessarily committed to the federal government; the peculiar duration required for the functions of some of its departments; the peculiar distance of the seat of its proceedings from the great body of its constituents; and the peculiar difficulty of circulating an adequate knowledge of them through any other channel; will not these considerations, some or other of which produced other exceptions from the powers of ordinary governments, all together, account for the policy of binding the hand of the federal government, from touching the channel which alone can give efficacy to its responsibility to its constituents; and of leaving those who administer it, to a remedy for their injured reputations, under the same laws, and in the same tribunals, which protect their lives, their liberties, and their properties?

But the question does not turn either on the wisdom of the Constitution, or on the policy which gave rise to its particular organization. It turns on the actual meaning of the instrument; by which it has appeared, that a power over the press is clearly excluded, from the number of powers delegated to the federal government.

3. And in the opinion of the committee, well may it be said, as the resolution concludes with saying, that the unconstitutional power exercised over the press by the "sedition-act," ought "more than any other, to produce universal alarm; because it is levelled against that right of freely examining public characters and measures, and of free communication among the people thereon, which has ever been justly deemed the only effectual guardian of every other right."

Without scrutinizing minutely into all the provisions of the "sedition-act," it will be sufficient to cite so much of section 2, as follows: "And be it further enacted, that if any person shall write, print, utter, or publish, or shall cause or procure to be written, printed, uttered or published, or shall knowingly and willingly assist or aid in writing, printing, uttering or publishing any false, scandalous and malicious writing or writings against the government of the United States, or either house of the Congress of the United States, or the President of the United States, *with an intent to defame the said government, or either house of the said Congress, or the President, or to bring them, or either of them, into contempt or disrepute; or to excite against them, or either, or any of them, the hatred of the good people of the United States, &c. Then such person being thereof convicted before any court of the United States, having jurisdiction thereof, shall be punished by a fine not exceeding two thousand dollars, and by imprisonment not exceeding two years.*"

On this part of the act, the following observations present themselves:

1. The Constitution supposes that the President, the Congress, and each of its houses may not discharge their trusts, either from defect of judgment or other causes. Hence, they are all made responsible to their constituents, at the returning periods of election; and the President, who is singly entrusted with very great powers, is, as a further guard, subjected to an intermediate impeachment.

2. Should it happen, as the Constitution supposes it may happen, that either of these branches of the government may not have duly discharged its trust, it is natural and proper that, according to the cause and degree of their faults, they should be brought into contempt or disrepute, and incur the hatred of the people.

3. Whether it has, in any case, happened that the proceedings of either, or all of those branches, evince such a violation of duty as to justify a contempt, a disrepute or hatred among the people, can only be determined by a free examination thereof, and a free communication among the people thereon.

4. Whenever it may have actually happened, that proceedings of this sort are chargeable on all or either of the branches of the government, it is the duty as well as right of intelligent and faithful citizens, to discuss and promulge them freely, as well to control them by the censorship of the public opinion, as to promote a remedy according to the rules of the Constitution. And it cannot be avoided, that those who are to apply the remedy must feel, in some degree, a contempt or hatred against the transgressing party.

5. As the act was passed on July 14, 1798, and is to be in force until March 3, 1801, it was of course, that during its continuance, two elections of the entire House of Representatives, an election of a part of the Senate, and an election of a President, were to take place.

6. That consequently, during all these elections, intended by the Constitution to preserve the purity, or to purge the faults of the administration, the great remedial rights of the people were to be exercised, and the responsibility of their public agents to be screened, under the penalties of this act.

May it not be asked of every intelligent friend to the liberties of his country, whether the power exercised in such an act as this, ought not to produce great and universal alarm? Whether a rigid execution of such an act, in time past, would not have repressed that information and communication among the people, which is indispensable to the just exercise of their electoral rights? And whether such an act, if made perpetual, and enforced with rigour, would not, in time to come, either destroy our free system of government, or prepare a convulsion that might prove equally fatal to it?

In answer to such questions, it has been pleaded that the writings and publications forbidden by the act, are those only which are false and malicious, and intended to defame; and merit is claimed for the privilege allowed to authors to justify, by proving the truth of their publications, and for the limitations to which the sentence of fine and imprisonment is subjected.

To those who concurred in the act, under the extraordinary belief that the option lay between the passing of such an act, and leaving in force the common law of libels, which punishes truth equally with falsehood, and submits the fine and imprisonment to the indefinite discretion of the court, the merit of good intentions ought surely not to be refused. A like merit may perhaps be due for the discontinuance of the *corporal punishment,* which the common law also leaves to the discretion of the court. This merit of *intention,* however, would have been greater, if the several mitigations had not been limited to so short a period; and the apparent inconsistency would have been avoided, between justifying the act at one time, by contrasting it with the rigors of the common law, otherwise in force, and at another time by appealing to the nature of the crisis, as requiring the temporary rigour exerted by the act.

But, whatever may have been the meritorious intentions of all or any who contributed to the sedition-act, a very few reflections will prove, that its baneful tendency is little diminished by the privilege of giving in evidence the truth of the matter contained in political writings.

In the first place, where simple and naked facts alone are in question, there is sufficient difficulty in some cases, and sufficient trouble and vexation in all, of meeting a prosecution from the government, with the full and formal proof necessary in a court of law.

But in the next place, it must be obvious to the plainest minds, that opinions, and inferences, and conjectural observations, are not only in many cases inseparable from the facts, but may often be more the objects of the prosecution than the facts themselves; or may even be altogether abstracted from particular facts; and that opinions and inferences, and conjectural observations, cannot be subjects of that kind of proof which appertains to facts, before a court of law.

Again: It is no less obvious, that the *intent* to defame or bring into contempt or disrepute, or hatred, which is made a condition of the offence created by the act, cannot prevent its pernicious influence on the freedom of the press. For, omitting the inquiry, how far the malice of the intent is an inference of the law from the mere publication, it is manifestly impossible to punish the intent to bring those who administer the government into disrepute or contempt, without striking at the right of freely discussing public characters and measures: because those who engage in such discussions, must expect and *intend* to excite these unfavourable sentiments, so far as they may be thought to be deserved. To prohibit, therefore, the intent to excite those unfavourable sentiments against those who administer the government, is equivalent to a prohibition of the actual excitement of them; and to prohibit the actual excitement of them, is equivalent to a prohibition of discussions having that tendency and effect; which, again, is equivalent to a protection of those who administer the government, if they should at any time deserve the contempt or hatred of the people, against being exposed to it, by free animadversions on their characters and conduct. Nor can there be a doubt, if those in public trust be shielded by penal laws from such strictures of the press, as may expose them to contempt or disrepute, or hatred, where they may deserve it, in exact proportion as they may deserve to be exposed, will be the certainty and criminality of the intent to expose them, and the vigilance of prosecuting and punishing it; nor a doubt, that a government thus intrenched in penal statutes, against the just and natural effects of a culpable administration, will easily evade the responsibility, which is essential to a faithful discharge of its duty.

Let it be recollected, lastly, that the right of electing the members of the government, constitutes more particularly the essence of a free and responsible government. The value and efficacy of this right, depends on the knowledge of the comparative merits and demerits of the candidates for public trust; and on the equal freedom, consequently, of examining and discussing these merits and demerits of the candidates respectively. It has been seen, that a number of important elections will take place whilst the act is in force, although it should not be continued beyond the term

to which it is limited. Should there happen, then, as is extremely probable in relation to some or other of the branches of the government, to be competitions between those who are, and those who are not, members of the government, what will be the situations of the competitors? Not equal; because the characters of the former will be covered by the "sedition-act" from animadversions exposing them to disrepute among the people; whilst the latter may be exposed to the contempt and hatred of the people, without a violation of the act. What will be the situation of the people? Not free; because they will be compelled to make their election between competitors, whose pretensions they are not permitted, by the act, equally to examine, to discuss, and to ascertain. And from both these situations, will not those in power derive an undue advantage for continuing themselves in it; which by impairing the right of election, endangers the blessings of the government founded on it?

It is with justice, therefore, that the General Assembly have affirmed in the resolution, as well that the right of freely examining public characters and measures, and free communication thereon, is the only effectual guardian of every other right, as that this particular right is levelled at, by the power exercised in the "sedition-act."

The resolution next in order is as follows:

That this state having by its convention, which ratified the federal Constitution, expressly declared, that among other essential rights, "the liberty of conscience and of the press cannot be cancelled, abridged, restrained or modified by any authority of the United States," and from its extreme anxiety to guard these rights from every possible attack of sophistry and ambition, having, with other states, recommended an amendment for that purpose, which amendment was, in due time, annexed to the Constitution, it would mark a reproachful inconsistency, and criminal degeneracy, if an indifference were now shown to the most palpable violation of one of the rights thus declared and secured; and the establishment of a precedent, which may be fatal to the other.

To place this resolution in its just light, it will be necessary to recur to the act of ratification by Virginia, which stands in the ensuing form:

We, the delegates of the people of Virginia, duly elected in pursuance of a recommendation from the General Assembly, and now met in convention, having fully and freely investigated and discussed the proceedings of the federal convention, and being prepared as well as the most mature deliberation hath enabled us to decide thereon, do, in the name and in behalf of the people of Virginia, declare and make known, that the powers granted under the Constitution, being derived from the people of the United States, may be resumed by them, whensoever the same shall be perverted to their injury or oppression; and that every power not granted thereby, remains with them, and at their will. That, therefore, no right of any denomination can be cancelled, abridged, restrained, or modified, by the Congress, by the Senate, or House of Representatives, acting in any capacity, by the President, or any department or officer of the United States, except in those instances in which power is given by the Constitution for those purposes; and that, among other essential rights, the liberty of conscience and of the press, cannot be cancelled, abridged, restrained, or modified, by any authority of the United States.

Here is an express and solemn declaration by the convention of the state, that they ratified the Constitution in the sense, that no right of any denomination can be cancelled, abridged, restrained, or modified by the government of the United States or any part of it; except in those instances in which power is given by the Constitution; and in the sense particularly, "that among other essential rights, the liberty of conscience and freedom of the press cannot be cancelled, abridged, restrained, or modified, by any authority of the United States."

Words could not well express, in a fuller or more forcible manner, the understanding of the convention, that the liberty of conscience and the freedom of the press, were *equally* and *completely* exempted from all authority whatever of the United States.

Under an anxiety to guard more effectually these rights against every possible danger, the convention, after ratifying the Constitution, proceeded to prefix to certain amendments proposed by them, a declaration of rights, in which are two articles providing, the one for the liberty of conscience, the other for the freedom of speech and of the press.

Similar recommendations having proceeded from a number of other states, and Congress, as has been seen, having in consequence thereof, and with a view to extend the ground of public confidence, proposed, among other declaratory and restrictive clauses, a clause expressly securing the liberty of conscience and of the press; and Virginia having concurred in the ratifications which made them a part of the Constitution, it will remain with a candid public to decide, whether it would not mark an inconsistency

and degeneracy, if an indifference were now shown to a palpable violation of one of those rights, the freedom of the press; and to a precedent therein, which may be fatal to the other, the free exercise of religion.

That the precedent established by the violation of the former of these rights, may, as is affirmed by the resolution, be fatal to the latter, appears to be demonstrable, by a comparison of the grounds on which they respectively rest; and from the scope of reasoning, by which the power over the former has been vindicated.

First. Both of these rights, the liberty of conscience and of the press, rest equally on the original ground of not being delegated by the Constitution, and consequently withheld from the government. Any construction, therefore, that would attack this original security for the one, must have the like effect on the other.

Secondly. They are both equally secured by the supplement to the Constitution; being both included in the same amendment; made at the same time, and by the same authority. Any construction or argument, then, which would turn the amendment into a grant or acknowledgment of power with respect to the press, might be equally applied to the freedom of religion.

Thirdly. If it be admitted that the extent of the freedom of the press, secured by the amendment, is to be measured by the common law on this subject, the same authority may be resorted to, for the standard which is to fix the extent of the "free exercise of religion." It cannot be necessary to say what this standard would be; whether the common law be taken solely as the unwritten, or as varied by the written law of England.

Fourthly. If the words and phrases in the amendment, are to be considered as chosen with a studied discrimination, which yields an argument for a power over the press, under the limitation that its freedom be not abridged, the same argument results from the same consideration, for a power over the exercise of religion, under the limitation that its freedom be not prohibited.

For, if Congress may regulate the freedom of the press, provided they do not abridge it, because it is said only "they shall not abridge it," and is not said, "they shall make no law respecting it," the analogy of reasoning is conclusive, that Congress may *regulate* and even *abridge* the free exercise of religion, provided they do not *prohibit* it, because it is said only "they shall not prohibit it," and is *not* said, "they shall make no law *respecting,* or no law *abridging* it."

The General Assembly were governed by the clearest reason, then, in considering the "sedition-act," which legislates on the freedom of the press, as establishing a precedent that may be fatal to the liberty of conscience; and it will be the duty of all, in proportion as they value the security of the latter, to take the alarm at every encroachment on the former.

The two concluding resolutions only remain to be examined. They are in the words following:

That the good people of this commonwealth, having ever felt and continuing to feel the most sincere affection for their brethren of the other states; the truest anxiety for establishing and perpetuating the union of all; and the most scrupulous fidelity to that Constitution, which is the pledge of mutual friendship, and the instrument of mutual happiness; the General Assembly doth solemnly appeal to the like dispositions in the other states, in confidence that they will concur with this commonwealth in declaring, as it does hereby declare, that the acts aforesaid are unconstitutional; and, that the necessary and proper measures will be taken by each, for co-operating with this state, in maintaining unimpaired the authorities, rights, and liberties reserved to the states respectively, or to the people.

That the governor be desired to transmit a copy of the foregoing resolutions to the executive authority of each of the other states, with a request that the same may be communicated to the legislature thereof; and that a copy be furnished to each of the senators and representatives representing this state in the Congress of the United States.

The fairness and regularity of the course of proceeding here pursued, have not protected it against objections even from sources too respectable to be disregarded.

It has been said, that it belongs to the judiciary of the United States, and not the state legislatures, to declare the meaning of the Federal Constitution.

But a declaration that proceedings of the Federal Government are not warranted by the Constitution, is a novelty neither among the citizens, nor among the legislatures of the states; nor are the citizens or the legislature of Virginia, singular in the example of it.

Nor can the declarations of either, whether affirming or denying the constitutionality of measures of the Federal Government, or whether made before or after judicial decisions thereon, be deemed, in any point of view, an assumption of the office of the judge. The declarations, in such cases, are expressions of opinion, unaccompanied with any other effect than what they may produce on opinion, by exciting reflection. The expositions of the judiciary, on the other hand, are carried into immediate effect by force. The former may lead to a change in the legislative expression of the general will; possibly to a change in the opinion of the judiciary; the latter enforces the general will, whilst that will and that opinion continue unchanged.

And if there be no impropriety in declaring the unconstitutionality of proceedings in the Federal Government, where can be the impropriety of communicating the declaration to other states, and inviting their concurrence in a like declaration? What is allowable for one, must be allowable for all; and a free communication among the states, where the Constitution imposes no restraint, is as allowable among the state governments as among other public bodies or private citizens. This consideration derives a weight, that cannot be denied to it, from the relation of the state legislatures to the federal legislature, as the immediate constituents of one of its branches.

The legislatures of the states have a right also to originate amendments to the Constitution, by a concurrence of two-thirds of the whole number, in applications to Congress for the purpose. When new states are to be formed by a junction of two or more states, or parts of states, the legislatures of the states concerned are, as well as Congress, to concur in the measure. The states have a right also to enter into agreements or compacts, with the consent of Congress. In all such cases, a communication among them results from the object which is common to them.

It is lastly to be seen, whether the confidence expressed by the resolution, that the *necessary and proper measures* would be taken by the other states for co-operating with Virginia in maintaining the rights reserved to the states, or to the people, be in any degree liable to the objections which have been raised against it.

If it be liable to objection, it must be because either the object or the means are objectionable.

The object being to maintain what the Constitution has ordained, is in itself a laudable object.

The means are expressed in the terms "the necessary and proper measures." A proper object was to be pursued, by means both necessary and proper.

To find an objection, then, it must be shown that some meaning was annexed to these general terms, which was not proper; and, for this purpose, either that the means used by the General Assembly were an example of improper means, or that there were no proper means to which the terms could refer.

In the example given by the state, of declaring the alien and sedition-acts to be unconstitutional, and of communicating the declaration to the other states, no trace of improper means has appeared. And if the other states had concurred in making a like declaration, supported, too, by the numerous applications flowing immediately from the people, it can scarcely be doubted, that these simple means would have been as sufficient, as they are unexceptionable.

It is no less certain that other means might have been employed, which are strictly within the limits of the Constitution. The legislatures of the states might have made a direct representation to Congress, with a view to obtain a rescinding of the two offensive acts; or, they might have represented to their respective senators in Congress their wish, that two-thirds thereof would propose an explanatory amendment to the Constitution; or two-thirds of themselves, if such had been their option, might, by an application to Congress, have obtained a convention for the same object.

These several means, though not equally eligible in themselves, nor probably, to the states, were all constitutionally open for consideration. And if the General Assembly, after declaring the two acts to be unconstitutional, the first and most obvious proceeding on the subject, did not undertake to point out to the other states a choice among the farther measures that might become necessary and proper, the reserve will not be misconstrued by liberal minds into any culpable imputation.

These observations appear to form a satisfactory reply to every objection which is not founded on a misconception of the terms employed in the resolutions. There is one other, however, which may be of too much importance not to be added. It cannot be forgotten, that among the arguments addressed to those who apprehended danger to liberty from the establishment of the General Government over so great a country, the appeal was emphatically made to the intermediate existence of the state governments, between the people and that government, to the vigilance with which they would descry the first symptoms of usurpation; and to the promptitude with which they would sound the alarm to the public. This argument was proba-

bly not without its effect; and if it was a proper one then, to recommend the establishment of the Constitution, it must be a proper one now, to assist in its interpretation.

The only part of the two concluding resolutions that remains to be noticed, is the repetition in the first, of that warm affection to the union and its members, and of that scrupulous fidelity to the Constitution, which have been invariably felt by the people of this state. As the proceedings were introduced with these sentiments, they could not be more properly closed than in the same manner. Should there be any so far misled as to call in question the sincerity of these professions, whatever regret may be excited by the error, the General Assembly cannot descend into a discussion of it. Those, who have listened to the suggestion, can only be left to their own recollection of the part which this state has borne in the establishment of our national independence, in the establishment of our national Constitution, and in maintaining under it the authority and laws of the Union, without a single exception of internal resistance or commotion. By recurring to these facts, they will be able to convince themselves, that the representatives of the people of Virginia, must be above the necessity of opposing any other shield to attacks on their national patriotism, than their own consciousness, and the justice of an enlightened public; who will perceive in the resolutions themselves, the strongest evidence of attachment both to the Constitution and to the Union, since it is only by maintaining the different governments and departments within their respective limits, that the blessings of either can be perpetuated.

The extensive view of the subject thus taken by the committee, has led them to report to the House, as the result of the whole, the following resolution:

Resolved, That the General Assembly, having carefully and respectfully attended to the proceedings of a number of the states, in answer to its resolutions of December 21, 1798, and having accurately and fully re-examined and reconsidered the latter, finds it to be its indispensable duty to adhere to the same, as founded in truth, as consonant with the Constitution, and as conducive to its preservation; and more especially to be its duty to renew, as it does hereby renew, its protest against "the alien and sedition-acts," as palpable and alarming infractions of the Constitution.

The Duty of Americans, at the Present Crisis

TIMOTHY DWIGHT

1798

Timothy Dwight (1752–1817) was a strict Calvinist minister, an author of patriotic songs and poems, president of Yale College, and secretary of the Hartford Convention that considered New England's grievances arising from the War of 1812 (see the next selection). The sermon reproduced here was preached on the Fourth of July, 1798, in the midst of the crisis rooted in American disagreements with the French revolutionary government.

The Duty of Americans, at the Present Crisis

Behold I come as a thief: Blessed is he that watcheth, and keepeth his garments, lest he walk naked, and they see his shame.

Revelation XVI. xv.

This passage is inserted as a parenthesis in the account of the sixth vial. To feel its whole force it will be necessary to recur to that account, and to examine it with some attention. It is given in these words.

V. 12. "And the sixth angel poured out his vial upon the great river Euphrates; and the water thereof was dried up, that the way of the king of the east might be prepared."

13. "And I saw three unclean spirits like frogs come out of the mouth of the dragon, and out of the mouth of the beast, and out of the mouth of the false prophet.["]

14. "For they are the spirits of * devils, working miracles, which go forth unto the kings of the earth, and of the whole world, to gather them to the battle of that great day of God Almighty."

15. "Behold I come as a thief: Blessed is he that watcheth, and keepeth his garments, lest he walk naked, and they see his shame."

16. "And he gathered them together into a place called in the Hebrew tongue Armageddon."

To this account is subjoined that of the seventh vial;

*Gr. Demons

at the effusion of which is accomplished a wonderful and most affecting convulsion of this guilty world, and the final ruin of the Antichristian empire. The circumstances of this amazing event are exhibited at large in the remainder of this, and in the three succeeding chapters.

Instead of employing the time, allowed by the present occasion, in stating the several opinions of commentators concerning this remarkable prophecy, opinions which you can examine at your leisure, I shall, as briefly as may be, state to you that, which appears to me to be its true meaning. This is necessary to be done, to prepare you for the use of it, which is now intended to be made.

In the 12th verse, under a natural allusion to the manner in which the ancient Babylon was destroyed, a description is given us of the measures, used by the Most High to prepare the way for the destruction of the spiritual Babylon. The river Euphrates surrounded the walls, and ran through the middle, of the ancient Babylon, and thus became the means of its wealth, strength and safety. When Cyrus and Cyaxares,† the kings of Persia and Media, or, in the Jewish phraseology, of the east, took this celebrated city, they dried up, or emptied, the waters of the Euphrates, out of its proper channel, by turning them into a lake, or more probably a sunken region of the country, above the city. They then entered by the channel which passed through the city, made themselves masters of it, and overturned the empire. The emptying, or drying up, of the waters of the real Euphrates thus prepared the way of the real kings of the east for the destruction of the city and empire of the real Babylon. The drying up of the waters of the figurative Euphrates in the like manner prepares the way of the figurative kings of the east for the destruction of the city and empire of the figurative Babylon. The terms *waters, Euphrates, kings, east, Babylon,* are all figurative or symbolical; and are not to be understood as denoting real kings, or a real east, any more than a real Euphrates, or a real

†The Darius of Daniel

Babylon. The whole meaning of the prophet is, I apprehend, that God will, under this vial, so diminish the wealth, strength, and safety, of the spiritual or figurative Babylon, as effectually to prepare the way for its destroyers.

In the remaining verses an event is predicted, of a totally different kind; which is also to take place in the same period. Three unclean spirits, like frogs, are exhibited as proceeding out of the mouth of the dragon or Devil, of the beast or Romish government, and of the false prophet, or, as I apprehend, of the regular clergy of that hierarchy. These spirits are represented as working miracles, as going forth to the kings, of the whole world, to gather them; and as actually gathering them together to the battle of that great day of God Almighty, described in the remainder of this chapter, and in the three succeeding ones. Of this vast enterprise the miserable end is strongly marked, in the name of the place, into which they are said to be gathered—Armageddon—the mountain of destruction and mourning.

The writer of this book will himself explain to us what he intended by the word *spirits* in this passage. In his 1st Epistle, ch. iv. v. 1. he says, "Beloved, believe not every spirit; but try the spirits, whether they be of God; because many false prophets are gone out into the world."

I.E. Believe not every teacher, or doctrine, professing to come from God; but examine all carefully, that ye may know whether they come from God, or not; for many false prophets, or teachers passing themselves upon the church for teachers of truth, but in reality teachers of false doctrines, are gone out into the world.

In the same sense, if I am not deceived, is the word used in the passage under consideration. One great characteristic and calamity of this period is, therefore, that unclean teachers, or teachers of unclean doctrines, will spread through the world, to unite mankind against God. They are said to be three; i.e. several; a definite number being used here, as in many other passages of this book, for an indefinite one; to *come out of the mouths* of the three evil agents abovementioned; i.e. to originate in those countries, where they have principally co-operated against the kingdom of God; to be *unclean; to resemble* frogs; i.e. to be lothesome, clamorous, impudent, and pertinacious; to be *the spirits of demons,* i.e. to be impious, malicious, proud, deceitful, and cruel; *to work miracles,* or wonders; and *to gather great multitudes of men to battle,* i.e. to embark them in an open, professed enterprise, against God Almighty.

Having thus summarily explained my views of this prophecy, I shall now for the purpose of presenting it in a more distinct and comprehensive view, draw together the several parts of it in a paraphrase.

In the sixth great division of the period of providence, denoted by the vials filled with divine judgments and emptied on the world, the wealth, strength and safety of the Antichristian empire will be greatly lessened, and thus effectual preparation will be made for its final overthrow.

In the meantime several teachers of false and immoral doctrines will arise in those countries, where the powers of the Antichristian empire have especially distinguished themselves, by corrupting the truth, and persecuting the followers, of Christ; the character of which teachers and their doctrines will be impure, lothesome, impudent, pertinacious, proud, deceitful, impious, malicious, and cruel.

These teachers will, by their doctrines and labours, openly, professedly, and in an unusual manner, contend against God, and against his kingdom in this world, and will strive to unite mankind in this opposition.

Nor will they fail of astonishing success; for they will actually unite a large part of the human race, particularly in Christendom, in this impious undertaking.

But they will only unite them to their destruction; a destruction most awfully accomplished at the effusion of the seventh vial.

From this explanation it is manifest, that the prediction consists of two great and distinct parts; *the preparation for the overthrow of the Antichristian empire; and the embarkation of men in a professed and unusual opposition to God, and to his kingdom, accomplished by means of false doctrines, and impious teachers.*

By the ablest commentators the fifth vial is considered as having been poured out at the time of the Reformation. The first is supposed, and with almost absolute certainty, to have begun to operate not long after the year 800. If we calculate from that period to the year 1517, the year in which the Reformation began in Germany, the four first vials will be found to have occupied about four times 180 years. 180 years may therefore be estimated as the greatest, and 170 years as the least, duration of a single vial. From the year 1517 to the year 1798 there are 281 years. If the fifth vial be supposed to have continued 180 years, its termination was in the year 1697; if 170, in 1687. Of course the sixth vial may be viewed as having been in operation more than 100 years.

You will now naturally ask, What events in the Providence of God, found in this period, verify the prediction?

To this question I answer, generally, that the whole complexion of things appears to me to have, in a manner surprisingly exact, corresponded with the prediction. The following particulars will evince with what propriety this answer is returned.

Within this period the Jesuits, who constituted the strongest branch, and the most formidable internal support, of the Romish hierarchy, have been suppressed.

Within this period various other orders of the regular Romish clergy have in some countries been suppressed, and in others greatly reduced. Their permanent possessions have been confiscated, and their wealth and power greatly lessened.

Within this period the Antichristian secular powers have been in most instances exceedingly weakened. Poland as a body politic is nearly annihilated. Austria has deeply suffered. Venice and the popish part of Switzerland as bodies politic have vanished. The Sardinian monarchy is on the eve of dissolution. Spain, Naples, Tuscany, and Genoa, are sorely wounded; and Portugal totters to its fall. By the treaty, now on the tapis in Germany, the Romish archbishoprics and bishoprics, in that empire, are proposed to be secularized, and as distinct governments to be destroyed. As the strength of these powers was the foundation, on which the hierarchy rested; so their destruction, or diminution, is a final preparation for its ruin.

In France, Belgium, the Italian, and Cis-rhenane republics, a new form of government has been instituted, the effect of which, whether it shall prove permanent, or not, must be greatly and finally to diminish the strength of the hierarchy.

In France, and in Belgium, the whole power and influence of the clergy of all descriptions have, in a sense, been destroyed; and their immense wealth has been diverted into new channels. In France, also, an open, violent, and inveterate war has been made upon the hierarchy, and carried on with unexampled bitterness and cruelty.*

Within this period, also, the revenues of the pope have been greatly curtailed; the territory of Avignon has been taken out of his hands; and his general weight and authority have exceedingly declined.

Within the present year his person has been seized, his secular government overturned, a republic formed out of his dominions, and an apparent and at least temporary end put to his dominion.

To all these mighty preparations for the ruin of the Antichristian empire may be added, as of the highest efficacy, that great change of character, of views, feelings, and habits, throughout many Antichristian countries, which assures us completely, that its former strength can never return.

Thus has the first part of this remarkable prophecy been accomplished. Not less remarkable has been the fulfilment of the second.

About the year 1728, Voltaire, so celebrated for his wit and brilliancy, and not less distinguished for his hatred of christianity and his abandonment of principle, formed a systematical design to destroy christianity, and to introduce in its stead a general diffusion of irreligion and atheism. For this purpose he associated with himself Frederic the II, king of Prussia, and Mess. D'Alembert and Diderot, the principal compilers of the Encyclopedie; all men of talents, atheists, and in the like manner abandoned. The principal parts of this system were, 1st. The compilation of the Encyclopedie;† in which with great art and insidiousness the doctrines of natural as well as Christian theology were rendered absurd and ridiculous; and the mind of the reader was insensibly steeled against conviction and duty. 2. The overthrow of the religious orders in Catholic countries; a step essentially necessary to the destruction of the religion professed in those countries. 3. The establishment of a sect of philosophists to serve, it is presumed, as a conclave, a rallying point, for all their followers. 4. The appropriation to themselves, and their disciples, of the places and honours of members of the French Academy, the most respectable literary society in France, and always considered as containing none but men of prime learning and talents. In this way they designed to hold out themselves, and their

*In the mention of all these evils brought on the Romish hierarchy, I beg it may be remembered, that I am far from justifying the iniquitous conduct of their persecutors. I know not that any person holds it, and all other persecution, more in abhorence. Neither have I a doubt of the integrity and piety of multitudes of the unhappy sufferers. In my view they claim, and I trust will receive, the commiseration, and, as occasion offers, the kind offices of all men possessed even of common humanity.

†The celebrated French Dictionary of Arts and Sciences, in which articles of theology were speciously and decently written, but, by references artfully made to other articles, all the truth of the former was entirely and insidiously overthrown to most readers, by the sophistry of the latter.

friends, as the only persons of great literary and intellectual distinction in that country, and to dictate all literary opinions to the nation.* 5. The fabrication of books of all kinds against christianity, especially such as excite doubt, and generate contempt and derision. Of these they issued, by themselves and their friends, who early became numerous, an immense number; so printed, as to be purchased for little or nothing, and so written, as to catch the feelings, and steal upon the approbation, of every class of men. 6. The formation of a secret academy, of which Voltaire was the standing president, and in which books were formed, altered, forged, imputed as posthumous to deceased writers of reputation, and sent abroad with the weight of their names. These were printed and circulated, at the lowest price, through all classes of men, in an uninterrupted succession, and through every part of the kingdom.

Nor were the labours of this academy confined to religion. They attacked also morality and government, unhinged gradually the minds of men, and destroyed their reverence for every thing heretofore esteemed sacred.

In the mean time, the Masonic societies, which had been originally instituted for convivial and friendly purposes only, were, especially in France and Germany, made the professed scenes of debate concerning religion, morality, and government, by these philosophists†, who had in great numbers become Masons. For such debate the legalized existence of Masonry, its profound secrecy, its solemn and mystic rites and symbols, its mutual correspondence, and its extension through most civilized countries, furnished the greatest advantages. All here was free, safe, and calculated to encourage the boldest excursions of restless opinion and impatient ardour, and to make and fix the deepest impressions. Here, and in no other place, under such arbitrary governments, could every innovator in these important subjects utter every sentiment, however daring, and attack every doctrine and institution, however guarded by law or sanctity. In the secure and unrestrained debates of the lodge, every novel, licentious, and alarming opinion was resolutely advanced. Minds, already tinged with philosophism, were here speedily blackened with a deep and deadly die; and those, which came fresh and innocent to the scene of contamination, became early and irremediably corrupted. A stubborn incapacity of conviction, and a flinty insensibility to every moral and natural tie, grew of course out of this combination of causes; and men were surely prepared, before themselves were aware, for every plot and perpetration. In these hot beds were sown the seeds of that astonishing Revolution, and all its dreadful appendages, which now spreads dismay and horror throughout half the globe.

While these measures were advancing the great design with a regular and rapid progress, Doctor Adam Weishaupt, professor of the canon law in the University of Ingolstadt, a city of Bavaria (in Germany) formed, about the year 1777, the order of Illuminati. This order is professedly a higher order of Masons, originated by himself, and grafted on ancient Masonic institutions. The secresy, solemnity, mysticism, and correspondence of Masonry, were in this new order preserved and enhanced; while the ardour of innovation, the impatience of civil and moral restraints, and the aims against government, morals, and religion, were elevated, expanded, and rendered more systematical, malignant, and daring.

In the societies of Illuminati doctrines were taught, which strike at the root of all human happiness and virtue; and every such doctrine was either expressly or implicitly involved in their system.

The being of God was denied and ridiculed.

Government was asserted to be a curse, and authority a mere usurpation.

Civil society was declared to be the only apostasy of man.

The possession of property was pronounced to be robbery.

Chastity and natural affection were declared to be nothing more than groundless prejudices.

Adultery, assassination, poisoning, and other crimes of the like infernal nature, were taught as lawful, and even as virtuous actions.

---

*So far was this carried, that a Mr. Beauzet, a layman, but a sincere christian, who was one of the forty members, once asked D'Alembert how they came to admit him among them? D'Alembert answered, without hesitation, "I am sensible, this must seem astonishing to you; but we wanted a skilful grammarian, and among our party, not one had acquired a reputation in this line. We know that you believe in God, but, being a good sort of man, we cast our eyes upon you, for want of a philosopher to supply your place." Brit. Crit. Art. Barruel's Memoirs of the History of Jacobinism. August 1797.

†The words *philosophism* and *philosophists* may in our opinion, be happily adapted, from this work, to designate the doctrines of the deistical sect; and thus to rescue the honourable terms of philosophy and philosopher from the abuse, into which they have fallen. Philosophism is the love of sophisms and thus completely describes the sect of Voltaire. A philosophist is a lover of sophists. Brit. Crit. Ibid.

To crown such a system of falshood and horror all means were declared to be lawful, provided the end was good.

In this last doctrine men are not only loosed from every bond, and from every duty; but from every inducement to perform any thing which is good, and, abstain from any thing which is evil; and are set upon each other, like a company of hellhounds to worry, rend, and destroy. Of the goodness of the end every man is to judge for himself; and most men, and all men who resemble the Illuminati, will pronounce every end to be good, which will gratify their inclinations. The great and good ends proposed by the Illuminati, as the ultimate objects of their union, are the overthrow of religion, government, and human society civil and domestic. These they pronounce to be so good, that murder, butchery, and war, however extended and dreadful, are declared by them to be completely justifiable, if necessary for these great purposes. With such an example in view, it will be in vain to hunt for ends, which can be evil.

Correspondent with this summary was the whole system. No villainy, no impiety, no cruelty, can be named, which was not vindicated; and no virtue, which was not covered with contempt.

The names by which this society was enlarged, and its doctrines spread, were of every promising kind. With unremitted ardour and diligence the members insinuated themselves into every place of power and trust, and into every literary, political and friendly society; engrossed as much as possible the education of youth, especially of distinction; became licensers of the press, and directors of every literary journal; waylaid every foolish prince, every unprincipled civil officer, and every abandoned clergyman; entered boldly into the desk, and with unhallowed hands, and satanic lips, polluted the pages of God; inlisted in their service almost all the booksellers, and of course the printers, of Germany; inundated the country with books, replete with infidelity, irreligion, immorality, and obscenity; prohibited the printing, and prevented the sale, of books of the contrary character; decried and ridiculed them when published in spite of their efforts; panegyrized and trumpeted those of themselves and their coadjutors; and in a word made more numerous, more diversified, and more enormous exertions, than an active imagination would have preconceived.

To these exertions their success has been proportioned. Multitudes of the Germans, notwithstanding the gravity, steadiness, and sobriety of their national character, have become either partial or entire converts to these wretched doctrines; numerous societies have been established among them; the public faith and morals have been unhinged; and the political and religious affairs of that empire have assumed an aspect, which forebodes its total ruin. In France, also, Illuminatism has been eagerly and extensively adopted; and those men, who have had, successively, the chief direction of the public affairs of that country, have been members of this society. Societies have also been erected in Switzerland and Italy, and have contributed probably to the success of the French, and to the overthrow of religion and government, in those countries. Mentz was delivered up to Custine by the Illuminati; and that general appears to have been guillotined, because he declined to encourage the same treachery with respect to Manheim.

Nor have England and Scotland escaped the contagion. Several societies have been erected in both of those countries. Nay in the private papers, seized in the custody of the leading members in Germany, several such societies are recorded as having been erected in America, before the year 1786.

It is a remarkable fact, that a large proportion of the sentiments, here stated, have been publicly avowed and applauded in the French legislature. The being and providence of God have been repeatedly denied and ridiculed. Christ has been mocked with the grossest insult. Death, by a solemn legislative decree has been declared to be an eternal sleep. Marriage has been degraded to a farce, and the community, by the law of divorce, invited to universal prostitution. In the school of public instruction atheism is professedly taught; and at an audience before the legislature, Nov. 30, 1793, the head scholar declared, that he and his schoolfellows detested a God; a declaration received by the members with unbounded applause, and rewarded with the fraternal kiss of the president, and with the honors of the sitting.

I presume I have sufficiently proved the fulfilment of the second part of this remarkable prophesy; and shewn, that doctrines and teachers, answering to the description, have arisen in the very countries specified, and that they are rapidly spreading through the world, to engage mankind in an open and professed war against God. I shall only add, that the titles of these philosophistical books have, in various instances, been too obscene to admit of a translation by a virtuous man, and in a decent state of society. So fully are these teachers entitled to the epithet unclean.

Assuming now as just, for the purposes of this discourse, the explanation, which has been given, I shall proceed to consider the import of the text.

The text is an affectionate address of the Redeemer to his children, teaching them that conduct, which he wills them especially to pursue in this alarming season. It is the great practical remark, drawn by infinite wisdom and goodness from a most solemn sermon, and cannot fail therefore to merit our highest attention. Had he not, while recounting the extensive and dreadful convulsion, described in the context, made a declaration of this nature, there would have been little room for the exercise of any emotions, beside those of terror and despair. The gloom would have been universal and entire; a blank midnight without a star to cheer the solitary darkness. But here a hope, a promise, is furnished to such as obey the injunction, by which it is followed; a luminary like that, which shone to the wise men of the east, is lighted up to guide our steps to the Author of peace and salvation.

Blessed, even in this calamitous season, saith the Saviour of men, *is he that watcheth, and keepeth his garments, lest he walk naked and they see his shame.*

Sin is the nakedness and shame of the scriptures, and righteousness the garment which covers it. To watch and keep the garments is, of course, so to observe the heart and the life, so carefully to resist temptation and abstain from sin, and so faithfully to cultivate holiness and perform duty, that the heart and the life shall be adorned with the white robes of evangelical virtue, the unspotted attire of spiritual beauty.

The cautionary precept given to us by our Lord is, therefore,

That we should be eminently watchful to perform our duty faithfully, in the trying period, in which our lot is cast.

To those, who obey, a certain blessing is secured by the promise of the Redeemer.

[I.] The great and general object, aimed at by this command, and by every other, is private, personal obedience and reformation of life; personal piety, righteousness, and temperance.

To every man is by his Creator especially committed the care of himself; of his time, his talents, and his soul. He knows, or may know, better than any other man, his wants, his sins, and his dangers, and of course the means of relief, reformation, and escape. No one, so well as he, can watch the approach of temptation, so feelingly pray for divine assistance, or so profitably resolve on future obedience. In truth no resolutions, no prayers, no watchfulness of others, will profit him at all, unless seconded by his own. No other person can make any useful impressions on our hearts, or our lives, unless by rousing in us the necessary exertions. All extraneous labours terminate in this single point: it is the end of every doctrine, exhortation, and reproof, of every moral and religious institution.

The manner, in which such obedience is to be performed, and such reformation accomplished, is described to you weekly in the desk, and daily in the scriptures. A detail of it, therefore, will not be necessary, nor expected, on the present occasion. You already know what is to be done, and the manner in which it is to be done. You need not be told, that you are to use all efforts of your own, and to look humbly and continually to God to render those efforts successful; that you are to resist carefully and faithfully every approaching temptation, and every rising sin; that you are to resolve on newness of life, and to seize every occasion, as it presents itself, to honour God, and to bless your fellow men; that you are strenuously to contend against evil habits, and watchfully to cherish good ones; and that you are constantly to aim at uniformity and eminency in a holy life, and to "adorn the doctrine of God our Saviour in all things."

But it may be necessary to remind you, that personal obedience and reformation is the foundation, and the sum, of all national worth and prosperity. If each man conducts himself aright, the community cannot be conducted wrong. If the private life be unblamable, the public state must be commendable and happy.

Individuals are often apt to consider their own private conduct as of small importance to the public welfare. This opinion is wholly erroneous and highly mischievous. No man can adopt it, who believes, and remembers, the declarations of God. If "one sinner destroyeth much good," if "the effectual fervent prayer of a righteous man availeth much," if ten righteous persons, found in the polluted cities of the vale of Siddim, would have saved them from destruction, the personal conduct of no individual can be insignificant to the safety and happiness of a nation. On the contrary, the advantages to the public of private virtue, faithful prayer and edifying example, cannot be calculated. No one can conjecture how many will be made better, safer, and happier, by the virtue of one.

Wherever wealth, politeness, talents, and office, lend their aid to the inherent efficacy of virtue, its influence is proportionally greater. In this case the example is seen by greater numbers, is regarded with more respectful attention, and felt with greater force. The piety of Hezekiah reformed and saved a nation. Men far inferior in station to kings, and possessed of far humbler means of doing good, may still easily circulate through multitudes both virtue and happiness. The beggar on the dunghill may become a public blessing. Every parent, if a faithful one, is a public blessing of course. How delightful a path of patriotism is this?

It is also to be remembered, that this is the way, in which the chief good, ever placed in the power of most persons, is to be done. If this opportunity of serving God, and befriending mankind, be lost, no other will by the great body of men ever be found. Few persons can be concerned in settling systems of faith, moulding forms of government, regulating nations, or establishing empires. But almost all can train up a family for God, instil piety, justice, kindness and truth, distribute peace and comfort around a neighbourhood, receive the poor and the outcast into their houses, tend the bed of sickness, pour balm into the wounds of pain, and awaken a smile in the aspect of sorrow. In the secret and lowly vale of life, virtue in its most lovely attire delights to dwell. There God, with peculiar complacency, most frequently finds the inestimable ornament of a meek and quiet spirit; and there the morning and the evening incense ascends with peculiar fragrance to heaven. When angels became the visitors, and the guests, of Abraham, he was a simple husbandman.

Besides, this is the great mean of personal safety and happiness. No good man was ever forgotten, or neglected, of God. To him duty is always safety. Around the tabernacle of every one, that feareth God, the angel of protection will encamp, and save him from the impending evil.

II. Among the particular duties required by this precept, and at the present time, none holds a higher place than the observation of the Sabbath.

The Sabbath and its ordinances have ever been the great means of all moral good to mankind. The faithful observation of the sabbath is, therefore, one of the chief duties

and interests of men; but the present time furnishes reasons, peculiar, at least in degree, for exemplary regard to this divine institution. The enemies of God have by private argument, ridicule, and influence, and by public decrees, pointed their especial malignity against the Sabbath; and have expected, and not without reason, that, if they could annihilate it, they should overthrow christianity. From them we cannot but learn its importance. Enemies usually discern, with more sagacity, the most promising point of attack, than those who are to be attacked. In this point are they to be peculiarly opposed. Here, peculiarly, are their designs to be baffled. If they fail here, they will finally fail. Christianity cannot fall, but by the neglect of the Sabbath.

I have been credibly informed, that, some years before the Revolution, an eminent philosopher of this country, now deceased, declared to David Hume, that Christianity would be exterminated from the American colonies within a century from that time. The opinion has doubtless been often declared and extensively imbibed; and has probably furnished our enemies their chief hopes of success. Where religion prevails, their system cannot succeed. Where religion prevails, Illuminatism cannot make disciples, a French directory cannot govern, a nation cannot be made slaves, nor villains, nor atheists, nor beasts. To destroy us, therefore, in this dreadful sense, our enemies must first destroy our Sabbath, and seduce us from the house of God.

Religion and Liberty are the two great objects of defensive war. Conjoined, they unite all the feelings, and call forth all the energies, of man. In defense of them, nations contend with the spirit of the Maccabees; "one will chase a thousand, and two put ten thousand to flight." The Dutch, in defense of them, few and feeble as they were in their infancy, assumed a gigantic courage, and grew like the fabled sons of Alous to an instantaneous and gigantic strength, broke the arms of the Spanish empire, swept its fleets from the ocean, pulled down its pride, plundered its treasures, captivated its dependencies, and forced its haughty monarch to a peace on their own terms. Religion and liberty are the meat and the drink of the body politic. Withdraw one of them, and it languishes, consumes, and dies. If indifference to either at any time becomes the prevailing character of a people, one half of their motives to vigorous defense is lost, and the hopes of their enemies are proportionally increased. Here, eminently, they are inseparable. Without religion we may possibly retain the freedom of savages, bears, and wolves; but not the freedom of New-England. If our religion were gone, our state of society would perish with it; and nothing would be left, which would be worth defending. Our children of course, if not ourselves, would be prepared, as the ox for the slaughter, to become the victims of conquest, tyranny, and atheism.

The Sabbath, with its ordinances, constitutes the bond of union to christians; the badge by which they know each other; their rallying point; the standard of their host. Beside public worship they have no means of effectual discrimination. To preserve this is to us a prime interest and duty. In no way can we so preserve, or so announce to others, our character as christians; or to effectually prevent our nakedness and shame from being seen by our enemies. Now, more than ever, we are "not to be ashamed of the gospel of Christ." Now, more than ever, are we to stand forth to the eye of our enemies, and of the world, as open, determined christians; as the followers of Christ; as the friends of God. Every man, therefore, who loves his country, or his religion, ought to feel, that he serves, or injures, both, as he celebrates, or neglects, the Sabbath. By the devout observation of this holy day he will reform himself, increase his piety, heighten his love to his country, and confirm his determination to defend all that merits his regard. He will become a better man, and a better citizen.

The house of God is also the house of social prayer. Here nations meet with God to ask, and to receive, national blessings. On the Sabbath, and in the sanctuary, the children of the Redeemer will, to the end of the world, assemble for this glorious end. Here he is ever present to give more than they can ask. If we faithfully unite, here, in seeking his protection, "no weapon formed against us will prosper."

3. Another duty, to which we are also eminently called, is an entire separation from our enemies. Among the moral duties of man some hold a higher rank than political ones, and among our own political duties none is more plain, or more absolute, than that which I have now mentioned.

In the eighteenth chapter of this prophecy, in which the dreadful effects of the seventh vial are particularly described, this duty is expressly enjoined on christians by a voice from heaven. "And I heard another voice from heaven, saying, Come out of her, my people, that ye be not partakers of her sins, and that ye receive not of her plagues." Under the evils and dangers of the sixth vial, the command in the text was given; under those of the seventh, the command which we are now considering. The world is already far advanced in the period of the sixth. In the text we are informed, that the Redeemer will hasten the progress of his vengeance on the enemies of his church, during the effusion of the two last vials. If, therefore, the judgments of the seventh are not already begun, a fact of which I am doubtful, they certainly cannot be distant. The present time is, of course, the very period for which this command was given.

The two great reasons for the command are subjoined to it by the Saviour—"that ye be not partakers of her sins; and that ye receive not of her plagues"; and each is a reason of incomprehensible magnitude.

The sins of these enemies of Christ, and Christians, are of numbers and degrees, which mock account and description. All that the malice and atheism of the dragon, the cruelty and rapacity of the beast, and the fraud and deceit of the false prophet, can generate, or accomplish, swell the list. No personal, or national, interest of man has been uninvaded; no impious sentiment, or action, against God has been spared; no malignant hostility against Christ, and his religion, has been unattempted. Justice, truth, kindness, piety, and moral obligation universally, have been not merely trodden under foot; this might have resulted from vehemence and passion; but ridiculed, spurned, and insulted, as the childish bugbears of drivelling idiocy. Chastity and decency have been alike turned out of doors; and shame and pollution called out of their dens to the hall of distinction, and the chair of state. Nor has any art, violence, or means, been unemployed to accomplish these evils.

For what end shall we be connected with men, of whom this is the character and conduct? Is it that we may assume the same character, and pursue the same conduct? Is it, that our churches may become temples of reason, our Sabbath a decade, and our psalms of praise Marseillois hymns? Is it, that we may change our holy worship into a dance of Jacobin phrenzy, and that we may behold a strumpet personating a goddess on the altars of Jehovah? Is it that we may see the Bible cast into a bonfire, the vessels of the sacramental supper borne by an ass in public procession, and our children, either wheedled or terrified, uniting in the mob, chanting mockeries against God, and hailing in the sounds of Ca ira the ruin of their religion, and the loss of their souls? Is it, that we may see our wives and daughters the victims of legal prostitution; soberly dishonoured; speciously polluted; the outcasts of delicacy and virtue, and the lothing of God and man? Is it, that we may see, in our public papers, a solemn comparison drawn by an American Mother club between the Lord Jesus Christ and a new Marat; and the fiend of malice and fraud exalted above the glorious Redeemer?

Shall we, my brethren, become partakers of these sins? Shall we introduce them into our government, our schools, our families? Shall our sons become the disciples of Voltaire, and the dragoons of Marat,* or our daughters the concubines of the Illuminati?

Some of my audience may perhaps say, "We do not believe such crimes to have existed." The people of Jerusalem did not believe, that they were in danger, until the Chaldeans surrounded their walls. The people of Laish were secure, when the children of Dan lay in ambush around their city. There are in every place, and in every age, persons "who are settled upon their lees," who take pride in disbelief, and "who say in their heart, the Lord will not do good, neither will he do evil." Some persons disbelieve through ignorance; some choose not to be informed; and some determine not to be convinced. The two last classes cannot be persuaded. The first may, perhaps, be at least ashamed, when they are told, that the evidence of all this, and much more, is complete, that it has been produced to the public, and may with a little pains-taking be known by themselves.

There are others, who, admitting the fact, deny the danger. "If others," say they, "are ever so abandoned, we need not adopt either their principles, or their practices." Common sense has however declared, two thousand years ago, and God has sanctioned the declaration, that "Evil communications corrupt good manners." Of this truth all human experience is one continued and melancholy proof. I need only add, that these persons are prepared to become the first victims of the corruption by this very self-confidence and security.

Should we, however, in a forbidden connection with these enemies of God, escape, against all hope, from moral ruin, we shall still receive our share of their plagues. This is the certain dictate of the prophetical injunction; and our own experience, and that of nations most intimately connected with them, has already proved its truth.

Look for conviction to Belgium; sunk into the dust of insignificance and meanness, plundered, insulted, forgotten, never to rise more. See Batavia wallowing in the same dust; the butt of fraud, rapacity, and derision, struggling in the last stages of life, and searching anxiously to find a quiet grave. See Venice sold in the shambles, and made the small change of a political bargain. Turn your eyes to Switzerland, and behold its happiness, and its hopes, cut off at a single stroke: happiness, erected with the labour and the wisdom of three centuries; hopes, that not long since hailed the blessings of centuries yet to come. What have they spread, but crimes and miseries; Where have they trodden, but to waste, to pollute, and to destroy?

All connection with them has been pestilential. Among ourselves it has generated nothing but infidelity, irreligion, faction, rebellion, the ruin of peace, and the loss of property. In Spain, in the Sardinian monarchy, in Genoa, it has sunk the national character, blasted national independence, rooted out confidence, and forerun destruction.

But France itself has been the chief seat of the evils, wrought by these men. The unhappy and ever to be pitied inhabitants of that country, a great part of whom are doubtless of a character similar to that of the peaceable citizens of other countries, and have probably no voluntary concern in accomplishing these evils, have themselves suffered far more from the hands of philosophists, and their followers, than the inhabitants of any other country. General Danican, a French officer, asserts in his memoirs, lately published, that three millions of Frenchmen have perished in the Revolution. Of this amazing destruction the causes by which it was produced, the principles on which it was founded, and the modes in which it was conducted, are an aggravation, that admits no bound. The butchery of the stall, and the slaughter of the stye, are scenes of deeper remorse, and softened with more sensibility. The siege of Lyons, and the judicial massacres at Nantes, stand, since the crucifixion, alone in the volume of human crimes. The misery of man never before reached the extreme of agony, nor the infamy of man its consummation. Collot D. Herbois and his satellites, Carrier and his associates, would claim eminence in a world of fiends, and will be marked

---

*See a four years Residence in France, lately published by Mr. Cornelius Davis of New-York. This is a most valuable and interesting work, and exhibits the French Revolution in a far more perfect light than any book I have seen. *It ought to be read by every American.*

with distinction in the future hissings of the universe. No guilt so deeply died in blood, since the phrenzied malice of Calvary, will probably so amaze the assembly of the final day; and Nantes and Lyons may, without a hyperbole, obtain a literal immortality in a remembrance revived beyond the grave.

In which of these plagues, my brethren, are you willing to share? Which of them will you transmit as a legacy to your children?

Would you escape, you must separate yourselves. Would you wholly escape, you must be wholly separated. I do not intend, that you must not buy and sell, or exhibit the common offices of justice and good will; but you are bound by the voice of reason, of duty, of safety, and of God, to shun all such connection with them, as will interweave your sentiments or your friendship, your religion or your policy, with theirs. You cannot otherwise fail of partaking in their guilt, and receiving of their plagues.

4thly. Another duty, to which we are no less forcibly called, is union among ourselves.

The same divine Person, who spoke in the text, hath also said, "A house, a kingdom, divided against itself cannot stand." A divided family will destroy itself. A divided nation will anticipate ruin, prepared by its enemies. Switzerland, Geneva, Genoa, Venice, the Sardinian territories, Belgium, and Batavia, are melancholy examples of the truth of this declaration of our Saviour; beacons, which warn, with a gloomy and dreadful light, the nations who survive their ruin.

The great bond of union to every people is its government. This destroyed, or distrusted, there is no center left of intelligence, counsel, or action; no system of purposes, or measures; no point of rallying, or confidence. When a nation is ready to say, "What part have we in David, or what inheritance in the son of Jesse?" it will naturally subjoin, "Every man to his tent, O Israel!"

The candour and uprightness, with which our own government has acted in the progress of the present controversy, have forced encomiums even from its most bitter opposers, and excited the warmest approbation and applause of all its friends. Few objects could be more important, auspicious, or gratifying to christians, than to see the conduct of their rulers such, as they can, with boldness of access, bring before their God, and fearlessly commend to his favour and protection.

In men, possessed of similar candour, adherence to our government, in the present crisis, may be regarded as a thing of course. They need not be informed, that the existing rulers must be the directors of our public affairs, and the only directors; that their views and measures will not and cannot always accord with the judgment of individuals, as the opinions of individuals accord no better with each other; that the officers of government are possessed of better information than private persons can be; that, if they had the same information, they would probably coincide with the opinions of their rulers; that confidence must be placed in men, imperfect as they are, in all human affairs, or no important business can be done; and that men of known and tried probity are fully deserving of that confidence.

At the present time this adherence ought to be unequivocally manifested. In a land of universal suffrage, where every individual is possessed of much personal consequence as in ours, the government ought, especially in great measures, to be as secure, as may be, of the harmonious and cheerful co-operation of the citizens. All success, here, depends on the hearty concurrence of the community; and no occasion ever called for it more.

But there are, even in this state, persons, who are opposed to the government. To them I observe, That the government of France has destroyed the independence of every nation, which has confided in it.

That every such nation has been ruined by its internal divisions, especially by the separation of the people from their government.

That they have attempted to accomplish our ruin by the same means, and will certainly accomplish it, if they can;

That the miseries suffered by the subjugated nations have been numberless and extreme, involving the loss of national honour, the immense plunder of public and private property, the conflagration of churches and dwellings, the total ruin of families, the butchery of great multitudes of fathers and sons, and the most deplorable dishonour of wives and daughters;

That the same miseries will be repeated here, if in their power.

That there is, under God, no mean of escaping this ruin, but union among ourselves, and unshaken adherence to the existing government;

That themselves have an infinitely higher interest in preserving the independence of their country, than in any thing, which *can* exist, should it be conquered;

That they must stand, or fall, with their country; since the French, like all other conquerors, though they may for a little time regard them, as aids and friends, with a seeming partiality, will soon lose that partiality in a general contempt and hatred for them, as Americans. That should they, contrary to all experience, escape these evils, their children will suffer them as extensively as those of their neighbours; and

That to oppose, or neglect, the defence of their country, is to stab the breast, from which they have drawn their life.

I know not that even these considerations will prevail: if they do not, nothing can be suggested by me, which will have efficacy. I must leave them, therefore, to their consciences, and their God.

In the mean time, since the great facts, of which this controversy has consisted, have not, during the preceding periods, been thoroughly known, or believed, by all; and since all questions of expediency will be viewed differently by different eyes; I cannot but urge a general spirit of conciliation. To men labouring under mere mistakes, and prejudices void of malignity, hard names are in most cases unhappily applied, and unkindness is unwisely exhibited. Multitudes, heretofore attached to France with great ardour, have, from full conviction of the necessity of changing their sentiments and their conduct, come forth in the most decisive language, and determined conduct, of defenders of their country. More are daily exhibiting the same spirit and measures. Almost all native Americans will, I doubt not, speedily appear in the same ranks; and none should, in my opinion, be discouraged by useless obloquy.

5. Another duty, injoined in the text, and highly incumbent on us at this time, is unshaken firmness in our opposition.

A steady and invincible firmness is the chief instrument of great achievements. It is the prime mean of great wealth, learning, wisdom, power and virtue; and without it nothing noble or useful is usually accomplished. Without it our separation from our enemies, and our union among ourselves, will avail to no end. The cause is too complex, the object too important, to be determined by a single effort. It is infinitely too important to be given up, let the consequence be what it may. No evils, which can flow from resistance, can be as great as those, which must flow from

submission. Great sacrifices of property, of peace, and of life, we may be called to make, but they will fall short of complete ruin. If they should not, it will be more desirable, beyond computation, to fall in the honourable and faithful defence of our families, our country, and our religion, than to survive, the melancholy, debased, and guilty spectators of the ruin of all. We contend for all that is, or ought to be, dear to man. Our cause is eminently that, in which "he who seeketh to save his life shall lose it, and he who loseth it," in obedience to the command of his Master, "shall find it" beyond the grave. To our enemies we have done no wrong. Unspotted justice looks down on all our public measures with a smile. We fight for that, for which we can pray. We fight for the lives, the honor, the safety, of our wives and children, for the religion of our fathers, and for the liberty, "with which Christ hath made us free." "We jeopard our lives," that our children may inherit these glorious blessings, be rescued from the grinding insolence of foreign despotism, and saved from the corruption and perdition of foreign atheism. I am a father. I feel the usual parental tenderness for my children. I have long soothed the approach of declining years with the fond hope of seeing my sons serving God and their generation around me. But from cool conviction I declare in this solemn place, I would far rather follow them one by one to an untimely grave, than to behold them, however prosperous, the victims of philosophism. What could I then believe, but that they were "nigh unto cursing, and that their end was to be burned."

From two sources only are we in danger of irresolution; *avarice, and a reliance on those fair professions,* which our enemies have began to make, and which they will doubtless continue to make, in degrees, and with insidiousness, still greater.

On the first of these sources I observe, that, if we grudge a part of our property in the defence of our country, we lose the whole; and not only the whole of our property, but all our comforts, and all our hopes. Every enjoyment of life, every solace of sorrow, will be offered up in one vast hecatomb at the shrine of pride, plunder, impurity, and atheism. Those "who fear not God, regard not man." All interests, beside their own, are in the view of such men the sport of wantonness, of insolence, and of a heart of millstone. They and their engines will soon tell you, if you do not put it out of their power, as one of the same engines told the miserable inhabitants of Neuwied (in Germany) unhappily placing confidence in their professions. Hear the story, in the words of Professor Robison,

> If ever there was a spot upon earth, where men may be happy in a state of cultivated society, it was the little principality of Neuwied. I saw it in 1770. The town was neat, and the palace handsome and in good state. But the country was beyond conception delightful; not a cottage that was out of repair; not a hedge out of order. It had been the hobby of the prince (pardon me the word) who made it his daily employment to go through his principality, and assist every householder, of whatever condition, with his advice and with his purse; and when a freeholder could not of himself put things into a thriving condition, the prince sent his workmen and did it for him. He endowed schools for the common people and two academies for the gentry and the people of business. He gave little portions to the daughters, and prizes to the well-behaving sons of the labouring people. His own houshold was a pattern of elegance and oeconomy; his sons were sent to Paris, to learn elegance, and to England, to learn science and agriculture. In short the whole was like a romance, and was indeed romantic. I heard it spoken of with a smile at the table of the bishop of Treves, and was induced to see it the next day as a curiosity. Yet even here the fanaticism of Knigge (one of the founders of the Illuminati) would distribute his poison, and tell the blinded people that they were in a state of sin and misery, that their prince was a despot, and that they would never be happy 'till he was made to fly, and 'till they were made all equal.

> They got their wish. The swarm of French locusts sat down at Neuwied's beautiful fields, in 1793, and intrenched themselves; and in three months prince's and farmers' houses, and cottages, and schools, and academies, all vanished. When they complained of their miseries to the French general, René le Grand, he replied, with a contemptuous and cutting laugh, "All is ours. We have left you your eyes to cry."

Will you you trust such professions? Have not your enemies made them to every country, which they have subjugated? Have they fulfilled them to one? Will they prove more sincere to you? Have they not deceived you in every expectation hitherto? On what grounds can you rely on them hereafter?

Will you grudge your property for the defence of itself, of your families, of yourselves. Will you preserve it to pay the price of a Dutch loan? to have it put in requisition by the French Directory? to label it on your doors, that they may, without trouble and without a tax bill, send their sol-diers and take it for the use of the Republic? Will you keep it to assist them to pay their fleets and armies for subduing you? and to maintain their forts and garrisons for keeping you in subjection? Shall it become the purchase of a French fete, holden to commemorate the massacres of the 10th of August, the butcheries of the 3d of September, or the murder of Louis the 16th, your former benefactor? Shall it furnish the means for *representatives of the people* to roll through your streets on the wheels of splendour, to imprison your sons and fathers; to seize on all the comforts, which you have earned with toil, and laid up with care; and to gather your wives, sisters, and daughters, into their brutal seraglios? Shall it become the price of the guillotine, and pay the expense of cleansing your streets from brooks of human blood?

Will you rely on men whose *principles justify falshood, injustice, and cruelty?* Will you trust philosophists? men who set truth at nought, who make justice a butt of mockery, who deny the being and providence of God, and laugh at the interests and sufferings of men? Think not that such men can change. They can scarcely be worse. There is not a hope that they will become better.

But perhaps you may be alarmed by the power, and the successes, of your enemies. I am warranted to declare, that the ablest judge of this subject in America has said, that, if we are united, firm, and faithful to ourselves, neither France, nor all Europe, can subdue these states. Against other nations they contended with great and decisive advantages. Those nations were near to them, were divided, feeble, corrupted, seduced by philosophists, slaves of despotism, and separated from their government. None of these characters can be applied to us, unless we voluntarily retain those, which depend on ourselves. Three thousand miles of ocean spread between us and our enemies, to enfeeble and disappoint their efforts. They will not here contend with silken Italians, with divided Swissers, nor with self-surrendered Belgians and Batavians. They will find a hardy race of freemen, uncorrupted by luxury, unbroken by despotism; enlightened to understand their privileges, glowing with independence, and determined to be free, or to die: men who love, and who will defend, their families, their country, and their religion: men fresh from triumph, and strong in a recent and victorious Revolution. Doubled, since that Revolution began, in their numbers, and quadrupled in their resources and advantages, at home, in a country formed to disappoint invasion, and to prosper defence, under leaders skilled in all the arts and duties of war, trained in the path of success, they have, if united, firm, and faithful, every thing to hope, and, beside the common evils of war, nothing to fear.

Think not that I trust in chariots and in horses. My own reliance is, I hope, I ardently hope yours is, also, on the Lord our God. All these are his most merciful blessings, and, as such, most supporting consolations to us. They are the very means, which he has provided for our safety, and our hope. Stupidity, sloth, and ingratitude, can alone be blind to them as tokens for good. We are not, my brethren, to look for miracles, nor to expect God to accomplish them. We are to trust in him for the blessings of a regular and merciful providence. Such a providence is over us for good. I have recited abundant proofs, and could easily recite many more. All these are means, with which we are to plant, and to water, and in answer to our prayers God will certainly give the increase.

But I am peculiarly confident in the promised blessing of the text. Our contention is a plain duty to God. The same glorious Person, who has commanded it, has promised to crown our obedience with his blessing, and has thus illumined this gloomy prediction, and shed the dawn of hope and comfort over this melancholy period.

To you the promise is eminently supporting. He has won your faith by the great things he has already done for your fathers, and for you. The same Almighty Hand, which destroyed the fleet of Chebucto by the storm, and whelmed it in the deep; which conducted into the arms of Manly, and of Mugford, those means of war, which for the time saved your country; which raised up your Washington to guide your armies and your councils; which united you with your brethren against every expectation and hope; which disappointed the devices of enemies without, and traitors within; which made the winds and the waves fight for you at Yorktown; which has, in later periods, repeatedly disclosed the machinations of your enemies, and which has now roused a noble spirit of resistance to intrigue and to terror; will accomplish for you a final deliverance from the hand of those, "who seek your hurt." He has been your fathers' God, and he will be yours.

Look through the history of your country. You will find scarcely less glorious and wonderful proofs of divine protection and deliverance, uniformly administered through every period of our existence as a people, than shone to the people of Israel in Egypt, in the wilderness, and in Canaan.

Can it be believed, can it be, that Christianity has been so planted here, the church of God so established, so happy a government constituted, and so desirable a state of society begun, merely to shew them to the world, and then destroy them? No instance can be found in the providence of God, in which a nation so wonderfully established, and preserved, has been overthrown, until it had progressed farther in corruption. We may be cast down, but experience only will prove to me, that we shall be destroyed.

But the consideration, which ought of itself to decide your opinions and your conduct, and which adds immense weight to all the others, is that the alternative, as exhibited in the prediction, and in providence, is beyond measure dreadful, and is at hand. "Behold," saith the Saviour, "I come as a thief"—suddenly, unexpectedly, alarmingly—as that wasting enemy, the burglar, breaks up the house in the hour of darkness, when all the inhabitants are lost in sleep and security. How strongly do the great events of the present day shew this awful advent of the King of Kings to be at the doors?

Turn your eyes, for a moment, to the face of providence, and mark its new and surprising appearance. The Jews, for the first time since the destruction of Jerusalem by Adrian, have, in these states, been admitted to the rights of citizenship; and have since been admitted to the same rights in Prussia. They have also, as we are informed, appointed a solemn delegation to examine the evidences of Christianity. In the Austrian dominions, it is asserted, they have agreed to observe the Christian Sabbath; and in England, have in considerable numbers embraced the Christian religion. New and unprecedented efforts have been made, and are fast increasing, in England, Scotland, Germany, and the United States, for the conversion of the heathen. Measures have, in Europe, and in America, been adopted, and are still enlarging, for putting an end to the African slavery, which will within a moderate period bring it to an end. Mohammedism is nearly extinct in Persia, one of the chief supports of that imposture. In Turkey, its other great support, the throne totters to its fall. The great calamities of the present period have fallen, also, almost exclusively upon the Antichristian empire; and almost every part of that empire has drunk deeply of the cup. France, Belgium, Spain, Ireland, the Sardinian monarchy, the Austrian dominions, Venice, Genoa, popish Switzerland, the Ecclesiastical State, popish Germany, Poland, and the French West-Indies, have all been visited with judgments wonderful and terrible; and in exact accordance with prophecy have furthered their own ruin. The kings, or states, of this empire are now plainly "hating the whore, eating her flesh, and burning her with fire." Batavia, protestant Switzerland, some parts of protestant Germany, and Geneva, have most unwisely, not to say wickedly, refused "to come out" and have therefore "partaken of the sins, and received of the plagues," of their enemies. To the same unhappy cause our own smartings may all be traced; but blessed be God, there is reason to hope, that "we are escaping from the snare of the fowler."

So sudden, so unexpected, so alarming a state of things has not existed since the deluge. Every mouth proclaims, every eye looks its astonishment. Wonders daily succeed wonders, and are beginning to be regarded as the standing course of things. As they are of so many kinds, exist in so many places, and respect so many objects; kinds, places and objects, all marked out in prophecy, exhibited as parts of one closely united system, and to be expected at the present time; they shew that this affecting declaration is even now fulfilling in a surprising manner, and that the advent of Christ is at least at our doors. Think how awful this period is. Think what convulsions, what calamities, are portended by that great Voice out of the temple of heaven from the Throne—"It is done!" by the voices and thunderings and lightnings, by the unprecedented shaking of the earth, the unexampled plague of hailstones, the fleeing of the islands, the vanishing of the mountains, the rending asunder of the Antichristian empire, the united ascent of all its sins before God, the falling of the cities of the nations, the general embattling of mankind against their Maker, and their final overthrow, in such immense numbers, that "all the fowls shall be filled with their flesh."

"God is jealous, and the Lord revengeth; the Lord revengeth and is furious; the Lord will take vengeance on his adversaries, he reserveth wrath for his enemies. The Lord is slow to anger, and great in power, and will not at all acquit the wicked. The Lord hath his way in the whirlwind, and in the storm, and the clouds are the dust of his feet. The mountains quake at him, and the hills melt; and the earth is burnt at his presence, yea the world, and all that dwell therein. Who can stand before his indignation? Who can abide in the fierceness of his anger?"

In this amazing conflict, amidst this stupendous and immeasurable ruin, how transporting the thought, that safety and peace may be certainly found. O thou God of our fathers! our own God! and the God of our children! enable us so to watch, and keep our garments, in this solemn day, that our shame appear not, and that both we and our posterity may be entitled to the blessing which thou hast promised.

AMEN

Report of the Hartford Convention

1815

On December 15, 1814, a group of delegates from states and counties in New England met in Hartford, Connecticut, to discuss problems arising from the War of 1812. The convention secretary was Timothy Dwight. New England had consistently opposed the war with Great Britain. The Federalist Party, which remained strong in this region despite its losses elsewhere, had opposed the federal government's embargo of British shipping, and the New England states had refused to allow the federal government to take over control of local militia. While several members of this convention had publicly considered seeking a separate peace between Great Britain and New England, effectively severing ties of union to the United States, the convention produced a more moderate report.

Report of the Hartford Convention

The Delegates from the Legislatures of the States of Massachusetts, Connecticut, and Rhode-Island, and from the Counties of Grafton and Cheshire in the State of New-Hampshire and the County of Windham in the State of Vermont, assembled in Convention, beg leave to report the following result of their conference

The Convention is deeply impressed with a sense of the arduous nature of the commission which they were appointed to execute, of devising the means of defence against dangers, and of relief from oppressions proceeding from the act of their own Government, without violating constitutional principles, or disappointing the hopes of a suffering and injured people. To prescribe patience and firmness to those who are already exhausted by distress, is sometimes to drive them to despair, and the progress towards reform by the regular road, is irksome to those whose imaginations discern, and whose feelings prompt, to a shorter course.—But when abuses, reduced to system and accumulated through a course of years have pervaded every department of Government, and spread corruption through every region of the State; when these are clothed with the forms of law, and enforced by an Executive whose will is their source, no summary means of relief can be applied without recourse to direct and open resistance. This experiment, even when justifiable, cannot fail to be painful to the good citizen; and the success of the effort will be no security against the danger of the example. Precedents of resistance to the worst administration, are eagerly seized by those who are naturally hostile to the best. Necessity alone can sanction a resort to this measure; and it should never be extended in duration or degree beyond the exigency, until the people, not merely in the fervour of sudden excitement, but after full deliberation, are determined to change the Constitution.

It is a truth, not to be concealed, that a sentiment prevails to no inconsiderable extent, that Administration have given such constructions to that instrument, and practised so many abuses under colour of its authority, that the time for a change is at hand. Those who so believe, regard the evils which surround them as intrinsic and incurable defects in the Constitution. They yield to a persuasion, that no change, at any time, or on any occasion, can aggravate the misery of their country. This opinion may ultimately prove to be correct. But as the evidence on which it rests is not yet conclusive, and as measures adopted upon the assumption of its certainty might be irrevocable, some general considerations are submitted, in the hope of reconciling all to a course of moderation and firmness, which may save them from the regret incident to sudden decisions, probably avert the evil, or at least insure consolation and success in the last resort.

The Constitution of the United States, under the auspices of a wise and virtuous Administration, proved itself competent to all the objects of national prosperity, comprehended in the views of its framers. No parallel can be found in history, of a transition so rapid as that of the United States from the lowest depression to the highest felicity—from the condition of weak and disjointed republics, to that of a great, united, and prosperous nation.

Although this high state of public happiness has undergone a miserable and afflicting reverse, through the prevalence of a weak and profligate policy, yet the evils and afflictions which have thus been induced upon the country, are not peculiar to any form of Government. The lust and caprice of power, the corruption of patronage, the oppression of the weaker interests of the community by the stronger, heavy taxes, wasteful expenditures, and unjust and ruinous wars, are the natural offspring of bad Administrations, in all ages and countries. It was indeed to be hoped, that the rulers of these States would not make such disastrous haste to involve their infancy in the embarrassments of old and rotten institutions. Yet all this have they done; and their conduct calls loudly for their dismission and disgrace. But to attempt upon every abuse of power to change the Constitution, would be to perpetuate the evils of revolution.

Again, the experiment of the powers of the Constitution, to regain its vigour, and of the people to recover from their delusions, has been hitherto made under the greatest possible disadvantages arising from the state of the world. The fierce passions which have convulsed the nations of Europe, have passed the Ocean, and finding their way to the bosoms of our citizens, have afforded to Administration the means of perverting public opinion, in respect to our foreign relations, so as to acquire its aid in the indulgence of their animosities, and the increase of their adherents. Further, a reformation of public opinion, resulting from dear bought experience, in the Southern Atlantic States, at least, is not to be despaired of. They will have felt, that the Eastern States cannot be made exclusively the victims of a capricious and impassioned policy. —They will have seen that the great and essential interests of the people, are common to the South and to the East. They will realize the fatal errors of a system, which seeks revenge for commercial injuries in the sacrifice of commerce, and aggravates by needless wars, to an immeasurable extent, the injuries it professes to redress. They may discard the influence of visionary theorists, and recognize the benefits of a practical policy. Indications of this desirable revolution of opinion, among our brethren in those States, are already manifested.—While a hope remains of its ultimate completion, its progress should not be retarded or stopped, by exciting fears which must check these favourable tendencies, and frustrate the efforts of the wisest and best men in those States, to accelerate this propitious change.

Finally, if the Union be destined to dissolution, by reason of the multiplied abuses of bad administrations, it should, if possible, be the work of peaceable times, and deliberate consent.—Some new form of confederacy should be substituted among those States, which shall intend to maintain a federal relation to each other.—Events may prove that the causes of our calamities are deep and permanent. They may be found to proceed, not merely from the blindness of prejudice, pride of opinion, violence of party spirit, or the confusion of the times; but they may be traced to implacable combinations of individuals, or of States, to monopolize power and office, and to trample without remorse upon the rights and interests of commercial sections of the Union. Whenever it shall appear that these causes are radical and permanent, a separation by equitable arrangement, will be preferable to an alliance by constraint, among nominal friends, but real enemies, inflamed by mutual hatred and jealousy, and inviting by intestine divisions, contempt, and aggression from abroad. But a severance of the Union by one or more States, against the will of the rest, and especially in a time of war, can be justified only by absolute necessity. These are among the principal objections against precipitate measures tending to disunite the States, and when examined in connection with the farewell address of the Father of his country, they must, it is believed, be deemed conclusive.

Under these impressions, the Convention have proceeded to confer and deliberate upon the alarming state of public affairs, especially, as affecting the interests of the people who have appointed them for this purpose, and they are naturally led to a consideration, in the first place, of the dangers and grievances which menace an immediate or speedy pressure, with a view of suggesting means of present relief; in the next place, of such as are of a more remote and general description, in the hope of attaining future security.

Among the subjects of complaint and apprehension, which might be comprised under the former of these propositions, the attention of the Convention has been occupied with the claims and pretensions advanced, and the authority exercised over the militia, by the executive and legislative departments of the National Government. Also, upon the destitution of the means of defence in which the Eastern States are left; while at the same time they are doomed to heavy requisitions of men and money for national objects.

The authority of the National Government over the

militia is derived from those clauses in the Constitution which give power to Congress "to provide for calling forth the militia to execute the laws of the Union, suppress insurrections and repel invasions"—Also "to provide for organizing, arming and disciplining the militia, and for governing such parts of them as may be employed in the service of the United States, reserving to the States respectively the appointment of the officers, and the authority of training the militia according to the discipline prescribed by Congress." Again, "The President shall be Commander in Chief of the army and navy of the United States, and of the militia of the several States, *when called into the actual service of the United States.*" In these specified cases only, has the National Government any power over the militia; and it follows conclusively that for all general and ordinary purposes, this power belongs to the States respectively, and to them alone. It is not only with regret, but with astonishment, the Convention perceive that under colour of an authority conferred with such plain and precise limitations, a power is arrogated by the executive government, and in some instances sanctioned by the two Houses of Congress, of controul over the militia, which if conceded, will render nugatory the rightful authority of the individual States over that class of men, and by placing at the disposal of the National Government the lives and services of the great body of the people, enable it at pleasure to destroy their liberties, and erect a military despotism on the ruins.

An elaborate examination of the principles assumed for the basis of these extravagant pretensions, of the consequences to which they lead, and of the insurmountable objections to their admission, would transcend the limits of this Report. A few general observations, with an exhibition of the character of these pretensions, and a recommendation of a strenuous opposition to them, must not however be omitted.

It will not be contended that by the terms used in the constitutional compact, the power of the National Government to call out the militia is other than a power expressly limited to three cases. One of these must exist as a condition precedent to the exercise of that power—Unless the laws shall be opposed, or an insurrection shall exist, or an invasion shall be made, Congress, and of consequence the President as their organ, has no more power over the militia than over the armies of a foreign nation.

But if the declaration of the President should be admitted to be an unerring test of the existence of these cases, this important power would depend, not upon the truth of the fact, but upon executive infallibility. And the limitation of the power would consequently be nothing more than merely nominal, as it might always be eluded. It follows therefore that the decision of the President in this particular cannot be conclusive. It is as much the duty of the State authorities to watch over the rights *reserved,* as of the United States to exercise the powers which are *delegated.*

The arrangement of the United States into military districts, with a small portion of the regular force, under an officer of high rank of the standing army, with power to call for the militia, as circumstances in his judgment may require; and to assume the command of them, is not warranted by the Constitution or any law of the United States. It is not denied that Congress may delegate to the President of the United States the power to call forth the militia in the cases which are within their jurisdiction—But he has no authority to substitute military prefects throughout the Union, to use their own discretion in such instances. To station an officer of the army in a military district without troops corresponding to his rank, for the purpose of taking command of the militia that may be called into service, is a manifest evasion of that provision of the Constitution which expressly reserves to the States the appointment of the officers of the militia; and the object of detaching such officer cannot be well conceived to be any other than that of superseding the Governour or other officers of the militia in their right to command.

The power of dividing the militia of the States into classes and obliging such classes to furnish by contract or draft, able bodied men, to serve for one or more years for the defence of the frontier, is not delegated to Congress. If a claim to draft the militia for one year for such general object be admissible, no limitation can be assigned to it, but the discretion of those who make the law. Thus with a power in Congress to authorize such a draft or conscription, and in the Executive to decide conclusively upon the existence and continuance of the emergency, the whole militia may be converted into a standing army disposable at the will of the President of the United States.

The power of compelling the militia and other citizens of the United States by a forcible draft or conscription to serve in the regular armies as proposed in a late official letter of the Secretary of War, is not delegated to Congress by the Constitution, and the exercise of it would be not less dangerous to their liberties, than hostile to the sovereignty of the States. The effort to deduce this power from the right of raising armies, is a flagrant attempt to pervert the sense of the clause in the Constitution which confers that right, and is incompatible with other provisions in that instrument. The armies of the United States have always been raised by contract, never by conscription, and nothing more can be wanting to a Government possessing the power thus claimed to enable it to usurp the entire controul of the militia, in derogation of the authority of the State, and to convert it by impressment into a standing army.

It may be here remarked, as a circumstance illustrative of the determination of the Executive to establish an absolute controul over all descriptions of citizens, that the right of impressing seamen into the naval service is expressly asserted by the Secretary of the Navy in a late report. Thus a practice, which in a foreign government has been regarded with great abhorrence by the people, finds advocates among those who have been the loudest to condemn it.

The law authorizing the enlistment of minors and apprentices into the armies of the United States, without the consent of parents and guardians, is also repugnant to the spirit of the Constitution. By a construction of the power to raise armies, as applied by our present rulers, not only persons capable of contracting are liable to be impressed into the army, but those who are under legal disabilities to make contracts, are to be invested with this capacity, in order to enable them to annul at pleasure contracts made in their behalf by legal guardians. Such an interference with the municipal laws and rights of the several States, could never have been contemplated by the framers of the Constitution. It impairs the salutary controul and influence of the parent over his child—the master over his servant— the guardian over his ward—and thus destroys the most important relations in society, so that by the conscription of the father, and the seduction of the son, the power of the Executive over all the effective male population of the United States is made complete.

Such are some of the odious features of the novel system proposed by the rulers of a free country, under the limited powers derived from the Constitution. What portion of them will be embraced in acts finally to be passed, it is yet impossible to determine. It is, however, sufficiently alarming to perceive, that these projects emanate from the highest authority, nor should it be forgotten, that by the plan of the Secretary of War, the classification of the militia embraced the principle of direct taxation upon the white population only; and that, in the House of Representatives, a motion to apportion the militia among the white popula-

tion exclusively, which would have been in its operation a direct tax, was strenuously urged and supported.

In this whole series of devices and measures for raising men, this Convention discern a total disregard for the Constitution, and a disposition to violate its provisions, demanding from the individual States a firm and decided opposition. An iron despotism can impose no harder servitude upon the citizen, than to force him from his home and his occupation, to wage offensive wars, undertaken to gratify the pride or passions of his master. The example of France has recently shewn that a cabal of individuals assuming to act in the name of the people, may transform the great body of citizens into soldiers, and deliver them over into the hands of a single tyrant. No war, not held in just abhorrence by a people, can require the aid of such stratagems to recruit an army. Had the troops already raised, and in great numbers sacrificed upon the frontier of Canada, been employed for the defence of the country, and had the millions which have been squandered with shameless profusion, been appropriated to their payment, to the protection of the coast, and to the naval service, there would have been no occasion for unconstitutional expedients. Even at this late hour, let Government leave to New-England the remnant of her resources, and she is ready and able to defend her territory, and to resign the glories and advantages of the border war, to those who are determined to persist in its prosecution.

That acts of Congress in violation of the Constitution are absolutely void, is an undeniable position. It does not, however, consist with the respect and forbearance due from a confederate State towards the General Government, to fly to open resistance upon every infraction of the Constitution. The mode and the energy of the opposition, should always conform to the nature of the violation, the intention of its authors, the extent of the injury inflicted, the determination manifested to persist in it, and the danger of delay. But in cases of deliberate, dangerous, and palpable infractions of the Constitution, affecting the sovereignty of a State, and liberties of the people; it is not only the right but the duty of such a State to interpose its authority for their protection, in the manner best calculated to secure that end. When emergencies occur which are either beyond the reach of the judicial tribunals, or too pressing to admit of the delay incident to their forms, States, which have no common umpire, must be their own judges, and execute their own decisions. It will thus be proper for the several States to await the ultimate disposal of the obnoxious measures, recommended by the Secretary of War, or pending before Congress, and so to use their power according to the character these measures shall finally assume, as effectually to protect their own sovereignty, and the rights and liberties of their citizens.

The next subject which has occupied the attention of the Convention, is the means of defence against the common enemy. This naturally leads to the inquiries, whether any expectation can be reasonably entertained, that adequate provision for the defence of the Eastern States will be made by the National Government? Whether the several States can, from their own resources, provide for self-defence and fulfil the requisitions which are to be expected for the national Treasury? and, generally what course, of conduct ought to be adopted by those States, in relation to the great object of defence?

Without pausing at present to comment upon the causes of the war, it may be assumed as a truth, officially announced, that to achieve the conquest of Canadian territory, and to hold it as a pledge for peace, is the deliberate purpose of Administration. This enterprize, commenced at a period when Government possessed the advantage of selecting the time and occasion for making a sudden descent upon an unprepared enemy, now languishes in the third year of the war. It has been prosecuted with various fortune, and occasional brilliancy of exploit, but without any solid acquisition. The British armies have been recruited by veteran regiments. Their navy commands Ontario. The American ranks are thinned by the casualties of war. Recruits are discouraged by the unpopular character of the contest, and by the uncertainty of receiving their pay.

In the prosecution of this favourite warfare, Administration have left the exposed and vulnerable parts of the country destitute of all efficient means of defence. The main body of the regular army has been marched to the frontier.—The navy has been stripped of a great part of its sailors for the service of the Lakes. Meanwhile the enemy scours the sea-coast, blockades our ports, ascends our bays and rivers, makes actual descents in various and distant places, holds some by force, and threatens all that are assailable, with fire and sword. The sea-board of four of the New-England States, following its curvatures, presents an extent of more than seven hundred miles, generally occupied by a compact population, and accessible by a naval force, exposing a mass of people and property to the devastation of the enemy, which bears a great proportion to the residue of the maritime frontier of the United States. This extensive shore has been exposed to frequent attacks, repeated contributions, and constant alarms. The regular forces detached by the national Government for its defence, are mere pretexts for placing officers of high rank in command. They are besides confined to a few places, and are too insignificant in number to be included in any computation.

These States have thus been left to adopt measures for their own defence. The militia have been constantly kept on the alert, and harassed by garrison duties, and other hardships, while the expenses, of which the National Government decline the reimbursement, threaten to absorb all the resources of the States. The President of the United States has refused to consider the expense of the militia detached by State authority, for the indispensable defence of the State, as chargeable to the Union, on the ground of a refusal by the Executive of the State, to place them under the command of officers of the regular army. Detachments of militia placed at the disposal of the General Government, have been dismissed either without pay, or with depreciated paper. The prospect of the ensuing campaign is not enlivened by the promise of any alleviation of these grievances. From authentic documents, extorted by necessity from those whose inclination might lead them to conceal the embarrassments of the Government, it is apparent that the treasury is bankrupt, and its credit prostrate. So deplorable is the state of the finances, that those who feel for the honour and safety of the country, would be willing to conceal the melancholy spectacle, if those whose infatuation has produced this state of fiscal concerns, had not found themselves compelled to unveil it to public view.

If the war be continued, there appears no room for reliance upon the national government for the supply of those means of defence, which must become indispensable to secure these States from desolation and ruin. Nor is it possible that the States can discharge this sacred duty from their own resources, and continue to sustain the burden of the national taxes. The Administration, after a long perseverance in plans to baffle every effort of commercial enterprize, had fatally succeeded in their attempts at the epoch of the war. Commerce, the vital spring of New-England's prosperity, was annihilated. Embargoes, restrictions, and the rapacity of revenue officers, had completed its destruction. The various objects for the employment of productive labour, in the branches of business dependent on commerce, have disappeared. The fisheries have shared its fate. Manufactures, which Government has professed an intention to favour and to cherish, as an indemnity for the failure of these branches of business, are doomed to struggle in their infancy with taxes and obstructions, which cannot fail most seriously to affect their growth. The specie is withdrawn from circulation. The landed interest, the last to feel these burdens, must prepare to become their principal support, as all other sources of revenue must be exhausted. Under these circumstances, taxes, of a description and amount unprecedented in this country, are in a train of imposition, the burden of which must fall with the heaviest pressure upon the States east of the Potowmac. The amount of these taxes for the ensuing year, cannot be estimated at less than five millions of dollars upon the New-England States, and the expenses of the last year for defence, in Massachusetts alone, approaches to one million of dollars.

From these facts, it is almost superfluous to state the irresistible inference that these States have no capacity of defraying the expense requisite for their own protection, and, at the same time, of discharging the demands of the national treasury.

The last inquiry, what course of conduct ought to be adopted by the aggrieved States, is in a high degree momentous. When a great and brave people shall feel themselves deserted by their Government, and reduced to the necessity either of submission to a foreign enemy, or of appropriating to their own use, those means of defence which are indispensable to self-preservation, they cannot consent to wait passive spectators of approaching ruin, which it is in their power to avert, and to resign the last remnant of their industrious earnings, to be dissipated in support of measures destructive of the best interests of the nation.

This Convention will not trust themselves to express their conviction of the catastrophe to which such a state of things inevitably tends. Conscious of their high responsibility to God and their country, solicitous for the continuance of the Union, as well as the sovereignty of the States, unwilling to furnish obstacles to peace—resolute never to submit to a foreign enemy, and confiding in the Divine care and protection, they will, until the last hope shall be extinguished, endeavour to avert such consequences.

With this view they suggest an arrangement, which may at once be consistent with the honour and interest of the National Government, and the security of these States. This it will not be difficult to conclude, if that government should be so disposed. By the terms of it these States might be allowed to assume their own defence, by the militia or other troops. A reasonable portion, also, of the taxes raised in each State might be paid into its treasury, and credited to the United States, but to be appropriated to the defence of such State, to be accounted for with the United States. No doubt is entertained that by such an arrangement, this portion of the country could be defended with greater effect, and in a mode more consistent with economy, and the public convenience, than any which has been practised.

Should an application for these purposes, made to Congress by the State Legislatures, be attended with success, and should peace upon just terms appear to be unattainable, the people would stand together for the common defence, until a change of Administration, or of disposition in the enemy, should facilitate the occurrence of that auspicious event. It would be inexpedient for this Convention to diminish the hope of a successful issue to such an application, by recommending, upon supposition of a contrary event, ulterior proceedings. Nor is it indeed within their province. In a state of things so solemn and trying as may then arise, the Legislatures of the States, or Conventions of the whole people, or delegates appointed by them for the express purpose in another Convention, must act as such urgent circumstances may then require.

But the duty incumbent on this Convention will not have been performed, without exhibiting some general view of such measures as they deem essential to secure the nation against a relapse into difficulties and dangers, should they, by the blessing of Providence, escape from their present condition, without absolute ruin. To this end a concise retrospect of the state of this nation under the advantages of a wise Administration, contrasted with the miserable abyss into which it is plunged by the profligacy and folly of political theorists, will lead to some practical conclusions. On this subject, it will be recollected, that the immediate influence of the Federal Constitution upon its first adoption, and for twelve succeeding years, upon the prosperity and happiness of the nation, seemed to countenance a belief in the transcendency of its perfection over all other human institutions. In the catalogue of blessings which have fallen to the lot of the most favoured nations, none could be enumerated from which our country was excluded—A free Constitution, administered by great and incorruptible statesmen, realized the fondest hopes of liberty and independence—The progress of agriculture was stimulated by the certainty of value in the harvest—and commerce, after traversing every sea, returned with the riches of every clime.—A revenue, secured by a sense of honour, collected without oppression, and paid without murmurs, melted away the national debt; and the chief concern of the public creditor arose from its too rapid diminution.—The wars and commotions of the European nations, and the interruptions of their commercial intercourse afforded to those who had not promoted, but who would have rejoiced to alleviate their calamities, a fair and golden opportunity, by combining themselves to lay a broad foundation for national wealth.—Although occasional vexations to commerce, arose from the furious collisions of the powers at war, yet the great and good men of that time conformed to the force of circumstances which they could not controul, and preserved their country in security from the tempests which overwhelmed the old world, and threw the wreck of their fortunes on these shores.—Respect abroad, prosperity at home, wise laws made by honoured legislators, and prompt obedience yielded by a contented people, had silenced the enemies of republican institutions.—The arts flourished—the sciences were cultivated—the comforts and conveniences of life were universally diffused—and nothing remained for succeeding administrations, but to reap the advantages, and cherish the resources, flowing from the policy of their predecessors.

But no sooner was a new administration established in the hands of the party opposed to the Washington policy, than a fixed determination was perceived and avowed of changing a system which had already produced these substantial fruits. The consequences of this change, for a few years after its commencement, were not sufficient to counteract the prodigious impulse towards prosperity, which had been given to the nation. But a steady perseverance in the new plans of administration, at length developed their weakness and deformity, but not until a majority of the people had been deceived by flattery, and inflamed by passion, into blindness to their defects. Under the withering influence of this new system, the declension of the nation has been uniform and rapid. The richest advantages for securing the great objects of the Constitution have been wantonly rejected. While Europe reposes from the convulsions that had shaken down her ancient institutions, she beholds with amazement this remote country, once so happy and so envied, involved in a ruinous war, and excluded from intercourse with the rest of the world.

To investigate and explain the means whereby this fatal reverse has been effected, would require a voluminous discussion. Nothing more can be attempted in this Report, than a general allusion to the principal outlines of the policy which has produced this vicissitude. Among these may be enumerated

First.—A deliberate and extensive system for effecting a combination among certain States, by exciting local jealousies and ambition, so as to secure to popular leaders in one section of the Union, the controul of public affairs in perpetual succession. To which primary object most other characteristics of the system may be reconciled.

Secondly.—The political intolerance displayed and avowed, in excluding from office men of unexceptionable merit, for want of adherence to the executive creed.

Thirdly.—The infraction of the judiciary authority and rights, by depriving judges of their offices in violation of the Constitution.

Fourthly.—The abolition of existing Taxes, requisite to prepare the Country for those changes to which nations are always exposed, with a view to the acquisition of popular favour.

Fifthly.—The influence of patronage in the distribution of offices, which in these States has been almost invariably made among men the least intitled to such distinction, and who have sold themselves as ready instruments for distracting public opinion, and encouraging administration to hold in contempt the wishes and remonstrances of a people thus apparently divided.

Sixthly.—The admission of new States into the Union, formed at pleasure in the western region, has destroyed the balance of power which existed among the original States, and deeply affected their interest.

Seventhly.—The easy admission of naturalized foreigners, to places of trust, honour or profit, operating as an inducement to the malcontent subjects of the old world to come to these States, in quest of executive patronage, and to repay it by an abject devotion to executive measures.

Eighthly.—Hostility to Great-Britain, and partiality to the late government of France, adopted as coincident with popular prejudice, and subservient to the main object, party power. Connected with these must be ranked erroneous and distorted estimates of the power and resources of those nations, of the probable results of their controversies, and of our political relations to them respectively.

Lastly and principally.—A visionary and superficial theory in regard to commerce, accompanied by a real hatred but a feigned regard to its interests, and a ruinous perseverance in efforts to render it an instrument of coercion and war.

But it is not conceivable that the obliquity of any administration could, in so short a period, have so nearly consummated the work of national ruin, unless favoured by defects in the Constitution.

To enumerate all the improvements of which that instrument is susceptible, and to propose such amendments as might render it in all respects perfect, would be a task, which this Convention has not thought proper to assume. —They have confined their attention to such as experience has demonstrated to be essential, and even among these, some are considered entitled to a more serious attention than others. They are suggested without any intentional disrespect to other States, and are meant to be such as all shall find an interest in promoting. Their object is to strengthen, and if possible to perpetuate, the Union of the States, by removing the grounds of existing jealousies, and providing for a fair and equal representation and a limitation of powers, which have been misused.

The first amendment proposed, relates to the apportionment of Representatives among the slave holding States. This cannot be claimed as a right. Those States are entitled to the slave representation, by a constitutional compact. It is therefore merely a subject of agreement, which should be conducted upon principles of mutual interest and accomodation, and upon which no sensibility on either side should be permitted to exist. It has proved unjust and unequal in its operation. Had this effect been foreseen, the privilege would probably not have been demanded; certainly not conceded. Its tendency in future will be adverse to that harmony and mutual confidence, which are more conducive to the happiness and prosperity of every confederated State, than a mere preponderance of power, the prolific source of jealousies and controversy, can be to any one of them. The time may therefore arrive, when a sense of magnanimity and justice will reconcile those States to acquiesce in a revision of this article, especially as a fair equivalent would result to them in the apportionment of taxes.

The next amendment relates to the admission of new States into the union.

This amendment is deemed to be highly important, and in fact indispensable. In proposing it, it is not intended to recognize the right of Congress to admit new States without the original limits of the United States, nor is any idea entertained of disturbing the tranquillity of any State already admitted into the union. The object is merely to restrain the constitutional power of Congress in admitting new States. At the adoption of the Constitution, a certain balance of power among the original parties was considered to exist, and there was at that time, and yet is among those parties, a strong affinity between their great and general interests.—By the admission of these States that balance has been materially affected, and unless the practice be modified, must ultimately be destroyed. The Southern States will first avail themselves of their new confederates to govern the East, and finally the Western States multiplied in number, and augmented in population, will controul the interests of the whole. Thus for the sake of present power, the Southern States will be common sufferers with the East, in the loss of permanent advantages. None of the old States can find an interest in creating prematurely an overwhelming Western influence, which may hereafter discern (as it has heretofore) benefits to be derived to them by wars and commercial restrictions.

The next amendments proposed by the Convention, relate to the powers of Congress, in relation to Embargo and the interdiction of commerce.

Whatever theories upon the subject of commerce, have hitherto divided the opinions of statesmen, experience has at last shewn that it is a vital interest in the United States, and that its success is essential to the encouragement of agriculture and manufactures, and to the wealth, finances, defence, and liberty of the nation. Its welfare can never interfere with the other great interests of the State, but must promote and uphold them. Still those who are immediately concerned in the prosecution of commerce, will of necessity be always a minority of the nation. They are, however, best qualified to manage and direct its course by the advantages of experience, and the sense of interest. But they are entirely unable to protect themselves against the sudden and injudicious decisions of bare majorities, and the mistaken or oppressive projects of those who are not actively concerned in its pursuits. Of consequence, this interest is always exposed to be harassed, interrupted, and entirely destroyed, upon pretence of securing other interests. Had the merchants of this nation been permitted, by their own government, to pursue an innocent and lawful commerce, how different would have been the state of the treasury and of public credit! How short-sighted and miserable is the policy which has annihilated this order of men, and doomed their ships to rot in the docks, their capital to waste unemployed, and their affections to be alienated from the Government which was formed to protect them! What security for an ample and unfailing revenue can ever be had, comparable to that which once was realized in the good faith, punctuality, and sense of honour, which attached the mercantile class to the interests of the Government! Without commerce, where can be found the aliment for a navy; and without a navy, what is to constitute the defence, and ornament, and glory of this nation! No union can be durably cemented, in which every great interest does not find itself reasonably secured against the encroachment and combinations of other interests. When, therefore, the past system of embargoes and commercial restrictions shall have been reviewed—when the fluctuation and inconsistency of public measures, betraying a want of information as well as feeling in the majority, shall have been considered, the reasonableness of some restrictions upon the power of a bare majority to repeat these oppressions, will appear to be obvious.

The next amendment proposes to restrict the power of making offensive war. In the consideration of this amendment, it is not necessary to inquire into the justice of the present war. But one sentiment now exists in relation to its expediency, and regret for its declaration is nearly universal. No indemnity can ever be attained for this terrible calamity, and its only palliation must be found in obstacles to its future recurrence. Rarely can the state of this country call for or justify offensive war. The genius of our institutions is unfavourable to its successful prosecution; the felicity of our situation exempts us from its necessity.—In this case, as in the former, those more immediately exposed to its fatal effects are a minority of the nation. The commercial towns, the shores of our seas and rivers, contain the population, whose vital interests are most vulnerable by a foreign enemy. Agriculture, indeed, must feel at last, but this appeal to its sensibility comes too late. Again, the immense population which has swarmed into the West, remote from immediate danger, and which is constantly augmenting, will not be averse from the occasional distur-

bances of the Atlantic States. Thus interest may not unfrequently combine with passion and intrigue, to plunge the nation into needless wars, and compel it to become a military, rather than a happy and flourishing people. These considerations which it would be easy to augment, call loudly for the limitation proposed in the amendment.

Another amendment, subordinate in importance, but still in a high degree expedient, relates to the exclusion of foreigners, hereafter arriving in the United States, from the capacity of holding offices of trust, honour or profit.

That the stock of population already in these States, is amply sufficient to render this nation in due time sufficiently great and powerful, is not a controvertible question—Nor will it be seriously pretended, that the national deficiency in wisdom, arts, science, arms or virtue, needs to be replenished from foreign countries. Still, it is agreed, that a liberal policy should offer the rights of hospitality, and the choice of settlement, to those who are disposed to visit the country.—But why admit to a participation in the government aliens who were no parties to the compact —who are ignorant of the nature of our institutions, and have no stake in the welfare of the country, but what is recent and transitory? It is surely a privilege sufficient, to admit them after due probation to become citizens, for all but political purposes.—To extend it beyond these limits, is to encourage foreigners to come to these states as candidates for preferment. The Convention forbear to express their opinion upon the inauspicious effects which have already resulted to the honour and peace of this nation, from this misplaced and indiscriminate liberality.

The last amendment respects the limitation of the office of President, to a single constitutional term, and his eligibility from the same State two terms in succession.

Upon this topic, it is superfluous to dilate. The love of power is a principle in the human heart which too often impels to the use of all practicable means to prolong its duration. The office of President has charms and attractions which operate as powerful incentives to this passion. The first and most natural exertion of a vast patronage is directed towards the security of a new election. The interest of the country, the welfare of the people, even honest fame and respect for the opinion of posterity, are secondary considerations. All the engines of intrigue; all the means of corruption, are likely to be employed for this object. A President whose political career is limited to a single election, may find no other interest than will be promoted by making it glorious to himself, and beneficial to his country. But the hope of reelection is prolific of temptations, under which these magnanimous motives are deprived of their principal force. The repeated election of the President of the United States from any one State, affords inducements and means for intrigue, which tend to create an undue local influence, and to establish the domination of particular States. The justice, therefore, of securing to every State a fair and equal chance for the election of this officer from its own citizens is apparent, and this object will be essentially promoted by preventing an election from the same State twice in succession.

Such is the general view which this Convention has thought proper to submit, of the situation of these States, of their dangers and their duties. Most of the subjects which it embraces have separately received an ample and luminous investigation, by the great and able assertors of the rights of their Country, in the National Legislature; and nothing more could be attempted on this occasion, than a digest of general principles, and of recommendations, suited to the present state of public affairs. The peculiar difficulty and delicacy of performing, even this undertaking, will be appreciated by all who think seriously upon the crisis. Negotiations for Peace, are at this hour supposed to be pending, the issue of which must be deeply interesting to all. No measures should be adopted, which might unfavorably affect that issue; none which should embarrass the Administration, if their professed desire for peace is sincere; and none, which on supposition of their insincerity, should afford them pretexts for prolonging the war, or relieving themselves from the responsibility of a dishonorable peace. It is also devoutly to be wished, that an occasion may be afforded to all friends of the country, of all parties, and in all places, to pause and consider the awful state to which pernicious counsels, and blind passions, have brought this people. The number of those who perceive, and who are ready to retrace errors, must it is believed be yet sufficient to redeem the nation. It is necessary to rally and unite them by the assurance that no hostility to the Constitution is meditated, and to obtain their aid, in placing it under guardians, who alone can save it from destruction. Should this fortunate change be effected, the hope of happiness and honor may once more dispel the surrounding gloom. Our nation may yet be great, our union durable. But should this prospect be utterly hopeless, the time will not have been lost, which shall have ripened a general

sentiment of the necessity of more mighty efforts to rescue from ruin, at least some portion of our beloved Country.

THEREFORE RESOLVED—

That it be and hereby is recommended to the Legislatures of the several States represented in this Convention, to adopt all such measures as may be necessary effectually to protect the citizens of said States from the operation and effects of all acts which have been or may be passed by the Congress of the United States, which shall contain provisions, subjecting the militia or other citizens to forcible drafts, conscriptions, or impressments, not authorised by the Constitution of the United States.

Resolved, That it be and hereby is recommended to the said Legislatures, to authorize an immediate and earnest application to be made to the Government of the United States, requesting their consent to some arrangement, whereby the said States may, separately or in concert, be empowered to assume upon themselves the defence of their territory against the enemy; and a reasonable portion of the taxes, collected within said States, may be paid into the respective treasuries thereof, and appropriated to the payment of the balance due said States, and to the future defence of the same. The amount so paid into the said treasuries to be credited, and the disbursements made as aforesaid to be charged to the United States.

Resolved, That it be, and it hereby is, recommended to the Legislatures of the aforesaid States, to pass laws (where it has not already been done) authorizing the Governours or Commanders in Chief of their militia to make detachments from the same, or to form voluntary corps, as shall be most convenient and conformable to their Constitutions, and to cause the same to be well armed, equipped and disciplined, and held in readiness for service; and upon the request of the Governour of either of the other States to employ the whole of such detachment or corps, as well as the regular forces of the State, or such part thereof as may be required and can be spared consistently with the safety of the State, in assisting the State, making such request to repel any invasion thereof which shall be made or attempted by the public enemy.

Resolved, That the following amendments of the Constitution of the United States, be recommended to the

States represented as aforesaid, to be proposed by them for adoption by the State Legislatures, and, in such cases as may be deemed expedient, by a Convention chosen by the people of each State.

And it is further recommended, that the said States shall persevere in their efforts to obtain such amendments, until the same shall be effected.

First. Representatives and direct taxes shall be apportioned among the several States which may be included within this union, according to their respective numbers of free persons, including those bound to serve for a term of years and excluding Indians not taxed, and all other persons.

Second. No new State shall be admitted into the union by Congress in virtue of the power granted by the Constitution, without the concurrence of two thirds of both Houses.

Third. Congress shall not have power to lay any embargo on the ships or vessels of the citizens of the United States, in the ports or harbours thereof, for more than sixty days.

Fourth. Congress shall not have power, without the concurrence of two thirds of both Houses, to interdict the commercial intercourse between the United States and any foreign nation or the dependencies thereof.

Fifth. Congress shall not make or declare war, or authorize acts of hostility against any foreign nation without the concurrence of two thirds of both Houses, except such acts of hostility be in defence of the territories of the United States when actually invaded.

Sixth. No person who shall hereafter be naturalized, shall be eligible as a member of the Senate or House of Representatives of the United States, nor capable of holding any civil office under the authority of the United States.

Seventh. The same person shall not be elected President of the United States a second time; nor shall the President be elected from the same State two terms in succession.

Resolved. That if the application of these States to the government of the United States, recommended in a foregoing Resolution, should be unsuccessful, and peace should not be concluded, and the defence of these States should be neglected, as it has been since the commencement of the war, it will in the opinion of this Convention be expedient for the Legislatures of the several States to appoint Delegates to another Convention, to meet at Boston, in the State of Massachusetts, on the third Thursday of June next, with such powers and instructions as the exigency of a crisis so momentous may require.

Resolved, That the Hon. George Cabot, the Hon. Chauncey Goodrich, and the Hon. Daniel Lyman, or any two of them, be authorized to call another meeting of this Convention, to be holden in Boston, at any time before new Delegates shall be chosen, as recommended in the above Resolution, if in their judgment the situation of the Country shall urgently require it.

HARTFORD, January 4th, 1814.

George Cabot,	James Hillhouse,
Nathan Dane,	John Treadwell,
William Prescott,	Zephaniah Swift,
Harrison G. Otis,	Nathaniel Smith,
Timothy Bigelow,	Calvin Goddard,
Joshua Thomas,	Roger M. Sherman,
Samuel S. Wilde,	Daniel Lyman,
Joseph Lyman,	Samuel Ward,
Stephen Longfellow, Jr.	Edward Manton,
Daniel Waldo,	Benjamin Hazard,
Hodijah Baylies,	Benjamin West,
George Bliss,	Mills Olcott,
Chauncey Goodrich,	William Hall, Jr.

Commentaries on the Constitution of the United States

JOSEPH STORY

1833

A Familiar Exposition of the Constitution of the United States

JOSEPH STORY

1840

Seven years after the first publication of *Commentaries on the Constitution of the United States,* Story published a version for high school and college students under the title *A Familiar Exposition of the Constitution of the United States.* Selections here, taken from both the *Commentaries* and *Familiar Exposition,* concern the Constitution's Supremacy Clause—establishing that federal laws shall be accepted as the law of the land whenever they come in conflict with any state's laws.

Commentaries on the Constitution of the United States

Supremacy of Laws

§ 1830. The next clause [in the Constitution] is "This constitution, and the laws of the United States, which shall be made in pursuance thereof, and all treaties made, or which shall be made, under the authority of the United States, shall be the supreme law of the land. And the judges in every state shall be bound thereby, any thing in the constitution or laws of any state to the contrary notwithstanding."[1]

§ 1831. The propriety of this clause would seem to result from the very nature of the constitution. If it was to establish a national government, that government ought, to the extent of its powers and rights, to be supreme. It would

---

1. See Journal of Convention, p. 222, 282, 293.

be a perfect solecism to affirm, that a national government should exist with certain powers; and yet, that in the exercise of those powers it should not be supreme. What other inference could have been drawn, than of their supremacy, if the constitution had been totally silent? And surely a positive affirmance of that, which is necessarily implied, cannot in a case of such vital importance be deemed unimportant. The very circumstance, that a question might be made, would irresistibly lead to the conclusion, that it ought not to be left to inference. A law, by the very meaning of the term, includes supremacy. It is a rule, which those, to whom it is prescribed, are bound to observe. This results from every political association. If individuals enter into a state of society, the laws of that society must be the supreme regulator of their conduct. If a number of political societies enter into a larger political society, the laws, which the latter may enact, pursuant to the powers entrusted to it by its constitution, must necessarily be supreme over those societies, and the individuals, of whom they are composed. It would otherwise be a mere treaty, dependent upon the good faith of the parties, and not a government, which is only another name for political power and supremacy. But it will not follow, that acts of the larger society, which are not pursuant to its constitutional powers, but which are invasions of the residuary authorities of the smaller societies, will become the supreme law of the land. They will be merely acts of usurpation, and will deserve to be treated as such. Hence we perceive, that the above clause only declares a truth, which flows immediately and necessarily from the institution of a national government.[2] It will be observed, that the supremacy of the laws is attached to those only, which are made in pursuance of the constitution; a caution very proper in itself, but in fact the limitation would have arisen by irresistible implication, if it had not been expressed.[3]

§ 1832. In regard to treaties, there is equal reason, why they should be held, when made, to be the supreme law of the land. It is to be considered, that treaties constitute solemn compacts of binding obligation among nations; and unless they are scrupulously obeyed, and enforced, no foreign nation would consent to negotiate with us; or if it did, any want of strict fidelity on our part in the discharge of the treaty stipulations would be visited by reprisals, or war.[4] It is, therefore, indispensable, that they should have the obligation and force of a law, that they may be executed by the judicial power, and be obeyed like other laws. This will not prevent them from being cancelled or abrogated by the nation upon grave and suitable occasions; for it will not be disputed, that they are subject to the legislative power, and may be repealed, like other laws, at its pleasure;[5] or they may be varied by new treaties. Still, while they do subsist, they ought to have a positive binding efficacy as laws upon all the states, and all the citizens of the states. The peace of the nation, and its good faith, and moral dignity, indispensably require, that all state laws should be subjected to their supremacy. The difference between considering them as laws, and considering them as executory, or executed contracts, is exceedingly important in the actual administration of public justice. If they are supreme laws, courts of justice will enforce them directly in all cases, to which they can be judicially applied, in opposition to all state laws, as we all know was done in the case of the British debts secured by the treaty of 1783, after the constitution was adopted.[6] If they are deemed but solemn compacts, promissory in their nature and obligation, courts of justice may

be embarrassed in enforcing them, and may be compelled to leave the redress to be administered through other departments of the government.[7] It is notorious, that treaty stipulations (especially those of the treaty of peace of 1783) were grossly disregarded by the states under the confederation. They were deemed by the states, not as laws, but like requisitions, of mere moral obligation, and dependent upon the good will of the states for their execution. Congress, indeed, remonstrated against this construction, as unfounded in principle and justice.[8] But their voice was not heard. Power and right were separated; the argument was all on one side; but the power was on the other.[9] It was probably to obviate this very difficulty, that this clause was inserted in the constitution;[10] and it would redound to the immortal honour of its authors, if it had done no more, than thus to bring treaties within the sanctuary of justice, as laws of supreme obligation.[11] There are, indeed, still cases, in which courts of justice can administer no effectual redress; as when the terms of a stipulation import a contract, when either of the parties engages to perform a particular act the treaty addresses itself to the political, and not to the judicial, department; and the legislature must execute the contract, before it can become a rule for the courts.[12]

§ 1833. It is melancholy to reflect, that, conclusive as this

7. See Iredell J.'s reasoning in *Ware* v. *Hylton*, 3 Dall. R. 270 to 277; 5 Marshall's Life of Washington, ch. 8, p. 652, 656; 1 Wait's State Papers, 45, 47, 71, 81, 145; Serg. on Const. ch. 21, p. 217, 218, ch. 33, p. 396, 397, (2d edit. ch. 21, p. 218, 219, ch. 34, p. 406, 407.)—"A treaty," said the Supreme Court, in *Foster* v. *Neilson*, 2 Peters's R. 314, "is in its nature a contract between two nations, not a legislative act. It does not generally effect of itself the object to be accomplished, especially so far, as its operation is infraterritorial; but is carried into execution by the sovereign power of the respective parties to the instrument. In the United States a different principle is established. Our constitution declares a treaty to be the law of the land. It is consequently to be regarded by courts of justice as equivalent to an act of the legislature, whenever it operates of itself without the aid of any legislative provision."

8. Circular Letter of Congress, 13th April, 1787; 12 Journ. of Congress, 32 to 36.

9. See the opinion of Iredell J. in *Ware* v. *Hylton*, 3 Dall. 270 to 277.

10. Id. 276, 277. See Journal of Convention, p. 222, 282, 283, 293.

11. The importance of this power has been practically illustrated by the redress afforded by courts of law in cases pending before them upon treaty stipulations. See *United States* v. *The Peggy*, 1 Cranch, 103; *Ware* v. *Hylton*, 3 Dall. R. 199, 244, 261; *United States* v. *Arradondo*, 6 Peters's R. 691; *Soulard* v. *Smith*, 4 Peters's Sup. R. 511; Case of *Jonathan Robbins*, 1 Hall's Journ. of Jurisp. 25; Bees Adm'rs Rep. 263; 5 Wheat. Rep. App.

12. *Foster* v. *Neilson*, 2 Peters's Sup. R. 254, 314. See also the Bello Corunnes, 6 Wheat. R. 171; Serg. on Const. ch. 33, p. 397, 398, 399, (ch. 34, p. 407, 408, 409, 410, 2d edit.)

2. The Federalist, No. 33. See *Gibbons* v. *Ogden*, 9 Wheat. R. 210, 211; *McCulloch* v. *Maryland*, 4 Wheat. R. 405, 406.—This passage from the Federalist (No. 33) has been, for another purpose, already cited in Vol. I. § 340; but it is necessary to be here repeated to give due effect to the subsequent passages.

3. Ibid. See also 1 Tuck. Black. Comm. App. 369, 370.

4. See The Federalist, No. 64.

5. See Act of Congress, 7th July, 1798, ch. 84; *Talbot* v. *Seeman*, 1 Cranch, 1; *Ware* v. *Hylton*, 3 Dall. 361, Per Iredell J.

6. *Ware* v. *Hylton*, 3 Dall. R. 199. See also *Gibbons* v. *Ogden*, 9 Wheat. R. 210, 211; Letter of Congress of 13th April, 1787; 12 Journ. of Congress, 32.

view of the subject is in favour of the supremacy clause, it was assailed with great vehemence and zeal by the adversaries of the constitution; and especially the concluding clause, which declared the supremacy, "any thing in the constitution or laws of any state to the contrary notwithstanding."[13] And yet this very clause was but an expression of the necessary meaning of the former clause, introduced from abundant caution, to make its obligation more strongly felt by the state judges. The very circumstance, that any objection was made, demonstrated the utility, nay the necessity of the clause, since it removed every pretence, under which ingenuity could, by its miserable subterfuges, escape from the controlling power of the constitution.

§ 1834. To be fully sensible of the value of the whole clause, we need only suppose for a moment, that the supremacy of the state constitutions had been left complete by a saving clause in their favour. "In the first place, as these constitutions invest the state legislatures with absolute sovereignty, in all cases not excepted by the existing articles of confederation, all the authorities contained in the proposed constitution, so far as they exceed those enumerated in the confederation, would have been annulled, and the new congress would have been reduced to the same impotent condition with their predecessors. In the next place, as the constitutions of some of the states do not even expressly and fully recognize the existing powers of the confederacy, an express saving of the supremacy of the former would, in such states, have brought into question every power contained in the proposed constitution. In the third place, as the constitutions of the states differ much from each other, it might happen, that a treaty or national law, of great and equal importance to the states, would interfere with some, and not with other constitutions, and would consequently be valid in some of the states, at the same time, that it would have no effect in others. In fine, the world would have seen, for the first time, a system of government founded on an inversion of the fundamental principles of all government; it would have seen the authority of the whole society everywhere subordinate to the authority of the parts; it would have seen a monster, in which the head was under the direction of the members."[14]

§ 1835. At an early period of the government a question arose, how far a treaty could embrace commercial regulations, so as to be obligatory upon the nation, and upon

congress. It was debated with great zeal and ability in the house of representatives.[15] On the one hand it was contended, that a treaty might be made respecting commerce, as well as upon any other subject; that it was a contract between the two nations, which, when made by the president, by and with the consent of the senate, was binding upon the nation; and that a refusal of the house of representatives to carry it into effect was breaking the treaty, and violating the faith of the nation. On the other hand, it was contended, that the power to make treaties, if applicable to every object, conflicted with powers, which were vested exclusively in congress; that either the treaty making power must be limited in its operation, so as not to touch objects committed by the constitution to congress; or the assent and co-operation of the house of representatives must be required to give validity to any compact, so far as it might comprehend these objects: that congress was invested with the exclusive power to regulate commerce; that therefore, a treaty of commerce required the assent and co-operation of the house of representatives; that in every case, where a treaty required an appropriation of money, or an act of congress to carry it into effect, it was not in this respect obligatory, till congress had agreed to carry it into effect; and, that they were at free liberty to make, or withhold such appropriation, or act, without being chargeable with violating the treaty, or breaking the faith of the nation. In the result, the house of representatives adopted a resolution declaring, that the house of representatives do not claim any agency in making treaties; but when a treaty stipulates regulations on any of the subjects submitted to the power of congress, it must depend for its execution, as to such stipulations, on a law or laws to be passed by congress; and that it is the constitutional right and duty of the house of representatives, in all such cases, to deliberate on the expediency or inexpediency of carrying such treaty into effect, and to determine and act thereon, as in their judgment may be most conducive to the public good. It is well known, that the president and the senate, on that occasion, adopted a different doctrine, maintaining, that a treaty once ratified became the law of the land, and congress were constitutionally bound to carry it into effect.[16]

13. See The Federalist, No. 44, 64.
14. The Federalist, No. 44.

15. The question arose in the debate for carrying into effect the British Treaty of 1794.
16. See Journal of House of Representatives, 6th April, 1796; 5 Marshall's Life of Washington, ch. 8, p. 650 to 659; Serg. on Const. ch. 33, p. 401, (2d edit. ch. 34, p. 410, 411); 1 Debates on British Treaty, by F. Bache, 1796, p. 374 to 386; 4 Elliot's Deb. 244 to 248.—President

At the distance of twenty years, the same question was again presented for the consideration of both houses, upon a bill to carry into effect a clause in the treaty of 1815 with Great Britain, abolishing discriminating duties; and, upon that occasion, it was most ably debated. The result was, that a declaratory clause was adopted, instead of a mere enacting clause, so that the binding obligation of treaties was affirmatively settled.[17]

§ 1836. From this supremacy of the constitution and laws and treaties of the United States, within their constitutional scope, arises the duty of courts of justice to declare any unconstitutional law passed by congress or by a state legislature void. So, in like manner, the same duty arises, whenever any other department of the national or state governments exceeds its constitutional functions.[18] But the judiciary of the United States has no general jurisdiction to declare acts of the several states void, unless they are repugnant to the constitution of the United States, notwithstanding they are repugnant to the state constitution.[19] Such a power belongs to it only, when it sits to administer the local law of a state, and acts exactly, as a state tribunal is bound to act.[20] But upon this subject it seems unnecessary to dwell, since the right of all courts, state as well as national, to declare unconstitutional laws void, seems settled beyond the reach of judicial controversy.[21]

A Familiar Exposition of the Constitution of the United States

General Power to make Necessary and Proper Laws

§ 206. The next power of Congress is, "to make all laws, which shall be necessary and proper for carrying into execution the foregoing powers, and all other powers vested by this Constitution in the government of the United States, or in any department, or officer thereof."

§ 207. This clause is merely declaratory of a truth, which would have resulted by necessary implication from the act of establishing a National Government, and investing it with certain powers. If a power to do a thing is given, it includes the use of the means, necessary and proper, to execute it. If it includes any such means, it includes all such means; for none can, more correctly than others, be said exclusively to appertain to the power; and the choice must depend upon circumstances, to be judged of by Congress. What is a power, but the ability or faculty of doing a thing? What is the ability to do a thing, but the power of employing the *means* necessary to its execution? What is a legislative power, but a power of making laws? What are the means to execute a legislative power, but laws? What is the power, for instance, of laying and collecting taxes, but a legislative power, or a power to make laws to lay and collect taxes? What are the proper means of executing such a power, but necessary and proper laws? In truth, the constitutional operation of the government would be precisely the same, if the clause were obliterated, as if it were repeated in every article. It would otherwise result, that the power could never be exercised; that is, the end would be required, and yet no means allowed. This would be a perfect absurdity. It would be to create powers, and compel them to remain for ever in a torpid, dormant, and paralytic state. It cannot, therefore, be denied, that the powers, given by the Constitution, imply the ordinary means of execution; for, without the substance of the power, the Constitution would be a dead letter. If it should be asked, why,

Washington, on this occasion, refused to deliver the papers respecting the British Treaty of 1794, called for by the house of representatives; and asserted the obligatory force of the treaty upon congress in the most emphatic terms. He added, that he knew, that this was understood in the convention to be the intended interpretation, and he referred to the Journal of the Convention (see Journal of Convention, p. 284, 325, 326, 339, 342, 343) to show, that a proposition was made, "that no treaty should be binding on the United States, which was not ratified by a law;" and that it was explicitly rejected. (5 Marshall's Life of Washington, ch. 8, p. 654 to 658.) At a much earlier period, viz. in 1790, the same point came before the cabinet of President Washington in a treaty proposed with the Creek Indians. Upon that occasion, there seems to have been no doubt in the minds of any of his cabinet of the conclusiveness of a treaty containing commercial stipulations. Mr. Jefferson, on that occasion, firmly maintained it. A treaty, (said he,) made by the president with the concurrence of two thirds of the senate is the law of the land, and a law of a superior order, because it not only repeals past laws, *but cannot itself be repealed by future ones.* The treaty then will legally control the duty act, and the act for securing traders in this particular instance. Yet Mr. Jefferson afterwards, (in Nov. 1793,) seems to have fluctuated in opinion, and to have been unsettled, as to the nature and extent of the treaty-making power. 4 Jefferson's Corresp. 497, 498.

17. Serg. on Const. ch. 33, p. 402, (2d edit. ch. 34, p. 411) 2 Elliot's Deb. 273 to 279.—Upon this occasion, a most admirable speech was delivered by the late William Pinkney, in which his great powers of reasoning and juridical learning had an ample scope. See Wheaton's Life of Pinkney, p. 517.

18. *Marbury* v. *Madison,* 1 Cranch, 137, 176.

19. *Calder* v. *Bull,* 3 Dall. R. 386; S. C. 1 Peters's Cond. R. 172, 177.

20. *Satterlee* v. *Matthewson,* 2 Peters's Sup. R. 380, 413.

21. See Serg. on Const. ch. 33, p. 391, (2d edit. ch. 34, p. 401); 1 Kent's Comm. Lect. 20, p. 420, 421, (2d edit. p. 448, 449, 450.)

then, was the clause inserted in the Constitution; the answer is, that it is peculiarly useful, in order to avoid any doubt, which ingenuity or jealousy might raise upon the subject. There was also a clause in the Articles of Confederation, which restrained the authority of Congress to powers *expressly* granted; and, therefore, it was highly expedient to make an explicit declaration, that that rule of interpretation, which had been the source of endless embarrassments under the Confederation, should no longer prevail. The Continental Congress had been compelled, in numerous instances, to disregard that limitation, in order to escape from the most absurd and distressing consequences. They had been driven to the dangerous experiment of violating the Confederation, in order to preserve it.

§ 208. The plain import of the present clause is, that Congress shall have all the incidental and instrumental powers, necessary and proper to carry into execution the other express powers; not merely such as are indispensably necessary in the strictest sense, (for then the word "proper" ought to have been omitted,) but such also as are appropriate to the end required. Indeed, it would otherwise be difficult to give any rational interpretation to the clause; for it can scarcely be affirmed, that one means only exists to carry into effect any of the given powers; and if more than one should exist, then neither could be adopted, because neither could be shown to be indispensably necessary. The clause, in its just sense, then, does not enlarge any other power, specifically granted; nor is it the grant of any new power. It is merely a declaration, to remove all uncertainty, that every power is to be so interpreted, as to include suitable means to carry it into execution. The very controversies, which have since arisen, and the efforts, which have since been made, to narrow down the just interpretation of the clause, demonstrate its wisdom and propriety. The practice of the government, too, has been in conformity to this view of the matter. There is scarcely a law of Congress, which does not include the exercise of implied powers and means. This might be illustrated by abundant examples. Under the power "to establish post offices and post roads," Congress have proceeded to make contracts for the carriage of the mail, have punished offences against the establishment, and have made an infinite variety of subordinate provisions, not one of which is found expressly authorized in the Constitution. A still more striking case of implied power is, that the United States, as a government, have no express authority given to make any contracts; and yet it is plain, that the government could not go on for an hour without this implied power.

§ 209. There are many other cases, in which Congress have acted upon implied powers, some of which have given rise to much political discussion, and controversy; but it is not within the design of this work to examine those cases, or to express any opinion respecting them. It is proper, however, that the reader should be apprized, that among them, are the questions respecting the power of Congress to establish a national bank; to make national roads, canals, and other internal national improvements; to purchase cessions of foreign territory, (such, for example, as Louisiana and Florida;) to lay embargoes, without any fixed limitation of the time of their duration; and to prohibit intercourse or commerce with a foreign nation for an unlimited period.

§ 210. And here terminates the eighth section of the Constitution professing to enumerate the powers of Congress. But there are other clauses, delegating express powers, which, though detached from their natural connection in that instrument, should be here brought under review, in order to complete the enumeration.

Prohibitions on the United States

§ 221. We next come to the consideration of the prohibitions and limitations upon the powers of Congress, which are contained in the ninth section of the first article, passing by such, as have been already incidentally discussed.

§ 222. The first clause is, "The migration or importation of such persons, as any of the States now existing shall think proper to admit, shall not be prohibited by the Congress, prior to the year eighteen hundred and eight. But a tax or duty may be imposed upon such importation, not exceeding ten dollars for each person."

§ 223. This clause, as is manifest from its language, was designed solely to reserve to the Southern States, for a limited period, the right to import slaves. It is to the honor of America, that she should have set the first example of interdicting and abolishing the slave trade, in modern times. It is well known, that it constituted a grievance, of which some of the Colonies complained, before the Revolution, that the introduction of slaves was encouraged by the parent country, and that the prohibitory laws, passed by the Colonies, were negatived by the Crown. It was, doubtless, desirable, that the importation of slaves should have been at once interdicted throughout the Union. But it was indispensable to yield something to the prejudices, the wishes, and the supposed interests of the South. And it ought to be considered as a great point gained, in favor of humanity, that a period of twenty years should enable Congress to terminate, in America, (as Congress in fact have terminated the African slave trade,) a traffic, which has so long and so loudly upbraided the morals and justice of modern nations.

§ 224. The next clause is, "The privilege of the writ of *habeas corpus* shall not be suspended, unless when, in cases of rebellion or invasion, the public safety may require it." In order to understand the exact meaning of the terms here used, recourse must be had to the common law. The writ of *habeas corpus,* here spoken of, is a writ known to the common law, and used in all cases of confinement, or imprisonment of any party, in order to ascertain whether it is lawful or not. The writ commands the person, who detains the party, to produce his body, with the day and cause of his detention, before the Court or Judge, who issues the writ, to do, submit to, and receive, whatever the Court or Judge shall direct at the hearing. It is hence called the writ of *habeas corpus ad subjiciendum,* from the effective words of the writ, (when it was issued, as it originally was, in the Latin language) that you (the person, detaining the party,) have the body (*habeas corpus*) to submit (*ad subjiciendum*) to the order of the Court or Judge. And if the cause of detention is found to be insufficient, or illegal, the party is immediately set at liberty by the order of the Court or Judge. It is justly, therefore, esteemed the great bulwark of personal liberty, and is grantable, as a matter of right, to the party imprisoned. But as it had often, for frivolous reasons of state, been suspended or denied in the parent country, to the grievous oppression of the subject, it is made a matter of constitutional right in all cases, except when the public safety may, in cases of rebellion or invasion, require it. The exception is reasonable, since cases of great urgency may arise, in which the suspension may be indispensable for the preservation of the liberties of the country against traitors and rebels.

§ 225. The next clause is, "No bill of attainder, or *ex post facto* law, shall be passed." A bill of attainder, in its technical sense, is an act passed by the legislature, convicting a person of some crime, for which it inflicts upon him, without any trial, the punishment of death. If it inflicts a milder

punishment, it is usually called a bill of pains and penalties. Such acts are in the highest degree objectionable, and tyrannical, since they deprive the party of any regular trial by jury, and deprive him of his life, liberty, and property, without any legal proof of his guilt. In a republican government, such a proceeding is utterly inconsistent with first principles. It would be despotism in its worst form, by arming a popular Legislature with the power to destroy, at its will, the most virtuous and valuable citizens of the state.

§ 226. To the same class, belong *ex post facto* laws, that is, (in a literal interpretation of the phrase,) laws made after the act is done. In a general sense, all retrospective laws are *ex post facto;* but the phrase is here used to designate laws to punish, as public offences, acts, which, at the time when they were done, were lawful, or were not public crimes, or, if crimes, which were not liable to so severe a punishment. It requires no reasoning to establish the wisdom of a prohibition, which puts a fixed restraint upon such harsh legislation. In truth, the existence of such a power in a legislature is utterly incompatible with all just notions of the true ends and objects of a republican government.

§ 227. The next clause (not already commented on) is, "No money shall be drawn from the treasury, but in consequence of appropriations made by law. And a regular statement and account of the receipts and expenditures of all public money shall be published from time to time." The object of this clause is, to secure regularity, punctuality, fidelity, and responsibility, in the keeping and disbursement of the public money. No money can be drawn from the treasury by any officer, unless under appropriations made by some act of Congress. As all the taxes raised from the people, as well as the revenues arising from other sources, are to be applied to the discharge of the expenses, and debts, and other engagements of the government, it is highly proper, that Congress should possess the power to decide, how and when any money should be applied for these purposes. If it were otherwise, the Executive would possess an unbounded power over the public purse of the nation; and might apply all its monied resources at his pleasure. The power to control and direct the appropriations, constitutes a most useful and salutary check upon profusion and extravagance, as well as upon corrupt influence and public peculation In arbitrary governments, the prince levies what money he pleases from his subjects, disposes of it, as he thinks proper, and is beyond responsibility or reproof. It is wise, in a republic, to interpose every restraint, by which the public treasure, the common fund of all, should be applied, with unshrinking honesty, to such objects, as legitimately belong to the common defence, and the general welfare. Congress is made the guardian of this treasure; and, to make their responsibility complete and perfect, a regular account of the receipts and expenditures is required to be published, that the people may know, what money is expended, for what purposes, and by what authority.

§ 228. The next clause is, "No title of nobility shall be granted by the United States; and no person, holding any office of profit or trust under them, shall, without the consent of the Congress, accept of any present, emolument, office, or title, of any kind whatever, from any king, prince, or foreign state." A perfect equality of rights, privileges, and rank, being contemplated by the Constitution among all citizens, there is a manifest propriety in prohibiting Congress from creating any titles of nobility. The other prohibition, as to presents, emoluments, offices, and titles from foreign governments, besides aiding the same general object, subserves a more important policy, founded on the just jealousy of foreign corruption and undue influence exerted upon our national officers. It seeks to destroy, in their origin, all the blandishments from foreign favors, and foreign titles, and all the temptations to a departure from official duty by receiving foreign rewards and emoluments. No officer of the United States can without guilt wear honors borrowed from foreign sovereigns, or touch for personal profit any foreign treasure.

Prohibitions on the States

§ 229. Such are the prohibitions upon the government of the United States. And we next proceed to the prohibitions upon the States, which are not less important in themselves, or less necessary to the security of the Union. They are contained in the tenth section of the first article.

§ 230. The first clause is, "No State shall enter into any treaty, alliance, or confederation; grant letters of marque or reprisal; coin money; emit bills of credit; make any thing but gold or silver coin a tender in payment of debts; pass any bill of attainder, *ex post facto* law, or law impairing the obligation of contracts; or grant any title of nobility."

§ 231. The prohibition against a State's entering into any treaty, alliance or confederation, is indispensable to the preservation of the rights and powers of the National Gov-

ernment. A State might otherwise enter into engagements with foreign governments, utterly subversive of the policy of the National Government, or injurious to the rights and interests of the other States. One State might enter into a treaty or alliance with France, and another with England, and another with Spain, and another with Russia,—each in its general objects inconsistent with the other; and thus, the seeds of discord might be spread over the whole Union.

§ 232. The prohibition to "grant letters of marque and reprisal" stands on the same ground. This power would hazard the peace of the Union by subjecting it to the passions, resentments, or policy of a single State. If any State might issue letters of marque or reprisal at its own mere pleasure, it might at once involve the whole Union in a public war; or bring on retaliatory measures by the foreign government, which might cripple the commerce, or destroy the vital interests of other States. The prohibition is, therefore, essential to the public safety.

§ 233. The prohibition to "coin money" is necessary to our domestic interests. The existence of the power in the States would defeat the salutary objects intended, by confiding the like power to the National Government. It would have a tendency to introduce a base and variable currency, perpetually liable to frauds, and embarrassing to the commercial intercourse of the States.

§ 234. The prohibition to "emit bills of credit."— Bills of credit are a well-known denomination of paper money, issued by the Colonies before the Revolution, and afterwards by the States, in a most profuse degree. These bills of credit had no adequate funds appropriated to redeem them; and though on their face they were often declared payable in gold and silver, they were in fact never so paid. The consequence was, that they became the common currency of the country, in a constantly depreciating state, ruinous to the commerce and credit, and disgraceful to the good faith of the country. The evils of the system were of a most aggravated nature, and could not be cured, except by an entire prohibition of any future issues of paper money. And, indeed, the prohibition to coin money would be utterly nugatory, if the States might still issue a paper currency for the same purpose.

§ 235. But the inquiry here naturally occurs; What is the true meaning of the phrase "bills of credit" in the Constitution? In its enlarged, and perhaps in its literal sense, it may comprehend any instrument, by which a State engages to pay money at a future day, (and, of course, for which it obtains a present credit;) and thus it would include a certificate given for money borrowed. But the language of the Constitution itself, and the mischief to be prevented, which we know from the history of our country, equally limit the interpretation of the terms. The word "emit" is never employed in describing those contracts, by which a State binds itself to pay money at a future day for services actually received, or for money borrowed for present use. Nor are instruments, executed for such purposes, in common language denominated "bills of credit." To emit bills of credit, conveys to the mind the idea of issuing paper, intended to circulate through the community for ordinary purposes, as money, which paper is redeemable at a future day. This is the sense, in which the terms of the Constitution have been generally understood. The phrase (as we have seen) was well known, and generally used to indicate the paper currency, issued by the States during their colonial dependence. During the war of our Revolution, the paper currency issued by Congress was constantly denominated, in the acts of that body, bills of credit; and the like appellation was applied to similar currency issued by the States. The phrase had thus acquired a determinate and appropriate meaning. At the time of the adoption of the Constitution, bills of credit were universally understood to signify a paper medium intended to circulate between individuals, and between government and individuals, for the ordinary purposes of society. Such a medium has always been liable to considerable fluctuation. Its value is continually changing; and these changes, often great and sudden, expose individuals to immense losses, are the sources of ruinous speculations, and destroy all proper confidence between man and man. In no country, more than our own, had these truths been felt in all their force. In none, had more intense suffering, or more wide-spreading ruin accompanied the system. It was, therefore, the object of the prohibition to cut up the whole mischief by the roots, because it had been deeply felt throughout all the States, and had deeply affected the prosperity of all. The object of the prohibition was not to prohibit the thing, when it bore a particular name; but to prohibit the thing, whatever form or name it might assume. If the words are not merely empty sounds, the prohibition must comprehend the emission of any paper medium by a State government for the purposes of common circulation. It would be preposterous to suppose, that the Constitution meant solemnly to prohibit an issue under one denomination, leaving the power complete to issue the same thing under another. It can never be seriously contended, that the Constitution means to prohibit names, and not things; to deal with shadows, and to leave substances. What would be the consequence of such a construction? That a very important act, big with great and ruinous mischief, and on that account forbidden by words the most appropriate for its description, might yet be performed by the substitution of a name. That the Constitution, even in one of its vital provisions, might be openly evaded by giving a new name to an old thing. Call the thing a bill of credit, and it is prohibited. Call the same thing a certificate, and it is constitutional.

§ 236. Connected with this, is the prohibition, No State shall "make any thing but gold and silver coin a tender in payment of debts." The history of the State laws on this subject, while we were Colonies, as well as during the Revolution, and afterwards before the adoption of the Constitution, is startling at once to our morals, to our patriotism, and to our sense of justice. In the intermediate period between the commencement of the Revolutionary War, and the adoption of the Constitution, the system had attained its most appalling character. Not only was paper money declared to be a tender in payment of debts; but other laws, having the same general object, and interfering with private debts, under the name of appraisement laws, instalment laws, and suspension laws, thickened upon the statute book of many States in the Union, until all public confidence was lost, and all private credit and morals were prostrated. The details of the evils, resulting from this source, can scarcely be comprehended in our day. But they were so enormous, that the whole country seemed involved in a general bankruptcy; and fraud and chicanery obtained an undisputed mastery. Nothing but an absolute prohibition, like that contained in the Constitution, could arrest the overwhelming flood; and it was accordingly hailed with the most sincere joy by all good citizens. It has given us that healthy and sound currency, and that solid private credit, which constitute the true foundation of our prosperity, industry, and enterprise.

§ 237. The prohibition, to "pass any bill of attainder, *ex post facto* law, or law impairing the obligation of contracts," requires scarcely any vindication or explanation, beyond what has been already given. The power to pass bills of attainder, and *ex post facto* laws, (the nature of which has been already sufficiently explained,) is quite as unfit to be intrusted to the States, as to the General Government. It was exercised by the States during the Revolutionary War, in the shape of confiscation laws, to an extent, which, upon cool reflection, every sincere patriot must regret. Laws "impairing the obligation of contracts" are still more objectionable. They interfere with, and disturb, and destroy, private rights, solemnly secured by the plighted faith of the parties. They bring on the same ruinous effects, as paper tender laws, instalment laws, and appraisement laws, which are but varieties of the same general noxious policy. And they have been truly described, as contrary to the first principles of the social compact and to every principle of sound legislation.

§ 238. Although the language of this clause, "law impairing the obligation of contracts," would seem, at first view, to be free from any real ambiguity; yet there is not perhaps a single clause of the Constitution, which has given rise to more acute and vehement controversy. What is a contract? What is the obligation of a contract? What is impairing a contract? To what classes of laws does the prohibition apply? To what extent does it reach, so as to control prospective legislation on the subject of contracts? These and many other questions, of no small nicety and intricacy, have vexed the legislative halls, as well as the judicial tribunals, with an uncounted variety and frequency of litigation and speculation.

§ 239. In the first place, What is to be deemed a contract, in the constitutional sense of this clause? A contract is an agreement to do, or not to do, a particular thing; or (as was said on another occasion) a contract is a compact between two or more persons. A contract is either executory, or executed. An executory contract is one, in which a party binds himself to do, or not to do, a particular thing. An executed contract is one, in which the object of the contract is performed. This differs in nothing from a grant; for a contract executed conveys a thing in possession; a contract executory conveys only a thing in action. Since, then, a grant is in fact a contract executed, the obligation of which continues; and since the Constitution uses the general term, *contract*, without distinguishing between those, which are executory, and those, which are executed; it must be construed to comprehend the former, as well as the latter. A State law, therefore, annulling conveyances between individuals, and declaring, that the grantors shall stand seized of their former estates, notwithstanding those grants, would be as repugnant to the Constitution, as a State law, discharging the vendors from the obligation of

executing their contracts of sale by conveyances. It would be strange, indeed, if a contract to convey were secured by the Constitution, while an absolute conveyance remained unprotected. That the contract, while executory, was obligatory; but when executed, might be avoided.

§ 240. Contracts, too, are express, or implied. Express contracts are, where the terms of the agreement are openly avowed, and uttered at the time of the making of them. Implied contracts are such, as reason and justice dictate from the nature of the transaction, and which, therefore, the law presumes, that every man undertakes to perform. The Constitution makes no distinction between the one class of contracts and the other. It then equally embraces, and equally applies to both. Indeed, as by far the largest class of contracts in civil society, in the ordinary transactions of life, are implied, there would be very little object in securing the inviolability of express contracts, if those, which are implied, might be impaired by State legislation. The Constitution is not chargeable with such folly, or inconsistency. Every grant, in its own nature, amounts to an extinguishment of the right of the grantor, and implies a contract not to reassert it. A party is, therefore, always estopped by his own grant. How absurd would it be to provide, that an express covenant by a party, as a muniment attendant upon the estate, should bind him for ever, because executory, and resting in action; and yet, that he might reassert his title to the estate, and dispossess his grantee, because there was only an implied covenant not to reassert it.

§ 241. In the next place, What is the obligation of a contract? It seems agreed, that, when the obligation of contracts is spoken of in the Constitution, we are to understand, not the mere moral, but the legal obligation of contracts. The moral obligation of contracts is, so far as human society is concerned, of an imperfect kind, which the parties are left free to obey or not, as they please. It is addressed to the conscience of the parties, under the solemn admonitions of accountability to the Supreme Being. No human lawgiver can either impair, or reach it. The Constitution has not in contemplation any such obligations, but such only, as might be impaired by a State, if not prohibited. It is the civil obligation of contracts, which it is designed to reach, that is, the obligation, which is recognised by, and results from, the law of the State, in which it is made. If, therefore, a contract, when made, is by the law of the State declared to be illegal, or deemed to be a nullity, or a *naked pact,* or promise, it has no civil obligation; because the law, in such cases, forbids its having any binding efficacy, or force. It confers no legal right on the one party, and no correspondent legal duty on the other. There is no means allowed, or recognised to enforce it; for the maxim is, that from a mere naked promise no action arises. But when it does not fall within the predicament of being either illegal, or void, its obligatory force is coextensive with its stipulations.

§ 242. Nor is this obligatory force so much the result of the positive declarations of the municipal law, as of the general principles of natural, or (as it is sometimes called) universal, law. In a state of nature, independent of the obligations of positive law, contracts may be formed, and their obligatory force be complete. Between independent nations, treaties and compacts are formed, which are deemed universally obligatory; and yet in no just sense can they be deemed dependent on municipal law. Nay, there may exist (abstractly speaking) a perfect obligation in contracts, where there is no known and adequate means to enforce them. As, for instance, between independent nations, where their relative strength and power preclude the possibility, on the side of the weaker party, of enforcing them. So, in the same government, where a contract is made by a State with one of its own citizens, which yet its laws do not permit to be enforced by any action or suit. In this predicament are the United States, who are not suable on any contract made by themselves; but no one doubts, that these are still obligatory on the United States. Yet their obligation is not recognised by any positive municipal law, in a great variety of cases. It depends altogether upon principles of public or universal law. Still, in these cases, there is a right in the one party to have the contract performed, and a duty on the other side to perform it. But, generally speaking, when we speak of the obligation of a contract, we include in the idea some known means acknowledged by the municipal law to enforce it. Where all such means are absolutely denied, the obligation of the contract is understood to be impaired, although it may not be completely annihilated. Rights may, indeed, exist, without any present adequate correspondent remedies between private persons. Thus, a State may refuse to allow imprisonment for debt; and the debtor may have no property. But still the right of the creditor remains; and he may enforce it against the future property of the debtor. So, a debtor may die without leaving any known estate, or without any known

representative. In such cases, we should not say, that the right of the creditor was gone; but only, that there was nothing, on which it could presently operate. But suppose an administrator should be appointed, and property in contingency should fall in, the right might then be enforced to the extent of the existing means.

§ 243. The civil obligation of a contract, then, although it can never arise, or exist, contrary to positive law, may arise or exist independently of it; and it may be, exist, notwithstanding there may be no present adequate remedy to enforce it. Wherever the municipal law recognises an absolute duty to perform a contract, there the obligation to perform it is complete, although there may not be a perfect remedy.

§ 244. In the next place, What may properly be deemed impairing the obligation of contracts, in the sense of the Constitution? It is perfectly clear, that any law, which enlarges, abridges, or in any manner changes the intention of the parties, resulting from the stipulations in the contract, necessarily impairs it. The manner or degree, in which this change is effected, can in no respect influence the conclusion; for, whether the law affect the validity, the construction, the duration, the discharge, or the evidence of the contract, it impairs its obligation, although it may not do so, to the same extent, in all the supposed cases. Any deviation from its terms, by postponing, or accelerating the period of performance, which it prescribes, or by imposing conditions not expressed in the contract, or by dispensing with the performance of those, which are a part of the contract, however minute, or apparently immaterial in their effects upon it, impairs its obligation. *A fortiori,* a law, which makes the contract wholly invalid, or extinguishes, or releases it, is a law impairing it. Nor is this all. Although there is a distinction between the obligation of a contract, and a remedy upon it; yet if there are certain remedies existing at the time, when it is made, all of which are afterwards wholly extinguished by new laws, so that there remain no means of enforcing its obligation, and no redress for its violation; such an abolition of all remedies, operating immediately, is also an impairing of the obligation of such contract. But every change and modification of the remedy does not involve such a consequence. No one will doubt, that the Legislature may vary the nature and extent of remedies, so always, that some substantive remedy be in fact left. Nor can it be doubted, that the Legislature may prescribe the times and modes, in which remedies may be pursued; and bar suits, not brought within such periods, and not pursued in such modes. Statutes of limitations are of this nature; and have never been supposed to destroy the obligation of contracts, but to prescribe the times, within which that obligation shall be enforced by a suit; and in default thereof, to deem it either satisfied, or abandoned. The obligation to perform a contract is coeval with the undertaking to perform it. It originates with the contract itself, and operates anterior to the time of performance. The remedy acts upon the broken contract, and enforces a preexisting obligation. And a State Legislature may discharge a party from imprisonment upon a judgement in a civil case of contract, without infringing the Constitution; for this is but a modification of the remedy, and does not impair the obligation of the contract. So, if a party should be in jail, and give a bond for the prison liberties, and to remain a true prisoner, until lawfully discharged, a subsequent discharge by an act of the Legislature would not impair the contract; for it would be a lawful discharge in the sense of the bond.

§ 245. These general considerations naturally conduct us to some more difficult inquiries growing out of them; and upon which there has been a very great diversity of judicial opinion. The great object of the framers of the Constitution undoubtedly was, to secure the inviolability of contracts. This principle was to be protected in whatever form it might be assailed. No enumeration was attempted to be made of the modes, by which contracts might be impaired. It would have been unwise to have made such an enumeration, since it might have been defective; and the intention was to prohibit every mode or device for such purpose. The prohibition was universal.

§ 246. The question has arisen, and has been most elaborately discussed, how far the States may constitutionally pass an insolvent law, which shall discharge the obligation of contracts. It is not doubted, that the States may pass insolvent laws, which shall discharge the person, or operate in the nature of a *cessio bonorum,* or a surrender of all the debtor's property, provided such laws do not discharge, or intermeddle with, the obligation of contracts. Nor is it denied, that insolvent laws, which discharge the obligation of contracts, made antecedently to their passage, are unconstitutional. But the question is how far the States may constitutionally pass insolvent laws, which shall operate upon, and discharge contracts, which are made subsequently to their passage. After the most ample argument, it has at length been settled, by a majority of the Supreme Court, that the States may constitutionally pass such laws operating upon *future* contracts, although not upon *past.*

§ 247. The remaining prohibition is, to "grant any title of nobility," which is supported by the same reasoning as that already suggested, in considering the like prohibition upon the National Government.

§ 248. The next clause, omitting the prohibition (already cited) to lay any imposts or duties on imports or exports, is, "No State shall, without the consent of Congress, lay any duty on tonnage; keep troops, or ships of war, in time of peace; enter into any agreement or compact with another State, or with a foreign power; or engage in war unless actually invaded, or in such imminent danger, as will not admit of delay." That part, which respects tonnage duties, has been already considered. The other parts have the same general policy in view, which dictated the preceding restraints upon State power. To allow the States to keep troops, or ships of war, in time of peace, might be hazardous to the public peace or safety, or compel the National Government to keep up an expensive corresponding force. To allow the States to enter into agreements with each other, or with foreign nations, might lead to mischievous combinations, injurious to the general interests, and bind them into confederacies of a geographical or sectional character. To allow the States to engage in war, unless compelled so to do in self-defence and upon sudden emergencies, would be (as has been already stated) to put the peace and safety of all the States in the power and discretion of any one of them. But an absolute prohibition of all these powers might, in certain exigencies, be inexpedient, and even mischievous; and, therefore, Congress may, by their consent, authorize the exercise of any of them, whenever, in their judgement, the public good shall require it.

§ 249. We have thus passed through the positive prohibitions introduced upon the powers of the States. It will be observed, that they divide themselves into two classes; those, which are political in their character, as an exercise of sovereignty; and those, which more especially regard the private rights of individuals. In the latter, the prohibition is absolute and universal. In the former, it is sometimes absolute, and sometimes subjected to the consent of Congress. It will, at once, be perceived, how full of difficulty and delicacy the task was, to reconcile the jealous tenacity of the States over their own sovereignty, with the permanent security of the National Government, and the inviolability of private rights. The task has been accomplished with eminent success. If every thing has not been accomplished, which a wise forecast might have deemed proper for the preservation of our national rights and liberties in all political events, much has been done to guard us against the most obvious evils, and to secure a wholesome administration of private justice. To have attempted more, would probably have endangered the whole fabric; and thus might have perpetuated the dominion of misrule and imbecility.

§ 250. It has been already seen, and it will hereafter more fully appear, that there are implied, as well as express, prohibitions in the Constitution upon the power of the States. Among the former, one clearly is, that no State can control, or abridge, or interfere with the exercise of any authority under the National Government. And it may be added, that State laws, as, for instance, State statutes of limitations, and State insolvent laws, have no operation upon the rights or contracts of the United States.

§ 251. And here end our commentaries upon the first article of the Constitution, embracing the organization and powers of the Legislative department of the government, and the prohibitions upon the State and National Governments. If we here pause, but for a moment, we cannot but be struck with the reflection, how admirably this division and distribution of legislative powers between the State and National Governments is adapted to preserve of the liberty, and to promote the happiness of the people of the United States. To the General Government are assigned all those powers, which relate to the common interests of all the States, as comprising one confederated nation; while to each State is reserved all those powers, which may affect, or promote its own domestic interests, its peace, its prosperity, its policy, and its local institutions. At the same time, such limitations and restraints are imposed upon each government, as experience has demonstrated to be wise to control any public functionaries, or as are indispensable to secure the harmonious operations of the Union.

PART EIGHT Forging a Nation

Daniel Webster, senator from Massachusetts. © Corbis/Bettmann

Robert Y. Hayne, senator from South
Carolina. Courtesy of the Governor's Mansion,
South Carolina

Jackson Forever!

The Hero of Two Wars and of Or'eans!

The Man of the People!

HE WHO COULD NOT BARTER NOR BARGAIN FOR THE

PRESIDENCY!

Who, although "*A Military Chieftain*," valued the purity of Elections and of the
Electors, **MORE** than the Office of **PRESIDENT** itself! Although the greatest
in the gift of his countrymen, and the highest in point of dignity of any in the world,

BECAUSE

It should be derived from the

PEOPLE!

No Gag Laws! No Black Cockades! No Reign of Terror! No Standing Army
or Navy Officers, when under the pay of Government, to browbeat, or

KNOCK DOWN

Old Revolutionary Characters, or our Representatives while in the discharge of
their duty. To the Polls then, and vote for those who will support

OLD HICKORY

AND THE ELECTORAL LAW.

Election poster for Andrew Jackson's presidential campaign. © Bettmann/CORBIS

The clear continuities in American politics and culture played an important role in the development of the Republic but do not overshadow the significant developments brought about by the Revolution and the construction of a new, independent government for the United States. Furthermore, America changed significantly with such events as Jefferson's Louisiana Purchase, by which the United States gained vast new territories and trade routes, and the effects of immigration and economic development, along with internal improvements such as roads, harbors, and canals, which vastly increased American population and commerce.

As America's size and population increased—at times exponentially—new issues arose and old issues were transformed in character by new circumstances. New parties and coalitions arose, committed to greater and more widely spread political participation, to greater federal efforts on behalf of commercial growth, and to the spread of commercial habits and virtues. Issues of federal control and influence over commerce, taxation, and internal improvements often centered on particular events, such as the chartering of a national bank to hold deposits of the federal government. But they continued to raise nagging questions of the proper relationship between the state and the federal governments, as well as the proper size and scope of government in general, and the nature and purpose of America and her people.

Opinion against the Constitutionality of a National Bank

THOMAS JEFFERSON

February 15, 1791

Opinion as to the Constitutionality of the Bank of the United States

ALEXANDER HAMILTON

February 23, 1791

Alexander Hamilton served as President Washington's secretary of the treasury. One of his early legislative proposals was for the formation of a Bank of the United States. The bank would take deposits from and lend money to the federal government, as well as establish a common currency for use in commerce between the states and between American and foreign companies and governments. The new nation had no such bank at this time. Many supported the idea as a means by which to encourage commerce and bind the states together. Others opposed it as an unconstitutional exercise of federal power and a threat to the states and their people. Washington, a careful man, sought opinions on the proposal's constitutionality from his secretary of state (Thomas Jefferson) and his attorney general (Edmund Randolph) as well as Hamilton. The opinions of Jefferson and Hamilton, reproduced here, flesh out questions of how far the Constitution's Necessary and Proper Clause expands the powers expressly granted to the federal government and how far the central government's power of regulating commerce extended.

Opinion against the Constitutionality of a National Bank

The bill for establishing a National Bank undertakes among other things:—

1. To form the subscribers into a corporation.
2. To enable them in their corporate capacities to receive grants of land; and so far is against the laws of *Mortmain*.[1]

3. To make alien subscribers capable of holding lands; and so far is against the laws of *alienage*.
4. To transmit these lands, on the death of a proprietor, to a certain line of successors; and so far changes the course of *Descents*.
5. To put the lands out of the reach of forfeiture or escheat; and so far is against the laws of *Forfeiture and Escheat*.
6. To transmit personal chattels to successors in a certain line; and so far is against the laws of *Distribution*.
7. To give them the sole and exclusive right of banking under the national authority; and so far is against the laws of Monopoly.
8. To communicate to them a power to make laws paramount to the laws of the States; for so they must be construed, to protect the institution from the control of the State legislatures; and so, probably, they will be construed.

I consider the foundation of the Constitution as laid on this ground: That "all powers not delegated to the United States, by the Constitution, nor prohibited by it to the States, are reserved to the States or to the people." [XIIth amendment.] To take a single step beyond the boundaries thus specially drawn around the powers of Congress, is to

---

1. Though the Constitution controls the laws of Mortmain so far as to permit Congress itself to hold land for certain purposes, yet not so far as to permit them to communicate a similar right to other corporate bodies.

take possession of a boundless field of power, no longer susceptible of any definition.

The incorporation of a bank, and the powers assumed by this bill, have not, in my opinion, been delegated to the United States, by the Constitution.

I. They are not among the powers specially enumerated: for these are: 1st. A power to lay taxes for the purpose of paying the debts of the United States; but no debt is paid by this bill, nor any tax laid. Were it a bill to raise money, its origination in the Senate would condemn it by the Constitution.

2d. "To borrow money." But this bill neither borrows money nor ensures the borrowing it. The proprietors of the bank will be just as free as any other money holders, to lend or not to lend their money to the public. The operation proposed in the bill, first, to lend them two millions, and then to borrow them back again, cannot change the nature of the latter act, which will still be a payment, and not a loan, call it by what name you please.

3d. To "regulate commerce with foreign nations, and among the States, and with the Indian tribes." To erect a bank, and to regulate commerce, are very different acts. He who erects a bank, creates a subject of commerce in its bills; so does he who makes a bushel of wheat, or digs a dollar out of the mines; yet neither of these persons regulates commerce thereby. To make a thing which may be bought and sold, is not to prescribe regulations for buying and selling. Besides, if this was an exercise of the power of regulating commerce, it would be void, as extending as much to the internal commerce of every State, as to its external. For the power given to Congress by the Constitution does not extend to the internal regulation of the commerce of a State, (that is to say of the commerce between citizen and citizen,) which remain exclusively with its own legislature; but to its external commerce only, that is to say, its commerce with another State, or with foreign nations, or with the Indian tribes. Accordingly the bill does not propose the measure as a regulation of trade, but as "productive of considerable advantages to trade." Still less are these powers covered by any other of the special enumerations.

II. Nor are they within either of the general phrases, which are the two following:—

1. To lay taxes to provide for the general welfare of the United States, that is to say, "to lay taxes for *the purpose* of providing for the general welfare." For the laying of taxes is the *power,* and the general welfare the *purpose* for which the power is to be exercised. They are not to lay taxes *ad libitum for any purpose they please;* but only *to pay the debts or provide for the welfare of the Union.* In like manner, they are not *to do anything they please* to provide for the general welfare, but only to *lay taxes* for that purpose. To consider the latter phrase, not as describing the purpose of the first, but as giving a distinct and independent power to do any act they please, which might be for the good of the Union, would render all the preceding and subsequent enumerations of power completely useless.

It would reduce the whole instrument to a single phrase, that of instituting a Congress with power to do whatever would be for the good of the United States; and, as they would be the sole judges of the good or evil, it would be also a power to do whatever evil they please.

It is an established rule of construction where a phrase will bear either of two meanings, to give it that which will allow some meaning to the other parts of the instrument, and not that which would render all the others useless. Certainly no such universal power was meant to be given them. It was intended to lace them up straitly within the enumerated powers, and those without which, as means, these powers could not be carried into effect. It is known that the very power now proposed *as a means* was rejected as *an end* by the Convention which formed the Constitution. A proposition was made to them to authorize Congress to open canals, and an amendatory one to empower them to incorporate. But the whole was rejected, and one of the reasons for rejection urged in debate was, that then they would have a power to erect a bank, which would render the great cities, where there were prejudices and jealousies on the subject, adverse to the reception of the Constitution.

2. The second general phrase is, "to make all laws *necessary* and proper for carrying into execution the enumerated powers." But they can all be carried into execution without a bank. A bank therefore is not *necessary,* and consequently not authorized by this phrase.

It has been urged that a bank will give great facility or convenience in the collection of taxes. Suppose this were true: yet the Constitution allows only the means which are "*necessary,*" not those which are merely "convenient" for effecting the enumerated powers. If such a latitude of construction be allowed to this phrase as to give any non-enumerated power, it will go to every one, for there is not one which ingenuity may not torture into a *convenience* in some instance *or other,* to *some one* of so long a list of enumerated powers. It would swallow up all the delegated powers, and reduce the whole to one power, as before observed. Therefore it was that the Constitution restrained them to the *necessary* means, that is to say, to those means without which the grant of power would be nugatory.

But let us examine this convenience and see what it is. The report on this subject, page 3, states the only *general* convenience to be, the preventing the transportation and re-transportation of money between the States and the treasury (for I pass over the increase of circulating medium, ascribed to it as a want, and which, according to my ideas of paper money, is clearly a demerit). Every State will have to pay a sum of tax money into the treasury; and the treasury will have to pay, in every State, a part of the interest on the public debt, and salaries to the officers of government resident in that State. In most of the States there will still be a surplus of tax money to come up to the seat of government for the officers residing there. The payments of interest and salary in each State may be made by treasury orders on the State collector. This will take up the great export of the money he has collected in his State, and consequently prevent the great mass of it from being drawn out of the State. If there be a balance of commerce in favor of that State against the one in which the government resides, the surplus of taxes will be remitted by the bills of exchange drawn for that commercial balance. And so it must be if there was a bank. But if there be no balance of commerce, either direct or circuitous, all the banks in the world could not bring up the surplus of taxes, but in the form of money. Treasury orders then, and bills of exchange may prevent the displacement of the main mass of the money collected, without the aid of any bank; and where these fail, it cannot be prevented even with that aid.

Perhaps, indeed, bank bills may be a more *convenient* vehicle than treasury orders. But a little *difference* in the degree of *convenience,* cannot constitute the necessity which the constitution makes the ground for assuming any non-enumerated power.

Besides; the existing banks will, without a doubt, enter into arrangements for lending their agency, and the more favorable, as there will be a competition among them for it; whereas the bill delivers us up bound to the national bank, who are free to refuse all arrangement, but on their own terms, and the public not free, on such refusal, to employ any other bank. That of Philadelphia, I believe, now does this business, by their post-notes, which, by an arrangement with the treasury, are paid by any State collector to whom they are presented. This expedient alone suffices to prevent the existence of that *necessity* which may justify the assumption of a non-enumerated power as a means for carrying into effect an enumerated one. The thing may be done, and has been done, and well done, without this assumption; therefore, it does not stand on that degree of *necessity* which can honestly justify it.

It may be said that a bank whose bills would have a currency all over the States, would be more convenient than one whose currency is limited to a single State. So it would be still more convenient that there should be a bank, whose bills should have a currency all over the world. But it does not follow from this superior conveniency, that there exists anywhere a power to establish such a bank; or that the world may not go on very well without it.

Can it be thought that the Constitution intended that for a shade or two of *convenience,* more or less, Congress should be authorized to break down the most ancient and fundamental laws of the several States; such as those against Mortmain, the laws of Alienage, the rules of descent, the acts of distribution, the laws of escheat and forfeiture, the laws of monopoly? Nothing but a necessity invincible by any other means, can justify such a prostitution of laws, which constitute the pillars of our whole system of jurisprudence. Will Congress be too straitlaced to carry the Constitution into honest effect, unless they may pass over the foundation-laws of the State government for the slightest convenience of theirs?

The negative of the President is the shield provided by the Constitution to protect against the invasions of the legislature: 1. The right of the Executive. 2. Of the Judiciary. 3. Of the States and State legislatures. The present is the case of a right remaining exclusively with the States, and consequently one of those intended by the Constitution to be placed under its protection.

It must be added, however, that unless the President's mind on a view of everything which is urged for and against this bill, is tolerably clear that it is unauthorized by the Constitution; if the pro and the con hang so even as to balance his judgment, a just respect for the wisdom of the legislature would naturally decide the balance in favor of their opinion. It is chiefly for cases where they are clearly misled by error, ambition, or interest, that the Constitution has placed a check in the negative of the President.

Opinion as to the Constitutionality of the Bank of the United States

The Secretary of the Treasury having perused with attention the papers containing the opinions of the Secretary of State and Attorney-General, concerning the constitutionality of the bill for establishing a National Bank, proceeds, according to the order of the President, to submit the reasons which have induced him to entertain a different opinion.

It will naturally have been anticipated, that in performing this task, he would feel uncommon solicitude. Personal considerations alone, arising from the reflection that the measure originated with him, would be sufficient to produce it. The sense which he has manifested of the great importance of such an institution to the successful administration of the department under his particular care, and an expectation of serious ill consequences to result from a failure of the measure, do not permit him to be without anxiety on public accounts. But the chief solicitude arises from a firm persuasion, that principles of construction like those espoused by the Secretary of State and Attorney-General, would be fatal to the just and indispensable authority of the United States.

In entering upon the argument, it ought to be premised that the objections of the Secretary of State and Attorney-General are founded on a general denial of the authority of the United States to erect corporations. The latter, indeed, expressly admits, that if there be any thing in the bill which is not warranted by the Constitution, it is the clause of incorporation.

Now it appears to the Secretary of the Treasury that this *general principle* is *inherent* in the very *definition* of government, and *essential* to every step of the progress to be made by that of the United States, namely: That every power vested in a government is in its nature *sovereign,* and includes, by *force* of the *term,* a right to employ all the *means* requisite and fairly applicable to the attainment of the *ends* of such power, and which are not precluded by restrictions and exceptions specified in the Constitution, or

not immoral, or not contrary to the *essential ends* of political society.

This principle, in its application to government in general, would be admitted as an axiom; and it will be incumbent upon those who may incline to deny it, to prove a distinction, and to show that a rule which, in the general system of things, is essential to the preservation of the social order, is inapplicable to the United States.

The circumstance that the powers of sovereignty are in this country divided between the National and State governments, does not afford the distinction required. It does not follow from this, that each of the portion of *powers* delegated to the one or to the other, is not sovereign with *regard to its proper objects.* It will only *follow* from it, that each has sovereign power as to *certain things,* and not as to *other things.* To deny that the government of the United States has sovereign power, as to its declared purposes and trusts, because its power does not extend to all cases, would be equally to deny that the State governments have sovereign power in any case, because their power does not extend to every case. The tenth section of the first article of the Constitution exhibits a long list of very important things which they may not do. And thus the United States would furnish the singular spectacle of a *political society* without *sovereignty,* or of a *people governed,* without *government.*

If it would be necessary to bring proof to a proposition so clear, as that which affirms that the powers of the federal government, as to *its objects,* were sovereign, there is a clause of its Constitution which would be decisive. It is that which declares that the Constitution, and the laws of the United States made in pursuance of it, and all treaties made, or which shall be made, under their authority, shall be the *supreme law of the land.* The power which can create the *supreme law of the land* in *any case,* is doubtless *sovereign* as to such case.

This general and indisputable principle puts at once an end to the *abstract* question, whether the United States have power to erect a *corporation;* that is to say, to give a *legal* or *artificial capacity* to one or more persons, distinct from the *natural.* For it is unquestionably incident to *sovereign power* to erect corporations, and consequently to *that* of the United States, in *relation* to the *objects* intrusted to the management of the government. The difference is this: where the authority of the government is general, it can create corporations in *all cases;* where it is confined to certain branches of legislation, it can create corporations *only* in those cases.

Here then, as far as concerns the reasonings of the Secretary of State and the Attorney General, the affirmative of the constitutionality of the bill might be permitted to rest. It will occur to the President, that the principle here advanced has been untouched by either of them.

For a more complete elucidation of the point, nevertheless, the arguments which they had used against the power of the government to erect corporations, however foreign they are to the great and fundamental rule which has been stated, shall be particularly examined. And after showing that they do not tend to impair its force, it shall also be shown that the power of incorporation, incident to the government in certain cases, does fairly extend to the particular case which is the object of the bill.

The first of these arguments is, that the foundation of the Constitution is laid on this ground: "That all powers not delegated the United States by the Constitution, nor prohibited to it by the States, are reserved for the States, or to the people." Whence it is meant to be inferred, that Congress can in no case exercise any power not included in those not enumerated in the Constitution. And it is affirmed, that the power of erecting a corporation is not included in any of the enumerated powers.

The main proposition here laid down, in its true signification is not to be questioned. It is nothing more than a consequence of this republican maxim, that all government is a delegation of power. But how much is delegated in each case, is a question of fact, to be made out by fair reasoning and construction, upon the particular provisions of the Constitution, taking as guides the general principles and general ends of governments.

It is not denied that there are *implied,* as well as *express powers,* and that the *former* are as effectually delegated as the *latter.* And for the sake of accuracy it shall be mentioned, that there is another class of powers, which may be properly denominated *resulting powers.* It will not be doubted, that if the United States should make a conquest of any of the territories of its neighbors, they would possess sovereign jurisdiction over the conquered territory. This would be rather a result, from the whole mass of the powers of the government, and from the nature of political society, than a consequence of either of the powers specially enumerated.

But be this as it may, it furnishes a striking illustration of the general doctrine contended for; it shows an extensive case, in which a power of erecting corporations is either implied in, or would result from, some or all of the powers vested in the national government. The jurisdiction acquired over such conquered country would certainly be competent to any species of legislation.

To return:—It is conceded that *implied powers* are to be considered as delegated equally with *express ones.* Then it follows, that as a power of erecting a corporation may as well be *implied* as any other thing, it may as well be employed as an *instrument* or *mean* of carrying into execution any of the specified powers, as any other *instrument* or *mean* whatever. The only question must be, in this, as in every other case, whether the mean to be employed, or in this instance, the corporation to be erected, has a natural relation to any of the acknowledged objects or lawful ends of the government. Thus a corporation may not be erected by Congress for superintending the police of the city of Philadelphia, because they are not authorized to *regulate* the *police* of that city. But one may be erected in relation to the collection of taxes, or to the trade with foreign countries, or to the trade between the States, or with the Indian tribes; because it is the province of the federal government to *regulate* those objects, and because it is incident to a general *sovereign* or *legislative* power to *regulate* a thing, to employ all the means which relate to its regulation to the best and greatest advantage. . . .

Through this mode of reasoning respecting the right of employing all the means requisite to the execution of the specified powers of the government, it is objected, that none but necessary and proper means are to be employed; and the Secretary of State maintains, that no means are to be considered as *necessary* but those without which the grant of the power would be *nugatory.* Nay, so far does he go in his restrictive interpretation of the *word,* as even to make the case of *necessity* which shall warrant the constitutional exercise of the power to depend on *casual* and *temporary* circumstances; an idea which alone refutes the construction. The *expediency* of exercising a particular power, at a particular time, must, indeed, depend on circumstances; but the constitutional right of exercising it must be uniform and invariable, the same to-day as to-morrow.

All the arguments, therefore, against the constitutionality of the bill derived from the accidental existence of certain State banks,—institutions which happen to exist to-day, and, for aught that concerns the government of the United States, may disappear to-morrow,—must not only be rejected as fallacious, but must be viewed as demonstrative that there is a *radical* source of error in the reasoning.

It is essential to the being of the national government, that so erroneous a conception of the meaning of the word *necessary* should be exploded.

It is certain, that neither the grammatical nor popular sense of the term requires that construction. According to both, *necessary* often means no more than *needful, requisite, incidental, useful,* or *conducive to.* It is a common mode of expression to say, that it is *necessary* for a government or a person to do this or that thing, when nothing more is intended or understood, than that the interests of the government or person require, or will be promoted by, the doing of this or that thing. The imagination can be at no loss for exemplifications of the use of the word in this sense. And it is the true one in which it is to be understood as used in the Constitution. The whole turn of the clause containing it indicates, that it was the intent of the Convention, by that clause, to give a liberal latitude to the exercise of the specified powers. The expressions have peculiar comprehensiveness. They are, "to make all *laws* necessary and proper for *carrying into execution* the *foregoing powers,* and *all other powers* vested by the Constitution in the *government* of the United States, or in any *department* or *officer* thereof."

To understand the word as the Secretary of State does, would be to depart from its obvious and popular sense, and to give it a restrictive operation, an idea never before entertained. It would be to give it the same force as if the word *absolutely* or *indispensably* had been prefixed to it.

Such a construction would beget endless uncertainty and embarrassment. The cases must be palpable and extreme, in which it could be pronounced, with certainty, that a measure was absolutely necessary, or one, without which, the exercise of a given power would be nugatory. There are few measures of any government which would stand so severe a test. To insist upon it, would be to make the criterion of the exercise of any implied power, a *case of extreme necessity;* which is rather a rule to justify the overleaping of the bounds of constitutional authority, than to govern the ordinary exercise of it.

It may be truly said of every government, as well as of that of the United States, that it has only a right to pass such laws as are necessary and proper to accomplish the objects intrusted to it. For no government has a right to do *merely what it pleases.* Hence, by a process of reasoning similar to that of the Secretary of State, it might be proved that neither of the State governments has a right to incorporate a bank. It might be shown that all the public business of the state could be performed without a bank, and inferring thence that it was unnecessary, it might be argued that it could not be done, because it is against the rule which has been just mentioned. A like mode of reasoning would prove that there was no power to incorporate the inhabitants of a town, with a view to a more perfect police. For it is certain that an incorporation may be dispensed with, though it is better to have one. It is to be remembered that there is no *express* power in any State constitution to erect corporations.

The *degree* in which a measure is necessary, can never be a *test* of the legal right to adopt it; that must be a matter of opinion, and can only be a *test* of expediency. The *relation* between the *measure* and the *end;* between the *nature* of the *mean* employed towards the execution of a power, and the object of that power, must be the criterion of constitutionality, not the more or less of *necessity* or *utility.*

The practice of the government is against the rule of construction advocated by the Secretary of State. Of this, the Act concerning light-houses, beacons, buoys, and public piers, is a decisive example. This, doubtless, must be referred to the powers of regulating trade, and is fairly relative to it. But it cannot be affirmed that the exercise of that power in this instance was strictly *necessary,* or that the power itself would be *nugatory,* without that of regulating establishments of this nature.

This restrictive interpretation of the word *necessary* is also contrary to this sound maxim of construction; namely, that the powers contained in a constitution of government, especially those which concern the general administration of the affairs of a country, its finances, trade, defence, &c., ought to be construed liberally in advancement of the public good. This rule does not depend on the particular form of a government, or on the particular demarkation of the boundaries of its powers, but on the nature and objects of government itself. The means by which national exigencies are to be provided for, national inconveniences obviated, national prosperity promoted, are of such infinite variety, extent, and complexity, that there must of necessity be great latitude of discretion in the selection and application of those means. Hence, consequently, the necessity and propriety of exercising the authorities intrusted to a government on principles of liberal construction.

The Attorney-General admits the *rule,* but takes a distinction between a State and the Federal Constitution. The latter, he thinks, ought to be construed with greater strictness, because there is more danger of error in defining *partial* than *general* powers. But the reason of the *rule* forbids such a distinction. This reason is, the variety and extent of public exigencies, a far greater proportion of which, and of a far more critical kind, are objects of *National* than of *State* administration. The greater danger of error, as far as it is supposable, may be a prudent reason for caution in practice, but it cannot be a rule of restrictive interpretation.

In regard to the clause of the Constitution immediately under consideration, it is admitted by the Attorney-General, that no *restrictive* effect can be ascribed to it. He defines the word *necessary* thus: "To be *necessary* is to be *incidental,* and may be denominated the natural means of executing a power."

But while on the one hand the construction of the Secretary of State is deemed inadmissible, it will not be contended, on the other, that the clause in question gives any *new* or *independent* power. But it gives an explicit sanction to the doctrine of *implied powers,* and is equivalent to an admission of the proposition that the government, as to its *specified powers* and *objects,* has plenary and sovereign authority, in some cases paramount to the States; in others, co-ordinate with it. For such is the plain import of the declaration, that it may pass all *laws* necessary and proper to carry into execution those powers.

It is no valid objection to the doctrine to say, that it is calculated to extend the power of the general government throughout the entire sphere of State legislation. The same thing has been said, and may be said, with regard to every exercise of power by *implication* or *construction.*

The moment the literal meaning is departed from, there is a chance of error and abuse. And yet an adherence to the letter of its powers would at once arrest the motions of government. It is not only agreed, on all hands, that the exercise of constructive powers is indispensable, but every act which has been passed is more or less an exemplification of it. One has been already mentioned—that relating to light-houses, &c.—that which declares the power of the President to remove officers at pleasure, acknowledges the same truth in another and a signal instance.

The truth is, that difficulties on this point are inherent in the nature of the Federal Constitution; they result inevitably from a division of the legislative power. The consequence of this division is, that there will be cases clearly within the power of the national government; others, clearly without its powers; and a third class, which will leave room for controversy and difference of opinion, and concerning which a reasonable latitude of judgment must be allowed.

But the doctrine which is contended for is not chargeable with the consequences imputed to it. It does not affirm that the national government is sovereign in all respects, but that it is sovereign to a certain extent; that is, to the extent of the objects of its specified powers.

It leaves, therefore, a criterion of what is constitutional, and of what is not so. This criterion is the *end,* to which the measure relates as a *mean.* If the *end* be clearly comprehended within any of the specified powers, and if the measure have an obvious relation to that *end,* and is not forbidden by any particular provision of the Constitution, it may safely be deemed to come within the compass of the national authority. There is also this further criterion, which may materially assist the decision: Does the proposed measure a bridge a pre-existing right of any State or of any individual? If it does not, there is a strong presumption in favor of its constitutionality, and slighter relations to any declared object of the Constitution may be permitted to turn the scale.

The general objections, which are to be inferred from the reasonings of the Secretary of State and Attorney-General, to the doctrine which has been advanced, have been stated, and it is hoped satisfactorily answered. Those of a more particular nature shall now be examined.

The Secretary of State introduces his opinion with an observation, that the proposed incorporation undertakes to create certain capacities, properties, or attributes, which are against the laws of *alienage, descents, escheat,* and *forfeiture, distribution* and *monopoly,* and to confer a power to make laws paramount to those of the States. And nothing, says he, in another place, but *necessity, invincible* by *other means,* can justify such a *prostration* of laws, which constitute the pillars of our whole system of jurisprudence, and are the foundation laws of the State governments. If these are truly the foundation laws of the several States, then have most of them subverted their own foundations. For there is scarcely one of them which has not, since the establishment of its particular constitution, made material alterations in some of those branches of its jurisprudence, especially the law of descents. But it is not conceived how any thing can be called the fundamental law of a State government which is not established in its constitution, unalterable by the ordinary legislature. And, with regard to the question of necessity, it has been shown that this can only constitute a question of expediency, not of right.

To erect a corporation, is to substitute a *legal* or *artificial* to a *natural* person, and where a number are concerned, to give them *individuality*. To that *legal* or *artificial* person, once created, the common law of every State, of itself, annexes all those incidents and attributes which are represented as a prostration of the main pillars of their jurisprudence.

It is certainly not accurate to say, that the erection of a corporation is *against* those different *heads* of the State laws; because it is rather to create a kind of person or entity, to which they are inapplicable, and to which the general rule of those laws assign a different regimen. The laws of alienage cannot apply to an artificial person, because it can have no country; those of descent cannot apply to it, because it can have no heirs; those of escheat are foreign from it, for the same reason; those of forfeiture, because it cannot commit a crime; those of distribution, because, though it may be dissolved, it cannot die.

As truly might it be said, that the exercise of the power of prescribing the rule by which foreigners shall be naturalized, is against the law of alienage, while it is, in fact, only to put them in a situation to cease to be the subject of that law. To do a thing which is against a law, is to do something which it forbids, or which is a violation of it.

But if it were even to be admitted that the erection of a corporation is a direct alteration of the stated laws, in the enumerated particulars, it would do nothing towards proving that the measure was unconstitutional. If the government of the United States can do no act which amounts to an alteration of a State law, all its powers are nugatory; for almost every new law is an alteration, in some way or other, of an *old law,* either *common* or *statute.*

There are laws concerning bankruptcy in some States. Some States have laws regulating the values of foreign coins. Congress are empowered to establish uniform laws concerning bankruptcy throughout the United States, and to regulate the values of foreign coins. The exercise of either of these powers by Congress, necessarily involves an alteration of the laws of those States.

Again. Every person, by the common law of each State, may export his property to foreign countries, at pleasure. But Congress, in pursuance of the power of regulating trade, may *prohibit* the exportation of commodities; in doing which, they would alter the common law of each State, in abridgment of individual right.

It can therefore never be good reasoning to say this or that act is unconstitutional, because it alters this or that law of a State. It must be shown that the act which makes the alteration is unconstitutional on other accounts; not *because* it makes the alteration.

There are two points in the suggestions of the Secretary of State, which have been noted, that are peculiarly incorrect. One is, that the proposed incorporation is against the laws of monopoly, because it stipulates an exclusive right of banking under the national authority; the other, that it gives power to the institution to make laws paramount to those of the States.

But, with regard to the first point: The bill neither prohibits any State from erecting as many banks as they please, nor any number of individuals from associating to carry on the business, and consequently, is free from the charge of establishing a monopoly; for monopoly implies a *legal impediment* to the carrying on of the trade by others than those to whom it is granted.

And with regard to the second point, there is still less foundation. The by-laws of such an institution as a bank can operate only on its own members—can only concern the disposition of its own property, and must essentially resemble the rules of a private mercantile partnership. They are expressly not to be contrary to law; and law must here mean the law of a State, as well as of the United States. There never can be a doubt, that a law of a corporation, if contrary to a law of a State, must be overruled as void, unless the law of the State is contrary to that of the United States, and then the question will not be between the law of the State and that of the corporation, but between the law of the State and that of the United States. . . .

Most of the arguments of the Secretary of State, which have not been considered in the foregoing remarks, are of a nature rather to apply to the expediency than to the constitutionality of the bill. They will, however, be noticed in the discussions which will be necessary in reference to the particular heads of the powers of the government which are involved in the question.

Those of the Attorney-General will now properly come under view.

His first objection is, that the power of incorporation is not *expressly* given to Congress. This shall be conceded, but in *this sense only,* that it is not declared in *express terms* that Congress may erect a corporation. But this cannot mean, that there are not certain *express powers* which *necessarily* include it. For instance, Congress have express power to exercise exclusive legislation, in all cases whatsoever, over such *district* (not exceeding ten miles square) as may, by cession of particular States and the acceptance of Congress, become the seat of the government of the United States; and to exercise *like authority* over all places purchased, by consent of the legislature of the State in which the same shall be, for the erection of forts, arsenals, dockyards, and other needful buildings. Here, then, is express power to exercise *exclusive legislation,* in *all cases whatsoever,* over *certain places;* that is, to do, in respect to those places, all that any government whatsoever may do. For language does not afford a more complete designation of sovereign power than in those comprehensive terms. It is, in other words, a power to pass all laws whatsoever, and, consequently, to pass laws for erecting corporations, as well as for any other purpose which is the proper object of law in a free government.

Surely it can never be believed that Congress, with *exclusive powers of legislation in all cases* whatsoever, cannot erect a corporation within the district which shall become the seat of government, for the better regulation of its police. And yet there is an unqualified denial of the power to erect corporations in every case, on the part both of the Secretary of State and of the Attorney-General; the former, indeed, speaks of that power in these emphatical terms: That it is a *right remaining exclusively with the States.*

As far, then, as there is an *express power* to do any *particular act of legislation,* there is an *express one* to erect a corporation in the case above described. But, accurately speaking, no *particular power* is more than *that implied in a general one.* Thus the power to lay a duty on a *gallon of rum* is only a particular *implied* in the general power to lay

and collect taxes, duties, imposts, and excises. This serves to explain in what sense it may be said that Congress have not an express power to make corporations.

This may not be an improper place to take notice of an argument which was used in debate in the House of Representatives. It was there argued, that if the Constitution intended to confer so important a power as that of erecting corporations, it would have been expressly mentioned. But the case which has been noticed is clearly one in which such a power exists, and yet without any specification or express grant of it, further than as every *particular implied* in a general power can be said to be so granted.

But the argument itself is founded upon an exaggerated and erroneous conception of the nature of the power. It has been shown that it is not of so transcendent a kind as the reasoning supposes, and that, viewed in a just light, it is a mean, which ought to have been left to *implication,* rather than an *end,* which ought to have been expressly granted.

Having observed that the power of erecting corporations is not expressly granted to Congress, the Attorney-General proceeds thus:—

"If it can be exercised by them, it must be—

1. Because the nature of the federal government implies it.

2. Because it is involved in some of the specified powers of legislation.

3. Because it is necessary and proper to carry into execution some of the specified powers."

To be implied in the *nature* of the *federal government,* says he, would beget a doctrine so indefinite as to grasp at every power.

This proposition, it ought to be remarked, is not precisely, or even substantially, that which has been relied upon. The proposition relied upon is, that the *specified powers of Congress* are in their nature *sovereign.* That it is incident to sovereign power to erect corporations, and that therefore Congress have a right, within the *sphere* and in *relation* to the *objects of their power,* to erect corporations. It shall, however, be supposed that the Attorney-General would consider the two propositions in the same light, and that the objection made to the one would be made to the other.

To this objection an answer has been already given. It is this, that the doctrine is stated with this *express qualifi-*

cation, that the right to erect corporations does *only* extend to *cases* and *objects* within the *sphere* of the *specified powers* of the *government.* A *general* legislative authority implies a power to erect corporations in *all cases.* A *particular* legislative power implies authority to erect corporations in relation to cases arising under *that power only.* Hence the affirming that, as *incident* to sovereign power, Congress may erect a corporation in relation to the *collection* of their taxes, is no more than to affirm that they may do whatever else they please,—than the saying that they have a power to regulate trade, would be to affirm that they have a power to regulate religion; or than the maintaining that they have sovereign power as to taxation, would be to maintain that they have sovereign power as to every thing else.

The Attorney-General undertakes in the next place to show, that the power of erecting corporations is not involved in any of the specified powers of legislation confided to the national government. In order to this, he has attempted an enumeration of the particulars, which he supposes to be comprehended under the several heads of the *powers* to lay and collect taxes, &c.; to borrow money on the credit of the United States; to regulate commerce with sovereign nations; between the States, and with the Indian tribes; to dispose of and make all needful rules and regulations respecting the territory or other property belonging to the United States. The design of which enumeration is to show, *what* is included under those different heads of power, and negatively, that the power of erecting corporations is not included.

The truth of this inference or conclusion must depend on the accuracy of the enumeration. If it can be shown that the enumeration is *defective,* the inference is destroyed. To do this will be attended with no difficulty.

The heads of the power to lay and collect taxes are stated to be:

1. To stipulate the sum to be lent.

2. An interest or no interest to be paid.

3. The time and manner of repaying, unless the loan be placed on an irredeemable fund.

This enumeration is liable to a variety of objections. It omits in the first place, the *pledging* or *mortgaging* of a fund for the security of the money lent, an usual, and in most cases an essential ingredient.

The idea of a stipulation of an *interest* or no *interest* is too confined. It should rather have been said, to stipulate

the *consideration* of the loan. Individuals often borrow on considerations other than the payment of interest, so may governments, and so they often find it necessary to do. Every one recollects the lottery tickets and other douceurs often given in Great Britain as collateral inducements to the lending of money to the government. There are also frequently collateral conditions, which the enumeration does not contemplate. Every contract which has been made for moneys borrowed in Holland, induces stipulations that the sum due shall be *free* from *taxes,* and from sequestration in time of war, and mortgages all the land and property of the United States for the reimbursement.

It is also known that a lottery is a common expedient for borrowing money, which certainly does not fall under either of the enumerated heads.

The heads of the power to regulate commerce with foreign nations, are stated to be:

1. To prohibit them or their commodities from our ports.

2. To impose duties on *them,* where none existed before, or to increase *existing* duties on them.

3. To subject *them* to any species of custom-house regulation.

4. To grant *them* any exemptions or privileges which policy may suggest.

This enumeration is far more exceptionable than either of the former. It omits *every thing* that relates to the *citizens' vessels,* or *commodities* of the United States.

The following palpable omissions occur at once:

1. Of the power to prohibit the exportation of commodities, which not only exists at all times, but which in time of war it would be necessary to exercise, particularly with relation to naval and warlike stores.

2. Of the power to prescribe rules concerning the *characteristics* and privileges of an American bottom; how she shall be navigated, or whether by citizens or foreigners, or by a proportion of each.

3. Of the power of regulating the manner of contracting with seamen; the police of ships on their voyages, &c., of which the Act for the government and regulation of seamen, in the merchants' service, is a specimen. . . .

The last enumeration relates to the power to dispose of, and make all *needful rules* and *regulations* respecting the territory or *other property* belonging to the United States.

The heads of this power are said to be:

1. To exert an ownership over the territory of the United States, which may be properly called the property of the United States, as in the western territory, and to *institute a government therein,* or

2. To exert an ownership over the other property of the United States.

The idea of exerting an ownership over the territory or other property of the United States, is particularly indefinite and vague. It does not at all satisfy the conception of what must have been intended by a power to make all *needful rules* and *regulations,* nor would there have been any use for a special clause, which authorized nothing more. For the right of exerting an ownership is implied in the very definition of property. It is admitted, that in regard to the western territory, something more is intended; even the institution of a government, that is, the creation of a body politic, or corporation of the highest nature; one which, in its maturity, will be able itself to create other corporations. Why, then, does not the same clause authorize the erection of a corporation, in respect to the regulation or disposal of any other of the property of the United States?

This idea will be enlarged upon in another place.

Hence it appears, that the enumerations which have been attempted by the Attorney-General, are so imperfect, as to authorize no conclusion whatever; they therefore have no tendency to disprove that each and every of the powers, to which they relate, includes that of erecting corporations, which they certainly do, as the subsequent illustrations will more and more evince.

It is presumed to have been satisfactorily shown in the course of the preceding observations:

1. That the power of the government, *as* to the objects intrusted to its management, is, in its nature, sovereign.

2. That the right of erecting corporations is one inherent in, and inseparable from, the idea of sovereign power.

3. That the position, that the government of the United States can exercise no power but such as is delegated to it by its Constitution, does not militate against this principle.

4. That the word *necessary,* in the general clause, can have no *restrictive* operation derogating from the force of this principle; indeed, that the degree in which a measure is or is not *necessary,* cannot be a *test* of *constitutional right,* but of *expediency only.*

5. That the power to erect corporations is not to be considered as an *independent* or *substantive* power, but as

an *incidental* and *auxiliary* one, and was therefore more properly left to implication, than expressly granted.

6. That the principle in question does not extend the power of the government beyond the prescribed limits, because it only affirms a power to *incorporate* for purposes *within the sphere* of the *specified powers.*

And lastly, that the right to exercise such a power in certain cases is unequivocally granted in the most *positive* and *comprehensive* terms. To all which it only remains to be added, that such a power has actually been exercised in two very eminent instances; namely, in the erection of two governments; one northwest of the River Ohio, and the other southwest—the last independent of any antecedent compact. And these result in a full and complete demonstration, that the Secretary of State and Attorney-General are mistaken when they deny generally the power of the national government to erect corporations.

It shall now be endeavored to be shown that there is a power to erect one of the kind proposed by the bill. This will be done by tracing a natural and obvious relation between the institution of a bank and the objects of several of the enumerated powers of the government; and by showing that, *politically* speaking, it is necessary to the effectual execution of one or more of those powers.

In the course of this investigation, various instances will be stated, by way of illustration of a right to erect corporations under those powers.

Some preliminary observations may be proper.

The proposed bank is to consist of an association of persons, for the purpose of creating a joint capital, to be employed chiefly and essentially in loans. So far the object is not only lawful, but it is the mere exercise of a right which the law allows to every individual. The Bank of New-York, which is not incorporated, is an example of such an association. The bill proposes in addition, that the government shall become a joint proprietor in this undertaking, and that it shall permit the bills of the company, payable on demand, to be receivable in its revenues; and stipulates that it shall not grant privileges, similar to those which are to be allowed to this company, to any others. All this is incontrovertibly within the compass of the discretion of the government. The only question is, whether it has a right to incorporate this company, in order to enable it the more effectually to accomplish ends which are in themselves lawful.

To establish such a right, it remains to show the relation

of such an institution to one or more of the specified powers of the government. Accordingly it is affirmed that it has a relation, more or less direct, to the power of collecting taxes, to that of borrowing money, to that of regulating trade between the States, and to those of raising and maintaining fleets and armies. To the two former the relation may be said to be immediate; and in the last place it will be argued, that it is clearly within the provision which authorizes the making of all *needful rules and regulations* concerning the *property* of the United States, as the same has been practised upon by the government.

A bank relates to the collection of taxes in two ways—*indirectly,* by increasing the quantity of circulating medium and quickening circulation, which facilitates the means of paying directly, by creating a *convenient species* of medium in which they are to be paid.

To designate or appoint the *money* or *thing* in which taxes are to be paid, is not only a proper, but a *necessary exercise* of the power of collecting them. Accordingly Congress, in the law concerning the collection of the duties on imposts and tonnage, have provided that they shall be paid in gold and silver. But while it was an indispensable part of the work to say in what they should be paid, the choice of the specific thing was mere matter of discretion. The payment might have been required in the commodities themselves. Taxes in kind, however ill-judged, are not without precedents, even in the United States; or it might have been in the paper money of the several States, or in the bills of the Bank of North America, New-York and Massachusetts, all or either of them; or it might have been in bills issued under the authority of the United States.

No part of this can, it is presumed, be disputed. The appointment, then, of the *money* or *thing* in which the taxes are to be paid, is an incident to the power of collection. And among the expedients which may be adopted, is that of bills issued under the authority of the United States.

Now the manner of issuing these bills is again matter of discretion. The government might doubtless proceed in the following manner:

It might provide that they should be issued under the direction of certain officers, payable on demand; and, in order to support their credit, and give them a ready circulation, it might, besides giving them a currency in its taxes, set apart, out of any moneys in its treasury, a given sum, and appropriate it, under the direction of those officers, as a fund for answering the bills, as presented for payment.

The constitutionality of all this would not admit of a question, and yet it would amount to the institution of a bank, with a view to the more convenient collection of taxes. For the simplest and most precise idea of a bank is, a deposit of coin, or other property, as a fund for *circulating a credit* upon it, which is to answer the purpose of money. That such an arrangement would be equivalent to the establishment of a bank, would become obvious, if the place where the fund to be set apart was kept should be made a receptacle of the moneys of all other persons who should incline to deposit them there for safe-keeping; and would become still more so, if the officers charged with the direction of the fund were authorized to make discounts at the usual rate of interest, upon good security. To deny the power of the government to add these ingredients to the plan, would be to refine away all government.

A further process will still more clearly illustrate the point. Suppose, when the species of bank which has been described was about to be instituted, it was to be urged that, in order to secure to it a due degree of confidence, the fund ought not only to be set apart and appropriated generally, but ought to be specifically vested in the officers who were to have the direction of it, and in their *successors* in office, to the end that it might acquire the character of *private property,* incapable of being resumed without a violation of the sanctions by which the rights of property are protected, and occasioning more serious and general alarm—the apprehension of which might operate as a check upon the government. Such a proposition might be opposed by arguments against the expediency of it, or the solidity of the reason assigned for it, but it is not conceivable what could be urged against its constitutionality; and yet such a disposition of the thing would amount to the erection of a corporation; for the true definition of a corporation seems to be this: It is a *legal* person, or a person created by act of law, consisting of one or more natural persons authorized to hold property, or a franchise in succession, in a legal, as contradistinguished from natural, capacity.

Let the illustration proceed a step further. Suppose a bank of the nature which has been described, with or without incorporation, had been instituted, and that experience had evinced, as it probably would, that, being wholly under a public direction, it possessed not the confidence requisite to the credit of the bills. Suppose, also, that, by some of those adverse conjunctures which occasionally attend nations, there had been a very great drain of the specie of the country, so as not only to cause general distress for want of an adequate medium of circulation, but to produce, in consequence of that circumstance, considerable defalcations in the public revenues. Suppose, also, that there was no bank instituted in any State; in such a posture of things, would it not be most manifest, that the incorporation of a bank like that proposed by the bill would be a measure immediately relative to the *effectual collection* of the taxes, and completely within the province of the sovereign power of providing, by all laws necessary and proper, for that collection? If it be said, that such a state of things would render that necessary, and therefore constitutional, which is not so now, the answer to this, and a solid one it doubtless is, must still be that which has been already stated—circumstances may affect the expediency of the measure, but they can neither add to nor diminish its constitutionality.

A bank has a direct relation to the power of borrowing money, because it is an usual, and in sudden emergencies an essential, instrument in the obtaining of loans to government.

A nation is threatened with a war; large sums are wanted on a sudden to make the requisite preparations. Taxes are laid for the purpose, but it requires time to obtain the benefit of them. Anticipation is indispensable. If there be a bank, the supply can at once be had. If there be none, loans from individuals must be sought. The progress of these is often too slow for the exigency; in some situations they are not practicable at all. Frequently, when they are, it is of great consequence to be able to anticipate the product of them by advance from a bank.

The essentiality of such an institution as an instrument of loans, is exemplified at this very moment. An Indian expedition is to be prosecuted. The only fund, out of which the money can arise, consistently with the public engagements, is a tax, which only begins to be collected in July next. The preparations, however, are instantly to be made. The money must, therefore, be borrowed—and of whom could it be borrowed if there were no public banks?

It happens that there are institutions of this kind, but if there were none, it would be indispensable to create one.

Let it then be supposed that the necessity existed, (as but for a casualty would be the case,) that proposals were made for obtaining a loan; that a number of individuals came forward and said, we are willing to accommodate the government with the money; with what we have in hand,

and the credit we can raise upon it, we doubt not of being able to furnish the sum required; but in order to this, it is indispensable that we should be incorporated as a bank. This is essential towards putting it in our power to do what is desired, and we are obliged on that account to make it the *consideration* or *condition* of the loan.

Can it be believed that a compliance with this proposition would be unconstitutional? Does not this alone evince the contrary? It is a necessary part of a power to borrow, to be able to stipulate the consideration or conditions of a loan. It is evident, as has been remarked elsewhere, that this is not confined to the mere stipulation of a *franchise*. If it may, and it is not perceived why it may not, then the grant of a corporate capacity may be stipulated as a consideration of the loan. There seems to be nothing unfit or foreign from the nature of the thing in giving individuality, or a corporate capacity to a number of persons, who are willing to lend a sum of money to the government, the better to enable them to do it, and make them an ordinary instrument of loans in future emergencies of the state. But the more general view of the subject is still more satisfactory. The legislative power of borrowing money, and of making all laws necessary and proper for carrying into execution that power, seems obviously competent to the appointment of the *organ*, through which the abilities and wills of individuals may be most efficaciously exerted for the accommodation of the government by loans.

The Attorney-General opposes to this reasoning the following observation:—"Borrowing money presupposes the accumulation of a fund to be lent, and is secondary to the creation of an ability to lend." This is plausible in theory, but is not true in fact. In a great number of cases, a previous accumulation of a fund equal to the whole sum required does not exist. And nothing more can be actually presupposed, than that there exists resources, which, put into activity to the greatest advantage by the nature of the operation with the government, will be equal to the effect desired to be produced. All the provisions and operations of government must be presumed to contemplate as they *really* are.

The institution of a bank has also a natural relation to the regulation of trade between the States, in so far as it is conducive to the creation of a convenient medium of *exchange* between them, and to the keeping up a full circulation, by preventing the frequent displacement of the metals in reciprocal remittances. Money is the very hinge on which commerce turns. And this does not merely mean gold and silver; many other things have served the purpose, with different degrees of utility. Paper has been extensively employed.

It cannot, therefore, be admitted, with the Attorney-General, that the regulation of trade between the States, as it concerns the medium of circulation and exchange, ought to be considered as confined to coin. It is even supposable that the whole, or the greatest part, of the coin of the country might be carried out of it.

The Secretary of State objects to the relation here insisted upon, by the following mode of reasoning:—To erect a bank, says he, and to regulate commerce, are very different acts. He who creates a bank, creates a subject of commerce; so does he who makes a bushel of wheat, or digs a dollar out of the mines; yet neither of these persons regulate commerce thereby. To make a thing which may be bought and sold, is not to prescribe regulations for *buying* and *selling*.

This making the regulation of commerce to consist in prescribing rules for *buying* and *selling*—this, indeed, is a species of regulation of trade, but is one which falls more aptly within the province of the local jurisdictions than within that of the general government, whose care they must be presumed to have been intended to be directed to those general political arrangements concerning trade on which its aggregate interests depend, rather than to the details of *buying* and *selling*. Accordingly, such only are the regulations to be found in the laws of the United States, whose objects are to give encouragement to the enterprise of our own merchants, and to advance our navigation and manufactures. And it is in reference to these general relations of commerce, that an establishment which furnishes facilities to circulation, and a convenient medium of exchange and alienation, is to be regarded as a regulation of trade.

The Secretary of State further argues, that if this was a regulation of commerce, it would be void, as *extending as much to the internal commerce of every State as to its external.* But what regulation of commerce does not extend to the internal commerce of every State? What are all the duties upon imported articles, amounting to prohibitions, but so many bounties upon domestic manufactures, affecting the interests of different classes of citizens, in different ways? What are all the provisions in the Coasting Act which relate to the trade between district and district of the same State? In short, what regulation of trade between the States but must affect the internal trade of each State? What can operate upon the whole but must extend to every part?

The relation of a bank to the execution of the powers that concern the common defence, has been anticipated. It has been noted, that, at this very moment, the aid of such an institution is essential to the measures to be pursued for the protection of our frontiers.

It now remains to show, that the incorporation of a bank is within the operation of the provision which authorizes Congress to make all needful rules and regulations concerning the property of the United States. But it is previously necessary to advert to a distinction which has been taken by the Attorney-General.

He admits that the word *property* may signify personal property, however acquired, and yet asserts that it cannot signify money arising from the sources of revenue pointed out in the Constitution, "because," says he, "the disposal and regulation of money is the final cause for raising it by taxes."

But it would be more accurate to say that the *object* to which money is intended to be applied is the *final cause* for raising it, than that the disposal and regulation of it is *such*.

The support of government—the support of troops for the common defence—the payment of the public debt, are the true *final causes* for raising money. The disposition and regulation of it, when raised, are the steps by which it is applied to the *ends* for which it was raised, not the *ends* themselves. Hence, therefore, the money to be raised by taxes, as well as any other personal property, must be supposed to come within the meaning, as they certainly do within the letter, of authority to make all needful rules and regulations concerning the property of the United States.

A case will make this plainer. Suppose the public debt discharged, and the funds now pledged for it liberated. In some instances it would be found expedient to repeal the taxes; in others, the repeal might injure our own industry, our agriculture and manufactures. In these cases they would, of course, be retained. Here, then, would be moneys arising from the authorized sources of revenue, which would not fall within the rule by which the Attorney-General endeavors to except them from other personal property, and from the operation of the clause in question. The moneys being in the coffers of government, what is to hinder such a disposition to be made of them as is contemplated in the bill; or what an incorporation of the parties concerned, under the clause which has been cited?

It is admitted, that with regard to the western territory

they give a power to erect a corporation—that is, to institute a government; and by what rule of construction can it be maintained, that the same words in a constitution of government will not have the same effect when applied to one species of property as to another, as far as the subject is capable of it?—Or that a legislative power to make all needful rules and regulations, or to pass all laws necessary and proper, concerning the public property, which is admitted to authorize an incorporation in one case, will not authorize it in another?—will justify the institution of a government over the western territory, and will not justify the incorporation of a bank for the more useful management of the moneys of the United States? If it will do the last, as well as the first, then, under this provision alone, the bill is constitutional, because it contemplates that the United States shall be joint proprietors of the stock of the bank.

There is an observation of the Secretary of State to this effect, which may require notice in this place:—Congress, says he, are not to lay taxes *ad libitum, for any purpose they please,* but only to pay the debts or provide for the welfare of the Union. Certainly no inference can be drawn from this against the power of applying their money for the institution of a bank. It is true that they cannot without breach of trust lay taxes for any other purpose than the general welfare; but so neither can any other government. The welfare of the community is the only legitimate end for which money can be raised on the community. Congress can be considered as under only one restriction which does not apply to other governments,—they cannot rightfully apply the money they raise to any purpose merely or purely local. But, with this exception, they have as large a discretion in relation to the application of money as any legislature whatever. The constitutional *test* of a right application must always be, whether it be for a purpose of *general* or *local* nature. If the former, there can be no want of constitutional power. The quality of the object, as how far it will really promote or not the welfare of the Union, must be matter of conscientious discretion, and the arguments for or against a measure in this light must be arguments concerning expediency or inexpediency, not constitutional right. Whatever relates to the general order of the finances, to the general interests of trade, &c., being general objects, are constitutional ones for the *application of money.*

A bank, then, whose bills are to circulate in all the revenues of the country, is *evidently* a *general* object, and, for that very reason, a constitutional one, as far as regards the appropriation of money to it. Whether it will really be a beneficial one or not, is worthy of careful examination, but is no more a constitutional point, in the particular referred to, than the question, whether the western lands shall be sold for twenty or thirty cents per acre.

A hope is entertained that it has, by this time, been made to appear, to the satisfaction of the President, that a bank has a natural relation to the power of collecting taxes—to that of regulating trade—to that of providing for the common defence—and that, as the bill under consideration contemplates the government in the light of a joint proprietor of the stock of the bank, it brings the case within the provision of the clause of the Constitution which immediately respects the property of the United States.

Under a conviction that such a relation subsists, the Secretary of the Treasury, with all deference, conceives, that it will result as a necessary consequence from the position, that all the specified powers of government are sovereign, as to the proper objects; that the incorporation of a bank is a constitutional measure; and that the objections taken to the bill, in this respect, are ill-founded.

But, from an earnest desire to give the utmost possible satisfaction to the mind of the President, on so delicate and important a subject, the Secretary of the Treasury will ask his indulgence, while he gives some additional illustrations of cases in which a power of erecting corporations may be exercised, under some of those heads of the specified powers of the government, which are alleged to include the right of incorporating a bank.

1. It does not appear susceptible of a doubt, that if Congress had thought proper to provide, in the collection laws, that the bonds to be given for the duties should be given to the collector of the district, A or B, as the case might require, to ensure to him and his successors in office, in trust for the United States, that it would have been consistent with the Constitution to make such an arrangement; and yet this, it is conceived, would amount to an incorporation.

2. It is not an unusual expedient of taxation to form particular branches of revenue—that is, to mortgage or sell the product of them for certain definite sums, leaving the collection to the parties to whom they are mortgaged or sold. There are even examples of this in the United States. Suppose that there was any particular branch of revenue which it was manifestly expedient to place on this

footing, and there were a number of persons willing to engage with the government, upon condition that they should be incorporated, and the sums vested in them, as well for their greater safety, as for the more convenient recovery and management of the taxes. Is it supposable that there could be any constitutional obstacle to the measure? It is presumed that there could be none. It is certainly a mode of collection which it would be in the discretion of the government to adopt, though the circumstances must be very extraordinary that would induce the Secretary to think it expedient.

3. Suppose a new and unexplored branch of trade should present itself, with some foreign country. Suppose it was manifest, that to undertake it with advantage required an union of the capitals of a number of individuals, and that those individuals would not be disposed to embark without an incorporation, as well to obviate that consequence of a private partnership which makes every individual liable in his whole estate for the debts of the company, to their utmost extent, as for the more convenient management of the business—what reason can there be to doubt that the national government would have a constitutional right to institute and incorporate such a company? None. They possess a general authority to regulate trade with foreign countries. This is a mean, which has been practised to that end, by all the principal commercial nations, who have trading companies to this day, which have subsisted for centuries. Why may not the United States, *constitutionally,* employ the *means* usual in other countries, for attaining the *ends* intrusted to them?

A power to make all needful rules and regulations concerning territory, has been construed to mean a power to erect a government. A power to regulate trade, is a power to make all needful rules and regulations concerning trade. Why may it not, then, include that of erecting a trading company, as well as, in other cases, to erect a government?

It is remarkable that the State conventions, who had proposed amendments in relation to this point, have most, if not all of them, expressed themselves nearly thus: Congress shall not grant monopolies, nor *erect any company* with exclusive advantages of commerce! Thus, at the same time, expressing their sense, that the power to erect trading companies or corporations was inherent in Congress, and objecting to it no further than as to the grant of *exclusive* privileges.

The Secretary entertains all the doubts which prevail concerning the utility of such companies, but he cannot fashion to his own mind a reason, to induce a doubt, that there is a constitutional authority in the United States to establish them. If such a reason were demanded, none could be given, unless it were this: That Congress cannot erect a corporation. Which would be no better than to say, they cannot do it, because they cannot do it—first presuming an inability, without reason, and then assigning that inability as the cause of itself. Illustrations of this kind might be multiplied without end. They shall, however, be pursued no further.

There is a sort of evidence on this point, arising from an aggregate view of the Constitution, which is of no inconsiderable weight: the very general power of laying and collecting taxes, and appropriating their proceeds—that of borrowing money indefinitely—that of coining money, and regulating foreign coins—that of making all needful rules and regulations respecting the property of the United States. These powers combined, as well as the reason and nature of the thing, speak strongly this language: that it is the manifest design and scope of the Constitution to vest in Congress all the powers requisite to the effectual administration of the finances of the United States. As far as concerns this object, there appears to be no parsimony of power.

To suppose, then, that the government is precluded from the employment of so usual and so important an instrument for the administration of its finances as that of a bank, is to suppose what does not coincide with the general tenor and complexion of the Constitution, and what is not agreeable to impressions that any new spectator would entertain concerning it.

Little less than a prohibitory clause can destroy the strong presumptions which result from the general aspect of the government. Nothing but demonstration should exclude the idea that the power exists.

In all questions of this nature, the practice of mankind ought to have great weight against the theories of individuals.

The fact, for instance, that all the principal commercial nations have made use of trading corporations or companies, for the purpose of *external commerce,* is a satisfactory proof that the establishment of them is an incident to the regulation of the commerce.

This other fact, that banks are an usual engine in the administration of national finances, and an ordinary and the most effectual instrument of loan, and one which, in this country, has been found essential, pleads strongly against the supposition that a government, clothed with most of the most important prerogatives of sovereignty in relation to its revenues, its debts, its credits, its defence, its trade, its intercourse with foreign nations, is forbidden to make use of that instrument as an appendage to its own authority.

It has been stated as an auxiliary test of constitutional authority to try whether it abridges any pre-existing right of any State, or any individual. The proposed investigation will stand the most severe examination on this point. Each State may still erect as many banks as it pleases. Every individual may still carry on the banking business to any extent he pleases.

Another criterion may be this: whether the institution or thing has a more direct relation, as to its uses, to the objects of the reserved powers of the State governments than to those of the powers delegated by the United States. This rule, indeed, is less precise than the former; but it may still serve as some guide. Surely a bank has more reference to the objects intrusted to the national government than to those left to the care of the State governments. The common defence is decisive in this comparison.

It is presumed that nothing of consequence in the observations of the Secretary of State, and Attorney-General, has been left unnoticed.

There are, indeed, a variety of observations of the Secretary of State designed to show that the utilities ascribed to a bank, in relation to the collection of taxes, and to trade, could be obtained without it; to analyze which, would prolong the discussion beyond all bounds. It shall be forborne for two reasons. First, because the report concerning the bank, may speak for itself in this respect; and secondly, because all those observations are grounded on the erroneous idea that the *quantum* of necessity or utility is the *test* of a constitutional exercise of power.

One or two remarks only shall be made. One is, that he has taken no notice of a very essential advantage to trade in general, which is mentioned in the report, as peculiar to the existence of a bank circulation, equal in the public es-

timation to gold and silver. It is this that renders it unnecessary to lock up the money of the country, to accumulate for months sucessively, in order to the periodical payment of interest. The other is this: that his arguments to show that treasury orders and bills of exchange, from the course of trade, will prevent any considerable displacement of the metals, are founded on a particular view of the subject. A case will prove this. The sums collected in a State may be small in comparison with the debt due to it; the balance of its trade, direct and circuitous with the seat of government, may be even, or nearly so; here, then, without bank bills, which in that State answer the purpose of coin, there must be a displacement of the coin, in proportion to the difference between the sum collected in the State, and that to be paid in it. With bank bills, no such displacement would take place, or as far as it did, it would be gradual and insensible. In many other ways, also, would there be at least a temporary and inconvenient displacement of the coin, even where the course of trade would eventually return it to its proper channels.

The difference of the two situations in point of convenience to the treasury, can only be appreciated by one, who experiences the embarrassments of making provision for the payment of the interest on a stock, continually changing place in thirteen different places.

One thing which has been omitted, just occurs, although it is not very material to the main argument. The Secretary of State affirms that the bill only contemplates a repayment, not a loan, to the government. But here he is certainly mistaken. It is true the government invests in the stock of the bank a sum equal to that which it receives on loan. But let it be remembered, that it does not, therefore, cease to be a proprietor of the stock, which would be the case, if the money received back were in the nature of a payment. It remains a proprietor still, and will share in the profit or loss of the institution, according as the dividend is more or less than the interest it is to pay on the sum borrowed. Hence that sum is manifestly, and in the strictest sense, a loan.

Veto Message

ANDREW JACKSON

July 10, 1832

It was Jefferson's close ally and presidential successor, James Madison, who oversaw the chartering of a second Bank of the United States after the first bank's charter expired in 1811. Madison had supported the first bank and, after the War of 1812 left inflation and a large national debt, won support for a second bank. But financial panic during the 1820s and an increasing hostility toward financial interests cut into the popularity and public prestige of this second Bank of the United States. During this era, increasing numbers of American men were given the vote; requirements that voters own some form of property were becoming increasingly uncommon. With the election of Andrew Jackson, the conflict between small landholders, particularly in the South and West, and manufacturing and financial interests (including many mechanics and artisans) in the North became increasingly pronounced. Powerful politicians supporting the American system of high tariffs and federally controlled internal improvements sought to gain an extension of the bank's charter in 1832, and they won sufficient votes to secure legislation to that effect. But Jackson saw that bank as an undemocratic tool of monied interests—including foreigners. Presidential vetoes of legislation passed by Congress were extremely rare at this time, and almost always cited the bill's violation of the Constitution as the reason for refusing to sign it into law. Amos Kendall, a leading adviser to Jackson, is generally credited with having taken the lead in drafting this message.

Veto Message

The bill "to modify and continue" the act entitled "An act to incorporate the subscribers to the Bank of the United States" was presented to me on the 4th July instant. Having considered it with the solemn regard to the principles of the Constitution which the day was calculated to inspire, and come to the conclusion that it ought not to become a law, I herewith return it to the Senate, in which it originated, with my objections.

A bank of the United States is in many respects convenient for the Government and useful to the people. Entertaining this opinion, and deeply impressed with the belief that some of the powers and privileges possessed by the existing bank are unauthorized by the Constitution, subversive of the rights of the States, and dangerous to the liberties of the people, I felt it my duty at an early period of my Administration to call the attention of Congress to the practicability of organizing an institution combining all its advantages and obviating these objections. I sincerely regret that in the act before me I can perceive none of those modifications of the bank charter which are necessary, in my opinion, to make it compatible with justice, with sound policy, or with the Constitution of our country.

The present corporate body, denominated the president, directors, and company of the Bank of the United States, will have existed at the time this act is intended to take effect twenty years. It enjoys an exclusive privilege of banking under the authority of the General Government, a monopoly of its favor and support, and, as a necessary consequence, almost a monopoly of the foreign and domestic exchange. The powers, privileges, and favors bestowed upon it in the original charter, by increasing the value of the stock far above its par value, operated as a gratuity of many millions to the stockholders.

An apology may be found for the failure to guard against this result in the consideration that the effect of the original act of incorporation could not be certainly foreseen at the time of its passage. The act before me proposes another gratuity to the holders of the same stock, and in many cases to the same men, of at least seven millions more. This donation finds no apology in any uncertainty as to the effect of the act. On all hands it is conceded that its passage will increase at least 20 or 30 percent more the market price of the stock, subject to the payment of the annuity of $200,000 per year secured by the act, thus adding in a moment one-fourth to its par value. It is not our own citizens only who are to receive the bounty of our Government. More than eight millions of the stock of this bank are held by foreigners. By this act the American Republic proposes virtually to make them a present of some millions of dollars. For these gratuities to foreigners and to some of our own opulent citizens the act secures no equivalent whatever. They are the certain gains of the present stockholders under the operation of this act, after making full allowance for the payment of the bonus.

Every monopoly and all exclusive privileges are granted at the expense of the public, which ought to receive a fair equivalent. The many millions which this act proposes to bestow on the stockholders of the existing bank must come directly or indirectly out of the earnings of the American people. It is due to them, therefore, if their Government sell monopolies and exclusive privileges, that they should at least exact for them as much as they are worth in open market. The value of the monopoly in this case may be correctly ascertained. The twenty-eight millions of stock would probably be at an advance of 50 percent, and command in market at least $42 million subject to the payment of the present bonus. The present value of the monopoly, therefore, is $17 million and this the act proposes to sell for three millions, payable in fifteen annual installments of $200,000 each.

It is not conceivable how the present stockholders can have any claim to the special favor of the Government. The present corporation has enjoyed its monopoly during the period stipulated in the original contract. If we must have such a corporation, why should not the Government sell out the whole stock and thus secure to the people the full market value of the privileges granted? Why should not Congress create and sell twenty-eight millions of stock, incorporating the purchasers with all the powers and privileges secured in this act and putting the premium upon the sales into the Treasury?

But this act does not permit competition in the purchase of this monopoly. It seems to be predicated on the erroneous idea that the present stockholders have a prescriptive right not only to the favor but to the bounty of Government. It appears that more than a fourth part of the stock is held by foreigners and the residue is held by a few hundred of our own citizens, chiefly of the richest class. For their benefit does this act exclude the whole American people from competition in the purchase of this monop-

oly and dispose of it for many millions less than it is worth. This seems the less excusable because some of our citizens not now stockholders petitioned that the door of competition might be opened, and offered to take a charter on terms much more favorable to the Government and country.

But this proposition, although made by men whose aggregate wealth is believed to be equal to all the private stock in the existing bank, has been set aside, and the bounty of our Government is proposed to be again bestowed on the few who have been fortunate enough to secure the stock and at this moment wield the power of the existing institution. I can not perceive the justice or policy of this course. If our Government must sell monopolies, it would seem to be its duty to take nothing less than their full value, and if gratuities must be made once in fifteen or twenty years let them not be bestowed on the subjects of a foreign government nor upon a designated and favored class of men in our own country. It is but justice and good policy, as far as the nature of the case will admit, to confine our favors to our own fellow-citizens, and let each in his turn enjoy an opportunity to profit by our bounty. In the bearings of the act before me upon these points I find ample reasons why it should not become a law.

It has been urged as an argument in favor of rechartering the present bank that the calling in of its loans will produce great embarrassment and distress. The time allowed to close its concerns is ample, and if it has been well managed its pressure will be light, and heavy only in case its management has been bad. If, therefore, it shall produce distress, the fault will be its own, and it would furnish a reason against renewing a power which has been so obviously abused. But will there ever be a time when this reason will be less powerful? To acknowledge its force is to admit that the bank ought to be perpetual, and as a consequence the present stockholders and those inheriting their rights as successors be established a privileged order, clothed both with great political power and enjoying immense pecuniary advantages from their connection with the Government.

The modifications of the existing charter proposed by this act are not such, in my view, as make it consistent with the rights of the States or the liberties of the people. The qualification of the right of the bank to hold real estate, the limitation of its power to establish branches, and the power reserved to Congress to forbid the circulation of small notes are restrictions comparatively of little value or importance. All the objectionable principles of the existing corporation, and most of its odious features, are retained without alleviation.

The fourth section provides

> that the notes or bills of the said corporation, although the same be, on the faces thereof, respectively made payable at one place only, shall nevertheless be received by the said corporation at the bank or at any of the offices of discount and deposit thereof if tendered in liquidation or payment of any balance or balances due to said corporation or to such office of discount and deposit from any other incorporated bank.

This provision secures to the State banks a legal privilege in the Bank of the United States which is withheld from all private citizens. If a State bank in Philadelphia owe the Bank of the United States and have notes issued by the St. Louis branch, it can pay the debt with those notes, but if a merchant, mechanic, or other private citizen be in like circumstances he can not by law pay his debt with those notes, but must sell them at a discount or send them to St. Louis to be cashed. This boon conceded to the State banks, though not unjust in itself, is most odious because it does not measure out equal justice to the high and the low, the rich and the poor. To the extent of its practical effect it is a bond of union among the banking establishments of the nation, erecting them into an interest separate from that of the people, and its necessary tendency is to unite the Bank of the United States and the State banks in any measure which may be thought conducive to their common interest.

The ninth section of the act recognizes principles of worse tendency than any provision of the present charter.

It enacts that "the cashier of the bank shall annually report to the Secretary of Treasury the names of all stockholders who are not resident citizens of the United States, and on the application of the treasurer of any State shall make out and transmit to such treasurer a list of stockholders residing in or citizens of such State, with the amount of stock owned by each." Although this provision, taken in connection with a decision of the Supreme Court, surrenders, by its silence, the right of the States to tax the banking institutions created by this corporation under the name of branches throughout the Union, it is evidently intended to be construed as a concession of their right to tax that portion of the stock which may be held by their own citizens and residents. In this light, if the act becomes a law, it will be understood by the States, who will probably proceed to levy a tax equal to that paid upon the stock of banks incorporated by themselves. In some States that tax is now 1 percent, either on the capital or on the shares, and that may be assumed as the amount which all citizen or resident stockholders would be taxed under the operation of this act. As it is only the stock *held* in the States and not that *employed* within them which would be subject to taxation, and as the names of foreign stockholders are not to be reported to the treasurers of the States, it is obvious that the stock held by them will be exempt from this burden. Their annual profits will therefore be 1 percent more than the citizen stockholders, and as the annual dividends of the bank may be safely estimated at 7 percent, the stock will be worth 10 or 15 percent more to foreigners than to citizens of the United States. To appreciate the effects which this state of things will produce, we must take a brief review of the operations and present condition of the Bank of the United States.

By documents submitted to Congress at the present session it appears that on the 1st of January 1832, of the twenty-eight millions of private stock in the corporation, $8,405,500 were held by foreigners, mostly of Great Britain. The amount of stock held in the nine Western and Southwestern States is $140,200, and in the four Southern States is $5,623,100, and in the Middle and Eastern States is about $13,522,000. The profits of the bank in 1831, as shown in a statement to Congress, were about $3,455,598; of this there accrued in the nine Western States about $1,640,048; in the four Southern States about $352,507, and in the Middle and Eastern States about $1,463,041. As little stock is held in the West, it is obvious that the debt of the people in that section to the bank is principally a debt to the Eastern and foreign stockholders; that the interest they pay upon it is carried into the Eastern States and into Europe, and that it is a burden upon their industry and a drain of their currency, which no country can bear without inconvenience and occasional distress. To meet this burden and equalize the exchange operations of the bank, the amount of specie drawn from those States through its branches within the last two years, as shown by its official reports, was about $6 million. More than half a million of this amount does not stop in the Eastern States, but passes on to Europe to pay the dividends of the foreign stockholders. In the principle of taxation recognized by this act the Western States find no adequate compensation for this perpetual burden on their industry and drain of their currency. The branch bank at Mobile made last year $95,140, yet under the provisions of this act the State of Alabama can raise no revenue from these profitable operations, because not a share of the stock is held by any of her citizens. Mississippi and Missouri are in the same condition in relation to the branches at Natchez and St. Louis, and such, in a greater or less degree, is the condition of every Western State. The tendency of the plan of taxation which this act proposes will be to place the whole United States in the same relation to foreign countries which the Western States now bear to the Eastern. When by a tax on resident stockholders the stock of this bank is made worth 10 or 15 percent more to foreigners than to residents, most of it will inevitably leave the country.

Thus will this provision in its practical effect deprive the Eastern as well as the Southern and Western States of the means of raising a revenue from the extension of business and great profits of this institution. It will make the American people debtors to aliens in nearly the whole amount due to this bank, and send across the Atlantic from two to five millions of specie every year to pay the bank dividends.

In another of its bearings this provision is fraught with danger. Of the twenty-five directors of this bank five are chosen by the Government and twenty by the citizen stockholders. From all voice in these elections the foreign stockholders are excluded by the charter. In proportion, therefore, as the stock is transferred to foreign holders the extent of suffrage in the choice of directors is curtailed. Already is almost a third of the stock in foreign hands and not represented in elections. It is constantly passing out of the country, and this act will accelerate its departure. The entire control of the institution would necessarily fall into the hands of a few citizen stockholders, and the ease with which the object would be accomplished would be a temptation to designing men to secure that control in their own hands by monopolizing the remaining stock. There is danger that a president and directors would then be able to elect themselves from year to year, and without responsibility or control manage the whole concerns of the bank during the existence of its charter. It is easy to conceive that great evils to our country and its institutions might flow from such a concentration of power in the hands of a few men irresponsible to the people.

Is there no danger to our liberty and independence in a bank that in its nature has so little to bind it to our country? The president of the bank has told us that most of the State banks exist by its forbearance. Should its influence become concentered, as it may under the operation of such an act as this, in the hands of a self-elected directory whose interests are identified with those of the foreign stockholders, will there not be cause to tremble for the purity of our elections in peace and for the independence of our country in war? Their power would be great whenever they might choose to exert it; but if this monopoly were regularly renewed every fifteen or twenty years on terms proposed by themselves, they might seldom in peace put forth their strength to influence elections or control the affairs of the nation. But if any private citizen or public functionary should interpose to curtail its powers or prevent a renewal of its privileges, it can not be doubted that he would be made to feel its influence.

Should the stock of the bank principally pass into the hands of the subjects of a foreign country, and we should unfortunately become involved in a war with that country, what would be our condition? Of the course which would be pursued by a bank almost wholly owned by the subjects of a foreign power, and managed by those whose interests, if not affections, would run in the same direction there can be no doubt. All its operations within would be in aid of the hostile fleets and armies without. Controlling our currency, receiving our public moneys, and holding thousands of our citizens in dependence, it would be more formidable and dangerous than the naval and military power of the enemy.

If we must have a bank with private stockholders, every consideration of sound policy and every impulse of American feeling admonishes that it should be *purely American*. Its stockholders should be composed exclusively of our own citizens, who at least ought to be friendly to our Government and willing to support it in times of difficulty and danger. So abundant is domestic capital that competition in subscribing for the stock of local banks has recently led almost to riots. To a bank exclusively of American stockholders, possessing the powers and privileges granted by this act, subscriptions for $200 million could be readily obtained. Instead of sending abroad the stock of the bank in which the Government must deposit its funds and on which it must rely to sustain its credit in times of emergency, it would rather seem to be expedient to prohibit its sale to aliens under penalty of absolute forfeiture.

It is maintained by the advocates of the bank that its constitutionality in all its features ought to be considered as settled by precedent and by the decision of the Supreme Court. To this conclusion I can not assent. Mere precedent is a dangerous source of authority, and should not be regarded as deciding questions of constitutional power except where the acquiescence of the people and the States can be considered as well settled. So far from this being the case on this subject, an argument against the bank might be based on precedent. One Congress, in 1791, decided in favor of a bank; another, in 1811, decided against it. One Congress, in 1815, decided against a bank; another, in 1816, decided in its favor. Prior to the present Congress, therefore, the precedents drawn from that source were equal. If we resort to the States, the expressions of legislative, judicial, and executive opinions against the bank have been probably to those in its favor as 4 to 1. There is nothing in precedent, therefore, which, if its authority were admitted, ought to weigh in favor of the act before me.

If the opinion of the Supreme Court covered the whole ground of this act, it ought not to control the coordinate authorities of this Government. The Congress, the Executive, and the Court must each for itself be guided by its own opinion of the Constitution. Each public officer who takes an oath to support the Constitution swears that he will support it as he understands it, and not as it is understood by others. It is as much the duty of the House of Representatives, of the Senate, and of the President to decide upon the constitutionality of any bill or resolution which may be presented to them for passage or approval as it is of the supreme judges when it may be brought before them for judicial decision. The opinion of the judges has no more authority over Congress than the opinion of Congress has over the judges, and on that point the President is independent of both. The authority of the Supreme Court must not, therefore, be permitted to control the Congress or the Executive when acting in their legislative capacities, but to have only such influence as the force of their reasoning may deserve.

But in the case relied upon the Supreme Court have not decided that all the features of this corporation are compatible with the Constitution. It is true that the court have said that the law incorporating the bank is a constitutional exercise of power by Congress; but taking into view the whole opinion of the court and the reasoning by which they have come to that conclusion, I understand them to

have decided that inasmuch as a bank is an appropriate means for carrying into effect the enumerating powers of the General Government, therefore the law incorporating it is in accordance with that provision of the Constitution which declares that Congress shall have power "to make all laws which shall be necessary and proper for carrying those powers into execution." Having satisfied themselves that the word "*necessary*" in the Constitution means "*needful,*" "*requisite,*" "*essential,*" "*conducive to,*" and that "a bank" is a convenient, a useful, and essential instrument in the prosecution of the Government's "fiscal operations," they conclude that to "use one must be within the discretion of Congress" and that "the act to incorporate the Bank of the United States is a law made in pursuance of the Constitution"; "but," say they, "*where the law is not prohibited and is really calculated to effect any of the objects intrusted to the Government, to undertake here to inquire into the degree of its necessity would be to pass the line which circumscribes the judicial department and to tread on legislative ground.*"

The principle here affirmed is that the "degree of its necessity," involving all the details of a banking institution, is a question exclusively for legislative consideration. A bank is constitutional, but it is the province of the Legislature to determine whether this or that particular power, privilege, or exemption is "necessary and proper" to enable the bank to discharge its duties to the Government, and from their decision there is no appeal to the courts of justice. Under the decision of the Supreme Court, therefore, it is the exclusive province of Congress and the President to decide whether the particular features of this act are *necessary* and *proper* in order to enable the bank to perform conveniently and efficiently the public duties assigned to it as a fiscal agent, and therefore constitutional, or *unnecessary* and *improper,* and therefore unconstitutional.

Without commenting on the general principle affirmed by the Supreme Court, let us examine the details of this act in accordance with the rule of legislative action which they have laid down. It will be found that many of the powers and privileges conferred on it can not be supposed necessary for the purpose for which it is proposed to be created, and are not, therefore, means necessary to attain the end in view, and consequently not justified by the Constitution.

The original act of incorporation, section 21, enacts "that no other bank shall be established by any future law of the United States during the continuance of the corporation hereby created, for which the faith of the United

States is hereby pledged: *Provided,* Congress may renew existing charters for banks within the District of Columbia not increasing the capital thereof, and may also establish any other bank or banks in said District with capitals not exceeding in the whole $6 million if they shall deem it expedient." This provision is continued in force by the act before me fifteen years from the 3d of March 1836.

If Congress possessed the power to establish one bank, they had power to establish more than one if in their opinion two or more banks had been "necessary" to facilitate the execution of the powers delegated to them in the Constitution. If they possessed the power to establish a second bank, it was a power derived from the Constitution to be exercised from time to time, and at any time when the interests of the country or the emergencies of the Government might make it expedient. It was possessed by one Congress as well as another, and by all Congresses alike, and alike at every session. But the Congress of 1816 have taken it away from their successors for twenty years, and the Congress of 1832 proposes to abolish it for fifteen years more. It can not be "*necessary*" or "*proper*" for Congress to barter away or divest themselves of any of the powers vested in them by the Constitution to be exercised for the public good. It is not "*necessary*" to the efficiency of the bank, nor is it "*proper*" in relation to themselves and their successors. They may *properly* use the discretion vested in them, but they may not limit the discretion of their successors. This restriction on themselves and grant of a monopoly to the bank is therefore unconstitutional.

In another point of view this provision is a palpable attempt to amend the Constitution by an act of legislation. The Constitution declares that "the Congress shall have power to exercise exclusive legislation in all cases whatsoever" over the District of Columbia. Its constitutional power, therefore, to establish banks in the District of Columbia and increase their capital at will is unlimited and uncontrollable by any other power than that which gave authority to the Constitution. Yet this act declares that Congress shall *not* increase the capital of existing banks, nor create other banks with capitals exceeding in the whole $6 million. The Constitution declares that Congress *shall* have power to exercise exclusive legislation over this District "*in all cases whatsoever,*" and this act declares they shall not. Which is the supreme law of the land? This provision can not be "*necessary*" or "*proper*" or *constitutional* unless the absurdity be admitted that whenever it be

"necessary and proper" in the opinion of Congress they have a right to barter away one portion of the powers vested in them by the Constitution as a means of executing the rest.

On two subjects only does the Constitution recognize in Congress the power to grant exclusive privileges or monopolies. It declares that "Congress shall have power to promote the progress of science and useful arts by securing for limited times to authors and inventors the exclusive right to their respective writings and discoveries." Out of this express delegation of power have grown our laws of patents and copyrights. As the Constitution expressly delegates to Congress the power to grant exclusive privileges in these cases as the means of executing the substantive power "to promote the progress of science and useful arts," it is consistent with the fair rules of construction to conclude that such a power was not intended to be granted as a means of accomplishing any other end. On every other subject which comes within the scope of Congressional power there is an ever-living discretion in the use of proper means, which can not be restricted or abolished without an amendment of the Constitution. Every act of Congress, therefore, which attempts by grants of monopolies or sale of exclusive privileges for a limited time, or a time without limit, to restrict or extinguish its own discretion in the choice of means to execute its delegated powers is equivalent to a legislative amendment of the Constitution, and palpably unconstitutional.

This act authorizes and encourages transfers of its stock to foreigners and grants them an exemption from all State and national taxation. So far from being "*necessary and proper*" that the bank should possess this power to make it a safe and efficient agent of the Government in its fiscal operations, it is calculated to convert the Bank of the United States into a foreign bank, to impoverish our people in time of peace, to disseminate a foreign influence through every section of the Republic, and in war to endanger our independence.

The several States reserved the power at the formation of the Constitution to regulate and control titles and transfers of real property, and most, if not all, of them have laws disqualifying aliens from acquiring or holding lands within their limits. But this act, in disregard of the undoubted right of the States to prescribe such disqualifications, gives to alien stockholders in this bank an interest and title, as members of the corporation, to all the real property it may acquire within any of the States of this Union. This privilege granted to aliens is not "*necessary*" to enable the bank to perform its public duties, nor in any sense "*proper,*" because it is vitally subversive of the rights of the States.

The Government of the United States have no constitutional power to purchase lands within the States except "for the erection of forts, magazines, arsenals, dockyards, and other needful buildings," and even for these objects only "by the consent of the legislature of the State in which the same shall be." By making themselves stockholders in the bank and granting to the corporation the power to purchase lands for other purposes they assume a power not granted in the Constitution and grant to others what they do not themselves possess. It is not "*necessary*" to the receiving, safe-keeping, or transmission of the funds of the Government that the bank should possess this power, and it is not "*proper*" that Congress should thus enlarge the powers delegated to them in the Constitution.

The old Bank of the United States possessed a capital of only $11 million, which was found fully sufficient to enable it with dispatch and safety to perform all the functions required of it by the Government. The capital of the present bank is $35 million—at least twenty-four more than experience has proved to be *necessary* to enable a bank to perform its public functions. The public debt which existed during the period of the old bank and on the establishment of the new has been nearly paid off, and our revenue will soon be reduced. This increase of capital is therefore not for public but for private purposes.

The Government is the only "*proper*" judge where its agents should reside and keep their offices, because it best knows where their presence will be "*necessary.*" It can not, therefore, be "*necessary*" or "*proper*" to authorize the bank to locate branches where it pleases to perform the public service, without consulting the Government, and contrary to its will. The principle laid down by the Supreme Court concedes that Congress can not establish a bank for purposes of private speculation and gain, but only as a means of executing the delegated powers of the General Government. By the same principle a branch bank can not constitutionally be established for other than public purposes. The power which this act gives to establish two branches in any State, without the injunction or request of the Government and for other than public purposes, is not "*necessary*" to the due *execution* of the powers delegated to Congress.

The bonus which is exacted from the bank is a confession upon the face of the act that the powers granted by it are greater than are "*necessary*" to its character of a fiscal agent. The Government does not tax its officers and agents for the privilege of serving it. The bonus of a million and a half required by the original charter and that of three millions proposed by this act are not exacted for the privilege of granting "the necessary facilities for transferring the public funds from place to place within the United States or the Territories thereof, and for distributing the same in payment of the public creditors without charging commission or claiming allowance on account of the difference of exchange," as required by the act of incorporation, but for something more beneficial to the stockholders. The original act declares that it (the bonus) is granted "in consideration of the exclusive privileges and benefits conferred by this act upon the said bank," and the act before me declares it to be "in consideration of the exclusive benefits and privileges continued by this act to the said corporation for fifteen years, as aforesaid." It is therefore for "exclusive privileges and benefits" conferred for their own use and emolument, and not for the advantage of the Government, that a bonus is exacted. These surplus powers for which the bank is required to pay can not surely be "*necessary*" to make it the fiscal agent of the Treasury. If they were, the exaction of a bonus for them would not be "*proper.*"

It is maintained by some that the bank is a means of executing the constitutional power "to coin money and regulate the value thereof." Congress have established a mint to coin money and passed laws to regulate the value thereof. The money so coined, with its value so regulated, and such foreign coins as Congress may adopt are the only currency known to the Constitution. But if they have other power to regulate the currency, it was conferred to be exercised by themselves, and not to be transferred to a corporation. If the bank be established for that purpose, with a charter unalterable without its consent, Congress have parted with their power for a term of years, during which the Constitution is a dead letter. It is neither necessary nor proper to transfer its legislative power to such a bank, and therefore unconstitutional.

By its silence, considered in connection with the decision of the Supreme Court in the case of McCulloch against the State of Maryland, this act takes from the States the power to tax a portion of the banking business carried on within their limits, in subversion of one of the strongest barriers which secured them against Federal encroachments. Banking, like farming, manufacturing, or any other occupation or profession, is a *business,* the right to follow which is not originally derived from the laws. Every citizen and every company of citizens in all of our States possessed the right until the State legislatures deemed it good policy to prohibit private banking by law. If the prohibitory State laws were now repealed, every citizen would again possess the right. The State banks are a qualified restoration of the right which has been taken away by the laws against banking, guarded by such provisions and limitations as in the opinion of the State legislatures the public interest requires. These corporations, unless there be an exemption in their charter, are, like private bankers and banking companies, subject to State taxation. The manner in which these taxes shall be laid depends wholly on legislative discretion. It may be upon the bank, upon the stock, upon the profits, or in any other mode which the sovereign power shall will.

Upon the formation of the Constitution the States guarded their taxing power with peculiar jealousy. They surrendered it only as it regards imports and exports. In relation to every other object within their jurisdiction, whether persons, property, business, or professions, it was secured in as ample a manner as it was before possessed. All persons, though United States officers, are liable to a poll tax by the States within which they reside. The lands of the United States are liable to the usual land tax, except in the new States, from whom agreements that they will not tax unsold lands are exacted when they are admitted into the Union. Horses, wagons, any beasts or vehicles, tools, or property belonging to private citizens, though employed in the service of the United States, are subject to State taxation. Every private business, whether carried on by an officer of the General Government or not, whether it be mixed with public concerns or not, even if it be carried on by the Government of the United States itself, separately or in partnership, falls within the scope of the taxing power of the State. Nothing comes more fully within it than banks and the business of banking, by whomsoever instituted and carried on. Over this whole subject-matter it is just as absolute, unlimited, and uncontrollable as if the Constitution had never been adopted, because in the formation of that instrument it was reserved without qualification.

The principle is conceded that the States can not rightfully tax the operations of the General Government. They can not tax the money of the Government deposited in the State banks, nor the agency of those banks in remitting it; but will any man maintain that their mere selection to perform this public service for the General Government would exempt the State banks and their ordinary business from State taxation? Had the United States, instead of establishing a bank at Philadelphia, employed a private banker to keep and transmit their funds, would it have deprived Pennsylvania of the right to tax his bank and his usual banking operations? It will not be pretended. Upon what principle, then, are the banking establishments of the Bank of the United States and their usual banking operations to be exempted from taxation? It is not their public agency or the deposits of the Government which the States claim a right to tax, but their banks and their banking powers, instituted and exercised within State jurisdiction for their private emolument—those powers and privileges for which they pay a bonus, and which the States tax in their own banks. The exercise of these powers within a State, no matter by whom or under what authority, whether by private citizens in their original right, by corporate bodies created by the States, by foreigners or the agents of foreign governments located within their limits, forms a legitimate object of State taxation. From this and like sources, from the persons, property, and business that are found residing, located, or carried on under their jurisdiction, must the States, since the surrender of their right to raise a revenue from imports and exports, draw all the money necessary for the support of their governments and the maintenance of their independence. There is no more appropriate subject of taxation than banks, banking, and bank stocks, and none to which the States ought more pertinaciously to cling.

It can not be *necessary* to the character of the bank as a fiscal agent of the Government that its private business should be exempted from that taxation to which all the State banks are liable, nor can I conceive it "*proper*" that the substantive and most essential powers reserved by the States shall be thus attacked and annihilated as a means of executing the powers delegated to the General Government. It may be safely assumed that none of those sages who had an agency in forming or adopting our Constitution ever imagined that any portion of the taxing power of the States not prohibited to them nor delegated to Congress was to be swept away and annihilated as a means of executing certain powers delegated to Congress.

If our power over means is so absolute that the Supreme Court will not call in question the constitutionality of an act of Congress the subject of which "is not prohibited, and is really calculated to effect any of the objects intrusted to the Government," although, as in the case before me, it takes away powers expressly granted to Congress and rights scrupulously reserved to the States, it becomes us to proceed in our legislation with the utmost caution. Though not directly, our own powers and the rights of the States may be indirectly legislated away in the use of means to execute substantive powers. We may not enact that Congress shall not have the power of exclusive legislation over the District of Columbia, but we may pledge the faith of the United States that as a means of executing other powers it shall not be exercised for twenty years or forever. We may not pass an act prohibiting the States to tax the banking business carried on within their limits, but we may, as a means of executing our powers over other objects, place that business in the hands of our agents and then declare it exempt from State taxation in their hands. Thus may our own powers and the rights of the States, which we can not directly curtail or invade, be frittered away and extinguished in the use of means employed by us to execute other powers. That a bank of the United States, competent to all the duties which may be required by the Government, might be so organized as not to infringe on our own delegated powers or the reserved rights of the States I do not entertain a doubt. Had the Executive been called upon to furnish the project of such an institution, the duty would have been cheerfully performed. In the absence of such a call it was obviously proper that he should confine himself to pointing out those prominent features in the act presented which in his opinion make it incompatible with the Constitution and sound policy. A general discussion will now take place, eliciting new light and settling important principles; and a new Congress, elected in the midst of such discussion, and furnishing an equal representation of the people according to the last census, will bear to the Capitol the verdict of public opinion, and, I doubt not, bring this important question to a satisfactory result.

Under such circumstances the bank comes forward and asks a renewal of its charter for a term of fifteen years upon conditions which not only operate as a gratuity to the stockholders of many millions of dollars, but will sanction any abuses and legalize any encroachments.

Suspicions are entertained and charges are made of gross abuse and violation of its charter. An investigation unwillingly conceded and so restricted in time as necessarily to make it incomplete and unsatisfactory discloses enough to excite suspicion and alarm. In the practices of the principal bank partially unveiled, in the absence of important witnesses, and in numerous charges confidently made and as yet wholly uninvestigated there was enough to induce a majority of the committee of investigation—a committee which was selected from the most able and honorable members of the House of Representatives—to recommend a suspension of further action upon the bill and a prosecution of the inquiry. As the charter had yet four years to run, and as a renewal now was not necessary to the successful prosecution of its business, it was to have been expected that the bank itself, conscious of its purity and proud of its character, would have withdrawn its application for the present, and demanded the severest scrutiny into all its transactions. In their declining to do so there seems to be an additional reason why the functionaries of the Government should proceed with less haste and more caution in the renewal of their monopoly.

The bank is professedly established as an agent of the executive branch of the Government, and its constitutionality is maintained on that ground. Neither upon the propriety of present action nor upon the provisions of this act was the Executive consulted. It has had no opportunity to say that it neither needs nor wants an agent clothed with such powers and favored by such exemptions. There is nothing in its legitimate functions which makes it necessary or proper. Whatever interest or influence, whether public or private, has given birth to this act, it can not be found either in the wishes or necessities of the executive department, by which present action is deemed premature, and the powers conferred upon its agent not only unnecessary, but dangerous to the Government and country.

It is to be regretted that the rich and powerful too often bend the acts of Government to their selfish purposes. Distinctions in society will always exist under every just government. Equality of talents, of education, or of wealth can not be produced by human institutions. In the full enjoyment of the gifts of Heaven and the fruits of superior industry, economy, and virtue, every man is equally entitled to protection by law; but when the laws undertake to add to these natural and just advantages artificial distinctions, to grant titles, gratuities, and exclusive privileges, to make the rich richer and the potent more powerful, the humble members of society—the farmers, mechanics, and laborers—who have neither the time nor the means of securing like favors to themselves, have a right to complain of the injustice of their Government. There are no necessary evils in government. Its evils exist only in its abuses. If it would confine itself to equal protection, and, as Heaven does its rains, shower its favors alike on the high and the low, the rich and the poor, it would be an unqualified blessing. In the act before me there seems to be a wide and unnecessary departure from these just principles.

Nor is our Government to be maintained or our Union preserved by invasions of the rights and powers of the several States. In thus attempting to make our General Government strong we make it weak. Its true strength consists in leaving individuals and States as much as possible to themselves—in making itself felt, not in its power, but in its beneficence; not in its control, but in its protection; not in binding the States more closely to the center, but leaving each to move unobstructed in its proper orbit.

Experience should teach us wisdom. Most of the difficulties our Government now encounters and most of the dangers which impend over our Union have sprung from an abandonment of the legitimate objects of Government by our national legislation, and the adoption of such principles as are embodied in this act. Many of our rich men have not been content with equal protection and equal benefits, but have besought us to make them richer by act of Congress. By attempting to gratify their desires we have in the results of our legislation arrayed section against section, interest against interest, and man against man, in a fearful commotion which threatens to shake the foundations of our Union. It is time to pause in our career to review our principles, and if possible revive that devoted patriotism and spirit of compromise which distinguished the sages of the Revolution and the fathers of our Union. If we can not at once, in justice to interests vested under improvident legislation, make our Government what it ought to be, we can at least take a stand against all new grants of monopolies and exclusive privileges, against any prostitution of our Government to the advancement of the few at the expense of the many, and in favor of compromise and gradual reform in our code of laws and system of political economy.

I have now done my duty to my country. If sustained by my fellow-citizens, I shall be grateful and happy; if not, I shall find in the motives which impel me ample grounds for contentment and peace. In the difficulties which surround us and the dangers which threaten our institutions there is cause for neither dismay nor alarm. For relief and deliverance let us firmly rely on that kind Providence which I am sure watches with peculiar care over the destinies of our Republic, and on the intelligence and wisdom of our countrymen. Through *His* abundant goodness and *their* patriotic devotion our liberty and Union will be preserved.

Veto Message

JAMES MADISON

March 3, 1817

Madison split with Jefferson in supporting a national bank. But Madison held to Jefferson's strict construction of the powers granted the federal government by the Constitution in regard to internal improvements—the building of federal roads, canals, and the like. The bill for which this veto message was delivered provided that the federal government's bonus and dividends from the Bank of the United States should fund internal improvements.

Veto Message

To the House of Representatives of the United States:

Having considered the bill this day presented to me entitled "An act to set apart and pledge certain funds for internal improvements," and which sets apart and pledges funds "for constructing roads and canals, and improving the navigation of water courses, in order to facilitate, promote, and give security to internal commerce among the several States, and to render more easy and less expensive the means and provisions for the common defense," I am constrained by the insuperable difficulty I feel in reconciling the bill with the Constitution of the United States to return it with that objection to the House of Representatives, in which it originated.

The legislative powers vested in Congress are specified and enumerated in the eighth section of the first article of the Constitution, and it does not appear that the power proposed to be exercised by the bill is among the enumerated powers, or that it falls by any just interpretation within the power to make laws necessary and proper for carrying into execution those or other powers vested by the Constitution in the Government of the United States.

"The power to regulate commerce among the several States" can not include a power to construct roads and canals, and to improve the navigation of water courses in order to facilitate, promote, and secure such a commerce without a latitude of construction departing from the ordinary import of the terms strengthened by the known inconveniences which doubtless led to the grant of this remedial power to Congress.

To refer the power in question to the clause "to provide for the common defense and general welfare" would be contrary to the established and consistent rules of interpretation, as rendering the special and careful enumeration of powers which follow the clause nugatory and improper. Such a view of the Constitution would have the effect of giving to Congress a general power of legislation instead of the defined and limited one hitherto understood to belong to them, the terms "common defense and general welfare" embracing every object and act within the purview of a legislative trust. It would have the effect of subjecting both the Constitution and laws of the several States in all cases not specifically exempted to be superseded by laws of Congress, it being expressly declared "that the Constitution of the United States and laws made in pursuance thereof shall be the supreme law of the land, and the judges of every State shall be bound thereby, anything in the constitution or laws of any State to the contrary notwithstanding." Such a view of the Constitution, finally, would have the effect of excluding the judicial authority of the United States from its participation in guarding the boundary between the legislative powers of the General and the State Governments, inasmuch as questions relating to the general welfare, being questions of policy and expediency, are unsusceptible of judicial cognizance and decision.

A restriction of the power "to provide for the common defense and general welfare" to cases which are to be provided for by the expenditure of money would still leave within the legislative power of Congress all the great and most important measures of Government, money being the ordinary and necessary means of carrying them into execution.

If a general power to construct roads and canals, and to improve the navigation of water courses, with the train of powers incident thereto, be not possessed by Congress, the assent of the States in the mode provided in the bill cannot confer the power. The only cases in which the consent and cession of particular States can extend the power of Congress are those specified and provided for in the Constitution.

I am not unaware of the great importance of roads and canals and the improved navigation of water courses, and that a power in the National Legislature to provide for them might be exercised with signal advantage to the general prosperity. But seeing that such a power is not expressly given by the Constitution, and believing that it can not be deduced from any part of it without an inadmissible latitude of construction and a reliance on insufficient precedents; believing also that the permanent success of the Constitution depends on a definite partition of powers between the General and the State Governments, and that no adequate landmarks would be left by the constructive extension of the powers of Congress as proposed in the bill, I have no option but to withhold my signature from it, and to cherishing the hope that its beneficial objects may be attained by a resort for the necessary powers to the same wisdom and virtue in the nation which established the Constitution in its actual form and providently marked out in the instrument itself a safe and practicable mode of improving it as experience might suggest. . . .

Commentaries on the Constitution of the United States

JOSEPH STORY

1833

In these sections of *Commentaries,* Story spells out the view that the commerce power is exclusive rather than concurrent; that because Congress has the power to regulate commerce the states cannot have that same power. In addition, Story interprets the Constitution as supporting national tariffs aimed at protecting domestic companies entering into the manufacturing business.

Commentaries on the Constitution of the United States

Power to Borrow Money, and Regulate Commerce

§ 162. The next power of Congress is, "to borrow money on the credit of the United States." This power, also, seems indispensable to the sovereignty and existence of the National Government; for otherwise, in times of great public dangers, or severe public calamities, it might be impossible to provide, adequately, for the public exigencies. In times of peace, it may not, ordinarily, be necessary for the expenditures of a nation to exceed its revenues. But the experience of all nations must convince us, that, in times of war, the burdens and expenses of a single year may more than equal the ordinary revenue of ten years. And, even in times of peace, there are occasions, in which loans may be the most facile, convenient, and economical means of supplying any extraordinary expenditure. The experience of the United States, has already shown the importance of the power, both in peace and in war. Without this resource, neither the war of Independence, nor the more recent war with Great Britain could have been successfully carried on, or terminated. And the purchase of Louisiana was by the same means promptly provided for, without being felt by the nation, in its ordinary fiscal concerns.

§ 168. The next power of Congress is, "to regulate commerce with foreign nations, and among the several States, and with the Indian tribes." The want of this power to regulate commerce was, as has been already suggested, a leading defect of the Confederation. In the different States, the most opposite and conflicting regulations existed; each pursued its own real or supposed local interests; each was jealous of the rivalry of its neighbors; and each was successively driven to retaliatory measures, in order to satisfy public clamor, or to alleviate private distress. In the end, however, all their measures became utterly nugatory, or mischievous, engendering mutual hostilities, and prostrating all their commerce at the feet of foreign nations. It is hardly possible to exaggerate the oppressed and degraded state of domestic commerce, manufactures, and agriculture, at the time of the adoption of the Constitution. Our ships were almost driven from the ocean; our work-shops were nearly deserted; our mechanics were in a starving condition; and our agriculture was sunk to the lowest ebb. These were the natural results of the inability of the General Government to regulate commerce, so as to prevent the injurious monopolies and exclusions of foreign nations, and the conflicting, and often ruinous regulations of the different States. If duties were laid by one State, they were rendered ineffectual by the opposite policy of another. If one State gave a preference to its own ships or commerce, it was counteracted by another. If one State endeavored to foster its own manufactures by any measures of protection, that made it an object of jealousy to others; and brought upon it the severe retaliation of foreign governments. If one State was peculiarly favored in its agricultural products, that constituted an inducement with others to load them with some restrictions, which should redress the inequality. It was easy to foresee, that this state of things could not long exist, without bringing on a border warfare, and a deep-rooted hatred, among neighboring States, fatal to the Union, and, of course, fatal also to the liberty of every member of it.

§ 164. The power "to regulate foreign commerce," enabled the government at once to place the whole country upon an equality with foreign nations; to compel them to abandon their narrow and selfish policy towards us; and to protect our own commercial interests against their injurious competitions. The power to regulate commerce "among the several States," in like manner, annihilated the causes of domestic feuds and rivalries. It compelled every State to regard the interests of each, as the interests of all; and thus diffused over all the blessings of a free, active, and rapid exchange of commodities, upon the footing of perfect equality. The power to regulate commerce "with the Indian tribes," was equally necessary to the peace and safety of the frontier States. Experience had shown the utter impracticability of escaping from sudden wars, and invasions, on the part of these tribes; and the dangers were immeasurably increased by the want of uniformity of regulations and control in the intercourse with them. Indeed, in nothing has the profound wisdom of the framers of the Constitution been more displayed, than in the grant of this power to the Union. By means of it, the country has risen from poverty to opulence; from a state of narrow and scanty resources to an ample national revenue; from a feeble, and disheartening intercourse and competition with foreign nations, in agriculture, commerce, manufactures, and population, to a proud, and conscious independence in arts, in numbers, in skill, and in civil polity.

§ 165. In considering this clause of the Constitution, several important inquiries are presented. In the first place, what is the natural import of the terms; in the next place, how far the power is exclusive of that of the States; in the third place, to what purposes and for what objects the power may be constitutionally applied; and in the fourth place, what are the true nature and extent of the power to regulate commerce with the Indian tribes.

§ 166. In the first place, then, what is the constitutional meaning of the words, "to regulate commerce;" for the Constitution being (as has been aptly said) one of enumeration, and not of definition, it becomes necessary, in order to ascertain the extent of the power, to ascertain the meaning of the words. The power is, to regulate; that is, to prescribe the rule, by which commerce is to be governed. The subject to be regulated, is commerce. Is that limited to traffic, to buying and selling, or the interchange of commodities? Or does it comprehend navigation and intercourse? If the former construction is adopted, then a general term, applicable to many objects, is restricted to one of its significations. If the latter, then a general term is retained in its general sense. To adopt the former, without some guiding grounds furnished by the context, or the nature of the power, would be improper. The words being general, the sense must be general, also, and embrace all subjects comprehended under them, unless there be some obvious mischief, or repugnance to other clauses, to limit them. In the present case, there is nothing to justify such a limitation. Commerce undoubtedly is traffic; but it is something more. It is intercourse. It describes the commercial intercourse between nations, and parts of nations, in all its branches; and is regulated by prescribing rules for carrying on that intercourse. The mind can scarcely conceive a system for regulating commerce between nations, which shall exclude all laws concerning navigation; which shall be silent on the admission of the vessels of one nation into the ports of another; and be confined to prescribing rules for the conduct of individuals in the actual employment of buying and selling, or barter. It may, therefore, be safely affirmed, that the terms of the Constitution have, at all times, been understood to include a power over navigation, as well as over trade, over intercourse, as well as over traffic. It adds no small strength to this interpreation, that the practice of all foreign countries, as well as of our own, has uniformly conformed to this view of the subject.

§ 167. The next inquiry is, whether this power to regulate commerce, is like that to lay taxes. The latter, may well be concurrent, while the former, is exclusive, resulting from the different nature of the two powers. The power of Congress in laying taxes is not necessarily, or naturally inconsistent with that of the States. Each may lay a tax on the same property, without interfering with the action of the other; for taxation is but taking small portions from the mass of property, which is susceptible of almost infinite division. In imposing taxes for State purposes, a State is not doing what Congress is empowered to do. Congress is not empowered to tax for those purposes, which are within the exclusive province of the States. When, then, each government exercises the power of taxation, neither is exercising the power of the other. But when a State proceeds to regulate commerce with foreign nations, or among the several States, it is exercising the very power, which is granted to Congress; and is doing the very thing, which Congress is authorized to do. There is no analogy, then, between the power of taxation, and the power of regulating commerce.

§ 168. Nor can any power be inferred in the States, to regulate commerce, from other clauses in the Constitution, or the acknowledged rights exercised by the States. The Constitution has prohibited the States from laying any impost or duty on imports or exports; but this does not admit, that the State might otherwise have exercised the power, as a regulation of commerce. The laying of such imposts and duties may be, and indeed often is, used, as a mere regulation of commerce, by governments possessing that power. But the laying of such imposts and duties is as certainly, and more usually, a right exercised as a part of the power to lay taxes; and with this latter power the States are clearly intrusted. So that the prohibition is an exception from the acknowledged power of the State to lay taxes, and not from the questionable power to regulate commerce. Indeed, the Constitution treats these as distinct and independent powers. The same remarks apply to a duty on tonnage.

§ 169. In the next place, to what extent, and for what objects and purposes, the power to regulate commerce may be constitutionally applied.

§ 170. And first, among the States. It is not doubted, that it extends to the regulation of navigation, and to the coasting trade and fisheries, within, as well as without any State, wherever it is connected with the commerce or intercourse with any other State, or with foreign nations. It extends to the regulation and government of seamen on board of American ships; and to conferring privileges upon ships built and owned in the United States, in domestic, as well as in foreign trade. It extends to quarantine laws, and pilotage laws, and wrecks of the sea. It extends, as well to the navigation of vessels engaged in carrying passengers, and whether steam vessels or of any other description, as to the navigation of vessels engaged in traffic and general coasting business. It extends to the laying of embargoes, as well on domestic, as on foreign voyages. It extends to the construction of lighthouses, the placing of buoys and beacons, the removal of obstructions to navigation in creeks, rivers, sounds, and bays, and the establishment of securities to navigation against the inroads of the ocean. It extends also to the designation of a particular port or ports of entry and delivery for the purposes of foreign commerce. These powers have been actually exerted by the National Government under a system of laws, many of which commenced with the early establishment of the Constitution; and they have continued unquestioned unto our day, if not to the utmost range of their reach, at least to that of their ordinary application.

§ 171. Many of the like powers have been applied in the regulation of foreign commerce. The commercial system of the United States has also been employed sometimes for the purpose of revenue; sometimes for the purpose of prohibition; sometimes for the purpose of retaliation and commercial reciprocity; sometimes to lay embargoes; sometimes to encourage domestic navigation, and the shipping and mercantile interest, by bounties, by discriminating duties, and by special preferences and privileges; and sometimes to regulate intercourse with a view to mere political objects, such as to repel aggressions, increase the pressure of war, or vindicate the rights of neutral sovereignty. In all these cases, the right and duty have been conceded to the National Government by the unequivocal voice of the people.

§ 172. It may be added, that Congress have also, from the earliest period of the government, applied the same power of regulating commerce for the purpose of encouraging and protecting domestic manufactures; and although this application of it has been recently contested, yet Congress have never abandoned the exercise of it for such a purpose. Indeed, if Congress does not possess the power to encourage domestic manufactures, by regulations of commerce, it is a power, that is utterly annihilated; for it is admitted, on all sides, that the States do not possess it. And America would then present the singular spectacle of a nation voluntarily depriving itself, in the exercise of its admitted rights of sovereignty, of all means of promoting some of its most vital interests.

§ 173. In respect to trade with the Indian tribes. Antecedently to the American Revolution, the authority to regulate trade and intercourse with the Indian tribes, whether they were within, or without the boundaries of the Colonies, was understood to belong to the prerogative of the British crown. And after the American Revolution, the like power would naturally fall to the Federal Government, with a view to the general peace and interests of all the States. Two restrictions, however, upon the power, were, by express terms, incorporated into the Confederation, which occasioned endless embarrassments and doubts. The power of Congress was restrained to Indians, not members of any of the States; and was not to be exercised so as to violate or infringe the legislative right of any State, within its own limits. What description of Indians were to be deemed members of a State, was never settled under the Confederation; and was a question of frequent perplexity and contention in the federal councils. And how the trade with Indians, though not members of a State, yet residing within its legislative jurisdiction, was to be regulated by an external authority, without so far intruding on the internal rights of legislation, was absolutely incomprehensible. In this case, as in some other cases, the Articles of Confederation inconsiderately endeavored to accomplish impossibilities; to reconcile a partial sovereignty in the Union, with complete sovereignty in the States; to subvert a mathematical axiom, by taking away a part, and letting the whole remain. The Constitution has wisely disembarrassed the power of these two limitations; and has thus given to Congress, as the only safe and proper depositary, the exclusive power, which belonged to the Crown in the ante-revolutionary times; a power indispensable to the peace of the States, and to the just preservation of the rights and territory of the Indians.

Naturalization, Bankruptcy, and Coinage of Money

§ 174. The next power of Congress is, "to establish a uniform rule of naturalization, and uniform laws on the subject of bankruptcies throughout the States." The power of naturalization is, with great propriety, confided to Congress, since, if left to the States, they might naturalize foreigners upon very different, and even upon opposite systems; and, as the citizens of all the States have common privileges in all, it would thus be in the power of any one State to defeat the wholesome policy of all the others in regard to this most important subject. Congress alone can have power to pass uniform laws, obligatory on all the States; and thus to adopt a system, which shall secure all of them against any dangerous results from the indiscriminate admission of foreigners to the right of citizenship upon their first landing on our shores. And, accordingly, this power is exclusive in Congress.

§ 175. The power to pass bankrupt laws is equally important, and proper to be intrusted to Congress, although it is greatly to be regretted, that it has not, except for a very brief period, been acted upon by Congress. Bankrupt and insolvent laws, when properly framed, have two great ob-

jects in view; first, to secure to honest but unfortunate debtors a discharge from debts, which they are unable to pay, and thus to enable them to begin anew in the career of industry, without the discouraging fear, that it will be wholly useless; secondly, to secure to creditors a full surrender, and equal participation, of and in the effects of their debtors, when they have become bankrupt, or failed in business. On the one hand, such laws relieve the debtor from perpetual bondage to his creditors, in the shape, either of an unlimited imprisonment for his debts, or of an absolute right to appropriate all his future earnings. The latter course obviously destroys all encouragement to future enterprise and industry, on the part of the debtor; the former is, if possible, more harsh, severe, and indefensible; for it makes poverty, in itself sufficiently oppressive, the cause or occasion of penalties and punishments.

§ 176. It is obvious, that no single State is competent to pass a uniform system of bankruptcy, which shall operate throughout all of them. It can have no power to discharge debts, contracted in other States; or to bind creditors in other States. And it is hardly within the range of probability, that the same system should be universally adopted, and persevered in permanently, by all the States. In fact, before, as well as since the adoption of the Constitution, the States have had very different systems on the subject, exhibiting a policy as various and sometimes as opposite, as could well be imagined. The future will, in all human probability, be, as the past. And the utter inability of any State to discharge contracts made within its own territorial limits, before the passage of its own laws, or to discharge any debts whatever, contracted in other States, or due to the citizens thereof, must perpetually embarrass commercial dealings, discourage industry, and diminish private credit and confidence. The remedy is in the hands of Congress. It has been given for wise ends, and has hitherto been strangely left without any efficient operation.

§ 177. The next power of Congress is, to "coin money, regulate the value thereof, and of foreign coins, and fix the standard of weights and measures." The object of the power over the coinage and currency of the country is, to produce uniformity in the value of money throughout the Union, and thus to save us from the embarrassments of a perpetually fluctuating and variable currency. If each State might coin money, as it pleased, there would be no security for any uniform coinage, or any uniform standard of value; and a great deal of base and false coin, would constantly be thrown into the market. The evils from this cause are abundantly felt among the small principalities of continental Europe. The power to fix the standard of weights and measures is a matter of great public convenience, although it has hitherto remained in a great measure dormant. The introduction of the decimal mode of calculation, in dollars and cents, instead of the old and awkward system of pounds, shillings, and pence, has been found of great public convenience, although it was at first somewhat unpopular. A similar system in weights and measures has been thought by many statesmen to have advantages equally great and universal. At all events, the power is safe in the hands of Congress, and may hereafter be acted upon, whenever either our foreign, or our domestic intercourse, shall imperiously require a new system.

§178. The next power of Congress is, "to provide for the punishment of counterfeiting the securities, and current coin of the United States." This is a natural, and, in a just view, an indispensable appendage to the power to borrow money, and to coin money. Without it, there would be no adequate means for the General Government to punish frauds or forgeries, detrimental to its own interests, and subversive of public and private confidence. . . .

§1073. A question has been recently made, whether congress have a constitutional authority to apply the power to regulate commerce for the purpose of encouraging and protecting domestic manufactures. It is not denied, that congress may, incidentally, in its arrangements for revenue, or to countervail foreign restrictions, encourage the growth of domestic manufactures. But it is earnestly and strenuously insisted, that, under the colour of regulating commerce, congress have no right permanently to prohibit any importations, or to tax any unreasonably for the purpose of securing the home market to the domestic manufacturer, as they thereby destroy the commerce entrusted to them to regulate, and foster an interest, with which they have no constitutional power to interfere.[1] This opinion constitutes the leading doctrine of several states in the Union at the present moment; and is maintained, as vital to the existence of the Union. On the other hand, it is as earnestly and strenuously maintained, that congress does possess the constitutional power to encourage and protect manufactures by appropriate regulations of commerce;

1. See Address of the Philadelphia Free Trade Convention, in September and October 1831.

and that the opposite opinion is destructive of all the purposes of the Union, and would annihilate its value.

§1074. Under such circumstances, it becomes indispensable to review the grounds, upon which the doctrine of each party is maintained, and to sift them to the bottom; since it cannot be disguised, that the controversy still agitates all America, and marks the divisions of party by the strongest lines, both geographical and political, which have ever been seen since the establishment of the national government.

§1075. The reasoning, by which the doctrine is maintained, that the power to regulate commerce cannot be constitutionally applied, as a means, directly to encourage domestic manufactures, has been in part already adverted to in considering the extent of the power to lay taxes. It is proper, however, to present it entire in its present connexion. It is to the following effect.—The constitution is one of limited and enumerated powers; and none of them can be rightfully exercised beyond the scope of the objects, specified in those powers. It is not disputed, that, when the power is given, all the appropriate means to carry it into effect are included. Neither is it disputed, that the laying of duties is, or may be an appropriate means of regulating commerce. But the question is a very different one, whether, under pretence of an exercise of the power to regulate commerce, congress may in fact impose duties for objects wholly distinct from commerce. The question comes to this, whether a power, exclusively for the regulation of commerce, is a power for the regulation of manufactures? The statement of such a question would seem to involve its own answer. Can a power, granted for one purpose, be transferred to another? If it can, where is the limitation in the constitution? Are not commerce and manufactures as distinct, as commerce and agriculture? If they are, how can a power to regulate one arise from a power to regulate the other? It is true, that commerce and manufactures are, or may be, intimately connected with each other. A regulation of one may injuriously or beneficially affect the other. But that is not the point in controversy. It is, whether congress has a right to regulate that, which is not committed to it, under a power, which is committed to it, simply because there is, or may be an intimate connexion between the powers. If this were admitted, the enumeration of the powers of congress would be wholly unnecessary and nugatory. Agriculture, colonies, capital, machinery, the wages of labour, the profits of stock, the rents of land, the punctual performance of contracts, and the diffusion of knowledge would all be within the scope of the power; for all of them bear an intimate relation to commerce. The result would be, that the powers of congress would embrace the widest extent of legislative functions, to the utter demolition of all constitutional boundaries between the state and national governments. When duties are laid, not for purposes of revenue, but of retaliation and restriction, to countervail foreign restrictions, they are strictly within the scope of the power, as a regulation of commerce. But when laid to encourage manufactures, they have nothing to do with it. The power to regulate manufactures is no more confided to congress, than the power to interfere with the systems of education, the poor laws, or the road laws of the states. It is notorious, that, in the convention, an attempt was made to introduce into the constitution a power to encourage manufactures; but it was withheld.[2] Instead of granting the power to congress, permission was given to the states to impose duties, with the consent of that body, to encourage their own manufactures; and thus, in the true spirit of justice, imposing the burthen on those, who were to be benefited. It is true, that congress may, incidentally, when laying duties for revenue, consult the other interests of the country. They may so arrange the details, as indirectly to aid manufactures. And this is the whole extent, to which congress has ever gone until the tariffs, which have given rise to the present controversy. The former precedents of congress are not, even if admitted to be authoritative, applicable to the question now presented.[3]

§ 1076. The reasoning of those, who maintain the doctrine, that congress has authority to apply the power to regulate commerce to the purpose of protecting and encouraging domestic manufactures, is to the following effect. The power to regulate commerce, being in its terms unlimited, includes all means appropriate to the end, and all means, which have been usually exerted under the power. No one can doubt or deny, that a power to regulate trade involves a power to tax it. It is a familiar mode, recognised in the practice of all nations, and was known and admitted by the United States, while they were colonies, and has ever since been acted upon without opposition or question. The American colonies wholly denied the authority of the British parliament to tax them, except as a regulation of commerce; but they admitted this exercise of power, as legitimate and unquestionable. The distinction was with difficulty maintained in practice between laws for the regulation of commerce by way of taxation, and laws, which were made for mere monopoly, or restriction, when they incidentally produced revenue.[4] And it is certain, that the main and admitted object of parliamentary regulations of trade with the colonies was the encouragement of manufactures in Great-Britain. Other nations have, in like manner, for like purposes, exercised the like power. So, that there is no novelty in the use of the power, and no stretch in the range of the power.

§ 1077. Indeed, the advocates of the opposite doctrine admit, that the power may be applied, so as incidentally to give protection to manufactures, when revenue is the principal design; and that it may also be applied to countervail the injurious regulations of foreign powers, when there is no design of revenue. These concessions admit, then, that the regulations of commerce are not wholly for purposes of revenue, or wholly confined to the purposes of commerce, considered *per se*. If this be true, then other objects may enter into commercial regulations; and if so, what restraint is there, as to the nature or extent of the objects, to which they may reach, which does not resolve itself into a question of expediency and policy? It may be admitted, that a power, given for one purpose, cannot be perverted to purposes wholly opposite, or beside its legitimate scope. But what perversion is there in applying a power to the very purposes, to which it has been usually applied? Under such circumstances, does not the grant of the power without restriction concede, that it may be legitimately applied to such purposes? If a different intent had existed, would not that intent be manifested by some corresponding limitation?

2. A proposition was referred to the committee of Details and Revision "to establish public institutions, rewards, and immunities, for the promotion of agriculture, commerce, trade, and manufactures." The committee never reported on it. Journ. of Convention, p. 261.

3. The above arguments and reasoning have been gathered, as far as could be, from documents admitted to be of high authority by those, who maintain the restrictive doctrine. See the Exposition and Protest of the South Carolina legislature, in Dec. 1828, attributed to Mr. Vice President Calhoun; the Address of the Free Trade Convention at Philadelphia, in Oct. 1831, attributed to Mr. Attorney General Berrien; the Oration of the Hon. Mr. Drayton, on the 4th of July, 1831; and the Speech of Mr. Senator Hayne, 9th of Jan. 1832. See also 4 Jefferson's Corresp. 421.

4. See Mr. Madison's Letter to Mr. Cabell, 18th Sept. 1828; Mr. Verplanck's Letter to Col. Drayton, in 1831; Address of the New-York Convention in favour of Domestic Industry, November, 1831, p. 12, 13, 14; 9 Wheat. R. 202; 1 Pitk. Hist. ch. 3, p. 93 to 106.

§ 1078. Now it is well known, that in commercial and manufacturing nations, the power to regulate commerce has embraced practically the encouragement of manufactures. It is believed, that not a single exception can be named. So, in an especial manner, the power has always been understood in Great-Britain, from which we derive our parentage, our laws, our language, and our notions upon commercial subjects. Such was confessedly the notion of the different states in the Union under the confederation, and before the formation of the present constitution. One known object of the policy of the manufacturing states then was, the protection and encouragement of their manufactures by regulations of commerce.[5] And the exercise of this power was a source of constant difficulty and discontent; not because improper of itself; but because it bore injuriously upon the commercial arrangements of other states. The want of uniformity in the regulations of commerce was a source of perpetual strife and dissatisfaction, of inequalities, and rivalries, and retaliations among the states. When the constitution was framed, no one ever imagined, that the power of protection of manufactures was to be taken away from all the states, and yet not delegated to the Union. The very suggestion would of itself have been fatal to the adoption of the constitution. The manufacturing states would never have acceded to it upon any such terms; and they never could, without the power, have safely acceded to it; for it would have sealed their ruin. The same reasoning would apply to the agricultural states; for the regulation of commerce, with a view to encourage domestic agriculture, is just as important, and just as vital to the interests of the nation, and just as much an application of the power, as the protection or encouragement of manufactures. It would have been strange indeed, if the people of the United States had been solicitous solely to advance and encourage commerce, with a total disregard of the interests of agriculture and manufactures, which had, at the time of the adoption of the constitution, an unequivocal preponderance throughout the Union. It is manifest from contemporaneous documents, that one object of the constitution was, to encourage manufactures and agriculture by this very use of the power.[6]

§ 1079. The terms, then, of the constitution are sufficiently large to embrace the power; the practice of other nations, and especially of Great-Britain and of the American states, has been to use it in this manner; and this exercise of it was one of the very grounds, upon which the establishment of the constitution was urged and vindicated. The argument, then, in its favour would seem to be absolutely irresistible under this aspect. But there are other very weighty considerations, which enforce it.

§ 1080. In the first place, if congress does not possess the power to encourage domestic manufactures by regulations of commerce, the power is annihilated for the whole nation. The states are deprived of it. They have made a voluntary surrender of it; and yet it exists not in the national government. It is then a mere nonentity. Such a policy, voluntarily adopted by a free people, in subversion of some of their dearest rights and interests, would be most extraordinary in itself, without any assignable motive or reason for so great a sacrifice, and utterly without example in the history of the world. No man can doubt, that domestic agriculture and manufactures may be most essentially promoted and protected by regulations of commerce. No man can doubt, that it is the most usual, and generally the most efficient means of producing those results. No man can question, that in these great objects the different states of America have as deep a stake, and as vital interests, as any other nation. Why, then, should the power be surrendered and annihilated? It would produce the most serious mischiefs at home; and would secure the most complete triumph over us by foreign nations. It would introduce and perpetuate national debility, if not national ruin. A foreign nation might, as a conqueror, impose upon us this restraint, as a badge of dependence, and a sacrifice of sovereignty, to subserve its own interests; but that we should impose it upon ourselves, is inconceivable. The achievement of our independence was almost worthless, if such a system was to be pursued. It would be in effect a perpetuation of that very system of monopoly, of encouragement of foreign manufactures, and depression of domestic industry, which was so much complained of during our colonial dependence; and which kept all America in a state of poverty, and slavish devotion to British interests. Under such circumstances, the constitution would be established, not for the purposes avowed in the preamble, but for the exclusive benefit and advancement of foreign nations, to aid their manufactures, and sustain their agriculture. Suppose cotton, rice, tobacco, wheat, corn, sugar, and other

5. 1 American Museum, 16.

6. 1 Elliot's Debates, 74, 75, 76, 77, 115; 3 Elliot's Debates, 31, 32, 33; 2 Amer. Museum, 371, 372, 373; 3 Amer. Museum, 62, 554, 556, 557; The Federalist, No. 12, 41; 1 Tuck. Black. Comm. App. 237, 238; 1 American Museum, 16, 282, 289, 429, 432; Id. 434, 436; Hamilton's Report on Manufactures, in 1791; 4 Elliot's Debates, App. 351 to 354.

raw materials could be, or should hereafter be, abundantly produced in foreign countries, under the fostering hands of their governments, by bounties and commercial regulations, so as to become cheaper with such aids than our own; are all our markets to be opened to such products without any restraint, simply because we may not want revenue, to the ruin of our products and industry? Is America ready to give every thing to Europe, without any equivalent; and take in return whatever Europe may choose to give, upon its own terms? The most servile provincial dependence could not do more evils. Of what consequence would it be, that the national government could not tax our exports, if foreign governments might tax them to an unlimited extent, so as to favour their own, and thus to supply us with the same articles by the overwhelming depression of our own by foreign taxation? When it is recollected, with what extreme discontent and reluctant obedience the British colonial restrictions were enforced in the manufacturing and navigating states, while they were colonies, it is incredible, that they should be willing to adopt a government, which should, or might entail upon them equal evils in perpetuity. Commerce itself would ultimately be as great a sufferer by such a system, as the other domestic interests. It would languish, if it did not perish. Let any man ask himself, if New-England, or the Middle states would ever have consented to ratify a constitution, which would afford no protection to their manufactures or home industry. If the constitution was ratified under the belief, sedulously propagated on all sides, that such protection was afforded, would it not now be a fraud upon the whole people to give a different construction to its powers?

§ 1081. It is idle to say, that with the consent of congress, the states may lay duties on imports or exports, to favour their own domestic manufactures. In the first place, if congress could constitutionally give such consent for such a purpose, which has been doubted;[7] they would have a right to refuse such consent, and would certainly refuse it, if the result would be what the advocates of free trade contend for. In the next place, it would be utterly impracticable with such consent to protect their manufactures by any such local regulations. To be of any value they must be general, and uniform through the nation. This is not a matter of theory. Our whole experience under the confederation established beyond all controversy the utter lo-

cal futility, and even the general mischiefs of independent state legislation upon such a subject. It furnished one of the strongest grounds for the establishment of the constitution.[8]

§ 1082. In the next place, if revenue be the sole legitimate object of an impost, and the encouragement of domestic manufactures be not within the scope of the power of regulating trade, it would follow, (as has been already hinted,) that no monopolizing or unequal regulations of foreign nations could be counteracted. Under such circumstances, neither the staple articles of subsistence, nor the essential implements for the public safety, could be adequately ensured or protected at home by our regulations of commerce. The duty might be wholly unnecessary for revenue; and incidentally, it might even check revenue. But, if congress may, in arrangements for revenue, incidentally and designedly protect domestic manufactures, what ground is there to suggest, that they may not incorporate this design through the whole system of duties, and select and arrange them accordingly? There is no constitutional measure, by which to graduate, how much shall be assessed for revenue, and how much for encouragement of home industry. And no system ever yet adopted has attempted, and in all probability none hereafter adopted will attempt, wholly to sever the one object from the other. The constitutional objection in this view is purely speculative, regarding only future possibilities.

§ 1083. But if it be conceded, (as it is,) that the power to regulate commerce includes the power of laying duties to countervail the regulations and restrictions of foreign nations, then, what limits are to be assigned to this use of the power?[9] If their commercial regulations, either designedly or incidentally, do promote their own agriculture and manufactures, and injuriously affect ours, why may not congress apply a remedy coextensive with the evil? If congress have, as cannot be denied, the choice of the means, they may countervail the regulations, not only by the exercise of the *lex talionis* in the same way, but in any other way conducive to the same end. If Great Britain by commercial regulations restricts the introduction of our staple products and manufactures into her own territories, and levies prohibitory duties, why may not congress apply the same rule to her staple products and manufactures, and secure

7. See Mr. Madison's Letter to Mr. Cabell, 18th Sept. 1828; 4 Elliot's Debates, App. 345.

8. Mr. Madison's Letter to Mr. Cabell, 18th Sept. 1828; 4 Elliot's Debates, App. 345.
9. See the Federalist, No. 11, 12.

the same market to ourselves? The truth is, that as soon as the right to retaliate foreign restrictions or foreign policy by commercial regulations is admitted, the question, in what manner, and to what extent, it shall be applied, is a matter of legislative discretion, and not of constitutional authority. Whenever commercial restrictions and regulations shall cease all over the world, so far as they favour the nation adopting them, it will be time enough to consider, what America ought to do in her own regulations of commerce, which are designed to protect her own industry and counteract such favoritism. It will then become a question, not of power, but of policy. Such a state of things has never yet existed. In fact the concession, that the power to regulate commerce may embrace other objects, than revenue, or even than commerce itself, is irreconcilable with the foundation of the argument on the other side.

§ 1084. Besides; the power is to regulate commerce. And in what manner regulate it? Why does the power involve the right to lay duties? Simply, because it is a common means of executing the power. If so, why does not the same right exist as to all other means equally common and appropriate? Why does the power involve a right, not only to lay duties, but to lay duties for *revenue,* and not merely for the regulation and restriction of commerce, considered *per se?* No other answer can be given, but that revenue is an incident to such an exercise of the power. It flows from, and does not create the power. It may constitute the motive for the exercise of the power, just as any other cause may; as for instance, the prohibition of foreign trade, or the retaliation of foreign monopoly; but it does not constitute the power.

§ 1085. Now, the motive of the grant of the power is not even alluded to in the constitution. It is not even stated, that congress shall have power to promote and encourage domestic navigation and trade. A power to regulate commerce is not necessarily a power to advance its interests. It may in given cases suspend its operations and restrict its advancement and scope. Yet no man ever yet doubted the right of congress to lay duties to promote and encourage domestic navigation, whether in the form of tonnage duties, or other preferences and privileges, either in the foreign trade, or coasting trade, or fisheries.[10] It is as certain, as any thing human can be, that the sole object of congress, in securing the vast privileges to American built ships, by

such preferences, and privileges, and tonnage duties, was, to encourage the domestic manufacture of ships, and all the dependent branches of business.[11] It speaks out in the language of all their laws, and has been as constantly avowed, and acted on, as any single legislative policy ever has been. No one ever dreamed, that revenue constituted the slightest ingredient in these laws. They were purely for the encouragement of home manufactures, and home artisans, and home pursuits. Upon what grounds can congress constitutionally apply the power to regulate commerce to one great class of domestic manufactures, which does not involve the right to encourage all? If it be said, that navigation is a part of commerce, that is true. But a power to regulate navigation no more includes a power to encourage the manufacture of ships by tonnage duties, than any other manufacture. Why not extend it to the encouragement of the growth and manufacture of cotton and hemp for sails and rigging; of timber, boards, and masts; of tar, pitch, and turpentine; of iron and wool; of sheetings and shirtings; of artisans and mechanics, however remotely connected with it? There are many products of agriculture and manufactures, which are connected with the prosperity of commerce as intimately, as domestic ship building. If the one may be encouraged, as a primary motive in regulations of commerce, why may not the others? The truth is, that the encouragement of domestic ship building is within the scope of the power to regulate commerce, simply, because it is a known and ordinary means of exercising the power. It is one of many, and may be used like all others according to legislative discretion. The motive to the exercise of a power can never form a constitutional objection to the exercise of the power.

§ 1086. Here, then, is a case of laying duties, an ordinary means used in executing the power to regulate commerce; how can it be deemed unconstitutional? If it be said, that the motive is not to collect revenue, what has that to do with the power? When an act is constitutional, as an exercise of a power, can it be unconstitutional from the motives, with which it is passed? If it can, then the constitutionality of an act must depend, not upon the power, but upon the motives of the legislature. It will follow, as a consequence, that the same act passed by one legislature will be constitutional, and by another unconstitutional. Nay, it might be unconstitutional, as well from its omissions as its enactments, since if its omissions were to favour

10. See Mr. Jefferson's Report on the Fisheries, 1st Feb. 1791, 10 Amer. Mus. App. 1, &c., 8, &c.

11. See Mr. Williamson's Speech in Congress, 8 Amer. Mus. 140.

manufactures, the motive would contaminate the whole law. Such a doctrine would be novel and absurd. It would confuse and destroy all the tests of constitutional rights and authorities. Congress could never pass any law without an inquisition into the motives of every member; and even then, they might be re-examinable. Besides; what possible means can there be of making such investigations? The motives of many of the members may be, nay must be utterly unknown, and incapable of ascertainment by any judicial or other inquiry: they may be mixed up in various manners and degrees; they may be opposite to, or wholly independent of each other. The constitution would thus depend upon processes utterly vague, and incomprehensible; and the written intent of the legislature upon its words and acts, the *lex scripta,* would be contradicted or obliterated by conjecture, and parol declarations, and fleeting reveries, and heated imaginations. No government on earth could rest for a moment on such a foundation. It would be a constitution of sand heaped up and dissolved by the flux and reflux of every tide of opinion. Every act of the legislature must therefore be judged of from its object and intent, as they are embodied in its provisions; and if the latter are within the scope of admitted powers, the act must be constitutional, whether the motive for it were wise, or just, or otherwise. The manner of applying a power may be an abuse of it; but this does not prove, that it is unconstitutional.

§ 1087. Passing by these considerations, let the practice of the government and the doctrines maintained by those, who have administered it, be deliberately examined; and they will be found to be in entire consistency with this reasoning. The very first congress, that ever sat under the constitution, composed in a considerable degree of those, who had framed, or assisted in the discussion of its provisions in the state conventions, deliberately adopted this view of the power. And what is most remarkable, upon a subject of deep interest and excitement, which at the time occasioned long and vehement debates, not a single syllable of doubt was breathed from any quarter against the constitutionality of protecting agriculture and manufactures by laying duties, although the intention to protect and encourage them was constantly avowed.[12] Nay, it was con-

tended to be a paramount duty, upon the faithful fulfilment of which the constitution had been adopted, and the omission of which would be a political fraud, without a whisper of dissent from any side.[13] It was demanded by the people from various parts of the Union; and was resisted by none.[14] Yet, state jealousy was never more alive than at this period, and state interests never more actively mingled in the debates of congress. The two great parties, which afterwards so much divided the country upon the question of a liberal and strict construction of the constitution, were then distinctly formed, and proclaimed their opinions with firmness and freedom. If, therefore, there had been a point of doubt, on which to hang an argument, it cannot be questioned, but that it would have been brought into the array of opposition. Such a silence, under such circumstances, is most persuasive and convincing.

§ 1088. The very preamble of this act[15] (the second passed by congress) is, "Whereas it is necessary for the support of the government, for the discharge of the debts of the United States, and *the encouragement and protection of manufactures,* that duties be laid on goods, wares, and merchandises imported, Be it enacted," &c.[16] Yet, not a solitary voice was raised against it. The right, and the duty, to pass such laws was, indeed, taken so much for granted, that in some of the most elaborate expositions of the government upon the subject of manufactures, it was scarcely alluded to.[17] The Federalist itself, dealing with every shadow of objection against the constitution, never once alludes to such a one; but incidentally commends this power; as leading to beneficial results on all domestic interests.[18] Every successive congress since that time has constantly acted upon the system through all the changes of party and local interests. Every successive executive has sanctioned laws on the subject; and most of them have actively recommended the encouragement of manufactures to congress.[19] Until a very recent period, no person in the

13. See 1 Lloyd's Deb. 24, 160, 161, 243, 244; 4 Elliot's Deb. App. 351, 352.

14. See Grimké's Speech, in Dec. 1828, p. 58, 59, 63.

15. Act of 4th July, 1789.

16. It is not a little remarkable, that the culture of cotton was just then beginning in South Carolina; and her statesmen then thought a protecting duty to aid agriculture was in all respects proper, and constitutional. 1 Lloyd's Deb. 79; Id. 210, 211, 212, 244.

17. Hamilton's Report on Manufacturers in 1791.

18. The Federalist, No. 10, 35, 41.

19. See 4 Elliot's Debates, App. 353, 354.

12. See 1 Lloyd's Deb. 17, 19, 22, 23, 24, 26, 27, 28, 31, 34, 39, 43, 46, 47, 50, 51, 52, 55, 64 to 69, 71, 72, 74 to 83, 94, 95, 97, 109, 116, 145, 160, 161, 211, 212, 243, 244, 254; Id. 144, 183, 194, 206, 207. See also 5 Marshall's Wash. ch. 3, p. 189, 190.

public councils seriously relied upon any constitutional difficulty. And even now, when the subject has been agitated, and discussed with great ability and zeal throughout the Union, not more than five states have expressed an opinion against the constitutional right, while it has received an unequivocal sanction in the others with an almost unexampled degree of unanimity. And this too, when in most other respects these states have been in strong opposition to each other upon the general system of politics pursued by the government.

§ 1089. If ever, therefore, contemporaneous exposition, and the uniform and progressive operations of the government itself, in all its departments, can be of any weight to settle the construction of the constitution, there never has been, and there never can be more decided evidence in favour of the power, than is furnished by the history of our national laws for the encouragement of domestic agriculture and manufactures. To resign an exposition so sanctioned, would be to deliver over the country to interminable doubts; and to make the constitution not a written system of government, but a false and delusive text, upon which every successive age of speculatists and statesmen might build any system, suited to their own views and opinions. But if it be added to this, that the constitution gives the power in the most unlimited terms, and neither assigns motives, nor objects for its exercise; but leaves these wholly to the discretion of the legislature, acting for the common good, and the general interests; the argument in its favour becomes as absolutely irresistible, as any demonstration of a moral or political nature ever can be. Without such a power, the government would be absolutely worthless, and made merely subservient to the policy of foreign nations, incapable of self-protection or self-support;[20] with it, the country will have a right to assert its equality, and dignity, and sovereignty among the other nations of the earth.[21]

§ 1089. In regard to the rejection of the proposition in the convention "to establish *institutions, rewards,* and *immunities* for the promotion of agriculture, commerce, trades, and manufactures,"[22] it is manifest, that it has no bearing on the question. It was a power much more broad in its extent and objects, than the power to encourage manufactures by the exercise of another granted power. It might be contended with quite as much plausibility, that the rejection was an implied rejection of the right to encourage commerce, for that was equally within the scope of the proposition. In truth, it involved a direct power to establish *institutions, rewards,* and *immunities* for all the great interests of society, and was, on that account, deemed too broad and sweeping. It would establish a general, and not a limited power of government.

§ 1090. Such is a summary (necessarily imperfect) of the reasoning on each side of this contested doctrine. The reader will draw his own conclusions; and these Commentaries have no further aim, than to put him in possession of the materials for a proper exercise of his judgment.

§ 1091. When the subject of the regulation of commerce was before the convention, the first draft of the constitution contained an article, that "no navigation act shall be passed, without the assent of two thirds of the members present in each house."[23] This article was afterwards recommended in a report of a committee to be stricken out. In the second revised draft it was left out; and a motion, to insert such a restriction to have effect until the year 1808, was negatived by the vote of seven states against three.[24] Another proposition, that no act, regulating the commerce of the United States with foreign powers, should be passed without the assent of two thirds of the members of each house, was rejected by the vote of seven states against four.[25] The rejection was, probably, occasioned by two leading reasons. First, the general impropriety of allowing the minority in a government to control, and in effect to govern all the legislative powers of the majority. Secondly, the especial inconvenience of such a power in regard to regulations of commerce, where the proper remedy for

20. 4 Jefferson's Correspondence, 280, 281; 1 Pitkin's Hist. ch. 3, p. 93 to 106.

21. The foregoing summary has been principally abstracted from the Letter of Mr. Madison to Mr. Cabell, 18th Sept. 1828; 4 Elliot's Deb. 345; Mr. Grimké's Speech in Dec. 1828, in the South Carolina senate; Mr. Huger's Speech in the South Carolina legislature, in Dec. 1830; Address of the New York Convention of the Friends of Domestic Industry, in Oct. 1831; Mr. Verplanck's Letter to Col. Drayton, in 1831; Mr. Clay's Speech in the senate, in Feb. 1832; Mr. Edward Everett's Address to the American Institute, in Oct. 1831; Mr. Hamilton's Report on Manufac-

tures, in 1791; Mr. Jefferson's Report on the Fisheries, in 1791. See, also, 4 Jefferson's Correspondence, 280, 281.

22. Journal of Convention, p. 261.

23. Journal of Convention, p. 222.

24. Journal of Convention, 222, 285, 286, 293, 358, 387. See, also, 3 American Museum, 62, 419, 420; 2 American Museum, 553; 2 Pitkin's Hist. 261.

25. Journal of Convention, 306.

grievances of the worst sort might be withheld from the navigating and commercial states by a very small minority of the other states.[26] A similar proposition was made, after the adoption of the constitution, by some of the states; but it was never acted upon.[27]

§ 1092. The power of congress also extends to regulate commerce with the Indian tribes. This power was not contained in the first draft of the constitution. It was afterwards referred to the committee on the constitution (among other propositions) to consider the propriety of giving to congress the power "to regulate affairs with the Indians, as well within, as without the limits of the United States." And, in the revised draft, the committee reported the clause, "and with the Indian Tribes," as it now stands.[28]

§ 1093. Under the confederation, the continental congress were invested with the sole and exclusive right and power "of regulating the trade and managing all affairs with the Indians, not *members* of any of the states, provided, that the legislative right of any state within its own limits be not infringed or violated."[29]

Admission of New States—Government of Territories

§ 216. The first clause of the fourth article declares, "New States may be admitted by the Congress into this Union. But no new State shall be formed or erected within the jurisdiction of any other State; nor any State be formed by the junction of two or more States, or parts of States, without the consent of the Legislatures of the States concerned, as well as of the Congress." It was early foreseen, from the extent of the territory of some States, that a division thereof into several States might become important and convenient to the inhabitants thereof, as well as add to the security of the Union. And it was also obvious, that new States would spring up in the then vacant western territory, which had been ceded to the Union, and that such new States could not long be retained in a state of dependence upon the National Government. It was indispensable, therefore, to make some suitable provisions for both these emergencies. On the one hand, the integrity of any of the States ought not to be severed without their own

consent; for their sovereignty would, otherwise, be at the mere will of Congress. On the other hand, it was equally clear, that no State ought to be admitted into the Union without the consent of Congress; for, otherwise, the balance, equality, and harmony of the existing States might be destroyed. Both of these objects are, therefore, united in the present clause. To admit a new State into the Union, the consent of Congress is necessary; to form a new State within the boundaries of an old one, the consent of the latter is also necessary. Under this clause, besides Vermont, three new States formed within the boundaries of the old States, viz. Kentucky, Tennessee, and Maine; and nine others, viz. Ohio, Indiana, Illinois, Mississippi, Alabama, Louisiana, Missouri, Arkansas, and Michigan, formed within the territories ceded to the United States, have been already admitted into the Union. Thus far, indeed, the power has been most propitious to the general welfare of the Union, and has realized the patriotic anticipation, that the parents would exult in the glory and prosperity of their children.

§ 217. The second clause of the same section is, "The Congress shall have power to dispose of, and make all needful rules and regulations respecting the territory, or other property, belonging to the United States. And nothing in this Constitution shall be so construed, as to prejudice any claims of the United States, or of any particular State." As the General Government possesses the right to acquire territory by cession and conquest, it would seem to follow, as a natural incident, that it should possess the power to govern and protect, what it had acquired. At the time of the adoption of the Constitution, it had acquired the vast region included in the Northwestern Territory; and its acquisitions have since been greatly enlarged by the purchase of Louisiana and Florida. The two latter Territories, (Louisiana and Florida,) subject to the treaty stipulations, under which they were acquired, are of course under the general regulation of Congress, so far as the power has not been or may not be parted with by erecting them into States. The Northwestern Territory has been peopled under the admirable Ordinance of the Continental Congress of the 13th of July, 1787, which we owe to the wise forecast and political wisdom of a man, whom New England can never fail to reverence.[1]

§ 218. The main provisions of this Ordinance, which

26. See The Federalist, No. 22; 1 Tucker's Black. Comm. App. 253, 375.

27. 1 Tucker's Black. Comm. App. 253, 375.

28. Journal of Convention, 220, 260, 356.

29. Art. 9.

1. The late Hon. Nathan Dane, of Beverly, Massachusetts.

constitute the basis of the Constitutions and Governments of all the States and Territories organized within the Northwestern Territory, deserve here to be stated, as the ordinance is equally remarkable for the beauty and exactness of its text, and for its masterly display of the fundamental principles of civil and religious and political liberty. It begins, by providing a scheme for the descent and distribution of estates equally among all the children, and their representatives, or other relatives of the deceased in equal degree, making no distinction between the whole and the half blood; and for the mode of disposing of real estate by will, and by conveyances. It then proceeds to provide for the organization of the territorial governments, according to their progress in population, confiding the whole power to a Governor and Judges, in the first instance, subject to the control of Congress. As soon as the Territory contains five thousand inhabitants, it provides for the establishment of a general Legislature, to consist of three branches, a Governor, a Legislative Council, and a House of Representatives; with a power to the Legislature to appoint a delegate to Congress. It then proceeds to state certain fundamental articles of compact between the original States, and the people and States in the Territory, which are to remain unalterable, unless by common consent. The first provides for the freedom of religious opinion and worship. The second provides for the right to the writ of *habeas corpus;* for the trial by jury; for a proportionate representation in the Legislature; for judicial proceedings according to the course of the common law; for capital offences being bailable; for fines being moderate, and punishments not being cruel or unusual; for no man's being deprived of his liberty or property, but by the judgement of his peers, or the law of the land; for full compensation for property taken, or services demanded, for the public exigencies; "and, for the just preservation of rights and property, that no law ought ever to be made, or have force in the said Territory, that shall, in any manner whatever, *interfere with, or affect private contracts or engagements, bona fide,* and without fraud, previously formed." The third provides for the encouragement of religion, and education, and schools, and for good faith and due respect for the rights and property of the Indians. The fourth provides, that the Territory, and States formed therein, shall for ever remain a part of the Confederacy, subject to the constitutional authority of Congress; that the inhabitants shall be liable to be taxed proportionately for the public ex-

penses; that the Legislatures in the Territory shall never interfere with the primary disposal of the soil by Congress, nor with their regulations for securing the title to the soil to purchasers; that no tax shall be imposed on lands, the property of the United States; and non-resident proprietors shall not be taxed more than residents; that the navigable waters leading into the Mississippi and St. Lawrence, and the carrying places between the same, shall be common highways, and for ever free. The fifth provides, that there shall be formed in the Territory not less than three, nor more than five States, with certain boundaries; and whenever any of the said States shall contain sixty thousand free inhabitants, such State shall (and may not before) be admitted, by its delegates, into Congress, on an equal footing with the original States in all respects whatever, and shall be at liberty to form a permanent Constitution and State government, provided it shall be republican, and in conformity to these articles of compact. The sixth and last provides, that there shall be neither slavery nor involuntary servitude in the said Territory, otherwise than in the punishment of crimes; but fugitives from other States, owing service therein, may be reclaimed. Such is a brief outline of this most important ordinance, the effects of which upon the destinies of the country have already been abundantly demonstrated in the Territory, by an almost unexampled prosperity and rapidity of population, by the formation of republican governments, and by an enlightened system of jurisprudence. Already five States, composing a part of that Territory, have been admitted into the Union; and others are fast advancing towards the same grade of political dignity.

§ 219. The proviso, reserving the claims of the Union, as well as of the several States, was adopted from abundant caution, to quiet public jealousies upon the subject of the contested titles, which were then asserted by some of the States to some parts of the Western Territory. Happily, these sources of alarm and irritation have long since been dried up.

§ 220. And here is closed our Review of the express powers conferred upon Congress. There are other incidental and implied powers, resulting from other provisions of the Constitution, which will naturally present themselves to the mind in our future examination of those provisions. At present, it may suffice to say, that, with reference to due energy in the General Government, to due protection of the national interests, and to due security to the Union, fewer powers could scarcely have been granted, without jeoparding the existence of the whole system. Without the power to lay and collect taxes, to provide for the common defence, and promote the general welfare, the whole system would have been vain and illusory. Without the power to borrow money upon sudden or unexpected emergencies, the National Government might have been embarrassed, and sometimes have been incapable of performing its own proper functions and duties. Without the power to declare war and raise armies, and provide a navy, the whole country would have been placed at the mercy of foreign nations, or of invading foes, who should trample upon our rights and liberties. Without the power exclusively to regulate commerce, the intercourse between the States would have been liable to constant jealousies, rivalries, and dissensions; and the intercourse with foreign nations would have been liable to mischievous interruptions, from secret hostilities, or open retaliatory restrictions. The other powers are principally auxiliary to these; and are dictated by an enlightened policy, a devotion to justice, and a regard to the permanence of the Union. The wish of every patriot must be, that the system thus formed may be perpetual, and that the powers thus conferred may be constantly used for the purposes, for which they were originally given, for the promotion of the true interests of all the States, and not for the gratification of party spirit, or the aggrandizement of rulers at the expense of the people.

Prohibitions on the United States

§ 1801. The next clause is as follows: "A person charged in any state with treason, felony, or other crime, who shall flee from justice, and be found in another state, shall, on demand of the executive authority of the state, from which he fled, be delivered up, to be removed to the state having jurisdiction of the crime." A provision, substantially the same, existed under the confederation.[1]

§ 1802. It has been often made a question, how far any nation is, by the law of nations, and independent of any treaty stipulations, bound to surrender upon demand fugitives from justice, who, having committed crimes in another country, have fled thither for shelter. Mr. Chancellor Kent considers it clear upon principle, as well as authority, that every state is bound to deny an asylum to criminals,

and, upon application and due examination of the case, to surrender the fugitive to the foreign state, where the crime has been committed.[2] Other distinguished judges and jurists have entertained a different opinion.[3] It is not uncommon for treaties to contain mutual stipulations for the surrender of criminals; and the United States have sometimes been a party to such an arrangement.[4]

§ 1803. But, however the point may be, as to foreign nations, it cannot be questioned, that it is of vital importance to the public administration of criminal justice, and the security of the respective states, that criminals, who have committed crimes therein, should not find an asylum in other states; but should be surrendered up for trial and punishment. It is a power most salutary in its general operation, by discouraging crimes, and cutting off the chances of escape from punishment. It will promote harmony and good feelings among the states; and it will increase the general sense of the blessings of the national government. It will, moreover, give strength to a great moral duty, which neighbouring states especially owe to each other, by elevating the policy of the mutual suppression of crimes into a legal obligation. Hitherto it has proved as useful in practice, as it is unexceptionable in its character.[5]

§ 1804. The next clause is, "No person held to service or labor in one state under the laws thereof, escaping into another, shall in consequence of any law or regulation therein be discharged from such service or labour; but shall be delivered up on the claim of the party, to whom such service or labour may be due."[6]

§ 1805. This clause was introduced into the constitution solely for the benefit of the slave-holding states, to enable them to reclaim their fugitive slaves, who should have escaped into other states, where slavery was not tolerated. The want of such a provision under the confederation was felt, as a grievous inconvenience, by the slave-holding

1. Confederation, Art. 4.

2. 1 Kent's Comm. Lect. 2, p. 36, (2 edit. p. 36, 37); Matter of Washburn, 4 John. Ch. R. 106; *Rex* v. *Ball,* 1 Amer. Jurist, 297; Vattel, B. 2, § 76, 77; Rutherforth, Inst. B. 2, ch. 9, § 12.

3. *Com'th.* v. *Deacon,* 10 Sergeant & Rawle, R. 125; 1 American Jurist. 297.

4. See Treaty with Great Britain of 1794, art. 27; *United States* v. *Nash,* Bees, Adm. R. 266.

5. See 1 Kent's Comm. Lect. 2, p. 36, (2 edit. p. 36.) See Journ. of Convention, 222, 304.

6. This clause in its substance was unanimously adopted by the Convention. Journ. of Convention, 307.

states,[7] since in many states no aid whatsoever would be allowed to the owners; and sometimes indeed they met with open resistance. In fact, it cannot escape the attention of every intelligent reader, that many sacrifices of opinion and feeling are to be found made by the Eastern and Middle states to the peculiar interests of the south. This forms no just subject of complaint; but it should for ever repress the delusive and mischievous notion, that the south has not at all times had its full share of benefits from the Union.

§ 1806. It is obvious, that these provisions for the arrest and removal of fugitives of both classes contemplate summary ministerial proceedings, and not the ordinary course of judicial investigations, to ascertain, whether the complaint be well founded, or the claim of ownership be established beyond all legal controversy. In cases of suspected crimes the guilt or innocence of the party is to be made out at his trial; and not upon the preliminary inquiry, whether he shall be delivered up. All, that would seem in such cases to be necessary, is, that there should be *primâ facie* evidence before the executive authority to satisfy its judgment, that there is probable cause to believe the party guilty, such as upon an ordinary warrant would justify his commitment for trial.[8] And in the cases of fugitive slaves there would seem to be the same necessity of requiring only *primâ facie* proofs of ownership, without putting the party to a formal assertion of his rights by a suit at the common law. Congress appear to have acted upon this opinion; and, accordingly, in the statute upon this subject have authorized summary proceedings before a magistrate, upon which he may grant a warrant for a removal.[9]

---

7. 1 Tuck, Black. Comm. App. 366. See also Serg. on Const. ch. 31 p. 385, (ch. 33, p. 394 to 398, 2d edit.) *Glen* v. *Hodges,* 9 John. R. 67; *Commonwealth* v. *Halloway,* 2 Serg. & Rawle R. 306.

8. See Serg. on Const. ch. 31 p. 385, (2d edit. ch. 33, p. 394.)

9. Act of 12 Feb. 1793, ch. 51, (ch. 7); Serg. on Const. ch. 31, p. 387, (2d edit. ch. 33, p. 397, 398); *Glen* v. *Hodges,* 9 John. R. 62; *Wright* v. *Deacon,* 5 Serg. & R. 62; *Commonwealth* v. *Griffin,* 2 Pick. R. 11.

Address to the Young Men's Lyceum of Springfield, Illinois

ABRAHAM LINCOLN

January 27, 1838

Address to the Wisconsin State Agricultural Society, Milwaukee, Wisconsin

ABRAHAM LINCOLN

September 30, 1859

Lincoln began his political career as an Illinois Whig—as a member of a political party devoted to high tariffs and internal improvements. Born and raised on the frontier, his life was in large measure spent attempting to tame it—to spread law (his chosen profession) and commerce throughout the United States.

Lincoln's address to the Young Men's Lyceum, titled "The Perpetuation of Our Political Institutions," aims to quell mob violence and lynching through the spread of a "political religion" devoted to the Constitution, its authors, and the revolution that spawned it. His "Address to the Wisconsin State Agricultural Society" paints a picture of economic progress and individual betterment in which all who are willing to work might participate and profit from labor and commerce.

Address to the Young Men's Lyceum of Springfield, Illinois

The Perpetuation of Our Political Institutions

As a subject for the remarks of the evening, *the perpetuation of our political institutions,* is selected.

In the great journal of things happening under the sun, we, the American People, find our account running, under date of the nineteenth century of the Christian era. We find ourselves in the peaceful possession, of the fairest portion of the earth, as regards extent of territory, fertility of soil, and salubrity of climate. We find ourselves under the government of a system of political institutions, conduc-

ing more essentially to the ends of civil and religious liberty, than any of which the history of former times tells us. We, when mounting the stage of existence, found ourselves the legal inheritors of these fundamental blessings. We toiled not in the acquirement or establishment of them—they are a legacy bequeathed us, by a *once* hardy, brave, and patriotic, but *now* lamented and departed race of ancestors. Their's was the task (and nobly they performed it) to possess themselves, and through themselves, us, of this goodly land; and to uprear upon its hills and its valleys, a political edifice of liberty and equal rights; 'tis ours only, to transmit these, the former, unprofaned by the foot of an invader; the latter, undecayed by the lapse of time, and untorn by usurpation—to the latest generation that fate shall permit the world to know. This task of gratitude to our fathers, justice to ourselves, duty to posterity, and love for our species in general, all imperatively require us faithfully to perform.

How, then, shall we perform it? At what point shall we expect the approach of danger? By what means shall we fortify against it? Shall we expect some transatlantic military giant, to step the Ocean, and crush us at a blow? Never! All the armies of Europe, Asia and Africa combined, with all the treasure of the earth (our own excepted) in their military chest; with a Buonaparte for a commander, could not by force, take a drink from the Ohio, or make a track on the Blue Ridge, in a trial of a thousand years.

At what point then is the approach of danger to be expected? I answer, if it ever reach us, it must spring up amongst us. It cannot come from abroad. If destruction be our lot, we must ourselves be its author and finisher. As a nation of freemen, we must live through all time, or die by suicide.

I hope I am over wary; but if I am not, there is, even now, something of ill-omen amongst us. I mean the increasing disregard for law which pervades the country; the growing disposition to substitute the wild and furious passions, in lieu of the sober judgement of Courts; and the worse than savage mobs, for the executive ministers of justice. This disposition is awfully fearful in any community; and that it now exists in ours, though grating to our feelings to admit, it would be a violation of truth, and an insult to our intelligence, to deny. Accounts of outrages committed by mobs, form the every-day news of the times. They have pervaded the country, from New England to Louisiana;—they are neither peculiar to the eternal snows of the former, nor the burning suns of the latter;—they are not the creature of climate—neither are they confined to the slaveholding, or the non-slaveholding States. Alike, they spring up among the pleasure hunting masters of Southern slaves, and the order loving citizens of the land of steady habits. Whatever, then, their cause may be, it is common to the whole country.

It would be tedious, as well as useless, to recount the horrors of all of them. Those happening in the State of Mississippi, and at St. Louis, are, perhaps, the most dangerous in example, and revolting to humanity. In the Mississippi case, they first commenced by hanging the regular gamblers: a set of men, certainly not following for a livelihood, a very useful, or very honest occupation; but one which, so far from being forbidden by the laws, was actually licensed by an act of the Legislature, passed but a single year before. Next, negroes, suspected of conspiring to raise an insurrection, were caught up and hanged in all parts of the State: then, white men, supposed to be leagued with the negroes; and finally, strangers, from neighboring States, going thither on business, were, in many instances, subjected to the same fate. Thus went on this process of hanging, from gamblers to negroes, from negroes to white citizens, and from these to strangers; till, dead men were seen literally dangling from the boughs of trees upon every road side; and in numbers almost sufficient, to rival the native Spanish moss of the country, as a drapery of the forest.

Turn, then, to that horror-striking scene at St. Louis.

A single victim was only sacrificed there. His story is very short; and is, perhaps, the most highly tragic, of any thing of its length, that has ever been witnessed in real life. A mulatto man, by the name of McIntosh, was seized in the street, dragged to the suburbs of the city, chained to a tree, and actually burned to death; and all within a single hour from the time he had been a freeman, attending to his own business, and at peace with the world.

Such are the effects of mob law; and such are the scenes, becoming more and more frequent in this land so lately famed for love of law and order; and the stories of which, have even now grown too familiar, to attract any thing more, than an idle remark.

But you are, perhaps, ready to ask, "What has this to do with the perpetuation of our political institutions?" I answer, it has much to do with it. Its direct consequences are, comparatively speaking, but a small evil; and much of its danger consists, in the proneness of our minds, to regard its direct, as its only consequences. Abstractly considered, the hanging of the gamblers at Vicksburg, was of but little consequence. They constitute a portion of population, that is worse than useless in any community; and their death, if no pernicious example be set by it, is never matter of reasonable regret with any one. If they were annually swept, from the stage of existence, by the plague or small pox, honest men would, perhaps, be much profited, by the operation. Similar too, is the correct reasoning, in regard to the burning of the negro at St. Louis. He had forfeited his life, by the perpetration of an outrageous murder, upon one of the most worthy and respectable citizens of the city; and had he not died as he did, he must have died by the sentence of the law, in a very short time afterwards. As to him alone, it was as well the way it was, as it could otherwise have been. But the example in either case, was fearful. When men take it in their heads to day, to hang gamblers, or burn murderers, they should recollect, that, in the confusion usually attending such transactions, they will be as likely to hang or burn some one, who is neither a gambler nor a murderer as one who is; and that, acting upon the example they set, the mob of to-morrow, may, and probably will, hang or burn some of them, by the very same mistake. And not only so; the innocent, those who have ever set their faces against violations of law in every shape, alike with the guilty, fall victims to the ravages of mob law; and thus it goes on, step by step, till all the walls erected for the defence of the persons and property of individuals, are trodden down, and disregarded. But all this even, is not the full extent of the evil. By such examples, by instances of the perpetrators of such acts going unpunished, the lawless in spirit, are encouraged to become lawless in practice; and having been used to no restraint, but dread of punishment, they thus become, absolutely unrestrained. Having ever regarded Government as their deadliest bane, they make a jubilee of the suspension of its operations; and pray for nothing so much, as its total annihilation. While, on the other hand, good men, men who love tranquility, who desire to abide by the laws, and enjoy their benefits, who would gladly spill their blood in the defence of their country; seeing their property destroyed; their families insulted, and their lives endangered; their persons injured; and seeing nothing in prospect that forebodes a change for the better; become tired of, and disgusted with, a Government that offers them no protection; and are not much averse to a change in which they imagine they have nothing to lose. Thus, then, by the operation of this mobocratic spirit, which all must admit, is now abroad in the land, the strongest bulwark of any Government, and particularly of those constituted like ours, may effectually be broken down and destroyed—I mean the *attachment* of the People. Whenever this effect shall be produced among us; whenever the vicious portion of population shall be permitted to gather in bands of hundreds and thousands, and burn churches, ravage and rob provision stores, throw printing presses into rivers, shoot editors, and hang and burn obnoxious persons at pleasure, and with impunity; depend on it, this Government cannot last. By such things, the feelings of the best citizens will become more or less alienated from it; and thus it will be left without friends, or with too few, and those few too weak, to make their friendship effectual. At such a time and under such circumstances, men of sufficient talent and ambition will not be wanting to seize the opportunity, strike the blow, and overturn that fair fabric, which for the last half century, has been the fondest hope, of the lovers of freedom, throughout the world.

I know the American People are *much* attached to their Government;—I know they would suffer *much* for its sake;—I know they would endure evils long and patiently, before they would ever think of exchanging it for another. Yet, notwithstanding all this, if the laws be continually despised and disregarded, if their rights to be secure in their persons and property, are held by no better tenure than the caprice of a mob, the alienation of their affections from the Government is the natural consequence; and to that, sooner or later, it must come.

Here then, is one point at which danger may be expected.

The question recurs "how shall we fortify against it?" The answer is simple. Let every American, every lover of liberty, every well wisher to his posterity, swear by the blood of the Revolution, never to violate in the least particular, the laws of the country; and never to tolerate their violation by others. As the patriots of seventy-six did to the support of the Declaration of Independence, so to the support of the Constitution and Laws, let every American pledge his life, his property, and his sacred honor;—let every man remember that to violate the law, is to trample on the blood of his father, and to tear the character of his own, and his children's liberty. Let reverence for the laws, be breathed by every American mother, to the lisping babe, that prattles on her lap—let it be taught in schools, in seminaries, and in colleges;—let it be written in Primmers, spelling books, and in Almanacs;—let it be preached from the pulpit, proclaimed in legislative halls, and enforced in courts of justice. And, in short, let it become the *political religion* of the nation; and let the old and the young, the rich and the poor, the grave and the gay, of all sexes and tongues, and colors and conditions, sacrifice unceasingly upon its altars.

While ever a state of feeling, such as this, shall universally, or even, very generally prevail throughout the nation, vain will be every effort, and fruitless every attempt, to subvert our national freedom.

When I so pressingly urge a strict observance of all the laws, let me not be understood as saying there are no bad laws, nor that grievances may not arise, for the redress of which, no legal provisions have been made. I mean to say no such thing. But I do mean to say, that, although bad laws, if they exist, should be repealed as soon as possible, still while they continue in force, for the sake of example, they should be religiously observed. So also in unprovided cases. If such arise, let proper legal provisions be made for them with the least possible delay; but, till then, let them if not too intolerable, be borne with.

There is no grievance that is a fit object of redress by mob law. In any case that arises, as for instance, the promulgation of abolitionism, one of two positions is necessarily true; that is, the thing is right within itself, and therefore deserves the protection of all law and all good citizens; or, it is wrong, and therefore proper to be prohibited by legal enactments; and in neither case, is the interposition of mob law, either necessary, justifiable, or excusable.

But, it may be asked, why suppose danger to our political institutions? Have we not preserved them for more than fifty years? And why may we not for fifty times as long?

We hope there is no *sufficient* reason. We hope all dangers may be overcome; but to conclude that no danger may ever arise, would itself be extremely dangerous. There are now, and will hereafter be, many causes, dangerous in their tendency, which have not existed heretofore; and which are not too insignificant to merit attention. That our government should have been maintained in its original form from its establishment until now, is not much to be wondered at. It had many props to support it through that period, which now are decayed, and crumbled away. Through that period, it was felt by all, to be an undecided experiment; now, it is understood to be a successful one. Then, all that sought celebrity and fame, and distinction, expected to find them in the success of that experiment. Their *all* was staked upon it:—their destiny was *inseparably* linked with it. Their ambition aspired to display before an admiring world, a practical demonstration of the truth of a proposition, which had hitherto been considered, at best no better, than problematical; namely, *the capability of a people to govern themselves.* If they succeeded, they were to be immortalized; their names were to be transferred to counties and cities, and rivers and mountains; and to be revered and sung, and toasted through all time. If they failed, they were to be called knaves and fools, and fanatics for a fleeting hour; then to sink and be forgotten. They succeeded. The experiment is successful; and thousands have won their deathless names in making it so. But the game is caught; and I believe it is true, that with the catching, end the pleasures of the chase. This field of glory is harvested, and the crop is already appropriated. But new reapers will arise, and *they,* too, will seek a field. It is to deny, what the history of the world tells us is true, to suppose that men of ambition and talents will not continue to spring up amongst us. And, when they do, they will as naturally seek the gratification of their ruling passion, as others have *so* done before them. The question then, is, can that gratification be found in supporting and maintaining an edifice that has been erected by others? Most certainly it cannot. Many great and good men sufficiently qualified for any task they should undertake, may ever be found, whose ambition would aspire to nothing beyond a seat in Congress, a gubernatorial or a presidential chair; *but such belong not to the family of the lion, or the tribe of the eagle.* What! think you these places would satisfy an Alexander, a Caesar, or a Napoleon? Never! Towering genius disdains a beaten path. It seeks regions hitherto unexplored. It sees *no distinction* in adding story to story, upon the monuments of fame, erected to the memory of others. It *denies* that it is glory enough to serve under any chief. It *scorns* to tread in the footsteps of *any* predecessor, however illustrious. It thirsts and burns for distinction; and, if possible, it will have it, whether at the expense of emancipating slaves, or enslaving freemen. Is it unreasonable then to expect, that some man possessed of the loftiest genius, coupled with ambition sufficient to push it to its utmost stretch, will at some time, spring up among us? And when such a one does, it will require the people to be united with each other, attached to the government and laws, and generally intelligent, to successfully frustrate his designs.

Distinction will be his paramount object; and although he would as willingly, perhaps more so, acquire it by doing good as harm; yet, that opportunity being past, and nothing left to be done in the way of building up, he would set boldly to the task of pulling down.

Here then, is a probable case, highly dangerous, and such a one as could not have well existed heretofore.

Another reason which *once was;* but which, to the same extent, is *now no more,* has done much in maintaining our institutions thus far. I mean the powerful influence which the interesting scenes of the revolution had upon the *passions* of the people as distinguished from their judgment. By this influence, the jealousy, envy, and avarice, incident to our nature, and so common to a state of peace, prosperity, and conscious strength, were, for the time, in a great measure smothered and rendered inactive; while the deep rooted principles of *hate,* and the powerful motive of *revenge,* instead of being turned against each other, were directed exclusively against the British nation. And thus, from the force of circumstances, the basest principles of our nature, were either made to lie dormant, or to become the active agents in the advancement of the noblest of cause—that of establishing and maintaining civil and religious liberty.

But this state of feeling *must fade, is fading, has faded,* with the circumstances that produced it.

I do not mean to say, that the scenes of the revolution *are now* or *ever will be* entirely forgotten; but that like every thing else, they must fade upon the memory of the world, and grow more and more dim by the lapse of time. In history, we hope, they will be read of, and recounted, so long as the bible shall be read;—but even granting that they will, their influence *cannot be* what it heretofore has been. Even then, they *cannot be* so universally known, nor so vividly felt, as they were by the generation just gone to rest. At the close of that struggle, nearly every adult male had been a participator in some of its scenes. The consequence was, that of those scenes, in the form of a husband, a father, a son or a brother, a *living history was* to be found in every family—a history bearing the indubitable testimonies of its own authenticity, in the limbs mangled, in the scars of wounds received, in the midst of the very scenes related—a history, too, that could be read and understood alike by all, the wise and the ignorant, the learned and the unlearned. But *those* histories are gone. They *can* be read no more forever. They *were* a fortress of strength; but, what invading foemen could *never do,* the silent artillery of time *has done;* the levelling of its walls. They are gone. They *were* a forest of giant oaks; but the all resistless hurricane has swept over them, and left only, here and there, a lonely trunk, despoiled of its verdure, shorn of its foliage; unshading and unshaded, to murmur in a few more gentle breezes, and to combat with its mutilated limbs, a few more ruder storms, then to sink, and be no more.

They *were* the pillars of the temple of liberty; and now, that they have crumbled away, that temple must fall, unless we, their descendants, supply their places with other pillars, hewn from the solid quarry of sober reason. Passion has helped us; but can do so no more. It will in future be our enemy. Reason, cold, calculating, unimpassioned reason, must furnish all the materials for our future support and defence. Let those materials be moulded into *general intelligence, sound morality* and, in particular, *a reverence for the constitution and laws;* and, that we improved to the last; that we remained free to the last; that we revered his name to the last; that, during his long sleep, we permitted no hostile foot to pass over or desecrate his resting place;

shall be that which to learn the last trump shall awaken our WASHINGTON.

Upon these let the proud fabric of freedom rest, as the rock of its basis; and as truly as has been said of the only greater institution, *"the gates of hell shall not prevail against it."*

Address to the Wisconsin State Agricultural Society, Milwaukee, Wisconsin

Members of the Agricultural Society and Citizens of Wisconsin:

Agricultural Fairs are becoming an institution of the country; they are useful in more ways than one; they bring us together, and thereby make us better acquainted, and better friends than we otherwise would be. From the first appearance of man upon the earth, down to very recent times, the words *"stranger"* and *"enemy"* were *quite* or *almost,* synonymous. Long after civilized nations had defined robbery and murder as high crimes, and had affixed severe punishments to them, when practiced among and upon their own people respectively, it was deemed no offence, but even meritorious, to rob, and murder, and enslave *strangers,* whether as nations or as individuals. Even yet, this has not totally disappeared. The man of the highest moral cultivation, in spite of all which abstract principle can do, likes him whom he *does* know, much better than him whom he does *not* know. To correct the evils, great and small, which spring from want of sympathy, and from positive enmity, among *strangers,* as nations, or as individuals, is one of the highest functions of civilization. To this end our Agricultural Fairs contribute in no small degree. They make more pleasant, and more strong, and more durable, the bond of social and political union among us. Again, if, as Pope declares, "happiness is our being's end and aim," our Fairs contribute much to that end and aim, as occasions of recreation—as holidays. Constituted as man is, he has positive need of occasional recreation; and whatever can give him this, associated with virtue and advantage, and free from vice and disadvantage, is a positive good. Such recreation our Fairs afford. They are a present pleasure, to be followed by no pain, as a consequence; they are a present pleasure, making the future more pleasant.

But the chief use of agricultural fairs is to aid in improving the great calling of *agriculture,* in all it's departments, and minute divisions—to make mutual exchange of agricultural discovery, information, and knowledge; so that, at the end, *all* may know every thing, which may have been known to but *one,* or to but a *few,* at the beginning—to bring together especially all which is supposed to not be generally known, because of recent discovery, or invention.

And not only to bring together, and to impart all which has been *accidentally* discovered or invented upon ordinary motive; but, by exciting emulation, for premiums, and for the pride and honor of success—of triumph, in some sort—to stimulate that discovery and invention into extraordinary activity. In this, these Fairs are kindred to the patent clause in the Constitution of the United States; and to the department, and practical system, based upon that clause.

One feature, I believe, of every fair, is a regular *address.* The Agricultural Society of the young, prosperous, and soon to be, great State of Wisconsin, has done me the high honor of selecting me to make that address upon this occasion—an honor for which I make my profound, and grateful acknowledgement.

I presume I am not expected to employ the time assigned me, in the mere flattery of the farmers, as a class. My opinion of them is that, in proportion to numbers, they are neither better nor worse than other people. In the nature of things they are more numerous than any other class; and I believe there really are more attempts at flattering them than any other; the reason of which I cannot perceive, unless it be that they can cast more votes than any other. On reflection, I am not quite sure that there is not cause of suspicion against you, in selecting me, in some sort a politician, and in no sort a farmer, to address you.

But farmers, being the most numerous class, it follows that their interest is the largest interest. It also follows that that interest is most worthy of all to be cherished and cultivated—that if there be inevitable conflict between that interest and any other, that other should yield.

Again, I suppose it is not expected of me to impart to you much specific information on Agriculture. You have no reason to believe, and do not believe, that I possess it—if that were what you seek in this address, any one of your own number, or class, would be more able to furnish it.

You, perhaps, do expect me to give some general interest to the occasion; and to make some general suggestions, on practical matters. I shall attempt nothing more. And in

such suggestions by me, quite likely very little will be new to you, and a large part of the rest possibly already known to be erroneous.

My first suggestion is an inquiry as to the effect of greater *thoroughness* in all the departments of Agriculture than now prevails in the North-West—perhaps I might say in America. To speak entirely within bounds, it is known that fifty bushels of wheat, or one hundred bushels of Indian corn can be produced from an acre. Less than a year ago I saw it stated that a man, by extraordinary care and labor, had produced of wheat, what was equal to two hundred bushels from an acre. But take fifty of wheat, and one hundred of corn, to be the *possibility,* and compare with it the actual crops of the country. Many years ago I saw it stated in a Patent Office Report that eighteen bushels was the average crop throughout the wheat growing region of the United States; and this year an intelligent farmer of Illinois, assured me that he did not believe the land harvested in that State this season, had yielded more than an average of eight bushels to the acre. The brag crop I heard of in our vicinity was two thousand bushels from ninety acres. Many crops were thrashed, producing no more than three bushels to the acre; much was cut, and then abandoned as not worth threshing; and much was abandoned as not worth cutting. As to Indian corn, and, indeed, most other crops, the case has not been much better. For the last four years I do not believe the ground planted with corn in Illinois, has produced an average of twenty bushels to the acre. It is true, that heretofore we have had better crops, with no better cultivators; but I believe it is also true that the soil has never been pushed up to one-half of its capacity.

What would be the effect upon the farming interest, to push the soil up to something near its full capacity? Unquestionably it will take more labor to produce *fifty* bushels from an acre, than it will to produce *ten* bushels from the same acre. But will it take more labor to produce fifty bushels from *one* acre, than from *five?* Unquestionably, thorough cultivation will require more labor to the *acre;* but will it require more to the *bushel?* If it should require just as *much* to the bushel, there are some *probable,* and several *certain,* advantages in favor of the thorough practice. It is probable it would develope those unknown causes, or develope unknown cures for those causes, which of late years have cut down our crops below their former average. It is almost certain, I think, that in the deeper plowing, analysis of soils, experiments with manures, and varieties of seeds, observance of seasons, and the like, these cases would be found. It is certain that thorough cultivation would spare half or more than half, the cost of land, simply because the same product would be got from half, or from less than half the quantity of land. This proposition is self-evident, and can be made no plainer by repetitions or illustrations. The cost of land is a great item, even in new countries; and constantly grows greater and greater, in comparison with other items, as the country grows older.

It also would spare a large proportion of the making and maintaining of inclosures—the same, whether these inclosures should be hedges, ditches, or fences. This again, is a heavy item—heavy at first, and heavy in its continual demand for repairs. I remember once being greatly astonished by an apparently authentic exhibition of the proportion the cost of inclosures bears to all the other expenses of the farmer; though I can not remember exactly what that proportion was. Any farmer, if he will, can ascertain it in his own case, for himself.

Again, a great amount of "locomotion" is spared by thorough cultivation. Take fifty bushels of wheat, ready for the harvest, standing upon a *single* acre, and it can be harvested in any of the known ways, with less than half the labor which would be required if it were spread over *five* acres. This would be true, if cut by the old hand sickle; true, to a greater extent if by the scythe and cradle; and to a still greater extent, if by the machines now in use. These machines are chiefly valuable, as a means of substituting animal power for the power of men in this branch of farm work. In the highest degree of perfection yet reached in applying the horse power to harvesting, fully nine-tenths of the power is expended by the animal in carrying himself and dragging the machine over the field, leaving certainly not more than one-tenth to be applied directly to the only end of the whole operation—the gathering in the grain, and clipping of the straw. When grain is very thin on the ground, it is always more or less intermingled with weeds, chess and the like, and a large part of the power is expended in cutting these. It is plain that when the crop is very thick upon the ground, the larger proportion of the power is directly applied to gathering in and cutting it; and the smaller, to that which is totally useless as an end. And what I have said of harvesting is true, in a greater or less de-

gree of mowing, plowing, gathering in of crops generally, and, indeed, of almost all farm work.

The effect of thorough cultivation upon the farmer's own mind, and, in reaction through his mind, back upon his business, is perhaps quite equal to any other of its effects. Every man is proud of what he does *well;* and no man is proud of what he does *not* do well. With the former, his heart is in his work; and he will do twice as much of it with less fatigue. The latter performs a little imperfectly, looks at it in disgust, turns from it, and imagines himself exceedingly tired. The little he has done, comes to nothing, for want of finishing.

The man who produces a good full crop will scarcely ever let any part of it go to waste. He will keep up the enclosure about it, and allow neither man nor beast to trespass upon it. He will gather it in due season and store it in perfect security. Thus he labors with satisfaction, and saves himself the whole fruit of his labor. The other, starting with no purpose for a full crop, labors less, and with less satisfaction; allows his fences to fall, and cattle to trespass; gathers not in due season, or not at all. Thus the labor he has performed, is wasted away, little by little, till in the end, he derives scarcely anything from it.

The ambition for broad acres leads to poor farming, even with men of energy. I scarcely ever knew a mammoth farm to sustain itself; much less to return a profit upon the outlay. I have more than once known a man to spend a respectable fortune upon one; fail and leave it; and then some man of more modest aims, get a small fraction of the ground, and make a good living upon it. Mammoth farms are like tools or weapons, which are too heavy to be handled. Ere long they are thrown aside, at a great loss.

The successful application of *steam power,* to farm work is a *desideratum*—especially a Steam Plow. It is not enough, that a machine operated by steam, will really plow. To be successful, it must, all things considered, plow *better* than can be done with animal power. It must do all the work as well, and *cheaper;* or more *rapidly,* so as to get through more perfectly *in season;* or in some way afford an advantage over plowing with animals, else it is no success. I have never seen a machine intended for a Steam Plow. Much praise, and admiration, are bestowed upon some of them; and they may be, for aught I know, already successful; but I have not perceived the demonstration of it. I have thought a good deal, in an abstract way, about a Steam

Plow. That one which shall be so contrived as to apply the larger proportion of its power to the cutting and turning the soil, and the smallest, to the moving itself over the field, will be the best one. A very small stationary engine would draw a large gang of plows through the ground from a short distance to itself; but when it is not stationary, but has to move along like a horse, dragging the plows after it, it must have additional power to carry itself; and the difficulty grows by what is intended to overcome it; for what adds power also adds size, and weight to the machine, thus increasing again, the demand for power. Suppose you should construct the machine so as to cut a succession of short furrows, say a rod in length, transversely to the course the machine is locomoting, something like the shuttle in weaving. In such case the whole machine would move North only the width of a furrow, while in length, the furrow would be a rod from East to West. In such case, a very large proportion of the power, would be applied to the actual plowing. But in this, too, there would be a difficulty, which would be the getting of the plow *into,* and *out of,* the ground, at the ends of all these short furrows.

I believe, however, ingenious men will, if they have not already, overcome the difficulty I have suggested. But there is still another, about which I am less sanguine. It is the supply of *fuel,* and especially of *water,* to make steam. Such supply is clearly practicable, but can the expense of it be borne? Steamboats live upon the water, and find their fuel at stated places. Steam mills, and other stationary steam machinery, have their stationary supplies of fuel and water. Railroad locomotives have their regular wood and water station. But the steam plow is less fortunate. It does not live upon the water; and if it be once at a water station, it will work away from it, and when it gets away can not return, without leaving its work, at a great expense of its time and strength. It will occur that a wagon and horse team might be employed to supply it with fuel and water; but this, too, is expensive; and the question recurs, "can the expense be borne?" When this is added to all other expenses, will not the plowing cost more than in the old way?

It is to be hoped that the steam plow will be finally successful, and if it shall be, "*thorough cultivation*"—putting the soil to the top of its capacity—producing the largest crop possible from a given quantity of ground—will be most favorable to it. Doing a large amount of work upon a small quantity of ground, it will be, as nearly as possible,

stationary while working, and as free as possible from locomotion; thus expending its strength as much as possible upon its work, and as little as possible in travelling. Our thanks, and something more substantial than thanks, are due to every man engaged in the effort to produce a successful steam plow. Even the unsuccessful will bring something to light, which, in the hands of others, will contribute to the final success. I have not pointed out difficulties, in order to discourage, but in order that being seen, they may be the more readily overcome.

The world is agreed that *labor* is the source from which human wants are mainly supplied. There is no dispute upon this point. From this point, however, men immediately diverge. Much disputation is maintained as to the best way of applying and controlling the labor element. By some it is assumed that labor is available only in connection with capital—that nobody labors, unless somebody else, owning capital, somehow, by the use of that capital, induces him to do it. Having assumed this, they proceed to consider whether it is best that capital shall *hire* laborers, and thus induce them to work by their own consent; or *buy* them, and drive them to it without their consent. Having proceeded so far they naturally conclude that all laborers are necessarily either *hired* laborers, or *slaves.* They further assume that whoever is once a *hired* laborer, is fatally fixed in that condition for life; and thence again that his condition is as bad as, or worse than that of a slave. This is the "*mud-sill*" theory.

But another class of reasoners hold the opinion that there is no *such* relation between capital and labor, as assumed; and that there is no such thing as a freeman being fatally fixed for life, in the condition of a hired laborer, that both these assumptions are false, and all inferences from them groundless. They hold that labor is prior to, and independent of, capital; that, in fact, capital is the fruit of labor, and could never have existed if labor had not *first* existed—that labor can exist without capital, but that capital could never have existed without labor. Hence they hold that labor is the superior—greatly the superior—of capital.

They do not deny that there is, and probably always will be, *a* relation between labor and capital. The error, as they hold, is in assuming that the *whole* labor of the world exists within that relation. A few men own capital; and that few avoid labor themselves, and with their capital, hire, or buy, another few to labor for them. A large majority belong to neither class—neither work for others, nor have others working for them. Even in all our slave States, except South Carolina, a majority of the whole people of all colors, are neither slaves nor masters. In these Free States, a large majority are neither *hirers* nor *hired.* Men, with their families—wives, sons and daughters—work for themselves, on their farms, in their houses and in their shops, taking the whole product to themselves, and asking no favors of capital on the one hand, nor of hirelings or slaves on the other. It is not forgotten that a considerable number of persons mingle their own labor with capital; that is, labor with their own hands, and also buy slaves or hire freemen to labor for them; but this is only a *mixed,* and not a *distinct* class. No principle stated is disturbed by the existence of this mixed class. Again, as has already been said, the opponents of the "*mud-sill*" theory insist that there is not, of necessity, any such thing as the free hired laborer being fixed to that condition for life. There is demonstration for saying this. Many independent men, in this assembly, doubtless a few years ago were hired laborers. And their case is almost if not quite the general rule.

The prudent, penniless beginner in the world, labors for wages awhile, saves a surplus with which to buy tools or land, for himself; then labors on his own account another while, and at length hires another new beginner to help him. This, say its advocates, is *free* labor—the just and generous, and prosperous system, which opens the way for all—gives hope to all, and energy, and progress, and improvement of condition to all. If any continue through life in the condition of the hired laborer, it is not the fault of the system, but because of either a dependent nature which prefers it, or improvidence, folly, or singular misfortune. I have said this much about the elements of labor generally, as introductory to the consideration of a new phase which that element is in process of assuming. The old general rule was that *educated* people did not perform manual labor. They managed to eat their bread, leaving the toil of producing it to the uneducated. This was not an insupportable evil to the working bees, so long as the class of drones remained very small. But *now,* especially in these free States, nearly all are educated—quite too nearly all, to leave the labor of the uneducated, in any wise adequate to the support of the whole. It follows from this that henceforth educated people must labor. Otherwise, education itself would become a positive and intolerable evil.

No country can sustain, in idleness, more than a small percentage of its numbers. The great majority must labor at something productive. From these premises the problem springs, "How can *labor* and *education* be the most satisfactorily combined?"

By the "*mud-sill*" theory it is assumed that labor and education are incompatible; and any practical combination of them impossible. According to that theory, a blind horse upon a tread-mill, is a perfect illustration of what a laborer should be—all the better for being blind, that he could not tread out of place, or kick understandingly. According to that theory, the education of laborers, is not only useless, but pernicious, and dangerous. In fact, it is, in some sort, deemed a misfortune that laborers should have heads at all. Those same heads are regarded as explosive materials, only to be safely kept in damp places, as far as possible from that peculiar sort of fire which ignites them. A Yankee who could invent a strong *handed* man without a head would receive the everlasting gratitude of the "mud-sill" advocates.

But Free Labor says "no!" Free Labor argues that, as the Author of man makes every individual with one head and one pair of hands, it was probably intended that heads and hands should cooperate as friends; and that that particular head, should direct and control that particular pair of hands. As each man has one mouth to be fed, and one pair of hands to furnish food, it was probably intended that that particular pair of hands should feed that particular mouth—that each head is the natural guardian, director, and protector of the hands and mouth inseparably connected with it; and that being so, every head should be cultivated, and improved, by whatever will add to its capacity for performing its charge. In one word Free Labor insists on universal education.

I have so far stated the opposite theories of "*Mud-Sill*" and "Free Labor" without declaring any preference of my own between them. On an occasion like this I ought not to declare any. I suppose, however, I shall not be mistaken, in assuming as a fact, that the people of Wisconsin prefer free labor, with its natural companion, education.

This leads to the further reflection, that no other human occupation opens so wide a field for the profitable and agreeable combination of labor with cultivated thought, as agriculture. I know of nothing so pleasant to the mind, as the discovery of anything which is at once *new* and *valuable*—nothing which so lightens and sweetens toil, as the hopeful pursuit of such discovery. And how vast, and how varied a field is agriculture, for such discovery. The mind, already trained to thought, in the country school, or higher school, cannot fail to find there an exhaustless source of profitable enjoyment. Every blade of grass is a study; and to produce two, where there was but one, is both a profit and a pleasure. And not grass alone; but soils, seeds, and seasons—hedges, ditches, and fences, draining, droughts, and irrigation—plowing, hoeing, and harrowing—reaping, mowing, and threshing—saving crops, pests of crops, diseases of crops, and what will prevent or cure them—implements, utensils, and machines, their relative merits, and how to improve them—hogs, horses, and cattle—sheep, goats, and poultry—trees, shrubs, fruits, plants, and flowers—the thousand things of which these are specimens—each a world of study within itself.

In all this, book-learning is available. A capacity, and taste, for reading, gives access to whatever has already been discovered by others. It is the key, or one of the keys, to the already solved problems. And not only so. It gives a relish, and facility, for successfully pursuing the yet unsolved ones. The rudiments of science, are available, and highly valuable. Some knowledge of Botany assists in dealing with the vegetable world—with all growing crops. Chemistry assists in the analysis of soils, selection, and application of manures, and in numerous other ways. The mechanical branches of Natural Philosophy, are ready help in almost everything; but especially in reference to implements and machinery.

The thought recurs that education—cultivated thought—can best be combined with agricultural labor, or any labor, on the principle of *thorough* work—that careless, half performed, slovenly work, makes no place for such combination. And thorough work, again, renders sufficient, the smallest quantity of ground to each man. And this again, conforms to what must occur in a world less inclined to wars, and more devoted to the arts of peace, than heretofore. Population must increase rapidly—more rapidly than in former times—and ere long the most valuable of all arts, will be the art of deriving a comfortable subsistence from the smallest area of soil. No community whose every member possesses this art, can ever be the victim of oppression in any of its forms. Such community will be alike independent of crowned-kings, money-kings, and land-kings.

But, according to your programme, the awarding of premiums awaits the closing of this address. Considering the deep interest necessarily pertaining to that performance, it would be no wonder if I am already heard with some impatience. I will detain you but a moment longer. Some of you will be successful, and such will need but little philosophy to take them home in cheerful spirits; others will be disappointed, and will be in a less happy mood. To such, let it be said, "Lay it not too much to heart." Let them adopt the maxim, "Better luck next time;" and then, by renewed exertion, make that better luck for themselves.

And by the successful, and the unsuccessful, let it be remembered, that while occasions like the present, bring their sober and durable benefits, the exultations and mortifications of them, are but temporary; that the victor shall soon be the vanquished, if he relax in his exertion; and that the vanquished this year, may be victor the next, in spite of all competition.

It is said an Eastern monarch once charged his wise men to invent him a sentence, to be ever in view, and which should be true and appropriate in all times and situations. They presented him the words: "*And this, too, shall pass away.*" How much it expresses! How chastening in the hour of pride!—how consoling in the depths of affliction! "And this, too, shall pass away." And yet let us hope it is not *quite* true. Let us hope, rather, that by the best cultivation of the physical world, beneath and around us; and the intellectual and moral world within us, we shall secure an individual, social, and political prosperity and happiness, whose course shall be onward and upward, and which, while the earth endures, shall not pass away.

Newspaper Editorials

WILLIAM LEGGETT

William Leggett (1801–39) was a newspaper editor in New York City at a time when many papers vied for readership, party patronage, and political influence through their pages. Leggett's forceful editorials calling for equal rights, economic liberty, and the reduction of government programs were influential during his lifetime and long after his death. They also caused embarrassment within Leggett's own Jacksonian Democratic-Republican Party. Leggett was a strong supporter of Jackson and saw himself as a defender of the Jeffersonian tradition of democracy and limited government that Jackson so admired. But Leggett's attacks on government agencies and regulations were aimed at Jacksonians as well as their opponents.

"Direct Taxation"

No reflecting mind can consider the mode of raising revenue in this country for the support of the Government, in connexion with the great principle on which that Government is founded, without being struck with the anomaly it presents. The fundamental principle of our political institutions is that the great body of the people are honest and intelligent, and fully capable of self-government. Yet so little confidence is really felt in their virtue and intelligence, that we dare not put them to the test of asking them, openly and boldly, to contribute, each according to his means, to defray the necessary expenses of the Government; but resort, instead, to every species of indirection and arbitrary restriction on trade. This is true, not only of the General Government, but of every State Government, and every municipal corporation. The General Government raises its revenue by a tax on foreign commerce, giving rise to the necessity of a fleet of revenue vessels, and an army of revenue officers. The State Governments raise their funds by a tax on auction sales, bonuses on banks, tolls on highways, licenses, excise, &c. The municipal corporations descend a step in this prodigious scale of legislative swindling, and derive their resources from impositions on grocers, from steamboat, and stage-coach licenses, and from a tax on beef, wood, coal, and nearly every prime necessary of life. This whole complicated system is invented and persevered in for the purpose of deriving the expenses of Government from a people whose virtue and intelligence constitute the avowed basis of our institutions! What an absurdity does not a mere statement of the fact present?

Has any citizen, rich or poor, the least idea of the amount which he annually pays for the support of the government? The thing is impossible. No arithmetician, not even Babbit with his calculating machine, could compute the sum. He pays a tax on every article of clothing he wears, on every morsel of food he eats, on the fuel that warms him in winter, on the light which cheers his home in the evening, on the implements of his industry, on the amusements which recreate his leisure. There is scarcely an article produced by human labour or ingenuity which does not bear a tax for the support of one of the three governments under which every individual lives.

We have heretofore expressed the hope, and most cordially do we repeat it, that the day will yet come when we shall see the open and honest system of direct taxation resorted to. It is the only democratic system. It is the only method of taxation by which the people can know how much their government costs them. It is the only method which does not give the lie to the great principle on which we profess to have established all our political institutions. It is the only method, moreover, in consonance with the doctrines of that magnificent science, which, the twin-sister, as it were, of democracy, is destined to make this country the pride and wonder of the earth.

There are many evils which almost necessarily flow from our complicated system of indirect taxation. In the first place, taxes fall on the people very unequally. In the second place, it gives rise to the creation of a host of useless officers, and there is no circumstance which exercises such a vitiating and demoralizing influence on politics, as the converting of elections into a strife of opposite parties for place instead of principles. Another bad effect of the system is that it strengthens the government at the expense of the rights of the people, induces it to extend its powers to objects which were not contemplated in its original institution, and renders it every year less and less subject to the popular will. The tendency of the system is to build up and foster monopolies of various kinds, and to impose all sorts of restrictions on those pursuits which should be left wholly to the control of the laws of trade. We are well satisfied, and have long been so, that the only way to preserve economy in government, to limit it to its legitimate purposes, and to keep aroused the necessary degree of vigilance on the part of the people, is by having that government dependent for its subsistence on a direct tax on property.

If the fundamental principle of democracy is not a cheat and a mockery, a mere phrase of flattery, invented to gull the people—if it is really true that popular intelligence and virtue are the true source of all political power and the true basis of Government—if these positions are admitted, we can conceive no possible objection to a system of direct taxation which at all counterbalances any of the many important and grave considerations that may be urged in its favour.

For our own part, we profess ourselves to be democrats in the fullest and largest sense of the word. We are for free trade and equal rights. We are for a strictly popular Government. We have none of those fears, which some of our writers, copying the slang of the English aristocrats, profess to entertain of an "unbalanced democracy." We believe when government in this country shall be a true reflection of public sentiment; when its duties shall be strictly confined to its only legitimate ends, the equal protection of the whole community in life, person, and property; when all restrictions on trade shall be abolished, and when the funds necessary for the support of the government and the defence of the country are derived directly from taxation on property—we believe when these objects are brought about, we shall then present to the admiration of the world a nation founded as the hills, free as the air, and prosperous as a fruitful soil, a genial climate, and industry, enterprise, temperance and intelligence can render us.

"Chief Justice Marshall"

We perceive with pleasure that public and spontaneous demonstrations of respect for the character and talents of the late Judge Marshall have taken place in every part of the country where the tidings of his death have been received. These tributes to the memory of departed excellence have a most salutary effect on the living; and few men have existed in our republic who so entirely deserved to be thus distinguished as examples, by a universal expression of sorrow at their death, as he whose loss the nation now laments. Possessed of a vast hereditary fortune, he had none of the foolish ostentation or arrogance which are the usual companions of wealth. Occupying an office too potent—lifted too high above the influence of popular will—there was no man who in his private intercourse and habits, exhibited a more general and equal regard for the people. He was accessible to men of all degrees, and "familiar, but by no means vulgar" in his bearing, he was distinguished as much in the retired walks of life by his unaffected simplicity and kindness, as in public by the exercise of his great talents and acquirements.

The death of such a man, of great wisdom and worth, whose whole life has been passed in the public service, and whose history is interwoven with that of our country in some of its brightest and most interesting passages, furnishes a proper occasion for the expression of general respect and regret. In these sentiments we most fully join; but at the same time we cannot so far lose sight of those great principles of government which we consider essential to the permanent prosperity of man, as to neglect the occasion offered by the death of Judge Marshall to express our satisfaction that the enormous powers of the Supreme tribunal of the country will no longer be exercised by one whose cardinal maxim in politics inculcated distrust of popular intelligence and virtue, and whose constant object, in the decision of all constitutional questions, was to strengthen government at the expense of the people's rights. . . .

There is no journalist who entertained a truer respect for the virtues of Judge Marshall than ourselves; there is none who believed more fully in the ardour of his patriotism, or the sincerity of his political faith. But according to our firm opinion, the articles of his creed, if carried into practise, would prove destructive of the great principle of human liberty, and compel the many to yield obedience to the few. The principles of government entertained by Marshall were the same as those professed by Hamilton, and not widely different from those of the elder Adams. That both these illustrious men, as well as Marshall, were sincere lovers of their country, and sought to effect, through the means of government, the greatest practicable amount of human happiness and prosperity, we do not entertain, we never have entertained a doubt. Nor do we doubt that among those who uphold the divine right of kings, and wish to see a titled aristocracy and hierarchy established, there are also very many solely animated by a desire to have a government established adequate to self-preservation and the protection of the people. Yet if one holding a political creed of this kind, and who, in the exercise of high official functions, had done all in his power to change the character of the government from popular to monarchical, should be suddenly cut off by death, would it be unjustifiable in those who deprecated his opinions to allude to them and their tendency, while paying a just tribute to his intellectual and moral worth? . . .

Of Judge Marshall's spotless purity of life, of his many estimable qualities of heart, and of the powers of his mind, we record our hearty tribute of admiration. But sincerely believing that the principles of democracy are identical with the principles of human liberty, we cannot but experience joy that the chief place in the supreme tribunal of the Union will no longer be filled by a man whose political doctrines led him always to pronounce such decision of Constitutional questions as was calculated to strengthen government at the expense of the people. We lament the death of a good and exemplary man, but we cannot grieve that the cause of aristocracy has lost one of its chief supports.

"The Despotism of the Majority"

Words undergo variations in their meaning to accommodate them to the varying usages of men. Despotism, though originally confined, according to its derivation, to the government of a single ruler, and considered a term of honour, rather than reproach, is now employed to signify unlimited tyranny, whether exercised by one or legion, whether by a single autocrat, wielding all the power of the state, or by the majority of a community, combined under strict party organization, and ruling the minority with dictatorial and imperious sway. The two most prominent instances which the world now presents of these different classes of despotism, is that of a single tyrant in Russia, and that of a multitudinous tyrant in America; and it is a question which some seem to think not easily answered which is the worse, that of an autocracy, or that of a majority.

The intolerance, the bitter, persecuting intolerance, often displayed by a majority in this country, on questions of stirring political interest, towards the rights and feelings of the minority, has come to be a subject of comment by enlightened minds in Europe, that are eagerly watching the results of our great democratic experiment, and drawing arguments in favour of aristocratic government from every imperfection we exhibit. Thus, in the eloquent speech recently delivered by Sir Robert Peel, at Glasgow, there are some allusions to the intolerance of dominant parties in this country, which no candid person can peruse without admitting they contain enough of truth to give great point and sharpness to their sarcasms.

We cannot be suspected of any sympathy with Sir Robert Peel in the purpose with which he made this reference to America. Our love for the democratic principle is too sincere and unbounded, to allow us to have a feeling in common with those who desire to conserve aristocratic institutions. The democratic principle is the only principle which promises equal liberty, and equal prosperity to mankind. We yearn with intense longing for the arrival of that auspicious day in the history of the human race, when it shall everywhere take the place of the aristocratic principle, and knit all the families of mankind together in the bonds of equal brotherhood. Then shall the worn out nations sit down at last in abiding peace, and the old earth, which has so long drunk the blood of encountering millions, grow young again in a millenial holiday.

No American, having sense and soul to feel and appreciate the ineffable blessings of equal liberty, would answer Sir Robert Peel's interrogatory as he supposes. The effeminate popinjays, whom the land, overcloyed with their insipid sweetness, yearly sends abroad to foreign travel, and who prefer the glitter of courtly pomp to the widely diffused and substantial blessings of freedom, might utter such a dissuasion against the adoption of democratic principles. But no honest and manly American, worthy of that name, with intelligence enough to know, and heart enough to feel, that the best and loftiest aim of government is, not to promote excessive and luxurious refinement among a few, but the general good of all—"the greatest good of the greatest number"—would ever lisp a syllable to dissuade England from adopting the glorious democratic principle of equal political rights.

But while we thus differ from Sir Robert Peel in the tenor and purpose of the remarks we have quoted, we are forced to admit that there is but too much truth in the charge of despotism against the majority in our political divisions. The right of the majority to rule, is a maxim which lies at the bottom of democratic government; but a maxim of still higher obligation makes it their duty so to rule, as to preserve inviolate the equal rights of all. This rule of paramount authority is not always obeyed. We have seen numerous and frightful instances of its violation, in those outbreaks of "popular indignation," which men have drawn upon themselves by the fatal temerity of expressing their views on a subject of deep interest to every American, on which their sentiments differed from those of the majority. The wild excesses of riot are not chargeable alone to the madness and brutality of those who take part in them, but to the approval of others, who set on the human bulldogs to bait the abolitionists, by calling the latter all sorts of opprobrious names; and encouraging the former by bestowing laudatory appellations on their ferocity. They are "true friends of the Constitution," they are men "who appreciate the blessings of liberty," they are "champions of union," they are patriots and heroes; while those against whom their drunken rage is directed are pointed out as fanatics, of the most diabolical temper; as incendiaries, ready to burn to the ground the temple of freedom; as murderers, ready to incite the negro against his master, and incarnadine the whole south with the blood of promiscuous and discriminate slaughter.

But to descend from the terrible instances of despotism, which the conduct of the majority on the slave question displays, we see the consequences of the same tyranny in a thousand matters of less startling moment. Does not our newspaper press show marks of the iron rule of despotism, as exercised by a majority? Whence comes its subserviency? Whence comes it that each journal goes with its party in all things, and to all lengths approving what the party approves, whether men or measures, and condemning what it condemns? Why is it that no journalist dares, in the exercise of true independence, to act with his party in what he deems conformable with its political tenets, and censure its course when it varies from them? Why is it that if, forgetting for a moment that he is not a freeman, he honestly blames some erroneous step, or fails to approve it, his reproach, or his very silence, is made the occasion of persecution, and he finds himself suddenly stripped of support? Whence comes this we ask, but from the despotism of a majority, from that bitter intolerance of the mass, which now supplies an argument to the monarchists and aristocrats of the old world, against the adoption of the principles of popular government?

The book press of our country is not less overcrowed by the despotism of the majority than the newspapers. The very work from which Sir Robert Peel makes his quotation affords us a ready illustration. Thousands are burning to read the production of De Tocqueville, and a hundred publishers are anxious to gratify the desire. But they dare not. The writer has not hesitated to express his opinions of slavery; and such is the despotism of a majority, that it will not suffer men to read nor speak upon that subject; and it would hinder them, if it could, even from the exercise of thought.

There are some bold spirits yet in the land, who are determined to battle against this spirit of despotism, and to assert and defend their rights of equal freedom, let the struggle cost what it may. They will speak with a voice that the roar of tumult cannot drown, and maintain their ground with a firmness that opposition cannot move; and if forced at last to surrender, it will be their lives, not their liberty, they will yield, considering it better to die freemen, than live slaves to the most cruel of all despots—a despotic majority.

"Morals of Legislation"

If Jeremy Bentham were alive now, the doings of our legislature would furnish him with some fine subjects for an additional chapter to his "Principles and Morals of Legislation." There is no subject too high or low for the ken of that sapient and potential body. It undertakes to regulate by statute all sorts of business and all sorts of opinions. A man must neither do anything, nor think anything, except as the law provides. We may eat no meat, burn no fuel, chew no tobacco, nor even visit a theatre, unless such meat, fuel, tobacco, and playhouse, are all stamped with the signet of the law. If you offer a banknote of a certain denomination, you violate a law and incur a penalty. If you receive it from another, you are no less guilty. If a friend desires to borrow money from you, and to accommodate him you withdraw it from a business where it is yielding you twenty percent, you must lend it to him at the rate of seven, or otherwise incur the liability of being sent to prison for your kindness. The good old notion that the world is governed too much, is laughed at as an absurdity by our modern Solons, who act upon the converse of the French merchants' request, to let trade alone, and undertake to regulate it in every particular.

We learn from Albany that Judge Soule's bill of abominations is likely to be adopted in the Senate by as large a majority, proportionally, as passed it in the other house. By the way, the orthoepy of this wise lawgiver's name seems to be a matter of dispute, for while some contend that it should be so pronounced as to rhyme with *foul,* others think the word *fool* presents the proper symphony. These last perhaps are governed by an analogy which has respect to something more than sound. But whatever difference of opinion there may be as to the gentleman's name, there is none whatever, in this quarter, as to the true character and effect of his proposed law. It is universally execrated by men acquainted with those laws which should alone regulate financial matters.

The motive which we hear alleged for the concurrence this bill is likely to receive in the Senate is a desire *to force* capital into the old channel of loans on bonds and mortgages. The forcing system is the only system for which our legislature seems to have any fondness. All its business is conducted on the hothouse plan. It first forces credit out of its natural channel, by suddenly acceding to the wishes of dishonest speculators, and multiplying the fatal brood of specially privileged banks. When the floods of paper money which these institutions force upon the community have produced their inevitable consequence, and forced the attention of the community from the regular modes of business to extravagant schemes of speculation, the legislature then undertakes to force things back again to their old positions, heedless of the ruin and distress which these compulsory and contradictory processes may occasion. We trust the day is at hand when the people will exert their moral force, and force the legislature to confine itself to the few and simple objects which alone properly belong to government, leaving men free to make their own bargains, and follow their own pursuits.

We do not believe that any great practical evil will follow immediately from the passing of Judge Soule's usury law. It but compels men to do, what the bad state of things brought about by the opposite forcing system of the legislature was already causing them to do, with an obligation stronger than legal compulsion. The bubble of credit had been inflated to bursting by the prodigal creation of bank monopolies, and astounded by its sudden explosion, the confidence of avarice is too much shaken to allow of his being any longer allured by the bait of three per cent a month. They who have money to lend are now afraid to lend it to men who offer to pay large rates of interest, and capital is on the natural reflux to those borrowers who offer smaller profits and larger securities. The proposed law of Judge Draco, therefore, may do little present harm—it may be, to a great extent, practically inoperative. But it is founded on utterly false principles, and on that account deserves the most earnest opposition. It is not the business of the legislature to make laws for the present hour, framed according to the supposed requirements of instant expediency. It is its business to draw up its code in accordance with the eternal principles of right, so that it may apply with equal justice to-day, to-morrow, and forever. This making a law to force capital one way now, and next winter making a new one to force it another, is the height of legislative folly and injustice. Had the wishes of the people, as emphatically expressed "against all monopolies" four years ago, been respected by their servants; had Andrew Jackson's veto of the charter of the United States Bank been followed, in the principal commercial states, by legislative measures of a kindred spirit; or had this state alone removed the restrictions on trade, and simply instituted a general corporation partnership law instead, leaving the community to pursue what traffick they pleased, to what extent and in what mode they pleased, we should not, at this time, stand amidst such a scene of financial desolation, having nothing but disorder and ruin to contemplate.

We all know and acknowledge the value of political and religious freedom; and we shall yet learn that commercial freedom is the next best blessing that man can enjoy. We shall yet learn, we trust, to practise, as well as to declaim, the noble and just sentiment of Jefferson, that the sum of a good government is to restrain men from injuring one another; to leave them otherwise free to regulate their own pursuits of industry and improvement; and not to take from the mouth of labour the bread it has earned.

"The Morals of Politics"

Public moralists have long noticed with regret, that the political contests of this country are conducted with intemperance wholly unsuited to conflicts of reason, and decided, in a great measure, by the efforts of the worst class of people. We apply this phrase, not to those whom the aristocracy designate as the "lower orders;" but to those only, whether well or ill dressed, and whether rich or poor, who enter into the struggle without regard for the inherent dignity of politics, and without reference to the permanent interests of their country and of mankind; but animated by selfish objects, by personal preferences or prejudices, the desire of office, or the hope of accomplishing private ends through the influence of party. Elections are commonly looked upon as mere game, on which depends the division of party spoils, the distribution of chartered privileges, and the allotment of pecuniary rewards. The antagonist principles of government, which should constitute the sole ground of controversy, are lost sight of in the eagerness of sordid motives; and the struggle, which should

be one of pure reason, with no aim but the achievement of political truth, and the promotion of the greatest good of the greatest number, sinks into a mere brawl, in which passion, avarice, and profligacy, are the prominent actors.

If the questions of government could be submitted to the people in the naked dignity of abstract propositions, men would reason upon them calmly, and frame their opinions according to the preponderance of truth. There is nothing in the intrinsic nature of politics that appeals to the passions of the multitude. It is an important branch of morals, and its principles, like those of private ethics, address themselves to the sober judgment of men. A strange spectacle would be presented, should we see mathematicians kindle into wrath in the discussion of a problem, and call on their hearers, in the angry terms of demagogues, to decide on the relative merits of opposite modes of demonstration.

The same temperance and moderation which characterize the investigation of truth in the exact sciences, belong not less to the inherent nature of politics, when confined within the proper field.

The object of all politicians, in the strict sense of the expression, is happiness—the happiness of a state—the greatest possible sum of happiness of which the social condition admits to those individuals who live together under the same political organization.

It may be asserted, as an undeniable proposition, that it is the duty of every intelligent man to be a politician. This is particularly true of a country, the institutions of which admit every man to the exercise of equal suffrage. All the duties of life are embraced under the three heads of religion, politics, and morals. The aim of religion is to regulate the conduct of man with reference to happiness in a future state of being; of politics, to regulate his conduct with reference to the happiness of communities; and of morals, to regulate his conduct with reference to individual happiness.

Happiness, then, is the end and aim of these three great and comprehensive branches of duty; and no man perfectly discharges the obligations imposed by either, who neglects those which the others enjoin. The right ordering of a state affects, for weal or wo, the interests of multitudes of human beings; and every individual of those multitudes has a direct interest, therefore, in its being ordered aright. "I am a man," says Terence, in a phrase as beautiful for the harmony of its language, as the benevolence and universal truth of its sentiment, "and nothing can be indifferent to me which affects humanity."

The sole legitimate object of politics, then, is the happiness of communities. They who call themselves politicians, having other objects, are not politicians, but demagogues. But is it in the nature of things, that the sincere and single desire to promote such a system of government as would most effectually secure the greatest amount of general happiness, can draw into action such violent passions, prompt such fierce declamation, authorize such angry criminations, and occasion such strong appeals to the worst motives of the venal and base, as we constantly see and hear in every conflict of the antagonist parties of our country? Or does not this effect arise from causes improperly mixed with politics, and with which they have no intrinsic affinity? Does it not arise from the fact, that government, instead of seeking to promote the greatest happiness of the community, by confining itself rigidly within its true field of action, has extended itself to embrace a thousand objects which should be left to the regulation of social morals, and unrestrained competition, one man with another, without political assistance or check? Are our elections, in truth, a means of deciding mere questions of government, or does not the decision of numerous questions affecting private interests, schemes of selfishness, rapacity, and cunning, depend upon them, even more than cardinal principles of politics?

It is to this fact, we are persuaded, that the immorality and licentiousness of party contests are to be ascribed. If government were restricted to the few and simple objects contemplated in the democratic creed, the mere protection of person, life, and property; if its functions were limited to the mere guardianship of the equal rights of men, and its action, in all cases, were influenced, not by the paltry suggestions of present expediency, but the eternal principles of justice; we should find reason to congratulate ourselves on the change, in the improved tone of public morals, as well as in the increased prosperity of trade.

The religious man, then, as well as the political and social moralist, should exert his influence to bring about the auspicious reformation. Nothing can be more self-evident than the demoralizing influence of special legislation. It degrades politics into a mere scramble for rewards obtained by a violation of the equal rights of the people; it perverts the holy sentiment of patriotism; induces a fever-

ish avidity for sudden wealth; fosters a spirit of wild and dishonest speculation; withdraws industry from its accustomed channels of useful occupation; confounds the established distinctions between virtue and vice, honour and shame, respectability and degradation; pampers luxury; and leads to intemperance, dissipation, and profligacy, in a thousand forms.

The remedy is easy. It is to confine government within the narrowest limits of necessary duties. It is to disconnect bank and state. It is to give freedom to trade, and leave enterprise, competition, and a just public sense of right to accomplish by their natural energies, what the artificial system of legislative checks and balances has so signally failed in accomplishing. The federal government has nothing to do, but to hold itself entirely aloof from banking, having no more connexion with it, than if banks did not exist. It should receive its revenues in nothing not recognized as money by the Constitution, and pay nothing else to those employed in its service. The state governments should repeal their laws imposing restraints on the free exercise of capital and credit. They should avoid, for the future, all legislation not in the fullest accordance with the letter and spirit of that glorious maxim of democratic doctrine, which acknowledges the equality of man's political rights. These are the easy steps by which we might arrive at the consummation devoutly to be wished.

The steps are easy; but passion, ignorance, and selfishness, are gathered round them, and oppose our ascent. Agrarian, leveller, and visionary, are the epithets, more powerful than arguments, with which they resist us. Shall we yield, discouraged, and submit to be always governed by the worst passions of the worst portions of mankind; or by one bold effort, shall we regenerate our institutions, and make government, indeed, not the dispenser of privileges to a few for their efforts in subverting the rights of the many, but the beneficent promoter of the equal happiness of all? The monopolists are prostrated by the explosion of their overcharged system; they are wrecked by the regurgitation of their own flood of mischief; they are buried beneath the ruins of the baseless fabric they had presumptuously reared to such a towering height.

Now is the time for the friends of freedom to bestir themselves. Let us accept the invitation of this glorious opportunity to establish, on an enduring foundation, the true principles of political and economic freedom.

We may be encountered with clamorous revilings: but

they only betray the evil temper which ever distinguishes wilful error and baffled selfishness. We may be denounced with opprobrious epithets; but they only show the want of cogent arguments. The worst of these is only the stale charge of *ultraism,* which is not worthy of our regard. To be ultra is not necessarily to be wrong. Extreme opinions are justly censurable only when they are erroneous; but who can be reprehended for going too far towards the right?

"If the two extremes," says Milton, in answer to the same poor objection, "be vice and virtue, falsehood and truth, the greater extremity of virtue and superlative truth we run into, the more virtuous and the more wise we become; and he that, flying from degenerate corruption, fears to shoot himself too far into the meeting embraces of a divinely warranted reformation, might better not have run at all."

Speech on Electioneering

DAVY CROCKETT

1848

David "Davy" Crockett (1786–1836) had little education, but his personal charm, romantic background, and storytelling ability made him a powerful political figure. He opposed his fellow Tennesseean Andrew Jackson's policies against internal improvements and sought, against Jackson's wishes, to grant lands to squatters in Tennessee. His positions and flair for political drama won him fame and consideration for the Whig Party's presidential nomination. But in the end, Jackson's Democratic machine ousted Crockett from political office. It was then that Crockett sought adventure in Texas, where he died in the Battle of the Alamo.

Crockett's life served as the basis for many stories—some based on fact and some wholly fictional. He added to this blurring of fact and fiction by, like many politicians before and after him, claiming authorship of several works written or heavily edited by others. In addition, almanacs relating folk wisdom and tall tales as well as spurious autobiographies came out under his name. Among these latter was *Colonel Crockett's Exploits and Adventures in Texas,* which was probably written by Richard Penn Smith. Whether written by Crockett or not, these works were extremely popular and helped entrench the populist notion of the brave frontiersman, and the values of independence and equality, in the public mind.

Speech on Electioneering

"Attend all public meetings," says I, "and get some friends to move that you take the chair; if you fail in this attempt, make a push to be appointed secretary; the proceedings of course will be published, and your name is introduced to the public. But should you fail in both undertakings, get two or three acquaintances, over a bottle of whiskey, to pass some resolutions, no matter on what subject; publish them even if you pay the printer—it will answer the purpose of breaking the ice, which is the main point in these matters. Intrigue until you are elected an officer of the militia; this is the second step towards promotion, and

can be accomplished with ease, as I know an instance of an election being advertised, and no one attending, the innkeeper at whose house it was to be held, having a military turn, elected himself colonel of his regiment." Says I, "You may not accomplish your ends with as little difficulty, but do not be discouraged—Rome wasn't built in a day.

"If your ambition or circumstances compel you to serve your country, and earn three dollars a day, by becoming a member of the legislature, you must first publicly avow that the constitution of the state is a shackle upon free and liberal legislation; and is, therefore, of as little use in the present enlightened age, as an old almanac of the year in which the instrument was framed. There is policy in this measure, for by making the constitution a mere dead letter, your headlong proceedings will be attributed to a bold and unshackled mind; whereas, it might otherwise be thought they arose from sheer mulish ignorance. 'The Government' has set the example in his attack upon the constitution of the United States, and who should fear to follow where 'the Government' leads?

"When the day of election approaches, visit your constituents far and wide. Treat liberally, and drink freely, in order to rise in their estimation, though you fall in your own. True, you may be called a drunken dog by some of the clean shirt and silk stocking gentry, but the real rough necks will style you a jovial fellow, their votes are certain, and frequently count double. Do all you can to appear to advantage in the eyes of the women. That's easily done—you have but to kiss and slabber their children, wipe their noses, and pat them on the head; this cannot fail to please their mothers, and you may rely on your business being done in that quarter.

"Promise all that is asked," said I, "and more if you can think of any thing. Offer to build a bridge or a church, to divide a county, create a batch of new offices, make a turnpike, or any thing they like. Promises cost nothing, therefore deny nobody who has a vote or sufficient influence to obtain one.

"Get up on all occasions, and sometimes on no occasion at all, and make long-winded speeches, though composed of nothing else than wind—talk of your devotion to your country, your modesty and disinterestedness, or on any such fanciful subject. Rail against taxes of all kinds, office-holders, and bad harvest weather; and wind up with a flourish about the heroes who fought and bled for our liberties in the times that tried men's souls. To be sure you run the risk of being considered a bladder of wind, or an empty barrel, but never mind that, you will find enough of the same fraternity to keep you in countenance.

"If any charity be going forward, be at the top of it, provided it is to be advertised publicly; if not, it isn't worth your while. None but a fool would place his candle under a bushel on such an occasion.

"These few directions," said I, "if properly attended to, will do your business; and when once elected, why a fig for the dirty children, the promises, the bridges, the churches, the taxes, the offices, and the subscriptions, for it is absolutely necessary to forget all these before you can become a thorough-going politician, and a patriot of the first water."

Speech before the U.S. Senate

DANIEL WEBSTER

January 20, 1830

Speech before the U.S. Senate

ROBERT Y. HAYNE

January 27, 1830

The following two speeches are taken from what has become known as the Webster-Hayne Debate. This series of speeches took place in January of 1830 between Robert Y. Hayne, senator from South Carolina, and Daniel Webster, senator from Massachusetts. It began on January 19, when Hayne made a speech on the Senate floor. That speech concerned a proposal to limit the sale of federally owned lands to those that were already on the market. In it, Hayne sided with Sen. Thomas Hart Benton of Missouri, who characterized the land proposal as a scheme by northeastern states to restrain westward migration. The goal, in Benton's view, was to keep the population in eastern states concentrated and poor, forcing the people to take difficult, low-paying manufacturing jobs. Hayne seized on this argument and added his own view that the national tariff, discouraging imports by artificially increasing their price, was another means by which northeastern interests were using their power at the federal level to serve their own interests at the expense of other sections of the nation. Webster responded on January 20 by painting the Northeastern states as the true friends of the West, but the major issues of the debate concerned Webster's and Hayne's differing conceptions of the nature and purpose of the union. Whereas Hayne sought to defend Southern interests by supporting policies that favored agriculture and states' rights, Webster sought to defend northeastern interests through "The American System"—a high tariff and stronger national government aiming to promote manufacturing.

Speech of Mr. Webster, of Massachusetts

The following resolution, moved by Mr. Foot, of Connecticut, being under consideration:

"Resolved, That the Committee on Public Lands be instructed to inquire and report the quantity of the public lands remaining unsold within each State and Territory, and whether it be expedient to limit, for a certain period, the sales of the public lands to such lands only as have heretofore been offered for sale, and are now subject to entry at the minimum price. And, also, whether the office of Surveyor General, and some of the Land Offices, may not be abolished without detriment to the public interest; or whether it be expedient to adopt measures to hasten the sales, and extend more rapidly the surveys of the public lands."

Mr. Webster said, on rising, that nothing had been further from his intention than to take any part in the discussion of this resolution. It proposed only an inquiry, on a subject of much importance, and one in regard to which it might strike the mind of the mover, and of other gentlemen, that inquiry and investigation would be useful. Although [said Mr. W.] I am one of those who do not perceive any particular utility in instituting the inquiry, I have, nevertheless, not seen that harm would be likely to result from adopting the resolution. Indeed, it gives no new powers, and hardly imposes any new duty on the Committee. All that the resolution proposes should be done, the Committee is quite competent, without the resolution, to do, by virtue of its ordinary powers. But, sir, although I have felt quite indifferent about the passing of the resolution, yet opinions were expressed yesterday on the general subject of the public lands, and on some other subjects, by the gentleman from South Carolina, so widely different from my own, that I am not willing to let the occasion pass without some reply. If I deemed the resolution, as originally proposed, hardly necessary, still less do I think it either necessary or expedient to adopt it, since a second branch has been added to it to-day. By this second branch, the Committee is to be instructed to inquire whether it be expedient to adopt measures to hasten the sales, and extend more rapidly the surveys of the public lands. Now, it appears that, in forty years, we have sold no more than about twenty millions of acres of public lands. The annual sales do not now exceed, and never have exceeded, one million of acres. A million a year is, according to our experience, as much as the increase of population can bring into settlement. And it appears also, that we have, at this moment, sir, surveyed and in the market, ready for sale, two hundred and ten millions of acres, or thereabouts. All this vast mass, at this moment, lies on our hands, for mere want of purchasers. Can any man, looking to the real interests of the country and the people, seriously think of inquiring whether we ought not still faster to hasten the public surveys, and to bring, still more and more rapidly, other vast quantities into the market? The truth is, that, rapidly as population has increased, the surveys have, nevertheless, outran our wants. There are more lands than purchasers. They are now sold at low prices, and taken up as fast as the increase of people furnishes hands to take them up. It is obvious, that no artificial regulation, no forcing of sales, no giving away of the lands even, can produce any great and sudden augmentation of population. The ratio of increase, though great, has yet its bounds. Hands for labor are multiplied only at a certain rate. The lands cannot be settled but by settlers; nor faster than settlers can be found. A system, if now adopted, of forcing sales at whatever prices, may have the effect of throwing large quantities into the hands of individuals, who would, in this way, in time, become themselves competitors with the Government in the sale of land. My own opinion has uniformly been, that the public lands should be offered freely, and at low prices; so as to encourage settlement and cultivation as rapidly as the increasing population of the country is competent to extend settlement and cultivation. Every actual settler should

be able to buy good land, at a cheap rate; but, on the other hand, speculation by individuals, on a large scale, should not be encouraged, nor should the value of all lands, sold and unsold, be reduced to nothing, by throwing new and vast quantities into the market at prices merely nominal.

I now proceed, sir, to some of the opinions expressed by the gentleman from South Carolina. Two or three topics were touched by him, in regard to which he expressed sentiments in which I do not at all concur.

In the first place, sir, the honorable gentleman spoke of the whole course and policy of the Government towards those who have purchased and settled the public lands and seemed to think this policy wrong. He held it to have been, from the first, hard and rigorous; he was of opinion that the United States had acted towards those who had subdued the Western wilderness, in the spirit of a stepmother, that the public domain had been improperly regarded as a source of revenue; and that we had rigidly compelled payment for that which ought to have been given away. He said we ought to have followed the analogy of other Governments, which had acted on a much more liberal system than ours, in planting colonies. He dwelt particularly upon the settlement of America by colonists from Europe; and reminded us that their governments had not exacted from those colonists payment for the soil; with them, he said, it had been thought that the conquest of the wilderness was, itself, an equivalent for the soil; and he lamented that we had not followed the example, and pursued the same liberal course towards our own emigrants to the West.

Now, sir, I deny altogether, that there has been any thing harsh or severe in the policy of the Government towards the new States of the West. On the contrary, I maintain that it has uniformly pursued towards those States, a liberal and enlightened system, such as its own duty allowed and required, and such as their interests and welfare demanded. The Government has been no step-mother to the new States; she has not been careless of their interests, nor deaf to their requests; but from the first moment, when the Territories which now form those States, were ceded to the Union, down to the time in which I am now speaking, it has been the invariable object of the Government to dispose of the soil, according to the true spirit of the obligation under which it received it; to hasten its settlement and cultivation, as far and as fast as practicable; and to rear the new communities into equal and independent States, at the earliest moment of their being able, by their numbers, to form a regular government.

I do not admit sir, that the analogy to which the gentleman refers is just, or that the cases are at all similar. There is no resemblance between the cases upon which a statesman can found an argument. The original North American colonists either fled from Europe, like our New England ancestors, to avoid persecution, or came hither at their own charges, and often at the ruin of their fortunes, as private adventurers. Generally speaking, they derived neither succor nor protection from their governments at home. Wide, indeed, is the difference between those cases and ours. From the very origin of the Government, these Western lands, and the just protection of those who had settled or should settle on them, have been the leading objects in our policy, and have led to expenditures, both of blood and treasure, not inconsiderable; not indeed exceeding the importance of the object, and not yielded grudgingly or reluctantly certainly; but yet not inconsiderable, though necessary sacrifices, made for high proper ends. The Indian title has been extinguished at the expense of many millions. Is that nothing? There is still a much more material consideration. These colonists, if we are to call them so, in passing the Alleghany, did not pass beyond the care and protection of their own Government. Wherever they went, the public arm was still stretched over them. A parental Government at home was still ever mindful of their condition, and their wants; and nothing was spared which a just sense of their necessities required. Is it forgotten that it was one of the most arduous duties of the Government, in its earliest years, to defend the frontiers against the Northwestern Indians? Are the sufferings and misfortunes under Harmar and St. Clair not worthy to be remembered? Do the occurrences connected with these military efforts show an unfeeling neglect of Western interests? And here, sir, what becomes of the gentleman's analogy? What English armies accompanied our ancestors to clear the forests of a barbarous foe? What treasures of the exchequer were expended in buying up the original title to the soil? What governmental arm held its aegis over our fathers' heads, as they pioneered their way in the wilderness? Sir, it was not till General Wayne's victory, in 1794, that it could be said we had conquered the savages. It was not till that period that the Government could have considered itself as having established an entire ability to protect those who should undertake the conquest of the

wilderness. And here, sir, at the epoch of 1794, let us pause, and survey the scene. It is now thirty-five years since that scene actually existed. Let us, sir, look back, and behold it. Over all that is now Ohio, there then stretched one vast wilderness, unbroken, except by two small spots of civilized culture, the one at Marietta, and the other at Cincinnati. At these little openings, hardly each a pin's point upon the map, the arm of the frontiersman had leveled the forest, and let in the sun. These little patches of earth, and themselves almost shadowed by the over hanging boughs of that wilderness, which had stood and perpetuated itself, from century to century, ever since the creation, were all that had then been rendered verdant by the hand of man. In an extent of hundreds and thousands of square miles, no other surface of smiling green attested the presence of civilization. The hunter's path crossed mighty rivers, flowing in solitary grandeur, whose sources lay in remote and unknown regions of the wilderness. It struck, upon the North, on a vast inland sea, over which the wintry tempests raged as on the ocean; all around was bare creation. It was a fresh, untouched, unbounded, magnificent wilderness! And, sir, what is it now? Is it imagination only, or can it possibly be fact, that presents such a change, as surprises and astonishes us, when we turn our eyes to what Ohio now is? Is it reality, or a dream, that, in so short a period even as thirty-five years, there has sprung up, on the same surface, an independent State, wth a million of people? A million of inhabitants! an amount of population greater than that of all the cantons of Switzerland; equal to one third of all the people of the United States, when they undertook to accomplish their independence. This new member of the republic has already left far behind her a majority of the old States. She is now by the side of Virginia and Pennsylvania; and in point of numbers, will shortly admit no equal but New York herself. If, sir, we may judge of measures by their results, what lessons do these facts read us upon the policy of the Government? What inferences do they authorize, upon the general question of kindness, or unkindness? What convictions do they enforce, as to the wisdom and ability, on the one hand, or the folly and incapacity, on the other, of our general administration of Western affairs? Sir, does it not require some portion of self-respect in us, to imagine that, if our light had shone on the path of government, if our wisdom could have been consulted in its measures, a more rapid advance to strength and prosperity would have been experienced? For my own part, while I am struck with wonder at the success, I also look with admiration at the wisdom and foresight which originally arranged and prescribed the system for the settlement of the public domain. Its operation has been, without a moment's interruption, to push the settlement of the Western country to the full extent of our utmost means.

But, sir, to return to the remarks of the honorable member from South Carolina. He says that Congress has sold these lands, and put the money into the treasury, while other Governments, acting in a more liberal spirit, gave away their lands; and that we ought, also, to have given ours away. I shall not stop to state an account between our revenues derived from land, and our expenditures in Indian treaties and Indian wars. But, I must refer the honorable gentleman to the origin of our own title to the soil of these territories, and remind him that we received them on conditions, and under trusts, which would have been violated by giving the soil away. For compliance with those conditions, and the just execution of those trusts, the public faith was solemnly pledged. The public lands of the United States have been derived from four principal sources. First, Cessions made to the United States by individual States, on the recommendation or request of the old Congress. Second, The compact with Georgia, in 1802. Third, The purchase of Louisiana, in 1802. Fourth, The purchase of Florida, in 1819. Of the first class, the most important was the cession by Virginia, of all her right and title, as well of soil as jurisdiction, to all the territory within the limits of her charter, lying to the Northwest of the river Ohio. It may not be ill-timed to recur to the causes and occasions of this and the other similar grants.

When the war of the Revolution broke out, a great difference existed in different States in the proportion between people and Territory. The Northern and Eastern States, with very small surfaces, contained comparatively a thick population, and there was generally within their limits, no great quantity of waste lands belonging to the Government, or the Crown of England. On the contrary, there were in the Southern States, in Virginia and in Georgia for example, extensive public domains, wholly unsettled and belonging to the Crown. As these possessions would necessarily fall from the crown, in the event of a prosperous issue of the war, it was insisted that they ought to devolve on the United States, for the good of the whole. The war, it was argued, was undertaken, and carried on, at the common expense of all the colonies; its benefits, if successful, ought also to be common; and the property of the common enemy, when vanquished, ought to be regarded as the general acquisition of all. While yet the war was raging, it was contended that Congress ought to have the power to dispose of vacant and unpatented lands commonly called Crown lands, for defraying the expenses of the war, and for other public and general purposes. "Reason and justice," said the Assembly of New Jersey, in 1778, "must decide, that the property which existed in the Crown of Great Britain, previous to the present Revolution, ought now to belong to Congress, in trust for the use and benefit of the United States. They have fought and bled for it, in proportion to their respective abilities, and therefore the reward ought not to be predilectionally distributed. Shall such States as are shut out, by situation, from availing themselves of the least advantage from this quarter, be left to sink under an enormous debt, whilst others are enabled, in a short period, to replace all their expenditures from the hard earnings of the whole confederacy?"

Moved by these considerations, and these addresses, Congress took up the subject, and in September, 1780, recommended to the several States in the Union, having claims to Western Territory, to make liberal cessions of a portion thereof to the United States; and on the 10th of October, 1780, Congress resolved, "That any lands, so ceded in pursuance of their preceding recommendation, should be disposed of for the common benefit of the United States; should be settled and formed into distinct republican States, to become members of the Federal Union, with the same rights of sovereignty, freedom, and independence, as the other States; and that the lands should be granted or settled, at such times, and under such regulations, as should be agreed on by Congress." Again, in September, 1783, Congress passed another resolution, expressing the conditions on which cessions from States should be received; and in October following, Virginia made her cession, reciting the resolution, or act, of September preceding, and then transferring her title to her Northwestern Territory to the United States, upon the express condition "that the lands, so ceded, should be considered as a common fund for the use and benefit of such of the United States as had become or should become members of the confederation, Virginia inclusive, and should be faithfully and *bona fide* disposed of for that purpose, and for no other use or purpose whatsoever." The grants from other States were on similar conditions. Massachusetts and Connecticut both had claims to western lands, and both relinquished them to the United States in the same manner. These grants were all made on three substantial conditions or trusts: First, that the ceded territories should be formed into States, and admitted in due time into the union, with all the rights belonging to other States. Second, that the lands should form a common fund, to be disposed of for the general benefit of all the States. Third, that they should be sold and settled, at such time and in such manner as Congress should direct.

Now, sir, it is plain that Congress never has been, and is not now, at liberty to disregard these solemn conditions. For the fulfilment of all these trusts, the public faith was, and is, fully pledged. How, then, would it have been possible for Congress, if it had been so disposed, to give away these public lands? How could they have followed the example of other Governments, if there had been such, and considered the conquest of the wilderness an equivalent compensation for the soil? The States had looked to this territory, perhaps too sanguinely, as a fund out of which means were to come to defray the expenses of the war. It had been received as a fund—as a fund Congress had bound itself to apply it. To have given it away, would have defeated all the objects which Congress, and particular States, had had in view, in asking and obtaining the cession, and would have plainly violated the conditions which the ceding States attached to their own grants.

The gentleman admits that the lands cannot be given away until the national debt is paid, because, to a part of that debt they stand pledged. But this is not the original pledge. There is, so to speak, an earlier mortgage. Before the debt was funded, at the moment of the cession of the lands, and by the very terms of that cession, every State in the Union obtained an interest in them, as in a common fund. Congress has uniformly adhered to this condition. It has proceeded to sell the lands, and to realize as much from them as was compatible with the other trusts created by the same deeds of cession. One of these deeds of trust, as I have already said, was, that the lands should be sold and settled, "at such time and manners as Congress shall direct." The Government has always felt itself bound, in regard to sale and settlement, to exercise its own best judgment, and not to transfer the discretion to others. It has not felt itself at liberty to dispose of the soil, therefore, in large masses, to individuals, thus leaving to them the time and manner of settlement. It had stipulated to use its own judgment. If, for instance, in order to rid itself of the trouble of forming a system for the sale of those lands, and going into detail, it had sold the whole of what is now Ohio, in one mass, to individuals, or companies, it would clearly have departed from its just obligations. And who can now tell, or conjecture, how great would have been the evil of such a course? Who can say what mischiefs would have ensued, if Congress had thrown these territories into the hands of private speculation? Or who, on the other hand, can now foresee what the event would be, should the Government depart from the same wise course hereafter, and, not content with such constant absorption of the public lands as the natural growth of our population may accomplish, should force great portions of them, at nominal or very low prices, into private hands, to be sold and settled, as and when such holders might think would be most for their own interest? Hitherto, sir, I maintain Congress has acted wisely, and done its duty on this subject. I hope it will continue to do it. Departing from the original idea, so soon as it was found practicable and convenient, of selling by townships, Congress has disposed of the soil in smaller and still smaller portions, till, at length, it sells in parcels of no more than eighty acres; thus putting it into the power of every man in the country, however poor, but who has health and strength, to become a freeholder if he desires, not of barren acres, but of rich and fertile soil. The Government has performed all the conditions of the grant. While it has regarded the public lands as a common fund, and has sought to make what reasonably could be made of them, as a source of revenue, it has also applied its best wisdom to sell and settle them, as fast and as happily as possible; and whensoever numbers would warrant it, each territory has been successively admitted into the Union, with all the rights of an independent State. Is there, then, sir, I ask, any well founded charge of hard dealing; any just accusation for negligence, indifference, or parsimony, which is capable of being sustained against the Government of the country, in its conduct towards the new States? Sir, I think there is not.

But there was another observation of the honorable member, which, I confess, did not a little surprise me. As a reason for wishing to get rid of the public lands as soon as we could, and as we might, the honorable gentleman said, he wanted no permanent sources of income. He wished to see the time when the Government should not possess a shilling of permanent revenue. If he could speak a magical word, and by that word convert the whole capital into gold, the word should not be spoken. The administration of a fixed revenue, [he said] only consolidates the Government, and corrupts the people! Sir, I confess I heard these sentiments uttered on this floor not without deep regret and pain.

I am aware that these, and similar opinions, are espoused by certain persons out of the capitol, and out of this Government; but I did not expect so soon to find them here. Consolidation!—that perpetual cry, both of terror and delusion—consolidation! Sir, when gentlemen speak of the effects of a common fund, belonging to all the States, as having a tendency to consolidation, what do they mean? Do they mean, or can they mean, any thing more than that the Union of the States will be strengthened, by whatever continues or furnishes inducements to the people of the States to hold together? If they mean merely this, then, no doubt, the public lands as well as every thing else in which we have a common interest, tends to consolidation; and to this species of consolidation every true American ought to be attached; it is neither more nor less than strengthening the Union itself. This is the sense in which the framers of the constitution use the word consolidation; and in which sense I adopt and cherish it. They tell us, in the letter submitting the constitution to the consideration of the country, that, "in all our deliberations on this subject, we kept steadily in our view that which appears to us the greatest interest of every true American—the consolidation of our Union—in which is involved our prosperity, felicity, safety; perhaps our national existence. This important consideration, seriously and deeply impressed on our minds, led each State in the Convention to be less rigid, on points of inferior magnitude, than might have been otherwise expected."

This, sir, is General Washington's consolidation. This is the true constitutional consolidation. I wish to see no new powers drawn to the General Government; but I confess I rejoice in whatever tends to strengthen the bond that unites us, and encourages the hope that our Union may be perpetual. And, therefore, I cannot but feel regret at the expression of such opinions as the gentleman has avowed; because I think their obvious tendency is to weaken the bond of our connexion. I know that there are some persons in the part of the country from which the honorable member comes, who habitually speak of the Union in terms of indifference, or even of disparagement. The honorable member himself is not, I trust, and can never be, one of these. They significantly declare, that it is time to calculate the value of the Union; and their aim seems to be to enumerate, and to magnify all the evils, real and imaginary, which the Government under the Union produces.

The tendency of all these ideas and sentiments is obviously to bring the Union into discussion, as a mere question of present and temporary expediency; nothing more than a mere matter of profit and loss. The Union to be preserved, while it suits local and temporary purposes to preserve it; and to be sundered whenever it shall be found to thwart such purposes. Union, of itself, is considered by the disciples of this school as hardly a good. It is only regarded as a possible means of good; or on the other hand, as a possible means of evil. They cherish no deep and fixed regard for it, flowing from a thorough conviction of its absolute and vital necessity to our welfare. Sir, I deprecate and deplore this tone of thinking and acting. I deem far otherwise of the Union of the States; and so did the framers of the constitution themselves. What they said I believe; fully and sincerely believe, that the Union of the States is essential to the prosperity and safety of the States. I am a Unionist, and in this sense a National Republican. I would strengthen the ties that hold us together. Far, indeed, in my wishes, very far distant be the day, when our associated and fraternal stripes shall be severed asunder, and when that happy constellation under which we have risen to so much renown, shall be broken up, and seen sinking, star after star, into obscurity and night!

Among other things, the honorable member spoke of the public debt. To that he holds the public lands pledged, and has expressed his usual earnestness for its total discharge. Sir, I have always voted for every measure for reducing the debt, since I have been in Congress. I wish it paid, because it is a debt; and, so far, is a charge upon the industry of the country, and the finances of the Government. But, sir, I have observed that, whenever the subject of the public debt is introduced into the Senate, a morbid sort of fervor is manifested in regard to it, which I have been sometimes at a loss to understand. The debt is not now large, and is in a course of most rapid reduction. A very few years will see it extinguished. Now I am not entirely able to persuade myself that it is not certain supposed incidental tendencies and effects of this debt, rather than its pressure and charge as a debt, that cause so much anxiety to get rid of it. Possibly it may be regarded as in some degree a tie, holding the different parts of the country together by considerations of mutual interest. If this be one of its effects, the effect itself is, in my opinion, not to be lamented. Let me not be misunderstood. I would not continue the debt for the sake of any collateral or consequential advantage, such as I have mentioned. I only mean to say, that that consequence itself is not one that I regret. At the same time, that if there are others who would, or who do regret it, I differ from them.

As I have already remarked, sir, it was one among the reasons assigned by the honorable member for his wish to be rid of the public lands altogether, that the public disposition of them, and the revenues derived from them, tends to corrupt the people. This, sir, I confess, passes my comprehension. These lands are sold at public auction, or taken up at fixed prices, to form farms and freeholds. Whom does this corrupt? According to the system of sales, a fixed proportion is every where reserved, as a fund for education. Does education corrupt? Is the schoolmaster a corrupter of youth? the spelling book, does it break down the morals of the rising generation? and the Holy Scriptures, are they fountains of corruption? or if, in the exercise of a provident liberality, in regard to its own property as a great landed proprietor, and to high purposes of utility towards others, the Government gives portions of these lands to the making of a canal, or the opening of a road, in the country where the lands themselves are situated, what alarming and overwhelming corruption follows from all this? Can there be nothing pure in government, except the exercise of mere control? Can nothing be done without corruption, but the imposition of penalty and restraint? Whatever is positively beneficent, whatever is actively good, whatever spreads abroad benefits and blessings which all can see, and all can feel, whatever opens intercourse, augments population, enhances the value of property, and diffuses knowledge—must all this be rejected and reprobated as a dangerous and obnoxious policy, hurrying us to the double ruin of a Government, turned into despotism by the mere exercise of acts of beneficence, and of a people, corrupted, beyond hope of rescue, by the improvement of their condition?

The gentleman proceeded, sir, to draw a frightful picture of the future. He spoke of the centuries that must elapse, before all the lands could be sold, and the great hardships that the States must suffer while the United States reserved to itself, within their limits, such large portions of soil, not liable to taxation. Sir, this is all, or mostly, imagination. If these lands were leasehold property, if they were held by the United States on rent, there would be much in the idea. But they are wild lands, held only till they can be sold; reserved no longer than till somebody will take them up, at low prices. As to their not being taxed, I would ask whether the States themselves, if they owned them, would tax them before sale? Sir, if in any case any State can show that the policy of the United States retards her settlement, or prevents her from cultivating the lands within her limits, she shall have my vote to alter that policy. But I look upon the public lands as a public fund, and that we are no more authorized to give them away gratuitously than to give away gratuitously the money in the treasury. I am quite aware that the sums drawn annually from the Western States make a heavy drain upon them, but that is unavoidable. For that very reason, among others, I have always been inclined to pursue towards them a kind and most liberal policy; but I am not at liberty to forget, at the same time, what is due to others, and to the solemn engagements under which the Government rests.

I come now to that part of the gentleman's speech which has been the main occasion of my addressing the Senate. The East! the obnoxious, the rebuked, the always reproached East! We have come in, sir, on this debate, for even more than a common share of accusation and attack. If the honorable member from South Carolina was not our original accuser, he has yet recited the indictment against us, with the air and tone of a public prosecutor. He has summoned us to plead on our arraignment; and he tells us we are charged with the crime of a narrow and selfish policy; of endeavoring to restrain emigration to the West, and, having that object in view, of maintaining a steady opposition to Western measures and Western interests. And the cause of all this narrow and selfish policy, the gentleman finds in the tariff. I think he called it the accursed policy of the tariff. This policy, the gentleman tells us, requires multitudes of dependent laborers, a population of paupers, and that it is to secure these at home that the East opposes whatever may induce to Western emigration. Sir, I rise to defend the East. I rise to repel, both the charge itself, and the cause assigned for it. I deny that the East has, at any time, shown an illiberal policy towards the West. I pronounce the whole accusation to be without the least foundation in any facts, existing either now, or at any previous time. I deny it in the general, and I deny each and all its particulars. I deny the sum total, and I deny the detail. I deny that the East has ever manifested hostility to the West, and I deny that she has adopted any policy that would naturally have led her in such a course. But the tariff! the tariff!! Sir, I beg to say, in regard to the East, that the original policy of the tariff is not hers, whether it be wise or unwise. New England is not its author. If gentlemen will recur to the tariff of 1816, they will find that that was not carried by New England votes. It was truly more a Southern than an Eastern measure. And what votes carried the tariff of 1824? Certainly, not those of New England. It is known to have been made matter of reproach, especially against Massachusetts, that she would not aid the tariff of 1824; and a selfish motive was imputed to her for that also. In point of fact, it is true that she did, indeed, oppose the tariff of 1824. There were more votes in favor of that law in the House of Representatives, not only in each of a majority of the Western States, but even in Virginia herself also, than in Massachusetts. It was literally forced upon New England; and this shows how groundless, how void of all probability any charge must be, which imputes to her hostility to the growth of the Western States, as naturally flowing from a cherished policy of her own. But leaving all conjectures about causes and motives, I go at once to the fact, and I meet it with one broad, comprehensive, and emphatic negative. I deny that, in any part of her history, at any period of the Government, or in relation to any leading subject, New England has manifested such hostility as is charged upon her. On the contrary, I maintain that, from the day of the cession of the territories by the States to Congress, no portion of the country has acted, either with more liberality or more intelligence, on the subject of the Western lands in the new States, than New England. This statement, though strong, is no stronger than the strictest truth will warrant. Let us look at the historical facts. So soon as the cessions were obtained, it became necessary to make provision for the government and disposition of the territory—the country was to be governed. This, for the present, it was obvious, must be by some territorial system of administration. But the soil, also, was to be granted and settled. Those immense regions, large enough almost for an empire, were to be appropriated to private ownership. How was this best to be done? What system for sale and disposition should be adopted? Two modes for conducting the sales presented

themselves; the one a Southern, and the other a Northern mode. It would be tedious, sir, here, to run out these different systems into all their distinctions, and to contrast their opposite results. That which was adopted was the Northern system, and is that which we now see in successful operation in all the new States. That which was rejected, was the system of warrants, surveys, entry, and location; such as prevails South of the Ohio. It is not necessary to extend these remarks into invidious comparisons. This last system is that which, as has been emphatically said, has shingled over the country to which it was applied with so many conflicting titles and claims. Every body acquainted with the subject knows how easily it leads to speculation and litigation—two great calamities in a new country. From the system actually established, these evils are banished. Now, sir, in effecting this great measure, the first important measure on the whole subject, New England acted with vigor and effect, and the latest posterity of those who settled Northwest of the Ohio, will have reason to remember, with gratitude, her patriotism and her wisdom. The system adopted was her own system. She knew, for she had tried and proved its value. It was the old fashioned way of surveying lands, before the issuing of any title papers, and then of inserting accurate and precise descriptions in the patents or grants, and proceeding with regular reference to metes and bounds. This gives to original titles, derived from Government, a certain and fixed character; it cuts up litigation by the roots, and the settler commences his labors with the assurance that he has a clear title. It is easy to perceive, but not easy to measure, the importance of this in a new country. New England gave this system to the West; and while it remains, there will be spread over all the West one monument of her intelligence in matters of government, and her practical good sense.

At the foundation of the constitution of these new Northwestern States, we are accustomed, sir, to praise the lawgivers of antiquity; we help to perpetuate the fame of Solon and Lycurgus; but I doubt whether one single law of any lawgiver, ancient or modern, has produced effects of more distinct, marked, and lasting character, than the ordinance of '87. That instrument was drawn by Nathan Dane, then, and now, a citizen of Massachusetts. It was adopted, as I think I have understood, without the slightest alteration; and certainly it has happened to few men, to be the authors of a political measure of more large and enduring consequence. It fixed, forever, the character of the population in the vast regions Northwest of the Ohio, by excluding from them involuntary servitude. It impressed on the soil itself, while it was yet a wilderness, an incapacity to bear up any other than free men. It laid the interdict against personal servitude, in original compact, not only deeper than all local law, but deeper, also, than all local constitutions. Under the circumstances then existing, I look upon this original and seasonable provision, as a real good attained. We see its consequences at this moment, and we shall never cease to see them, perhaps, while the Ohio shall flow. It was a great and salutary measure of prevention. Sir, I should fear the rebuke of no intelligent gentleman of Kentucky, were I to ask whether, if such an ordinance could have been applied to his own State, while it yet was a wilderness, and before Boone had passed the gap of the Alleghany, he does not suppose it would have contributed to the ultimate greatness of that Commonwealth? It is, at any rate, not to be doubted, that, where it did apply, it has produced an effect not easily to be described, or measured in the growth of the States, and the extent and increase of their population. Now, sir, this great measure again was carried by the North, and by the North alone. There were, indeed, individuals elsewhere favorable to it; but it was supported, as a measure, entirely by the votes of the Northern States. If New England had been governed by the narrow and selfish views now ascribed to her, this very measure was, of all others, the best calculated to thwart her purposes. It was, of all things, the very means of rendering certain a vast emigration from her own population to the West. She looked to that consequence only to disregard it. She deemed the regulation a most useful one to the States that would spring up on the territory, and advantageous to the country at large. She adhered to the principle of it perseveringly, year after year, until it was finally accomplished.

Leaving, then, sir, these two great and leading measures, and coming down to our own times, what is there in the history of recent measures of Government that exposes New England to this accusation of hostility to Western interests? I assert, boldly, that in all measures conducive to the welfare of the West, since my acquaintance here, no part of the country has manifested a more liberal policy. I beg to say, sir, that I do not state this with a view of claiming for her any special regard on that account. Not at all. She does not place her support of measures on the ground of favor conferred; far otherwise. What she has done has

been consonant to her view of the general good, and, therefore, she has done it. She has sought to make no gain of it; on the contrary, individuals may have felt, undoubtedly, some natural regret at finding the relative importance of their own States diminished by the growth of the West. But New England has regarded that as in the natural course of things, and has never complained of it. Let me see, sir, any one measure favorable to the West which has been opposed by New England, since the Government bestowed its attention to these Western improvements. Select what you will, if it be a measure of acknowledged utility, I answer for it, it will be found that not only were New England votes for it, but that New England votes carried it. Will you take the Cumberland Road? Who has made that? Will you take the Portland Canal? Whose support carried that bill? Sir, at what period beyond the Greek kalends could these measures, or measures like these, have been accomplished, had they depended on the votes of Southern gentlemen? Why, sir, we know that we must have waited till the constitutional notions of those gentlemen had undergone an entire change. Generally speaking, they have done nothing, and can do nothing. All that has been effected has been done by the votes of reproached New England. I undertake to say, sir, that if you look to the votes on any one of these measures, and strike out from the list of ayes the names of New England members, it will be found that in every case the South would then have voted down the West, and the measure would have failed. I do not believe that any one instance can be found where this is not strictly true. I do not believe that one dollar has been expended for these purposes beyond the mountains, which could have been obtained without cordial co-operation and support from New England. Sir, I put the gentleman to the West itself. Let gentlemen who have sat here ten years, come forth and declare by what aids, and by whose votes, they have succeeded in measures deemed of essential importance to their part of the country. To all men of sense and candor, in or out of Congress, who have any knowledge on the subject, New England may appeal, for refutation of the reproach now attempted to be cast upon her in this respect. I take liberty to repeat that I make no claim, on behalf of New England, or on account of that which I have not stated. She does not profess to have acted out of favor: for it would not have become her so to have acted. She solicits for no especial thanks; but, in the consciousness of having done her duty in these things, uprightly and honestly, and with a fair and liberal spirit, be assured she will repel, whenever she thinks the occasion calls for it, an unjust and groundless imputation of partiality and selfishness.

The gentleman alluded to a report of the late Secretary of the Treasury, which, according to his reading or construction of it, recommended what he called the tariff policy, or a branch of that policy; that is, the restraining of emigration to the West, for the purpose of keeping hands at home to carry on the manufactures. I think, sir, that the gentleman misapprehended the meaning of the Secretary, in the interpretation given to his remarks. I understand him only as saying, that, since the low price of lands at the West acts as a constant and standing bounty to agriculture, it is, on that account, the more reasonable to provide encouragement for manufactures. But, sir, even if the Secretary's observation were to be understood as the gentleman understands it, it would not be a sentiment borrowed from any New England source. Whether it be right or wrong, it does not originate in that quarter.

In the course of these remarks, I have spoken of the supposed desire, on the part of the Atlantic States, to check, or at least not to hasten, Western emigration, as a narrow policy. Perhaps I ought to have qualified the expression; because, sir, I am now about to quote the opinions of one to whom I would impute nothing narrow. I am now about to refer you to the language of a gentleman, of much and deserved distinction, now a member of the other House, and occupying a prominent situation there. The gentleman, sir, is from South Carolina. In 1825, a debate arose, in the House of Representatives, on the subject of the Western road. It happened to me to take some part in that debate. I was answered by the honorable gentleman to whom I have alluded; and I replied. May I be pardoned, sir, if I read a part of this debate?

"The gentleman from Massachusetts has urged, [said Mr. McDuffie] as one leading reason why the Governments should make roads to the West, that these roads have a tendency to settle the public lands; that they increase the inducements to settlement; and that this is a national object. Sir, I differ entirely from his views on the subject. I think that the public lands are settling quite fast enough; that our people need want no stimulus to urge them thither but want rather a check, at least on that artificial tendency to Western settlement which we have created by our own laws.

"The gentleman says that the great object of Government, with respect to those lands, is not to make them a source of revenue, but to get them settled. What would have been thought of this argument in the old thirteen States? It amounts to this, that these States are to offer a bonus for their own impoverishment—to create a vortex to swallow up our floating population. Look, sir, at the present aspect of the Southern States. In no part of Europe will you see the same indications of decay. Deserted villages, houses falling into ruin, impoverished lands thrown out of cultivation. Sir, I believe that, if the public lands had never been sold, the aggregate amount of the national wealth would have been greater at this moment. Our population, if concentrated in the old States, and not ground down by tariffs, would have been more prosperous and more wealthy. But every inducement has been held out to them to settle in the West, until our population has become sparse; and then the effects of this sparseness are now to be counteracted by another artificial system. Sir, I say if there is any object worthy the attention of this Government, it is a plan which shall limit the sale of the public lands. If those lands were sold according to their real value, be it so. But while the Government continues, as it now does, to give them away, they will draw the population of the older States, and still farther increase the effect which is already distressingly felt, and which must go to diminish the value of all those States possess. And this, sir, is held out to us as a motive for granting the present appropriation. I would not, indeed, prevent the formation of roads on these considerations, but I certainly would not encourage it. Sir, there is an additional item in the account of the benefits which this Government has conferred on the Western States. It is the sale of the public lands at the minimum price. At this moment we are selling to the people of the West, lands at one dollar and twenty-five cents an acre, which are fairly worth fifteen, and which would sell at that price if the markets were not glutted.

"Mr. W. observed, in reply, that the gentleman from South Carolina had mistaken him if he supposed that it was his wish so to hasten the sales of the public lands, as to throw them into the hands of purchasers who would sell again. His idea only went as far as this: that the price should be fixed as low as not to prevent the settlement of the lands, yet not so low as to tempt speculators to purchase. Mr. W. observed that he could not at all concur with the gentleman from South Carolina, in wishing to restrain the laboring classes of population in the Eastern States from going to any part of our territory, where they could better their condition; nor did he suppose that such an idea was any where entertained. The observations of the gentleman had opened to him new views of policy on their subject, and he thought he now could perceive why some of our States continued to have such bad roads; it must be for the purpose of preventing people from going out of them. The gentleman from South Carolina supposes that, if our population had been confined to the old thirteen States, the aggregate wealth of the country would have been greater than it now is. But, sir, it is an error that the increase of the aggregate of the national wealth is the object chiefly to be pursued by Government. The distribution of the national wealth is an object quite as important as its increase. He was not surprised that the old States were not increasing in population so fast as was expected (for he believed nothing like a decrease was pretended) should be an idea by no means agreeable to gentlemen from those States; we are all reluctant in submitting to the loss of relative importance: but this was nothing more than the natural condition of a country densely populated in one part, and possessing, in another, a vast tract of unsettled lands. The plan of the gentleman went to reverse the order of nature, vainly expecting to retain men within a small and comparatively unproductive territory, 'who have all the world before them where to choose.' For his own part, he was in favor of letting population take its own course; he should experience no feeling of mortification if any of his constituents liked better to settle on the Kansas, or the Arkansas, or the Lord knows where, within our territory; let them go, and be happier, if they could. The gentleman says our aggregate of wealth would have been greater, if our population had been restrained within the limits of the old States; but does he not consider population to be wealth? And has not this been increased by the settlement of a new and fertile country? Such a country presents the most alluring of all prospects to a young and laboring man; it gives him a freehold; it offers to him weight and respectability in society; and, above all, it presents to him a prospect of a permanent provision for his children. Sir, these are inducements which never were resisted, and never will be; and, were the whole extent of country filled with population up to the Rocky Mountains, these inducements would carry that population forward to the shores of the Pacific Ocean. Sir, it is in vain to

talk; individuals will seek their own good, and not any artificial aggregate of the national wealth. A young, enterprising, and hardy agriculturist can conceive of nothing better to him than plenty of good, cheap land."

Sir, with the reading of these extracts, I leave the subject. The Senate will bear me witness that I am not accustomed to allude to local opinions, nor to compare nor contrast different portions of the country. I have often suffered things to pass which I might, properly enough, have considered as deserving a remark, without any observation. But I have felt it my duty, on this occasion, to vindicate the State I represent from charges and imputations on her public character and conduct, which I know to be undeserved and unfounded. If advanced elsewhere, they might be passed, perhaps, without notice. But whatever is said here, is supposed to be entitled to public regard, and to deserve public attention; it derives importance and dignity from the place where it is uttered. As a true Representative of the State which has sent me here, it is my duty, and a duty which I shall fulfil, to place her history and her conduct, her honor and her character, in their just and proper light, so often as I think an attack is made upon her so respectable as to deserve to be repelled.

Speech of Mr. Hayne, of South Carolina

The resolution of Mr. Foot, of Connecticut, relative to the public lands, being under consideration, Mr. Hayne addressed the Chair as follows:

I do not rise at this late hour,[*] Mr. President, to go at large into the controverted questions between the Senator from Massachusetts and myself, but merely to correct some very gross errors into which he has fallen, and to afford explanations on some points, which, after what has fallen from that gentleman, may perhaps be considered as requiring explanation. The gentleman has attempted, through the whole course of his argument, to throw upon me the blame of having provoked this discussion. Though stand-

[*] The lateness of the hour when Mr. W. resumed his seat, compelled Mr. H. to curtail his remarks in reply, especially those which related to the Constitutional question. In the Speech as here reported, the arguments omitted are supplied. The great importance of the question, makes it desirable, that nothing should be omitted necessary to its elucidation.

ing himself at the very head and source of this angry controversy, which has flowed from him down to me, he insists that I have troubled the waters. In order to give color to this charge, (wholly unfounded, Sir, as every gentleman of this body will bear witness,) he alludes to my excitement when I first rose to answer the gentleman, after he had made his attack upon the South. He charges me with having then confessed that I had something rankling in my bosom which I desired to discharge. Sir, I have no recollection of having used that word. If it did escape me, however, in the excitement of the moment, it was not indicative of any personal hostility towards that Senator—for in truth, Sir, I felt none—but proceeded from a sensibility, which could not but be excited by what I had a right to consider as an unprovoked and most unwarrantable attack upon the South, through me.

The gentleman boasts that he has escaped unhurt in the conflict. The shaft, it seems, was shot by too feeble an arm to reach its destination. Sir, I am glad to hear this. Judging from the *actions* of the gentleman, I had feared that the arrow had penetrated even more deeply than I could have wished. From the beating of his breast, and the tone and manner of the gentleman, I should fear he *is* most sorely wounded. In a better spirit, however, I will say, I hope his wounds may heal kindly, and leave no scars behind; and let me assure the gentleman, that however deeply the arrow may have penetrated, its point was not envenomed. It was shot in fair and manly fight, and with the twang of the bow, have fled the feelings which impelled it. The gentleman indignantly repels the charge of having avoided the Senator from Missouri, (Mr. BENTON) and selected me as his adversary, from any apprehension of being overmatched. Sir, when I found the gentleman passing over in silence the arguments of the Senator from Missouri, which had charged the East with hostility towards the West, and directing his artillery against me, who had made no such charge, I had a right to inquire into the causes of so extraordinary a proceeding. I suggested some as probable, and among them, that to which the gentleman takes such strong exception. Sir, has he now given any sufficient reason for the extraordinary course of which I have complained? At one moment he tells us that "he did not hear the whole of the argument of the gentleman from Missouri," and again, "that having found a responsible indorser of the bill, he did not think proper to pursue the drawer." Well, Sir, if the gentleman answered the arguments which he did not hear, why attribute them to me, whom he did hear, and by whom they were certainly not urged? If he was determined to pursue the parties to the bill, why attempt to throw the responsibility on one who was neither the drawer nor the indorser? Let me once more, Sir, put this matter on its true footing. I will not be forced to assume a position in which I have not chosen to place myself. Sir, I disclaim any intention whatever in my original remarks on the public lands, to impute to the East hostility towards the West. I imputed none. I did not utter one word to that effect. I said nothing that could be tortured into an attack upon the East.

I did not mention the "accursed tariff"—a phrase which the gentleman has put into my mouth. I did not even impute the policy of Mr. Rush to New England. In alluding to that policy I noticed its source, and spoke of it as I thought it deserved. Sir, I am aware that a gentleman who rises without premeditation, to throw out his ideas on a question before the House, may use expressions of the force and extent of which he may, at the time, not be fully aware. I should not, therefore, rely so confidently on my own recollections, but for the circumstance, that I have not found one gentleman who heard my remarks, [except the Senator from Massachusetts himself,] who supposed that one word had fallen from my lips that called for a reply of the tone and character of that which the gentleman from Massachusetts thought proper to pronounce—not one, who supposed that I had thrown out any imputations against the East, or justly subjected myself or the South to rebuke, unless, indeed, the principles for which I contended were so monstrous, as to demand unmeasured reprobation. Now, Sir, what were those principles? I have already shown, that, whether sound or unsound, they are not separated by a "hair's breadth" from those contended for by the gentleman himself in 1825, and, therefore, that he, of all men, had the least right to take exception to them.

Sir, the gentleman charges me with having unnecessarily introduced the slave question; with what justice, let those determine who heard that gentleman pointing out the superiority of Ohio over Kentucky, and attributing it to that happy stroke of New England policy, by which slavery was forever excluded North of the Ohio river. Sir, I was wholly at a loss to conceive why that topic had been introduced here at all, until the gentleman followed it up by an attack upon the principles and policy of the South. When that was done, the object was apparent, and it became my duty to take up the gauntlet which the gentleman had thrown down, and to come out, without reserve, in defence of our institutions, and our principles. The gentleman charges us with a morbid sensibility on this subject. Sir, it is natural and proper that we should be sensitive on that topic, and we must continue so, just so long as those who do not live among us, shall be found meddling with a subject, with which they have nothing to do, and about which they know nothing. But, Sir, we will agree, now, henceforth, and forever, to avoid the subject altogether, never even to mention the word *slavery* on this floor, if gentlemen on the other side will only consent not to intrude it upon us, by forcing it unnecessarily into debate. When introduced, however, whether by a hint, or a sneer, by the imputation of weakness to slave holding States, or in any other way, we must be governed entirely by our own discretion, as to the manner in which the attack must be met. When the proposition was made here, to appropriate the public lands to emancipation, I met it with a protest. I have now met an attack of a different character by an argument.

The gentleman in alluding to the Hartford Convention, told us that he had nothing to do with it, and had nothing to say either for or against it, and yet he undertook, at the same time, to recommend that renowned assembly as a precedent to the South.

Sir, unkind as my allusion to the Hartford Convention has been considered by its supporters, I apprehend that this disclaimer of the gentleman's will be regarded as "the unkindest cut of all." When the gentleman spoke of the Carolina Conventions, of Colleton and Abbeville, let me tell him, that he spoke of that which never had existence, except in his own imagination. There have, indeed, been meetings of the people in those districts, composed Sir, of as high-minded and patriotic men as any country can boast of; but we have had no "convention" as yet; and when South Carolina shall resort to such a measure for the redress of her grievances, let me tell the gentleman that, of all the assemblies that have ever been convened in this country, the Hartford Convention is the very last we shall consent to take as an example; nor will it find more favor in our eyes, from being recommended to us by the Senator from Massachusetts. Sir, we would scorn to take advantage of difficulties created by a foreign war, to wring from the federal government a redress even of our griev-

ances. We are standing up for our constitutional rights in a time of profound peace; but if the country should, unhappily be involved in a war tomorrow, we should be found flying to the standard of our country—first driving back the common enemy, and then insisting upon the restoration of our rights.

The gentleman, speaking of the tariff and internal improvements, said, that in supporting these measures, he had but followed "a Carolina lead." He also quoted, with high encomium, the opinion of the present Chairman of the Committee of Ways and Means, of the other House, in relation to the latter subject. Now, Sir, it is proper that the Senator from Massachusetts should be, once for all, informed, that South Carolina acknowledges no leaders, whom she is willing blindly to follow, in any course of policy. The "Carolina doctrines" in relation to the "American system," have been expounded to us by the resolutions of her legislature, and the remonstrances of her citizens, now upon your table; and when the gentleman shows us one of her distinguished sons expressing different sentiments, he neither changes her principles, nor subjects the State to a charge of inconsistency. Sir, no man can entertain a higher respect than I do, for the distinguished talents, high character, and manly independence of the gentleman alluded to, (Mr. McDuffie;) but if he now entertains the opinions attributed to him, in relation to internal improvements and the public lands, there can be no doubt that his sentiments, in these respects, differ widely from those of a large majority of the people of South Carolina; while in relation to the tariff, and other questions of vital importance, he not only goes heart and hand with us, but is himself a host.

The gentleman considers the tariff of 1816, and the bonus bill, as the foundations of the American system, and intimates, that the former would not have prevailed, but for South Carolina votes. Now, Sir, as to the Tariff of 1816, I think a great mistake prevails throughout the country, in regarding it as the commencement of the existing policy. That was not a bill for *increasing*, but for *reducing duties*. During the war, double duties had been resorted to, for raising the revenue necessary for its prosecution. Manufactures had sprung up under the protection incidentally afforded by the restrictive measures, and the war.—On the restoration of peace, a scale of duties was to be established, adapted to the situation in which the country was, by that event, placed. All agreed that the duties were to be reduced, and that this reduction must be gradual. We had a debt on our hands of $140 or $150,000,000. Admonished by recent experience, a Navy was to be built up, and an extensive system of fortifications to be commenced. The operation, too, of a sudden reduction of duties upon the manufactures which had been forced into existence by the war, and which then bore their full proportion of the direct taxes, was also to be taken into consideration; and under all of these circumstances, it was determined to reduce the duties gradually, until they should reach the lowest amount necessary for revenue in time of peace. Such, Sir, was the true character of the tariff law of 1816. By that bill (reported, Sir, by the lamented Lowndes, a steady opponent of the protecting system,) the duties on woollen and cotton goods were at once *reduced* to 25 per cent, with a provision, that they should, in the course of three years, *be further reduced* to twenty per cent., while, by the tariff of 1824, the duties on the same articles were at once *increased* to 30 per cent., and were to go on increasing to 37½ per cent.; and by the tariff of 1828, have been carried much higher. And yet the tariff of 1816 is now quoted as an authority for the tariffs of 1824 and 1828; by which, duties admitted to be already high enough for all the purposes of revenue, are to go on increasing, year after year, for the avowed purpose of promoting domestic manufactures, by preventing importations. Suppose, Sir, the New England gentlemen were now to join the South in going back to a tariff for revenue, and were to propose to us gradually to reduce all the existing duties, so that they should come down, in two or three years, to fifteen or twenty per cent —would the gentleman consider us as sending in our adhesion to the American system, by voting for such a reduction? And if not, how can he charge the supporters of the tariff of 1816 with being the fathers of that system? In this view of the subject, it is not at all material, whether the Representatives from South Carolina voted for that measure or not; or whether the passage of the bill depended on their votes. On looking into the journals, however, it will be found that the bill actually passed the House of Representatives, by a vote of 88 to 54; and would have succeeded, if every member from South Carolina had voted against it.

The gentleman next mentions the "Bonus Bill" as the first step in the system of Internal Improvement. That was a bill, Sir, not appropriating, but setting apart a fixed sum (the Bank Bonus) for Internal Improvements, to be dis-

tributed among the States, on principles of perfect equality, and to be applied "by consent of the States" themselves. Though Mr. Madison put his veto on that bill, it was supposed, at the time, to be in the spirit of his own message; and though I must express my dissent from the measure, no doubt can exist, that if the system of Internal Improvement had been prosecuted on the principles of that bill, much of the inequality and injustice that have since taken place would have been avoided. But, Sir, I am by no means disposed to deny, or to conceal the fact, that a considerable change has taken place in the Southern States, and in South Carolina in particular, in relation to Internal Improvements, since that measure was first broached, at the close of the last war. Sir, when we were restored to a state of peace, the attention of our prominent statesmen was directed to plans for the restoration of the country from the wounds of the war, and the public mind received a strong impulse towards Internal Improvements. The minds of the eminent men of the South had, by the events of that war, received for the time a direction rather favorable to the enlargement of the powers of the Government. They had seen the public arm paralyzed by the opposition to that war, and it was quite natural that they should at that time rather be disposed to strengthen than to weaken the powers of the Federal Government. Internal Improvements sprang up in that heated soil, and I have no doubt that as a new question, hardly examined, and very little understood, the people of the South, for a short period, took up the belief that, to a certain extent, and under certain guards, the system could be beneficially and constitutionally pursued. But, Sir, before time had been allowed for the formation of any fixed and settled opinions, the evils of the system were so fully developed, the injustice, the inequality, the corruption flowing from it, and the alarming extent of powers claimed for the Federal Government by its supporters, became so manifest, as thoroughly to satisfy the South, that the system of Internal Improvement, on the principles on which it was to be administered, was not only unequal and unjust, but a most alarming innovation on the Constitution.

The gentleman has alluded to my own vote on the survey bill of 1824. Sir, I have to return him my thanks for having afforded me, by that allusion, an opportunity of explaining my conduct in relation to the system of Internal Improvements. At the time that I was called to a seat in this

House, I had been for many years removed from political life, and engaged in the arduous pursuit of a profession, which abstracted me almost entirely from the examination of political questions. The gentleman tells us he had not made up his own mind on this subject as late as 1817. Sir, I had not even fully examined it in 1823. But even at that time, I entertained doubts, both as to the constitutionality and expediency of the system. I came here with these feelings, and before I was yet warm in my seat, the survey bill of 1824 was brought up. We were then expressly told by its advocates, that its object was not to establish a system of Internal Improvements, but merely to present to Congress and the country a full view of the whole ground, leaving it hereafter to be decided whether the system should be prosecuted, and if so, on what principles? Sir, I was induced to believe, that no great work would be undertaken until the objects of that survey bill should be accomplished—that is to say, until the President should submit the whole scheme in one connected view, so that we should have before us at once all the measures deemed to be of "national importance," to which the attention of Congress might be directed.

Sir, I did suppose that a few great works, in which all the States would have a common interest, and which might therefore be considered as of "national importance," were alone intended to be embraced in that bill, and that in one or two years, the whole of the surveys would be completed, when Congress would have it in their power to decide whether the system should be carried on at all, and if so, on what principles. Sir, I know that more than one gentleman who voted for the survey bill of 1824, expressly stated at the time, that they did not intend to commit themselves on the general question; and I was one of that number. And it was expressly because I did not consider that bill, as committing those who supported it, for or against any system of Internal Improvement, that I voted against every amendment, calculated to give any expression of opinion, one way or the other. I was unwilling to deprive it of the character which it bore on its face, as a measure intended merely to bring before the public in a single view, the entire scheme, so as to enable us to judge of its practicability and expediency. Sir, in all these views and expectations, I was deceived. By the year 1826, it came to be fully understood that these surveys were never to be finished, and that $50,000 per annum was to be appropriated, merely to give popularity to the system, by feeding the hopes of the people in all parts of the country. In the mean time, too, appropriations were made and new works commenced, just as if no surveys were going on. Sir, as soon as I discovered the true character of the survey bill, I opposed it openly on this floor, and have since constantly voted against all appropriations for surveys. Sir, as to the system of Internal Improvement, my first impressions against it were fully confirmed, very soon after I took my seat here, and (except in cases which I consider as exceptions from the general rule,) I have uniformly voted against all appropriations for Internal Improvements, against the Cumberland Road, the Chesapeake and Delaware Canal, and all other works of a similar character. But Sir, if the South, or the statesmen of the South, had committed themselves ever so deeply on this subject, does the gentleman from Massachusetts suppose it would afford any excuse for their continued support of a system conducted on principles which now manifestly appear to be as unconstitutional as they are unequal and unjust? Surely not.

The gentleman has made his defence for his conduct in relation to the tariff of 1828. He considers the country as being committed by the tariff of 1824 to go on with the system. Sir, we wholly deny that the country is in any way committed, or that Congress could commit it on such a subject, much less to the support of a ruinous, unjust, and unconstitutional policy. But how, if such a committal were possible, could the imposition of a duty of 20 or 30 per cent. commit us to the imposition of duties of 50 or 100? The gentleman is mistaken in supposing that I charged him with having, in 1820, denounced the tariff as "utterly unconstitutional;" I stated that he had called its constitutionality in question. I have now before me the proceedings of the Boston meeting, to which I referred, and will read them, that there may be no mistake on the subject. In the resolutions reported by a committee, (of which Mr. W. was a member,) it was, among other things,

1. "*Resolved,* That no objection ought ever to be made to any amount of taxes equally apportioned, and imposed for the purpose of raising revenue, necessary for the support of government, but that taxes imposed on the people, for the benefit of any one class of men, (the manufacturers,) are equally inconsistent with *the principles of the Constitution,* and with sound policy."

2. "*Resolved,* That, in our opinion, the proposed tariff,

and the principles on which it is avowedly founded, would, if adopted, have a tendency, however different may be the motives of those who recommend them, to diminish the industry, impede the prosperity, and corrupt the morals of the people."

In support of these anti-tariff resolutions, (which were unanimously adopted,) Mr. Webster said:

"There is a power in names; and those who had pressed the tariff on Congress, and on the country, had represented it as immediately, and almost exclusively, connected with *domestic industry,* and national independence. In his opinion, no measure could prove more injurious to the industry of the country, and nothing was more fanciful than the opinion that national independence rendered such a measure necessary. He certainly thought it might be doubted, whether Congress would not be acting somewhat against *the spirit and intention of the Constitution,* in exercising the power to control essentially the pursuits and occupations of individuals, not as incidental to the exercise of any other power, but as a substantial and direct power. If such changes were wrought incidentally only, and were the necessary consequence of such impost as Congress, for the leading purpose of revenue, should enact, then they could not be complained of. But he doubted whether Congress fairly possessed the power of turning the incident into the principal; and instead of leaving manufactures to the protection of such laws as should be passed with a primary regard to revenue, of enacting laws, with the avowed object of giving a preference to particular manufactures, &c."

Sir, these are good sound "South Carolina doctrines," and if the gentleman finds reason to abandon them now, we cannot consent to go with him.

We have been often reproached, Sir, with lending our aid to some of the most obnoxious provisions of the Tariff of 1828. What was the fact? Not an amendment was put into that bill here, which did not go to reduce the duties. That bill came to the Senate in a form in which it was known that it could not pass. Gentlemen who would not vote for it, in that shape,—but who wished it to pass, called upon us to aid them in amending it, to suit their own purposes. Sir, if we had lent our aid to such an object, we would have deserved any fate that could have befallen us. We proceeded throughout on the open and avowed ground of hostility to the whole system, and acted accordingly.

To disprove my observations, that the New England members, generally, did not support *Internal Improvements* in the west, before that memorable era, the winter of 1825, the gentleman quoted two votes in 1820 and 1821, reducing the price, or extending the time of payment for the *Public Lands.* Now, Sir, the only objection to his authority, is, that it has no manner of relation to the point in dispute. I stated that New England did not support Internal Improvements, as a branch of the American system, before 1825. The gentleman proves, that on two occasions, they voted for certain measures in relation to the Public Lands—measures which I had always supposed had been forced upon Congress by motives of interest,—but which, whatever may have been their character, do not touch the point in dispute in the smallest degree. I think this mode of meeting my argument, however creditable to the gentleman's ingenuity, amounts to an acknowledgment that it is unanswerable.

The gentleman complains of his arguments having been misunderstood in relation to consolidation. He thinks my misapprehension almost miraculous in treating his as an argument in favor of the "consolidation of the government." Now, Sir, what was the point in dispute between us? I had deprecated the consolidation of the government. I said not one word against "the consolidation of the Union." I went further, and pointed out and deprecated some of the means, by which this consolidation was to be brought about. The gentleman gets up and attacks me and my argument at every point, ridicules our fears about "consolidation," and finally reads a passage from a letter of General Washington's, stating that one of the objects of the Constitution was, "the consolidation of the Union." Surely, Sir, under these circumstances, I was not mistaken in saying, that the authority quoted did not apply to the case, as the point in dispute was the "consolidation of the government," and not of "the Union." But, Sir, the gentleman has relieved me from all embarrassment on this point, by going fully into the examination of the Virginia doctrines of '98, and while he denounces them, giving us his own views of the powers of the Federal Government; views which, in my humble judgment, stop nothing short of the consolidation of all power in the hands of the Federal Government. Sir, when I last touched on this topic, I did little more than quote the high authorities on which our doctrines rest; but after the elaborate argument which we have just heard from the gentleman from Massachusetts, it cannot be supposed, that I can suffer them to go to the world unanswered. I entreat the Senate therefore to bear with me, while I go over as briefly as possible *the most prominent arguments of the gentleman.*

The proposition which I laid down and from which the gentleman dissents, is taken from the Virginia resolutions of '98, and is in these words, "that in case of a deliberate, palpable, and dangerous exercise by the Federal Government *of powers not granted* by the compact [the constitution] the States who are parties thereto, *have a right to interpose,* for arresting the progress of the evil, and for maintaining within their respective limits, the authorities, rights and liberties appertaining to them." The gentleman insists that the States have no right to decide whether the constitution has been violated by acts of Congress or not,—but *that the Federal Government is the exclusive judge of the extent of its own powers;* and that in case of a violation of the constitution, however "deliberate, palpable and dangerous," a State has no constitutional redress, except where the matter can be brought before the Supreme Court, whose decision must be final and conclusive on the subject. Having thus distinctly stated the points in dispute between the gentleman and myself, I proceed to examine them. And here it will be necessary to go back to the origin of the Federal Government. It cannot be doubted, and is not denied, that before the formation of the constitution, each State was an independent sovereignty, possessing all the rights and powers appertaining to independent nations; nor can it be denied that, after the constitution was formed, they remained equally sovereign and independent, as to all powers, not expressly delegated to the Federal Government. This would have been the case even if no positive provision to that effect had been inserted in that instrument. But to remove all doubt it is expressly declared, by the 10th article of the amendment of the constitution, "that the powers not delegated to the States, by the constitution, nor prohibited by it to the States, are reserved to the States respectively, or to the people." The true nature of the Federal constitution, therefore, is, (in the language of Mr. Madison,) "a compact to which the States are parties," a compact by which each State, acting in its sovereign capacity, has entered into an agreement with the other States, by which they have consented that certain designated powers shall be exercised by the United States, in the manner prescribed in the instrument. Nothing can be clearer, than that, under such a system, the Federal Government, exercising strictly delegated powers, can have no right to act beyond the pale of its authority; and that all such acts are void. A State, on the contrary, retaining all powers not expressly given away, may lawfully act in all cases where she has not voluntarily imposed restrictions on herself. Here then is a case of a compact between sovereigns, and the question arises—what is the remedy for a clear violation of its express terms by one of the parties? And here the plain obvious dictate of common sense, is in strict conformity with the understanding of mankind, and the practice of nations in all analogous cases—"that where resort can be had to no common superior, the parties to the compact must, themselves, be the rightful judges whether the bargain has been pursued or violated." (Madison's Report, p. 20.) When it is insisted by the gentleman that one of the parties "has the power of deciding ultimately and conclusively upon the extent of its own authority," I ask for the grant of such a power. I call upon the gentleman to shew it to me in the constitution. It is not to be found there. If it is to be inferred from the nature of the compact, I aver, that not a single argument can be urged in support of such an inference, in favor of the United States, which would not apply, with at least equal force, in favor of a State. All sovereigns are of necessity equal, and any one State, however small in population or territory, has the same rights as the rest, just as the most insignificant nation in Europe is as much sovereign as France, or Russia, or England.

The very idea of a division of power by compact, is destroyed by a right claimed and exercised by either to be the exclusive interpreter of the instrument. Power is not divided, where one of the parties can arbitrarily determine its limits. A compact between two, with a right reserved to one, to expound the instrument according to his own pleasure, is no compact at all, but an absolute surrender of the whole subject matter to the arbitrary discretion of the party who is constituted the judge. This is so obvious, that, in the conduct of human affairs between man and man, a common superior is always looked to as the expounder of contracts. But if there be no common superior, it results, from the very nature of things, that the parties *must be their own judges.* This is admitted to be the case where treaties are formed between independent nations, and if the same rule does not apply to the federal compact, it must be because the Federal is superior to the State Government, or because the States have surrendered their sovereignty. Neither branch of this proposition can be maintained for a moment. I have already shewn that all sovereigns must, as such, be equal. It only remains, therefore, to inquire whether the States have surrendered their sovereignty, and consented to reduce themselves to mere corporations. The whole form and structure of the Federal Government, the opinions of the framers of the Constitution, and the organization of the State Governments, demonstrate that though the States have surrendered certain specific powers, they have not surrendered their sovereignty. They have each an independent Legislature, Executive, and Judiciary, and exercise jurisdiction over the lives and property of their citizens. They have, it is true, voluntarily restrained themselves from doing certain acts, but, in all other respects, they are as omnipotent as any independent nation whatever. Here, however, we are met by the argument that the Constitution was not formed by *the States,* in their sovereign capacity, but by *the People,* and it is therefore inferred that the Federal Government, being created by all the People, must be supreme, and though it is not contended that the Constitution may be rightfully violated, yet it is insisted that from the decisions of the Federal Government there can be no appeal. It is obvious that this argument rests on the idea of State inferiority. Considering the Federal Government as one whole, and the States merely as component parts, it follows, of course, that the former is as much superior to the latter, as the whole is to the parts of which it is composed. Instead of deriving power by delegation from the States to the Union, this scheme seems to imply that the individual States derive their power from the United States, just as petty corporations may exercise so much power, and no more, as their superior may permit them to enjoy. This notion is entirely at variance with all our conceptions of State rights, as those rights were understood by Mr. Madison and others, at the time the Constitution was framed. I deny that the Constitution was framed by the People in the sense in which that word is used on the other side, and insist that it was framed by the States acting in their sovereign capacity. When, in the preamble of the Constitution, we find the words "we, the People of the United States," it is clear, they can only relate to the People as citizens of the several States, because the Federal Government was not then in existence.

We accordingly find, in every part of that instrument, that the people are always spoken of in that sense. Thus, in the 2d section of the 1st article, it is declared, "That the House of Representatives shall be composed of members chosen every second year, by the people of the several States." To show, that, in entering into this compact, the States acted in their sovereign capacity, and not merely as parts of one great community, what can be more conclusive than the historical fact, that, when every State had consented to it except one, she was not held to be bound. A majority of the people in any State bound that State, but nine-tenths of all the people of the United States could not bind the people of Rhode Island, until Rhode Island, as a State, had consented to the compact. It cannot be denied, that, at the time the Constitution was framed, the people of the United States were members of regularly organized governments, citizens of independent States; and, unless these State governments had been dissolved, it was impossible that the people could have entered into any compact but as citizens of these States. Suppose an assent to the Constitution had been given by all the people within a certain district of any State, but that the State, in its sovereign capacity, had refused its assent, would the people of that district have become citizens of the United States? Surely not. It is clear, then, that, in adopting the Constitution, the people did not act, and could not have acted in any other character than as citizens of their respective states. And if, on the adoption of the Constitution, they became citizens of the United States, it was only by virtue of that clause in the Constitution which declares "that the citizens of each State shall be entitled to all the privileges and immunities of citizens of the several States." In choosing members to the Convention, the States acted through their Legislatures, by whose authority the Constitution, when framed, was submitted for ratification to Conventions of the People, the usual and most appropriate organ of the sovereign will. I am not disposed to dwell longer on this point, which does appear to my mind to be too clear to admit of controversy. But I will quote from Mr. Madison's report, which goes the whole length in support of the doctrines for which I have contended:

"The other position involved in this branch of the resolution, namely, 'that the States are parties to the Constitution or compact,' is, in the judgment of the committee, equally free from objection. It is, indeed, true, that the term 'States' is sometimes used in a vague sense, and sometimes in different senses, according to the subject to which it is applied. Thus, it sometimes means the separate sections of territory occupied by the political societies within each; sometimes the particular governments established by those societies; sometimes those societies as organized into those particular governments; and, lastly, it means *the people composing those political societies, in their highest sovereign capacity.* Although it might be wished that the perfection of language admitted less diversity in the signification of the same words, yet little inconvenience is produced by it, where the true sense can be collected with certainty from the different applications. In the present instance, whatever different constructions of the term 'States,' in the resolution, may have been entertained, all will at least concur in that last mentioned; because, in that sense the Constitution was submitted to the 'States'; in that sense the 'States' ratified it; and in that sense of the term 'States,' they are consequently parties to the compact, from which the powers of the Federal Government result."

Having now established the position that the Constitution was a compact between sovereign and independent States, having no common superior, "it follows of necessity," (to borrow the language of Mr. Madison,) "that there can be no tribunal above their authority to decide in the last resort, whether the compact made by them be violated, and consequently, that, as the parties to it, they must themselves decide, in the last resort, such questions as may be of sufficient magnitude to require their interposition."

But, the gentleman insists that the tribunal provided by the Constitution, for the decision of controversies between the States and the Federal Government, is the Supreme Court. And here again I call for the authority on which the gentleman rests the assertion, that the Supreme Court has any jurisdiction whatever over questions of sovereignty between the States and the United States. When we look into the Constitution, we do not find it there. I put entirely out of view any act of Congress on the subject. We are not looking into the laws, but the Constitution.

It is clear that questions of sovereignty are not the proper subjects of *judicial investigation.* They are much too large, and of too delicate a nature, to be brought within the jurisdiction of a Court of justice. Courts, whether supreme or subordinate, are the mere creatures of the sovereign power, designed to expound and carry into effect its sovereign will. No independent state ever yet submitted to a Judge on the bench the true construction of a compact between itself and another sovereign. All Courts may incidentally take cognizance of treaties, where rights are claimed under them, but who ever heard of a Court making an inquiry into the authority of the agents of the high contracting parties to make the treaty,—whether its terms had been fulfilled, or whether it had become void, on account of a breach of its condition on either side? All these are political, and not judicial questions. Some reliance has been placed on those provisions of the Constitution which constitute "one Supreme Court," which provide, "that the judicial power shall extend to all cases in law and equity arising under this Constitution, the laws of the United States and treaties," and which declare "that the Constitution, and the laws of the United States *which shall be made in pursuance thereof,* and all treaties, &c. shall be the supreme law of the land," &c. Now, as to the name of the *Supreme Court,* it is clear that the term has relation only to its supremacy over the inferior Courts provided for by the Constitution, and has no reference whatever to any supremacy over the sovereign States. The words are, "the judicial power of the United States shall be vested in one Supreme Court, and such inferior Courts as Congress may from time to time establish," &c. Though jurisdiction is given "in cases arising under the Constitution," yet it is expressly limited to "cases in law and equity," shewing conclusively that this jurisdiction was incidental merely to the ordinary administration of justice, and not intended to touch high questions of conflicting sovereignty. When it is declared that the Constitution and the laws of the United States "made in pursuance thereof, shall be the supreme law of the land," it is manifest that no indication is given either as to the power of the Supreme Court, to bind the States by its decisions, nor as to the *course to be pursued in the event of laws being passed not in pursuance of the Constitution.* And I beg leave to call gentlemen's attention to the striking fact, that the powers of the Supreme Court in relation to questions arising under "the laws and the Constitution," are co-extensive with those arising under treaties. In all of these cases the power is limited to questions arising "in law and equity," that is to say, to cases where jurisdiction is incidentally acquired in the ordinary administration of justice. But as with regard to treaties, the Supreme Court has never assumed jurisdiction over questions arising between the sovereigns who are parties to it; so under the Constitution, they cannot assume jurisdiction over questions arising between the individual States and the United States.

If they should do so, they would be acting entirely out of their sphere. *Umpires* are indeed sometimes appointed by special agreement; but in the case before us, there can be no pretence that the Supreme Court have been specially constituted umpires. But if the Judiciary are, from their character and the peculiar scope of their duties, unfit for the high office of deciding questions of sovereignty, much more strongly is the Supreme Court disqualified from assuming the umpirage between the States and the United States, because it is created by, and is indeed merely one of the departments of the Federal Government. The United States have a Supreme Court; each State has also a Supreme Court. Both of them, in the ordinary administration of justice, must, of necessity, decide on the constitutionality of laws; but when it becomes a question of sovereignty between these two independent Governments, the subject matter is equally removed from the jurisdiction of both. If the Supreme Court of the United States can take cognizance of such a question, so can the Supreme Courts of the States. But, Sir, can it be supposed for a moment, that when the States proceeded to enter into the compact, called the Constitution of the United States, they could have designed, nay, that they could, under any circumstances, have consented to leave to a court to be created by the Federal Government the power to decide, finally, on the extent of the powers of the latter, and the limitations on the powers of the former. If it had been designed to do so, it would have been so declared, and assuredly some provision would have been made to secure, as umpires, a tribunal somewhat differently constituted from that whose appropriate duty is the ordinary administration of justice. But to prove, as I think, conclusively, that the Judiciary were not designed to act as umpires, it is only necessary to observe that, in a great majority of cases, that court could manifestly not take jurisdiction of the matters in dispute. Whenever it may be designed by the Federal Government to commit a violation of the Constitution, it can be done, and always will be done in such a manner as to deprive the court of all jurisdiction over the subject. Take the case of the Tariff and Internal Improvements, whether constitutional or unconstitutional, it is admitted that the Supreme Court *have no jurisdiction.* Suppose Congress should, for the acknowledged purpose of making an equal distribution of the property of the country, among States or individuals, proceed to lay taxes to the amount of $50,000,000 a year. Could the Supreme Court take cognizance of the act laying the tax, or making the distribution? Certainly not.

Take another case which is very likely to occur. Congress have the *unlimited power of taxation.* Suppose them also to assume an *unlimited power of appropriation.* Appropriations of money are made to establish presses, promote education, build and support churches, create an order of nobility, or for any other unconstitutional object; it is manifest that, in none of these cases, could the constitutionality of the laws making those grants be tested before the Supreme Court. It would be in vain, that a State should come before the Judges with an act appropriating money to any of these objects, and ask of the Court to decide whether these grants were constitutional. They could not even be heard; the Court would say, they had nothing to do with it; and they would say rightly. It is idle, therefore, to talk of the Supreme Court affording any security to the States, in cases where their rights may be violated by the exercise of unconstitutional powers on the part of the Federal Government. On this subject Mr. Madison, in his report says: "But it is objected, that the judicial authority is to be regarded as the sole expositor of the Constitution in the last resort; and it may be asked, for what reason, the declaration by the General Assembly, supposing it to be theoretically true, could be required at the present day, and in so solemn a manner.

"On this objection it might be observed, first: that there may be instances of usurped power, which the forms of the Constitution would never draw within the control of the Judicial Department: Secondly, that if the decision of the Judiciary be raised above the authority of the sovereign parties to the Constitution, the decisions of the other Departments, not carried by the forms of the Constitution before the Judiciary, must be equally authoritative and final with the decisions of that Department. But the proper answer to the objection is, that the resolution of the General Assembly relates to those great and extraordinary cases in which all the forms of the Constitution may prove ineffectual against infractions dangerous to the essential rights of the parties to it. The resolution supposes that dangerous powers not delegated, may not only be usurped and executed by the other Departments, but that the Judicial Departments also, may exercise or sanction dangerous powers beyond the grant of the Constitution, and consequently, that the ultimate right of the parties to the Constitution to judge whether the compact has been dangerously violated, must extend to violations by one delegated authority, as well as by another—by the Judiciary, as well as by the Executive or Legislative.

"However true, therefore, it may be, that the Judicial Department is, in all questions submitted to it by the forms of the Constitution, to decide in the last resort, this resort must necessarily be deemed the last in relation to the authorities of the other Departments of the Government; not in relation *to the rights of the parties to the constitutional compact,* from which the judicial as well as the other Departments, hold their delegated trusts. On any other hypothesis, the delegation of Judicial power would annul the authority delegating it; and the concurrence of this Department with the others in usurped powers, might subvert forever, and beyond the possible reach *of any rightful remedy,* the very Constitution which all were instituted to preserve."

If, then, the Supreme Court are not, and from their organization, can not be the umpires in questions of conflicting sovereignty, the next point to be considered is, whether Congress themselves possess the right of deciding conclusively on the extent of their own powers. This, I know, is a popular notion, and it is founded on the idea, that as all the States are represented here, nothing can prevail which is not in conformity with the will of the majority—and it is supposed to be a republican maxim "that the majority must govern." Now, Sir, I admit that much care has been taken to secure the States and the People from rash and unadvised legislation. The organization of two houses, the one the representatives of the States, and the other of the people, manifest an anxiety to secure equality and justice in the operation of the Federal System. But all this has done no more than to secure us against any laws, but such as should be assented to by a majority of the representatives in the two Houses of Congress.

Now will any one contend that it is the true spirit of this Government, that the *will of a majority of Congress* should, in all cases, be *the supreme law?* If no security was intended to be provided for the rights of the States, and the liberty of the citizen, beyond the mere organization of the Federal Government, we should have had no written Constitution, but Congress would have been authorized to legislate for us, in all cases whatsoever; and the acts of our State Legislatures, like those of the present legislative councils in

the Territories, would have been subjected to the revision and control of Congress. If the will of a majority of Congress is to be the supreme law of the land, it is clear the Constitution is a dead letter, and has utterly failed of the very object for which it was designed—the protection of the rights of the minority. But when, by the very terms of the compact, strict limitations are imposed on every branch of the Federal Government, and it is, moreover, expressly declared, that all powers, not granted to them, "are reserved to the States or the People," with what show of reason can it be contended, that the Federal Government is to be the exclusive judge of the extent of its own powers? A *written Constitution* was resorted to in this country, as a great experiment, for the purpose of ascertaining how far the rights of a minority could be secured against the encroachments of majorities—often acting under party excitement, and not unfrequently under the influence of strong interests. The moment that Constitution was formed, the will of the majority ceased to be the law, except in cases that should be acknowledged by the parties to it to be *within the Constitution,* and to have been thereby submitted to their will. But when Congress, (exercising a delegated and strictly limited authority) pass beyond these limits, their acts become null and void; and must be declared to be so by the Courts, in cases within their jurisdiction; and may be pronounced to be so, by the States themselves, in cases not within the jurisdiction of the Courts, or of *sufficient importance to justify such an interference.* I will put the case strongly. Suppose, in the language of Mr. Jefferson, the Federal Government, in its three ruling branches, should, (at some future day,) be found "to be in combination to strip their colleagues, the State authorities, of the powers reserved by them, and to exercise themselves all powers, foreign and domestic," would there be no constitutional remedy against such an usurpation? If so, then Congress is supreme, and your Constitution is not worth the parchment on which it is written. What the gentleman calls the right of revolution would exist, and could be exerted as well without a Constitution as with it.

It is in vain to tell us, that all the States are represented here. Representation may, or may not, afford security to the people. The only practical security against oppression, in representative governments, is to be found in this, that *those who impose the burthens,* are compelled to *share them.* Where there are conflicting interests, however, and a *majority* are enabled to impose burthens on the *minority,* for their own advantage, it is obvious that representation, on the part of that minority, can have no other effect than to "furnish an apology for the injustice." What security would a representation of the American colonies, in the British Parliament, have afforded to our ancestors? What would be the value of a West India representation there now? Of what value is *our representation here,* on questions connected with the "American system;" where, (to use the strong language of a distinguished statesman) the "imposition is laid, not by the representatives of those who *pay the tax,* but by the representatives of those who are *to receive the bounty?*" Sir, representation will afford us ample security if the Federal Government shall be strictly confined within the limits prescribed by the constitution, and if, limiting its action to matters in which all have a common interest, the system shall be made to operate equally over the whole country. But it will afford us none, if the will of an interested majority shall be the supreme law, and Congress shall undertake to legislate for us, in all cases whatsoever. Before I leave this branch of the subject, I must remark, that, while gentlemen admit, as they do, that the Courts may nullify an act of Congress, by declaring it to be unconstitutional, it is impossible for them to contend, that *Congress are the final judges* of the extent of their own powers.

I think I have now shown, that the right of a State to judge of infractions of the constitution, on the part of the Federal Government, results from the very nature of the compact; and that, neither by the express provisions of that instrument, nor by any fair implication, is such a power exclusively reserved to the Federal Government, or any of its departments—executive, legislative, or judicial. But I go farther, and contend, that the power in question may be fairly considered as reserved to the States, by that clause of the constitution before referred to, which provides, "that all powers not delegated to the United States, are reserved to the States, respectively, or to the people."

No doubt can exist, that, before the States entered into the compact, they possessed the right to the fullest extent, of determining the limits of their own powers—it is incident to all sovereignty. Now, have they given away that right, or agreed to limit or restrict it in any respect? Assuredly not. They have agreed, that certain specific powers shall be exercised by the Federal Government; but the moment that Government steps beyond the limits of its charter, the right of the States "to interpose for arresting the

progress of the evil, and for maintaining within their respective limits the authorities, rights, and liberties, appertaining to them," is as full and complete as it was before the Constitution was formed. It was plenary then, and never having been surrendered, must be plenary now. But what then? asks the gentleman. A State is brought into collision with the United States, in relation to the exercise of unconstitutional powers: who is to decide between them? Sir, it is the common case of difference of opinion between sovereigns, as to the true construction of a compact. Does such a difference of opinion necessarily produce war? No. And if not, among rival nations, why should it do so among friendly States? In all such cases, some mode must be devised by mutual agreement, for settling the difficulty; and most happily for us, that mode is clearly indicated in the Constitution itself, and results indeed from the very form and structure of the Government. The creating power is three fourths of the States. By their decision, the parties to the compact have agreed to be bound, even to the extent of changing the entire form of the Government itself; and it follows of necessity, that in case of a deliberate and settled difference of opinion between the parties to the compact, as to the extent of the powers of either, resort must be had to their common superior—(that power which may give any character to the Constitution they may think proper,) viz: three-fourths of the States. This is the view of the matter taken by Mr. Jefferson himself, who in 1821, expressed himself in this emphatic manner: "It is a fatal heresy to suppose, that either our State Governments are superior to the Federal, or the Federal to the State; neither is authorized literally to decide what belongs to itself, or its copartner in government, in differences of opinion between their different sets of public servants: the appeal is to neither, but to their employers, peaceably assembled by their representatives in convention."

But it has been asked, Why not compel a State, objecting to the constitutionality of a law, to appeal to her sister States, by a proposition to amend the constitution? I answer, because, such a course would, in the first instance, admit the exercise of an unconstitutional authority, which the States are not bound to submit to, even for a day, and because it would be absurd to suppose that any redress would ever be obtained by such an appeal, even if a State were at liberty to make it. If a majority of both Houses of Congress should, from any motive, be induced deliberately, to exercise "powers not granted," what prospect would there be of "arresting the progress of the evil," by a vote of three fourths? But the constitution does not permit a minority to submit to the people a proposition for an amendment of the constitution. Such a proposition can only come from "two-thirds of the two Houses of Congress, or the Legislatures of two-thirds of the States." It will be seen therefore, at once, that a minority, whose constitutional rights are violated, can have no redress by an amendment of the constitution. When any State is brought into direct collision with the Federal Government, in the case of an attempt, by the latter, to exercise unconstitutional powers, the appeal must be made by Congress, (the party proposing to exert the disputed power,) in order to have it expressly conferred, and, until so conferred, the exercise of such authority must be suspended. Even in cases of doubt, such an appeal is due to the peace and harmony of the Government. On this subject our present Chief Magistrate, in his opening message to Congress, says: "I regard *an appeal to the source of power,* in cases of real doubt, and where its exercise is deemed indispensable to the general welfare, as among *the most sacred of all our obligations.* Upon this country, more than any other, has, in the providence of God, been cast the special guardianship of the great principle of adherence to *written constitutions.* If it fail here all hope in regard to it will be extinguished. That this was intended to be a government of limited and specific, and not general powers, must be admitted by all; and it is our duty to preserve for it the character intended by its framers. The scheme has worked well. It has exceeded the hopes of those who devised it, and became an object of admiration to the world. Nothing is clearer, in my view, than that we are chiefly indebted for the success of the constitution under which we are now acting, to the watchful and auxiliary operation of the State authorities. This is not the reflection of a day, but belongs to the most deeply rooted convictions of my mind. I cannot, therefore, too strongly or too earnestly, for my own sense of its importance, warn you against all encroachments upon the legitimate sphere of State sovereignty. Sustained by its healthful and invigorating influence, the Federal system can never fail."

But the gentleman apprehends that this will "make the Union a rope of sand." Sir, I have shown that it is a power indispensably necessary to the preservation of the constitutional rights of the States, and of the people. I now proceed to show that it is perfectly safe, and will practically have no effect but to keep the Federal Government within the limits of the constitution, and prevent those unwarrantable assumptions of power, which cannot fail to impair the rights of the States, and finally destroy the Union itself. This is a government of checks and balances. All free governments must be so. The whole organization and regulation of every department of the Federal, as well as of the State Governments, establish, beyond a doubt, that it was the first object of the great fathers of our federal system to interpose effectual checks to prevent that over-action, which is the besetting sin of all governments, and which has been the great enemy to freedom over all the world. There is an obvious and wide distinction, between the power of acting, and of preventing action, a distinction running through the whole of our system. No one can question, that in all really doubtful cases, it would be extremely desirable to leave things as they are. And how happy would it be for mankind, and how greatly would it contribute to the peace and tranquillity of this country, and to that mutual harmony on which the preservation of the Union must depend, that the Federal Government (confining its operations to subjects clearly federal,) should only be felt in the blessings which it dispenses. Look, Sir, at our system of checks. The House of Representatives checks the Senate, the Senate checks the House, the Executive checks both, the Judiciary checks the whole; and it is in the true spirit of this system, that the States should check the Federal Government, at least so far as to preserve the constitution from "gross, palpable and deliberate violations," and to compel an appeal to the amending power, in cases of real doubt and difficulty. That the States possess this right, seems to be acknowledged by Alexander Hamilton himself. In the 51st No. of the Federalist, he says, "that in a single republic all the powers surrendered by the people, are submitted to the administration of a single government, and usurpations are guarded against by a division of the government into separate departments. In the compound republic of America, the power surrendered by the people is first divided between two distinct governments, and then the portion allotted to each sub-divided into separate departments; hence a double security arises to the rights of the people. The different governments *will control each other,* at the same time each will be controlled by itself."

I have already shown, that it has been fully recognized by the Virginia resolutions of '98, and by Mr. Madison's report on these resolutions, that it is not only "the right, but the duty of the States," to "judge of infractions of the constitution," and "to interpose for *maintaining within their limits the authorities, rights, and liberties, appertaining to them.*"

Mr. Jefferson, on various occasions, expressed himself in language equally strong. In the Kentucky resolutions of '98, prepared by him, it is declared that the federal government "was not made the exclusive and final judge of the extent of the powers delegated to itself since that would have made its discretion, and not the Constitution the measure of its powers, but that, as in all other cases of compact among parties having no common judge, each party has an equal right *to judge for itself, as well of infractions as the mode and measure of redress.*"

In the Kentucky resolutions of '99, it is even more explicitly declared, "that the several States which formed the Constitution, being sovereign and independent, have the unquestionable right *to judge of its infraction,* and that *a nullification* by those sovereignties of all unauthorized acts done under color of that instrument is *the rightful remedy.*"

But the gentleman says, this right will be dangerous. Sir, I insist, that of all the checks that have been provided by the Constitution, this is by far the safest, and the least liable to abuse. It is admitted by the gentleman, that the Supreme Court may declare a law to be unconstitutional, and check your further progress. The Supreme Court consists of only seven judges: four are a quorum, three of whom are a majority, and may exercise this mighty power. Now, the Judges of this Court are without any direct responsibility, in matters of opinion, and may certainly be governed by any of the motives, which it is supposed will influence a State in opposing the acts of the Federal Government. Sir, it is not my desire to excite prejudice against the Supreme Court. I not only entertain the highest respect for the individuals who compose that tribunal, but I believe they have rendered important services to the country; and that, confined within their appropriate sphere, (the decision of questions "of law and equity,") they will constitute a fountain from which will forever flow the streams of pure and undefiled justice, diffusing blessings throughout the land. I object only to the assumption of political power by the Supreme Court, a power which belongs not to them, and which they cannot safely exercise. But, surely, a power which the gentleman is willing to confide to *three Judges of the Supreme Court,* may safely be entrusted to *a sovereign State.* Sir, there are so many powerful motives to restrain a

State from taking such high ground as to interpose her sovereign power to protect her citizens from unconstitutional laws, that the danger is not that this power will be wantonly exercised, but that she will fail to exert it, even on proper occasions.

A State will be restrained by a sincere love of the Union. The People of the United States cherish a devotion to the Union, so pure, so ardent, that nothing short of intolerable oppression, can ever tempt them to do any thing that may possibly endanger it. Sir, there exists, moreover, a deep and settled conviction of the benefits, which result from a close connexion of all the States, for purposes of mutual protection and defence. This will co-operate with the feelings of patriotism to induce a State to avoid any measures calculated to endanger that connexion. A State will always feel the necessity of consulting public opinion, both at home and abroad, before she resorts to any measures of such a character. She will know that if she acts rashly, she will be abandoned even by her own citizens, and will utterly fail in the object she has in view. If, as is asserted in the declaration of independence, all experience has proved that mankind are more disposed to suffer while evils are sufferable, than to resort to measures for redress, why should this case be an exception, where so many additional motives must always be found for forbearance? Look at our own experience on this subject. Virginia and Kentucky, so far back as '98, avowed the principles for which I have been contending—principles which have never since been abandoned; and no instance has yet occurred, in which it has been found necessary, practically to exert the power asserted in those resolutions.

If the alien and sedition laws had not been yielded to the force of public opinion, there can be no doubt, that the State of Virginia would have interposed to protect her citizens from its operation. And if the apprehension of such an interposition by a State, should have the effect of restraining the Federal Government from acting, except in cases clearly within the limits of their authority, surely no one can doubt the beneficial operation of such a restraining influence. Mr. Jefferson assures us, that the embargo was actually yielded up, rather than force New England into open opposition to it. And it was right to yield it, Sir, to honest convictions of its unconstitutionality, entertained by so large a portion of our fellow citizens. If the knowledge that the States possess the Constitutional right to interpose, in the event "of gross, deliberate, and palpable violations of the Constitution," should operate to prevent a perseverance in such violations, surely the effect would be greatly to be desired. But there is one point of view, in which this matter presents itself to my mind with irresistible force. The Supreme Court, it is admitted, may nullify an act of Congress, by declaring it to be unconstitutional. Can Congress, after such a nullification, proceed to enforce the law, even if they should differ in opinion from the Court? What then would be the effect of such a decision? And what would be the remedy in such a case? Congress would be *arrested in the exercise of the disputed power,* and the only remedy would be, *an appeal to the creating power,* three-fourths of the States, for an amendment of the Constitution. And by whom must such an appeal be made? It must be made by the party proposing to exercise the disputed power. Now I will ask, whether a sovereign State may not be safely entrusted with the exercise of a power, operating merely as a check, which is admitted to belong to the Supreme Court, and which may be exercised every day, by any three of its members? Sir, no ideas that can be formed of arbitrary power on the one hand, and abject dependence on the other, can be carried further, than to suppose, that three individuals, mere men, "subject to like passions with ourselves," may be safely entrusted with the power to nullify an act of Congress, because they conceive it to be unconstitutional; but that a sovereign and independent State, even the great State of New York, is bound, implicitly, to submit to its operation, even where it violates, in the grossest manner, her own rights, or the liberties of her citizens. But we do not contend that a common case would justify the interposition.

This is "the extreme medicine of the State," and cannot become our daily bread.

Mr. Madison, in his report, says, "It does not follow, however, that because the States, as sovereign parties to their constitutional compact, must ultimately decide whether it has been violated, that such a decision ought to be interposed, either in a hasty manner, or on doubtful and inferior occasions. Even in the case of ordinary conventions between different nations, where, by the strict rule of interpretation, a breach of a part may be deemed a breach of the whole, every part being deemed a condition of every other part, and of the whole, it is always laid down, that the breach must be both wilful and material to justify an application of the rule. But in the case of an intimate and Constitutional Union, like that of the United

States, it is evident, that the interposition of the parties, in their sovereign capacity, can be called for by occasions only, deeply and essentially affecting the vital principles of their political system.

"The resolution has, accordingly, guarded against any misapprehension of its object, by expressly requiring, for such an interposition, 'the case of a deliberate, palpable, and dangerous breach of the Constitution, by the exercise of powers not granted by it.' 'It must be a case, not of a light and transient nature, but of a nature dangerous to the great purposes for which the Constitution was established.' It must be a case, moreover, not obscure or doubtful in its construction, but plain and palpable. Lastly, it must be a case, not resulting from a partial consideration, or hasty determination; but a case stamped with a final consideration, and deliberate adherence. It is not necessary, because the resolution does not require that the question should be discussed, how far the exercise of any particular power, ungranted by the Constitution, would justify the interposition of the parties to it. As cases might easily be stated, which none would contend ought to fall within that description; and cases, on the other hand, might, with equal ease, be stated, so flagrant and so fatal, as to unite every opinion in placing them within the description.

"But the resolution has done more than guard against misconstruction, by expressly referring to cases of a deliberate, palpable, and dangerous nature. It specifies *the object of the interposition* which it contemplates to be solely that of *arresting the progress of the evil of usurpation,* and of maintaining the authorities, rights, and liberties appertaining to the States, as parties to the Constitution."

No one can read this, without perceiving that Mr. Madison goes the whole length, in support of the principles for which I have been contending.

The gentleman has called upon us to carry out our scheme *practically.* Now, Sir, if I am correct in my view of this matter, then it follows, of course, that the right of a State being established, the Federal Government is *bound to acquiesce* in a solemn decision of a state, acting in its sovereign capacity, at least so far as to make an appeal to the People for an amendment of the Constitution. This solemn decision of a State, (made either through its Legislature or a Convention, as may be supposed to be the proper organ of its sovereign will—a point I do not propose now to discuss) binds the Federal Government under the highest constitutional obligation, not to resort to any means of coercion against the citizens of the dissenting State. How then can any collision ensue between the Federal and State Governments, unless indeed, the former should determine to enforce the law by unconstitutional means? What could the Federal Government do in such a case?—Resort, says the Gentleman, to the courts of justice. Now, can any man believe, that in the face of a solemn decision of a State, that an act of Congress is "a gross, palpable, and deliberate violation of the Constitution," and the interposition of its sovereign authority, to protect its citizens from the usurpation, that juries could be found ready, merely to register the decrees of the Congress, wholly regardless of the unconstitutional character of their acts? Will the gentleman contend that juries are to be coerced to find verdicts at the point of the bayonet? And, if not, how are the United States to enforce an act, solemnly pronounced to be unconstitutional? But if the attempt should be made to carry such a law into effect, by force, in what would the case differ, from an attempt to carry into effect an act nullified by the Courts, or to do any other unlawful and unwarrantable act? Suppose Congress should pass an agrarian law, or a law emancipating our slaves, or should commit any other gross violation of our constitutional rights, will any gentleman contend that the decision of every branch of the Federal Government in favor of such laws could prevent the States from declaring them null and void, and protecting their citizens from their operation?

Sir, if Congress should ever attempt to enforce any such laws, they would put themselves so clearly in the wrong, that no one could doubt the right of the State to exert its protecting power.

Sir, the gentleman has alluded to that portion of the Militia of South Carolina with which I have the honor to be connected; and asked how they would act in the event of the nullification of the tariff law by the State of South Carolina? The tone of the gentleman on this subject did not seem to me as respectful as I could have desired. I hope, Sir, no imputation was intended.

[Mr. Webster—"Not at all; just the reverse."]

Well, Sir, the gentleman asks what their leaders would be able to read to them out of Coke upon Littleton, or any other law book, to justify their enterprise? Sir, let me assure the gentleman, that when any attempt shall be made from any quarter, to enforce *unconstitutional laws,* clearly violating our essential rights, our leaders, (whoever they

may be) will not be found reading black letter from the musty pages of old law books. They will look to the Constitution, and when called upon by the sovereign authority of the State to preserve and protect the rights secured to them by the charter of their liberties, they will succeed in defending them, or "perish in the last ditch." Sir, I will put the case home to the gentleman. Is there any violation of the constitutional rights of the States, and the liberties of the citizen, (sanctioned by Congress and the Supreme Court,) which he would believe it to be the right and duty of a State to resist? Does he contend for the doctrine "of passive obedience and non-resistance"? Would he justify an open resistance to an act of Congress sanctioned by the Courts, which should abolish the trial by jury, or destroy the freedom of religion, or the freedom of the press? Yes, Sir, he would advocate resistance in such cases; and so would I, and so would all of us. But such resistance would, according to his doctrine, be *revolution;* it would be *rebellion.* According to my opinion it would be just, legal, and *constitutional resistance.* The whole difference between us, then, consists in this: The gentleman would make force the only arbiter in all cases of collision between the States and the Federal Government. I would resort to a peaceful remedy—the interposition of the State to "arrest the progress of the evil," until such times as "a Convention, (assembled at the call of Congress or two-thirds of the States,) shall decide to which they mean to give an authority claimed by two of their organs." Sir, I say with Mr. Jefferson, (whose words I have here borrowed) that "it is the peculiar wisdom and felicity of our Constitution, to have provided this *peaceable appeal,* where that of other nations," (and I may add that of the gentleman) "is at once *to force.*"

The gentleman has made an eloquent appeal to our hearts in favor of union. Sir, I cordially respond to that appeal. I will yield to no gentleman here in sincere attachment to the Union,—but it is a Union *founded on the Constitution,* and not such a Union as that gentleman would give us, that is dear to my heart. If this is to become one great "consolidated government," swallowing up the rights of the States, and the liberties of the citizen, "riding and ruling over the plundered ploughman, and beggared yeomanry," the Union will not be worth preserving. Sir it is because South Carolina loves the Union, and would preserve it forever, that she is opposing now, while there is hope, those usurpations of the Federal Government, which, once established, will, sooner or later, tear this Union into fragments. The gentleman is for marching under a banner studded all over with stars, and bearing the inscription *Liberty* and *Union*. I had thought, sir, the gentleman would have borne a standard, displaying in its ample folds a brilliant sun, extending its golden rays from the centre to the extremities, in the brightness of whose beams, the "little stars hide their diminished heads." Our's, Sir, is the banner of the Constitution, the twenty-four stars are there in all their undiminished lustre, on it is inscribed, *Liberty—the Constitution—Union*. We offer up our fervent prayers to the Father of all mercies, that it may continue to wave for ages yet to come, over a free, a happy, and a united people.

Fort Hill Address

JOHN C. CALHOUN

July 26, 1831

John C. Calhoun (1782–1850) was a congressman and senator from South Carolina who also served as vice president under President Andrew Jackson. An early supporter of a strong national government, he also supported the War of 1812 and, in the beginning, the American system of tariffs and internal improvements. However, over time Calhoun changed his position in regard to federal authority. Thus, in 1828, he wrote (anonymously) the South Carolina Exposition and Protest—a document protesting high tariffs as an attack on Southern interests and asserting the right of states to refuse to accede to federal laws they deemed unjust.

The selection reproduced here is often called the "Fort Hill Address" because Calhoun wrote it at his home, a relatively small plantation which he called Fort Hill. In it, Calhoun elaborates the doctrine of nullification first laid out in the Virginia and Kentucky Resolutions.

Fort Hill Address

*On the relation which the States and
General Government bear to each other*

The question of the relation which the States and General Government bear to each other is not one of recent origin. From the commencement of our system, it has divided public sentiment. Even in the Convention, while the Constitution was struggling into existence, there were two parties as to what this relation should be, whose different sentiments constituted no small impediment in forming that instrument. After the General Government went into operation, experience soon proved that the question had not terminated with the labors of the Convention. The great struggle that preceded the political revolution of 1801, which brought Mr. Jefferson into power, turned essentially on it, and the doctrines and arguments on both sides were embodied and ably sustained;— on the one, in the Virginia and Kentucky Resolutions, and the Report to the Virginia Legislature;—and on the other, in the replies of the Legislature of Massachusetts and some of the other States. These Resolutions and this Report, with the decision of the Supreme Court of Pennsylvania about the same time (particularly in the case of Cobbett, delivered by Chief Justice M'Kean, and concurred in by the whole bench), contain what I believe to be the true doctrine on this important subject. I refer to them in order to avoid the necessity of presenting my views, with the reasons in support of them, in detail.

As my object is simply to state my opinions, I might pause with this reference to documents that so fully and ably state all the points immediately connected with this deeply-important subject; but as there are many who may not have the opportunity or leisure to refer to them, and as it is possible, however clear they may be, that different persons may place different interpretations on their meaning, I will, in order that my sentiments may be fully known, and to avoid all ambiguity, proceed to state, summarily, the doctrines which I conceive they embrace.

The great and leading principle is, that the General Government emanated from the people of the several States, forming distinct political communities, and acting in their separate and sovereign capacity, and not from all of the people forming one aggregate political community; that the Constitution of the United States is, in fact, a compact, to which each State is a party, in the character already described; and that the several States, or parties, have a right to judge of its infractions; and in case of a deliberate, palpable, and dangerous exercise of power not delegated, they have the right, in the last resort, to use the language of the Virginia Resolutions, "*to interpose for arresting the progress of the evil, and for maintaining, within their respective limits, the authorities, rights, and liberties appertaining to them.*" This right of interposition, thus solemnly asserted by the State of Virginia, be it called what it may,—State-right, veto, nullification, or by any other name,—I conceive to be the fundamental principle of our system, resting on facts historically as certain as our revolution itself, and deductions as simple and demonstrative as that of any political or moral truth whatever; and I firmly believe that on its recognition depend the stability and safety of our political institutions.

I am not ignorant that those opposed to the doctrine have always, now and formerly, regarded it in a very different light, as anarchical and revolutionary. Could I believe such, in fact, to be its tendency, to me it would be no recommendation. I yield to none, I trust, in a deep and sincere attachment to our political institutions and the union of these States. I never breathed an opposite sentiment; but, on the contrary, I have ever considered them the great instruments of preserving our liberty, and promoting the happiness of ourselves and our posterity; and next to these I have ever held them most dear. Nearly half my life has been passed in the service of the Union, and whatever public reputation I have acquired is indissolubly identified with it. To be too national has, indeed, been considered by many, even of my friends, my greatest political fault. With these strong feelings of attachment, I have examined, with the utmost care, the bearing of the doctrine in question; and, so far from anarchical or revolutionary, I solemnly believe it to be the only solid foundation of our system, and of the Union itself; and that the opposite doctrine, which denies to the States the right of protecting their reserved powers, and which would vest in the General Government (it matters not through what department) the right of determining, exclusively and finally, the powers delegated to it, is incompatible with the sovereignty of the States, and of the Constitution itself, considered as the basis of a Federal Union. As strong as this language is, it is not stronger than that used by the illustrious Jefferson, who said, to give to the General Government the final and exclusive right to judge of its powers, is to make "*its discretion,* and *not the Constitution, the measure of its powers;*" and that, "*in all cases of compact between parties having no common judge, each party has an equal right to judge for itself, as well of the infraction as of the mode and measure of redress.*" Language cannot be more explicit, nor can higher authority be adduced.

That different opinions are entertained on this subject, I consider but as an additional evidence of the great diversity of the human intellect. Had not able, experienced, and patriotic individuals, for whom I have the highest respect, taken different views, I would have thought the right too clear to admit of doubt; but I am taught by this, as well as by many similar instances, to treat with deference opinions differing from my own. The error may, possibly, be with me; but if so, I can only say that, after the most mature and conscientious examination, I have not been able to detect it. But, with all proper deference, I must think that theirs is the error who deny what seems to be an essential attribute of the conceded sovereignty of the States, and who attribute to the General Government a right utterly incompatible with what all acknowledge to be its limited and restricted character: an error originating principally, as I must think, in not duly reflecting on the nature of our institutions, and on what constitutes the only rational object of all political constitutions.

It has been well said by one of the most sagacious men of antiquity, that the object of a constitution is, to *restrain the government, as that of laws* is to restrain *individuals.* The remark is correct; nor is it less true where the government is vested in a majority, than where it is in a single or a few individuals—in a republic, than a monarchy or aristocracy. No one can have a higher respect for the maxim that the majority ought to govern than I have, taken in its proper sense, subject to the restrictions imposed by the Constitution, and confined to objects in which every portion of the community have similar interests; but it is a great error to suppose, as many do, that the right of a majority to govern is a natural and not a conventional right, and therefore absolute and unlimited. By nature, every individual has the right to govern himself; and governments, whether founded on majorities or minorities, must derive their right from the assent, expressed or implied, of the governed, and be subject to such limitations as they may impose. Where the interests are the same, that is, where the laws that may benefit one will benefit all, or the reverse, it is just and proper to place them under the control of the majority; but where they are dissimilar, so that the law that may benefit one portion may be ruinous to another, it would be, on the contrary, unjust and absurd to subject them to its will; and such I conceive to be the theory on which our Constitution rests.

That such dissimilarity of interests may exist, it is impossible to doubt. They are to be found in every community, in a greater or less degree, however small or homogeneous; and they constitute every where the great difficulty of forming and preserving free institutions. To guard against the unequal action of the laws, when applied to dissimilar and opposing interests, is, in fact, what mainly renders a constitution indispensable; to overlook which, in reasoning on our Constitution, would be to omit the principal element by which to determine its character. Were there no contrariety of interests, nothing would be more simple and easy than to form and preserve free institutions. The right of suffrage alone would be a sufficient guarantee. It is the conflict of opposing interests which renders it the most difficult work of man.

Where the diversity of interests exists in separate and distinct classes of the community, as is the case in England, and was formerly the case in Sparta, Rome, and most of the free States of antiquity, the rational constitutional provision is, that each should be represented in the government, as a separate estate, with a distinct voice, and a negative on the acts of its co-estates, in order to check their encroachments. In England, the Constitution has assumed expressly this form, while in the governments of Sparta and Rome, the same thing was effected under different, but not much less efficacious forms. The perfection of their organization, in this particular, was that which gave to the constitutions of these renowned States all their celebrity, which secured their liberty for so many centuries, and raised them to so great a height of power and prosperity. Indeed, a constitutional provision giving to the great and separate interests of the community the right of self-protection, must appear, to those who will duly reflect on the subject, not less essential to the preservation of liberty than the right of suffrage itself. They, in fact, have a common object, to effect which the one is as necessary as the other to secure *responsibility; that is, that those who make and execute the laws should be accountable to those on whom the laws in reality operate—the only solid and durable foundation of liberty.* If, without the right of suffrage, our rulers would oppress us, so, without the right of self-protection, the major would equally oppress the minor interests of the community. The absence of the former would make the governed the slaves of the rulers; and of the latter, the feebler interests, the victim of the stronger.

Happily for us, we have no artificial and separate classes of society. We have wisely exploded all such distinctions; but we are not, on that account, exempt from all contrariety of interests, as the present distracted and dangerous condition of our country, unfortunately, but too clearly proves. With us they are almost exclusively geographical, resulting mainly from difference of climate, soil, situation,

industry, and production; but are not, therefore, less necessary to be protected by an adequate constitutional provision, than where the distinct interests exist in separate classes. The necessity is, in truth, greater, as such separate and dissimilar geographical interests are more liable to come into conflict, and more dangerous, when in that state, than those of any other description: so much so, that *ours is the first instance on record where they have not formed, in an extensive territory, separate and independent* communities, *or subjected the whole to despotic sway.* That such may not be our unhappy fate also, must be the sincere prayer of every lover of his country.

So numerous and diversified are the interests of our country, that they could not be fairly represented in a single government, organized so as to give to each great and leading interest a separate and distinct voice, as in governments to which I have referred. A plan was adopted better suited to our situation, but perfectly novel in its character. The powers of government were divided, not, as heretofore, in reference to classes, but geographically. One General Government was formed for the whole, to which were delegated all the powers supposed to be necessary to regulate the interests common to all the States, leaving others subject to the separate control of the States, being, from their local and peculiar character, such that they could not be subject to the will of a majority of the whole Union, without the certain hazard of injustice and oppression. It was thus that the interests of the whole were subjected, as they ought to be, to the will of the whole, while the peculiar and local interests were left under the control of the States separately, to whose custody only they could be safely confided. This distribution of power, settled solemnly by a constitutional compact, to which all the States are parties, constitutes the peculiar character and excellence of our political system. It is truly and emphatically *American, without example or parallel.*

To realize its perfection, we must view the General Government and those of the States as a whole, each in its proper sphere independent; each perfectly adapted to its respective objects; the States acting separately, representing and protecting the local and peculiar interests; and acting jointly through one General Government, with the weight respectively assigned to each by the Constitution, representing and protecting the interest of the whole; and thus perfecting, by an admirable but simple arrangement, the great principle of representation and responsibility, without which no government can be free or just. To preserve this sacred distribution as originally settled, by coercing each to move in its prescribed orbit, is the great and difficult problem, on the solution of which the duration of our Constitution, of our Union, and, in all probability, our liberty depends. How is this to be effected?

The question is new, when applied to our peculiar political organization, where the separate and conflicting interests of society are represented by distinct but connected governments; but it is, in reality, an old question under a new form, long since perfectly solved. Whenever separate and dissimilar interests have been separately represented in any government; whenever the sovereign power has been divided in its exercise, the experience and wisdom of ages have devised but one mode by which such political organization can be preserved,—the mode adopted in England, and by all governments, ancient and modern, blessed with constitutions deserving to be called free,—to give to each co-estate the right to judge of its powers, with a negative or veto on the acts of the others, in order to protect against encroachments the interests it particularly represents: a principle which all of our constitutions recognize in the distribution of power among their respective departments, as essential to maintain the independence of each; but which, to all who will duly reflect on the subject, must appear far more essential, for the same object, in that great and fundamental distribution of powers between the General and State Governments. So essential is the principle, that, to withhold the right from either, where the sovereign power is divided, is, in fact, *to annul the division* itself, and to *consolidate,* in the one left in the exclusive possession of the right, *all* powers of government; for it is not possible to distinguish, practically, between a government having all power, and one having the right to take what powers it pleases. Nor does it in the least vary the principle, whether the distribution of power be between co-estates, as in England, or between distinctly organized but connected governments, as with us. The reason is the same in both cases, while the necessity is greater in our case, as the danger of conflict is greater where the interests of a society are divided geographically than in any other, as has already been shown.

These truths do seem to me to be incontrovertible; and I am at a loss to understand how any one, who has maturely reflected on the nature of our institutions, or who has read history or studied the principles of free govern-ment to any purpose, can call them in question. The explanation must, it appears to me, be sought in the fact that, in every free State there are those who look more to the necessity of maintaining power than guarding against its abuses. I do not intend reproach, but simply to state a fact apparently necessary to explain the contrariety of opinions among the intelligent, where the abstract consideration of the subject would seem scarcely to admit of doubt. If such be the true cause, I must think the fear of weakening the government too much, in this case, to be in a great measure unfounded, or, at least, that the danger is much less from that than the opposite side. I do not deny that a power of so high a nature may be abused by a State; but when I reflect that the States unanimously called the General Government into existence with all its powers, which they freely delegated on their part, under the conviction that their common peace, safety, and prosperity required it; that they are bound together by a common origin, and the recollection of common suffering and common triumph in the great and splendid achievement of their independence; and that the strongest feelings of our nature, and among them the love of national power and distinction, are on the side of the Union, it does seem to me that the fear which would strip the States of their sovereignty, and degrade them, in fact, to mere dependent corporations, lest they should abuse a right indispensable to the peaceable protection of those interests which they reserved under their own peculiar guardianship when they created the General Government, is unnatural and unreasonable. If those who voluntarily created the system cannot be trusted to preserve it, who can?

So far from extreme danger, I hold that there never was a free State in which this great conservative principle, indispensable to all, was ever so safely lodged. In others, when the co-estates representing the dissimilar and conflicting interests of the community came into contact, the only alternative was compromise, submission, or force. Not so in ours. Should the General Government and a State come into conflict, we have a higher remedy: the power which called the General Government into existence, which gave it all its authority, and can enlarge, contract, or abolish its powers at its pleasure, may be invoked. The States themselves may be appealed to,—three fourths of which, in fact, form a power, whose decrees are the Constitution itself, and whose voice can silence all discontent. The utmost extent, then, of the power is, that a State, acting in its sovereign capacity as one of the parties to the constitutional compact, may compel the Government, created by that compact, to submit a question touching its infraction, to the parties who created it; to avoid the supposed dangers of which, it is proposed to resort to the novel, the hazardous, and, I must add, fatal project of giving to the General Government the sole and final right of interpreting the Constitution;—thereby reversing the whole system, making that instrument the creature of its will, instead of a rule of action impressed on it at its creation, and annihilating, in fact, the authority which imposed it, and from which the Government itself derives its existence.

That such would be the result, were the right in question vested in the Legislative or Executive branch of the Government, is conceded by all. No one has been so hardy as to assert that Congress or the President ought to have the right, or deny that, if vested finally and exclusively in either, the consequences which I have stated would necessarily follow; but its advocates have been reconciled to the doctrine, on the supposition that there is one department of the General Government which, from its peculiar organization, affords an independent tribunal, through which the Government may exercise the high authority which is the subject of consideration, with perfect safety to all.

I yield, I trust, to few in my attachment to the Judiciary Department. I am fully sensible of its importance, and would maintain it, to the fullest extent, in its constitutional powers and independence; but it is impossible for me to believe it was ever intended by the Constitution that it should exercise the power in question, or that it is competent to do so; and, if it were, that it would be a safe depository of the power.

Its powers are judicial, and not political; and are expressly confined by the Constitution "to all *cases* in law and equity arising under this Constitution, the laws of the United States, and the treaties made, or which shall be made, under its authority;" and which I have high authority in asserting excludes political questions, and comprehends those only where there are parties amenable to the process of the court.* Nor is its incompetency less clear than its want of constitutional authority. There may be

many, and the most dangerous infractions on the part of Congress, of which, it is conceded by all, the court, as a judicial tribunal, cannot, from its nature, take cognizance. The Tariff itself is a strong case in point; and the reason applies equally *to all others where Congress perverts a power from an object intended, to one not intended, the most insidious and dangerous of all infractions; and which may be extended to all of its powers, more especially to the taxing and appropriating.* But, supposing it competent to take cognizance of all infractions of every description, the insuperable objection still remains, that it would not be a safe tribunal to exercise the power in question.

It is a universal and fundamental political principle, that the power to protect can safely be confided only to those interested in protecting, or their responsible agents,—a maxim not less true in private than in public affairs. The danger in our system is, that the General Government, which represents the interests of the whole, may encroach on the States, which represent the peculiar and local interests, or that the latter may encroach on the former.

In examining this point, we ought not to forget that the Government, through all its departments, judicial as well as others, is administered by delegated and responsible agents; and that the *power which really controls, ultimately, all the movements, is not in the agents, but those who elect or appoint them.* To understand, then, its real character, and what would be the action of the system in any supposable case, we must raise our view from the mere agents to this high controlling power, which finally impels every movement of the machine. By doing so, we shall find all under the control of the will of a majority, compounded of the majority of the States, taken as political bodies, and the majority of the people of the States, estimated in federal numbers. These, united, constitute the real and final power which impels and directs the movements of the General Government. The majority of the States elect the majority of the Senate; of the people of the States, that of the House of Representatives; the two united, the President; and the President and a majority of the Senate appoint the judges: a majority of whom, and a majority of the Senate and House, with the President, really exercise all the powers of the Government, with the exception of the cases where the Constitution requires a greater number than a majority. The judges are, in fact, as truly the judicial representatives of this united majority, as the majority of Congress itself, or the President, is its legislative or

*I refer to the authority of Chief Justice Marshall, in the case of Jonathan Robbins. I have not been able to refer to the speech, and speak from memory.

executive representative; and to confide the power to the Judiciary to determine finally and conclusively what powers are delegated and what reserved, would be, in reality, to confide it to the majority, whose agents they are, and by whom they can be controlled in various ways; and, of course, to subject (against the fundamental principle of our system and all sound political reasoning) the reserved powers of the States, with all the local and peculiar interests they were intended to protect, to the will of the very majority against which the protection was intended. Nor will the tenure by which the judges hold their office, however valuable the provision in many other respects, materially vary the case. Its highest possible effect would be to *retard,* and not *finally* to *resist,* the will of a dominant majority.

But it is useless to multiply arguments. Were it possible that reason could settle a question where the passions and interests of men are concerned, this point would have been long since settled for ever by the State of Virginia. The report of her Legislature, to which I have already referred, has really, in my opinion, placed it beyond controversy. Speaking in reference to this subject, it says: "It has been objected" (to the right of a State to interpose for the protection of her reserved rights) "that the judicial authority is to be regarded as the sole expositor of the Constitution. On this objection it might be observed, first, that there may be instances of usurped powers which the forms of the Constitution could never draw within the control of the Judicial Department; secondly, that, if the decision of the judiciary be raised above the sovereign parties to the Constitution, the decisions of the other departments, not carried by the forms of the Constitution before the Judiciary, must be equally authoritative and final with the decision of that department. But the proper answer to the objection is, that the resolution of the General Assembly relates to those great and extraordinary cases, in which all the forms of the Constitution may prove ineffectual against infractions dangerous to the essential rights of the parties to it. The resolution supposes that dangerous powers, not delegated, may not only be usurped and executed by the other departments, but that the Judicial Department may also exercise or sanction dangerous powers, beyond the grant of the Constitution, and, consequently, that the ultimate right of the parties to the Constitution to judge whether the compact has been dangerously violated, must extend to violations by one delegated authority, as

well as by another,—by the judiciary, as well as by the executive or legislative."

Against these conclusive arguments, as they seem to me, it is objected that, if one of the parties has the right to judge of infractions of the Constitution, so has the other; and that, consequently, in cases of contested powers between a State and the General Government, each would have a right to maintain its opinion, as is the case when sovereign powers differ in the construction of treaties or compacts; and that, of course, it would come to be a mere question of force. The error is in the assumption that the General Government is a party to the constitutional compact. The States, as has been shown, formed the compact, acting as sovereign and independent communities. The General Government is but its creature; and though, in reality, a government, with all the rights and authority which belong to any other government, within the orbit of its powers, it is, nevertheless, a government emanating from a compact between sovereigns, and partaking, in its nature and object, of the character of a joint commission, appointed to superintend and administer the interests in which all are jointly concerned; but having, beyond its proper sphere, no more power than if it did not exist. To deny this would be to deny the most incontestable facts and the clearest conclusions; while to acknowledge its truth is, to destroy utterly the objection that the appeal would be to force, in the case supposed. For, if each party has a right to judge, then, under our system of government, the final cognizance of a question of contested power would be in the States, and not in the General Government. It would be the duty of the latter, as in all similar cases of a contest between one or more of the principals and a joint commission or agency, to refer the contest to the principals themselves. Such are the plain dictates of both reason and analogy. On no sound principle can the agents have a right to final cognizance, as against the principals, much less to use force against them to maintain their construction of their powers. Such a right would be monstrous, and has never, heretofore, been claimed in similar cases.

That the doctrine is applicable to the case of a contested power between the States and the General Government, we have the authority, not only of reason and analogy, but of the distinguished statesman already referred to. Mr. Jefferson, at a late period of his life, after long experience and mature reflection, says, "With respect to our State and

Federal Governments, I do not think their relations are correctly understood by foreigners. They suppose the former are subordinate to the latter. This is not the case. They are co-ordinate departments of one simple and integral whole. But you may ask, If the two departments should claim each the same subject of power, where is the umpire to decide between them? In cases of little urgency or importance, the prudence of both parties will keep them aloof from the questionable ground; but, if it can neither be avoided nor compromised, a convention of the States must be called to ascribe the doubtful power to that department which they may think best."

It is thus that our Constitution, by authorizing amendments, and by prescribing the authority and mode of making them, has, by a simple contrivance, with its characteristic wisdom, provided a power which, in the last resort, supersedes effectually the necessity, and even the pretext for force: a power to which none can fairly object; with which the interests of all are safe; which can definitively close all controversies in the only effectual mode, by freeing the compact of every defect and uncertainty, by an amendment of the instrument itself. It is impossible for human wisdom, in a system like ours, to devise another mode which shall be safe and effectual, and, at the same time, consistent with what are the relations and acknowledged powers of the two great departments of our Government. It gives a beauty and security peculiar to our system, which, if duly appreciated, will transmit its blessings to the remotest generations; but, if not, our splendid anticipations of the future will prove but an empty dream. Stripped of all its covering, the naked question is, whether ours is a federal or a consolidated government; a constitutional or absolute one; a government resting ultimately on the solid basis of the sovereignty of the States or on the unrestrained will of a majority; a form of government, as in all other unlimited ones, in which injustice, and violence, and force must finally prevail. *Let it never be forgotten that, where the majority rules without restriction, the minority is the subject;* and that, if we should absurdly attribute to the former the exclusive right of construing the Constitution, there would be, in fact, between the sovereign and subject, under such a government, no Constitution, or, at least, nothing deserving the name, or serving the legitimate object of so sacred an instrument.

How the States are to exercise this high power of interposition, which constitutes so essential a portion of their reserved rights that it *cannot be delegated without an entire surrender of their sovereignty,* and converting our system from a *federal* into a *consolidated* Government, is a question that the States only are competent to determine. The arguments which prove that they possess the power, equally prove that they are, in the language of Jefferson, *"the rightful judges of the mode and measure of redress."* But the spirit of forbearance, as well as the nature of the right itself, forbids a recourse to it, except in cases of dangerous infractions of the Constitution; and then only in the last resort, when all reasonable hope of relief from the ordinary action of the Government has failed; when, if the right to interpose did not exist, the alternative would be submission and oppression on one side, or resistance by force on the other. That our system should afford, in such extreme cases, an intermediate point between these dire alternatives, by which the Government may be brought to a pause, and thereby an interval obtained to compromise differences, or, if impracticable, be compelled to submit the question to a constitutional adjustment, through an appeal to the States themselves, is an evidence of its high wisdom: an element not, as is supposed by some, of weakness, but of strength; not of anarchy or revolution, but of peace and safety. *Its general recognition would of itself, in a great measure, if not altogether, supersede the necessity of its exercise, by impressing on the movements of the Government that moderation and justice so essential to harmony and peace, in a country of such vast extent and diversity of interests as ours;* and would, if controversy should come, turn the resentment of the aggrieved from the system to those who had abused its powers (a point all-important), and cause them to seek redress, *not in revolution or overthrow, but in reformation.* It is, in fact, properly understood, *a substitute,—where the alternative would be force,—tending to prevent, and, if that fails, to correct peaceably the aberrations to which all systems are liable, and which, if permitted to accumulate without correction, must finally end in a general catastrophe.*

I have now said what I intended in reference to the abstract question of the relation of the States to the General Government, and would here conclude, did I not believe that a mere general statement on an abstract question, without including that which may have caused its agitation, would be considered by many imperfect and unsatisfactory. Feeling that such would be justly the case, I am compelled, reluctantly, to touch on the Tariff, so far, at least, as may be necessary to illustrate the opinions which I have already advanced. Anxious, however, to intrude as little as possible on the public attention, I will be as brief as possible; and with that view will, as far as may be consistent with my object, avoid all debatable topics.

Whatever diversity of opinion may exist in relation to the principle, or the effect on the productive industry of the country, of the present, or any other Tariff of protection, there are certain political consequences flowing from the present which none can doubt, and all must deplore. It would be in vain to attempt to conceal, that it has divided the country into two great geographical divisions, and arrayed them against each other, in opinion at least, if not interests also, on some of the most vital of political subjects,—on its finance, its commerce, and its industry,—subjects calculated, above all others, in time of peace, to produce excitement, and in relation to which the Tariff has placed the sections in question in deep and dangerous conflict. If there be any point on which the (I was going to say, southern section, but to avoid, as far as possible, the painful feelings such discussions are calculated to excite, I shall say) weaker of the two sections is unanimous, it is, that its prosperity depends, in a great measure, on free trade, light taxes, economical, and, as far as possible, equal disbursements of the public revenue, and unshackled industry;—leaving them to pursue whatever may appear most advantageous to their interests. From the Potomac to the Mississippi, there are few, indeed, however divided on other points, who would not, if dependent on their volition, and if they regarded the interest of their particular section only, remove from commerce and industry every shackle, reduce the revenue to the lowest point that the wants of the Government fairly required, and restrict the appropriations to the most moderate scale consistent with the peace, the security, and the engagements of the public; and who do not believe that the opposite system is calculated to throw on them an unequal burden, to repress their prosperity, and to encroach on their enjoyment.

On all these deeply-important measures, the opposite opinion prevails, if not with equal unanimity, with at least a greatly preponderating majority, in the other and stronger section; so much so, that no two distinct nations ever entertained more opposite views of policy than these two sections do, on all the important points to which I have referred. Nor is it less certain that this unhappy conflict, flowing directly from the Tariff, has extended itself to the halls of legislation, and has converted the deliberations of Congress into an annual struggle between the two sections; the stronger to maintain and increase the superiority it has already acquired, and the other to throw off or diminish its burdens: a struggle in which all the noble and generous feelings of patriotism are gradually subsiding into sectional and selfish attachments.* Nor has the effect of this dangerous conflict ended here. It has not only divided the two sections on the important point already stated, but on the deeper and more dangerous questions, the constitutionality of a protective Tariff, and the general principles and theory of the Constitution itself: the stronger, in order to maintain their superiority, giving a construction to the instrument which the other believes would convert the General Government into a consolidated, irresponsible government, with the total destruction of liberty; and the weaker, seeing no hope of relief with such assumption of powers, turning its eye to the reserved sovereignty of the States, as the only refuge from oppression. I shall not extend these remarks, as I might, by showing that, while the effect of the system of protection was rapidly alienating one section, it was not less rapidly, by its necessary operation, distracting and corrupting the other; and, between the two, subjecting the administration to violent and sudden changes, totally inconsistent with all stability and wisdom in the management of the affairs of the nation, of which we already see fearful symptoms. Nor do I deem it necessary to inquire whether this unhappy conflict grows out of true or mistaken views of interest on either or both sides. Regarded in either light, it ought to admonish us of the extreme danger to which our system is exposed, and the great moderation and wisdom necessary to preserve it. If it comes from mistaken views,—if the interests of the two sections, as affected by the Tariff, be really the same, and the system, instead of acting unequally, in reality diffuses equal blessings, and imposes equal burdens on every part,—it ought to teach us how liable those who are differently situated, and who view their interests under different aspects, are to come to different conclusions, even when their interests are strictly the same; and,

---

*The system, if continued, must end, not only in subjecting the industry and property of the weaker section to the control of the stronger, but in proscription and political disfranchisement. It must finally control elections and appointments to offices, as well as acts of legislation, to the great increase of the feelings of animosity, and of the fatal tendency to a complete alienation between the sections.

consequently, with what extreme caution any system of policy ought to be adopted, and with what a spirit of moderation pursued, in a country of such great extent and diversity as ours. But if, on the contrary, the conflict springs really from contrariety of interests,—if the burden be on one side and the benefit on the other,—then are we taught a lesson not less important, how little regard we have for the interests of others while in pursuit of our own; or, at least, how apt we are to consider our own interest the interest of all others; and, of course, how great the danger, in a country of such acknowledged diversity of interests, of the oppression of the feebler by the stronger interest, and, in consequence of it, of the most fatal sectional conflicts. But whichever may be the cause, the real or supposed diversity of interest, it cannot be doubted that the political consequences of the prohibitory system, be its effects in other respects beneficial or otherwise, are really such as I have stated; nor can it be doubted that a conflict between the great sections, on questions so vitally important, indicates a condition of the country so distempered and dangerous, as to demand the most serious and prompt attention. It is only when we come to consider of the remedy, that, under the aspect I am viewing the subject, there can be, among the informed and considerate, any diversity of opinion.

Those who have not duly reflected on its dangerous and inveterate character, suppose that the disease will cure itself; that events ought to be left to take their own course; and that experience, in a short time, will prove that the interest of the whole community is the same in reference to the Tariff, or, at least, whatever diversity there may now be, time will assimilate. Such has been their language from the beginning, but, unfortunately, the progress of events has been the reverse. The country is now more divided than in 1824, and then more than in 1816. The majority may have increased, but the opposite sides are, beyond dispute, more determined and excited than at any preceding period. Formerly, the system was resisted mainly as inexpedient; but now, as unconstitutional, unequal, unjust, and oppressive. Then, relief was sought exclusively from the General Government; but now, many, driven to despair, are raising their eyes to the reserved sovereignty of the States as the only refuge. If we turn from the past and present to the future, we shall find nothing to lessen, but much to aggravate the danger. The increasing embarrassment and distress of the staple States, the growing conviction, from experience, that they are caused by the prohibitory system principally, and that, under its continued operation, their present pursuits must become profitless, and with a conviction that their great and peculiar agricultural capital cannot be diverted from its ancient and hereditary channels without ruinous losses,—all concur to increase, instead of dispelling, the gloom that hangs over the future. In fact, to those who will duly reflect on the subject, the hope that the disease will cure itself must appear perfectly illusory. The question is, in reality, one between the exporting and non-exporting interests of the country. *Were there no exports, there would be no tariff.* It would be perfectly useless. On the contrary, so long as there are States which raise the great agricultural staples with the view of obtaining their supplies, and which must depend on the general market of the world for their sales, the conflict must remain if the system should continue, and the disease become more and more inveterate. Their interest, and that of those who, by high duties, would confine the purchase of their supplies to the home market, must, from the nature of things, in reference to the Tariff, be in conflict. Till, then, we cease to raise the great staples, cotton, rice, and tobacco, for the general market, and till we can find some other profitable investment for the immense amount of capital and labor now employed in their production, the present unhappy and dangerous conflict cannot terminate, unless with the prohibitory system itself.

In the mean time, while idly waiting for its termination through its own action, the progress of events in another quarter is rapidly bringing the contest to an immediate and decisive issue. We are fast approaching a period very novel in the history of nations, and bearing directly and powerfully on the point under consideration—the final payment of a long-standing funded debt—a period that cannot be greatly retarded, or its natural consequences eluded, without proving disastrous to those who attempt either, if not to the country itself. When it arrives, the Government will find itself in possession of a surplus revenue of $10,000,000 or $12,000,000, if not previously disposed of,—which presents the important question, What previous disposition ought to be made? a question which must press urgently for decision at the very next session of Congress. It cannot be delayed longer without the most distracting and dangerous consequences.

The honest and obvious course is, to prevent the accumulation of the surplus in the Treasury by a timely and judicious reduction of the imposts; and thereby to leave the money in the pockets of those who made it, and from whom it cannot be honestly nor constitutionally taken, unless required by the fair and legitimate wants of the Government. If, neglecting a disposition so obvious and just, the Government should attempt to keep up the present high duties, when the money is no longer wanted, or to dispose of this immense surplus by enlarging the old, or devising new schemes of appropriations; or, finding that to be impossible, it should adopt the most dangerous, unconstitutional, and absurd project ever devised by any government, of dividing the surplus among the States,—a project which, if carried into execution, would not fail to create an antagonist interest between the States and General Government on all questions of appropriations, which would certainly end in reducing the latter to a mere office of collection and distribution,—either of these modes would be considered, by the section suffering under the present high duties, as a fixed determination to perpetuate for ever what it considers the present unequal, unconstitutional, and oppressive burden; and from that moment it would cease to look to the General Government for relief. This deeply-interesting period, which must prove so disastrous should a wrong direction be given, but so fortunate and glorious, should a right one, is just at hand. The work must commence at the next session, as I have stated, or be left undone, or, at least, be badly done. The succeeding session would be too short, and too much agitated by the presidential contest, to afford the requisite leisure and calmness; and the one succeeding would find the country in the midst of the crisis, when it would be too late to prevent an accumulation of the surplus; which I hazard nothing in saying, judging from the nature of men and government, if once permitted to accumulate, would create an interest strong enough to perpetuate itself; supported, as it would be, by others so numerous and powerful; and thus would pass away a moment, never to be quietly recalled, so precious, if properly used, to lighten the public burden; to equalize the action of the Government; to restore harmony and peace; and to present to the world the illustrious example, which could not fail to prove most favorable to the great cause of liberty every where, of a nation the freest, and, at the same time, the best and most cheaply governed; of the highest earthly blessing at the least possible sacrifice.

As the disease will not, then, heal itself, we are brought to the question, Can a remedy be applied? and if so, what ought it to be?

To answer in the negative would be to assert that our Union has utterly failed; and that the opinion, so common before the adoption of our Constitution, that a free government could not be practically extended over a large country, was correct; and that ours had been destroyed by giving it limits so great as to comprehend, not only dissimilar, but irreconcilable interests. I am not prepared to admit a conclusion that would cast so deep a shade on the future; and that would falsify all the glorious anticipations of our ancestors, while it would so greatly lessen their high reputation for wisdom. Nothing but the clearest demonstration founded on actual experience, will ever force me to a conclusion so abhorrent to all my feelings. As strongly as I am impressed with the great dissimilarity, and, as I must add, as truth compels me to do, contrariety of interests in our country, resulting from the causes already indicated, and which are so great that they cannot be subjected to the unchecked will of a majority of the whole without defeating the great end of government, and without which it is a curse—justice—yet I see in the Union, as ordained by the Constitution, the means, if wisely used, not only of reconciling all diversities, but also the means, and the only effectual one, of securing to us justice, peace, and security, at home and abroad, and with them that national power and renown, the love of which Providence has implanted, for wise purposes, so deeply in the human heart: in all of which great objects every portion of our country, widely extended and diversified as it is, has a common and identical interest. If we have the wisdom to place a proper relative estimate on these more elevated and durable blessings, the present and every other conflict of like character may be readily terminated; but if, reversing the scale, each section should put a higher estimate on its immediate and peculiar gains, and, acting in that spirit, should push favorite measures of mere policy, without some regard to peace, harmony, or justice, our sectional conflicts would then, indeed, without some constitutional check, become interminable, except by the dissolution of the Union itself. That we have, in fact, so reversed the estimate, is too certain to be doubted, and the result is our present distempered and dangerous condition. The cure must commence in the correction of the error; and not to admit that we have erred would be the worst possible symptom. It would prove the disease to be incurable, through the regular and ordinary process of legislation; and would compel, finally, a resort to extraordinary, but I still trust, not only constitutional, but safe remedies.

No one would more sincerely rejoice than myself to see the remedy applied from the quarter where it could be most easily and regularly done. It is the only way by which those, who think that it is the only quarter from which it may constitutionally come, can possibly sustain their opinion. To omit the application by the General Government, would compel even them to admit the truth of the opposite opinion, or force them to abandon our political system in despair; while, on the other hand, all their enlightened and patriotic opponents would rejoice at such evidence of moderation and wisdom, on the part of the General Government, as would supersede a resort to what they believe to be the higher powers of our political system, as indicating a sounder state of public sentiment than has ever heretofore existed in any country; and thus affording the highest possible assurance of the perpetuation of our glorious institutions to the latest generation. For, as a people advance in knowledge, in the same degree they may dispense with mere artificial restrictions in their government; and we may imagine (but dare not expect to see) a state of intelligence so universal and high, that all the guards of liberty may be dispensed with, except an enlightened public opinion, acting through the right of suffrage; but it presupposes a state where every class and every section of the community are capable of estimating the effects of every measure, not only as it may affect itself, but every other class and section; and of fully realizing the sublime truth that the highest and wisest policy consists in maintaining justice, and promoting peace and harmony; and that, compared to these, schemes of mere gain are but trash and dross. I fear experience has already proved that we are far removed from such a state; and that we must, consequently, rely on the old and clumsy, but approved mode of checking power, in order to prevent or correct abuses; but I do trust that, though far from perfect, we are, at least, so much so as to be capable of remedying the present disorder in the ordinary way; and thus to prove that, with us, public opinion is so enlightened, and our political machine so perfect, as rarely to require for its preservation the intervention of the power that created it. How is this to be effected?

The application may be painful, but the remedy, I conceive, is certain and simple. There is but one effectual cure —an honest reduction of the duties to a fair system of revenue, adapted to the just and constitutional wants of the Government. Nothing short of this will restore the country to peace, harmony, and mutual affection. There is already a deep and growing conviction in a large section of the country, that the impost, even as a revenue system, is extremely unequal, and that it is mainly paid by those who furnish the means of paying the foreign exchanges of the country on which it is laid; and that the case would not be varied, taking into the estimate the entire action of the system, whether the producer or consumer pays in the first instance.

I do not propose to enter formally into the discussion of a point so complex and contested; but, as it has necessarily a strong practical bearing on the subject under consideration in all its relations, I cannot pass it without a few general and brief remarks.

If the producer, in reality, pays, none will doubt but the burden would mainly fall on the section it is supposed to do. The theory that the consumer pays, in the first instance, renders the proposition more complex, and will require, in order to understand where the burden, in reality, ultimately falls, on that supposition, to consider the protective, or, as its friends call it, the American System, under its threefold aspect of taxation, of protection, and of distribution,—or as performing, at the same time, the several functions of giving a revenue to the Government, of affording protection to certain branches of domestic industry, and furnishing means to Congress of distributing large sums through its appropriations: all of which are so blended in their effects, that it is impossible to understand its true operation without taking the whole into the estimate.

Admitting, then, as supposed, that he who consumes the article pays the tax in the increased price, and that the burden falls wholly on the consumers, without affecting the producers as a class (which, by the by, is far from being true, except in the single case, if there be such a one, where the producers have a monopoly of an article so indispensable to life that the quantity consumed cannot be affected by any increase of price), and that, considered in the light of a tax merely, the impost duties fall equally on every section in proportion to its population, still, when combined with its other effects, the burden it imposes as a tax may be so transferred from one section to the other as to take it from one and place it wholly on the other. Let us apply the remark first to its operation as a system of protection:

The tendency of the tax or duty on the imported article is not only to raise its price, but also, in the same proportion, that of the domestic article of the same kind, for which purpose, when intended for protection, it is, in fact, laid; and, of course, in determining where the system ultimately places the burden in reality, this effect, also, must be taken into the estimate. If one of the sections exclusively produces such domestic articles and the other purchases them from it, then it is clear that, to the amount of such increased prices, the tax or duty on the consumption of foreign articles would be transferred from the section producing the domestic articles to the one that purchased and consumed them;—unless the latter, in turn, be indemnified by the increased price of the objects of its industry, which none will venture to assert to be the case with the great staples of the country, which form the basis of our exports, the price of which is regulated by the foreign, and not the domestic market. To those who grow them, the increased price of the foreign and domestic articles both, in consequence of the duty on the former, is in reality, and in the strictest sense, a tax, while it is clear that the increased price of the latter acts as a bounty to the section producing them; and that, as the amount of such increased prices on what it sells to the other section is greater or less than the duty it pays on the imported articles, the system will, in fact, operate as a bounty or tax: if greater, the difference would be a bounty; if less, a tax.

Again, the operation may be equal in every other respect, and yet the pressure of the system, relatively, on the two sections, be rendered very unequal by the appropriations or distribution. If each section receives back what it paid into the treasury, the equality, if it previously existed, will continue; but if one receives back less, and the other proportionably more than is paid, then the difference in relation to the sections will be to the former a loss, and to the latter a gain; and the system, in this aspect, would operate to the amount of the difference, as a contribution from the one receiving less than it paid to the other that receives more. Such would be incontestably its general effects, taken in all its different aspects, even on the theory supposed to be most favorable to prove the equal action of the system, that the consumer pays, in the first instance, the whole amount of the tax.

To show how, on this supposition, the burden and advantages of the system would actually distribute themselves between the sections, would carry me too far into details; but I feel assured, after full and careful examination, that they are such as to explain, what otherwise would seem inexplicable, that one section should consider its repeal a calamity, and the other a blessing; and that such opposite views should be taken by them as to place them in a state of determined conflict in relation to the great fiscal and commercial interest of the country. Indeed, were there no satisfactory explanation, the opposite views that prevail in the two sections, as to the effects of the system, ought to satisfy all of its unequal action. There can be no safer, or more certain rule, than to suppose each portion of the country equally capable of understanding their respective interests, and that each is a much better judge of the effects of any system or measures on its peculiar interests than the other can possibly be.

But, whether the opinion of its unequal action be correct or erroneous, nothing can be more certain than that the impression is widely extending itself, that the system, under all its modifications, is essentially unequal; and if to this be added a conviction still deeper and more universal, that every duty imposed *for the purpose of protection is not only unequal, but also unconstitutional,* it would be a fatal error to suppose that any remedy, short of that which I have stated, can heal our political disorders.

In order to understand more fully the difficulty of adjusting this unhappy contest on any other ground, it may not be improper to present a general view of the constitutional objection, that it may be clearly seen how hopeless it is to expect that it can be yielded by those who have embraced it.

They believe that all the powers vested by the Constitution in Congress are, not only restricted by the limitations expressly imposed, but also by the nature and object of the powers themselves. Thus, though the power to impose duties on imports be granted in general terms, without any other express limitations but that they shall be equal, and no preference shall be given to the ports of one State over those of another, yet, as being a portion of the taxing power given with the view of raising revenue, it is, from its nature, restricted to that object, as much so as if the Convention had expressly so limited it; and that to use it to effect any other purpose not specified in the Constitution, is an infraction of the instrument in its most dangerous form—an infraction by perversion, more easily made, and more difficult to resist, than any other. The same view is believed to be applicable to the power of regulating commerce, as well as all the other powers. To surrender this important principle, it is conceived, would be to surrender all power, and to render the Government unlimited and despotic; and to yield it up, in relation to the particular power in question, would be, in fact, to surrender the control of the whole industry and capital of the country to the General Government, and would end in placing the weaker section in a colonial relation towards the stronger. For nothing are more dissimilar in their nature, or may be more unequally affected by the same laws, than different descriptions of labor and property; and if taxes, by increasing the amount and changing the intent only, may be perverted, in fact, into a system of penalties and rewards, it would give all the power that could be desired to subject the labor and property of the minority to the will of the majority, to be regulated without regarding the interest of the former in subserviency to the will of the latter. Thus thinking, it would seem unreasonable to expect, that any adjustment, based on the recognition of the correctness of a construction of the Constitution which would admit the exercise of such a power, would satisfy the weaker of two sections, particularly with its peculiar industry and property, which experience has shown may be so injuriously affected by its exercise. Thus much for one side.

The just claim of the other ought to be equally respected. Whatever excitement the system has justly caused in certain portions of our country, I hope and believe all will conceive that the change should be made with the least possible detriment to the interests of those who may be liable to be affected by it; consistently, with what is justly due to others, and the principles of the Constitution. To effect this will require the kindest spirit of conciliation and the utmost skill; but, even with these, it will be impossible to make the transition without a shock, greater or less, though I trust, if judiciously effected, it will not be without many compensating advantages. That there will be some such cannot be doubted. It will, at least, be followed by greater stability, and will tend to harmonize the manufacturing with all the other great interests of the country, and bind the whole in mutual affection. But these are not all. Another advantage of essential importance to the ulti-

mate prosperity of our manufacturing industry will follow. *It will cheapen production;* and, in that view, the loss of any one branch will be nothing like in proportion to the reduction of duty on that particular branch. Every reduction will, in fact, operate as a bounty to every other branch except the one reduced; and thus the effect of a general reduction will be to cheapen, universally, the price of production, by cheapening living, wages, and material, so as to give, if not equal profits after the reduction—profits by no means reduced proportionally to the duties—an effect which, as it regards the foreign markets, is of the utmost importance. It must be apparent, on reflection, that the means adopted to secure the home market for our manufactures are precisely the opposite of those necessary to obtain the foreign. In the former, the increased expense of production, in consequence of a system of protection, may be more than compensated by the increased price at home of the article protected; but in the latter, this advantage is lost; and, as there is no other corresponding compensation, the increased cost of production must be a dead loss in the foreign market. But whether these advantages, and many others that might be mentioned, will ultimately compensate to the full extent or not the loss to the manufacturers, on the reduction of the duties, certain it is, that we have approached a point at which a great change cannot be much longer delayed; and that the more promptly it may be met, the less excitement there will be, and the greater leisure and calmness for a cautious and skilful operation in making the transition; and which it becomes those more immediately interested duly to consider. Nor ought they to overlook, in considering the question, the different character of the claims of the two sides. The one asks from Government no advantage, but simply to be let alone in the undisturbed possession of their natural advantages, and to secure which, as far as was consistent with the other objects of the Constitution, was one of their leading motives in entering into the Union; while the other side claims, for the advancement of their prosperity, the positive interference of the Government. In such cases, on every principle of fairness and justice, such interference ought to be restrained within limits strictly compatible with the natural advantages of the other. He who looks to all the causes in operation—the near approach of the final payment of the public debt—the growing disaffection and resistance to the system in so large a section of the country—the deeper principles on which opposition to it is gradually turning—must be, indeed, infatuated not to see a great change is unavoidable; and that the attempt to elude or much longer delay it must, finally, but increase the shock and disastrous consequences which may follow.

In forming the opinions I have expressed, I have not been actuated by an unkind feeling towards our manufacturing interest. I now am, and ever have been, decidedly friendly to them, though I cannot concur in all of the measures which have been adopted to advance them. I believe considerations higher than any question of mere pecuniary interest forbade their use. But subordinate to these higher views of policy, I regard the advancement of mechanical and chemical improvements in the arts with feelings little short of enthusiasm; not only as the prolific source of national and individual wealth, but as the great means of enlarging the domain of man over the material world, and thereby of laying the solid foundation of a highly-improved condition of society, morally and politically. I fear not that we shall extend our power too far over the great agents of nature; but, on the contrary, I consider such enlargement of our power as tending more certainly and powerfully to better the condition of our race, than any one of the many powerful causes now operating to that result. With these impressions, I not only rejoice at the general progress of the arts in the world, but in their advancement in our own country; and as far as protection may be incidentally afforded, in the fair and honest exercise of our constitutional powers, I think now, as I have always thought, that sound policy, connected with the security, independence, and peace of the country, requires it should be done; but that we cannot go a single step beyond without jeopardizing our peace, our harmony and our liberty—considerations of infinitely more importance to us than any measure of mere policy can possibly be.

In thus placing my opinions before the public, I have not been actuated by the expectation of changing the public sentiment. Such a motive, on a question so long agitated, and so beset with feelings of prejudice and interest, would argue, on my part, an insufferable vanity, and a profound ignorance of the human heart. To avoid, as far as possible, the imputation of either, I have confined my statement, on the many and important points on which I have been compelled to touch, to a simple declaration of my opinion, without advancing any other reasons to sustain them than what appeared to me to be indispensable to the full understanding of my views; and if they should, on any point, be thought to be not clearly and explicitly developed, it will, I trust, be attributed to my solicitude to avoid the imputations to which I have alluded, and not from any desire to disguise my sentiments, nor the want of arguments and illustrations to maintain positions, which so abound in both, that it would require a volume to do them any thing like justice. I can only hope the truths which, I feel assured, are essentially connected with all that we ought to hold most dear, may not be weakened in the public estimation by the imperfect manner in which I have been, by the object in view, compelled to present them.

With every caution on my part, I dare not hope, in taking the step I have, to escape the imputation of improper motives; though I have, without reserve, freely expressed my opinions, not regarding whether they might or might not be popular. I have no reason to believe that they are such as will conciliate public favor, but the opposite, which I greatly regret, as I have ever placed a high estimate on the good opinion of my fellow-citizens. But, be that as it may, I shall, at least, be sustained by feelings of conscious rectitude. I have formed my opinions after the most careful and deliberate examination, with all the aids which my reason and experience could furnish; I have expressed them honestly and fearlessly, regardless of their effects personally, which, however interesting to me individually, are of too little importance to be taken into the estimate, where the liberty and happiness of our country are so vitally involved.

PART NINE Prelude to War

Engraving of Abraham Lincoln, sixteenth president of the
United States. © Bettmann/CORBIS

Americans' regional differences date from the earliest colonial settlements. Furthermore, such factors as climate; soil; and early political, economic, and religious structure soon formed distinct regional American communities and characters. Such regional diversity helped persuade revolutionary leaders that, in forming a new government, they must retain the colonies-become-states, not merely as departments of the national government, but as sovereign states, governing themselves in all matters not requiring united action.

But the balance between local control and national vigor was never easy to maintain. The question continually recurred: Who shall be the final judge of whether a law should be followed or struck down as a violation of the people's accustomed rights? Most of British history up through the eighteenth century is the story of battles over the answer to this question, and the same could be said of much of the history of the United States up through the Civil War.

Regional differences complicated this issue. For example, Southerners saw the federal tariff as a device forcing them to pay higher prices for manufactured goods so that Northern companies would profit. They also saw federal improvements on roads, canals, and bridges as a subsidy for Northern interests that would profit from easier trade routes.

Northerners, for their part, complained of federal actions favoring the South. Most important in that area was legislation concerning slavery. During the seventeenth century, an increasing number of black Africans were brought to the American colonies as slaves. At first, they joined white indentured servants who had purchased passage to the New World by selling their labor for a set number of years. But the distinction between someone working off a debt and someone condemned to a life of involuntary service, with his descendants condemned to the same fate, made this coexistence difficult. Further, Northern colonies had less use for slavery than those in the South, owing to their relative lack of large farms where slave labor could be used most effectively—and on which slaves could most effectively be kept as a separate, subordinate group.

Thus, slavery increasingly became a Southern institution. And Southerners insisted that this institution, and its importance to the South, be respected in the North. Constitutional provisions counting slaves as part-persons for purposes of representation and laws committing all states to help find and hand over runaway slaves were the most obvious attempts to protect Southern interests. More systemic problems arose from America's increasing population and territory. These factors caused concern over how best to maintain a balance of power and interests between slave-holding and non-slave-holding sections of the country, particularly as new territories in the West were opened to settlement and statehood.

Changes in laws regarding fugitive slaves, the ability of residents of American territories to choose whether to allow slavery, and regional boundaries all were attempts to keep the United States together in one union. But diverging visions of what kind of life a good American should expect and lead made such compromises difficult and short-lived. Moreover, disagreements regarding the inherently difficult system of competing sovereignties rendered debates over national power and regional character stronger, more divisive, and, in the end, explosive.

Laws Regulating Servants and Slaves, 1630–1852

Massachusetts Law on Capture and Protection of Servants

1630–41

Maryland Law Deeming Runaway Apprentices to Be Felons

March 26, 1642

North Carolina Law against Entertaining Runaways

1741

Connecticut Law Regarding Escape of Negroes and Servants

[no date given]

First Fugitive Slave Law

February 12, 1793

Maryland Resolutions Protesting against Pennsylvanians

December 17, 1821

Alabama Slave Code

1852

Americans were concerned with the problem of runaway servants before their colonies contained significant numbers of black African slaves. Apprenticeship and the practice of indentured servitude created a class of persons who might see it in their self-interest to run away. Thus, colonial laws early on took notice of the need to recapture runaway servants, though they sometimes recognized the possibility that the master's cruelty might be the root cause of the servant's flight. As time went on, these laws became tougher and more far-reaching in their drive to enlist the community in recapturing runaways. These laws did not prevent a significant number of bystanders from refusing to assist and even from interfering with attempts at recapture.

Massachusetts — Capture and Protection of Servants

1630–41

Acts respecting Masters, Servants, and Labourers. Sec. 3. It is also ordered, that when any servants shall run from their masters, or any other inhabitants shall privily go away with suspicion of evil intentions, it shall be lawful for the next magistrate, or the constable and two of the chief inhabitants where no magistrate is, to press men and boats or pinnaces at the publick charge, to pursue such persons by sea and land, and bring them back by force of arms. . . . Sec. 6. It is ordered, and by this court declared; that if any servant shall flee from the tyranny and cruelty of his or her master to the house of any freeman of the same town, they shall be there protected and sustained till due order be taken for their relief; provided due notice thereof be speedily given to their master from whom they fled, and to the next magistrate or constable where the party so fled is harboured.

Maryland — Runaway Apprentices Felons

March 26, 1642

Act against Fugitives.—It shall be felony in any apprentice Servant to depart away secretly from his or her Master or dame then being with intent to convey him or her Selfe away out of the Province. And on any other person that shall wittingly accompany such Servant in such unlawfull departure as aforesaid. And the offendors therein shall suffer paines of death, and after his due debts paid shall forfeit all his Lands, goods, & Chattels within the Province. Provided, that in Case his Lordship or his Leivt't-Generall shall at the request of the partie so condemned exchange such pains of death into Servitude, that then such exchange shall not exceed the term of Seaven years, and that the Master or dame of the parties so pardoned of death shall first be satisfied for the terme of such parties Service unexpired from the day of such unlawfull departure, and for double the time of his absence dureing his said departure.

North Carolina—Entertainment of Runaways

1741

XXVII. Any person harbouring a runaway shall be prosecuted and compelled to pay the sum of twenty-five pounds or serve the owner of the slave or his assigns five years. If he actually carry away the slave, he shall be convicted of felony and suffer accordingly. XXVIII. Seven shillings and sixpence, Proclamation money, reward for taking up runaways. For every mile over ten, threepence. XXXIV. Runaways when taken up shall be whipped. XXXV. Constables must give a receipt for runaway. Any failure shall be fined twenty shillings, Proclamation money, to be paid the church warden. XXXVI. Sheriff who shall hold a runaway longer than the act directs shall forfeit five pounds. Sheriff who allows a runaway to escape is liable to action from the party grieved. XXXVIII. This article takes up the fees of the jailor, etc.

Connecticut—Escape of Negroes and Servants

[no date given]

An Act to prevent the Running away of Indian and Negro Servants. Be it enacted by the Governour, Council, and Representatives, in General Court assembled, and by the Authority of the same, that whatsoever Negro or Indian Servant or Servants shall at any time after the publication hereof be found wandering out of the Town Bounds, or Place to which they belong, without a Ticket or Pass in writing under the Hand of some Assistant or Justice of the Peace, or under the Hand of the Master or Owner of such Negro or Indian Servant or Servants, shall be deemed and accounted to be Run-a-ways; and every person Inhabiting in this Colony, finding or meeting with any such Negro or Indian Servant or Servants, not having a Ticket as aforesaid, is hereby impowered to seize and secure him or them, and bring him or them before the next authority, to be examined and returned to his or their Master or Owner,

who shall satisfy the charge accruing thereby; and all Ferrymen within this Colony are hereby required not to suffer any Indian or Negro Servant, without Certificate as aforesaid, to pass over their respective Ferrys, by assisting of them therein directly or indirectly, on penalty of paying a fine of Twenty Shillings for every such Offence to the County Treasury, to be levied on their estates upon nonpayment, by warrant from any one Assistant or Justice of the Peace: And the like methods shall or may be used and observed as to Vagrant or Suspected Persons, found wandring from Town to Town, having no Certificate as aforesaid, who shall be seized and conveyed before the next Authority to be Examined and Disposed of according to Law: And if any Free Negroes shall travel without such Certificate or Pass, and be stopped, seized, or taken up, they shall pay all Charges arising thereby.

First Fugitive Slave Law

February 12, 1793

An Act respecting fugitives from justice and persons escaping from the service of their masters

SECTION 1. *Be it enacted by the Senate and House of Representatives of the United States of America in Congress assembled,* That whenever the executive authority of any state in the Union, or of either of the territories northwest or south of the river Ohio, shall demand any person as a fugitive from justice, of the executive authority of any such state or territory to which such person shall have fled, and shall moreover produce the copy of an indictment found, or an affidavit made before a magistrate of any state or territory as aforesaid, charging the person so demanded, with having committed treason, felony or other crime, certified as authentic by the governor or chief magistrate of the state or territory from whence the person so charged fled, it shall be the duty of the executive authority of the state or territory to which such person shall have fled, to cause him or her to be arrested and secured, and notice of the arrest to be given to the executive authority making such demand, or to the agent of such authority appointed to receive the fugitive, and to cause the fugitive to be delivered to such agent when he shall appear: But if no such agent shall appear within six months from the time of the arrest, the prisoner may be discharged. And all costs or expenses incurred in the apprehending, securing, and transmitting such fugitive to the state or territory making such demand, shall be paid by such state or territory.

SEC. 2. *And be it further enacted,* That any agent, appointed as aforesaid, who shall receive the fugitive into his custody, shall be empowered to transport him or her to the state or territory from which he or she shall have fled. And if any person or persons shall by force set at liberty, or rescue the fugitive from such agent while transporting, as aforesaid, the person or persons so offending shall, on conviction, be fined not exceeding five hundred dollars, and be imprisoned not exceeding one year.

SEC. 3. *And be it also enacted,* That when a person held to labour in any of the United States, or in either of the territories on the northwest or south of the river Ohio, under the laws thereof, shall escape into any other of the said states or territory, the person to whom such labour or service may be due, his agent or attorney, is hereby empowered to seize or arrest such fugitive from labour, and to take him or her before any judge of the circuit or district courts of the United States, residing or being within the state, or before any magistrate of a county, city or town corporate, wherein such seizure or arrest shall be made, and upon proof to the satisfaction of such judge or magistrate, either by oral testimony or affidavit taken before and certified by a magistrate of any such state or territory, that the person so seized or arrested, doth, under the laws of the state or territory from which he or she fled, owe service or labour to the person claiming him or her, it shall be the duty of such judge or magistrate to give a certificate thereof to such claimant, his agent or attorney, which shall be sufficient warrant for removing the said fugitive from labour, to the state or territory from which he or she fled.

SEC. 4. *And be it further enacted,* That any person who shall knowingly and willingly obstruct or hinder such claimant, his agent or attorney, in so seizing or arresting such fugitive from labour, or shall rescue such fugitive from such claimant, his agent or attorney when so arrested pursuant to the authority herein given or declared; or shall harbor or conceal such person after notice that he or she was a fugitive from labour, as aforesaid, shall, for either of the said offences, forfeit and pay the sum of five hundred dollars. Which penalty may be recovered by and for the benefit of such claimant, by action of debt, in any court proper to try the same; saving moreover to the person claiming such labour or service, his right of action for or on account of the said injuries or either of them.

Maryland Resolutions Protesting against Pennsylvanians

December 17, 1821

Mr. Wright laid before the House an attested copy of a resolution passed by the General Assembly of the State of Maryland, complaining of the protection offered by the citizens of Pennsylvania to the slaves of the citizens of Maryland, who abscond and go into that State, and declaring that it is the duty of Congress to enact such a law as will prevent a continuance of the evils complained of; which resolution was referred to the Committee on the Judiciary.

Alabama Slave Code

1852

CHAPTER III.

Patrols

§ 983. All white male owners of slaves, below the age of sixty years, and all other free white persons, between the ages of eighteen and forty-five years, who are not disabled by sickness or bodily infirmity, except commissioned officers in the militia, and persons exempt by law from the performance of militia duty, are subject to perform patrol duty.

§ 984. During the second week of the month of March, in each year, the justices of each precinct in the state, must make out a complete list of all the persons within their precinct, subject to patrol duty; and make division of the whole number, into detachments of not less than four, nor more than six, one of which number must be designated leader of the patrol.

§ 985. After such enumeration and division is made, a record must be made thereof, which must be retained by the senior justice, who must cause lists to be made of the names of the persons composing each detachment, with the leader thereof, numbering the list from number one, consecutively, and designating, on each list, when the term of service of the detachment will commence; each detachment being required to serve as patrol, not less than two nor more than three weeks.

§ 986. The list, so made out, must be delivered to the constable, during the second week in March, and must be by him served on the leader of each detachment, within ten days thereafter, either personally, or by leaving the list at his place of residence.

§ 987. If the leader of the patrol is sick or absent, the constable must notify the next person on the list, informing him that he is the leader of the patrol detachment.

§ 988. When the term of service of all the detachments is exhausted, the justice must again cause notice to be given by the constable, to the leader of each detachment, stating when the term of service of each detachment will commence; which must be served in the same manner as the previous notice.

§ 989. Upon receiving such notice with a list of the persons comprising the detachment, the leader must within five days thereafter, notify each member thereof, personally, or by leaving written notice at his place of residence; and designate the time and place of the meeting of the patrol.

§ 990. Each detachment must patrol such parts of the precinct as in their judgment is necessary, at least once a week at night, during their term of service, and oftener, when required so to do by a justice of the peace; or when informed, by a credible person, of evidences of insubordination, or threatened outbreak, or insurrection of the slaves; or of any contemplated unlawful assembly of slaves or free negroes.

§ 991. Any member of a patrol detachment may send a substitute, who, if accepted by the leader, may patrol in his stead.

§ 992. The patrol has power to enter, in a peaceable manner, upon any plantation; to enter by force, if necessary, all negro cabins or quarters, kitchens and out houses, and to apprehend all slaves who may there be found, not belonging to the plantation or household, without a pass from their owner or overseer; or strolling from place to place, without authority.

§ 993. The patrol has power to punish slaves found under the circumstances recited in the preceding section, by stripes, not exceeding thirty-nine.

§ 994. It is the duty of the patrol, on receiving information that any person is harboring a runaway slave, to make search for such slave, and if found, to apprehend and take him before a justice of the peace, who, if the owner is unknown, must commit him to jail.

§ 995. If the patrol find any slave from home without a pass, and under circumstances creating the belief that he is a runaway, they must detain him in custody, and give in-formation thereof to the owner, if known; and if unknown, or without their precinct, deliver him up to a justice, who must commit him to jail for safe keeping.

§ 996. If there is but one justice in the precinct, he must perform all the duties required by this chapter; and if there be no justices in office in the precinct on the second Monday in March, the duties here enjoined must be performed the week succeeding his election.

§ 997. The leader, or any member of the detachment, failing to appear according to the notice, and perform patrol duty, must be fined ten dollars by the justice of the precinct.

§ 998. The leader of each patrol must, at the expiration of each term of service, make report in writing, and upon oath, to the justice, of the number of times his detachment has patrolled, and of the absence, without sufficient excuse, of any member of the detachment at the times designated for patrolling, and failure to perform patrol duty; and thereupon it is the duty of the justice to cite such delinquents to appear at a time and place designated by him, and show cause why a fine should not be imposed against him; and upon their failure to appear, or to render a sufficient excuse, they must each be fined ten dollars for each omission, for which execution may issue.

§ 999. If the leader of the patrol fails to make such report, within one month after the expiration of his term of service, he is guilty of a misdemeanor, and, on conviction, must be fined in a sum not less than twenty dollars, at the discretion of the jury.

§ 1000. The justice must make report in writing, to the solicitor of his circuit, of all omissions on the part of patrol leaders, to make the reports referred to in the two preceding sections.

§ 1001. Every person appointed a leader of the patrol, who refuses, without sufficient excuse, to act as such, must be fined twenty dollars by the justice appointing him; being first cited to appear and show cause against it.

§ 1002. Every justice and constable failing or refusing to perform any of the duties required of them by this chapter, are guilty of a misdemeanor, and, on conviction, must be fined, the justice not less than fifty, and the constable not less than twenty dollars, at the discretion of the jury.

§ 1003. All fines collected for a violation of the provisions of this chapter, must be paid by the justice or constable collecting it, into the county treasury; and failing to do so, may be proceeded against by motion in the name of the county treasurer, as for other money collected in their official capacity.

§ 1004. The patrol, if sued for any act done in the performance of patrol duty, may give this law in evidence under the general issue; but are liable in damages, to any person aggrieved, for any unnecessary violence committed under color of performing patrol duty, either by unnecessarily breaking or entering houses, or for excessive punishment inflicted on any slave.

CHAPTER IV.

Slaves and Free Negroes

ARTICLE I
Slaves

§ 1005. No master, overseer, or other person having the charge of a slave, must permit such slave to hire himself to another person, or to hire his own time, or to go at large, unless in a corporate town, by consent of the authorities thereof, evidenced by an ordinance of the corporation; and every such offence is a misdemeanor, punishable by fine not less than twenty nor more than one hundred dollars.

§ 1006. No master, overseer, or head of a family must permit any slave to be or remain at his house, out house, or kitchen, without leave of the owner or overseer, above four hours at any one time; and for every such offence he forfeits ten dollars, to be recovered before any justice of the peace, by any person who may sue for the same.

§ 1007. Any owner or overseer of a plantation, or householder, who knowingly permits more than five negroes, other than his own, to be and remain at his house, plantation, or quarter, at any one time, forfeits ten dollars for each and every one over that number, to the use of any one who may sue for the same, before any justice of the peace; unless such assemblage is for the worship of almighty God, or for burial service, and with the consent of the owner or overseer of such slaves.

§ 1008. No slave must go beyond the limits of the plantation on which he resides, without a pass, or some letter or token from his master or overseer, giving him authority to go and return from a certain place; and if found violating this law, may be apprehended and punished, not exceeding twenty stripes, at the discretion of any justice before whom he may be taken.

§ 1009. If any slave go upon the plantation, or enter the house or out house of any person, without permission in writing from his master or overseer, or in the prosecution of his lawful business, the owner or overseer of such plantation or householder may give, or order such slave to be given ten lashes on his bare back.

§ 1010. Any railroad company in whose car or vehicle, and the master or owner of any steamboat, or vessel, in which a slave is transported or carried, without the written authority of the owner or person in charge of such slave, forfeits to the owner the sum of fifty dollars; and if such slave is lost, is liable for his value, and all reasonable expenses attending the prosecution of the suit.

§ 1011. In any action under the preceding section, it devolves on the defendant to prove that the owner has regained possession of the slave.

§ 1012. No slave can keep or carry a gun, powder, shot, club, or other weapon, except the tools given him to work with, unless ordered by his master or overseer to carry such weapon from one place to another. Any slave found offending against the provisions of this section, may be seized, with such weapon, by any one, and carried before any justice, who, upon proof of the offence, must condemn the weapon to the use of such person, and direct that the slave receive thirty-nine lashes on his bare back.

§ 1013. Any justice of the peace may, within his own county, grant permission in writing to any slave, on the application of his master or overseer, to carry and use a gun and ammunition within his master's plantation.

§ 1014. No slave can, under any pretence, keep a dog; and for every such offence must be punished by any justice of the peace with twenty stripes on his bare back. If such dog is kept with the consent of the owner or overseer, he must pay five dollars for every dog so kept, to the use of any person who will sue for the same before any justice: and is also liable to any person for any injury committed by said dogs.

§ 1015. Riots, routs, unlawful assemblies, trespasses, and seditious speeches by a slave, are punished, by the direction of any justice before whom he may be carried, with stripes not exceeding one hundred.

§ 1016. Any person having knowledge of the commission of any offence by a slave against the law, may apprehend him, and take him before a justice of the peace for trial.

§ 1017. Any slave fire hunting in the night time, must be punished with thirty-nine lashes, by order of any justice before whom he may be carried. If such fire hunting by the slave is by the command of the master or overseer, the slave must not be punished, but the master or overseer forfeits the sum of fifty dollars, one half to the county, and the other half to any person who may sue for the same before any justice of the peace.

§ 1018. No slave can own property, and any property purchased or held by a slave, not claimed by the master or owner, must be sold by order of any justice of the peace; one half the proceeds of the sale, after the payment of costs and necessary expenses, to be paid to the informer, and the residue to the county treasury.

§ 1019. Any slave who writes for, or furnishes any other slave with any pass or free paper, on conviction before any justice of the peace, must receive one hundred lashes on his bare back.

§ 1020. Not more than five male slaves shall assemble together at any place off the plantation, or place to which they belong, with or without passes or permits to be there, unless attended by the master or overseer of such slaves, or unless such slaves are attending the public worship of God, held by white persons.

§ 1021. It is the duty of all patrols, and all officers, civil and military, to disperse all such unlawful assemblies; and each of the slaves constituting such unlawful assembly, must be punished by stripes, not exceeding ten; and for the second offence, may be punished with thirty-nine stripes, at the discretion of any justice of the peace before whom he may be brought.

§ 1022. Any slave who preaches, exhorts, or harangues any assembly of slaves, or of slaves and free persons of color, without a license to preach or exhort from some religious society of the neighborhood, and in the presence of five slave-holders, must, for the first offence, be punished with thirty-nine lashes, and for the second, with fifty lashes; which punishment may be inflicted by any officer of a patrol company, or by the order of any justice of the peace.

§ 1023. Runaway slaves may be apprehended by any person, and carried before any justice of the peace, who must either commit them to the county jail, or send them to the owner, if known; who must, for every slave so apprehended, pay the person apprehending him six dollars, and all reasonable charges.

§ 1024. Any justice of the peace receiving information that three or more runaway slaves are lurking and hid in swamps, or other obscure places, may, by warrant, reciting the names of the slaves, and their owners, if known, direct a leader of the patrol of the district, and if there be none, then any other suitable person, to summon, and take with him such power as may be necessary to apprehend such runaway; and if taken, to deliver them to the owner or commit them to the jail of his proper county.

§ 1025. For such apprehension and delivery to the owner, or committal to jail, the parties so apprehending shall be entitled to twenty dollars for each slave, to be paid by the owner.

§ 1026. The justice committing a runaway, must endeavor to ascertain from the slave, and from all other sources within his reach, the true name of the slave, and his owner's name, and residence; and must include all such information in the commitment, which must be preserved and filed by the justice.

§ 1027. On the reception of a runaway slave, the sheriff must, without delay, cause advertisement to be made in a newspaper, published in the county, if there be one, if not, in the one published nearest to the court house of such county, giving an accurate description of the person of the slave, his supposed age, the information contained in the warrant in relation to the slave, and his owner, and such other facts important to the identification of the slave, as the sheriff may be able to obtain from the slave, or from any other source, which must be continued for six months, once a week, if the slave is not sooner reclaimed by the owner.

§ 1028. If the slave is not reclaimed within six months, the sheriff must advertise and sell him for cash, in the manner slaves are sold under execution. The proceeds of the sale, after all expenses are paid, must be paid to the county treasurer for the use of the county.

§ 1029. The owner may regain the possession of the slave before sale, or the proceeds after sale, by appearing before the judge of probate of the county, and proving, by an impartial witness, his title to the slave; which proof must be reduced to writing, sworn to, subscribed, and filed in the office of the probate judge.

§ 1030. Thereupon, and upon the payment by the owner of the costs of advertising, and all other expenses attending the imprisonment, the judge of probate must, by order in writing, direct the jailor, if the slave has not been sold, to deliver him to the applicant. If he has been sold, then the order must be directed to the county treasurer, to pay him over the proceeds of such sale received in the treasury.

§ 1031. The title of the purchaser of such slave is not

affected by the claim of the owner, or by an irregularity in the advertisement or sale.

§ 1032. The fee of probate judge is two dollars, and the sheriff is allowed the same commissions as on sales under execution.

ARTICLE II
Free Negroes

§ 1033. Every free colored person who has come to this state since the first day of February, one thousand eight hundred and thirty-two, and has been admonished by any sheriff, justice of the peace, or other judicial officer, that he cannot, by law, remain in this state; and does not, within thirty days, depart therefrom, must, on conviction, be punished by imprisonment in the penitentiary for two years; and shall have thirty days after his discharge from the penitentiary to leave the state; and on failing to do so, must be imprisoned in the penitentiary for five years.

§ 1034. All sheriffs, justices of the peace, and other judicial officers, knowing of any free person of color being within the state, contrary to the provisions of the preceding section, are hereby required to give the warning therein prescribed.

§ 1035. If any free person of color is at any time found at an unlawful assembly of slaves, he forfeits twenty dollars, to any person who will sue for the same, before any justice of the peace; and for the second offence, must, in addition thereto, be punished with ten stripes. All justices of the peace, sheriffs, and constables, are charged with the execution of this law.

§ 1036. No free person of color must retail, or assist in retailing, or vending, spirituous or vinous liquors; and for every such offence, forfeits twenty dollars, to be recovered before any justice of the peace, by any one who will sue for the same; and for the second offence, having been once convicted and fined, must be punished by stripes, not exceeding twenty-five, at the discretion of the justice.

§ 1037. The preceding sections of this article do not apply to, or affect any free person of color, who, by the treaty between the United States and Spain, became a citizen of the United States, or the descendants of such.

§ 1038. Any free person of color who writes for, or furnishes a slave with a pass, is guilty of a misdemeanor, and, on conviction, must be fined not less than fifty dollars, and be imprisoned not less than six months.

§ 1039. Any free person of color who writes for, or furnishes any slave a pass, with the intent to enable such slave to escape from his master, is guilty of a felony, and, on conviction, must be imprisoned in the penitentiary not less than three, nor more than seven years.

§ 1040. Any free person of color imprisoned in the penitentiary, must leave the state in one month after his discharge, unless pardoned; and failing to do so, or having left returns again, on conviction, must be imprisoned in the penitentiary five years.

§ 1041. Any free person of color, who buys of, or sells to, any slave, any article, or commodity whatever, without a written permission from the master, or overseer of such slave, designating the article so to be bought, or sold, is guilty of a misdemeanor, and must, upon conviction, before any justice of the peace of the county where such offence is committed, be punished with thirty-nine stripes.

§ 1042. Any free person of color, found in company with any slave, in any kitchen, out house, or negro quarter, without a written permission from the owner, or overseer of such slave, must, for every such offence, receive fifteen lashes; and for every subsequent offence, thirty-nine lashes; which may be inflicted by the owner or overseer of the slave, or by any officer or member of any patrol company.

§ 1043. If any free person of color permits a slave to be, or remain in his house, or out house, or about his premises, without permission, in writing, from the owner, or overseer of the slave, he shall be punished as provided in the preceding section.

§ 1044. Any free person of color, who preaches, exhorts, or harangues any assembly of slaves, or of slaves and free persons of color, unless in the presence of five slaveholders, and licensed to preach or exhort by some religious society of the neighborhood, must, for the first offence, receive thirty-nine lashes, and for the second offence, fifty lashes, by the order of any justice of the county, before whom the offender may be carried.

"Slavery"

"Agriculture and the Militia"

JOHN TAYLOR OF CAROLINE

1818

John Taylor (1753–1824) lived the bulk of his life in Caroline County, Virginia, taking time from his plantation to serve as a state legislator and member of the U.S. Senate. He worked against ratification of the Constitution, introduced James Madison's Resolutions against the Alien and Sedition Acts in the Virginia House of Delegates, fought for religious disestablishment in Virginia, and argued against federal restrictions on the expansion of slavery into the territories. In addition to a number of works outlining the theory of American constitutional government, Taylor wrote extensively on agricultural topics.

Slavery

Negro slavery is a misfortune to agriculture, incapable of removal, and only within the reach of palliation. The state legislatures, hopeless of removing all its inconveniences, have been led by their despair to suffer all; and among them, one of a magnitude sufficient to affect deeply the prosperity of agriculture, and threaten awfully the safety of the country; I allude to the policy of introducing by law into society, a race, or nation of people between the masters and slaves, having rights extremely different from either, called free negroes and mulattoes. It is not my intention to consider the peril to which this policy exposes the safety of the country, by the excitement to insurrection, with which it perpetually goads the slaves, the channels for communication it affords, and the reservoir for recruits it provides. I shall only observe, that it was this very policy, which first doomed the whites, and then the mulattoes themselves, to the fate suffered by both in St. Domingo; and which contributes greatly to an apprehension so often exhibited. Being defined by experience in that country, and by expectation in this, it is unnecessary for me to consider the political consequences of this policy.

My present object is to notice its influence on agriculture. This so entirely depends on slaves in a great proportion of the union, that it must be deeply affected by whatever shall indispose them to labour, render them intractable, or entice them into a multitude of crimes and irregularities. A free negro and mulatto class is exactly calculated to effect all these ends. They live upon agriculture as agents or brokers for disposing of stolen products, and diminish its capital, both to the extent of these stolen products, and also to the amount of the labour lost in carrying on the trade.

They wound agriculture in the two modes of being an unproductive class living upon it, like a stock-jobber or capitalist class, and of diminishing the utility of the slaves. This latter mode might be extended to a multitude of particulars, among which rendering the slaves less happy, compelling masters to use more strictness, disgusting them with agriculture itself, and greatly diminishing their ability to increase the comforts, and of course the utility of slaves, would be items deeply trenching upon its prosperity. It is however unnecessary to prove what every agriculturist in the slave states experimentally knows, namely, that his operations are greatly embarrassed, and his efforts retarded, by circumstances having the class of free negroes for their cause.

The only remedy is to get rid of it. This measure ought to be settled by considerations of a practical moral nature, and not by a moral hypothesis, resembling several mechanical inventions incarcerated at Washington, beautiful and ingenious, but useless. It is substantial, not balloon morality, by which the questions ought to be considered; whether a severance of the free negro class from the whites and slaves, will benefit or injure either of the three classes; or whether it will benefit or injure a majority of them as constituting one body? The situation of the free negro class is exactly calculated to force it into every species of vice. Cut off from most of the rights of citizens, and from all the allowances of slaves, it is driven into every species of crime for subsistence; and destined to a life of idleness, anxiety and guilt. The slaves more widely share in its guilt, than in its fraudulent acquisitions. They owe to it the perpetual pain of repining at their own condition by having an object of comparison before their eyes, magnified by its idleness and thefts with impunity, into a temptation the most alluring to slaves; and will eventually owe to it the consequences of their insurrections. The whites will reap also a harvest of consequences from the free negro class, and throughout all their degrees of rank suffer much in their morals from the two kinds of intercourse maintained with it. If vice is misery, this middle class is undoubtedly placed in a state of misery itself, and contributes greatly to that of the other two. The interest of virtue, therefore, as well as sound policy, is allied with the interest of agriculture, in recommending the proposed severance. If it should not benefit every individual of the three classes, as is probable, no doubt can exist of its benefiting a majority of each, and a very great majority of the whole. No injury, but much good to the whites and slaves is perceivable in the measure. And relief from the disadvantages of inferior rights, from the necessity of living in a settled course of vice, and from the dangers portended by it to a commotion among the slaves, promises great benefits to the free negro class itself from a severance.

It may be easily effected by purchasing of Congress lands sufficient for their subsistence in states where slavery is not allowed, and giving them the option of removing to those lands, or emigrating wherever they please. Perhaps both the national safety and prosperity would justify a harsher measure. To advance both by bestowing rewards, cannot be severe, unjust or illiberal.

At least it will be admitted by those acquainted with the subject, that the prosperity of agriculture is considerably influenced by the circumstances alluded to in this number.

Slavery, Continued

Societies are instituted to control and diminish the imperfections of human nature, because without them it generates ignorance, savageness and depravity of manners. Those best constituted, cannot however cure it of a disposition to command, and to live by the labour of others; it is eternally forming sub-societies for acquiring power and wealth, and to these perfidious, ambitious, avaricious or unconstitutional sub-societies, the liberty and property of the rest of the body politic has universally fallen a prey. They are of a civil or military complexion, or of both, as the circumstances of the case may require fraud or force. Anciently, the general ignorance of mankind, caused the frauds of superstition to suffice for working the ends of traiterous sub-societies. As these became exploded, the more intricate pecuniary frauds were resorted to. Now, on account of the increasing knowledge and more prying temper of mankind, military force is united with pecuniary frauds. And hitherto the most perfect society for the public good, has never been able to defend itself against sub-societies in some form for advancing the wealth or power of a faction or a particular interest. Combine with this universal experience, that it is impossible to conceive a form of society better calculated to excite and foster factions or sub-societies, than one constituted of distinct colours, incurable prejudices, and inimicable interests, and the inferences are unavoidable. If the badges of foolish names can drive men into phrenzy without cause, will not those which powerfully assail both reason and the senses, create deadly factions.

The attempt will undoubtedly terminate according to the nature of man, as it has once already terminated; but its catastrophe ought rather to be courted than avoided if the author of the notes on Virginia* is right in the following quotations. "The whole commerce between master and slave," says he, "is a perpetual exercise of the most boisterous passions, the most unremitting despotism on one part, and degrading submissions on the other. The parent storms, the child looks on, catches the lineaments of wrath, puts on the same airs in the circle of smaller slaves, gives a loose to his worst of passions, and thus nursed, educated and daily exercised in tyranny, cannot but be stamped by it with odious peculiarities. The man must be a prodigy who can retain his manners and morals undepraved by such circumstances. The Almighty has no attribute which can take side with us in such a contest." Such is the picture exhibited in the Notes on Virginia of "the manners" of the people, without a single palliating circumstance; and Winterbotham in his history of America has quoted and varnished it anew.

*Thomas Jefferson.—B. F.

No man has been less accustomed than the author of the Notes on Virginia to paint his opinions, for the same reason that an Indian paints his body; and yet from reading the whole chapter on the manners of that state, a stranger would hardly form a more correct idea of them, than a stranger to Indians would of their colour, on seeing one painted coal black. Circumstances affect the mind, as weather does beer, and frequently produces a sort of moral fermentation, which throws up bubbles of prismatic splendor, whilst they are played upon by the rays of some temporary effervescence, but destined to burst when the fermentation ceases. The Notes on Virginia were written in the heat of a war for liberty; the human mind was made still hotter by the French revolution; and let those who were insensible of the mental fermentations and moral bubbles generated by these causes, censure Mr. Jefferson. I should be unjust to do it.

If Mr. Jefferson's assertions are correct, it is better to run the risque of national extinction, by liberating and fighting the blacks, than to live abhorred of God, and consequently hated of man. If they are erroneous, they ought not to be admitted as arguments for the emancipating policy. The considerations, which this chapter of impassioned censure of slave holders, inspire, are too extensive for a hasty essay, but a few of them may be noticed. I shall pass over the enlistment of the Deity in the question with an humble hope, that his justice and mercy do not require the whites and blacks to be placed in such a relative situation, as that one colour must extinguish the other; and as inclining to think the enrolment of his name on the side of the slaves, somewhat like a charge of inattention to his own attributes, apparently siding with masters throughout all ages and among most nations hitherto, the liberating St. Domingo masters excepted; and not a little tinged with impiety. Slavery was carried farther among the Greeks and Romans than among ourselves, and yet these two nations produced more great and good patriots and citizens, than, probably, all the rest of the world. In the United States it is also probable that the public and private character of individuals is as good, as in the countries where locomotive liberty and slavery to a faction, exist; nor do the slave states seem less productive of characters in whom the nation is willing to confide than the others. Even the author of the quotation himself may be fairly adduced as an instance which refutes every syllable of his chapter on Virginia manners, unless indeed this refutation, and an abundance of others like it, can be evaded by forming the best citizens into a class of prodigies or monsters, to evade the force of eminent virtues towards the refutation of erroneous assertions.

These facts are referred to the consideration of the physiologist. To me it seems, that slaves are too far below, and too much in the power of the master, to inspire furious passions; that such are nearly as rare and disgraceful towards slaves as towards horses; that slaves are more frequently the objects of benevolence than of rage; that children from their nature are inclined to soothe, and hardly ever suffered to tyrannize over them; that they open instead of shut the sluices of benevolence in tender minds; and that fewer good public or private characters have been raised in countries enslaved by some faction or particular interest, than in those where personal slavery existed.

I conjecture the cause of this to be, that vicious and mean qualities become despicable in the eyes of freemen from their association with the character of slaves. Character, like condition is contrasted, and as one contrast causes us to love liberty better, so the other causes us to love virtue better. Qualities odious in themselves, become more contemptible, when united with the most degraded class of men, than when seen in our equals; and pride steps in to aid the struggles of virtue. Instead therefore of fearing that children should imbibe the qualities of slaves, it is probable, that the circumstance of seeing bad qualities in slaves will contribute to their virtue.

For the same reason the submission and flattery of slaves will be despised, and cause us rather to hate servility than to imbibe a dictatorial arrogance; and only inspire the same passion with the submission and flattery of a spaniel. It is the submission and flattery of equals, which fills men with the impudent and wicked wish to dictate, and an impatience of free opinion and fair discussion. This reprehensible temper is a sound objection against any species of human policy, which generates it, and applies most forcibly against that conferring on an individual a power, so to dispense money and honours, as to procure submission and flattery from the highest ranks and conditions in society, a thousand times more genial to pride, than the submission and flattery of a poor slave; and ten thousand times more pernicious to nations.

Virtue and vice are naturally and unavoidably coexistent in the moral world, as beauty and deformity are in the animal; one is the only mirror in which the other can be seen, and therefore, in the present state of man, one cannot be destroyed without the other. It may be thus that personal slavery has constantly reflected the strongest rays of civil liberty and patriotism. Perhaps it is suffered by the Deity to perform an office without which these rays are gradually obscured and finally obliterated by charters and partial laws. Perhaps the sight of slavery and its vices may inspire the mind with an affection for liberty and virtue, just as the climates and deserts of Arabia, would make it think Italy a paradise.

Let it not be supposed that I approve of slavery because I do not aggravate its evils, or prefer a policy which must terminate in a war of extermination. The chapter on the manners of slave-holders before quoted, concludes with an intimation, that the consent of the masters to a general emancipation, or their own extirpation, were the alternatives between which they had to choose. Such a hint from a profound mind is awful. It admits an ability in the blacks, though shackled by slavery, to extirpate the whites, and proposes to increase this ability by knocking off their shackles. Such a hint adds force to the recommendation in the previous essay for separating the enslaved and free blacks, as some security against the prognosticated extirpation. And after such a hint, "with what execration should the statesman be loaded" who thus forewarned, should produce the destruction of the most civilized portion of society, and re-people half the world with savages. If England and America would erect and foster a settlement of free negroes in some fertile part of Africa, it would soon subsist by its own energies. Slavery might then be gradually re-exported, and philanthropy gratified by a slow reanimation of the virtue, religion and liberty of the negroes, instead of being again afflicted with the effects of her own rash attempts suddenly to change human nature.

Agriculture and the Militia

The rocks of our salvation; as they are called by legislatures, presidents, governors, and toast-makers, throughout the United States; and hard rocks indeed they need be, to withstand the saws, wedges, and chisels, made by law, to cut, split and chip them to pieces. It is probable that more talents were wasted upon the bank of the United States, at each of its epochs, than have been expended for the im-

provement of these national fortresses, for securing wealth and independence, since the revolution. Edifice, after edifice, has been raised upon their ruins; but the new structures resemble the venerable fabricks from whence they are torn, as the modern huts raised of its ruins resemble the ancient city of Palmyra.

A pernicious little army (pernicious as constituting a reason for neglecting the militia), a species of marine preparation, whose most striking features are decay, imbecility and expense; and an awful unconstitutional precedent, for resorting to a volunteer militia, officered by the President instead of the States, have dismantled one fortress, and all the arts to enrich capital and speculation legerdemain, by paper, at the expense of property and industry, as practised in England, are playing upon the other.

When the future historian of our republick, shall search for acts of patriotism, and matter for biography, the contrast between the heroes who have created, and the politicians who have ruined a nation, will afford him ample room for exhausting the strongest phrases of eulogy and censure. The first was not effected by enfeebling the heart, nor will the second be avoided by impoverishing the soil and its cultivators; by beguiling the militia of its power and importance, with substitutions founded in the pretext of diminishing its duty, but preparing the means of usurpation for some ambitious president; and by taxing agriculture in various crafty modes, under pretence of enriching it, but in fact to enrich capitalists at its expense.

The patriots of the revolution have chiefly retired to the enjoyment of a treasure, deposited beyond the schemes of craft, leaving to their successors two specious fields as productive of glory, as the field of war was to them. Far from exhausting the resources for gaining the transporting consciousness of having benefited our country, they left for these successors the creation of a proud militia and a fertile country, as equally meriting national admiration and gratitude, with the feats which secured our independence, and placed prosperity within our reach. But of what avail is it, that one set of patriots should have cut away the causes which enfeebled our militia, and impoverished our agriculture, if another does not enable us to reap from their valour the rewards which excited it? After wading through the calamities of war near to these rewards, to reject them, one by neglect, and the other by the preference of a harpy which always eats and never feeds, seems only consistent with the policy of the British parliament, which excited the resistance of the revolutionary heroes. Had they been told that they were fighting to destroy the militia, and to make agriculture food for charter and paper capital, they would have discerned no reason for making themselves food for powder.

It would be easy to shew that agriculture never can experience fair treatment without a sound militia, but it is a subject too extensive and important to be considered in this light way, and therefore they are only exhibited in union, in the concluding essay, to remind the reader, that they are political twins, one of whom never lives long free, after the other dies.

Executive, legislative and festive encomiums of these twins, which ought to be called "Liberty and prosperity," though the unhappy delusions of fervour, produce the knavish effects of flattery; they prevent us from acquiring a militia and an agriculture, which deserve praise (false praise always excludes real merit), and keep us without laws for raising either to mediocrity, much less to perfection. I do not believe that these encomiums are generally the artifices of deliberate vice and secret purpose, to impose upon the enthusiastic and unwary, in pursuance of the precedents so often exhibited by rapacious priests clothed in the garb of sanctity; but yet rapacity may sometimes assume the language of patriotism, to keep the people blind to the dangers which threaten, and to the measures which can save them.

The good humour of the festive board will bear illustrations of these assertions, with less discomfort than cold design, or deluded negligence; and therefore, however inconsistent it may be with the gravity and importance of our subject, an aversion for giving pain to any one, induces me to supply it with the following toasts.

THE MILITIA . . . The Rock of our Liberty.
Unarmed, undisciplined, and without uniformity, substituted by an ineffectual navy, an ineffectual army, and paper volunteers, officered by the president.
Unpatronized even at the expense of a gun boat.
Flattered and despised.
Taught self contempt, instead of a proud and erect spirit. *Nine cheers.*

AGRICULTURE . . . The fountain of our wealth.
A land killer.
A payer of bounties and receiver of none.

A beautifier of towns and a sacrificer of the country.
A cultivator for stock, without stock for cultivation.
Giving its money to those who will give it flattery.
A weight in the legislative scales of the United States, as much heavier than a feather, as a feather is heavier than nothing.
Its labour steeped in an infusion of thievery, dissatisfaction and sedition, by a mixture of bond and free negroes.
Producing 40,000,000 dollars annually for exportation, bearing most taxes for publick benefit, and taxed in various modes for the private benefit of 300,000,000 dollars worth of capitalists who pay no taxes.
Out of a remnant of the 40,000,000 dollars exported, compelled by protecting duties to pay heavy bounties for the encouragement of manufactures, already amounting to above 150,000,000 dollars annually. *Nine cheers more.*

A few words, at parting, to the reader, will close these essays. If he is of the courteous nature which loves to give and to receive flattery; or if his interest tugs him violently against them, he may disbelieve the plainest truths they contain, or at least reject them as being told in too blunt a style. If he is ignorant of agriculture or a devotee of a party or an idol, he will rather presume, that our agriculture is perfect and undefrauded, than take the trouble of enabling himself to judge; or silently swallow the grossest errours, than give up his superstition. These papers never contemplated the desperate hope of obtaining the attention of any one of these characters. Half the profit of agriculture, must undoubtedly convince the several tribes of capitalists, that it flourishes exceedingly. The idolator will rather embrace the stake than truth, and the agriculturist who prefers ignorance to knowledge, though these hasty essays constituted a complete system of husbandry, would be as little benefited by them, as a lawyer or a physician who practised by deputy, would be by the reports of Coke, or the dispensatory of Cullen.* Yet to those who would think and inquire, opinions slowly and cautiously admitted, upon various views of national interest, without a motive likely to mislead or deceive, might afford suggestions capable of becoming subservient to better talents, awakened to the discussion of subjects so momentous to national happiness. To awaken such, was the summit of the author's design.

*William Cullen (1710–90), Scots physician, noted teacher and diagnostician.—B. F.

The Missouri Compromise

1820–21

The Missouri Territory sought to enter the union as a state in 1818. Because its proposed constitution allowed slavery, this would have given slave-holding states a numerical advantage in the U.S. Senate, then evenly divided between slave-holding and non-slave-holding states. James Tallmadge, a congressman from New York, sought to insert in Missouri's constitution a provision freeing slaves born there after admission into the union and prohibiting importation of slaves into that state. An angry stalemate ensued when this amendment was defeated in the U.S. Senate. Only after Maine applied for admission as a free state did members of Congress from the North signal approval of Missouri's application as a slave state. But this approval itself had a catch: In the rest of the territory of the Louisiana Purchase, slavery would not be allowed north of the line marking Missouri's southern border. Moreover, Missouri was not made a state until it accepted the further condition that it not deny free blacks their rights under the U.S. Constitution.

The Missouri Compromise

An act to authorize the People of the Missouri Territory to form a Constitution and State Government, and for the admission of such State into the Union on an equal footing with the original States, and to prohibit Slavery in certain Territories

Sec. 1. *Be it enacted by the Senate and House of Representatives of the United States of America in Congress assembled,* That the inhabitants of that portion of the Missouri Territory included within the boundaries hereinafter designated, be, and they are hereby authorized to form for themselves a Constitution and State Government; and to assume such name as they shall deem proper; and the said State, when formed, shall be admitted into the Union, upon an equal footing with the original States, in all respects whatsoever. . . .

Sec. 8. *And be it further enacted,* That in all that territory ceded by France to the United States, under the name of Louisiana, which lies north of thirty-six degrees and thirty minutes north latitude, not included within the limits of the State contemplated by this act, slavery and involuntary servitude, otherwise than in the punishment of crimes, whereof the parties shall have been duly convicted, shall be, and is hereby forever prohibited; *Provided always,* That any person escaping into the same, from whom labor or service is lawfully claimed, in any state or territory of the United States, such fugitive may be lawfully reclaimed and conveyed to the person claiming his or her labor or service as aforesaid. . . .

Resolution providing for the Admission of the State of Missouri into the Union, on a certain Condition

2 March, 1821

Resolved by the Senate and House of Representatives of the United States of America in Congress assembled, That Missouri shall be admitted into this Union on an equal footing with the original States, in all respects whatever, upon the fundamental condition, that the fourth clause of the 26th section of the third article of the constitution submitted on the part of said state to Congress, shall never be construed to authorize the passage of any law, and that no law shall be passed in conformity thereto, by which any citizen, of either of the states in this Union, shall be excluded from the enjoyment of any of the privileges and immunities to which such citizen is entitled under the constitution of the United States: *Provided,* That the legislature of the said state, by a solemn public act, shall declare the assent of the said state to the said fundamental condition, and shall transmit to the President of the United States, on or before the fourth Monday in November next, an authentic copy of the said act; upon the receipt whereof, the President, by proclamation, shall announce the fact; whereupon, and without any further proceedings on the part of Congress, the admission of the said state into this Union shall be considered as complete.

Newspaper Editorials

WILLIAM LEGGETT

"Governor McDuffie's Message"

February 10, 1835

"The Question of Slavery Narrowed
to a Point"

April 15, 1837

"'Abolition Insolence'"

July 29, 1837

Leggett believed that his opposition to slavery was the logical
extension of Jacksonian principles of liberty and equality. But
his willingness to discuss the abolition of slavery and defend the
rights of abolitionists caused significant problems within Jackson's Democratic Republican Party. In New York, a small wing
of radical democrats called the loco-focos went so far as to form
a short-lived splinter party to support Leggett's principles. Leggett himself sought reform within his party and refused to accept
the loco-foco nomination for mayor of New York.

"Governor McDuffie's Message"

Governor McDuffie, in his late message to the Legislature
of South Carolina, has promulgated various errors in relation to the views and principles of the democracy of the
middle and northern states, which might excite astonishment at his ignorance, or regret at his insincerity, did we
not know that they are founded on the misrepresentations
of the Bank tory organs of this part of the world. Great
pains have been taken by these to persuade the people
of the south, that all the violent anathemas uttered against
the system of slavery, by enthusiasts and fanatics in this
quarter, and all their dangerous zeal for immediate emancipation, originate with the democracy. The charge of
agrarianism, also, which has with such marvellous propriety been urged against this journal, because it supports the
doctrine, not of an equalization of property, which is an

impracticable absurdity, but because it maintains the principle of equal political rights, seems to have excited the sensitive apprehensions of the Governor of South Carolina,
and prompted him to the utterance of sentiments which
we are sorry to see avowed on such a public and grave occasion, as that of addressing the legislature in his official
capacity.

We must beg leave to set Governor McDuffie right on
these points. In the first place, what is called agrarianism
by the Bank tory presses is nothing more than the great
principle which has always been maintained with peculiar
earnestness by the southern states, and most especially by
Virginia and South Carolina. It is simply an opposition to
all partial and exclusive legislation, which gives to one profession, one class of industry, one section of the Union,
or one portion of the people, privileges and advantages
denied to the others, or of which, from the nature of their
situation and circumstances, they cannot partake. It is
opposition to bounties, protections, incorporations, and
perpetuities of all kinds, under whatever mask they may
present themselves. It is neither more nor less in short,
than a denial of the legislative authority to grant any partial or exclusive privileges under pretence of the "general
welfare," the "wants of the community," "sound policy,"
"sound action," "developing the resources and stimulating
the industry of the community," or any other undefinable
pretence, resorted to as a subterfuge by avarice and ambition. This is what the whig papers, as they style themselves,
hold up to the South as a dangerous doctrine, calculated
to unsettle the whole system of social organization, and
subject the rights of property to the arbitrary violence of a
hungry and rapacious populace! . . .

Governor McDuffie is still more misled in his ideas of
the part taken by the democracy of this and the eastern
states in the mad and violent schemes of the immediate
abolitionists, as they are called. He may be assured that the
abettors and supporters of Garrison,[1] and other itinerant
orators who go about stigmatizing the people of the south

---

1. William Lloyd Garrison, leading advocate of the immediate abolition of slavery.—Ed.

as "men stealers," are not the organs or instruments of the democracy of the north, but of the aristocracy—of that party which has always been in favour of encroaching on the rights of the white labourers of this quarter. It is so in Europe, and so is it here. There, the most violent opponents of the rights of the people of England, are the most loud in their exclamations against the wrongs of the people of Africa, as if they sought to quiet their consciences, for oppressing one colour, by becoming the advocates of the freedom of the other. Daniel O'Connell[2] is one of the few exceptions, and even he, in one of his speeches, with the keenest and most bitter irony, taunted these one-sided philanthropists with perpetuating the long enduring system of oppression in Ireland, while they were affecting the tenderest sympathy for the blacks of the West Indies. Was Rufus King,[3] the great leader on the Missouri question, a representative of the democracy of the north? and were not the interests of the planters of the south sustained by the democracy alone?

Governor McDuffie may make himself perfectly easy on the score of the democracy of the north. They are not agrarians, nor fanatics, nor hypocrites. They make a trade neither of politics, nor philanthropy. They know well that admitting the slaves of the south to an equality of civil and social rights, however deeply it might affect the dignity and interests of the rich planters of that quarter, would operate quite as injuriously, if not more so, on themselves. The civil equality might affect both equally, but the social equality would operate mainly to the prejudice of the labouring classes among the democracy of the north. It is here the emancipated slaves would seek a residence and employment, and aspire to the social equality they could never enjoy among their ancient masters. If they cannot bring themselves up to the standard of the free labouring white men, they might pull the latter down to their own level, and thus lower the condition of the white labourer by association, if not by amalgamation.

Not only this, but the labouring classes of the north, which constitute the great mass of the democracy, are not so short-sighted to consequences, that they cannot see, that the influx of such a vast number of emancipated slaves would go far to throw them out of employment, or at least depreciate the value of labour to an extent that would be fatal to their prosperity. This they know, and this will forever prevent the democracy of the north from advocating or encouraging any of those ill-judged, though possibly well-intended schemes for a general and immediate emancipation, or indeed for any emancipation, that shall not both receive the sanction and preserve the rights of the planters of the south, and, at the same time, secure the democracy of the north against the injurious, if not fatal consequences, of a competition with the labour of millions of manumitted slaves.

If any class of people in this quarter of the Union have an interest in this question, independent of the broad principle of humanity, it is the aristocracy. It is not those who labour and have an interest in keeping up its price, but those who employ labour and have an interest in depressing it. These last would receive all the benefits of a great influx of labourers, which would cause the supply to exceed the demand, and consequently depress the value of labour; while the former would not only experience the degradation of this competition, but become eventually its victims. . . .

Again we assure Governor McDuffie, and all those who imagine they see in the democracy of the north, the enemies to their rights of property, and the advocates of principles dangerous to the safety and prosperity of the planters of the south, that they may make themselves perfectly easy on these heads. The danger is not in the democratic, but the aristocratic ascendancy. The whole is a scheme of a few ill-advised men, which certain whig politicians have used to set the republicans of the south against the democracy of the north, and thus, by dividing, conquer them both.

"The Question of Slavery Narrowed to a Point"

————Farewell remorse!
Evil be thou my good! By thee, at least,
—I more than half, perhaps, will reign.
                              Milton

The temperate and well-considered sentiments of Mr. Rives[1] on the subject of slavery, as expressed in the Senate

2. Member of Parliament from Ireland, well known for agitation on behalf of the rights of Roman Catholics and repeal of Ireland's union with England.—Ed.

3. Whig Senator from New York who led anti-slavery opposition to the Missouri Compromise of 1820.—Ed.

1. William C. Rives, senator from Virginia—Ed.

last winter, when certain petitions against slavery in the District of Columbia were under consideration, do not meet with much approval in the southern states. But the violent language of Mr. Calhoun[2] is applauded to the echo. Mr. Rives, it will be remembered, admitted, in the most explicit manner, that "slavery is an evil, moral, social, and political;" while Mr. Calhoun, on the other hand, maintained that "it is a good—a great good."

We have a paragraph lying before us, from the *New-Orleans True American,* in which the sentiments of Mr. Calhoun are responded to with great ardour, and the admission that slavery is an evil is resisted as giving up the whole question in dispute. The writer says:

"If the principle be once acknowledged, that slavery is an evil, the success of the fanatics is certain. We are with Mr. Calhoun on this point. He insists that slavery is a *positive good* in our present social relations—that no power in the Union can touch the construction of southern society, without actual violation of all guaranteed and unalienated rights. This is the threshold of our liberties. If once passed, the tower must fall."

Reader, contemplate the picture presented to you in this figurative language: the tower of liberty erected on the prostrate bodies of three millions of slaves. Worthy foundation of such an edifice! And appropriately is the journal which displays such anxiety for its stability termed the *True American.*

"Evil, be thou my good," is the exclamation of Mr. Calhoun, and myriads of true Americans join in worship of the divinity thus set up. But truth has always been a great iconoclast, and we think this idol of the slaveholders would fare little better in her hands than the images of pagan idolatry.

If the question of the abolition of slavery is to be narrowed down to the single point whether slavery is an evil or not, it will not take long to dispose of it. Yet it would perhaps not be an easy thing to prove that slavery is an evil, for the same reason that it would not be easy to prove that one and one are two; because the proposition is so elementary and self-evident, that it would itself be taken for a logical axiom as readily as any position by which we might seek to establish it. The great fundamental maxim of democratic faith is the natural equality of rights of all mankind. This is one of those truths which, in our Declaration of Independence, the Bill of Rights of this Confederacy, we claim to be self-evident. Those who maintain that slavery is not an evil must repudiate this maxim. They must be content to denounce the attempts to abolish slavery on the same ground that Gibbon * denounced the petitions to the British Parliament against the slave trade, because there was "a leaven of democratical principles in them, wild ideas of the rights and natural equality of man," and they must join that full-faced aristocrat in execrating "the fatal consequences of democratical principles, which lead by a path of flowers to the abyss of hell." If they admit man's natural equality, they at once admit slavery to be an evil. "In a future day," says Dymond, in his admirable work on morals,[3] "it will probably become a subject of wonder how it could have happened that, on such a subject as slavery, men could have inquired and examined and debated, year after year; and that many years could have passed before the minds of a nation were so fully convinced of its enormity, and of their consequent duty to abolish it, as to suppress it to the utmost of their power. This will probably be a subject of wonder, because the question is so simple, that he who simply applies the requisitions of the moral law finds no time for reasoning or for doubt. The question as soon as it is proposed is decided."

But if we shut our eyes upon the moral law, and decide whether slavery is a good or an evil with sole reference to the test of utility; if we consider it merely a question of political economy, and one in which the interests of humanity and the rights of nature, as they affect the slave, are not to be taken into account, but the mere advantage of the masters alone regarded, we shall still come to the same conclusion. The relative condition of any two states of this Confederacy, taking one where slavery exists, and one where it does not, illustrates the truth of this remark. But it would not be difficult to prove, by a process of statistical arguments, that slave labour is far more costly than free, wretchedly as the wants and comforts of the slaves are provided for in most of the southern states. So that, limiting the inquiry to the mere question of pecuniary profit, it could be demonstrated that slavery is an evil. But this is a view of the subject infinitely less important than its malign influence in social and political respects, still regarding the

* See his letter to Lord Sheffield, Miscellaneous Works, vol. I, p. 349.

3. A reference to Jonathan Dymond's *On the Applicability of the Pacific Principles of the New Testament to the Conduct of States,* the first American edition of which was published in 1832.—Ed.

2. John C. Calhoun, senator from South Carolina.—Ed.

prosperity of the whites as alone deserving consideration. When the social and political effects on three millions of black men are superadded as proper subjects of inquiry, the evil becomes greatly increased.

But to enter seriously into an argument to prove that slavery is an evil would be a great waste of time. They who assert the contrary do so under the influence of such feelings as are evinced by the ruined archangel, in the words from Milton which we have quoted at the head of these remarks. They do so in a tone of malignant defiance, and their own hearts, as they make the declaration, throb with a degrading consciousness of its falsehood.

The position that no power in the Union can touch the construction of southern society without violating guaranteed rights, will no more bear the test of examination, than the assertion that slavery is not an evil. There is no power, we concede, in the federal government to abolish slavery in any state, and none in any state to abolish it except within its own limits. But in as far as a free and full discussion of slavery, in all its characteristics and tendencies, may be considered as touching the construction of southern society, the right belongs to every citizen; and it is by this mode of touching it that it is hoped eventually to do away entirely with the deplorable evil. It cannot always exist against the constant attrition of public opinion.

The right to discuss slavery exists in various forms. It is claimed, in the first place, that Congress has absolute authority over that subject, so far as it relates to the District of Columbia. Every state, also, has authority over it within its own limits. And the people of the United States have absolute authority over it, so far as it presents a question to be considered in reference to any proposed amendment of the federal constitution. Suppose, for example, it should be desired by any portion of the people, to change the basis of southern representation in Congress, on the ground that slaves, being allowed to have no political rights, but being considered mere property, ought not to be enumerated in the political census, any more than the cattle and sheep of northern graziers and woolgrowers. The Constitution is amenable in this, as in every other respect, with the single exception of the equal representation of every state in the federal Senate; and it is consequently a legitimate subject of discussion. Yet the discussion of this subject involves, naturally and necessarily, a consideration of slavery in all its relations and influences. Suppose, again, any portion of the citizens of a state where negroes are not

held to bondage, but are not admitted to equal suffrage, as in this state, should desire those distinctive limitations to be removed. This is a legitimate question to be discussed, and the discussion of this brings up the whole subject of slavery. Or suppose, thirdly, that any persons in a free state should desire to re-instate negro slavery. The south would scarcely quarrel with them for seeking to carry their wishes into effect; yet they could only hope to do so through the means of a discussion which would legitimately embrace every topic connected with slavery, nearly or remotely.

It is by discussion alone that those who are opposed to slavery seek to effect a reconstruction of southern society; and the means, we think, if there is any virtue in truth, will yet be found adequate to the end. If slavery is really no evil, the more it is discussed, the greater will be the number of its advocates; but if it is "an evil, moral, social and political," as Mr. Rives has had the manliness to admit, in the very teeth of Mr. Calhoun's bravado, it will gradually give way before the force of sound opinion.

"Abolition Insolence"

The oppression which our fathers suffered from Great Britain was nothing in comparison with that which the negroes experience at the hands of the slaveholders. It may be "abolition insolence" to say these things; but as they are truths which justice and humanity authorize us to speak, we shall not be too dainty to repeat them whenever a fitting occasion is presented. Every American who, in any way, authorizes or countenances slavery, is derelict to his duty as a christian, a patriot, and a man. Every one does countenance and authorize it, who suffers any opportunity of expressing his deep abhorrence of its manifold abominations to pass by unimproved. If the freemen of the north and west would but speak out on this subject in such terms as their consciences prompt, we should soon have to rejoice in the complete enfranchisement of our negro brethren of the south.

If an extensive and well-arranged insurrection of the blacks should occur in any of the slave states, we should probably see the freemen of this quarter of the country rallying around that "glorious emblem" [1] which is so magniloquently spoken of in the foregoing extract, and marching

1. Namely, the American flag.—Ed.

beneath its folds to take sides with the slaveholders, and reduce the poor negroes, struggling for liberty, to heavier bondage than they endured before. It may be "abolition insolence" to call this "glorious emblem" the standard of oppression, but, at all events, it is unanswerable truth. For our part, we call it so in a spirit, not of insolence, not of pride speaking in terms of petulant contempt, but of deep humility and abasement. We confess, with the keenest mortification and chagrin, that the banner of our country is the emblem, not of justice and freedom, but of oppression; that it is the symbol of a compact which recognizes, in palpable and outrageous contradiction of the great principle of liberty, the right of one man to hold another as property; and that we are liable at any moment to be required, under all our obligations of citizenship, to array ourselves beneath it, and wage a war, of extermination if necessary, against the slave, for no crime but asserting his right of equal humanity—the self-evident truth that all men are created equal, and have an unalienable right of life, liberty, and the pursuit of happiness. Would we comply with such a requisition? No! rather would we see our right arm lopped from our body, and the mutilated trunk itself gored with mortal wounds, than raise a finger in opposition to men struggling in the holy cause of freedom. The obligations of citizenship are strong, but those of justice, humanity and religion stronger. We earnestly trust that the great contest of opinion which is now going on in this country may terminate in the enfranchisement of the slaves, without recourse to the strife of blood; but should the oppressed bondmen, impatient of the tardy progress of truth urged only in discussion, attempt to burst their chains by a more violent and shorter process, they should never encounter our arm, nor hear our voice, in the ranks of their opponents. We should stand a sad spectator of the conflict; and whatever commiseration we might feel for the discomfiture of the oppressors, we should pray that the battle might end in giving freedom to the oppressed.

Senate Speeches on the Compromise of 1850

Speech on the Slavery Question

JOHN C. CALHOUN

March 4, 1850

The Constitution and the Union

DANIEL WEBSTER

March 7, 1850

Both of the speeches reproduced here were originally delivered on the floor of the U.S. Senate. Calhoun was too ill to deliver his own speech but was carried into the chamber to hear it read for him. He appeared despite his grave illness (he would die only days later) because of the importance he, like Webster, attached to the issues under consideration. Those issues stemmed from legislation that came to be known as the Compromise of 1850.

In 1850, America's acquisition of vast new territories from its war with Mexico threatened to upset the uneasy balance of sectional forces. Western territories were not likely places for the expansion of slavery, yet they promised to produce significant numbers of new states. Under the Compromise, California was allowed to enter the union as a free state, and inhabitants of New Mexico and Utah were allowed to decide for themselves whether to allow slavery. In exchange, Texas was paid $10 million for abandoning its claims to (vast) territories in the west and Congress passed a more expansive and strict Fugitive Slave Law. The Compromise also enacted a ban on the slave trade in the District of Columbia, a long-held goal of Northern interests.

Calhoun opposed the measures in the Compromise. Webster, along with Henry Clay and Stephen Douglas, sponsored them.

Speech on the Slavery Question, Delivered in the Senate

March 4th, 1850

I have, Senators, believed from the first that the agitation of the subject of slavery would, if not prevented by some timely and effective measure, end in disunion. Entertaining this opinion, I have, on all proper occasions, endeavored to call the attention of both the two great parties which divide the country to adopt some measure to prevent so great a disaster, but without success. The agitation has been permitted to proceed, with almost no attempt to resist it, until it has reached a point when it can no longer be disguised or denied that the Union is in danger. You have thus had forced upon you the greatest and the gravest question that can ever come under your consideration— How can the Union be preserved?

To give a satisfactory answer to this mighty question, it is indispensable to have an accurate and thorough knowledge of the nature and the character of the cause by which the Union is endangered. Without such knowledge it is impossible to pronounce, with any certainty, by what measure it can be saved; just as it would be impossible for a physician to pronounce, in the case of some dangerous disease, with any certainty, by what remedy the patient could be saved, without similar knowledge of the nature and character of the cause which produced it. The first question, then, presented for consideration, in the investigation I propose to make, in order to obtain such knowledge, is—What is it that has endangered the Union?

To this question there can be but one answer,—that the immediate cause is the almost universal discontent which pervades all the States composing the Southern section of the Union. This widely-extended discontent is not of recent origin. It commenced with the agitation of the slavery question, and has been increasing ever since. The next question, going one step further back, is—What has caused this widely diffused and almost universal discontent?

It is a great mistake to suppose, as is by some, that it originated with demagogues, who excited the discontent with the intention of aiding their personal advancement, or with the disappointed ambition of certain politicians, who resorted to it as the means of retrieving their fortunes. On the contrary, all the great political influences of the section were arrayed against excitement, and exerted to the utmost to keep the people quiet. The great mass of the people of the South were divided, as in the other section, into Whigs and Democrats. The leaders and the presses of both parties in the South were very solicitous to prevent excitement and to preserve quiet; because it was seen that the effects of the former would necessarily tend to weaken, if not destroy, the political ties which united them with their respective parties in the other section. Those who know the strength of party ties will readily appreciate the immense force which this cause exerted against agitation, and in favor of preserving quiet. But, great as it was, it was not sufficient to prevent the wide-spread discontent which now pervades the section. No; some cause, far deeper and more powerful than the one supposed, must exist, to account for discontent so wide and deep. The question then recurs—What is the cause of this discontent? It will be found in the belief of the people of the Southern States, as prevalent as the discontent itself, that they cannot remain, as things now are, consistently with honor and safety, in the Union. The next question to be considered is—What has caused this belief?

One of the causes is, undoubtedly, to be traced to the long-continued agitation of the slave question on the part of the North, and the many aggressions which they have made on the rights of the South during the time. I will not enumerate them at present, as it will be done hereafter in its proper place.

There is another lying back of it—with which this is intimately connected—that may be regarded as the great and primary cause. This is to be found in the fact that the equilibrium between the two sections, in the Government as it stood when the constitution was ratified and the Government put in action, has been destroyed. At that time there was nearly a perfect equilibrium between the two, which afforded ample means to each to protect itself against the aggression of the other; but, as it now stands, one section has the exclusive power of controlling the Government, which leaves the other without any adequate means of protecting itself against its encroachment and oppression. To place this subject distinctly before you, I have, Senators, prepared a brief statistical statement, showing the relative weight of the two sections in the Government under the first census of 1790 and the last census of 1840.

According to the former, the population of the United States, including Vermont, Kentucky, and Tennessee, which then were in their incipient condition of becoming States, but were not actually admitted, amounted to 3,929,827. Of this number the Northern States had 1,997,899, and the Southern 1,952,072, making a difference of only 45,827 in favor of the former States. The number of States, including Vermont, Kentucky, and Tennessee, were sixteen; of which eight, including Vermont, belonged to the Northern section, and eight, including Kentucky and Tennessee, to the Southern,—making an equal division of the States between the two sections under the first census. There was a small preponderance in the House of Representatives, and in the Electoral College, in favor of the Northern, owing to the fact that, according to the provisions of the constitution, in estimating federal numbers five slaves count but three; but it was too small to affect sensibly the perfect equilibrium which, with that exception, existed at the time. Such was the equality of the two sections when the States composing them agreed to enter into a Federal Union. Since then the equilibrium between them has been greatly disturbed.

According to the last census the aggregate population of the United States amounted to 17,063,357, of which the Northern section contained 9,728,920, and the Southern 7,334,437, making a difference, in round numbers, of 2,400,000. The number of States had increased from sixteen to twenty-six, making an addition of ten States. In the mean time the position of Delaware had become doubtful as to which section she properly belonged. Considering her as neutral, the Northern States will have thirteen and the Southern States twelve, making a difference in the Senate of two Senators in favor of the former. According to the apportionment under the census of 1840, there were two hundred and twenty-three members of the House of Representatives, of which the Northern States had one hundred and thirty-five, and the Southern States (considering Delaware as neutral) eighty-seven, making a difference in favor of the former in the House of Representatives of forty-eight. The difference in the Senate of two members, added to this, gives to the North, in the electoral college, a majority of fifty. Since the census of 1840, four States have been added to the Union—Iowa, Wisconsin, Florida, and Texas. They leave the difference in the Senate as it stood when the census was taken; but add two to the side of the North in the House, making the present majority in the House in its favor fifty, and in the electoral college fifty-two.

The result of the whole is to give the Northern section a predominance in every department of the Government, and thereby concentrate in it the two elements which constitute the Federal Government,—majority of States, and a majority of their population, estimated in federal numbers. Whatever section concentrates the two in itself possesses the control of the entire Government.

But we are just at the close of the sixth decade, and the commencement of the seventh. The census is to be taken this year, which must add greatly to the decided preponderance of the North in the House of Representatives and in the electoral college. The prospect is, also, that a great increase will be added to its present preponderance in the Senate, during the period of the decade, by the addition of new States. Two territories, Oregon and Minnesota, are already in progress, and strenuous efforts are making to bring in three additional States from the territory recently conquered from Mexico; which, if successful, will add three other States in a short time to the Northern section, making five States; and increasing the present number of its States from fifteen to twenty, and of its Senators from thirty to forty. On the contrary, there is not a single territory in progress in the Southern section, and no certainty that any additional State will be added to it during the decade. The prospect then is, that the two sections in the Senate, should the efforts now made to exclude the South from the newly acquired territories succeed, will stand, before the end of the decade, twenty Northern States to

fourteen Southern (considering Delaware as neutral), and forty Northern Senators to twenty-eight Southern. This great increase of Senators, added to the great increase of members of the House of Representatives and the electoral college on the part of the North, which must take place under the next decade, will effectually and irretrievably destroy the equilibrium which existed when the Government commenced.

Had this destruction been the operation of time, without the interference of Government, the South would have had no reason to complain; but such was not the fact. It was caused by the legislation of this Government, which was appointed, as the common agent of all, and charged with the protection of the interests and security of all. The legislation by which it has been effected, may be classed under three heads. The first is, that series of acts by which the South has been excluded from the common territory belonging to all the States as members of the Federal Union —which have had the effect of extending vastly the portion allotted to the Northern section, and restricting within narrow limits the portion left the South. The next consists in adopting a system of revenue and disbursements, by which an undue proportion of the burden of taxation has been imposed upon the South, and an undue proportion of its proceeds appropriated to the North; and the last is a system of political measures, by which the original character of the Government has been radically changed. I propose to bestow upon each of these, in the order they stand, a few remarks, with the of view of showing that it is owing to the action of this Government, that the equilibrum between the two sections has been destroyed, and the whole powers of the system centered in a sectional majority.

The first of the series of acts by which the South was deprived of its due share of the territories, originated with the confederacy which preceded the existence of this Government. It is to be found in the provision of the ordinance of 1787. Its effect was to exclude the South entirely from that vast and fertile region which lies between the Ohio and the Mississippi rivers, now embracing five States and one territory. The next of the series is the Missouri compromise, which excluded the South from that large portion of Louisiana which lies north of 36° 30′, excepting what is included in the State of Missouri. The last of the series excluded the South from the whole of the Oregon Territory. All these, in the slang of the day, were what are called slave territories, and not free soil; that is, territories belonging to slaveholding powers and open to the emigration of masters with their slaves. By these several acts, the South was excluded from 1,238,025 square miles—an extent of country considerably exceeding the entire valley of the Mississippi. To the South was left the portion of the Territory of Louisiana lying south of 36° 30′, and the portion north of it included in the State of Missouri, with the portion lying south of 36° 30′, including the States of Louisiana and Arkansas, and the territory lying west of the latter, and south of 36° 30′, called the Indian country. These, with the Territory of Florida, now the State, make, in the whole, 283,503 square miles. To this must be added the territory acquired with Texas. If the whole should be added to the Southern section, it would make an increase of 325,520, which would make the whole left to the South, 609,023. But a large part of Texas is still in contest between the two sections, which leaves it uncertain what will be the real extent of the portion of territory that may be left to the South.

I have not included the territory recently acquired by the treaty with Mexico. The North is making the most strenuous efforts to appropriate the whole to herself, by excluding the South from every foot of it. If she should succeed, it will add to that from which the South has already been excluded, 526,078 square miles, and would increase the whole which the North has appropriated to herself, to 1,764,023, not including the portion that she may succeed in excluding us from in Texas. To sum up the whole, the United States, since they declared their independence, have acquired 2,373,046 square miles of territory, from which the North will have excluded the South, if she should succeed in monopolizing the newly acquired territories, about three-fourths of the whole, leaving to the South but about one-fourth.

Such is the first and great cause that has destroyed the equilibrium between the two sections in the Government.

The next is the system of revenue and disbursements which has been adopted by the Government. It is well known that the Government has derived its revenue mainly from duties on imports. I shall not undertake to show that such duties must necessarily fall mainly on the exporting States, and that the South, as the great exporting portion of the Union, has in reality paid vastly more than her due proportion of the revenue; because I deem it unnecessary, as the subject has on so many occasions been fully discussed. Nor shall I, for the same reason, undertake to show that a far greater portion of the revenue has been disbursed at the North, than its due share; and that the joint effect of these causes has been, to transfer a vast amount from South to North, which, under an equal system of revenue and disbursements, would not have been lost to her. If to this be added, that many of the duties were imposed, not for revenue, but for protection,—that is, intended to put money, not in the treasury, but directly into the pocket of the manufacturers,—some conception may be formed of the immense amount which, in the long course of sixty years, has been transferred from South to North. There are no data by which it can be estimated with any certainty; but it is safe to say, that it amounts to hundreds of millions of dollars. Under the most moderate estimate, it would be sufficient to add greatly to the wealth of the North, and thus greatly increase her population by attracting emigration from all quarters to that section.

This, combined with the great primary cause, amply explains why the North has acquired a preponderance in every department of the Government by its disproportionate increase of population and States. The former, as has been shown, has increased, in fifty years, 2,400,000 over that of the South. This increase of population, during so long a period, is satisfactorily accounted for, by the number of emigrants, and the increase of their descendants, which have been attracted to the Northern section from Europe and the South, in consequence of the advantages derived from the causes assigned. If they had not existed —if the South had retained all the capital which has been extracted from her by the fiscal action of the Government; and, if it had not been excluded by the ordinance of 1787 and the Missouri compromise, from the region lying between the Ohio and the Mississippi rivers, and between the Mississippi and the Rocky Mountains north of 36° 30′ —it scarcely admits of a doubt, that it would have divided the emigration with the North, and by retaining her own people, would have at least equalled the North in population under the census of 1840, and probably under that about to be taken. She would also, if she had retained her equal rights in those territories, have maintained an equality in the number of States with the North, and have preserved the equilibrium between the two sections that existed at the commencement of the Government. The loss, then, of the equilibrium is to be attributed to the action of this Government.

But while these measures were destroying the equilibrium between the two sections, the action of the Government was leading to a radical change in its character, by concentrating all the power of the system in itself. The occasion will not permit me to trace the measures by which this great change has been consummated. If it did, it would not be difficult to show that the process commenced at an early period of the Government; and that it proceeded, almost without interruption, step by step, until it absorbed virtually its entire powers; but without going through the whole process to establish the fact, it may be done satisfactorily by a very short statement.

That the Government claims, and practically maintains the right to decide in the last resort, as to the extent of its powers, will scarcely be denied by any one conversant with the political history of the country. That it also claims the right to resort to force to maintain whatever power it claims, against all opposition, is equally certain. Indeed it is apparent, from what we daily hear, that this has become the prevailing and fixed opinion of a great majority of the community. Now, I ask, what limitation can possibly be placed upon the powers of a government claiming and exercising such rights? And, if none can be, how can the separate governments of the States maintain and protect the powers reserved to them by the constitution—or the people of the several States maintain those which are reserved to them, and among others, the sovereign powers by which they ordained and established, not only their separate State Constitutions and Governments, but also the Constitution and Government of the United States? But, if they have no constitutional means of maintaining them against the right claimed by this Government, it necessarily follows, that they hold them at its pleasure and discretion, and that all the powers of the system are in reality concentrated in it. It also follows, that the character of the Government has been changed in consequence, from a federal republic, as it originally came from the hands of its framers, into a great national consolidated democracy. It has indeed, at present, all the characteristics of the latter, and not one of the former, although it still retains its outward form.

The result of the whole of these causes combined is— that the North has acquired a decided ascendency over every department of this Government, and through it a control over all the powers of the system. A single section governed by the will of the numerical majority, has now, in fact, the control of the Government and the entire powers of the system. What was once a constitutional federal republic, is now converted, in reality, into one as absolute as that of the Autocrat of Russia, and as despotic in its tendency as any absolute government that ever existed.

As, then, the North has the absolute control over the Government, it is manifest, that on all questions between it and the South, where there is a diversity of interests, the interest of the latter will be sacrificed to the former, however oppressive the effects may be; as the South possesses no means by which it can resist, through the action of the Government. But if there was no question of vital importance to the South, in reference to which there was a diversity of views between the two sections, this state of things might be endured, without the hazard of destruction to the South. But such is not the fact. There is a question of vital importance to the Southern section, in reference to which the views and feelings of the two sections are as opposite and hostile as they can possibly be.

I refer to the relation between the two races in the Southern section, which constitutes a vital portion of her social organization. Every portion of the North entertains views and feelings more or less hostile to it. Those most opposed and hostile, regard it as a sin, and consider themselves under the most sacred obligation to use every effort to destroy it. Indeed, to the extent that they conceive they have power, they regard themselves as implicated in the sin, and responsible for not suppressing it by the use of all and every means. Those less opposed and hostile, regard it as a crime—an offence against humanity, as they call it; and, although not so fanatical, feel themselves bound to use all efforts to effect the same object; while those who are least opposed and hostile, regard it as a blot and a stain on the character of what they call the Nation, and feel themselves accordingly bound to give it no countenance or support. On the contrary, the Southern section regards the relation as one which cannot be destroyed without subjecting the two races to the greatest calamity, and the section to poverty, desolation, and wretchedness; and accordingly they feel bound, by every consideration of interest and safety, to defend it.

This hostile feeling on the part of the North towards the social organization of the South long lay dormant, but it only required some cause to act on those who felt most intensely that they were responsible for its continuance, to call it into action. The increasing power of this Government, and of the control of the Northern section over all its departments, furnished the cause. It was this which made an impression on the minds of many, that there was little or no restraint to prevent the Government from doing whatever it might choose to do. This was sufficient of itself to put the most fanatical portion of the North in action, for the purpose of destroying the existing relation between the two races in the South.

The first organized movement towards it commenced in 1835. Then, for the first time, societies were organized, presses established, lecturers sent forth to excite the people of the North, and incendiary publications scattered over the whole South, through the mail. The South was thoroughly aroused. Meetings were held every where, and resolutions adopted, calling upon the North to apply a remedy to arrest the threatened evil, and pledging themselves to adopt measures for their own protection, if it was not arrested. At the meeting of Congress, petitions poured in from the North, calling upon Congress to abolish slavery in the District of Columbia, and to prohibit, what they called, the internal slave trade between the States—announcing at the same time, that their ultimate object was to abolish slavery, not only in the District, but in the States and throughout the Union. At this period, the number engaged in the agitation was small, and possessed little or no personal influence.

Neither party in Congress had, at that time, any sympathy with them or their cause. The members of each party presented their petitions with great reluctance. Nevertheless, small and contemptible as the party then was, both of the great parties of the North dreaded them. They felt, that though small, they were organized in reference to a subject which had a great and a commanding influence over the Northern mind. Each party, on that account, feared to oppose their petitions, lest the opposite party should take advantage of the one who might do so, by favoring them. The effect was, that both united in insisting that the petitions should be received, and that Congress should take jurisdiction over the subject. To justify their course, they took the extraordinary ground, that Congress was bound to receive petitions on every subject, however objectionable they might be, and whether they had, or had not, jurisdiction over the subject. These views prevailed in the House of Representatives, and partially in the Senate; and thus the party succeeded in their first movements, in gaining what they proposed—a position in Congress, from which agitation could be extended over the whole Union. This was the commencement of the agitation, which has

ever since continued, and which, as is now acknowledged, has endangered the Union itself.

As for myself, I believed at that early period, if the party who got up the petitions should succeed in getting Congress to take jurisdiction, that agitation would follow, and that it would in the end, if not arrested, destroy the Union. I then so expressed myself in debate, and called upon both parties to take grounds against assuming jurisdiction; but in vain. Had my voice been heeded, and had Congress refused to take jurisdiction, by the united votes of all parties, the agitation which followed would have been prevented, and the fanatical zeal that gives impulse to the agitation, and which has brought us to our present perilous condition, would have become extinguished, from the want of fuel to feed the flame. *That* was the time for the North to have shown her devotion to the Union; but, unfortunately, both of the great parties of that section were so intent on obtaining or retaining party ascendency, that all other considerations were overlooked or forgotten.

What has since followed are but natural consequences. With the success of their first movement, this small fanatical party began to acquire strength; and with that, to become an object of courtship to both the great parties. The necessary consequence was, a further increase of power, and a gradual tainting of the opinions of both of the other parties with their doctrines, until the infection has extended over both; and the great mass of the population of the North, who, whatever may be their opinion of the original abolition party, which still preserves its distinctive organization, hardly ever fail, when it comes to acting, to co-operate in carrying out their measures. With the increase of their influence, they extended the sphere of their action. In a short time after the commencement of their first movement, they had acquired sufficient influence to induce the legislatures of most of the Northern States to pass acts, which in effect abrogated the clause of the constitution that provides for the delivery up of fugitive slaves. Not long after, petitions followed to abolish slavery in forts, magazines, and dockyards, and all other places where Congress had exclusive power of legislation. This was followed by petitions and resolutions of legislatures of the Northern States, and popular meetings, to exclude the Southern States from all territories acquired, or to be acquired, and to prevent the admission of any State hereafter into the Union, which, by its constitution, does not prohibit slavery. And Congress is invoked to do all this, expressly with the view to the final abolition of slavery in the States. That has been avowed to be the ultimate object from the beginning of the agitation until the present time; and yet the great body of both parties of the North, with the full knowledge of the fact, although disavowing the abolitionists, have co-operated with them in almost all their measures.

Such is a brief history of the agitation, as far as it has yet advanced. Now I ask, Senators, what is there to prevent its further progress, until it fulfils the ultimate end proposed, unless some decisive measure should be adopted to prevent it? Has any one of the causes, which has added to its increase from its original small and contemptible beginning until it has attained its present magnitude, diminished in force? Is the original cause of the movement—that slavery is a sin, and ought to be suppressed—weaker now than at the commencement? Or is the abolition party less numerous or influential, or have they less influence with, or control over the two great parties of the North in elections? Or has the South greater means of influencing or controlling the movements of this Government now, than it had when the agitation commenced? To all these questions but one answer can be given: No—no—no. The very reverse is true. Instead of being weaker, all the elements in favor of agitation are stronger now than they were in 1835, when it first commenced, while all the elements of influence on the part of the South are weaker. Unless something decisive is done, I again ask, what is to stop this agitation, before the great and final object at which it aims—the abolition of slavery in the States—is consummated? Is it, then, not certain, that if something is not done to arrest it, the South will be forced to choose between abolition and secession? Indeed, as events are now moving, it will not require the South to secede, in order to dissolve the Union. Agitation will of itself effect it, of which its past history furnishes abundant proof—as I shall next proceed to show.

It is a great mistake to suppose that disunion can be effected by a single blow. The cords which bound these States together in one common Union, are far too numerous and powerful for that. Disunion must be the work of time. It is only through a long process, and successively, that the cords can be snapped, until the whole fabric falls asunder. Already the agitation of the slavery question has snapped some of the most important, and has greatly weakened all the others, as I shall proceed to show.

The cords that bind the States together are not only many, but various in character. Some are spiritual or ecclesiastical; some political; others social. Some appertain to the benefit conferred by the Union, and others to the feeling of duty and obligation.

The strongest of those of a spiritual and ecclesiastical nature, consisted in the unity of the great religious denominations, all of which originally embraced the whole Union. All these denominations, with the exception, perhaps, of the Catholics, were organized very much upon the principle of our political institutions. Beginning with smaller meetings, corresponding with the political divisions of the country, their organization terminated in one great central assemblage, corresponding very much with the character of Congress. At these meetings the principal clergymen and lay members of the respective denominations, from all parts of the Union, met to transact business relating to their common concerns. It was not confined to what appertained to the doctrines and discipline of the respective denominations, but extended to plans for disseminating the Bible—establishing missions, distributing tracts—and of establishing presses for the publication of tracts, newspapers, and periodicals, with a view of diffusing religious information—and for the support of their respective doctrines and creeds. All this combined contributed greatly to strengthen the bonds of the Union. The ties which held each denomination together formed a strong cord to hold the whole Union together; but, powerful as they were, they have not been able to resist the explosive effect of slavery agitation.

The first of these cords which snapped, under its explosive force, was that of the powerful Methodist Episcopal Church. The numerous and strong ties which held it together, are all broken, and its unity gone. They now form separate churches; and, instead of that feeling of attachment and devotion to the interests of the whole church which was formerly felt, they are now arrayed into two hostile bodies, engaged in litigation about what was formerly their common property.

The next cord that snapped was that of the Baptists—one of the largest and most respectable of the denominations. That of the Presbyterian is not entirely snapped, but some of its strands have given way. That of the Episcopal Church is the only one of the four great Protestant denominations which remains unbroken and entire.

The strongest cord, of a political character, consists of the many and powerful ties that have held together the two great parties which have, with some modifications, existed from the beginning of the Government. They both extended to every portion of the Union, and strongly contributed to hold all its parts together. But this powerful cord has fared no better than the spiritual. It resisted, for a long time, the explosive tendency of the agitation, but has finally snapped under its force—if not entirely, in a great measure. Nor is there one of the remaining cords which has not been greatly weakened. To this extent the Union has already been destroyed by agitation, in the only way it can be, by sundering and weakening the cords which bind it together.

If the agitation goes on, the same force, acting with increased intensity, as has been shown, will finally snap every cord, when nothing will be left to hold the States together except force. But, surely, that can, with no propriety of language, be called a Union, when the only means by which the weaker is held connected with the stronger portion is *force*. It may, indeed, keep them connected; but the connection will partake much more of the character of subjugation, on the part of the weaker to the stronger, than the union of free, independent, and sovereign States, in one confederation, as they stood in the early stages of the Government, and which only is worthy of the sacred name of Union.

Having now, Senators, explained what it is that endangers the Union, and traced it to its cause, and explained its nature and character, the question again recurs—How can the Union be saved? To this I answer, there is but one way by which it can be—and that is—by adopting such measures as will satisfy the States belonging to the Southern section, that they can remain in the Union consistently with their honor and their safety. There is, again, only one way by which this can be effected, and that is—by removing the causes by which this belief has been produced. Do *this,* and discontent will cease—harmony and kind feelings between the sections be restored—and every apprehension of danger to the Union removed. The question, then, is—How can this be done? But, before I undertake to answer this question, I propose to show by what the Union cannot be saved.

It cannot, then, be saved by eulogies on the Union, however splendid or numerous. The cry of "Union, Union— the glorious Union!" can no more prevent disunion than the cry of "Health, health—glorious health!" on the part of the physician, can save a patient lying dangerously ill. So long as the Union, instead of being regarded as a protector, is regarded in the opposite character, by not much less than a majority of the States, it will be in vain to attempt to conciliate them by pronouncing eulogies on it.

Besides this cry of Union comes commonly from those whom we cannot believe to be sincere. It usually comes from our assailants. But we cannot believe them to be sincere; for, if they loved the Union, they would necessarily be devoted to the constitution. It made the Union,—and to destroy the constitution would be to destroy the Union. But the only reliable and certain evidence of devotion to the constitution is, to abstain, on the one hand, from violating it, and to repel, on the other, all attempts to violate it. It is only by faithfully performing these high duties that the constitution can be preserved, and with it the Union.

But how stands the profession of devotion to the Union by our assailants, when brought to this test? Have they abstained from violating the constitution? Let the many acts passed by the Northern States to set aside and annul the clause of the constitution providing for the delivery up of fugitive slaves answer. I cite this, not that it is the only instance (for there are many others), but because the violation in this particular is too notorious and palpable to be denied. Again: have they stood forth faithfully to repel violations of the constitution? Let their course in reference to the agitation of the slavery question, which was commenced and has been carried on for fifteen years, avowedly for the purpose of abolishing slavery in the States—an object all acknowledged to be unconstitutional—answer. Let them show a single instance, during this long period, in which they have denounced the agitators or their attempts to effect what is admitted to be unconstitutional, or a single measure which they have brought forward for that purpose. How can we, with all these facts before us, believe that they are sincere in their profession of devotion to the Union, or avoid believing their profession is but intended to increase the vigor of their assaults and to weaken the force of our resistance?

Nor can we regard the profession of devotion to the Union, on the part of those who are not our assailants, as sincere, when they pronounce eulogies upon the Union, evidently with the intent of charging us with disunion, without uttering one word of denunciation against our assailants. If friends of the Union, their course should be to unite with us in repelling these assaults, and denouncing the authors as enemies of the Union. Why they avoid this, and pursue the course they do, it is for them to explain.

Nor can the Union be saved by invoking the name of the illustrious Southerner whose mortal remains repose on the western bank of the Potomac. He was one of us—a slaveholder and a planter. We have studied his history, and find nothing in it to justify submission to wrong. On the contrary, his great fame rests on the solid foundation, that, while he was careful to avoid doing wrong to others, he was prompt and decided in repelling wrong. I trust that, in this respect, we profited by his example.

Nor can we find any thing in his history to deter us from seceding from the Union, should it fail to fulfil the objects for which it was instituted, by being permanently and hopelessly converted into the means of oppressing instead of protecting us. On the contrary, we find much in his example to encourage us, should we be forced to the extremity of deciding between submission and disunion.

There existed then, as well as now, a union—that between the parent country and her then colonies. It was a union that had much to endear it to the people of the colonies. Under its protecting and superintending care, the colonies were planted and grew up and prospered, through a long course of years, until they became populous and wealthy. Its benefits were not limited to them. Their extensive agricultural and other productions, gave birth to a flourishing commerce, which richly rewarded the parent country for the trouble and expense of establishing and protecting them. Washington was born and grew up to manhood under that union. He acquired his early distinction in its service, and there is every reason to believe that he was devotedly attached to it. But his devotion was a rational one. He was attached to it, not as an end, but as a means to an end. When it failed to fulfil its end, and, instead of affording protection, was converted into the means of oppressing the colonies, he did not hesitate to draw his sword, and head the great movement by which that union was for ever severed, and the independence of these States established. This was the great and crowning glory of his life, which has spread his fame over the whole globe, and will transmit it to the latest posterity.

Nor can the plan proposed by the distinguished Senator from Kentucky, nor that of the administration save the Union. I shall pass by, without remark, the plan proposed by the Senator, and proceed directly to the consideration of that of the administration. I however assure the distinguished and able Senator, that, in taking this course, no disrespect whatever is intended to him or his plan. I have adopted it, because so many Senators of distinguished abilities, who were present when he delivered his speech, and explained his plan, and who were fully capable to do justice to the side they support, have replied to him.

The plan of the administration cannot save the Union, because it can have no effect whatever, towards satisfying the States composing the southern section of the Union, that they can, consistently with safety and honor, remain in the Union. It is, in fact, but a modification of the Wilmot Proviso. It proposes to effect the same object,—to exclude the South from all territory acquired by the Mexican treaty. It is well known that the South is united against the Wilmot Proviso, and has committed itself by solemn resolutions, to resist, should it be adopted. Its opposition *is not to the name,* but that which it *proposes to effect.* That, the Southern States hold to be unconstitutional, unjust, inconsistent with their equality as members of the common Union, and calculated to destroy irretrievably the equilibrium between the two sections. These objections equally apply to what, for brevity, I will call the Executive Proviso. There is no difference between it and the Wilmot, except in the mode of effecting the object; and in that respect, I must say, that the latter is much the least objectionable. It goes to its object openly, boldly, and distinctly. It claims for Congress unlimited power over the territories, and proposes to assert it over the territories acquired from Mexico, by a positive prohibition of slavery. Not so the Executive Proviso. It takes an indirect course, and in order to elude the Wilmot Proviso, and thereby avoid encountering the united and determined resistance of the South, it denies, by implication, the authority of Congress to legislate for the territories, and claims the right as belonging exclusively to the inhabitants of the territories. But to effect the object of excluding the South, it takes care, in the mean time, to let in emigrants freely from the Northern States and all other quarters, except from the South, which it takes special care to exclude by holding up to them the danger of having their slaves liberated under the Mexican laws. The necessary consequence is to exclude the South from the territory, just as effectually as would the Wilmot Proviso. The only difference in this respect is, that what one proposes to effect directly and openly, the other proposes to effect indirectly and covertly.

But the Executive Proviso is more objectionable than the Wilmot, in another and more important particular. The latter, to effect its object, inflicts a dangerous wound upon the constitution, by depriving the Southern States, as joint partners and owners of the territories, of their rights in them; but it inflicts no greater wound than is absolutely necessary to effect its object. The former, on the contrary, while it inflicts the same wound, inflicts others equally great, and, if possible, greater, as I shall next proceed to explain.

In claiming the right for the inhabitants, instead of Congress, to legislate for the territories, the Executive Proviso, assumes that the sovereignty over the territories is vested in the former: or to express it in the language used in a resolution offered by one of the Senators from Texas (General Houston, now absent), they have "the same inherent right of self-government as the people in the States." The assumption is utterly unfounded, unconstitutional, without example, and contrary to the entire practice of the Government, from its commencement to the present time, as I shall proceed to show.

The recent movement of individuals in California to form a constitution and a State government, and to appoint Senators and Representatives, is the first fruit of this monstrous assumption. If the individuals who made this movement had gone into California as adventurers, and if, as such, they had conquered the territory and established their independence, the sovereignty of the country would have been vested in them, as a separate and independent community. In that case, they would have had the right to form a constitution, and to establish a government for themselves; and if, afterwards, they thought proper to apply to Congress for admission into the Union as a sovereign and independent State, all this would have been regular, and according to established principles. But such is not the case. It was the United States who conquered California and finally acquired it by treaty. The sovereignty, of course, is vested in them, and not in the individuals who have attempted to form a constitution and a State without their consent. All this is clear, beyond controversy unless it can be shown that they have since lost or been divested of their sovereignty.

Nor is it less clear, that the power of legislating over the acquired territory is vested in Congress, and not, as is as-
sumed, in the inhabitants of the territories. None can deny that the Government of the United States has the power to acquire territories, either by war or treaty; but if the power to acquire exists, it belongs to Congress to carry it into execution. On this point there can be no doubt, for the constitution expressly provides, that Congress shall have power "to make all laws which shall be necessary and proper to carry into execution the foregoing powers" (those vested in Congress), "and all other powers vested by this constitution in *the Government* of the United States, or in *any department* or *officer* thereof." It matters not, then, where the power is vested; for, if vested at all in the Government of the United States, or any of its departments, or officers, the power of carrying it into execution is clearly vested in Congress. But this important provision, while it gives to Congress the power of legislating over territories, imposes important limitations on its exercise, by restricting Congress to passing laws necessary and proper for carrying the power into execution. The prohibition extends, not only to all laws not suitable or appropriate to the object of the power, but also to all that are unjust, unequal, or unfair,—for all such laws would be unnecessary and improper, and, therefore, unconstitutional.

Having now established, beyond controversy, that the sovereignty over the territories is vested in the United States,—that is, in the several States composing the Union, —and that the power of legislating over them is expressly vested in Congress, it follows, that the individuals in California who have undertaken to form a constitution and a State, and to exercise the power of legislating without the consent of Congress, have usurped the sovereignty of the State and the authority of Congress, and have acted in open defiance of both. In other words, what they have done is revolutionary and rebellious in its character, anarchical in its tendency, and calculated to lead to the most dangerous consequences. Had they acted from premeditation and design, it would have been, in fact, actual rebellion; but such is not the case. The blame lies much less upon them than upon those who have induced them to take a course so unconstitutional and dangerous. They have been led into it by language held here, and the course pursued by the Executive branch of the Government.

I have not seen the answer of the Executive to the calls made by the two Houses of Congress for information as to the course which it took, or the part which it acted, in reference to what was done in California. I understand the answers have not yet been printed. But there is enough known to justify the assertion, that those who profess to represent and act under the authority of the Executive, have advised, aided, and encouraged the movement, which terminated in forming, what they call a constitution and a State. General Riley, who professed to act as civil Governor, called the convention—determined on the number, and distribution of the delegates—appointed the time and place of its meeting—was present during the session—and gave its proceedings his approbation and sanction. If he acted without authority, he ought to have been tried, or at least reprimanded, and his course disavowed. Neither having been done, the presumption is, that his course has been approved. This, of itself, is sufficient to identify the Executive with his acts, and to make it responsible for them. I touch not the question, whether General Riley was appointed, or received the instructions under which he professed to act from the present Executive, or its predecessor. If from the former, it would implicate the preceding, as well as the present administration. If not, the responsibility rests exclusively on the present.

It is manifest from this statement, that the Executive Department has undertaken to perform acts preparatory to the meeting of the individuals to form their so called constitution and government, which appertain exclusively to Congress. Indeed, they are identical, in many respects, with the provisions adopted by Congress, when it gives permission to a territory to form a constitution and government, in order to be admitted as a State into the Union.

Having now shown that the assumption upon which the Executive, and the individuals in California, acted throughout this whole affair, is unfounded, unconstitutional, and dangerous; it remains to make a few remarks, in order to show that what has been done, is contrary to the entire practice of the Government, from the commencement to the present time.

From its commencement until the time that Michigan was admitted, the practice was uniform. Territorial governments were first organized by Congress. The Government of the United States appointed the governors, judges, secretaries, marshals, and other officers; and the inhabitants of the territory were represented by legislative bodies, whose acts were subject to the revision of Congress. This state of things continued until the government of a territory applied to Congress to permit its inhabitants to form a constitution and government, preparatory to

admission into the Union. The act preliminary to giving permission was, to ascertain whether the inhabitants were sufficiently numerous to authorize them to be formed into a State. This was done by taking a census. That being done, and the number proving sufficient, permission was granted. The act granting it, fixed all the preliminaries—the time and place of holding the convention; the qualification of the voters; establishment of its boundaries, and all other measures necessary to be settled previous to admission. The act giving permission necessarily withdraws the sovereignty of the United States, and leaves the inhabitants of the incipient State as free to form their constitution and government as were the original States of the Union after they had declared their independence. At this stage, the inhabitants of the territory became, for the first time, a people, in legal and constitutional language. Prior to this, they were, by the old acts of Congress, called inhabitants, and not people. All this is perfectly consistent with the sovereignty of the United States, with the powers of Congress, and with the right of a people to self-government.

Michigan was the first case in which there was any departure from the uniform rule of acting. Hers was a very slight departure from established usage. The ordinance of 1787 secured to her the right of becoming a State, when she should have 60,000 inhabitants. Owing to some neglect, Congress delayed taking the census. In the mean time her population increased, until it clearly exceeded more than twice the number which entitled her to admission. At this stage, she formed a constitution and government, without a census being taken by the United States, and Congress waived the omission, as there was no doubt she had more than a sufficient number to entitle her to admission. She was not admitted at the first session she applied, owing to some difficulty respecting the boundary between her and Ohio. The great irregularity, as to her admission, took place at the next session—but on a point which can have no possible connection with the case of California.

The irregularities in all other cases that have since occurred, are of a similar nature. In all, there existed territorial governments established by Congress, with officers appointed by the United States. In all, the territorial government took the lead in calling conventions, and fixing the preliminaries preparatory to the formation of a constitution and admission into the Union. They all recognized the sovereignty of the United States, and the authority of

Congress over the territories; and wherever there was any departure from established usage, it was done on the presumed consent of Congress, and not in defiance of its authority, or the sovereignty of the United States over the territories. In this respect California stands alone, without usage or a single example to cover her case.

It belongs now, Senators, to you to decide what part you will act in reference to this unprecedented transaction. The Executive has laid the paper purporting to be the Constitution of California before you, and asks you to admit her into the Union as a State; and the question is, will you or will you not admit her? It is a grave question, and there rests upon you a heavy responsibility. Much, very much, will depend upon your decision. If you admit her, you indorse and give your sanction to all that has been done. Are you prepared to do so? Are you prepared to surrender your power of legislation for the territories—a power expressly vested in Congress by the constitution, as has been fully established? Can you, consistently with your oath to support the constitution, surrender the power? Are you prepared to admit that the inhabitants of the territories possess the sovereignty over them, and that any number, more or less, may claim any extent of territory they please; may form a constitution and government, and erect it into a State, without asking your permission? Are you prepared to surrender the sovereignty of the United States over whatever territory may be hereafter acquired to the first adventurers who may rush into it? Are you prepared to surrender virtually to the Executive Department all the powers which you have heretofore exercised over the territories? If not, how can you, consistently with your duty and your oaths to support the constitution, give your assent to the admission of California as a State, under a pretended constitution and government? Again, can you believe that the project of a constitution which they have adopted has the least validity? Can you believe that there is such a State in reality as the State of California? No; there is no such State. It has no legal or constitutional existence. It has no validity, and can have none, without your sanction. How, then, can you admit it as a *State,* when, according to the provision of the constitution, your power is limited to admitting new *States.* To be admitted, it must be a State,—and an existing State, independent of your sanction, before you can admit it. When you give your permission to the inhabitants of a territory to form a constitution and a State, the constitution and State they form, derive their author-

ity from the people, and not from you. The State, before it is admitted is actually a State, and does not become so by the *act of admission,* as would be the case with California, should you admit her contrary to the constitutional provisions and established usage heretofore.

The Senators on the other side of the Chamber must permit me to make a few remarks in this connection particularly applicable to them,—with the exception of a few Senators from the South, sitting on the other side of the Chamber.—When the Oregon question was before this body, not two years since, you took (if I mistake not) universally the ground, that Congress had the sole and absolute power of legislating for the territories. How, then, can you now, after the short interval which has elapsed, abandon the ground which you took, and thereby virtually admit that the power of legislating, instead of being in Congress, is in the inhabitants of the territories? How can you justify and sanction by your votes the acts of the Executive, which are in direct derogation of what you then contended for? But to approach still nearer to the present time, how can you, after condemning, little more than a year since, the grounds taken by the party which you defeated at the last election, wheel round and support by your votes the grounds which, as explained recently on this floor by the candidate of the party in the last election, are identical with those on which the Executive has acted in reference to California? What are we to understand by all this? Must we conclude that there is no sincerity, no faith in the acts and declarations of public men, and that all is mere acting or hollow profession? Or are we to conclude that the exclusion of the South from the territory acquired from Mexico is an object of so paramount a character in your estimation, that right, justice, constitution and consistency must all yield, when they stand in the way of our exclusion?

But, it may be asked, what is to be done with California, should she not be admitted? I answer, remand her back to the territorial condition, as was done in the case of Tennessee, in the early stage of the Government. Congress, in her case, had established a territorial government in the usual form, with a governor, judges, and other officers, appointed by the United States. She was entitled, under the deed of cession, to be admitted into the Union as a State as soon as she had sixty thousand inhabitants. The territorial government, believing it had that number, took a census, by which it appeared it exceeded it. She then formed a constitution, and applied for admission. Congress refused to admit her, on the ground that the census should be taken by the United States, and that Congress had not determined whether the territory should be formed into one or two States, as it was authorized to do under the cession. She returned quietly to her territorial condition. An act was passed to take a census by the United States, containing a provision that the territory should form one State. All afterwards was regularly conducted, and the territory admitted as a State in due form. The irregularities in the case of California are immeasurably greater, and offer much stronger reasons for pursuing the same course. But, it may be said, California may not submit. That is not probable; but if she should not, when she refuses, it will then be time for us to decide what is to be done.

Having now shown what cannot save the Union, I return to the question with which I commenced, How can the Union be saved? There is but one way by which it can with any certainty; and that is, by a full and final settlement, on the principle of justice, of all the questions at issue between the two sections. The South asks for justice, simple justice, and less she ought not to take. She has no compromise to offer, but the constitution; and no concession or surrender to make. She has already surrendered so much that she has little left to surrender. Such a settlement would go to the root of the evil, and remove all cause of discontent, by satisfying the South, she could remain honorably and safely in the Union, and thereby restore the harmony and fraternal feelings between the sections, which existed anterior to the Missouri agitation. Nothing else can, with any certainty, finally and for ever settle the questions at issue, terminate agitation, and save the Union.

But can this be done? Yes, easily; not by the weaker party, for it can of itself do nothing—not even protect itself—but by the stronger. The North has only to will it to accomplish it—to do justice by conceding to the South an equal right in the acquired territory, and to do her duty by causing the stipulations relative to fugitive slaves to be faithfully fulfilled—to cease the agitation of the slave question, and to provide for the insertion of a provision in the constitution, by an amendment, which will restore to the South, in substance, the power she possessed of protecting herself, before the equilibrium between the sections was destroyed by the action of this Government. There will be no difficulty in devising such a provision—one that will protect the South, and which, at the same time, will improve and strengthen the Government, instead of impairing and weakening it.

But will the North agree to this? It is for her to answer the question. But, I will say, she cannot refuse, if she has half the love of the Union which she professes to have, or without justly exposing herself to the charge that her love of power and aggrandizement is far greater than her love of the Union. At all events, the responsibility of saving the Union rests on the North, and not on the South. The South cannot save it by any act of hers, and the North may save it without any sacrifice whatever, unless to do justice, and to perform her duties under the constitution, should be regarded by her as a sacrifice.

It is time, Senators, that there should be an open and manly avowal on all sides, as to what is intended to be done. If the question is not now settled, it is uncertain whether it ever can hereafter be; and we, as the representatives of the States of this Union, regarded as governments, should come to a distinct understanding as to our respective views, in order to ascertain whether the great questions at issue can be settled or not. If you, who represent the stronger portion, cannot agree to settle them on the broad principle of justice and duty, say so; and let the States we both represent agree to separate and part in peace. If you are unwilling we should part in peace, tell us so, and we shall know what to do, when you reduce the question to submission or resistance. If you remain silent, you will compel us to infer by your acts what you intend. In that case, California will become the test question. If you admit her, under all the difficulties that oppose her admission, you compel us to infer that you intend to exclude us from the whole of the acquired territories, with the intention of destroying, irretrievably, the equilibrium between the two sections. We would be blind not to perceive in that case, that your real objects are power and aggrandizement, and infatuated not to act accordingly.

I have now, Senators, done my duty in expressing my opinions fully, freely, and candidly, on this solemn occasion. In doing so, I have been governed by the motives which have governed me in all the stages of the agitation of the slavery question since its commencement. I have exerted myself, during the whole period, to arrest it, with the intention of saving the Union, if it could be done; and if it could not, to save the section where it has pleased Providence to cast my lot, and which I sincerely believe has justice and the constitution on its side. Having faithfully done my duty to the best of my ability, both to the Union and my section, throughout this agitation, I shall have the consolation, let what will come, that I am free from all responsibility.

The Constitution and the Union

March 7, 1850

Mr. PRESIDENT,—I wish to speak to-day, not as a Massachusetts man, nor as a Northern man, but as an American, and a member of the Senate of the United States. It is fortunate that there is a Senate of the United States; a body not yet moved from its propriety, not lost to a just sense of its own dignity and its own high responsibilities, and a body to which the country looks, with confidence, for wise, moderate, patriotic, and healing counsels. It is not to be denied that we live in the midst of strong agitations, and are surrounded by very considerable dangers to our institutions and government. The imprisoned winds are let loose. The East, the North, and the stormy South combine to throw the whole sea into commotion, to toss its billows to the skies, and disclose its profoundest depths. I do not affect to regard myself, Mr. President, as holding, or as fit to hold, the helm in this combat with the political elements; but I have a duty to perform, and I mean to perform it with fidelity, not without a sense of existing dangers, but not without hope. I have a part to act, not for my own security or safety, for I am looking out for no fragment upon which to float away from the wreck, if wreck there must be, but for the good of the whole, and the preservation of all; and there is that which will keep me to my duty during this struggle, whether the sun and the stars shall appear, or shall not appear for many days. I speak to-day for the preservation of the Union. "Hear me for my cause." I speak to-day, out of a solicitous and anxious heart, for the restoration to the country of that quiet and that harmony which make the blessings of this Union so rich, and so dear to us all. These are the topics that I propose to myself to discuss; these are the motives, and the sole motives, that influence me in the wish to communicate my opinions to the Senate and the country; and if I can do any thing, however little, for the promotion of these ends, I shall have accomplished all that I expect.

Mr. President, it may not be amiss to recur very briefly to the events which, equally sudden and extraordinary, have brought the country into its present political condition. In May, 1846, the United States declared war against Mexico. Our armies, then on the frontiers, entered the provinces of that republic, met and defeated all her troops, penetrated her mountain passes, and occupied her capital. The marine force of the United States took possession of her forts and her towns, on the Atlantic and on the Pacific. In less than two years a treaty was negotiated, by which Mexico ceded to the United States a vast territory, extending seven or eight hundred miles along the shores of the Pacific, and reaching back over the mountains, and across the desert, until it joins the frontier of the State of Texas. It so happened, in the distracted and feeble condition of the Mexican government, that, before the declaration of war by the United States against Mexico had become known in California, the people of California, under the lead of American officers, overthrew the existing Mexican provincial government, and raised an independent flag. When the news arrived at San Francisco that war had been declared by the United States against Mexico, this independent flag was pulled down, and the stars and stripes of this Union hoisted in its stead. So, Sir, before the war was over, the forces of the United States, military and naval, had possession of San Francisco and Upper California, and a great rush of emigrants from various parts of the world took place into California in 1846 and 1847. But now behold another wonder.

In January of 1848, a party of Mormons made a discovery of an extraordinarily rich mine of gold, or rather of a great quantity of gold, hardly proper to be called a mine, for it was spread near the surface, on the lower part of the south, or American, branch of the Sacramento. They attempted to conceal their discovery for some time; but soon another discovery of gold, perhaps of greater importance, was made, on another part of the American branch of the Sacramento, and near Sutter's Fort, as it is called. The fame of these discoveries spread far and wide. They inflamed more and more the spirit of emigration towards California, which had already been excited; and adventurers crowded into the country by hundreds, and flocked towards the Bay of San Francisco. This, as I have said, took place in the winter and spring of 1848. The digging commenced in the spring of that year, and from that time to this the work of searching for gold has been prosecuted with a success not heretofore known in the history of this globe. You recollect, Sir, how incredulous at first the American public was at the accounts which reached us of these discoveries; but we all know, now, that these accounts received, and continue to receive, daily confirmation, and down to the present moment I suppose the assurance is as strong, after the experience of these several months, of the existence of deposits of gold apparently inexhaustible in the regions near San Francisco, in California, as it was at any period of the earlier dates of the accounts.

It so happened, Sir, that although, after the return of peace, it became a very important subject for legislative consideration and legislative decision to provide a proper territorial government for California, yet differences of opinion between the two houses of Congress prevented the establishment of any such territorial government at the last session. Under this state of things, the inhabitants of California, already amounting to a considerable number, thought it to be their duty, in the summer of last year, to establish a local government. Under the proclamation of General Riley, the people chose delegates to a convention, and that convention met at Monterey. It formed a constitution for the State of California, which, being referred to the people, was adopted by them in their primary assemblages. Desirous of immediate connection with the United States, its Senators were appointed and representatives chosen, who have come hither, bringing with them the authentic constitution of the State of California; and they now present themselves, asking, in behalf of their constituents, that it may be admitted into this Union as one of the United States. This constitution, Sir, contains an express prohibition of slavery, or involuntary servitude, in the State of California. It is said, and I suppose truly, that, of the members who composed that convention, some sixteen were natives of, and had been residents in, the slave-holding States, about twenty-two were from the non-slave-holding States, and the remaining ten members were either native Californians or old settlers in that country. This prohibition of slavery, it is said, was inserted with entire unanimity.

It is this circumstance, Sir, the prohibition of slavery, which has contributed to raise, I do not say it has wholly raised, the dispute as to the propriety of the admission of California into the Union under this constitution. It is not to be denied, Mr. President, nobody thinks of denying, that, whatever reasons were assigned at the commencement of the late war with Mexico, it was prosecuted for the purpose of the acquisition of territory, and under the alleged argument that the cession of territory was the only form

in which proper compensation could be obtained by the United States from Mexico, for the various claims and demands which the people of this country had against that government. At any rate, it will be found that President Polk's message, at the commencement of the session of December, 1847, avowed that the war was to be prosecuted until some acquisition of territory should be made. As the acquisition was to be south of the line of the United States, in warm climates and countries, it was naturally, I suppose, expected by the South, that whatever acquisitions were made in that region would be added to the slave-holding portion of the United States. Very little of accurate information was possessed of the real physical character, either of California or New Mexico, and events have not turned out as was expected. Both California and New Mexico are likely to come in as free States; and therefore some degree of disappointment and surprise has resulted. In other words, it is obvious that the question which has so long harassed the country, and at some times very seriously alarmed the minds of wise and good men, has come upon us for a fresh discussion; the question of slavery in these United States.

Now, Sir, I propose, perhaps at the expense of some detail and consequent detention of the Senate, to review historically this question, which, partly in consequence of its own importance, and partly, perhaps mostly, in consequence of the manner in which it has been discussed in different portions of the country, has been a source of so much alienation and unkind feeling between them.

We all know, Sir, that slavery has existed in the world from time immemorial. There was slavery, in the earliest periods of history, among the Oriental nations. There was slavery among the Jews; the theocratic government of that people issued no injunction against it. There was slavery among the Greeks; and the ingenious philosophy of the Greeks found, or sought to find, a justification for it exactly upon the grounds which have been assumed for such a justification in this country; that is, a natural and original difference among the races of mankind, and the inferiority of the black or colored race to the white. The Greeks justified their system of slavery upon that idea, precisely. They held the African and some of the Asiatic tribes to be inferior to the white race; but they did not show, I think, by any close process of logic, that, if this were true, the more intelligent and the stronger had therefore a right to subjugate the weaker.

The more manly philosophy and jurisprudence of the

Romans placed the justification of slavery on entirely different grounds. The Roman jurists, from the first and down to the fall of the empire, admitted that slavery was against the natural law, by which, as they maintained, all men, of whatsoever clime, color, or capacity, were equal; but they justified slavery, first, upon the ground and authority of the law of nations, arguing, and arguing truly, that at that day the conventional law of nations admitted that captives in war, whose lives, according to the notions of the times, were at the absolute disposal of the captors, might, in exchange for exemption from death, be made slaves for life, and that such servitude might descend to their posterity. The jurists of Rome also maintained, that, by the civil law, there might be servitude or slavery, personal and hereditary; first, by the voluntary act of an individual, who might sell himself into slavery; secondly, by his being reduced into a state of slavery by his creditors, in satisfaction of his debts; and, thirdly, by being placed in a state of servitude or slavery for crime. At the introduction of Christianity, the Roman world was full of slaves, and I suppose there is to be found no injunction against that relation between man and man in the teachings of the Gospel of Jesus Christ or of any of his Apostles. The object of the instruction imparted to mankind by the founder of Christianity was to touch the heart, purify the soul, and improve the lives of individual men. That object went directly to the first fountain of all the political and social relations of the human race, as well as of all true religious feeling, the individual heart and mind of man.

Now, Sir, upon the general nature and influence of slavery there exists a wide difference of opinion between the northern portion of this country and the southern. It is said on the one side, that, although not the subject of any injunction or direct prohibition in the New Testament, slavery is a wrong; that it is founded merely in the right of the strongest; and that it is an oppression, like unjust wars, like all those conflicts by which a powerful nation subjects a weaker to its will; and that, in its nature, whatever may be said of it in the modifications which have taken place, it is not according to the meek spirit of the Gospel. It is not "kindly affectioned"; it does not "seek another's, and not its own"; it does not "let the oppressed go free." These are sentiments that are cherished, and of late with greatly augmented force, among the people of the Northern States. They have taken hold of the religious sentiment of that part of the country, as they have, more or less, taken hold of the religious feelings of a considerable portion of mankind.

The South, upon the other side, having been accustomed to this relation between the two races all their lives, from their birth, having been taught, in general, to treat the subjects of this bondage with care and kindness, and I believe, in general, feeling great kindness for them, have not taken the view of the subject which I have mentioned. There are thousands of religious men, with consciences as tender as any of their brethren at the North, who do not see the unlawfulness of slavery; and there are more thousands, perhaps, that, whatsoever they may think of it in its origin, and as a matter depending upon natural right, yet take things as they are, and, finding slavery to be an established relation of the society in which they live, can see no way in which, let their opinions on the abstract question be what they may, it is in the power of the present generation to relieve themselves from this relation. And candor obliges me to say, that I believe they are just as conscientious, many of them, and the religious people, all of them, as they are at the North who hold different opinions.

The honorable Senator from South Carolina* the other day alluded to the separation of that great religious community, the Methodist Episcopal Church. That separation was brought about by differences of opinion upon this particular subject of slavery. I felt great concern, as that dispute went on, about the result. I was in hopes that the difference of opinion might be adjusted, because I looked upon that religious denomination as one of the great props of religion and morals throughout the whole country, from Maine to Georgia, and westward to our utmost western boundary. The result was against my wishes and against my hopes. I have read all their proceedings and all their arguments; but I have never yet been able to come to the conclusion that there was any real ground for that separation; in other words, that any good could be produced by that separation. I must say I think there was some want of candor and charity. Sir, when a question of this kind seizes on the religious sentiments of mankind, and comes to be discussed in religious assemblies of the clergy and laity, there is always to be expected, or always to be feared, a great degree of excitement. It is in the nature of man, manifested by his whole history, that religious disputes are apt to become warm in proportion to the strength of the convictions which men entertain of the magnitude of the questions at issue. In all such disputes, there will sometimes be found men with whom every thing is absolute;

*Mr. Calhoun.

absolutely wrong, or absolutely right. They see the right clearly; they think others ought so to see it, and they are disposed to establish a broad line of distinction between what is right and what is wrong. They are not seldom willing to establish that line upon their own convictions of truth and justice; and are ready to mark and guard it by placing along it a series of dogmas, as lines of boundary on the earth's surface are marked by posts and stones. There are men who, with clear perceptions, as they think, of their own duty, do not see how too eager a pursuit of one duty may involve them in the violation of others, or how too warm an embracement of one truth may lead to a disregard of other truths equally important. As I heard it stated strongly, not many days ago, these persons are disposed to mount upon some particular duty, as upon a war-horse, and to drive furiously on and upon and over all other duties that may stand in the way. There are men who, in reference to disputes of that sort, are of opinion that human duties may be ascertained with the exactness of mathematics. They deal with morals as with mathematics; and they think what is right may be distinguished from what is wrong with the precision of an algebraic equation. They have, therefore, none too much charity towards others who differ from them. They are apt, too, to think that nothing is good but what is perfect, and that there are no compromises or modifications to be made in consideration of difference of opinion or in deference to other men's judgment. If their perspicacious vision enables them to detect a spot on the face of the sun, they think that a good reason why the sun should be struck down from heaven. They prefer the chance of running into utter darkness to living in heavenly light, if that heavenly light be not absolutely without any imperfection. There are impatient men; too impatient always to give heed to the admonition of St. Paul, that we are not to "do evil that good may come"; too impatient to wait for the slow progress of moral causes in the improvement of mankind. They do not remember that the doctrines and the miracles of Jesus Christ have, in eighteen hundred years, converted only a small portion of the human race; and among the nations that are converted to Christianity, they forget how many vices and crimes, public and private, still prevail, and that many of them, public crimes especially, which are so clearly offences against the Christian religion, pass without exciting particular indignation. Thus wars are waged, and unjust wars. I do not deny that there may be just wars. There certainly are; but

it was the remark of an eminent person, not many years ago, on the other side of the Atlantic, that it is one of the greatest reproaches to human nature that wars are sometimes just. The defence of nations sometimes causes a just war against the injustice of other nations. In this state of sentiment upon the general nature of slavery lies the cause of a great part of those unhappy divisions, exasperations, and reproaches which find vent and support in different parts of the Union.

But we must view things as they are. Slavery does exist in the United States. It did exist in the States before the adoption of this Constitution, and at that time. Let us, therefore, consider for a moment what was the state of sentiment, North and South, in regard to slavery, at the time this Constitution was adopted. A remarkable change has taken place since; but what did the wise and great men of all parts of the country think of slavery then? In what estimation did they hold it at the time when this Constitution was adopted? It will be found, Sir, if we will carry ourselves by historical research back to that day, and ascertain men's opinions by authentic records still existing among us, that there was then no diversity of opinion between the North and the South upon the subject of slavery. It will be found that both parts of the country held it equally an evil, a moral and political evil. It will not be found that, either at the North or at the South, there was much, though there was some, invective against slavery as inhuman and cruel. The great ground of objection to it was political; that it weakened the social fabric; that, taking the place of free labor, society became less strong and labor less productive; and therefore we find from all the eminent men of the time the clearest expression of their opinion that slavery is an evil. They ascribed its existence here, not without truth, and not without some acerbity of temper and force of language, to the injurious policy of the mother country, who, to favor the navigator, had entailed these evils upon the Colonies. I need hardly refer, Sir, particularly to the publications of the day. They are matters of history on the record. The eminent men, the most eminent men, and nearly all the conspicuous politicians of the South, held the same sentiments; that slavery was an evil, a blight, a scourge, and a curse. There are no terms of reprobation of slavery so vehement in the North at that day as in the South. The North was not so much excited against it as the South; and the reason is, I suppose, that there was much less of it at the North, and the people did not see, or think they saw, the evils so prominently as they were seen, or thought to be seen, at the South.

Then, Sir, when this Constitution was framed, this was the light in which the Federal Convention viewed it. That body reflected the judgment and sentiments of the great men of the South. A member of the other house, whom I have not the honor to know, has, in a recent speech, collected extracts from these public documents. They prove the truth of what I am saying, and the question then was, how to deal with it, and how to deal with it as an evil. They came to this general result. They thought that slavery could not be continued in the country if the importation of slaves were made to cease, and therefore they provided that, after a certain period, the importation might be prevented by the act of the new government. The period of twenty years was proposed by some gentleman from the North, I think, and many members of the Convention from the South opposed it as being too long. Mr. Madison especially was somewhat warm against it. He said it would bring too much of this mischief into the country to allow the importation of slaves for such a period. Because we must take along with us, in the whole of this discussion, when we are considering the sentiments and opinions in which the constitutional provision originated, that the conviction of all men was, that, if the importation of slaves ceased, the white race would multiply faster than the black race, and that slavery would therefore gradually wear out and expire. It may not be improper here to allude to that, I had almost said, celebrated opinion of Mr. Madison. You observe, Sir, that the term *slave,* or *slavery,* is not used in the Constitution. The Constitution does not require that "fugitive slaves" shall be delivered up. It requires that persons held to service in one State, and escaping into another, shall be delivered up. Mr. Madison opposed the introduction of the term *slave,* or *slavery,* into the Constitution; for he said that he did not wish to see it recognized by the Constitution of the United States of America that there could be property in men.

Now, Sir, all this took place in the Convention in 1787; but connected with this, concurrent and contemporaneous, is another important transaction, not sufficiently attended to. The Convention for framing this Constitution assembled in Philadelphia in May, and sat until September, 1787. During all that time the Congress of the United States was in session at New York. It was a matter of design, as we know, that the Convention should not assemble in the same city where Congress was holding its sessions. Almost all the public men of the country, therefore, of distinction and eminence, were in one or the other of these two assemblies; and I think it happened, in some instances, that the same gentlemen were members of both bodies. If I mistake not, such was the case with Mr. Rufus King, then a member of Congress from Massachusetts. Now, at the very time when the Convention in Philadelphia was framing this Constitution, the Congress in New York was framing the Ordinance of 1787, for the organization and government of the territory northwest of the Ohio. They passed that Ordinance on the 13th of July, 1787, at New York, the very month, perhaps the very day, on which these questions about the importation of slaves and the character of slavery were debated in the Convention at Philadelphia. So far as we can now learn, there was a perfect concurrence of opinion between these two bodies; and it resulted in this Ordinance of 1787, excluding slavery from all the territory over which the Congress of the United States had jurisdiction, and that was all the territory northwest of the Ohio. Three years before, Virginia and other States had made a cession of that great territory to the United States; and a most munificent act it was. I never reflect upon it without a disposition to do honor and justice, and justice would be the highest honor, to Virginia, for the cession of her northwestern territory. I will say, Sir, it is one of her fairest claims to the respect and gratitude of the country, and that, perhaps, it is only second to that other claim which belongs to her; that from her counsels, and from the intelligence and patriotism of her leading statesmen, proceeded the first idea put into practice of the formation of a general constitution of the United States. The Ordinance of 1787 applied to the whole territory over which the Congress of the United States had jurisdiction. It was adopted two years before the Constitution of the United States went into operation; because the Ordinance took effect immediately on its passage, while the Constitution of the United States, having been framed, was to be sent to the States to be adopted by their Conventions; and then a government was to be organized under it. This Ordinance, then, was in operation and force when the Constitution was adopted, and the government put in motion, in April, 1789.

Mr. President, three things are quite clear as historical truths. One is, that there was an expectation that, on the ceasing of the importation of slaves from Africa, slavery would begin to run out here. That was hoped and expected.

Another is, that, as far as there was any power in Congress to prevent the spread of slavery in the United States, that power was executed in the most absolute manner, and to the fullest extent. An honorable member,* whose health does not allow him to be here to-day—

A SENATOR. He is here.

I am very happy to hear that he is; may he long be here, and in the enjoyment of health to serve his country! The honorable member said, the other day, that he considered this Ordinance as the first in the series of measures calculated to enfeeble the South, and deprive them of their just participation in the benefits and privileges of this government. He says, very properly, that it was enacted under the old Confederation, and before this Constitution went into effect; but my present purpose is only to say, Mr. President, that it was established with the entire and unanimous concurrence of the whole South. Why, there it stands! The vote of every State in the Union was unanimous in favor of the Ordinance, with the exception of a single individual vote, and that individual vote was given by a Northern man. This Ordinance prohibiting slavery for ever northwest of the Ohio has the hand and seal of every Southern member in Congress. It was therefore no aggression of the North on the South. The other and third clear historical truth is, that the Convention meant to leave slavery in the States as they found it, entirely under the authority and control of the States themselves.

This was the state of things, Sir, and this the state of opinion, under which those very important matters were arranged, and those three important things done; that is, the establishment of the Constitution of the United States with a recognition of slavery as it existed in the States; the establishment of the ordinance for the government of the Northwestern Territory, prohibiting, to the full extent of all territory owned by the United States, the introduction of slavery into that territory, while leaving to the States all power over slavery in their own limits; and creating a power, in the new government, to put an end to the importation of slaves, after a limited period. There was entire coincidence and concurrence of sentiment between the North and the South, upon all these questions, at the period of the adoption of the Constitution. But opinions, Sir, have changed, greatly changed; changed North and changed South. Slavery is not regarded in the South now as it was then. I see an honorable member of this body paying me the honor of listening to my remarks;[†] he brings to my mind, Sir, freshly and vividly, what I have learned of his great ancestor, so much distinguished in his day and generation, so worthy to be succeeded by so worthy a grandson, and of the sentiments he expressed in the Convention in Philadelphia.[‡]

Here we may pause. There was, if not an entire unanimity, a general concurrence of sentiment running through the whole community, and especially entertained by the eminent men of all parts of the country. But soon a change began, at the North and the South, and a difference of opinion showed itself; the North growing much more warm and strong against slavery, and the South growing much more warm and strong in its support. Sir, there is no generation of mankind whose opinions are not subject to be influenced by what appear to them to be their present emergent and exigent interests. I impute to the South no particularly selfish view in the change which has come over her. I impute to her certainly no dishonest view. All that has happened has been natural. It has followed those causes which always influence the human mind and operate upon it. What, then, have been the causes which have created so new a feeling in favor of slavery in the South, which have changed the whole nomenclature of the South on that subject, so that, from being thought and described in the terms I have mentioned and will not repeat, it has now become an institution, a cherished institution, in that quarter; no evil, no scourge, but a great religious, social, and moral blessing, as I think I have heard it latterly spoken of? I suppose this, Sir, is owing to the rapid growth and sudden extension of the COTTON plantations of the South. So far as any motive consistent with honor, justice, and general judgment could act, it was the COTTON interest that gave a new desire to promote slavery, to spread it, and to use its labor. I again say that this change was produced by causes which must always produce like effects. The whole interest of the South became connected, more or less, with the extension of slavery. If we look back to the history of the commerce of this country in the early years of this government, what were our exports? Cotton was hardly, or but to a very limited extent, known. In 1791 the first parcel of cotton of the growth of the United States was exported, and

*Mr. Calhoun.

† Mr. Mason of Virginia.
‡ See Madison Papers, Vol. III. pp. 1390, 1428, *et seq.*

amounted only to 19,200 pounds.* It has gone on increasing rapidly, until the whole crop may now, perhaps, in a season of great product and high prices, amount to a hundred millions of dollars. In the years I have mentioned, there was more of wax, more of indigo, more of rice, more of almost every article of export from the South, than of cotton. When Mr. Jay negotiated the treaty of 1794 with England, it is evident from the twelfth article of the treaty, which was suspended by the Senate, that he did not know that cotton was exported at all from the United States.

Well, Sir, we know what followed. The age of cotton became the golden age of our Southern brethren. It gratified their desire for improvement and accumulation, at the same time that it excited it. The desire grew by what it fed upon, and there soon came to be an eagerness for other territory, a new area or new areas for the cultivation of the cotton crop; and measures leading to this result were brought about rapidly, one after another, under the lead of Southern men at the head of the government, they having a majority in both branches of Congress to accomplish their ends. The honorable member from South Carolina† observed that there has been a majority all along in favor of the North. If that be true, Sir, the North has acted either very liberally and kindly, or very weakly; for they never exercised that majority efficiently five times in the history of the government, when a division or trial of strength arose. Never. Whether they were out-generalled, or whether it was owing to other causes, I shall not stop to consider; but no man acquainted with the history of the Union can deny that the general lead in the politics of the country, for three fourths of the period that has elapsed since the adoption of the Constitution, has been a Southern lead.

In 1802, in pursuit of the idea of opening a new cotton region, the United States obtained a cession from Georgia of the whole of her western territory, now embracing the rich and growing States of Alabama and Mississippi. In 1803 Louisiana was purchased from France, out of which the States of Louisiana, Arkansas, and Missouri have been framed, as slave-holding States. In 1819 the cession of Florida was made, bringing in another region adapted to cultivation by slaves. Sir, the honorable member from South Carolina thought he saw in certain operations of the gov-

ernment, such as the manner of collecting the revenue, and the tendency of measures calculated to promote emigration into the country, what accounts for the more rapid growth of the North than the South. He ascribes that more rapid growth, not to the operation of time, but to the system of government and administration established under this Constitution. That is matter of opinion. To a certain extent it may be true; but it does seem to me that, if any operation of the government can be shown in any degree to have promoted the population, and growth, and wealth of the North, it is much more sure that there are sundry important and distinct operations of the government, about which no man can doubt, tending to promote, and which absolutely have promoted, the increase of the slave interest and the slave territory of the South. It was not time that brought in Louisiana; it was the act of men. It was not time that brought in Florida; it was the act of men. And lastly, Sir, to complete those acts of legislation which have contributed so much to enlarge the area of the institution of slavery, Texas, great and vast and illimitable Texas, was added to the Union as a slave State in 1845; and that, Sir, pretty much closed the whole chapter, and settled the whole account.

That closed the whole chapter and settled the whole account, because the annexation of Texas, upon the conditions and under the guaranties upon which she was admitted, did not leave within the control of this government an acre of land, capable of being cultivated by slave labor, between this Capitol and the Rio Grande or the Nueces, or whatever is the proper boundary of Texas; not an acre. From that moment, the whole country, from this place to the western boundary of Texas, was fixed, pledged, fastened, decided, to be slave territory for ever, by the solemn guaranties of law. And I now say, Sir, as the proposition upon which I stand this day, and upon the truth and firmness of which I intend to act until it is overthrown, that there is not at this moment within the United States, or any territory of the United States, a single foot of land, the character of which, in regard to its being free territory or slave territory, is not fixed by some law, and some irrepealable law, beyond the power of the action of the government. Is it not so with respect to Texas? It is most manifestly so. The honorable member from South Carolina, at the time of the admission of Texas, held an important post in the executive department of the government; he was Secretary of State. Another eminent person of great

---

* Seybert's Statistics, p. 92. A small parcel of cotton found its way to Liverpool from the United States in 1784, and was refused admission, on the ground that it could not be the growth of the United States.

† Mr. Calhoun.

activity and adroitness in affairs, I mean the late Secretary of the Treasury,* was a conspicuous member of this body, and took the lead in the business of annexation, in coöperation with the Secretary of State; and I must say that they did their business faithfully and thoroughly; there was no botch left in it. They rounded it off, and made as close joinerwork as ever was exhibited. Resolutions of annexation were brought into Congress, fitly joined together, compact, efficient, conclusive upon the great object which they had in view, and those resolutions passed.

Allow me to read a part of these resolutions. It is the third clause of the second section of the resolution of the 1st of March, 1845, for the admission of Texas, which applies to this part of the case. That clause is as follows:—

> New States, of convenient size, not exceeding four in number, in addition to said State of Texas, and having sufficient population, may hereafter, by the consent of said State, be formed out of the territory thereof, which shall be entitled to admission under the provisions of the Federal Constitution. And such States as may be formed out of that portion of said territory lying south of thirty-six degrees thirty minutes north latitude, commonly known as the Missouri Compromise line, shall be admitted into the Union with or without slavery, as the people of each State asking admission may desire; and in such State or States as shall be formed out of said territory north of said Missouri Compromise line, slavery or involuntary servitude (except for crime) shall be prohibited.

Now, what is here stipulated, enacted, and secured? It is, that all Texas south of 36° 30′, which is nearly the whole of it, shall be admitted into the Union as a slave State. It was a slave State, and therefore came in as a slave State; and the guaranty is, that new States shall be made out of it, to the number of four, in addition to the State then in existence and admitted at that time by these resolutions, and that such States as are formed out of that portion of Texas lying south of 36° 30′ may come in as slave States. I know no form of legislation which can strengthen this. I know no mode of recognition that can add a tittle of weight to it. I listened respectfully to the resolutions of my honorable friend from Tennessee.† He proposed to recognize that stipulation with Texas. But any additional recognition would weaken the force of it; because it stands here on the ground of a contract, a thing done for a consideration. It

is a law founded on a contract with Texas, and designed to carry that contract into effect. A recognition now, founded not on any consideration or any contract, would not be so strong as it now stands on the face of the resolution. I know no way, I candidly confess, in which this government, acting in good faith, as I trust it always will, can relieve itself from that stipulation and pledge, by any honest course of legislation whatever. And therefore I say again, that, so far as Texas is concerned, in the whole of that State south of 36° 30′, which, I suppose, embraces all the territory capable of slave cultivation, there is no land, not an acre, the character of which is not established by law; a law which cannot be repealed without the violation of a contract, and plain disregard of the public faith.

I hope, Sir, it is now apparent that my proposition, so far as it respects Texas, has been maintained, and that the provision in this article is clear and absolute; and it has been well suggested by my friend from Rhode Island,‡ that that part of Texas which lies north of 36° 30′ of north latitude, and which may be formed into free States, is dependent, in like manner, upon the consent of Texas, herself a slave State.

Now, Sir, how came this? How came it to pass that within these walls, where it is said by the honorable member from South Carolina that the free States have always had a majority, this resolution of annexation, such as I have described it, obtained a majority in both houses of Congress? Sir, it obtained that majority by the great number of Northern votes added to the entire Southern vote, or at least nearly the whole of the Southern vote. The aggregate was made up of Northern and Southern votes. In the House of Representatives there were about eighty Southern votes and about fifty Northern votes for the admission of Texas. In the Senate the vote for the admission of Texas was twenty-seven, and twenty-five against it; and of those twenty-seven votes, constituting the majority, no less than thirteen came from the free States, and four of them were from New England. The whole of these thirteen Senators, constituting within a fraction, you see, one half of all the votes in this body for the admission of this immeasurable extent of slave territory, were sent here by free States.

Sir, there is not so remarkable a chapter in our history of political events, political parties, and political men as is afforded by this admission of a new slave-holding terri-

*Mr. Walker.
†Mr. Bell.

‡Mr. Greene.

tory, so vast that a bird cannot fly over it in a week. New England, as I have said, with some of her own votes, supported this measure. Three fourths of the votes of liberty-loving Connecticut were given for it in the other house, and one half here. There was one vote for it from Maine, but, I am happy to say, not the vote of the honorable member who addressed the Senate the day before yesterday,* and who was then a Representative from Maine in the House of Representatives; but there was one vote from Maine, ay, and there was one vote for it from Massachusetts, given by a gentleman then representing, and now living in, the district in which the prevalence of Free Soil sentiment for a couple of years or so has defeated the choice of any member to represent it in Congress. Sir, that body of Northern and Eastern men who gave those votes at that time are now seen taking upon themselves, in the nomenclature of politics, the appellation of the Northern Democracy. They undertook to wield the destinies of this empire, if I may give that name to a republic, and their policy was, and they persisted in it, to bring into this country and under this government all the territory they could. They did it, in the case of Texas, under pledges, absolute pledges, to the slave interest, and they afterwards lent their aid in bringing in these new conquests, to take their chance for slavery or freedom. My honorable friend from Georgia,[†] in March, 1847, moved the Senate to declare that the war ought not to be prosecuted for the conquest of territory, or for the dismemberment of Mexico. The whole of the Northern Democracy voted against it. He did not get a vote from them. It suited the patriotic and elevated sentiments of the Northern Democracy to bring in a world from among the mountains and valleys of California and New Mexico, or any other part of Mexico, and then quarrel about it; to bring it in, and then endeavor to put upon it the saving grace of the Wilmot Proviso. There were two eminent and highly respectable gentlemen from the North and East, then leading gentlemen in the Senate, (I refer, and I do so with entire respect, for I entertain for both of those gentlemen, in general, high regard, to Mr. Dix of New York and Mr. Niles of Connecticut,) who both voted for the admission of Texas. They would not have that vote any other way than as it stood; and they would have it as it did stand. I speak of the vote upon the annexation of Texas. Those two gentlemen would have the resolution of annexation just as it is, without amendment; and they voted for it just as it is, and their eyes were all open to its true character. The honorable member from South Carolina who addressed us the other day was then Secretary of State. His correspondence with Mr. Murphy, the Chargé d'Affaires of the United States in Texas, had been published. That correspondence was all before those gentlemen, and the Secretary had the boldness and candor to avow in that correspondence, that the great object sought by the annexation of Texas was to strengthen the slave interest of the South. Why, Sir, he said so in so many words—

MR. CALHOUN. Will the honorable Senator permit me to interrupt him for a moment?

Certainly.

MR. CALHOUN. I am very reluctant to interrupt the honorable gentleman; but, upon a point of so much importance, I deem it right to put myself *rectus in curia*. I did not put it upon the ground assumed by the Senator. I put it upon this ground: that Great Britain had announced to this country, in so many words, that her object was to abolish slavery in Texas, and, through Texas, to accomplish the abolition of slavery in the United States and the world. The ground I put it on was, that it would make an exposed frontier, and, if Great Britain succeeded in her object, it would be impossible that that frontier could be secured against the aggressions of the Abolitionists; and that this government was bound, under the guaranties of the Constitution, to protect us against such a state of things.

That comes, I suppose, Sir, to exactly the same thing. It was, that Texas must be obtained for the security of the slave interest of the South.

MR. CALHOUN. Another view is very distinctly given.

That was the object set forth in the correspondence of a worthy gentleman not now living,[‡] who preceded the honorable member from South Carolina in the Department of State. There repose on the files of the Department, as I have occasion to know, strong letters from Mr. Upshur to the United States minister in England, and I believe there are some to the same minister from the honorable Senator himself, asserting to this effect the sentiments of this gov-

*Mr. Hamlin.
†Mr. Berrien.

‡Mr. Upshur.

ernment; namely, that Great Britain was expected not to interfere to take Texas out of the hands of its then existing government and make it a free country. But my argument, my suggestion, is this; that those gentlemen who composed the Northern Democracy when Texas was brought into the Union saw clearly that it was brought in as a slave country, and brought in for the purpose of being maintained as slave territory, to the Greek Kalends. I rather think the honorable gentleman who was then Secretary of State might, in some of his correspondence with Mr. Murphy, have suggested that it was not expedient to say too much about this object, lest it should create some alarm. At any rate, Mr. Murphy wrote to him that England was anxious to get rid of the constitution of Texas, because it was a constitution establishing slavery; and that what the United States had to do was to aid the people of Texas in upholding their constitution; but that nothing should be said which should offend the fanatical men of the North. But, Sir, the honorable member did avow this object himself, openly, boldly, and manfully; he did not disguise his conduct or his motives.

MR. CALHOUN. Never, never.

What he means he is very apt to say.

MR. CALHOUN. Always, always.

And I honor him for it.

This admission of Texas was in 1845. Then, in 1847, *flagrante bello* between the United States and Mexico, the proposition I have mentioned was brought forward by my friend from Georgia, and the Northern Democracy voted steadily against it. Their remedy was to apply to the acquisitions, after they should come in, the Wilmot Proviso. What follows? These two gentlemen,* worthy and honorable and influential men, (and if they had not been they could not have carried the measure,) these two gentlemen, members of this body, brought in Texas, and by their votes they also prevented the passage of the resolution of the honorable member from Georgia, and then they went home and took the lead in the Free Soil party. And there they stand, Sir! They leave us here, bound in honor and conscience by the resolutions of annexation; they leave us here, to take the odium of fulfilling the obligations in fa-

* Messrs. Niles of Connecticut and Dix of New York.

vor of slavery which they voted us into, or else the greater odium of violating those obligations, while they are at home making capital and rousing speeches for free soil and no slavery. And therefore I say, Sir, that there is not a chapter in our history, respecting public measures and public men, more full of what would create surprise, more full of what does create, in my mind, extreme mortification, than that of the conduct of the Northern Democracy on this subject.

Mr. President, sometimes, when a man is found in a new relation to things around him and to other men, he says the world has changed, and that he has not changed. I believe, Sir, that our self-respect leads us often to make this declaration in regard to ourselves when it is not exactly true. An individual is more apt to change, perhaps, than all the world around him. But, under the present circumstances, and under the responsibility which I know I incur by what I am now stating here, I feel at liberty to recur to the various expressions and statements, made at various times, of my own opinions and resolutions respecting the admission of Texas, and all that has followed. Sir, as early as 1836, or in the early part of 1837, there was conversation and correspondence between myself and some private friends on this project of annexing Texas to the United States; and an honorable gentleman with whom I have had a long acquaintance, a friend of mine, now perhaps in this chamber, I mean General Hamilton, of South Carolina, was privy to that correspondence. I had voted for the recognition of Texan independence, because I believed it to be an existing fact, surprising and astonishing as it was, and I wished well to the new republic; but I manifested from the first utter opposition to bringing her, with her slave territory, into the Union. I happened, in 1837, to make a public address to political friends in New York, and I then stated my sentiments upon the subject. It was the first time that I had occasion to advert to it; and I will ask a friend near me to have the kindness to read an extract from the speech made by me on that occasion. It was delivered in Niblo's Garden, in 1837.

(Mr. Greene then read the following extract from the speech of Mr. Webster to which he referred:—)

Gentlemen, we all see that, by whomsoever possessed, Texas is likely to be a slave-holding country; and I frankly avow my entire unwillingness to do any thing which shall extend the slavery of the African race on this continent, or add other slave-holding States to the Union. When I say that I regard slavery in itself as a great moral, social, and political evil, I only use language which has been adopted by distinguished men, themselves citizens of slave-holding States. I shall do nothing, therefore, to favor or encourage its further extension. We have slavery already amongst us. The Constitution found it in the Union; it recognized it, and gave it solemn guaranties. To the full extent of these guaranties we are all bound, in honor, in justice, and by the Constitution. All the stipulations contained in the Constitution in favor of the slave-holding States which are already in the Union ought to be fulfilled, and, so far as depends on me, shall be fulfilled, in the fulness of their spirit, and to the exactness of their letter. Slavery, as it exists in the States, is beyond the reach of Congress. It is a concern of the States themselves; they have never submitted it to Congress, and Congress has no rightful power over it. I shall concur, therefore, in no act, no measure, no menace, no indication of purpose, which shall interfere or threaten to interfere with the exclusive authority of the several States over the subject of slavery as it exists within their respective limits. All this appears to me to be matter of plain and imperative duty.

But when we come to speak of admitting new States, the subject assumes an entirely different aspect. Our rights and our duties are then both different. . . .

I see, therefore, no political necessity for the annexation of Texas to the Union; no advantages to be derived from it; and objections to it of a strong, and, in my judgment, decisive character.

I have nothing, Sir, to add to, or to take from, those sentiments. That speech, the Senate will perceive, was made in 1837. The purpose of immediately annexing Texas at that time was abandoned or postponed; and it was not revived with any vigor for some years. In the mean time it happened that I had become a member of the executive administration, and was for a short period in the Department of State. The annexation of Texas was a subject of conversation, not confidential, with the President and heads of departments, as well as with other public men. No serious attempt was then made, however, to bring it about. I left the Department of State in May, 1843, and shortly after I learned, though by means which were no way connected with official information, that a design had been taken up of bringing Texas, with her slave territory and population, into this Union. I was in Washington at the time, and persons are now here who will remember that we had an arranged meeting for conversation upon it. I went home to Massachusetts and proclaimed the existence of that pur-

pose, but I could get no audience and but little attention. Some did not believe it, and some were too much engaged in their own pursuits to give it any heed. They had gone to their farms or to their merchandise, and it was impossible to arouse any feeling in New England, or in Massachusetts, that should combine the two great political parties against this annexation; and, indeed, there was no hope of bringing the Northern Democracy into that view, for their leaning was all the other way. But, Sir, even with Whigs, and leading Whigs, I am ashamed to say, there was a great indifference towards the admission of Texas, with slave territory, into this Union.

The project went on. I was then out of Congress. The annexation resolutions passed on the 1st of March, 1845; the legislature of Texas complied with the conditions and accepted the guaranties; for the language of the resolution is, that Texas is to come in "upon the conditions and under the guaranties herein prescribed." I was returned to the Senate in March, 1845, and was here in December following, when the acceptance by Texas of the conditions proposed by Congress was communicated to us by the President, and an act for the consummation of the union was laid before the two houses. The connection was then not completed. A final law, doing the deed of annexation ultimately, had not been passed; and when it was put upon its final passage here, I expressed my opposition to it, and recorded my vote in the negative; and there that vote stands, with the observations that I made upon that occasion.* Nor is this the only occasion on which I have expressed myself to the same effect. It has happened that, between 1837 and this time, on various occasions, I have expressed my entire opposition to the admission of slave States, or the acquisition of new slave territories, to be added to the United States. I know, Sir, no change in my own sentiments, of my own purposes, in that respect. I will now ask my friend from Rhode Island to read another extract from a speech of mine made at a Whig Convention in Springfield, Massachusetts, in the month of September, 1847. (Mr. Greene here read the following extract:—)

We hear much just now of a *panacea* for the dangers and evils of slavery and slave annexation, which they call the "Wilmot Proviso." That certainly is a just sentiment, but it is not a sentiment to found any new party upon. It is not a sentiment on which Massachusetts Whigs differ. There is not a

*See the remarks on the Admission of Texas, Volume IX. p. 55.

man in this hall who holds to it more firmly than I do, nor one who adheres to it more than another.

I feel some little interest in this matter, Sir. Did not I commit myself in 1837 to the whole doctrine, fully, entirely? And I must be permitted to say that I cannot quite consent that more recent discoverers should claim the merit and take out a patent.

I deny the priority of their invention. Allow me to say, Sir, it is not their thunder. . . .

We are to use the first and the last and every occasion which offers to oppose the extension of slave power.

But I speak of it here, as in Congress, as a political question, a question for statesmen to act upon. We must so regard it. I certainly do not mean to say that it is less important in a moral point of view, that it is not more important in many other points of view; but as a legislator, or in any official capacity, I must look at it, consider it, and decide it as a matter of political action.

On other occasions, in debates here, I have expressed my determination to vote for no acquisition, or cession, or annexation, north or south, east or west. My opinion has been, that we have territory enough, and that we should follow the Spartan maxim, "Improve, adorn what you have," seek no further. I think that it was in some observations that I made on the three-million loan bill that I avowed this sentiment. In short, Sir, it has been avowed quite as often, in as many places, and before as many assemblies, as any humble opinions of mine ought to be avowed.

But now that, under certain conditions, Texas is in the Union, with all her territory, as a slave State, with a solemn pledge, also, that, if she shall be divided into many States, those States may come in as slave States south of 36° 30', how are we to deal with this subject? I know no way of honest legislation, when the proper time comes for the enactment, but to carry into effect all that we have stipulated to do. I do not entirely agree with my honorable friend from Tennessee,* that, as soon as the time comes when she is entitled to another representative, we should create a new State. On former occasions, in creating new States out of territories, we have generally gone upon the idea that, when the population of the territory amounts to about sixty thousand, we would consent to its admission as a State. But it is quite a different thing when a State is divided, and two or more States made out of it. It does not follow in

*Mr. Bell.

such a case that the same rule of apportionment should be applied. That, however, is a matter for the consideration of Congress, when the proper time arrives. I may not then be here; I may have no vote to give on the occasion; but I wish it to be distinctly understood, that, according to my view of the matter, this government is solemnly pledged, by law and contract, to create new States out of Texas, with her consent, when her population shall justify and call for such a proceeding, and, so far as such States are formed out of Texan territory lying south of 36° 30', to let them come in as slave States. That is the meaning of the contract which our friends, the Northern Democracy, have left us to fulfil; and I, for one, mean to fulfil it, because I will not violate the faith of the government. What I mean to say is, that the time for the admission of new States formed out of Texas, the number of such States, their boundaries, the requisite amount of population, and all other things connected with the admission, are in the free discretion of Congress, except this; to wit, that, when new States formed out of Texas are to be admitted, they have a right, by legal stipulation and contract, to come in as slave States.

Now, as to California and New Mexico, I hold slavery to be excluded from those territories by a law even superior to that which admits and sanctions it in Texas. I mean the law of nature, of physical geography, the law of the formation of the earth. That law settles for ever, with a strength beyond all terms of human enactment, that slavery cannot exist in California or New Mexico. Understand me, Sir; I mean slavery as we regard it; the slavery of the colored race as it exists in the Southern States. I shall not discuss the point, but leave it to the learned gentlemen who have undertaken to discuss it; but I suppose there is no slavery of that description in California now. I understand that *peonism,* a sort of penal servitude, exists there, or rather a sort of voluntary sale of a man and his offspring for debt, an arrangement of a peculiar nature known to the law of Mexico. But what I mean to say is, that it is as impossible that African slavery, as we see it among us, should find its way, or be introduced, into California and New Mexico, as any other natural impossibility. California and New Mexico are Asiatic in their formation and scenery. They are composed of vast ridges of mountains, of great height, with broken ridges and deep valleys. The sides of these mountains are entirely barren; their tops capped by perennial snow. There may be in California, now made free by its constitution, and no doubt there are, some tracts of valuable land. But it is not so in New Mexico. Pray, what is the evidence which every gentleman must have obtained on this subject, from information sought by himself or communicated by others? I have inquired and read all I could find, in order to acquire information on this important subject. What is there in New Mexico that could, by any possibility, induce any body to go there with slaves? There are some narrow strips of tillable land on the borders of the rivers; but the rivers themselves dry up before mid-summer is gone. All that the people can do in that region is to raise some little articles, some little wheat for their *tortillas,* and that by irrigation. And who expects to see a hundred black men cultivating tobacco, corn, cotton, rice, or any thing else, on lands in New Mexico, made fertile only by irrigation?

I look upon it, therefore, as a fixed fact, to use the current expression of the day, that both California and New Mexico are destined to be free, so far as they are settled at all, which I believe, in regard to New Mexico, will be but partially for a great length of time; free by the arrangement of things ordained by the Power above us. I have therefore to say, in this respect also, that this country is fixed for freedom, to as many persons as shall ever live in it, by a less repealable law than that which attaches to the right of holding slaves in Texas; and I will say further, that, if a resolution or a bill were now before us, to provide a territorial government for New Mexico, I would not vote to put any prohibition into it whatever. Such a prohibition would be idle, as it respects any effect it would have upon the territory; and I would not take pains uselessly to reaffirm an ordinance of nature, nor to reënact the will of God. I would put in no Wilmot Proviso for the mere purpose of a taunt or a reproach. I would put into it no evidence of the votes of superior power, exercised for no purpose but to wound the pride, whether a just and a rational pride, or an irrational pride, of the citizens of the Southern States. I have no such object, no such purpose. They would think it a taunt, an indignity; they would think it to be an act taking away from them what they regard as a proper equality of privilege. Whether they expect to realize any benefit from it or not, they would think it at least a plain theoretic wrong; that something more or less derogatory to their character and their rights had taken place. I propose to inflict no such wound upon any body, unless something

essentially important to the country, and efficient to the preservation of liberty and freedom, is to be effected. I repeat, therefore, Sir, and, as I do not propose to address the Senate often on this subject, I repeat it because I wish it to be distinctly understood, that, for the reasons stated, if a proposition were now here to establish a government for New Mexico, and it was moved to insert a provision for a prohibition of slavery, I would not vote for it.

Sir, if we were now making a government for New Mexico, and any body should propose a Wilmot Proviso, I should treat it exactly as Mr. Polk treated that provision for excluding slavery from Oregon. Mr. Polk was known to be in opinion decidedly averse to the Wilmot Proviso; but he felt the necessity of establishing a government for the Territory of Oregon. The proviso was in the bill, but he knew it would be entirely nugatory; and, since it must be entirely nugatory, since it took away no right, no describable, no tangible, no appreciable right of the South, he said he would sign the bill for the sake of enacting a law to form a government in that Territory, and let that entirely useless, and, in that connection, entirely senseless, proviso remain. Sir, we hear occasionally of the annexation of Canada; and if there be any man, any of the Northern Democracy, or any one of the Free Soil party, who supposes it necessary to insert a Wilmot Proviso in a territorial government for New Mexico, that man would of course be of opinion that it is necessary to protect the everlasting snows of Canada from the foot of slavery by the same overspreading wing of an act of Congress. Sir, wherever there is a substantive good to be done, wherever there is a foot of land to be prevented from becoming slave territory, I am ready to assert the principle of the exclusion of slavery. I am pledged to it from the year 1837; I have been pledged to it again and again; and I will perform those pledges; but I will not do a thing unnecessarily that wounds the feelings of others, or that does discredit to my own understanding.

Now, Mr. President, I have established, so far as I proposed to do so, the proposition with which I set out, and upon which I intend to stand or fall; and that is, that the whole territory within the former United States, or in the newly acquired Mexican provinces, has a fixed and settled character, now fixed and settled by law which cannot be repealed; in the case of Texas without a violation of public faith, and by no human power in regard to California or New Mexico; that, therefore, under one or other of these laws, every foot of land in the States or in the Territories has already received a fixed and decided character.

Mr. President, in the excited times in which we live, there is found to exist a state of crimination and recrimination between the North and South. There are lists of grievances produced by each; and those grievances, real or supposed, alienate the minds of one portion of the country from the other, exasperate the feelings, and subdue the sense of fraternal affection, patriotic love, and mutual regard. I shall bestow a little attention, Sir, upon these various grievances existing on the one side and on the other. I begin with complaints of the South. I will not answer, further than I have, the general statements of the honorable Senator from South Carolina, that the North has prospered at the expense of the South in consequence of the manner of administering this government, in the collecting of its revenues, and so forth. These are disputed topics, and I have no inclination to enter into them. But I will allude to other complaints of the South, and especially to one which has in my opinion just foundation; and that is, that there has been found at the North, among individuals and among legislators, a disinclination to perform fully their constitutional duties in regard to the return of persons bound to service who have escaped into the free States. In that respect, the South, in my judgment, is right, and the North is wrong. Every member of every Northern legislature is bound by oath, like every other officer in the country, to support the Constitution of the United States; and the article of the Constitution* which says to these States that they shall deliver up fugitives from service is as binding in honor and conscience as any other article. No man fulfils his duty in any legislature who sets himself to find excuses, evasions, escapes from this constitutional obligation. I have always thought that the Constitution addressed itself to the legislatures of the States or to the States themselves. It says that those persons escaping to other States "shall be delivered up," and I confess I have always been of the opinion that it was an injunction upon the States themselves. When it is said that a person escaping into another State, and coming therefore within the jurisdiction of that State, shall be delivered up, it seems to me the import of the clause is, that the State itself, in obedience to the Constitution, shall cause him to be delivered up. That

is my judgment. I have always entertained that opinion, and I entertain it now. But when the subject, some years ago, was before the Supreme Court of the United States, the majority of the judges held that the power to cause fugitives from service to be delivered up was a power to be exercised under the authority of this government. I do not know, on the whole, that it may not have been a fortunate decision. My habit is to respect the result of judicial deliberations and the solemnity of judicial decisions. As it now stands, the business of seeing that these fugitives are delivered up resides in the power of Congress and the national judicature, and my friend at the head of the Judiciary Committee† has a bill on the subject now before the Senate, which, with some amendments to it, I propose to support, with all its provisions, to the fullest extent. And I desire to call the attention of all sober-minded men at the North, of all conscientious men, of all men who are not carried away by some fanatical idea or some false impression, to their constitutional obligations. I put it to all the sober and sound minds at the North as a question of morals and a question of conscience. What right have they, in their legislative capacity or any other capacity, to endeavor to get round this Constitution, or to embarrass the free exercise of the rights secured by the Constitution to the persons whose slaves escape from them? None at all; none at all. Neither in the forum of conscience, nor before the face of the Constitution, are they, in my opinion, justified in such an attempt. Of course it is a matter for their consideration. They probably, in the excitement of the times, have not stopped to consider of this. They have followed what seemed to be the current of thought and of motives, as the occasion arose, and they have neglected to investigate fully the real question, and to consider their constitutional obligations; which, I am sure, if they did consider, they would fulfil with alacrity. I repeat, therefore, Sir, that here is a well-founded ground of complaint against the North, which ought to be removed, which it is now in the power of the different departments of this government to remove; which calls for the enactment of proper laws authorizing the judicature of this government, in the several States, to do all that is necessary for the recapture of fugitive slaves and for their restoration to those who claim them. Wherever I go, and whenever I speak on the subject, and when I speak here I desire to speak to the

---

*Art. IV. Sect. 2, § 2.

†Mr. Mason.

whole North, I say that the South has been injured in this respect, and has a right to complain; and the North has been too careless of what I think the Constitution peremptorily and emphatically enjoins upon her as a duty.

Complaint has been made against certain resolutions that emanate from legislatures at the North, and are sent here to us, not only on the subject of slavery in this District, but sometimes recommending Congress to consider the means of abolishing slavery in the States. I should be sorry to be called upon to present any resolutions here which could not be referable to any committee or any power in Congress; and therefore I should be unwilling to receive from the legislature of Massachusetts any instructions to present resolutions expressive of any opinion whatever on the subject of slavery, as it exists at the present moment in the States, for two reasons: first, because I do not consider that the legislature of Massachusetts has any thing to do with it; and next, because I do not consider that I, as her representative here, have any thing to do with it. It has become, in my opinion, quite too common; and if the legislatures of the States do not like that opinion, they have a great deal more power to put it down than I have to uphold it; it has become, in my opinion, quite too common a practice for the State legislatures to present resolutions here on all subjects and to instruct us on all subjects. There is no public man that requires instruction more than I do, or who requires information more than I do, or desires it more heartily; but I do not like to have it in too imperative a shape. I took notice, with pleasure, of some remarks made upon this subject, the other day, in the Senate of Massachusetts, by a young man of talent and character, of whom the best hopes may be entertained. I mean Mr. Hillard. He told the Senate of Massachusetts that he would vote for no instructions whatever to be forwarded to members of Congress, nor for any resolutions to be offered expressive of the sense of Massachusetts as to what her members of Congress ought to do. He said that he saw no propriety in one set of public servants giving instructions and reading lectures to another set of public servants. To his own master each of them must stand or fall, and that master is his constituents. I wish these sentiments could become more common. I have never entered into the question, and never shall, as to the binding force of instructions. I will, however, simply say this: if there be any matter pending in this body, while I am a member of it, in which Massachusetts has an interest of her own not adverse to the general interests of the country, I shall pursue her instructions with gladness of heart and with all the efficiency which I can bring to the occasion. But if the question be one which affects her interest, and at the same time equally affects the interests of all the other States, I shall no more regard her particular wishes or instructions than I should regard the wishes of a man who might appoint me an arbitrator or referee to decide some question of important private right between him and his neighbor, and then *instruct* me to decide in his favor. If ever there was a government upon earth it is this government, if ever there was a body upon earth it is this body, which should consider itself as composed by agreement of all, each member appointed by some, but organized by the general consent of all, sitting here, under the solemn obligations of oath and conscience, to do that which they think to be best for the good of the whole.

Then, Sir, there are the Abolition societies, of which I am unwilling to speak, but in regard to which I have very clear notions and opinions. I do not think them useful. I think their operations for the last twenty years have produced nothing good or valuable. At the same time, I believe thousands of their members to be honest and good men, perfectly well-meaning men. They have excited feelings; they think they must do something for the cause of liberty; and, in their sphere of action, they do not see what else they can do than to contribute to an Abolition press, or an Abolition society, or to pay an Abolition lecturer. I do not mean to impute gross motives even to the leaders of these societies, but I am not blind to the consequences of their proceedings. I cannot but see what mischiefs their interference with the South has produced. And is it not plain to every man? Let any gentleman who entertains doubts on this point recur to the debates in the Virginia House of Delegates in 1832, and he will see with what freedom a proposition made by Mr. Jefferson Randolph for the gradual abolition of slavery was discussed in that body. Every one spoke of slavery as he thought; very ignominious and disparaging names and epithets were applied to it. The debates in the House of Delegates on that occasion, I believe, were all published. They were read by every colored man who could read, and to those who could not read, those debates were read by others. At that time Virginia was not unwilling or afraid to discuss this question, and to let that part of her population know as much of the discussion as they could learn. That was in 1832. As has been said by the honorable member from South Carolina, these Abolition societies commenced their course of action in 1835. It is said, I do not know how true it may be, that they sent incendiary publications into the slave States; at any rate, they attempted to arouse, and did arouse, a very strong feeling; in other words, they created great agitation in the North against Southern slavery. Well, what was the result? The bonds of the slaves were bound more firmly than before, their rivets were more strongly fastened. Public opinion, which in Virginia had begun to be exhibited against slavery, and was opening out for the discussion of the question, drew back and shut itself up in its castle. I wish to know whether any body in Virginia can now talk openly as Mr. Randolph, Governor McDowell, and others talked in 1832, and sent their remarks to the press? We all know the fact, and we all know the cause; and every thing that these agitating people have done has been, not to enlarge, but to restrain, not to set free, but to bind faster, the slave population of the South.*

Again, Sir, the violence of the Northern press is complained of. The press violent! Why, Sir, the press is violent everywhere. There are outrageous reproaches in the North against the South, and there are reproaches as vehement in the South against the North. Sir, the extremists of both parts of this country are violent; they mistake loud and violent talk for eloquence and for reason. They think that he who talks loudest reasons best. And this we must expect, when the press is free, as it is here, and I trust always will be; for, with all its licentiousness and all its evil, the entire and absolute freedom of the press is essential to the preservation of government on the basis of a free constitution. Wherever it exists there will be foolish and violent paragraphs in the newspapers, as there are, I am sorry to say, foolish and violent speeches in both houses of Congress. In truth, Sir, I must say that, in my opinion, the vernacular tongue of the country has become greatly vitiated, depraved, and corrupted by the style of our Congressional debates. And if it were possible for those debates to vitiate the principles of the people as much as they have depraved their tastes, I should cry out, "God save the Republic!"

Well, in all this I see no solid grievance, no grievance presented by the South, within the redress of the government, but the single one to which I have referred; and that

*See Note at the end of the Speech.

is, the want of a proper regard to the injunction of the Constitution for the delivery of fugitive slaves.

There are also complaints of the North against the South. I need not go over them particularly. The first and gravest is, that the North adopted the Constitution, recognizing the existence of slavery in the States, and recognizing the right, to a certain extent, of the representation of slaves in Congress, under a state of sentiment and expectation which does not now exist; and that, by events, by circumstances, by the eagerness of the South to acquire territory and extend her slave population, the North finds itself, in regard to the relative influence of the South and the North, of the free States and the slave States, where it never did expect to find itself when they agreed to the compact of the Constitution. They complain, therefore, that, instead of slavery being regarded as an evil, as it was then, an evil which all hoped would be extinguished gradually, it is now regarded by the South as an institution to be cherished, and preserved, and extended; an institution which the South has already extended to the utmost of her power by the acquisition of new territory.

Well, then, passing from that, every body in the North reads; and every body reads whatsoever the newspapers contain; and the newspapers, some of them, especially those presses to which I have alluded, are careful to spread about among the people every reproachful sentiment uttered by any Southern man bearing at all against the North; every thing that is calculated to exasperate and to alienate; and there are many such things, as every body will admit, from the South, or some portion of it, which are disseminated among the reading people; and they do exasperate, and alienate, and produce a most mischievous effect upon the public mind at the North. Sir, I would not notice things of this sort appearing in obscure quarters; but one thing has occurred in this debate which struck me very forcibly. An honorable member from Louisiana addressed us the other day on this subject. I suppose there is not a more amiable and worthy gentleman in this chamber, nor a gentleman who would be more slow to give offence to any body, and he did not mean in his remarks to give offence. But what did he say? Why, Sir, he took pains to run a contrast between the slaves of the South and the laboring people of the North, giving the preference, in all points of condition, and comfort, and happiness, to the slaves of the South. The honorable member, doubtless, did not suppose that he gave any offence, or did any injustice. He was merely expressing his opinion. But does he know how remarks of that sort will be received by the laboring people of the North? Why, who are the laboring people of the North? They are the whole North. They are the people who till their own farms with their own hands; freeholders, educated men, independent men. Let me say, Sir, that five sixths of the whole property of the North is in the hands of the laborers of the North; they cultivate their farms, they educate their children, they provide the means of independence. If they are not freeholders, they earn wages; these wages accumulate, are turned into capital, into new freeholds, and small capitalists are created. Such is the case, and such the course of things, among the industrious and frugal. And what can these people think when so respectable and worthy a gentleman as the member from Louisiana undertakes to prove that the absolute ignorance and the abject slavery of the South are more in conformity with the high purposes and destiny of immortal, rational human beings, than the educated, the independent free labor of the North?

There is a more tangible and irritating cause of grievance at the North. Free blacks are constantly employed in the vessels of the North, generally as cooks or stewards. When the vessel arrives at a Southern port, these free colored men are taken on shore, by the police or municipal authority, imprisoned, and kept in prison till the vessel is again ready to sail. This is not only irritating, but exceedingly unjustifiable and oppressive. Mr. Hoar's mission, some time ago, to South Carolina, was a well-intended effort to remove this cause of complaint. The North thinks such imprisonments illegal and unconstitutional; and as the cases occur constantly and frequently, they regard it as a great grievance.

Now, Sir, so far as any of these grievances have their foundation in matters of law, they can be redressed, and ought to be redressed; and so far as they have their foundation in matters of opinion, in sentiment, in mutual crimination and recrimination, all that we can do is to endeavor to allay the agitation, and cultivate a better feeling and more fraternal sentiments between the South and the North.

Mr. President, I should much prefer to have heard from every member on this floor declarations of opinion that this Union could never be dissolved, than the declaration of opinion by any body, that, in any case, under the pressure of any circumstances, such a dissolution was possible.

I hear with distress and anguish the word "secession," especially when it falls from the lips of those who are patriotic, and known to the country, and known all over the world, for their political services. Secession! Peaceable secession! Sir, your eyes and mine are never destined to see that miracle. The dismemberment of this vast country without convulsion! The breaking up of the fountains of the great deep without ruffling the surface! Who is so foolish, I beg every body's pardon, as to expect to see any such thing? Sir, he who sees these States, now revolving in harmony around a common centre, and expects to see them quit their places and fly off without convulsion, may look the next hour to see the heavenly bodies rush from their spheres, and jostle against each other in the realms of space, without causing the wreck of the universe. There can be no such thing as a peaceable secession. Peaceable secession is an utter impossibility. Is the great Constitution under which we live, covering this whole country, is it to be thawed and melted away by secession, as the snows on the mountain melt under the influence of a vernal sun, disappear almost unobserved, and run off? No, Sir! No, Sir! I will not state what might produce the disruption of the Union; but, Sir, I see as plainly as I see the sun in heaven what that disruption itself must produce; I see that it must produce war, and such a war as I will not describe, *in its twofold character.*

Peaceable secession! Peaceable secession! The concurrent agreement of all the members of this great republic to separate! A voluntary separation, with alimony on one side and on the other. Why, what would be the result? Where is the line to be drawn? What States are to secede? What is to remain American? What am I to be? An American no longer? Am I to become a sectional man, a local man, a separatist, with no country in common with the gentlemen who sit around me here, or who fill the other house of Congress? Heaven forbid! Where is the flag of the republic to remain? Where is the eagle still to tower? or is he to cower, and shrink, and fall to the ground? Why, Sir, our ancestors, our fathers and our grandfathers, those of them that are yet living amongst us with prolonged lives, would rebuke and reproach us; and our children and our grandchildren would cry out shame upon us, if we of this generation should dishonor these ensigns of the power of the government and the harmony of that Union which is every day felt among us with so much joy and gratitude. What is to become of the army? What is to become of the navy?

What is to become of the public lands? How is each of the thirty States to defend itself? I know, although the idea has not been stated distinctly, there is to be, or it is supposed possible that there will be, a Southern Confederacy. I do not mean, when I allude to this statement, that any one seriously contemplates such a state of things. I do not mean to say that it is true, but I have heard it suggested elsewhere, that the idea has been entertained, that, after the dissolution of this Union, a Southern Confederacy might be formed. I am sorry, Sir, that it has ever been thought of, talked of, or dreamed of, in the wildest flights of human imagination. But the idea, so far as it exists, must be of a separation, assigning the slave States to one side and the free States to the other. Sir, I may express myself too strongly, perhaps, but there are impossibilities in the natural as well as in the physical world, and I hold the idea of a separation of these States, those that are free to form one government, and those that are slave-holding to form another, as such an impossibility. We could not separate the States by any such line, if we were to draw it. We could not sit down here to-day and draw a line of separation that would satisfy any five men in the country. There are natural causes that would keep and tie us together, and there are social and domestic relations which we could not break if we would, and which we should not if we could.

Sir, nobody can look over the face of this country at the present moment, nobody can see where its population is the most dense and growing, without being ready to admit, and compelled to admit, that ere long the strength of America will be in the Valley of the Mississippi. Well, now, Sir, I beg to inquire what the wildest enthusiast has to say on the possibility of cutting that river in two, and leaving free States at its source and on its branches, and slave States down near its mouth, each forming a separate government? Pray, Sir, let me say to the people of this country, that these things are worthy of their pondering and of their consideration. Here, Sir, are five millions of freemen in the free States north of the river Ohio. Can any body suppose that this population can be severed, by a line that divides them from the territory of a foreign and an alien government, down somewhere, the Lord knows where, upon the lower banks of the Mississippi? What would become of Missouri? Will she join the *arrondissement* of the slave States? Shall the man from the Yellow Stone and the Platte be connected, in the new republic, with the man who lives on the southern extremity of the Cape of Florida? Sir, I am ashamed to pursue this line of remark. I dislike it, I have

an utter disgust for it. I would rather hear of natural blasts and mildews, war, pestilence, and famine, than to hear gentlemen talk of secession. To break up this great government! to dismember this glorious country! to astonish Europe with an act of folly such as Europe for two centuries has never beheld in any government or any people! No, Sir! no, Sir! There will be no secession! Gentlemen are not serious when they talk of secession.

Sir, I hear there is to be a convention held at Nashville. I am bound to believe that, if worthy gentlemen meet at Nashville in convention, their object will be to adopt conciliatory counsels; to advise the South to forbearance and moderation, and to advise the North to forbearance and moderation; and to inculcate principles of brotherly love and affection, and attachment to the Constitution of the country as it now is. I believe, if the convention meet at all, it will be for this purpose; for certainly, if they meet for any purpose hostile to the Union, they have been singularly inappropriate in their selection of a place. I remember, Sir, that, when the treaty of Amiens was concluded between France and England, a sturdy Englishman and a distinguished orator, who regarded the conditions of the peace as ignominious to England, said in the House of Commons, that, if King William could know the terms of that treaty, he would turn in his coffin! Let me commend this saying of Mr. Windham, in all its emphasis and in all its force, to any persons who shall meet at Nashville for the purpose of concerting measures for the overthrow of this Union over the bones of Andrew Jackson!

Sir, I wish now to make two remarks, and hasten to a conclusion. I wish to say, in regard to Texas, that if it should be hereafter, at any time, the pleasure of the government of Texas to cede to the United States a portion, larger or smaller, of her territory which lies adjacent to New Mexico, and north of 36° 30' of north latitude, to be formed into free States, for a fair equivalent in money or in the payment of her debt, I think it an object well worthy the consideration of Congress, and I shall be happy to concur in it myself, if I should have a connection with the government at that time.

I have one other remark to make. In my observations upon slavery as it has existed in this country, and as it now exists, I have expressed no opinion of the mode of its extinguishment or melioration. I will say, however, though I have nothing to propose, because I do not deem myself so competent as other gentlemen to take any lead on this subject, that if any gentleman from the South shall propose a scheme, to be carried on by this government upon a large scale, for the transportation of free colored people to any colony or any place in the world, I should be quite disposed to incur almost any degree of expense to accomplish that object. Nay, Sir, following an example set more than twenty years ago by a great man,* then a Senator from New York, I would return to Virginia, and through her to the whole South, the money received from the lands and territories ceded by her to this government, for any such purpose as to remove, in whole or in part, or in any way to diminish or deal beneficially with, the free colored population of the Southern States. I have said that I honor Virginia for her cession of this territory. There have been received into the treasury of the United States eighty millions of dollars, the proceeds of the sales of the public lands ceded by her. If the residue should be sold at the same rate, the whole aggregate will exceed two hundred millions of dollars. If Virginia and the South see fit to adopt any proposition to relieve themselves from the free people of color among them, or such as may be made free, they have my full consent that the government shall pay them any sum of money out of the proceeds of that cession which may be adequate to the purpose.

And now, Mr. President, I draw these observations to a close. I have spoken freely, and I meant to do so. I have sought to make no display. I have sought to enliven the occasion by no animated discussion, nor have I attempted any train of elaborate argument. I have wished only to speak my sentiments, fully and at length, being desirous, once and for all, to let the Senate know, and to let the country know, the opinions and sentiments which I entertain on all these subjects. These opinions are not likely to be suddenly changed. If there be any future service that I can render to the country, consistently with these sentiments and opinions, I shall cheerfully render it. If there be not, I shall still be glad to have had an opportunity to disburden myself from the bottom of my heart, and to make known every political sentiment that therein exists.

And now, Mr. President, instead of speaking of the possibility or utility of secession, instead of dwelling in those caverns of darkness, instead of groping with those ideas so full of all that is horrid and horrible, let us come out into the light of day; let us enjoy the fresh air of Liberty and Union; let us cherish those hopes which belong to us; let us devote ourselves to those great objects that are fit for our

*Mr. Rufus King.

consideration and our action; let us raise our conceptions to the magnitude and the importance of the duties that devolve upon us; let our comprehension be as broad as the country for which we act, our aspirations as high as its certain destiny; let us not be pigmies in a case that calls for men. Never did there devolve on any generation of men higher trusts than now devolve upon us, for the preservation of this Constitution and the harmony and peace of all who are destined to live under it. Let us make our generation one of the strongest and brightest links in that golden chain which is destined, I fondly believe, to grapple the people of all the States to this Constitution for ages to come. We have a great, popular, constitutional government, guarded by law and by judicature, and defended by the affections of the whole people. No monarchical throne presses these States together, no iron chain of military power encircles them; they live and stand under a government popular in its form, representative in its character, founded upon principles of equality, and so constructed, we hope, as to last for ever. In all its history it has been beneficent; it has trodden down no man's liberty; it has crushed no State. Its daily respiration is liberty and patriotism; its yet youthful veins are full of enterprise, courage, and honorable love of glory and renown. Large before, the country has now, by recent events, become vastly larger. This republic now extends, with a vast breadth, across the whole continent. The two great seas of the world wash the one and the other shore. We realize, on a mighty scale, the beautiful description of the ornamental border of the buckler of Achilles:—

Now, the broad shield complete, the artist crowned
With his last hand, and poured the ocean round;
In living silver seemed the waves to roll,
And beat the buckler's verge, and bound the whole.

NOTE
Page 90

Letter from Mr. Webster to the Editors of the National Intelligencer, inclosing Extracts from a Letter of the late Dr. Channing.

Washington, February 15th, 1851.
Messrs. Gales & Seaton:—

Having occasion recently to look over some files of letters written several years ago, I happened to fall on one from the late Rev. Dr. W. E. Channing. It contains passages which I think, coming from such a source, and written at such a time, would be interesting to the country. I have therefore extracted them, and send them to you for publication in your columns. Yours respectfully,

DANIEL WEBSTER.

Boston, May 14th, 1828.

My dear Sir:—

I wish to call your attention to a subject of general interest.

A little while ago, Mr. Lundy of Baltimore, the editor of a paper called "The Genius of Universal Emancipation," visited this part of the country, to stir us up to the work of abolishing slavery at the South, and the intention is to organize societies for this purpose. I know few objects into which I should enter with more zeal, but I am aware how cautiously exertions are to be made for it in this part of the country. I know that our Southern brethren interpret every word from this region on the subject of slavery as an expression of hostility. I would ask if they cannot be brought to understand us better, and if we can do any good till we remove their misapprehensions. It seems to me that, before moving in this matter, we ought to say to them distinctly, "We consider slavery as your calamity, not your crime, and we will share with you the burden of putting an end to it. We will consent that the public lands shall be appropriated to this object; or that the general government shall be clothed with power to apply a portion of revenue to it."

I throw out these suggestions merely to illustrate my views. We must first let the Southern States see that we are their *friends* in this affair; that we sympathize with them, and, from principles of patriotism and philanthropy, are willing to share the toil and expense of abolishing slavery, or I fear our interference will avail nothing. I am the more sensitive on this subject from my increased solicitude for the preservation of the Union. I know no public interest so important as this. I ask from the general government hardly any other boon than that it will hold us together, and preserve pacific relations and intercourse among the States. I deprecate every thing which sows discord and exasperates sectional animosities. If it will simply keep us at peace, and will maintain in full power the national courts, for the purpose of settling quietly among citizens of different States questions which might otherwise be settled by arms, I shall be satisfied.

My fear in regard to our efforts against slavery is, that we shall make the case worse by rousing sectional pride and passion for its support, and that we shall only break the country into two great parties, which may shake the foundations of government.

I have written to you because your situation gives you advantages which perhaps no other man enjoys for ascertaining the method, if any can be devised, by which we may operate beneficially and safely in regard to slavery. Appeals will probably be made soon to the people here, and I wish that wise men would save us from the rashness of enthusiasts, and from the perils to which our very virtues expose us.

With great respect, your friend,

WM. E. CHANNING.

HON. DANIEL WEBSTER.

Second Fugitive Slave Law

September 18, 1850

Ableman v. Booth

ROGER TANEY

1858

The Fugitive Slave Law of 1793 was never well enforced in North-ern states. As time went on and abolitionist sentiment grew, a number of states went so far as to forbid their officers to assist those hunting runaways and to enact personal liberty laws, which guaranteed jury trials for persons accused of being runaway slaves. The strengthened Fugitive Slave Law of 1850 was intended to stop this resistance. It imposed heavy fines on those who as-sisted runaway slaves and set up federal court procedures that many found highly prejudicial to the accused runaway.

These new rules only increased the level of conflict between those seeking to recapture and those seeking to protect run-aways. Sherman Booth, an abolitionist newspaper editor in Wis-consin, led a mob that broke an accused runaway out of a federal jail so that he could escape to Canada. When Booth was prose-cuted under the Fugitive Slave Law, he sought protection from the Wisconsin courts. In two sets of legal proceedings spanning eight years, the Wisconsin Supreme Court freed Booth; asserted its authority to interfere with, stop, and overrule federal court proceedings; and declared the Fugitive Slave Law of 1850 to be unconstitutional. The U.S. Supreme Court overturned the Wis-consin Court on all counts.

Second Fugitive Slave Law

September 18, 1850

An Act to amend, and supplementary to, the Act entitled "An Act respecting Fugitives from Justice, and Persons escaping from the Service of their Masters," approved February twelfth, one thousand seven hundred and ninety-three.

Be it enacted by the Senate and House of Representatives of the United States of America in Congress assembled, That the per-sons who have been, or may hereafter be, appointed com-missioners, in virtue of any act of Congress, by the Circuit Courts of the United States, and who, in consequence of such appointment, are authorized to exercise the powers that any justice of the peace, or other magistrate of any of the United States, may exercise in respect to offenders for any crime or offence against the United States, by arrest-ing, imprisoning, or bailing the same under and by virtue of the thirty-third section of the act of the twenty-fourth of September seventeen hundred and eighty-nine, entitled "An Act to establish the judicial courts of the United States," shall be, and are hereby, authorized and required to exer-cise and discharge all the powers and duties conferred by this act.

SEC. 2. *And be it further enacted,* That the Superior Court of each organized Territory of the United States shall have the same power to appoint commissioners to take ac-knowledgments of bail and affidavits, and to take deposi-tions of witnesses in civil causes, which is now possessed by the Circuit Court of the United States; and all commis-sioners who shall hereafter be appointed for such purposes by the Superior Court of any organized Territory of the United States, shall possess all the powers, and exercise all the duties, conferred by law upon the commissioners ap-pointed by the Circuit Courts of the United States for sim-ilar purposes, and shall moreover exercise and discharge all the powers and duties conferred by this act.

SEC. 3. *And be it further enacted,* That the Circuit Courts of the United States, and the Superior Courts of each or-ganized Territory of the United States, shall from time to time enlarge the number of commissioners, with a view to afford reasonable facilities to reclaim fugitives from labor, and to the prompt discharge of the duties imposed by this act.

SEC. 4. *And be it further enacted,* That the commissioners above named shall have concurrent jurisdiction with the judges of the Circuit and District Courts of the United States, in their respective circuits and districts within the several States, and the judges of the Superior Courts of the Territories, severally and collectively, in term-time and vacation; and shall grant certificates to such claimants, upon satisfactory proof being made, with authority to take and remove such fugitives from service or labor, under the restrictions herein contained, to the State or Territory from which such persons may have escaped or fled.

SEC. 5. *And be it further enacted,* That it shall be the duty of all marshals and deputy marshals to obey and execute all warrants and precepts issued under the provisions of this act, when to them directed; and should any marshal or deputy marshal refuse to receive such warrant, or other process, when tendered, or to use all proper means diligently to execute the same, he shall, on conviction thereof, be fined in the sum of one thousand dollars, to the use of such claimant, on the motion of such claimant by the Circuit or District Court for the district of such marshall; and after arrest of such fugitive, by such marshal or his deputy, or whilst at any time in his custody under the provisions of this act, should such fugitive escape, whether with or without the assent of such marshal or his deputy, such marshal shall be liable, on his official bond, to be prosecuted for the benefit of such claimant, for the full value of the service or labor of said fugitive in the State, Territory, or District whence he escaped: and the better to enable the said commissioners, when thus appointed, to execute their duties faithfully and efficiently, in conformity with the requirements of the Constitution of the United States and of this act, they are hereby authorized and empowered, within their counties respectively, to appoint, in writing under their hands, any one or more suitable persons, from time to time, to execute all such warrants and other process as may be issued by them in the lawful performance of their respective duties; with authority to such commissioners, or the persons to be appointed by them, to execute process as aforesaid, to summon and call to their aid the bystanders, or *posse comitatus* of the proper county, when necessary to insure a faithful observance of the clause of the Constitu-

tion referred to, in conformity with the provisions of this act; and all good citizens are hereby commanded to aid and assist in the prompt and efficient execution of this law, whenever their services may be required, as aforesaid, for that purpose; and said warrants shall run, and be executed by said officers, anywhere in the State within which they are issued.

SEC. 6. *And be it further enacted,* That when a person held to service or labor in any State or Territory of the United States, has heretofore or shall hereafter escape into another State or Territory of the United States, the person or persons to whom such service or labor may be due, or his, her, or their agent or attorney, duly authorized, by power of attorney, in writing, acknowledged and certified under the seal of some legal officer or court of the State or Territory in which the same may be executed, may pursue and reclaim such fugitive person, either by procuring a warrant from some one of the courts, judges, or commissioners aforesaid, of the proper circuit, district, or county, for the apprehension of such fugitive from service or labor, or by seizing and arresting such fugitive, where the same can be done without process, and by taking, or causing such person to be taken, forthwith before such court, judge, or commissioner, whose duty it shall be to hear and determine the case of such claimant in a summary manner; and upon satisfactory proof being made, by deposition or affidavit, in writing, to be taken and certified by such court, judge, or commissioner, or by other satisfactory testimony, duly taken and certified by some court, magistrate, justice of the peace, or other legal officer authorized to administer an oath and take depositions under the laws of the State or Territory from which such person owing service or labor may have escaped, with a certificate of such magistracy or other authority, as aforesaid, with the seal of the proper court or officer thereto attached, which seal shall be sufficient to establish the competency of the proof, and with proof, also by affidavit, of the identity of the person whose service or labor is claimed to be due as aforesaid, that the person so arrested does in fact owe service or labor to the person or persons claiming him or her, in the State or Territory from which such fugitive may have escaped as aforesaid, and that said person escaped, to make out and deliver to such claimant, his or her agent or attorney, a certificate setting forth the substantial facts as to the service or labor due from such fugitive to the claimant, and of his or her escape from the State or Territory in which such service or labor was due, to the State or Territory in which he or she was arrested, with authority to such claimant, or his or her agent or attorney, to use such reasonable force and restraint as may be necessary, under the circumstances of the case, to take and remove such fugitive person back to the State or Territory whence he or she may have escaped as aforesaid. In no trial or hearing under this act shall the testimony of such alleged fugitive be admitted in evidence; and the certificates in this and the first [fourth] section mentioned, shall be conclusive of the right of the person or persons in whose favor granted, to remove such fugitive to the State or Territory from which he escaped, and shall prevent all molestation of such person or persons by any process issued by any court, judge, magistrate, or other person whomsoever.

Sec. 7. *And be it further enacted,* That any person who shall knowingly and willingly obstruct, hinder, or prevent such claimant, his agent or attorney, or any person or persons lawfully assisting him, her, or them, from arresting such a fugitive from service or labor, either with or without process as aforesaid, or shall rescue, or attempt to rescue, such fugitive from service or labor, from the custody of such claimant, his or her agent or attorney, or other person or persons lawfully assisting as aforesaid, when so arrested, pursuant to the authority herein given and declared; or shall aid, abet, or assist such person so owing service or labor as aforesaid, directly or indirectly, to escape from such claimant, his agent or attorney, or other person or persons legally authorized as aforesaid; or shall harbor or conceal such fugitive, so as to prevent the discovery and arrest of such person, after notice or knowledge of the fact that such person was a fugitive from service or labor as aforesaid, shall, for either of said offences, be subject to a fine not exceeding one thousand dollars, and imprisonment not exceeding six months, by indictment and conviction before the District Court of the United States for the district in which such offence may have been committed, or before the proper court of criminal jurisdiction, if committed within any one of the organized Territories of the United States; and shall moreover forfeit and pay, by way of civil damages to the party injured by such illegal conduct, the sum of one thousand dollars, for each fugitive so lost as aforesaid, to be recovered by action of debt, in any of the District or Territorial Courts aforesaid, within whose jurisdiction the said offence may have been committed.

Sec. 8. *And be it further enacted,* That the marshals, their deputies, and the clerks of the said District and Territorial Courts, shall be paid, for their services, the like fees as may be allowed to them for similar services in other cases; and where such services are rendered exclusively in the arrest, custody, and delivery of the fugitive to the claimant, his or her agent or attorney, or where such supposed fugitive may be discharged out of custody for the want of sufficient proof as aforesaid, then such fees are to be paid in the whole by such claimant, his agent or attorney; and in all cases where the proceedings are before a commissioner, he shall be entitled to a fee of ten dollars in full for his services in each case, upon the delivery of the said certificate to the claimant, his or her agent or attorney; or a fee of five dollars in cases where the proof shall not, in the opinion of such commissioner, warrant such certificate and delivery, inclusive of all services incident to such arrest and examination, to be paid, in either case, by the claimant, his or her agent or attorney. The person or persons authorized to execute the process to be issued by such commissioners for the arrest and detention of fugitives from service or labor as aforesaid, shall also be entitled to a fee of five dollars each for each person he or they may arrest and take before any such commissioner as aforesaid, at the instance and request of such claimant, with such other fees as may be deemed reasonable by such commissioner for such other additional services as may be necessarily performed by him or them; such as attending at the examination, keeping the fugitive in custody, and providing him with food and lodging during his detention, and until the final determination of such commissioner; and, in general, for performing such other duties as may be required by such claimant, his or her attorney or agent, or commissioner in the premises, such fees to be made up in conformity with the fees usually charged by the officers of the courts of justice within the proper district or county, as near as may be practicable, and paid by such claimants, their agents or attorneys, whether such supposed fugitives from service or labor be ordered to be delivered to such claimants by the final determination of such commissioners or not.

Sec. 9. *And be it further enacted,* That, upon affidavit made by the claimant of such fugitive, his agent or attorney, after such certificate has been issued, that he has reason to apprehend that such fugitive will be rescued by force from his or their possession before he can be taken beyond the limits of the State in which the arrest is made, it shall be the duty of the officer making the arrest to retain such fugitive in his custody, and to remove him to the State whence he fled, and there to deliver him to said claimant, his agent, or attorney. And to this end, the officer aforesaid is hereby authorized and required to employ so many persons as he may deem necessary to overcome such force, and to retain them in his service so long as circumstances may require. The said officer and his assistants, while so employed, to receive the same compensation, and to be allowed the same expenses, as are now allowed by law for transportation of criminals, to be certified by the judge of the district within which the arrest is made, and paid out of the treasury of the United States.

SEC. 10. *And be it further enacted,* That when any person held to service or labor in any State or Territory, or in the District of Columbia, shall escape therefrom, the party to whom such service or labor shall be due, his, her, or their agent or attorney, may apply to any court of record therein, or judge thereof in vacation, and make satisfactory proof to such court, or judge in vacation, of the escape aforesaid, and that the person escaping owed service or labor to such party. Whereupon the court shall cause a record to be made of the matters so proved, and also a general description of the person so escaping, with such convenient certainty as may be; and a transcript of such record, authenticated by the attestation of the clerk and of the seal of the said court, being produced in any other State, Territory, or district in which the person so escaping may be found, and being exhibited to any judge, commissioner, or other officer authorized by the law of the United States to cause persons escaping from service or labor to be delivered up, shall be held and taken to be full and conclusive evidence of the fact of escape, and that the service or labor of the person escaping is due to the party in such record mentioned. And upon the production by the said party of other and further evidence if necessary, either oral or by affidavit, in addition to what is contained in the said record of the identity of the person escaping, he or she shall be delivered up to the claimant. And the said court, commissioner, judge, or other person authorized by this act to grant certificates to claimants of fugitives, shall, upon the production of the record and other evidences aforesaid, grant to such claimant a certificate of his right to take any such person identified and proved to be owing service or labor as aforesaid, which certificate shall authorize such claimant to seize or arrest and transport such person to the State or Territory from which he escaped: *Provided,* That nothing herein contained shall be construed as requiring the production of a transcript of such record as evidence as aforesaid. But in its absence the claim shall be heard and determined upon other satisfactory proofs, competent in law.

Approved, September 18, 1850.

Ableman v. Booth (62 US 506)

Stephen V. R. Ableman v. Sherman M. Booth; and The United States v. Sherman M. Booth

Mr. Chief Justice Taney delivered the opinion of the court.

The plaintiff in error in the first of these cases is the marshal of the United States for the district of Wisconsin, and the two cases have arisen out of the same transaction, and depend, to some extent, upon the same principles. On that account, they have been argued and considered together; and the following are the facts as they appear in the transcripts before us:

Sherman M. Booth was charged before Winfield Smith, a commissioner duly appointed by the District Court of the United States for the district of Wisconsin, with having, on the 11th day of March, 1854, aided and abetted, at Milwaukee, in the said district, the escape of a fugitive slave from the deputy marshal, who had him in custody under a warrant issued by the district judge of the United States for that district, under the act of Congress of September 18, 1850.

Upon the examination before the commissioner, he was satisfied that an offence had been committed as charged, and that there was probable cause to believe that Booth had been guilty of it; and thereupon held him to bail to appear and answer before the District Court of the United States for the district of Wisconsin, on the first Monday in July then next ensuing. But on the 26th of May his bail or surety in the recognisance delivered him to the marshal, in the presence of the commissioner, and requested the commissioner to recommit Booth to the custody of the marshal; and he having failed to recognise again for his appearance before the District Court, the commissioner committed him to the custody of the marshal, to be delivered to the keeper of the jail until he should be discharged by due course of law.

Booth made application on the next day, the 27th of May, to A. D. Smith, one of the justices of the Supreme Court of the State of Wisconsin, for a writ of *habeas corpus,* stating that he was restrained of his liberty by Stephen V. R. Ableman, marshal of the United States for that district, under the warrant of commitment hereinbefore mentioned; and alleging that his imprisonment was illegal, because the act of Congress of September 18, 1850, was unconstitutional and void; and also that the warrant was defective, and did not describe the offence created by that act, even if the act were valid.

Upon this application, the justice, on the same day, issued the writ of *habeas corpus,* directed to the marshal, requiring him forthwith to have the body of Booth before him, (the said justice,) together with the time and cause of his imprisonment. The marshal thereupon, on the day above mentioned, produced Booth, and made his return, stating that he was received into his custody as marshal on the day before, and held in custody by virtue of the warrant of the commissioner above mentioned, a copy of which he annexed to and returned with the writ.

To this return Booth demurred, as not sufficient in law to justify his detention. And upon the hearing the justice decided that his detention was illegal, and ordered the marshal to discharge him and set him at liberty, which was accordingly done.

Afterwards, on the 9th of June, in the same year, the marshal applied to the Supreme Court of the State for a *certiorari,* setting forth in his application the proceedings hereinbefore mentioned, and charging that the release of Booth by the justice was erroneous and unlawful, and praying that his proceedings might be brought before the Supreme Court of the State for revision.

The *certiorari* was allowed on the same day; and the writ was accordingly issued on the 12th of the same month, and returnable on the third Tuesday of the month; and on the 20th the return was made by the justice, stating the proceedings, as hereinbefore mentioned.

The case was argued before the Supreme Court of the State, and on the 19th of July it pronounced its judgment, affirming the decision of the associate justice discharging Booth from imprisonment, with costs against Ableman, the marshal.

Afterwards, on the 26th of October, the marshal sued out a writ of error, returnable to this court on the first Monday of December, 1854, in order to bring the judg-

ment here for revision; and the defendant in error was regularly cited to appear on that day; and the record and proceedings were certified to this court by the clerk of the State court in the usual form, in obedience to the writ of error. And on the 4th of December, Booth, the defendant in error, filed a memorandum in writing in this court, stating that he had been cited to appear here in this case, and that he submitted it to the judgment of this court on the reasoning in the argument and opinions in the printed pamphlets therewith sent.

After the judgment was entered in the Supreme Court of Wisconsin, and before the writ of error was sued out, the State court entered on its record, that, in the final judgment it had rendered, the validity of the act of Congress of September 18, 1850, and of February 12, 1793, and the authority of the marshal to hold the defendant in his custody, under the process mentioned in his return to the writ of *habeas corpus,* were respectively drawn in question, and the decision of the court in the final judgment was against their validity, respectively.

This certificate was not necessary to give this court jurisdiction, because the proceedings upon their face show that these questions arose, and how they were decided; but it shows that at that time the Supreme Court of Wisconsin did not question their obligation to obey the writ of error, nor the authority of this court to re-examine their judgment in the cases specified. And the certificate is given for the purpose of placing distinctly on the record the points that were raised and decided in that court, in order that this court might have no difficulty in exercising its appellate power, and pronouncing its judgment upon all of them.

We come now to the second case. At the January term of the District Court of the United States for the district of Wisconsin, after Booth had been set at liberty, and after the transcript of the proceedings in the case above mentioned had been returned to and filed in this court, the grand jury found a bill of indictment against Booth for the offence with which he was charged before the commissioner, and from which the State court had discharged him. The indictment was found on the 4th of January, 1855. On the 9th a motion was made, by counsel on behalf of the accused, to quash the indictment, which was overruled by the court; and he thereupon pleaded not guilty, upon which issue was joined. On the 10th a jury was called and appeared in court, when he challenged the array; but the challenge was overruled and the jury empanelled. The trial, it appears, continued from day to day, until the 13th, when the jury found him guilty in the manner and form in which he stood indicted in the fourth and fifth counts. On the 16th he moved for a new trial and in arrest of judgment, which motions were argued on the 20th, and on the 23d the court overruled the motions, and sentenced the prisoner to be imprisoned for one month, and to pay a fine of $1,000 and the costs of prosecution; and that he remain in custody until the sentence was complied with.

We have stated more particularly these proceedings, from a sense of justice to the District Court, as they show that every opportunity of making his defence was afforded him, and that his case was fully heard and considered.

On the 26th of January, three days after the sentence was passed, the prisoner by his counsel filed his petition in the Supreme Court of the State, and with his petition filed a copy of the proceedings in the District Court, and also affidavits from the foreman and one other member of the jury who tried him, stating that their verdict was, guilty on the fourth and fifth counts, and not guilty on the other three; and stated in his petition that his imprisonment was illegal, because the fugitive slave law was unconstitutional; that the District Court had no jurisdiction to try or punish him for the matter charged against him, and that the proceedings and sentence of that court were absolute nullities in law. Various other objections to the proceedings are alleged, which are unimportant in the questions now before the court, and need not, therefore, be particularly stated. On the next day, the 27th, the court directed two writs of *habeas corpus* to be issued—one to the marshal, and one to the sheriff of Milwaukee, to whose actual keeping the prisoner was committed by the marshal, by order of the District Court. The *habeas corpus* directed each of them to produce the body of the prisoner, and make known the cause of his imprisonment, immediately after the receipt of the writ.

On the 30th of January the marshal made his return, not acknowledging the jurisdiction, but stating the sentence of the District Court as his authority; that the prisoner was delivered to, and was then in the actual keeping of the sheriff of Milwaukee county, by order of the court, and he therefore had no control of the body of the prisoner; and if the sheriff had not received him, he should have so reported to the District Court, and should have conveyed him to some other place or prison, as the court should command.

On the same day the sheriff produced the body of Booth before the State court, and returned that he had been committed to his custody by the marshal, by virtue of a transcript, a true copy of which was annexed to his return, and which was the only process or authority by which he detained him.

This transcript was a full copy of the proceedings and sentence in the District Court of the United States, as hereinbefore stated. To this return the accused, by his counsel, filed a general demurrer.

The court ordered the hearing to be postponed until the 2d of February, and notice to be given to the district attorney of the United States. It was accordingly heard on that day, and on the next, (February 3d,) the court decided that the imprisonment was illegal, and ordered and adjudged that Booth be, and he was by that judgment, forever discharged from that imprisonment and restraint, and he was accordingly set at liberty.

On the 21st of April next following, the Attorney General of the United States presented a petition to the Chief Justice of the Supreme Court, stating briefly the facts in the case, and at the same time presenting an exemplification of the proceedings hereinbefore stated, duly certified by the clerk of the State court, and averring in his petition that the State court had no jurisdiction in the case, and praying that a writ of error might issue to bring its judgment before this court to correct the error. The writ of error was allowed and issued, and, according to the rules and practice of the court, was returnable on the first Monday of December, 1855, and a citation for the defendant in error to appear on that day was issued by the Chief Justice at the same time.

No return having been made to this writ, the Attorney General, on the 1st of February, 1856, filed affidavits, showing that the writ of error had been duly served on the clerk of the Supreme Court of Wisconsin, at his office, on the 30th of May, 1855, and the citation served on the defendant in error on the 28th of June, in the same year. And also the affidavit of the district attorney of the United States for the district of Wisconsin, setting forth that when he served the writ of error upon the clerk, as above mentioned, he was informed by the clerk, and has also been informed by one of the justices of the Supreme Court, which released Booth, "*that the court had directed the clerk to make no return to the writ of error, and to enter no order upon the journals or records of the court concerning the same.*" And, upon these proofs, the Attorney General moved the court for an order upon the clerk to make return to the writ of error, on or before the first day of the next ensuing term of this court. The rule was accordingly laid, and on the 22d of July, 1856, the Attorney General filed with the clerk of this court the affidavit of the marshal of the district of Wisconsin, that he had served the rule on the clerk on the 7th of the month above mentioned; and no return having been made, the Attorney General, on the 27th of February, 1857, moved for leave to file the certified copy of the record of the Supreme Court of Wisconsin, which he had produced with his application for the writ of error, and to docket the case in this court, in conformity with a motion to that effect made at the last term. And the court thereupon, on the 6th of March, 1857, ordered the copy of the record filed by the Attorney General to be received and entered on the docket of this court, to have the same effect and legal operation as if returned by the clerk with the writ of error, and that the case stand for argument at the next ensuing term, without further notice to either party.

The case was accordingly docketed, but was not reached for argument in the regular order and practice of the court until the present term.

This detailed statement of the proceedings in the different courts has appeared to be necessary in order to form a just estimate of the action of the different tribunals in which it has been heard, and to account for the delay in the final decision of a case, which, from its character, would seem to have demanded prompt action. The first case, indeed, was reached for trial two terms ago. But as the two cases are different portions of the same prosecution for the same offence, they unavoidably, to some extent, involve the same principles of law, and it would hardly have been proper to hear and decide the first before the other was ready for hearing and decision. They have accordingly been argued together, by the Attorney General of the United States, at the present term. No counsel has in either case appeared for the defendant in error. But we have the pamphlet arguments filed and referred to by Booth in the first case, as hereinbefore mentioned, also the opinions and arguments of the Supreme Court of Wisconsin, and of the judges who compose it, in full, and are enabled, therefore, to see the grounds on which they rely to support their decisions.

It will be seen, from the foregoing statement of facts, that a judge of the Supreme Court of the State of Wisconsin in the first of these cases, claimed and exercised the right to supervise and annul the proceedings of a commissioner of the United States, and to discharge a prisoner, who had been committed by the commissioner for an offence against the laws of this Government, and that this exercise of power by the judge was afterwards sanctioned and affirmed by the Supreme Court of the State.

In the second case, the State court has gone a step further, and claimed and exercised jurisdiction over the proceedings and judgment of a District Court of the United States, and upon a summary and collateral proceeding, by *habeas corpus,* has set aside and annulled its judgment, and discharged a prisoner who had been tried and found guilty of an offence against the laws of the United States, and sentenced to imprisonment by the District Court.

And it further appears that the State court have not only claimed and exercised this jurisdiction, but have also determined that their decision is final and conclusive upon all the courts of the United States, and ordered their clerk to disregard and refuse obedience to the writ of error issued by this court, pursuant to the act of Congress of 1789, to bring here for examination and revision the judgment of the State court.

These propositions are new in the jurisprudence of the United States, as well as of the States; and the supremacy of the State courts over the courts of the United States, in cases arising under the Constitution and laws of the United States, is now for the first time asserted and acted upon in the Supreme Court of a State.

The supremacy is not, indeed, set forth distinctly and broadly, in so many words, in the printed opinions of the judges. It is intermixed with elaborate discussions of different provisions in the fugitive slave law, and of the privileges and power of the writ of *habeas corpus.* But the paramount power of the State court lies at the foundation of these decisions; for their commentaries upon the provisions of that law, and upon the privileges and power of the writ of *habeas corpus,* were out of place, and their judicial action upon them without authority of law, unless they had the power to revise and control the proceedings in the criminal case of which they were speaking; and their judgments, releasing the prisoner, and disregarding the writ of error from this court, can rest upon no other foundation.

If the judicial power exercised in this instance has been reserved to the States, no offence against the laws of the United States can be punished by their own courts, without the permission and according to the judgment of the courts of the State in which the party happens to be imprisoned; for, if the Supreme Court of Wisconsin possessed the power it has exercised in relation to offences against the act of Congress in question, it necessarily follows that they must have the same judicial authority in relation to any other law of the United States; and, consequently, their supervising and controlling power would embrace the whole criminal code of the United States, and extend to offences against our revenue laws, or any other law intended to guard the different departments of the General Government from fraud or violence. And it would embrace all crimes, from the highest to the lowest; including felonies, which are punished with death, as well as misdemeanors, which are punished by imprisonment. And, moreover, if the power is possessed by the Supreme Court of the State of Wisconsin, it must belong equally to every other State in the Union, when the prisoner is within its territorial limits; and it is very certain that the State courts would not always agree in opinion; and it would often happen, that an act which was admitted to be an offence, and justly punished, in one State, would be regarded as innocent, and indeed as praiseworthy, in another.

It would seem to be hardly necessary to do more than state the result to which these decisions of the State courts must inevitably lead. It is, of itself, a sufficient and conclusive answer; for no one will suppose that a Government which has now lasted nearly seventy years, enforcing its laws by its own tribunals, and preserving the union of the States, could have lasted a single year, or fulfilled the high trusts committed to it, if offences against its laws could not have been punished without the consent of the State in which the culprit was found.

The judges of the Supreme Court of Wisconsin do not distinctly state from what source they suppose they have derived this judicial power. There can be no such thing as judicial authority, unless it is conferred by a Government or sovereignty; and if the judges and courts of Wisconsin possess the jurisdiction they claim, they must derive it either from the United States or the State. It certainly has not been conferred on them by the United States; and it is equally clear it was not in the power of the State to confer it, even if it had attempted to do so; for no State can authorize one of its judges or courts to exercise judicial power, by *habeas corpus* or otherwise, within the jurisdiction of another and independent Government. And although the

State of Wisconsin is sovereign within its territorial limits to a certain extent, yet that sovereignty is limited and restricted by the Constitution of the United States. And the powers of the General Government, and of the State, although both exist and are exercised within the same territorial limits, are yet separate and distinct sovereignties, acting separately and independently of each other, within their respective spheres. And the sphere of action appropriated to the United States is as far beyond the reach of the judicial process issued by a State judge or a State court, as if the line of division was traced by landmarks and monuments visible to the eye. And the State of Wisconsin had no more power to authorize these proceedings of its judges and courts, than it would have had if the prisoner had been confined in Michigan, or in any other State of the Union, for an offence against the laws of the State in which he was imprisoned.

It is, however, due to the State to say, that we do not find this claim of paramount jurisdiction in the State courts over the courts of the United States asserted or countenanced by the Constitution or laws of the State. We find it only in the decisions of the judges of the Supreme Court. Indeed, at the very time these decisions were made, there was a statute of the State which declares that a person brought up on a *habeas corpus* shall be remanded, if it appears that he is confined:

"1st. By virtue of process, by any court or judge of the United States, in a case where such court or judge has exclusive jurisdiction; or,

"2d. By virtue of the final judgment or decree of any competent court of civil or criminal jurisdiction." (Revised Statutes of the State of Wisconsin, 1849, ch. 124, page 629.)

Even, therefore, if these cases depended upon the laws of Wisconsin, it would be difficult to find in these provisions such a grant of judicial power as the Supreme Court claims to have derived from the State.

But, as we have already said, questions of this kind must always depend upon the Constitution and laws of the United States, and not of a State. The Constitution was not formed merely to guard the States against danger from foreign nations, but mainly to secure union and harmony at home; for if this object could be attained, there would be but little danger from abroad; and to accomplish this purpose, it was felt by the statesmen who framed the Constitution, and by the people who adopted it, that it was necessary that many of the rights of sovereignty which the States then possessed should be ceded to the General Government; and that, in the sphere of action assigned to it, it should be supreme, and strong enough to execute its own laws by its own tribunals, without interruption from a State or from State authorities. And it was evident that anything short of this would be inadequate to the main objects for which the Government was established; and that local interests, local passions or prejudices, incited and fostered by individuals for sinister purposes, would lead to acts of aggression and injustice by one State upon the rights of another, which would ultimately terminate in violence and force, unless there was a common arbiter between them, armed with power enough to protect and guard the rights of all, by appropriate laws, to be carried into execution peacefully by its judicial tribunals.

The language of the Constitution, by which this power is granted, is too plain to admit of doubt or to need comment. It declares that "this Constitution, and the laws of the United States which shall be passed in pursuance thereof, and all treaties made, or which shall be made, under the authority of the United States, shall be the supreme law of the land, and the judges in every State shall be bound thereby, anything in the Constitution or laws of any State to the contrary notwithstanding."

But the supremacy thus conferred on this Government could not peacefully be maintained, unless it was clothed with judicial power, equally paramount in authority to carry it into execution; for if left to the courts of justice of the several States, conflicting decisions would unavoidably take place, and the local tribunals could hardly be expected to be always free from the local influences of which we have spoken. And the Constitution and laws and treaties of the United States, and the powers granted to the Federal Government, would soon receive different interpretations in different States, and the Government of the United States would soon become one thing in one State and another thing in another. It was essential, therefore, to its very existence as a Government, that it should have the power of establishing courts of justice, altogether independent of State power, to carry into effect its own laws; and that a tribunal should be established in which all cases which might arise under the Constitution and laws and treaties of the United States, whether in a State court or a court of the United States, should be finally and conclusively decided.

Without such a tribunal, it is obvious that there would be no uniformity of judicial decision; and that the supremacy, (which is but another name for independence,) so carefully provided in the clause of the Constitution above referred to, could not possibly be maintained peacefully, unless it was associated with this paramount judicial authority.

Accordingly, it was conferred on the General Government, in clear, precise, and comprehensive terms. It is declared that its judicial power shall (among other subjects enumerated) extend to all cases in law and equity arising under the Constitution and laws of the United States, and that in such cases, as well as the others there enumerated, this court shall have appellate jurisdiction both as to law and fact, with such exceptions and under such regulations as Congress shall make. The appellate power, it will be observed, is conferred on this court in all cases or suits in which such a question shall arise. It is not confined to suits in the inferior courts of the United States, but extends to all cases where such a question arises, whether it be in a judicial tribunal of a State or of the United States. And it is manifest that this ultimate appellate power in a tribunal created by the Constitution itself was deemed essential to secure the independence and supremacy of the General Government in the sphere of action assigned to it; to make the Constitution and laws of the United States uniform, and the same in every State; and to guard against evils which would inevitably arise from conflicting opinions between the courts of a State and of the United States, if there was no common arbiter authorized to decide between them.

The importance which the framers of the Constitution attached to such a tribunal, for the purpose of preserving internal tranquillity, is strikingly manifested by the clause which gives this court jurisdiction over the sovereign States which compose this Union, when a controversy arises between them. Instead of reserving the right to seek redress for injustice from another State by their sovereign powers, they have bound themselves to submit to the decision of this court, and to abide by its judgment. And it is not out of place to say, here, that experience has demonstrated that this power was not unwisely surrendered by the States; for in the time that has already elapsed since this Government came into existence, several irritating and angry controversies have taken place between adjoining States, in relation to their respective boundaries, and which have sometimes threatened to end in force and violence, but for the power vested in this court to hear them and decide between them.

The same purposes are clearly indicated by the different language employed when conferring supremacy upon the laws of the United States, and jurisdiction upon its courts. In the first case, it provides that "this Constitution, and the laws of the United States *which shall be made in pursuance thereof,* shall be the supreme law of the land, and obligatory upon the judges in every State." The words in italics show the precision and foresight which marks every clause in the instrument. The sovereignty to be created was to be limited in its powers of legislation, and if it passed a law not authorized by its enumerated powers, it was not to be regarded as the supreme law of the land, nor were the State judges bound to carry it into execution. And as the courts of a State, and the courts of the United States, might, and indeed certainly would, often differ as to the extent of the powers conferred by the General Government, it was manifest that serious controversies would arise between the authorities of the United States and of the States, which must be settled by force of arms, unless some tribunal was created to decide between them finally and without appeal.

The Constitution has accordingly provided, as far as human foresight could provide, against this danger. And in conferring judicial power upon the Federal Government, it declares that the jurisdiction of its courts shall extend to all cases arising under "this Constitution" and the laws of the United States—leaving out the words of restriction contained in the grant of legislative power which we have above noticed. The judicial power covers every legislative act of Congress, whether it be made within the limits of its delegated powers, or be an assumption of power beyond the grants in the Constitution.

This judicial power was justly regarded as indispensable, not merely to maintain the supremacy of the laws of the United States, but also to guard the States from any encroachment upon their reserved rights by the General Government. And as the Constitution is the fundamental and supreme law, if it appears that an act of Congress is not pursuant to and within the limits of the power assigned to the Federal Government, it is the duty of the courts of the United States to declare it unconstitutional and void. The grant of judicial power is not confined to the administration of laws passed in pursuance to the provisions of the Constitution, nor confined to the interpretation of such laws; but, by the very terms of the grant, the Constitution is under their view when any act of Congress is brought before them, and it is their duty to declare the law void, and refuse to execute it, if it is not pursuant to the legislative powers conferred upon Congress. And as the final appellate power in all such questions is given to this court, controversies as to the respective powers of the United States and the States, instead of being determined by military and physical force, are heard, investigated, and finally settled, with the calmness and deliberation of judicial inquiry. And no one can fail to see, that if such an arbiter had not been provided, in our complicated system of government, internal tranquillity could not have been preserved; and if such controversies were left to arbitrament of physical force, our Government, State and National, would soon cease to be Governments of laws, and revolutions by force of arms would take the place of courts of justice and judicial decisions.

In organizing such a tribunal, it is evident that every precaution was taken, which human wisdom could devise, to fit it for the high duty with which it was intrusted. It was not left to Congress to create it by law; for the States could hardly be expected to confide in the impartiality of a tribunal created exclusively by the General Government, without any participation on their part. And as the performance of its duty would sometimes come in conflict with individual ambition or interests, and powerful political combinations, an act of Congress establishing such a tribunal might be repealed in order to establish another more subservient to the predominant political influences or excited passions of the day. This tribunal, therefore, was erected, and the powers of which we have spoken conferred upon it, not by the Federal Government, but by the people of the States, who formed and adopted that Government, and conferred upon it all the powers, legislative, executive, and judicial, which it now possesses. And in order to secure its independence, and enable it faithfully and firmly to perform its duty, it engrafted it upon the Constitution itself, and declared that this court should have appellate power in all cases arising under the Constitution and laws of the United States. So long, therefore, as this Constitution shall endure, this tribunal must exist with it, deciding in the peaceful forms of judicial proceeding the angry and irritating controversies between sovereignties, which in other countries have been determined by the arbitrament of force.

These principles of constitutional law are confirmed and

illustrated by the clause which confers legislative power upon Congress. That power is specifically given in article 1, section 8, paragraph 18, in the following words:

"To make all laws which shall be necessary and proper to carry into execution the foregoing powers, and all other powers vested by this Constitution in the Government of the United States, or in any department or officer thereof."

Under this clause of the Constitution, it became the duty of Congress to pass such laws as were necessary and proper to carry into execution the powers vested in the judicial department. And in the performance of this duty, the First Congress, at its first session, passed the act of 1789, ch. 20, entitled *"An act to establish the judicial courts of the United States."* It will be remembered that many of the members of the Convention were also members of this Congress, and it cannot be supposed that they did not understand the meaning and intention of the great instrument which they had so anxiously and deliberately considered, clause by clause, and assisted to frame. And the law they passed to carry into execution the powers vested in the judicial department of the Government proves, past doubt, that their interpretation of the appellate powers conferred on this court was the same with that which we have now given; for by the 25th section of the act of 1789, Congress authorized writs of error to be issued from this court to a State Court, whenever a right had been claimed under the Constitution or laws of the United States, and the decision of the State court was against it. And to make this appellate power effectual, and altogether independent of the action of State tribunals, this act further provides, that upon writs of error to a State court, instead of remanding the cause for a final decision in the State court, this court may at their discretion, if the cause shall have been once remanded before, proceed to a final decision of the same, and award execution.

These provisions in the act of 1789 tell us, in language not to be mistaken, the great importance which the patriots and statesmen of the First Congress attached to this appellate power, and the foresight and care with which they guarded its free and independent exercise against interference or obstruction by States or State tribunals.

In the case before the Supreme Court of Wisconsin, a right was claimed under the Constitution and laws of the United States, and the decision was against the right claimed; and it refuses obedience to the writ of error, and regards its own judgment as final. It has not only reversed and annulled the judgment of the District Court of the United States, but it has reversed and annulled the provisions of the Constitution itself, and the act of Congress of 1789, and made the superior and appellate tribunal the inferior and subordinate one.

We do not question the authority of State court, or judge, who is authorized by the laws of the State to issue the writ of *habeas corpus,* to issue it in any case where the party is imprisoned within its territorial limits, provided it does not appear, when the application is made, that the person imprisoned is in custody under the authority of the United States. The court or judge has a right to inquire, in this mode of proceeding, for what cause and by what authority the prisoner is confined within the territorial limits of the State sovereignty. And it is the duty of the marshal, or other person having the custody of the prisoner, to make known to the judge or court, by a proper return, the authority by which he holds him in custody. This right to inquire by process of *habeas corpus,* and the duty of the officer to make a return, grows, necessarily, out of the complex character of our Government, and the existence of two distinct and separate sovereignties within the same territorial space, each of them restricted in its powers, and each within its sphere of action, prescribed by the Constitution of the United States, independent of the other. But, after the return is made, and the State judge or court judicially apprized that the party is in custody under the authority of the United States, they can proceed no further. They then know that the prisoner is within the dominion and jurisdiction of another Government, and that neither the writ of *habeas corpus,* nor any other process issued under State authority, can pass over the line of division between the two sovereignties. He is then within the dominion and exclusive jurisdiction of the United States. If he has committed an offence against their laws, their tribunals alone can punish him. If he is wrongfully imprisoned, their judicial tribunals can release him and afford him redress. And although, as we have said, it is the duty of the marshal, or other person holding him, to make known, by a proper return, the authority under which he detains him, it is at the same time imperatively his duty to obey the process of the United States, to hold the prisoner in custody under it, and to refuse obedience to the mandate or process of any other Government. And consequently it is his duty not to take the prisoner, nor suffer him to be taken, before a State judge or court upon a *habeas corpus* issued under State authority. No State judge or court, after they are judicially informed that the party is imprisoned under the authority of the United States, has any right to interfere with him, or to require him to be brought before them. And if the authority of a State, in the form of judicial process or otherwise, should attempt to control the marshal or other authorized officer or agent of the United States, in any respect, in the custody of his prisoner, it would be his duty to resist it, and to call to his aid any force that might be necessary to maintain the authority of law against illegal interference. No judicial process, whatever form it may assume, can have any lawful authority outside of the limits of the jurisdiction of the court or judge by whom it is issued; and an attempt to enforce it beyond these boundaries is nothing less than lawless violence.

Nor is there anything in this supremacy of the General Government, or the jurisdiction of its judicial tribunals, to awaken the jealousy or offend the natural and just pride of State sovereignty. Neither this Government, nor the powers of which we are speaking, were forced upon the States. The Constitution of the United States, with all the powers conferred by it on the General Government, and surrendered by the States, was the voluntary act of the people of the several States, deliberately done, for their own protection and safety against injustice from one another. And their anxiety to preserve it in full force, in all its powers, and to guard against resistance to or evasion of its authority, on the part of a State, is proved by the clause which requires that the members of the State Legislatures, and all executive and judicial officers of the several States, (as well as those of the General Government,) shall be bound, by oath or affirmation, to support this Constitution. This is the last and closing clause of the Constitution, and inserted when the whole frame of Government, with the powers hereinbefore specified, had been adopted by the Convention; and it was in that form, and with these powers, that the Constitution was submitted to the people of the several States, for their consideration and decision.

Now, it certainly can be no humiliation to the citizen of a republic to yield a ready obedience to the laws as administered by the constituted authorities. On the contrary, it is among his first and highest duties as a citizen, because free government cannot exist without it. Nor can it be inconsistent with the dignity of a sovereign State to observe faithfully, and in the spirit of sincerity and truth, the compact into which it voluntarily entered when it became a State of this Union. On the contrary, the highest honor of sovereignty is untarnished faith. And certainly no faith could be more deliberately and solemnly pledged than that which every State has plighted to the other States to support the Constitution as it is, in all its provisions, until they shall be altered in the manner which the Constitution itself prescribes. In the emphatic language of the pledge required, it is *to support this Constitution*. And no power is more clearly conferred by the Constitution and laws of the United States, than the power of this court to decide, ultimately and finally, all cases arising under such Constitution and laws; and for that purpose to bring here for revision, by writ of error, the judgment of a State court, where such questions have arisen, and the right claimed under them denied by the highest judicial tribunal in the State.

We are sensible that we have extended the examination of these decisions beyond the limits required by any intrinsic difficulty in the questions. But the decisions in question were made by the supreme judicial tribunal of the State; and when a court so elevated in its position has pronounced a judgment which, if it could be maintained, would subvert the very foundations of this Government, it seemed to be the duty of this court, when exercising its appellate power, to show plainly the grave errors into which the State court has fallen, and the consequences to which they would inevitably lead.

But it can hardly be necessary to point out the errors which followed their mistaken view of the jurisdiction they might lawfully exercise; because, if there was any defect of power in the commissioner, or in his mode of proceeding, it was for the tribunals of the United States to revise and correct it, and not for a State court. And as regards the decision of the District Court, it had exclusive and final jurisdiction by the laws of the United States; and neither the regularity of its proceedings nor the validity of its sentence could be called in question in any other court, either of a State or the United States, by *habeas corpus* or any other process.

But although we think it unnecessary to discuss these questions, yet, as they have been decided by the State court, and are before us on the record, and we are not willing to be misunderstood, it is proper to say that, in the judgment of this court, the act of Congress commonly called the fugitive slave law is, in all of its provisions, fully authorized by the Constitution of the United States; that the commissioner had lawful authority to issue the warrant and commit the party, and that his proceedings were regular and conformable to law. We have already stated the opinion and judgment of the court as to the exclusive jurisdiction of the District Court, and the appellate powers which this court is authorized and required to exercise. And if any argument was needed to show the wisdom and necessity of this appellate power, the cases before us sufficiently prove it, and at the same time emphatically call for its exercise.

The judgment of the Supreme Court of Wisconsin must therefore be reversed in each of the cases now before the court.

Scott v. Sandford

ROGER TANEY

1856

Dred Scott was the slave of John Emerson, an army doctor who took Scott with him for extended stays in Illinois and the Territory of Wisconsin—both of which banned slavery. On Emerson's death, Scott became the property of his widow, whom he sued for his freedom in 1846. While the case was still in the courts, Mrs. Emerson transferred ownership of Scott to her brother, F. A. Sanford. Sanford, whose name was misspelled "Sandford" by a court official, became the defendant in Scott's suit for his freedom.

Scott claimed that, because he had been taken to a state and a territory where slavery was illegal, he had, in effect, been freed. After making its way through both Missouri and federal courts, the case finally came to the United States Supreme Court in 1856. The Court did not decide the case immediately, instead scheduling rearguments for after the presidential election of 1856. After the reargument, the Court issued a sweeping opinion, not merely deciding on Scott's case, but also declaring it impossible for a black man to be a citizen of the United States and declaring the Missouri Compromise, which banned slavery in a number of federal territories, to be unconstitutional.

Dred Scott v. Sandford (60 US 393)

Mr. Chief Justice Taney delivered the opinion of the court.

The question is simply this: Can a negro, whose ancestors were imported into this country, and sold as slaves, become a member of the political community formed and brought into existence by the Constitution of the United States, and as such become entitled to all the rights, and privileges, and immunities, guarantied by that instrument to the citizen? One of which rights is the privilege of suing in a court of the United States in the cases specified in the Constitution.

It will be observed, that the plea applies to that class of persons only whose ancestors were negroes of the African race, and imported into this country, and sold and held as slaves. The only matter in issue before the court, therefore, is, whether the descendants of such slaves, when they shall be emancipated, or who are born of parents who had become free before their birth, are citizens of a State, in the sense in which the word citizen is used in the Constitution of the United States. And this being the only matter in dispute on the pleadings, the court must be understood as speaking in this opinion of that class only, that is, of those persons who are the descendants of Africans who were imported into this country, and sold as slaves.

The situation of this population was altogether unlike that of the Indian race. The latter, it is true, formed no part of the colonial communities, and never amalgamated with them in social connections or in government. But although they were uncivilized, they were yet a free and independent people, associated together in nations or tribes, and governed by their own laws. Many of these political communities were situated in territories to which the white race claimed the ultimate right of dominion. But that claim was acknowledged to be subject to the right of the Indians to occupy it as long as they thought proper, and neither the English nor colonial Governments claimed or exercised any dominion over the tribe or nation by whom it was occupied, nor claimed the right to the possession of the territory, until the tribe or nation consented to cede it. These Indian Governments were regarded and treated as foreign Governments, as much so as if an ocean had separated the red man from the white; and their freedom has constantly been acknowledged, from the time of the first emigration to the English colonies to the present day, by the different Governments which succeeded each other. Treaties have been negotiated with them, and their alliance sought for in war; and the people who compose these Indian political communities have always been treated as foreigners not living under our Government. It is true that the course of events has brought the Indian tribes within the limits of the United States under subjection to the white race; and it has been found necessary, for their sake as well as our own, to regard them as in a state of pupilage, and to legislate to a certain extent over them and the territory they occupy. But they may, without doubt, like the subjects of any other foreign Government, be naturalized by the authority of Congress, and become citizens of a State, and of the United States; and if an individual should leave his nation or tribe, and take up his abode among the white population, he would be entitled to all the rights and privileges which would belong to an emigrant from any other foreign people.

We proceed to examine the case as presented by the pleadings.

The words "people of the United States" and "citizens" are synonymous terms, and mean the same thing. They both describe the political body who, according to our republican institutions, form the sovereignty, and who hold the power and conduct the Government through their representatives. They are what we familiarly call the "sovereign people," and every citizen is one of this people, and a constituent member of this sovereignty. The question before us is, whether the class of persons described in the plea in abatement compose a portion of this people, and are constituent members of this sovereignty? We think they are not, and that they are not included, and were not intended to be included, under the word "citizens" in the Constitution, and can therefore claim none of the rights and privileges which that instrument provides for and secures to citizens of the United States. On the contrary, they were at that time considered as a subordinate and inferior class of beings, who had been subjugated by the dominant race, and, whether emancipated or not, yet remained subject to their authority, and had no rights or privileges but such as those who held the power and the Government might choose to grant them.

It is not the province of the court to decide upon the justice or injustice, the policy or impolicy, of these laws. The decision of that question belonged to the political or law-making power; to those who formed the sovereignty and framed the Constitution. The duty of the court is, to interpret the instrument they have framed, with the best lights we can obtain on the subject, and to administer it as we find it, according to its true intent and meaning when it was adopted.

In discussing this question, we must not confound the rights of citizenship which a State may confer within its own limits, and the rights of citizenship as a member of the Union. It does not by any means follow, because he has all the rights and privileges of a citizen of a State, that he must be a citizen of the United States. He may have all of the rights and privileges of the citizen of a State, and yet not be entitled to the rights and privileges of a citizen in any other State. For, previous to the adoption of the Constitution of the United States, every State had the undoubted right to confer on whomsoever it pleased the character of citizen, and to endow him with all its rights. But this character of course was confined to the boundaries of the State, and gave him no rights or privileges in other States beyond those secured to him by the laws of nations and the comity of States. Nor have the several States surrendered the power of conferring these rights and privileges by adopting the Constitution of the United States. Each State may still confer them upon an alien, or any one it thinks proper, or upon any class or description of persons; yet he would not be a citizen in the sense in which that word is used in the Constitution of the United States, nor entitled to sue as such in one of its courts, nor to the privileges and immunities of a citizen in the other States. The rights which he would acquire would be restricted to the State which gave them. The Constitution has conferred on Congress the right to establish an uniform rule of naturalization, and this right is evidently exclusive, and has always been held by this court to be so. Consequently, no State, since the adoption of the Constitution, can by naturalizing an alien invest him with the rights and privileges secured to a citizen of a State under the Federal Government, although, so far as the State alone was concerned, he would undoubtedly be entitled to the rights of a citizen, and clothed with all the rights and immunities which the Constitution and laws of the State attached to that character.

It is very clear, therefore, that no State can, by any act or law of its own, passed since the adoption of the Constitution, introduce a new member into the political community created by the Constitution of the United States. It cannot make him a member of this community by making him a member of its own. And for the same reason it cannot introduce any person, or description of persons, who were not intended to be embraced in this new political family, which the Constitution brought into existence, but were intended to be excluded from it.

The question then arises, whether the provisions of the Constitution, in relation to the personal rights and privileges to which the citizen of a State should be entitled, embraced the negro African race, at that time in this country, or who might afterwards be imported, who had then or should afterwards be made free in any State; and to put it in the power of a single State to make him a citizen of the United States, and endue him with the full rights of citizenship in every other State without their consent? Does the Constitution of the United States act upon him whenever he shall be made free under the laws of a State, and raised there to the rank of a citizen, and immediately clothe him with all the privileges of a citizen in every other State, and in its own courts?

The court think the affirmative of these propositions cannot be maintained. And if it cannot, the plaintiff in error could not be a citizen of the State of Missouri, within the meaning of the Constitution of the United States, and, consequently, was not entitled to sue in its courts.

It is true, every person, and every class and description of persons, who were at the time of the adoption of the Constitution recognised as citizens in the several States, became also citizens of this new political body; but none other; it was formed by them, and for them and their posterity, but for no one else. And the personal rights and privileges guarantied to citizens of this new sovereignty were intended to embrace those only who were then members of the several State communities, or who should afterwards by birthright or otherwise become members, according to the provisions of the Constitution and the principles on which it was founded. It was the union of those who were at that time members of distinct and separate political communities into one political family, whose power, for certain specified purposes, was to extend over the whole territory of the United States. And it gave to each citizen rights and privileges outside of his State which he did not before possess, and placed him in every other State upon a perfect equality with its own citizens as to rights of person and rights of property; it made him a citizen of the United States.

It becomes necessary, therefore, to determine who were citizens of the several States when the Constitution was adopted. And in order to do this, we must recur to the Governments and institutions of the thirteen colonies, when they separated from Great Britain and formed new sovereignties, and took their places in the family of independent nations. We must inquire who, at that time, were recognised as the people or citizens of a State, whose rights and liberties had been outraged by the English Government; and who declared their independence, and assumed the powers of Government to defend their rights by force of arms.

In the opinion of the court, the legislation and histories of the times, and the language used in the Declaration of Independence, show, that neither the class of persons who had been imported as slaves, nor their descendants, whether they had become free or not, were then acknowledged as a part of the people, nor intended to be included in the general words used in that memorable instrument.

It is difficult at this day to realize the state of public opinion in relation to that unfortunate race, which prevailed in the civilized and enlightened portions of the world at the time of the Declaration of Independence, and when the Constitution of the United States was framed and adopted. But the public history of every European nation displays it in a manner too plain to be mistaken.

They had for more than a century before been regarded as beings of an inferior order, and altogether unfit to associate with the white race, either in social or political relations; and so far inferior, that they had no rights which the white man was bound to respect; and that the negro might justly and lawfully be reduced to slavery for his benefit. He was bought and sold, and treated as an ordinary article of merchandise and traffic, whenever a profit could be made by it. This opinion was at that time fixed and universal in the civilized portion of the white race. It was regarded as an axiom in morals as well as in politics, which no one thought of disputing, or supposed to be open to dispute; and men in every grade and position in society daily and habitually acted upon it in their private pursuits, as well as in matters of public concern, without doubting for a moment the correctness of this opinion.

And in no nation was this opinion more firmly fixed or more uniformly acted upon than by the English Government and English people. They not only seized them on the coast of Africa, and sold them or held them in slavery for their own use; but they took them as ordinary articles of merchandise to every country where they could make a profit on them, and were far more extensively engaged in this commerce than any other nation in the world.

The opinion thus entertained and acted upon in England was naturally impressed upon the colonies they founded on this side of the Atlantic. And, accordingly, a negro of the African race was regarded by them as an article of property, and held, and bought and sold as such, in every one of the thirteen colonies which united in the Declaration of Independence, and afterwards formed the Constitution of the United States. The slaves were more or less numerous in the different colonies, as slave labor was found more or less profitable. But no one seems to have doubted the correctness of the prevailing opinion of the time.

The legislation of the different colonies furnishes positive and indisputable proof of this fact.

It would be tedious, in this opinion, to enumerate the various laws they passed upon this subject. It will be sufficient, as a sample of the legislation which then generally prevailed throughout the British colonies, to give the laws of two of them; one being still a large slaveholding State, and the other the first State in which slavery ceased to exist.

The province of Maryland, in 1717, (ch. 13, s. 5,) passed a law declaring "that if any free negro or mulatto intermarry with any white woman, or if any white man shall intermarry with any negro or mulatto woman, such negro or mulatto shall become a slave during life, excepting mulattoes born of white women, who, for such intermarriage, shall only become servants for seven years, to be disposed of as the justices of the county court, where such marriage so happens, shall think fit; to be applied by them towards the support of a public school within the said county. And any white man or white woman who shall intermarry as aforesaid, with any negro or mulatto, such white man or white woman shall become servants during the term of seven years, and shall be disposed of by the justices as aforesaid, and be applied to the uses aforesaid."

The other colonial law to which we refer was passed by Massachusetts in 1705, (chap. 6.) It is entitled "An act for the better preventing of a spurious and mixed issue," &c.; and it provides, that "if any negro or mulatto shall presume to smite or strike any person of the English or other Christian nation, such negro or mulatto shall be severely whipped, at the discretion of the justices before whom the offender shall be convicted."

And "that none of her Majesty's English or Scottish subjects, nor of any other Christian nation, within this province, shall contract matrimony with any negro or mulatto; nor shall any person, duly authorized to solemnize marriage, presume to join any such in marriage, on pain of forfeiting the sum of fifty pounds; one moiety thereof to her Majesty, for and towards the support of the Government within this province, and the other moiety to him or them

that shall inform and sue for the same, in any of her Majesty's courts of record within the province, by bill, plaint, or information."

We give both of these laws in the words used by the respective legislative bodies, because the language in which they are framed, as well as the provisions contained in them, show, too plainly to be misunderstood, the degraded condition of this unhappy race. They were still in force when the Revolution began, and are a faithful index to the state of feeling towards the class of persons of whom they speak, and of the position they occupied throughout the thirteen colonies, in the eyes and thoughts of the men who framed the Declaration of Independence and established the State Constitutions and Governments. They show that a perpetual and impassable barrier was intended to be erected between the white race and the one which they had reduced to slavery, and governed as subjects with absolute and despotic power, and which they then looked upon as so far below them in the scale of created beings, that intermarriages between white persons and negroes or mulattoes were regarded as unnatural and immoral, and punished as crimes, not only in the parties, but in the person who joined them in marriage. And no distinction in this respect was made between the free negro or mulatto and the slave, but this stigma, of the deepest degradation, was fixed upon the whole race.

We refer to these historical facts for the purpose of showing the fixed opinions concerning that race, upon which the statesmen of that day spoke and acted. It is necessary to do this, in order to determine whether the general terms used in the Constitution of the United States, as to the rights of man and the rights of the people, was intended to include them, or to give to them or their posterity the benefit of any of its provisions.

The language of the Declaration of Independence is equally conclusive:

It begins by declaring that, "when in the course of human events it becomes necessary for one people to dissolve the political bands which have connected them with another, and to assume among the powers of the earth the separate and equal station to which the laws of nature and nature's God entitle them, a decent respect for the opinions of mankind requires that they should declare the causes which impel them to the separation."

It then proceeds to say: "We hold these truths to be self-evident: that all men are created equal; that they are endowed by their Creator with certain unalienable rights; that among them is life, liberty, and the pursuit of happiness; that to secure these rights, Governments are instituted, deriving their just powers from the consent of the governed."

The general words above quoted would seem to embrace the whole human family, and if they were used in a similar instrument at this day would be so understood. But it is too clear for dispute, that the enslaved African race were not intended to be included, and formed no part of the people who framed and adopted this declaration; for if the language, as understood in that day, would embrace them, the conduct of the distinguished men who framed the Declaration of Independence would have been utterly and flagrantly inconsistent with the principles they asserted; and instead of the sympathy of mankind, to which they so confidently appealed, they would have deserved and received universal rebuke and reprobation.

Yet the men who framed this declaration were great men—high in literary acquirements—high in their sense of honor, and incapable of asserting principles inconsistent with those on which they were acting. They perfectly understood the meaning of the language they used, and how it would be understood by others; and they knew that it would not in any part of the civilized world be supposed to embrace the negro race, which, by common consent, had been excluded from civilized Governments and the family of nations, and doomed to slavery. They spoke and acted according to the then established doctrines and principles, and in the ordinary language of the day, and no one misunderstood them. The unhappy black race were separated from the white by indelible marks, and laws long before established, and were never thought of or spoken of except as property, and when the claims of the owner or the profit of the trader were supposed to need protection.

This state of public opinion had undergone no change when the Constitution was adopted, as is equally evident from its provisions and language.

The brief preamble sets forth by whom it was formed, for what purposes, and for whose benefit and protection. It declares that it is formed by the *people* of the United States; that is to say, by those who were members of the different political communities in the several States; and its great object is declared to be to secure the blessings of liberty to themselves and their posterity. It speaks in general terms of the *people* of the United States, and of *citizens* of the several States, when it is providing for the exercise of

the powers granted or the privileges secured to the citizen. It does not define what description of persons are intended to be included under these terms, or who shall be regarded as a citizen and one of the people. It uses them as terms so well understood, that no further description or definition was necessary.

But there are two clauses in the Constitution which point directly and specifically to the negro race as a separate class of persons, and show clearly that they were not regarded as a portion of the people or citizens of the Government then formed.

One of these clauses reserves to each of the thirteen States the right to import slaves until the year 1808, if it thinks proper. And the importation which it thus sanctions was unquestionably of persons of the race of which we are speaking, as the traffic in slaves in the United States had always been confined to them. And by the other provision the States pledge themselves to each other to maintain the right of property of the master, by delivering up to him any slave who may have escaped from his service, and be found within their respective territories. By the first above-mentioned clause, therefore, the right to purchase and hold this property is directly sanctioned and authorized for twenty years by the people who framed the Constitution. And by the second, they pledge themselves to maintain and uphold the right of the master in the manner specified, as long as the Government they then formed should endure. And these two provisions show, conclusively, that neither the description of persons therein referred to, nor their descendants, were embraced in any of the other provisions of the Constitution; for certainly these two clauses were not intended to confer on them or their posterity the blessings of liberty, or any of the personal rights so carefully provided for the citizen.

No one of that race had ever migrated to the United States voluntarily; all of them had been brought here as articles of merchandise. The number that had been emancipated at that time were but few in comparison with those held in slavery; and they were identified in the public mind with the race to which they belonged, and regarded as a part of the slave population rather than the free. It is obvious that they were not even in the minds of the framers of the Constitution when they were conferring special rights and privileges upon the citizens of a State in every other part of the Union.

Indeed, when we look to the condition of this race in

the several States at the time, it is impossible to believe that these rights and privileges were intended to be extended to them.

It is very true, that in that portion of the Union where the labor of the negro race was found to be unsuited to the climate and unprofitable to the master, but few slaves were held at the time of the Declaration of Independence; and when the Constitution was adopted, it had entirely worn out in one of them, and measures had been taken for its gradual abolition in several others. But this change had not been produced by any change of opinion in relation to this race; but because it was discovered, from experience, that slave labor was unsuited to the climate and productions of these States: for some of the States, where it had ceased or nearly ceased to exist, were actively engaged in the slave trade, procuring cargoes on the coast of Africa, and transporting them for sale to those parts of the Union where their labor was found to be profitable, and suited to the climate and productions. And this traffic was openly carried on, and fortunes accumulated by it, without reproach from the people of the States where they resided. And it can hardly be supposed that, in the States where it was then countenanced in its worst form—that is, in the seizure and transportation—the people could have regarded those who were emancipated as entitled to equal rights with themselves.

And we may here again refer, in support of this proposition, to the plain and unequivocal language of the laws of the several States, some passed after the Declaration of Independence and before the Constitution was adopted, and some since the Government went into operation. . . .

Thus, Massachusetts, in 1786, passed a law similar to the colonial one of which we have spoken. The law of 1786, like the law of 1705, forbids the marriage of any white person with any negro, Indian, or mulatto, and inflicts a penalty of fifty pounds upon any one who shall join them in marriage; and declares all such marriages absolutely null and void, and degrades thus the unhappy issue of the marriage by fixing upon it the stain of bastardy. And this mark of degradation was renewed, and again impressed upon the race, in the careful and deliberate preparation of their revised code published in 1836. This code forbids any person from joining in marriage any white person with any Indian, negro, or mulatto, and subjects the party who shall offend in this respect, to imprisonment, not exceeding six months, in the common jail, or to hard labor, and to a fine

of not less than fifty nor more than two hundred dollars; and, like the law of 1786, it declares the marriage to be absolutely null and void. It will be seen that the punishment is increased by the code upon the person who shall marry them, by adding imprisonment to a pecuniary penalty.

So, too, in Connecticut. We refer more particularly to the legislation of this State, because it was not only among the first to put an end to slavery within its own territory, but was the first to fix a mark of reprobation upon the African slave trade. The law last mentioned was passed in October, 1788, about nine months after the State had ratified and adopted the present Constitution of the United States; and by that law it prohibited its own citizens, under severe penalties, from engaging in the trade, and declared all policies of insurance on the vessel or cargo made in the State to be null and void. But, up to the time of the adoption of the Constitution, there is nothing in the legislation of the State indicating any change of opinion as to the relative rights and position of the white and black races in this country, or indicating that it meant to place the latter, when free, upon a level with its citizens. And certainly nothing which would have led the slaveholding States to suppose, that Connecticut designed to claim for them, under the new Constitution, the equal rights and privileges and rank of citizens in every other State.

The first step taken by Connecticut upon this subject was as early as 1774, when it passed an act forbidding the further importation of slaves into the State. But the section containing the prohibition is introduced by the following preamble:

"And whereas the increase of slaves in this State is injurious to the poor, and inconvenient."

This recital would appear to have been carefully introduced, in order to prevent any misunderstanding of the motive which induced the Legislature to pass the law, and places it distinctly upon the interest and convenience of the white population—excluding the inference that it might have been intended in any degree for the benefit of the other.

And in the act of 1784, by which the issue of slaves, born after the time therein mentioned, were to be free at a certain age, the section is again introduced by a preamble assigning a similar motive for the act. It is in these words:

"Whereas sound policy requires that the abolition of slavery should be effected as soon as may be consistent with the rights of individuals, and the public safety and welfare"—showing that the right of property in the master was to be protected, and that the measure was one of policy, and to prevent the injury and inconvenience, to the whites, of a slave population in the State.

And still further pursuing its legislation, we find that in the same statute passed in 1774, which prohibited the further importation of slaves into the State, there is also a provision by which any negro, Indian, or mulatto servant, who was found wandering out of the town or place to which he belonged, without a written pass such as is therein described, was made liable to be seized by any one, and taken before the next authority to be examined and delivered up to his master—who was required to pay the charge which had accrued thereby. And a subsequent section of the same law provides, that if any free negro shall travel without such pass, and shall be stopped, seized, or taken up, he shall pay all charges arising thereby. And this law was in full operation when the Constitution of the United States was adopted, and was not repealed till 1797. So that up to that time free negroes and mulattoes were associated with servants and slaves in the police regulations established by the laws of the State.

And again, in 1833, Connecticut passed another law, which made it penal to set up or establish any school in that State for the instruction of persons of the African race not inhabitants of the State, or to instruct or teach in any such school or institution, or board or harbor for that purpose, any such person, without the previous consent in writing of the civil authority of the town in which such school or institution might be.

And it appears by the case of Crandall *v.* The State, reported in 10 Conn. Rep., 340, that upon an information filed against Prudence Crandall for a violation of this law, one of the points raised in the defence was, that the law was a violation of the Constitution of the United States; and that the persons instructed, although of the African race, were citizens of other States, and therefore entitled to the rights and privileges of citizens in the State of Connecticut. But Chief Justice Dagget, before whom the case was tried, held, that persons of that description were not citizens of a State, within the meaning of the word citizen in the Constitution of the United States, and were not therefore entitled to the privileges and immunities of citizens in other States. . . .

We have made this particular examination into the legislative and judicial action of Connecticut, because, from the early hostility it displayed to the slave trade on the coast of Africa, we may expect to find the laws of that State as lenient and favorable to the subject race as those of any other State in the Union; and if we find that at the time the Constitution was adopted, they were not even there raised to the rank of citizens, but were still held and treated as property, and the laws relating to them passed with reference altogether to the interest and convenience of the white race, we shall hardly find them elevated to a higher rank anywhere else.

A brief notice of the laws of two other States, and we shall pass on to other considerations.

By the laws of New Hampshire, collected and finally passed in 1815, no one was permitted to be enrolled in the militia of the State, but free white citizens; and the same provision is found in a subsequent collection of the laws, made in 1855. Nothing could more strongly mark the entire repudiation of the African race. The alien is excluded, because, being born in a foreign country, he cannot be a member of the community until he is naturalized. But why are the African race, born in the State, not permitted to share in one of the highest duties of the citizen? The answer is obvious; he is not, by the institutions and laws of the State, numbered among its people. He forms no part of the sovereignty of the State, and is not therefore called on to uphold and defend it.

Again, in 1822, Rhode Island, in its revised code, passed a law forbidding persons who were authorized to join persons in marriage, from joining in marriage any white person with any negro, Indian, or mulatto, under the penalty of two hundred dollars, and declaring all such marriages absolutely null and void; and the same law was again re-enacted in its revised code of 1844. So that, down to the last-mentioned period, the strongest mark of inferiority and degradation was fastened upon the African race in that State.

It would be impossible to enumerate and compress in the space usually allotted to an opinion of a court, the various laws, marking the condition of this race, which were passed from time to time after the Revolution, and before and since the adoption of the Constitution of the United States. In addition to those already referred to, it is sufficient to say, that Chancellor Kent, whose accuracy and research no one will question, states in the sixth edition of his Commentaries, (published in 1848, 2 vol., 258, note *b,*) that in no part of the country except Maine, did the African race, in point of fact, participate equally with the whites in the exercise of civil and political rights.

The legislation of the States therefore shows, in a manner not to be mistaken, the inferior and subject condition of that race at the time the Constitution was adopted, and long afterwards, throughout the thirteen States by which that instrument was framed; and it is hardly consistent with the respect due to these States, to suppose that they regarded at that time, as fellow-citizens and members of the sovereignty, a class of beings whom they had thus stigmatized; whom, as we are bound, out of respect to the State sovereignties, to assume they had deemed it just and necessary thus to stigmatize, and upon whom they had impressed such deep and enduring marks of inferiority and degradation; or, that when they met in convention to form the Constitution, they looked upon them as a portion of their constituents, or designed to include them in the provisions so carefully inserted for the security and protection of the liberties and rights of their citizens. It cannot be supposed that they intended to secure to them rights, and privileges, and rank, in the new political body throughout the Union, which every one of them denied within the limits of its own dominion. More especially, it cannot be believed that the large slaveholding States regarded them as included in the word citizens, or would have consented to a Constitution which might compel them to receive them in that character from another State. For if they were so received, and entitled to the privileges and immunities of citizens, it would exempt them from the operation of the special laws and from the police regulations which they considered to be necessary for their own safety. It would give to persons of the negro race, who were recognised as citizens in any one State of the Union, the right to enter every other State whenever they pleased, singly or in companies, without pass or passport, and without obstruction, to sojourn there as long as they pleased, to go where they pleased at every hour of the day or night without molestation, unless they committed some violation of law for which a white man would be punished; and it would give them the full liberty of speech in public and in private upon all subjects upon which its own citizens might speak; to hold public meetings upon political affairs, and to keep and carry arms wherever they went. And all of this would be done in the face of the subject race of the same color, both free and slaves, and inevitably producing discontent and insubordination among them, and endangering the peace and safety of the State.

It is impossible, it would seem, to believe that the great men of the slaveholding States, who took so large a share in framing the Constitution of the United States, and exercised so much influence in procuring its adoption, could have been so forgetful or regardless of their own safety and the safety of those who trusted and confided in them.

Besides, this want of foresight and care would have been utterly inconsistent with the caution displayed in providing for the admission of new members into this political family. For, when they gave to the citizens of each State the privileges and immunities of citizens in the several States, they at the same time took from the several States the power of naturalization, and confined that power exclusively to the Federal Government. No State was willing to permit another State to determine who should or should not be admitted as one of its citizens, and entitled to demand equal rights and privileges with their own people, within their own territories. The right of naturalization was therefore, with one accord, surrendered by the States, and confided to the Federal Government. And this power granted to Congress to establish an uniform rule of *naturalization* is, by the well-understood meaning of the word, confined to persons born in a foreign country, under a foreign Government. It is not a power to raise to the rank of a citizen any one born in the United States, who, from birth or parentage, by the laws of the country, belongs to an inferior and subordinate class. And when we find the States guarding themselves from the indiscreet or improper admission by other States of emigrants from other countries, by giving the power exclusively to Congress, we cannot fail to see that they could never have left with the States a much more important power—that is, the power of transforming into citizens a numerous class of persons, who in that character would be much more dangerous to the peace and safety of a large portion of the Union, than the few foreigners one of the States might improperly naturalize. The Constitution upon its adoption obviously took from the States all power by any subsequent legislation to introduce as a citizen into the political family of the United States any one, no matter where he was born, or what might be his character or condition; and it gave to Congress the power to confer this character upon those only who were born outside of the dominions of the United States. And no law of a State, therefore, passed since the Constitution was adopted, can give any right of citizenship outside of its own territory.

A clause similar to the one in the Constitution, in relation to the rights and immunities of citizens of one State in the other States, was contained in the Articles of Confederation. But there is a difference of language, which is worthy of note. The provision in the Articles of Confederation was, "that the *free inhabitants* of each of the States, paupers, vagabonds, and fugitives from justice, excepted, should be entitled to all the privileges and immunities of free citizens in the several States."

It will be observed, that under this Confederation, each State had the right to decide for itself, and in its own tribunals, whom it would acknowledge as a free inhabitant of another State. The term *free inhabitant,* in the generality of its terms, would certainly include one of the African race who had been manumitted. But no example, we think, can be found of his admission to all the privileges of citizenship in any State of the Union after these Articles were formed, and while they continued in force. And, notwithstanding the generality of the words "free inhabitants," it is very clear that, according to their accepted meaning in that day, they did not include the African race, whether free or not: for the fifth section of the ninth article provides that Congress should have the power "to agree upon the number of land forces to be raised, and to make requisitions from each State for its quota in proportion to the number of *white* inhabitants in such State, which requisition should be binding."

Words could hardly have been used which more strongly mark the line of distinction between the citizen and the subject; the free and the subjugated races. The latter were not even counted when the inhabitants of a State were to be embodied in proportion to its numbers for the general defence. And it cannot for a moment be supposed, that a class of persons thus separated and rejected from those who formed the sovereignty of the States, were yet intended to be included under the words "free inhabitants," in the preceding article, to whom privileges and immunities were so carefully secured in every State.

But although this clause of the Articles of Confederation is the same in principle with that inserted in the Constitution, yet the comprehensive word *inhabitant,* which might be construed to include an emancipated slave, is omitted; and the privilege is confined to *citizens* of the State. And this alteration in words would hardly have been made, unless a different meaning was intended to be conveyed, or a possible doubt removed. The just and fair inference is, that as this privilege was about to be placed under the protection of the General Government, and the words expounded by its tribunals, and all power in relation to it taken from the State and its courts, it was deemed prudent to describe with precision and caution the persons to whom this high privilege was given—and the word *citizen* was on that account substituted for the words *free inhabitant.* The word citizen excluded, and no doubt intended to exclude, foreigners who had not become citizens of some one of the States when the Constitution was adopted; and also every description of persons who were not fully recognised as citizens in the several States. This, upon any fair construction of the instruments to which we have referred, was evidently the object and purpose of this change of words.

To all this mass of proof we have still to add, that Congress has repeatedly legislated upon the same construction of the Constitution that we have given. Three laws, two of which were passed almost immediately after the Government went into operation, will be abundantly sufficient to show this. The two first are particularly worthy of notice, because many of the men who assisted in framing the Constitution, and took an active part in procuring its adoption, were then in the halls of legislation, and certainly understood what they meant when they used the words "people of the United States" and "citizen" in that well-considered instrument.

The first of these acts is the naturalization law, which was passed at the second session of the first Congress, March 26, 1790, and confines the right of becoming citizens *"to aliens being free white persons."*

Now, the Constitution does not limit the power of Congress in this respect to white persons. And they may, if they think proper, authorize the naturalization of any one, of any color, who was born under allegiance to another Government. But the language of the law above quoted, shows that citizenship at that time was perfectly understood to be confined to the white race; and that they alone constituted the sovereignty in the Government.

Congress might, as we before said, have authorized the naturalization of Indians, because they were aliens and foreigners. But, in their then untutored and savage state, no one would have thought of admitting them as citizens in a civilized community. And, moreover, the atrocities they had but recently committed, when they were the allies of Great Britain in the Revolutionary war, were yet fresh in the recollection of the people of the United States, and they were even then guarding themselves against the threatened renewal of Indian hostilities. No one supposed then that any Indian would ask for, or was capable of enjoying, the privileges of an American citizen, and the word white was not used with any particular reference to them.

Neither was it used with any reference to the African race imported into or born in this country; because Congress had no power to naturalize them, and therefore there was no necessity for using particular words to exclude them.

It would seem to have been used merely because it followed out the line of division which the Constitution has drawn between the citizen race, who formed and held the Government, and the African race, which they held in subjection and slavery, and governed at their own pleasure.

Another of the early laws of which we have spoken, is the first militia law, which was passed in 1792, at the first session of the second Congress. The language of this law is equally plain and significant with the one just mentioned. It directs that every "free able-bodied white male citizen" shall be enrolled in the militia. The word *white* is evidently used to exclude the African race, and the word "citizen" to exclude unnaturalized foreigners; the latter forming no part of the sovereignty, owing it no allegiance, and therefore under no obligation to defend it. The African race, however, born in the country, did owe allegiance to the Government, whether they were slave or free; but it is repudiated, and rejected from the duties and obligations of citizenship in marked language.

The third act to which we have alluded is even still more decisive; it was passed as late as 1813, (2 Stat., 809,) and it provides: "That from and after the termination of the war in which the United States are now engaged with Great Britain, it shall not be lawful to employ, on board of any public or private vessels of the United States, any person or persons except citizens of the United States, *or* persons of color, natives of the United States."

Here the line of distinction is drawn in express words.

Persons of color, in the judgment of Congress, were not included in the word citizens, and they are described as another and different class of persons, and authorized to be employed, if born in the United States.

And even as late as 1820, (chap. 104, sec. 8,) in the charter to the city of Washington, the corporation is authorized "to restrain and prohibit the nightly and other disorderly meetings of slaves, free negroes, and mulattoes," thus associating them together in its legislation; and after prescribing the punishment that may be inflicted on the slaves, proceeds in the following words: "And to punish such free negroes and mulattoes by penalties not exceeding twenty dollars for any one offence; and in case of the inability of any such free negro or mulatto to pay any such penalty and cost thereon, to cause him or her to be confined to labor for any time not exceeding six calendar months." And in a subsequent part of the same section, the act authorizes the corporation "to prescribe the terms and conditions upon which free negroes and mulattoes may reside in the city."

This law, like the laws of the States, shows that this class of persons were governed by special legislation directed expressly to them, and always connected with provisions for the government of slaves, and not with those for the government of free white citizens. And after such an uniform course of legislation as we have stated, by the colonies, by the States, and by Congress, running through a period of more than a century, it would seem that to call persons thus marked and stigmatized, "citizens" of the United States, "fellow-citizens," a constituent part of the sovereignty, would be an abuse of terms, and not calculated to exalt the character of an American citizen in the eyes of other nations.

The conduct of the Executive Department of the Government has been in perfect harmony upon this subject with this course of legislation. The question was brought officially before the late William Wirt, when he was the Attorney General of the United States, in 1821, and he decided that the words "citizens of the United States" were used in the acts of Congress in the same sense as in the Constitution; and that free persons of color were not citizens, within the meaning of the Constitution and laws; and this opinion has been confirmed by that of the late Attorney General, Caleb Cushing, in a recent case, and acted upon by the Secretary of State, who refused to grant passports to them as "citizens of the United States."

But it is said that a person may be a citizen, and entitled to that character, although he does not possess all the rights which may belong to other citizens; as, for example, the right to vote, or to hold particular offices; and that yet, when he goes into another State, he is entitled to be recognised there as a citizen, although the State may measure his rights by the rights which it allows to persons of a like character or class resident in the State, and refuse to him the full rights of citizenship.

This argument overlooks the language of the provision in the Constitution of which we are speaking.

Undoubtedly, a person may be a citizen, that is, a member of the community who form the sovereignty, although he exercises no share of the political power, and is incapacitated from holding particular offices. Women and minors, who form a part of the political family, cannot vote; and when a property qualification is required to vote or hold a particular office, those who have not the necessary qualification cannot vote or hold the office, yet they are citizens.

So, too, a person may be entitled to vote by the law of the State, who is not a citizen even of the State itself. And in some of the States of the Union foreigners not naturalized are allowed to vote. And the State may give the right to free negroes and mulattoes, but that does not make them citizens of the State, and still less of the United States. And the provision in the Constitution giving privileges and immunities in other States, does not apply to them.

Neither does it apply to a person who, being the citizen of a State, migrates to another State. For then he becomes subject to the laws of the State in which he lives, and he is no longer a citizen of the State from which he removed. And the State in which he resides may then, unquestionably, determine his *status* or condition, and place him among the class of persons who are not recognised as citizens, but belong to an inferior and subject race; and may deny him the privileges and immunities enjoyed by its citizens.

But so far as mere rights of person are concerned, the provision in question is confined to citizens of a State who are temporarily in another State without taking up their residence there. It gives them no political rights in the State, as to voting or holding office, or in any other respect. For a citizen of one State has no right to participate in the government of another. But if he ranks as a citizen in the State to which he belongs, within the meaning of the Constitution of the United States, then, whenever he goes into another State, the Constitution clothes him, as to the rights of person, with all the privileges and immunities which belong to citizens of the State. And if persons of the African race are citizens of a State, and of the United States, they would be entitled to all of these privileges and immunities in every State, and the State could not restrict them; for they would hold these privileges and immunities under the paramount authority of the Federal Government, and its courts would be bound to maintain and enforce them, the Constitution and laws of the State to the contrary notwithstanding. And if the States could limit or restrict them, or place the party in an inferior grade, this clause of the Constitution would be unmeaning, and could have no operation; and would give no rights to the citizen when in another State. He would have none but what the State itself chose to allow him. This is evidently not the construction or meaning of the clause in question. It guaranties rights to the citizen, and the State cannot withhold them. And these rights are of a character and would lead to consequences which make it absolutely certain that the African race were not included under the name of citizens of a State, and were not in the contemplation of the framers of the Constitution when these privileges and immunities were provided for the protection of the citizen in other States.

The case of Legrand *v.* Darnall (2 Peters, 664) has been referred to for the purpose of showing that this court has decided that the descendant of a slave may sue as a citizen in a court of the United States; but the case itself shows that the question did not arise and could not have arisen in the case.

It appears from the report, that Darnall was born in Maryland, and was the son of a white man by one of his slaves, and his father executed certain instruments to manumit him, and devised to him some landed property in the State. This property Darnall afterwards sold to Legrand, the appellant, who gave his notes for the purchase-money. But becoming afterwards apprehensive that the appellee had not been emancipated according to the laws of Maryland, he refused to pay the notes until he could be better satisfied as to Darnall's right to convey. Darnall, in the mean time, had taken up his residence in Pennsylvania, and brought suit on the notes, and recovered judgment in the Circuit Court for the district of Maryland.

The whole proceeding, as appears by the report, was an

amicable one; Legrand being perfectly willing to pay the money, if he could obtain a title, and Darnall not wishing him to pay unless he could make him a good one. In point of fact, the whole proceeding was under the direction of the counsel who argued the case for the appellee, who was the mutual friend of the parties, and confided in by both of them, and whose only object was to have the rights of both parties established by judicial decision in the most speedy and least expensive manner.

Legrand, therefore, raised no objection to the jurisdiction of the court in the suit at law, because he was himself anxious to obtain the judgment of the court upon his title. Consequently, there was nothing in the record before the court to show that Darnall was of African descent, and the usual judgment and award of execution was entered. And Legrand thereupon filed his bill on the equity side of the Circuit Court, stating that Darnall was born a slave, and had not been legally emancipated, and could not therefore take the land devised to him, nor make Legrand a good title; and praying an injunction to restrain Darnall from proceeding to execution on the judgment, which was granted. Darnall answered, averring in his answer that he was a free man, and capable of conveying a good title. Testimony was taken on this point, and at the hearing the Circuit Court was of opinion that Darnall was a free man and his title good, and dissolved the injunction and dismissed the bill; and that decree was affirmed here, upon the appeal of Legrand.

Now, it is difficult to imagine how any question about the citizenship of Darnall, or his right to sue in that character, can be supposed to have arisen or been decided in that case. The fact that he was of African descent was first brought before the court upon the bill in equity. The suit at law had then passed into judgment and award of execution, and the Circuit Court, as a court of law, had no longer any authority over it. It was a valid and legal judgment, which the court that rendered it had not the power to reverse or set aside. And unless it had jurisdiction as a court of equity to restrain him from using its process as a court of law, Darnall, if he thought proper, would have been at liberty to proceed on his judgment, and compel the payment of the money, although the allegations in the bill were true, and he was incapable of making a title. No other court could have enjoined him, for certainly no State equity court could interfere in that way with the judgment of a Circuit Court of the United States.

But the Circuit Court as a court of equity certainly had equity jurisdiction over its own judgment as a court of law, without regard to the character of the parties; and had not only the right, but it was its duty—no matter who were the parties in the judgment—to prevent them from proceeding to enforce it by execution, if the court was satisfied that the money was not justly and equitably due. The ability of Darnall to convey did not depend upon his citizenship, but upon his title to freedom. And if he was free, he could hold and convey property, by the laws of Maryland, although he was not a citizen. But if he was by law still a slave, he could not. It was therefore the duty of the court, sitting as a court of equity in the latter case, to prevent him from using its process, as a court of common law, to compel the payment of the purchase-money, when it was evident that the purchaser must lose the land. But if he was free, and could make a title, it was equally the duty of the court not to suffer Legrand to keep the land, and refuse the payment of the money, upon the ground that Darnall was incapable of suing or being sued as a citizen in a court of the United States. The character or citizenship of the parties had no connection with the question of jurisdiction, and the matter in dispute had no relation to the citizenship of Darnall. Nor is such a question alluded to in the opinion of the court.

Besides, we are by no means prepared to say that there are not many cases, civil as well as criminal, in which a Circuit Court of the United States may exercise jurisdiction, although one of the African race is a party; that broad question is not before the court. The question with which we are now dealing is, whether a person of the African race can be a citizen of the United States, and become thereby entitled to a special privilege, by virtue of his title to that character, and which, under the Constitution, no one but a citizen can claim. It is manifest that the case of Legrand and Darnall has no bearing on that question, and can have no application to the case now before the court.

This case, however, strikingly illustrates the consequences that would follow the construction of the Constitution which would give the power contended for to a State. It would in effect give it also to an individual. For if the father of young Darnall had manumitted him in his lifetime, and sent him to reside in a State which recognised him as a citizen, he might have visited and sojourned in Maryland when he pleased, and as long as he pleased, as a citizen of the United States; and the State officers and tribunals would be compelled, by the paramount authority of the Constitution, to receive him and treat him as one of its citizens, exempt from the laws and police of the State in relation to a person of that description, and allow him to enjoy all the rights and privileges of citizenship, without respect to the laws of Maryland, although such laws were deemed by it absolutely essential to its own safety.

The only two provisions which point to them and include them, treat them as property, and make it the duty of the Government to protect it; no other power, in relation to this race, is to be found in the Constitution; and as it is a Government of special, delegated, powers, no authority beyond these two provisions can be constitutionally exercised. The Government of the United States had no right to interfere for any other purpose but that of protecting the rights of the owner, leaving it altogether with the several States to deal with this race, whether emancipated or not, as each State may think justice, humanity, and the interests and safety of society, require. The States evidently intended to reserve this power exclusively to themselves.

No one, we presume, supposes that any change in public opinion or feeling, in relation to this unfortunate race, in the civilized nations of Europe or in this country, should induce the court to give to the words of the Constitution a more liberal construction in their favor than they were intended to bear when the instrument was framed and adopted. Such an argument would be altogether inadmissible in any tribunal called on to interpret it. If any of its provisions are deemed unjust, there is a mode prescribed in the instrument itself by which it may be amended; but while it remains unaltered, it must be construed now as it was understood at the time of its adoption. It is not only the same in words, but the same in meaning, and delegates the same powers to the Government, and reserves and secures the same rights and privileges to the citizen; and as long as it continues to exist in its present form, it speaks not only in the same words, but with the same meaning and intent with which it spoke when it came from the hands of its framers, and was voted on and adopted by the people of the United States. Any other rule of construction would abrogate the judicial character of this court, and make it the mere reflex of the popular opinion or passion of the day. This court was not created by the Constitution for such purposes. Higher and graver trusts have been confided to it, and it must not falter in the path of duty.

What the construction was at that time, we think can hardly admit of doubt. We have the language of the Declaration of Independence and of the Articles of Confederation, in addition to the plain words of the Constitution itself; we have the legislation of the different States, before, about the time, and since, the Constitution was adopted; we have the legislation of Congress, from the time of its adoption to a recent period; and we have the constant and uniform action of the Executive Department, all concurring together, and leading to the same result. And if anything in relation to the construction of the Constitution can be regarded as settled, it is that which we now give to the word "citizen" and the word "people."

And upon a full and careful consideration of the subject, the court is of opinion, that, upon the facts stated in the plea in abatement, Dred Scott was not a citizen of Missouri within the meaning of the Constitution of the United States, and not entitled as such to sue in its courts; and, consequently, that the Circuit Court had no jurisdiction of the case, and that the judgment on the plea in abatement is erroneous.

We are aware that doubts are entertained by some of the members of the court, whether the plea in abatement is legally before the court upon this writ of error; but if that plea is regarded as waived, or out of the case upon any other ground, yet the question as to the jurisdiction of the Circuit Court is presented on the face of the bill of exception itself, taken by the plaintiff at the trial; for he admits that he and his wife were born slaves, but endeavors to make out his title to freedom and citizenship by showing that they were taken by their owner to certain places, hereinafter mentioned, where slavery could not by law exist, and that they thereby became free, and upon their return to Missouri became citizens of that State.

Now, if the removal of which he speaks did not give them their freedom, then by his own admission he is still a slave; and whatever opinions may be entertained in favor of the citizenship of a free person of the African race, no one supposes that a slave is a citizen of the State or of the United States. If, therefore, the acts done by his owner did not make them free persons, he is still a slave, and certainly incapable of suing in the character of a citizen.

The principle of law is too well settled to be disputed, that a court can give no judgment for either party, where it has no jurisdiction; and if, upon the showing of Scott himself, it appeared that he was still a slave, the case ought to have been dismissed, and the judgment against him and in favor of the defendant for costs, is, like that on the plea in abatement, erroneous, and the suit ought to have been dismissed by the Circuit Court for want of jurisdiction in that court. . . .

The case, as he himself states it, on the record brought here by his writ of error, is this:

The plaintiff was a negro slave, belonging to Dr. Emerson, who was a surgeon in the army of the United States. In the year 1834, he took the plaintiff from the State of Missouri to the military post at Rock Island, in the State of Illinois, and held him there as a slave until the month of April or May, 1836. At the time last mentioned, said Dr. Emerson removed the plaintiff from said military post at Rock Island to the military post at Fort Snelling, situate on the west bank of the Mississippi river, in the Territory known as Upper Louisiana, acquired by the United States of France, and situate north of the latitude of thirty-six degrees thirty minutes north, and north of the State of Missouri. Said Dr. Emerson held the plaintiff in slavery at said Fort Snelling, from said last-mentioned date until the year 1838.

In the year 1835, Harriet, who is named in the second count of the plaintiff's declaration, was the negro slave of Major Taliaferro, who belonged to the army of the United States. In that year, 1835, said Major Taliaferro took said Harriet to said Fort Snelling, a military post, situated as hereinbefore stated, and kept her there as a slave until the year 1836, and then sold and delivered her as a slave, at said Fort Snelling, unto the said Dr. Emerson hereinbefore named. Said Dr. Emerson held said Harriet in slavery at said Fort Snelling until the year 1838.

In the year 1836, the plaintiff and Harriet intermarried, at Fort Snelling, with the consent of Dr. Emerson, who then claimed to be their master and owner. Eliza and Lizzie, named in the third count of the plaintiff's declaration, are the fruit of that marriage. Eliza is about fourteen years old, and was born on board the steamboat Gipsey, north of the north line of the State of Missouri, and upon the river Mississippi. Lizzie is about seven years old, and was born in the State of Missouri, at the military post called Jefferson Barracks.

In the year 1838, said Dr. Emerson removed the plaintiff and said Harriet, and their said daughter Eliza, from said Fort Snelling to the State of Missouri, where they have ever since resided.

Before the commencement of this suit, said Dr. Emerson sold and conveyed the plaintiff, and Harriet, Eliza, and Lizzie, to the defendant, as slaves, and the defendant has ever since claimed to hold them, and each of them, as slaves.

In considering this part of the controversy, two questions arise: 1. Was he, together with his family, free in Missouri by reason of the stay in the territory of the United States hereinbefore mentioned? And 2. If they were not, is Scott himself free by reason of his removal to Rock Island, in the State of Illinois, as stated in the above admissions?

We proceed to examine the first question.

The act of Congress, upon which the plaintiff relies, declares that slavery and involuntary servitude, except as a punishment for crime, shall be forever prohibited in all that part of the territory ceded by France, under the name of Louisiana, which lies north of thirty-six degrees thirty minutes north latitude, and not included within the limits of Missouri. And the difficulty which meets us at the threshold of this part of the inquiry is, whether Congress was authorized to pass this law under any of the powers granted to it by the Constitution; for if the authority is not given by that instrument, it is the duty of this court to declare it void and inoperative, and incapable of conferring freedom upon any one who is held as a slave under the laws of any one of the States.

The counsel for the plaintiff has laid much stress upon that article in the Constitution which confers on Congress the power "to dispose of and make all needful rules and regulations respecting the territory or other property belonging to the United States;" but, in the judgment of the court, that provision has no bearing on the present controversy, and the power there given, whatever it may be, is confined, and was intended to be confined, to the territory which at that time belonged to, or was claimed by, the United States, and was within their boundaries as settled by the treaty with Great Britain, and can have no influence upon a territory afterwards acquired from a foreign Government. It was a special provision for a known and particular territory, and to meet a present emergency, and nothing more. . . .

The Constitution has always been remarkable for the felicity of its arrangement of different subjects, and the perspicuity and appropriateness of the language it uses. But if this clause is construed to extend to territory acquired by the present Government from a foreign nation, outside of the limits of any charter from the British Government to a colony, it would be difficult to say, why it was deemed necessary to give the Government the power to sell any vacant lands belonging to the sovereignty which might be found within it; and if this was necessary, why the grant of this power should precede the power to legislate over it and establish a Government there; and still more difficult to say, why it was deemed necessary so specially and particularly to grant the power to make needful rules and regulations in relation to any personal or movable property it might acquire there. For the words, *other property* necessarily, by every known rule of interpretation, must mean property of a different description from territory or land. And the difficulty would perhaps be insurmountable in endeavoring to account for the last member of the sentence, which provides that "nothing in this Constitution shall be so construed as to prejudice any claims of the United States or any particular State," or to say how any particular State could have claims in or to a territory ceded by a foreign Government, or to account for associating this provision with the preceding provisions of the clause, with which it would appear to have no connection.

The words "needful rules and regulations" would seem, also, to have been cautiously used for some definite object. They are not the words usually employed by statesmen, when they mean to give the powers of sovereignty, or to establish a Government, or to authorize its establishment. Thus, in the law to renew and keep alive the ordinance of 1787, and to reestablish the Government, the title of the law is: "An act to provide for the government of the territory northwest of the river Ohio." And in the Constitution, when granting the power to legislate over the territory that may be selected for the seat of Government independently of a State, it does not say Congress shall have power "to make all needful rules and regulations respecting the territory"; but it declares that "Congress shall have power to exercise exclusive legislation in all cases whatsoever over such District (not exceeding ten miles square) as may, by cession of particular States and the acceptance of Congress, become the seat of the Government of the United States."

The words "rules and regulations" are usually employed in the Constitution in speaking of some particular specified power which it means to confer on the Government, and not, as we have seen, when granting general powers of legislation. As, for example, in the particular power to Congress "to make rules for the government and regulation of the land and naval forces, or the particular and specific power to regulate commerce"; "to establish an uniform

rule of naturalization"; "to coin money and *regulate* the value thereof." And to construe the words of which we are speaking as a general and unlimited grant of sovereignty over territories which the Government might afterwards acquire, is to use them in a sense and for a purpose for which they were not used in any other part of the instrument. But if confined to a particular Territory, in which a Government and laws had already been established, but which would require some alterations to adapt it to the new Government, the words are peculiarly applicable and appropriate for that purpose.

The necessity of this special provision in relation to property and the rights or property held in common by the confederated States, is illustrated by the first clause of the sixth article. This clause provides that "all debts, contracts, and engagements entered into before the adoption of this Constitution, shall be as valid against the United States under this Government as under the Confederation." This provision, like the one under consideration, was indispensable if the new Constitution was adopted. The new Government was not a mere change in a dynasty, or in a form of government, leaving the nation or sovereignty the same, and clothed with all the rights, and bound by all the obligations of the preceding one. But, when the present United States came into existence under the new Government, it was a new political body, a new nation, then for the first time taking its place in the family of nations. It took nothing by succession from the Confederation. It had no right, as its successor, to any property or rights of property which it had acquired, and was not liable for any of its obligations. It was evidently viewed in this light by the framers of the Constitution. And as the several States would cease to exist in their former confederated character upon the adoption of the Constitution, and could not, in that character, again assemble together, special provisions were indispensable to transfer to the new Government the property and rights which at that time they held in common; and at the same time to authorize it to lay taxes and appropriate money to pay the common debt which they had contracted; and this power could only be given to it by special provisions in the Constitution. The clause in relation to the territory and other property of the United States provided for the first, and the clause last quoted provided for the other. They have no connection with the general powers and rights of sovereignty delegated to the new Government, and can neither enlarge nor diminish them. They were inserted to meet a present emergency, and not to regulate its powers as a Government.

Indeed, a similar provision was deemed necessary, in relation to treaties made by the Confederation; and when in the clause next succeeding the one of which we have last spoken, it is declared that treaties shall be the supreme law of the land, care is taken to include, by express words, the treaties made by the confederated States. The language is: "and all treaties made, or which shall be made, under the authority of the United States, shall be the supreme law of the land."

Whether, therefore, we take the particular clause in question, by itself, or in connection with the other provisions of the Constitution, we think it clear, that it applies only to the particular territory of which we have spoken, and cannot, by any just rule of interpretation, be extended to territory which the new Government might afterwards obtain from a foreign nation. Consequently, the power which Congress may have lawfully exercised in this Territory, while it remained under a Territorial Government, and which may have been sanctioned by judicial decision, can furnish no justification and no argument to support a similar exercise of power over territory afterwards acquired by the Federal Government. We put aside, therefore, any argument, drawn from precedents, showing the extent of the power which the General Government exercised over slavery in this Territory, as altogether inapplicable to the case before us. . . .

This brings us to examine by what provision of the Constitution the present Federal Government, under its delegated and restricted powers, is authorized to acquire territory outside of the original limits of the United States, and what powers it may exercise therein over the person or property of a citizen of the United States, while it remains a Territory, and until it shall be admitted as one of the States of the Union.

There is certainly no power given by the Constitution to the Federal Government to establish or maintain colonies bordering on the United States or at a distance, to be ruled and governed at its own pleasure; nor to enlarge its territorial limits in any way, except by the admission of new States. That power is plainly given; and if a new State is admitted, it needs no further legislation by Congress, because the Constitution itself defines the relative rights and powers, and duties of the State, and the citizens of the State, and the Federal Government. But no power is given

to acquire a Territory to be held and governed permanently in that character.

And indeed the power exercised by Congress to acquire territory and establish a Government there, according to its own unlimited discretion, was viewed with great jealousy by the leading statesmen of the day. And in the Federalist, (No. 38,) written by Mr. Madison, he speaks of the acquisition of the Northwestern Territory by the confederated States, by the cession from Virginia, and the establishment of a Government there, as an exercise of power not warranted by the Articles of Confederation, and dangerous to the liberties of the people. And he urges the adoption of the Constitution as a security and safeguard against such an exercise of power.

We do not mean, however, to question the power of Congress in this respect. The power to expand the territory of the United States by the admission of new States is plainly given; and in the construction of this power by all the departments of the Government, it has been held to authorize the acquisition of territory, not fit for admission at the time, but to be admitted as soon as its population and situation would entitle it to admission. It is acquired to become a State, and not to be held as a colony and governed by Congress with absolute authority; and as the propriety of admitting a new State is committed to the sound discretion of Congress, the power to acquire territory for that purpose, to be held by the United States until it is in a suitable condition to become a State upon an equal footing with the other States, must rest upon the same discretion. It is a question for the political department of the Government, and not the judicial; and whatever the political department of the Government shall recognise as within the limits of the United States, the judicial department is also bound to recognise, and to administer in it the laws of the United States, so far as they apply, and to maintain in the Territory the authority and rights of the Government and also the personal rights and rights of property of individual citizens, as secured by the Constitution. All we mean to say on this point is, that, as there is no express regulation in the Constitution defining the power which the General Government may exercise over the person or property of a citizen in a Territory thus acquired, the court must necessarily look to the provisions and principles of the Constitution, and its distribution of powers, for the rules and principles by which its decision must be governed.

Taking this rule to guide us, it may be safely assumed

that citizens of the United States who migrate to a Territory belonging to the people of the United States, cannot be ruled as mere colonists, dependent upon the will of the General Government, and to be governed by any laws it may think proper to impose. The principle upon which our Governments rest, and upon which alone they continue to exist, is the union of States, sovereign and independent within their own limits in their internal and domestic concerns, and bound together as one people by a General Government, possessing certain enumerated and restricted powers, delegated to it by the people of the several States, and exercising supreme authority within the scope of the powers granted to it, throughout the dominion of the United States. A power, therefore, in the General Government to obtain and hold colonies and dependent territories, over which they might legislate without restriction, would be inconsistent with its own existence in its present form. Whatever it acquires, it acquires for the benefit of the people of the several States who created it. It is their trustee acting for them, and charged with the duty of promoting the interests of the whole people of the Union in the exercise of the powers specifically granted.

At the time when the Territory in question was obtained by cession from France, it contained no population fit to be associated together and admitted as a State; and it therefore was absolutely necessary to hold possession of it, as a Territory belonging to the United States, until it was settled and inhabited by a civilized community capable of self-government, and in a condition to be admitted on equal terms with the other States as a member of the Union. But, as we have before said, it was acquired by the General Government, as the representative and trustee of the people of the United States, and it must therefore be held in that character for their common and equal benefit; for it was the people of the several States, acting through their agent and representative, the Federal Government, who in fact acquired the Territory in question, and the Government holds it for their common use until it shall be associated with the other States as a member of the Union.

But until that time arrives, it is undoubtedly necessary that some Government should be established, in order to organize society, and to protect the inhabitants in their persons and property; and as the people of the United States could act in this matter only through the Government which represented them, and through which they spoke

and acted when the Territory was obtained, it was not only within the scope of its powers, but it was its duty to pass such laws and establish such a Government as would enable those by whose authority they acted to reap the advantages anticipated from its acquisition, and to gather there a population which would enable it to assume the position to which it was destined among the States of the Union. The power to acquire necessarily carries with it the power to preserve and apply to the purposes for which it was acquired. The form of government to be established necessarily rested in the discretion of Congress. It was their duty to establish the one that would be best suited for the protection and security of the citizens of the United States, and other inhabitants who might be authorized to take up their abode there, and that must always depend upon the existing condition of the Territory, as to the number and character of its inhabitants, and their situation in the Territory. In some cases a Government, consisting of persons appointed by the Federal Government, would best subserve the interests of the Territory, when the inhabitants were few and scattered, and new to one another. In other instances, it would be more advisable to commit the powers of self-government to the people who had settled in the Territory, as being the most competent to determine what was best for their own interests. But some form of civil authority would be absolutely necessary to organize and preserve civilized society, and prepare it to become a State; and what is the best form must always depend on the condition of the Territory at the time, and the choice of the mode must depend upon the exercise of a discretionary power by Congress, acting within the scope of its constitutional authority, and not infringing upon the rights of person or rights of property of the citizen who might go there to reside, or for any other lawful purpose. It was acquired by the exercise of this discretion, and it must be held and governed in like manner, until it is fitted to be a State.

But the power of Congress over the person or property of a citizen can never be a mere discretionary power under our Constitution and form of Government. The powers of the Government and the rights and privileges of the citizen are regulated and plainly defined by the Constitution itself. And when the Territory becomes a part of the United States, the Federal Government enters into possession in the character impressed upon it by those who created it. It enters upon it with its powers over the citizen strictly defined, and limited by the Constitution, from which it derives its own existence, and by virtue of which alone it continues to exist and act as a Government and sovereignty. It has no power of any kind beyond it; and it cannot, when it enters a Territory of the United States, put off its character, and assume discretionary or despotic powers which the Constitution has denied to it. It cannot create for itself a new character separated from the citizens of the United States, and the duties it owes them under the provisions of the Constitution. The Territory being a part of the United States, the Government and the citizen both enter it under the authority of the Constitution, with their respective rights defined and marked out; and the Federal Government can exercise no power over his person or property, beyond what that instrument confers, nor lawfully deny any right which it has reserved.

A reference to a few of the provisions of the Constitution will illustrate this proposition.

For example, no one, we presume, will contend that Congress can make any law in a Territory respecting the establishment of religion, or the free exercise thereof, or abridging the freedom of speech or of the press, or the right of the people of the Territory peaceably to assemble, and to petition the Government for the redress of grievances.

Nor can Congress deny to the people the right to keep and bear arms, nor the right to trial by jury, nor compel any one to be a witness against himself in a criminal proceeding.

These powers, and others, in relation to rights of person, which it is not necessary here to enumerate, are, in express and positive terms, denied to the General Government; and the rights of private property have been guarded with equal care. Thus the rights of property are united with the rights of person, and placed on the same ground by the fifth amendment to the Constitution, which provides that no person shall be deprived of life, liberty, and property, without due process of law. And an act of Congress which deprives a citizen of the United States of his liberty or property, merely because he came himself or brought his property into a particular Territory of the United States, and who had committed no offence against the laws, could hardly be dignified with the name of due process of law.

So, too, it will hardly be contended that Congress could by law quarter a soldier in a house in a Territory without the consent of the owner, in time of peace; nor in time of war, but in a manner prescribed by law. Nor could they by law forfeit the property of a citizen in a Territory who was convicted of treason, for a longer period than the life of the person convicted; nor take private property for public use without just compensation.

The powers over person and property of which we speak are not only not granted to Congress, but are in express terms denied, and they are forbidden to exercise them. And this prohibition is not confined to the States, but the words are general, and extend to the whole territory over which the Constitution gives it power to legislate, including those portions of it remaining under Territorial Government, as well as that covered by States. It is a total absence of power everywhere within the dominion of the United States, and places the citizens of a Territory, so far as these rights are concerned, on the same footing with citizens of the States, and guards them as firmly and plainly against any inroads which the General Government might attempt, under the plea of implied or incidental powers. And if Congress itself cannot do this—if it is beyond the powers conferred on the Federal Government—it will be admitted, we presume, that it could not authorize a Territorial Government to exercise them. It could confer no power on any local Government, established by its authority, to violate the provisions of the Constitution.

It seems, however, to be supposed, that there is a difference between property in a slave and other property, and that different rules may be applied to it in expounding the Constitution of the United States. And the laws and usages of nations, and the writings of eminent jurists upon the relation of master and slave and their mutual rights and duties, and the powers which Governments may exercise over it, have been dwelt upon in the argument.

But in considering the question before us, it must be borne in mind that there is no law of nations standing between the people of the United States and their Government, and interfering with their relation to each other. The powers of the Government, and the rights of the citizen under it, are positive and practical regulations plainly written down. The people of the United States have delegated to it certain enumerated powers, and forbidden it to exercise others. It has no power over the person or property of a citizen but what the citizens of the United States have granted. And no laws or usages of other nations, or reasoning of statesmen or jurists upon the relations of master and slave, can enlarge the powers of the Government, or take from the citizens the rights they have reserved. And if the Constitution recognises the right of property of the master in a slave, and makes no distinction between that description of property and other property owned by a citizen, no tribunal, acting under the authority of the United States, whether it be legislative, executive, or judicial, has a right to draw such a distinction, or deny to it the benefit of the provisions and guarantees which have been provided for the protection of private property against the encroachments of the Government.

Now, as we have already said in an earlier part of this opinion, upon a different point, the right of property in a slave is distinctly and expressly affirmed in the Constitution. The right to traffic in it, like an ordinary article of merchandise and property, was guarantied to the citizens of the United States, in every State that might desire it, for twenty years. And the Government in express terms is pledged to protect it in all future time, if the slave escapes from his owner. This is done in plain words—too plain to be misunderstood. And no word can be found in the Constitution which gives Congress a greater power over slave property, or which entitles property of that kind to less protection than property of any other description. The only power conferred is the power coupled with the duty of guarding and protecting the owner in his rights.

Upon these considerations, it is the opinion of the court that the act of Congress which prohibited a citizen from holding and owning property of this kind in the territory of the United States north of the line therein mentioned, is not warranted by the Constitution, and is therefore void; and that neither Dred Scott himself, nor any of his family, were made free by being carried into this territory; even if they had been carried there by the owner, with the intention of becoming a permanent resident.

We have so far examined the case, as it stands under the Constitution of the United States, and the powers thereby delegated to the Federal Government.

But there is another point in the case which depends on State power and State law. And it is contended, on the part of the plaintiff, that he is made free by being taken to Rock Island, in the State of Illinois, independently of his residence in the territory of the United States; and being so made free, he was not again reduced to a state of slavery by being brought back to Missouri.

Our notice of this part of the case will be very brief; for the principle on which it depends was decided in this court, upon much consideration, in the case of Strader et al. *v.* Graham, reported in 10th Howard, 82. In that case, the slaves had been taken from Kentucky to Ohio, with the consent of the owner, and afterwards brought back to Kentucky. And this court held that their *status* or condition, as free or slave, depended upon the laws of Kentucky, when they were brought back into that State, and not of Ohio; and that this court had no jurisdiction to revise the judgment of a State court upon its own laws. This was the point directly before the court, and the decision that this court had not jurisdiction turned upon it, as will be seen by the report of the case.

So in this case. As Scott was a slave when taken into the State of Illinois by his owner, and was there held as such, and brought back in that character, his *status,* as free or slave, depended on the laws of Missouri, and not of Illinois.

It has, however, been urged in the argument, that by the laws of Missouri he was free on his return, and that this case, therefore, cannot be governed by the case of Strader et al. *v.* Graham, where it appeared, by the laws of Kentucky, that the plaintiffs continued to be slaves on their return from Ohio. But whatever doubts or opinions may, at one time, have been entertained upon this subject, we are satisfied, upon a careful examination of all the cases decided in the State courts of Missouri referred to, that it is now firmly settled by the decisions of the highest court in the State, that Scott and his family upon their return were not free, but were, by the laws of Missouri, the property of the defendant; and that the Circuit Court of the United States had no jurisdiction, when, by the laws of the State, the plaintiff was a slave, and not a citizen. . . .

Upon the whole, therefore, it is the judgment of this court, that it appears by the record before us that the plaintiff in error is not a citizen of Missouri, in the sense in which that word is used in the Constitution; and that the Circuit Court of the United States, for that reason, had no jurisdiction in the case, and could give no judgment in it. Its judgment for the defendant must, consequently, be reversed, and a mandate issued, directing the suit to be dismissed for want of jurisdiction.

The Relative Position and Treatment of the Negroes

The Abolitionists—Consistency of Their Labors

GEORGE S. SAWYER

1858

As the struggle over slavery and its position within the United States intensified, abolitionist statements concerning the evils of slavery were met with statements by Southerners—and also by some Northerners—defending the institution. George S. Sawyer, a Southern slaveholder and lawyer, compared his idyllic picture of slave life with a nightmare vision of non-slave societies—including Great Britain, the source of much antislavery writing. According to this so-called mud-sill theory, Northern industrial institutions subjected workers of whatever color to worse deprivations than slavery, particularly because Northern workers lacked a master whose own interest dictated that he look after theirs. Selections here are taken from Sawyer's *Southern Institutes, or, an inquiry into the Origin and Early prevalence of slavery and the Slave-trade: with an analysis of the laws, history, and government of the institution in the principal nations, ancient and modern, from the earliest ages down to the present time. With notes and comments in Defence of the southern institutions.*

The Relative Position and Treatment of the Negroes

No government has ever existed in the civilized world that placed the black and the white man upon an equal footing as to all the rights and privileges of citizens. In their political and social condition, universally among the Caucasian race, the negro lives under many social and civil disabilities. Lord Mansfield said, in the decision of Sommersett's case, that such was the odium that existed against them among the English people, that they could not live in the enjoyment of any social or civil privileges in England. In France they can never attain to the rights of citizens. The fundamental principles of our Federal and State governments place these privileges all beyond the reach of the negro in America. The Constitution of the United States and that of nearly all the States, say, that every *free white* male citizen, &c., shall be a duly qualified elector; and such only are eligible to any office of honor, profit, or trust, or to be admitted generally to civil functions, to seats in the churches, public schools, places of general assembly, or private circles of society; all intermarriages between the white and the black races is prohibited by law. This all goes to show that the negro race, by universal consent of the civilized world, are considered a separate and distinct race of beings, suited only to their own peculiar state and condition.[1] Their freedom is but a name, an unmeaning sound; they are by nature totally incapacitated to enjoy the rights and privileges of freemen, except in secluded communities of their own kindred blood, which ever have been, and ever will be, sooner or later, when left to themselves, in a state of barbarism. Their condition among the whites is necessarily that of pupilage and dependence.

Considerations of this kind first induced civilized nations to purchase them as slaves. Slavery . . . had its origin

---

1. These truths are set forth in a striking light in the very learned and masterly opinion of the Supreme Court of the United States in the Dred Scott case. See 19 Hou. Rep. p. 408–410. It is there decided that the descendants of African slaves are not citizens of the United States within the meaning of the Constitution, even though they be free.

in the stern yet merciful dictates of humanity; the very word from which they take their name in the Latin language, indicates the act of mercy that spared their lives.[2] Slavery originated from the same cause, and existed by the same laws in Africa.[3] This principle of national law that governed the whole ancient world, took effect there also; and thousands and millions of the hapless wretches who fell into the hands of their otherwise merciless captors, were by its benign influence snatched, as it were, from the jaws of death. But by the barbarous customs of the country, their blood was spared but for a time; till the anniversary of some funeral rites or festive occasion, to water the graves of the ancestors of their victors. Wars and revolutions had destroyed and enslaved nations, till one-sixth owned and held the other five-sixths of the entire population in bondage. The less the demand for these preserved captives as merchandize, the less value and consequence they became to their African owners, and even burdensome to support; and hence the greater number could be sacrificed on all occasions, and the more shocking these scenes of carnage and bloodshed became to glut the bloodthirsty mania of these African savages.

Such was the condition of all the slave regions of Africa when the first English slave ship found its way to her coast. She arrived there upon a mission of mercy; to be (as Commander Forbes, of the British navy in 1850, tells us he was at one of their sacrifices),[4] the unworthy instrument, in the hands of Divine Providence, in saving the lives of *some* of these miserable creatures doomed to the knife of the executioner; to transport them from this thraldom of heathen darkness into the light and knowledge of the one living and true God.

Humanity and Christian benevolence every where plead for mercy to the wretched African captive. It was originally the same spirit that induced Moses to retain the foreign fugitive who had escaped from a heathen master to some one of the tribes of Israel: actuated by the noblest impulse of the human heart, he could not suffer the stranger to be denied the blessings that had been vouchsafed to his own countrymen, and remanded back into a land of heathen darkness. The same motives touched the cord of true philanthropy in the heart of Queen Elizabeth, and moved her at first to permit, encourage, and patronize John Hawkins and other English merchants to engage in the traffic. It was the same spirit that first moved the enlightened and philanthropic body of the British Parliament to charter the Royal African, and afterwards the West India Company, for the same purpose. It was in the Christian hope of benefiting these wretched beings in Africa, that the pious John Newton, of Liverpool, fitted a slave ship, and actually commanded her for several trips in the Guinea Trade. It was the same spirit that moved the pen of the celebrated Jonathan Edwards in defence of the African slave trade, and prompted him to dedicate one of his master-pieces of logic to that object. It also quieted the conscience of the renowned Cotton Mather to hold them as slaves; and also that of the Rev. Dr. Styles, one of the early presidents of Yale College, to export a barrel of rum to the coast of Africa to buy him a slave. . . .

This originally beneficent scheme of ransoming these prisoners from destruction, and making them as comfortable and happy in a Christian land as their character and the nature of their condition will admit, is no more accountable for the horrid abuses that have been consequent upon it, than the Christian religion itself is for the oceans of human blood that have flowed in its footsteps. And the question of suppression of the slave trade by law at the present day is one of national policy, and pure expediency, as to whether, in consequence of the avarice and wickedness of mankind, it is not productive of more evil than good to Africa, and the world at large. It is not my purpose to enter into any discussion of this question; but there is a fair question that may be asked by every true philanthropist, Whether these attempts at suppression do not aggravate the sufferings of the African slaves, both in their native country and on their passage, when smuggled away for a foreign port? It is conceded by the best-informed upon this subject, that nothing but the entire conquest of Africa can ever abolish this trade; and the question may be conscientiously asked, whether the ineffectual and fruitless attempts at present being made at suppression are, on the whole, productive of any good.

2. *Serve* or *Servare,* to preserve, not slay their captives. Inst. Just. lib. i. t. 2. c. 3.

3. Wheat's Elements of Inter. Law, p. 194. The slave trade is not prohibited by the code of nations; this principle of national law is still in force in Africa, and in all nations where it has not been abolished by municipal regulations. Op. cit. (in loco.), Case of Diana Stowell, 1 Dod. p. 95.

4. Africa and the American Flag, by Foote.

Every human being with African blood in his veins, who has escaped from this maelstrom of African slavery and of human misery, lived through the horrors of the *middle passage,* and is now alive in a Christian land, owes his existence, and that of his posterity to the merciful interposition of the African slave trade. But for this, the life-blood that now flows freely through the swelling pulsations of his heart, and animates his system, would have long since drenched the grave of some barbaric prince, or person of rank, upon a heathen soil.

The same principle of national law that permitted Abraham to bring back the women, and also the people from the slaughter of Chederlaomer and the kings that were with him at the battle of Shaveh, to pay tithes of all to Melchisedec, the Jewish High Priest; and to divide the spoils with the king of Sodom and give him the people;[5] the same principle of national law that permitted the Hebrew slave-dealers under the Mosaic code to purchase the captives of the heathen round about them; the same principle that permitted governor Winthrop to brand the captive Pequods on the shoulder, and send them with the negroes to the West Indies for slaves, has also, from the earliest ages, prevailed in Africa, as well as all other nations.[6] By this law of captivity, the custom of sparing the lives of their captives made them their property, as it did in ancient Greece, Rome, and all the nations of Europe. This law, as we have before remarked, was founded in mercy; it was one step in the progress of civilization; it was enacted in favor of human life.

In Africa, as in all nations, these captives were lawful articles of commerce; the right of the African owner to sell them was perfect and indefeasible, and (as we shall show more fully hereafter), has been universally so held by the judicial tribunals of all civilized nations. Therefore, slaves were originally procured from Africa in a regular and lawful course of trade; it was a legal commerce, carried on by many pious men, under the permission and patronage of Christian sovereigns. As in all other commercial enterprises, companies were chartered by the British Parliament to promote this kind of trade with Africa. At length, bad men engaged in the trade, perverted its original purpose, and abused this privilege.

Origin of Slavery in the United States

Some of the English, Spanish, and other slave ships, at length found their way to the West Indies, and the coast of America. Slavery was not legislated into the British Colonies in America; it flowed in there freely as the wind that bloweth where it listeth, for the reason that it was then a regular and lawful commerce, and there was no law in the colonies to prohibit it. New England was for a long time a great importing emporium for African slaves; some of the principal places along her coast owe their origin to the wealth derived from this trade. Newport was not alone; other places contributed their portion. Many of these slaves were retained as domestics, and for other service in the New England States, but they were mostly reshipped at these places for the West Indies and Southern markets.[7] England, France, Spain, and Portugal, were, for a long time, and some still are, deeply engaged in this traffic. The British Colonies in America made several ineffectual attempts to suppress it, but were always overpowered by the authority of the mother country.

Feeling a natural aversion to negro labor and negro society, the colonial authorities frequently remonstrated against its introduction into the colonies. But every voice was put to silence, and every effort to remedy this evil frustrated, by the overwhelming power of English despotism; and the trade was continued for years under the favor of foreign influence and foreign power. Hence arose the numerous class of slave population in the United States.

In Virginia, several efforts were made to prohibit the importation of slaves, but the British Government constantly checked all their efforts. South Carolina passed a similar law, which was rejected by the king in council upon the plea that slavery was beneficial to the country as a source of protection, &c. Massachusetts was the first of the colonies to participate in this trade; yet, when she would stop, Governor Hutchinson, acting under the direction of the Crown of England, rejected all her efforts. The importation of slaves into Georgia was early prohibited for twenty years, that this State might be peopled with a sturdy white population, and thus become a strong barrier of protection against the inroad of Spanish incursions

---

5. Gen. 14:12, 16.
6. Wheat's Elements International Law, p. 194.

7. Peterson's His. Rho., pp. 22, 24.

from the South.[8] The slave population continued to increase during the colonial existence of the States; till, at the formation and adoption of the Federal Constitution, twelve of the thirteen were slave-holding States.[9]

This class of population was forced upon the colonists against their will in great numbers, and as they existed in all the original States but one, some provision necessarily had to be agreed upon in the Constitution for their recognition and government. The idea is held up by Abolitionists among people not well informed upon this subject, that the African progenitors of the present slave population in this country were originally stolen from Africa; and hence their present owners and holders are denounced as partakers of stolen property, known to be such.

This is but one of the multiplicity of errors that lie at the foundation of all the misguided zeal and fanaticism that prevail in different States and places upon this subject.

But is not the same true of the East India company? look at the horrors and abuse of the opium trade, and others, which will be more fully set forth hereafter. The following passage, it is said, was originally inserted in the Declaration of Independence, by Mr. Jefferson. Speaking of the king of England, he says, "He has waged a cruel war against human nature itself, violating its most sacred rights of life and liberty in the persons of a distant people who never offended him; capturing and carrying them away into slavery in another hemisphere, or to incur a miserable death in their transportation thither. This piratical warfare, the opprobrium of infidel powers, is the warfare of the Christian king of Great Britain. Determined to keep open a market where men should be bought and sold, he has prostituted his negative for the suppressing of every legislative attempt to prohibit or restrain this execrable commerce." In the first place, it can hardly be said that the British nation waged a war against human nature in permitting and encouraging the African slave trade; it was, as we have said, in its real design, or as patronized by government, dictated by humanity. In the second place, it violated no rights of life or liberty by capturing and carrying away a distant people

into slavery; it found them already in slavery and doomed to inevitable destruction in their native country. It found them lawfully held and owned by their native masters, and purchased them in a fair and legitimate course of trade; capturing and kidnapping were never sanctioned by royal authority. Neither was it "the opprobrium of infidel powers." Africa has been visited by the slave merchant of nearly every nation of the earth, as a lawful commerce; and the traffic is given up by African potentates at this day, with the greatest reluctance. It is even the source of a violent prejudice in Africa against those who have abolished it, and becomes a great obstacle to their commerce with those nations.

This groundless assertion of Thomas Jefferson is as unfounded a scandal upon the government of Great Britain, as his blasphemous remark upon the story of the Virgin Mary was upon the inspired author of St. Matthew's Gospel. He finally became ashamed of it himself, and concluded to suppress it, from a delicacy of feeling towards some gentlemen of the South; and, as he intimates, from the same feeling towards some of the delegates from the North, then engaged in the Guinea trade. This language, at the organization of the Federal Government, became as applicable to the government of the United States and the framers of its constitution, as to the king of Great Britain —since it is provided by that instrument that the importation of African slaves shall not be prohibited by Congress prior to the year 1808. For eighteen years then, this nefarious war against human nature, as termed by Mr. Jefferson, was continued under the direct sanction of the framers and adopters of the Constitution of the United States. Thus was this scandal of Mr. Jefferson upon not only the English but American nation, silently yet severely rebuked by the united voice of the American people. Thomas Jefferson himself turns a perfect somersault in sentiment, and wages this same war against human nature, by taking the oath to support the Constitution as President of the United States, and that, too, before the time of this provisional sanction of the African slave trade had elapsed. If he was sincere in what he uttered against the king of England with regard to this traffic, what a paragon of absurdity does his biography here present!

Thomas Jefferson was a true patriot and a great man, but he was extremely fond of strange eccentricities, quaint expressions, glaring paradoxes, and sweeping assertions. And he displays this peculiarity in a singular degree in

8. Bancroft's Hist. U.S., vol. 2, p. 17. Stephens' Hist. Ga., vol. 1, pp. 285, 6, 7, and 8. Tuck's Black. vol. 1, part 2d, pp. 49–51. Appendix to Mad. State Papers, 3, 1390. Walsh's Appeal, 327. South Carolina Statutes, 2:526. Stephens' Journal, 3:281. Encl. Am., tit. Slavery, vol. 2, p. 429. Jefferson's Corresp., 146:2. Illiot's Debates, 335. Story's Const. U.S.; 3d, p. 203:132.

9. Census U.S. 1850.

some of his expressions in the Declaration of Independence. He there asserts that "all men are created equal, and endowed by their Creator with certain inalienable rights," &c.[10] In the first place, all men are not *created* at all; it is contended by some that there never was but one man *created,* and by others that each type of man had its origin in a separate creation. But if it is to be understood that all men are *born* equal, its absurdity in a literal sense is none the less apparent (as we have endeavored to show above). In the second place, men have no inalienable rights either naturally or politically. What natural or political right has a man, that he may not voluntarily or involuntarily forfeit or transfer to the body politic? It is one of the fundamental principles in the science of human government, that it derives its just and full powers from the consent of the governed; and this consent consists in a voluntary alienation of a portion for the more safe and certain protection of the balance. Hence government becomes a kind of compromise or compact between the rulers and the ruled; and every individual subject may forfeit his liberty, and even his life, in various ways. He may do it by the voluntary commission of crime, or by enlisting into the army, &c. Again, he may involuntarily forfeit it by such a concourse of circumstances as to render it necessary; to avoid a death by fire, he may jump into the ocean; the calls of his country may require too "the poor offering of his life, and the victim must be ready at the appointed hour of sacrifice." Physical disabilities and worldly misfortunes may throw him upon the cold charities of the world, and confine him to the prison limits of public alms. Mental infirmities and derangements may consign him to a lunatic asylum; what then becomes of his inalienable right to life, liberty, and the pursuit of happiness?

But let us inquire into what claim Mr. Jefferson had to originality in this particular. Alexander Hamilton, speaking of the British colonies in America, long prior to the Declaration of Independence, used the following language:

"We are threatened with the most abject slavery. It has been proven that resistance by remonstrance will be without effect. Were not the disadvantages of slavery too obvious to stand in need of it, I might enumerate the tedious train of calamities inseparable from it. I might show that it is fatal to religion and morality, that it tends to debase the mind and corrupt its noblest springs of action."[11] "That Americans are entitled to freedom is manifest upon every rational principle; *all men have a common original, they participate in a common nature and consequently have a common right;* no valid reason can be assigned why one man should exercise more power or pre-eminence over his fellow men than another, unless they have voluntarily vested him with that right. Since, then, Americans have not by any act of theirs empowered the British Parliament to make laws for them, it follows," &c.[12] It will not be pretended that Mr. Hamilton, in the use of the above language, had reference to any other than British subjects, or the Anglo-Saxon race; he is speaking of their condition in America, and assigns this as a reason why they were, and ought to be, free and independent. He could not have intended to convey the fantastical idea that seems to have been taken from it by the writer of the Declaration of Independence, or that it should apply to negroes, Indians,[13] &c. If so, he could not have been so inconsistent as to sit as chairman of a committee of three, in 1788, during the existence of the Confederation, consisting of Mr. Hamilton, Mr. Madison, and Mr. Sedgewick, who reported a resolution to Congress strongly recommending the necessity and propriety of negotiating a treaty with the King of Spain for the restitution of fugitive slaves who escaped from the States adjoining into his territory, to which we shall refer more particularly hereafter. Besides, he was one of the most lucid and logical commentators upon the Constitution of the United States and one of the most successful advocates for its adoption with all its pro-slavery provisions.

But Mr. Jefferson seized upon this restricted remark, metamorphosed it into an ecumenical proposition, and brandished it in his usual sweeping and random manner in the Declaration of Independence. But public opinion, in this instance, too, gave a negative to his startling hypothesis, by adopting the idea as it was intended by its original

10. In justice to the real author of this sentiment, it should be observed that this was intended to apply only to political men, members of the body politic;—for to what others did the Declaration of Independence relate?

11. Hamilton's Works, vol. ii. p. 9.

12. Ibid., vol. ii. p. 3.

13. The Supreme Court of the United States have recently decided that negroes are not citizens of the United States within the meaning of the Constitution of the U.S.; that the principles of our government do not apply to them; that the government of the United States was designed for the white man, and that slaves are lawful property. (Dred Scott Case.)

author; and in the subsequent formation and adoption of the Constitution of the United States, held that only free white male citizens have a common right, and that negroes might be held as slaves, and restored to their owners when they escaped.[14] The framers carried out the full meaning and spirit of this much-abused and misconstrued clause in the Declaration of Independence, in the provisions of the Constitution of the United States, by thus adopting its true and original meaning. It related only to the hereditary claims to prominence and power of the Anglo-Saxon race over one another; hence it provided that there should be no titles of nobility, no established class, rank or religion, that "no man should be deprived of his life, liberty, or property, without due process of law," &c. This covered the whole original doctrine of this celebrated clause in the Declaration of Independence.

At the adoption of the Constitution of the United States, twelve of the thirteen were slave-holding States; and, indeed, it might be said that all were of that character, for although there do not appear to have been any slaves actually held in Massachusetts, yet, as we shall see, but a short time previous that State held many, and there never was any law there abolishing it, except the force of public opinion, unexpressed by any direct legislative enactment. There were, at that date, in the several States, about seven hundred thousand slaves. This number could not have been estimated at a value less than three hundred millions of dollars. This vast amount of property had been originally acquired in a legitimate course of trade; the right of the owners was perfect and indefeasible by any act of legislation without remuneration. How, then, could the subject be disposed of in the formation of the present government? It must be tolerated or abolished. But were the United States able, at the close of a protracted and expensive war, with a bankrupt treasury, to pay this amount as a remuneration to the owners for the loss of property and damages sustained by the abolition of slavery?

It must, therefore, be tolerated, and its existence provided for as a matter of right. The policy adopted by the framers of the Constitution was (as we shall show more fully hereafter), for Congress to abstain from all interference with this subject, directly or indirectly, and to leave it exclusively to the governments of the several States in which it existed.

14. See opinion of Supreme Court in Dred Scott case.

The Position and Treatment of Slaves

The definition of "a slave, is one who is subject to the power of a master, and who belongs to him in such a manner that the master may sell him, dispose of his person, his industry, and his labor; and who can do nothing, possess nothing, nor acquire anything, but that may belong to his master."[15]

Many of the features of this definition have but a nominal existence, without any practical effect. It will be seen that the slave belongs to his master only for certain specific purposes. The idea of property in his person (as we shall show more fully hereafter) is but a fiction of law. The power to sell, alienate, and transfer, is not only an essential requisite to the existence of the present relation between master and slave, but greatly enhances the value of that relation; and when not abused, is a source of great comfort and blessing to the slave. By this provision of law, the master who cruelly treats his slave can be compelled to transfer him to another master. Besides, the slave who is dissatisfied with his master can select another more congenial to his notion, and by requesting the change, the master will generally find it to his interest to grant his request, as the value of the slave's services consists, in a great measure, in his being contented and satisfied with his master. For this reason, slaves are seldom sold except in families. The idea is prevalent among the misinformed upon this subject, that no heed is given to the desires of the slave in this particular; but this the universal experience of every man acquainted with the management of slaves will contradict. Though the slave's right to property is not known *de jure,* yet it exists, and is practically recognised *de facto*—as much so as the property of a free person; and in their intercourse with the world it is universally observed and respected. Like the Roman slaves they have their *peculium,* to which the master lays no claim.[16] And many a one, by industry and economy, acquires sufficient means to purchase his freedom. But comparatively few are willing to invest it in that way. The remark of an industrious and economical negro man, belonging to a friend of mine, illustrates their general ideas of freedom. It was generally supposed that he had accu-

15. Civil code of La., Art. 35, Domat. tom. 2, sect. 97; ff. D. lib. 1, 5, 1. 4, s. 1, et Tit. 6, 1. 1, sect. 1. This definition does not make a slave, but presupposes his existence. A thing cannot be defined that has no existence.

16. Civil Code of Louisiana, Art. 175.

mulated a considerable amount of money. I asked him one day, in the presence of his master, why he did not purchase his freedom, to which he replied that negro property was so fluctuating that he considered it a poor investment, and he was looking out for a better speculation.

This shows the utter contempt and ridicule in which the more intelligent portion of the slave population hold the subject of liberty, accompanied with all the disabilities and disadvantages which the negro must suffer in all parts of the country. He feels and realizes the fact that he enjoys all the freedom that the nature of his character and condition in society will possibly admit. He sees thousands around him nominally free, but who are actually in a worse slavery than himself, and with whom he would not exchange situations. He concludes that, after all, this boasted liberty is but a sound, an unmeaning thing, and that slavery is the happiest condition that the black population in this country can enjoy.[17]

The numerous classifications and divisions of labor peculiar to Roman slavery, are unknown to the American system in the United States. They are here divided into but two classes or divisions, known as the house or family servants and the plantation hands. These latter are generally under the management of an overseer, who corresponds to the Roman villicus, having the superintendence of all the affairs immediately connected with the plantation. This is a necessary regulation, and one enforced by law where the proprietor does not reside on the plantation. It is as necessary for the safety and peace of the neighborhood as for the good order and regulation of the plantation. From fifty to one hundred negroes dwelling together in a single village or quarter (which is about the average number), without the immediate supervision of some white man, to regulate them and keep them in order, would be as dangerous a foe to the surrounding plantations, as well as their own, as a

camp of Camanche Indians to the border settlements upon our frontier.

There are in the slave-holding States a numerous class of persons who make this a regular profession, and follow it constantly for a livelihood. Their reputation and success in business, like all other professions, depends upon their skill and judgment in discipline and good management. Many of the most prominent citizens of these States have commenced life by this kind of employment, and risen from it to wealth and distinction. The duties of an overseer are those of any other general superintendent of any particular branch of business. He is invested with all necessary authority to secure the services of those under his charge, and to preserve good discipline and order in the quarter.

All those barbarous modes of punishment, such as wearing the *furca,* the cross, hanging them up by the hands with weights to their feet to be whipped, have all been done away. In turbulent and unmanageable cases, corporeal punishment is still allowed. But this, among all humane and judicious managers, is resorted to with reason and discretion, and not unfrequently with great reluctance.

The instrument generally used for inflicting this punishment is a soft buckskin thong, from four to six inches in length, and from a half to an inch in width, attached to the end of a common whip. All excessive punishments are discountenanced; the greatest dissatisfaction is generally felt by the owner at the breaking of the skin in the course of such punishment; and, should it happen, not unfrequently the manager is discharged for the violation of this fixed rule. Confinement in the stocks is also sometimes resorted to in the most desperate cases, and for certain criminal offences. The idea generally held up by the Abolitionists, that the slaves are all brutally beaten and whipped without discretion or mercy, is false and unfounded. Nothing is a more certain source of dissatisfaction, on the part of the owner, than the cruel treatment or neglect of his overseer to his slaves. That instances of cruelty and neglect, from brutal and unprincipled managers, do sometimes occur, cannot be denied; but these are rare, and generally meet with the severest rebuke from public opinion, and, if possible, are visited with the penalty of the law. There is no object of human sympathy upon which it is more keenly alive, in the Southern States, than that of neglect and cruel treatment to slaves. Their helpless and dependent condition renders them peculiarly the objects of sympathy in this particular.

17. A Returning Penitent.—Our readers may remember an advertisement of a runaway that appeared in our columns some three years since, and excited some characteristic comments from the New York Tribune. No information was elicited by the advertisement concerning the fugitive, who was a very intelligent and valuable servant, that had been well treated and well regarded. We have now before us, however, a letter written by the servant referred to, who addresses a friend and relative, enclosing an appeal to his mistress, and begging permission to return to servitude and safety. He addresses earnest and emphatic assurances of penitence and regret to his "dear mistress," and begs her to receive and permit the return of her "dear servant." The New York Tribune will notice, of course.—*Charleston Courier.*

Their tasks of labor must not be beyond their strength, their constitution, and ability to perform; if humanity, law, and the force of public opinion should all fail to regulate this matter within its proper bounds, pecuniary interest, always the last and most sordid appeal to the motives of the master, would restrain him from over-working his slave.

The plantation hands generally reside in a little hamlet or cluster of cottages, apart and some distance from the master's residence, when that is on the plantation; this is called the "*quarter.*" It consists of a group of cabins numbering in proportion to the number of inhabitants, arranged in rows at some distance apart, with a yard or playground intervening, generally beset with large shade trees. This little cluster, when adorned with its usual hues of snow, ensconced beneath and within the verdant shades of some retired grove, looming out with its glimmerings of white through the green boughs of the trees, presents a scene to the view of the traveller approaching the distant heights of the back-ground, that, were he not accustomed to the optical illusion, he might mistake for a respectable New England village. The hands leave the quarter in the morning at the ringing of the bell, and are in the field in the busy season as soon as daylight will enable them to work. When the distance from the quarter will not admit of their returning to their meals, they are carried to them in the field. They continue at their work till towards noon; when it is time to feed the teams, the plough-boys then return to the stables for that purpose, and the balance, commonly known as the hoehands, take from one to three hours' recess according to the heat of the weather and the condition of the crop. During the hottest part of the summer it is common for them to take three hours' recess in the middle of the day. This time they spend in lounging and sleeping in the cooling retreat of some adjacent grove of shade trees upon the borders of the field; after which, they again resume their labors and continue till dark; when they return to the quarter, get their suppers, and retire for the night. Such is the regular routine of their daily labors during the planting and busy season for the week till Saturday noon; then, if the condition of the crop will admit of it, they are discharged from labor till Monday morning. This portion of the day they usually spend in cultivating their small "patches" for themselves. And those of the men who are too indolent to improve this opportunity, as many of them are, they are compelled to it by their managers.

The women spend their time thus allowed them in washing and repairing their clothes, and preparing to resume their labor on the following week. It is a privilege commonly given to those of the men who will improve it, to plant and cultivate small portions or "patches" (as they term them) for themselves. From these they not unfrequently realize from thirty to fifty bushels of corn; this, with the fodder that they can save, they can sell to their masters, their neighbors, or haul to a neighboring town, for from thirty to forty dollars. They also have the privilege of raising poultry and of selling their eggs, chickens, ducks, and turkeys, besides all they can realize from odd jobs and overwork, for which they are as regularly paid as hired laborers. I know of many plantations where book accounts are kept with the slaves, and every item, that belongs to their debt and credit, is as formally and regularly entered as in the account-books of country merchants.[18] . . .

Thus, any slave, who has been well disciplined and enured to habits of industry and economy, who will improve his opportunity, may actually save as much for himself, besides the service that his master claims, as the majority of laborers in the free States, who labor for from ten to fifteen dollars per month, clothe themselves, and sustain all losses from sickness, want of employment, &c.

Where can there be found a class of agricultural hirelings who actually save, on an average, more than from fifty to one hundred dollars, annually, for any number of years from their earnings? On the other hand, how many thousands are there who but just live and support their families from hand to mouth by their daily labor, without being able to save one dollar at the year's end;—a class who must be constantly weighed down with cares and anxieties for the welfare of themselves and families in sickness and other misfortunes.

The slave is relieved from all this oppressive burden of troubles; he is comforted by the pleasing consolation, if he has any thought for his family, that they have a sure support, in sickness and health, in infancy and old age. He is

18. One of the "Horrors of Slavery."—The Norfolk (Va.) Herald states that, a few days ago, several free negroes were put up at auction, in Norfolk County, and sold to labor for a term sufficient to liquidate their taxes. Singular to relate, four of them were purchased by a slave in Portsmouth, who felt quite proud of the distinction, and made known his determination to get the full value of his money out of them, or know the reason why. This is a development under our "Institutions" which the apostles of free society would do well to make a note of.

relieved of all those dark forebodings of the future that so weigh down and depress the spirits of the poor laborer of the free States.[19] All that the slave makes is his own; he has nothing to pay out for the necessaries of life, though in strictness of law all that he has belongs to his master; yet this is but a nominal provision; it is all included, like a wheel within a wheel, in his possessions. But he is the proprietor of his slave's *peculium* only as his representative, guardian, and protector, to see that he is not wronged, and that he does not apply his means inconsistent with his duties as a servant. It is given in charge by the law to the master for the same reason that the slave's person is, and that is because he is incapable of managing it himself.

As to their food and clothing, it compares well with that of any class of free laborers with whom I have become acquainted. They are generally allowed plenty of the most substantial and wholesome articles of diet. It is generally estimated that it requires as many barrels of mess-pork, of two hundred pounds each, as there are slaves, big and little, to furnish them with meat for one year. It is true, that the planter is not always at the expense of purchasing that amount, for the reason that he has other sources of supply; but the amount of meat annually consumed, on every well-managed plantation, is equal to this estimate.

For breadstuffs, an allowance is made of a bushel of meal, per month, for each slave. In addition to this, they generally have sweet-potatoes and milk; besides, all the poultry, vegetables, and other articles which they may raise, or purchase themselves. They have also privileges by which they are enabled to supply themselves with sugar and coffee; their tobacco and molasses are furnished for them by their masters. For clothing, the general rule is two suits a year, one for summer and one for winter. Their winter suits are made of heavy goods manufactured from cotton and wool, called jeans; they have, also, for winter, one blanket, overcoat, and flannel under-shirts. They wear a kind of wool, or glazed hat; they have, also, two pairs of shoes, or, more frequently, a pair of shoes and a pair of boots. Their summer suits are made of a kind of cotton goods called Osnaburgs, or Lowells. These keep them well clad for their labor during the year; they have separate suits for Sundays, for

19. Although the negro race are naturally more disposed to idiocy and insanity, yet among the slaves of the South, the like are almost wholly unknown, an evidence of their happy state of mind. For statistics on this point, see Essay on Political Slavery, post, p. 367.

which, and the few articles of luxury that they buy, they generally spend their savings during the year.

It is now Christmas; the cotton-picking season is over; the slaves have finished their year's work, and are now enjoying their holidays. They have a week to themselves before resuming the labors of another year. While I sit penning this chapter, the town is thronged with hundreds of the black people from the neighboring plantations. They have come to town to sell their "truck" (as they term it), which they have raised during the year, and to buy articles of family luxuries, and fine clothing, as they may fancy. They spend this week in visiting, feasting, frolicking, dancing, and such other amusements as they most enjoy. When it has passed, they cheerfully make preparations for another crop.

The house slaves or servants have nothing to do with the plantation; they are retained as waiting servants, and their duties are confined to the more immediate wants of the family. One has charge of the sleeping-rooms, and the various apartments of the house; others of the culinary department; others of the laundry; others again, of the horses kept for family uses, and pleasure carriages. This class of servants have their houses usually in the back yard, or somewhere near the family residence, and eat at what may be called the second table, after the white members of the family. Like all white servants throughout the free States: in all families of respectability they are kept neatly clad; and often for a Sunday garb, or ball dress, put on what would, in a Quaker village, be called a rich and extravagant costume. . . .

It is asserted by Abolition writers and speakers that the slaves enjoy no religious privileges. This is another one of the numerous popular errors resulting from ignorance and misrepresentation, that help to fan the flame of popular fanaticism that pervades the Abolition crusade of the North against the South. By the rules of church discipline, slaves are admitted as, and actually become, members of all Evangelical churches throughout the slave-holding States. In all towns and neighborhoods where there is regular preaching they are generally privileged to attend, and one exercise of the Sabbath is usually devoted to their express benefit. Plantations and settlements remote from these privileges, are generally supplied by itinerant preachers either of the Methodist Episcopal Conference, or by those appointed by the several denominations to take charge of the different stations of the African Mission. Not unfrequently, settlements support local preachers for the benefit of the colored population. It is true, some masters object to having preaching on their plantations, and to their slaves attending church; but such men are not peculiar to the slave States.

Child-like in their intellectual capacity, predisposed to superstition, credulity, and imitation; confiding in their superiors, without reason or reflection, they become the most willing and ready pretenders to religious notions. But these have very little practical effect upon their moral character. They are generally the most zealous and enthusiastic converts of the faith; but their zeal, unfortunately, is not according to their knowledge. This misfortune, however, is not peculiar to the slave population. They are more passionate and flaming in their pretensions to religious observances, than scrupulous and exact in the discharge of their practical obligations; more vehement and boisterous in their devotional exercises, than penitent and humble for their remissness of duty. But we fear that even these remarks cannot be confined to the colored population.

Marriage rites and ceremonies are as strictly observed among them, and the relation of husband and wife, parent and child, as firmly protected, generally, as their character and condition will possibly admit. These are essentially under the supervision and direction of the master, for without the influence of his immediate interposition and regulation, such relations could no more exist among African slaves in America, than in their native country. The proper regulation of the matrimonial connection, is the cause of more difficulty, trouble, and anxiety to the master, than perhaps any other subject connected with the management of his slaves. Upon this subject the males and females are mutually unfortunate and ill-adapted in their nature to the security of family tranquillity. We hear much prating and rhodomontade among anti-slavery writers and speakers, about female virtue; much about the heavenly boon guaranteed to all females in the protection of their chastity. And when they preach and write about enlightening the South upon the evils of slavery, they would have us believe that this is dearer than life to the female slave; that it is the pearl of great price, and pure as the driven snow. They would also teach us that it may be involuntarily prostituted to open shame by the wanton authority and control of the master with impunity. But this is the result of ignorance and bad philosophy. This is the most indeli-

cate and objectionable part of our subject; yet with the high precedent of the modern Sto(we)ic philosophy before us, we need feel no qualms of delicacy or self-reproach in entering upon a brief consideration of the subject.

The relation of master and slave puts the latter in his power only for certain specified purposes; and he cannot, by virtue of that relation, exercise any more power or control over the slave than is implied as necessary to secure the object for which the servant has been intrusted to the charge of the master. Hence nature, law, and public opinion, all cry out and remonstrate with an unwavering voice against the usurpation of any illegitimate and unnatural authority over the slave for dissolute and abandoned purposes. Nature has wisely regulated the government of the passions in both man and beast, with a view to the protection of the weaker sex. And when the master approaches even the negro wench for the purpose of improper familiarity, nature disarms him of all superiority over her; and he must not only meet her upon grounds of equality, but humble himself at her feet. And thus conscious of his own guilty position, like the cowardly thief in the night, he loses all courage for the exercise of authority or resistance, and if she has but the disposition, she may, with perfect impunity, spurn his proffered kindness with contempt. And the master, so far from entertaining feelings of revenge, would value the slave higher and praise her the more for her strict adherence to virtuous principles. Every slaveholder knows, if not, he will soon learn by sad experience, that just in proportion as he practises or permits and encourages dissolute habits among his slaves, he loses the confidence of the males as a master, and the reverence and respect of the females as a superior. And these are the only effective sources of authority and good government over them. The man who would violate his trust and prostitute his authority to overcome the chaste and virtuous habits of a helpless and defenceless female slave, is as much a monster in human shape, as he who is guilty of incest within the circle of his own domestic fireside. And though violations of the natural, civil, and moral law, in both these instances, may, and do, sometimes occur, yet they show the offender equally as unfit to have charge of the personal subjects of the outrage in one instance as in the other. They are both alike responsible to the law, responsible to public opinion, and above and beyond responsible to their God and the tribunal of their own bed and board. This last responsibility, when all others fail, operates as the chief of terrors to all such evil-doers. We hear it said that in the case of the slave there is none to avenge the wrong; but the culprit can never escape the horrors of a guilty conscience or the dread of exposure. In most cases he would call upon the rocks and the mountains to fall upon him, and hide him from the day of wrath and the terrible revelation of household vengeance that awaits him in a day of retribution. Thus the injured female servant feels conscious of the protection of the domestic tribunal to which she can safely resort for redress. And this is an arbitress that, it is universally acknowledged, in matters of this kind, "beareth not the sword in vain."

What evils are there, then, in this particular, peculiar to the relation of master and slave? or that do not apply with equal force to the condition of hired servants? We shall, perhaps, be told that one has redress at law, while the other has not; but what privilege is that to the destitute servant girl, who is struggling, as it were, between life and death, with the task of three slaves imposed upon her, for the pitiful compensation of one dollar and a half per week— a sum not sufficient to keep her in decent clothes, to say nothing of her liability to sickness and other contingent expenses—without friends, without money, and liable, at the least displeasure of her employer, to be turned out upon the cold charities of the world, and there to incur the uncertainty and difficulty of obtaining another situation, or go to the almshouse for a support. No such fears, no such dread or anxiety operates upon the mind of the female slave; she knows that she has a protector, to whom she can resort with impunity. But does the law afford no protection to the slave in this particular? I answer, yes; the culprit is just as amenable and liable to its penalties, for any violence or outrage, in the one instance as in the other. The female slave has as strong inducements, and as much encouragement to lead a virtuous life, as the hired servant girl, if she had the disposition; and she has quite as strong a shield of protection thrown around her, both by nature and by law, if she chooses to avail herself of the privilege. But the predominance of the animal passions superinduces the loose, easy and reckless habits, in this respect, natural to the negro wench. Her character, in this particular, forms a striking contrast to the deathly tenacity of her virtue, peculiar, of all savages, to the Indian squaw. . . .

Again, we hear of long and windy appeals to the sympathies of anti-slavery people, about the horrors of separating man and wife, parent and child, as though this was necessary to the relation of master and slave, and peculiar to that institution. Here is another of those popular errors blazoned forth by ignorant and malicious brawlers, to inflame the prejudices and excite the hostilities of one section of the Union against the other.

To the native African, a wife or a child, as to any of those cares, anxieties, and tender regards that exist in the bosom of civilized man, is wholly unknown. By the force of habit and imitation, they imbibe these feelings to some extent in their connexion with civilized society; yet even then they often cherish a morbid insensibility to all ties of family and kindred that is truly derogatory to human nature. Horrid as the idea of an owner and master may seem to the Abolitionist, the poor wife is often glad to appeal to his merciful protection against the cruelties and brutal treatment of her husband. So also is the child against the neglect and abuses of the mother. The authoress of Uncle Tom's Cabin has kindly informed us that emotions of parental and kindred attachment are ardent and strong in the hearts of the negro race, but my experience and observation have led me to form a very different conclusion upon that subject. Lust and beastly cruelty are the strong passions that glow in the negro's bosom. "There is no flesh in his obdurate heart; it does not feel for man," or beast. I have often witnessed scenes of his cruelties to animals, that would make the heart of civilized man bleed at every pore. This is natural to his race in their native country; it results from the peculiar physical conformation of the head, and the consequent predominance of the animal passions. All travellers agree in bearing testimony to the truth of this fact. But it is the interest, as well as the duty of the master, to improve the character of his slaves in this particular, as the value of their services will be greatly enhanced thereby.

Though the slave, like a minor, cannot marry without the permission of those under whose authority he may be, yet no control is exercised by the master over their choice of a companion. When married, each family has its separate house or apartment, where they are required to live together decently and faithfully as man and wife. These houses, as we have before said, are situated together in clusters of cottages in some pleasant and retired situation. In building them, they are generally raised from two to four feet from the ground to give a free circulation of air under them, and thus render them as cool and comfortable as possible. These cottages are generally frame buildings (though sometimes of brick and sometimes of logs) of one story in height, and two rooms from sixteen to twenty feet square, finished with a view to health, convenience and comfort. We often hear of their living in miserable huts, with no floor but the earth, without bedding, &c. It is true, there are instances of this kind, as there are in every community where poor, destitute and improvident people can be found. But why should these exceptions be heralded forth to the world as one of the evils of slavery? With the same plausibility might such facts be urged against the present organization of society. "The poor ye have always with you." No traveller can pass through the laboring communities of the Northern States, and observe the condition of thousands of the poor and destitute, without seeing and feeling the inconsistency and injustice of such slanderous imputations upon the condition of the slave population of the South. But more of this anon. . . .

It is for the interest, as well as the duty of the master, to cultivate the tender sensibilities, and improve the character and condition of his slaves in this respect, as the value of their services will thereby be greatly enhanced. Interest, then, as well as humanity and duty, plead against the separation of husband and wife, parent and child, and the breaking up of families. This sentiment so pervades public opinion, that such instances but seldom occur. Observe the list of notices of the sales of negroes throughout the Southern States, and almost universally you will see the specification that families are not to be separated. It may be boldly asserted, in the hearing of all Southern men, and those best acquainted with the system, that such is the law and the state of public opinion, that there is not a slaveholder in the country, of respectable standing in the community where he lives, who would consent to sell a family of slaves separately. And I venture to say, further, that you may travel from Pittsburg to New Orleans, and from Baltimore to Corpus Christi, and try every man in both routes, and not be able to purchase a child under ten years of age without its mother, if alive.[20] But are the laws of slavery the only laws that permit the separation of husband and wife, &c.? I appeal to maritime and martial laws, the regulations of the army and navy, commerce, California gold, and the Mexican and foreign wars, for an answer to this question. Why is it, then, that this system is alone singled out as the peculiar object of calumny and vituperation?

If there is one spark of true philanthropy, if there is

20. The law prohibits it.

one sincere emotion of friendship and kind regard for the welfare of the slave, known to the Anglo-Saxon race, that exists in its greatest purity and most unalloyed state in the benevolent heart of the Southern master. I have become convinced of this truth from a somewhat long and familiar acquaintance with real facts. The many instances of kind regard and mutual attachment that I have witnessed between masters and superannuated servants, who have long passed their days of usefulness and profit, and become helpless, have satisfied me that the truest friends to the black man are those who have been raised by, and among them, and best know his character and condition, and best understand his interests and his wants.

When age and infirmities have rendered them unfit for the daily duties of regular hands, the men are assigned some light task about the garden or the quarter, suited to their ability; and the old women are left to attend to the children, knit, sew, or spin, and sometimes, when they are able, to cook. They are generally spoken to by all the white members of the family in terms of kindness and due respect, generally addressed by the epithet of uncle or aunt. I have known of great devotion and regard for the welfare of these aged and helpless people; and by all masters of good breeding they are kindly treated. . . .

We often see striking manifestations of a kindred sentiment towards even the animal creation; some faithful old dog or horse, that has long since passed his days of usefulness, is long nurtured by the kind and compassionate attention of the owner, not for what he may hope from them in future, but in gratitude for the good they have done in the past. This example is not instanced to compare man with beast; but to show that it is but the natural impulse of the human heart, when thrown into long association with man, or even beast, to contract feelings of attachment, of kindness and compassion for their misfortunes. And when those feelings are not repulsed and eradicated by the vicious and refractory character of the negro slave, they beget for him a friendship and compassionate regard for his welfare, that can be found nowhere so sincere and so warm as in the heart of a kind and benevolent Southern master. In confirmation of this truth, instances by thousands might be enumerated of the heroic devotion of masters and mistresses to the health, safety, and comfort of their slaves, even at the hazard and loss of their lives in times of great pestilential peril. But our limits will only permit us to mention but few. An instance of this kind, often related to me, and of which there are many living witnesses, now occurs as suitable to give as an illustration. It is an account of the heroic devotion of a distinguished lady who lived in the parish, and near the place where the bloody scene of Uncle Tom's death was laid. It occurred during the terrible ravages of the cholera through the Red River country, and the different parts of the South, in 1833.

Already it had stricken down its thousands in and around this section of the State of Louisiana. Already its bloody footprints might be traced high up upon the banks of this stream, and wide over the face of this devoted section of country; it sped its course bearing a trail like "the destroying angel that walketh in darkness and wasteth at noonday." At length, it broke out in the numerous household of the subject of this narrative; her husband was absent; its victims were falling thick and fast around her; moved by compassion for the suffering and helpless condition of the servants in her charge, this heroine left the family residence, and a group of darling children smiling around her, and rushed, as it were, into the jaws of death, to try to administer to the comfort and relief of her distressed slaves. There she continued her labors of mercy among them, night and day, till in turn, she herself fell a victim to this deathly scourge and a martyr to the benevolence and magnanimity of a true Christian heart. . . .

What would have been the fate of these unfortunate beings had they been in the boasted land of freedom? Who would have cared for them had they been conveyed by some subterranean railroad scheme to the heart of an abolition community? Ye boasting philanthropists, read the following facts, and weep tears of blood over the truth! . . .

Need I refer to the shocking scenes of suffering that necessarily occur among the free population, in all large cities, that have not the means to secure their own comfort during the prevalence of these terrible epidemics?—a state of things that gives rise to the various bodies of charitable associations for their relief. How much better in this respect, as well as in all other helpless situations, is the condition of the slave! This feeling of confidence and assurance that he will be provided for in all times of need; that in all times of trial he can fall back upon the sympathy and compassion of a benevolent master, like a child upon a parent, is a great source of comfort and consolation to the slave. It renders him always cheerful and happy. No anxieties and troubles about himself or his family, no dark and fearful forebodings of the future, weigh down and depress his spirits. He

is never subjected to such fits of gloom and despondency as we often see depicted upon the countenances of thousands in the land of liberty. A gloomy and depressed state of mind is altogether unnatural to a negro slave. With perfect deference to your position, with perfect confidence in your sympathy, kindness, and compassion towards him, he will always approach you with a smile of familiarity, freedom, and cheerfulness, totally unknown to the privileges of a negro in any other part of the country. None of that arrogance of superiority, none of that stern and relentless scorn peculiar to the people of the free States, in their intercourse with the negro race, ever finds place in the chivalric heart of a Southern master.

The cause of this is in the different relation and relative position in which the parties are placed with regard to one another. Ever conscious and ever taught to feel his inferiority in both capacity and condition, the slave regulates his manners and intercourse with his superiors accordingly. He always appeals to their generosity and magnanimity of soul, not to do him a wrong or an injustice, in his comparatively helpless and defenceless condition. This cannot fail to win the sympathy and compassion for his misfortunes, of every ingenuous heart.

On the other hand, the negro of the free States pretends to no inferiority. With a bold, defying, and arrogant air, he attempts to intrude himself upon the white man upon perfect grounds of equality; a sentiment utterly abhorred by the nature, the morals, politics, and religion of the Anglo-Saxon race in all parts of the world. And hence their entire want of social sympathy; their cold, distant, and repulsive feeling for the negro race in the free States. This will be found universal in all those States and in Europe, except in instances of hypocritical and dogmatical pretensions, by a few misguided enthusiasts, as a false pretence to consistency. There is no such friendly intercourse, no such sympathy for their welfare and social familiarity existing between the black and white population of the free States, except in the instances above cited, as there is between the Southern slave-holder and the well-behaved free colored people around him. The secret of it all is that these people are less assuming in their manners, and less arrogant in their pretensions.

In Louisiana, the better class of the free colored people frequently attain to great wealth and comparative respectability. They live side by side with the white people, and are good neighbors together; and in some instances upon terms of great intimacy and friendship, except in some of the more reserved social and family intercourse, in regard to which there always exist mutual and friendly concessions.[21]

Whoever wishes to see the most striking instances of the mutual feelings of regard that exist between the master and slave, should take a trip down the Mississippi river in company with a number of Southern planters returning from a summer tour at the North, and witness their meeting after a long absence. See them as they drop out at their several plantations along upon the river bank, first met by a group of jubilant slaves, with joy sparkling in their eyes and beaming from their countenances, each impatient for his turn to greet him with a welcome "*How dy, Massa?*" and a fond shake of the hand. One on witnessing such scenes cannot but be reminded of the strange spectacle that would be presented in the streets of Philadelphia, New York, or Boston, to see some aristocratic millionaire beset by a crowd of dirty negroes, each waiting an opportunity to shake him by the hand.

Much of the misapprehension and the wrong impressions of those not well-informed upon the subject in regard to the true character of slavery, or slavery as it really is in America, arise from a wrong idea of its fundamental precepts. All anti-slavery agitation is predicated upon the hypothesis that the slave-holder and the slave, are naturally of equal rank and capacity, as in the case of Hebrew, Greek, and Roman slavery;—that slavery is an obstacle to the rise, progress, and improvement of the slaves. But every one familiar with the subject knows that the very reverse of this hypothesis is the truth. Instead of preventing the slave's improvement, it has converted him from a savage to a state of partial civilization; instead of obstructing his improvement, it prevents him from degenerating into his native barbarism, as he has universally tended when left to himself.[22]

The history of the present and the past proves that the condition of the American slave is the happiest one that he is capable of enjoying. In no age or nation have the same number of Africans attained to so high an elevation in their character and condition. Nowhere else have they enjoyed so many of the blessings of Christian society and the privileges of civilized life. They are well fed, well clothed, well cared for in sickness and in health, in infancy and old age. Enjoying religious privileges in common with the free white population, they are wholly devoid of cares and anxieties for themselves and their families.

The gayety, hilarity, and joy often manifested by these people while at their labor, or at their dwellings, present scenes truly romantic to the traveller as he approaches a well-managed plantation upon a pleasant evening of spring. His advent is first noticed by some one or more huge mastiffs occupying the position of the Roman janitors at the gate of the castle. Their loud barking gives note of the approaching stranger. He is next observed by a group of curly-headed young urchins who scamper away to their hiding-places, or some more distant and safe retreat, to stand and gaze at what they deem a lawless intrusion upon their premises. The sun is reclining towards the western ocean of forests, the earth is clad in her verdant mantle, and vegetation glows in tints of living green. The herds and flocks are grazing upon the open fields, and the birds are making melody through the groves with their evening song. The yard teems with every species of ducks, geese, turkeys, chickens, goats, cats, and dogs of various sizes, castes, colors, and descriptions. In the distance he hears the merry song of the plough-boys and hands that "stalk afield," and the shrill tones of the *k-e-s-o-o-k! k-e-s-o-o-k!* of the old stock-"minder," at the sound of which a hundred forest grunters come squealing and growling up from the adjacent woods to the accustomed spot of rendezvous to receive their daily rations. A ceremony repeated from evening to evening, to enable this faithful old patriarch and feeder of flocks and herds, to ascertain if any lawless marauder or prowling vermin have invaded their ranks

21. In many instances, these free people of color hold hundreds of slaves, and are universally the most cruel and oppressive masters; but these are mixed bloods, or not of the real negro type.

22. "A CANDID CONFESSION.—The British Governor of Jamaica, in his address at the opening of the Provincial Legislature, *recommends the transportation of the fugitive slaves from our Southern States, who have taken refuge in Canada,* to the island of Jamaica, for the following reasons: 'The people who may, if matters be properly represented to them, be induced to come hither from America, are precisely the sort of industrial population we require; besides, they are admirably adapted to the climate of this island. Bringing with them an amount of *civilization far higher than that of the generality of the laboring population of this island,* and acquainted as they are to a much greater extent with agriculture and mechanical arts—two of the greatest desiderata in Jamaica

—the black and colored people of America are not only admirably calculated to develop the innumerable resources of the island to a far greater extent than the natives are at present capable of, but they will, to a certainty, if brought here, be the means of improving our native peasantry, by continually presenting, to a people so imitative, examples worthy for them to follow.'

"This is a striking testimony, as the New York Express justly remarks, to the humanizing and elevating influences with which the African is surrounded in the United (Southern) States."—*Richmond (Va.) Dispatch.*

and diminished their number. But should the traveller be belated and not reach this rural village till after night, frequently, as he approaches, he hears the far-off echoes of music, and the sounds of jubilant voices in dancing, rejoicings and merriment, as though they were celebrating some festive occasion. Where can there be found a class of agricultural laborers so independent of the world, so bountifully supplied with all the comforts of life? Where can there be found a class of hired laborers of this description whose families are furnished with one barrel of meat to each member per year, and one bushel of meal to each per month? and besides this from fifty to one hundred dollars of their wages saved for their contingent expenses. It may be safely asserted that such a class of hired laborers cannot be found within the territory of the United States, and much less in Europe. And every man who has experienced the hardship of supporting a family from his daily labors will respond to the truth of the assertion.

The negroes, as we have seen, never have, and never can, as a people, attain to equal rights and privileges with the whites without a miracle; they can never live upon grounds of equality with them in the same community. Inferiority is the position in which nature has placed them; and so long as they are in the same community with the whites, laws and institutions necessarily have been, and must be adapted to them in that condition. It is not the statute law that creates the slavery, but it is rather an adaptation of itself to the previous condition in which it finds the slave. All statute law upon that subject in its very provisions presupposes the condition of slavery, and is designed only for its good government and regulation. This we have seen, and shall see, is true from the nature, history, government and laws of the institution. Each sovereignty ever has been, and ever will be, its own arbiter of its own government and laws upon this subject. Slavery is always anterior to all its statute laws; and its very existence is always the cause and gives rise to the necessity of all political interference and regulations of the institution. This point we shall illustrate more fully hereafter. But we are told that slavery is a sin; that the very institution is a *malum in se,* a great moral and political evil; that the very relation of master and slave is necessarily wrong in itself; and that no government can legislate to uphold a sin, &c.

After what we have said upon the connexion of the constitution and laws of the Jewish nation with Hebrew slavery, of the relation of those laws to that institution, and their force and effect upon the same, we think we might justly leave this question between the modern Stoic philosophers and the Author of the Ten Commandments.

We sometimes hear of the sin of slavery in the abstract, but the idea is beyond my comprehension. Slavery in the abstract, to my understanding, is a perfect contradiction in terms. Slavery is but a relation, and that can never constitute an abstract idea, except it be between two abstract ideas or existences. But, in this instance, the relation is between two material and positive subjects, without which it has no conceivable form, and is therefore necessarily an idea in the concrete.

Its moral character, therefore, must always depend upon the condition of the subjects to which it relates, and the circumstances under which it exists. The slavery of one man to another may be wrong in one instance, and right in another; there can be no general principle of universal application to determine its character. In what, then, does the sin consist? In the forcible subjection of one man to another, says one, and the compulsion to labor without compensation. In depriving the slave of his natural rights, says another. But this definition of the evil would condemn civil government, and all its coercive measures. Besides, the idea of laboring without compensation supposes an impossibility; the food and raiment necessary to the existence of the slave is an essential compensation. Its adequacy has no reference to the definition. Therefore we must seek for some other definition of the sin of this relation. It consists, says another, in unjustly depriving the slave of his liberty; but this is but another form of the same idea, and in part the *petitio principii.* The question of justice or injustice in depriving any subject of his liberty, is one to be determined with reference to the rights of all parties, and the end and object of all government. But, says another, its sin consists in degrading the slave to a chattel, and making him liable to be bought and sold as an article of merchandize. But who is responsible for this? We have shown that government and law do not *place,* but *find* him in that condition —a condition, in many instances, from which they are incapable of extricating him, as in case of the negro in the Slave States. But this point we shall consider more fully hereafter.

If slavery in America is an evil, it is a necessary one, resulting from the peculiar character of the negro race, the condition of the country, and growing out of the imperfections of human nature. Civil government, with all its penal laws, prison discipline, and system of coercive measures, is in violation of the natural rights of man, and, in that sense, may be called an evil; but it is a relative one, and relates to the simple fact that mankind are as they are, rather than as they should be. If the world was perfect, penal laws would be unknown.

It will perhaps be said that government, on the part of freemen, is a voluntary surrendering of their natural rights; that they are parties to the compact, and may, therefore, justly incur the penalties of its laws: but that the slave has no voice, part or lot in the matter, except unconditional subjection and obedience. This is true, but it arises from his presumed incapacity for civil functions, as in the case of minors and women. In neither case does the law create the cause of their disability, but ever strives to adapt itself to their condition.

The same principles that would abolish the relation of master and slave, and remove all restraint imposed by that relation upon the liberties of the entire mass of the slave population in this country, would also, if carried out to their necessary results, abolish all restraint imposed by penal codes, prison discipline, and poor laws, upon the balance of the population. These restraints, in both instances, arise from the same cause, are founded upon the same reasons, and exist from the same necessity. One of the principal reasons that sustains them, and renders them both alike necessary, is the peace, prosperity and safety of society; or, in other words, the greatest amount of good to the greatest number. To this end all governments have a right, and it is their leading object, to shape their laws. All governments have the right, and it is their object, to secure, first, their own permanency, preservation and perpetuity; and second, the best possible state of society in the best possible manner. They must, therefore, be their own judges of the manner in which this end shall be obtained, and have the right to employ the most expedient measures to secure the same. Hence, the right of any independent government to regulate and uphold the institution of slavery, so long as it may be deemed expedient, and conducive to the common defence and general welfare of the State, is indisputable.

This relation imposes reciprocal obligations and duties upon both the master and slave. It is the duty of the master, imposed upon him by the law of the land, as well as that of humanity, to refrain from imposing excessive labor and from cruel treatment; to protect the objects of his trust, in sickness and in health, in infancy and helpless old age; to clothe the naked and feed the hungry, and to treat them, under all circumstances, with as much kindness and compassion as the welfare of society, his own interests and safety, and the disposition, character and position of the slave, will safely admit. In the words of St. Paul, to "give them that which is just and equitable."

On the other hand, it is the duty of the slave to "*obey his master with fear and trembling,*" *i.e.* with a high sense of reverence for their superiors; and "*with singleness of heart,*" *i.e.* with a willingness and sincerity; "*as unto Christ,*" *i.e.* they owe, in a degree, the same faithful obedience, reverence and devotion to their earthly, that they do to their Heavenly Master; "*not with eye-service, as men-pleasers, but as the servants of Christ, doing the will of God from the heart;*" "*with good will doing service as to the Lord, and not to men.*"

The doctrine of Christian resignation and obedience here inculcated by St. Paul, must for ever stand opposed to the teachings, preaching and practice of a class of the false and pretended friends of freedom in our sister States. It is a chapter direct upon the duties of servants and masters; it teaches them to be reconciled, sincere and faithful. "Art thou called to be a servant, care not for it." And though it exists not in the form of a statute law, yet I trust it is equally as imperious and as important as a statute. And though we weep over the remissness of these Christian duties, both by the master and the slave, yet surely we will not, for this reason alone, rashly dissolve this Gospel relation between them, and thus put for ever beyond the power of either to do "*the will of God*" in that capacity.

The Abolitionists—Consistency of Their Labors

This Essay will be confined to that school of Abolitionists who pretend to confine their labors to moral and religious means. Their political aspect will form a distinct topic, to be considered hereafter.

The fundamental principle in the creed of this class of "latter day" reformers, is, that the relation between master and slave is an usurpation of unjustifiable power, wrong *ab initio,* and ought to be abolished, irrespective of consequences.

It is wrong, say they, because it deprives its subjects of their natural rights. But so do civil government, penal codes, poor laws, and lunatic asylums. It is wrong because it denies the slave the means of religious instruction. This is a misrepresentation of facts; they enjoy these in common with the free population. It is wrong because it permits the vilest monster of a man to have as many slaves as he can get, and abuse and maltreat them with impunity. This is also a misrepresentation; the law protects the slave against cruel treatment (as we shall show). But the law also permits this same monster to have a wife, and as many children as may be added to his family, over whom he has as much control as he has over his slaves.

But slavery is wrong because it has a deleterious influence upon the moral and religious character of the community where it exists; and it should, therefore, be condemned. But, from what we have said in another place in this book, it would seem that the Founder of the Christian religion, and his Apostles, had the misfortune to differ with these "*latter day saints*" upon this subject. At best, such a position can be but a matter of opinion; as is true of the influence of great cities; great manufacturing communities; large collections of people for extensive public works; the army; the navy; the marine laws and regulations, and a thousand other collections and associations that might be mentioned. To be consistent, these fastidious conservators of public morals, who believe in their deleterious influences upon morals and religion, should wage the same war of extermination against them all.

But slavery is condemned by the golden rule, "Whatsoever ye would that men should do to you do ye even so to them." This, we have endeavored to show, imposes no obligation upon the master to liberate his slave, but directly the reverse. But it denies the slave all means of education and hope of improvement, and thus puts an interdict on his advancement. This position is one of the fundamental errors in the creed of the Abolitionists. The relation of the slave to his master, and his association with civilized life, instead of denying him the sources of education and means of improvement, is a constant source of education and means of improving his character and condition; instead of interdicting his advancement it prevents him from degenerating into his native barbarism.[1]

But slavery is wrong because it reduces men to things, and allows them to be bought and sold. This is also a misrepresentation, from which an egregious error pervades

public opinion throughout the free States. The idea of property in the person of the slave is an absurdity, which we shall explain more fully hereafter.[2]

But slavery must be wrong from the scenes of cruelty and incidents of abuse of the murderous treatment of the slaves, that are so frequently paraded before the public. But if the relation of master and servant is to be condemned on this ground alone, consistency calls for the condemnation of all the individual relations of persons whence arise abuses of authority and cruel treatment. And why is slavery singled out as the special object of calumny and vituperation for this reason? If abolition is the work of love, charity, and Christian benevolence, why is it that all the most revolting scenes of cruelty, misery, and wretchedness, arising from other relations, always escape their notice? If they condemn slavery for this, why not condemn those also?

The same reason would abolish the relation between husband and wife, parent and child, guardian and ward, tutor and pupil, master and apprentice, and every other instance of the individual authority of one person over another. No honest philosopher can fail to see the analogy of these relations in this particular. It is said, that in the association of husband and wife, and parent and child, there is a natural guarantee for the discharge of reciprocal duties and for kind treatment in the incentive for conjugal and parental affection, that is unknown to any other relation. But this conclusion, it will be readily seen, rests upon false premises. The relation itself furnishes no more assurance in one instance than in the other of the discharge of these reciprocal duties. On the contrary, where the domestic relation is unfortunate, the very reverse of this is true.

History is full of instances to show that misery is often the result of matrimonial connection. We all sympathize with Socrates in his trials with Xantippe and the Greek sophists. Juvenal tells us that those Roman matrons who had no affection for their husbands, kept their hired miscreants to torture their slaves. The greatest source of grief to the creator of the Lady in Comus was his misfortunes in his domestic relations. And thus was the Laureate of Eve enabled to write the best treatise on divorce. The face of one of England's earliest and best linguists is reported to have exhibited crimson marks, traced by loving fingers; and Greek, Hebrew, Latin, and English, must often have met

---

1. Compare the condition of the negro in America with that in Africa, and tell me what has been the cause of the difference. Or, compare the condition of the American slave with that of a St. Domingo freeman, or an emancipated slave of Jamaica, and answer the same question.

2. See Essay on the Political Aspect of Slavery, &c., post, 312, et seq.

and run together in his brain, as he reeled beneath the confusing ring of a fair hand knocking at his ears. Look at the helpmates of Whitelocke, Bishop Cooper, and Addison; they were tempestuous viragoes, endowed with a genius for scolding and trouble that constantly haunted the midnight visions of their husbands. The wives of Rousseau, Molière, Montaigne, Dante, Byron, Dryden, and Steele, were acute vixens, with tempers composed of vinegar and saltpetre, and tongues tipped with lunar caustic and as explosive as gun-cotton. Their husbands might as well sit to a bundle of lucifer-matches; for, at the least rub, they would ignite into a flame of hell-fire and blue blazes that would scorch their earlocks till they were glad to beat a retreat and make their escape. Some betook themselves to their gin-cup and club meetings, and others spent their lives in tears, solitude, and repentance. But how many modern Mrs. Caudles, whose "Curtain Lectures" are suppressed, and forever kept a secret from the world, while their poor submissive husbands are buffeting the storms of their household eloquence with hearts cheered by its pleasing consolations, and sleep sweetened by its soothing accents. And these miserable beings, with no source of earthly comfort left, in attempting to drown their sorrows, drown themselves in that liquid current, that is sweeping millions to a premature grave.

Were one willing to prostitute his pen to the capacity of a moral scavenger, and gather up the dregs that float only in the filthy sewers of society, and parade them all into a tale of the cares and misfortunes of matrimonial connections, he might present a picture that would put to the blush, and shame even the seared face of the author of Uncle Tom's Cabin. He could not only vary its figure with scars and stripes, but he could dye the ground-work of the picture crimson, with human blood.

But we forbear; we will present but few instances of the fruits of matrimony that have, in the last few weeks, come under our notice, as an offset to the fictitious parts of Uncle Tom, which, according to the modern Stoic and Abolition philosophers, are just grounds for condemning the institution.

"A Monster in human shape.—A German, named Jacob Brenigar, is now awaiting his trial in Wyoming County, Va., charged with a series of offences that surpass in horror any of the tales which old wives tell bad children to keep them quiet, of giants that lived "once upon a time." This Brenigar was formerly a Baptist preacher in North Carolina. While residing there, he attempted an outrage upon his own daughter. His wife made the fact known, and Brenigar, with his family, moved over into Wyoming. There he made another attempt at a rape upon his daughter. Shortly after, being desirous of obtaining his license to preach, which had been taken away from him in North Carolina, he applied to his wife to retract the charge she had brought against him, and admit that she had sworn falsely. This she refused to do, notwithstanding he inflicted frequent and severe beatings upon her. At last, finding neither persuasion, threats, nor beatings, would have any influence, one night he pulled his wife from the bed and dragged her over a piece of new ground full of stumps, so that she died in a short time after giving premature birth to a child. Mrs. Brenigar, at first, refused to tell the mode of receiving her injuries, but, finding that death was inevitable, made some of her neighbors acquainted with the facts. The husband was arrested, but released on bail. While under bonds he made an attempt to decoy his niece, a married woman, into some woods at the back of her residence, but she told her husband, who pursued the ruffian, and would have killed him, but his gun missed fire."—*Abington Democrat,* 1854.

"Singular Case.—Rev. Joseph Johnson is on trial at Kingston, Ulster Co., N.Y., on a charge of having murdered his wife and child. The evidence thus far tends to prove that the *Reverend gentleman* was in love with some other woman than his wife, and he got rid of the latter by drowning her in order to marry the former, which he did a few months ago. This miscreant escaped the just penalty of the law for a time by a defect in the indictment."—*Times, July,* 1854. . . .

"Total Depravity.—The Evansville Journal contains an account of a brute in human form, living in that place, who left his house early one Monday morning, and went sporting in the woods with his gun and dog, leaving a wife and child locked up in the house, both of whom were dangerously sick, without food or drink of any description within their reach. The inhuman wretch remained away all day, and until nearly 12 o'clock that night. About 10 o'clock in the evening some of the neighbors were alarmed by the groans of the woman, and the crying of the child—heard cries for food, water, &c., &c. The doors were forced open, and a horrible sight presented itself. The woman was in the last agonies of death, the immediate cause of which was undoubtedly neglect and starvation. She died in about one hour after being discovered. The child, about a year and six months old, was cared for by the neighbors, and exhibited painful symptoms of hunger, disease, and most wanton and brutal neglect. The wretch of a father returned before his wife died, but could give no excuse for his unpardonable absence, or for leaving his family in such a destitute condition."—*Louisville Democrat*. . . .

Whoever heard "of sorrows like these," of misery in such grim and horrid forms, among the slaves? One would suppose that consistency would arm the whole Abolition host in the panoply of war against the institution whence such scenes arose. And we see that the women, always the most sincere and guileless followers of consistency, are beginning to take action in this matter; they are about getting up an insurrection of spirits and others to abolish the abominable institution of marriage. It would seem, by the following extracts, that their present head-quarters was at Hope Dale, Milford, Massachusetts.

"WOMAN'S RIGHTS CONVENTION.—A notice of the forthcoming Annual Convention for the consideration of Woman's Rights, will be found in another column of our paper, and we call attention to it, hoping that some of our readers will thereby be induced to attend it. It is an important movement, this 'Woman's Rights' movement—one of the most important of the age—and all who feel interested in the welfare of the *whole* human race, should seriously consider the subject. Many women—as well as men—are not conscious of the necessity of it—not *now*—not feeling wronged by popular usages, having favored positions, or being content to be the mere appendages of men, if not their slaves. Into some women's souls, however, the iron has entered, and here follows a record of wrongs endured by a few which we take from THE UNA for the present month. They are extracts from letters addressed to Mrs. Davis, whose editorial comments follow them."   W. H. F.

"*Letter No.* 1.—Please do not send the 'Una' any more—I cannot receive it. My husband tore the last one from my hands and burned it. Oh, for an hour of peace, of rest! A blessing which I shall never again enjoy, till I hear 'the songs of angels round the Throne.' Sometimes I wish my ears were duller than they are, I hear so many heart-grieving, wrath-provoking things; but patience, patience, says my proud, firm heart. 'To *bear,* is to conquer our *fate.*'

"*No.* 2.—It is evident to me, my dear Madam, that the iron has never entered into your soul. You have never felt yourself a dependant, a slave in your husband's house—not daring to use one cent of money without his knowledge; and, at the same time, knowing he will not permit you to do, even with your own, what you desire. I brought my husband twenty thousand dollars. I have been three months trying to get one dollar to send you for your paper. My children, born in this relation, are a curse; for their inharmonious organizations are constantly a reproach to me. They are ill-looking and sickly, while we both have excellent constitutions. . . .

"*No.* 4.—A man may beat his wife, maltreat his servants, and ruin his children; that is nobody's concern. Society regards those things that are injurious to it, but meddles in nothing else, so it says. Do you not think, if society had any true regard for itself, it would prevent nine-tenths of the marriages, simply that criminals might not be born. I am quite certain that no circumstances can so ruin a good organization, that it may not be redeemable. While in these loathed, hated unions, good ones cannot be produced. I know I am a slave, and Mr. _____ is my lord. He can bind my body, tie my hands, but with my will he can do nothing. Do you ask why I am in this position? I was educated to get a husband—and was flattered and urged into a marriage at seventeen, that was thought to be very advantageous, and I thought that I loved. But I now see that misplaced affection differs as much from a right state of feeling, as truth from falsehood; and the living a lie is terrible. You have seen me always immersed in gaiety, but I felt that you looked below the surface and saw that this was not sufficient for me. I shall be a devotee when I am passé. Dorcas Societies, Ragged Schools, Boriaboula Missions anything to kill time, and make me forget my degradation; for I am a legalized—bah—I cannot write the word. God help us, for there is no other 'arm mighty to save.' . . ."

It may be pertinently asked why there is not more sympathy for the cause of the poor oppressed and down-trodden women of Hope Dale? There is not a slave on the Southern plantations but that has more liberty than they; they are struggling between life and death to assert their rights, and to throw off the galling yoke of matrimony, an institution upon which they remark as follows: "But so radical is the question of marriage itself, so deep is the hell of the marriage institution, '*as it is,*' and so sore therefore does every body feel in relation to the question, that the very proposition to discuss it is considered by some as tantamount to licentiousness."

It seems that this natural guarantee, so often spoken of for the protection of the wife and children, fails of its object among the "Christian Socialists" of Massachusetts. They are laboring and longing for the millennium of "Free Loveism" (as they term it). The only security for conjugal attachment, fidelity, and happiness, consists not in the respect of the relation itself, but in the kind and amiable disposition of the parties. But will the same cause secure no kind treatment to the slave? Whatever secures family peace, prosperity and happiness, secures also kind and humane treatment to him. When all other motives fail, the slave has the security, for food and raiment, at least, from the love of gain and pecuniary considerations of his master, an incentive ever opposed to the claims of the wife and children upon his clemency. Another school of Abolitionists, in carrying out their principles to their legitimate results, lay the axe at the root of all government and laws that forcibly deprive men of their liberty in their administration and execution. They stand upon the broad platform of abolition, non-resistance, and the *anti-coercitione regni*. Among the thousand ludicrous extracts that might be made from their publications, we submit only the following letter of Thomas Haskell to Adam Ballou, editor of the *Practical Christian*.

"*Gloucester, September* 10, 1854.

"BROTHER BALLOU:—I intended to have been at your annual meeting, but circumstances are such that I cannot conveniently attend; so I will send you my thoughts upon the present human governments. I have been thinking lately of the complete resemblance they bear to the 'Man of sin' spoken of by the Apostle, 'who opposeth and exalteth himself above all that is called God, or that is worshipped, so that he, as God, sitteth in the temple of God showing himself that he is God.' Does not our Government fully answer this description? Look at the Fugitive Slave Law, read the debates they had upon it, and see with what contempt and scorn they treated the thought that there was any higher law than their own enactments. Perhaps this Government is as complete a resemblance of a Righteous Government, as is possible for Satan to transform himself into an Angel of Light.

"Mankind are governed by one or the other of those two great principles, *love* and *fear*. This Government, both State and National, is founded upon the latter. We are not required to do or not to do certain acts because they

are right or wrong, but because they are the enactments of Government, and must be obeyed, or we must suffer certain forfeitures and penalties for disobedience. All who willingly sustain this Government of fear and violence, are willing slaves. They try to oppose chattel slavery, but they are sustaining a system equally degrading and inhuman. What greater degradation can be heaped upon us, than to be forbidden to give a starving brother a piece of bread under the penalty of one thousand dollars fine and six months imprisonment. Yet such is the institution we are taught we must sustain to protect the weak from the oppression of the strong, the righteous from the tyranny of the wicked."

But if the abuse of any privilege, right, or institution, is to determine its character, suppose one was to adopt the uncharitable course of the Abolitionists in judging a tree by its fruits, and should sketch faithfully the annals of the Church for the last half century, write the biography of the numerous backslidden saints, and the dark catalogue of crimes and misdemeanors that have stained its sacred history; and in the book he should devote a single chapter exclusively to the clergy, and hold all sincere Christians accountable for the black calendar of iniquities in the lives of all the murderers and miscreants that have invaded the ranks of this holy order, and condemn them all as of the same type of character; and, finally, denounce the Church and all its priesthood as a posthumous bantling of the devil. Could he be judged less consistent, and less charitable towards them, than the Northern slanderers and persecutors are towards the people of the South?

We are not of that school of moralists or logicians who would attempt to justify one evil by the existence of another. But we do say, that if one institution is to be condemned in consequence of the abuse of its privileges, and the bad fruits that thus result from it, all others must fall for a like reason. And we repeat the question, why are the Southern people selected as the special objects of calumny and vituperation? pursued, persecuted and denounced, with all the malice, clamor and indignation of public enemies? Is human nature so perfect, is the world so free from cruelty and abuses to the helpless of mankind, in every other portion, that there are no objects of sympathy, no cause of suffering deserving of this fanfaronade of Northern philanthropy, but the slaves of the South?

"SUICIDE TO AVOID THE CAT.—James Ransom, an able seaman of the Valorous, 16 (paddle), Captain Buckle, in the Baltic, committed suicide on the 5th of August last, by jumping overboard. It appears that the unfortunate poor fellow had been sentenced to receive three dozen lashes for some offence. While the gratings were being rigged for this punishment, he pleaded hard to the captain for mercy, and subsequently to the first lieutenant, to intercede in obtaining some other punishment; but finding these officers determined to let the punishment be inflicted, jumped overboard and was drowned."— *Plymouth (Eng.) Mail.*

"CRUELTY.—An American young woman, 19 years old, says the Newark (N.J.) Advertiser of the 20th, came to the office of the Overseer of the Poor last evening, and stated that she had been living, since she was three years old, with a family in Clinton township; and that on Tuesday last, the family compelled her to remain in a cold shed to do her washing, refusing her any opportunity of warming herself, so that at night her feet were badly frozen. Yesterday, seeing that she was crippled so as to be of no further service to them, they sent her to Newark. The Overseer of the Poor bestowed all requisite attention upon her, and this morning, after making an affidavit of the above facts before Justice Baldwin, she was taken to the Almshouse. Her feet are so badly frozen that is probable both must be amputated."

These very people were undoubtedly loudest in their denunciations of slavery, and were contributing their mite to support the cause of the poor slave at the South.

From personal observation I can assert the fact, and challenge a contradiction by any well-informed person, that there are to-day, May 12th, 1857, fifty thousand people in the city of New York, and twenty thousand in Boston, whose condition, as to the enjoyment of all the pleasures and comforts of life, will bear no comparison to the general condition of the slave population of the South.

The scenes of beggary, squalid poverty, and wretchedness, that force themselves upon the sight of the traveller in all the large cities of the Free States, forcibly remind him of the truth of the old maxim, that true charity should always begin its work at home.

"'WHITE SLAVE.'—This is the self-assumed title of white persons in New York. The New York Tribune contains a letter from a person who signs herself 'The Wife of a White Slave.' She complains that her husband, a glass-blower, is compelled to work without the rest that is allowed 'the slave on the plantation.' She very piteously inquires, 'While there are so many to employ their talents in behalf of the colored slave, is there not one to speak a word for the white?' Alluding to the severity of the labor of her husband and his fellow-workmen, and the little relaxation allowed them, she inquires, 'Who can wonder, however much they may deplore the error, that such men should recruit their exhausted energies with an artificial stimulus?'

"It is astonishing, that with such examples at their doors, the enthusiasts restrict their efforts to schemes for intermeddling with slavery at the South. But it is always so. Fanaticism prefers that far-reaching sort of sympathy, which manifests itself towards a distant people, and which can be indulged along with that kind of pomp and circumstance which is so grateful to its followers. They prefer that the dollar they give should be wasted upon impracticable schemes that make a noise in the world, rather than it should be given to the complaining 'White Slave' (as he calls himself) at their very doors."

But distance seems to lend enchantment to the cause of the Abolitionists. If philanthropy was their real motto, and humanity their real theme, and they were sincerely toiling in its spirit, and laboring in its hope, why do they not adopt the spirit of universal charity and benevolence of "Him who went about doing good," and in their labors of love breathe the brotherly spirit of St. Paul in his Epistle to the slave-holder Philemon? Like moral monomaniacs, there is no evil in their sight but the far-off wrongs of the Southern slave; there is no oppression that moves their compassion, no suffering that reaches their sympathy, but his. Thousands of their fellow-beings around may live in the most abject poverty and wretchedness, and die of starvation and distress, yet they have remembered not the wants of the poor and needy in the day of their distress. And whosoever of the Abolitionists does not clothe the naked and feed the hungry at home, the same is a hollow-hearted hypocrite, a liar, and the truth is not in him.

But "a prophet is not without honor, save in his own country"; therefore these Abolitionists and fomenters of disaffection and disunion, have to look to a foreign land in hope of reward. They must go to Great Britain for sympathy, to receive the congratulations and praises of the oppressive and tyrannical aristocracy of England. There are treasured up for them *crowns* of glory, and honors immortal. And Great Britain herself, with a laboring population literally weltering in their own grim misery, starvation and despair, is sending back her emissaries, professedly to aid in this great work of freedom and humanity; like Satan reproving sin, to preach liberty and emancipation to the American people.

British Slavery

A plantation of well-fed and well-clothed negro slaves shocks humanity, and calls down the vengeance of heaven upon the head of the slave-holder. But a press-gang may perform its heart-rending work in perfect consistency with the free and glorious institutions of Britain. One of the most repulsive features of the general system of British slavery is their laws relative to impressment. By these, peaceable and unoffending men are doomed to her vessels of war to serve at the pleasure and bidding of her naval officers. In this practice there are some of the most distressing instances of the sundering of kindred ties of home and friends. Here the husband is torn from the wife, the father from the child, the brother from the sister, by the press-gang, the kidnappers and slave-hunters of England—a custom that never has prevailed in any other civilized nation, ancient or modern. Anciently, some of the maritime nations condemned men to the galleys for crime.[3]

After a long and laborious voyage in a merchant vessel, the sun-burned seaman arrives in sight of home. His wife and children, who have long bewailed his absence, and feared for his life, stand with joyous countenances upon the shore, eager to embrace the returning wanderer. Perhaps a government vessel, on the search for seamen, then sends its barbarous press-gang aboard the ship, and forces the husband and father once more from the presence of the beloved ones. Long protracted years will pass away before he will be allowed to return. Then his wife may be dead, his children at the mercy of the parish. Yet England preaches freedom and humanity! . . .

Whoever wishes to see another faithful and life-like picture of this species of British slavery, should read the novel of Jacob Faithful, by Capt. Marryatt. Could we but follow the history of Jacob and Thomas, the watermen, or bring them up to tell their own tales of the "cat," and the horrors of naval discipline aboard of British men-of-war, we might then institute a comparison between the condition of this species of British, and American, slaves.

Slavery is any system of involuntary servitude, by which the time, service, and toil of one person becomes the property of another by compulsion. This has been the fundamental requisite of the institution in all ages of the world. But it has existed in different forms and under modified features in different nations and at different times. The power of life and death over the slave peculiar to some nations, is not an essential requisite to its existence; neither is the right to sell and alienate the services accompanied by a compulsory right to control the person of the slave in that manner (or, in other words, by a fiction of law to sell the slave). He who is compelled to labor without adequate compensation, without the ability to escape, to acquire property in the soil, or representation in legislation, is a slave! SLAVERY OF THE AGRICULTURAL PEASANTRY OF BRITAIN. Yet, such is the real condition of the mass of the laboring population of Great Britain.

The land-tenant is compelled to labor, and is subject to the will of his lord, because he fixes the price of rent, shares in the products of the soil and the proceeds of the poor man's labor, *ad libitum,* always leaving him a scant subsistence of the necessaries of life. He cannot escape from this condition; "once a peasant in England, and the man must remain a peasant forever."[4]

This is evident from the general policy of the nation upon this subject, which is to reduce the number of land proprietors and concentrate them all in the hands of a few who may hold the reins of government. In the United Kingdom, the land is divided into immense estates, constantly retained in the hands of a few; and the tendency of the existing laws of entail and primogeniture is to reduce even the number of these proprietors. There are 77,007,048 acres of land in the United Kingdom, including the small adjacent islands. Of this quantity, 28,227,435 acres are uncultivated. The number of proprietors of all this land is about 50,000. While the people of the United Kingdom number, at least, 28,000,000.[5] What a tremendous major-

---

3. See McCulloch, Dict. Com. (Impressment), where he coolly discusses the expediency of the laws.

4. London Times, 1844. Said Mr. Kay, of Trinity College, Cambridge: "Unless the English peasant has the means, and will consent to tear himself from his relations, friends, and early associations, and either transplant himself into a town or a distant colony, he has no chance of improving his condition." See White Slaves of England, p. 14.

5. See McCulloch, Dict. Com. "Britain."

ity, then, own not a foot of soil! And such are the policy and laws of England, that they never can, to any considerable number, own one foot of land, but must remain thereon, at the will and mercy of these few lords of the soil, and subject to a government in which they have no voice, and in which their interests are not represented.

"Mankind," says Aristotle, "are divided into freemen and slaves";[6] look, then, at the condition of the British peasantry, and say if they are freemen?

Look at the effects of the landed aristocracy in England. The Rev. Mr. Henry Worsley states, that in the year 1770, there were in England 250,000 freehold estates in the hands of 250,000 different families; and that, in 1815, the whole of the lands of England were concentrated in the hands of only 32,000 proprietors!

The effects of this system are obvious, according to the old maxim, "the big fish eat up the little ones," which is particularly true of all landed proprietors in all countries. As fast as the smaller estates come into market they are bought up by this landed aristocracy, the more wealthy and opulent proprietors outbidding the smaller ones, and thus monopolizing land at any cost. "The consequence is," says a distinguished lawyer of Westmoreland and Cumberland Counties in 1849, "for some time past, the number of small estates has been rapidly diminishing in all parts of the country. In a short time, none of them will remain, but all be merged in the great estates. The consequence is, that the peasant's position, instead of being what it once was, one of hope, is fast becoming one of despair. Unless he emigrates, it is now impossible for him ever to rise above a peasant."[7] But what chance have the majority of the peasantry of Great Britain to emigrate, when their year's labor is scarcely sufficient to keep soul and body together. The distressing policy of this monopoly of the British aristocracy, by swallowing these small estates, is to turn thousands upon thousands adrift upon the country without houses, or means of support. If one of the great landholders prefers the pursuit of grazing to that of farming, he may sweep away the homes of his laborers, turning the poor wretches

upon the country as wandering paupers, or drive them into the cities to overstock the workshops, and thus reduce the wages of the poor mechanic, which are now too small to afford him and his family the necessaries of life. The country, by this means, is filled with beggary, misery, and distress; the poor-houses peopled to overflowing with helpless paupers; till, at length, the government is driven to the desperate alternative of emptying them by transportation to the shores of America.

But we propose to present a few of the leading sketches and astounding facts, to show the condition of the white slaves that remain, and of their condition, generally, under British domination.

Mr. John Fox, medical officer of the Cerne Union, in Dorsetshire, says: "Most of the cottages of the agricultural laborers in Devon, Somerset, Dorset, and Wiltshire, are of the worst description; some are mere mud-hovels, and situated in low and damp places, with cesspools, or accumulations of filth, close to the doors. The mud floors of many are much below the level of the road, and, in wet seasons, are little better than so much clay. In many of them, the bed stood on the ground-floor, which was damp three parts of the year; scarcely one had a fireplace in the bedroom; and one had a single pane of glass stuck in the mud wall as its only window. Persons living in these cottages are generally poor, very dirty, and usually in rags, living almost wholly on bread and potatoes, scarcely ever tasting animal food, and, consequently, highly susceptible of disease, and very unable to contend with it." . . .

"Slaves cannot breathe in England," said the English jurist; "that moment their lungs receive our air, their shackles fall." But, turn to Catholic Ireland, with her quintuple population, in rags and wretchedness, staining the sweetest scenery ever eye reposed on! Scenery that hath wreathed the immortal shamrock around the brow of painting, poetry, and eloquence. Talk of ancient miseries in the mines of Laurian; talk of the tears and groans of the Roman Ergastula; talk of the bondage and chains of the Ottoman's slave, of the degradation and sufferings of the subjects of Moslem power!

But the crowning scene to this picture of human misery may be drawn from the beautiful Emerald Isle. A people whose very life-blood has been trampled out by the oppressive system of British slavery; whose miseries have gone forth upon the wings of song and in themes of elo-

---

6. οἰκία δὲ τελείος ἐκ δούλων καὶ ἐλευθέρων. De Rep. I:3. He says, in another place, that some were born to rule and others to serve; are not the peasants born to serve?

7. See White Slaves of England, p. 15. This most excellent work contains a compilation of testimony and facts collected entirely from foreign sources of the most reliable kind.

quence, till they have kindled the sympathies of all nations save their oppressors.

It is the universal and concurrent testimony of all travellers, that in consequence of this system of organized oppression, Ireland has become the home of miseries that scarce have a parallel upon the face of the earth. "Everywhere in Ireland a traveller as he passes along the road will see on the road-side and in the fields, places that look like mounds of earth and sods, with a higher heap of sods upon the top, out of which smoke is curling upwards; and with two holes in the side of the heap next the road, one of which is used as a door, and the other as the window of the hovel. These are the homes of the peasantry! Entering, you will find it to contain but one room, formed by the mud walls; and in these places, upon the mud floor, the families of the peasants live. Men, women, boys, and girls, live and sleep together, and herd with the wallowing pig.

Gaunt, ragged figures crawl out of these hovels and plant the ground around with potatoes, which constitute the only food of the inmates during the year, or swarm the roads and thoroughfares as wretched beggars. But the tenure even of these miserable hovels is insecure. The tenants are subject to the tender mercies of the lay proctor of some absent lord, and if they do not pay their rent at a proper time, they are liable to be turned adrift even in the middle of the night. And they have no appeal except to the court of heaven. Kay says, that in 1849, more than 50,000 families were evicted and turned as beggars upon the community.[8]

Here was a striking illustration of the effects of immediate emancipation in all its wretchedness. Think of the heart-rending scenes of misery and distress that must have followed the turning out near half a million of people, pennyless, upon the charities of Great Britain! Thousands of these poor wretches after wandering about for a time like the ghosts of Aeneas, starved to death and perished by the road-side, the victims of the murderous policy of the humane and benevolent landed aristocracy of Britain.[9] . . .

The dearest ties of family are sundered by the force of want, like a company of shipwrecked wanderers in an open boat, who see no possible means of deliverance. The lot must fall upon some to perish, that, peradventure, some may be saved. The husband can, perhaps, pay his own pas-

sage to America, but the wife and children must remain paupers in the land of their hereditary misery.

But the evil consequences of British slavery do not end with the miseries and sufferings of the agricultural laborers or tenants of the soil. There are London, Liverpool, Manchester, Birmingham, Glasgow, Dublin, and many other cities and towns, with their crowds of slaves either in the factories and workshops, or in the streets as beggars, paupers, and criminals. There are said to be four millions of paupers in the United Kingdom! Can such an amount of wretchedness be found in any other country upon the face of the globe? To what cause can this be attributed save to the oppressive system of the landed aristocracy and the laws that favor them. How else could there be eleven millions of acres of good tillable land unoccupied, save for some of the pleasure purposes of these aristocrats, and four millions of perishing paupers? It is said that more than two millions of people were kept from starving in England and Wales, in 1848, by relief doled out to them from public and private sources.[10]

So scant are the earnings of those who labor day and night in the cities and towns, that they may become paupers if thrown out of employment a single week. Upon an average a hard-working peasant can earn five shillings a week; two of which must go for rent, leaving him only three shillings to buy his food and raiment. The slaves of Great Britain are not attached to the soil, and bought and sold with it like the serfs of Russia, or the negroes of the United States; but far better would it be for them were such their destiny. Then the rich landlord who enjoys the labor of his hundred, would also incur the responsibility of their maintenance in sickness, and in infancy and old age. But they are called freemen to enable their lords to detach them from the soil at will, and after spending long and faithful lives in their service, till they have passed their days of usefulness, then to turn them adrift and drive them forth to starve, perish, or become paupers at public charge, without incurring any penalties for their cruelties, such as the slave-holders of other countries would suffer. The Russian, the Spanish, and the North American slave-holder must support his slaves in sickness and helpless old age,

8. White Slaves of England, p. 22.
9. See great Speech of Sir Robert Peel, on Ireland, 1849.

10. How much of this was the proceeds of the slave labor of the South, contributed as thousands were by the people of the Southern States for the relief of starving Ireland?

or suffer the penalties of the law for his neglect. But the British slave-holder is exempt from such a tax; he may leave them to perish by thousands with impunity. His Irish slaves may be saved from starvation by American bounty, but neither American or any other human law can punish the offender. Truly then did Southey write:

"To talk of English happiness is to talk of Spartan freedom; the *Helots* are overlooked. In no country can such riches be acquired by commerce, but it is the one who grows rich by the labor of the hundred. The hundred human beings like himself, as wonderfully fashioned by nature, gifted with like capacities, and equally destined for immortality, are sacrificed *body and soul.*

"Horrible as it may seem, the assertion is true to the very letter. They are deprived in childhood of all instruction and all enjoyments — of the sports in which childhood instinctively indulges — of fresh air by day and natural sleep by night. Their health, physical and moral, is alike destroyed; they die of diseases induced by unremitting taskwork, by too close confinement in the impure atmosphere of crowded rooms, by the particles of metallic or vegetable dust which they are constantly inhaling; or they live to grow up without decency, without comfort, and with-

out hope — without morals, without religion, and without shame, and bring forth *slaves* like themselves to tread in the same path of misery."

Again, this same distinguished Englishman says: "The English boast of their liberty; but there is *no liberty in England for the poor.* They are no longer sold with the soil (as formerly), it is true; but they cannot leave the parish of their nativity if they are liable to become chargeable. In such a case, if they endeavor to remove to some situation where they hope more easily to maintain themselves, where work is more plentiful or provisions cheaper, the overseers are alarmed, the intruder is apprehended as if he were a criminal, and sent back to his own parish. Wherever a pauper dies, the parish must be at the expense of his burial. Instances therefore have not been wanting of wretches, in the last stage of disease, having been hurried away in an open cart, and dying upon the road. Nay, even women in the pains of labor have been driven out, and perished by the way-side, because the birthplace of the child would be its parish." [11]

11. Whoever has a desire to pursue this subject more in detail, may refer to the White Slaves of England, by Cobden, or to the original sources of information from which these facts are compiled.

What Is Slavery?

Slavery Is Despotism

1853

HARRIET BEECHER STOWE

Harriet Beecher Stowe (1811–96) was the daughter of the famous New England minister Lyman Beecher. She is the author of *Uncle Tom's Cabin,* an abolitionist novel written in response to the Fugitive Slave Law of 1850. The book sold more than 300,000 copies in its first year. Two years later, Stowe published *A key to Uncle Tom's cabin; presenting the original facts and documents upon which the story is founded. Together with corroborative statements verifying the truth of the work.* Selections reproduced here are taken from that work. In it, Stowe sought to answer critics who charged her with exaggerating the plight of black slaves.

What Is Slavery?

The author will now enter into a consideration of slavery as it stands revealed in slave law.

What is it according to the definition of law-books and legal interpreters? "A slave," says the law of Louisiana, "is one who is in the power of a master to whom he belongs. The master may sell him, dispose of his person, his industry, and his labour; he can do nothing, possess nothing, nor acquire anything, but what must belong to his master." South Carolina says: "Slaves shall be deemed, sold, taken, reputed, and adjudged in law, to be chattels personal in the hands of their owners and possessors, and their executors, administrators, and assigns, TO ALL INTENTS, CONSTRUCTIONS AND PURPOSES WHATSOEVER." The law of Georgia is similar.

Let the reader reflect on the extent of the meaning in this last clause. Judge Ruffin, pronouncing the opinion of the Supreme Court of North Carolina, says a slave is "one doomed in his own person, and his posterity, to live without knowledge, and without the capacity to make anything his own, and to toil that another may reap the fruits."

This is what slavery *is,* this is what it is to be a slave!

The slave-code, then, of the Southern States, is designed to keep millions of human beings in the condition of chattels personal; to keep them in a condition in which the master may sell them, dispose of their time, person, and labour; in which they can do nothing, possess nothing, and acquire nothing, except for the benefit of the master; in which they are doomed in themselves and in their posterity to live without knowledge, without the power to make anything their own, to toil that another may reap. The laws of the slave-code are designed to work out this problem, consistently with the peace of the community, and the safety of that superior race which is constantly to perpetrate this outrage.

From this simple statement of what the laws of slavery are designed to do—from a consideration that the class thus to be reduced, and oppressed, and made the subjects of a perpetual robbery, are *men* of like passions with our own, men originally made in the image of God as much as ourselves, men partakers of that same humanity of which Jesus Christ is the highest ideal and expression—when we consider that the material thus to be acted upon is that fearfully explosive element, the soul of man; that soul elastic, upspringing, immortal, whose free will even the Omnipotence of God refuses to coerce, we may form some idea of the tremendous force which is necessary to keep this mightiest of elements in the state of repression which is contemplated in the definition of slavery.

Of course, the system necessary to consummate and perpetuate such a work, from age to age, must be a fearfully stringent one; and our readers will find that it is so. Men who make the laws, and men who interpret them, may be fully sensible of their terrible severity and inhumanity; but if they are going to preserve the THING, they have no resource but to make the laws and to execute them faithfully after they are made. They may say with the Hon. Judge

Ruffin, of North Carolina, when solemnly from the bench announcing this great foundation principle of slavery, that "THE POWER OF THE MASTER MUST BE ABSOLUTE, TO RENDER THE SUBMISSION OF THE SLAVE PERFECT"—they may say with him, "I most freely confess my sense of the harshness of this proposition; I feel it as deeply as any man can; and, as a principle of moral right, every person in his retirement must repudiate it;" but they will also be obliged to add, with him, "But in the *actual condition* of things IT MUST BE SO. . . . This discipline belongs to the state of slavery. . . . It is INHERENT in the relation of master and slave."

And, like Judge Ruffin, men of honour, men of humanity, men of kindest and gentlest feelings, are *obliged* to interpret these severe laws with inflexible severity. In the perpetual reaction of that awful force of human passion and human will, which necessarily meets the compressive power of slavery—in that seething, boiling tide, never wholly repressed, which rolls its volcanic stream underneath the whole framework of society so constituted, ready to find vent at the least rent or fissure or unguarded aperture—there is a constant necessity which urges to severity of law, and inflexibility of execution. So Judge Ruffin says, "We cannot allow the *right* of the master to be brought into discussion in the courts of justice. The slave, to remain a slave, must be made sensible that there is NO APPEAL FROM HIS MASTER." Accordingly, we find in the more southern States, where the slave population is most accumulated, and slave property most necessary and valuable, and, of course, the determination to abide by the system the most decided, *there* the enactments are most severe, and the interpretation of Courts the most inflexible.* And, when legal decisions of a contrary character begin to be made, it would appear that it is a symptom of leaning towards emancipation. So abhorrent is the slave-code to every feeling of humanity, that just as soon as there is any hesitancy in the community about perpetuating the institution of slavery, judges begin to listen to the voice of their more honourable nature, and by favourable interpretations to soften its necessary severities.

Such decisions do not commend themselves to the professional admiration of legal gentlemen. But in the workings of the slave system, when the irresponsible power

* We except the State of Louisiana. Owing to the influence of the French code in that State, more really humane provisions prevail there. How much these provisions avail in point of fact will be shown when we come to that part of the subject.

which it guarantees comes to be used by men of the most brutal nature, cases sometimes arise for trial where the consistent exposition of the law involves results so loathsome and frightful that the judge prefers to be illogical, rather than inhuman. Like a spring out-gushing in the desert, some noble man, now and then, from the fulness of his own better nature, throws out a legal decision, generously inconsistent with every principle and precedent of slave jurisprudence, and we bless God for it. All we wish is that there were more of them, for then should we hope that the day of redemption was drawing nigh.

The reader is now prepared to enter with us on the proof of this proposition: That the slave-code is designed *only for the security of the master, and not with regard to the welfare of the slave.*

This is implied in the whole current of law-making and law-administration, and is often asserted in distinct form, with a precision and clearness of legal accuracy which, in a literary point of view, are quite admirable. Thus, Judge Ruffin, after stating that considerations restricting the power of the master had often been drawn from a comparison of slavery with the relation of parent and child, master and apprentice, tutor and pupil, says distinctly:

> The Court does not recognise their application. There is no likeness between the cases. They are in opposition to each other, and there is an impassable gulf between them. . . . In the one [case], the end in view is the *happiness of the youth,* born to equal rights with that governor on whom the duty devolves of training the young to usefulness, in a station which he is afterwards to assume among freemen. . . . With slavery it is far otherwise. The *end is the profit of the master* his security and the public safety.

Not only is this principle distinctly asserted in so many words, but it is more distinctly implied in multitudes of the arguings and reasonings which are given as grounds of legal decisions. Even such provisions as seem to be for the benefit of the slave we often find carefully interpreted so as to show that it is only on account of his property value to his master that he is thus protected, and not from any consideration of humanity towards himself. Thus it has been decided that a master can bring no action for assault and battery on his slave, *unless the injury be such as to produce a loss of service.*

The spirit in which this question is discussed is worthy of remark. We give a brief statement of the case, as presented in Wheeler, p. 239.

It was an action for assault and battery committed by Dale on one Cornfute's slave. It was contended by Cornfute's counsel that it was not necessary to *prove loss of service,* in order that the action should be sustained; that an action might be supported for beating plaintiff's *horse;* and that the lord might have an action for the battery of his villein, which is founded on this principle, that, as the villein could not support the action, *the injury would be without redress unless the lord could.* On the other side, it was said that Lord Chief Justice Raymond had decided that an assault on a horse was no cause of action, unless accompanied with *a special damage of the animal,* which would impair his value.

Chief Justice Chase decided that no redress could be obtained in the case, because the value of the slave had not been impaired; *without injury or wrong to the master* no action could be sustained; and assigned this among other reasons for it, that there was no reciprocity in the case, as the master was not liable for assault and battery committed by his slave, neither could he gain redress for one committed upon his slave.

Let any reader now imagine what an amount of wanton cruelty and indignity may be heaped upon a slave man or woman or child without actually impairing their power to do service to the master, and he will have a full sense of the cruelty of this decision.

In the same spirit it has been held in North Carolina that patrols (night watchmen) are not liable to the master for inflicting punishment on the slave, unless their conduct clearly demonstrates *malice against the master.*

The cool-bloodedness of some of these legal discussions is forcibly shown by two decisions in Wheeler's Law of Slavery, p. 243. On the question whether the criminal offence of assault and battery can be committed on a slave, there are two decisions of the two States of South and North Carolina; and it is difficult to say which of these decisions has the pre-eminence for cool legal inhumanity. That of South Carolina reads thus. Judge O'Neill says:

> The criminal offence of assault and battery cannot, at common law, be committed upon the person of a slave. For notwithstanding (for some purposes) a slave is regarded by law as a *person,* yet generally he is a mere chattel personal, and his right or personal protection belongs to his master, who can maintain an action of trespass for the battery of his slave. There can be therefore no offence against the State for a *mere beating of a slave unaccompanied with any circumstances of cru-*

elty (!!), or an attempt to kill and murder. The peace of the State *is not thereby broken;* for a slave is not generally regarded as legally capable of being within the peace of the State. He is not a citizen, and is not in that character entitled to her protection.

What declaration of the utter indifference of the State to the sufferings of the slave could be more elegantly cool and clear? But in North Carolina it appears that the case is argued still more elaborately.

Chief Justice Taylor thus shows that, after all, there are reasons why an assault and battery upon the slave may, on the whole, have some such general connection with the comfort and security of the community, that it may be construed into a breach of the peace, and should be treated as an indictable offence.

> The instinct of a slave may be, and generally is, tamed into subservience to his master's will, and from him he receives chastisement, whether it be merited or not, with perfect submission; for he knows the extent of the dominion assumed over him, and that the law ratifies the claim. But when the same authority is wantonly usurped by a stranger, Nature is disposed to assert her rights, and to prompt the slave to a resistance, often momentarily successful, sometimes fatally so. The public peace is thus broken, as much as if a free man had been beaten; for the party of the aggressor is always the strongest, and such contests usually terminate by overpowering the slave, and inflicting on him a severe chastisement, without regard to the original cause of the conflict. There is, consequently, as much reason for making such offences indictable as if a white man had been the victim. A wanton injury committed on a slave is a great provocation to the owner, awakens his resentment, and has a direct tendency to a breach of the peace, by inciting him to seek immediate vengeance. If resented in the heat of blood, it would probably extenuate a homicide to manslaughter, upon the same principle with the case stated by Lord Hale that if, A riding on the road, B had whipped his horse out of the track, and then A had alighted and killed B. These offences are usually committed by men of dissolute habits, hanging loose upon society, who, being repelled from association with well-disposed citizens, take refuge in the company of coloured persons and slaves, whom they deprave by their example, embolden by their familiarity, and then beat, under the expectation that a slave dare not resent a blow from a white man. If such offences may be committed with impunity, the public peace will not only be rendered extremely insecure, but the value of slave property must be much impaired, for the offenders can seldom make any

reparation in damages. Nor is it necessary, in any case, that a person who has received an injury, real or imaginary, from a slave, should carve out his own justice; for the law has made ample and summary provision for the punishment of all trivial offences committed by slaves, by carrying them before a justice, who is authorised to pass sentence for their being publicly whipped. This provision, while it excludes the necessity of private vengeance, would seem to forbid its legality, since it effectually protects all persons from the insolence of slaves, even where their masters are unwilling to correct them upon complaint being made. The common law has often been called into efficient operation, for the punishment of public cruelty inflicted upon animals, for needless and wanton barbarity exercised even by masters upon their slaves, and for various violations of decency, morals, and comfort. Reason and analogy seem to require that a human being, although the subject of property, should be so far protected as the public might be injured through him.

For all purposes necessary to enforce the obedience of the slave, and to render him useful as property, the law secures to the master a complete authority over him, and it will not lightly interfere with the relation thus established. It is a more effectual guarantee of his right of property, when the slave is protected from wanton abuse from those who have no power over him; for it cannot be disputed that a slave is rendered less capable of performing his master's service, when he finds himself exposed by the law to the capricious violence of every turbulent man in the community.

If this is not a scrupulous disclaimer of all humane intention in the decision, as far as the slave is concerned, and an explicit declaration that he is protected only out of regard to the comfort of the community, and his property value to his master, it is difficult to see how such a declaration could be made. After all this cold-blooded course of remark, it is somewhat curious to come upon the following certainly most unexpected declaration, which occurs in the very next paragraph:—

Mitigated as slavery is by the *humanity of our laws,* the refinement of manners, and by *public opinion, which revolts at every instance of cruelty towards* them, it would be an anomaly in the system of police which affects them, if the offence stated in the verdict were not indictable.

The reader will please to notice that this remarkable declaration is made of the State of North Carolina. We shall have occasion again to refer to it by and by, when we extract from the statute-book of North Carolina some specimens of these humane laws.

In the same spirit it is decided, under the law of Louisiana, that if an individual injures another's slave so as to make him *entirely useless,* and the owner recovers from him the full value of the slave, the slave by that act becomes thenceforth the property of the person who injured him.

A decision to this effect is given in Wheeler's Law of Slavery, p. 249. A woman sued for an injury done to her slave by the slave of the defendant. The injury was such as to render him entirely useless, his *only* eye being put out. The parish court decreed that she should recover 1200 dollars, that the defendant should pay a further sum of 25 dollars a month from the time of the injury; also the physician's bill, and 200 dollars for the sustenance of the slave during his life, and that he should remain for ever in the possession of his mistress.

The case was appealed. The judge reversed the decision, and delivered the slave into the possession of the man whose slave had committed the outrage. In the course of the decision, the judge remarks, with that calm legal explicitness for which many decisions of this kind are remarkable, that—

The principle of humanity, which would lead us to suppose that the mistress, whom he had long served, would treat her miserable blind slave with more kindness than the defendant, to whom the judgment ought to transfer him, cannot be taken into consideration in deciding this case.

Observe, now, the following case of Jennings *v.* Fundeberg. It seems Jennings brings an action of trespass against Fundeberg for killing his slave. The case was thus:—Fundeberg, with others, being out hunting runaway negroes, surprised them in their camp, and, as the report says, "*fired his gun towards them,* as they were running away, *to induce them to stop.*" One of them being shot through the head was thus *induced to stop*—and the master of the boy brought action for trespass against the firer for killing his slave.

The decision of the inferior Court was as follows:—

The Court "thought the killing accidental, and that the defendant ought not to be made answerable as a trespasser. . . . When one is lawfully interfering with the property of another, and accidentally destroys it, he is no trespasser, and ought not to be answerable for the value of the property. In this case, the defendant was engaged in a lawful and *meritorious* service, and if he really fired his gun in the manner stated, it was an allowable act."

The superior judge reversed the decision, on the ground

that in dealing with another person's property one is responsible for any injury which he could have avoided by any degree of circumspection. "The firing . . . was *rash and incautious.*" Does not the whole spirit of this discussion speak for itself?

See also the very next case in Wheeler's Law. Richardson *v.* Dukes, p. 202.

> Trespass for killing the plaintiff's slave. It appeared the slave was stealing potatoes from a bank near the defendant's house. The defendant fired upon him with a gun loaded with buck-shot, and killed him. The jury found a verdict for plaintiff for one dollar. Motion for a new trial.
>
> *The Court, Nott J.,* held, there must be a new trial; that the jury ought to have given the plaintiff the value of the slave. That if the jury were of opinion the slave was of bad character, some deduction from the usual price ought to be made, but the plaintiff was certainly entitled to his actual damage for killing his slave. Where property is in question, the value of the article, as nearly as it can be ascertained, furnishes a rule from which they are not at liberty to depart.

It seems that the value of this unfortunate piece of property was somewhat reduced from the circumstance of his "stealing potatoes." Doubtless he had his own best reasons for this; so, at least, we should infer from the following remark, which occurs in one of the reasonings of Judge Taylor of North Carolina.

> The act of 1786 (Iredell's Revisal, p. 588) does, in the pre-amble, recognise the fact, that many persons, *by cruel treatment to their slaves, cause* them to commit crimes for which they are executed. . . . The cruel treatment here alluded to must consist in *withholding from them the necessaries of life;* and the crimes thus resulting are such as are calculated to *furnish them with food and raiment.*

Perhaps "stealing potatoes" in this case was one of the class of crimes alluded to.

Again we have the following case:—

> The defendants went to the plantation of Mrs. Whitsell for the purpose of hunting for runaway negroes; there being many in the neighbourhood, and the place in considerable alarm. As they approached the house with loaded guns, a negro ran from the house, or near the house, towards a swamp, when they fired and killed him.
>
> The judge charged the jury, that such circumstances might exist, by the excitement and alarm of the neighbourhood, as to authorise the killing of a negro without the sanction of the magistrate.

This decision was reversed in the Superior Court, in the following language:

> By the statute of 1740, any white man may apprehend and moderately correct any slave who may be found out of the plantation at which he is employed, and if the slave assaults the white person, *he may be killed;* but a slave who is merely flying away cannot be killed. Nor can the defendants be justified by common law, if *we consider the negro as a person;* for they were not clothed with the authority of the law to apprehend him as a felon, and without such authority he could not be killed.

If *we consider the negro a person,* says the judge; and, from his decision in the case, he evidently intimates that he has a strong leaning to his opinion, though it has been contested by so many eminent legal authorities that he puts forth his sentiments modestly, and in an hypothetical form. The reader, perhaps, will need to be informed that the question whether the slave is to be considered a person or a human being in any respect has been extensively and ably argued on both sides in legal courts, and it may be a comfort to know that the balance of legal opinion inclines in favour of the slave. Judge Clarke, of Mississippi, is quite clear on the point, and argues very ably and earnestly, though, as he confesses, against very respectable legal authorities, that the slave *is* a person—that he *is* a reasonable creature. The reasoning occurs in the case State of Mississippi *v.* Jones, and is worthy of attention as a literary curiosity.

It seems that a case of murder of a slave had been clearly made out and proved in the lower Court, and that judgment was arrested, and the case appealed on the ground whether, in that State, murder could be committed on a slave. Judge Clarke thus ably and earnestly argues:—

> The question in this case is, whether murder can be committed on a slave. Because individuals may have been deprived of many of their rights by society, it does not follow that they have been deprived of all their rights. In some respects, slaves may be considered as chattels; but in others they are regarded as men. The law views them as capable of committing crimes. This can only be upon the principle, that they are *men* and rational beings. The Roman law has been much relied on by the counsel of the defendant. That law was confined to the Roman empire, giving the power of life and death over captives in war, as slaves; but it no more extended here, than the similar power given to parents over the lives of their children. Much stress has also been laid, by the defendant's counsel, on

the case cited from Taylor's Reports, decided in North Carolina; yet, in that case, two judges against one were of opinion, that killing a slave was murder. Judge Hall, who delivered the dissenting opinion in the above case, based his conclusions, as we conceive, upon erroneous principles, by considering the laws of Rome applicable here. His inference, also, that a person cannot be condemned capitally, because he may be liable in a civil action, is not sustained by reason or authority, but appears to us to be in direct opposition to both. At a very early period in Virginia, the power of life over slaves was given by statute; but Tucker observes, that as soon as these statutes were repealed, it was at once considered by their Courts that the killing of a slave might be murder. (Commonwealth *v.* Dolly Chapman: indictment for maliciously stabbing a slave, under a statute.) It has been determined in Virginia that slaves are persons. In the constitution of the United States, slaves are expressly designated as "persons." In this State the legislature have considered slaves as reasonable and accountable beings; and it would be a stigma upon the character of the State, and a reproach to the administration of justice, if the life of a slave could be taken with impunity, or if he could be murdered in cold blood, without subjecting the offender to the highest penalty known to the criminal jurisprudence of the country. Has the slave no rights, because he is deprived of his freedom? He is still a human being, and possesses all those rights of which he is not *deprived by the positive provisions of the law;* but in vain shall we look for any law passed by the enlightened and philanthropic legislature of this State, giving even to the master, much less to a stranger, power over the life of a slave. Such a statute would be worthy the age of Draco or Caligula, and would be condemned by the unanimous voice of the people of this State, where even cruelty to slaves, much [more] the taking away of life, meets with universal reprobation. By the provisions of our law, a slave may commit murder, and be punished with death; why, then, is it not murder to kill a slave? Can a mere chattel commit murder, and be subject to punishment? . . .

The right of the master exists not by force of the law of nature or nations, but by virtue only of the positive law of the State; and although that gives to the master the right to command the services of the slave, requiring the master to feed and clothe the slave from infancy till death, yet it gives the master no right to take the life of the slave; and, if the offence be not murder, it is not a crime, and subjects the offender to no punishment.

The taking away the life of a reasonable creature, under the king's peace, with malice aforethought, expressed or implied, is murder at common law. Is not a slave a reasonable creature —is he not a human being? And the meaning of this phrase, "reasonable creature," is a human being. For the killing a lu-

natic, an idiot, or even a child unborn, is murder, as much as the killing a philosopher; and has not the slave as much reason as a lunatic, an idiot, or an unborn child?

Thus triumphantly, in this nineteenth century of the Christian era, and in the State of Mississippi, has it been made to appear that the slave is a reasonable creature—a human being!

What sort of system, what sort of a public sentiment, was that which made this argument *necessary!*

And let us look at some of the admissions of this argument with regard to the *nature* of slavery. According to the judge, it is depriving human beings of *many of their rights.* Thus he says: "Because individuals may have been deprived of many of their rights by society, it does not follow that they have been deprived of *all* their rights." Again, he says of the slave: "He is still a human being, and possesses all those *rights* of which he is not deprived by *positive provisions of the law.*" Here he admits that the provisions of law deprive the slave of natural *rights.* Again he says: "The right of the master exists not by force of the law of nature or of nations, but by virtue only of the positive law of the State." According to the decision of this judge, therefore, slavery exists by the same right that robbery or oppression of any kind does—the right of *ability.* A gang of robbers associated into a society have rights over all the neighbouring property that they can acquire, of precisely the same kind.

With the same unconscious serenity does the law apply that principle of force and robbery which is the essence of slavery, and show how far the master may proceed in appropriating another human being as his property.

The question arises, May a master give a woman to one person, and her *unborn children* to another one? Let us hear the case argued. The unfortunate mother, selected as the test point of this interesting legal principle, comes to our view in the will of one Samuel Marksbury, under the style and denomination of "my negro wench, Pen." Said Samuel states in his will that, for the good-will and love he bears to his *own* children, he gives said negro wench, Pen, to son Samuel, and all her future increase to daughter Rachael. When daughter Rachael, therefore, marries, her husband sets up a claim for this increase, as it is stated, quite off-hand, that the "wench had several children." Here comes a beautifully interesting case, quite stimulating to legal acumen. Inferior Court decides that Samuel Marksbury could not have given away unborn children, on the strength of the legal maxim, "*Nemo dat quod non ha-*

bet"—*i.e.,* "Nobody can give what he has not got"—which certainly one should think sensible and satisfactory enough. The case, however, is appealed, and reversed in the superior Court; and now let us hear the reasoning.

The judge acknowledges the force of the maxim above quoted—says, as one would think any man might say, that it is quite a correct maxim—the only difficulty being that it does not at all apply to the present case. Let us hear him:

> He who is the absolute owner of a *thing* owns all its faculties for profit or increase; and he may, no doubt, grant the profits or increase, as well as the *thing* itself. Thus, it is every day's practice to grant the future rents or profits of real estate; and it is held that a man may grant the wool of a flock of sheep for years.

See also p. 33, Fanny *v.* Bryant, 4 J. J. Marshall's Rep., 368. In this almost precisely the same language is used. If the reader will proceed, he will find also this principle applied with equal clearness to the hiring, selling, mortgaging of unborn children; and the perfect legal *nonchalance* of these discussions is only comparable to running a dissecting-knife through the course of all the heart-strings of a living subject, for the purpose of demonstrating the laws of nervous contraction.

Judge Stroud, in his sketch of the slave-laws, page 99, lays down for proof the following assertion:—That the penal codes of the slave States bear much more severely on slaves than on white persons. He introduces his consideration of this proposition by the following humane and sensible remarks:—

> A being, ignorant of letters, unenlightened by religion, and deriving but little instruction from good example, cannot be supposed to have right conceptions as to the nature and extent of moral or political obligations. This remark, with but a slight qualification, is applicable to the condition of the slave. It has been just shown that the benefits of education are not conferred upon him, while his *chance* of acquiring a knowledge of the precepts of the gospel is so remote as scarcely to be appreciated. He may be regarded, therefore, as almost without the capacity to comprehend the force of laws; and on this account, such as are designed for his government should be recommended by their simplicity and mildness.
>
> His condition suggests another motive for tenderness on his behalf in these particulars. *He is unable to read;* and holding little or no communication with those who are better informed than himself, how is he to become acquainted with the fact that a law for his observance has been made? To exact obedience to a law which has not been promulgated, which is unknown to the subject of it, has ever been deemed most unjust and tyrannical. The reign of Caligula, were it obnoxious to no other reproach than this, would never cease to be remembered with abhorrence.
>
> The lawgivers of the slave-holding States seem, in the formation of their penal codes, to have been uninfluenced by these claims of the slave upon their compassionate consideration. The *hardened convict* moves their sympathy, and is to be *taught* the laws *before* he is expected to obey them; yet the *guiltless slave* is subjected to an extensive system of cruel enactments, of no part of which probably has he ever heard.
>
> Parts of this system apply to the slave exclusively, and for every infraction a large retribution is demanded; while with respect to offences for which whites as well as slaves are amenable, *punishments of much greater severity are inflicted upon the latter* than upon the former.

This heavy charge of Judge Stroud is sustained by twenty pages of proof, showing the very great disproportion between the number of offences made capital for slaves, and those that are so for whites. Concerning this, we find the following cool remark in Wheeler's Law of Slavery, page 222, note.

> Much has been said of the disparity of punishment between the white inhabitants and the slaves and negroes of the same State; that slaves are punished with much more severity, for the commission of similar crimes, by white persons, than the latter. The charge is undoubtedly true to a considerable extent. It must be remembered that the primary object of the enactment of penal laws is the protection and security of those who make them. The slave has no agency in making them. He is, indeed, one cause of the apprehended evils to the other class, which those laws are expected to remedy. That he should be held amenable for a violation of those rules established for the security of the other is the natural result of the state in which he is placed. And the severity of those rules will always bear a relation to that danger, real or ideal, of the other class.
>
> It has been so among all nations, and will ever continue to be so, while the disparity between bond and free remains.

A striking example of a legal decision to this purport is given in Wheeler's Law of Slavery, page 224. The case, apart from legal technicalities, may be thus briefly stated:—

The defendant, Mann, had hired a slave-woman for a year. During this time the slave committed some slight offence, for which the defendant undertook to chastise her.

While in the act of doing so, the slave ran off, whereat he shot at and wounded her. The judge in the inferior Court charged the jury that if they believed the punishment was cruel and unwarrantable, and disproportioned to the offence, in law the defendant was guilty, *as he had only a special property in the slave.* The jury finding evidence that the punishment *had* been cruel, unwarrantable, and *disproportioned to the offence,* found verdict against the defendant. But on what ground? Because, according to the law of North Carolina, cruel, unwarrantable, disproportionate punishment of a slave from a master, is an indictable offence? No. They decided against the defendant, not because the punishment was cruel and unwarrantable, but because *he* was not the person who had the right to inflict it, "as he had only a SPECIAL *right of property in the slave.*"

The defendant appealed to a higher Court, and the decision was reversed, on the ground that the hirer has for the time being all the rights of the master. The remarks of Judge Ruffin are so characteristic, and so strongly express the conflict between the feelings of the humane judge and the logical necessity of a strict interpreter of slave-law, that we shall quote largely from it. One cannot but admire the unflinching calmness with which a man, evidently possessed of honourable and humane feelings, walks through the most extreme and terrible results and conclusions, in obedience to the laws of legal truth. Thus he says:—

A judge cannot but lament when such cases as the present are brought into judgment. It is impossible that the reasons on which they go can be appreciated, but where institutions similar to our own exist, and are *thoroughly understood.* The struggle, too, in the judge's own breast, between the feelings of the man and the duty of the magistrate, is a severe one, presenting strong temptations to put aside such questions, if it be possible. It is useless, however, to complain of things inherent in our political state; and it is criminal in a Court to avoid any responsibility which the laws impose. With whatever reluctance, therefore, it is done, the Court is compelled to express an opinion upon the extent of the dominion of the master over the slave in North Carolina. The indictment charges a battery on Lydia, a slave of Elizabeth Jones. . . . The inquiry here is, whether a cruel and unreasonable battery on a slave by the hirer is indictable. The judge below instructed the jury that it is. He seems to have put it on the ground that the defendant had but a special property. Our laws uniformly treat the master, or other person having the possession and command of the slave, as entitled to the same extent of authority.

The object is the same, the service of the slave; and the same powers must be confided. In a criminal proceeding, and, indeed, in reference to all other persons but the general owner, the hirer and possessor of the slave, in relation to both rights and duties, is, for the time being, the owner. . . . But upon the general question whether the owner is answerable *criminaliter* for a battery upon his own slave, or other exercise of authority of force not forbidden by the statute, the Court entertains but little doubt. That he is so liable has never been decided; nor, as far as is known, been hitherto contended. There has been no prosecution of the sort. The established habits and uniform practice of the country in this respect is the best evidence of the portion of power deemed by the whole community requisite to the preservation of the master's dominion. If we thought differently, we could not set our notions in array against the judgment of everybody else, and say that this or that authority may be safely lopped off. This has indeed been assimilated at the bar to the other domestic relations; and arguments drawn from the well-established principles, which confer and restrain the authority of the parent over the child, the tutor over the pupil, the master over the apprentice, have been pressed on us.

The Court does not recognise their application; there is no likeness between the cases; they are in opposition to each other, and there is an impassable gulf between them. The difference is that which exists between freedom and slavery, and a greater cannot be imagined. In the one, the end in view is the happiness of the youth, born to equal rights with that governor on whom the duty devolves of training the young to usefulness in a station which he is afterwards to assume among freemen. To such an end, and with such a subject, moral and intellectual instruction seem the natural means, and, for the most part, they are found to suffice. Moderate force is superadded only to make the others effectual. If that fail, it is better to leave the party to his own headstrong passions, and the ultimate correction of the law, than to allow it to be immoderately inflicted by a private person. With slavery it is far otherwise. The end is the profit of the master, his security, and the public safety; the subject, one doomed, in his own person and his posterity, to live without knowledge, and without the capacity to make anything his own, and to toil that another may reap the fruits. What moral considerations shall be addressed to such a being to convince him, what it is impossible but that the most stupid must feel and know can never be true, that he is thus to labour upon a principle of natural duty, or for the sake of his own personal happiness? Such services can only be expected from one who has no will of his own; who surrenders his will in implicit obedience to that of another. Such obedience is the consequence only of uncontrolled authority over the body. There is nothing else which can operate to produce the effect. THE POWER OF THE MASTER MUST BE ABSOLUTE, TO RENDER THE SUBMISSION TO THE SLAVE PERFECT. I most freely confess my sense of the harshness of this proposition. I feel it as deeply as any man can; and as a principle of moral right, every person in his retirement must repudiate it; but, in the actual condition of things, it must be so; there is no remedy. This discipline belongs to the state of slavery. They cannot be disunited without abrogating at once the rights of the master, and absolving the slave from his subjection. It constitutes the curse of slavery to both the bond and the free portions of our population; but it is *inherent in the relation* of master and slave. That there may be particular instances of cruelty and deliberate barbarity, where in conscience the law might properly interfere, is most probable. The difficulty is to determine where *a Court* may properly begin. Merely in the abstract, it may well be asked which power of the master accords with right. The answer will probably sweep away all of them. But we cannot look at the matter in that light. The truth is, that we are forbidden to enter upon a train of general reasoning on the subject. We cannot allow the right of the master to be brought into discussion in the courts of justice. The slave, to remain a slave, must be made sensible that there is no appeal from his master; that his power is, in no instance, usurped, but is conferred by the laws of man at least, if not by the law of God. The danger would be great, indeed, if the tribunals of justice should be called on to graduate the punishment appropriate to every temper and every dereliction of menial duty.

No man can anticipate the many and aggravated provocations of the master which the slave would be constantly stimulated by his own passions, or the instigation of others, to give; or the consequent wrath of the master, prompting him to bloody vengeance upon the turbulent traitor; a vengeance *generally practised with impunity, by reason of its privacy.* The Court, therefore, disclaims the power of changing the relation in which these parts of our people stand to each other. . . .

I repeat, that I would gladly have avoided this ungrateful question; but being brought to it, the Court is compelled to declare that while slavery exists amongst us in its present state, or until it shall seem fit to the legislature to interpose express enactments to the contrary, it will be the imperative *duty* of the judges *to recognise the full dominion of the owner over the slave,* except where the exercise of it is forbidden by statute.

And this we do upon the ground that *this dominion is essential to the value of slaves as property, to the security of the master and the public tranquillity, greatly dependant upon their subordination;* and, in fine, as most effectually securing the general protection and comfort of the slaves themselves. Judgment below reversed; and judgment entered for the defendant.

No one can read this decision, so fine and clear in expression, so dignified and solemn in its earnestness, and so dreadful in its results, without feeling at once deep respect for the man and horror for the system. The man, judging him from this short specimen, which is all the author knows, has one of that high order of minds which looks straight through all verbiage and sophistry to the heart of every subject which it encounters. He has, too, that noble scorn of dissimulation, that straightforward determination not to call a bad thing by a good name, even when most popular, and reputable, and legal, which it is to be wished could be more frequently seen, both in our Northern and Southern States. There is but one sole regret; and that is, that such a man, with such a mind, should have been merely an *expositor,* and not a *reformer* of law.

Slavery Is Despotism

It is always important, in discussing a thing, to keep before our minds exactly what it is.

The only means of understanding precisely what a civil institution is, are an examination of the laws which regulate it. In different ages and nations, very different things have been called by the name of slavery. Patriarchal servitude was one thing, Hebrew servitude was another, Greek and Roman servitude still a third; and these institutions differed very much from each other. What, then, is American slavery, as we have seen it exhibited by law, and by the decision of Courts?

Let us begin by stating what it is not:—

1. It is not apprenticeship.
2. It is not guardianship.
3. It is in no sense a system for the education of a weaker race by a stronger.
4. The happiness of the governed is in no sense its object.
5. The temporal improvement or the eternal well-being of the governed is in no sense its object.

The object of it has been distinctly stated in one sentence by Judge Ruffin—"The end is the profit of the master, his security, and the public safety."

Slavery, then, is absolute despotism, of the most unmitigated form.

It would, however, be doing injustice to the absolutism of any *civilised* country to liken American slavery to it. The absolute governments of Europe none of them pretend to be founded on a *property* right of the governor to the persons and entire capabilities of the governed.

This is a form of despotism which exists only in some of the most savage countries of the world; as, for example, in Dahomey.

The European absolutism or despotism, now, does, to some extent, recognise the happiness and welfare of the *governed* as the foundation of government; and the ruler is considered as invested with power *for the benefit of the people;* and his right to rule is supposed to be in somewhat predicated upon the idea that he better understands how to promote the good of the people than they themselves do. No government in the *civilised* world now presents the pure despotic idea, as it existed in the old days of the Persian and Assyrian rule.

The arguments which defend slavery must be substantially the same as those which defend despotism of any other kind; and the objections which are to be urged against it are precisely those which can be urged against despotism of any other kind. The customs and practices to which it gives rise are precisely those to which despotisms in all ages have given rise.

Is the slave suspected of a crime? His master has the power to examine him by torture (see State *v.* Castleman). His master has, in fact, in most cases, the power of life and death, owing to the exclusion of the slave's evidence. He has the power of banishing the slave, at any time, and without giving an account to anybody, to an exile as dreadful as that of Siberia, and to labours as severe as those of the galleys. He has also unlimited power over the character of his slave. He can accuse him of any crime, yet withhold from him all right of trial or investigation, and sell him into captivity, with his name blackened by an unexamined imputation.

These are all abuses for which despotic governments are blamed. They are powers which good men who are despotic rulers are beginning to disuse; but, under the flag of every slaveholding State, and under the flag of the whole United States in the District of Columbia, they are committed indiscriminately to men of any character.

But the worst kind of despotism has been said to be that which extends alike over the body and over the soul; which can bind the liberty of the conscience, and deprive a man of all right of choice in respect to the manner in which he shall learn the will of God, and worship him. In other days, kings on their thrones, and cottagers by their firesides, alike trembled before a despotism which declared itself able to bind and to loose, to open and to shut the kingdom of heaven.

Yet this power to control the conscience, to control the religious privileges, and all the opportunities which man has of acquaintanceship with his Maker, and of learning to do his will, is, under the flag of every slave State, and under the flag of the United States, placed in the hands of any men of any character who can afford to pay for it.

It is a most awful and most solemn truth that the greatest republic in the world does sustain under her national flag the worst system of despotism which can possibly exist.

With regard to one point to which we have adverted—the power of the master to deprive the slave of a legal trial while accusing him of crime—a very striking instance has occurred in the District of Columbia, within a year or two. The particulars of the case, as stated at the time, in several papers, were briefly these: A gentleman in Washington, our national capital—an elder in the Presbyterian church —held a female slave, who had, for some years, supported a good character in a Baptist church of that city. He accused her of an attempt to poison his family, and immediately placed her in the hands of a slave-dealer, who took her over and imprisoned her in the slave-pen at Alexandria, to await the departure of a coffle. The poor girl had a mother, who felt as any mother would naturally feel.

When apprised of the situation of her daughter she flew to the pen, and, with tears, besought an interview with her only child; but she was cruelly repulsed, and told to be gone! She then tried to see the elder, but failed. She had the promise of money sufficient to purchase her daughter, but the owner would listen to no terms of compromise.

In her distress, the mother repaired to a lawyer in the city, and begged him to give form to her petition in writing. She stated to him what she wished to have said, and he arranged it for her in such a form as she herself might have presented it in, had not the benefits of education been denied her. The following is the letter:—

Washington, July 25, 1851.

SIR,—I address you as a rich Christian freeman and father, while I am myself but a poor slave-mother. I come to plead with you for an only child whom I love, who is a professor of the Christian religion with yourself, and a member of a Christian church; and who, by your act of ownership, now pines in her imprisonment in a loathsome man-warehouse, where she is held for sale. I come to plead with you for the exercise of that blessed law, "Whatsoever ye would that men should do unto you, do ye even so to them."

With great labour, I have found friends who are willing to aid me in the purchase of my child, to save us from a cruel separation. You, as a father, can judge of my feelings when I was told that you had decreed her banishment to distant as well as to hopeless bondage!

For nearly six years my child has done for you the hard labour of a slave; from the age of sixteen to twenty-two she has done the hard work of your chamber, kitchen, cellar, and stables. By night and by day, your will and your commands have been her highest law; and all this has been unrequited toil. If in all this time her scanty allowance of tea and coffee has been sweetened, it has been at the cost of her slave-mother, and not at yours.

You are an office-bearer in the church, and a man of prayer. As such, and as the absolute owner of my child, I ask candidly whether she has enjoyed such mild and gentle treatment, and amiable example, as she ought to have had, to encourage her in her monotonous bondage? Has she received at your hands, in faithful religious instruction in the Word of God, a full and fair compensation for all her toil? It is not to me alone that you must answer these questions. You acknowledge the high authority of His laws who preached a deliverance to the captive, and who commands you to give to your servant "that which is just and equal." Oh, I entreat you, withhold not, at this trying hour, from my child that which will cut off her last hope, and which may endanger your own soul!

It has been said that you charge my daughter with crime. Can this be really so? Can it be that you would set aside the obligations of honour and good citizenship—that you would dare to sell the guilty one away for money, rather than bring her to trial, which you know she is ready to meet? What would you say, if you were accused of guilt and refused a trial? Is not her fair name as precious to her, in the church to which she belongs, as yours can be to you?

Suppose, now, for a moment, that your daughter, whom you love, instead of mine, was in these hot days incarcerated in a negro-pen, subject to my control, fed on the coarsest food, committed to the entire will of a brute, denied the privilege commonly allowed even to the murderer—that of seeing the face of his friends? Oh, then you would FEEL!—feel soon, then, for a poor slave-mother and her child, and do for us as you shall wish you had done when we shall meet before the Great Judge, and when it shall be your greatest joy to say, "I *did* let the oppressed free!"

ELLEN BROWN

Mr. —————.

The girl, however, was sent off to the Southern market.

The writer has received these incidents from the gentleman who wrote the letter. Whether the course pursued by the master was strictly legal is a point upon which we are not entirely certain; that it was a course in which the law did not in fact interfere, is quite plain, and it is also very apparent that it was a course against which public sentiment did not remonstrate. The man who exercised this power was a professedly religious man, enjoying a position of importance in a Christian church; and it does not appear, from any movements in the Christian community about him, that they did not consider his course a justifiable one.

Yet is not this kind of power the very one at which we are so shocked when we see it exercised by foreign despots?

Do we not read with shuddering that in Russia, or in Austria, a man accused of crime is seized upon, separated from his friends, allowed no opportunities of trial or of self-defence, but hurried off to Siberia, or some other dreaded exile?

Why is despotism any worse in the governor of a State than in a private individual?

There is a great controversy now going on in the world between the despotic and the republican principle. All the common arguments used in support of slavery are arguments that apply with equal strength to despotic government, and there are some arguments in favour of despotic governments that do not apply to individual slavery.

There are arguments, and quite plausible ones, in favour of despotic government. Nobody can deny that it possesses a certain kind of efficiency, compactness, and promptness of movement, which cannot, from the nature of things, belong to a republic. Despotism has established and sustained much more efficient systems of police than ever a republic did. The late King of Prussia, by the possession of absolute despotic power, was enabled to carry out a much more efficient system of popular education than we ever have succeeded in carrying out in America. He districted his kingdom in the most thorough manner, and obliged every parent, whether he would or not, to have his children thoroughly educated.

If we reply to all this, as we do, that the possession of absolute power in a man qualified to use it right is undoubtedly calculated for the good of the state, but that there are so few men that know how to use it, that this form of government is not, on the whole, a safe one, then we have stated an argument that goes to overthrow slavery as much as it does a despotic government; for certainly the chances are much greater of finding one man, in the course of fifty years, who is capable of wisely using this power, than of finding thousands of men every day in our streets, who can be trusted with such power. It is a painful and most serious fact, that America trusts to the hands of the most brutal men of her country, equally with the best, that despotic power which she thinks an unsafe thing even in the hands of the enlightened, educated, and cultivated Emperor of the Russias.

With all our republican prejudices, we cannot deny that Nicholas is a man of talent, with a mind liberalised by education; we have been informed, also, that he is a man of serious and religious character; he certainly, acting as he does in the eye of all the world, must have great restraint upon him from public opinion, and a high sense of character. But who is the man to whom American laws intrust powers more absolute than those of Nicholas of Russia, or Ferdinand of Naples? He may have been a pirate on the high seas; he may be a drunkard; he may, like Souther, have been convicted of a brutality at which humanity turns pale; but, for all that, American slave-law will none the less trust him with this irresponsible power,—power over the body, and power over the soul.

On which side, then, stands the American nation, in the great controversy which is now going on between self-government and despotism? On which side does America stand, in the great controversy for liberty of conscience?

Do foreign governments exclude their population from the reading of the Bible? The slave of America is excluded by the most effectual means possible. Do we say, "Ah! but we read the Bible to our slaves, and present the gospel orally?" This is precisely what religious despotism in Italy says. Do we say that we have no objection to our slaves reading the Bible, if they will stop there; but that with this there will come in a flood of general intelligence, which will upset the existing state of things? This is precisely what is said in Italy.

Do we say we should be willing that the slave should read his Bible, but that he, in his ignorance, will draw false and erroneous conclusions from it, and for that reason we prefer to impart its truths to him orally? This, also, is precisely what the religious despotism of Europe says.

Do we say in our vainglory that despotic government dreads the coming in of anything calculated to elevate and educate the people? And is there not the same dread through all the despotic slave governments of America?

On which side, then, does the American nation stand, in the great, last QUESTION of the age?

Kansas-Nebraska Act

1856

Fifth Lincoln-Douglas Debate

October 7, 1858

The line drawn by the Missouri Compromise, forbidding slavery north of Missouri's southern border in territory from the Louisiana Purchase, brought on bloody conflict between pro- and antislavery forces; this effectively stopped the admission of new states from the area. Finally, in 1854, Illinois senator Stephen A. Douglas proposed legislation to split the Nebraska territory in two. Passed as two identical acts, one each for Nebraska and the new territory of Kansas, this legislation provided that, counter to the provisions of the Missouri Compromise, Congress would have no say in whether slavery was allowed in either territory. Instead, inhabitants of both Nebraska and Kansas would decide for themselves whether to allow slavery. The Missouri Compromise was declared inoperative and void.

Douglas was the incumbent senator from Illinois when Lincoln decided to run for that office and when Lincoln challenged Douglas to a series of debates. The ensuing debates focused on issues arising from what became known as the Kansas-Nebraska Act. Lincoln's performance did not win him a Senate seat. It did, however, launch him to national prominence as the man who had shown himself able to hold his own in public debate with Douglas. Douglas was reelected by the state legislature, but in 1860, in a highly splintered election, lost his bid for the presidency to Lincoln.

Kansas-Nebraska Act

SEC. 14. That the Constitution and all the laws of the United States which are not locally inapplicable shall have the same force and effect within the said Territory of Nebraska (or Kansas, the language being the same in reference to both,) as elsewhere within the United States, except the 8th section of the act, preparatory to the admission of Missouri into the Union, approved March sixth, eighteen hundred and twenty, which, being inconsistent with the principles of non-intervention by Congress with slavery in the States and Territories, as recognised by the legislation of eighteen hundred and fifty, commonly called the compromise measures, is hereby declared inoperative and void; it being the true intent and meaning of this act not to legislate slavery into any Territory or State, nor to exclude it therefrom, but to leave the people thereof perfectly free to form and regulate their domestic institutions in their own way, subject only to the Constitution of the United States. *Provided,* That nothing herein contained shall be construed to revive or put in force any law or regulation which may have existed prior to the act of 6th March, 1820, either protecting, establishing, prohibiting, or abolishing slavery.

Fifth Joint Debate, at Galesburg

Mr. Douglas's Speech

LADIES AND GENTLEMEN: Four years ago I appeared before the people of Knox County for the purpose of defending my political action upon the Compromise Measures of 1850 and the passage of the Kansas-Nebraska bill. Those of you before me who were present then will remember that I vindicated myself for supporting those two measures by the fact that they rested upon the great fundamental principle that the people of each State and each Territory of this Union have the right, and ought to be permitted to exercise the right, of regulating their own domestic concerns in their own way, subject to no other limitation or restriction than that which the Constitution of the United States imposes upon them. I then called upon the people of Illinois to decide whether that principle of self-government was right or wrong. If it was and is right, then the Compromise Measures of 1850 were right, and consequently, the Kansas and Nebraska bill, based upon the same principle, must necessarily have been right.

The Kansas and Nebraska bill declared, in so many words, that it was the true intent and meaning of the Act not to legislate slavery into any State or Territory, nor to exclude it therefrom, but to leave the people thereof perfectly free to form and regulate their domestic institutions in their own way, subject only to the Constitution of the United States. For the last four years I have devoted all my energies, in private and public, to commend that principle to the American people. Whatever else may be said in condemnation or support of my political course, I apprehend that no honest man will doubt the fidelity with which, under all circumstances, I have stood by it.

During the last year a question arose in the Congress of the United States whether or not that principle would be violated by the admission of Kansas into the Union under the Lecompton Constitution. In my opinion, the attempt to force Kansas in under that constitution was a gross violation of the principle enunciated in the Compromise Measures of 1850, and Kansas and Nebraska bill of 1854, and therefore I led off in the fight against the Lecompton Constitution, and conducted it until the effort to carry that constitution through Congress was abandoned. And I can appeal to all men, friends and foes, Democrats and Republicans, Northern men and Southern men, that during the whole of that fight I carried the banner of Popular Sovereignty aloft, and never allowed it to trail in the dust, or lowered my flag until victory perched upon our arms.

When the Lecompton Constitution was defeated, the question arose in the minds of those who had advocated it what they should next resort to in order to carry out their views. They devised a measure known as the English bill, and granted a general amnesty and political pardon to all men who had fought against the Lecompton Constitution, provided they would support that bill. I for one did not choose to accept the pardon, or to avail myself of the amnesty granted on that condition. The fact that the supporters of Lecompton were willing to forgive all differences of opinion at that time in the event those who opposed it favored the English bill, was an admission they did not think that opposition to Lecompton impaired a man's standing in the Democratic party.

Now, the question arises, What was that English bill which certain men are now attempting to make a test of political orthodoxy in this country? It provided, in substance, that the Lecompton Constitution should be sent back to the people of Kansas for their adoption or rejection, at an election which was held in August last, and in case they refused admission under it, that Kansas should be kept out of the Union until she had 93,420 inhabitants. I was in favor of sending the constitution back in order to enable the people to say whether or not it was their act and deed, and embodied their will; but the other proposition, that if they refused to come into the Union under it, they should be kept out until they had double or treble the population they then had, I never would sanction by my vote. The reason why I could not sanction it is to be found in the fact that by the English bill, if the people of Kansas had only agreed to become a slaveholding State under the Lecompton Constitution, they could have done so with 35,000 people, but if they insisted on being a Free State, as they had a right to do, then they were to be punished by being kept out of the Union until they had nearly three times that population. I then said in my place in the Senate, as I now say to you, that whenever Kansas has population enough for a Slave State, she has population enough for a Free State. I have never yet given a vote, and I never intend to record one, making an odious and unjust distinction between the different States of this Union. I hold it to be a fundamental principle in our Republican form of government that all the States of this Union, old and new, free and slave, stand on an exact equality.

Equality among the different States is a cardinal principle on which all our institutions rest. Wherever, therefore, you make a discrimination, saying to a Slave State that it shall be admitted with 35,000 inhabitants, and to a Free State that it shall not be admitted until it has 93,000 or 100,000 inhabitants, you are throwing the whole weight of the Federal Government into the scale in favor of one class of States against the other. Nor would I, on the other hand, any sooner sanction the doctrine that a Free State could be admitted into the Union with 35,000 people, while a Slave State was kept out until it had 93,000. I have always declared in the Senate my willingness, and I am willing now to adopt the rule, that no Territory shall ever become a State until it has the requisite population for a member of Congress, according to the then existing ratio. But while I have always been, and am now, willing to adopt that general rule, I was not willing and would not consent to make an exception of Kansas, as a punishment for her obstinacy in demanding the right to do as she pleased in the formation of her constitution. It is proper that I should remark here, that my opposition to the Lecompton Constitution did not rest upon the peculiar position taken by Kansas on the subject of slavery. I held then, and hold now, that if the people of Kansas want a Slave State, it is their right to make one, and be received into the Union under it; if, on the contrary, they want a Free State, it is their right to have it, and no man should ever oppose their admission because they ask it under the one or the other. I hold to that great principle of self-government which asserts the right of every people to decide for themselves the nature and character of the domestic institutions and fundamental law under which they are to live.

The effort has been and is now being made in this State by certain postmasters and other Federal office-holders to make a test of faith on the support of the English bill. These men are now making speeches all over the State against me and in favor of Lincoln, either directly or indirectly, because I would not sanction a discrimination between Slave and Free States by voting for the English bill. But while that bill is made a test in Illinois for the purpose of breaking up the Democratic organization in this State, how is it in the other States? Go to Indiana, and there you find English himself, the author of the English bill, who is a candidate for re-election to Congress, has been forced by public opinion to abandon his own darling project, and to give a promise that he will vote for the admission of Kansas at once, whenever she forms a constitution in pursuance of law, and ratifies it by a majority vote of her people. Not only is this the case with English himself, but I am informed that every Democratic candidate for Congress in Indiana takes the same ground. Pass to Ohio, and there you find that Groesbeck, and Pendleton, and Cox, and all the other anti-Lecompton men who stood shoulder to shoulder with me against the Lecompton Constitution, but voted for the English bill, now repudiate it and take the same ground that I do on that question. So it is with the Joneses and others of Pennsylvania, and so it is with every other Lecompton Democrat in the Free States. They now abandon even the English bill, and come back to the true platform which I proclaimed at the time in the Senate, and upon which the Democracy of Illinois now stand.

And yet, notwithstanding the fact that every Lecompton and anti-Lecompton Democrat in the Free States has abandoned the English bill, you are told that it is to be made a test upon me, while the power and patronage of the Government are all exerted to elect men to Congress in the other States who occupy the same position with reference to it that I do. It seems that my political offense consists in the fact that I first did not vote for the English bill, and thus pledge myself to keep Kansas out of the Union until she has a population of 93,420, and then return home, violate that pledge, repudiate the bill, and take the opposite ground. If I had done this, perhaps the Administration would now be advocating my re-election, as it is that of the others who have pursued this course. I did not choose to give that pledge, for the reason that I did not intend to carry out that principle. I never will consent, for the sake of conciliating the frowns of power, to pledge myself to do that which I do not intend to perform. I now submit the question to you, as my constituency, whether I was not right, first, in resisting the adoption of the Lecompton Constitution, and, secondly, in resisting the English bill. I repeat that I opposed the Lecompton Constitution because it was not the act and deed of the people of Kansas, and did not embody their will. I denied the right of any power on earth, under our system of government, to force a constitution on an unwilling people. There was a time when some men could pretend to believe that the Lecompton Constitution embodied the will of the people of Kansas; but that time has passed. The question was referred to the people of Kansas under the English bill last August, and then, at a fair election, they rejected the Lecompton Constitution by a vote of from eight to ten against it to one in its favor. Since it has been voted down by so overwhelming a majority, no man can pretend that it was the act and deed of that people.

I submit the question to you whether or not, if it had not been for me, that constitution would have been crammed down the throats of the people of Kansas against their consent. While at least ninety-nine out of every hundred people here present agree that I was right in defeating that project, yet my enemies use the fact that I did defeat it by doing right, to break me down and put another man in the United States Senate in my place. The very men who acknowledge that I was right in defeating Lecompton now form an alliance with Federal office-holders, professed Lecompton men, to defeat me, because I did right. My political opponent, Mr. Lincoln, has no hope on earth, and has never dreamed that he had a chance of success, were it not for the aid that he is receiving from Federal office-holders, who are using their influence and the patronage of the Government against me in revenge for my having defeated the Lecompton Constitution.

What do you Republicans think of a political organization that will try to make an unholy and unnatural combination with its professed foes to beat a man merely because he has done right? You know that such is the fact with regard to your own party. You know that the axe of decapitation is suspended over every man in office in Illinois, and the terror of proscription is threatened every Democrat by the present Administration, unless he supports the Republican ticket in preference to my Democratic associates and myself. I could find an instance in the postmaster of the city of Galesburg, and in every other postmaster in this vicinity, all of whom have been stricken down simply because they discharged the duties of their offices honestly, and supported the regular Democratic ticket in this State in the right. The Republican party is availing itself of every unworthy means in the present contest to carry the election, because its leaders know that if they let this chance slip they will never have another, and their hopes of making this a Republican State will be blasted forever.

Now, let me ask you whether the country has any interest in sustaining this organization known as the Republican party. That party is unlike all other political organizations in this country. All other parties have been national in their character,—have avowed their principles alike in the Slave and Free States, in Kentucky, as well as Illinois, in Louisiana as well as in Massachusetts. Such was the case with the old Whig party, and such was and is the case with the Democratic party. Whigs and Democrats could proclaim their principles boldly and fearlessly in the North and in the South, in the East and in the West, wherever the Constitution ruled, and the American flag waved over American soil.

But now you have a sectional organization, a party which appeals to the Northern section of the Union against the Southern, a party which appeals to Northern passion, Northern pride, Northern ambition, Northern prejudices, against Southern people, the Southern States, and Southern institutions. The leaders of that party hope that they will be able to unite the Northern States in one great sectional party; and inasmuch as the North is the strongest section, that they will thus be enabled to out-vote, conquer, govern and control the South. Hence you find that they now make speeches advocating principles and measures

which cannot be defended in any slaveholding State of this Union. Is there a Republican residing in Galesburg who can travel into Kentucky and carry his principles with him across the Ohio? What Republican from Massachusetts can visit the Old Dominion without leaving his principles behind him when he crosses Mason and Dixon's line? Permit me to say to you in perfect good humor, but in all sincerity, that no political creed is sound which cannot be proclaimed fearlessly in every State of this Union where the Federal Constitution is the supreme law of the land.

Not only is this Republican party unable to proclaim its principles alike in the North and in the South, in the Free States and in the Slave States, but it cannot even proclaim them in the same forms and give them the same strength and meaning in all parts of the same State. My friend Lincoln finds it extremely difficult to manage a debate in the center part of the State, where there is a mixture of men from the North and the South. In the extreme northern part of Illinois he can proclaim as bold and radical Abolitionism as ever Giddings, Lovejoy, or Garrison enunciated; but when he gets down a little farther south he claims that he is an Old Line Whig, a disciple of Henry Clay, and declares that he still adheres to the Old Line Whig creed, and has nothing whatever to do with Abolitionism, or negro equality, or negro citizenship. I once before hinted this of Mr. Lincoln in a public speech, and at Charleston he defied me to show that there was any difference between his speeches in the North and in the South, and that they were not in strict harmony. I will now call your attention to two of them, and you can then say whether you would be apt to believe that the same man ever uttered both. In a speech in reply to me at Chicago in July last, Mr. Lincoln, in speaking of the equality of the negro with the white man, used the following language:—

> I should like to know, if, taking this old Declaration of Independence, which declares that all men are equal upon principle, and making exceptions to it, where will it stop? If one man says it does not mean a negro, why may not another man say it does not mean another man? If the Declaration is not the truth, let us get the statute book in which we find it, and tear it out. Who is so bold as to do it? If it is not true, let us tear it out.

You find that Mr. Lincoln there proposed that if the doctrine of the Declaration of Independence, declaring all men to be born equal, did not include the negro and put him on an equality with the white man, that we should take the statute book and tear it out. He there took the ground that the negro race is included in the Declaration of Independence as the equal of the white race, and that there could be no such thing as a distinction in the races, making one superior and the other inferior. I read now from the same speech:—

My friends [he says], I have detained you about as long as I desire to do, and I have only to say, let us discard all this quibbling about this man and the other man, this race and that race and the other race being inferior, and therefore they must be placed in an inferior position, discarding our standard that we have left us. Let us discard all these things, and unite as one people throughout this land, until we shall once more stand up declaring that all men are created equal.

[Voices: "That's right," etc.]

Yes, I have no doubt that you think it is right; but the Lincoln men down in Coles, Tazewell, and Sangamon counties *do not* think it is right. In the conclusion of the same speech, talking to the Chicago Abolitionists, he said: "I leave you, hoping that the lamp of liberty will burn in your bosoms until there shall no longer be a doubt that all men are created free and equal." [Voices: "Good, good."] Well, you say good to that, and you are going to vote for Lincoln because he holds that doctrine. I will not blame you for supporting him on that ground; but I will show you, in immediate contrast with that doctrine, what Mr. Lincoln said down in Egypt in order to get votes in that locality, where they do not hold to such a doctrine. In a joint discussion between Mr. Lincoln and myself, at Charleston, I think, on the 18th of last month, Mr. Lincoln, referring to this subject, used the following language:—

I will say, then, that I am not, nor ever have been, in favor of bringing about in any way the social and political equality of the white and black races; that I am not, nor ever have been, in favor of making voters of the free negroes, or jurors, or qualifying them to hold office, or having them to marry with white people. I will say, in addition, that there is a physical difference between the white and black races which, I suppose, will forever forbid the two races living together upon terms of social and political equality; and inasmuch as they cannot so live, that while they do remain together there must be the position of superior and inferior, that I, as much as any other man, am in favor of the superior position being assigned to the white man.

[Voices: "Good for Mr. Lincoln."]

Fellow-citizens, here you find men hurrahing for Lincoln, and saying that he did right, when in one part of the State he stood up for negro equality; and in another part, for political effect, discarded the doctrine, and declared that there always must be a superior and inferior race. Abolitionists up North are expected and required to vote for Lincoln because he goes for the equality of the races, holding that by the Declaration of Independence the white man and the negro were created equal, and endowed by the divine law with that equality; and down South he tells the old Whigs, the Kentuckians, Virginians, and Tennesseeans, that there is a physical difference in the races, making one superior and the other inferior, and that he is in favor of maintaining the superiority of the white race over the negro.

Now, how can you reconcile those two positions of Mr. Lincoln? He is to be voted for in the South as a pro-slavery man, and he is to be voted for in the North as an Abolitionist. Up here he thinks it is all nonsense to talk about a difference between the races, and says, that we must "discard all quibbling about this race and that race and the other race being inferior, and therefore they must be placed in an inferior position." Down South he makes this "quibble" about this race and that race and the other race being inferior as the creed of his party, and declares that the negro can never be elevated to the position of the white man. You find that his political meetings are called by different names in different counties in the State. Here they are called Republican meetings; but in old Tazewell, where Lincoln made a speech last Tuesday, he did not address a *Republican* meeting, but "a grand rally of the *Lincoln men.*" There are very few Republicans there, because Tazewell County is filled with old Virginians and Kentuckians, all of whom are Whigs or Democrats; and if Mr. Lincoln had called an Abolition or Republican meeting there, he would not get many votes.

Go down into Egypt, and you find that he and his party are operating under an alias there, which his friend Trumbull has given them, in order that they may cheat the people. When I was down in Monroe County a few weeks ago, addressing the people, I saw handbills posted announcing that Mr. Trumbull was going to speak in behalf of Lincoln; and what do you think the name of his party was there? Why the "*Free Democracy.*" Mr. Trumbull and Mr. Jehu

Baker were announced to address the Free Democracy of Monroe County, and the bill was signed, "Many Free Democrats." The reason that Lincoln and his party adopted the name of "Free Democracy" down there was because Monroe County has always been an old-fashioned Democratic county, and hence it was necessary to make the people believe that they were Democrats, sympathized with them, and were fighting for Lincoln as Democrats.

Come up to Springfield, where Lincoln now lives and always has lived, and you find that the Convention of his party which assembled to nominate candidates for Legislature, who are expected to vote for him if elected, dare not adopt the name of Republican, but assembled under the title of "all opposed to the Democracy." Thus you find that Mr. Lincoln's creed cannot travel through even one half of the counties of this State, but that it changes its hues and becomes lighter and lighter as it travels from the extreme north, until it is nearly white when it reaches the extreme south end of the State.

I ask you, my friends, why cannot Republicans avow their principles alike everywhere? I would despise myself if I thought that I was procuring your votes by concealing my opinions, and by avowing one set of principles in one part of the State, and a different set in another part. If I do not truly and honorably represent your feelings and principles, then I ought not to be your senator; and I will never conceal my opinions, or modify or change them a hair's breadth, in order to get votes. I will tell you that this Chicago doctrine of Lincoln's—declaring that the negro and the white man are made equal by the Declaration of Independence and by Divine Providence—is a monstrous heresy. The signers of the Declaration of Independence never dreamed of the negro when they were writing that document. They referred to white men, to men of European birth and European descent, when they declared the equality of all men. I see a gentleman there in the crowd shaking his head. Let me remind him that when Thomas Jefferson wrote that document, he was the owner, and so continued until his death, of a large number of slaves. Did he intend to say in that Declaration that his negro slaves, which he held and treated as property, were created his equals by divine law, and that he was violating the law of God every day of his life by holding them as slaves? It must be borne in mind that when that Declaration was put forth, every one of the thirteen Colonies, were slaveholding

Colonies, and every man who signed that instrument represented a slaveholding constituency. Recollect, also, that no one of them emancipated his slaves, much less put them on an equality with himself, after he signed the Declaration. On the contrary, they all continued to hold their negroes as slaves during the Revolutionary War. Now, do you believe—are you willing to have it said—that every man who signed the Declaration of Independence declared the negro his equal, and then was hypocrite enough to continue to hold him as a slave, in violation of what he believed to be the divine law? And yet when you say that the Declaration of Independence includes the negro, you charge the signers of it with hypocrisy.

I say to you, frankly, that in my opinion this Government was made by our fathers on the white basis. It was made by white men for the benefit of white men and their posterity forever, and was intended to be administered by white men in all time to come. But while I hold that under our Constitution and political system the negro is not a citizen, cannot be a citizen, and ought not to be a citizen, it does not follow by any means that he should be a slave. On the contrary, it does follow that the negro, as an inferior race, ought to possess every right, every privilege, every immunity, which he can safely exercise, consistent with the safety of the society in which he lives. Humanity requires, and Christianity commands, that you shall extend to every inferior being, and every dependent being, all the privileges, immunities, and advantages which can be granted to them, consistent with the safety of society. If you ask me the nature and extent of these privileges, I answer that that is a question which the people of each State must decide for themselves. Illinois has decided that question for herself. We have said that in this State the negro shall not be a slave, nor shall he be a citizen; Kentucky holds a different doctrine. New York holds one different from either, and Maine one different from all. Virginia, in her policy on this question, differs in many respects from the others, and so on, until there are hardly two States whose policy is exactly alike in regard to the relation of the white man and the negro. Nor can you reconcile them and make them alike. Each State must do as it pleases. Illinois had as much right to adopt the policy which we have on that subject as Kentucky had to adopt a different policy. The great principle of this Government is, that each State has the right to do as it pleases on all these questions, and no other State or power on earth has the right to interfere with us, or complain of us merely because our system differs from theirs. In the Compromise Measures of 1850, Mr. Clay declared that this great principle ought to exist in the Territories as well as in the States, and I reasserted his doctrine in the Kansas and Nebraska bill in 1854.

But Mr. Lincoln cannot be made to understand, and those who are determined to vote for him, no matter whether he is a pro-slavery man in the South and a negro-equality advocate in the North, cannot be made to understand how it is that in a Territory the people can do as they please on the slavery question under the Dred Scott decision. Let us see whether I cannot explain it to the satisfaction of all impartial men. Chief Justice Taney has said, in his opinion in the Dred Scott case, that a negro slave, being property, stands on an equal footing with other property, and that the owner may carry them into United States territory the same as he does other property. Suppose any two of you, neighbors, should conclude to go to Kansas, one carrying $100,000 worth of negro slaves, and the other $100,000 worth of mixed merchandise, including quantities of liquors. You both agree that under that decision you may carry your property to Kansas; but when you get it there, the merchant who is possessed of the liquors is met by the Maine liquor law, which prohibits the sale or use of his property, and the owner of the slaves is met by equally unfriendly legislation, which makes his property worthless after he gets it there. What is the right to carry your property into the Territory worth to either, when unfriendly legislation in the Territory renders it worthless after you get it there? The slaveholder when he gets his slaves there finds that there is no local law to protect him in holding them, no slave code, no police regulation maintaining and supporting him in his right, and he discovers at once that the absence of such friendly legislation excludes his property from the Territory just as irresistibly as if there was a positive Constitutional prohibition excluding it.

Thus you find it is with any kind of property in a Territory: It depends for its protection on the local and municipal law. If the people of a Territory want slavery, they make friendly legislation to introduce it; but if they do not want it, they withhold all protection from it, and then it cannot exist there. Such was the view taken on the subject by different Southern men when the Nebraska bill passed. See the speech of Mr. Orr, of South Carolina, the present

speaker of the House of Representatives of Congress, made at that time; and there you will find this whole doctrine argued out at full length. Read the speeches of other Southern Congressmen, Senators and Representatives, made in 1854, and you will find that they took the same view of the subject as Mr. Orr,—that slavery could never be forced on a people who did not want it. I hold that in this country there is no power on the face of the globe that can force any institution on an unwilling people. The great fundamental principle of our Government is that the people or each State and each Territory shall be left perfectly free to decide for themselves what shall be the nature and character of their institutions. When this Government was made, it was based on that principle. At the time of its formation there were twelve slaveholding States and one Free State in this Union.

Suppose this doctrine of Mr. Lincoln and the Republicans, of uniformity of laws of all the States on the subject of slavery, had prevailed; suppose Mr. Lincoln himself had been a member of the Convention which framed the Constitution, and that he had risen in that august body, and, addressing the father of his country, had said as he did at Springfield: "A house divided against itself cannot stand. I believe this Government cannot endure permanently, half Slave and half Free. I do not expect the Union to be dissolved; I do not expect the house to fall; but I do expect it will cease to be divided. It will become all one thing or all the other." What do you think would have been the result? Suppose he had made that Convention believe that doctrine, and they had acted upon it, what do you think would have been the result? Do you believe that the one Free State would have outvoted the twelve slaveholding States, and thus abolished slavery? On the contrary, would not the twelve slaveholding States have outvoted the one Free State, and under his doctrine have fastened slavery by an irrevocable constitutional provision upon every inch of the American Republic?

Thus you see that the doctrine he now advocates, if proclaimed at the beginning of the Government, would have established slavery everywhere throughout the American continent; and are you willing, now that we have the majority section, to exercise a power which we never would have submitted to when we were in the minority? If the Southern States had attempted to control our institutions, and make the States all Slave, when they had the power, I ask, Would you have submitted to it? If you would not, are you willing, now that we have become the strongest under that great principle of self-government that allows each State to do as it pleases, to attempt to control the Southern institutions? Then, my friends, I say to you that there is but one path of peace in this Republic, and that is to administer this Government as our fathers made it, divided into Free and Slave States, allowing each State to decide for itself whether it wants slavery or not. If Illinois will settle the slavery question for herself, and mind her own business and let her neighbors alone, we will be at peace with Kentucky and every other Southern State. If every other State in the Union will do the same, there will be peace between the North and the South, and in the whole Union.

Mr. Lincoln's Reply

My Fellow-Citizens: A very large portion of the speech which Judge Douglas has addressed to you has previously been delivered and put in print. I do not mean that for a hit upon the Judge at all. If I had not been interrupted, I was going to say that such an answer as I was able to make to a very large portion of it, had already been more than once made and published. There has been an opportunity afforded to the public to see our respective views upon the topics discussed in a large portion of the speech which he has just delivered. I make these remarks for the purpose of excusing myself for not passing over the entire ground that the Judge has traversed. I however desire to take up some of the points that he has attended to, and ask your attention to them, and I shall follow him backwards upon some notes which I have taken, reversing the order, by beginning where he concluded.

The Judge has alluded to the Declaration of Independence, and insisted that negroes are not included in that Declaration; and that it is a slander upon the framers of that instrument to suppose that negroes were meant therein; and he asks you: Is it possible to believe that Mr. Jefferson, who penned the immortal paper, could have supposed himself applying the language of that instrument to the negro race, and yet held a portion of that race in slavery? Would he not at once have freed them?

I only have to remark upon this part of the Judge's speech (and that, too, very briefly, for I shall not detain myself, or you, upon that point for any great length of time,) that I believe the entire records of the world, from the date of the Declaration of Independence up to within three years

ago, may be searched in vain for one single affirmation, from one single man, that the negro was not included in the Declaration of Independence; I think I may defy Judge Douglas to show that he ever said so, that Washington ever said so, that any President ever said so, that any member of Congress ever said so, or that any living man upon the whole earth ever said so, until the necessities of the present policy of the Democratic party, in regard to slavery, had to invent that affirmation. And I will remind Judge Douglas and this audience that while Mr. Jefferson was the owner of slaves, as undoubtedly he was, in speaking upon this very subject he used the strong language that "he trembled for his country when he remembered that God was just;" and I will offer the highest premium in my power to Judge Douglas if he will show that he, in all his life, ever uttered a sentiment at all akin to that of Jefferson.

The next thing to which I will ask your attention is the Judge's comments upon the fact, as he assumes it to be, that we cannot call our public meetings as Republican meetings; and he instances Tazewell County as one of the places where the friends of Lincoln have called a public meeting and have not dared to name it a Republican meeting. He instances Monroe County as another, where Judge Trumbull and Jehu Baker addressed the persons whom the Judge assumes to be the friends of Lincoln, calling them the "Free Democracy." I have the honor to inform Judge Douglas that he spoke in that very County of Tazewell last Saturday, and I was there on Tuesday last; and when he spoke there, he spoke under a call not venturing to use the word "Democrat." [Turning to Judge Douglas:] What think you of this?

So, again, there is another thing to which I would ask the Judge's attention upon this subject. In the contest of 1856 his party delighted to call themselves together as the "National Democracy;" but now, if there should be a notice put up anywhere for a meeting of the "National Democracy," Judge Douglas and his friends would not come. They would not suppose themselves invited. They would understand that it was a call for those hateful postmasters whom he talks about.

Now a few words in regard to these extracts from speeches of mine which Judge Douglas has read to you, and which he supposes are in very great contrast to each other. Those speeches have been before the public for a considerable time, and if they have any inconsistency in them, if there is any conflict in them, the public have been able to detect it. When the Judge says, in speaking on this subject, that I make speeches of one sort for the people of the northern end of the State, and of a different sort for the southern people, he assumes that I do not understand that my speeches will be put in print and read north and south. I knew all the while that the speech that I made at Chicago, and the one I made at Jonesboro, and the one at Charleston, would all be put in print, and all the reading and intelligent men in the community would see them and know all about my opinions. And I have not supposed, and do not now suppose, that there is any conflict whatever between them.

But the Judge will have it that if we do not confess that there is a sort of inequality between the white and the black races which justifies us in making them slaves, we must then insist that there is a degree of equality that requires us to make them our wives. Now, I have all the while taken a broad distinction in regard to that matter; and that is all there is in these different speeches which he arrays here; and the entire reading of either of the speeches will show that that distinction was made. Perhaps by taking two parts of the same speech he could have got up as much of a conflict as the one he has found. I have all the while maintained that in so far as it should be insisted that there was an equality between the white and black races that should produce a perfect social and political equality, it was an impossibility. This you have seen in my printed speeches, and with it I have said that in their right to "life, liberty, and the pursuit of happiness," as proclaimed in that old Declaration, the inferior races are our equals. And these declarations I have constantly made in reference to the abstract moral question, to contemplate and consider when we are legislating about any new country which is not already cursed with the actual presence of the evil,—slavery.

I have never manifested any impatience with the necessities that spring from the actual presence of black people amongst us, and the actual existence of slavery amongst us where it does already exist; but I have insisted that, in legislating for new countries where it does not exist, there is no just rule other than that of moral and abstract right! With reference to those new countries, those maxims as to the right of a people to "life, liberty, and the pursuit of happiness" were the just rules to be constantly referred to. There is no misunderstanding this, except by men interested to misunderstand it. I take it that I have to address an intelligent and reading community, who will peruse what I say, weigh it, and then judge whether I advance improper or

unsound views, or whether I advance hypocritical, and deceptive, and contrary views in different portions of the country. I believe myself to be guilty of no such thing as the latter, though, of course, I cannot claim that I am entirely free from all error in the opinions I advance.

The Judge has also detained us a while in regard to the distinction between his party and our party. His he assumes to be a national party,—ours a sectional one. He does this in asking the question whether this country has any interest in the maintenance of the Republican party? He assumes that our party is altogether sectional,—that the party to which he adheres is national; and the argument is, that no party can be a rightful party—can be based upon rightful principles—unless it can announce its principles everywhere. I presume that Judge Douglas could not go into Russia and announce the doctrine of our national Democracy; he could not denounce the doctrine of kings and emperors and monarchies in Russia; and it may be true of this country that in some places we may not be able to proclaim a doctrine as clearly as the truth of Democracy, because there is a section so directly opposed to it that they will not tolerate us in doing so. Is it the true test of the soundness of a doctrine that in some places people won't let you proclaim it? Is that the way to test the truth of any doctrine? Why, I understood that at one time the people of Chicago would not let Judge Douglas preach a certain favorite doctrine of his. I commend to his consideration the question, whether he takes that as a test of the unsoundness of what he wanted to preach?

There is another thing to which I wish to ask attention for a little while on this occasion. What has always been the evidence brought forward to prove that the Republican party is a sectional party? The main one was that in the Southern portion of the Union the people did not let the Republicans proclaim their doctrines amongst them. That has been the main evidence brought forward,—that they had no supporters, or substantially none, in the Slave States. The South have not taken hold of our principles as we announce them; nor does Judge Douglas now grapple with those principles.

We have a Republican State Platform, laid down in Springfield in June last, stating our position all the way through the questions before the country. We are now far advanced in this canvass. Judge Douglas and I have made perhaps forty speeches apiece, and we have now for the fifth time met face to face in debate, and up to this day I have not found either Judge Douglas or any friend of his taking hold of the Republican platform, or laying his finger upon anything in it that is wrong. I ask you to recollect that. Judge Douglas turns away from the platform of principles to the fact that he can find people somewhere who will not allow us to announce those principles. If he had great confidence that our principles were wrong, he would take hold of them and demonstrate them to be wrong. But he does not do so. The only evidence he has of their being wrong is in the fact that there are people who won't allow us to preach them. I ask again, is that the way to test the soundness of a doctrine?

I ask his attention also to the fact that by the rule of nationality he is himself fast becoming sectional. I ask his attention to the fact that his speeches would not go as current now south of the Ohio River as they have formerly gone there. I ask his attention to the fact that he felicitates himself to-day that all the Democrats of the Free States are agreeing with him, while he omits to tell us that the Democrats of any Slave State agree with him. If he has not thought of this, I commend to his consideration the evidence in his own declaration, on this day, of his becoming sectional too. I see it rapidly approaching. Whatever may be the result of this ephemeral contest between Judge Douglas and myself, I see the day rapidly approaching when his pill of sectionalism, which he has been thrusting down the throats of Republicans for years past, will be crowded down his own throat.

Now, in regard to what Judge Douglas said (in the beginning of his speech) about the Compromise of 1850 containing the principle of the Nebraska bill, although I have often presented my views upon that subject, yet as I have not done so in this canvass, I will, if you please, detain you a little with them. I have always maintained, so far as I was able, that there was nothing of the principle of the Nebraska bill in the Compromise of 1850 at all,—nothing whatever. Where can you find the principle of the Nebraska bill in that Compromise? If anywhere, in the two pieces of the Compromise organizing the Territories of New Mexico and Utah. It was expressly provided in these two Acts that when they came to be admitted into the Union, they should be admitted with or without slavery, as they should choose, by their own constitutions. Nothing was said in either of those Acts as to what was to be

done in relation to slavery during the Territorial existence of those Territories, while Henry Clay constantly made the declaration (Judge Douglas recognizing him as a leader) that, in his opinion, the old Mexican laws would control that question during the Territorial existence, and that these old Mexican laws excluded slavery.

How can that be used as a principle for declaring that during the Territorial existence as well as at the time of framing the constitution, the people, if you please, might have slaves if they wanted them? I am not discussing the question whether it is right or wrong; but how are the New Mexican and Utah laws patterns for the Nebraska bill? I maintain that the organization of Utah and New Mexico *did not* establish a general principle at all. It had no feature of establishing a general principle. The Acts to which I have referred were a part of a general system of Compromises. They did not lay down what was proposed as a regular policy for the Territories, only an agreement in this particular case to do in that way, because other things were done that were to be a compensation for it. They were allowed to come in in that shape, because in another way it was paid for,—considering that as a part of that system of measures called the Compromise of 1850, which finally included half-a-dozen Acts. It included the admission of California as a Free State, which was kept out of the Union for half a year because it had formed a free constitution. It included the settlement of the boundary of Texas, which had been undefined before, which was in itself a slavery question; for if you pushed the line farther west, you made Texas larger, and made more slave territory; while, if you drew the line toward the east, you narrowed the boundary and diminished the domain of slavery, and by so much increased free territory. It included the abolition of the slave trade in the District of Columbia. It included the passage of a new Fugitive-Slave law.

All these things were put together, and though passed in separate Acts, were nevertheless, in legislation (as the speeches of the time will show), made to depend upon each other. Each got votes, with the understanding that the other measures were to pass, and by this system of Compromise, in that series of measures, those two bills—the New Mexico and Utah bills—were passed: and I say for that reason they could not be taken as models, framed upon their own intrinsic principle, for all future Territories. And I have the evidence of this in the fact that Judge Douglas, a year afterward, or more than a year afterward, perhaps, when he first introduced bills for the purpose of framing new Territories, did not attempt to follow these bills of New Mexico and Utah; and even when he introduced this Nebraska bill, I think you will discover that he did not exactly follow them. But I do not wish to dwell at great length upon this branch of the discussion. My own opinion is, that a thorough investigation will show most plainly that the New Mexico and Utah bills were part of a system of compromise, and not designed as patterns for future Territorial legislation; and that this Nebraska bill did not follow them as a pattern at all.

The Judge tells us, in proceeding, that he is opposed to making any odious distinction between Free and Slave States. I am altogether unaware that the Republicans are in favor of making any odious distinctions between the Free and Slave States. But there is still a difference, I think, between Judge Douglas and the Republicans in this. I suppose that the real difference between Judge Douglas and his friends, and the Republicans on the contrary is, that the Judge is not in favor of making any difference between slavery and liberty, that he is in favor of eradicating, of pressing out of view, the questions of preference in this country for free or slave institutions; and consequently every sentiment he utters discards the idea that there is any wrong in slavery. Everything that emanates from him or his co-adjutors in their course of policy carefully excludes the thought that there is anything wrong in slavery. All their arguments, if you will consider them, will be seen to exclude the thought that there is anything whatever wrong in slavery. If you will take the Judge's speeches, and select the short and pointed sentences expressed by him,—as his declaration that he "do n't care whether slavery is voted up or down," you will see at once that this is perfectly logical, if you do not admit that slavery is wrong. If you do admit that it is wrong, Judge Douglas cannot logically say he do n't care whether a wrong is voted up or down.

Judge Douglas declares that if any community want slavery, they have a right to have it. He can say that logically, if he says that there is no wrong in slavery; but if you admit that there is a wrong in it, he cannot logically say that anybody has a right to do wrong. He insists that, upon the score of equality, the owners of slaves and owners of property—of horses and every other sort of property—should be alike, and hold them alike in a new Territory. That is perfectly logical if the two species of property are alike and are equally founded in right. But if you admit that one of them is wrong, you cannot institute any equality between

right and wrong. And from this difference of sentiment,—the belief on the part of one that the institution is wrong, and a policy springing from that belief which looks to the arrest of the enlargement of that wrong; and this other sentiment, that it is no wrong, and a policy sprung from that sentiment, which will tolerate no idea of preventing the wrong from growing larger, and looks to there never being an end of it through all the existence of things,—arises the real difference between Judge Douglas and his friends on the one hand, and the Republicans on the other.

Now, I confess myself as belonging to that class in the country who contemplate slavery as a moral, social, and political evil, having due regard for its actual existence amongst us and the difficulties of getting rid of it in any satisfactory way, and to all the constitutional obligations which have been thrown about it; but, nevertheless, desire a policy that looks to the prevention of it as a wrong, and looks hopefully to the time when as a wrong it may come to an end.

Judge Douglas has again, for, I believe, the fifth time, if not the seventh, in my presence, reiterated his charge of a conspiracy or combination between the National Democrats and Republicans. What evidence Judge Douglas has upon this subject I know not, inasmuch as he never favors us with any.

I have said upon a former occasion, and I do not choose to suppress it now, that I have no objection to the division in the Judge's party. He got it up himself. It was all his and their work. He had, I think, a great deal more to do with the steps that led to the Lecompton Constitution than Mr. Buchanan had; though at last, when they reached it, they quarreled over it, and their friends divided upon it. I am very free to confess to Judge Douglas that I have no objection to the division; but I defy the Judge to show any evidence that I have in any way promoted that division, unless he insists on being a witness himself in merely saying so. I can give all fair friends of Judge Douglas here to understand exactly the view that Republicans take in regard to that division. Do n't you remember how two years ago the opponents of the Democratic party were divided between Fremont and Fillmore? I guess you do. Any Democrat who remembers that division will remember also that he was at the time very glad of it, and then he will be able to see all there is between the National Democrats and the Republicans. What we now think of the two divisions of Democrats, you then thought of the Fremont and Fillmore divisions. That is all there is of it.

But if the Judge continues to put forward the declaration that there is an unholy and unnatural alliance between the Republicans and the National Democrats, I now want to enter my protest against receiving him as an entirely competent witness upon that subject. I want to call to the Judge's attention an attack he made upon me in the first one of these debates, at Ottawa, on the 21st of August. In order to fix extreme Abolitionism upon me, Judge Douglas read a set of resolutions which he declared had been passed by a Republican State Convention, in October, 1854, at Springfield, Illinois, and he declared I had taken part in that Convention. It turned out that although a few men calling themselves an anti-Nebraska State Convention had sat at Springfield about that time, yet neither did I take any part in it, nor did it pass the resolutions or any such resolutions as Judge Douglas read. So apparent had it become that the resolutions which he read had not been passed at Springfield at all, nor by a State Convention in which I had taken part, that seven days afterward, at Freeport, Judge Douglas declared that he had been misled by Charles H. Lanphier, editor of the *State Register,* and Thomas L. Harris, member of Congress in that District, and he promised in that speech that when he went to Springfield he would investigate the matter. Since then Judge Douglas has been to Springfield, and I presume has made the investigation; but a month has passed since he has been there, and, so far as I know, he has made no report of the result of his investigation. I have waited as I think a sufficient time for the report of that investigation, and I have some curiosity to see and hear it. A fraud, an absolute forgery was committed, and the perpetration of it was traced to the three,—Lanphier, Harris, and Douglas. Whether it can be narrowed in any way so as to exonerate any one of them, is what Judge Douglas's report would probably show.

It is true that the set of resolutions read by Judge Douglas were published in the Illinois *State Register* on the 16th of October, 1854, as being the resolutions of an anti-Nebraska Convention which had sat in that same month of October, at Springfield. But it is also true that the publication in the *Register* was a forgery then, and the question is still behind, which of the three, if not all of them, committed that forgery? The idea that it was done by mistake, is absurd. The article in the Illinois *State Register* contains part of the real proceedings of that Springfield Convention, showing that the writer of the article had the real proceedings before him, and purposely threw out the genuine resolutions passed by the Convention, and fraudulently substituted the others. Lanphier then, as now, was the editor of the *Register,* so that there seems to be but little room for his escape. But then it is to be borne in mind that Lanphier had less interest in the object of that forgery than either of the other two. The main object of that forgery at that time was to beat Yates and elect Harris to Congress, and that object was known to be exceedingly dear to Judge Douglas at that time. Harris and Douglas were both in Springfield when the Convention was in session, and although they both left before the fraud appeared in the *Register,* subsequent events show that they have both had their eyes fixed upon that Convention.

The fraud having been apparently successful upon the occasion, both Harris and Douglas have more than once since then been attempting to put it to new uses. As the fisherman's wife, whose drowned husband was brought home with his body full of eels, said when she was asked, "What was to be done with him?" "*Take the eels out and set him again,*" so Harris and Douglas have shown a disposition to take the eels out of that stale fraud by which they gained Harris's election, and set the fraud again more than once. On the 9th of July, 1856, Douglas attempted a repetition of it upon Trumbull on the floor of the Senate of the United States, as will appear from the Appendix of the *Congressional Globe* of that date.

On the 9th of August, Harris attempted it again upon Norton in the House of Representatives, as will appear by the same document,—the Appendix to the *Congressional Globe* of that date. On the 21st of August last, all three—Lanphier, Douglas, and Harris—reattempted it upon me at Ottawa. It has been clung to and played out again and again as an exceedingly high trump by this blessed trio. And now that it has been discovered publicly to be a fraud, we find that Judge Douglas manifests no surprise at it at all. He makes no complaint of Lanphier, who must have known it to be a fraud from the beginning. He, Lanphier, and Harris are just as cozy now, and just as active in the concoction of new schemes as they were before the general discovery of this fraud. Now, all this is very natural if they are all alike guilty in that fraud, and it is very unnatural if any one of them is innocent. Lanphier perhaps insists that the rule of honor among thieves does not quite require him to take all upon himself, and consequently my friend Judge Douglas finds it difficult to make a satisfactory report upon his investigation. But meanwhile the three are agreed that each is "*a most honorable man.*"

Judge Douglas requires an indorsement of his truth and honor by a re-election to the United States Senate, and he makes and reports against me and against Judge Trumbull, day after day, charges which we know to be utterly untrue, without for a moment seeming to think that this one unexplained fraud, which he promised to investigate, will be the least drawback to his claim to belief. Harris ditto. He asks a re-election to the lower House of Congress without seeming to remember at all that he is involved in this dishonorable fraud. The Illinois *State Register,* edited by Lanphier, then, as now, the central organ of both Harris and Douglas, continues to din the public ear with these assertions, without seeming to suspect that they are at all lacking in title to belief.

After all, the question still recurs upon us, How did that fraud originally get into the *State Register?* Lanphier then, as now, was the editor of that paper. Lanphier knows. Lanphier cannot be ignorant of how and by whom it was originally concocted. Can he be induced to tell, or, if he has told, can Judge Douglas be induced to tell how it originally was concocted? It may be true that Lanphier insists that the two men for whose benefit it was originally devised, shall at least bear their share of it! How that is, I do not know, and while it remains unexplained, I hope to be pardoned if I insist that the mere fact of Judge Douglas making charges against Trumbull and myself is not quite sufficient evidence to establish them!

While we were at Freeport, in one of these joint discussions, I answered certain interrogatories which Judge Douglas had propounded to me, and then in turn propounded some to him, which he in a sort of way answered. The third one of these interrogatories I have with me, and wish now to make some comments upon it. It was in these words: "If the Supreme Court of the United States shall decide that States cannot exclude slavery from their limits, are you in favor of acquiescing in, adopting, and following such decision as a rule of political action?"

To this interrogatory Judge Douglas made no answer in any just sense of the word. He contented himself with sneering at the thought that it was possible for the Supreme Court ever to make such a decision. He sneered at me for propounding the interrogatory. I had not propounded it without some reflection, and I wish now to address to this audience some remarks upon it.

In the second clause of the sixth article, I believe it is, of the Constitution of the United States, we find the following language: "This Constitution and the laws of the United States which shall be made in pursuance thereof; and all treaties made, or which shall be made, under the authority of the United States, shall be the supreme law of the land; and the judges in every State shall be bound thereby, anything in the Constitution or laws of any State to the contrary, notwithstanding."

The essence of the Dred Scott case is compressed into the sentence which I will now read: "Now, as we have already said in an earlier part of this opinion, upon a different point, the right of property in a slave is distinctly and expressly affirmed in the Constitution." I repeat it, "The right of property in a slave is distinctly and expressly affirmed in the Constitution."

What is it to be *"affirmed"* in the Constitution? Made firm in the Constitution,—so made that it cannot be separated from the Constitution without breaking the Constitution; durable as the Constitution, and part of the Constitution. Now, remembering the provision of the Constitution which I have read; affirming that that instrument is the supreme law of the land; that the Judges of every State shall be bound by it, any law or constitution of any State to the contrary notwithstanding; that the right of property in a slave is affirmed in that Constitution, is made, formed into, and cannot be separated from it without breaking it; durable as the instrument; part of the instrument;—what follows as a short and even syllogistic argument from it? I think it follows, and I submit to the consideration of men capable of arguing, whether as I state it, in syllogistic form, the argument has any fault in it?

Nothing in the Constitution or laws of any State can destroy a right distinctly and expressly affirmed in the Constitution of the United States.

The right of property in a slave is distinctly and expressly affirmed in the Constitution of the United States.

Therefore, nothing in the Constitution or laws of any State can destroy the right of property in a slave.

I believe that no fault can be pointed out in that argument; assuming the truth of the premises, the conclusion, so far as I have capacity at all to understand it, follows inevitably. There is a fault in it as I think, but the fault is not in the reasoning: the falsehood in fact is a fault in the premises.

I believe that the right of property in a slave *is not* distinctly and expressly affirmed in the Constitution, and

Judge Douglas thinks it *is*. I believe that the Supreme Court and the advocates of that decision may search in vain for the place in the Constitution where the right of property in a slave is distinctly and expressly affirmed. I say, therefore, that I think one of the premises is not true in fact. But it is true with Judge Douglas. It is true with the Supreme Court who pronounced it. They are estopped from denying it, and being estopped from denying it the conclusion follows that, the Constitution of the United States being the supreme law, no constitution or law can interfere with it. It being affirmed in the decision that the right of property in a slave is distinctly and expressly affirmed in the Constitution, the conclusion inevitably follows that no State law or constitution can destroy that right.

I then say to Judge Douglas and to all others, that I think it will take a better answer than a sneer to show that those who have said that the right of property in a slave is distinctly and expressly affirmed in the Constitution, are not prepared to show that no constitution or law can destroy that right. I say I believe it will take a far better argument than a mere sneer to show to the minds of intelligent men that whoever has so said, is not prepared, whenever public sentiment is so far advanced as to justify it, to say the other. This is but an opinion, and the opinion of one very humble man; but it is my opinion that the Dred Scott decision, as it is, never would have been made in its present form if the party that made it had not been sustained previously by the elections. My own opinion is, that the new Dred Scott decision, deciding against the right of the people of the States to exclude slavery will never be made, if that party is not sustained by the elections. I believe, further, that it is just as sure to be made as to-morrow is to come, if that party shall be sustained.

I have said, upon a former occasion, and I repeat it now, that the course of argument that Judge Douglas makes use of upon this subject (I charge not his motives in this), is preparing the public mind for that new Dred Scott decision. I have asked him again to point out to me the reasons for his first adherence to the Dred Scott decision as it is. I have turned his attention to the fact that General Jackson differed with him in regard to the political obligation of a Supreme Court decision. I have asked his attention to the fact that Jefferson differed with him in regard to the political obligation of a Supreme Court decision. Jefferson said that "Judges are as honest as other men, and not more so." And he said, substantially, that "whenever a free people should give up in absolute submission to any department of government, retaining for themselves no appeal from it, their liberties were gone." I have asked his attention to the fact that the Cincinnati platform upon which he says he stands, disregards a time-honored decision of the Supreme Court, in denying the power of Congress to establish a National Bank. I have asked his attention to the fact that he himself was one of the most active instruments at one time in breaking down the Supreme Court of the State of Illinois, because it had made a decision distasteful to him, —a struggle ending in the remarkable circumstance of his sitting down as one of the new Judges who were to overslaugh that decision; getting his title of Judge in that very way.

So far in this controversy I can get no answer at all from Judge Douglas upon these subjects. Not one can I get from him, except that he swells himself up and says, "All of us who stand by the decision of the Supreme Court are the friends of the Constitution; all you fellows that dare question it in any way, are the enemies of the Constitution." Now, in this very devoted adherence to this decision, in opposition to all the great political leaders whom he has recognized as leaders, in opposition to his former self and history, there is something very marked. And the manner in which he adheres to it,—not as being right upon the merits, as he conceives (because he did not discuss that at all), but as being absolutely obligatory upon every one, simply because of the source from whence it comes,—as that which no man can gainsay, whatever it may be; this is another marked feature of his adherence to that decision. It marks it in this respect that it commits him to the next decision whenever it comes, as being as obligatory as this one, since he does not investigate it, and won't inquire whether this opinion is right or wrong. So he takes the next one without inquiring whether it is right or wrong. He teaches men this doctrine, and in so doing prepares the public mind to take the next decision when it comes, without any inquiry.

In this I think I argue fairly (without questioning motives at all) that Judge Douglas is most ingeniously and powerfully preparing the public mind to take that decision when it comes; and not only so, but he is doing it in various other ways. In these general maxims about liberty, in his assertions that he "do n't care whether slavery is voted up or voted down;" that "whoever wants slavery has a right to have it;" that "upon principles of equality it should be allowed to go everywhere;" that "there is no inconsistency between free and slave institutions." In this he is also preparing (whether purposely or not) the way for making the institution of slavery national! I repeat again, for I wish no misunderstanding, that I do not charge that he means it so; but I call upon your minds to inquire, if you were going to get the best instrument you could, and then set it to work in the most ingenious way, to prepare the public mind for this movement, operating in the Free States, where there is now an abhorrence of the institution of slavery, could you find an instrument so capable of doing it as Judge Douglas, or one employed in so apt a way to do it?

I have said once before, and I will repeat it now, that Mr. Clay, when he was once answering an objection to the Colonization Society, that it had a tendency to the ultimate emancipation of the slaves, said that "those who would repress all tendencies to liberty and ultimate emancipation must do more than put down the benevolent efforts of the Colonization Society,—they must go back to the era of our liberty and independence, and muzzle the cannon that thunders its annual joyous return; they must blot out the moral lights around us; they must penetrate the human soul, and eradicate the light of reason and the love of liberty!" And I do think —I repeat, though I said it on a former occasion—that Judge Douglas and whoever, like him, teaches that the negro has no share, humble though it may be, in the Declaration of Independence, is going back to the era of our liberty and independence, and, so far as in him lies, muzzling the cannon that thunders its annual joyous return; that he is blowing out the moral lights around us, when he contends that whoever wants slaves has a right to hold them; that he is penetrating, so far as lies in his power, the human soul, and eradicating the light of reason and the love of liberty, when he is in every possible way preparing the public mind, by his vast influence, for making the institution of slavery perpetual and national.

There is, my friends, only one other point to which I will call your attention for the remaining time that I have left me, and perhaps I shall not occupy the entire time that I have, as that one point may not take me clear through it.

Among the interrogatories that Judge Douglas propounded to me at Freeport, there was one in about this language: "Are you opposed to the acquisition of any further territory to the United States, unless slavery shall first be prohibited therein?" I answered, as I thought, in this way, that I am not generally opposed to the acquisition of additional territory, and that I would support a proposition for the acquisition of additional territory according as my supporting it was or was not calculated to aggravate this slavery question amongst us. I then proposed to Judge Douglas another interrogatory, which was correlative to that; "Are you in favor of acquiring additional territory, in disregard of how it may affect us upon the slavery question?" Judge Douglas answered,—that is, in his own way he answered it. I believe that, although he took a good many words to answer it, it was a little more fully answered than any other. The substance of his answer was, that this country would continue to expand; that it would need additional territory; that it was as absurd to suppose that we could continue upon our present territory, enlarging in population as we are, as it would be to hoop a boy twelve years of age, and expect him to grow to man's size without bursting the hoops. I believe it was something like that. Consequently, he was in favor of the acquisition of further territory as fast as we might need it, in disregard of how it might affect the slavery question.

I do not say this as giving his exact language, but he said so substantially; and he would leave the question of slavery where the territory was acquired, to be settled by the people of the acquired territory. [Voice: "That's the doctrine."] May be it is; let us consider that for a while. This will probably, in the run of things, become one of the concrete manifestations of this slavery question. If Judge Douglas's policy upon this question succeeds, and gets fairly settled down, until all opposition is crushed out, the next thing will be a grab for the territory of poor Mexico, an invasion of the rich lands of South America, then the adjoining islands will follow, each one of which promises additional slave-fields. And this question is to be left to the people of those countries for settlement. When we shall get Mexico, I do n't know whether the Judge will be in favor of the Mexican people that we get with it settling that question for themselves and all others; because we know the Judge has a great horror for mongrels, and I understand that the people of Mexico are most decidedly a race of mongrels. I understand that there is not more than one person there out of eight who is pure white, and I suppose from the Judge's previous declaration that when we get Mexico or any considerable portion of it, he will be in favor of these mongrels settling the question, which would bring him somewhat into collision with his horror of an inferior race.

It is to be remembered, though, that this power of acquiring additional territory is a power confided to the President and Senate of the United States. It is a power not under the control of the representatives of the people any further than they, the President and the Senate, can be considered the representatives of the people. Let me illustrate that by a case we have in our history. When we acquired the territory from Mexico in the Mexican war, the House of Representatives, composed of the immediate representatives of the people, all the time insisted that the territory thus to be acquired should be brought in upon condition that slavery should be forever prohibited therein, upon the terms and in the language that slavery had been prohibited from coming into this country. That was insisted upon constantly and never failed to call forth an assurance that any territory thus acquired should have that prohibition in it, so far as the House of Representatives was concerned. But at last the President and Senate acquired the territory without asking the House of Representatives anything about it, and took it without that prohibition. They have the power of acquiring territory without the immediate representatives of the people being called upon to say anything about it, and thus furnishing a very apt and powerful means of bringing new territory into the Union, and when it is once brought into the country, involving us anew in this slavery agitation.

It is, therefore, as I think, a very important question for the consideration of the American people, whether the policy of bringing in additional territory, without considering at all how it will operate upon the safety of the Union in reference to this one great disturbing element in our national politics, shall be adopted as the policy of the country. You will bear in mind that it is to be acquired, according to the Judge's view, as fast as it is needed, and the indefinite part of this proposition is that we have only Judge Douglas and his class of men to decide how fast it is needed. We have no clear and certain way of determining or demonstrating how fast territory is needed by the necessities of the country. Whoever wants to go out filibustering, then, thinks that more territory is needed. Whoever wants wider slave-fields, feels sure that some additional territory is needed as slave-territory. Then it is as easy to show the necessity of additional slave-territory as it is to assert anything that is incapable of absolute demonstration. Whatever motive a man or a set of men may have for making annexation of property or territory, it is very easy to assert, but much less easy to disprove, that it is necessary for the wants of the country.

And now it only remains for me to say that I think it is a very grave question for the people of this Union to consider, whether, in view of the fact that this slavery question has been the only one that has ever endangered our Republican institutions, the only one that has ever threatened or menaced a dissolution of the Union, that has ever disturbed us in such a way as to make us fear for the perpetuity of our liberty,—in view of these facts, I think it is an exceedingly interesting and important question for this people to consider whether we shall engage in the policy of acquiring additional territory, discarding altogether from our consideration, while obtaining new territory, the question how it may affect us in regard to this, the only endangering element to our liberties and national greatness.

The Judge's view has been expressed. I, in my answer to his question, have expressed mine. I think it will become an important and practical question. Our views are before the public. I am willing and anxious that they should consider them fully; that they should turn it about and consider the importance of the question, and arrive at a just conclusion as to whether it is or not wise in the people of this Union, in the acquisition of new territory, to consider whether it will add to the disturbance that is existing amongst us,—whether it will add to the one only danger that has ever threatened the perpetuity of the Union or our own liberties. I think it is extremely important that they shall decide, and rightly decide, that question before entering upon that policy.

And now, my friends, having said the little I wish to say upon this head, whether I have occupied the whole of the remnant of my time or not, I believe I could not enter upon any new topic so as to treat it fully, without transcending my time, which I would not for a moment think of doing. I give way to Judge Douglas.

Mr. Douglas's Rejoinder

GENTLEMEN: The highest compliment you can pay me during the brief half-hour that I have to conclude is by observing a strict silence. I desire to be heard rather than to be applauded.

The first criticism that Mr. Lincoln makes on my speech was that it was in substance what I have said everywhere else in the State where I have addressed the people. I wish I could only say the same of his speech. Why, the reason I complain of him is because he makes one speech north, and another south. Because he has one set of sentiments for the Abolition counties, and another set for the counties opposed to Abolitionism. My point of complaint against him is that I cannot induce him to hold up the same standard, to carry the same flag, in all parts of the State. He does not pretend, and no other man will, that I have one set of principles for Galesburg, and another for Charleston. He does not pretend that I hold to one doctrine in Chicago, and an opposite one in Jonesboro. I have proved that he has a different set of principles for each of these localities. All I asked of him was that he should deliver the speech that he has made here to-day in Coles County instead of in old Knox. It would have settled the question between us in that doubtful county. Here I understand him to reaffirm the doctrine of negro equality, and to assert that by the Declaration of Independence the negro is declared equal to the white man. He tells you to-day that the negro was included in the Declaration of Independence when it asserted that all men were created equal.

[Voices: "We believe it."] Very well.

Mr. Lincoln asserts to-day, as he did at Chicago, that the negro was included in that clause of the Declaration of Independence which says that all men were created equal, and endowed by the Creator with certain inalienable rights, among which are life, liberty, and the pursuit of happiness. If the negro was made his equal and mine, if that equality was established by divine law, and was the negro's inalienable right, how came he to say at Charleston to the Kentuckians residing in that section of our State that the negro was physically inferior to the white man, belonged to an inferior race, and he was for keeping him always in that inferior condition? I wish you to bear these things in mind. At Charleston he said that the negro belonged to an inferior race, and that he was for keeping him in that inferior condition. There he gave the people to understand that there was no moral question involved, because, the inferiority, being established, it was only a question of degree, and not a question of right; here, to-day, instead of making it a question of degree, he makes it a moral question, says that it is a great crime to hold the negro in that inferior condition. [Voices: "He's right."] Is he right now, or was he right in Charleston? [Voice: "Both."] He is right then, sir, in your estimation, not because he is consistent, but because he can trim his principles any way, in any section, so as to secure votes. All I desire of him is that he will declare the same principles in the south that he does in the north.

But did you notice how he answered my position that a man should hold the same doctrines throughout the length and breadth of this Republic? He said, "Would Judge Douglas go to Russia and proclaim the same principles he does here?" I would remind him that Russia is not under the American Constitution. If Russia was a part of the American Republic, under our Federal Constitution, and I was sworn to support the Constitution, I would maintain the same doctrine in Russia that I do in Illinois. The slaveholding States are governed by the same Federal Constitution as ourselves, and hence a man's principles, in order to be in harmony with the Constitution, must be the same in the South as they are in the North, the same in the Free States as they are in the Slave States. Whenever a man advocates one set of principles in one section, and another set in another section, his opinions are in violation of the spirit of the Constitution which he has sworn to support. When Mr. Lincoln went to Congress in 1847, and, laying his hand upon the Holy Evangelists, made a solemn vow, in the presence of high Heaven, that he would be faithful to the Constitution, what did he mean,—the Constitution as he expounds it in Galesburg, or the Constitution as he expounds it in Charleston?

Mr. Lincoln has devoted considerable time to the circumstance that at Ottawa I read a series of resolutions as having been adopted at Springfield, in this State, on the 4th or 5th of October, 1854, which happened not to have been adopted there. He has used hard names; has dared to talk about fraud, about forgery, and has insinuated that there was a conspiracy between Mr. Lanphier, Mr. Harris, and myself to perpetrate a forgery. Now, bear in mind that he does not deny that these resolutions were adopted in a majority of all the Republican counties of this State in that year; he does not deny that they were declared to be the platform of this Republican party in the first Congressional District, in the second, in the third, and in many counties of the fourth, and that they thus became the platform of his party in a majority of the counties upon which he now relies for support; he does not deny the truthfulness of the resolutions, but takes exception to the *spot* on which they were adopted. He takes to himself great merit because he thinks they were not adopted on the right spot for me to use them against him, just as he was very severe in Congress upon the Government of his country when he thought that he had discovered that the Mexican war was not begun in the right *spot,* and was therefore unjust. He tries very hard to make out that there is something very extraordinary in the place where the thing was done, and not in the thing itself.

I never believed before that Abraham Lincoln would be guilty of what he has done this day in regard to those resolutions. In the first place, the moment it was intimated to me that they had been adopted at Aurora and Rockford instead of Springfield, I did not wait for him to call my attention to the fact, but led off, and explained in my first meeting after the Ottawa debate what the mistake was, and how it had been made. I supposed that for an honest man, conscious of his own rectitude, that explanation would be sufficient. I did not wait for him, after the mistake was made, to call my attention to it, but frankly explained it at once as an honest man would. I also gave the authority on which I had stated that these resolutions were adopted by the Springfield Republican Convention; that I had seen them quoted by Major Harris in a debate in Congress, as having been adopted by the first Republican State Convention in Illinois, and that I had written to him and asked him for the authority as to the time and place of their adoption; that, Major Harris being extremely ill, Charles H. Lanphier had written to me, for him, that they were adopted at Springfield on the 5th of October, 1854, and had sent me a copy of the Springfield paper containing them. I read them from the newspaper just as Mr. Lincoln reads the proceedings of meetings held years ago from the newspapers. After giving that explanation, I did not think there was an honest man in the State of Illinois who doubted that I had been led into the error, if it was such, innocently, in the way I detailed; and I will now say that I do not now believe that there is an honest man on the face of the globe who will not regard with abhorrence and disgust Mr. Lincoln's insinuations of my complicity in that forgery, if it was a forgery. Does Mr. Lincoln wish to push these things to the point of personal difficulties here? I commenced this contest by treating him courteously and kindly; I always spoke of him in words of respect; and in return he has sought, and is now seeking to divert public attention from the enormity of his revolutionary principles by impeaching men's sincerity and integrity, and inviting personal quarrels.

I desired to conduct this contest with him like a gentleman; but I spurn the insinuation of complicity and fraud made upon the simple circumstance of an editor of a newspaper having made a mistake as to the place where a thing was done, but not as to the thing itself. These resolutions were the platform of this Republican party of Mr. Lincoln's of that year. They were adopted in a majority of the Republican counties in the State; and when I asked him at Ottawa whether they formed the platform upon which he stood, he did not answer, and I could not get an answer out of him. He then thought, as I thought, that those resolutions were adopted at the Springfield Convention, but excused himself by saying that he was not there when they were adopted, but had gone to Tazewell court in order to avoid being present at the Convention. He saw them published as having been adopted at Springfield, and so did I, and he knew that if there was a mistake in regard to them, that I had nothing under heaven to do with it. Besides, you find that in all these northern counties where the Republican candidates are running pledged to him, that the Conventions which nominated them adopted that identical platform.

One cardinal point in that platform which he shrinks from is this: that there shall be no more Slave States admitted into the Union, even if the people want them. Lovejoy stands pledged against the admission of any more Slave States. [Voices: "Right, so do we."] So do you, you say. Farnsworth stands pledged against the admission of any more Slave States. Washburne stands pledged the same way. The candidate for the Legislature who is running on Lincoln's ticket in Henderson and Warren, stands committed by his vote in the Legislature to the same thing; and I am informed, but do not know of the fact, that your candidate here is also so pledged. [Voices: "Hurrah for him! good!"]

Now, you Republicans all hurrah for him, and for the doctrine of "no more Slave States," and yet Lincoln tells you that his conscience will not permit him to sanction that doctrine, and complains because the resolutions I read at Ottawa made him, as a member of the party, responsible for sanctioning the doctrine of no more Slave States. You are one way, you confess, and he is, or pretends to be, the other; and yet you are both governed by *principle* in supporting one another. If it be true, as I have shown it is, that the whole Republican party in the northern part of the State stands committed to the doctrine of no more Slave States, and that this same doctrine is repudiated by the Republicans in the other part of the State, I wonder whether Mr. Lincoln and his party do not present the case which he cited from the Scriptures, of a house divided against itself which cannot stand!

I desire to know what are Mr. Lincoln's principles and the principles of his party? I hold, and the party with which I am identified holds, that the people of each State, old and new, have the right to decide the slavery question for themselves; and when I used the remark that I did not care whether slavery was voted up or down, I used it in the connection that I was for allowing Kansas to do just as she pleased on the slavery question. I said that I did not care whether they voted slavery up or down, because they had the right to do as they pleased on the question, and therefore my action would not be controlled by any such consideration. Why cannot Abraham Lincoln, and the party with which he acts, speak out their principles so that they may be understood? Why do they claim to be one thing in one part of the State, and another in the other part? Whenever I allude to the Abolition doctrines, which he considers a slander to be charged with being in favor of, you all endorse them, and hurrah for them, not knowing that your candidate is ashamed to acknowledge them.

I have a few words to say upon the Dred Scott decision, which has troubled the brain of Mr. Lincoln so much. He insists that that decision would carry slavery into the Free States, notwithstanding that the decision says directly the opposite, and goes into a long argument to make you believe that I am in favor of, and would sanction, the doctrine that would allow slaves to be brought here and held as slaves contrary to our Constitution and laws. Mr. Lincoln knew better when he asserted this; he knew that one newspaper, and, so far as is within my knowledge, but one, ever asserted that doctrine, and that I was the first man in either House of Congress that read that article in debate, and denounced it on the floor of the Senate as Revolutionary. When the Washington *Union,* on the 17th of last November, published an article to that effect, I branded it at once, and denounced it; and hence the *Union* has been pursuing me ever since. Mr. Toombs, of Georgia, replied to me, and said that there was not a man in any of the Slave States south of the Potomac River that held any such doctrine.

Mr. Lincoln knows that there is not a member of the Supreme Court who holds that doctrine; he knows that every one of them, as shown by their opinions, holds the reverse. Why this attempt, then, to bring the Supreme Court into disrepute among the people? It looks as if there was an effort being made to destroy public confidence in the highest judicial tribunal on earth. Suppose he succeeds in destroying public confidence in the court, so that the people will not respect its decisions but will feel at liberty to disregard them and resist the laws of the land, what will he have gained? He will have changed the Government from one of laws into that of a mob, in which the strong arm of violence will be substituted for the decisions of the courts of justice. He complains because I did not go into an argument reviewing Chief Justice Taney's opinion, and the other opinions of the different judges, to determine whether their reasoning is right or wrong on the questions of law. What use would that be?

He wants to take an appeal from the Supreme Court to this meeting, to determine whether the questions of law were decided properly. He is going to appeal from the Supreme Court of the United States to every town meeting, in the hope that he can excite a prejudice against that court, and on the wave of that prejudice ride into the Senate of the United States, when he could not get there on his own principles or his own merits. Suppose he should succeed in getting into the Senate of the United States, what then will he have to do with the decision of the Supreme Court in the Dred Scott case? Can he reverse that decision when he gets there? Can he act upon it? Has the Senate any right to reverse it or revise it? He will not pretend that it has. Then why drag the matter into this contest, unless for the purpose of making a false issue, by which he can direct public attention from the real issue.

He has cited General Jackson in justification of the war he is making on the decision of the court. Mr. Lincoln misunderstands the history of the country if he believes there is any parallel in the two cases. It is true that the Supreme Court once decided that if a Bank of the United States was a necessary fiscal agent of the Government, it was constitutional, and if not, that it was unconstitutional, and also, that whether or not it was necessary for that purpose, was a political question for Congress, and not a judicial one for the courts to determine. Hence the court would not determine the bank unconstitutional. Jackson respected the decision, obeyed the law, executed it, and carried it into effect during its existence; but after the charter of the bank expired, and a proposition was made to create a new bank, General Jackson said, "It is unnecessary and improper, and therefore I am against it on constitutional grounds as well as those of expediency." Is Congress bound to pass every Act that is constitutional? Why, there are a thousand things that are constitutional, but yet are inexpedient and unnecessary, and you surely would not vote for them merely because you had the right to? And because General Jackson would not do a thing which he had a right to do, but did not deem expedient or proper, Mr. Lincoln is going to justify himself in doing that which he has no right to do.

I ask him whether he is not bound to respect and obey the decisions of the Supreme Court as well as I? The Constitution has created that court to decide all constitutional questions in the last resort; and when such decisions have been made, they become the law of the land, and you, and he, and myself, and every other good citizen, are bound by them. Yet he argues that I am bound by their decisions, and he is not. He says that their decisions are binding on Democrats, but not on Republicans. Are not Republicans bound by the laws of the land as well as Democrats? And when the court has fixed the construction of the Constitution on the validity of a given law, is not their decision binding upon Republicans as well as upon Democrats? Is it possible that you Republicans have the right to raise your mobs and oppose the laws of the land and the constituted authorities, and yet hold us Democrats bound to obey them?

My time is within half a minute of expiring, and all I have to say is, that I stand by the laws of the land. I stand by the Constitution as our fathers made it, by the laws as they are enacted, and by the decisions of the courts, upon all points within their jurisdiction as they are pronounced by the highest tribunal on earth; and any man who resists these must resort to mob law and violence to overturn the government of laws.

Bibliography

In addition to *The Congressional Record* and its antecedents, and federal statutes available in *Statutes at Large,* the following sources were used in preparing selections reproduced in this volume. Selection titles, where not self-evident, are given after their sources.

Adams, John. *The Works of John Adams, Second President of the United States.* Boston: Little, Brown, 1851–65. "Braintree Instructions."

Allen, W. B. *George Washington: A Collection.* Indianapolis: Liberty Fund, 1988. "Farewell Address," "Thanksgiving Proclamation," "Letter to the United Baptist Churches in Virginia," "Letter to the Roman Catholics in the United States of America," "Letter to the Hebrew Congregation in Newport."

Belz, Herman, ed. *The Webster-Hayne Debate on the Nature of the Union: Selected Documents.* Indianapolis: Liberty Fund, 2000. Speech of Daniel Webster, Speech of Robert Y. Hayne.

Boucher, Jonathan. *A View of the Causes and Consequences of the American Revolution; in Thirteen Discourses, Preached in North America between the years 1763 and 1775.* London: G. G. and J. Robinson, 1797. "On Civil Liberty, Passive Obedience, and Non-resistance."

Calhoun, John C. *Speeches of John C. Calhoun,* ed. Richard K. Cralle. New York: D. Appleton and Company, 1853–54. "Fort Hill Address," "Speech on Slavery."

Carey, George W., and James McClellan, eds. *The Federalist.* Indianapolis: Liberty Fund, 2001. Selections are taken from the Gideon edition of 1818.

Crockett, Davy. *Colonel Crockett's Exploits and Adventures in Texas.* New York: Wm. H. Graham, 1848.

Force, Peter, ed. *Tracts and Other Papers Relating Principally to the Origin, Settlement, and Progress of the Colonies in North America from the Discovery of the Country to the Year 1776.* Vol. IV. Washington, D.C.: Peter Force, 1846. "An Account of the Late Revolution in New England together with the Declaration of the Gentlemen, Merchants, and Inhabitants of Boston and the Country Adjacent."

Ford, Paul Leicester, ed. *Pamphlets on the Constitution of the United States, Published during its Discussion by the People, 1787–88.* Chicago, 1894. "An Examination of the Leading Principles of the Federal Constitution."

Hall, Michael G., Lawrence H. Leder, and Michael G. Kammen, eds. *The Glorious Revolution in America: Documents on the Colonial Crisis of 1689.* Chapel Hill: University of North Carolina Press, 1964.

House Miscellaneous Documents, 53rd Congress, Second Session, 1893–94, II, 576–91. Andrew Jackson "Veto Message."

Hutchinson, Thomas. *History of Massachusetts Bay.* Vol. 1. Boston: Fleet, 1764. John Cotton, "Copy of a Letter from Mr. Cotton to Lord Say and Seal."

Hyneman, Charles S., and Donald S. Lutz, eds. *American Political Writing during the Founding Era: 1760–1805.* Indianapolis: Liberty Fund, 1983. *Worcestriensis* Number IV, "A Discourse at the Dedication of the Tree of Liberty," "Thoughts on Government," "Memorial and Remonstrance against Religious Assessments," "Virginia Bill for Establishing Religious Freedom."

Kennedy, John Pendleton, ed. *Journals of the House of Burgesses of Virginia, 1761–65.* Richmond: E. Waddey, 1907. Resolutions in the Virginia House of Burgesses.

Labaree, Leonard W., ed. *The Papers of Benjamin Franklin.* New Haven: Yale University Press, 1962. Albany Plan of Union.

Lincoln, Abraham. *Complete Works of Abraham Lincoln,* ed. John G. Nicolay and John Hay. New York: Lamb Publishing, 1905. Lincoln Speeches.

Lipscomb, Andrew, and Albert Bergh, eds. *The Writings of Thomas Jefferson.* Vol. VII. Washington, D.C.: Thomas Jefferson Memorial Association, 1903–4. "Letter to the Danbury Baptist Association," "Opinion against the Constitutionality of a National Bank," "A Bill for Establishing Religious Freedom."

Lutz, Donald S., ed. *Colonial Origins of the American Constitution: A Documentary History.* Indianapolis: Liberty Fund, 1998. Colonial Documents: Articles, Laws, and Orders, Divine, Politic, and Martial for the Colony in Virginia, The Mayflower Compact, Fundamental Orders of Connecticut, Massachusetts Body of Liberties, Charter of Liberties and Frame of Government of the Province of Pennsylvania in America, Dorchester Agreement, Maryland Act for Swearing Allegiance, Plymouth Oath of Allegiance and Fidelity, Providence Agreement, Maryland Act for Church Liberties, Pennsylvania Act for Freedom of Conscience.

McClellan, James. *Liberty, Order, and Justice: An Introduction to the Constitutional Principles of American Government.* Indianapolis: Liberty Fund, 2000. Magna Charta, Petition of Right, English Bill of Rights, Declaration and Resolves of the First Continental Congress, Virginia Bill of Rights, Declaration of Independence, Articles of Confederation, Northwest Ordinance, Virginia and New Jersey Plans, Constitution of the United States of America.

McDonald, Forrest, ed. *Empire and Nation.* New York: Prentice-Hall, 1962. "Letters from a Farmer in Pennsylvania," Letters V and IX; "Letters from the Federal Farmer," Letter III.

McDougall, Marion Gleason. *Fugitive Slaves.* Boston: Ginn & Company, 1891. Laws Relating to Fugitives.

Madison, James. *The Writings of James Madison,* ed. Gaillard Hunt. New York: G. P. Putnam's Sons, 1908. James Madison "Veto Message."

Mather, Cotton. *Magnalia Christi Americana.* London: T. Parkhurst, 1702. "A Platform of Church Discipline."

New York *Journal,* October 18, 1787, December 13, 1787. "Brutus," Essays I and IV.

Ormond, John J., Arthur P. Bagby, and George Goldthwaite. *The Code of Alabama.* Montgomery: Brittan and De Wolf, Alabama State Printers, 1852. Alabama Slave Code.

Otis, James. *The Rights of the British Colonists Asserted and Proved.* In "Some Political Writings of James Otis," ed. C. F. Mullett, *University of Missouri Studies* 4 (1929).

Paine, Thomas. *Common Sense.* Philadelphia: W. and T. Bradford, 1776.

Pennsylvania Packet and Daily Advertiser, "Address of the Minority of the Pennsylvania Convention," December 18, 1787.

Philadelphia *Independent Gazetteer,* October 5, 1787. "Centinel," Letter I.

Pickering, Danby, ed. *The Statutes at Large,* XXVI, XXVII. The Stamp Act, Act Repealing the Stamp Act, Declaratory Act.

Political Speeches and Debates of Abraham Lincoln and Stephen A. Douglas, 1844–1861. Chicago: Foresman & Co., 1896. Lincoln-Douglas Debate.

Proceedings of a Convention of Delegates from the States of Massachusetts, Connecticut, and Rhode Island, the Counties of Cheshire and Grafton in the State of New-Hampshire and the County of Windham, in the State of Vermont Convened at Hartford in the State of Connecticut, December 15, 1814. Hartford, Conn.: Andrus and Starr, 1815.

Proceedings of the Congress at New York. Annapolis, Md.: Jonas Green, 1766. Declarations of the Stamp Act Congress.

Result of the Convention of Delegates Holden at Ipswich in the County of Essex, Who Were Deputed to Take into Consideration the Constitution and Form of Government, Proposed by the Convention of the State of Massachusetts-Bay. Newbury Port: John Mycall, 1778. The Essex Result.

Sandoz, Ellis, ed. *Political Sermons of the American Founding Era: 1730–1805.* Indianapolis: Liberty Fund, 1991. "The Rights of Conscience Inalienable," "The Duty of Americans, at the Present Crisis."

Sawyer, George S. *Southern Institutes.* Philadelphia: J. B. Lippincott and Co., 1858.

Story, Joseph. *Commentaries on the Constitution of the United States.* Boston: Brown, Shattuck and Co., 1833.

———. *A Familiar Exposition of the Constitution of the United States.* Boston: Marsh, Capen, Lyon and Webb, 1840.

Stowe, Harriet Beecher. *A Key to Uncle Tom's Cabin.* Boston: J. P. Jewett and Co., 1853. "What Is Slavery?" "Slavery Is Despotism."

Taylor, John. *Arator: Being a Series of Agricultural Essays, Practical and Political: In Sixty-Four Numbers.* Indianapolis: Liberty Fund, 1977. "Slavery," "Agriculture and the Militia."

Virginia Report of 1799–1800 Touching the Alien and Sedition Laws; Together with the Virginia Resolutions of December 21, 1798, The Debate and Proceedings Thereon in the House of Delegates of Virginia, and Several other Documents illustrative of The Report and Resolutions. Richmond: J. W. Randolph, 1850. Alien and Sedition Laws, Virginia Resolutions, Kentucky Resolutions, Madison's "Report on the Virginia Resolutions," Other States' Resolutions.

Webster, Daniel. *The Writings and Speeches of Daniel Webster.* Boston: Little, Brown, 1903. "Slavery and the Constitution."

White, Lawrence H., ed. *Democratick Editorials: Essays in Jacksonian Political Economy by William Leggett.* Indianapolis: Liberty Fund, 1984.

Williams, Roger. *The Bloody Tenent, of Persecution, for Cause of Conscience, discussed, in a Conference Between Truth and Peace.* London, 1644.

Winthrop, Robert C., ed. *Life and Letters of John Winthrop.* Boston: Ticknor and Fields, 1864–67. "Little Speech on Liberty."

This book is set in Adobe Garamond, a modern adaptation by Robert Slimbach of the typeface originally cut around 1540 by the French typographer and printer Claude Garamond. The Garamond face, with its small lowercase height and restrained contrast between thick and thin strokes, is a classic "old-style" face and has long been one of the most influential and widely used typefaces.

Printed on paper that is acid free and meets the requirements of the American National Standard for Permanence of Paper for Printed Library Materials, z39.48-1992. ∞

Book design by Sandra Hudson, Athens, Georgia
Typography by G & S Typesetters, Austin, Texas
Printed and bound by Edwards Brothers, Inc., Ann Arbor, Michigan